D0989726

Encyclopedia of British Football

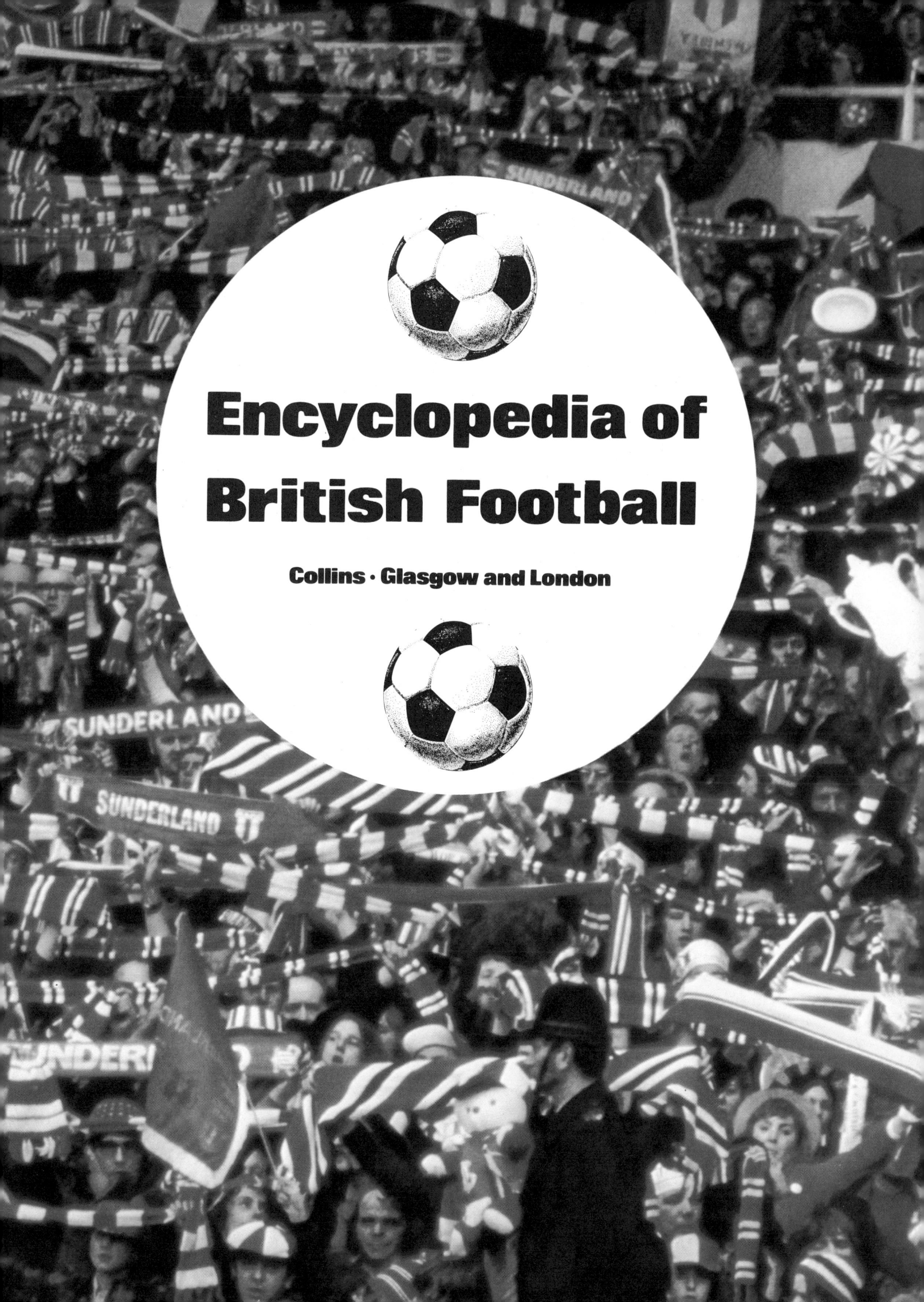

Encyclopedia of British Football

Collins · Glasgow and London

First published in this edition 1974
Published by William Collins Sons and Company Limited, Glasgow and London
© 1974 Marshall Cavendish Limited

The greater part of the material published in this book
was first published by Marshall Cavendish Limited
in *Book of Football*

Printed in Great Britain
ISBN 0 00 106181 X

Contents

Edited by Martin Tyler and Phil Soar

Additional artwork by Paul Buckle

Additional photographs supplied by:
P2 Sunderland fans by Ray Green
P8 Wembley by Syndication International
P42 Ian Storey-Moore by Colorsport
P44 Turnstile by Alan Duns
P46 Derek Dougan by Fotosports
P137 Colin Waldron by Ray Green
P153 Dudley Tyler by Colorsport

The Story of Football

CHAOS AT CUP-TIE FINAL. WHO WAS TO BLAME? SEE P.

The Daily Mirror

24 PAGES

NET SALE MUCH THE LARGEST OF ANY DAILY PICTURE NEWSPAPER

No. 6,079.　Registered at the G.P.O. as a Newspaper.　MONDAY, APRIL 30, 1923　One Penny.

POLICE v. CROWD: WEMBLEY'S FIRST CUP FINAL

A remarkable photograph, taken from the air, of the Stadium at Wembley, with spectators swarming over the playing pitch, while hundreds more are clustered outside.

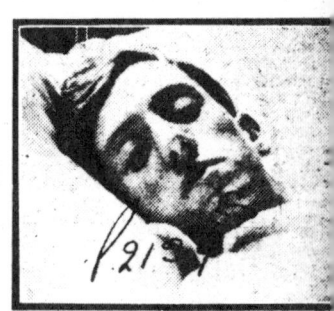

Robert Bruce at Willesden Hospital with a crushed chest.

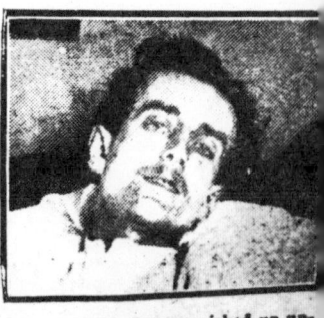

Mr. L. Hall, who was picked up unconscious, in Willesden Hospital.

Police pushing back part of the crowd on the pitch from the neighbourhood of one goal.

Official records will claim that the first contest to be staged at the Empire Stadium, Wembley, was the final for the Football Association Challenge Cup between West Ham United and Bolton Wanderers. Those who were present last Saturday will, however, long retain the memory of an earlier struggle in which the opposing elements were police and public, the ultimate victory resting with the force. (See also pages 12 and 24.)

Above *A familiar scene, dating back to seventeenth-century Italy.*
Opposite *Events yet undreamed of.*

The game that nobody invented

Nobody invented football. As soon as an Egyptian, or Assyrian, or Chinese had first kicked or bounced or rolled an object to a companion the seeds of football had been sown. Once the war-games of Greek youths had been adapted to include a ball, all the principles of the modern game had been established—a conflict in which one crowd of combatants tries to force the ball through the territory and into the base guarded by an opposing crowd of combatants. It really is as simple as that, and always has been, whether Association or Rugby, American or Gaelic, Australian Rules or the Eton Wall Game.

Football is, at its simplest, so instinctive and attractive a pastime that it is not surprising to find it growing at numerous points quite independently. Both in China and in ancient Mexico they played a sort of target football, kicking or heading a ball with immense skill through holes in silk screens or through rings set high in a wall. These were games played at royal command, for military training, or at religious festivals. To win a

casket of gold and jewellery was not unknown, though the equivalent of the loser's medal was often even more striking—occasionally the losing team was executed on the spot.

Acrobatic artistry and delicate skills still survive in a charming game played in Burma, where groups of men kick a wicker-work ball between them, the ball never stopping, never touching the ground: there are no goals, no winners or losers—just applause and appreciation of the grace and ball control involved.

Did football arrive with the kicking of a severed head?

The war-games of the Greeks were very different in spirit; they were adapted, as so many things Greek, by the empire-building Romans and were eventually spread throughout the Empire under the name of *harpastum*: two teams on a rectangle of land trying to kick or carry a ball over their rivals' base line.

Inevitably, the game came to Britain. The Britons and Celts adapted it in their own way—there is the legend that the first game played among the Anglo-Saxons was a victory celebration, using the severed head of a defeated Dane as a ball. And so British football evolved in a form that was barely to change for 1,500 years. Every Shrove Tuesday at Ashbourne, in Derbyshire, they still play the ferocious cross-country village game that some historians have traced back as far as the year AD 217. Conflicts of this sort, between hordes of players representing two neighbouring villages or, as in the case of Ashbourne, two halves of the same town, were the norm until the call for stricter and more uniform rules came towards the end of the 18th century.

The Normans, too, had a tradition of football, also adapted from the time of the Roman occupation, which they brought over with them. And within 100 years of William the Conqueror's arrival football had taken root both as a pastime among the Norman ruling elite and as a rampage among their subjects.

In medieval times the game developed very slowly, if at all. Skills took second place to vigour, and no one seems to have been anxious to establish real rules. Twice, between 1280 and 1325, it is recorded that footballers died through falling on their daggers; it is not recorded whether this was done on purpose after conceding a goal, nor whether the daggers were worn as part of the conventional football kit of the day, for discreet use in the thick of the scrimmage.

The only rules the game attracted simply banned it!

Indeed, the only rules that the game did attract at this time were those expressly forbidding it. Edward III, Richard II and Henry IV, all of them concerned with maintaining a strong army against the French, each decreed that football was bad training for battle and that, in any case, its popularity was getting in the way of regular archery practice. The game was banned time and again, both in England and Scotland, without any lasting effect. Then, as the years passed, the game became a natural target for the killjoys; the Puritans furiously condemned the 'bloody and murthering practice'; one Philip Stubbs, in proclaiming that the end of the world was just round the corner, put a fair measure of the blame on 'football playing and other

9

RADIO TIMES HULTON PICTURE LIBRARY

MANSELL COLLECTION

develishe pastimes' on the Sabbath.

But the game survived—as 'football' in the English towns and villages, as 'hurling' in Cornwall, and 'knappan' in parts of Wales. It became accepted as part of the English scene on holidays and at festival time. And, by about 1800, football can be said to have reached the threshold of the modern game— the rules still non-existent, the game itself still rough and punishing, but a game that would be understood and appreciated (though probably not enjoyed) by a present-day crowd at Wembley or Twickenham.

It was the public schools that gave the world football

The game, too, had acquired a respectability—not yet the aristocratic backing that cricket was already enjoying, but the respectability that always follows a good spectator sport. The gentry did not yet play the game, but they came along to watch, to lay an occasional bet, and even to raise a subdued cheer.

It was about now that football received the shot in the arm that was eventually to make it the most popular game in the world. The early 19th century saw a tremendous upsurge in education for the privileged; it was the era of the public schools, whose teaching methods impressed the aristocracy and the new industrialists alike. The boys at these schools had little time and even fewer facilities for the more extravagant pastimes of country-house living—no riding, no fishing,

no hunting, no horse-racing. But they quickly adapted the principles of the town and village games —all they needed were two teams and a ball—to the fields or yards round their school buildings; and they played these games at every opportunity.

And, conveniently for the game, this passion among the boys for the rough, invigorating games of the 'lower classes' coincided with the triumphant peak in the career of that great educationalist, Dr Thomas Arnold of Rugby School. Arnold himself was not a great supporter of the games cult but, seeing that the boys were determined to organize and play games, he brought discipline and a sense of purpose into their pursuit, just as he had done into every other facet of school life. Arnold's followers, and there were many of them, accepted the idea of organized games with enthusiasm. So suddenly, after centuries of official censure and puritan disapproval, people were actually *encouraging* boys to play football!

There was no stopping the game now. In every great public school football of one kind or another became part of the tradition. The rules, as yet, varied drastically from school to school. There was no such thing as the inter-school match, so there was absolutely no need for any one school to play the game to anything like the same rules as the school in the next county. Some of the games that evolved were bizarre in the extreme. At Charterhouse, 20-a-side matches were played in the only space available—a long brick cloister, open at one end, blocked in by a wall at the other:

no long kicks were allowed, no handling the ball, no passing forward—dribbling was the order of the day. At Harrow, where the game had to be adapted to the veritable bog that the winter rains formed in the fields below the hill on which the school stands, a big heavy ball was needed, and rules that encouraged movement. The ground was comparatively big—some 150 yards by 100 yards, and high kicking and catching the ball (though not carrying) were permitted.

Eton's Wall Game —only two goals in seventy years

At Eton, of course, the Wall Game flourished—on an extraordinary pitch 120 yards long and just six yards wide, with, in the early days, 18 or 20 on each side; the goals were a tree at one end and a garden door at the other; progress upfield was painfully slow and very muddy, tries (or 'shies' as Etonians called them) were rare, and converted goals much rarer. The Wall Game still appears to give a lot of Etonians and a lot of newspaper photographers pleasure at the annual St Andrew's Day match; but only two goals have been scored this century!

And at Rugby, too, football was steeped in tradition even before Dr Arnold—a wide-running game with plenty of space, long scrimmages, 'offside' given against a player getting in front of the ball, handling allowed only for a fair catch...

Until, that is, the afternoon in

1823 when a Manchester-born boy called William Webb Ellis, later a clergyman and later still to die in obscurity in the South of France, broke all the conventions by catching the ball, tucking it under his arm, and running with it to the opponents' goal line.

This little act of defiance, which might very easily have been shrugged off and forgotten, caused a lot of hard thinking at Rugby School. Eventually, 'running in', as it was called, was accepted into their rules and, in time, led to the basic distinction between the two codes of football.

While boys were still at school, the fact that they played to a strange set of rules hardly mattered. When, however, they left for the universities or for business in the provinces, it became clear that if they were to continue playing football they were going to need a universal set of rules, acceptable to all teams. Up until the 1850s, two teams at, say, Oxford, would only be playing on familiar ground if every player had been to the same school; as things turned out, a major game was often preceded by a long correspondence and lengthy argument about the conventions. Was handling to be allowed? How many players on each side? How long should the pitch be? How wide the goals? Would carrying the ball be permitted? ('Yes', would say all the Old Rugbeians; 'No', would say almost everyone else). And even when the game got under way, confusion and protests would necessitate long midfield conferences between the two captains.

In time it became usual for the Rugby men, and their small but

SUE GOODERS

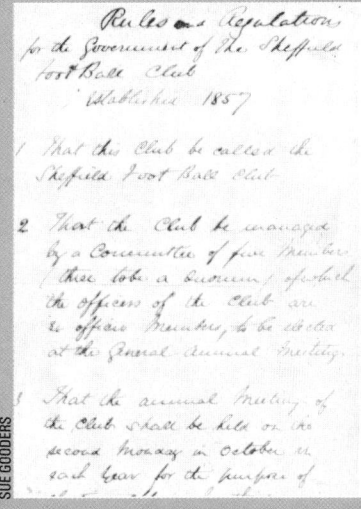

JACKDAW PUBLICATIONS

MANSELL COLLECTION

Far left *The early forerunners of modern day matches were generally timeless brawls between two neighbouring villages or parts of the same town. This London street game of around 1300 looks gentler than most.*
Above left *500 years on and the game has hardly changed. This print of a soldiers' friendly is dated 1827.*
Left *The first vestiges of organization; this school game of around 1850 at least has goalposts and approximately the same number on either side. The rules, however, obviously still allow handling and hacking.*
Above *The first minutes of the world's very first 'football club', Sheffield FC. Although the date is given as 1857, it is likely that the club's first members formed a team as early as 1854.*

posts), another great Victorian educationalist, J. C. Thring, issued the rules for what he called *The Simplest Game.* They were indeed very simple, and provided a very straightforward game—no violence, no kicking at the ball in the air, nobody allowed in front of the ball, etc. They were unadventurous, but they provoked great interest, and a number of schools agreed to adopt them.

And at Cambridge, things were moving again. The rules for a match between Cambridge Old Etonians and Cambridge Old Harrovians, in November 1862, specified 11-a-side, an umpire from each side plus a neutral referee, goals 12ft across and up to 20ft high, an hour and a quarter's play only, and the three-man offside rule. These rules were said to have worked well; in the following year they formed a vital part of the revised Cambridge Rules and, in the following months, those of the newly formed Football Association.

Rugby breaks away —over hacking, not handling

In the month of October 1863 football, in the South at least, came of age. The eager young gentlemen of Cambridge University issued their definitive set of rules, but almost at once the control of the game passed from the scholars to the clubs, where it has remained ever since.

The formation of the Football Association was bitter and often ill-tempered, and a certain stubbornness on both sides ensured that the split between the Rugby code and the dribbling code became too wide ever to be mended. The real divergence was not over running with the ball, but over 'hacking'. Rugby men felt it was manly and courageous to tackle an opponent by kicking him on the shin; the dribbling men did not, and voted it out. The Rugby men called the dribbling men cowards, and walked out of the Football Association for ever.

In 1863, football was still far from the game we know today. Every player was still allowed to handle the ball, and when he caught it he could 'make a mark' and so win a free kick; there was, in the first FA laws, a 'touch-down' rule, allowing a free kick at goal after a ball had been kicked over the opposing goal line and touched down (the Rugby 'try', in fact); there was still considerable disagreement over offside, and the FA started off with the Rugby-style 'no one interfering with play in front of the ball' rule.

But within a few years soccer rejected all the distinctive Rugby conventions. Soon only the goalkeeper could handle the ball, the touchdown was abolished, forward passing became the essence of good attacking play and of good entertainment for the spectators. By the early 1870s, England and Scotland were playing internationals and the FA Cup had begun its distinguished and glamorous career. It was only a matter of time before football was to become the most popular pursuit that Britain—and the world—had ever known.

growing company of followers from other schools, to play on their own, and for the others, from Westminster, Charterhouse, Shrewsbury, Harrow and so on, to come to some compromise over the rules of the 'dribbling' game.

Few of these early codes of rules have come down to us intact, but snatches from them give a clear idea of the patterns of the early game, and in particular how boring it must have been to stand in the cold and watch.

In almost every case the game was won or lost (if indeed any goals at all were scored in the one, or two, or three afternoons laid aside for it) in the interminable, seething scrimmage. The aim of the game was, by dint of skilful footwork, to dribble the ball solo through the opposing team, who would all gang up in a scrum to defend. If one man was tackled (and tackling was usually unceremonious and often brutal), another would gather the ball and perform his own solo run until possession was lost and the opposition forwards started the same process in reverse. There may have been the odd instance of inspired, high-speed wing play in the Matthews-Finney tradition, but it is obvious, especially as there was virtually no forward passing, that the games were liable to bog down in the mud. Individual ball-players made as much progress with their lone dribbling as a man trying to push a loaded wheelbarrow into Anfield just as the Kop are on their way out.

The Rugby code may have had too much handling for the purists, but the long kicks and daring runs with the ball might have made it, in those days at any rate, a far more enjoyable afternoon's sport.

The first serious attempts at laying down the rules of football went some way to improving it as a spectacle. In 1848, at Cambridge, 14 men representing Eton, Harrow, Winchester, Rugby and various other public schools, after a seven-hour session, produced the so-called 'Cambridge Rules'—rules that were adapted and tightened up twice in the 1850s.

Under 1848 rules catching the ball was still allowed

Goals were awarded for balls kicked between the flag posts and under the string; goal kicks and throw-ins were given much as today (though throw-ins, taken with one hand only, might travel as far as a kick); catching the ball direct from the foot was allowed, provided the catcher kicked it immediately (no running with the ball, despite that delegate from Rugby); and there was a much more workable offside law—a man could play a ball passed to him from behind, so long as there were *three* opponents between him and the goal.

The game was now established on a common foundation. Competition was possible, and winning became important. By 1855 rules like these were the basis of inter-university matches, and the legendary inter-school matches of public school fiction had begun to blossom.

Amid all this activity in the leisurely atmosphere of the universities and the public schools there

emerged, almost out of the blue, the first recognizable 'football club'.

The old, hard, ruthless town football had been played in Sheffield for many years, but sometime in 1854 or 1855 (though the oldest existing rulebook is dated 1857), after Sheffield Cricket Club had inaugurated a new ground at Bramall Lane, one of the cricketers—William Prest—and some friends from the Collegiate School in Sheffield formed the Sheffield Football Club.

They wrote a constitution and a set of rules (not unlike the Cambridge Rules, though a bit rougher—pushing with the hands was allowed) and specified that every member should have two caps—one red, one dark blue—to distinguish the teams in games played among themselves.

This small band of old school acquaintances, with no apparent encouragement from the gentlemanly scholars from 'down South', had laid the foundations of football in the North of England. Within five years there were 15 different clubs in the Sheffield area, and an 1861 match between the two great local rivals, Sheffield and Hallam, drew a gate of 600 spectators. (Seventy-five years later, at that same Bramall Lane, Sheffield United crammed in 68,000-plus for a Cup-tie.)

Meanwhile, back among the lawmakers, rules and regulations were being hammered out, published, revised, re-negotiated and re-published in a thoroughly confusing burst of activity. At Uppingham School in Rutland, where football was distinguished by an enormously wide goal (with, incidentally, a crossbar rather than tapes between the

COURTESY OF MR BRIAN BELK

The birth of the FA Cup

THE STORY OF FOOTBALL

The most important date in the history of football is 26 October 1863. That was the day on which the Football Association came into being and the point at which 'modern' football can be said to have begun.

In a sense, the most interesting thing about that meeting in the Freemason's Tavern, Great Queen Street, Holborn, was not the teams that were represented but those that were not. There was, for instance, no one from the main provincial centres of the game—Sheffield and Nottingham—nor, more surprisingly, from Cambridge, where the first formal laws had been drawn up in 1848. As a result it was 14 years before the whole country accepted uniform procedures.

The thirteen laws that were eventually approved are indicative of the origins of the men who drew them up. They were, basically, the laws of the game as played at Harrow and by the teams of Harrovian Old Boys—particularly No Names (of Kilburn) and Forest School, who became the famous Wanderers in 1864.

The Blackheath Club, which played to the rules of the game at Rugby, had broken away by the end of 1863, though that alternative game did leave behind it one significant innovation—the more precise name for its competitor. The story may not be true, but one Charles Wreford-Brown, who later became a notable official of the FA, was asked by some friends at Oxford whether he would join them for a game of 'rugger'. He refused, claiming that he was going to play 'soccer'—evidently a play on the word associa-

tion. The name caught on.

There was no immediate attempt by the new Football Association to integrate all the various other codes around the country. Not until Charles Alcock, who had been at Harrow from 1855 to 1859, joined the committee did some sort of impetus build up. The rigorous offside law, basically that still employed in rugby, was revised when Westminster and Charterhouse schools joined, but the most important step was the arrival of Yorkshire representatives in 1867.

Yorkshire is the home of the oldest of all football clubs—Sheffield FC. The first written evidence of the club's existence dates from 1857—though it may have been founded by Old Boys of the Collegiate School in Sheffield as early as 1854. By the later date, however, it had its own rules and its secretary approached the newly formed FA in 1863 with a view to integration. The FA did not even bother to reply.

The north Midlands generally was to the provinces what Harrow was to the Home Counties. It was here that the first of the present League clubs originated—Notts County (often referred to as Nottingham before 1882) in 1862, Nottingham Forest in 1865 and Chesterfield in 1866. There have been suggestions that a Stoke club was established by a group of Old Carthusians in 1863—but nineteenth century records give the date as no earlier than 1867.

The first hint of a game that the modern supporter might be able to identify with was the Notts County–Nottingham Forest clash of 1866. The only score of the day came at the end of a 'negative scoreless afternoon' (shades of the present day) when 'there was a sort of steeplechase across the goal-line and over the grandstand railings . . . where W H Revis, of the Forest, touched down. The place-kick, 15 yards at right angles from the goal-line was taken by the same player.' The ball had merely to go between the posts as there was no cross-bar.

As can be deduced, the Nottingham game was a hybrid, relying on a mixture of Rugby, Sheffield and London rules, but with the expansion

COURTESY OF THE TIMES

FOOTBALL.—Last evening a meeting of the captains or other representatives of the football clubs of the metropolis was held at the Freemasons' Tavern, Great Queen-street, Lincoln's Inn-fields. Mr. Pember, N. N. Kilburn Club, having been voted to the chair, observed that the adoption of a certain set of rules by all football players was greatly to be desired, and said that the meeting had been called to carry that object into effect as far as practicable. Mr. E. C. Morley (Barnes) moved, and Mr. Mackenzie (Forest Club, Leytonstone) seconded, the following resolution :—"That it is advisable that a football association should be formed for the purpose of settling a code of rules for the regulation of the game of football." Mr. B. F. Hartshorne said that though he felt it was most desirable that a definite set of rules for football should be generally adopted, yet, as the representative of the Charterhouse School, he could not pledge himself to any course of action without seeing more clearly what other schools would do in the matter. On the part of the Charterhouse he would willingly coalesce if other public schools would do the same. Probably, at a more advanced stage of the association, the opinion of the generality of the great schools would be obtained. The chairman said every association must have a beginning, and they would be very happy to have the co-operation of the last speaker at a future meeting. The resolution for the formation of the association was then put and carried. The officers were elected as follows :—Mr. A. Pember, President ; Mr. E. C. Morley (Barnes), Hon. Secretary; Mr. F. M. Campbell (Blackheath), Treasurer. The annual subscription was fixed at one guinea, all clubs being eligible if of one year's standing, and to be entitled to send two representatives to the yearly meeting, to be held in the last week in September, when the rules would be revised, and the general business arrangements carried out.

ST. GEORGE'S-IN-THE-EAST.—The arrangement which has been for some time past in progress for an exof the FA to accommodate Sheffield uniformity was not far away. As Alcock himself wrote, '... the objects of the Association are to still further remove the barriers which prevent the accomplishment of one universal game.'

By 1870 Alcock, now secretary of the FA, had established unofficial internationals between England and Scotland (or rather a team of Scots resident in London) and a regular London-Sheffield encounter. The growing competitiveness of the game encouraged him to add another suggestion in 1871—a challenge cup 'for which all clubs belonging to the Football Association should be invited to compete'. The idea was unashamedly based on the interhouse knock-out competition at Harrow—the winners being refered to as the 'Cock House'.

The Cup holders chose where the Final was played

The holders of the new trophy, known as the FA Challenge Cup, were to enjoy two invaluable advantages—they were exempt until the Final and they could choose where it was played. Fifteen clubs entered in the first year, though only twelve competed. Of these, two, Maidenhead and Marlow, have entered in each and every subsequent year. The real attraction was the appearance of Queen's Park, the Glasgow side that had been formed in 1867 and had still not had a single goal scored against them. Because of the distance they had to travel they were exempt until the semi-final, when they drew with the Wanderers at the Oval. Unfortunately they could not afford to return for a replay and the Wanderers went on to beat Royal Engineers in the Final at the same venue. The only goal of the match was scored by M P Betts, playing under the assumed name of A H Chequer—meaning that he was a member of the Old Harrovian side Harrow Chequers—and 2,000 people paid the not insubstantial sum of one shilling to watch. Captain of the Wanderers was one Charles W Alcock.

The Wanderers won again the following year, beating Oxford University at the early hour of 11 am so that the event would not clash with the Boat Race. The days of football pre-eminence were still far in the future! Queen's Park again had to withdraw at the semi-final stage. The Cup was dominated for a dozen years by a handful of southern clubs —Wanderers, Royal Engineers, Oxford University, Old Etonians and Clapham Rovers—but the writing was on the wall for these gentlemen amateurs as early as 1877.

In that year, as a result of correspondence between Manchester FC and Marlborough College, the authority of the FA rules was generally accepted throughout the country. Thus the Sheffield version passed into oblivion, but not before it had had a significant effect on the game. The throw-in was used in Yorkshire some five years before the FA accepted it and the free-kick was an innovation from Sheffield; so was the cross-bar. Before 1866 there had been no height

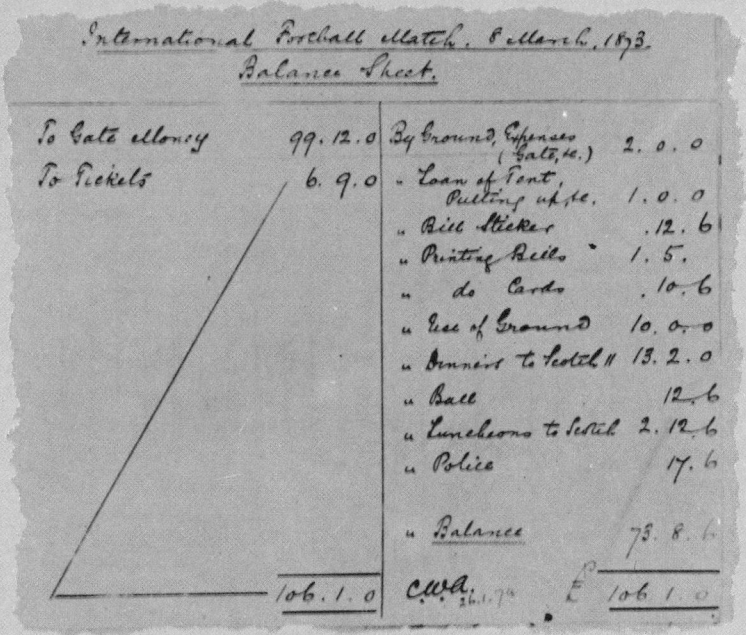

COURTESY OF FOOTBALL ASSOCIATION

Opposite page top The major problem facing the embryonic Football Association was the vast divergence of rules in operation all over the country. At Uppingham in 1862 teams numbered 15-a-side and attacked a goal stretched right across the pitch. Uppingham was one of the first codes to employ a crossbar but, at this time, still penalized kicking at the ball in the air.
Opposite page bottom Organized football arrives. Yet the foundation of the FA warranted just three column inches in The Times of 27 October 1863.
Above The balance sheet from England's very first 'home' international— against Scotland in 1873. The initials CWA are those of Charles Alcock, then secretary of the FA and the man who created the FA Cup competition.
Below Local rivalry in the Midlands. Stoke did not add 'City' until 1925.

STAFFORDSHIRE FOOTBALL ASSOCIATION.

Grand Football Match.

FINAL TIE for COUNTY CHALLENGE CUP,
VALUE 50 GUINEAS.

Winners to receive GOLD MEDALS; Losers, Silver Medals.

STOKE
v.
WEST BROMWICH ALBION.

Stoke Team.		West Bromwich Albion.	
H. WILDIN (Goal).		R. ROBERTS (Goal).	
T. STANFORD,	Backs.	H. BELL,	Backs.
M. MELLOR,		J. STANTON,	
H. R. BROWN,	Half Backs.	E. HORTON,	
F. BETTANY,		F. BUNN,	Half Backs.
F. JOHNSON,		J. WHITE,	
F. POWELL,		H. ASTON,	
G. SHUTT,	Forwards.	J. WHITEHOUSE,	
P. FENNELL,		G. TIMMINS,	
W. MYATT,		G. BELL,	Forwards.
F. BENNETT.		W. BISSEKER.	

Stoke have scored 42 goals to 3; West Brom ... competition. Special trains from all parts. Kick-off at 6 o'clock.
ADMISSION, 6d. and 1s.
AT STOKE, SATURDAY NEXT, APRIL 21st.
Tickets to be obtained on the way to the ground.

West Bromwich Albion have only been beaten once this season, and are in for the Final of the Wednesbury Charity Cup.
Stoke have played 30 matches—won 19, lost 7, drawn 4, and have scored 111 goals and lost 50. They hold the North Stafford Charity Cup for last Season.

ALLBUT AND DANIEL, PERCY STREET PRINTING WORKS, HANLEY

JACKDAW PUBLICATIONS

restriction on the goal at all—as was seen in that first Nottingham match.

The duration of the game had finally been determined at 90 minutes by 1877, and handling the ball had been restricted to the goalkeeper. In addition neutral referees and umpires (later linesmen) were now an established part of the game and even more so a year later when the familiar blast of the referee's whistle was heard for the first time during a match between Nottingham Forest and Sheffield Norfolk. Before 1878 officials had been forced to attract attention in any way they could—usually by waving a handkerchief.

It is never easy defining the exact moment when a new trend affected any discipline. Yet a casual observer could not fail to have been struck by unusual qualities of the 1878-79 FA Cup competition. It was won by Old Etonians, who beat Clapham Rovers 1-0, but there was nothing remarkable in that fact. A glance at the earlier rounds, however, reveals one very significant feature—the success of two provincial clubs. Nottingham Forest reached the semifinals and beat Old Harrovians, the real successors to the previous year's Cup winners Wanderers, who had lost most of their players to the Old Boy's clubs on the way.

But the real interest was reserved for Old Etonians' fourth-round tie with Darwen. The Lancashire side were trailing 5-1 with only 15 minutes left, suddenly came to life with a four-goal burst, and were robbed of their likely reward when the Etonians refused to play extra-time. £175 was raised to dispatch Darwen back to London—the result being a 2-2 draw and a second replay which the southerners won 6-2. Darwen had in their ranks two Scots—James Love and Fergus Suter—who were reputedly two of the first players to 'find money in their boots'. They had first appeared in Darwen as members of a Partick team playing a friendly match, and had been persuaded to stay. Lancashire had made its mark and the tide was on the turn.

Football finally takes hold in the industrial North

Football came late to the major industrial conurbations. Aston Villa came into being in 1874 with neighbours Small Heath (to be renamed Birmingham) following a year later. In Lancashire Blackburn and Bolton both saw the light of day in 1874 and the great Newton Heath side (later Manchester United) was founded at the Lancashire and Yorkshire Railway Company's engine depot of that name in 1878.

It was a time of hope for Lancashire. After the near starvation of the 1860s—when cotton supplies were cut off during the American Civil War—and the economic depression of the early 1870s, an industrial boom was absorbing all who needed work. Immigrants flocked in from the agricultural areas and the Celtic fringes and football turned this to its advantage. Advertisements in the Glasgow papers attracted the Scottish 'professors' who taught the English the 'passing' as opposed to 'dribbling' game. Some teams took on so many

Scots that English players felt positively lonely and it is to this era and not the reign of Shankly at Liverpool that we owe the oft-repeated cry of the overlooked, 'you need to wear a kilt to get into that team.'

There were, of course, inducements. A Scot named J J Lang claimed he was the first ever professional when Sheffield Wednesday paid him to move from Glasgow in 1876. By 1880, while most of the players had other jobs, they received substantial remuneration from playing the game—not unlike the 'shamateurs' of the 1960s and, in consequence, football was taken much more seriously than in the south. The days of the gentlemen amateur were almost over.

The 1881 Cup Final—between Old Etonians and Old Carthusians—was the last of the all-amateur finals and, indeed, the last all-southern Final until Spurs met Chelsea in 1967. Old Carthusians later went on to become the first club to win both the FA Cup (1881) and the Amateur Cup (1894 and 1897).

While Etonians managed to defeat Blackburn Rovers the following year, the inevitable happened in 1883 when Blackburn Olympic became the first club to take the trophy out of the Home Counties. It would have been difficult to devise a better pair of teams to illustrate the differences between the game, and the life, in the South and the North. The Old Etonians speak for themselves—representatives of all that was privileged in the South of England; gentlemen amateurs with the time and income to allow their devotion to the game when they thought fit. Blackburn Olympic came from one of the most industrialized areas in the world at that time —the dingy terraces that crawl like centipedes up and down the valleys of the mid-Lancashire weaving towns breeding many of the players that were not imported from Scotland.

Olympic even had a manager, once a travelling organizer of exhibition matches, one Jack Hunter. Like many managers after him, he took his team away to Blackpool to prepare for the Final. Of the players, two were weavers, one a spinner, one a plumber, one a metal-worker and two had no apparent means of support— apart from football.

The Cup retired to Blackburn for all of four years

'The blossom might be in the South, but the roots are in the North' goes the old economic adage, but in football the reverse was nearer the truth. Had the FA not wisely decided to accept professionalism the game must have developed very differently and might even have fallen into the sad split that has contributed to rugby's never having become a world-wide game. The North could never have competed with the South had it accepted the amateur strictures. A working man at the top of his craft might earn £2 for a six-day week; a farm labourer no more than 15/- (75p) at the time. Without some sort of financial inducement no working man could devote the requisite time and energy to the game. The vital decision was approaching; either the

Top *The North's first FA Cup success—Blackburn Olympic's victory in 1883.* **Above** *The Graphic's impression of the first soccer international in 1872.*

South accepted professionalism and kept the game under a single authority or insisted on the amateur ethic and caused the inevitable split.

As it happened the South had very little say on the field for a long time. The Cup stayed in Blackburn for four years—Blackburn Rovers following up the short-lived Olympic's success and equalling Wanderers' three successive wins. The Old Etonian success in 1882 was the last by a southern club until Spurs dramatic intervention in 1901. In fact, between Etonians' last win and Spurs 'double' in 1961, the Cup returned south on only seven occasions. Oddly enough the next eleven seasons saw six Lon-

don successes.

But to return North. The problem of 'professionalism' so worried the Lancashire FA that they forbade the signing-on of Scots in 1881 and in 1883 Accrington were expelled from the FA for giving an inducement to a particular player. Matters came to a head after a drawn Cup game between Preston North End and Upton Park on 19 January 1884. The London club protested that Preston had paid and played professionals and the Lilywhites were thrown out of the competition. Suspensions on members of the playing staffs followed for Great Lever and Burnley in Lancashire, Walsall and Birming-

ham St George's in the Midlands and Hearts in Scotland.

William Sudell, the founder of Preston North End, proposed the formation of a British Football Association as a result of these suspensions. In October 1884 he received the support of 26 Lancashire clubs plus Aston Villa and Sunderland.

It was a strange forerunner of the similar situation which was to confront the Rugby Union in Huddersfield a decade later, only on the latter occasion the parent body decided that amateurism was more important than unity and the Northern Football Union (Rugby League) was the result.

The *Manchester Guardian* read the crisis of 1884 thus: 'The first effect of any change (the legalization of professionalism) will be to make the Rugby game the aristocratic one, and the Association game will probably almost die out in the south of England, where it is already declining in favour.'

Unity was more important than staying amateur

By the start of the 1885-86 season a special general meeting of the FA had legalized the payment of players, basically on the same lines of those employed in cricket (Alcock was also secretary of Surrey CCC).

But it was not harmony everywhere. The Scots banned all professionals from ever playing north of the border and eventually took things further when, in 1887, they decreed that 'clubs belonging to this (the Scottish) Association shall not be members of any other National Association.'

It was something of a blow for the better Glasgow sides—Queen's Park had reached the Cup Final in 1884 and 1885 and the emerging Rangers had been beaten by Aston Villa in an 1887 semi-final at, of all places, Crewe. It was sad in another way for had the Scots maintained contact for just another year that utopia of so many administrators—a British League—might have come into being.

The Scots, nevertheless, had done a great deal for the English game. Before 1872 it was a 'dribbling' game. The public school boy had been taught to exhibit his individual excellence by simply running at the opposition until he lost the ball. As a result most English sides played with a goalkeeper, two backs and eight 'dribbling' forwards. The early contacts with the Scots showed just how inefficient the English system was. Though Royal Engineers and Sheffield had both been noted for a 'combination' style of operation, it was the Scots who had elevated the 'passing' game to a fine and impressive art, depending more on skill and perception than mere force and speed.

The south quickly adopted the 'passing' game and the first twenty years of organized football thus showed tremendous developments in every direction. The amateur dribblers of the 1860s could no more have lived with the professionals of the 1880s than the average League player in 1950 could have found a place in Arsenal's double winning side of 1971.

It is somehow appropriate that William McGregor, founder and first president of the Football League, should have come from Aston Villa, appropriate because this fine Midland club dominated the early years of the League as no club except the Arsenal of the 30's has done since.

Secure in their vast redbrick mausoleum north of Birmingham—'worth a goal start every home game' one manager said of it—Villa won the Championship six times before the First World War and the FA Cup five times in the same period.

Control of that era fell to very few clubs; primarily Aston Villa and Sunderland, with Manchester United, Newcastle United and the two club sides in both Sheffield and Liverpool providing the main opposition. The first 27 Championships were shared by only ten clubs—those eight plus Preston and Blackburn Rovers. It was to be some years before there was a significant shift of power towards the South. By the end of the First World War, London's trio of Arsenal, Chelsea and Spurs had at last all made their mark and the Southern League was absorbed as the Third Division in 1920.

William McGregor writes his now famous letter

But all this was in the future when Villa director William McGregor sent his famous letter to Blackburn, Bolton, Preston, West Bromwich and the secretary of his own club, Villa, on 2 March 1888. It had become increasingly difficult for the major clubs to guarantee fixtures; opponents either failed to turn up or were forced to complete postponed or replayed cup ties on dates which were already booked. The real concern, of course, was that gates were dropping off as a result. McGregor saw the great need for a definite list of fixtures

£10 REWARD.

STOLEN!

From the Shop Window of W. Shillcock, Football Outfitter, Newtown Row, Birmingham, between the hour of 9-30 p.m. on Wednesday, the 11th September, and 7-30 a.m., on Thursday, the 12th inst., the

ENGLISH CUP,

the property of Aston Villa F.C. The premises were broken into between the hours named, and the Cup, together with cash in drawer, stolen.

The above Reward will be paid for the recovery of the Cup, or for information as may lead to the conviction of the thieves.

Information to be given to the Chief of Police, or to Mr. W. Shillcock, 73, Newtown Row.

—as well as the added attraction of competitive football—which would guarantee spectators the game they expected to see.

The initial meeting was held on the eve of the Cup Final, Friday 23 March 1888, at Anderton's Hotel, in London. McGregor's suggestion for a name, the Association Football Union, was rejected because of a possible confusion with the rugby code while McGregor's own objections to the name Football League (because he thought it would be confused with the unpopular and politically extreme Irish National and Land Leagues) were felt to be irrelevant.

No southern club took any part in the foundation

The business was not concluded until 17 April at the Royal Hotel in Manchester, a far more appropriate setting as no southern club had taken any part in the discussions. There it was found that no more than 22 dates could be set aside for fixtures and the League would therefore have to be confined to 12 members. Thus Nottingham Forest, the Wednesday from Sheffield (who did not adopt the present title until 1929) and a long since defunct Lancashire League club called Halliwell went away empty handed while the remaining 12 became the founder members of the oldest League in the world.

Six were from Lancashire, Accring-

Left In 1895 Aston Villa won the FA Cup—and lost it. It was stolen from a shop window and never recovered. Villa were fined £25, and the money was used to purchase the new trophy.
Below The Aston Villa team that did the Double by winning the FA Cup and First Division Championship in 1897. It was 64 years before the feat was repeated—by Tottenham Hotspur.

JACKDAW PUBLICATIONS

PRESS ASSOCIATION

15

RADIO TIMES HULTON PICTURE LIBRARY

ton, Blackburn Rovers, Bolton Wanderers, Burnley, Everton and Preston North End, five from the loosely-defined Midlands, Aston Villa, Derby County, Notts County, West Bromwich Albion and Wolverhampton Wanderers and one, Stoke, came from the no-man's-land between the two. The twelve have been remarkably durable—only Accrington and Notts County spending the greater part of the first 80 years outside the First Division.

'Proud Preston' get through a season without defeat

McGregor explained: 'It appeared to me that a fixed programme of home-and-away matches between the leading clubs in the country, such fixtures to be kept inviolate, would produce football of a far more interesting nature than we then saw.' It was a fitting prologue.

The first season was dominated by Preston North End; 'Proud Preston', the 'Old Invincibles' that had emerged from the North End Cricket Club in 1881 and whose president was the William Sudell who had forced the professionalism issue with his openly illegal payments.

Sudell's team consisted largely of talented Scots, but in John Goodall he had the finest English centre-

forward of his day. Preston's inaugural double was completed without losing a game in the League or conceding a goal in the Cup. They thus became the first—and most likely the last—League side to go through a season without losing a game. But it was a brief flowering. Though they won the Championship the following season, Preston have not won it since, and have only one other Cup success to their credit, in 1938, and then it took a last minute penalty which went in off the bar to take a trophy back to Deepdale.

The Aston Villa story has its similarities, but they were always a far grander club than Preston. Between 1892 and 1905 Villa won five Championships and reached four Cup Finals, winning three of them. That included a double—in 1896-97— which, for 64 years, seemed destined to be the last of all time. Despite all the trophies they won in this period Villa are probably better remembered for one they lost—the FA Cup. After beating neighbours West Bromwich in the 1895 Final, Villa allowed a local boot and shoe manufacturer, William Shillcock, to display it in his shop window. It disappeared on the night of 11 September, and never reappeared in any recognizable form. The FA fined Villa £25, and used the money to buy a new trophy.

The midlanders' great rivals in this period were Sunderland. The

north-easterners' rise to fame was astonishingly fast. They relied on Scottish players who cost them no more than a signing-on fee, but the most famous Scotsman to join their ranks proved more expensive. Ned Doig—Arbroath's goalkeeper—was deemed ineligible after his first match, and Sunderland forfeited £50 and two points. The problem was resolved, and Doig proved his worth —between the start of the 1890-91 and 1896-97 seasons they lost only one home game. The results of such defensive excellence were the League Championships of 1892, 1893 and 1895, followed by further successes in 1902 and 1913.

Villa were beaten by a dream that came true

On the last of those five occasions Sunderland finally managed to reach their first Cup Final—only to see their double hopes disappear with a Tom Barber header that gave the trophy to rivals Villa. Early on in the game Clem Stephenson—the Villa forward who was later to captain the great Huddersfield side of the 1920s —told Sunderland's Charlie Buchan that he had dreamed Barber would head the only goal. As well as being accurate it was appropriate—neither club had much more than dreams to

live on for the next 60 years.

The Cup had been growing in importance since the founding of the League. By 1893 Surrey County Cricket Club, worried about the size of the crowds, had to withdraw the Oval as the venue and that year the Final was played at Fallowfield, Manchester. The official attendance was 45,000, though at least twice that number managed to get in. Wolves won for the first time, defeating Everton, despite having lost a League game 4-2 to a team of Everton reserves the previous week. The 1894 Final was played at Goodison, Notts County becoming the first Second Division side to take the trophy, but the season after that the wide open spaces of Crystal Palace staged the game for the first time.

Londoners still tended to be a little scathing about the whole event. This was partially because of the sudden invasion from the alien North ('a northern horde of uncouth garb and strange oaths' as the Pall Mall Gazette described Blackburn Rovers' supporters in 1885), but largely because southern clubs had little say in affairs.

But in 1901 Tottenham Hotspur, of the Southern League, became the first and only non-Football League team to win a post-1888 Cup Final— and an amazing affair it turned out to be. The 114,815 crowd still stands as the third largest attendance (after

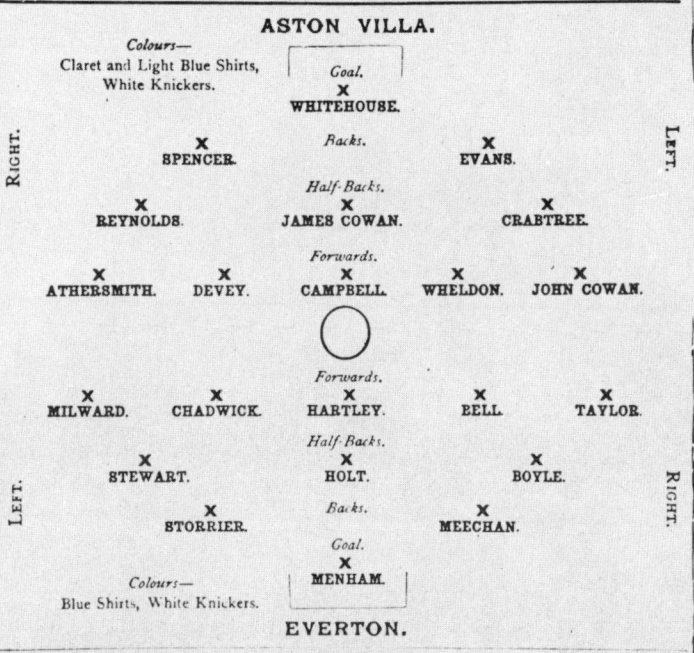

NOTHING BETTER THAN
John Piggott's Cup Tie Football PRICE 9/3

JOHN PIGGOTT.
Please send for my Football and General Lists.
117, CHEAPSIDE, AND MILK STREET, E.C.

HIT OF THE SEASON.
John Piggott's Surrey Driver Bat PRICE 15/9

SCOTCH WHISKY,
"BERTRAM BLEND."
EIGHT YEARS OLD.
Per 42/- Dozen.
Bottles and Case included.
Sample Flasks on the Ground, 1/-.
BERTRAM & CO., LONDON & LEITH, N.B.

MANFIELD'S BOOTS.

WHITE **CRICKET** BOOTS,
WITH STOUT DAMP-PROOF SOLES.
LEATHER LINED. 13/6.

THE "M" **CYCLING** SHOES,
4/11, 5/11, 8/11, 10/6.
PHOTO PRICE LISTS FREE.
SAMPLE PAIR POST FREE.

67 & 68, CHEAPSIDE; 376 & 377, STRAND,
ETC., ETC.
AND IN ALL LARGE TOWNS.

**WELCOME ALWAYS,
KEEP IT HANDY,
GRANT'S MORELLA
CHERRY BRANDY.**
The best Tonic for Football Players
(See Captain Boyton's letter.)
MOST COMFORTING IN CHILLY WEATHER.
Ask for GRANT'S and don't be put off with
inferior makes.

CRYSTAL PALACE.
Saturday, April 10th, 1897.
FINAL TIE
FOR THE
CHALLENGE CUP of the FOOTBALL ASSOCIATION.

ASTON VILLA.
Colours—
Claret and Light Blue Shirts,
White Knickers.

Goal.
X
WHITEHOUSE.

RIGHT.   LEFT.

Backs.
X   X
SPENCER.   EVANS.

Half-Backs.
X   X   X
REYNOLDS.   JAMES COWAN.   CRABTREE.

Forwards.
X   X   X   X   X
ATHERSMITH. DEVEY. CAMPBELL. WHELDON. JOHN COWAN.

◯

Forwards.
X   X   X   X   X
MILWARD. CHADWICK. HARTLEY. BELL.   TAYLOR.

Half-Backs.
X   X   X
STEWART.   HOLT.   BOYLE.

LEFT.   RIGHT.

Backs.
X   X
STORRIER.   MEECHAN.

Goal.
X
MENHAM.

Colours—
Blue Shirts, White Knickers.

EVERTON.

Referee—J. LEWIS (Lancashire).   Linesmen—J. HOWCROFT (Redcar).   A. SCRAGG (Crewe).

Official Programme.   ONE PENNY.

ELLIMAN'S FOR BRUISES

ACHES AND PAINS.
Miss ROSE ALPHONSINE, Spiral Ascensionist, writes:
"When doing my Spiral Ascension at the Jardin de
Paris my feet and knees became swollen and very sore.
I tried your Embrocation, and after two good rubbings
I was able to perform. I now use it after every ascension,
and will always keep same by me."
23, Helix Gardens, Brixton Hill, S.W., London,
October 29th, 1894.

1d. ARE YOU A FOOTBALLER? 1d.
We presume so, or you wouldn't
be at this Match!

Perhaps you also run a bike?
WELL
SPORTS
IS THE PAPER YOU WANT.
(Illustrated. 32 pages.)
People Swear by it,
Rivals Swear at it,
Agents Pant for it.
The Public Fight for it.
And you can Buy it EVERYWHERE.
Nothing succeeds like ——
SPORTS!

CARTERS
Used at Lord's, Oval,
Crystal Palace, Aston Villa, etc.
GRASS
237, 238, & 87,
HIGH HOLBORN, LONDON.
LISTS POST FREE
SEEDS.

Spurs of the Southern League win the FA Cup

As *The Times*, in typically subdued fashion, said, '. . . the result was not a true reflection of the run of the game. The second goal by Sheffield was the chief incident of the match. Clawley (the Spurs goalkeeper) fumbled a shot slightly but got it away. The referee decided that the ball was over the line and therefore a goal. Clawley says that this was impossible as he must have been behind his line for a goal to have been scored . . .' Most of the crowd it seemed, agreed with Clawley. The game ended at 2-2, but justice was seen to be done at Bolton when Spurs won the replay 3-1. To be fair, the Spurs team consisted of one Irishman, two Welshmen, three northern-Englishmen and five Scots and can hardly be credited with reviving football south of the Trent.

That distinction belongs more fairly to Arsenal. Founded in 1886 by a Scotsman called David Danskin and a group of workmates at the Woolwich Arsenal, the club was originally called Dial Square. The name was changed to Royal Arsenal, then Woolwich Arsenal, The Arsenal and, finally, plain Arsenal. Adopting professionalism in 1891, they found that the southern opposition was simply not strong enough and began to organize fixtures against teams from further north. In 1893 Arsenal became the first southern club to be elected to the Football League.

In 1892 the League had absorbed the rival Football Alliance and now had two divisions and 28 clubs, none south of Birmingham. Until 1898 there was no automatic system of promotion and relegation—the bottom clubs in the First Division and the top clubs in the Second playing 'test' matches to decide which were worthy of the premier places. In that year Stoke and Burnley reasoned that a draw in the last of these test matches would give them both First Division places. The resulting goalless game aroused more than a few suspicions and the system was abolished.

Arsenal's election to the Second Division in 1893 was followed by promotion to the First eleven years later. The subsequent relegation in 1913 proved a blessing in disguise for it led to Henry Norris, then chairman of Fulham, taking an interest in the club. He persuaded them to move right across London, from south of the river Plumstead to Highbury. Their arrival incurred the wrath not only of the local residents, who thought Arsenal an utterly undesirable neighbour, but of nearby Tottenham, to whom the Gunners were not only undesirable but a positive threat.

Norris's machinations gained Arsenal admittance to the First Division after the First World War and joining them were the third of London's great trio, Chelsea. Created out of nothing by the son of a builder —H. A. Mears—Chelsea FC started with a ground in 1905, bought a team and then began looking for someone to play.

The League took in Chelsea—as a brand new club

The Football League were somehow persuaded that it was in their best interests to take in a club that had yet to play a game—and in two years Chelsea had been promoted. 'Chelsea will stagger humanity!' wrote one journalist—though he was referring to the ground. Built in the style of the great Glasgow stadia, with hopes that it would hold 100,000, Stamford Bridge was privileged to hold the first three post-war Cup Finals but has rarely staggered anyone. In fact it had few rivals as the least appealing of the First Division grounds over 60 years later.

The same could never be said about

Left A cavalcade of fans leaving Kingsway, London, bound for the Cup Final of 1906, between Everton and Newcastle United, staged at Crystal Palace. Everton won the game 1-0.
Above The programme of the historic 1897 Cup Final which gave Aston Villa the Double. They beat Everton 3-2. Campbell, Devey and Crabtree scored for Villa, Bell and Hartley for Everton.

Manchester United's new stadium. In 1910 they finally moved across Manchester from Clayton—where the grandstand expressed its dismay and collapsed soon afterwards—to Old Trafford where, bettering Chelsea, it was hoped to seat 100,000. United had finally emerged as the major force they were to remain, winning the League in 1908 and 1911 and the Cup in 1909. The quality of Old Trafford was also soon realized. It staged the 'Khaki' Final (so called because of all the soldiers in the crowd) in 1915, the only time in the twentieth century that the Final has been initially fought for outside London.

The last few years before the First World War have aptly been called 'those strange years of hysteria'. Though Victoria was dead, the era contained the dying vestiges of Victoriana. All in all, it was a very bizarre period. These were the years of the suffragettes, the first great

the 1913 and 1923 Finals) at a football match under any code in England and they were treated to one of football's most celebrated disputed goals.

nationwide strikes, a state of open warfare between the political parties over Ireland, the first feeble attempts to create a welfare state and, of course, the inexorable approach of the corporate madness that was the First World War. In its small, strange way football somehow managed to reflect the atmosphere of that era.

When Oldham almost won the Championship

If Oldham Athletic, of all clubs, had won their last game of the 1914-15 season they would have become League Champions. In the Cup Bristol City were finalists in 1909, Barnsley in 1910 and then Bradford City and Barnsley both won the trophy, in 1911 and 1912. None of those four clubs had done anything of note before and none has done anything since. It was a strange time, but it was also a tribute to the strength in depth of the football of the times and a comment on the inability of the bigger clubs—like Villa—to automatically buy success.

There were replays in 1910, 1911 and 1912 and extra time was therefore instituted in 1913. It was fifty-eight years before another replay was needed. Another reflection of the mood of the times was the re-establishment of the Football Players and Trainers' Union. Though the players joined the Federation of Trades Unions in 1909 the Football Association remained violently opposed to any form of organized labour within football. This was a fair indication of the politics of that august body, but, to be fair, there were grounds for fears that football might unwittingly be involved in a

general strike. Several players, notably Charlie Roberts of Manchester United, felt that their international careers suffered because of support for the FPTU for the Football Association did not look lightly on the strike that was threatened for the beginning of the 1909-10 season. Most League clubs signed enough amateurs to be sure of fulfilling their fixtures, but nothing came of the threat and the union's real strength can be gauged from the maximum wage legislation, introduced in 1901, which remained in existence until the Eastham case a full six decades later.

A basic structure that has lasted for over 50 years

After the war, in 1920, the Southern League, founded by the professional club at Millwall, became the new Third Division. A year later a northern section was added, initially of 20 clubs but increased to 22 in 1923 and the League structure still in existence half a century later had been established.

Centre A Sunderland team line-up reproduced on a lapel badge for the Supporters Club. This was one of the earliest occurrences of what was to become a popular feature 60 years later. The north-easterners were second only to Aston Villa in the pre-First World War era. Depending largely on Scots who cost no more than a signing-on fee they won the League for the fourth time in 1902.
Below The legendary Billy Meredith (centre) in action for Manchester United against Queen's Park Rangers in September 1908.

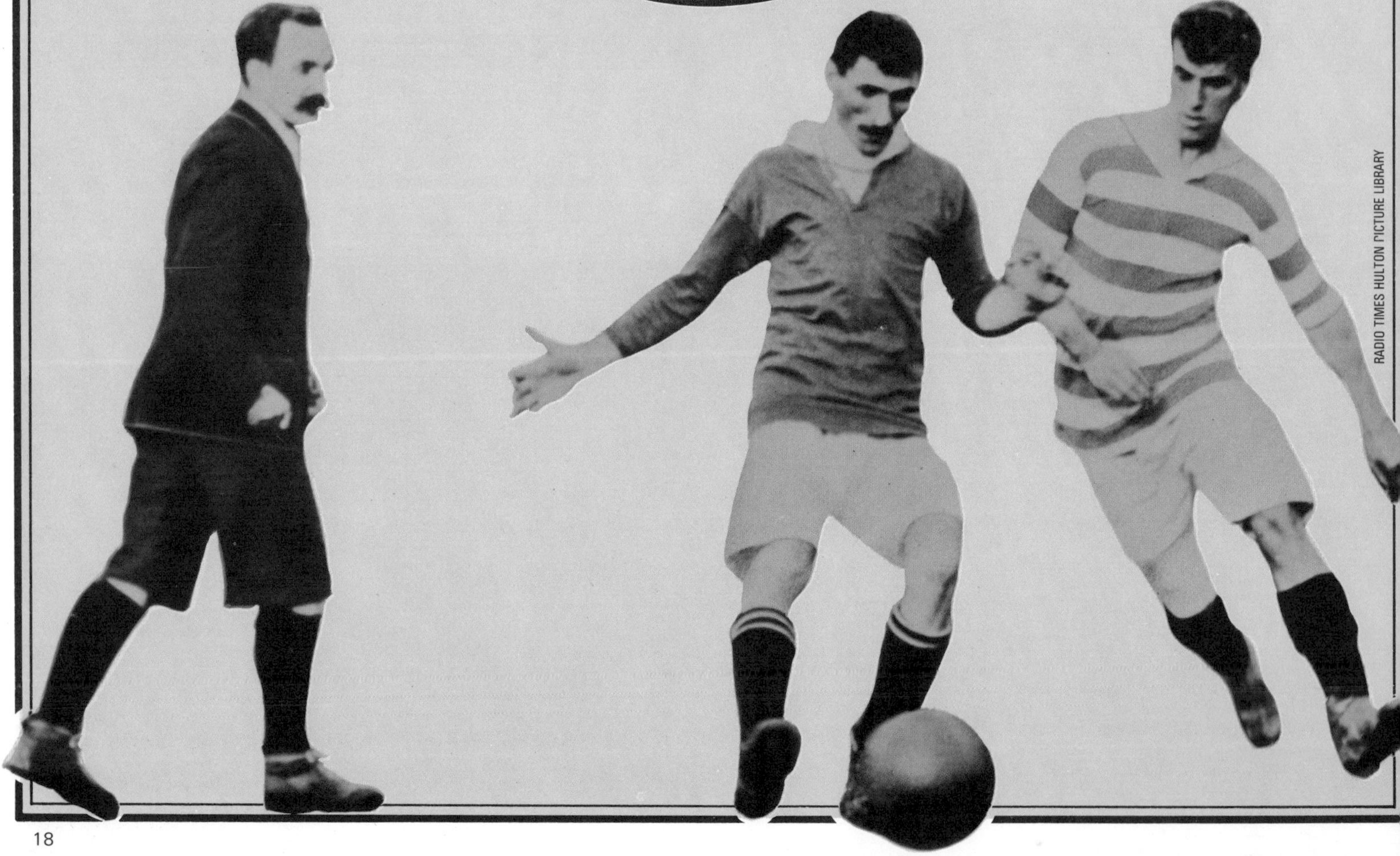

THE GROWTH OF THE FOOTBALL LEAGUE

Period	Seasons	I	II	III	IIIN	IIIS	IV	Total
1888-91	3	12						12
1891-92	1	14						14
1892-93	1	16	12					28
1893-94	1	16	15					31
1894-98	4	16	16					32
1898-05	7	18	18					36
1905-15	10	20	20					40
1919-20	1	22	22					44
1920-21	1	22	22	22				66
1921-23	2	22	22		20	22		86
1923-39	16	22	22		22	22		88
1946-50	4	22	22		22	22		88
1950-58	8	22	22		24	24		92
1958-74	16	22	22	24			24	92
	75							

SUNDERLAND F.C. 1901-2

BY COURTESY OF WILLIAM HEINEMANN LIMITED

RADIO TIMES HULTON PICTURE LIBRARY

The history of Scottish football, to be brutal, is the history of three very great clubs, of an epic series of internationals against the old enemy England, of a constant stream of talent leaving the country for richer rewards south of the border, and of very little else.

Despite occasional flashes from lesser clubs, Celtic and Rangers have dominated the field since the 1890s. And before the turn of the century, Queen's Park, perhaps the greatest amateur football club of all time, *was* Scottish football. They organized football north of the border from the first; excelled at it; beat the English, virtually on their own, time and again, and stamped their high-principled personality on the Scottish game.

Football had flourished in Scotland, of course, long before Queen's Park Football Club was founded. The Scottish game had grown in concert with that of Wales and Ireland and the English countryside, a game of violent celtic fervour characterized by uncompromising battles between neighbouring villages—clan against clan, as often as not, and with plenty of heads broken in the process.

As in England, the game provoked its share of royal disfavour. James I, James II, James III and James IV liberally scattered statutes banning football across the 15th century, and James VI, on ascending the English throne, expressly forbade his son Henry from 'rough and violent exercises at the foot-ball'. (James V was a notable absentee from this bunch of anti-football monarchs, but then he was only one year old when he succeeded to the throne.) Yet football never lost its popularity. By the beginning of the 19th century, while the schools were beginning to take up the game in England, Scottish football found a working champion in the novelist Sir Walter Scott, a fervent supporter of the traditional inter-village game.

'The old clannish spirit is too apt to break out'

Indeed, Scott was himself much in evidence at the most famous of all the matches to be held in football's Dark Ages north of the border. Sir Walter not only backed (financially) the Men of Selkirk against the Men of Yarrow (themselves backed, incidentally, by the Earl of Home)—he also wrote a ballad specially for the day. The game (in two legs, rather like the European Cup) ended even—one leg each; and the food and drink lying ready for the teams dissuaded them from playing a decider. At this date (1815), though, football in Scotland was generally recognized to be in decline, and even Scott himself was declaring that 'it was not always safe to have even the game of football between villages; the old clannish spirit is too apt to break out.'

Nevertheless, football survived in Scotland not through the influence of the public schools as it did in the south of England, but through the young artisans and professional men who recognized the game for the simple, energetic and enjoyable

Scotland before the old firm

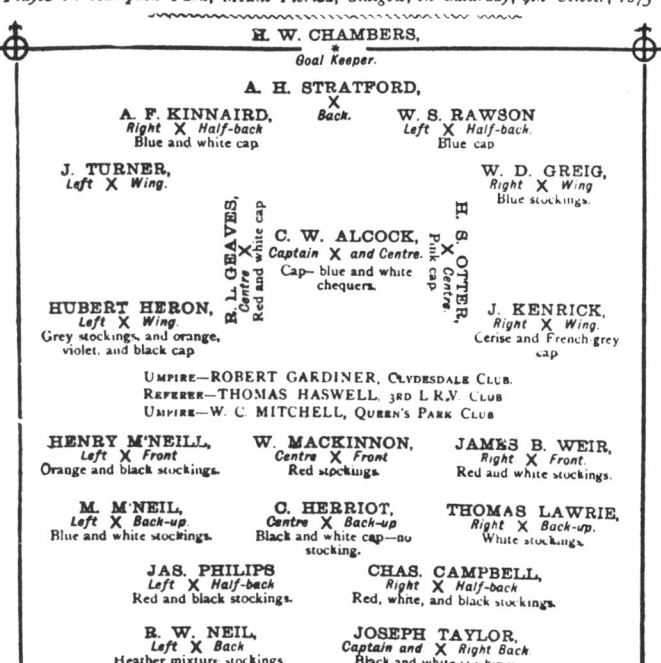

Top *A ticket for the first international football match, at Partick in 1872.*
Above *The programme for an 1875 friendly between Queen's Park and the Wanderers. As players did not wear numbers, they were identified by the colour of their caps or stockings. Queen's Park, despite their strange 2-2-3-3 formation had still not lost a game since their formation 8 years earlier.*

pastime that it was. The game had its greatest following in the industrial areas of Scotland's central lowlands, and in Glasgow the keenest players eventually gravitated, in the mid 1860s, to one of the city's three public parks—Queen's Park.

On 9 July 1867, together with YMCA members and caber-tossing Highlanders who also used the park for recreation, they met to form the 'Queen's Park Football Club', thus

officially establishing the game in Scotland and founding a tradition in Glasgow which, for single-minded fanaticism, would be difficult to parallel anywhere but in Rio de Janeiro.

The early history of Queen's Park is one of virtually undiluted success. Between their formation in 1867 and 1872 not a single goal was scored against them; they did not lose a single match until February 1876, when they were beaten by London's Wanderers, and only in December of the same year, by which time Scottish competition had become extremely fierce, did they go down at home.

Queen's Park lay down their own rules

In the very early years, Queen's Park were so dominant that not only did they attract the best players and consequently the best results—they also laid down the rules, which were obediently followed by early local opponents such as Thistle, Hamilton Gymnasium and Airdrie (all of whom, incidentally, played their football in the summer months).

In 1870, however, Queen's Park's reputation ensured the acceptance of Scottish football on the national map. Charles Alcock, the recently elected Secretary of the FA wrote a letter to the *Glasgow Herald* announcing that teams of English and Scottish players were to meet at Kennington Oval (the headquarters of Surrey County Cricket Club, but then also the premier football ground in London). He invited nominations from Scotland with a stirring call to arms: 'In Scotland, once essentially the land of football, there should still be a spark left of the old fire, and I confidently appeal to Scotsmen.... etc. etc.'

It was a stroke of genius on Alcock's part. No one, least of all a gentleman footballer, could resist a provocative challenge like that. Queen's Park nominated one Robert Smith, a member of a famous Queen's Park family now based in London, as their player, and the teams met on 19 November 1870, England winning 1-0.

This was not, as yet, international football, or anything like it. The Scottish team was in reality composed of a lot of well-heeled young men who owed family name and background to Scotland, but who were all living in or near, London, and had time on their hands. One of their number was an Old Rugbeian, who had presumably learnt his football in the handling tradition; another was the son of the Prime Minister W E Gladstone, and was himself an MP at the time of the match; yet another was Quintin Hogg, the grandfather of a later Lord Chancellor.

And, most illustrious of all, the Old Etonian A F Kinnaird, aristocrat, football patriarch, successful banker, later Lord High Commissioner of the Church of Scotland—and a football fanatic, who played whenever he possibly could, and whose personality swayed the Football Association for five decades. His influence on the game is

19

incalculable; that it came unscathed through the early troubled years of professionalism into the heyday of popularity in the years before World War I is in considerable part due to this remarkable Scot and his 33 years as President of the Football Association.

This first encounter between 'England' and 'London Scottish', was followed by repeat performances on roughly the same lines, twice in 1871 (a 1-1 draw and 2-1 win to 'England') and once in February 1872 (1-0 to 'England'). .

It was the Queen's Park visit to London for the semi-final of the first FA Cup competition that really formalized inter-national football. Donating a guinea (one sixth of that year's income) toward the purchase of the Cup, Queen's Park drew with Wanderers but could not afford to return for a replay. Nevertheless their style impressed everyone present and also made them aware that the 400 mile journey was not only feasible but might even be worthwhile. The result was the very first football international, played in 1872.

Alcock and Kinnaird probably had most to do with arranging the trip north—Alcock was originally chosen to play for England and Kinnaird for Scotland though neither actually performed—but, looking back, the most interesting feature was the patronizing attitude of the Londoners—that England were going north to show the Scots how to play the game.

Nothing could have been further from reality. Sadly lacking is a photograph of the teams—the players would not promise to buy prints so the official photographer refused to take any frames. At Kennington the following year there was more trouble over photographs —on that occasion they never materialized because the England players insisted on pulling faces.

The match was played at the West of Scotland Cricket Club's ground in Partick. The Scots included nine Queen's Park men (and two more, the brothers Smith, who had played for the club before moving to London a couple of seasons earlier). This provided an understanding between players that the scratch English team could not match, but skilfully though the Scotsmen played, neither side could score— and so the first England-Scotland match ended in a goalless draw. (It happened only twice more in the next century—in 1942 and in 1970).

A shilling entrance but 4,000 still came to watch

The success of the encounter— 4,000 spectators turned up, 'including many ladies'—led Queen's Park to search for a suitable ground to play further fixtures. The following season Glasgow Town Council agreed to let 'Hampden Park, Mount Florida' to the club. Ten years later railway construction forced them to move to another site in Hampden Park. The present stadium was completed on yet another site in 1903.

In the spring of 1873, Scotland travelled south to take on the English giants at Kennington. Again the majority of their side was composed of Queen's Park men and again the crowd was enormous by contemporary standards, 3,000 of them at a shilling a head. They saw a splendidly contested match, with England's powerful dribbling earning them a 2-0 lead, which Scotland equalized only to allow England to score twice more in the closing stages.

The following year, 1874, was a great one for Scottish football. In the first place, Scotland now had its own Football Association, formed in 1873 not specifically to run football north of the border (Queen's Park were doing that very effectively at that time without help from outside), but to institute their own cup competition for the 1873-4 season. Of the original eight SFA members, only Queen's Park now survives (the others were Clydesdale, Dumbreck, Easter, Granville, Rovers, Vale of Leven, and Third Lanark, the last to fade away as late as 1967). There were 16 entrants for the first Scottish Cup, which in 1874 was duly won by Queen's Park, as it was in the two following seasons as well.

And, on 7 March 1874, the Scots defeated England. There were 7000 spectators to watch the 2-1 triumph, and a game which, by all accounts, was notable for its 'beautiful and scientific play'. The English, as usual, excelled in individual brilliance. The Scots, also as usual, knew each other's play (seven men from Queen's Park), and bewildered their opponents with their accurate, defence-splitting passes. The home side's winning goal was described as '. . . a scene which can never be forgotten as long as internationals are played'; Harry McNeil, the midfield wizard, was carried shoulder-high to the pavilion; and the first of Scottish football's 'finest hours' was complete.

The pattern was to be repeated in the coming few years, all too often for the self respect of the English clubs. The two countries drew in 1875, Scotland won 3-0 in 1876, beat England in England for the first time in 1877, and thrashed them 7-2 at Hampden in 1878. Of the first eleven matches, from 1872 to 1882, England won two and Scotland seven; on four occasions Scotland scored five or more goals. There was no doubt about it, the Scots had taken on England at their own game and made them look silly.

Both sides were still, of course, amateur but Scotland were playing like professionals. There will always be a dispute about who first developed the passing game—the great Royal Engineers club, which had many successful seasons in London football in the 70s and 80s, claim some credit for 'the combination game', and Sheffield were also early to discover the weaknesses of the individualistic dribbling method, with eight forwards, one half-back, one back and one goalkeeper.

The passing game— not only effective but attractive too

But it is traditionally held that Queen's Park were the first club to perfect football as a *team* game, rather than a game played by a group of individuals. And while the English gentlemen footballers of the 70s and 80s were still vainly dribbling solo at the opposing defenders—just as they had done at school—their undoubted skills were quite impotent when faced with the understanding and team work built up by the Glaswegians.

And this skilled passing game was not only effective, it was attractive too for it increased the scope of the game and the speed of the attacks, and it led to more goals. No wonder they were packing 12,000 into Hampden Park for the internationals as early as 1880.

The popularity of football in Scotland at the start of the 1880s,

Above The Queen's Park side that won the first Scottish Cup in 1874.
Opposite top The Oval was the venue of the England-Scotland match for some years. Here England attack during the 1877 match—the first one they lost at home, Scotland winning 3-1.
Opposite bottom Dumbarton challenge Queen's Park in 1883. The Dunbartonshire side were one of the strongest in Scotland before 1900, winning two League Championships.

and the skill of the young footballers who flocked to the new clubs—long-forgotten names like Renton and Oxford Glasgow, still-familiar ones like Kilmarnock and Dumbarton—transformed the game. The non-London clubs were demanding universal laws. Rules for goal-kicks and corners were regularized into the form they have today; handling the ball was reserved for the goalkeeper alone; free kicks for infringements were accepted. After a series of squabbles between English and Scottish clubs, the Scottish throw-in was adopted all over the country.

Whereas before the English rule had allowed a one-armed hurl when the ball went out of play, the Scottish had favoured a two-armed throw from behind the head. Before the 1880 match the English refused to take the field unless the referee, a Mr Hamilton, agreed to let them take throws as they liked. He agreed, but as soon as the whistle had blown obviously suffered a kind of selective amnesia which led to him allowing only the 'Scottish' throw—basically that which we know today.

The rules were settled more or less amicably. The dispute over professionalism was not. The rumblings began at the end of the 1870s: rumours started over the alleged payment of players by some of the northern English clubs, and by the early 1880s a full-scale row was brewing. Teams with unashamed working-class origins were making themselves felt, especially as in many

tackling and foul temper. The next year (after a club called Rangers had reached the semi-finals of the FA Cup before going down to Aston Villa), the Scottish Association decreed that '. . . clubs belonging to this association shall not be members of any other national association.' Scotland had broken away, just as it seemed that the still-amateur South of England might be proposing to form a British League.

When the Scots decreed that they should separate

The decision of the Scottish clubs to form a Scottish League in 1891 (and so grant two seasons of glory to Dumbarton, who won the first two Championships) heralded the end of the first chapter in Scottish football. Although professionalism was still banned (until 1893, when the SFA bowed to the inevitable), payments to League players were made quite openly; Queen's Park, still fiercely amateur, refused to join the league until 1900, and the relentless advance of the hard, working-class clubs finally overshadowed these Scottish aristocrats. In 1896, the first year in which the 'Anglos' (the Scottish professionals playing in the English League) were allowed to be selected for Scotland, Queen's Park, for the first time, provided only one member of Scotland's team. But the balance was restored, Scotland's sorry run ended, and they started winning again. And there were 50,000 supporters there to see it.

For Queen's Park it had been a glorious run. In the years between their formation in 1867 and the coming of professionalism, they had, virtually alone, run Scottish football. Losing in two consecutive Finals, they had come closer than any Scottish team to taking the coveted FA Cup out of England; they had, again virtually alone, provided international teams to humble England; they had won the Scottish Cup nine times.

They had provided Scottish crowds with an attractive and fast-moving game which was supported with all the fervour of a new religion. What is more, it grew unopposed. Cricket had never really thrived in Scotland, and rugby was even more haughtily upper-class in Edinburgh and the Borders than it was in southern England. And against all odds and all predictions Queen's Park have remained both amateur and, relatively, talented. In the 1890s, with the advent of professionalism, Celtic and Rangers took over the commanding heights of Scottish football and, sadly perhaps, have shared the battle for supremacy ever since.

The Glaswegian duo owe a lot to Queen's Park—not least for the ground where they regularly contest cup finals and play their more attractive European club matches. And it is a profound commentary on the changing fortunes of a football club that Queen's Park, with a ground that has held 150,000, consider themselves to have a good attendance if they play before one-hundredth of that number.

parts of the country factories and offices were beginning to close after noon on Saturday, allowing the working man a full half-day's leisure every week. And the teams emerging in the North of England—Darwen and Preston, Blackburn and Accrington—often fielded more Scots than Englishmen.

At first, perhaps, the chance of a job in the prosperous factories of Lancashire was as much a lure as the prospect of a weekly shilling or two for playing football, but soon the northern clubs were competing for the services of the Scottish football names and talent scouts were scouring the parks of Glasgow for a likely catch.

The prevailing attitude towards both professionalism and Scots is best illustrated by the infamous story about Major Marindin, referee of the 1887 semi-final between West Brom and Preston. The midlanders won 3-1 and after the game Marindin asked whether they were all English. On being told the team had no Scots Marindin said 'Well then, I am pleased to present you with the ball . . . . I hope you win the Cup.' They didn't, losing to an Aston Villa led by a Scotsman, 2-0.

In 1885 England accepted professionalism, under strict supervision. Scotland held out against it for another eight years. It was a bad time for Scottish football. On the one hand their strong ideological principles forced them to reject the idea of paying sportsmen money; on the other, they saw quite clearly that

the English clubs were ready to snap up those footballers whose principles were less rigid, and Scottish football could only suffer in consequence.

The return of the Anglos—and the return of success

It is surprising, in fact, and a tribute to the deep wells of talent to be tapped in the Scottish Lowlands in those days, that the effect was not worse. The professionalism crisis soured the FA Cup, and the Scottish clubs who still competed. In 1886, the professionals of the fast-rising Preston North End thrashed the amateur Queen's Park 3-0 in Glasgow, and in a game of brutal

RANGERS FC

CELTIC FC

ALL OTHER TEAMS

SCOTTISH FA CUP 1893-73

Rangers: 20   Celtic: 21

LEAGUE CHAMPIONSHIP 1893-73

Celtic: 27   Rangers: 33

LEAGUE CUP 1946-73

Rangers: 7   Celtic: 7

THE STORY OF FOOTBALL

And the rest came nowhere

'You might as well attempt to stop the flow of Niagara with a kitchen chair as to endeavour to stem the tide of professionalism,' said the leading voice of one of the factions at the 1893 AGM of the Scottish Football Association. The speaker was J H McLaughlin of Celtic, a prime advocate of the issue at question, the legalization of professionalism in Scotland.

At that meeting—the third inside a year when the question of allowing professionalism was the main item on the agenda—the motion was finally carried. And from that day in May, the story of Scottish football has virtually become the story of Rangers and Celtic. Indeed, of the next 73 Scottish First Division championships contested, only seven different clubs on only 13 occasions took the title away from Glasgow's 'Old Firm.'

Looking back on the first day of 1974, a casual observer would see

that from 1893 Rangers and Celtic had been champions 60 times— Rangers 33, Celtic 27; their records in the Scottish Cup would be hardly less impressive—41 times they had lifted the trophy out of a possible 68 since the birth of professionalism, Celtic with 21 wins and Rangers 20.

Those figures reflect a situation that was prophesied as far back as 1890 by the almost clairvoyant members of the club which is now the last bastion of amateurism in the senior British game, Queen's Park.

In an aptly titled book, 'The Game for the Game's Sake' (the history of Queen's Park), Glasgow author Robert Crampsey depicts clearly and concisely the attitude of the Hampden club to professionalism at the time: 'Queen's also saw, and warned, that the certain effect of a moneyed game within Scotland would be to tip the scales far too heavily in favour of the big city clubs. As long as those intangible things

called honour and prestige were all that were at stake then a local lad might just as well play for his village or small town with which he at least had an affinity. Pay him, and he would sell his sword to the highest bidder.'

Queen's Park, of course, had a lot to lose. Up to the inception of legalized payments, they had been top dogs in Scotland, if not Britain. But it wasn't a mercenary urge to maintain their status that motivated a fierce opposition to professionalism. They were sincerely worried about the effect of financial incentives on the game in Scotland in general. Apart from their prediction about the 'big city clubs' (which they, to an extent, certainly were) they also foresaw the exodus to England, and the reaping of higher rewards available in a far more heavily-populated country, by the cream of Scotland's talent.

The principles which moved the members of Queen's at the time bear the closest scrutiny. Even before payments were legalized, many clubs were obviously practising a form of professionalism. Players would be paid for time off work and for travelling expenses, with sums that clearly exceeded what they were actually due. Queen's Park never did—and indeed still do not—hold with that sort of thing.

And while Queen's Park remained a drawing power right up till the Second World War—and old-time Hampdenites still talk nostalgic-

Above The two-horse race that has been Scottish football since the advent of professionalism in May 1893. Before that date the 'old firm' won only one of the first 20 Scottish Cup competitions. Aberdeen presented the most potent threat to the duo during the 1960s; *above right* Andy Georgehan, the Dons' keeper, loses the ball to Colin Stein at Ibrox while *right* Aberdeen captain Martin Buchan is effectively dispossessed by Celtic's Billy McNeill. By the end of the decade Aberdeen had not won a single trophy.

ally of the 'great' Queen's team of the late twenties—it is a fact that since 1893, when they held the Scottish Cup, they have not won a single major trophy.

So the signs of what was to come were manifestly clear to some way back at the very birth of professionalism. Fortunately Queen's Park were only partially right, for Aberdeen, the two Dundee clubs, Hearts and Hibs are also 'big city clubs'. So why have they never enjoyed a protracted run of success? And since there were six First Division teams in Glasgow—none of them, theoretically at least, enjoying a proportionate population advantage over the other cities—why have Partick Thistle, Clyde, Queen's Park and Third Lanark (sadly now defunct) not even taken a minor share of the 'Old Firm's' success?

The answer—in a word—must be religion. Rangers and Celtic very quickly became more than just foot-

Queen's Park	1893
St Bernard's	1895
Hearts	1896, 1901, 1906, 1956
Hibernian	1902
Third Lanark	1905
Dundee	1910
Falkirk	1913, 1957
Kilmarnock	1920, 1929
Partick Thistle	1921
Morton	1922
Airdrieonians	1924
St Mirren	1926, 1959
East Fife	1938
Clyde	1939, 1955, 1958
Aberdeen	1947, 1970
Motherwell	1952
Dunfermline	1961, 1968

Hearts	1894-95, 1896-97, 1957-58, 1959-60
Hibernian	1902-03, 1947-48, 1950-51, 1951-52
Third Lanark	1903-04
Motherwell	1931-32
Aberdeen	1954-55
Dundee	1961-62
Kilmarnock	1964-65
Aberdeen	1945-46, 1955-56
East Fife	47-48, 49-50, 53-54
Hibernian	1972-73
Motherwell	1950-51
Dundee	1951-52, 1952-53
Hearts	1954-55, 1958-59, 1959-60, 1962-63
Partick Thistle	1971-72

ball clubs. They were causes—to be fought for, defended, devoted to and, if the need arose, died for. And, but for the dedicated medical staff who man the casualty departments of Glasgow's infirmaries, the supreme sacrifice—martyrdom—would, over the years, have taken its toll of the city's population on many a drunken Saturday night.

Exactly when the religious rift between the two clubs occurred is strangely obscure. Certainly Celtic, founded in 1887 by Brother Walfrid, of the Catholic teaching order of Marist Brothers, had religious influences from the very first. Celtic Football and Athletic Club was formed principally to raise money for food for needy children in the missions of St Mary's, Sacred Heart and St Michael's in the impoverished east end of the city.

Rangers have no such deep-rooted affinity with Protestantism, although Ibrox Park, their wide-open stadium just south of the Clyde, has come to mean to Glasgow's Protestants almost what the Vatican means to the world's Catholics.

Rangers were founded by a group of enthusiastic rowers who used to 'kick the ball' after their strenuous work-outs on the Clyde. In fact, Rangers' first ground was at Glasgow Green, to this day the centre for rowing enthusiasts in the city. A Catholic is known to have played for Rangers in the twenties, and although they have since made 'mistakes' and signed one or two others (who were quickly released), the club now practises religious discrimination by refusing to sign a 'left-footer', to put it in Glaswegian vernacular.

Celtic, for their part, judge a man solely by his ability. Many of the greatest players in the club's history —John Thomson, Bobby Evans, Bobby Collins, Willie Fernie, and as many as four of the European Cup winning team of 1967 were Protestants. In fact Ronnie Simpson, the goalkeeper in the 1967 side, is the son of an ex-Rangers centre-half, Jimmy Simpson. And in 1965 Celtic appointed a Protestant team manager when they brought Jock Stein from Hibernian.

But for all that, Celtic's supporters are 99 per cent Catholic. Much more to the point, they are Irish Catholic—or of Irish extraction. Those 'needy children' for whom the club was founded were largely the offspring of the droves of Irish workers who came to Glasgow at the end of the last century looking for work and enough to live on.

Their descendants form the basis of Celtic's support nowadays, and on match days at Parkhead many of the songs to be heard are the Irish rebel songs, more suited, perhaps, to a Belfast rally than a Scottish football match.

Rangers fans counter by pledging their allegiance in song to the cause of Protestantism, or more correctly Irish Protestantism, and epitomized by their parody of the hit song 'Wand'rin Star'.

'I was born under a Union Jack, I was born under a Union Jack, Do I know where hell is? Hell is up the' Falls, Heaven is the Shankhill Road, we'll guard old Derry's Walls.'

How many of those Ibrox vocalists, one is tempted to ask, have ever seen Belfast's Shankhill Road or Londonderry's famous town walls?

The Pope, inevitably, comes in for his share of slandering, while William of Orange, England's William III, is the object of much derision from the terracing of Parkhead. Celtic fans insist 'There's only one King Billy—that's McNeill', surprising no one by feeling more for the Celtic captain of the 1960s, than for an English monarch of the seventeenth century.

With a background like that, of course, Rangers and Celtic are guaranteed the undying allegiance of tens of thousands. So has any provincial outfit a hope of competing with these two over the long term?

Nowadays, it seems extremely unlikely. Outside the 'Old Firm', with the occasional temporary exception, every club in Scotland faces an uphill struggle in the battle for economic survival. The money necessary to build, and maintain, a winning side just does not come in through the turnstiles anymore.

So every player in the country out-

23

side Ibrox and Parkhead is available for transfer. Players don't have to ask away. If somebody comes along to buy a provincial player, he'll be allowed to go if the price is right; those clubs just can't afford to turn down big money.

Nor can they afford to offer a youngster with potential star quality the same kind of money as Rangers or Celtic. So, as a direct result of the bitter rivalry between two clubs and their fans, Glasgow is generally able to skim the cream of the country's talent, either because of the financial aspect or because many a young fellow would gladly take a cut in wages to play for the club he has been brought up to idolize.

It wasn't always like that. In fact, until about 1960 the game was thriving in Scotland. It wasn't uncommon for crowds of 30,000 to turn up for a Third Lanark versus Hibs match at Cathkin Park. And, of course, in the years following the last War, the problem for most clubs was simply how quickly they could get people through the turnstiles. Yet Rangers and Celtic still managed to monopolize the top of the heap. The challenge presented by the provincials was often successful, but never lasted long enough to break the overall dominance enjoyed by the Firm.

Joint runners-up in the League Championship stakes to the big two are Hearts and Hibs, with four wins apiece. But two of Hearts' victories were gained in the 1890s, and the other two in 1958 and 1960. Hibs won the League in 1902-3, and then three times in their halcyon days between 1948 and 1952. In 1972 Hibs were still the only club outside Rangers and Celtic to win the title in successive years. Those great Edinburgh teams of the early and late fifties were the nearest anybody ever came to sustaining a serious threat to the Glasgow stranglehold. But even they didn't last long.

A Saturday exodus to the shrines of Glasgow

Hearts, for instance, with the near-legendary Dave Mackay at wing-half and the formidable inside trio of Conn, Bauld and Wardhaugh up front, looked invincible in their hey-day. But sandwiched between their two League titles was one by Rangers, who were only mediocre by comparison. The Old Firm refused to surrender.

Hearts did win a Scottish Cup and two League Cups as well as their League Championships, but never completed the big double in one season. So it was with Hibs. They won three League Championships in five years, with what many Scots still regard as the finest forward line in history (Smith, Johnston, Reilly, Turnbull and Ormond), but never won a cup. Indeed, in the 25 years since the Scottish League Cup became a major competition, only two seasons have gone by when the Old Firm failed to land one of the major trophies. They were 1951-52, when Hibs won the League, Motherwell the Scottish Cup, and Dundee the League Cup, and 1954-55 when Aberdeen won the League, Clyde the

Top *Rangers imports Gerhard Neef (in goal) and Johansen (2) hold off Dundee United forwards Wilson and Ken Cameron at United's Tannadice Park.*
Above *The game goes on but the real Rangers-Celtic struggle is off the field.*

Scottish Cup and Hearts the League Cup. Fifteen years later no one expected to see such a season again.

The hopelessness of the provincials was put in a nutshell by the late Tom Preston, chairman of Airdrie. Tom, a great talker who played in Airdrie's Scottish Cup winning team of 1924, rarely thought, never mind spoke, about anything but football. A distinguished Scottish journalist recalls a walk through Airdrie with Parker:—

'Two little boys about ten years old skipped past us. They were wearing Celtic scarves and woollen ski-hats. Tom spread his hands and said, "See that? That's what we've got to compete with." He was, of course, referring to the fact that here were two local boys who, even at their age, were leaving the town to follow

Celtic.' In the 1960s it was the same all over the country.

Every week managers and directors in Dundee, Edinburgh, Ayr, Kilmarnock, Fife and Aberdeen looked from their windows and saw busloads of Rangers and Celtic supporters departing—and watched their own fans trickle through the turnstiles in pitifully small numbers.

But the outlying districts of Scotland are relatively close examples of places where Rangers and Celtic enjoy huge support. There are registered supporters' clubs for this pair all over the world. Rangers have clubs in Mauritius, New Zealand and Australia, to say nothing of their innumerable devotees exiled in North America.

Ironically, Rangers' biggest supporters' club is in England. In Corby,

the steel town of Northamptonshire, the Rangers Supporters' Association secretary Duncan Perrat says that, with 800 members, the Corby branch is not only the biggest soccer supporters' club (in the genuine sense) in the country, but in the world.

Considered from a detached viewpoint, Scottish football often adopts the features of a farce. For instance, between the years 1905 and 1947 only once (1931-32) did a team outside the duo manage to win the Scottish First Division. The Motherwell of the thirties were generally regarded as the finest team in the country. Yet at the end of their purple patch that solitary League Championship was all they had to show. Rangers saw to that with an incredible eight wins in nine years. Motherwell were runners-up four times. It is almost as if the Scottish League had a rule prohibiting provincial clubs from even challenging Glasgow.

Unlike English football, where the 'greatest ever team' provokes a fertile discussion never likely to be concluded, Scotland has far fewer choices at its command. One possibility is the Celtic team of just after the First World War, which won three League titles and four Scottish Cups and which included Patsy Gallagher—dubbed by Celtic's late president, Sir Robert Kelly, 'pound for pound the greatest footballer I ever saw'—Tommy McInally, Jimmy 'Napoleon' McMenemy and Jimmy McGrory, whose goal-scoring feats are unlikely to ever be equalled.

A Protestant alternative is the magnificent Rangers team of the twenties and thirties which included, inevitably, the legendary Alan Morton. Even in the light of the achievements of the Celtic team of more recent years, old-timers still claim nobody before or since could hold a candle to Gallagher and Morton.

Are Stein's Celtic Scotland's best ever club side?

But no chronicle of the great teams could be complete without a look at the eleven moulded into the first British outfit to win the European Cup by Jock Stein in 1967. That Celtic side had everything, but Bertie Auld deserves special mention because the Scots believe he was probably the first British player to match the continentals at their own game—or beat them. Slowing it down to his own pace, cockily arrogant in everything he did, Auld had the opposition beaten in the dressing-room before every match with his unshakeable confidence.

Perhaps it was a confidence that should have surprised no one. With Birmingham City Auld was, on his own admission, a failure. On going to Celtic he joined a team that were on their way to a string of victories that would leave most fans hazy about the last time Celtic had *not* been League Champions. When you play for a team that is *that* successful, you would have to be a very odd character indeed to be anything but confident.

SCOTTISH LEAGUE CHAMPIONSHIP

Season	First	Pts	Second	Pts
1890-91	†Dumbarton	29	†Rangers	29
1891-92	Dumbarton	37	Celtic	35
1892-93	Celtic	29	Rangers	27
1893-94	Celtic	29	Hearts	26
1894-95	Hearts	31	Celtic	26
1895-96	Celtic	30	Rangers	26
1896-97	Hearts	28	Hibernian	26
1897-98	Celtic	33	Rangers	29
1898-99	Rangers	36	Hearts	26
1899-1900	Rangers	32	Celtic	25
1900-01	Rangers	35	Celtic	29
1901-02	Rangers	28	Celtic	26
1902-03	Hibernian	37	Dundee	31
1903-04	Third Lanark	43	Hearts	39
1904-05	‡Celtic	41	Rangers	41
1905-06	Celtic	49	Hearts	43
1906-07	Celtic	55	Dundee	48
1907-08	Celtic	55	Falkirk	51
1908-09	Celtic	51	Dundee	50
1909-10	Celtic	54	Falkirk	52
1910-11	Rangers	52	Aberdeen	48
1911-12	Rangers	51	Celtic	45
1912-13	Rangers	53	Celtic	49
1913-14	Celtic	65	Rangers	59
1914-15	Celtic	65	Hearts	61
1915-16	Celtic	67	Rangers	56
1916-17	Celtic	64	Morton	54
1917-18	Rangers	56	Celtic	55
1918-19	Celtic	58	Rangers	57
1919-20	Rangers	71	Celtic	68
1920-21	Rangers	76	Celtic	66
1921-22	Celtic	67	Rangers	66
1922-23	Rangers	55	Airdrieonians	50
1923-24	Rangers	59	Airdrieonians	50
1924-25	Rangers	60	Airdrieonians	57
1925-26	Celtic	58	Airdrieonians	50
1926-27	Rangers	56	Motherwell	51
1927-28	Rangers	60	*Celtic	55
1928-29	Rangers	67	Celtic	51
1929-30	Rangers	60	Motherwell	55
1930-31	Rangers	60	Celtic	58
1931-32	Motherwell	66	Rangers	61
1932-33	Rangers	62	Motherwell	59
1933-34	Rangers	66	Motherwell	62
1934-35	Rangers	55	Celtic	52
1935-36	Celtic	66	*Rangers	61
1936-37	Rangers	61	Aberdeen	54
1937-38	Celtic	61	Hearts	58
1938-39	Rangers	59	Celtic	48
1939-46	No competition			
1946-47	Rangers	46	Hibernian	44
1947-48	Hibernian	48	Rangers	46
1948-49	Rangers	46	Dundee	45
1949-50	Rangers	50	Hibernian	49
1950-51	Hibernian	48	Rangers	38
1951-52	Hibernian	45	Rangers	41
1952-53	*Rangers	43	Hibernian	43
1953-54	Celtic	43	Hearts	38
1954-55	Aberdeen	49	Celtic	46
1955-56	Rangers	52	Aberdeen	46
1956-57	Rangers	55	Hearts	53
1957-58	Hearts	62	Rangers	49
1958-59	Rangers	50	Hearts	48
1959-60	Hearts	54	Kilmarnock	50
1960-61	Rangers	51	Kilmarnock	50
1961-62	Dundee	54	Rangers	51
1962-63	Rangers	57	Kilmarnock	48
1963-64	Rangers	55	Kilmarnock	49
1964-65	*Kilmarnock	50	Hearts	50
1965-66	Celtic	57	Rangers	55
1966-67	Celtic	58	Rangers	55
1967-68	Celtic	63	Rangers	61
1968-69	Celtic	54	Rangers	49
1969-70	Celtic	57	Rangers	45
1970-71	Celtic	56	Aberdeen	54
1971-72	Celtic	60	Aberdeen	50
1972-73	Celtic	57	Rangers	56

† Shared after indecisive play-off (2-2). ‡ Celtic won play-off. *Goal average.

SCOTTISH LEAGUE CUP—FINAL TIES

Season	Venue	Winners		Runners-up	
1945-46	Hampden Park	Aberdeen	3	Rangers	2
1946-47	Hampden Park	Rangers	4	Aberdeen	0
1947-48	Hampden Park	East Fife	1:4	Falkirk	1:1
1948-49	Hampden Park	Rangers	2	Raith Rovers	0
1949-50	Hampden Park	East Fife	3	Dunfermline Ath	0
1950-51	Hampden Park	Motherwell	3	Hibernian	0
1951-52	Hampden Park	Dundee	3	Rangers	2
1952-53	Hampden Park	Dundee	2	Kilmarnock	0
1953-54	Hampden Park	East Fife	3	Partick Thistle	2
1954-55	Hampden Park	Hearts	4	Motherwell	2
1955-56	Hampden Park	Aberdeen	2	St Mirren	1
1956-57	Hampden Park	Celtic	0:3	Partick Thistle	0:0
1957-58	Hampden Park	Celtic	7	Rangers	1
1958-59	Hampden Park	Hearts	5	Partick Thistle	1
1959-60	Hampden Park	Hearts	2	Third Lanark	1
1960-61	Hampden Park	Rangers	2	Kilmarnock	0
1961-62	Hampden Park	Rangers	1:3	Hearts	1:1
1962-63	Hampden Park	Hearts	1	Kilmarnock	0
1963-64	Hampden Park	Rangers	5	Morton	0
1964-65	Hampden Park	Rangers	2	Celtic	1
1965-66	Hampden Park	Celtic	2	Rangers	1
1966-67	Hampden Park	Celtic	1	Rangers	0
1967-68	Hampden Park	Celtic	5	Dundee	3
1968-69	Hampden Park	Celtic	6	Hibernian	2
1969-70	Hampden Park	Celtic	1	St Johnstone	0
1970-71	Hampden Park	Rangers	1	Celtic	0
1971-72	Hampden Park	Partick Thistle	4	Celtic	1
1972-73	Hampden Park	Hibernian	2	Celtic	1

SCOTTISH FOOTBALL ASSOCIATION CUP FINAL TIES

Year	Venue	Winners		Runners-up	
1874	Hampden Park	Queen's Park	2	Clydesdale	0
1875	Hampden Park	Queen's Park	3	Renton	0
1876	Hampden Park	Queen's Park	1:2	Third Lanark	1:0
1877	Hampden Park	Vale of Leven	0:1:3	Rangers	0:1:2
1878	Hampden Park	Vale of Leven	1	Third Lanark	0
1879[1]	Hampden Park	Vale of Leven	1	Rangers	1
1880	Cathkin Park	Queen's Park	3	Thornlibank	0
1881[2]	Kinning Park	Queen's Park	3	Dumbarton	1
1882	Cathkin Park	Queen's Park	2:4	Dumbarton	2:1
1883	Hampden Park	Dumbarton	2:2	Vale of Leven	2:1
1884[3]	Hampden Park	Queen's Park		Vale of Leven	
1885	Hampden Park	Renton	0:3	Vale of Leven	0:1
1886	Cathkin Park	Queen's Park	3	Renton	1
1887	Hampden Park	Hibernian	2	Dumbarton	1
1888	Hampden Park	Renton	6	Cambuslang	1
1889[4]	Hampden Park	Third Lanark	2	Celtic	1
1890	Ibrox Park	Queen's Park	1:2	Vale of Leven	1:1
1891	Hampden Park	Hearts	1	Dumbarton	0
1892[5]	Ibrox Park	Celtic	5	Queen's Park	1
1893	Ibrox Park	Queen's Park	2	Celtic	1
1894	Hampden Park	Rangers	3	Celtic	1
1895	Ibrox Park	St Bernard's	2	Renton	1
1896	Logie Green	Hearts	3	Hibernian	1
1897	Hampden Park	Rangers	5	Dumbarton	1
1898	Hampden Park	Rangers	2	Kilmarnock	0
1899	Hampden Park	Celtic	2	Rangers	0
1900	Ibrox Park	Celtic	4	Queen's Park	3
1901	Ibrox Park	Hearts	4	Celtic	3
1902	Celtic Park	Hibernian	1	Celtic	0
1903	Celtic Park	Rangers	1:0:2	Hearts	1:0:0
1904	Hampden Park	Celtic	3	Rangers	2
1905	Hampden Park	Third Lanark	0:3	Rangers	0:1
1906	Ibrox Park	Hearts	1	Third Lanark	0
1907	Hampden Park	Celtic	3	Hearts	0
1908	Hampden Park	Celtic	5	St Mirren	1
1909[6]					
1910	Ibrox Park	Dundee	2:0:2	Clyde	2:0:1
1911	Ibrox Park	Celtic	0:2	Hamilton Acad	0:0
1912	Ibrox Park	Celtic	2	Clyde	0
1913	Celtic Park	Falkirk	2	Raith Rovers	0
1914	Ibrox Park	Celtic	0:4	Hibernian	0:1
1915	No competition				
1916	No competition				
1917	No competition				
1918	No competition				
1919	No competition				
1920	Hampden Park	Kilmarnock	3	Albion Rovers	2
1921	Celtic Park	Partick Thistle	1	Rangers	0
1922	Hampden Park	Morton	1	Rangers	0
1923	Hampden Park	Celtic	1	Hibernian	0
1924	Ibrox Park	Airdrieonians	2	Hibernian	0
1925	Hampden Park	Celtic	2	Dundee	1
1926	Hampden Park	St Mirren	2	Celtic	0
1927	Hampden Park	Celtic	3	East Fife	1
1928	Hampden Park	Rangers	4	Celtic	0
1929	Hampden Park	Kilmarnock	2	Rangers	0
1930	Hampden Park	Rangers	0:2	Partick Thistle	0:1
1931	Hampden Park	Celtic	2:4	Motherwell	2:2
1932	Hampden Park	Rangers	1:3	Kilmarnock	1:0
1933	Hampden Park	Celtic	1	Motherwell	0
1934	Hampden Park	Rangers	5	St Mirren	0
1935	Hampden Park	Rangers	2	Hamilton Acad	1
1936	Hampden Park	Rangers	1	Third Lanark	0
1937	Hampden Park	Celtic	2	Aberdeen	1
1938*	Hampden Park	East Fife	1:4	Kilmarnock	1:2
1939	Hampden Park	Clyde	4	Motherwell	0
1940	No competition				
1941	No competition				
1942	No competition				
1943	No competition				
1944	No competition				
1945	No competition				
1946	No competition				
1947	Hampden Park	Aberdeen	2	Hibernian	1
1948	Hampden Park	Rangers	1:1	Morton	1:0
1949	Hampden Park	Rangers	4	Clyde	1
1950	Hampden Park	Rangers	3	East Fife	0
1951	Hampden Park	Celtic	1	Motherwell	0
1952	Hampden Park	Motherwell	4	Dundee	0
1953	Hampden Park	Rangers	1:1	Aberdeen	1:0
1954	Hampden Park	Celtic	2	Aberdeen	1
1955	Hampden Park	Clyde	1:1	Celtic	1:0
1956	Hampden Park	Hearts	3	Celtic	1
1957*	Hampden Park	Falkirk	1:2	Kilmarnock	1:1
1958	Hampden Park	Clyde	1	Hibernian	0
1959	Hampden Park	St Mirren	3	Aberdeen	1
1960	Hampden Park	Rangers	2	Kilmarnock	0
1961	Hampden Park	Dunfermline Ath	0:2	Celtic	0:0
1962	Hampden Park	Rangers	2	St Mirren	0
1963	Hampden Park	Rangers	1:3	Celtic	1:0
1964	Hampden Park	Rangers	3	Dundee	1
1965	Hampden Park	Celtic	3	Dunfermline Ath	2
1966	Hampden Park	Rangers	0:1	Celtic	0:0
1967	Hampden Park	Celtic	2	Aberdeen	0
1968	Hampden Park	Dunfermline Ath	3	Hearts	1
1969	Hampden Park	Celtic	4	Rangers	0
1970	Hampden Park	Aberdeen	3	Celtic	1
1971	Hampden Park	Celtic	1:2	Rangers	1:1
1972	Hampden Park	Celtic	6	Hibernian	1
1973	Hampden Park	Rangers	3	Celtic	2

[1]Vale of Leven awarded the cup after Rangers failed to attend the replay.
[2]After Dumbarton protested the first game, which Queen's Park won 2-1.
[3]Queen's Park awarded the cup after Vale of Leven failed to attend the final.
[4]Replay order by Scottish FA because of the state of the pitch in the first game, won by Third Lanark 3-0.
[5]After Queen's Park protested at the first game, which Celtic won 1-0.
[6]Owing to riots the cup was withheld after two drawn games (2-2, 1-1) at Hampden.
*After extra time in the replay.

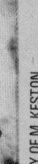

TOPIX

The Chapman Era

THE STORY
OF FOOTBALL

COURTESY OF M. KESTON

Above *Bowlers, boaters, trilbies and cloth caps mingle in a section of the crowd for the 1921 Cup Final at Stamford Bridge.*
Right *The cover of the programme for the same match. Spurs won 1-0.*
Top right *Complete with spectacles and plus-fours, Arsenal manager Herbert Chapman poses with his team at Hendon before the trip to Paris and the annual friendly with Racing Club.*
Inset *The bust of Herbert Chapman at Highbury—a memorial to the man who revolutionized football thinking.*

The twenty years between the First and Second World Wars has been called the era of the manager. That is not quite accurate. In truth it was the era of one manager; just one man, whose achievements found an appropriate setting halfway through two turbulent decades in the 1930 FA Cup Final. Those ninety minutes were, quite simply, a microcosm of the whole period.

The combatants were Huddersfield Town and Arsenal. Just eleven years earlier the Yorkshire club's directors had recommended that the organization move, lock, stock and barrel, to Leeds, support and success being sadly elusive in a Huddersfield obsessed with rugby league. The same year Arsenal crept into the First Division by means which could only be described as devious, being elected after finishing only sixth in the immediate pre-War Second Division.

Four years before the 1930 Final Huddersfield had become the first

club ever to win three consecutive League Championships and, five years after it, Arsenal did precisely the same thing. During their great years both were managed by the same man, Herbert Chapman and, appropriately enough, the game in question was won by the club he then managed, Arsenal, over the club he had left, Huddersfield.

Herbert Chapman was born in the very far south of Yorkshire, at Kiveton Park, in 1873. His professional career as a reserve with Spurs was distinguished only by the lemon coloured boots he wore. In 1907 he became manager of the Southern League side Northampton Town and later moved to Second Division Leeds City, who were ignominiously thrown out of the League in 1919 for making illegal payments to players. Their place was taken by Port Vale—who were to suffer exactly the same fate half a century later. Vale, however, were re-elected. Leeds were not and Chapman—sus-

pended though his only involvement was an alleged timely incineration of the club's books—took a partnership in an engineering firm.

Not for long though. Huddersfield, rather than move to Leeds as their directors were then threatening, managed to raise some cash and sign a number of players. When his suspension was lifted, Chapman joined Huddersfield as manager in September 1920. Here the story really begins. Chapman's first success was the FA Cup of 1922, albeit with a disputed Billy Smith penalty, and two years later Huddersfield won the League Championship on goal average from Cardiff. The next season they retained the title with a new defensive record—only 28 goals conceded—and went on to make it a hat-trick in 1926.

By that time, however, Chapman had gone. His success at Huddersfield was remarkable, for he had no great financial resources and the York-

shiremen, facing the fierce competition of rugby league, had never drawn large crowds. His team had few outstanding players—most notable was Alex Jackson, one of the Scottish 'Wembley Wizards' that crushed England 5-1 in 1928. Jackson was technically a right-winger, though he actually wandered all over the park more in the manner of an Alan Ball. England captains Clem Stephenson and Sam Wadsworth were valuable signings, while Sam Barkas was an excellent full-back partner for Wadsworth. Barkas, in fact, was one of Alf Ramsey's first boyhood idols.

COURTESY OF MRS M ALLSOP

COURTESY OF MRS M ALLSOP

Above Chapman (far left) with the Cup winning Huddersfield side of 1922. By 1925 he had set them on the way to a League hat-trick and left for Arsenal.

Chapman's ability lay in choosing and moulding his players as parts of a whole—not just allowing them to function as individuals in the well-defined grooves laid down when 'positional' play was strict. He chose well at Huddersfield, but he was perhaps lucky in that his formation came right immediately. When he moved to Arsenal in 1925 it took rather longer to build a Championship side.

In a sense it was an appropriate time to move, for 1925 was also the year of the most significant tactical development since the 'passing' game had superseded the 'dribbling' game in the 1870s.

The immediate cause was the change in the offside law on 12 June 1925, when the '. . . fewer than three players between the attacker and the goal' clause was changed to '. . . fewer than two . . .' The change had become desirable because so many teams were employing a very simple offside trap, bringing their defenders upfield to render lethargic forwards offside and sometimes confining play to a strip covering no more than 40 yards of the middle of the field.

The Notts County full-backs Morley and Montgomery had been guilty of this before the First World War, but it took their Newcastle counterparts McCracken and Hudspeth to elevate the 'offside game' to a fine art in the early 1920s. The pair became so identified with the ploy that when one side arrived at Newcastle Central station and a guard blew his whistle the centre-forward

was heard to remark 'Blimey, offside already!'

When the trend became unacceptable the International Board—the law making body—finally acted; and the results were startling. In the 1924-25 season 1192 goals were scored in the First Division. In the next season that figure read 1703—an increase of almost 50 per cent, or, more graphically, an extra goal for every match played.

But while the immediate result was to move the advantage from defence to attack, the long term effect was probably negative, for the tactical result was, at its simplest,

that one attacker became a defender.

Credit for devising the 'third-back game', as it became known, has never been adequately apportioned. Bob Gillespie of Queen's Park quickly made it his job to blot out the opposing centre-forward but folk-lore has it—with some concrete support—that the man behind the innovation was Herbert Chapman.

Chapman's first action on joining Arsenal had been to acquire a scheming inside-forward. His choice was Charlie Buchan from Sunderland, the .man selectors said was 'too clever to play for England'. The fee was an imaginative £2,000 down

and £100 for every goal he scored in the subsequent season. Buchan scored 19. But it was a transfer significant beyond its immediate impact and strange terms.

In 1929 Henry Norris, Arsenal's chairman, sued the FA for libel after he had been suspended for making illegal payments. The Buchan case was particularly mentioned and it was shown that Buchan had been offered other inducements to join the club. Norris lost his case and far more for, when he died in 1934, he was an exile from football and the club that he had dragged from obscurity.

Charlie Buchan's return to Arsenal, the club he had actually walked out on before the War over eleven shillings expenses, was not a very happy one. One of his, and Chapman's, earliest matches for the club was a humiliating 7-0 defeat at Newcastle on 6 October 1925. Buchan was so upset at such a return to his old home that he and Chapman organized an immediate tactical discussion. One or the other (accounts vary as to who it was) proposed that Arsenal's centre-half, Jack Butler, should adopt a purely defensive role and that one of the inside-forwards should drop back to supply the creative link between defence and attack that the centre-half could no longer provide.

Oddly enough Newcastle's centre-half, Charlie Spencer, claimed he had played just such a defensive role in that vital match, and the Arsenal plan may have come from observing Newcastle's success. Before 1925 the centre-half performed exactly the functions his title implied—he had played in the middle of the field helping in defence and instigating attacks.

Buchan expected to be given the creative inside-forward's job himself, but Chapman valued his goalscoring abilities too highly and detailed a reserve inside-forward, Andy Neil, to perform the midfield role at Upton Park the following week on Monday 8 October 1925. Arsenal won 4-0, with Buchan scoring twice.

Chapman gradually revised his team by pushing the full-backs out to mark the wingers, and using both his wing-halves (now free of their close-marking duties) to perform the midfield duties along with the withdrawn inside-forward. The scheme worked well enough, but was not perfected until Chapman purchased the vital creative link, Alex James, from Preston in 1929. Thus the team played in a formation which could loosely be described as 3-4-3 or 3-3-4, rather than the 2-3-5 of the pre-First World War era. Though most teams quickly copied Chapman's system, club programmes 45 years later were still putting down teams in the outdated 2-3-5 pattern.

One of the secrets of good management is, of course, fitting systems of play to the men available. Some successful managers, like Stan Cullis at Wolves, manage to find just the players to operate a stereotyped formation. Some, like Ramsey at Ipswich, devise a system which suits the limited skills of the players available. Chapman's way was a combination of both, and his spectacular dips into the transfer market were basically a means of filling very specific gaps in both team and system.

For over a decade Arsenal somehow _were_ football

Between 1925 and 1930 Chapman's team and tactics developed in step. Butler's successor as the 'policeman' centre-half was Herbie Roberts, acquired from Oswestry in 1926. His two full-backs were George Male and Eddie Hapgood, often partners for England. David Jack came from Bolton to replace Buchan for the first ever five figure fee (£10,370) in 1928 and, a year later, the key to the whole side arrived from Preston. Alex James was finally persuaded to adopt the midfield general role—spraying out long passes to the flying wingers Hulme and Bastin and to the unrefined but effective Jack Lambert at centre-forward.

That was essentially Chapman's great side of the early 1930s. Having lost the Cup Final of 1927, when Dan Lewis let the ball slide underneath his shiny new jumper and allowed Cardiff to take the Cup out of England for the first time, Arsenal returned to defeat Huddersfield 2-0 three years later.

The League was won for the first time in 1931 with 66 points (which remained a record until Leeds bettered it by one in 1969) and the following year Arsenal were at

Above Fanatical and colourful support in football is nothing new. West Ham followers are optimistic on their way to the 1923 Cup Final.
Right They would have been lucky to find a space. Some estimates say that 200,000 people got into Wembley for the first Final there.
Top right Germany's Graf Zeppelin has a view of Wembley and the 1930 Cup Final. It was the game of the inter-War period, between the only two clubs ever to win a hat-trick of Championships. Arsenal finally beat Huddersfield 2-0.
Far right Chapman's new approach to the whole field of club football prompted Daily Mail cartoonist Tom Webster to produce this strip in 1930.

RADIO TIMES HULTON PICTURE LIBRARY

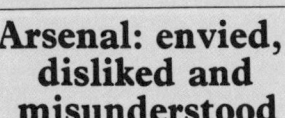

RADIO TIMES HULTON PICTURE LIBRARY

Wembley to lose by the famous 'over the line' goal to Newcastle: Allen's equalizing goal came from a cross which seemed well over the goal-line when Richardson made it. Between 1933 and 1935 Arsenal completed a hat-trick of League Championships, then beat Sheffield United in the Cup Final of 1936 and were champions again in 1938.

As Chapman died in 1934 he was neither with Huddersfield nor Arsenal when they completed their hat-tricks of Championships. He was succeeded at Highbury by George Allison, a radio commentator.

A simple recitation of Arsenal's successes in the 1930s, impressive though it is, tells only a part of the story. In a way that no other team, before or since, has ever approached, Arsenal somehow _were_ football for a decade. In almost every way the Gunners' influence on the game was all-pervasive and Chapman's remarkable success on the field should

never be allowed to conceal some remarkable achievements off it.

His skill as a public relations officer was certainly equal to his skill as a tactician. He claimed that as much energy had been expended getting the name of Gillespie Road tube station changed to Arsenal as had been exerted winning the Cup in 1930. He changed the name of the club from 'The Arsenal' to plain 'Arsenal' because, he explained, 'it will always be first in a list of clubs as well as on the field.' Appreciating the publicity value of the titled, he persuaded the board to accept Lord Lonsdale as one of their number and persuaded the Prince of Wales to open a new stand in 1932. He changed from the original Nottingham Forest colours to a red shirt with white sleeves because it was more distinctive, and later the red socks became blue and white hooped. This was so that the players could recognize each other without looking

up in a melee and not, as Chapman had kidded, because 'red runs in the wash.'

Arsenal: envied, disliked and misunderstood

Chapman was one of the first to experiment with numbering players—the FA finally accepted the idea for the 1933 Cup Final, five years after Chapman—and was in the forefront of schoolboy and youth training schemes.

In his trainer, Tom Whittaker, he appointed the first of the modern day physiotherapist coaches. Modern medical equipment, training routines and individual treatment all arrived at Highbury long before they had been considered anywhere else.

All in all, Arsenal were the very first of the wholly professional football clubs in the British Isles.

CENTRAL PRESS

mitment—one way or the other. Walsall's defeat of Arsenal in the third round of the Cup in 1933 was a cause of widespread celebration all over the country, and the economic conditions of the times go no small way to explaining the peculiar position that one match still holds in the game's folk-lore—it was the perfect example of the poor, underfed weakling rising to humiliate a Goliath which had all the advantages.

On reflection Arsenal gained their reputation not by winning everything going—though they won a lot —but by always being the team to beat. They were really the first professionals to invade a world of semi-amateurs. They disturbed the cosy unthinking mood of the time where even the leading clubs were happy to meander along, appointing an old player as manager, reaching the odd semi-final here, the top five of the League there. This was success, this was football. Arsenal were simply of another generation. Instead of putting down men in chess-board formation—centre forwards with iron foreheads and no feet, wingers on the touchline where they belonged —Arsenal experimented.

But Chapman's two great teams— Huddersfield and Arsenal—should not be allowed to disguise the fact that there were other sides of note in the inter-War period. Bolton, for instance, won the Cup in 1923, 1926 and again in 1929, the first being the occasion of the inaugural Wembley Final and the highest attendance ever at a British football match. West Bromwich won promotion from the Second Division and the FA Cup in 1931—a unique double—and the next year their promotion partners, Everton, went on to become only the second club to win the Second and First Division in consecutive seasons. With a Cup win in 1933, Everton were probably the closest rivals to Arsenal in the period. Dixie Dean had completed his remarkable 60-goal feat with a hat-trick in the last game of the 1927-28 season— against Arsenal—and went on to become a major attraction of the following decade.

The land that gave football to the world stood aloof

On a wider front Britain was barely aware. While Cuba and the Dutch East Indies battled for the World Cup the Home Countries stood aloof from FIFA. England did not enter until 1950, when a traumatic game against the United States showed how 20 years of isolation could take their toll. Chapman may have built the strongest club side in the world, but that was far removed from the true international success that was so long coming.

For the English, then, the era meant Arsenal and in the end that must be Chapman's epitaph. Mention the club in any soccer conscious country in the world and it will produce instant recognition. The word no longer means a place where arms are kept, but rather the club that Herbert Chapman built. The name is a permanent memorial to the achievements of one man—and the club that had the good sense to appoint him.

Make the Chelsea Team

PROGRESS. By TOM WEBSTER.

DAILY MAIL

Herein, perhaps, lies the key to the antipathy that followed, and still follows, the Gunners around the country. No story of the 1930s can be complete without considering this remarkable antagonism.

'Lucky Arsenal' was the cry that flitted across a decade. Time after time, Arsenal seemed happy to absorb the pressure of less talented attacks and win games by the simple expedient of the breakaway goal. It was difficult to convince the unsophisticated terraces or the ageing boardrooms of the 1930s that 80 minutes of unrewarded pressure was less valuable than one goal from a few sudden breaks by Hulme and Bastin. Indeed, it was to be another 30 years before British fans fully appreciated that the best of two teams is, by definition, the one that scores more goals.

It is, of course, impossible to view Arsenal out of historical perspective. The thirties were, for most of provincial Britain, arguably the worst decade for almost a century. In many of the textile towns unemployment reached a third of the workforce; in some places, like Jarrow, literally the whole town was on the dole for years on end. To these towns Arsenal came to represent the wealth, the affluence, and the unfair advantage that London seemed to have stolen from the rest of the country. It was not too unrealistic to see Arsenal as a symbol of the wealth earned in the north but spent and enjoyed in the south.

With the football ground being almost the only entertainment outlet available to the working-classes, it is not surprising that Arsenal became a subject of fierce emotional com-

29

The decline and death of amateur football

An FA decision on 19 October 1971 summed up the contemporary state of amateur football. The reigning Amateur Cup holders, Skelmersdale United, were fined £1500 for gross mismanagement after an investigation into the keeping of their accounts. They were alleged to have misused expense forms and made payments to players which were contrary to FA rules. Their chairman's final, cynical, comment was simply: 'The really annoying thing about these affairs is that some get caught and some don't.'

The amateur game had turned full circle; it had become a world of totally blurred distinctions. Apart from the notable exceptions like Corinthian Casuals, of the Isthmian League, few of the South's leading sides could claim to be innocent of illegal payments. Great Britain play in a supposedly amateur Olympic tournament, yet their opponents in a qualifying round for the 1972 Games, Bulgaria, were anything but amateur. All Eastern European countries refuse to distinguish between amateurs and professionals and so Bulgaria fielded seven of the team that played against Greece in a *full* international only a few weeks later.

In England the FA finally managed to put a stop to what had become a farce and called everyone 'players', despite resistance amongst senior clubs, many of whom wished to do nothing to threaten the FA Amateur Cup. For it is that competition where the money, the prestige and the glory had their home to the end of 1974.

The vital point in the split between amateurs and non-amateurs was 1883. That was the first year in which a club (Blackburn Olympic) that paid its players won the FA Cup. In the same year Accrington were expelled from the FA for paying illegal inducements and, on 19 January 1884, the celebrated FA Cup match between Preston and Upton Park took place. After the game the Londoners objected that Preston paid their players. William Sudell, the Preston manager, admitted as much and the Lancastrians were thrown out of the competition. That was the final splash of water that broke the dam. Sudell convened a meeting of similarly inclined clubs and threatened a breakaway movement. The result was that, in 1885, the FA, unable to beat such a movement, legalized professionalism and so avoided the terrible split the Rugby Union brought upon itself.

'Professionalism is an evil to be repressed'

There were, however, places where the decision to allow members to pay their players was not popular. Pierce Dix, speaking for the fiercely amateur Sheffield FC, the oldest club in existence, proclaimed: 'Professionalism in football is an evil and as such should be repressed.' The Scots agreed. They forbade members to sign anyone who had taken money in England and stayed aloof for another eight long years.

Oddly enough, what was to become the greatest of the amateur clubs had been formed only two years earlier. Being distressed at England's lack of success against Scotland, the famed 'Pa' (N L) Jackson created his exclusive all-amateur side with the express intent of building a team capable of beating the Scots. Composed largely of Oxford and Cambridge products, the Corinthians had an ethos more akin to Twickenham than to White Hart Lane, but for 20 years they proved a match for the best of the professionals. In 1884 that year's Cup winners, Blackburn Rovers, were crushed 8-1; in 1894 and 1895 the England teams against Wales were composed entirely of Corinthians. But perhaps their best known feat was a staggering 10-3 victory over Bury in 1904, only a year after Bury had achieved a record FA Cup Final win by beating Derby 6-0.

It is a revealing insight into the sort of people who ran football before the Second World War that even up to that date an amateur playing for England would receive a first class train ticket (a professional would only get a second) and often stayed at a better hotel than his paid teammates. Indeed, the Corinthians developed some of the greatest names the game knew before the First World War, including the ideal gentleman amateur C B Fry, England captain G O Smith, the Walters brothers, A M and P M (known inevitably as morning and afternoon) and perhaps the most famous of all, Charles Wreford-Brown, the man who is supposed to have invented the name 'soccer'.

It was eleven years after Old Etonians proved to be the last non-professional side to win the FA Cup that the amateur version began.

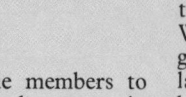

Below Crook Town, Amateur Cup winners in 1901. Crook were to wait until 1954 before taking the trophy again, but by 1964 they had appeared in five finals and won them all.
Right The Pegasus defence combines to clear a Bishop Auckland attack in the classic 1951 final. Between them these clubs won five Wembley finals in the space of seven years.
Right below Skelmersdale players refuse to watch a penalty taken against Enfield in 1967. It was missed, and the Lancastrians lost the replay.

Sheffield had suggested such a competition in 1891, but it was 1894 before Old Carthusians won the first final, beating Casuals 2-1 at Richmond. Carthusians, FA Cup winners in 1881, thus became the first club ever to have won both competitions. It is strange to think that a club with such a distinguished history now plays casual weekend old boys football.

London and the North-East: the amateur bastions

In fact Carthusians' success was a little misleading, for the competition tended to be dominated by the better organized sides from the North in the years leading up to the First World War.

The Home Counties and North-East have ruled the amateur game ever since with only occasional exceptions—the famous Pegasus side of the early 1950s and Skelmersdale in 1971 actually won the trophy, and such obscure performers as Swindon Victoria in 1921, Bournemouth Gasworks Athletic in 1930 and the more famous Marine of Liverpool in 1932 are the only other 'outsiders' to appear in post-1914 finals.

The first decade of the new competition was reasonably peaceful. But in 1905 the FA proposed that the London, Middlesex and Surrey Associations should take over the professional clubs in their areas. London was, at this time, the bastion of the amateur game, with only one of its clubs (Arsenal) having entered the Football League before 1900. The suggestion provoked several

SYNDICATION INTERNATIONAL

FOOTBALL ASSOCIATION AMATEUR CUP FINALS

Year	Venue	Winners		Runners-up	
1894	Richmond	Old Carthusians	2	Casuals	1
1895	Leeds	Middlesbrough	2	Old Carthusians	1
1896	Leicester	Bishop Auckland	1	R.A. (Portsmouth)	0
1897	Tufnell Park	[1]Old Carthusians	1:4	Stockton	1:1
1898	Crystal Palace	Middlesbrough	2	Uxbridge	1
1899	Middlesbrough	Stockton	1	Harwich & Parkeston	0
1900	Leicester	Bishop Auckland	5	Lowestoft Town	1
1901	Harwich	[2]Crook Town	1:3	King's Lynn	1:0
1902	Leeds	Old Malvernians	5	Bishop Auckland	1
1903	Reading	[1]Stockton	0:1	Oxford City	0:0
1904	Bradford	Sheffield	3	Ealing	1
1905	Shepherds Bush	West Hartlepool	3	Clapton	2
1906	Stockton	Oxford City	3	Bishop Auckland	0
1907	Chelsea	Clapton	2	Stockton	1
1908	Bishop Auckland	Depot Bn. R.E.	2	Stockton	1
1909	Ilford	Clapton	6	Eston United	0
1910	Bishop Auckland	R.M.L.I. (Gosport)	2	South Bank	1
1911	Herne Hill	Bromley	1	Bishop Auckland	0
1912	Middlesbrough	[3]Stockton	0:1	Eston United	0:0
1913	Reading	[4]South Bank	1:1	Oxford City	1:0
1914	Leeds	Bishop Auckland	1	Northern Nomads	0
1915	Millwall	Clapton	1	Bishop Auckland	0
1916-19		No competition			
1920	Millwall	*Dulwich Hamlet	1	Tufnell Park	0
1921	Middlesbrough	Bishop Auckland	4	Swindon Victoria	2
1922	Middlesbrough	*Bishop Auckland	5	South Bank	2
1923	Crystal Palace	*London Caledonians	2	Evesham Town	1
1924	Millwall	Clapton	3	Erith & Belvedere	0
1925	Millwall	Clapton	2	Southall	1
1926	Sunderland	Northern Nomads	7	Stockton	1
1927	Millwall	Leyton	3	Barking Town	1
1928	Middlesbrough	Leyton	3	Cockfield	2
1929	Arsenal	Ilford	3	Leyton	1
1930	West Ham	Ilford	5	Bournemouth Gasworks Athletic	1
1931	Arsenal	Wycombe Wanderers	1	Hayes	0
1932	West Ham	Dulwich Hamlet	7	Marine (Liverpool)	1
1933	Dulwich	[1]Kingstonian	1:4	Stockton	1:1
1934	West Ham	Dulwich Hamlet	2	Leyton	1
1935	Middlesbrough	[5]Bishop Auckland	0:2	Wimbledon	0:1
1936	Selhurst Park	[6]Casuals	1:2	Ilford	1:0
1937	West Ham	Dulwich Hamlet	2	Leyton	0
1938	Millwall	Bromley	1	Erith & Belvedere	0
1939	Sunderland	*Bishop Auckland	3	Willington	0
1940-45		No competition			
1946	Chelsea	Barnet	3	Bishop Auckland	2
1947	Arsenal	Leytonstone	2	Wimbledon	1
1948	Chelsea	Leytonstone	1	Barnet	0
1949	Wembley	Bromley	1	Romford	0
1950	Wembley	Willington	4	Bishop Auckland	0
1951	Wembley	Pegasus	2	Bishop Auckland	1
1952	Wembley	*Walthamstow Avenue	2	Leyton	1
1953	Wembley	Pegasus	6	Harwich & Parkeston	0
1954	Wembley	[7]Crook Town	2:2:1	Bishop Auckland	2:2:0
1955	Wembley	Bishop Auckland	2	Hendon	0
1956	Wembley	[3]Bishop Auckland	1:4	Corinthian Casuals	1:1
1957	Wembley	Bishop Auckland	3	Wycombe Wanderers	1
1958	Wembley	Woking	3	Ilford	0
1959	Wembley	[3]Crook Town	3	Barnet	2
1960	Wembley	Hendon	2	Kingstonian	1
1961	Wembley	Walthamstow Avenue	2	West Auckland Town	1
1962	Wembley	Crook Town	1:4	Hounslow Town	1:0
1963	Wembley	Wimbledon	4	Sutton United	2
1964	Wembley	[8]Crook Town	2	Enfield	1
1965	Wembley	Hendon	3	Whitby Town	1
1966	Wembley	Wealdstone	3	Hendon	1
1967	Wembley	Enfield	0:3	Skelmersdale United	0:0
1968	Wembley	Leytonstone	1	Chesham United	0
1969	Wembley	North Shields	2	Sutton United	1
1970	Wembley	Enfield	5	Dagenham	1
1971	Wembley	Skelmersdale United	4	Dagenham	1
1972	Wembley	Hendon	2	Enfield	0
1973	Wembley	Walton and Hersham	1	Slough Town	0

*After extra time
Replay at [1]Darlington, [2]Ipswich, [3]Middlesbrough, [4]Bishop Auckland, [5]Chelsea, [6]West Ham, [7]Newcastle and Middlesbrough, [8]Maine Road, Manchester

clubs to the belief that the FA was deliberately trying to minimize the influence of the amateurs and in fact effect a professional takeover of the Association.

As a result several clubs broke away to form the Amateur Football Association (later Alliance) in 1907. For a while the FA treated the rebels as total outcasts, even persuading the Scots to ban the traditional Corinthians-Queen's Park fixture and allow Northern Nomads to take the London side's place. A truce was not finally agreed until 1913, and the AFA was finally allowed a semi-independent existence in 1934. The FA had permitted amateur internationals since 1906—though against the wishes of the chairman Charles Clegg—but for 30 years insisted on having the teams selected by men who rarely saw an amateur match. An amateur selection committee was not introduced until 1935, and a Home International Championship for non-professionals only in 1954.

In the inter-War period the cup competition was largely a Home Counties affair, but the event really came into its own with the move to Wembley in 1949 and the emergence of the two great sides of the fifties—Pegasus and Bishop Auckland. The two met in what is probably the most famous and certainly the most romantic of all the Amateur Cup finals. Bishop Auckland eventually went on to win their tenth final—out of 18 appearances—in 1957, and made that occasion doubly memorable by becoming the first club ever to complete a hat-trick of victories. At the core of their side was the greatest of all the North Eastern half-back lines—Hardisty, Cresswell and Nimmins. Pegasus could hardly have been more different. Founded in 1948, almost as a rejuvenated Corinthians, the team's name combined the Oxford Centaur and Cambridge Falcon, and it was coached by Vic Buckingham of Spurs, later manager of WBA, Fulham and Barcelona.

The climax and decline of the Amateur Cup

Their style was copied from the great Spurs push-and-run League Championship side, and they put it to good effect before 100,000 in 1951 by beating the 'Bishops' 2-1. The next year they lost at home to Crook Town, but were back in 1953 to crush Harwich and Parkeston by the embarrassing margin of 6-0. Unfortunately, with the gradual disappearance of the players who had first created the team—many of whom went to the newly-amalgamated Corinthian Casuals—Pegasus declined. They were not helped by internecine quarrels between the two camps and some rather heavy-handed management. By the 1960s Pegasus had ceased to compete in the Amateur Cup—a sad end to a team which seemed to come straight out of the atmosphere of the nineteenth century.

Their decline was also accompanied by a slow decay of football in the North-East. The clubs up there —particularly Bishop Auckland and Crook Town—found it increasingly difficult to attract playing talent, most of which gravitated to minor League clubs. At the same time support dropped off dramatically. Where semi-finals had once attracted 40,000, by the mid-1960s they were drawing under 5,000; the 1970 Final was watched by only 33,000—a third of attendances 15 years before—despite the fact that both clubs came from the London area.

It is difficult to argue that the under-the-table payments with which most of the leading amateur clubs tried to buy success had not detracted from the appeal of those clubs. In addition private transport and television exposure have made it respectively easier and more attractive for a casual spectator in the Home Counties to travel to one of London's many League grounds or for one in Durham or Northumberland to travel to Newcastle.

When the reigning Amateur Cup holders Skelmersdale were fined £1500 and had their chairman Bill Gregson suspended *sine die*, it simply highlighted what had become an accepted fact. In amateur football only money could buy success. The dangers inherent in trying to impose amateurism had become all too apparent. As Percy Young, author of 'A History of British Football', has put it: 'To love the game beyond the prize is one of the most specious ideals ever smuggled into English ethics. Not because it is in itself bad, but because it is unworkable.' And so it proved. The 1974 Amateur Cup final was the last. After 80 years there was no more hypocrisy —only 'players'.

Hackney Marshes are a part of football folk-lore. Over 2,000 players, most of them only too genuinely amateur, desperately try to emulate their professional heroes every weekend.

![photograph of a sombre crowd of soldiers and spectators]

RADIO TIMES HULTON PICTURE LIBRARY

THE STORY OF FOOTBALL

All quiet on the Football front

A sombre atmosphere at Old Trafford before the 1915 Cup Final, known ever since as the 'Khaki Final'.

History tells us that the two World Wars of the 20th century were totally different in their impact on the British people. The first can be said to have crept up on them almost unawares.

For the century before 1914, wars had been something which happened in far-distant lands. They were invariably remote from both mind and body, unless a son went away to fight. News of border skirmishes and uprisings sometimes took weeks to reach England.

So, when an Austrian archduke was shot in Sarajevo, few people in Britain could foresee that this would be the trigger for a conflict which would touch almost every household in Europe.

The Second World War, which erupted only 21 years after the first one finished, was different. With the new emphasis on aerial power so clearly illustrated at Guernica, war was now total and immediate. When Britain entered the hostilities on 3 September 1939, everyone knew what it meant.

Because of the new awareness, organized sport came to an instant end with the call to arms by the Prime Minister, Neville Chamberlain. It had been so different in 1914. Then sport, and professional football in particular, continued almost as if nothing had happened.

By then the game had reached a kind of maturity after the birth-pangs, the squabbles over regulations, and the constant quarrels between the FA and the Football League.

In an age in which the divisions between rich and poor were still unbridgeably wide, the emergence of a class which worked, rather than merely existed, had brought the need for a popular entertainment.

Blazing, local rivalry was something with which the most downtrodden could identify. The local club gave men a sense of belonging, and it was something which could sustain them through the week. In 1913, when Aston Villa won the FA Cup for the fifth time by defeating Sunderland at Crystal Palace, the crowd reached a staggering 120,000.

The competition and the game itself were given royal approval when, the following year, King George V saw the Final between Burnley and Liverpool. The War was only three months away and, when it became clear that Britain was being dragged into the conflict by the maze of treaties she had signed in the previous decade, the FA and League had to decide whether they would be justified in keeping the game alive.

It was not long before football, like the country that gave birth to it, was fighting to survive. There were those who said that both players and spectators would be better employed on the war effort than on focusing their attention on the fate of a leather ball.

The desire and the intention to continue was one thing. But could the game remain viable? The result of an attendances survey was daunting in the extreme. Clubs all over the country reported that their receipts had gone down by more than half. The solution proposed by the League was as revolutionary as Robin Hood's legendary decision to rob the rich to help the poor. The wages of all players had to be cut by up to 15 per cent immediately. Under the scheme, the deducted percentage was to be posted weekly by cheque to the League and there form the basis of a fund from which the struggling clubs could gain assistance.

It soon became evident that football could not expect to continue in its pre-War form. The impending suspension of operations brought a case in which, to quote a League historian, 'the current of pure football had been interfered with or fouled'.

A group calling itself 'The Football Kings' offered a reward of fifty pounds to anyone who could produce evidence that a match between Manchester United and Liverpool on 2 April 1915 had been squared. The suggestion was that the players, believing that League football would soon be discontinued, had made a handsome profit by betting on the result.

The FA and the League set up a commission to inquire into the circumstances of the match, which United had won 2-0, and discovered that the cat had been let out of the bag by a player making a remark to another on the field. The upshot was an action for libel against the FA and the *Athletic News* by E J West, one of the players in the match. The authorities' evidence was, however, so comprehensive that West lost his case and subsequently admitted the truth of the charge.

Meanwhile, the FA Cup competition had proceeded throughout the 1914-15 season and Sheffield United and Chelsea qualified for the Final at Old Trafford, Manchester. It is a strange quirk of history that the ground was not to stage another Final until Chelsea won a replay

33

COLORSPORT

there in 1970.

The only wartime Final was played on a day of murky gloom in keeping with the atmosphere of a country nearing a second year of war. The usual exuberant Cup Final atmosphere was missing and, we are told, it was witnessed by a chastened, unostentatious crowd.

Chelsea, inconsistent even then, completely failed to reproduce the skill and method which had made them an attraction in the South. A mistake by their goalkeeper, Molyneux, gave Simmons United's first goal and two more came from Fazackerley and Kitchen. Chelsea, incidentally, fielded the only one-eyed player in Cup Final history—their centre-forward, Thomson.

At the end of the match, known ever since as the 'Khaki Final', Lord Derby presented the Cup to Utley, the United captain, with these stirring words: 'You have played with one another and against one another for the Cup, play with one another for England now!'

That was effectively the end of strictly organized football in England although, as in the Second World War, leagues were formed on a geographical basis. There were Midland and Lancashire sections, while Southern clubs joined a London combination. In Scotland, however, the leagues, although denuded of leading players, continued to operate because travelling was less of a problem. The results went into the official records, and so did one or two other oddities—with affairs conducted on a less formalized basis, Celtic managed to play twice in one day at the end of the 1915-16 season. On 15 April 1916 they beat Raith Rovers 6-0 at Celtic

Park in the afternoon and then travelled to Motherwell where they won an evening game 3-1.

The attitudes of both the English and Scottish FAs owed a lot to the widespread 'it'll be over by Christmas' optimism—a view shared, amongst others, by the Kaiser. When it became apparent that the War was to be no less than one of total commitment the Football Association threw itself wholeheartedly into the war effort. Payment of all players was suspended, no cups or medals were awarded, games were only played when they would not interfere with vital work.

The FA Cup tie played before no one at all!

Norwich and Bradford City replayed a Cup tie at Lincoln in 1915 behind closed gates so that production at local armament factories would not be affected. It is the only recorded instance of a first-class game without paying customers.

The FA offices in Russell Square were commandeered as headquarters of a 'Footballers' Battalion' and long after the War had the appearance of a beleaguered garrison with gas masks and tin helmets stacked in corners and falling out of cupboards. The entire Clapton Orient team joined the battalion—three died in Flanders, as did two sons of Lord Kinnaird, the FA President.

From the trenches, however, came rumours of the strange hold that football had upon half the world. At Christmas in 1914, the British and German armies had little stomach for the fight. There came a halt to the

terrible slaughter in which thousands died in attempting to wrest an extra 50 yards of worthless French or Belgian countryside.

It was then that a furtive and temporary flag of truce was raised on one side or the other and a ball mysteriously appeared. While governments hundreds of miles away plotted the annihilation of each other's youth, the men themselves were staging their own international matches. The following day they were back again trying to kill each other. But for a time football, the international language, brought enemies together, just as it had bound comrades to each other in the face of an increasingly inevitable death. The East Surrey Regiment kicked two footballs ahead when charging the enemy at Calmaison and, as one Yorkshire corps went over the top to face a bayonet charge, the leader cried out 'Come on lads, let's do this for Sheffield Wednesday.'

At home, the emergency leagues struggled on through two seasons, with players entitled only to expenses. Clubs had to contribute 20 per cent of all gates to a general pool, four per cent to charity and one per cent to the League.

When the armistice was signed, the FA and the League decided that, before normal wages could be paid, they and the clubs would have to get back to normal gates and normal teams.

Clubs were reminded of their duty to those 'who had played the game in the highest sense' for their country. The impression persists that, despite the millions who had died, the War was regarded in some quarters as a super-sporting event;

an Olympic Games with blood, perhaps, and one with lasting effects. After the war the FA refused to play any of the enemy powers (Germany, Hungary and Austria) for some time. When they finally did some of the results were 'unfortunate'—the Nazi salute given by the English team in Berlin in 1938 embarrasses the FA even today.

A year later, when the 1939-40 season began on 26 August, the war clouds were heavy all over Europe. The thousands who went to their local ground on the opening day tried to put their fears behind them, and they found ready support from their friends on the 'kops' (themselves named after a hill battle of the Boer War). Arsenal travelled to Molineux to play the spirited Wolves whom Major Frank Buckley had fashioned into a brilliant young side which had been runners up in the League and the Cup the previous season.

Newport County, the unexpected champions of the Third Division South were home to Southampton and celebrated their first Second Division match with a victory. The crisis was forgotten by the crowds which flocked everywhere on that summer day.

After the first three matches of the League programme in which, for the first time, players were numbered compulsorily, some unfashionable clubs were making the running. Blackpool, with three victories, were top of the First Division, Luton led the Second, Reading the Third Division South, and the now-forgotten Accrington the Third Division North.

Everton, the reigning champions, had three points and five goals, all

34

RADIO TIMES HULTON PICTURE LIBRARY

Opposite page The First World War 'Footballers' Battalion' had its headquarters at the FA offices in Russell Square. In the centre of the front row of this group is Major Frank Buckley (then a humble captain) who later managed Wolves during their successful spell at the end of the 1930s.
Left Aircraftman Stanley Matthews.

One of thanks for leaving me out, and one on behalf of Adam Little who had taken my place—I knew we'd do well to get away with less than five goals against.' Shankly was right—the Scots lost 8-0.

The curious nature of some of the wartime internationals is underlined by the fact that Stanley Mortensen, one of the many young stars who emerged during the period, played his first international match not for England, for whom he subsequently made many appearances, but for Wales. Early in a match at Wembley, Wales were reduced to 10 men by injury. Mortensen, an England reserve, came on as substitute in the red jersey of Wales. There was no fairy-tale debut for him, however. Wales were beaten 8-3 with Matthews again running riot.

In addition to demoralizing the likes of Scotland and Wales, Matthews found time to 'guest' for Blackpool, whom he was to join after the War for £11,500. In 1943, the 'Seasiders', having won the new Football League North, destroyed Arsenal, the pride of the South, in a war cup game. They won 4-2 in what was described with probable overstatement, as the 'greatest game in 30 years'.

Each year there was a national cup competition culminating in a Wembley final. The early rounds were played on a regional basis and, despite the problems of player release, the later games were played on a home-and-away two-legged basis.

Even so, there were problems, as a historic cup-tie at Cardiff demonstrated. At the end of 90 minutes of the second leg of a tie with Bristol City, the aggregate score was 3-3. Wartime regulations were that an extra ten minutes each way had to be played; if the match was still unresolved, the play had to continue until a goal was scored.

Normal extra time came and ended, and still the scores were level. Then came the marathon. Half an hour passed, then an hour as the players, now like drunken automatons, went through the farcical motions of a football match. When Billy Rees, Cardiff's Welsh international, finally ended the agony with a header, the time was 6.40 pm. The match had lasted 3 hours

40 minutes.

Many players lost the best years of their careers in the sterile desert of wartime football. Among these were Joe Bacuzzi, Fulham and England full-back, Willie Cook, Everton and Ireland, Maurice Edelston, the Reading and England amateur, Tory Gillick, Rangers and Scotland and Bryn Jones, for whom Arsenal had paid £14,000 to Wolves in 1938. He spent most of the War playing in the obscurity of the South Western League with Aberaman.

Others were, of course, among the tragic casualties of war: Joe Coen the Luton goalkeeper, Maurice Tomkins the captain of Fulham, Bob Anderson a Cardiff forward, George Bullock, Barnsley winger, Harry Goslin the Bolton captain, Cyril Tooze, Arsenal full-back, Bobby Daniel an Arsenal forward, and many others.

The players that did return were left wondering whether clubs who had found new stars during wartime, would want the 'old uns' back. The situation was further complicated by the fact that, as in 1914-1919, war had brought many clubs to the edge of financial ruin.

Barrow—the only club to make a profit—£8!

After the first wartime season, only four clubs in Scotland—Rangers, Dundee, Alloa and Raith—reported a profit. In England, the situation was infinitely worse. Only Barrow, profiting from the proximity of the dockyard, had a credit balance and that was only £8!

Derby, in terrible trouble, were rescued by the town corporation who arranged a series of charity matches. Early in the War, the club had almost died after a series of suspensions following financial irregularities detected by the FA. After being re-started Derby made such progress that they were able to win the first post-War Cup Final.

Assailed with doubts throughout its structure, football waited uneasily for the cessation of hostilities. The new dawn would bring immense problems, and it was for the administrators to find a system which would effectively bridge the giant stride from war to peace.

Then nobody knew that the brave new world which soccer faced so uneasily was to bring to the game the biggest boom it had ever known. The British serviceman, returning from the War, was to demonstrate that after home and family, football was the thing he had missed most.

---

scored by Tommy Lawton, the England centre-forward. Apart from his other accomplishments, Lawton had also scored all his club's goals in a season!

On Friday 1 September Germany invaded Poland and, though Prime Minister Chamberlain procrastinated, the die was cast. Players and spectators went home from the matches on the following day to help their wives put up blackout material. Within 24 hours, air raid sirens were sounding over London.

Organized football ended with the sharpness of a power cut. The assembling of crowds was prohibited by the government and, on 6 September, the Scottish FA suspended all players' contracts. Two days later, the English FA followed suit. The following day the government relaxed slightly because the expected aerial bombardment had not materialized, and decided to approve friendly soccer matches in select 'safe' areas and, on Monday 11 September, Arsenal played Cardiff at Ninian Park.

When Aldershot were the country's top football club

Events moved swiftly after that. The government, influenced by the soccer authorities, accepted that football had a beneficial effect on morale and, in October, competitive play resumed with eight regional leagues in England and two in Scotland.

English clubs were allowed to pay players thirty shillings a match while the Scots were able to pay ten shillings more. With contracts

suspended, players could play for any club they chose. There followed a remarkable shift in the balance of power in the game. The best clubs became those in areas where vast numbers of troops were quartered. So there emerged the great Aldershot side.

The manager of this modest Third Division club was Bill McCracken, the former Newcastle full-back of the 1920s, whose cunning tactics had brought a change in the offside law. The club's proximity to Britain's biggest army centre meant that suddenly he could call on all the greatest names in football. Among others, he had Tommy Lawton (Everton), Denis Compton (Arsenal), Stan Cullis (Wolves), Cliff Britton and Joe Mercer (Everton), Jimmy Hagan (Derby County) and Tommy Walker (Hearts and Scotland).

The experience some of these great players gained in playing together regularly enabled them to form the nucleus of what was described as one of the most outstanding England teams of all time.

One of that England side was Stanley Matthews who reached the high peak of his career during wartime. 'Picture Post', at the time Britain's biggest selling magazine, described him as 'a football equation without an answer'. Certainly, in the unending series of inter-service and international matches between the home countries played for charity, he seemed to mesmerize the opposition.

Many still claim that the England team which defeated Scotland at Maine Road in October 1943 was their best ever. Bill Shankly, then a Scottish regular, commented 'When I heard our team I said two prayers.

Regional Tournament Winners 1915-1919

	London	Lancashire	Midland	Champions after play-off
1915-16	Chelsea	Man City	Nottm Forest	Not contested
1916-17	West Ham	Liverpool	Leeds City	Not contested
1917-18	Chelsea	Stoke	Leeds City	Leeds City
1918-19	Brentford	Everton	Nottm Forest	Nottm Forest

Regional Tournament Winners 1940-1946

	League War Cup	North	South	South Scottish
1939-40	West Ham United	(League divided into 13 small groups)		
1940-41	Preston North End	Not held	Crystal Pal	Rangers
1941-42	Wolverhampton Wanderers	Blackpool	Leicester	Rangers
1942-43	Blackpool (N) & Arsenal (S)	Blackpool	Arsenal	Rangers
1943-44	Aston Villa (N) & Charlton (S)	Blackpool	Tottenham	Rangers
1944-45	Bolton (N) & Chelsea (S)	Huddersfield	Tottenham	Rangers
1945-46	Not held	Sheff Utd	Birmingham	Not held

**THE STORY
OF FOOTBALL**

The Golden Years

PRESS ASSOCIATION

Above *The first day of League football for seven long years; spectators cheerfully queue in the rain outside Stamford Bridge on 31 August 1946.*
Below *But enthusiasm for the game in the late 1940s was not all for the good. A sixth round FA Cup tie at Burnden Park between Bolton and Stoke on 9 March 1946 attracted so many fans that closing the gates had no effect at all. They were broken down by the thousands outside with the result that 33 people were killed and hundreds injured when a wall collapsed.*

It was an air of tremendous excitement which greeted the men who took the field for the first round of the FA Cup in 1945. It had been six long years since first-class football had been played in the British Isles, and many of the teams that appeared bore little resemblence to those that had played out the first three games of the 1939-40 season, a quickly aborted affair indeed.

Many great players would appear no more, overtaken by age and tiring muscles. Others had been killed during the war, men like Tommy Cooper the great Liverpool full-back who met his end as a despatch rider, Albert Clarke, Blackburn Rovers' gifted inside-forward killed in Normandy on D-Day, Harry Goslin, pre-War captain of Bolton Wanderers, killed in action in Italy, Coen, that fine Luton goalkeeper shot down in a raid over the Ruhr Valley on a RAF bombing raid, or youngsters just making their way in the game in 1939 like Reynolds, transferred from Charlton to Torquay United a few days before war began, called up and killed in action before he had ever kicked a ball for his new club.

Others again were scattered all over the country, indeed all over the world, retained in the Forces and in essential industries. Consequently clubs gave League chances to men who before the war and again to-day would not have been allowed to lace a boot in a League dressing room.

In 1946-47 in the frantic bid to find and mould a decent combination clubs called on more men than ever before or since. Arsenal had 31 men on first team duty during the season, Huddersfield Town 32. In the Second Division Newport County's League roll call reached the astonishing figure of 41 and Bury, Leicester City, Manchester City, Millwall, Nottingham Forest and Sheffield Wednesday, all topped the 30 mark. Beating them all were Hull City, in the Third North. They fielded 42 men.

PRESS ASSOCIATION

Right Bert Turner (third from left) deflects Dally Duncan's shot into his own net to give Derby the lead in the 1946 Cup Final. Less than a minute later Turner made amends by scoring at the other end for Charlton. The game had another memorable incident. In a radio interview before the match a prominent referee had been asked 'What are the chances of the ball bursting?' He gave the odds as a million to one. Strangely enough the ball burst early on and the same thing happened in the 1947 Final. Inferior wartime materials were blamed.

PRESS ASSOCIATION

Yet Saturday 31 August 1946 was a symbol to the British people that life was nearly back to normal. On that day a full programme of first class League fixtures was played in the British Isles for the first time since 2 September 1939. In fact the 1945-46 FA Cup competition had been completed under unique rules which required the games to be contested on a home-and-away basis. One resulting oddity was that Charlton became only the second side to reach the Final after undisputably *losing* an earlier game. Fulham beat them 2-1 in one of the Third Round matches but Charlton won on aggregate by taking the other match 3-1.

At the time hundreds of thousands of men were already demobbed with their gratuities burning a hole in their pockets and five or six years of their young lives to make up. Millions in factories and industry had been earning more money than ever before but as the war dragged on found less and less to spend it on. Now, with football back, there would be something exciting to help use up some of that cash, trips to be made by train and coach with meals to buy in towns not visited for many years, and wayside inns to dally at.

Years of austerity turn football into a rare luxury

Rationing still blanketed all the civilizing amenities of life, cars and television sets for all were still a dream, you could not have a house built because of a word called licence. Another period as long as the war they had come through lay ahead before austerity began to fade from people's lives. But in the meantime, there was sport. The fact that once the light evenings had gone the government banned midweek matches in the drive to put the national economy back into a peace time footing made the Saturday afternoon date all the more desirable.

Small wonder then that on 31 August 1946, when clubs opened their grounds to the public shortly after noon, there were long queues outside practically all of them. Small gates were the exceptions, not the rule. In the Third Division South, for example, only two clubs reported attendances of under 10,000. Crowds of 20,000 and 25,000 at this level were commonplace.

This was to be a unique season in many ways. The fixtures were a complete replica of those which had been made for the 1939-40 campaign—a season which died after just seven days. This heightened the illusion that life had been taken up where it had left off. Ahead lay the terrible winter of 1947, by far the worst of the century and at a time when food and fuel were still heavily restricted. The winter struck late, and with floodlighting still another future dream clubs could not get the alarming backlog of fixtures cleared. The season became the longest in history, lasting from 31 August to the following 14 June. The 1947-48 season began only 70 days later.

Both sides of the freeze-up, however, the crowds poured in. This was the time when a Jimmy Hill should have risen and forced through the no-maximum wage for footballers still 15 years or more in the future. Instead, after arbitration, the wage for the best First Division players was increased for the 1947-48 season to £12 a week maximum and £10 a week during the close season.

When the balance sheets for 1946-47 were presented all but half a dozen clubs reported profits, many of them substantial. Stoke City led the way with £32,207, Burnley made £18,000, Liverpool over £17,000, Middlesbrough £15,000 and Wolves nearly £11,000. In Scotland, Rangers made £12,500; Queen of the South, whose home town Dumfries has a population of only 26,000, topped £11,000.

But it was not these figures which created a sensation in the soccer world, rather the £15,000 paid by Derby County to Morton, the Scottish club, for inside forward Billy Steel to succeed Peter Doherty.

On the field the defensive techniques of future years had not even begun to put in an appearance. Clarrie Jordan scored 41 goals for Doncaster Rovers, Wally Ardron of Rotherham United 38; Don Clark (Bristol City) and Dick Yates (Chester) 36 each; four of the Wolves' forwards reached double figures—Dennis Westcott 37, Jesse Pye 20, Jimmy Mullen 12 and Johnny Hancocks 10. Charlie Wayman netted 30 times for Newcastle United. Freddie Steele got 29 for Stoke City, Stan Mortensen 28 for Blackpool with Reg Lewis and Ronnie Rooke getting 49 between them for Arsenal. Jack 'Gunner' Rowley thumped 26 for Manchester United.

There were great names abroad in the land but at the end of an historic and colourful first post-War season such an authority as the late Ivan Sharpe was moved to write: 'More and more players—that's the need to-day.'

The 1946-47 season attracted some 35,000,000 spectators but this record was left far behind in the second post-War campaign. When all the figures were in, the attendance total in first-class football alone topped 40,000,000. This was five million more than ever before and it represented the taking of £4,000,000 at the turnstiles. England won the Home International Championship and against foreign opposition were invincible. This made it possible for Lord Athlone, President of the Football Association to deliver a speech at the annual meeting which smacked faintly of 'showing the flag'.

'At a time when exports are of paramount importance', he said, 'football is far from being insignificant. A successful English referee in the Argentine or our international team in Italy is a way of speaking to other nations in a language ordinary people can understand.' For the first time the magic word 'television' came upon the scene. The FA was all for it, the Football League dead against it.

Two clubs dominated the English scene—Arsenal and Manchester United. United, for the first occasion in modern times, rose to a national eminence which has surrounded Old Trafford ever since. Colchester United, then members of the Southern League, had their first glorious hour when they knocked First Division Huddersfield Town out of the FA Cup. In Scotland Hibernian took the Championship to Edinburgh for the first time since 1903. The team included Gordon Smith, Alec Linwood, Willie Ormond, Eddie Turnbull and an Englishman, Bobby Combe. The most sensational transfer of the season came when Tommy Lawton, England's centre-forward, moved down to the Third Division, joining Notts County for a record £20,000 fee.

Surely 1948-49 could not see a new attendance record? In the event it did—easily. Leaving aside FA Cup games, internationals and the 30 major professional and amateur competitions outside the first class aegis the number of people who attended League matches reached the never surpassed total of 41,271,424.

At the end of it a move was made on the proposal of Plymouth Argyle to increase the minimum admission charge from 1/3d to 1/6d (6p to 7½p). It failed by two votes to go through. The League had just launched its new provident fund for players, railway fares were already 55 per cent up on the 1939 levels and hotel bills had increased by 75 per cent, but this was not passed on to the pub-

PRESS ASSOCIATION

DIAGRAM

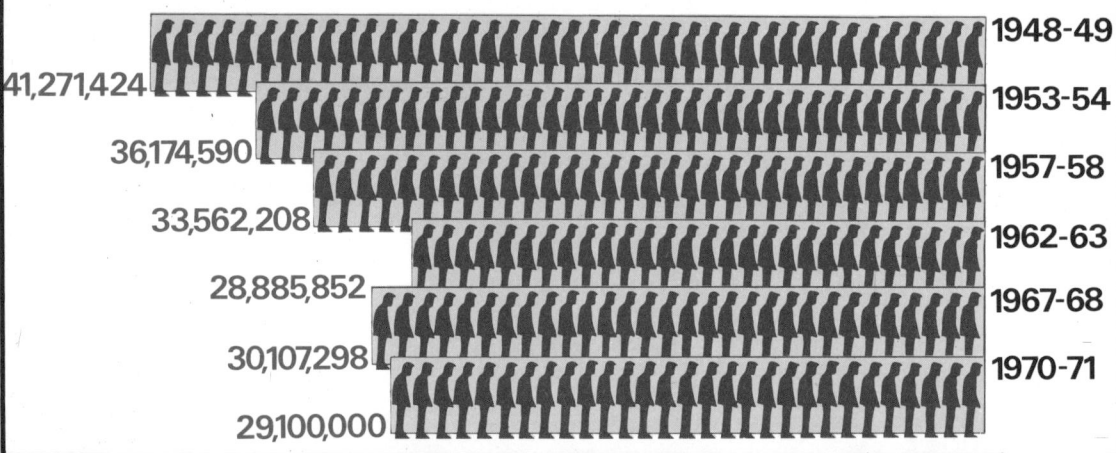

41,271,424	1948-49
36,174,590	1953-54
33,562,208	1957-58
28,885,852	1962-63
30,107,298	1967-68
29,100,000	1970-71

Left Tommy Lawton breaks away from Millwall's McMillen during a 1948 Third Division South match. Lawton, then still England's centre-forward, had caused a sensation by moving to Third Division Notts County for the first £20,000 fee a year before. Inspired by his leadership, County were the only club to score more than 100 League goals in 1948-49.

Left below The rise and fall of attendances in the 25 years after the Second World War. British football has never seen a period to compare with the immediate post-War seasons.

and drabness was disappearing. People could now think in terms of cars, clothes, furniture, new fabrics, new colours, television sets, holidays abroad. No longer did sport, and soccer in particular, represent one of the few worthwhile things on which to spend spare money and time. Perhaps some anglicized form of Dolce Vita was in the air.

The season's return for Football League attendances was still extremely good, topping 39,500,000 and it meant that in five campaigns the first class game in England and Wales alone had attracted some 197,000,000. But impressive as the figures for 1950-51 were they represented the first small hole in the dyke. Not only were they one million down on the previous season and nearly two million down on 1948-49, but the League was now bigger by four clubs.

Jackie Sewell— literally worth his weight in gold

In other respects the sky was still the limit. A few days before the transfer deadline in March 1951, Sheffield Wednesday persuaded Notts County to accept £34,000 for Jackie Sewell which made the player the first worth his weight in gold—literally. It caused a furore at the time yet exactly 19 years to the day Martin Peters moved across London from West Ham to Spurs for £200,000.

Talking of Tottenham, they were perhaps the first club to perceive the need to meet the new challenge from outside Britain which was about to engulf the national elevens of the four home countries. Arthur Rowe, Spurs manager, a silver haired Cockney had instituted a style called 'push and run'. Briefly it meant doing the simple things quickly and accurately and it showed the benefits of a higher work rate than previously thought necessary from all eleven members of a side. Newly promoted from Division Two they cast a shadow of the world wide greatness they were to earn a decade later by storming straight on to take the First Division title.

From that season the honeymoon between football and the fans was over. The game is still a crowd puller without parallel in any other form of activity known to twentieth-century man but it is unlikely ever to know again such a golden age at the turnstiles when in six years it was patronised by 236 million fans, a figure equivalent to the entire population of the United States or Russia. They were, indeed, the Golden Years.

lic. In what was the diamond jubilee season of the League the Victorian illusion of endless security and stability died hard. Goal scoring took a sharp downward trend, the figures dropping to 2.84 goals per match, almost as low as in the 1920s under the old offside law.

The defeat in the Cup of then mighty Sunderland by Yeovil Town of the Southern League on a sloping pitch down in Somerset was the most talked of event in the season. For the first time the Amateur Cup Final was staged at Wembley and a crowd of 95,000 payed over £20,000 to see Bromley beat Romford 1-0. Transfer fees continued to spiral upwards, Derby County paying Manchester United £25,000 for inside-forward Johnny Morris in March 1949.

As the twentieth century came up to its half way mark football reached a watershed. The boom was a long

way from over but 1949-50 was to be the last season in which total League attendances for a season topped 40,000,000. This, too, was the last season of the League in the form of 88 clubs equally divided into four sections, for at the annual meeting four new clubs—Colchester United, Gillingham, Scunthorpe and Lindsey United and Shrewsbury Town—were admitted, two each to both sections of Division Three. The election of Scunthorpe to the Northern group was one of the strangest quirks of post-War football. On the first ballot Shrewsbury were elected easily but Workington and Wigan Athletic tied for second place. Rather than just a straightforward vote between the two tied clubs, the League took it into its head to organize another open ballot—the result being that Scunthorpe defeated both of their seemingly stronger opponents. Workington replaced

New Brighton the following year but, twenty years later, Wigan were still trying to gain entry to the League.

Before this happened there was another very fine act to come. Portsmouth, who the season before had won the First Division Championship for the first time (conveniently in their jubilee year), successfully defended their title, but Wolves gave them a terrific fight which lasted until the final afternoon of the season, 6 May. Rangers were back in the box seat in Scotland taking both League and Cup. Arsenal won the FA Cup—without ever having to leave London! The cry 'Lucky Arsenal' was heard again in the land and perhaps not without justification.

The fifth post-War season, although it was not realised at the time, marked the real beginning in a change in public tastes and habits. At long last the all round austerity

DAILY EXPRESS

No. 17,949   FRIDAY FEBRUARY 7 1958   3 a.m. forecast: Cold; snow or sleet likely   Price 2½

ALIVE Blanchflower, Edwards, Berry, Scanlon, Morgans, Gregg, Wood, Charlton, Viollet, Foulkes; Busby

DEAD Byrne, Bent, Jones, Whelan, Colman, Pegg, and Tommy Taylor

SURVIVORS SPEAK

THREE TAKE-OFF ATTEMPTS—AND THEN DISASTER

EXPRESS Photo News

SEE PAGES 2, 5, 6, 7 AND 16

Matt Busby called out: It's my legs, my legs...

Express Staff Reporters

MANCHESTER United footballers told last night the stark, dramatic story of how the airliner bringing them home from Yugoslavia...

LONDON EXPRESS NEWS AND FEATURE SERVICES

THE STORY OF FOOTBALL

1966 and all that

February 1958; the story that stunned a soccer generation. Though the Daily Express *correctly reports Duncan Edwards as being alive he was to die a few days later.*

An Englishman looking at football since the Second World War will inevitably focus on one of two moments in time. One is the evening of 6 February 1958 when the plane carrying Manchester United, undisputably Britain's best club side, crashed on take-off from Munich airport. The other comes eight years later, the afternoon of 30 July 1966, when the country that gave the world the game finally took its place as more than an also-ran. After two decades of international mediocrity, a reputation had been re-established.

The World Cup win came at the midpoint of a decade which saw a complete change in the British game. The vital point was the abolition of the maximum wage in 1961. George Eastham had brought the whole question of players' conditions and contracts into the open and into the courts when Newcastle refused to give him a transfer. Victory for Eastham meant that men who had been restricted to a niggardly maximum wage of £20 a week could command three or four times that amount. Within a year Johnny Haynes, then captain of England, had become the first home footballer early £100 a week.

It was perhaps unfortunate that this players' revolution should have occurred just as two other forces were changing the fabric of the game, a little more slowly to be sure, but just as vitally. One was the growth of private transport and an effective road system, allowing anyone within forty miles of Manchester, say, to regard United as their local club.

The other factor was the introduction of regular televised games. This affected the game more subtly than the administrators had originally feared. Rather than simply staying at home to watch Spurs rather than going out to see Brentford—a matter of laziness—the really vital change was one of attitude. For spectators were persuaded that the football they wanted to see was that played by the major clubs and, in many cases, that alone.

Television has hardly affected the leading dozen or so clubs at all; it has come near to ruining many of the other 80. Youngsters reared on television have begun to think of Bobby Moore or George Best as the archetypal footballer—not the stunning exception. The local Third Division team—though they may be only 400 yards away—have become as remote from their conception of 'today's' football as Alex James or Dixie Dean.

And so the eventual effect of all these changes was to strengthen those already strong and to weaken those already weak. Great old clubs like Bolton and Blackburn found that their reputations meant nothing beside the pull of George Best at Old Trafford; and it is at that vast stadium that we find the greatest of all the great post-War clubs.

In 1971 Manchester United took a quite unprecedented step by making several of their League matches all-ticket. That was the result of 25 consecutive years as the greatest draw in Britain. Three times Sir Matt Busby built great sides—the 1948 combination that won the Cup, the 1958 'Babes' who died at Munich and the 1968 European Cup winning side. But it was not so much the success and hours of incomparable entertainment that has tied United to the hearts of the British people, rather it was a single incident at a German airfield when the team that has been called the greatest English club side ever was destroyed.

Over a decade later people who do not see a football match from one year to the next, religiously go along to their local ground when United play—simply because of the legend of Munich. It made United more than a football team—it made them an article of football faith.

There have been other good club sides—the orthodox fast-running Wolves of the 1950s who first introduced the British to European competition; the two North London 'double' sides of 1961 and 1971, so close geographically yet so far apart in style; Ipswich Town, the most unexpected winners in the history of the League and perfect proof that the age of method had arrived; Leeds United, 'the professionals', never giving anything away, never letting opponents relax, the worshippers of workrate yet destined to become seemingly eternal runners-up; Celtic, so utterly dominant under Stein's command in the 1960s that Scottish football became as predictable as the rising of the sun. And yet, for all this talent, British teams never made the impact they might have done in Europe.

In the first 18 years of the European Cup competition the trophy came to Britain only twice—with Celtic in 1967 and Manchester United in 1968. There was a little more success in the other competitions. Spurs won the Cup Winners Cup in 1963, West Ham in 1965, Manchester City in 1970 and Chelsea in 1971. Leeds won the Fairs Cup in 1968 and 1971, Newcastle United in 1969 and Arsenal in 1970. But all that cannot conceal that Britain could find no competitor for Real Madrid in the late 1950s, nor for Barcelona, Benfica and the two Milan clubs before 1965.

The first steps into Europe had been as painful as the Common Market negotiations. Though Hibernian entered the European Cup in its inaugural season (1955-56), reached the semi-finals and made £25,000 from the venture (a large sum for a Scottish club at the time), the Football League, in traditionally shortsighted fashion, had 'advised' Chelsea not to enter. It is worth remembering that the League had only just begun to allow floodlit fixtures at this time, and they 'advised' Manchester United the same way the following year. But Matt Busby was more farsighted than his superiors and took no notice.

Shortsighted and shabby—the FA's treatment of United

Revenge was swift. After the Munich crash in 1958 the organizing committee invited United to enter the European Cup the following year along with the League Champions, Wolves. A joint committee of the League and FA finally refused permission on the grounds that it was against the competition's rules (rules already waived by the organizers). It was the shabbiest paragraph in a truly parochial chapter.

Europe was a tremendous catalyst for the British. Not only did Football and Scottish League clubs come to adopt entry into European competition as a major goal, but it changed the face of the game in these somewhat isolated Isles. It was not long before club sides realized that the good old-fashioned tackle from behind and charge on the goalkeeper were not going to be tolerated by crowds, opponents or referees in European matches. The less physical game gradually crossed the Channel and its advantages led to a growing rejection of the intimidating behaviour so characteristic of the 1950s. By 1971 the charge on the goalkeeper was no more than a memory and the Football Association felt strongly enough to try and cut out the equally contentious tackle from behind.

So Britain finally came to accept the discipline of Europe, just as she came to accept a new concept in tactics and coaching and the widespread influx of supposedly 'continental' systems. The combination of an emphasis on sheer physical fitness, leading to the 'perpetual motion' players of whom Alan Ball was probably the best example, and the rejec-

Top *Part of the West Ham soccer school that was so prominent in the game at the beginning of 1972: From left to right: Jimmy Andrews (coach at Luton), Dave Sexton (Chelsea manager), Noel Cantwell (Coventry manager), Malcolm Allison (team manager at Manchester City), John Bond (Bournemouth manager) and Frank O'Farrell and Malcolm Musgrove (manager and coach at Manchester United) in an East End cafe.*
Centre *Geoff Hurst scores England's fourth goal in the 1966 World Cup final and the bench leaps up. The man still seated? Alf Ramsey.*
Bottom *An England squad train at Lilleshall under the eye of Harold Shepherdson.*

tion of the more strictly positional 'stopper' or '3-2-5' formation, with its familiar full-backs, inside-forwards and wingers, led to considerable confusion on the terraces in the 1960s.

That a man could wear a number 7 shirt and *not* patrol the right touchline seemed quite revolutionary to many used to watching Matthews and Finney. Dick Graham achieved some early success with an all-purpose Crystal Palace side—once threatening to number his players in alphabetical order as he claimed numbers did not count any more (which assumes that they once did of course)—and Matt Gillies and Bert Johnson took Leicester to the Cup Finals of 1961 and 1963 with similarly revolutionary concepts on how the game should be played.

But while Alf Ramsey achieved the most obvious success with methodical rather than inspired football—neither his Ipswich side of 1962 nor the England of 1966 will ever be categorized among the world's great entertainers—a more appealingly influential figure in the English game of the period was Ron Greenwood, manager of West Ham from 1961. This, in part, is a result of his willingness to allow journalists a view of the inner workings of the football world and his propensity to sit and discuss the game for hours with those who could take his views outside the dressing-room.

But more concrete evidence comes from a look at some of the 'graduates' from his Upton Park college. In 1971 Frank O'Farrell and Malcolm Musgrove, manager and coach at Manchester United, Malcolm Allison, team manager of Manchester City, Noel Cantwell of Coventry, Dave Sexton of Chelsea, Jimmy Bloomfield of Leicester and John Bond, young and startlingly successful manager of Bournemouth, all came into this 'graduate' category and there were several others. Greenwood's West Ham of the mid-sixties are still regarded in some quarters as the most entertaining team of the decade and it was that side that provided Alf Ramsey with the core of his World Cup winning team in Peters, Moore and Hurst.

Greenwood himself has often suggested that the real credit for the new ideas that gained so much currency in the 1960s should go to Walter Winterbottom. The Football Association's Chief Coach from 1946 to 1963, Winterbottom spent most of that period doubling-up as manager of England's various teams, roles whose compatability was not always obvious. While he is widely remembered for a relatively unspectacular spell as team manager, his work on the coaching side at Lilleshall is known only to those inside the game. His tactical appreciation, his encouragement of personal skills and his insistence on a team's corporate knowledge of its objectives are factors that no one who has taken an FA course could ignore. It was at Lilleshall, not Wembley, that the foundations of the 1966 World Cup win and the prospects for home football in the 1970s were laid.

For British football the two decades after 1950 were rather like a child's first few days at school. Suddenly it dawns that there is a lot more to life than his immediate family group, that there are other children from other families who are not only his equal but sometimes his superior.

So it was with football. It was not that whether Wolves or Manchester United won the League became less significant, more that the most important consequence was that success gained entrance to the European Cup. Whereas a climax used to occur every season—around the time of the Cup Final—it now seemed to occur only once every four years, at the time of the World Cup.

Before 1950 the British regarded the World Cup as an event competed for by foreigners. But the dispute with FIFA having been healed, the four home countries finally agreed to enter and FIFA accepted the Home International Championship as a qualifying competition. The first and second countries were to go through to the final rounds—virtually carte blanche for England and Scotland.

England 0 USA 1
The greatest shock
of all time?

In the event, it provided the Scots with a fine opportunity to display that shortsighted foolishness which has often made the English FA appear prophetic visionaries by comparison. England beat Scotland 1-0 at Hampden in the deciding match and the losers, coming only second in the Championship, refused to go to Brazil for the World Cup.

So England went alone and came back even lonelier. At Belo Horizonte they suffered a footballing humiliation not surpassed before or since. The game against the USA was expected to be a canter. That vast country had never adopted the world's most popular version of football, preferring instead its own brutal perversion. The American coach—irony of ironies—was a Scotsman, Bill Jeffrey, and the night before the game his team were up until the early hours at a party; the only unanswered question was the size of the defeat.

Instead they won 1-0; one British press agency assumed the score was a mistake and printed the result as 10-1. To be fair to England, it was one of those days that every team sometimes has—nothing would go right. Looking back, paradoxically, the outcome was more of a disappointment to the Americans than the English. The latter lost 1-0 to Spain in the next game and went home having not even reached the quarter-finals. But the Americans sincerely believed that their victory was going to be the spark that ignited the game across the Atlantic. They could not have been more wrong.

In England the result was not treated seriously—in fact it was dismissed as the fluke it undoubtedly was and the tower of English self-confidence survived, if only for another three years. The main reason for that pride was 80 years of internationals in which England had never lost at home to foreign opposition.

True, Eire had won a poor game 2-0 at Everton in 1949, but as nine of their side were regular Football League players they can hardly be regarded as aliens. That record was threatened in November 1951 when England drew 2-2 with Austria thanks to an Alf Ramsey penalty. In October 1953 they were 4-3 down to a FIFA side in a full international with only one minute left. Mortensen collided with an opponent and England were awarded a penalty ('although it was still two months to Christmas' as a reporter put it). Ramsey scored again and England's record was safe—but for just four weeks.

The moment of truth arrived on the afternoon of 25 November 1953. Ramsey later said that the game against Hungary had a profound effect on him; it could hardly have had any other. While the game against the USA could be dismissed as a freak the defeat by Hungary was without excuse. A far better team had shown England that reputation was no longer enough.

Eighteen years later that same England side were gathered at a function also attended by Ferenc Puskas. Ramsey greeted his full-back partner that day, Bill Eckersley, rather quizically; 'Hello, it is Bill isn't it?' and Puskas was heard to remark: 'It was like that when they played us—the team hardly seemed to know each other's names.'

England lost 6-3. Far worse, they had made no plans when, six months later, they played a return in Budapest. That one was lost 7-1. England were totally exposed by a side that shamed them in ability, fitness and, above all, in tactical awareness.

English football had entered a period in the doldrums from which it was not to emerge for a dozen years. In the 1954 World Cup the Uruguayan side that had defeated Scotland 7-0 also put out England 4-2. In 1958 England failed even to reach the quarter-finals, losing to the USSR in a group play-off. England's style was summed up by Vittorio Pozzo when he described a goal by Kevan as being scored with the 'outside of his head', implying that England were still not one of the world's more thoughtful soccer nations. That year, at least, Northern Ireland and Wales reached the quarter-finals.

In 1962 England went out 3-1 to Brazil, again in the quarter-finals; Scotland, Wales and Ireland failed to qualify. That was the end of Walter Winterbottom's reign as team manager. Alf Ramsey took over what ought to have been one of the best teams in the world. The first game after his appointment was against France, who declined in the 1960s to the Third Division of European football. England lost that game 5-2, Ramsey declared that they would win the World Cup anyway and the rest is history.

The World Cup victory is not to be denigrated—but what really stands out from 1966 is how sceptical about England's abilities (after previous World Cups) supporters had become and how little chance England were given of winning. Look at the facts. England played six games, all of them at Wembley. In nearly 60 years of internationals against foreign opposition, England had lost only four times at home—to Eire in 1949, to Hungary in 1953, to Sweden in 1959 and to Austria in 1965. Not even Brazil had managed to win at Wembley. Of the 40 full international games England had played against her six opponents, Uruguay, Mexico, France, Argentina, Portugal and West Germany, she had lost only 8. Not a single one of those had been at home and none of those six countries had managed even a draw at Wembley.

In fact the Germans, the other finalists, had never beaten England anywhere, managing just one draw back in Berlin in 1930. Quite simply each of those six matches should have been won and had they been ordinary mid-week 'friendlies' no one would have expected anything but the eventual results. But it is easy to be wise after the event. At the time there was always Brazil, seeking a hat-trick of victories, a rampant Hungarian attack, Eusebio in startling form and the ever-present threat of West Germany, Russia and Italy.

Ramsey's strength was in his free hand. At long last the FA had realized that the system devised by Stanley Rous during the Second World War—whereby he did everything—was the most effective available. Thus, although there was still an international committee technically in existence, Ramsey was the only man who did any selecting. When asked by one of this committee at a cocktail party exactly what its official duties were, Ramsey is reputed to have replied: 'To come to cocktail parties.'

How could England
have failed to win
the World Cup?

Being a defender himself, it is not surprising that Ramsey, like a successful First World War general, believed that defence was the key to victory. For the 1966 World Cup final England ended up with just two fulltime forwards, Hurst and Hunt, five defenders (Stiles playing an auxiliary defensive role wherever he was needed) and three providers.

The formation was substantially the same for the traumatic game in Leon four years later—except that now both Peters and Ball were required to be preoccupied in midfield—when it was proved beyond dispute that the best laid schemes of men, mice and Alf Ramsey can be thwarted by individual error.

Peter Bonetti, deputizing in goal for Banks, was adjudged to have been at fault for the first German goal and was possibly not blameless for the other two. It is sad that one display—albeit the most important of his career—will always be remembered before so many excellent ones elsewhere.

The years 1953 and 1966 must be considered the landmarks of the post-War era for English soccer. The former had the effect of an earthquake—it overthrew all the misconceptions English football had about itself, though it took ten years for all the lessons to filter through. The second date was notable for an atmosphere more akin to VE-day. That was not necessarily inappropriate for it was, after all, the day the national game came in from the cold.

The Seventies: A decade of disillusionment?

Even the sceptical League secretary Alan Hardaker cannot have enjoyed watching his own words come true. In October 1973, on the eve of the match against Poland which decided England's World Cup fate, he pronounced that: 'Defeat would not be the end of the world. In six weeks it would all be forgotten.'

England duly departed from the competition, amidst the expected and justified wailing. But barely had Mr Hardaker's promised six week rehabilitation elapsed when football, along with the rest of the nation, was plunged into its worst crisis since wartime. There was little time to ponder with melancholy on what might have been in the World Cup.

The shortage of electric power meant a ban on floodlighting, which immediately hit at the revenue from midweek fixtures so crucial to the majority of clubs. Kick-offs were tagged back to the almost medieval time of 1.45pm. Those clubs rich or resourceful enough to produce a generator of their own enjoyed a brief respite. Then a shortage of petrol removed the fuel needed to power the machinery. And the scarcity of the same commodity meant that spectators were reluctant to drive to games; and with a train strike running, or rather not running, along the same lines, the lack of transport had a drastic effect on attendances.

As the lights went out all over Europe . . .

Gates that were already falling plummeted. Once mighty Spurs played Stoke before 14,000. Old Trafford began to call 30,000 a good gate. The smaller clubs, already battling to survive, faced a full scale war. The plight of little Workington typified the crisis; for a

Left *The ill-fated Ian Storey-Moore, who became something of a symbol as the man most tipped to be included in Ramsey's next squad and yet won, in the end, just one cap. A goalscoring winger, he seemed the perfect answer to Ramsey's problems—to all but Ramsey. Cynics said it was because, with a Storey and a Moore in the team already, it would be too confusing to have a Storey-Moore as well. After an excellent decade with Nottingham Forest, Moore went to Manchester United for £200,000 but had to retire from the game because of continued ankle trouble after only a handful of games at Old Trafford— a sad end to a career that could have been one of the best of the post-war era.*

Fourth Division match on 15 December Exeter City made a round trip of 800 miles to be watched by 693 people. No wonder the Workington chairman (despite a 3-1 win) sadly admitted that it could be their last season in League football.

Joe Mercer called it 'the biggest battle in football history'. He encapsulated the feeling of the time when he added: 'I believe we still have a wonderful product. So let's start packaging it right and go out and sell it harder than ever before. People are creatures of habit. If they stop coming now, we may never get them back.'

But the structure of the Football League had been under stress throughout the seventies. The depression of December 1973 simply brought it to a head. The country had shown for some time its unwillingness to support 92 full-time League clubs. But the League itself seemed just as determined to reject any really meaningful change.

The problem, as ever, was basically financial. The abolition of the maximum wage had stretched resources from the beginning, but in the seventies the elastic showed severe signs of fraying. And a vicious circle continued to turn.

Players would not sign without a certain wage. This meant that clubs who once housed over 40 full-time professionals could only afford 17 or 18, making up their reserve teams, if they had one, with amateurs and apprentices. First team places became less competitive, and the supply of experienced players began to dry up. Costs did not go down, so the prices went up.

They reached a peak during a glut of spending in the 1972-73 season during which £6,000,000 changed clubs, with Derby County topping the lottery with their £250,000 purchase of Leicester City's David Nish. Crystal Palace and Manchester United led the cheque-waving charge, and their lack of playing success proved that there was no guarantee of a big fee being well spent.

To pay the inflated wages and transfer fees, there had to be an increase in revenue, and though most clubs employed fund-raising expertise, more had to be asked of the spectators. This came in two forms, more gate money and more matches. The former seemed less of a problem, though VAT added to the spectator's burden; even at 50p the live entertainment of a football match remained good value. But the increase in matches meant a different kind of problem.

With the Football League anxious to tempt sponsors without allowing

any firm to lend its name to the two plums, the League Championship and the League Cup, other competitions had to be created. Thus they spawned the Texaco and Watney Cups to spread even thinner the butter of interest on the bread of an increasingly apathetic public.

With Hardaker's own 'baby' the Football League Cup, eating into the first half of the season, plus a regular excursion of the more successful into Europe, the season was becoming more and more a test of endurance rather than a test of skill. Arsenal's double winning side played 64 matches in the 1970-71 season, apart from individual players' international calls.

At the end of the 1971-72 season what had been merely supposition became fact as one incident after another had 'exhaustion' labelled as the cause. Francis Lee went to hospital, instead of Berlin to play for England, because of physical strain. Alan Mullery wrote the finish to his international career because he was tired of all the travelling on top of his club commitments. Colin Todd and Alan Hudson earned themselves a less voluntary ban by refusing to go on an Under-23 tour.

Ultimately it was England, the national team, who got the thin end of a considerable wedge. And yet it was a decade that had begun with so much promise for Sir Alf Ramsey's squad. He assembled his ranks for the 1970 World Cup proudly announcing that this squad was more talented than the heroes of 1966. It probably was— but from Leon the path of the game in England was firmly down-hill.

Did Leon change the 1970 General Election result?

The incalculable failure in Mexico is well worn history. Ramsey's uneasy use of the substitute, glaringly exposed in the quarter-final tragedy in Leon, was to remain an achilles heel. But the thoroughness of his approach to the task of winning the game's major tournament at altitude deserved a better fate—even more so when their performance in a match lost at Leon was the best since 1966. The following week came the general election and a Prime Minister who had shaken Bobby Moore's hand as he received the World Cup was ousted. There are those who still insist that Edward Heath would never have been Prime Minister if England had beaten West Germany.

It was at home that Ramsey found himself in an unrelenting fight to turn England into a team, as they sought to prepare for the next challenge, the 1972 European Football Championship. Like any manager Ramsey needed to have access to his players, but this the clubs so often denied him. Many of his get-togethers prior to internationals were ravaged by non-attendance.

The selfishness of the clubs, who were unwilling to risk injuries to their stars during representative appearances, was as short-sighted as it was understandable. The 1966 triumph and the resultant boost in attendances indicated that a winning England team has a beneficial effect on all aspects of the game. That might have been worth remembering as medical certificates, quite remarkable for their convenience, were dispatched to Lancaster Gate marked 'for the attention of Sir A. Ramsey'.

Ramsey coped until the quarter-final of the European Championship, a two-legged affair against West Germany. For the first game at Wembley, Derby County announced that their centre-half Roy McFarland would not be fit for selection. Ramsey, having named his squad, was forced into a late compromise.

He chose Bobby Moore to play at centre-half with the loyal Norman Hunter alongside him. It was a duplication of talents in a situation that cried out for complementation. McFarland's absence proved a major factor in the 3-1 defeat, though even more important was Ramsey's failure to stifle the brilliant midfield talents of Gunter Netzer, whose performance that day was perhaps the best seen at Wembley since the Puskas of 1953.

McFarland's absence would have been written in the annals as sheer misfortune had not a most lively McFarland appeared for Derby County less than 48 hours later in a match which put them in with a strong chance of winning the First Division. Only the most romantic could not be cynical about McFarland's absence at Wembley.

There can be no excuse for the failure to beat Poland and Wales to qualify for the 1974 finals (the first time England had not qualified). But when Poland had to be beaten, there was no doubt who were the more prepared side. England had played just one international that season, against a poor Austrian side. Poland had all the cohesion of a club side, so much time had they spent together.

Even five days before a game

LONDON F.C.
LEA VALLEY STADIUM

HOME MATCHES
OCTOBER-NOVEMBER

DATE	OPPONENTS	LEAGUE	K.O.
SAT. 2	**INTER - A.C.**	EUROPEAN LEAGUE	15.00
SAT. 9	CARDIFF CITY	FOOTBALL COMBINATION	15.00
SUN. 17	**BENFICA**	EUROPEAN LEAGUE	15.00
SAT. 30	BRISTOL ROVERS	FOOTBALL COMBINATION	15.00
SAT. 6	**ANDERLECHT**	EUROPEAN LEAGUE	15.00
WED. 10	BRISTOL CITY	FOOTBALL COMBINATION	19.30
SAT. 13	SWINDON TOWN	FOOTBALL COMBINATION	15.00
SUN. 21	**MOSCOW**	EUROPEAN LEAGUE	15.00
SAT. 27	CHELSEA	FOOTBALL COMBINATION	15.00

Over 6,000 Unreserved seats available in the North Stand
price £1·60p, payment at the turnstiles only, on the day of the match

that important, the League had insisted on a full programme of matches. The question was justifiably asked: 'Does England deserve a successful team?' Scotland's magnificent defeat of Czechoslovakia and subsequent appearance in West Germany could only make things worse.

Bowing to a late goal from Capello, England fell to Italy the following month to round off the worst period in the history of the national team—defeats at home to West Germany, Northern Ireland and Italy and away to Poland and Italy. The army of anti-Ramsey critics pointed out that not a solitary important game, including the Mexico defeats by Brazil and West Germany, had been won in the first four years of the seventies.

If Ramsey has a can to carry, it must relate to his tactical attitudes. The 1966 triumph was founded on effort and running, and this has been the very essence of the English game since then. Such has been the competitiveness of the First Division that skill has been stifled. In terms of technique the English professional lags behind many European counterparts.

The physical side of football has always been an integral part of the game in England, if not so much Scotland. Lawrie McMenemy, then manager of Grimsby Town, summed it up concisely when, after watching the intricate, chess-board skills of an Ajax–Bayern Munich European Cup encounter, he said: 'Skillful it may be, but they would never watch it week after week in Grimsby.'

But there is a world of difference between honest physical play and cynical violence. And it was the latter which came under the scrutiny of the referees at the start of the 1971-72 season. In an orgy of bookings and sendings-off, the tackle from behind deserved and got particular scrutiny.

If violence on the field had detracted from the game's appeal to the spectators, violence amongst the fans had certainly been a deterrent to standing on the terraces. Gang warfare inside and outside the stadia, running battles at railway stations, scant regard for innocent bystanders, the wrecking of special trains; all were charges laid at the door of the football hooligan. More sordid cases involved assaults with weapons and, finally, a fatality at Coventry after a game against West Ham.

With the media always quick to report such newsworthy material football received unenviable publicity. The fear that a football ground is not a safe place to visit was undoubtedly another contributory factor to the decline in attendances.

Television has offered an alterna-

Opposite *A sign of things to come? Lots of people in the game thought so during the sixties, but then European match attendances began to fall even more steeply than Football League crowds and the possibility of a European Super-League quickly faded.*
Overleaf *Derek Dougan, Chairman of the PFA and sometime Wolves striker.*

tive for those who are prepared to take their spectator sport second hand. The BBC and ITV joined forces to present an organised negotiating front to screen matches and the result is a weekly output of recorded action that can add up to over two hours a week if you watch both channels. They, of course, pay for the privilege—a handsome annual fee, according to the television companies; a paltry sum if you are a member of the League management committee.

Television is both good and bad for the game. As an advertisement for the best (particularly the leading First Division clubs) it is a most powerful medium. But the tele-presenters are so skilled in their art that their edited weekend package can easily pass for the real thing—or, worse, become a more than satisfactory substitute for it.

On many weekends the dedicated viewer can see the goals and highlights of no less than five First Division matches. When the FA Cup is in its most intriguing stage sometimes six games reach the screen—all for the price of the electricity it takes to make the set work.

Even more pernicious—and far more subtle—is the risk that the young fan, weaned on many hours of *Match of the Day* and *The Big Match*, will be disappointed by the real thing when he is taken to a ground and discovers that goals do not arrive every three or four minutes, that there are no action replays, that a place on the terraces is not as comfortable as the sofa in front of the fire, and that Brian Clough does not miraculously appear to explain the finer points.

The subtle influence of goals every five minutes

What television has been able to do is to bring football's stars to the attention of the world. The age of the football super-star is exclusively a product of the polished media. But in the seventies George Best found that image too much to bear and decided to opt out. Best's genius has been matched by his immaturity, for which football is largely responsible. After several years of unreliability leading to indiscipline, he walked out on Manchester United in November 1972, and announced that at 26 he was retiring.

For nine months his immeasurable talent lay fallow, and perhaps wasted away. His, possibly inevitable, return in the September of the following year, a podgy caricature of himself, was welcomed but seemed doomed with an air of a toy needing new batteries. By January 1974 he was skipping training and, yet again, found himself on the transfer list. This time, significantly, the press took very little notice.

With the gradual decline of his contemporaries, like Geoff Hurst and Ron Davies, the replacing generation found it difficult to supply men who could put the ball in the net week in, week out. The problem was magnified at international level where Alf Ramsey

was continually shaking his head at sound team performances which fell short of success because no one could put the ball between the posts.

But even the seventies have offered some moments of magic. Arsenal became the fourth side in the history of the game to complete the League and Cup double. Their triumph in 1971 perhaps has more merit than the previous doubles of Preston, Aston Villa and Tottenham Hotspur. Their unceasing hounding of Leeds United in the League race and the character they showed in coming from behind to win the FA Cup in extra time (after even more of a tightrope performance against Stoke in the semi-final) somehow compensated for the steamrollering style which was often more effective than pretty.

Though the World Cup and the European Cup have emphasised England's lack of success at the highest international and club level, the minor European trophies have almost become resident in the boardrooms of the League clubs. Manchester City in 1970 and Chelsea the following year brought home the Cup Winners Cup, while the UEFA Cup, once the Fairs Cup, was successively with Leeds, Newcastle, Arsenal, Leeds, Spurs and Liverpool.

In domestic football, Stoke City added a little glitter to the League Cup when they beat Chelsea in the 1972 final. Appropriately enough for a team which has always recognised the value of age and experience, 35-year-old George Eastham shot the winning goal (his first for three years) and another veteran, Gordon Banks, won his first club medal.

But even Stoke's feat was eclipsed fourteen months later by Stoke's. As manager of Second Division Sunderland, Bob Stokoe was the key figure in the most dramatic of FA Cup Finals. A solidly struck goal by midfield player Ian Porterfield created the biggest upset of the century, by beating Leeds United the odds-on favourites. 1973 was the year of Sunderland. There was little else in football to celebrate.

For Leeds, certainly the club team of the seventies, it was another bewildering occasion when they failed on the fringe of the greatest prize. In four FA Cup Finals under Don Revie, they had only once won. Five times they had been runners-up in the First Division; winners again only once.

In many ways Leeds United are the microcosm of the problems of the seventies. Their gradual evolution into a strong team has been based on physical play with an emphasis on defence. They have been roundly accused of overstepping the mark in terms of what is called professionalism, of setting a bad example from the top. Their disciplinary record was appalling, and at the start of the 1972-73 season their ground was closed because of the bad behaviour of the crowd.

Yet there was a significant change at the start of the following campaign. The players, under the threat of the FA, behaved; not only did they win but they became a

free-scoring side. And in January they beat a League record by going their first 24 games unbeaten— and they did it in style!

Of the other club sides Celtic were the most notable—reaching a second European Cup final in 1970 but contributing to the game's lack of appeal north of the border by refusing to give up the League Championship. What had traditionally been a two horse race was now a walkover. In 1973 they won their record eighth consecutive title—a whole generation of spectators had grown up without realising that Celtic at the top of the League was not an immutable law. More interesting, perhaps, were their series of consecutive defeats in the first four League Cup finals of the decade.

Should Allison ever have bought Rodney Marsh?

Back south of the border there was only really Leeds. Derby shone intermittently, but finally fell to Brian Clough's showmanship when he resigned and all concerned acted out a parody of how not to run a football club. Manchester City, having reached their height in the 'After the Goal Rush' Final of 1969 when Neil Young's shot made Leicester runners-up for the fourth time in 20 years, declined gradually losing first Mercer, then Allison, then Johnny Hart through nervous exhaustion. Before he left in 1972, Allison at least made one of the most questionable decisions of the decade—buying the enigmatic Rodney Marsh when City seemed to have the Championship tied up. But the side fell apart, Derby crept through to the title, and Allison's reputation was scarred. As Joe Mercer commented: '£200,000 is a lot of money to spend just to lose the Championship'.

Elsewhere Spurs threatened to kill the League Cup singlehanded with two dreadful finals which they won with the greatest difficulty. Manchester United went through managers like most players go through chewing gum in an attempt to halt their decline. Half way through the 1973-74 season goalkeeper Alex Stepney remained their leading scorer—with 2 penalties and no George Best. Otherwise the North East looked the most likely source of the successor to Leeds. If not the improving Newcastle, or Cup winning Sunderland, then perhaps Jack Charlton's new Middlesbrough.

In 1974s economic crisis, gates of 13,000 for Burnley against Arsenal passed without comment. For a time games were played on Sundays and, when the idea proved a success, football's authorities surprised no one by abandoning the experiment. Almost as significant was a unique FA ruling which ordered a replay of the Newcastle-Nottingham Forest quarter-final after a crowd invasion when the home team were 3-1 down. The season ended in a sombre mood. The lights had come on again—but whether they would ever shine so brightly was another question.

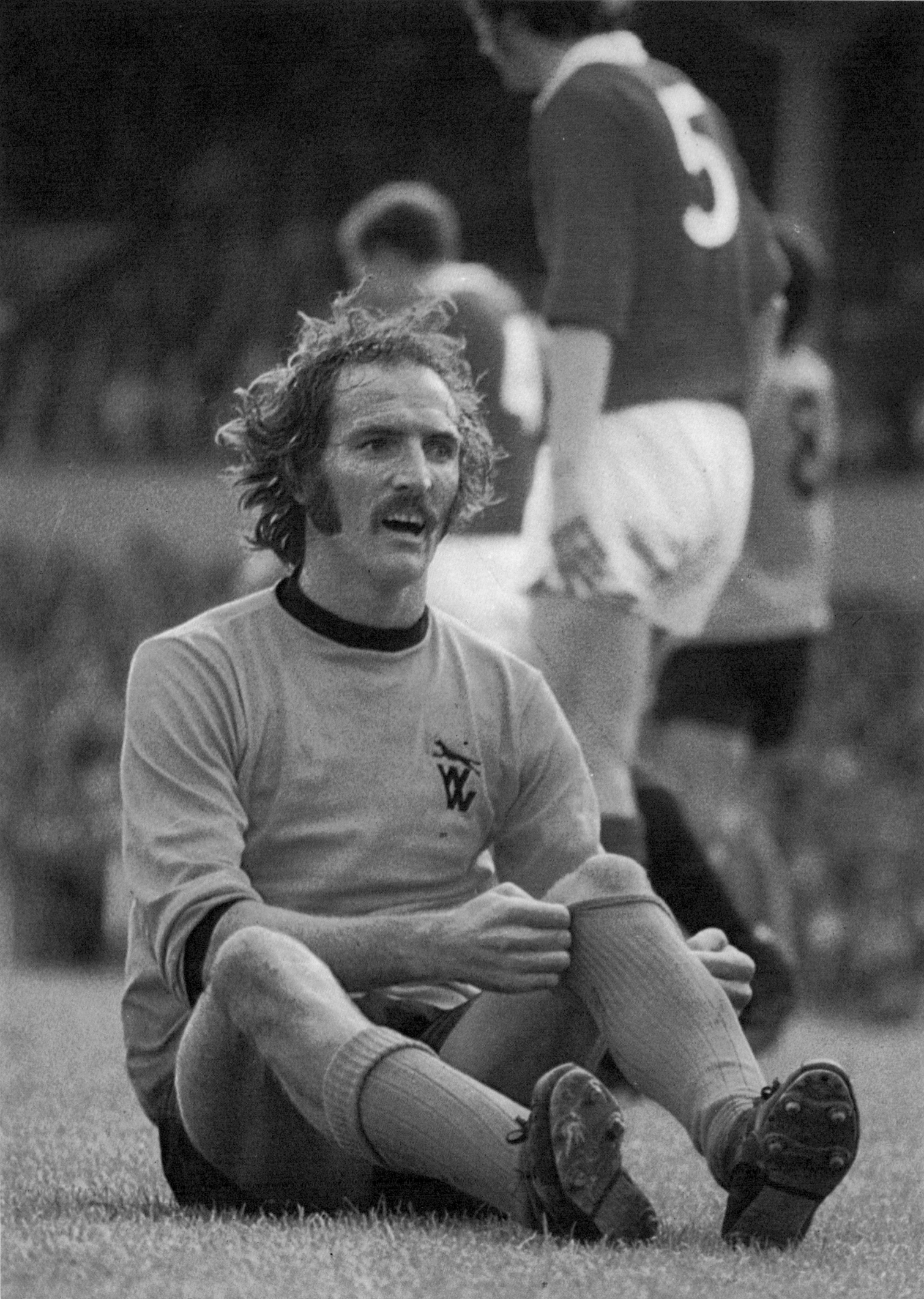

The Clubs

ALDERSHOT

Founded: 1927
Address: Recreation Ground, High Street, Aldershot
Telephone: Aldershot 20211
Ground capacity: 20,000 (2,000 seated)
Playing area: 117 by 76 yards
Record attendance: 19,138 v Carlisle United, FA Cup 4th round replay, 28.1.70
Record victory: 8-1 v Gateshead, Division IV, 1958-59
Record defeat: 0-9 v Bristol City, Division III(S), 28.12.46
Most League points: 56, Division IV, 1972-73
Most League goals: 83, Division IV, 1963-64
League scoring record: 23, Bobby Howfield, Division IV, 1961-62
　　　　　　　　　　　　　 Ron Fogg, Division IV, 1963-64
Record League aggregate: 127, Jack Howarth, 1965-1973
Most League appearances: 330, Len Walker, 1964-73
Most capped player: None

THE ALDERSHOT RECORD

	Division & place	Cup round reached
1933	SIII 17	5
1934	SIII 14	3
1935	SIII 18	3
1936	SIII 11	1
1937	SIII 22	1
1938	SIII 18	3
1939	SIII 10	2
1946		4
1947	SIII 20	2
1948	SIII 19	2
1949	SIII 21	3
1950	SIII 20	1
1951	SIII 18	3
1952	SIII 12	2
1953	SIII 19	1
1954	SIII 17	2
1955	SIII 14	2
1956	SIII 15	3
1957	SIII 19	1
1958	SIII 18	3
1959	IV 22	1
1960	IV 13	1
1961	IV 10	4
1962	IV 7	2
1963	IV 11	2
1964	IV 9	4
1965	IV 18	2
1966	IV 17	2
1967	IV 10	3
1968	IV 9	1
1969	IV 15	1
1970	IV 6	4
1971	IV 13	3
1972	IV 17	2
1973	IV 4P	2

S – Third Division South
P – promoted

Aldershot defend against Brentford at the Recreation Ground in 1972.

ARSENAL

Founded: 1886
Address: Arsenal Stadium, Highbury, London N.5
Telephone: (01) 226 3312
Ground capacity: 63,000 (17,500 seated)
Playing area: 110 by 71 yards
Record attendance: 73,295 v Sunderland, Division 1, 9.3.35
Record victory: 12-0 v Loughborough Town, Division II, 12.3.1900
Record defeat: 0-8 v Loughborough Town, Division II, 12.12.96
Most League points: 66, Division I, 1930-31
Most League goals: 127, Division I, 1930-31
League scoring record: 42, Ted Drake, Division I, 1934-35
Record League aggregate: 150, Cliff Bastin, 1930-1947
Most League appearances: 422, Bob John, 1922-1937
Most capped player: 44 (59 in all), Terry Neill, Northern Ireland

FA Cup	Year	Opponents	Score	Scorers
Winners	1930	Huddersfield Town	2-0	James, Lambert
	1936	Sheffield United	1-0	Drake
	1950	Liverpool	2-0	Lewis 2
	1971	Liverpool	*2-1	Kelly, George
Runners-up	1927	Cardiff City	0-1	
	1932	Newcastle United	1-2	John
	1952	Newcastle United	0-1	
	1972	Leeds United	0-1	
League Cup				
Runners-up	1968	Leeds United	0-1	
	1969	Swindon Town	*1-3	Gould

* – after extra time

THE ARSENAL RECORD

	Division & place	Cup round reached				
1890		q	1933	I 1C	3
1891		1	1934	I 1C	q-f
1892		1	1935	I 1C	q-f
1893		1	1936	I 6	Winners
1894	II 9	1	1937	I 3	q-f
1895	II 8	1	1938	I 1C	5
1896	II 7	1	1939	I 5	3
1897	II 10	q	1946		3
1898	II 5	1	1947	I 13	3
1899	II 7	1	1948	I 1C	3
1900	II 8	q	1949	I 5	4
1901	II 7	2	1950	I 6	Winners
1902	II 4	1	1951	I 5	5
1903	II 3	1	1952	I 3	Final
1904	II 2P	2	1953	I 1C	q-f
1905	I 10	1	1954	I 12	4
1906	I 12	s-f	1955	I 9	4
1907	I 7	s-f	1956	I 5	q-f
1908	I 14	1	1957	I 5	q-f
1909	I 6	2	1958	I 12	3
1910	I 18	2	1959	I 3	5
1911	I 10	2	1960	I 13	3
1912	I 10	1	1961	I 11	3
1913	I 20R	2	1962	I 10	4
1914	II 3	1	1963	I 7	5
1915	II 6P	2	1964	I 8	5
1920	I 11	2	1965	I 13	4
1921	I 9	1	1966	I 14	3
1922	I 17	q-f	1967	I 7	5
1923	I 11	1	1968	I 9	5
1924	I 19	2	1969	I 4	5
1925	I 20	1	1970	I 12	3
1926	I 2	q-f	1971	I 1C	Winners
1927	I 11	Final	1972	I 5	Final
1928	I 10	s-f	1973	I 2	s-f
1929	I 9	q-f			
1930	I 14	Winners			
1931	I 1C	4			
1932	I 2	Final			

q – qualifying rounds
P – promoted
R – relegated
C – Football League champions

ASTON VILLA

Founded: 1874
Address: Villa Park, Trinity Road, Birmingham 6
Telephone: (021) 327 6604
Ground capacity: 65,250 (11,750 seated)
Playing area: 115 by 75 yards
Record attendance: 76,588 v Derby County, FA Cup quarter-final, 2.3.46
Record victory: 13-0 v Wednesday Old Alliance, FA Cup 1st round, 30.10.86
Record defeat: 1-8 v Blackburn Rovers, FA Cup 3rd round, 1888-89
Most League points: 70, Division III, 1971-72
Most League goals: 128, Division I, 1930-31
League scoring record: 49, Pongo Waring, Division I, 1930-31
Record League aggregate: 213, Harry Hampton, 1904-1920
and Billy Walker, 1919-1934
Most League appearances: 480, Billy Walker, 1919-1934
Most capped player: 33 (out of 34), Peter McParland, Northern Ireland

FA Cup

	Year	Opponents	Score	Scorers
Winners	1887	West Bromwich Albion	2-0	Hodgetts, Hunter
	1895	West Bromwich Albion	1-0	Chatt
	1897	Everton	3-2	Campbell, Wheldon, Crabtree
	1905	Newcastle United	2-0	Hampton 2
	1913	Sunderland	1-0	Barber
	1920	Huddersfield Town	1-0	Kirton
	1957	Manchester United	2-1	McParland 2
Runners-up	1892	West Bromwich Albion	0-3	
	1924	Newcastle United	0-2	

League Cup

	Year	Opponents	Score	Scorers
Winners	1961	Rotherham United	A0-2	
			H3-0	O'Neill, Burrows, McParland
Runners-up	1963	Birmingham City	A1-3	Thomson
			H0-0	
	1971	Tottenham Hotspur	0-2	

THE VILLA RECORD

Year	Division & place	Cup round reached
1880		3
1881		4
1882		4
1883		q-f
1884		4
1885		3
1886		2
1887		Winners
1888		1
1889	I 2	q-f
1890	I 8	2
1891	I 9	2
1892	I 4	Final
1893	I 4	1
1894	I 1C	q-f
1895	I 3	Winners
1896	I 1C	1
1897	I 1C	Winners
1898	I 6	1
1899	I 1C	1
1900	I 1C	q-f
1901	I 15	s-f
1902	I 8	1
1903	I 2	s-f
1904	I 5	2
1905	I 4	Winners
1906	I 8	3
1907	I 5	2
1908	I 2	3
1909	I 7	1
1910	I 1C	3
1911	I 2	2
1912	I 6	2
1913	I 2	Winners
1914	I 2	s-f
1915	I 13	2
1920	I 9	Winners
1921	I 10	q-f
1922	I 5	q-f
1923	I 6	1
1924	I 6	Final
1925	I 15	3
1926	I 6	5
1927	I 10	3
1928	I 8	5
1929	I 3	s-f
1930	I 4	q-f
1931	I 2	3
1932	I 5	4
1933	I 2	4
1934	I 13	s-f
1935	I 13	3
1936	I 21R	3
1937	II 9	3
1938	II 1P	s-f
1939	I 12	4
1946		q-f
1947	I 8	3
1948	I 6	3
1949	I 10	4
1950	I 12	3
1951	I 15	4
1952	I 6	3
1953	I 11	q-f
1954	I 13	3
1955	I 6	4
1956	I 20	4
1957	I 10	Winners
1958	I 14	3
1959	I 21R	s-f
1960	II 1P	s-f
1961	I 9	5
1962	I 7	q-f
1963	I 15	4
1964	I 19	3
1965	I 16	5
1966	I 16	3
1967	I 21R	4
1968	II 16	4
1969	II 18	5
1970	II 21R	3
1971	III 4	1
1972	III 1P	1
1973	II 3	3

C — Football League champions
P — promoted
R — relegated

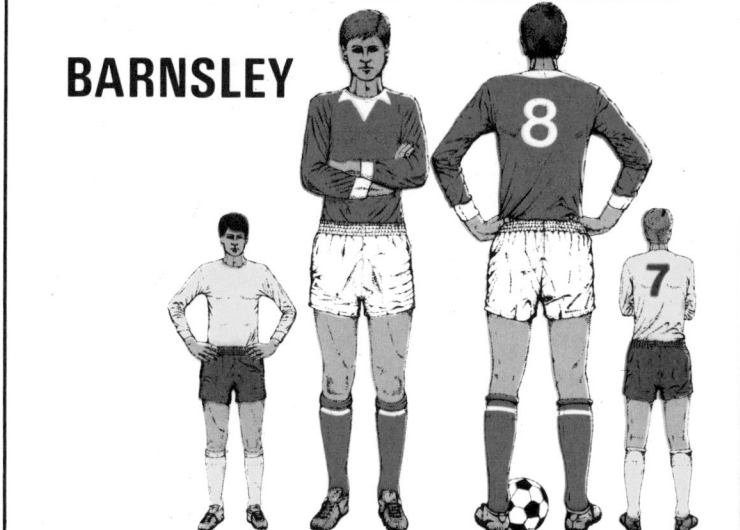

BARNSLEY

Formed: 1887 (as Barnsley St Peter's)
Address: Oakwell Ground, Grove Street, Barnsley, Yorkshire
Telephone: 0226 84113
Ground capacity: 38,500
Playing area: 111 by 75 yards
Record attendance: 40,255 v Stoke City, FA Cup 5th round, 15.2.36
Record victory: 9-0 v Loughborough Town, Division II, 28.1.1899
9-0 v Accrington Stanley, Division III(N), 3.2.34
Record defeat: 0-9 v Notts County, Division II, 19.11.27
Most League points: 67, Division III(N), 1938-39
Most League goals: 118, Division III(N), 1933-34
League scoring record: 33, Cecil McCormack, Division II, 1950-51
Record League aggregate: 123, Ernest Hine, 1921-1926 and 1934-1938
Most League appearances: 409, Eric Winstanley, 1961-1973
Most capped player: 9 (15 in all), Eddie McMorran, Ireland

FA Cup

	Year	Opponents	Score	Scorers
Winners	1912	West Bromwich Albion	0-0	
	Replay		1-0	Tufnell
Runners-up	1910	Newcastle United	1-1	Tufnell
	Replay		0-2	

THE BARNSLEY RECORD

Year	Division & place	Cup round reached
1895		1
1896		p
1897		1
1898		p
1899	II 11	1
1900	II 16	p
1901	II 15	p
1902	II 11	p
1903	II 8	2
1904	II 8	1
1905	II 7	1
1906	II 12	2
1907	II 8	q-f
1908	II 16	1
1909	II 17	1
1910	II 9	Final
1911	II 19	2
1912	II 6	Winners
1913	II 4	2
1914	II 5	1
1915	II 3	1
1920	II 12	2
1921	II 16	1
1922	II 3	3
1923	II 9	2
1924	II 11	1
1925	II 15	2
1926	II 18	1
1927	II 11	4
1928	II 14	3
1929	II 16	3
1930	II 17	3
1931	II 19	5
1932	II 21R	3
1933	NIII 8	3
1934	NIII 1P	1
1935	II 16	3
1936	II 20	q-f
1937	II 14	3
1938	II 21R	4
1939	NIII 1P	3
1946		5
1947	II 10	4
1948	II 12	3
1949	II 9	3
1950	II 13	3
1951	II 15	3
1952	II 20	4
1953	II 22R	4
1954	NIII 2	2
1955	NIII 1P	2
1956	II 18	4
1957	II 19	5
1958	II 14	3
1959	II 22R	3
1960	III 17	1
1961	III 8	q-f
1962	III 20	2
1963	III 18	3
1964	III 20	5
1965	III 24R	2
1966	IV 16	2
1967	IV 16	3
1968	IV 2P	1
1969	III 10	3
1970	III 7	2
1971	III 12	2
1972	III 22R	2
1973	IV 14	1

P — promoted
R — relegated
N — Third Division North
p — preliminary round

Numbers favour Villa in a two-to-one situation at Villa Park.

BIRMINGHAM CITY

Founded: 1875
Address: St Andrew's, Birmingham 9
Telephone: Birmingham 772 0101
Ground capacity: 55,000 (7,750 seated)
Playing area: 115 by 75 yards
Record attendance: 66,844 v Everton, FA Cup 5th round, 11.2.39
Record victory: 12-0 v Walsall Town Swifts, Division II, 4.1.03
12-0 v Doncaster Rovers, Division II, 11.4.03
Record defeat: 1-9 v Sheffield Wednesday, 13.12.30
Most League points: 59, Division II, 1947-48
Most League goals: 103, Division II, 1893-94
League scoring record: 29, Joe Bradford, Division I, 1927-28
Record League aggregate: 250, Joe Bradford, Division I, 1921-1935
Most capped player: 25, Harry Hibbs, England
Most League appearances: 486, Gil Merrick, 1946-1960

FA Cup	Year	Opponents	Score	Scorers
Runners-up	1931	West Bromwich Albion	1-2	Bradford
	1956	Manchester City	1-3	Kinsey
League Cup				
Winners	1963	Aston Villa	h3-1 a0-0	Leek 2, Bloomfield

THE BIRMINGHAM RECORD

	Division & place	Cup round reached
1889*		1
1890		2
1891		d
1892		2
1893	II 1	1
1894	II 2P	1
1895	II 12	1
1896	I 15R	1
1897	II 4	1
1898	II 6	q
1899	II 8	2
1900	II 3	q
1901	II 2P	3
1902	I 17R	p
1903	II 2P	1
1904	I 11	p
1905	I 7	1
1906†	I 7	4
1907	I 9	1
1908	I 20R	1
1909	II 11	1
1910	II 20	1
1911	II 16	1
1912	II 12	1
1913	II 3	3
1914	II 14	3
1915	II 5	3
1920	II 5	3
1921	II 1P	1
1922	II 18	§
1923	I 17	1
1924	I 14	2
1925	I 8	3
1926	I 14	4
1927	I 17	4
1928	I 11	5
1929	I 15	4
1930	I 11	4
1931	I 19	Final
1932	I 9	4
1933	I 13	6
1934	I 20	5
1935	I 19	6
1936	I 12	3
1937	I 11	3
1938	I 18	3
1939	I 21R	5
1946††		s-f
1947	II 3	q-f
1948	II 1P	3
1949	I 17	3
1950	I 22R	3
1951	II 4	s-f
1952	II 3	4
1953	II 6	q-f
1954	II 7	4
1955	II 1P	q-f
1956	I 6	Final
1957	I 12	s-f
1958	I 13	3
1959	I 9	5
1960	I 19	3
1961	I 19	5
1962	I 17	3
1963	I 20	3
1964	I 20	3
1965	I 22R	3
1966	II 10	4
1967	II 10	q-f
1968	II 4	s-f
1969	II 7	5
1970	II 18	3
1971	II 9	3
1972	II 2P	s-f
1973	I 10	3

q – qualifying round
p – preliminary round
P – promoted
R – relegated
* – as Small Heath until 1905
† – as Birmingham until 1945
†† – as Birmingham City
§ – did not enter
d – disqualified for fielding an ineligible player

BLACKBURN ROVERS

Founded: 1875
Address: Ewood Park, Blackburn
Telephone: Blackburn 55432
Ground capacity: 47,500 (7,000 seated)
Playing area: 110 by 75 yards
Record attendance: 61,783 v Bolton Wanderers, FA Cup quarter-final, 2.3.29
Record victory: 11-0 v Rossendale United, FA Cup, 1884-85
Record defeat: 0-8 v Arsenal, Division I, 25.2.33
Most League points: 56, Division II, 1957-58
Most League goals: 114, Division II, 1954-55
League scoring record: 43, Ted Harper, Division I, 1925-26
Record League aggregate: 140, Tom Briggs, 1952-1958
Most League appearances: 580, Ronnie Clayton, 1950-1969
Most capped player: 41, Bob Crompton, England

FA Cup	Year	Opponents	Score	Scorers
Winners	1884	Queen's Park	2-1	Brown, Forrest
	1885	Queen's Park	2-0	Forrest, Brown
	1886	West Bromwich Albion	0-0	
			2-0	Sowerbutts, Brown
	1890	Sheffield Wednesday	6-1	Dewar, Southworth, Lofthouse, Townley 3
	1891	Notts County	3-1	Dewar, Southworth, Townley
	1928	Huddersfield Town	3-1	Roscamp 2, McLean
Runners-up	1882	Old Etonians	0-1	
	1960	Wolverhampton Wanderers	0-3	

THE BLACKBURN RECORD

	Division & place	Cup round reached
1880		3
1881		2
1882		Final
1883		2
1884		Winners
1885		Winners
1886		Winners
1887		2
1888		2
1889	I 4	s-f
1890	I 3	Winners
1891	I 6	Winners
1892	I 9	2
1893	I 9	s-f
1894	I 4	s-f
1895	I 5	2
1896	I 8	1
1897	I 14	3
1898	I 15	1
1899	I 6	1
1900	I 4	2
1901	I 9	1
1902	I 4	1
1903	I 16	2
1904	I 15	3
1905	I 13	1
1906	I 9	1
1907	I 12	2
1908	I 14	1
1909	I 4	3
1910	I 3	3
1911	I 12	s-f
1912	I 1C	s-f
1913	I 5	q-f
1914	I 1C	3
1915	I 3	1
1920	I 20	1
1921	I 11	1
1922	I 15	3
1923	I 14	2
1924	I 8	1
1925	I 16	s-f
1926	I 12	4
1927	I 18	3
1928	I 12	Winners
1929	I 7	q-f
1930	I 6	5
1931	I 10	5
1932	I 16	4
1933	I 15	4
1934	I 8	3
1935	I 15	5
1936	I 15	5
1936	I 22R	4
1937	II 12	3
1938	II 16	3
1939	II 1P	q-f
1946		3
1947	I 17	5
1948	I 22R	4
1949	II 14	3
1950	II 16	3
1951	II 6	3
1952	II 14	s-f
1953	II 9	3
1954	II 3	4
1955	II 6	3
1956	II 4	5
1957	II 4	4
1958	II 2P	s-f
1959	I 10	4
1960	I 17	Final
1961	I 18	5
1962	I 16	q-f
1963	I 11	3
1964	I 7	5
1965	I 10	3
1966	I 22R	q-f
1967	II 4	3
1968	II 8	3
1969	II 19	5
1970	II 8	3
1971	II 21R	3
1972	III 10	1
1973	III 3	2

P – promoted
R – relegated

BLACKPOOL

Founded: 1887
Address: Bloomfield Road, Blackpool
Telephone: Blackpool 46118
Ground capacity: 38,000 (6,500 seated)
Playing area: 110 by 72 yards
Record attendance: 39,118 v Manchester United, Division I, 19.4.32
Record victory: 8-4 v Charlton, Division I, 27.9.52
Record defeat: 1-10 v Huddersfield Town, Division I, 13.12.30
Most League points: 58, Division II, 1929-30
Most League goals: 98, Division II, 1929-30
League scoring record: 45, Jimmy Hampson, Division II, 1929-30
Record League aggregate: 247, Jimmy Hampson, 1927-1938
Most League appearances: 568, Jimmy Armfield, 1952 1971
Most capped player: 43, Jimmy Armfield, England

FA Cup	Year	Opponents	Score	Scorers
Winners	1953	Bolton Wanderers	4-3	Mortensen 3, Perry
Runners-up	1948	Manchester United	2-4	Shimwell (pen), Mortensen
	1951	Newcastle United	0-2	

THE BLACKPOOL RECORD

	Division & place	Cup round reached				
1892		1	1933	I 22R	5	
1893		1	1934	II 11	4	
1894		p	1935	II 4	3	
1895		p	1936	II 3	4	
1896		1	1937	II 2P	3	
1897	II 8	1	1938	I 12	4	
1898	II 11	p	1939	I 15	3	
1899	II 16	2	1946		4	
1900*			1947	I 5	3	
1901	II 12	p	1948	I 9	Final	
1902	II 12	p	1949	I 16	4	
1903	II 14	q	1950	I 7	q-f	
1904	II 15		1951	I 3	Final	
1905	II 15	1	1952	I 9	3	
1906	II 14	3	1953	I 7	Winners	
1907	II 13	1	1954	I 6	5	
1908	II 15	1	1955	I 19	3	
1909	II 20	2	1956	I 2	3	
1910	II 12	1	1957	I 4	5	
1911	II 9	1	1958	I 7	3	
1912	II 14	2	1959	I 8	q-f	
1913	II 20	1	1960	I 11	4	
1914	II 16	1	1961	I 20	3	
1915	II 10	1	1962	I 13	3	
1920	II 4	2	1963	I 13	3	
1921	II 4	2	1964	I 18	3	
1922	II 19	1	1965	I 17	3	
1923	II 5	1	1966	I 13	3	
1924	II 4	2	1967	I 22R	3	
1925	II 17	q-f	1968	II 3	4	
1926	II 6	3	1969	II 8	3	
1927	II 9	3	1970	II 2P	4	
1928	II 19	3	1971	I 22R	4	
1929	II 8	3	1972	II 6	3	
1930	II 1P	4	1973	II 7	3	
1931	I 20	4				
1932	I 20	3				

P – promoted
R – relegated
p – preliminary round
q – qualifying round
* – failed to obtain re-election in 1899

Full-back Jimmy Armfield in 1970-71, his 17th season with Blackpool.

BOLTON WANDERERS

Founded: 1874
Address: Burnden Park, Bolton, BL5 2QR
Telephone: Bolton 21101
Ground capacity: 60,136 (8,000 seated)
Playing area: 113 by 76 yards
Record attendance: 69,912 v Manchester City, FA Cup 5th round, 18.2.33
Record victory: 13-0 v Sheffield United, FA Cup 2nd round, 1.2.1890
Record defeat: 0-7 v Manchester City, Division I, 21.3.36
Most League points: 56, Division II, 1934-35
Most League goals: 96, Division II, 1934-35
League scoring record: 38, Joe Smith, Division I, 1920-21
Record League aggregate: 255, Nat Lofthouse, 1946-1961
Most League appearances: 508, Eddie Hopkinson, 1956-1970
Most capped player: 33, Nat Lofthouse, England

FA Cup	Year	Opponents	Score	Scorers
Winners	1923	West Ham United	2-0	Jack, J R Smith
	1926	Manchester City	1-0	Jack
	1929	Portsmouth	2-0	Butler, Blackmore
	1958	Manchester United	2-0	Lofthouse (2)
Runners-up	1894	Notts County	1-4	Cassidy
	1904	Manchester City	0-1	
	1953	Blackpool	3-4	Lofthouse, Moir, Bell

THE BOLTON WANDERERS RECORD

	Division & place	Cup round reached				
1882		2	1927	I 4	5	
1883		3	1928	I 7	4	
1884		4	1929	I 14	Winners	
1885		q	1930	I 15	3	
1886		3	1931	I 14	4	
1887		q	1932	I 17	3	
1888		q	1933	I 21R	5	
1889	I 5	q	1934	II 3	q-f	
1890	I 9	s-f	1935	II 2P	s-f	
1891	I 5	1	1936	I 13	3	
1892	I 3	1	1937	I 20	5	
1893	I 5	1	1938	I 7	3	
1894	I 13	Final	1939	I 8	3	
1895	I 10	q-f	1946		s-f	
1896	I 4	s-f	1947	I 18	4	
1897	I 8	2	1948	I 17	3	
1898	I 11	q-f	1949	I 14	3	
1899	I 17R	1	1950	I 16	4	
1900	II 2P	1	1951	I 8	4	
1901	I 10	2	1952	I 5	3	
1902	I 12	2	1953	I 14	Final	
1903	I 18R	1	1954	I 5	q-f	
1904	II 7	Final	1955	I 18	4	
1905	II 2P	q-f	1956	I 8	4	
1906	I 6	1	1957	I 9	3	
1907	I 6	3	1958	I 15	Winners	
1908	I 19R	3	1959	I 4	q-f	
1909	II 1P	1	1960	I 6	4	
1910	I 20R	1	1961	I 18	4	
1911	II 2P	1	1962	I 11	3	
1912	I 4	3	1963	I 18	3	
1913	I 8	1	1964	I 21R	4	
1914	I 6	3	1965	II 3	5	
1915	I 17	s-f	1966	II 9	4	
1920	I 6	1	1967	II 9	4	
1921	I 3	1	1968	II 12	3	
1922	I 6	2	1969	II 17	4	
1923	I 13	Winners	1970	II 16	3	
1924	I 4	2	1971	II 22R	3	
1925	I 3	2	1972	III 8	4	
1926	I 8	Winners	1973	III 1P	5	

P – promoted
R – relegated
q – qualifying rounds

AFC BOURNEMOUTH

Founded: 1899 (as Boscombe)
Address: Dean Court, Bournemouth, Hampshire
Telephone: Bournemouth 35381
Ground capacity: 24,000
Playing area: 115 by 74 yards
Record attendance: 28,799 v Manchester United, FA Cup quarter-final, 2.3.57
Record victory: 11-0 v Margate, FA Cup 1st round, 20.11.71
Record defeat: 1-8 v Bradford City, Division III, 24.1.70
Most League points: 62, Division III, 1971-72
Most League goals: 88, Division III(S), 1956-57
League scoring record: 42, Ted Macdougall, 1970-71
Record League aggregate: 202, Ron Eyre, 1924-1933
Most League appearances: 412, Ray Bumstead, 1958-1970
Most capped player: 4 (13 in all), Tommy Godwin, Eire

THE BOURNEMOUTH RECORD

	Division & place	Cup round reached			Division & place	Cup round reached
1924	SIII 21	*		1952	SIII 14	1
1925	SIII 20	q		1953	SIII 9	1
1926	SIII 8	4		1954	SIII 19	2
1927	SIII 7	3		1955	SIII 17	3
1928	SIII 14	3		1956	SIII 9	1
1929	SIII 9	5		1957	SIII 5	q-f
1930	SIII 10	3		1958	SIII 9	2
1931	SIII 10	1		1959	III 12	1
1932	SIII 15	4		1960	III 10	4
1933	SIII 18	1		1961	III 19	3
1934	SIII 21	2		1962	III 3	1
1935	SIII 17	1		1963	III 5	1
1936	SIII 8	3		1964	III 4	1
1937	SIII 6	3		1965	III 11	2
1938	SIII 13	2		1966	III 18	3
1939	SIII 15	3		1967	III 20	2
1946		1		1968	III 12	3
1947	SIII 7	3		1969	III 4	2
1948	SIII 2	3		1970	III 21R	1
1949	SIII 3	3		1971	IV 2P	3
1950	SIII 12	4		1972	III 3	3
1951	SIII 9	2		1973	III 7	3

q – qualifying round
P – promoted   R – relegated
S – Third Division South
* – did not enter

BRADFORD CITY

Founded: 1903
Address: Valley Parade Ground, Bradford 8, Yorkshire
Telephone: Bradford 26565
Ground capacity: 24,500 (2,120 seated)
Playing area: 112 by 70 yards
Record attendance: 39,146 v Burnley, FA Cup 4th round, 11.3.11
Record victory: 11-1 v Rotherham United, Division III(N), 25.8.28
Record defeat: 1-9 v Colchester United, Division IV, 30.12.61
Most League points: 63, Division III(N), 1928-29
Most League goals: 128, Division III(N), 1928-29
League scoring record: 34, David Layne, Division IV, 1961-62
Record League aggregate: 88, Frank O'Rourke, 1906-1913
Most League appearances: 402, Bruce Stowell, 1958-1972
Most capped player: 9, H Hampton, Ireland

FA Cup	Year	Opponents	Score	Scorers
Winners	1911	Newcastle United	0-0	
	Replay		1-0	Spiers

THE BRADFORD CITY RECORD

	Division & place	Cup round reached			Division & place	Cup round reached
				1938	NIII 14	3
				1939	NIII 3	1
				1946		1
1904	II 10	p		1947	NIII 5	1
1905	II 8	p		1948	NIII 14	2
1906	II 11	3		1949	NIII 22	2
1907	II 5	3		1950	NIII 19	2
1908	II 1P	1		1951	NIII 7	1
1909	I 18	3		1952	NIII 15	2
1910	I 7	2		1953	NIII 16	2
1911	I 5	Winners		1954	NIII 5	1
1912	I 11	q-f		1955	NIII 21	3
1913	I 13	1		1956	NIII 8	2
1914	I 9	2		1957	NIII 9	1
1915	I 10	q-f		1958	NIII 3	3
1920	I 15	q-f		1959	III 11	4
1921	I 15	2		1960	III 19	5
1922	I 21R	2		1961	III 22R	2
1923	II 15	1		1962	IV 5	3
1924	II 18	1		1963	IV 23	3
1925	II 16	3		1964	IV 5	1
1926	II 16	3		1965	IV 19	1
1927	II 22R	3		1966	IV 23	1
1928	NIII 6	2		1967	IV 11	1
1929	NIII 1P	4		1968	IV 5	2
1930	II 18	5		1969	IV 4P	1
1931	II 10	4		1970	III 10	3
1932	II 7	3		1971	III 19	2
1933	II 11	3		1972	III 24R	1
1934	II 6	3		1973	IV 16	4
1935	II 20	4				
1936	II 12	5				
1937	II 21R	3				

P—promoted   R—relegated
N—Third Division North
p—preliminary round
q—qualifying round

BRENTFORD

Founded: 1888
Address: Griffin Park, Braemar Road, Brentford, Middlesex
Telephone: 01 560 2021
Ground capacity: 37,000 (4,500 seated)
Playing area: 114 by 75 yards
Record attendance: 39,626 v Preston North End, FA Cup quarter-final, 5.3.38
Record victory: 9-0 v Wrexham, Division III, 15.10.63
Record defeat: 0-7 v Swansea Town, Division III(S), 8.11.24
0-7 v Walsall, Division III(S), 19.1.57
Most League points: 62, Division III(S), 1932-33; Division IV, 1962-63
Most League goals: 98, Division IV, 1962-63
League scoring record: 36, John Holliday, Division III(S), 1932-33
Record League aggregate: 153, Jim Towers, 1954-1961
Most League appearances: 514, Ken Coote, 1949-1964
Most capped player: 12, Idris Hopkins, Wales

THE BRENTFORD RECORD

	Division & place	Cup round reached			Division & place	Cup round reached
				1950	II 9	3
				1951	II 9	3
				1952	II 10	4
1920		1		1953	II 17	4
1921	III 21	1		1954	II 21R	3
1922	SIII 9	1		1955	SIII 11	4
1923	SIII 14	p		1956	SIII 6	2
1924	SIII 17	p		1957	SIII 8	2
1925	SIII 21	p		1958	SIII 2	1
1926	SIII 18	2		1959	III 3	4
1927	SIII 11	5		1960	III 6	3
1928	SIII 12	3		1961	III 17	1
1929	SIII 13	2		1962	III 23R	1
1930	SII 2	1		1963	IV 1P	1
1931	SIII 3	4		1964	III 16	4
1932	SIII 5	4		1965	III 5	3
1933	SIII 1P	1		1966	III 23R	2
1934	II 4	3		1967	IV 9	3
1935	II 1P	3		1968	IV 14	2
1936	I 5	3		1969	IV 11	2
1937	I 6	4		1970	IV 5	1
1938	I 6	q-f		1971	IV 14	5
1939	I 18	3		1972	IV 3P	3
1946		q-f		1973	III 22R	1
1947	I 21R	4				
1948	II 15	4				
1949	II 18	q-f				

S – Third Division South
p – preliminary round
P – promoted
R – relegated

BRIGHTON AND HOVE ALBION

Founded: 1900
Address: Goldstone Ground, Old Shoreham Road, Hove, Sussex
Telephone: Brighton 739535
Ground capacity: 38,000 (3,400 seated)
Playing area: 112 by 75 yards
Record attendance: 36,747 v Fulham, Division II, 27.12.58
Record victory: 10-1 v Wisbech, FA Cup 1st round, 13.11.65
Record defeat: 0-9 v Middlesbrough, Division II, 23.8.58
Most League points: 65, Division III(S), 1955-56
Most League goals: 112, Division III(S), 1955-56
League scoring record: 30, H. Vallance, Division III(S), 1929-30
Record League aggregate: 113, Tommy Cook, 1922-1929
Most League appearances: 509, Tug Wilson, 1922-1936
Most capped player: 8, Jack Jenkins, Wales

THE BRIGHTON RECORD

Year	Division & place	Cup round reached
1906		2
1907		1
1908		2
1909		1
1910		1
1911		2
1912		1
1913		2
1914		3
1915		2
1920		p
1921	III 18	2
1922	SIII 19	2
1923	SIII 4	2
1924	SIII 5	3
1925	SIII 8	2
1926	SIII 5	1
1927	SIII 4	3
1928	SIII 4	2
1929	SIII 15	1
1930	SIII 5	5
1931	SIII 4	4
1932	SIII 8	3
1933	SIII 12	5
1934	SIII 10	4
1935	SIII 9	3
1936	SIII 7	3
1937	SIII 3	1
1938	SIII 5	3
1939	SIII 3	1
1946		5
1947	SIII 17	1
1948	SIII 22	3
1949	SIII 6	1
1950	SIII 8	1
1951	SIII 13	4
1952	SIII 5	1
1953	SIII 7	3
1954	SIII 2	2
1955	SIII 6	3
1956	SIII 2	2
1957	SIII 6	1
1958	SIII 1P	2
1959	II 12	3
1960	II 14	5
1961	II 16	4
1962	II 22R	3
1963	III 22R	1
1964	IV 8	1
1965	IV 1P	1
1966	III 15	2
1967	III 19	4
1968	III 10	2
1969	III 12	2
1970	III 5	2
1971	III 14	3
1972	III 2P	2
1973	II 22R	3

P – promoted
R – relegated
p – preliminary round
S – Third Division South

BRISTOL CITY

Founded: 1894
Address: Ashton Gate, Bristol 3S3 2EJ
Telephone: Bristol 664093
Ground capacity: 40,000
Playing area: 112 by 76 yards
Record attendance: 43,335 v Preston North End, FA Cup 5th round, 16.2.35
Record victory: 11-0 v Chichester, FA Cup 1st round, 5.11.60
Record defeat: 0-9 v Coventry City, Division III(S), 28.4.34
Most League points: 70, Division III(S), 1954-55
Most League goals: 104, Division III(S), 1926-27
League scoring record: 36, Don Clark, Division III(S), 1946-47
Record League aggregate: 315, John Atyeo, 1951-1966
Most League appearances: 597, John Atyeo, 1951-1966
Most capped player: 26, Billy Wedlock, England

FA Cup	Year	Opponents	Score
Runners-up	1909	Manchester United	0-1

THE CITY RECORD

Year	Division & place	Cup round reached
1899		1
1900		2
1901		q
1902	II 6	4q
1903	II 4	2
1904	II 4	1
1905	II 4	2
1906	II 1P	1
1907	I 2	2
1908	I 10	1
1909	I 8	Final
1910	I 16	2
1911	I 19R	1
1912	II 13	1
1913	II 16	1
1914	II 8	1
1915	II 13	2
1920	II 8	s-f
1921	II 3	1
1922	II 22R	1
1923	SIII 1P	2
1924	II 22R	3
1925	SIII 3	2
1926	SIII 4	3
1927	SIII 1P	2
1928	II 12	3
1929	II 20	3
1930	II 20	3
1931	II 16	3
1932	II 22R	4
1933	SIII 15	2
1934	SIII 19	3
1935	SIII 15	5
1936	SIII 13	1
1937	SIII 16	1
1938	SII 2	2
1939	SIII 8	1
1946		4
1947	SIII 3	2
1948	SIII 7	2
1949	SIII 16	3
1950	SIII 15	1
1951	SIII 10	5
1952	SIII 15	2
1953	SIII 5	1
1954	SIII 3	3
1955	SIII 1P	1
1956	II 11	3
1957	II 13	5
1958	II 17	5
1959	II 10	4
1960	II 22R	3
1961	III 14	4
1962	III 6	3
1963	III 14	3
1964	III 5	4
1965	III 2P	3
1966	II 5	3
1967	II 15	5
1968	II 19	5
1969	II 16	3
1970	II 14	3
1971	II 19	3
1972	II 8	3
1973	II 5	4

P – promoted   R – relegated   S – Third Division South   q – qualifying round

Above Brighton could not meet the challenge of the Second Division in 1972-73.
Right Gerry Gow, a bright prospect for Bristol City in the seventies.

BRISTOL ROVERS

Founded: 1883
Address: Bristol Stadium, Eastville, Bristol 5
Telephone: Bristol 558620/551905
Ground capacity: 39,333
Playing area: 112 by 76 yards
Record attendance: 38,472 v Preston North End, FA Cup 4th round, 30.1.60
Record victory: 15-1 v Weymouth, FA Cup preliminary round, 17.11.1900
Record defeat: 0-12 v Luton Town, Division III(S), 13.4.36
Most League points: 64, Division III(S), 1952-53
Most League goals: 92, Division III(S), 1952-53
League scoring record: 33, Geoff Bradford, Division III(S), 1952-53
Record League aggregate: 245, Geoff Bradford, 1949-1964
Most League appearances: 487, Harry Bamford, 1946-1958
Most capped player: 7, Matt O'Mahoney, 6 Eire, 1 Northern Ireland

THE BRISTOL ROVERS RECORD

Year	Division & place	Cup round reached	Year	Division & place	Cup round reached
1921	III 10	1	1951	SIII 6	6
1922	SIII 14	q	1952	SIII 7	4
1923	SIII 13	q	1953	SIII 1P	3
1924	SIII 9	q	1954	II 9	3
1925	SIII 17	1	1955	II 9	4
1926	SIII 19	1	1956	II 6	4
1927	SIII 10	3	1957	II 9	4
1928	SIII 19	2	1958	II 10	6
1929	SIII 19	2	1959	II 6	3
1930	SIII 20	3	1960	II 9	4
1931	SIII 15	4	1961	II 17	3
1932	SIII 18	2	1962	II 21R	3
1933	SIII 9	3	1963	III 19	1
1934	SIII 7	2	1964	III 12	4
1935	SIII 8	3	1965	III 6	3
1936	SIII 17	3	1966	III 16	1
1937	SIII 15	3	1967	III 5	3
1938	SIII 15	1	1968	III 15	3
1939	SIII 22	2	1969	III 16	5
1946		2	1970	III 3	2
1947	SIII 14	1	1971	III 6	2
1948	SIII 20	4	1972	III 6	3
1949	SIII 5	1	1973	III 5	1
1950	SIII 9	1			

P – promoted
R – relegated
q – qualifying rounds
S – Third Division South

BURNLEY

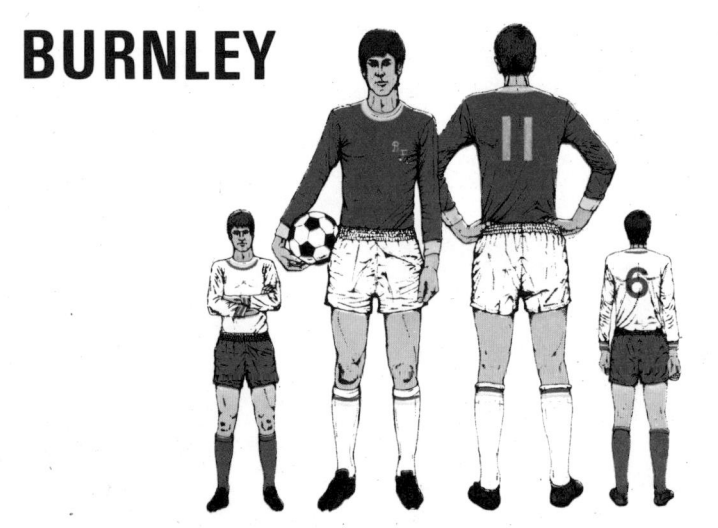

Founded: 1881
Address: Turf Moor, Burnley, Lancashire
Telephone: Burnley 27777
Ground capacity: 39,000 (4,500 seated)
Playing area: 117 by 76 yards
Record attendance: 54,775 v Huddersfield Town, FA Cup 3rd round, 23.2.24
Record victory: 9-0 v Darwen, Division I, 9.1.1892
9-0 v Crystal Palace, FA Cup 2nd round replay, 1908-09
9-0 v New Brighton, FA Cup 4th round, 26.1.57
Record defeat: 0-10 v Aston Villa, Division I, 29.8.25
0-10 v Sheffield United, Division I, 19.1.29
Most League points: 59, Division I, 1920-21
Most League goals: 102, Division I, 1960-61
League scoring record: 35, George Beel, Division I, 1927-28
Record League aggregate: 178, George Beel, 1923-1932
Most League appearances: 522, Jerry Dawson, 1906-1929
Most capped player: 51 (55 in all), Jimmy McIlroy, Northern Ireland

FA Cup	Year	Opponents	Score	Scorers
Winners	1914	Liverpool	1-0	Freeman
Runners-up	1947	Charlton Athletic	0-1	
	1962	Tottenham Hotspur	1-3	Robson

THE BURNLEY RECORD

Year	Division & place	Cup round reached	Year	Division & place	Cup round reached
1889	I 9	2	1931	II 8	4
1890	I 11	1	1932	II 19	3
1891	I 8	2	1933	II 19	q-f
1892	I 7	2	1934	II 13	3
1893	I 6	2	1935	II 12	s-f
1894	I 5	1	1936	II 15	3
1895	I 9	1	1937	II 13	5
1896	I 10	2	1938	II 6	4
1897	I 16R	1	1939	II 14	3
1898	II 1P	3	1946		3
1899	I 3	1	1947	II 2P	Final
1900	I 17R	1	1948	I 3	3
1901	II 3	2	1949	I 15	5
1902	II 9	1	1950	I 10	5
1903	II 18	q	1951	I 10	3
1904	II 5	q	1952	I 14	q-f
1905	II 11	q	1953	I 6	5
1906	II 9	1	1954	I 7	4
1907	II 7	1	1955	I 10	3
1908	II 7	1	1956	I 7	4
1909	II 14	q-f	1957	I 7	q-f
1910	II 14	2	1958	I 6	4
1911	II 8	q-f	1959	I 7	q-f
1912	II 3	1	1960	I 1C	q-f
1913	II 2P	s-f	1961	I 4	s-f
1914	I 12	Winners	1962	I 2	Final
1915	I 4	3	1963	I 3	4
1920	I 2	2	1964	I 9	q-f
1921	I 1C	3	1965	I 12	5
1922	I 3	1	1966	I 3	4
1923	I 15	1	1967	I 14	3
1924	I 17	s-f	1968	I 13	3
1925	I 19	1	1969	I 14	4
1926	I 20	3	1970	I 14	4
1927	I 5	5	1971	I 21R	3
1928	I 19	3	1972	II 7	3
1929	I 19	4	1973	II 1P	3
1930	I 21R	3			

q – qualifying rounds
P – promoted
R – relegated
C – Football League Champions

BURY

Founded: 1885
Address: Gigg Lane, Bury, Lancs
Telephone: (061) 764 4881
Ground capacity: 30,000 (7,000 seated)
Playing area: 112 by 73 yards
Record attendance: 35,000 v Bolton, FA Cup 3rd round, 9.1.60
Record victory: 12-1 v Stockton, FA Cup 1st round replay, 1896-97
Record defeat: 0-10 v Blackburn Rovers, FA Cup preliminary round, 1887-88
Most League points: 68, Division III, 1960-61
Most League goals: 108, Division III, 1960-61
League scoring record: 31, Norman Bullock, Division I, 1925-26
Record League aggregate: 124, Norman Bullock, 1920-1935
Most League appearances: 506, Norman Bullock, 1920-1935
Most capped player: 11 (14 in all), W Gorman, Republic of Ireland and 4, Northern Ireland

FA Cup	Year	Opponents	Score	Scorers
Winners	1900	Southampton	4-0	McLuckie 2, Wood, Plant
	1903	Derby County	6-0	Ross, Sagar, Leeming 2, Wood, Plant

THE BURY RECORD

Year	Division & place	Cup round reached
1895	II 1P	2
1896	I 11	q-f
1897	I 9	2
1898	I 14	1
1899	I 10	2
1900	I 12	Winners
1901	I 5	2
1902	I 7	q-f
1903	I 8	Winners
1904	I 12	2
1905	I 17	2
1906	I 17	1
1907	I 16	3
1908	I 7	2
1909	I 17	2
1910	I 13	2
1911	I 18	1
1912	I 20R	2
1913	II 11	2
1914	II 10	2
1915	II 11	2
1920	II 5	2
1921	II 11	1
1922	II 11	1
1923	II 6	3
1924	II 2P	1
1925	I 5	1
1926	I 4	4
1927	I 19	3
1928	I 5	4
1929	I 21R	5
1930	II 5	3
1931	II 13	4
1932	II 5	q-f
1933	II 4	4
1934	II 12	4
1935	II 10	3
1936	II 14	4
1937	II 3	4
1938	II 10	4
1939	II 16	3
1946		4
1947	II 17	3
1948	II 20	3
1949	II 12	3
1950	II 18	4
1951	II 20	3
1952	II 17	3
1953	II 20	4
1954	II 17	3
1955	II 13	3
1956	II 16	3
1957	II 21R	3
1958	NIII 4	2
1959	III 10	3
1960	III 7	3
1961	III 1P	1
1962	II 18	2
1963	II 8	4
1964	II 18	4
1965	II 16	3
1966	II 19	3
1967	II 22R	4
1968	III 2P	3
1969	II 21R	3
1970	III 19	1
1971	III 22R	2
1972	IV 8	3
1973	IV 13	1

P—promoted
R—relegated
N—Third Division North

CAMBRIDGE UNITED

Founded: 1919*
Address: Abbey Stadium, Newmarket Road, Cambridge
Telephone: Teversham 2170/2488
Ground capacity: 12,000 (1,200 seated)
Playing area: 115 by 75 yards
Record attendance: †8,691 v Grimsby Town, Division IV, 27.12.71
Record victory: 6-0 v Darlington, Division IV, 18.9.71
Record defeat: 0-5 v Colchester United, League Cup 1st round, 19.8.70
Most League points: 48, Division IV, 1971-72
Most League goals: 62, Division IV, 1971-72
League scoring record: 19, Brian Greenhalgh, 1971-72
Record League aggregate: 37, Brian Greenhalgh, 1972-73
Most League appearances: 127, Terry Eades, 1970-73
* as Abbey United. Changed name to Cambridge United in 1949
† ground record: 14,000 v Chelsea, Friendly, 1.5.70

THE CAMBRIDGE RECORD

Year	Division & place	Cup round reached
1971	IV 20	2
1972	IV 10	2
1973	IV 3P	1

P—promoted

CARDIFF CITY

Founded: 1899
Address: Ninian Park, Cardiff, CF1 8SX
Telephone: 0222 28501
Ground capacity: 58,000 (5,500 seated)
Playing area: 112 by 76 yards
Record attendance: *57,800 v Arsenal, Division I, 22.4.53
(*Ground record: 61,566, Wales v England, 14.10.61)
Record victory: 9-2 v Thames, Division III(S), 6.2.32
Record defeat: 2-11 v Sheffield United, Division I, 1.1.26
Most League points: 66, Division III(S), 1946-47
Most League goals: 93, Division III(S), 1946-47
League scoring record: 31, Stan Richards, Division III(S), 1946-47
Record League aggregate: 127, Len Davies, 1923-1929
Most League appearances: 445, Tom Farquharson, 1922-1935
Most capped player: 39 (41 in all), Alf Sherwood, Wales

FA Cup	Year	Opponents	Score	Scorer
Winners	1927	Arsenal	1-0	Ferguson
Runners-up	1925	Sheffield United	0-1	

THE CARDIFF RECORD

Year	Division & place	Cup round reached
1920		3
1921	II 2P	s-f
1922	I 4	q-f
1923	I 9	3
1924	I 2	q-f
1925	I 11	Final
1926	I 16	4
1927	I 14	Winners
1928	I 6	5
1929	I 22R	3
1930	II 8	4
1931	II 22R	3
1932	SIII 9	3
1933	SIII 19	1
1934	SIII 22	2
1935	SIII 19	1
1936	SIII 20	1
1937	SIII 18	3
1938	SIII 10	3
1939	SIII 13	4
1946		3
1947	SIII 1P	3
1948	II 5	3
1949	II 4	5
1950	II 10	5
1951	II 3	3
1952	II 2P	3
1953	I 12	3
1954	I 10	4
1955	I 20	3
1956	I 17	4
1957	I 21R	4
1958	II 15	5
1959	II 9	4
1960	II 2P	3
1961	I 15	3
1962	I 21R	3
1963	II 10	3
1964	II 15	3
1965	II 13	3
1966	II 20	4
1967	II 20	4
1968	II 13	3
1969	II 5	3
1970	II 7	3
1971	II 3	4
1972	II 19	5
1973	II 20	4

P – promoted
R – relegated
S – Third Division (South)

CARLISLE UNITED

Founded: 1903
Address: Brunton Park, Carlisle
Telephone: Carlisle 26237
Ground capacity: 25,500 (2,500 seated)
Playing area: 117 by 78 yards
Record attendance: 27,500 v Birmingham City, FA Cup 3rd round, 5.1.57
Record victory: 8-0 v Hartlepools United, Division III(N), 1.9.28
v Scunthorpe United, Division III(N), 25.12.52
Record defeat: 1-11 v Hull City, Division III(N), 14.1.39
Most League points: 62, Division III(N), 1950-51
Most League goals: 113, Division IV, 1963-64
League scoring record: 42, Jimmy McConnell, Division III(N), 1928-29
Record League aggregate: 126, Jimmy McConnell, 1928-1932
Most League appearances: 376, Ron Thompson, 1951-1965
Most capped player: 4, Eric Welsh, Northern Ireland

THE CARLISLE RECORD

	Division & place	Cup round reached
1929	NIII 8	2
1930	NIII 15	3
1931	NIII 8	3
1932	NIII 18	2
1933	NIII 19	2
1934	NIII 13	2
1935	NIII 22	1
1936	NIII 13	1
1937	NIII 10	3
1938	NIII 12	1
1939	NIII 19	1
1946		2
1947	NIII 16	3
1948	NIII 9	1
1949	NIII 15	1
1950	NIII 9	3
1951	NIII 3	3
1952	NIII 7	1
1953	NIII 9	1
1954	NIII 13	1
1955	NIII 20	2
1956	NIII 21	1
1957	NIII 15	3
1958	NIII 16	2
1959	IV 10	2
1960	IV 19	1
1961	IV 19	2
1962	IV 4P	3
1963	III 23R	3
1964	IV 2P	5
1965	III 1P	1
1966	II 14	4
1967	II 3	4
1968	II 10	4
1969	II 12	3
1970	II 12	5
1971	II 4	4
1972	II 10	3
1973	II 18	5

P—promoted R—relegated
N—Third Division North

Carlisle's Bobby Owen outjumps the red-shirted Orient defenders.

CHARLTON ATHLETIC

Founded: 1905
Address: The Valley, Floyd Road, Charlton, London SE7
Telephone: (01) 858 3711/3712
Ground capacity: 66,000 (2,900 seated)
Playing area: 112 by 73 yards
Record attendance: 75,031 v Aston Villa, FA Cup 5th round, 12.2.56
Record victory: 8-1 v Middlesbrough, Division I, 12.9.53
Record defeat: 1-11 v Aston Villa, Division II, 14.11.59
Most League points: 61, Division III(S), 1934-35
Most League goals: 107, Division II, 1957-58
League scoring record: 32, Ralph Allen, Division III(S), 1934-35
Record League aggregate: 153, Stuart Leary, 1953-62
Most League appearances: 583, Sam Bartram, 1934-56
Most capped player: 19, John Hewie, Scotland

FA Cup	Year	Opponents	Score	Scorers
Winners	1947	Burnley	1-0	Duffy
Runners-up	1946	Derby County	1-4	Turner H

THE CHARLTON RECORD

	Division & place	Cup round reached
1922	SIII 16	q
1923	SIII 12	4
1924	SIII 14	2
1925	SIII 15	p
1926	SIII 21	3
1927	SIII 13	2
1928	SIII 11	3
1929	SIII 1P	3
1930	II 13	4
1931	II 15	3
1932	II 10	3
1933	II 22R	3
1934	SIII 5	4
1935	SIII 1P	1
1936	II 2P	3
1937	I 2	3
1938	I 4	5
1939	I 3	3
1946		Final
1947	I 19	Winners
1948	I 13	5
1949	I 9	3
1950	I 20	4
1951	I 17	3
1952	I 10	3
1953	I 5	3
1954	I 9	3
1955	I 15	3
1956	I 14	5
1957	I 22R	3
1958	II 3	4
1959	II 8	4
1960	II 7	4
1961	II 10	3
1962	II 15	4
1963	II 20	4
1964	II 4	3
1965	II 18	4
1966	II 16	3
1967	II 19	3
1968	II 15	3
1969	II 3	4
1970	II 20	4
1971	II 20	3
1972	II 21R	3
1973	III 11	3

q — qualifying round
p — preliminary round
P — promotion
R — relegation
S — Third Division South

CHELSEA

Founded: 1905
Address: Stamford Bridge, London SW6
Telephone: (01) 385 5545
Ground capacity: 60,000 (15,500 seated)
Playing area: 114 by 71½ yards
Record attendance: 82,905 v Arsenal, Division I, 12.10.35
Record victory: 13-0 v Jeunesse Hautcharge, 1st Rd European Cup Winners Cup, 29.9.71
Record defeat: 1-8 v Wolverhampton Wanderers, Division I, 26.9.53
Most League points: 57, Division II, 1906-07
Most League goals: 98, Division I, 1960-61
League scoring record: 41, Jimmy Greaves, 1960-61
Record League aggregate: 164, Bobby Tambling, 1958-1970
Most League appearances: 467, Peter Bonetti, 1960-1973
Most capped player: 23, Eddie McCreadie, Scotland

FA Cup	Year	Opponents	Score	Scorers
Winners	1970	Leeds United	*2-2	Houseman, Hutchinson
			*2-1	Osgood, Webb
Runners-up	1915	Sheffield United	0-3	
	1967	Tottenham Hotspur	1-2	Tambling
League Cup				
Winners	1965	Leicester City	H3-2	Tambling, Venables (pen) McCreadie
			A0-0	
Runners-up	1972	Stoke City	1-2	Osgood

THE CHELSEA RECORD

Year	Division & place	F.A. Cup round reached	Year	Division & place	F.A. Cup round reached
1906	II 3	3q	1939	I 20	q-f
1907	II 2P	1	1946		5
1908	I 13	2	1947	I 15	4
1909	I 11	2	1948	I 18	4
1910	I 19R	2	1949	I 13	5
1911	II 3	s-f	1950	I 13	s-f
1912	II 2P	2	1951	I 20	5
1913	I 18	2	1952	I 19	s-f
1914	I 8	1	1953	I 19	5
1915	I 19	Final	1954	I 8	3
1920	I 3	s-f	1955	I 1C	5
1921	I 18	q-f	1956	I 16	5
1922	I 9	1	1957	I 12	4
1923	I 19	2	1958	I 11	4
1924	I 21R	1	1959	I 14	4
1925	II 5	1	1960	I 18	4
1926	II 3	4	1961	I 12	3
1927	II 4	q-f	1962	I 22R	3
1928	II 3	3	1963	II 2P	5
1929	II 9	5	1964	I 5	4
1930	II 2P	3	1965	I 3	s-f
1931	I 12	q-f	1966	I 5	s-f
1932	I 12	s-f	1967	I 9	Final
1933	I 18	3	1968	I 6	q-f
1934	I 19	5	1969	I 5	q-f
1935	I 12	3	1970	I 3	Winners
1936	I 8	5	1971	I 6	4
1937	I 13	4	1972	I 7	5
1938	I 10	3	1973	I 12	6

C — Football League Champions
P — promoted
R — relegated
q — qualifying round

THE CHESTER RECORD

Year	Division & place	Cup round reached	Year	Division & place	Cup round reached
1932	NIII 3	2	1955	NIII 24	1
1933	NIII 4	4	1956	NIII 17	1
1934	NIII 10	2	1957	NIII 21	1
1935	NIII 3	3	1958	NIII 21	2
1936	NIII 2	2	1959	IV 13	2
1937	NIII 3	4	1960	IV 20	2
1938	NIII 9	3	1961	IV 24	1
1939	NIII 6	4	1962	IV 23	2
1946		3	1963	IV 21	1
1947	NIII 3	4	1964	IV 12	2
1948	NIII 20	4	1965	IV 8	3
1949	NIII 18	2	1966	IV 7	3
1950	NIII 12	2	1967	IV 19	1
1951	NIII 13	1	1968	IV 22	2
1952	NIII 19	3	1969	IV 14	2
1953	NIII 20	1	1970	IV 11	4
1954	NIII 24	1	1971	IV 5	3
			1972	IV 20	1
			1973	IV 15	1

N — Third Division North

CHESTERFIELD

Founded: 1866
Address: Recreation Ground, Saltergate, Chesterfield, Derbyshire
Telephone: Chesterfield 2318
Ground capacity: 28,500 (3,000 seated)
Playing area: 114 by 72 yards
Record attendance: 30,968 v Newcastle United, Division II, 7.4.39
Record victory: 10-0 v Glossop North End, Division II, 17.1.03
Record defeat: 1-9 v Port Vale, Division II, 24.9.32
Most League points: 64, Division IV, 1969-70
Most League goals: 102, Division III(N), 1930-31
League scoring record: 44, Jimmy Cookson, Division III(N), 1925-26
Record League aggregate: 112, Herbert Munday, 1899-1909
Most League appearances: 613, Dave Blakey, 1948-1967
Most capped player: 4 (7 in all), Walter McMillen, Northern Ireland

CHESTER

Founded: 1884
Address: Sealand Road, Chester, Cheshire
Telephone: Chester 21048
Ground capacity: 20,500 (2,100 seated)
Playing area: 114 by 76 yards
Record attendance: 20,500 v Chelsea, FA Cup 3rd round replay, 16.1.52
Record victory: 12-0 v York City, Division III(N), 1.2.36
Record defeat: 2-11 v Oldham Athletic, Division III(N), 19.1.52
Most League points: 56, Division III(N), 1946-47; Division IV, 1964-65
Most League goals: 119, Division IV, 1964-65
League scoring record: 36, Dick Yates, Division III(N), 1946-47
Record League aggregate: 83, Gary Talbot, 1963-1967 and 1968-1970
Most League appearances: 408, Ray Gill, 1951-1962
Most capped player: 9 (30 in all), W Lewis, Wales

THE CHESTERFIELD RECORD

Year	Division & place	Cup round reached	Year	Division & place	Cup round reached
1900	II 7	p	1938	II 11	5
1901	II 14	1	1939	II 6	3
1902	II 16	p	1946		3
1903	II 6	p	1947	II 4	4
1904	II 11	p	1948	II 16	3
1905*	II 5	p	1949	II 6	3
1906*	II 18	2	1950	II 14	5
1907*	II 18	1	1951	II 21R	3
1908*	II 19	2	1952	NIII 13	2
1909*	II 19L	1	1953	NIII 12	2
1910		1	1954	NIII 6	4
1911		p	1955	NIII 6	1
1912		p	1956	NIII 6	2
1913		1	1957	NIII 6	3
1914		1	1958	NIII 8	1
1915		p	1959	III 16	3
1920		p	1960	III 18	1
1921		p	1961	III 24R	3
1922	NIII 13	p	1962	IV 19	2
1923	NIII 4	p	1963	IV 15	2
1924	NIII 3	p	1964	IV 16	3
1925	NIII 7	p	1965	IV 12	3
1926	NIII 4	3	1966	IV 20	1
1927	NIII 7	3	1967	IV 15	1
1928	NIII 16	1	1968	IV 7	3
1929	NIII 11	3	1969	IV 20	3
1930	NIII 4	3	1970	IV 1P	1
1931	NIII 1P	1	1971	III 5	2
1932	II 17	4	1972	III 13	3
1933	II 21R	5	1973	III 16	2
1934	NIII 2	3			
1935	NIII 10	3			
1936	NIII 1P	2			
1937	II 15	3			

P — promoted
R — relegated
p — preliminary round
L — not re-elected
N — Third Division North
* — as Chesterfield Town

COLCHESTER UNITED

Founded: 1937
Address: Layer Road, Colchester, Essex
Telephone: Colchester 74042
Ground capacity: 16,150 (1,205 seated)
Playing area: 110 by 73 yards
Record attendance: 19,072 v Reading, FA Cup 1st round, 27.11.48
Record victory: 9-1 v Bradford City, Division IV, 30.12.61
Record defeat: 0-7 v Leyton Orient, Division III(S), 5.1.52
0-7 v Reading, Division III(S), 18.9.57
Most League points: 58, Division III(S), 1956-57
Most League goals: 104, Division IV, 1961-62
League scoring record: 37, Bobby Hunt, Division IV, 1961-62
Record League aggregate: 131, Martyn King, 1959-1965
Most League appearances: 421, Peter Wright, 1952-1964
Most capped player: None

THE COLCHESTER RECORD						
	Division & place	Cup round reached	1960	III	9	1
			1961	III	23R	2
1946		p	1962	IV	2P	1
1947		1	1963	III	12	1
1948		5	1964	III	17	2
1949		1	1965	III	23R	2
1950		p	1966	IV	4P	1
1951	SIII	16	1	1967	III	13	2
1952	SIII	10	3	1968	III	22R	3
1953	SIII	22	3	1969	IV	6	2
1954	SIII	23	1	1970	IV	10	1
1955	SIII	24	1	1971	IV	6	q-f
1956	SIII	12	1	1972	IV	11	1
1957	SIII	3	1	1973	IV	22	2
1958	SIII	12	1	p — preliminary rounds
1959	III	5	4	P — promoted R — relegated
			S — Third Division South

COVENTRY CITY

Founded: 1883
Address: Highfield Road, Coventry
Telephone: Coventry 57171
Ground capacity: 54,000 (13,170 seated)
Playing area: 110 by 75 yards
Record attendance: 51,457 v Wolverhampton Wanderers, Division II, 29.4.67
Record victory: 9-0 v Bristol City, Division III(S), 28.4.34
Record defeat: 2-10 v Norwich City, Division III(S), 15.3.30
Most League points: 60, Division IV, 1958-59 & Division III, 1963-64
Most League goals: 108, Division III(S), 1931-32
League scoring record: 49, Clarrie Bourton, Division III(S), 1931-32
Record League aggregate: 171, Clarrie Bourton, 1931-1937
Most League appearances: 486, George Curtis, 1956-1970
Most capped player: 21 (34 in all), Dave Clements, Northern Ireland

THE COVENTRY RECORD					
	Division & place	Cup round reached	1946		3
			1947	II 8	4
			1948	II 10	4
1908		1	1949	II 16	3
1909		q	1950	II 12	3
1910		q-f	1951	II 7	3
1911		3	1952	II 21R	4
1912		2	1953	SIII 6	3
1913		1	1954	SIII 14	1
1914		4q	1955	SIII 9	3
1915		6q	1956	SIII 8	1
1920	II 20	1	1957	SIII 16	1
1921	II 21	6q	1958	SIII 19	2
1922	II 20	2	1959	IV 2P	2
1923	II 18	5q	1960	III 5	1
1924	II 19	1	1961	III 15	3
1925	II 22R	1	1962	III 14	2
1926	NIII 16	1	1963	III 4	q-f
1927	SIII 15	2	1964	III 1P	2
1928	SIII 20	1	1965	II 10	3
1929	SIII 11	1	1966	II 3	5
1930	SIII 6	3	1967	II 1P	3
1931	SIII 14	2	1968	I 20	4
1932	SIII 12	1	1969	I 20	4
1933	SIII 6	2	1970	I 6	3
1934	SIII 2	2	1971	I 10	3
1935	SIII 3	3	1972	I 18	4
1936	SIII 1P	1	1973	I 18	6
1937	II 8	5	P — promoted R — relegated
1938	II 4	3	S — Third Division South
1939	II 4	3	N — Third Division North
			q — qualifying round

CREWE ALEXANDRA

Founded: 1876
Address: Gresty Road, Crewe, Cheshire
Telephone: Crewe 3014
Ground capacity: 16,000
Playing area: 113 by 75 yards
Record attendance: 20,000 v Tottenham Hotspur, FA Cup 4th round, 30.1.60
Record victory: 8-0 v Rotherham United, Division III(N), 1.10.32
Record defeat: 2-13 v Tottenham Hotspur, FA Cup 4th round replay, 3.2.60
Most League points: 59, Division IV, 1962-63
Most League goals: 95, Division III(N), 1931-32
League scoring record: 34, Terry Harkin, Division IV, 1964-65
Record League aggregate: 126, Bert Swindells, 1928-1937
Most League appearances: 430, Peter Leigh, 1963-1972
Most capped player: 12 (30 in all), William Lewis, Wales

THE CREWE RECORD

Year	Division & place	Cup round reached
1886		3
1887		p
1888		s-f
1889		1
1890		p
1891		1
1892		1
1893	II 10	p
1894	II 12	p
1895	II 16	p
1896	II 16L	1
1897		p
1898		p
1899		p
1900		p
1901		p
1902		p
1903		p
1904		p
1905		p
1906		1
1907		1
1908		p
1909		p
1910		p
1911		2
1912		1
1913		p
1914		p
1915		p
1920		p
1921		p
1922	NIII 6	p
1923	NIII 6	p
1924	NIII 20	p
1925	NIII 15	p
1926	NIII 11	2
1927	NIII 15	3
1928	NIII 17	4
1929	NIII 9	1
1930	NIII 11	2
1931	NIII 18	2
1932	NIII 6	1
1933	NIII 10	2
1934	NIII 14	1
1935	NIII 13	1
1936	NIII 6	3
1937	NIII 20	3
1938	NIII 8	2
1939	NIII 8	2
1946		1
1947	NIII 8	1
1948	NIII 10	4
1949	NIII 12	3
1950	NIII 7	2
1951	NIII 9	2
1952	NIII 16	1
1953	NIII 10	1
1954	NIII 16	2
1955	NIII 22	1
1956	NIII 24	1
1957	NIII 24	1
1958	NIII 24	1
1959	IV 18	1
1960	IV 14	4
1961	IV 9	4
1962	IV 10	2
1963	IV 3P	2
1964	III 22R	1
1965	IV 10	1
1966	IV 14	4
1967	IV 5	3
1968	IV 4P	1
1969	III 23R	2
1970	IV 15	1
1971	IV 15	2
1972	IV 24	1
1973	IV 21	3

P—promoted
R—relegated
p—preliminary round
L—failed to gain re-election

THE PALACE RECORD

Year	Division & place	Cup round reached
1921	III 1P	2
1922	II 14	2
1923	II 16	1
1924	II 15	3
1925	II 21R	2
1926	SIII 13	5
1927	SIII 6	1
1928	SIII 5	2
1929	SIII 2	5
1930	SIII 9	3
1931	SIII 2	4
1932	SIII 4	2
1933	SIII 5	1
1934	SIII 12	4
1935	SIII 5	1
1936	SIII 6	2
1937	SIII 14	1
1938	SIII 7	3
1939	SIII 2	1
1946		3
1947	SIII 18	3
1948	SIII 13	3
1949	SIII 22	1
1950	SIII 7	1
1951	SIII 24	1
1952	SIII 19	1
1953	SIII 13	2
1954	SIII 22	1
1955	SIII 20	2
1956	SIII 23	1
1957	SIII 20	3
1958	SIII 14	3
1959	IV 7	3
1960	IV 8	3
1961	IV 2P	2
1962	III 15	3
1963	III 11	2
1964	III 2P	2
1965	II 7	q-f
1966	II 11	3
1967	II 7	3
1968	II 11	3
1969	II 2P	3
1970	I 20	5
1971	I 18	3
1972	I 20	3
1973	I 21R	4

P—promoted
R—relegated
S—Third Division South

CRYSTAL PALACE

Founded: 1905
Address: Selhurst Park, SE25 6PU
Telephone: 01-653 2223/4
Ground capacity: 51,000 (9,000 seated)
Playing area: 110 by 75 yards
Record attendance: 49,498 v Chelsea, Division I, 27.12.69
Record victory: 9-0 v Barrow, Division IV, 10.10.59
Record defeat: 4-11 v Manchester City, FA Cup 5th round, 20.2.26
Most League points: 64, Division IV, 1960-61
Most League goals: 110, Division IV, 1960-61
League scoring record: 46, Peter Simpson, Division III(S), 1930-31
Record League aggregate: 154, Peter Simpson, 1930-1936
Most League appearances: 432, Terry Long, 1956-1969
Most capped player: 5 (15 in all), J T Jones, Wales

Colin Sinclair of Darlington (10) is beaten by Chester keeper Taylor in September 1972. The attendance at Feethams was a dismal 1,401.

DARLINGTON

Founded: 1883
Address: Feethams Ground, Darlington, County Durham
Telephone: Darlington 650976
Ground capacity: 20,000
Playing area: 110 by 74 yards
Record attendance: 21,023 v Bolton Wanderers, League cup 3rd round, 14.11.60
Record victory: 9-2 v Lincoln City, Division III(N), 7.1.28
Record defeat: 0-10 v Doncaster Rovers, Division IV, 25.1.64
Most League points: 59, Division IV, 1965-66
Most League goals: 108, Division III(N), 1929-30
League scoring record: 39, Doug Brown, Division III(N), 1924-25
Record League aggregate: 74, Doug Brown, 1923-1926
Most League appearances: 442, Ron Greener, 1955-1967
Most capped player: None

THE DARLINGTON RECORD

Year	Division & place	Cup round reached
1911		3
1912		2
1913		p
1914		p
1915		1
1920		2
1921		1
1922	NIII 2	1
1923	NIII 9	p
1924	NIII 6	1
1925	NIII 1P	1
1926	II 15	2
1927	II 21R	4
1928	NIII 7	3
1929	NIII 19	3
1930	NIII 3	1
1931	NIII 11	1
1932	NIII 11	3
1933	NIII 22	4
1934	NIII 16	1
1935	NIII 5	2
1936	NIII 12	3
1937	NIII 22	4
1938	NIII 19	1
1939	NIII 18	2
1946		2
1947	NIII 17	2
1948	NIII 16	1
1949	NIII 4	3
1950	NIII 17	1
1951	NIII 18	1
1952	NIII 23	1
1953	NIII 21	1
1954	NIII 21	1
1955	NIII 15	3
1956	NIII 15	2
1957	NIII 18	2
1958	NIII 20	5
1959	IV 16	3
1960	IV 15	2
1961	IV 7	2
1962	IV 13	1
1963	IV 12	1
1964	IV 19	1
1965	IV 17	3
1966	IV 2P	2
1967	III 22R	2
1968	IV 16	1
1969	IV 5	2
1970	IV 22	1
1971	IV 12	2
1972	IV 19	2
1973	IV 24	1

P—promoted
R—relegated
p—preliminary round
N—Third Division North

DERBY COUNTY

Founded: 1884
Address: Baseball Ground, Shaftesbury Crescent, Derby DE3 8NB
Telephone: 0332 40105
Ground capacity: 40,500 (13,250 seated)
Playing area: 110 by 71 yards
Record attendance: 41,826 v Tottenham Hotspur, Division I, 20.9.69
Record victory: 9-0 v Wolverhampton Wanderers, Division I, 10.1.90 and v Sheffield Wednesday, Division I, 21.1.99
Record defeat: 2-11 v Everton, FA Cup 1st round, 18.1.90
Most League points: 63, Division II, 1968-69
Most League goals: 111, Division III (N), 1956-57
League scoring record: 37, Jack Bowers, Division I, 1930-31 and Ray Straw, Division III (N), 1956-57
Record League aggregate: 291, Steve Bloomer, 1892-1906 and 1910-1914
Most League appearances: 478, Jack Parry, 1949-1966
Most capped player: 26, Sammy Crooks, England

FA Cup	Year	Opponents	Score	Scorers
Winners	1946	Charlton Athletic	*4-1	Stamps 2, Doherty, og
Runners-up	1898	Nottingham Forest	1-3	Bloomer
	1899	Sheffield United	1-4	Boag
	1903	Bury	0-6	

*—after extra time

THE DERBY RECORD

	Division & place	Cup round reached
1885		1
1886		3
1887		2
1888		2
1889	I 10	2
1890	I 7	1
1891	I 11	2
1892	I 10	1
1893	I 13	1
1894	I 3	q-f
1895	I 15	1
1896	I 2	s-f
1897	I 3	s-f
1898	I 10	Final
1899	I 9	Final
1900	I 6	1
1901	I 12	1
1902	I 6	s-f
1903	I 9	Final
1904	I 14	s-f
1905	I 11	1
1906	I 15	2
1907	I 19R	3
1908	II 6	1
1909	II 5	s-f
1910	II 4	2
1911	II 6	q-f
1912	II 1P	2
1913	I 7	1
1914	I 20R	2
1915	II 1P	1
1920	I 18	1
1921	I 21R	2
1922	II 12	1
1923	II 14	s-f
1924	II 3	2
1925	II 3	1
1926	II 2P	4
1927	I 12	4
1928	I 4	4
1929	I 6	4
1930	I 2	4
1931	I 6	3
1932	I 15	5
1933	I 7	s-f
1934	I 4	5
1935	I 6	5
1936	I 2	q-f
1937	I 4	5
1938	I 13	3
1939	I 6	3
1946		Winners
1947	I 14	5
1948	I 4	s-f
1949	I 3	q-f
1950	I 11	q-f
1951	I 11	4
1952	I 17	3
1953	I 22R	3
1954	II 18	3
1955	II 22R	3
1956	NIII 2	2
1957	NIII 1P	2
1958	II 16	3
1959	II 7	3
1960	II 18	3
1961	II 12	3
1962	II 16	4
1963	II 18	4
1964	II 13	3
1965	II 9	3
1966	II 8	3
1967	II 17	3
1968	II 18	3
1969	II 1P	3
1970	I 4	5
1971	I 9	5
1972	I 1C	5
1973	I 7	6

P—promoted   R—relegated
N—Third Division North
C—League Champions

DONCASTER ROVERS

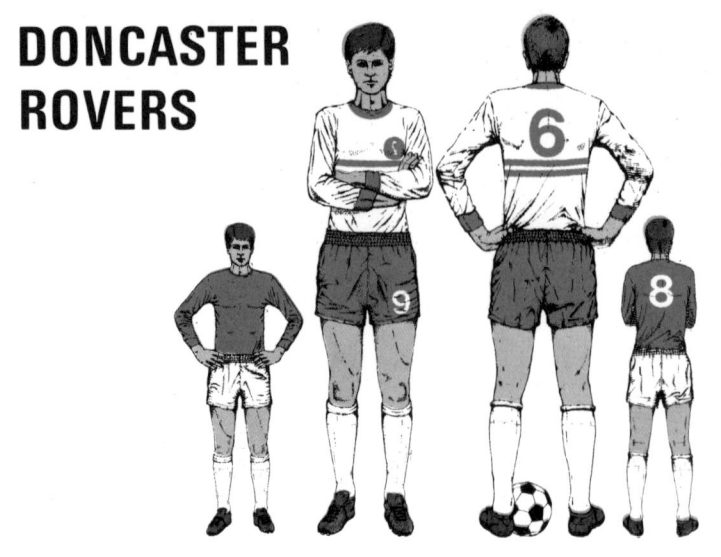

Founded: 1879
Address: Belle Vue Ground, Doncaster
Telephone: Doncaster 55281
Ground capacity: 44,382
Playing area: 119 by 79 yards
Record attendance: 37,149 v Hull City, Division III(N), 2.10.48
Record victory: 10-0 v Darlington, Division IV, 25.1.64
Record defeat: 0-12 v Small Heath, Division II, 11.4.03
Most League points: 72, Division III(N), 1946-47
Most League goals: 123, Division III(N), 1946-47
League scoring record: 42, Clarrie Jordan, Division III(N), 1946-47
Record League aggregate: 178, Tom Keetley, 1923-1929
Most League appearances: 441, Fred Emery, 1922-1936
Most capped player: 14, Len Graham, Northern Ireland

THE DONCASTER ROVERS RECORD

	Division & place	Cup round reached
1902	II 7	p
1903*	II 16	q
1905*	II 18	q
1924	NIII 9	q
1925	NIII 18	1
1926	NIII 10	2
1927	NIII 8	2
1928	NIII 4	1
1929	NIII 5	1
1930	NIII 14	4
1931	NIII 15	2
1932	NIII 15	2
1933	NIII 6	3
1934	NIII 7	3
1935	NIII 1P	1
1936	II 18	3
1937	II 22R	3
1938	NIII 2	3
1939	NIII 2	4
1946		1
1947	NIII 1P	3
1948	II 21R	3
1949	NIII 3	1
1950	NIII 1P	4
1951	II 11	3
1952	II 16	5
1953	II 13	3
1954	II 12	5
1955	II 18	5
1956	II 17	5
1957	II 14	3
1958	II 22R	3
1959	III 22R	3
1960	IV 17	3
1961	IV 11	1
1962	IV 21	1
1963	IV 16	2
1964	IV 14	3
1965	IV 9	3
1966	IV 1P	1
1967	III 23R	1
1968	IV 10	3
1969	IV 1P	3
1970	III 11	2
1971	III 23R	1
1972	IV 12	1
1973	IV 17	3

q—qualifying rounds
p—preliminary rounds
P—promoted
R—relegated
N—Third Division North
*Doncaster failed to gain re-election.
Elected in 1904 and 1923.

EVERTON

Founded: 1878
Address: Goodison Park, Liverpool 4
Telephone: (051) 525 5263/4
Ground capacity: 56,000 (25,000 seated)
Playing area: 112 by 75 yards
Record attendance: 78,299 v Liverpool, Division I, 18.8.48
Record victory: 11-2 v Derby County, FA Cup 1st round, 18.1.1890
Record defeat: 4-10 v Tottenham Hotspur, Division I, 11.10.58
Most League points: 66, Division I, 1969-70
Most League goals: 121, Division II, 1930-31
League scoring record: 60, Dixie Dean, Division I, 1927-28
Record League aggregate: 349, Dixie Dean, 1925-1937
Most League appearances: 465, Ted Sagar, 1929-1953
Most capped player: 37 (65 in all), Alan Ball, England

FA Cup	Year	Opponents	Score	Scorers
Winners	1906	Newcastle United	1-0	Young
	1933	Manchester City	3-0	Stein, Dean, Dunn
	1966	Sheffield Wednesday	3-2	Trebilcock 2, Temple
Runners-up	1893	Wolverhampton Wanderers	0-1	
	1897	Aston Villa	2-3	Bell, Boyle
	1907	Sheffield Wednesday	1-2	Sharp
	1968	West Bromwich Albion	*0-1	

*after extra time

THE EVERTON RECORD

Year	Division & place	Cup round reached	Year	Division & place	Cup round reached
1887		1	1929	I 18	3
1888		2	1930	I 22R	4
1889	I 8	q	1931	II 1P	s-f
1890	I 2	2	1932	I 1C	3
1891	I 1C	1	1933	I 11	Winners
1892	I 5	1	1934	I 14	3
1893	I 3	Final	1935	I 8	q-f
1894	I 6	1	1936	I 16	3
1895	I 2	q-f	1937	I 17	5
1896	I 3	q-f	1938	I 14	4
1897	I 7	Final	1939	I 1C	q-f
1898	I 4	s-f	1946		3
1899	I 4	2	1947	I 10	4
1900	I 11	1	1948	I 14	5
1901	I 7	2	1949	I 18	4
1902	I 2	1	1950	I 18	s-f
1903	I 12	q-f	1951	I 22R	3
1904	I 3	1	1952	II 7	3
1905	I 2	s-f	1953	II 16	s-f
1906	I 11	Winners	1954	II 2P	5
1907	I 3	Final	1955	I 11	4
1908	I 11	q-f	1956	I 15	q-f
1909	I 2	2	1957	I 15	5
1910	I 10	s-f	1958	I 16	4
1911	I 4	3	1959	I 16	5
1912	I 2	q-f	1960	I 15	3
1913	I 11	q-f	1961	I 5	3
1914	I 15	1	1962	I 4	5
1915	I 1C	s-f	1963	I 1C	5
1920	I 16	1	1964	I 3	5
1921	I 7	q-f	1965	I 4	4
1922	I 20	1	1966	I 11	Winners
1923	I 5	1	1967	I 6	q-f
1924	I 7	2	1968	I 5	Final
1925	I 17	3	1969	I 3	s-f
1926	I 11	3	1970	I 1C	3
1927	I 20	4	1971	I 14	s-f
1928	I 1C	4	1972	I 15	5
			1973	I 17	4

C – Football League Champions
P – promoted   R – relegated
q – qualifying competition

Founded: 1904
Address: St. James' Park, Exeter
Telephone: Exeter 54073
Ground capacity: 18,500 (1,940 seated)
Playing area: 114 by 73 yards
Record attendance: 20,984 v Sunderland, FA Cup 6th Rd. replay, 4.3.31
Record victory: 8-1 v Coventry City, Division III(S), 4.12.26
8-1 v Aldershot, Division III(S), 4.5.35
Record defeat: 0-9 v Notts County, Division III(S), 16.10.48, and
0-9 v Northampton Town, Division III(S), 12.4.58
Most League points: 58, Division III(S), 1932-33; Division IV, 1963-64
Most League goals: 88, Division III(S), 1932-33
League scoring record: 34, Fred Whitlow, Division III(S), 1932-33
Record League aggregate: 105, Alan Banks, 1963-66, 1967-1973
Most League appearances: 495, Arnold Mitchell, 1952-66
Most capped player: 1 (17 in all), Dermot Curtis, Eire

THE EXETER CITY RECORD

Year	Division & place	Cup round reached	Year	Division & place	Cup round reached
1909		2	1947	SIII 15	1
1910		5q	1948	SIII 11	1
1911		1	1949	SIII 12	3
1912		4q	1950	SIII 16	4
1913		4q	1951	SIII 14	4
1914		2	1952	SIII 23	2
1915		1	1953	SIII 17	1
1920		6q	1954	SIII 9	1
1921	SIII 19	1	1955	SIII 22	1
1922	SIII 21	5q	1956	SIII 16	3
1923	SIII 20	5q	1957	SIII 21	1
1924	SIII 16	2	1958	SIII 24	1
1925	SIII 7	1	1959	IV 5	1
1926	SIII 20	1	1960	IV 9	3
1927	SIII 12	3	1961	IV 21	1
1928	SIII 8	4	1962	IV 18	1
1929	SIII 21	3	1963	IV 17	1
1930	SIII 16	1	1964	IV 4P	2
1931	SIII 13	6	1965	III 17	2
1932	SIII 7	3	1966	III 22R	1
1933	SIII 2	1	1967	IV 14	1
1934	SIII 9	1	1968	IV 20	2
1935	SIII 11	2	1969	IV 17	3
1936	SIII 22	1	1970	IV 18	2
1937	SIII 21	5	1971	IV 9	1
1938	SIII 17	2	1972	IV 15	2
1939	SIII 14	1	1973	IV 8	1
1946		2			

P – promoted
R – relegated
q – qualifying round

EXETER CITY

FULHAM

Founded: 1880
Address: Craven Cottage, Stevenage Road, London SW6
Telephone: (01) 736 5621/7035
Ground capacity: 45,000 (9,000 seated)
Playing area: 110 by 75 yards
Record attendance: 49,335 v Millwall, Division II, 8.10.38
Record victory: 10-1 v Ipswich Town, Division I, 26.10.63
Record defeat: 0-9 v Wolverhampton Wanderers, Division I, 16.9.59
Most League points: 60, Division II, 1958-59 & Division III, 1970-71
Most League goals: 111, Division III(S), 1931-32
League scoring record: 41, Frank Newton, Division III(S), 1931-32
Record League aggregate: 156, Bedford Jezzard, 1948-1956
Most League appearances: 598, Johnny Haynes, 1952-1970
Most capped player: 56, Johnny Haynes, England

THE FULHAM RECORD

Year	Division & place	Cup round reached
1904		1
1905		q-f
1906		2
1907		2
1908	II 4	s-f
1909	II 10	2
1910	II 7	2
1911	II 10	1
1912	II 8	q-f
1913	II 9	1
1914	II 11	1
1915	II 12	2
1920	II 6	1
1921	II 9	3
1922	II 7	2
1923	II 10	1
1924	II 20	2
1925	II 12	2
1926	II 19	q-f
1927	II 18	4
1928	II 21R	3
1929	SIII 5	2
1930	SIII 7	4
1931	SIII 9	3
1932	SIII 1P	3
1933	II 3	3
1934	II 16	3
1935	II 7	3
1936	II 9	s-f
1937	II 11	3
1938	II 8	3
1939	II 12	4
1946		3
1947	II 15	3
1948	II 11	q-f
1949	II 1P	3
1950	I 17	3
1951	I 18	q-f
1952	I 22R	3
1953	II 8	3
1954	II 8	4
1955	II 14	3
1956	II 9	4
1957	II 11	4
1958	II 5	s-f
1959	II 2P	4
1960	I 10	4
1961	I 17	3
1962	I 20	s-f
1963	I 16	3
1964	I 15	4
1965	I 20	3
1966	I 20	3
1967	I 19	4
1968	I 22R	4
1969	II 22R	4
1970	III 4	1
1971	III 2P	1
1972	II 20	4
1973	II 9	3

P – promoted   R – relegated
S – Third Division South

THE GILLINGHAM RECORD

Year	Division & place	Cup round reached
1899*		1
1900		p
1901		p
1902		p
1903		p
1904		p
1905		p
1906		1
1907		2
1908		2
1909		p
1910		p
1911		1
1912		1
1913		1
1914		2
1915		1
1920		1
1921	III 22	p
1922	SIII 18	1
1923	SIII 16	p
1924	SIII 15	1
1925	SIII 13	p
1926	SIII 10	2
1927	SIII 20	2
1928	SIII 16	3
1929	SIII 22	1
1930	SIII 21	1
1931	SIII 16	2
1932	SIII 21	1
1933	SIII 7	2
1934	SIII 17	2
1935	SIII 20	1
1936	SIII 16	2
1937	SIII 11	2
1938†	SIII 22	1
1939		q
1946		q
1947		3
1948		3
1949		q
1950		2
1951	SIII 22	2
1952	SIII 22	2
1953	SIII 20	2
1954	SIII 10	1
1955	SIII 4	2
1956	SIII 10	1
1957	SIII 22	2
1958	SIII 22	3
1959	IV 11	1
1960	IV 7	3
1961	IV 15	3
1962	IV 20	1
1963	IV 5	3
1964	IV 1P	1
1965	III 7	2
1966	III 6	1
1967	III 11	2
1968	III 11	1
1969	III 20	2
1970	III 20	5
1971	III 24R	1
1972	IV 13	1
1973	IV 9	1

P – promoted   R – relegated
*New Brompton Excelsior until 1913
†Not re-elected
Re-elected 1950

GILLINGHAM

Founded: 1893
Address: Priestfield Stadium, Gillingham, Kent
Telephone: Medway 51854
Ground capacity: 22,000 (1,000 seated)
Playing area: 114 by 75 yards
Record attendance: 23,002 v Queen's Park Rangers, FA Cup 3rd round, 10.1.48
Record victory: 10-1 v Gorleston, FA Cup 1st round, 16.11.57
Record defeat: 2-9 v Nottingham Forest, Division III(S), 18.11.50
Most League points: 60, Division IV, 1963-64
Most League goals: 82, Division IV, 1958-59
League scoring record: 31, Ernie Morgan, Division III(S), 1954-55
Record League aggregate: 103, Brian Gibbs, 1962-1969
Most League appearances: 571, John Simpson, 1957-1972
Most capped player: 1, Frank Fox, England

GRIMSBY TOWN

Founded: 1878 (as Grimsby Pelham)
Address: Blundell Park, Cleethorpes, Lincolnshire
Telephone: Cleethorpes 61420/61803
Ground capacity: 28,000 (1800 seated)
Playing area: 111 by 74 yards
Record attendance: 31,657 v Wolves, FA Cup 5th round, 20.2.37
Record victory: 9-2 v Darwen, Division II, 15.4.1899
Record defeat: 1-9 v Arsenal, Division I, 28.1.31
Most League points: 68, Division III(N), 1955-56
Most League goals: 103, Division II, 1933-34
League scoring record: 42, Pat Glover, Division II, 1933-34
Record League aggregate: 182, Pat Glover, 1930-1939
Most League appearances: 448, Keith Jobling, 1953-1969
Most capped player: 7, Pat Glover, Wales

Gillingham's Bill Williams makes his presence felt against Mansfield.

George Best and Manchester United fell to Halifax in the 1971 Watney Cup.

THE GRIMSBY RECORD

	Division & place	Cup round reached		Division & place	Cup round reached
1893	II 4	2	1935	I 5	3
1894	II 5	1	1936	I 17	s-f
1895	II 5	p	1937	I 11	5
1896	II 3	2	1938	I 20	3
1897	II 3	1	1939	I 10	s-f
1898	II 12	1	1946		3
1899	II 10	1	1947	I 16	4
1900	II 6	1	1948	I 22R	3
1901	II 1P	p	1949	II 11	4
1902	I 15	1	1950	II 11	4
1903	I 17R	2	1951	II 22R	3
1904	II 6	1	1952	NIII 2	2
1905	II 13	1	1953	NIII 5	3
1906	II 8	1	1954	NIII 17	3
1907	II 11	1	1955	NIII 23	3
1908	II 18	q-f	1956	NIII 1P	3
1909	II 13	1	1957	II 16	3
1910	II 19L	1	1958	II 13	3
1911		3	1959	II 21R	4
1912	II 9	p	1960	III 4	2
1913	II 7	1	1961	III 6	1
1914	II 15	1	1962	III 2P	1
1915	II 17	1	1963	II 19	3
1920	II 22M	1	1964	II 21R	3
1921	III 13	2	1965	III 10	2
1922	NIII 3	1	1966	III 11	4
1923	NIII 14	p	1967	III 17	1
1924	NIII 11	1	1968	III 21R	1
1925	NIII 12	p	1969	IV 23	1
1926	NIII 1P	3	1970	IV 16	1
1927	II 17	3	1971	IV 19	1
1928	II 11	3	1972	IV 1P	1
1929	II 2P	3	1973	III 9	4
1930	I 18	3			
1931	I 13	5			
1932	I 21R	5			
1933	II 13	4			
1934	II 1P	4			

p—preliminary round
N—Third Division North
P—promoted
R—relegated
L—not re-elected
M—not re-elected to Second Division but invited to join newly formed Third Division.

HALIFAX TOWN

Founded: 1911
Address: Shay Ground, Halifax, Yorkshire
Telephone: Halifax 53423
Ground capacity: 25,000 (1,806 seated)
Playing area: 110 by 70 yards
Record attendance: 36,885 v Tottenham Hotspur, FA Cup 5th round, 14.2.53
Record victory: 7-0 v Bishop Auckland, FA Cup 2nd round replay, 10.1.67
Record defeat: 0-13 v Stockport County, Division III(N), 6.1.34
Most League points: 57, Division IV, 1968-69
Most League goals: 83, Division III(N), 1957-58
League scoring record: 34, Albert Valentine, Division III(N), 1934-35
Record League aggregate: 129, Ernest Dixon, 1922-1930
Most League appearances: 296, Alex South, 1956-1965
Most capped player: 1, Mick Meagan, Eire

THE HALIFAX RECORD

	Division & place	Cup round reached
1922	NIII 19	p
1923	NIII 7	1
1924	NIII 14	2
1925	NIII 9	p
1926	NIII 5	1
1927	NIII 4	1
1928	NIII 12	2
1929	NIII 13	1
1930	NIII 21	1
1931	NIII 17	2
1932	NIII 17	3
1933	NIII 15	5
1934	NIII 9	3
1935	NIII 2	1
1936	NIII 17	2
1937	NIII 7	1
1938	NIII 18	1
1939	NIII 12	3
1946		1
1947	NIII 22	2
1948	NIII 21	1
1949	NIII 19	1
1950	NIII 21	1
1951	NIII 22	1
1952	NIII 20	1
1953	NIII 14	5
1954	NIII 23	1
1955	NIII 14	1
1956	NIII 19	2
1957	NIII 11	1
1958	NIII 7	1
1959	III 9	2
1960	III 15	2
1961	III 9	2
1962	III 18	1
1963	III 24R	2
1964	IV 10	1
1965	IV 23	1
1966	IV 15	1
1967	IV 12	3
1968	IV 11	3
1969	IV 2P	4
1970	III 18	1
1971	III 3	1
1972	III 16	1
1973	III 20	2

P—promoted
R—relegated
p—preliminary round
N—Third Division North

HARTLEPOOL

Founded: 1908
Address: The Victoria Ground, Clarence Road, Hartlepool, Durham
Telephone: Hartlepool 2584/3492
Ground capacity: 19,500
Playing area: 113 by 75 yards
Record attendance: 17,426 v Manchester United, FA Cup 3rd round, 5.1.57
Record victory: 10-1 v Barrow, Division IV, 4.4.59
Record defeat: 1-10 v Wrexham, Division IV, 3.3.62
Most League points: 60, Division IV, 1967-68
Most League goals: 90, Division III(N), 1956-57
League scoring record: 28, Bill Robinson, Division III(N), 1927-28
Record League aggregate: 98, Ken Johnson, 1949-1964
Most League appearances 448, Watty Moore, 1948-1964
Most capped player: 1 (11 in all), Ambrose Fogarty, Eire

THE HARTLEPOOL RECORD

	Division & place	Cup round reached		Division & place	Cup round reached
			1951	NIII 16	2
			1952	NIII 9	3
1922	NIII 4	p	1953	NIII 17	2
1923	NIII 15	p	1954	NIII 18	1
1924	NIII 21	p	1955	NIII 5	4
1925	NIII 20	1	1956	NIII 4	3
1926	NIII 6	p	1957	NIII 2	3
1927	NIII 17	1	1958	NIII 17	2
1928	NIII 15	1	1959	IV 19	2
1929	NIII 21	1	1960	IV 19	1
1930	NIII 8	1	1961	IV 23	1
1931	NIII 20	1	1962	IV 22	3
1932	NIII 13	1	1963	IV 24	1
1933	NIII 14	2	1964	IV 23	1
1934	NIII 11	2	1965	IV 15	2
1935	NIII 12	2	1966	IV 18	3
1936	NIII 8	3	1967	IV 8	1
1937	NIII 6	2	1968	IV 3P	1
1938	NIII 20	2	1969	III 22R	1
1939	NIII 21	2	1970	IV 23	2
1946		1	1971	IV 23	1
1947	NIII 13	2	1972	IV 18	2
1948	NIII 19	2	1973	IV 20	1
1949	NIII 16	1			
1950	NIII 18	2			

p – preliminary round
N – Third Division North
P – promoted
R – relegated

HEREFORD UNITED

Founded: 1924
Address: Edgar Street, Hereford
Telephone: Hereford 4037
Ground capacity: 16,000 (2,000 seated)
Playing area: 111 by 80 yards
Record attendance: 18,114 v Sheffield Wednesday, FA Cup 3rd round, 4.1.58
Record victory: 11-0 v Thynnes, FA Cup qualifying rounds, September 1947
Record defeat: 2-9 v Yeovil Town, Southern League, April 1957
Most capped player: None

THE HEREFORD RECORD

	Division & place	Cup round reached	
1973	IV 2P	1	P—promoted

HUDDERSFIELD TOWN

Founded: 1908
Address: Leeds Road, Huddersfield
Telephone: Huddersfield 20335/6
Ground capacity: 48,000 (6,200 seated)
Playing area: 115 by 75 yards
Record attendance: 67,037 v Arsenal, FA Cup quarter-final, 27.2.32
Record victory: 10-1 v Blackpool, Division I, 13.12.30
Record defeat: 0-8 v Middlesbrough, Division I, 1950-51
Most League points: 64, Division II, 1919-20
Most League goals: 97, Division II, 1919-20
League scoring record: 35, George Brown, Division I, 1925-26
Record League aggregate: 142, George Brown, 1921-1929
Most League appearances: 494, Billy Smith, 1919-1934
Most capped player: 31 (41 in all), Jimmy Nicholson, Northern Ireland

FA Cup	Year	Opponents	Score	Scorers
Winners	1922	Preston North End	1-0	Smith (pen)
Runners-up	1920	Aston Villa	*0-1	
	1928	Blackburn Rovers	1-3	Jackson
	1930	Arsenal	0-2	
	1938	Preston North End	*0-1	

*after extra time

THE HUDDERSFIELD RECORD

	Division & place	Cup round reached
1911	II 13	
1912	II 17	1
1913	II 5	2
1914	II 13	2
1915	II 8	1
1920	II 2P	Final
1921	I 17	3
1922	I 14	Winners
1923	I 3	3
1924	I 1C	3
1925	I 1C	1
1926	I 1C	4
1927	I 2	3
1928	I 2	Final
1929	I 16	s-f
1930	I 10	Final
1931	I 5	3
1932	I 4	q-f
1933	I 6	4
1934	I 2	4
1935	I 16	3
1936	I 3	4
1937	I 15	3
1938	I 15	Final
1939	I 19	s-f
1946		3
1947	I 20	3
1948	I 19	3
1949	I 20	4
1950	I 15	3
1951	I 19	5
1952	I 21R	3
1953	II 2P	4
1954	I 3	3
1955	I 12	q-f
1956	I 21R	3
1957	II 12	5
1958	II 9	3
1959	II 14	3
1960	II 6	4
1961	II 20	4
1962	II 7	4
1963	II 6	3
1964	II 12	5
1965	II 8	4
1966	II 4	5
1967	II 6	3
1968	II 14	3
1969	II 6	4
1970	II 1P	3
1971	I 15	4
1972	I 22R	q-f
1973	I 21R	3

C – Football League champions
P – promoted   R – relegated

HULL CITY

Founded: 1904
Address: Boothferry Park, Hull HU4 6EU
Telephone: 0482 52195/6
Ground capacity: 42,000 (9,000 seated)
Playing area: 113 by 73 yards
Record attendance: 55,019 v Manchester United, FA Cup quarter-final, 26.2.49
Record victory: 11-1 v Carlisle United, Division III (N), 14.1.39
Record defeat: 0-8 v Wolverhampton Wanderers, Division II, 4.11.11
Most League points: 69, Division III, 1965-66
Most League goals: 109, Division III, 1965-66
League scoring record: 39, Bill McNaughton, Division III (N), 1932-33
Record League aggregate: 195, Chris Chilton, 1960-1971
Most League appearances: 511, Andy Davidson, 1947-1967
Most capped player: 15 (59 in all), Terry Neill, Northern Ireland

THE HULL RECORD

	Division & place	Cup round reached
1906	II 5	1
1907	II 9	1
1908	II 8	2
1909	II 4	1
1910	II 3	1
1911	II 5	3
1912	II 7	1
1913	II 12	2
1914	II 7	1
1915	II 7	q-f
1920	II 11	1
1921	II 13	q-f
1922	II 5	2
1923	II 12	1
1924	II 17	1
1925	II 10	3
1926	II 13	3
1927	II 7	5
1928	II 14	3
1929	II 12	3
1930	II 21R	s-f
1931	NIII 6	3
1932	NIII 8	3
1933	NIII 1P	3
1934	II 15	4
1935	II 13	3
1936	II 22R	3
1937	NIII 5	1
1938	NIII 3	3
1939	NIII 7	2
1947	NIII 11	3
1948	NIII 5	3
1949	NIII 1P	q-f
1950	II 7	4
1951	II 10	5
1952	II 18	4
1953	II 18	4
1954	II 15	5
1955	II 19	3
1956	II 22R	3
1957	NIII 8	3
1958	NIII 5	4
1959	III 2P	1
1960	II 21R	3
1961	III 11	3
1962	III 10	2
1963	III 10	3
1964	III 8	3
1965	III 4	2
1966	III 1P	q-f
1967	II 12	3
1968	II 17	3
1969	II 11	3
1970	II 13	3
1971	II 5	q-f
1972	II 12	5
1973	II 13	5

P — promoted   R — relegated
Did not compete in 1946 Cup

Ken Wagstaff, a prolific scorer for Hull City in the sixties and seventies.

IPSWICH TOWN

Founded: 1880
Address: Portman Road, Ipswich, Suffolk
Telephone: Ipswich 51306/57107
Ground capacity: 36,000 (5,500 seated)
Playing area: 112 by 75 yards
Record attendance: 34,636 v Arsenal, Division I, 10.3.73
Record victory: 10-0 v Floriana, Malta, European Cup, 1962-63
Record defeat: 1-10 v Fulham, Division I, 26.12.63
Most League points: 64, Division III(S), 1953-54 & 1955-56
Most League goals: 106, Division III(S), 1955-56
League scoring record: 41, Ted Phillips, Division III(S), 1956-57
Record aggregate: 203, Ray Crawford, 1958-1963 & 1966-1969
Most League appearances: 428, Tom Parker, 1946-1957
Most capped player: 13, (19 in all), Allan Hunter, Northern Ireland

THE IPSWICH RECORD

	Division & place	Cup round reached
1939	SIII 7	3
1946		2
1947	SIII 6	2
1948	SIII 4	1
1949	SIII 7	1
1950	SIII 17	3
1951	SIII 8	2
1952	SIII 17	3
1953	SIII 16	3
1954	SIII 1P	5
1955	II 21R	3
1956	SIII 3	1
1957	SIII 1P	3
1958	II 8	4
1959	II 16	5
1960	II 11	3
1961	II 1P	3
1962	I 1C	4
1963	I 17	4
1964	I 22R	4
1965	II 5	4
1966	II 15	3
1967	II 5	5
1968	II 1P	3
1969	I 12	3
1970	I 18	3
1971	I 19	5
1972	I 13	4
1973	I 4	4

C – Football League champions
P – promoted   R – relegated
S – Third Division South

LEEDS UNITED

Founded: 1904†
Address: Elland Road, Leeds 11 **Telephone:** 0532 76037/8
Ground capacity: 50,000 (12,000 seated) **Playing area:** 115 by 76 yards
Record attendance: 57,892 v Sunderland, FA Cup 5th round, 15.3.67
Record victory: 10-0 v Lyn Oslo, European Cup 1st Rd, 17.9.69
Record defeat: 1-8 v Stoke City, Division I, 27.8.34
Most League points: 67, Division I, 1968-69
Most League goals: 98, Division II, 1927-28
League scoring record: 42, John Charles, 1953-54
Record League aggregate: 154, John Charles, 1949-1957 & 1962
Most League appearances: 629, Jack Charlton, 1953-1973
Most capped player: 39, Billy Bremner, Scotland (start of 1973-74 season)

FA Cup	Year	Opponents	Score	Scorers
Winners	1972	Arsenal	1-0	Clarke
Runners-up	1965	Liverpool	*1-2	Bremner
	1970	Chelsea	*2-2	Charlton, Jones
			*1-2	Jones
	1973	Sunderland	0-1	
League Cup				
Winners	1968	Arsenal	1-0	Cooper

†as Leeds City. Reconstituted as Leeds United 1920   *after extra time

THE LEEDS RECORD

	Division & place	FA Cup round reached
1906†	II 6	
1907†	II 10	1
1908†	II 12	1
1909†	II 12	2
1910†	II 17	1
1911†	II 11	1
1912†	II 19	2
1913†	II 6	1
1914†	II 4	2
1915†	II 15	2
1920‡	II	
1921	II 14	1q
1922	II 8	1
1923	II 7	2
1924	II 1P	3
1925	I 18	1
1926	I 19	3
1927	I 21R	4
1928	II 2P	3
1929	I 13	4
1930	I 5	4
1931	I 21R	5
1932	II 2P	3
1933	I 8	5
1934	I 9	3
1935	I 18	4
1936	I 11	5
1937	I 19	3
1938	I 9	4
1939	I 13	4
1946		3
1947	I 22R	3
1948	II 18	3
1949	II 15	3
1950	II 5	q-f
1951	II 5	4
1952	II 6	5
1953	II 10	3
1954	II 10	3
1955	II 4	3
1956	II 2P	3
1957	I 8	3
1958	I 17	3
1959	I 15	3
1960	I 21R	3
1961	II 14	3
1962	II 19	3
1963	II 5	5
1964	II 1P	4
1965	I 2	Final
1966	I 2	4
1967	I 4	s-f
1968	I 4	s-f
1969	I 1C	3
1970	I 2	Final
1971	I 2	5
1972	I 2	Winners
1973	I 3	Final

C – Football League Champions
P – promoted
R – relegated
q – qualifying competition
†as Leeds City
‡Leeds expelled from the League after 8 matches. Fixtures transferred to Port Vale, who finished 13th.

LEICESTER CITY

Founded: 1884
Address: Filbert Street, Leicester
Telephone: Leicester 57111/2
Ground capacity: 42,000 (11,000 seated)
Playing area: 112 by 75 yards
Record attendance: 47,298 v Tottenham Hotspur, FA Cup 5th round, 18.2.28
Record victory: 10-0 v Portsmouth, Division I, 20.10.28
Record defeat: 0-12 v Nottingham Forest, Division I, 21.4.09
Most League points: 61, Division II, 1956-57
Most League goals: 109, Division II, 1956-57
League scoring record: 44, Arthur Rowley, Division II, 1956-57
Record League aggregate: 262, Arthur Chandler, 1923-1935
Most League appearances: 530, Adam Black, 1919-1935
Most capped player: 37 (73 in all), Gordon Banks, England

FA Cup	Year	Opponents	Score	Scorers
Runners-up	1949	Wolverhampton Wanderers	1-3	Griffiths
	1961	Tottenham Hotspur	0-2	
	1963	Manchester United	1-3	Keyworth
	1969	Manchester City	0-1	
League Cup				
Winners	1964	Stoke City	h1-1	Gibson
			a3-2	Stringfellow, Gibson, Riley
Runners-up	1965	Chelsea	a2-3	Appleton, Goodfellow
			h0-0	

THE LEICESTER RECORD

	Division & place	Cup round reached
1894		2
1895	II 4	1
1896	II 8	4q
1897	II 9	4q
1898	II 7	1
1899	II 3	4q
1900	II 5	1
1901	II 11	1
1902	II 14	p
1903	II 15	2q
1904	II 18	4q
1905	II 14	1
1906	II 7	1
1907	II 3	1
1908	II 2P	2
1909	I 20R	2
1910	II 5	q-f
1911	II 15	2
1912	II 10	2
1913	II 15	1
1914	II 18	1
1915	II 19	6q
1920	II 14	3
1921	II 12	1
1922	II 9	3
1923	II 3	2
1924	II 12	1
1925	II 1P	q-f
1926	I 17	3
1927	I 7	1
1928	I 3	5
1929	I 2	5
1930	I 8	3
1931	I 16	3
1932	I 19	5
1933	I 19	3
1934	I 17	s-f
1935	I 21R	4
1936	II 6	5
1937	II 1P	3
1938	I 16	4
1939	I 22R	4
1946		3
1947	II 9	5
1948	II 9	5
1949	II 19	Final
1950	II 15	3
1951	II 14	3
1952	II 5	3
1953	II 5	3
1954	II 1P	q-f
1955	I 21R	3
1956	II 5	4
1957	II 1P	3
1958	I 18	3
1959	I 19	4
1960	I 12	q-f
1961	I 6	Final
1962	I 14	3
1963	I 4	Final
1964	I 11	3
1965	I 18	q-f
1966	I 7	5
1967	I 8	3
1968	I 13	q-f
1969	I 21R	Final
1970	II 3	5
1971	II 1P	q-f
1972	I 12	4
1973	I 16	3

P – promoted   R – relegated
q – qualifying round
p – preliminary round

City manager Jimmy Bloomfield.

THE LINCOLN RECORD

	Division & place	Cup round reached
1885		3
1886		1
1887		1
1888		p
1889		p
1890		2
1891		1
1892		p
1893	II 9	p
1894	II 8	p
1895	II 13	q
1896	II 13	p
1897	II 16	p
1898	II 14	p
1899	II 12	p
1900	II 9	p
1901	II 8	p
1902	II 5	2
1903	II 10	1
1904	II 12	q
1905	II 9	1
1906	II 13	2
1907	II 19	2
1908	II 20L	1
1909		1
1910	II 15	p
1911	II 21L	p
1912		2
1913	II 8	p
1914	II 19	1
1915	II 16	1
1920	II 21L	1
1921		2
1922	NIII 14	p
1923	NIII 13	q
1924	NIII 19	3
1925	NIII 8	p
1926	NIII 15	1
1927	NIII 11	3
1928	NIII 2	3
1929	NIII 6	3
1930	NIII 5	2
1931	NIII 2	2
1932	NIII 1P	2
1933	II 18	3
1934	II 22R	3
1935	NIII 4	2
1936	NIII 4	1
1937	NIII 2	2
1938	NIII 7	2
1939	NIII 17	3
1946		2
1947	NIII 12	3
1948	NIII 1P	1
1949	II 22R	1
1950	NIII 4	1
1951	NIII 5	1
1952	NIII 1P	3
1953	II 15	3
1954	II 16	4
1955	II 16	3
1956	II 8	3
1957	II 18	3
1958	II 20	3
1959	II 19	3
1960	II 13	3
1961	II 22R	4
1962	III 22R	1
1963	IV 22	3
1964	IV 11	3
1965	IV 22	3
1966	IV 22	1
1967	IV 24	1
1968	IV 13	1
1969	IV 8	3
1970	IV 8	2
1971	IV 21	3
1972	IV 5	1
1973	IV 10	1

p – preliminary round
q – qualifying round
L – not re-elected
N – Third Division North
P – promoted   R – relegated

LINCOLN CITY

Founded: 1883
Address: Sincil Bank, Lincoln
Telephone: Lincoln 21912/21298
Ground capacity: 25,300 (3,000 seated)
Playing area: 110 by 75 yards
Record attendance: 25,000 v Wolverhampton Wanderers, FA Cup 3rd Rd, 4.1.58
Record victory: 11-1 v Crewe Alexandra, Division III(N), 29.9.51
Record defeat: 3-11 v Manchester City, Division II, 23.3.1895
Most League points: 69, Division III (N), 1951-52
Most League goals: 121, Division III (N), 1951-52
League scoring record: 42, Alan Hall, Division III(N), 1931-32
Record League aggregate: 144, Andy Graver, 1950-1954, 1958-1961
Most League appearances: 402, Tony Emery, 1946-1959
Most capped player: 3 (7 in all), David Pugh, Wales
  3 (6 in all), Con Moulson, Eire, 3, George Moulson, Eire
N.B. The symbol above is not Lincoln City's official club badge.

LIVERPOOL

Founded: 1892
Address: Anfield Road, Liverpool 4 **Telephone:** (051) 263 2361
Ground Capacity: 54,400 (11,100 seated)
Playing area: 110 by 75 yards
Record attendance: 61,905 v Wolverhampton Wanderers, FA Cup 4th round, 2.2.52
Record victory: 10-1 v Rotherham United, Division II, 18.2.96
Record defeat: 1-9 v Birmingham City, Division II, 11.12.54
Most League points: 62, Division II, 1961-62
Most League goals: 106, Division II, 1895-96
League scoring record: 41, Roger Hunt, Division II, 1961-62
Record League aggregate: 245, Roger Hunt, 1959-1969
Most League appearances: 492, Billy Liddell, 1946-1961
Most capped player: 34, Roger Hunt, England

FA Cup	Year	Opponents	Score	Scorers
Winners	1965	Leeds United	*2-1	Hunt, St John
Runners-up	1914	Burnley	0-1	
	1950	Arsenal	0-2	
	1971	Arsenal	*1-2	Heighway

THE LIVERPOOL RECORD

Year	Division & place	F.A. Cup round reached
1894	II 1P	q-f
1895	I 16R	2
1896	II 1P	2
1897	I 5	s-f
1898	I 9	q-f
1899	I 2	s-f
1900	I 10	2
1901	I 1C	1
1902	I 11	2
1903	I 5	1
1904	I 17R	1
1905	II 1P	1
1906	I 1C	s-f
1907	I 15	q-f
1908	I 8	3
1909	I 16	2
1910	I 2	1
1911	I 13	2
1912	I 17	2
1913	I 12	3
1914	I 16	Final
1915	I 14	2
1920	I 4	q-f
1921	I 4	2
1922	I 1C	2
1923	I 1C	3
1924	I 12	q-f
1925	I 4	q-f
1926	I 7	4
1927	I 9	5
1928	I 16	4
1929	I 5	4
1930	I 12	3
1931	I 9	3
1932	I 10	q-f
1933	I 14	3
1934	I 18	5
1935	I 7	4
1936	I 19	4
1937	I 18	3
1938	I 11	5
1939	I 11	5
1946		4
1947	I 1C	s-f
1948	I 11	4
1949	I 12	5
1950	I 8	Final
1951	I 9	3
1952	I 11	5
1953	I 17	3
1954	I 22R	3
1955	II 11	5
1956	II 3	5
1957	II 3	3
1958	II 4	q-f
1959	II 4	3
1960	II 3	4
1961	II 3	4
1962	II 1P	5
1963	I 8	s-f
1964	I 1C	q-f
1965	I 7	Winners
1966	I 1C	3
1967	I 5	5
1968	I 3	q-f
1969	I 2	5
1970	I 5	q-f
1971	I 5	Final
1972	I 3	4
1973	I 1C	q-f

C — Football League Champions
P — promoted
R — relegated

THE LUTON TOWN RECORD

Year	Division & place	Cup round reached
1898	II 8	1
1899	II 15	p
1900	II 17L	p
1921	SIII 9	3
1922	SIII 4	2
1923	SIII 5	1
1924	SIII 7	1
1925	SIII 16	1
1926	SIII 7	2
1927	SIII 8	3
1928	SIII 13	3
1929	SIII 7	3
1930	SIII 13	1
1931	SIII 7	2
1932	SIII 6	3
1933	SIII 14	q-f
1934	SIII 6	3
1935	SIII 4	4
1936	SIII 2	4
1937	SIII 1P	4
1938	II 12	5
1939	II 7	3
1946		3
1947	II 13	5
1948	II 13	5
1949	II 10	5
1950	II 17	3
1951	II 19	4
1952	II 8	q-f
1953	II 3	5
1954	II 6	3
1955	II 2P	5
1956	I 10	3
1957	I 16	3
1958	I 8	3
1959	I 17	Final
1960	I 22R	5
1961	II 13	5
1962	II 13	3
1963	II 22R	3
1964	III 18	3
1965	III 21R	2
1966	IV 6	2
1967	IV 17	2
1968	IV 1P	3
1969	III 3	3
1970	III 2P	2
1971	II 6	3
1972	II 13	3
1973	II 12	q-f

P—promoted R—relegated
S—Third Division South
L – not re-elected

LUTON TOWN

Founded: 1885
Address: 70 Kenilworth Road, Luton
Telephone: Luton 23151
Ground capacity: 31,000 (3,500 seated)
Playing area: 112 by 72 yards
Record attendance: 30,069 v Blackpool, FA Cup 6th round replay, 4.3.59
Record victory: 12-0 v Bristol Rovers, Division III(S), 13.4.36
Record defeat: 1-9 v Swindon Town, Division III(S), 28.8.21
Most League points: 66, Division IV, 1967-68
Most League goals: 103, Division III(S), 1936-37
League scoring record: 55, Joe Payne, Division III(S), 1936-37
Record League aggregate: 233, Gordon Turner, 1949-1964
Most appearances: 494, Bob Mortort, 1949-1964
Most capped player: 19, George Cummins, Eire

FA Cup	Year	Opponents	Score	Scorers
Runners-up	1959	Nottingham Forest	1-2	Pacey

MANCHESTER CITY

Founded: 1880
Address: Maine Road, Moss Side, Manchester 4
Telephone: (061) 226 1191/2
Ground capacity: 52,500
Playing area: 117 by 77 yards
Record attendance: 84,569 v Stoke City, FA Cup quarter-final, 3.3.34
Record victory: 11-3 v Lincoln City, Division II, 23.3.95
Record defeat: 1-9 v Everton, Division I, 3.9.06
Most League points: 62, Division II, 1946-47
Most League goals: 108, Division II, 1926-27
League scoring record: 38, Tom Johnson, Division I, 1928-29
Record League aggregate: 158, Tom Johnson, 1919-1930
Most League appearances: 508, Bert Trautmann, 1949-1965
Most capped player: 31, Colin Bell, England (at 1.1.74)

FA Cup	Year	Opponents	Score	Scorers
Winners	1904	Bolton Wanderers	1-0	Meredith
	1934	Portsmouth	2-1	Tilson 2
	1956	Birmingham City	3-1	Hayes, Dyson, Johnstone
	1969	Leicester City	1-0	Young
Runners-up	1926	Bolton Wanderers	0-1	
	1933	Everton	0-3	
	1955	Newcastle United	1-3	Johnstone
League Cup				
Winners	1970	West Bromwich Albion	2-1	Doyle, Pardoe

The sale of Malcolm Macdonald (right) saved Luton from bankruptcy in 1971.

Veteran Tony Book (right) led Manchester City to a succession of honours.

THE CITY RECORD

Year	Division & place	Cup round reached
1893†	II 5	
1894†	II 13	
1895	II 9	
1896	II 2	
1897	II 6	1
1898	II 3	2
1899	II 1P	2
1900	I 7	1
1901	I 11	1
1902	I 18R	2
1903	II 1P	1
1904	I 2	Winners
1905	I 3	2
1906	I 5	1
1907	I 17	1
1908	I 3	3
1909	I 19R	1
1910	II 1P	q-f
1911	I 17	2
1912	I 15	2
1913	I 6	2
1914	I 13	q-f
1915	I 5	3
1920	I 7	2
1921	I 2	1
1922	I 10	3
1923	I 8	1
1924	I 11	s-f
1925	I 10	1
1926	I 21R	Final
1927	II 3	3
1928	II 1P	5
1929	I 8	3
1930	I 3	5
1931	I 8	3
1932	I 14	s-f
1933	I 16	Final
1934	I 5	Winners
1935	I 4	3
1936	I 9	5
1937	I 1C	q-f
1938	I 21R	q-f
1939	II 5	4
1946		4
1947	II 1P	5
1948	I 10	5
1949	I 7	3
1950	I 21R	3
1951	II 2P	3
1952	I 15	3
1953	I 20	4
1954	I 17	4
1955	I 7	Final
1956	I 4	Winners
1957	I 18	3
1958	I 5	3
1959	I 20	3
1960	I 16	3
1961	I 13	4
1962	I 12	4
1963	I 21R	5
1964	II 6	3
1965	II 11	3
1966	II 1P	q-f
1967	I 15	q-f
1968	I 1C	4
1969	I 13	Winners
1970	I 9	4
1971	I 11	5
1972	I 4	3
1973	I 11	5

C – Football League Champions
P – promoted   R – relegated
†as Ardwick

THE UNITED RECORD

Year	Division & place	Cup round reached
1890†		1
1891†		
1892†		
1893†	I 16	1
1894†	I 16R	2
1895†	II 3	1
1896†	II 6	2
1897†	II 2	q-f
1898†	II 4	2
1899†	II 4	1
1900†	II 4	
1901†	II 10	1
1902†	II 15	
1903	II 5	2
1904	II 3	2
1905	II 3	
1906	II 2P	q-f
1907	I 8	1
1908	I 1C	q-f
1909	I 13	Winners
1910	I 5	1
1911	I 1C	3
1912	I 13	q-f
1913	I 4	3
1914	I 14	1
1915	I 18	1
1920	I 12	2
1921	I 13	1
1922	I 22R	1
1923	II 4	2
1924	II 14	1
1925	II 2P	1
1926	I 9	s-f
1927	I 15	3
1928	I 18	q-f
1929	I 12	4
1930	I 17	3
1931	I 22R	4
1932	II 12	3
1933	II 6	3
1934	II 20	3
1935	II 5	4
1936	II 1P	4
1937	I 21R	4
1938	II 2P	5
1939	I 14	3
1946		4
1947	I 2	5
1948	I 2	Winners
1949	I 2	s-f
1950	I 4	q-f
1951	I 2	q-f
1952	I 1C	3
1953	I 8	5
1954	I 4	3
1955	I 5	4
1956	I 1C	3
1957	I 1C	Final
1958	I 9	Final
1959	I 2	3
1960	I 7	5
1961	I 7	4
1962	I 15	s-f
1963	I 19	Winners
1964	I 2	s-f
1965	I 1C	s-f
1966	I 4	s-f
1967	I 1C	4
1968	I 2	3
1969	I 11	q-f
1970	I 8	s-f
1971	I 8	3
1972	I 8	4
1973	I 18	3

C – Football League champions
P – promoted   R – relegated
† – as Newton Heath

MANCHESTER UNITED

Founded: 1880
Address: Old Trafford, Stretford, Manchester 16
Telephone: (061) 872 1661/2
Ground capacity: 61,500 (18,500 seated)
Playing area: 116 by 76 yards
Record attendance: *70,504 v Aston Villa, Division I, 27.12.20
Record victory: 10-1 v Wolverhampton Wanderers, Division I, 15.10.1892
Record defeat: 0-7 v Aston Villa, Division I, 27.12.30
Most League points: 64, Division I, 1956-57
Most League goals: 103, Division I, 1956-57 & Division I, 1958-59
League scoring record: 32, Denis Viollet, Division I, 1959-60
Record League aggregate: 198, Bobby Charlton, 1956-1973
Most League appearances: 606, Bobby Charlton, 1956-1973
Most capped player: 106, Bobby Charlton, England

FA Cup	Year	Opponents	Score	Scorers
Winners	1909	Bristol City	1-0	Turnbull (A)
	1948	Blackpool	4-2	Rowley 2, Pearson, Anderson
	1963	Leicester City	3-1	Herd 2, Law
Runners-up	1957	Aston Villa	1-2	Taylor
	1958	Bolton Wanderers	0-2	

*ground record: 76,962 for Wolverhampton Wanderers v Grimsby Town, FA Cup semi-final, 25.3.39

MANSFIELD TOWN

Founded: 1905
Address: Field Mill Ground, Quarry Lane, Mansfield, Notts
Telephone: Mansfield 23567
Ground capacity: 20,500 (2,300 seated)
Playing area: 115 by 72 yards
Record attendance: 24,467 v Nottingham Forest, FA Cup 3rd round, 10.1.53
Record victory: 9-2 v Rotherham United, Division III(N), 27.12.32
9-2 v Hounslow Town, FA Cup 1st round replay, 5.11.62
Record defeat: 1-8 v Walsall, Division III(N), 19.1.33
Most League points: 64, Division III(N), 1950-51
Most League goals: 108, Division IV, 1962-63
League scoring record: 55, Ted Harston, Division III(N), 1936-37
Record League aggregate: 104, Harry Johnson, 1931-1936
Most League appearances: 386, Don Bradley, 1949-1962

THE MANSFIELD RECORD

Year	Division & place	Cup round reached
1932	SIII 20	1
1933	NIII 16	1
1934	NIII 17	1
1935	NIII 8	3
1936	NIII 19	1
1937	NIII 9	2
1938	SIII 14	3
1939	SIII 16	2
1946		3
1947	SIII 22	1
1948	NIII 8	3
1949	NIII 10	3
1950	NIII 8	2
1951	NIII 2	5
1952	NIII 6	1
1953	NIII 18	3
1954	NIII 7	1
1955	NIII 13	1
1956	NIII 18	2
1957	NIII 16	1
1958	NIII 6	3
1959	III 20	1
1960	III 22R	3
1961	IV 20	2
1962	IV 14	2
1963	IV 4P	3
1964	III 7	1
1965	III 3	2
1966	III 19	1
1967	III 9	4
1968	III 20	1
1969	III 15	q-f
1970	III 6	5
1971	III 7	2
1972	III 21R	2
1973	IV 6	1

P – promoted   R – relegated
S – Third Division South
N – Third Division North

MIDDLESBROUGH

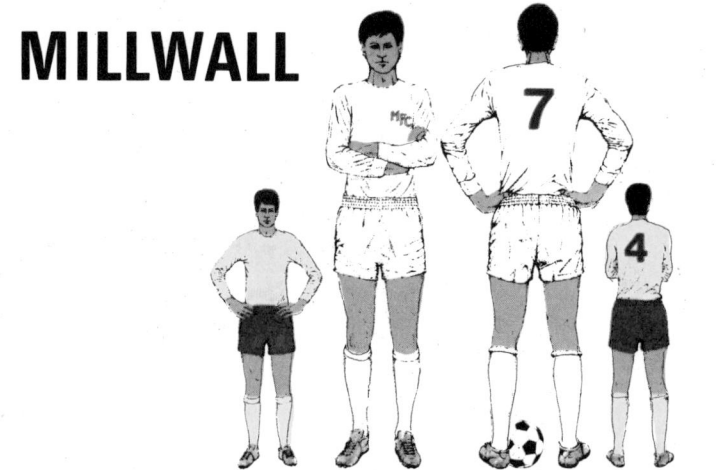

Founded: 1876
Address: Ayresome Park, Middlesbrough, Yorkshire
Telephone: Middlesbrough 89659
Ground capacity: 42,000 (10,200 seated)
Playing area: 115 by 75 yards
Record attendance: 53,596 v Sunderland, Division I, 27.12.49
Record victory: 10-3 v Sheffield United, Division I, 18.11.33
Record defeat: 0-9 v Blackburn Rovers, Division II, 6.11.54
Most League points: 62, Division II, 1926-27
Most League goals: 122, Division II, 1926-27
League scoring record: 59, George Camsell, Division II, 1926-27
Record League aggregate: 326, George Camsell, 1925-1939
Most League appearances: 563, Tim Williamson, 1902-1923
Most capped player: 26, Wilf Mannion, England

FA Amateur Cup	Year	Opponents	Score	Scorers
Winners	1895	Old Carthusians	2-1	Mullen, Nelmes
	1898	Uxbridge	2-1	Bishop, Kempley

THE MIDDLESBROUGH RECORD

	Division & place	Cup round reached		Division & place	Cup round reached
1888		q-f	1929	II 1P	4
1889		q	1930	I 16	5
1890		q	1931	I 7	3
1891		q	1932	I 18	3
1892		2	1933	I 17	5
1893		1	1934	I 16	3
1894		2	1935	I 20	3
1895		2q	1936	I 14	q-f
1896		1q	1937	I 7	3
1897		5q	1938	I 5	5
1898		2q	1939	I 4	4
1899			1946		5
1900	II 14	p	1947	I 11	q-f
1901	II 6	q-f	1948	I 16	5
1902	II 2P	1	1949	I 19	3
1903	I 13	p	1950	I 9	4
1904	I 10	q-f	1951	I 6	3
1905	I 15	1	1952	I 18	4
1906	I 18	3	1953	I 13	3
1907	I 11	2	1954	I 21R	3
1908	I 6	1	1955	II 12	3
1909	I 9	1	1956	II 14	4
1910	I 17	1	1957	II 6	4
1911	I 16	3	1958	II 7	4
1912	I 7	2	1959	II 13	3
1913	I 16	3	1960	II 5	3
1914	I 4	1	1961	II 5	3
1915	I 12	2	1962	II 12	5
1920	I 13	2	1963	II 4	4
1921	I 8	1	1964	II 10	3
1922	I 18	1	1965	II 17	5
1923	I 18	2	1966	II 21R	3
1924	I 22R	1	1967	III 2P	3
1925	II 13	1	1968	II 6	4
1926	II 10	4	1969	II 4	3
1927	II 1P	5	1970	II 4	q-f
1928	I 22R	5	1971	II 7	4
			1972	II 9	5
			1973	II 4	3

P – promoted   R – relegated
q – qualifying round   p – preliminary round

MILLWALL

Founded: 1885
Address: The Den, Cold Blow Lane, New Cross, London S.E.14
Telephone: 01-639 3143
Ground capacity: 40,000 (3,500 seated)
Playing area: 112 by 74 yards
Record attendance: 48,672 v Derby County, FA Cup 5th round, 20.2.37
Record victory: 9-1 v Torquay United, Division III(S), 29.8.27
9-1 v Coventry City, Division III(S), 19.11.27
Record defeat: 1-9 v Aston Villa, FA Cup 4th round, 28.1.46
Most League points: 65, Division III(S), 1927-28; Division III, 1965-66
Most League goals: 127, Division III(S), 1927-28
League scoring record: 37, Dick Parker, Division III(S), 1926-27
Record League aggregate: 79, Derek Possee, 1967-1973
Most League appearances: 374, Harry Cripps, 1961-1973
Most capped player: 26, (27 in all), Eamonn Dunphy, Eire

THE MILLWALL RECORD

	Division & place	Cup round reached		Division & place	Cup round reached
1895	1		1933	II 7	4
1896	1		1934	II 21R	4
1897	1		1935	SIII 12	4
1898	q		1936	SIII 12	3
1899	q		1937	SIII 8	s-f
1900	s-f		1938	SIII 1P	3
1901	1		1939	II 13	4
1902	p		1946		4
1903	s-f		1947	II 18	3
1904	1		1948	II 22R	3
1905	1		1949	SIII 8	2
1906	2		1950	SIII 22	1
1907	2		1951	SIII 5	4
1908	1		1952	SIII 4	2
1909	3		1953	SIII 2	3
1910	1		1954	SIII 12	2
1911	1		1955	SIII 5	3
1912	1		1956	SIII 22	1
1913	1		1957	SIII 17	5
1914	3		1958	SIII 23	2
1915	2		1959	IV 9	2
1920	1		1960	IV 5	1
1921	III 7	1	1961	IV 6	1
1922	SIII 12	q-f	1962	IV 1P	1
1923	SIII 6	2	1963	III 16	2
1924	SIII 3	1	1964	III 21R	1
1925	SIII 5	1	1965	IV 2P	4
1926	SIII 3	5	1966	III 2P	2
1927	SIII 3	q-f	1967	II 8	3
1928	SIII 1P	3	1968	II 7	3
1929	II 14	4	1969	II 10	4
1930	II 14	5	1970	II 10	3
1931	II 14	3	1971	II 8	3
1932	II 9	3	1972	II 3	4
			1973	II 11	5

P – promoted   R – relegated
S – Third Division South
q – qualifying round
p – preliminary round

Millwall's Alan Dorney wins a tussle with Birmingham City's Bob Hatton.

NEWCASTLE UNITED

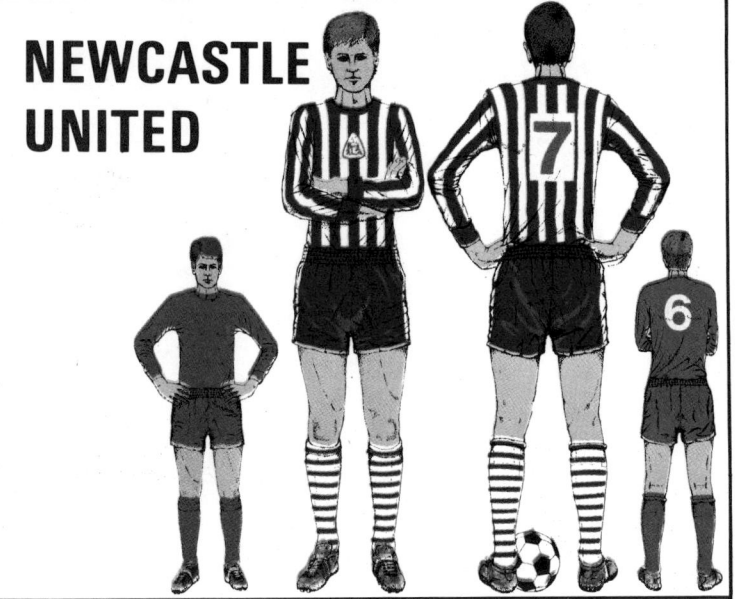

Founded: 1882
Address: St James' Park, Newcastle-on-Tyne, NE1 4ST
Telephone: (0632) 28361/2
Ground capacity: 56,000
Playing area: 115 by 75 yards
Record attendance: 68,386 v Chelsea, Division I, 3.9.30
Record victory: 13-0 v Newport County, Division II, 5.10.46
Record defeat: 0-9 v Burton Wanderers, Division II, 15.4.95
Most League points: 57, Division II, 1964-65
Most League goals: 98, Division I, 1951-52
League scoring record: 36, Hughie Gallacher, Division I, 1926-27
Record League aggregate: 178, Jackie Milburn, 1946-1957
Most League appearances: 432, Jim Lawrence, 1904-1922
Most capped player: 40, Alf McMichael, Northern Ireland

FA Cup	Year	Opponents	Score	Scorers
Winners	1910	Barnsley	*1-1	Rutherford
			2-0	Shepherd 2 (1 pen)
	1924	Aston Villa	2-0	Harris, Seymour
	1932	Arsenal	2-1	Allen 2
	1951	Blackpool	2-0	Milburn 2
	1952	Arsenal	1-0	Robledo (G)
	1955	Manchester City	3-1	Milburn, Mitchell, Hannah
Runners-up	1905	Aston Villa	0-2	
	1906	Everton	0-1	
	1908	Wolverhampton Wanderers	1-3	Howie
	1911	Bradford City	*0-0	
			0-1	

*After extra time.

THE NEWCASTLE RECORD

	Division & place	Cup round reached
1893		1
1894	II 4	2
1895	II 10	2
1896	II 5	2
1897	II 5	1
1898	II 2P	2
1899	I 13	2
1900	I 5	2
1901	I 6	1
1902	I 3	q-f
1903	I 14	1
1904	I 4	1
1905	I 1C	Final
1906	I 4	Final
1907	I 1C	1
1908	I 4	Final
1909	I 1C	s-f
1910	I 4	Winners
1911	I 8	Final
1912	I 3	1
1913	I 14	q-f
1914	I 11	1
1915	I 15	q-f
1920	I 8	2
1921	I 5	3
1922	I 7	2
1923	I 4	1
1924	I 9	Winners
1925	I 6	2
1926	I 10	5
1927	I 1C	5
1928	I 9	3
1929	I 10	3
1930	I 19	q-f
1931	I 17	4
1932	I 11	Winners
1933	I 5	3
1934	I 21R	3
1935	II 6	4
1936	II 8	5
1937	II 4	3
1938	II 19	3
1939	II 9	5
1946		3
1947	II 5	s-f
1948	II 2P	3
1949	I 4	3
1950	I 5	4
1951	I 4	Winners
1952	I 8	Winners
1953	I 16	4
1954	I 15	5
1955	I 8	Winners
1956	I 11	q-f
1957	I 17	4
1958	I 19	4
1959	I 11	3
1960	I 8	3
1961	I 21R	q-f
1962	II 11	3
1963	II 7	4
1964	II 8	3
1965	II 1P	3
1966	I 15	4
1967	I 20	4
1968	I 10	3
1969	I 9	4
1970	I 7	3
1971	I 11	3
1972	I 11	3
1973	I 9	4

P — promoted
R — relegated
C — Football League Champions

NEWPORT COUNTY

Founded: 1911
Address: Somerton Park, Newport, Monmouthshire
Telephone: Newport 71543/71271
Ground capacity: 22,060 (672 seated)
Playing area: 112 by 78 yards
Record attendance: 24,268 v Cardiff City, Division III(S), 16.10.37
Record victory: 10-0 v Merthyr Town, Division III(S), 10.4.30
Record defeat: 0-13 v Newcastle United, Division II, 5.10.46
Most League points: 56, Division IV, 1972-73
Most League goals: 85, Division IV, 1964-65
League scoring record: 34, Tudor Martin, Division III(S), 1929-30
Record League aggregate: 99, Reg Parker, 1948-1954
Most League appearances: 530, Ray Wilcox, 1946-1960
Most capped player: 2, Billy Thomas, Wales
2 (4 in all), Jack Nicholls, Wales
2 (9 in all), Freddie Cook, Wales
2 (41 in all), Alf Sherwood, Wales

THE NEWPORT RECORD

	Division & place	Cup round reached
1920		1
1921	III 15	q
1922	SIII 20	
1923	SIII 22	p
1924	SIII 10	q
1925	SIII 6	p
1926	SIII 17	2
1927	SIII 9	1
1928	SIII 9	1
1929	SIII 16	2
1930	SIII 18	2
1931	SIII 22	2
1932	*	
1933	SIII 21	2
1934	SIII 18	2
1935	SIII 22	1
1936	SIII 21	1
1937	SIII 19	2
1938	SIII 16	3
1939	SIII 1P	3
1946		3
1947	II 22R	3
1948	SIII 12	2
1949	SIII 15	5
1950	SIII 21	3
1951	SIII 11	4
1952	SIII 6	3
1953	SIII 15	3
1954	SIII 15	1
1955	SIII 19	1
1956	SIII 19	1
1957	SIII 12	4
1958	SIII 11	1
1959	III 17	4
1960	III 13	3
1961	III 13	1
1962	III 24R	2
1963	IV 20	1
1964	IV 15	4
1965	IV 16	3
1966	IV 9	1
1967	IV 18	1
1968	IV 12	3
1969	IV 22	1
1970	IV 21	3
1971	IV 22	1
1972	IV 14	1
1973	IV 5	2

q – qualifying round   p – preliminary
P – promoted   R – relegated
S – Third Division South
*Newport were not re-elected in
1931, and took Thames' place in 1932.

NORTHAMPTON TOWN

THE NORTHAMPTON RECORD

Founded: 1897
Address: County Ground, Abingdon Avenue, Northampton NN1 4PS
Telephone: Northampton 31553
Ground capacity: 21,000 (2,000 seated)
Playing area: 120 by 75 yards
Record attendance: 24,523 v Fulham, Division I, 23.4.66
Record victory: 10-0 v Walsall, Division III(S), 5.11.27
Record defeat: 0-10 v Bournemouth, Division III(S), 2.9.39
Most League points: 62, Division III(S), 1952-53 & Division III, 1962-63
Most League goals: 109, Division III(S), 1952-53 & Division III, 1962-63
League scoring record: 36, Cliff Holton, Division III, 1961-62
Record League aggregate: 135, Jack English, 1947-1960
Most League appearances: 521, Tommy Fowler, 1946-1961
Most capped player: 12 (16 in all), E Lloyd Davies, Wales

THE NORTHAMPTON RECORD

Year	Division & place	Cup round reached
1906		1
1907		1
1908		1
1909		1
1910		2
1911		2
1912		3
1913		1
1914		p
1915		2
1920		p
1921	III 14	1
1922	SIII 17	2
1923	SIII 8	p
1924	SIII 8	1
1925	SIII 9	1
1926	SIII 12	3
1927	SIII 18	2
1928	SIII 2	3
1929	SIII 3	3
1930	SIII 4	3
1931	SIII 6	1
1932	SIII 14	4
1933	SIII 8	2
1934	SIII 13	5
1935	SIII 7	3
1936	SIII 15	1
1937	SIII 7	1
1938	SIII 9	1
1939	SIII 17	1
1946		3
1947	SIII 13	3
1948	SIII 14	2
1949	SIII 20	2
1950	SIII 2	5
1951	SIII 21	4
1952	SIII 8	1
1953	SIII 3	2
1954	SIII 5	2
1955	SIII 13	1
1956	SIII 11	3
1957	SIII 14	1
1958	SIII 13	4
1959	IV 8	2
1960	IV 6	1
1961	IV 3P	3
1962	III 8	3
1963	III 1P	1
1964	II 11	3
1965	II 2P	3
1966	I 21R	3
1967	II 21R	3
1968	III 17	1
1969	III 21R	3
1970	IV 14	5
1971	IV 7	1
1972	IV 21	2
1973	IV 23	1

P — promoted   R — relegated
S — Third Division South
p — preliminary round

THE NORWICH RECORD

Year	Division & place	Cup round reached
1906		2
1907		2
1908		2
1909		3
1910		1
1911		2
1912		1
1913		2
1914		1
1915		3
1920		q-f
1921		1
1922	SIII 15	1
1923	SIII 18	1
1924	SIII 11	1
1925	SIII 12	2
1926	SIII 16	1
1927	SIII 16	3
1928	SIII 17	2
1929	SIII 17	3
1930	SIII 8	1
1931	SIII 21	2
1932	SIII 10	2
1933	SIII 3	1
1934	SIII 1P	1
1935	II 14	5
1936	II 11	3
1937	II 17	4
1938	II 14	3
1939	II 21R	3
1946		3
1947	SIII 21	2
1948	SIII 21	2
1949	SIII 9	2
1950	SIII 11	3
1951	SIII 2	5
1952	SIII 3	3
1953	SIII 4	2
1954	SIII 7	5
1955	SIII 11	2
1956	SIII 7	3
1957	SIII 24	1
1958	SIII 8	3
1959	III 4	s-f
1960	III 2P	1
1961	II 4	5
1962	II 17	5
1963	II 11	q-f
1964	II 17	3
1965	II 6	3
1966	II 13	5
1967	II 11	5
1968	II 9	4
1969	II 13	3
1970	II 11	3
1971	II 10	3
1972	II 1P	3
1973	I 20	3

P — promoted
R — relegated
S — Third Division South

NORWICH CITY

Founded: 1905
Address: Carrow Road, Norwich NOR 22
Telephone: 0603 21514/5
Ground capacity: 41,000 (4,850 seated)
Playing area: 114 by 74 yards
Record attendance: 43,984 v Leicester City, FA Cup quarter-final, 30.3.63
Record victory: 10-1 v Coventry City, Division III(S), 15.3.30
Record defeat: 0-7 v Walsall, Division III(S), 13.9.30
Most League points: 64, Division III(S), 1950-51
Most League goals: 99, Division III(S), 1952-53
League scoring record: 31, Ralph Hunt, Division III(S), 1955-56
Record League aggregate: 122, Johnny Gavin, 1945-1954 & 1955-1958
Most League appearances: 590, Ron Ashman, 1947-1964
Most capped player: 5 (24 in all), Ron Davies, Wales
5 (7 in all), Johnny Gavin, Republic of Ireland

League Cup	Year	Opponents	Score	Scorers
Winners	1962	Rochdale	A3-0	Lythgoe 2, Punton
			H1-0	Hill
Runners-up	1973	Tottenham Hotspur	0-1	

NOTTINGHAM FOREST

Founded: 1865
Address: City Ground, Nottingham
Telephone: Nottingham 868236
Ground capacity: 49,000 (6,222 seated)
Playing area: 115 by 78 yards
Record attendance: 49,946 v Manchester United, Division I, 28.10.67
Record victory: 14-0 v Clapton, FA Cup 1st round, 17.1.1891
Record defeat: 1-9 v Blackburn Rovers, Division II, 10.4.37
Most League points: 70, Division III(S), 1950-51
Most League goals: 110, Division III(S), 1950-51
League scoring record: 36, Wally Ardron, Division III(S), 1950-51
Record League aggregate: 199, Grenville Morris, 1898-1913
Most League appearances: 614, Bob McKinlay, 1951-1970
Most capped player: 16 (21 in all), Grenville Morris, Wales

FA Cup	Year	Opponents	Score	Scorers
Winners	1898	Derby County	3-1	Capes 2, McPherson
	1959	Luton Town	2-1	Dwight, Wilson

Forest's Doug Fraser and Sammy Chapman (right) defend against Crystal Palace.

THE FOREST RECORD

Year	Division & place	Cup round reached
1879		s-f
1880		s-f
1881		2
1882		1
1883		3
1884		2
1885		s-f
1886		3
1887		3
1888		5
1889		2
1890		1
1891		q-f
1892		s-f
1893	I 10	2
1894	I 7	q-f
1895	I 7	q-f
1896	I 13	1
1897	I 11	q-f
1898	I 8	Winners
1899	I 11	q-f
1900	I 8	s-f
1901	I 4	2
1902	I 5	s-f
1903	I 10	2
1904	I 9	2
1905	I 16	2
1906	I 19R	3
1907	II 1P	1
1908	I 9	1
1909	I 14	q-f
1910	I 14	3
1911	I 20R	1
1912	II 15	1
1913	II 17	2
1914	II 20	1
1915	II 18	1
1920	II 18	1
1921	II 18	1
1922	II 1P	3
1923	I 20	1
1924	I 20	1
1925	I 22R	2
1926	II 17	q-f
1927	II 5	4
1928	II 10	q-f
1929	II 11	3
1930	II 10	q-f
1931	II 17	3
1932	II 11	3
1933	II 5	3
1934	II 17	4
1935	II 9	5
1936	II 19	4
1937	II 19	3
1938	II 20	4
1939	II 20	3
1946		3
1947	II 11	5
1948	II 19	3
1949	II 21R	3
1950	SIII 4	2
1951	SIII 1P	2
1952	II 4	3
1953	II 7	4
1954	II 4	3
1955	II 15	5
1956	II 7	3
1957	II 2P	4
1958	I 10	4
1959	I 13	Winners
1960	I 20	4
1961	I 14	3
1962	I 19	4
1963	I 9	q-f
1964	I 13	3
1965	I 5	5
1966	I 18	4
1967	I 2	s-f
1968	I 11	4
1969	I 18	3
1970	I 15	3
1971	I 16	5
1972	I 21R	3
1973	II 14	3

P—promoted
R—relegated
S—Third Division South

THE COUNTY RECORD

Year	Division & place	Cup round reached
1878		1
1879		1
1880		1
1881		3
1882		3
1883		s-f
1884		s-f
1885		q-f
1886		5
1887		q-f
1888		q
1889	I 11	2
1890	I 10	3
1891	I 3	Final
1892	I 8	q
1893	I 14R	
1894	II 3	Winners
1895	II 2	1
1896	II 10	1
1897	II 1P	2
1898	I 13	1
1899	I 5	2
1900	I 15	2
1901	I 3	2
1902	I 13	1
1903	I 15	3
1904	I 13	1
1905	I 18	1
1906	I 16	1
1907	I 18	q-f
1908	I 18	2
1909	I 15	1
1910	I 19	1
1911	I 11	1
1912	I 16	2
1913	I 19R	1
1914	II 1P	1
1915	I 16	1
1920	I 21R	3
1921	I 6	2
1922	II 13	s-f
1923	II 1P	1
1924	I 10	2
1925	I 9	3
1926	I 22R	5
1927	II 16	3
1928	II 15	3
1929	II 5	3
1930	II 22R	3
1931	SIII 1P	4
1932	II 16	3
1933	II 15	3
1934	II 18	3
1935	II 22R	3
1936	SIII 9	3
1937	SIII 2	1
1938	SIII 11	4
1939	SIII 11	4
1946		2
1947	SIII 12	3
1948	SIII 6	4
1949	SIII 11	3
1950	SIII 1P	3
1951	II 17	3
1952	II 15	4
1953	II 19	4
1954	II 14	3
1955	II 7	q-f
1956	II 20	3
1957	II 20	3
1958	II 21R	4
1959	III 23R	1
1960	IV 2P	2
1961	III 5	2
1962	III 13	2
1963	III 7	1
1964	III 24R	2
1965	IV 13	2
1966	IV 8	1
1967	IV 20	1
1968	IV 17	1
1969	IV 19	1
1970	IV 7	1
1971	IV 1P	3
1972	III 4	4
1973	III 2P	3

P – promoted
R – relegated
S – Third Division South

NOTTS COUNTY

Founded: 1862
Address: Meadow Lane, Nottingham NG2 3HS
Telephone: Nottingham 864152
Ground capacity: 40,000 (4,470 seated)
Playing area: 117 by 74 yards
Record attendance: 47,301 v York City, FA Cup quarter-final, 12.3.55
Record victory: 15-0 v Thornhill United, 1st round Cup, 1884-85
Record defeat: 1-9 v Aston Villa, Division I, 29.9.1889
1-9 v Bristol Rovers, Division I, 16.11.1889
1-9 v Portsmouth, Division II, 9.4.27
Most League points: 69, Division IV, 1970-71
Most League goals: 107, Division IV, 1959-60
League scoring record: 39, Tom Keetley, Division III(S), 1930-31
Record League aggregate: 109, Tony Hateley, 1958-1963 and 1970-72
Most League appearances: 564, Albert Iremonger, 1904-1926
Most capped player: 7 (10 in all), Bill Fallon, Republic of Ireland

FA Cup	Year	Opponents	Score	Scorers
Winners	1894	Bolton Wanderers	4-1	Watson, Logan 3
Runners-up	1891	Blackburn Rovers	1-3	Oswald

OLDHAM ATHLETIC

Founded: 1894*
Address: Boundary Park, Oldham
Telephone: 061 624 4972
Ground capacity: 36,000 (3,500 seated)
Playing area: 110 by 74 yards
Record attendance: 47,671 v Sheffield Wednesday, FA Cup 4th round, 25.1.30
Record victory: 11-0 v Southport, Division IV, 26.12.62
Record defeat: 4-13 v Tranmere Rovers, Division III(N), 26.12.35
Most League points: 59, Division III(N), 1952-53
Division IV, 1962-63
Division IV, 1970-71
Most League goals: 95, Division IV, 1962-63
League scoring record: 33, Tommy Davis, Division III(N), 1936-37
Record League aggregate: 110, Eric Gemmell, 1947-1954
Most League appearances: 369, David Wilson, 1907-1921
Most capped player: 9 (24 in all), Albert Gray, Wales
*as Pine Villa, name changed to Oldham Athletic in 1899

THE OLDHAM RECORD

Year	Division & place	Cup round reached
1907		2
1908	II 3	2
1909	II 6	1
1910	II 2P	1
1911	I 7	2
1912	I 18	3
1913	I 9	s-f
1914	I 3	1
1915	I 2	q-f
1920	I 17	1
1921	I 19	1
1922	I 19	2
1923	I 22R	1
1924	II 7	2
1925	II 18	1
1926	II 7	3
1927	II 10	3
1928	II 7	4
1929	II 18	3
1930	II 3	4
1931	II 12	3
1932	II 16	3
1933	II 16	3
1934	II 9	4
1935	II 21R	3
1936	NIII 7	2
1937	NIII 4	3
1938	NIII 4	1
1939	NIII 5	1
1946		2
1947	NIII 19	2
1948	NIII 11	2
1949	NIII 6	3
1950	NIII 11	3
1951	NIII 15	3
1952	NIII 4	2
1953	NIII 1P	3
1954	II 22R	3
1955	NIII 10	2
1956	NIII 20	1
1957	NIII 19	2
1958	NIII 15	2
1959	IV 21	3
1960	IV 23	2
1961	IV 12	2
1962	IV 11	4
1963	IV 2P	1
1964	III 9	3
1965	III 20	3
1966	III 20	3
1967	III 10	3
1968	III 16	1
1969	III 24R	1
1970	IV 19	2
1971	IV 3P	1
1972	III 11	1
1973	III 4	1

P – promoted
R – relegated
N – Third Division North

THE ORIENT RECORD

Year	Division & place	Cup round reached
1906*	II 20	1
1907	II 17	q
1908	II 14	p
1909	II 15	1
1910	II 16	1
1911	II 4	1
1912	II 4	1
1913	II 14	1
1914	II 6	2
1915	II 9	1
1920	II 15	1
1921	II 7	1
1922	II 15	1
1923	II 19	1
1924	II 10	1
1925	II 11	1
1926	II 20	q-f
1927	II 20	3
1928	II 20	3
1929	II 22R	4
1930	SIII 12	4
1931	SIII 19	1
1932	SIII 16	2
1933	SIII 20	1
1934	SIII 11	3
1935	SIII 14	2
1936	SIII 14	4
1937	SIII 12	2
1938	SIII 19	2
1939	SIII 20	2
1946		1
1947†	SIII 19	1
1948	SIII 17	1
1949	SIII 19	2
1950	SIII 18	1
1951	SIII 17	1
1952	SI'I 16	5
1953	SIII 14	1
1954	SIII 11	q-f
1955	SIII 2	2
1956	SIII 1P	4
1957	II 15	3
1958	II 12	4
1959	II 17	3
1960	II 10	3
1961	II 19	5
1962	II 2P	4
1963	I 22R	5
1964	II 16	4
1965	II 19	3
1966	II 22	3
1967	III 14	2
1968‡	III 18	4
1969	III 18	1
1970	III 1P	1
1971	II 17	4
1972	II 17	q-f
1973	II 15	3

P – promoted   R – relegated
q – qualifying competition
p – preliminary round
S – Third Division South
* – as Clapton Orient 1881–1946
† – as Leyton Orient 1946–1968
‡ – as Orient 1968–

ORIENT

Founded: 1881
Address: Leyton Stadium, Brisbane Road, Leyton, London E10
Telephone: (01) 539 1368/6800
Ground capacity: 35,000 (3,600 seated)
Playing area: 110 by 80 yards
Record attendance: 34,345 v West Ham United, FA Cup 4th round, 28.1.64
Record victory: 9-2 v Aldershot, Division III(S), 2.2.34
    9-2 v Chester, League Cup 3rd round, 17.10.62
Record defeat: 0-8 v Aston Villa, FA Cup 4th round, 30.1.29
Most League points: 66, Division III(S), 1955-56
Most League goals: 106, Division III(S), 1955-56
League scoring record: 35, Tommy Johnston, Division II, 1957-58
Record League aggregate: 119, Tommy Johnston, 1956-1962
Most League appearances: 374, Alf Wood, 1921-1931
Most capped player: 3, Tommy Evans, Wales
    3 (4 in all), Ernest Morley, Wales

Birmingham's Bob Hatton holds off the Orient defence at Brisbane Road.

OXFORD UNITED

Founded: 1896*
Address: Manor Ground, Beech Road, Headington, Oxford
Telephone: Oxford 61503
Ground capacity: 18,000 (1,700 seated)
Playing area: 112 by 78 yards
Record attendance: 22,730 v Preston North End, FA Cup quarter-final, 29.2.64
Record victory: 7-0 v Barrow, Division IV, 19.12.64
Record defeat: 0-5 v Cardiff City, Division II, 8.2.69
Most League points: 61, Division IV, 1964-65
Most League goals: 87, Division IV, 1964-65
League Scoring record: 23, Colin Booth, Division IV, 1964-65
Record League aggregate: 73, Graham Atkinson, 1962-1973
Most League appearances: 385, Ron Atkinson, 1962-1971
Most capped player: 3, David Roberts, Wales
*as Headington United. Name changed to Oxford United 25.6.60

THE OXFORD RECORD

Year	Division & place	Cup round reached
1961		3
1962		1
1963	IV 18	3
1964	IV 18	q-f
1965	IV 4P	1
1966	III 14	1
1967	III 15	1
1968	III 1P	1
1969	II 20	3
1970	II 15	3
1971	II 14	5
1972	II 15	3
1973	II 8	4

P – promoted

PETERBOROUGH UNITED

Founded: 1934
Address: London Road, Peterborough, PEL 8AL
Telephone: 0733 3623
Ground capacity: 30,000 (3,000 seated)
Playing area: 113 by 76 yards
Record attendance: 30,096 v Swansea Town, FA Cup 5th round, 20.2.65
Record victory: 8-1 v Oldham Athletic, Division IV, 26.11.69
Record defeat: 1-8 v Northampton Town, FA Cup 2nd round, 1946-47
Most League points: 66, Division IV, 1960-61
Most League goals: 134, Division IV, 1960-61
League scoring record: 52, Terry Bly, Division IV, 1960-61
Record League aggregate: 81, Terry Bly, 1960-1962
Most League appearances: 273, Brian Wright, 1963-1971
Most capped player: 8 (17 in all), Tony Millington, Wales

THE POSH RECORD		
	Division & place	Cup round reached
1957		4
1958		1
1959		3
1960		4
1961	IV 1P	4
1962	III 5	4
1963	III 6	3
1964	III 10	1
1965	III 8	q-f
1966	III 13	2
1967	III 15	4
1968	III 24R	3
1969	IV 18	1
1970	IV 9	4
1971	IV 16	2
1972	IV 8	3
1973	IV 19	3

P—promoted
R—relegated (for illegal payments)
Actually finished ninth

PLYMOUTH ARGYLE

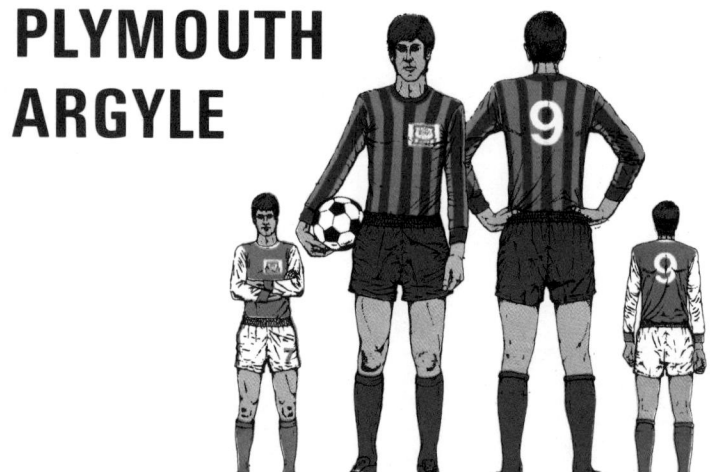

Founded: 1886
Address: Home Park, Plymouth, Devon
Telephone: Plymouth 52561
Ground capacity: 40,000 (3,700 seated)
Playing area: 112 by 75 yards
Record attendance: 43,596 v Aston Villa, Division II, 10.10.36
Record victory: 8-1 v Millwall, Division II, 16.1.32
Record defeat: 0-9 v Stoke City, Division II, 17.12.00
Most League points: 68, Division III(S), 1929-30
Most League goals: 107, Division III(S), 1925-26 and 1951-52
League scoring record: 32, Jack Cock, Division III(S), 1925-26
Record League aggregate: 180, Sammy Black, 1924-1938
Most League appearances: 470, Sammy Black, 1924-1938
Most capped player: 20 (23 in all), Moses Russell, Wales

THE PLYMOUTH RECORD		
	Division & place	Cup round reached
1904		1
1905		1
1906		2
1907		1
1908		2
1909		3
1910		1
1911		1
1912		1
1913		2
1914		2
1915		1
1920		3
1921	III 11	3
1922	SIII 2	1
1923	SIII 2	3
1924	SIII 2	1
1925	SIII 2	1
1926	SIII 2	3
1927	SIII 2	3
1928	SIII 3	1
1929	SIII 4	4
1930	SIII 1P	3
1931	II 18	3
1932	II 4	4
1933	II 14	3
1934	II 10	3
1935	II 8	4
1936	II 7	4
1937	II 5	4
1938	II 13	3
1939	II 15	3
1946		3
1947	II 19	3
1948	II 17	3
1949	II 20	3
1950	II 21R	3
1951	SIII 4	3
1952	SIII 1P	1
1953	II 4	5
1954	II 19	4
1955	II 20	3
1956	II 21R	3
1957	SIII 18	2
1958	SIII 3	3
1959	III 1P	3
1960	II 19	3
1961	II 11	3
1962	II 5	4
1963	II 12	3
1964	II 20	3
1965	II 15	4
1966	II 18	4
1967	II 16	3
1968	II 22R	3
1969	III 5	1
1970	III 17	2
1971	III 15	1
1972	III 8	1
1973	III 8	4

S – Third Division South
P – promoted
R – relegated

PORTSMOUTH

Founded: 1898
Address: Fratton Park, Frogmore Road, Portsmouth
Telephone: Portsmouth 31204/5
Ground capacity: 46,000 (6,750 seated)
Playing area: 116 by 73 yards
Record attendance: 51,385 v Derby County, FA Cup quarter-final, 26.2.49
Record victory: 9-1 v Notts County, Division II, 9.4.27
Record defeat: 0-10 v Leicester City, Division I, 20.10.28
Most League points: 65, Division III, 1961-62
Most League goals: 87, Division II, 1923-24, 1926-27; Division III, 1961-62
League scoring record: 40, Billy Haines, Division II, 1926-27
Record League aggregate: 194, Peter Harris, 1946-1960
Most League appearances: 764, Jimmy Dickinson, 1946-1965
Most capped player: 48, Jimmy Dickinson, England

FA Cup	Year	Opponents	Score	Scorers
Winners	1939	Wolverhampton Wanderers	4-1	Parker 2, Barlow, Anderson
Runners-up	1929	Bolton Wanderers	0-2	
	1934	Manchester City	1-2	Rutherford

THE PORTSMOUTH RECORD

Year	Division & place	Cup round reached
1900		1
1901		q-f
1902		q-f
1903		1
1904		1
1905		2
1906		1
1907		2
1908		3
1909		2
1910		2
1911		1
1912		2
1913		1
1914		1
1915		1
1920		1
1921	SIII 12	1
1922	SIII 3	1
1923	SIII 6	1
1924	SIII 1P	1
1925	II 4	2
1926	II 11	3
1927	II 2P	4
1928	I 20	3
1929	I 20	Final
1930	I 13	4
1931	I 4	5
1932	I 8	5
1933	I 9	3
1934	I 10	Final
1935	I 14	4
1936	I 10	3
1937	I 9	3
1938	I 19	4
1939	I 17	Winners
1946		3
1947	I 12	4
1948	I 8	4
1949	I 1C	s-f
1950	I 1C	5
1951	I 7	3
1952	I 4	q-f
1953	I 15	3
1954	I 14	5
1955	I 3	3
1956	I 12	4
1957	I 19	4
1958	I 20	4
1959	I 22R	5
1960	II 20	3
1961	II 21R	3
1962	III 1P	1
1963	II 16	4
1964	II 9	3
1965	II 20	3
1966	II 12	4
1967	II 14	4
1968	II 5	5
1969	II 15	4
1970	II 17	3
1971	II 16	4
1972	II 16	5
1973	II 17	3

P – promoted
R – relegated
S – Third Division South

THE PORT VALE RECORD

Year	Division & place	Cup round reached
1893*	II 11	q
1894*	II 7	q
1895*	II 15	q
1896*	II 14L	p
1897*		p
1898*		2
1899*	II 9	1
1900*	II 11	1
1901*	II 9	1
1902*	II 13	1
1903*	II 9	p
1904*	II 13	p
1905*	II 16	2
1906*	II 17	1
1907*	†II 16	2
1908*		p
1909*		p
1910*		p
1911*		p
1912*		p
1913*		p
1914		1
1915		q
1920	§II 13	1
1921	II 17	p
1922	II 18	1
1923	II 17	p
1924	II 16	p
1925	II 8	1
1926	II 8	3
1927	II 8	4
1928	II 9	5
1929	II 21R	3
1930	NIII 1P	2
1931	II 5	4
1932	II 20	4
1933	II 17	3
1934	II 8	3
1935	II 18	3
1936	II 21R	4
1937	NIII 11	3
1938	NIII 15	1
1939	SIII 18	2
1946		3
1947	SIII 10	4
1948	SIII 8	1
1949	SIII 13	1
1950	SIII 13	4
1951	SIII 12	3
1952	SIII 13	1
1953	NIII 2	2
1954	NIII 1P	s-f
1955	II 17	4
1956	II 12	4
1957	II 22R	3
1958	SIII 15	2
1959	IV 1P	1
1960	III 14	5
1961	III 7	3
1962	III 12	5
1963	III 3	4
1964	III 13	4
1965	III 22R	2
1966	IV 19	3
1967	IV 13	2
1968	‡IV 18	1
1969	IV 13	3
1970	IV 4P	2
1971	III 17	1
1972	III 15	3
1973	III 6	3

q – qualifying rounds
p – preliminary rounds
P – promoted
R – relegated
* – As Burslem Port Vale. Name changed in 1913
L – failed to obtain re-election
† – Burslem Port Vale resigned from the League
§ – Port Vale returned to the League, taking over the fixtures and record of Leeds City on 9 October 1919
‡ – Expelled from the League for financial irregularities and therefore technically finished 24th. Obtained re-election immediately.
N – Third Division North

PORT VALE

Founded: 1876
Address: Vale Park, Hamil Road, Burslem, Stoke-on-Trent
Telephone: Stoke-on-Trent 87626/85524
Ground capacity: 50,000 (7,700 seated)
Playing area: 114 by 78 yards
Record attendance: 50,000 v Aston Villa, FA Cup 5th round, 20.2.60
Record victory: 9-1 v Chesterfield, Division II, 24.9.32
Record defeat: 0-10 v Sheffield United, Division II, 10.12.1892
0-10 v Notts County, Division II, 26.2.1895
Most League points: 69, Division III(N), 1953-54
Most League goals: 110, Division IV, 1958-59
League scoring record: 38, Wilf Kirkham, Division II, 1926-27
Record League aggregate: 154, Wilf Kirkham, 1923-29, 1931-33
Most League appearances: 761, Roy Sproson, 1950-1972
Most capped player: 7, Sammy Morgan, Northern Ireland

Left David Munks, a utility player for Portsmouth in the seventies.
Below Graham Hawkins concentrating on a clearance for Preston.

PRESTON NORTH END

Founded: 1881
Address: Deepdale, Preston PR1 GRU
Telephone: Preston 53818/9
Ground capacity: 40,100
Playing area: 112 by 78 yards
Record attendance: 42,684 v Arsenal, Division I, 23.4.38
Record victory: 26-0 v Hyde, FA Cup 1st series 1st round, 15.10.1887
Record defeat: 0-7 v Blackpool, Division I, 1.5.48
Most League points: 61, Division III, 1970-71
Most League goals: 100, Division II, 1927-28 & Division I, 1957-58
League scoring record: 37, Ted Harper, Division II, 1932-33
Record League aggregate: 187, Tom Finney, 1946-1960
Most League appearances: 440, Willie Cunningham, 1949-1964
Most capped player: 76, Tom Finney, England

FA Cup	Year	Opponents	Score	Scorers
Winners	1889	Wolverhampton Wanderers	3-0	Dewhurst, Ross, Thompson
	1938	Huddersfield Town	*1-0	Mutch (pen)
Runners-up	1888	West Bromwich Albion	1-2	Goodall
	1922	Huddersfield Town	0-1	
	1937	Sunderland	1-3	O'Donnell (F)
	1954	West Bromwich Albion	2-3	Morrison, Wayman
	1964	West Ham United	2-3	Holden, Dawson

*after extra time

THE PRESTON RECORD

Year	Division & place	Cup round reached
1884		4
1885		†
1886		3
1887		s-f
1888		Final
1889	I 1C	Winners
1890	I 1C	q-f
1891	I 2	1
1892	I 2	q-f
1893	I 2	s-f
1894	I 14	2
1895	I 4	2
1896	I 9	1
1897	I 4	q-f
1898	I 12	1
1899	I 15	2
1900	I 16	q-f
1901	I 17R	1
1902	II 3	1
1903	II 7	2
1904	II 1P	2
1905	I 8	q-f
1906	I 2	1
1907	I 14	1
1908	I 12	1
1909	I 10	2
1910	I 12	1
1911	I 14	2
1912	I 19R	1
1913	II 1P	1
1914	I 19R	3
1915	II 2P	1
1920	I 19	3
1921	I 16	s-f
1922	I 16	Final
1923	I 16	2
1924	I 18	1
1925	I 21R	2
1926	II 12	3
1927	II 6	4
1928	II 4	3
1929	II 13	3
1930	II 16	3
1931	II 7	3
1932	II 13	5
1933	II 9	3
1934	II 2P	q-f
1935	I 11	q-f
1936	I 7	4
1937	I 14	Final
1938	I 3	Winners
1939	I 9	q-f
1946		5
1947	I 7	q-f
1948	I 7	q-f
1949	I 21R	4
1950	II 6	3
1951	II 1P	4
1952	I 7	3
1953	I 2	4
1954	I 11	Final
1955	I 14	4
1956	I 19	3
1957	I 3	5
1958	I 2	3
1959	I 12	5
1960	I 9	q-f
1961	I 22R	4
1962	II 10	q-f
1963	II 17	3
1964	II 3	Final
1965	II 12	4
1966	II 17	q-f
1967	II 13	3
1968	II 20	4
1969	II 14	4
1970	II 22R	3
1971	III 1P	1
1972	II 18	4
1973	II 19	3

C – Football League champions
P – promoted
R – relegated
† – Preston expelled by FA

THE QPR RECORD

Year	Division & place	Cup round reached
1900		2
1901		q
1902		q
1903		q
1904		q
1905		q
1906		1
1907		2
1908		1
1909		1
1910		q-f
1911		1
1912		1
1913		2
1914		q-f
1915		3
1920		1
1921	SIII 3	2
1922	SIII 5	1
1923	SIII 11	q-f
1924	SIII 22	1
1925	SIII 19	1
1926	SIII 22	2
1927	SIII 14	*
1928	SIII 10	1
1929	SIII 6	1
1930	SIII 3	3
1931	SIII 8	3
1932	SIII 13	4
1933	SIII 16	3
1934	SIII 4	3
1935	SIII 13	2
1936	SIII 4	1
1937	SIII 9	3
1938	SIII 3	2
1939	SIII 6	3
1946		5
1947	SIII 2	3
1948	SIII 1P	q-f
1949	II 13	3
1950	II 20	3
1951	II 16	3
1952	II 22R	3
1953	SIII 21	1
1954	SIII 18	1
1955	SIII 15	1
1956	SIII 18	1
1957	SIII 10	3
1958	SIII 10	2
1959	III 13	2
1960	III 8	2
1961	III 2	2
1962	III 4	3
1963	III 13	3
1964	III 15	3
1965	III 14	2
1966	III 3	3
1967	III 1P	3
1968	II 2P	3
1969	I 22R	3
1970	II 9	q-f
1971	II 10	3
1972	II 4	3
1973	II 2P	5

P – promoted
R – relegated
S – Third Division South
q – qualifying rounds
* – did not enter

QUEEN'S PARK RANGERS

Founded: 1885
Address: Ellerslie Road, Shepherd's Bush, London W12
Telephone: (01) 743 2618
Ground capacity: 37,000 (7,750 seated)
Playing area: 112 by 72 yards
Record attendance: 33,572 v Chelsea, FA Cup quarter-final, 21.2.70
Record victory: 9-2 v Tranmere Rovers, Division III, 4.12.60
Record defeat: 1-8 v Mansfield Town, Division III, 15.3.65
1-8 v Manchester United, Division I, 12.2.69
Most League points: 67, Division III, 1966-67
Most League goals: 111, Division III, 1961-62
League scoring record: 37, George Goddard, Division III(S), 1929-30
Record League aggregate: 172, George Goddard, 1926-1934
Most League appearances: 519, Tony Ingham, 1950-1963
Most capped player: 6, Ray Brady, Republic of Ireland

League Cup	Year	Opponents	Score	Scorers
Winners	1967	West Bromwich Albion	3-2	Morgan (R), Marsh, Lazarus

READING

Founded: 1871
Address: Elm Park, Norfolk Road, Reading
Telephone: Reading 57878/9/0
Ground capacity: 27,000 (3,200 seated)
Playing area: 112 by 77 yards
Record attendance: 33,042 v Brentford, FA Cup 5th round, 19.2.27
Record victory: 10-2 v Crystal Palace, Division III(S), 4.9.46
Record defeat: 0-18 v Preston North End, FA Cup 1st round, 1893-94
Most League points: 61, Division III(S), 1951-52
Most League goals: 112, Division III(S), 1951-52
League scoring record: 39, Ronnie Blackman, Division III(S), 1951-52
Record League aggregate: 156, Ronnie Blackman, 1947-1954
Most League appearances: 453, Dick Spiers, 1955-1970
Most capped player: 8, William McConnell, Ireland

Below Reading salute Barry Wagstaff's goal against Arsenal in the 1971-72 FA Cup.
Right Rochdale on the attack against Third Division rivals Port Vale.

THE READING RECORD

Year	Division & place	Cup round reached
1900		1
1901		3
1902		2
1903		1
1904		1
1905		1
1906		1
1907		1
1908		1
1909		1
1910		1
1911		q
1912		3
1913		3
1914		1
1915		1
1920		1
1921	III 20	1
1922	SIII 13	1
1923	SIII 19	1
1924	SIII 18	1
1925	SIII 14	2
1926	SIII 1P	3
1927	II 14	s-f
1928	II 18	4
1929	II 15	5
1930	II 19	3
1931	II 21R	3
1932	SIII 2	1
1933	SIII 4	3
1934	SIII 3	3
1935	SIII 2	5
1936	SIII 3	3
1937	SIII 5	3
1938	SIII 6	1
1939	SIII 5	1
1946		1
1947	SIII 9	3
1948	SIII 10	3
1949	SII 2	2
1950	SIII 10	3
1951	SIII 3	3
1952	SII 2	3
1953	SIII 11	1
1954	SIII 8	1
1955	SIII 18	3
1956	SIII 17	2
1957	SIII 13	3
1958	SIII 5	3
1959	III 6	1
1960	III 11	3
1961	III 18	3
1962	III 7	1
1963	III 20	1
1964	III 6	2
1965	III 13	4
1966	III 8	3
1967	III 4	2
1968	III 5	3
1969	III 14	3
1970	III 8	1
1971	III 21R	3
1972	III 16	4
1973	III 7	4

P – promoted
R – relegated
S – Third Division South

THE ROCHDALE RECORD

Year	Division & place	Cup round reached
1913		1
1914		p
1915		2
1920		1
1921		1
1922	NIII 20	p
1923	NIII 12	p
1924	NIII 2	p
1925	NIII 6	p
1926	NIII 3	2
1927	NIII 2	1
1928	NIII 13	2
1929	NIII 17	1
1930	NIII 10	1
1931	NIII 21	1
1932	NIII 21	1
1933	NIII 18	1
1934	NIII 22	1
1935	NIII 20	1
1936	NIII 20	1
1937	NIII 18	1
1938	NIII 17	1
1939	NIII 15	1
1946		3
1947	NIII 6	3
1948	NIII 12	2
1949	NIII 7	1
1950	NIII 3	2
1951	NIII 11	3
1952	NIII 21	3
1953	NIII 22	1
1954	NIII 19	1
1955	NIII 12	3
1956	NIII 12	1
1957	NIII 13	1
1958	NIII 10	1
1959	III 24R	1
1960	IV 12	2
1961	IV 17	1
1962	IV 12	2
1963	IV 7	1
1964	IV 20	2
1965	IV 6	1
1966	IV 21	2
1967	IV 21	1
1968	IV 19	1
1969	IV 3P	1
1970	III 9	1
1971	III 16	4
1972	III 18	1
1973	III 13	1

P – promoted
R – relegated
N – Third Division North
p – preliminary round

ROCHDALE

Founded: 1900
Address: Spotland, Willbutts Lane, Rochdale, Lancashire
Telephone: 0706 44648
Ground capacity: 28,000 (700 seated)
Playing area: 113 by 75 yards
Record attendance: 24,231 v Notts County, FA Cup 2nd round, 10.12.49
Record victory: 8-1 v Chesterfield, Division III(N), 18.12.26
Record defeat: 0-8 v Wrexham, Division III(N), 28.12.29
Most League points: 62, Division III(N), 1923-24
Most League goals: 105, Division III(N), 1926-27
League scoring record: 44, Albert Whitehurst, Division III(N), 1926-27
Record League aggregate: 117, Albert Whitehurst, 1923-1928
Most League appearances: 298, Ray Aspden, 1955-1967
Most capped player: None

League Cup

	Year	Opponents	Score
Runners-up	1962	Norwich City	h0-3 a0-1

ROTHERHAM UNITED

Founded: 1884
Address: Millmoor Ground, Rotherham, Yorkshire
Telephone: Rotherham 2434
Ground capacity: 24,000 (1,392 seated)
Playing area: 115 by 76 yards
Record attendance: 25,000 v Sheffield Wednesday, Division II, 26.1.52
25,000 v Sheffield United, Division II, 13.12.52
Record victory: 8-0 v Oldham Athletic, Division III(N), 26.5.47
Record defeat: 1-11 v Bradford City, Division III(N), 25.8.28
Most League points: 71, Division III(N), 1950-51
Most League goals: 114, Division III(N), 1946-47
League scoring record: 38, Wally Ardron, Division III(N), 1946-47
Record League aggregate: 130, Gladstone Guest, 1946-1956
Most League appearances: 459, Danny Williams, 1946-1962
Most capped player: 6, Harry Millership, Wales

League Cup

	Season	Opponents	Score	Scorers
Runners-up	1960-61	Aston Villa	H2-0 A0-3	Webster, Kirkman

THE ROTHERHAM RECORD

Year	Division & place	Cup round reached
1894*	II 14	q
1895*	II 12	q
1896*	II 15	1
1920†	II 17	q
1921†	II 19	q
1922†	II 16	q
1923†	II 21R	1
1924†	NIII 4	q
1925†	NIII 22	q
1926‡	NIII 14	3
1927	NIII 19	1
1928	NIII 14	3
1929	NIII 16	1
1930	NIII 20	3
1931	NIII 14	1
1932	NIII 19	1
1933	NIII 17	1
1934	NIII 21	3
1935	NIII 9	2
1936	NIII 11	2
1937	NIII 17	1
1938	NIII 6	2
1939	NIII 11	1
1946		4
1947	NIII 2	3
1948	NIII 2	3
1949	NIII 2	4
1950	NIII 6	3
1951	NIII 1P	4
1952	II 9	4
1953	II 12	5
1954	II 5	4
1955	II 3	4
1956	II 19	3
1957	II 17	3
1958	II 18	3
1959	II 20	3
1960	II 8	4
1961	II 15	4
1962	II 9	3
1963	II 14	3
1964	II 7	3
1965	II 14	4
1966	II 7	4
1967	II 18	4
1968	II 21R	5
1969	III 11	2
1970	III 14	3
1971	III 8	3
1972	III 5	4
1973	III 21R	2

P – promoted
R – relegated
N – Third Division North
q – qualifying round
* – Rotherham Town, who resigned from the League in 1896
† – Rotherham County elected to the League in 1919
‡ – Rotherham County and Rotherham Town amalgamated to form Rotherham United at the start of the 1925-26 season.

SCUNTHORPE UNITED

Founded: 1904
Address: Old Show Ground, Scunthorpe, Lincolnshire
Telephone: Scunthorpe 2954
Ground capacity: 25,000 (3,000 seated)
Playing area: 111 by 73 yards
Record attendance: 23,935 v Portsmouth, FA Cup 4th round, 30.1.54
Record victory: 9-0 v Boston United, FA Cup 1st round, 21.11.53
Record defeat: 0-8 v Carlisle United, Division III(N), 25.12.52
Most League points: 66, Division III(N), 1957-58
Most League goals: 88, Division III(N), 1957-58
League scoring record: 31, Barry Thomas, Division II, 1961-62
Record League aggregate: 92, Barry Thomas, 1959-1962, 1964-1966
Most League appearances: 600, Jack Brownsword, 1950-1965
Most capped player: None

THE SCUNTHORPE RECORD

	Division & place	Cup round reached			Division & place	Cup round reached
1951	NIII 12	q		1963	II 9	3
1952	NIII 14	3		1964	II 22R	3
1953	NIII 15	3		1965	III 18	1
1954	NIII 3	4		1966	III 4	1
1955	NIII 3	2		1967	III 18	2
1956	NIII 9	4		1968	III 23R	2
1957	NIII 14	2		1969	IV 16	1
1958	NIII 1P	5		1970	IV 12	5
1959	II 18	3		1971	IV 17	3
1960	II 15	4		1972	IV 4P	1
1961	II 9	4		1973	III 24R	3
1962	II 4	3				

P – promoted
R – relegated
N – Third Division North
q – qualifying round

Founded: 1889
Address: Bramall Lane, Sheffield S2 4SU
Telephone: 0742 25585
Ground Capacity: 55,000 (7,900 seated)
Playing area: 115 by 73 yards
Record attendance: 68,287 v Leeds United, FA Cup 5th round, 15.2.36
Record victory: 11-2 v Cardiff City, Division 1, 1.1.26
Record defeat: 0-13 v Bolton Wanderers, FA Cup 2nd round, 1.2.90
Most League points: 60, Division II, 1952–53
Most League goals: 102, Division I, 1925–26
League scoring record: 41, Jimmy Dunne, Division I, 1930-31
Record League aggregate: 205, Harry Johnson, 1919-1930
Most League appearances: 629, Joe Shaw, 1948-1966
Most capped player: 25, Billy Gillespie, Ireland

FA Cup	Year	Opponents	Score	Scorers
Winners	1899	Derby County	4-1	Bennett, Beers, Almond, Priest
	1902	Southampton	1-1	Common
			2-1	Hedley, Barnes
	1915	Chelsea	3-0	Simmons, Fazackerley, Kitchen
	1925	Cardiff City	1-0	Tunstall
Runners-up	1901	Tottenham Hotspur	2-2	Bennett, Priest
			1-3	Priest
	1936	Arsenal	0-1	

THE UNITED RECORD

	Division & place	Cup round reached			Division & place	Cup round reached
				1931	I 15	5
1890		2		1932	I 7	4
1891		1		1933	I 10	4
1892		2		1934	I 22R	3
1893	II 2P	2		1935	II 11	4
1894	I 10	1		1936	II 3	Final
1895	I 6	2		1937	II 7	4
1896	I 12	2		1938	II 3	4
1897	I 2	1		1939	II 2P	5
1898	I 1C	1		1946		4
1899	I 16	Winners		1947	I 6	q-f
1900	I 2	q-f		1948	I 12	3
1901	I 14	Final		1949	I 22R	4
1902	I 10	Winners		1950	II 3	4
1903	I 4	2		1951	II 8	4
1904	I 7	q-f		1952	II 11	q-f
1905	I 6	1		1953	II 1P	4
1906	I 13	2		1954	I 20	3
1907	I 4	1		1955	I 13	3
1908	I 17	1		1956	I 22R	5
1909	I 12	1		1957	II 7	3
1910	I 6	1		1958	II 6	5
1911	I 9	1		1959	II 3	q-f
1912	I 14	1		1960	II 4	q-f
1913	I 15	1		1961	II 2P	s-f
1914	I 10	s-f		1962	I 5	q-f
1915	I 6	Winners		1963	I 10	5
1920	I 14	2		1964	I 12	4
1921	I 20	1		1965	I 19	4
1922	I 11	1		1966	I 9	4
1923	I 10	s-f		1967	I 10	5
1924	I 5	1		1968	I 21R	q-f
1925	I 14	Winners		1969	II 9	3
1926	I 5	4		1970	II 6	4
1927	I 8	3		1971	II 2P	3
1928	I 13	s-f		1972	I 10	3
1929	I 11	3		1973	I 14	4
1930	I 20	4				

C – Football League champions
P – promoted
R – relegated

SHEFFIELD UNITED

SHEFFIELD WEDNESDAY

Founded: 1867
Address: Hillsborough, Sheffield 6
Telephone: Sheffield 343122
Ground capacity: 60,000 (24,500 seated)
Playing area: 115 by 75 yards
Record attendance: 72,841 v Manchester City, FA Cup 5th round, 17.2.34
Record victory: 12-0 v Halliwell, FA Cup 1st round, 17.1.1891
Record defeat: 0-10 v Aston Villa, Division I, 5.10.1912
Most League points: 62, Division II, 1958-59
Most League goals: 106, Division II, 1958-59
League scoring record: 46, Derek Dooley, Division II, 1951-52
Record League aggregate: 147, John Fantham, 1958-1969
Most League appearances: 465, Jack Brown, 1925-1937
Most capped player: 33, Ron Springett, England

FA Cup	Year	Opponents	Score	Scorers
Winners	1896	Wolverhampton Wanderers	2-1	Spiksley 2
	1907	Everton	2-1	Stewart, Simpson
	1935	West Bromwich Albion	4-2	Rimmer 2, Palethorpe, Hooper
Runners-up	1890	Blackburn Rovers	1-6	Bennett
	1966	Everton	2-3	McCalliog, Ford

THE WEDNESDAY RECORD

	Division & place	Cup round reached		Division & place	Cup round reached
1881		4	1929*	I 1C	4
1882		s-f	1930	I 1C	s-f
1883		4	1931	I 3	4
1884		2	1932	I 3	5
1885		3	1933	I 3	3
1886			1934	I 11	5
1887			1935	I 3	Winners
1888		q-f	1936	I 20	4
1889		q-f	1937	I 22R	4
1890		Final	1938	II 17	3
1891		q-f	1939	II 3	5
1892		q-f	1946		5
1893	I 12	q-f	1947	II 20	5
1894	I 12	s-f	1948	II 4	4
1895	I 8	s-f	1949	II 8	4
1896	I 7	Winners	1950	II 2P	3
1897	I 6	1	1951	I 21R	3
1898	I 5	2	1952	II 1P	3
1899	I 18R	1	1953	I 18	3
1900	II 1P	2	1954	I 19	s-f
1901	I 8	1	1955	I 22R	4
1902	I 9	1	1956	II 1P	3
1903	I 1C	1	1957	I 14	3
1904	I 1C	s-f	1958	I 22R	5
1905	I 9	s-f	1959	II 1P	3
1906	I 3	q-f	1960	I 5	s-f
1907	I 13	Winners	1961	I 2	q-f
1908	I 5	1	1962	I 6	5
1909	I 5	3	1963	I 6	4
1910	I 11	1	1964	I 6	3
1911	I 6	1	1965	I 8	3
1912	I 5	1	1966	I 17	Final
1913	I 3	3	1967	I 11	q-f
1914	I 18	q-f	1968	I 19	5
1915	I 7	3	1969	I 15	4
1920	I 22R	1	1970	I 22R	4
1921	II 10	2	1971	II 15	3
1922	II 10	1	1972	II 14	3
1923	II 8	3	1973	II 10	5
1924	II 8	2			
1925	II 14	2			
1926	II 1P	3			
1927	I 16	4			
1928	I 14	5			

P — promoted
R — relegated
*The club officially changed their name to Sheffield Wednesday in the summer of 1929. Before then they were known as The Wednesday.
†Did not enter

SHREWSBURY TOWN

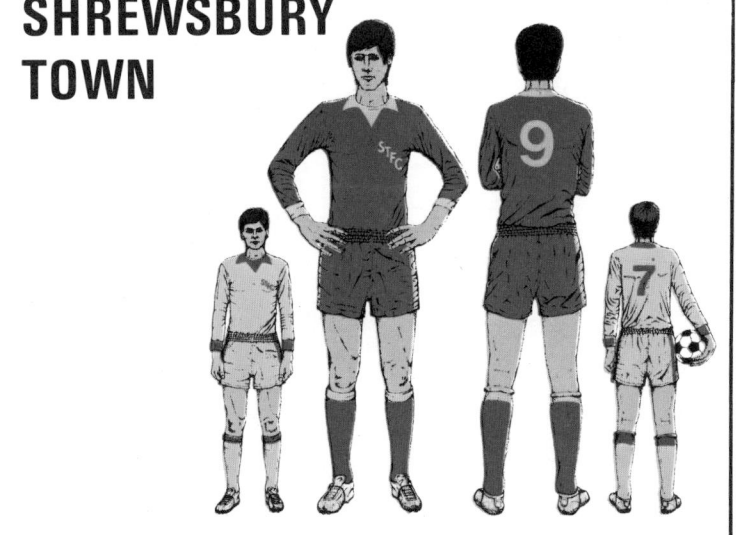

Founded: 1886
Address: Gay Meadow, Shrewsbury, Shropshire
Telephone: Shrewsbury 56068
Ground capacity: 20,050 (1,400 seated)
Playing area: 116 by 75 yards
Record attendance: 18,917 v Wallsall, Division III, 26.4.61
Record victory: 7-0 v Swindon Town, Division III(S), 1954-55
Record defeat: 1-8 v Norwich City, Division III(S), 1952-53
1-8 v Coventry City, Division III, 22.10.63
Most League points: 58, Division IV, 1958-59
Most League goals: 101, Division IV, 1958-59
League scoring record: 39, Alf Wood, Division III, 1971-72
Record League aggregate: 152, Arthur Rowley, 1958-1965
Most League appearances: 329, Joe Wallace, 1954-1963
Most capped player: 5 (12 in all), Jimmy McLaughlin, Northern Ireland

THE SHREWSBURY RECORD

	Division & place	Cup round reached		Division & place	Cup round reached
			1964	III 11	1
1951	NIII 20	*	1965	III 16	5
1952	SIII 20	1	1966	III 10	5
1953	SIII 23	4	1967	III 6	3
1954	SIII 21	1	1968	III 3	3
1955	SIII 16	1	1969	III 17	1
1956	SIII 13	2	1970	III 15	2
1957	SIII 9	1	1971	III 13	2
1958	SIII 17	1	1972	III 12	3
1959	IV 4P	2	1973	III 15	2
1960	III 3	1			
1961	III 10	3			
1962	III 19	4			
1963	III 15	3			

P — promoted
N — Third Division North
S — Third Division South
*Shrewsbury withdrew, refusing to play in the qualifying rounds after being elected to the Football League

SOUTHAMPTON

Founded: 1885
Address: The Dell, Milton Road, Southampton SO9 4XX
Telephone: Southampton 23408
Ground capacity: 31,000 (6,500 seated)
Playing area: 110 by 72 yards
Record attendance: 31,044 v Manchester United, Division I, 8.10.69
Record victory: 14-0 v Newbury, FA Cup 1st round, 10.9.94
Record defeat: 0-8 v Tottenham Hotspur, Division II, 28.3.36
0-8 v Everton, Division I, 20.11.71
Most League points: 61, Division III(S), 1921-22 & Division III, 1959-60
Most League goals: 112, Division III(S), 1957-58
League scoring record: 39, Derek Reeves, Division III, 1959-60
Record League aggregate: 159, Terry Paine, 1956-73
Most League appearances: 672, Terry Paine, 1956-73
Most capped player: 23 (28 in all), Ron Davies, Wales

FA Cup	Year	Opponents	Score	Scorers
Runners-up	1900	Bury	0-4	
	1902	Sheffield United	1-1	Wood
	Replay		1-2	Brown

Southampton's Mick Channon shows his most taunting form against Ipswich.

THE SAINTS RECORD

Year	Division & place	Cup round reached
1895	1	
1896	1	
1897	2	
1898	s-f	
1899	q-f	
1900	Final	
1901	1	
1902	Final	
1903	1	
1904	2	
1905	q-f	
1906	q-f	
1907	2	
1908	s-f	
1909	1	
1910	2	
1911	1	
1912	1	
1913		1
1914		1
1915		3
1920		1
1921	III 2	3
1922	SIII 1P	2
1923	II 11	q-f
1924	II 5	3
1925	II 7	s-f
1926	II 14	3
1927	II 13	s-f
1928	II 17	3
1929	II 4	3
1930	II 7	3
1931	II 9	3
1932	II 14	3
1933	II 12	3
1934	II 14	3
1935	II 19	4
1936	II 17	3
1937	II 18	3
1938	II 15	3
1939	II 18	3
1946		4
1947	II 14	4
1948	II 3	q-f
1949	II 3	3
1950	II 4	3
1951	II 12	4
1952	II 13	3
1953	II 21R	5
1954	SIII 6	1
1955	SIII 3	2
1956	SIII 14	2
1957	SIII 4	3
1958	SIII 6	2
1959	III 14	3
1960	III 1P	4
1961	II 8	4
1962	II 6	4
1963	II 13	s-f
1964	II 5	3
1965	II 4	4
1966	II 2P	3
1967	I 19	4
1968	I 15	4
1969	I 7	4
1970	I 11	4
1971	I 7	5
1972	I 19	3
1973	I 13	3

P – promoted
S – Third Division South
R – relegated

PRESS ASSOCIATION

Ted Bates, the manager who took Southampton into Division I in 1966.

THE SOUTHEND RECORD

Year	Division & place	Cup round reached
1910		2
1911		1
1912		q
1913		1
1914		1
1915		2
1920		1
1921	III 17	3
1922	SIII 22	2
1923	SIII 15	q
1924	SIII 19	2
1925	SIII 10	q
1926	SIII 11	5
1927	SIII 19	2
1928	SIII 7	2
1929	SIII 12	1
1930	SIII 11	2
1931	SIII 5	1
1932	SIII 3	2
1933	SIII 13	4
1934	SIII 16	3
1935	SIII 21	3
1936	SIII 18	3
1937	SIII 10	2
1938	SIII 12	3
1939	SIII 12	4
1946		1
1947	SIII 8	3
1948	SIII 9	1
1949	SIII 18	1
1950	SIII 3	3
1951	SIII 7	1
1952	SIII 9	5
1953	SIII 8	1
1954	SIII 16	2
1955	SIII 10	3
1956	SIII 4	4
1957	SIII 7	4
1958	SIII 7	3
1959	III 8	1
1960	III 12	2
1961	III 20	2
1962	III 16	1
1963	III 8	2
1964	III 14	1
1965	III 12	1
1966	III 21R	3
1967	IV 6	1
1968	IV 6	1
1969	IV 7	4
1970	IV 17	1
1971	IV 18	3
1972	IV 2P	2
1973	IV 14	1

R – relegated
S – Third Division South
q – qualifying competition

SOUTHPORT

Founded: 1881
Address: Haig Avenue, Southport
Telephone: 0704 5353
Ground capacity: 20,855 (1,855 seated)
Playing area: 113 by 77 yards
Record attendance: 20,010 v Newcastle United, FA Cup 4th round replay, 26.1.32
Record victory: 8-1 v Nelson, Division III(N), 1.1.31
Record defeat: 0-11 v Oldham Athletic, Division IV, 26.12.62
Most League points: 62, Division IV, 1972-73
Most League goals: 88, Division III(N), 1930-31
League scoring record: 32, Archie Waterston, Division III(N), 1930-31
Record League aggregate: 98, Alan Spence, 1962-1969
Most League appearances: 401, Arthur Peat, 1962-1972
Most capped player: 2 (4 in all), Terry Harkin, Northern Ireland

SOUTHEND UNITED

Founded: 1906
Address: Roots Hall Ground, Victoria Avenue, Southend-on-Sea, Essex
Telephone: Southend 40707
Ground capacity: 35,000 (3,000 seated)
Playing area: 110 by 74 yards
Record attendance: 28,059 v Birmingham City, FA Cup 4th round, 26.1.57
Record victory: 10-1 v Golders Green, FA Cup 1st round, 24.11.34
v Brentwood, FA Cup 2nd round, 2.12.68
Record defeat: 1-9 v Brighton, Division III, 27.11.65
Most League points: 60, Division IV, 1971-72
Most League goals: 92, Division III(S), 1950-51
League scoring record: 31, Jim Shankly, Division III(S), 1928-29 & Sammy McCrory, Division III(S), 1957-58
Record League aggregate: 122, Roy Hollis, 1953-1960
Most League appearances: 451, Sandy Anderson, 1950-1963
Most capped player: 9, George Mackenzie, Republic of Ireland

THE SOUTHPORT RECORD

Year	Division & place	Cup round reached
1922	NIII 9	1
1923	NIII 17	p
1924	NIII 7	p
1925	NIII 4	p
1926	NIII 20	3
1927	NIII 12	4
1928	NIII 8	4
1929	NIII 12	2
1930	NIII 9	1
1931	NIII 5	q-f
1932	NIII 7	4
1933	NIII 12	2
1934	NIII 18	1
1935	NIII 21	1
1936	NIII 21	1
1937	NIII 14	1
1938	NIII 16	1
1939	NIII 4	3
1946		1
1947	NIII 21	1
1948	NIII 15	1
1949	NIII 21	3
1950	NIII 16	3
1951	NIII 21	2
1952	NIII 17	2
1953	NIII 6	2
1954	NIII 11	2
1955	NIII 11	1
1956	NIII 5	2
1957	NIII 22	1
1958	NIII 23	1
1959	IV 24	1
1960	IV 21	1
1961	IV 14	3
1962	IV 17	3
1963	IV 13	1
1964	IV 21	2
1965	IV 20	3
1966	IV 10	5
1967	IV 2P	1
1968	III 14	3
1969	III 8	2
1970	III 22R	1
1971	IV 8	1
1972	IV 7	1
1973	IV 1P	1

P – promoted
R – relegated
N – Third Division North
p – preliminary round

STOCKPORT COUNTY

Founded: 1883
Address: Edgeley Park, Stockport, Cheshire
Telephone: Stockport 8888/9
Ground capacity: 24,900 (3,000 seated)
Playing area: 115 by 75 yards
Record attendance: 27,833 v Liverpool, FA Cup 5th round, 11.2.50
Record victory: 13-0 v Halifax Town, Division III(N), 6.1.34
Record defeat: 1-8 v Chesterfield, Division II, 19.4.02
Most League points: 64, Division IV, 1966-67
Most League goals: 115, Division III(N), 1933-34
League scoring record: 46, Alf Lythgoe, Division III(N), 1933-34
Record League aggregate: 132, Jack Connor, 1951-1956
Most League appearances: 465, Robert Murray, 1952-1963
Most capped player: 1, Harry Hardy, England

THE STOCKPORT RECORD

	Division & place	Cup round reached			
1901	II 17	q	1938	II 22R	3
1902	II 17	p	1939	NIII 9	4
1903	II 17	q	1946		1
1904	II 16	p	1947	NIII 4	3
1905*		p	1948	NIII 17	4
1906	II 10	1	1949	NIII 8	3
1907	II 12	1	1950	NIII 10	5
1908	II 13	1	1951	NIII 10	4
1909	II 18	2	1952	NIII 3	1
1910	II 13	2	1953	NIII 11	3
1911	II 17	p	1954	NIII 10	3
1912	II 16	1	1955	NIII 9	1
1913	II 19	1	1956	NIII 7	1
1914	II 12	p	1957	NIII 5	1
1915	II 14	1	1958	NIII 9	4
1920	II 16	1	1959	III 21R	3
1921	II 20R	1	1960	IV 10	2
1922	NIII 1P	p	1961	IV 13	4
1923	II 20	p	1962	IV 16	1
1924	II 13	p	1963	IV 19	1
1925	II 19	2	1964	IV 17	1
1926	II 22R	3	1965	IV 24	4
1927	NIII 6	1	1966	IV 13	2
1928	NIII 3	2	1967	IV 1P	1
1929	NIII 2	3	1968	III 13	1
1930	NIII 2	3	1969	III 9	3
1931	NIII 7	2	1970	III 24R	2
1932	NIII 12	1	1971	IV 11	1
1933	NIII 3	2	1972	IV 23	2
1934	NIII 3	2	1973	IV 11	3
1935	NIII 7	5			
1936	NIII 5	1			
1937	NIII 1P	1			

p – preliminary round
q – qualifying round
P – promoted R – relegated
N – Third Division North
*Failed to gain re-election in 1904.
Returned when Divsion II increased
from 19 to 20 clubs in 1905

STOKE CITY

Founded: 1863 (though no recorded reference before 1867)
Address: Victoria Ground, Stoke-on-Trent, Staffordshire
Telephone: 0782 44660
Ground capacity: 50,500 (10,000 seated)
Playing area: 116 by 75 yards
Record attendance: 51,380 v Arsenal, Division I, 29.3.37
Record victory: 10-3 v West Bromwich Albion, Division I, 4.2.37
Record defeat: 0-10 v Preston North End, Division I, 14.9.1889
Most League points: 63, Division III(N), 1926-27
Most League goals: 92, Division III(N), 1926-27
League scoring record: 33, Freddie Steele, Division I, 1936-37
Record League aggregate: 142, Freddie Steele, 1934-1939
Most League appearances: 502, John McCue, 1946-1960
Most capped player: 36 (73 in all), Gordon Banks, England

League Cup	Year	Opponents	Score	Scorers
Winners	1972	Chelsea	2-1	Conroy, Eastham
Runners-up	1964	Leicester City	1-1	Bebbington
		(aggregate)	2-3	Viollet, Kinnell

THE STOKE CITY RECORD

	Division & place	Cup round reached				
			1932	II 3	5	
			1933	II 1P	4	
1889	I 12	p	1934	I 12	q-f	
1890	I 12L	q-f	1935	I 10	3	
1891		q-f	1936	I 4	5	
1892	I 13	q-f	1937	I 10	4	
1893	I 7	1	1938	I 17	4	
1894	I 11	2	1939	I 7	3	
1895	I 14	2	1946		q-f	
1896	I 6	q-f	1947	I 4	5	
1897	I 13	2	1948	I 15	4	
1898	I 16	2	1949	I 11	5	
1899	I 12	s-f	1950	I 19	3	
1900	I 9	1	1951	I 13	5	
1901	I 16	1	1952	I 20	4	
1902	I 16	q-f	1953	I 21R	4	
1903	I 6	q-f	1954	II 11	4	
1904	I 16	1	1955	II 5	4	
1905	I 12	2	1956	II 13	5	
1906	I 10	2	1957	II 5	3	
1907	I 20R	1	1958	II 11	5	
1908*	II 10	q-f	1959	II 5	4	
1909		1	1960	II 17	3	
1910		1	1961	II 18	5	
1911		1	1962	II 8	4	
1912		p	1963	II 1P	3	
1913		1	1964	I 17	5	
1914		1	1965	I 11	4	
1915		p	1966	I 10	3	
1920	II 10	1	1967	I 12	3	
1921	II 20	1	1968	I 18	4	
1922	II 2P	3	1969	I 19	5	
1923	I 21R	2	1970	I 9	4	
1924	II 6	1	1971	I 13	s-f	
†1925	II 20	1	1972	I 17	s-f	
1926	II 21R	4	1973	I 15	3	
1927	NIII 1P	1				
1928	II 5	q-f				
1929	II 6	3				
1930	II 11	3				
1931	II 11	3				

P—promoted
R—relegated
L—not re-elected
p—preliminary round
*resigned from League
†name changed to Stoke City
in 1925

SUNDERLAND

Founded: 1879
Address: Roker Park Ground, Sunderland, Co. Durham
Telephone: Sunderland 72077/58638
Ground capacity: 58,000 (9,500 seated)
Playing area: 112 by 72 yards
Record attendance: 75,118 v Derby County, FA Cup quarter-final replay, 8.3.33
Record victory: 11-1 v Fairfield, FA Cup 1st round, 2.2.1895
Record defeat: 0-8 v West Ham United, Division 1, 19.10.68
Most League points: 61, Division II, 1963-64
Most League goals: 109, Division I, 1935-36
League scoring record: 43, David Halliday, Division I, 1928-29
Record League aggregate: 209, Charlie Buchan, 1911-1925
Most League appearances: 419, Ned Doig, 1890-1914
Most capped player: 33 (56 in all), Billy Bingham & 33, Martin Harvey, N. Ireland

FA Cup	Year	Opponents	Score	Scorers
Winners	1937	Preston North End	3-1	Gurney, Carter, Burbanks
	1973	Leeds United	1-0	Porterfield
Runners-up	1913	Aston Villa	0-1	

THE SUNDERLAND RECORD

Year	Division & place	Cup round reached
1890		1
1891	I 7	q-f
1892	I 1C	s-f
1893	I 1C	q-f
1894	I 2	2
1895	I 1C	s-f
1896	I 5	2
1897	I 15	2
1898	I 2	1
1899	I 7	2
1900	I 3	2
1901	I 2	1
1902	I 1C	2
1903	I 3	1
1904	I 6	1
1905	I 5	1
1906	I 14	3
1907	I 10	3
1908	I 16	1
1909	I 3	q-f
1910	I 8	3
1911	I 3	1
1912	I 8	3
1913	I 1C	Final
1914	I 7	q-f
1915	I 8	1
1920	I 5	3
1921	I 12	1
1922	I 12	1
1923	I 2	2
1924	I 3	1
1925	I 7	2
1926	I 3	5
1927	I 3	3
1928	I 15	4
1929	I 4	3
1930	I 9	5
1931	I 11	s-f
1932	I 13	4
1933	I 12	q-f
1934	I 6	4
1935	I 2	4
1936	I 1C	3
1937	I 8	Winners
1938	I 8	s-f
1939	I 16	5
1946		5
1947	I 9	3
1948	I 20	3
1949	I 8	4
1950	I 3	4
1951	I 12	q-f
1952	I 12	3
1953	I 9	4
1954	I 18	3
1955	I 4	s-f
1956	I 9	s-f
1957	I 20	4
1958	I 21R	3
1959	II 15	3
1960	II 16	3
1961	II 6	q-f
1962	II 3	4
1963	II 3	5
1964	II 2P	q-f
1965	I 15	4
1966	I 19	3
1967	I 17	5
1968	I 16	3
1969	I 17	3
1970	I 21R	3
1971	II 13	3
1972	II 5	4
1973	II 6	Winners

C — Football League Champions
P — promoted   R — relegated

THE SWANSEA RECORD

Year	Division & place	Cup round reached
1921	III 5	2
1922	SIII 10	3
1923	SIII 3	p
1924	SIII 4	2
1925	SIII 1P	2
1926	II 5	s-f
1927	II 12	q-f
1928	II 6	3
1929	II 19	4
1930	II 15	3
1931	II 20	3
1932	II 15	3
1933	II 10	3
1934	II 19	5
1935	II 17	4
1936	II 13	3
1937	II 16	5
1938	II 18	3
1939	II 19	3
1946		3
1947	II 21R	4
1948	SIII 5	3
1949	SIII 1P	2
1950	II 8	4
1951	II 18	3
1952	II 19	5
1953	II 11	3
1954	II 20	4
1955	II 10	5
1956	II 10	3
1957	II 10	3
1958	II 19	3
1959	II 11	3
1960	II 12	4
1961	II 7	5
1962	II 20	3
1963	II 15	4
1964	II 19	s-f
1965	II 22R	5
1966	III 17	1
1967	III 21R	4
1968	IV 15	4
1969	IV 10	3
1970*	IV 3P	3
1971	III 11	4
1972	III 13	4
1973	III 23R	1

P — promoted   R — relegated
S — Third Division South
*Name changed to Swansea City during 1969-70 season

SWANSEA CITY

Founded: 1900 (as Swansea Town)
Address: Vetch Field, Swansea
Telephone: Swansea 53633
Ground capacity: 35,500 (4,000 seated)
Playing area: 110 by 73 yards
Record attendance: 32,700 v Arsenal, FA Cup 4th round, 17.2.68
Record victory: 8-1 v Bristol Rovers, Division III(S), 15.4.22
8-1 v Bradford City, Division II, 22.2.26
Record defeat: 1-8 v Fulham, Division II, 22.1.38
Most League points: 62, Division III(S), 1948-49
Most League goals: 90, Division II, 1956-57
League scoring record: 35, Cyril Pearce, Division II, 1931-32
Record League aggregate: 166, Ivor Allchurch, 1949-1958, 1965-1968
Most League appearances: 585, Billy Milne, 1919-1937
Most capped player: 42 (68 in all), Ivor Allchurch, Wales

Juventus fall victim to Swindon Town, Anglo-Italian Cup winners in 1969.

SWINDON TOWN

Founded: 1881
Address: County Ground, Swindon, Wiltshire
Telephone: Swindon 22118
Ground capacity: 32,000 (8,500 seated)
Playing area: 117 by 78 yards
Record attendance: 32,000 v Arsenal, FA Cup 3rd round, 15.1.72
Record victory: 10-1 v Farnham United Brewery, FA Cup 1st round, 28.11.25
Record defeat: 1-10 v Manchester City, FA Cup 4th round replay, 25.1.30
Most League points: 64, Division III, 1968-69
Most League goals: 100, Division III(S), 1926-27
League scoring record: 47, Harry Morris, Division III(S), 1926-27
Record League aggregate: 216, Harry Morris, 1926-1933
Most League appearances: 554, Maurice Owen, 1946-1963
Most capped player: 30, Rod Thomas, Wales

League Cup	Year	Opponents	Score	Scorers
Winners	1969	Arsenal	*3-1	Smart, Rogers 2

*—after extra time

THE SWINDON RECORD

Year	Division & place	Cup round reached
1906		1
1907		q
1908		3
1909		1
1910		s-f
1911		q-f
1912		s-f
1913		3
1914		2
1915		1
1920		2
1921	III 4	2
1922	SIII 6	2
1923	SIII 9	1
1924	SIII 6	q-f
1925	SIII 4	1
1926	SIII 6	4
1927	SIII 6	1
1928	SIII 6	4
1929	SIII 10	5
1930	SIII 14	4
1931	SIII 12	1
1932	SIII 17	1
1933	SIII 22	3
1934	SIII 8	3
1935	SIII 16	4
1936	SIII 19	1
1937	SIII 13	2
1938	SIII 8	4
1939	SIII 9	2
1946		1
1947	SIII 4	2
1948	SIII 16	5
1949	SIII 4	3
1950	SIII 14	2
1951	SIII 17	2
1952	SIII 16	5
1953	SIII 18	3
1954	SIII 19	2
1955	SIII 21	1
1956	SIII 24	4
1957	SIII 23	2
1958	SIII 4	1
1959	III 15	2
1960	III 16	1
1961	III 16	2
1962	III 9	1
1963	III 2P	4
1964	II 14	5
1965	II 21R	3
1966	III 7	3
1967	III 8	5
1968	III 9	4
1969	III 2P	3
1970	II 5	q-f
1971	II 12	4
1972	II 11	3
1973	II 16	4

P — promoted   R — relegated
q — qualifying rounds
S — Third Division South

TORQUAY UNITED

Founded: 1898
Address: Plainmoor, Torquay, Devon
Telephone: Torquay 38666/7
Ground capacity: 22,000
Playing area: 112 by 74 yards
Record attendance: 21,908 v Huddersfield Town, FA Cup 4th round, 29.1.55
Record victory: 9-0 v Swindon Town, Division III(S), 8.3.52
Record defeat: 2-10 v Fulham, Division III(S), 7.9.31
2-10 v Luton Town, Division III(S), 2.9.33
Most League points: 60, Division IV, 1959-60
Most League goals: 89, Division III(S), 1956-57
League scoring record: 40, 'Sammy' Collins, Division III(S), 1955-56
Record League aggregate: 204, 'Sammy' Collins, 1948-1958
Most League appearances: 443, Dennis Lewis, 1947-1959
Most capped player: None

THE TORQUAY RECORD

	Division & place	Cup round reached
1928	SIII 22	Sc
1929	SIII 18	2
1930	SIII 19	1
1931	SIII 11	3
1932	SIII 19	1
1933	SIII 10	2
1934	SIII 20	2
1935	SIII 10	2
1936	SIII 10	2
1937	SIII 20	1
1938	SIII 20	1
1939	SIII 19	2
1946		1
1947	SIII 11	1
1948	SIII 18	3
1949	SIII 9	4
1950	SIII 5	2
1951	SIII 20	1
1952	SIII 11	2
1953	SIII 12	1
1954	SIII 13	1
1955	SIII 8	4
1956	SIII 5	3
1957	SIII 2	3
1958	SIII 21	2
1959	IV 12	3
1960	IV 3P	2
1961	III 12	2
1962	III 21R	2
1963	IV 6	2
1964	IV 6	2
1965	IV 11	3
1966	IV 3P	1
1967	III 7	1
1968	III 4	1
1969	III 6	2
1970	III 13	1
1971	III 10	4
1972	III 23R	3
1973	IV 18	2

Sc—scratched
P—promoted
R—relegated
S—Third Division South

Torquay's Dunne clears from Gillingham's Tydeman in a League game in 1969-70.

TOTTENHAM HOTSPUR

Founded: 1882
Address: White Hart Lane, Tottenham, N17
Telephone: (01) 808 1020
Ground capacity: 56,000 (10,000 seated)
Playing area: 111 by 73 yards
Record attendance: 75,038 v Sunderland, FA Cup, quarter-final, 5.3.38
Record victory: 13-2 v Crewe Alexandra, FA Cup 4th round, 3.2.60
Record defeat: 2-7 v Liverpool, Division I, 31.10.14
2-7 v Newcastle United, Division I, 1.9.51
2-7 v Blackburn Rovers, Division I, 7.9.63
Most League points: 70, Division II, 1919-20
Most League goals: 115, Division I, 1960-61
League scoring record: 37, Jimmy Greaves, Division I, 1962-63
Record League aggregate: 220, Jimmy Greaves, 1961-1970
Most League appearances: 418, Ted Ditchburn, 1946-1959
Most capped player: 46 (56 in all), Danny Blanchflower, Northern Ireland

	Year	Opponents	Score	Scorers
FA Cup Winners	1901	Sheffield United	2-2	Brown 2
			3-1	Cameron, Smith, Brown
	1921	Wolverhampton W	1-0	Dimmock
	1961	Leicester City	2-0	Smith, Dyson
	1962	Burnley	3-1	Greaves, Smith, Blanchflower (pen)
	1967	Chelsea	2-1	Robertson, Saul
League Cup Winners	1971	Aston Villa	2-0	Chivers 2
	1973	Norwich City	1-0	Coates

THE SPURS RECORD

	Division & place	F.A. Cup round reached
1895		4q
1896		1
1897		3q
1898		2q
1899		q-f
1900		1
1901		Winners
1902		1
1903		q-f
1904		q-f
1905		2
1906		3
1907		3
1908		1
1909	II 2P	3
1910	I 15	3
1911	I 15	2
1912	I 12	1
1913	I 17	2
1914	I 17	2
1915	I 20R	2
1920	II 1P	q-f
1921	I 6	Winners
1922	I 2	s-f
1923	I 12	q-f
1924	I 15	1
1925	I 12	3
1926	I 15	4
1927	I 13	3
1928	I 21R	5
1929	II 10	3
1930	II 12	3
1931	II 3	4
1932	II 8	3
1933	II 2P	4
1934	I 3	5
1935	I 22R	5
1936	II 5	q-f
1937	II 10	q-f
1938	II 5	q-f
1939	II 8	4
1946		3
1947	II 6	3
1948	II 8	s-f
1949	II 5	3
1950	II 1P	5
1951	I 1C	3
1952	I 2	4
1953	I 10	s-f
1954	I 16	q-f
1955	I 16	5
1956	I 18	s-f
1957	I 2	5
1958	I 3	4
1959	I 18	5
1960	I 3	5
1961	I 1C	Winners
1962	I 3	Winners
1963	I 2	3
1964	I 4	3
1965	I 6	5
1966	I 8	5
1967	I 3	Winners
1968	I 7	5
1969	I 6	q-f
1970	I 11	4
1971	I 3	q-f
1972	I 6	q-f
1973	I 8	4

C – Football League champions
P – promoted   R – relegated
q – qualifying round

TRANMERE ROVERS

Founded: 1883
Address: Prenton Park, 14 Prenton Road West, Birkenhead
Telephone: 051 608 3677/4194
Ground capacity: 24,500 (4,000 seated)
Playing area: 112 by 72 yards
Record attendance: 24,424 v Stoke City, FA Cup 4th round, 5.2.72
Record victory: 13-4 v Oldham Athletic, Division III(N), 26.12.35
Record defeat: 1-9 v Tottenham Hotspur, FA Cup 3rd round replay, 14.1.53
Most League points: 60, Division IV, 1964-65
Most League goals: 111, Division III(N), 1930-31
League scoring record: 35, Robert 'Bunny' Bell, Division III(N), 1933-34
Record League aggregate: 104, Robert 'Bunny' Bell, 1931-1936
Most League appearances: 595, Harold Bell, 1946-1964
Most capped player: 3 (4 in all), John Brown, Ireland;
　　　　　　　　　　　　3 (23 in all), Bert Gray, Wales

THE TRANMERE RECORD

	Division & place	Cup round reached
1922	NIII 18	q
1923	NIII 16	q
1924	NIII 12	p
1925	NIII 21	p
1926	NIII 7	p
1927	NIII 9	1
1928	NIII 5	3
1929	NIII 7	2
1930	NIII 12	1
1931	NIII 3	1
1932	NIII 4	3
1933	NIII 11	4
1934	NIII 7	4
1935	NIII 6	2
1936	NIII 3	4
1937	NIII 19	1
1938	NIII 1P	3
1939	II 22R	3
1946		2
1947	NIII 10	1
1948	NIII 18	2
1949	NIII 11	1
1950	NIII 5	2
1951	NIII 4	2
1952	NIII 11	4
1953	NIII 12	3
1954	NIII 14	3
1955	NIII 19	1
1956	NIII 16	2
1957	NIII 23	1
1958	NIII 11	3
1959	III 7	2
1960	III 20	1
1961	III 21R	2
1962	IV 15	1
1963	IV 8	3
1964	IV 7	1
1965	IV 5	1
1966	IV 5	1
1967	IV 4P	2
1968	III 19	5
1969	III 7	1
1970	III 16	4
1971	III 18	1
1972	III 19	4
1973	III 10	2

N – Third Division North
P – promotion
R – relegation
p – preliminary round
q – qualifying round

Ex-Liverpool star Ron Yeats became Tranmere's player-manager in 1971.

WALSALL

Founded: 1888 (as Walsall Town Swifts)
Address: Fellows Park, Walsall, Staffordshire
Telephone: Walsall 22791
Ground capacity: 24,100 (1,160 seated)
Playing area: 113 by 73 yards
Record attendance: 25,453 v Newcastle United, Division II, 29.8.61
Record victory: 10-0 v Darwen, Division II, 4.3.1899
Record defeat: 0-12 v Small Heath, Division II, 17.12.1892
　　　　　　　　　　0-12 v Darwen, Division II, 26.12.1896
Most League points: 65, Division IV, 1959-60
Most League goals: 102, Division IV, 1959-60
League scoring record: 39, Gilbert Alsop, Division III(N), 1933-34 and 1934-35
Record League aggregate: 184, Tony Richards, 1954-1963
Most League appearances: 459, Colin Taylor, 1958-1963, 1964-1968
　　　　　　　　　　　　　　and 1969-1973
Most capped player: 3, Albert Jones, England

THE WALSALL RECORD

	Division & place	Cup round reached
1893*	II 12	p
1894*	II 10	p
1895*	II 14L	q
1896		p
1897	II 12	p
1898	II 10	1
1899	II 6	p
1900	II 12	1
1901	II 16L	p
1922	NIII 8	1
1923	NIII 3	p
1924	NIII 17	p
1925	NIII 19	p
1926	NIII 21	1
1927	NIII 14	3
1928	SIII 18	1
1929	SIII 14	3
1930	SIII 17	4
1931	SIII 17	3
1932	NIII 16	1
1933	NIII 5	4
1934	NIII 4	2
1935	NIII 14	3
1936	NIII 10	3
1937	SIII 17	4
1938	SIII 21	2
1939	SIII 21	5
1946		1
1947	SIII 5	3
1948	SIII 3	3
1949	SIII 14	4
1950	SIII 19	1
1951	SIII 15	1
1952	SIII 24	1
1953	SIII 24	1
1954	SIII 24	3
1955	SIII 23	3
1956	SIII 20	3
1957	SIII 15	1
1958	SIII 20	1
1959	IV 6	1
1960	IV 1P	2
1961	III 2P	1
1962	II 14	4
1963	II 21R	3
1964	III 19	1
1965	III 19	1
1966	III 9	4
1967	III 12	3
1968	III 7	4
1969	III 13	3
1970	III 12	3
1971	III 20	2
1972	III 9	4
1973	III 17	2

L – not re-elected
P – promoted
R – relegated
N – Third Division North
S – Third Division South
* – as Walsall Town Swifts

WATFORD

Founded: 1898
Founded: 1898
Address: Vicarage Road, Watford, Hertfordshire
Telephone: Watford 21759
Ground capacity: 36,500 (4,000 seated)
Playing area: 113 by 73 yards
Record attendance: 34,099 v Manchester United, FA Cup 4th round, 3.2.69
Record victory: 10-1 v Lowestoft, FA Cup 1st round, 27.11.26
Record defeat: 0-10 v Wolverhampton Wanderers, FA Cup 1st round replay, 13.1.12
Most League points: 64, Division III, 1968-69
Most League goals: 92, Division IV, 1959-60
League scoring record: 42, Cliff Holton, Division IV, 1959-60
Record League aggregate: 144, Tommy Barnett, 1928-1939
Most League appearances: 398, Tommy Barnett, 1928-1939
Most capped player: 2, Frank Hoddinott, Wales
2 (44 in all), Pat Jennings, Northern Ireland

THE WATFORD RECORD

Year	Division & place	Cup round reached
1906		2
1907		1
1908		1
1909		1
1910		1
1911		1
1912		1
1913		p
1914		p
1915		p
1920		p
1921	III 6	2
1922	SIII 7	2
1923	SIII 10	1
1924	SIII 20	3
1925	SIII 11	1
1926	SIII 15	2
1927	SIII 21	2
1928	SIII 15	1
1929	SIII 8	4
1930	SIII 15	2
1931	SIII 18	5
1932	SIII 11	q-f
1933	SIII 11	3
1934	SIII 15	1
1935	SIII 6	2
1936	SIII 5	4
1937	SIII 4	1
1938	SIII 4	3
1939	SIII 4	3
1946		4
1947	SIII 16	2
1948	SIII 15	1
1949	SIII 17	1
1950	SIII 6	4
1951	SIII 23	1
1952	SIII 21	2
1953	SIII 10	2
1954	SIII 4	1
1955	SIII 7	3
1956	SIII 20	2
1957	SIII 11	2
1958	SIII 16	1
1959	IV 15	2
1960	IV 4P	5
1961	III 4	3
1962	III 17	3
1963	III 17	4
1964	III 3	2
1965	III 9	1
1966	III 12	2
1967	III 3	3
1968	III 6	3
1969	III 1P	4
1970	II 19	s-f
1971	II 18	4
1972	II 22R	3
1973	III 19	3

P – promoted
R – relegated
p – preliminary round
S – Third Division South

THE ALBION RECORD

Year	Division & place	Cup round reached
1885		q-f
1886		Final
1887		Final
1888		Winners
1889	I 6	s-f
1890	I 5	1
1891	I 12	s-f
1892	I 12	Winners
1893	I 8	1
1894	I 8	1
1895	I 13	Final
1896	I 16	q-f
1897	I 12	2
1898	I 7	q-f
1899	I 14	q-f
1900	I 13	q-f
1901	I 18R	s-f
1902	II 1P	1
1903	I 7	1
1904	I 18R	1
1905	II 10	p
1906	II 4	1
1907	II 4	s-f
1908	II 5	2
1909	II 3	2
1910	II 11	3
1911	II 1P	2
1912	I 9	Final
1913	I 10	1
1914	I 5	3
1915	I 11	1
1920	I 1C	1
1921	I 14	1
1922	I 13	3
1923	I 17	3
1924	I 16	q-f
1925	I 2	q-f
1926	I 13	4
1927	I 22R	3
1928	II 8	3
1929	II 7	q-f
1930	II 6	3
1931	II 2P	Winners
1932	I 6	3
1933	I 4	4
1934	I 7	3
1935	I 9	Final
1936	I 18	4
1937	I 16	s-f
1938	I 22R	4
1939	II 10	4
1946		4
1947	II 7	4
1948	II 7	4
1949	II 2P	q-f
1950	I 14	3
1951	I 16	3
1952	I 13	5
1953	I 4	4
1954	I 2	Winners
1955	I 17	4
1956	I 13	5
1957	I 11	s-f
1958	I 4	q-f
1959	I 5	5
1960	I 4	5
1961	I 10	3
1962	I 9	5
1963	I 14	4
1964	I 10	4
1965	I 14	3
1966	I 6	3
1967	I 13	4
1968	I 8	Winners
1969	I 10	s-f
1970	I 16	3
1971	I 17	4
1972	I 16	3
1973	I 22R	5

C – Football League Champions
P – promoted   R – relegated
p – preliminary rounds

WEST BROMWICH ALBION

Founded: 1879
Address: The Hawthorns, West Bromwich, Staffordshire
Telephone: (021) 553 0095
Ground capacity: 50,500 (10,600 seated)
Playing area: 115 by 75 yards
Record attendance: 64,815 v Arsenal, FA Cup quarter-final, 6.3.37
Record victory: 12-0 v Darwen, Division I, 4.3.1892
Record defeat: 3-10 v Stoke City, Division I, 4.2.37
Most League points: 60, Division I, 1919-20
Most League goals: 105, Division II, 1929-30
League scoring record: 39, William G Richardson, Division I, 1935-36
Record League aggregate: 208, Ronnie Allen, 1950-1961
Most League appearances: 455, Jesse Pennington, 1903-1922
Most capped player: 33 (43 in all), Stuart Williams, Wales

FA Cup

	Year	Opponents	Score	Scorers
Winners	1888	Preston North End	2-1	Bayliss, Woodhall
	1892	Aston Villa	3-0	Geddes, Nicholls, Reynolds
	1931	Birmingham City	2-1	W G Richardson 2
	1954	Preston North End	3-2	Allen 2, Griffin
	1968	Everton	*1-0	Astle
Runners-up	1886	Blackburn	0-0	
	replay		0-2	
	1887	Aston Villa	0-2	
	1895	Aston Villa	0-1	
	1912	Barnsley	0-0	
	replay		0-1	
	1935	Sheffield Wednesday	2-4	Boyes, Sandford

*after extra time

League Cup

	Year	Opponents	Score	Scorers
Winners	1966	West Ham United	(a) 1-2	Astle
			(h) 4-1	Kaye, Brown, Clark (C), Williams
Runners-up	1967	Queen's Park Rangers	2-3	Clark (C) 2
	1970	Manchester City	1-2	Astle

WEST HAM UNITED

Founded: 1900
Address: Boleyn Ground, Green Street, Upton Park, London E13
Telephone: (01) 472 0704
Ground capacity: 42,000 (8,750 seated)
Playing area: 112 by 72 yards
Record attendance: 42,322 v Tottenham Hotspur, Division I, 17.10.70
Record victory: 8-0 v Rotherham United, Division II, 8.3.58
8-0 v Sunderland, Division I, 19.10.68
Record defeat: 2-8 v Blackburn Rovers, Division I, 26.12.63
Most League points: 57, Division II, 1957-58
Most League goals: 101, Division II, 1957-58
League scoring record: 41, Vic Watson, Division I, 1929-30
Record League aggregate: 306, Vic Watson, 1920-1935
Most League appearances: 523, Bobby Moore, 1958-1973
Most capped player: 108, Bobby Moore, England (on 1 January 1974)

FA Cup

	Year	Opponents	Score	Scorers
Winners	1964	Preston North End	3-2	Sissons, Hurst, Boyce
Runners-up	1923	Bolton Wanderers	0-2	

League Cup

	Year	Opponents	Score	Scorers
Runners-up	1966	West Bromwich Albion	h2-1	Moore, Byrne
			a1-4	Peters

THE HAMMERS RECORD

Year	Division & place	Cup round reached
1913		2
1914		3
1915		1
1920	II 7	3
1921	H 5	1
1922	II 4	1
1923	II 2P	Final
1924	I 13	2
1925	I 13	3
1926	I 18	3
1927	I 6	4
1928	I 17	4
1929	I 17	q-f
1930	I 7	q-f
1931	I 18	3
1932	I 22R	4
1933	II 20	s-f
1934	II 7	4
1935	II 3	3
1936	II 4	3
1937	II 6	3
1938	II 9	3
1939	II 11	5
1946		4
1947	II 11	3
1948	II 6	3
1949	II 7	3
1950	II 19	4
1951	II 13	4
1952	II 12	4
1953	II 14	3
1954	II 13	4
1955	II 8	3
1956	II 16	q-f
1957	II 8	4
1958	II 1P	5
1959	I 6	3
1960	I 14	3
1961	I 16	3
1962	I 8	3
1963	I 12	q-f
1964	I 14	Winners
1965	I 9	4
1966	I 12	4
1967	I 16	3
1968	I 12	5
1969	I 8	5
1970	I 17	3
1971	I 20	3
1972	I 14	5
1973	I 6	4

P – promoted
R – relegated

THE WOLVES RECORD

Year	Division & place	Cup round reached
1884		2
1885		1
1886		4
1887		3
1888		3
1889	I 3	Final
1890	I 4	s-f
1891	I 4	q-f
1892	I 6	q-f
1893	I 11	Winners
1894	I 9	1
1895	I 11	q-f
1896	I 14	Final
1897	I 10	2
1898	I 3	2
1899	I 8	2
1900	I 4	1
1901	I 13	q-f
1902	I 14	1
1903	I 11	1
1904	I 8	2
1905	I 14	2
1906	I 20R	2
1907	II 6	1
1908	II 9	Winners
1909	II 7	1
1910	II 8	2
1911	II 9	3
1912	II 5	3
1913	II 10	2
1914	II 9	2
1915	II 4	2
1920	II 19	2
1921	II 15	Final
1922	II 17	1
1923	II 22R	2
1924	NIII 1P	3
1925	II 6	1
1926	II 4	3
1927	II 15	q-f
1928	II 16	4
1929	II 17	3
1930	II 9	3
1931	II 4	q-f
1932	II 1P	4
1933	I 20	3
1934	I 15	4
1935	I 17	4
1936	I 15	3
1937	I 5	q-f
1938	I 2	4
1939	I 2	Final
1946		4
1947	I 3	4
1948	I 5	4
1949	I 6	Winners
1950	I 2	5
1951	I 14	s-f
1952	I 16	4
1953	I 3	3
1954	I 1C	3
1955	I 2	q-f
1956	I 3	3
1957	I 6	4
1958	I 1C	q-f
1959	I 1C	4
1960	I 2	Winners
1961	I 3	4
1962	I 18	4
1963	I 5	3
1964	I 16	3
1965	I 21R	q-f
1966	II 6	5
1967	II 2P	4
1968	I 17	3
1969	I 16	4
1970	I 13	3
1971	I 4	4
1972	I 9	3
1973	I 5	s-f

C – Football League champions
R – relegated
P – promoted
N – Third Division North

WOLVERHAMPTON WANDERERS

Founded: 1876 (as St Luke's School, Blakenhall)
Address: Molineux, Wolverhampton, Staffordshire
Telephone: Wolverhampton 24053/4
Ground capacity: 53,500 (8,300 seated)
Playing area: 115 by 72 yards
Record attendance: 61,315 v Liverpool, FA Cup 5th round, 11.2.39
Record victory: 14-0 v Crosswell's Brewery, FA Cup qualifying rounds, 1886-87
Record defeat: 1-10 v Newton Heath, Division I, 15.10.1892
Most League points: 64, Division I, 1957-58
Most League goals: 115, Division II, 1931-32
League scoring record: 37, Dennis Westcott, Division I, 1946-47
Record League aggregate: 164, Billy Hartill, 1928-1935
Most League appearances: 491, Billy Wright, 1946-1959
Most capped player: 105, Billy Wright, England

FA Cup	Year	Opponents	Score	Scorers
Winners	1893	Everton	1-0	Allen
	1908	Newcastle United	3-1	Hunt, Hedley, Harrison
	1949	Leicester City	3-1	Pye 2, Smyth
	1960	Blackburn Rovers	3-0	McGrath (og), Deeley 2
Runners-up	1889	Preston North End	0-3	
	1896	Sheffield Wednesday	1-2	Black
	1921	Tottenham Hotspur	0-1	
	1939	Portsmouth	1-4	Dorsett

Veteran striker Derek Dougan discovered new life with Wolves in the seventies.

WORKINGTON

Founded: 1884
Address: Borough Park, Workington, Cumberland
Telephone: Workington 2871/3736
Ground capacity: 21,000 (1,200 seated)
Playing area: 112 by 76 yards
Record attendance: 21,500 v Manchester United, FA Cup 3rd round, 4.1.58
Record victory: 9-1 v Barrow, League Cup 1st round, 2.9.64
Record defeat: 0-8 v Wrexham, Division III(N), 24.10.53
Most League points: 59, Division IV, 1963-64
Most League goals: 93, Division III(N), 1956-57
League scoring record: 26, Jimmy Dailey, Division III(N), 1956-57
Record League aggregate: 84, Jimmy Dailey, 1953-1958
Most League appearances: 424, Bobby Brown, 1956-1968

THE WORKINGTON RECORD

Year	Division & place	Cup round reached
1952	NIII 24	3
1953	NIII 23	1
1954	NIII 20	2
1955	NIII 8	3
1956	NIII 10	2
1957	NIII 4	2
1958	NIII 19	3
1959	IV 17	1
1960	IV 16	3
1961	IV 8	1
1962	IV 8	3
1963	IV 10	2
1964	IV 3P	2
1965	III 15	3
1966	III 5	1
1967	III 24R	2
1968	IV 23	2
1969	IV 12	2
1970	IV 20	2
1971	IV 10	3
1972	IV 6	2
1973	IV 13	1

P – promoted   R – relegated
N – Third Division North

WREXHAM

Founded: 1873
Address: Racecourse Ground, Mold Road, Wrexham, Denbighshire
Telephone: Wrexham 2414
Ground capacity: 36,000 (5,500 seated)
Playing area: 117 by 75 yards
Record attendance: 34,445 v Manchester United, FA Cup 4th round, 26.1.57
Record victory: 10-1 v Hartlepools, Division IV, 3.3.62
Record defeat: 0-9 v Brentford, Division III, 15.10.63
Most League points: 61, Division IV, 1969-70
Most League goals: 106, Division III(N), 1932-33
League scoring record: 44, Tom Bamford, Division III(N), 1933-34
Record League aggregate: 175, Tom Bamford, 1928-1934
Most League appearances: 503, Alf Jones, 1923-1936
Most capped player: 22, Horace Blew, Wales

THE WREXHAM RECORD

Year	Division & place		Cup round reached
1922	NIII	12	2
1923	NIII	10	3
1924	NIII	16	2
1925	NIII	16	q
1926	NIII	19	1
1927	NIII	13	2
1928	NIII	11	4
1929	NIII	3	1
1930	NIII	17	4
1931	NIII	4	3
1932	NIII	10	1
1933	NIII	2	2
1934	NIII	6	1
1935	NIII	18	2
1936	NIII	18	1
1937	NIII	8	3
1938	NIII	10	2
1939	NIII	14	1
1946			3
1947	NIII	7	2
1948	NIII	3	2
1949	NIII	9	1
1950	NIII	20	2
1951	NIII	14	2
1952	NIII	18	2
1953	NIII	3	3
1954	NIII	8	3
1955	NIII	18	2
1956	NIII	14	1
1957	NIII	12	4
1958	NIII	12	1
1959	III	18	1
1960	III	23R	3
1961	IV	16	1
1962	IV	3P	3
1963	III	9	3
1964	III	23R	2
1965	IV	14	2
1966	IV	24	2
1967	IV	7	2
1968	IV	8	1
1969	IV	9	2
1970	IV	2P	4
1971	III	9	1
1972	III	16	3
1973	III	12	2

P – promoted R – relegated
N – Third Division North
q – qualifying competition

YORK CITY

Founded: 1922
Address: Bootham Crescent, York
Telephone: York 24447
Ground capacity: 24,500 (1,000 seated)
Playing area: 115 by 75 yards
Record attendance: 28,123 v Huddersfield Town, FA Cup 5th round, 5.3.38
Record victory: 9-1 v Southport, Division III(N), 2.2.57
Record defeat: 0-12 v Chester, Division III(N), 1.2.36
Most League points: 62, Division IV, 1964-65
Most League goals: 92, Division III(N), 1954-55
League scoring record: 31, Bill Fenton, Division III(N), 1951-52
31, Alf Bottom, Division III(N), 1955-56
Record League aggregate: 125, Norman Wilkinson, 1954-1966
Most League appearances: 481, Barry Jackson, 1958-1970
Most capped player: 1 (27 in all), Eamonn Dunphy, Eire

THE YORK RECORD

Year	Division & place		Cup round reached
1930	NIII	6	3
1931	NIII	12	3
1932	NIII	10	1
1933	NIII	20	1
1934	NIII	12	1
1935	NIII	15	3
1936	NIII	16	1
1937	NIII	12	4
1938	NIII	11	q-f
1939	NIII	20	3
1946			4
1947	NIII	15	1
1948	NIII	13	1
1949	NIII	14	2
1950	NIII	22	1
1951	NIII	17	3
1952	NIII	10	1
1953	NIII	4	1
1954	NIII	22	1
1955	NIII	4	s-f
1956	NIII	11	4
1957	NIII	7	2
1958	NIII	13	4
1959	IV	3P	1
1960	III	21R	3
1961	IV	5	3
1962	IV	6	1
1963	IV	14	3
1964	IV	22	1
1965	IV	3P	1
1966	III	24R	1
1967	IV	22	2
1968	IV	21	1
1969	IV	21	3
1970	IV	13	4
1971	IV	4P	4
1972	III	19	2
1973	III	18	3

N – Third Division North
P – promoted
R – relegated

Laurie Calloway of York City gives the seven-man wall of Bristol Rovers the full force of his left foot during a Third Division encounter in October 1972.

ABERDEEN

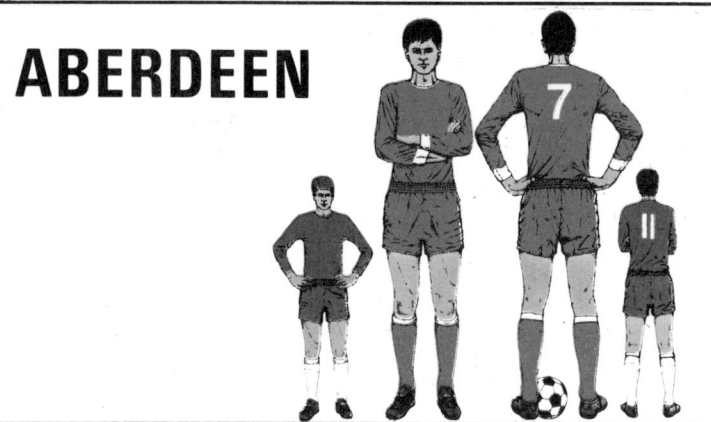

Founded: 1903
Address: Pittodrie Stadium, Aberdeen AB2 1QH
Telephone: 0224 21428
Ground capacity: 45,000 (10,000 seated)
Playing area: 110 by 71 yards
Record attendance: 46,061 v Heart of Midlothian, Scottish Cup 4th round, 13.3.54
Record victory: 13-0 v Peterhead, Scottish Cup 3rd round, 9.2.23
Record defeat: 2-9 v Dundee, Division 1, 17.4.09
Most League points: 61, Division I, 1935-36
Most League goals: 96, Division I, 1935-36
League scoring record: 38, Benny Yorston, Division I, 1929-30
Record League aggregate: 160, Harry Yorston, 1950-57
Most League appearances: *Not Available*
Most capped player: 16, Bobby Clark, Scotland

Scottish Cup	Year	Opponents	Score	Scorers
Winners	1947	Hibernian	2-1	Hamilton, Williams
	1970	Celtic	3-1	Harper, McKay 2
Runners-up	1937	Celtic	1-2	Armstrong
	1953	Rangers	1-1	Yorston
			0-1	
	1954	Celtic	1-2	Buckley
	1959	St Mirren	1-3	Baird
	1967	Celtic	0-2	
League Cup				
Winners	1946	Rangers	3-2	Baird, Williams, Taylor
	1956	St Mirren	2-1	og, Leggat
Runners-up	1947	Rangers	0-4	

THE ABERDEEN RECORD

	Division & place	Cup round reached		Division & place	Cup round reached
1906	I 12	2	1937	I 2	Final
1907	I 12	2	1938	I 6	3
1908	I 8	s-f	1939	I 3	s-f
1909	I 8	2	1947	I 3	Winners
1910	I 4	3	1948	I 10	3
1911	I 2	s-f	1949	I 13	1
1912	I 9	3	1950	I 8	q-f
1913	I 8	2	1951	I 5	q-f
1914	I 13	3	1952	I 11	q-f
1915	I 14		1953	I 11	Final
1916	I 11		1954	I 9	Final
1917	I 20		1955	I 1C	s-f
1918	†		1956	I 2	5
1919	†		1957	I 6	6
1920	I 17	4	1958	I 12	q-f
1921	I 11	3	1959	I 13	Final
1922	I 15	s-f	1960	I 15	2
1923	I 5	4	1961	I 6	3
1924	I 13	s-f	1962	I 12	3
1925	I 15	4	1963	I 6	q-f
1926	I 11	s-f	1964	I 9	3
1927	I 8	2	1965	I 12	1
1928	I 5	4	1966	I 8	s-f
1929	I 7	4	1967	I 4	Final
1930	I 3	3	1968	I 5	2
1931	I 6	q-f	1969	I 15	s-f
1932	I 7	1	1970	I 8	Winners
1933	I 5	2	1971	I 2	s-f
1934	I 5	q-f	1972	I 2	q-f
1935	I 6	s-f	1973	I 4	q-f
1936	I 3	q-f			

C—Scottish League Champions
† Aberdeen did not compete

AIRDRIEONIANS

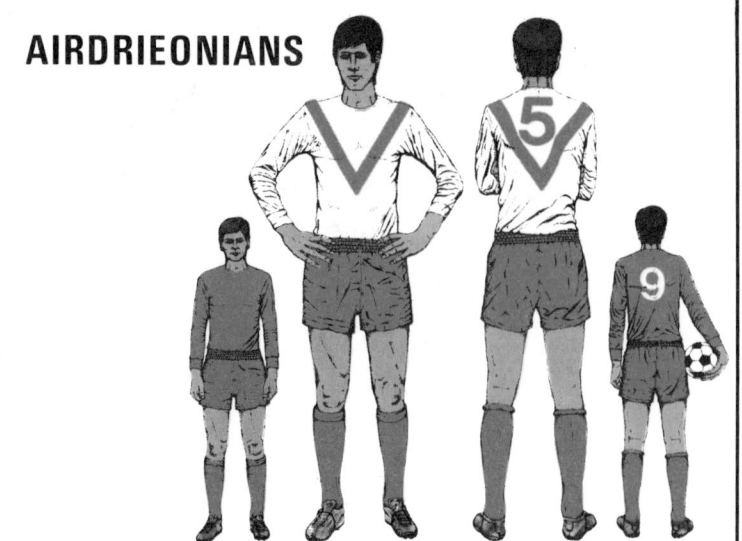

Founded: 1878
Address: Broomfield Park, Airdrie, Lanarkshire
Telephone: Airdrie 62067
Ground capacity: 26,000 (2,000 seated)
Playing area: 112 by 68 yards
Record attendance: 26,000 v Hearts, Scottish Cup 4th round, 8.3.52
Record victory: 11-1 v Falkirk, Division I, 28.4.51
Record defeat: 1-11 v Hibernian, Division I, 24.10.59
Most League points: 57, Division I, 1924-25
Most League goals: 107, Division II, 1965-66
League scoring record: 39, H G Yarnall, Division I, 1916-17
Most capped player: 9, Jimmy Crapnell, Scotland

Scottish Cup	Year	Opponents	Score	Scorers
Winners	1924	Hibernian	2-0	Russell 2

THE AIRDRIEONIANS RECORD

	Division & place	Cup round reached		Division & place	Cup round reached
1895	II 6	1	1931	I 9	2
1896	II 5	p	1932	I 14	s-f
1897	II 4	p	1933	I 18	2
1898	II 8	p	1934	I 18	1
1899	II 6	1	1935	I 14	q-f
1900	II 9	1	1936	I 19R	2
1901	II 2	1	1937	II 4	2
1902	II 4	1	1938	II 3	1
1903	II 1P	1	1939	II 4	2
1904	I 12	1	1947	II 2P	1
1905	I 4	s-f	1948	I 15R	q-f
1906	I 3	3	1949	II 3	1
1907	I 4	1	1950	II 2P	1
1908	I 6	1	1951	I 14	q-f
1909	I 5	3	1952	I 13	q-f
1910	I 9	2	1953	I 14	3
1911	I 11	2	1954	I 15R	1
1912	I 10	2	1955	II 1P	s-f
1913	I 4	3	1956	I 7	q-f
1914	I 6	3	1957	I 11	q-f
1915	I 10		1958	I 16	1
1916	I 14		1959	I 5	2
1917	I 4		1960	I 16	3
1918	I 15		1961	I 13	s-f
1919	I 13		1962	I 15	1
1920	I 7	1	1963	I 11	2
1921	I 10	1	1964	I 15	3
1922	I 16	3	1965	I 17R	2
1923	I 2	2	1966	II 2P	1
1924	I 2	Winners	1967	I 13	2
1925	I 2	3	1968	I 13	q-f
1926	I 2	q-f	1969	I 7	q-f
1927	I 4	2	1970	I 12	2
1928	I 13	3	1971	I 10	s-f
1929	I 15	3	1972	I 15	4
1930	I 12	3	1973	I 18R	q-f

P—promoted
R—relegated
p—preliminary round

ALBION ROVERS

Founded: 1881
Address: Cliftonhill Park, Coatbridge, Lanarkshire
Telephone: Coatbridge 21865
Ground capacity: 20,000 (580 seated)
Record attendance: 27,381 v Rangers, Scottish Cup 2nd round, 8.2.36
Record victory: 10-0 v Brechin City, Division II, 1937-38
Record defeat: 1-9 v Motherwell, Division I, 1936-37
Most League points: 54, Division II, 1929-30
Most League goals: 101, Division II, 1929-30
League scoring record: 41, Jim Renwick, Division II, 1932-33
Record League aggregate: *Not available*
Most League appearances: *Not available*
Most capped player: 1, Jock White, Scotland

Scottish Cup

	Year	Opponents	Score	Scorers
Runners-up	1920	Kilmarnock	2-3	Watson, Hillhouse

THE ALBION ROVERS RECORD

Year	Division & place	Cup round reached
1904	II 9	2
1905	II 8	p
1906	II 3	p
1907	II 6	p
1908	II 9	1
1909	II 10	1
1910	II 9	p
1911	II 3	p
1912	II 12	p
1913	II 9	p
1914	II 2	1
1915	II 9	
1916		
1917		
1918		
1919		
1920	*I 22	Final
1921	I 17	s-f
1922	I 11	2
1923	I 19R	1
1924	II 5	1
1925	II 14	1
1926	II 9	3
1927	II 16	1
1928	II 8	4
1929	II 4	3
1930	II 3	3
1931	II 9	2
1932	II 16	2
1933	II 5	q-f
1934	II 1P	q-f
1935	I 16	2
1936	I 16	2
1937	I 20R	2
1938	II 2P	3
1939	I 16R	1
1947	II 4	3
1948	II 2P	1
1949	I 16R	2
1950	II 11	2
1951	II 8	2
1952	II 14	3
1953	II 16	3
1954	II 7	2
1955	II 11	5
1956	II 17	4
1957	II 5	4
1958	II 17	2
1959	II 10	1
1960	II 10	2
1961	II 17	1
1962	II 18	2
1963	II 7	1
1964	II 9	3
1965	II 11	p
1966	II 7	1
1967	II 8	p
1968	II 8	p
1969	II 7	p
1970	II 11	1
1971	II 7	3
1972	II 18	3
1973	II 18	1

*Elected to First Division in 1919
P – promoted
R – relegated
p – preliminary round

Left *Aberdeen celebrate their unexpected win over Celtic in the 1970 Scottish Cup.*
Below *A few loyal fans see Albion's Dickson score against Queen's Park in 1972.*

ALLOA ATHLETIC

Founded: 1878
Address: Recreation Ground, Alloa, Clackmannanshire
Telephone: Alloa 2695
Ground capacity: 20,000
Record attendance: 13,000 v Dunfermline, Scottish Cup, 3rd round replay, 22.2.39
Record victory: 9-2 v Forfar Athletic, Division II, 18.3.33
Record defeat: 10-0 v Dundee, Division II, 8.3.47
Most League points: 60, Division II, 1921-22
Most League goals: 92, Division II, 1961-62
League scoring record: 29, Peter Smith, Division II, 1961-62
Most capped player: 1, Jock Hepburn, Scotland

THE ALLOA RECORD

Year	Division & place	Cup round reached
1920		2
1921		3
1922	II 1P	3
1923	I 20R	1
1924	II 16	2
1925	II 4	2
1926	II 16	2
1927	II 15	3
1928	II 15	3
1929	II 13	1
1930	II 19	1
1931	II 13	2
1932	II 13	1
1933	II 11	1
1934	II 15	2
1935	II 10	1
1936	II 4	1
1937	II 9	1
1938	II 11	1
1939	II 2	q-f
1947	II 5	1
1948	II 12	2
1949	II 14	2
1950	II 16	1
1951	II 16	1
1952	II 7	2
1953	II 9	2
1954	II 11	1
1955	II 15	5
1956	II 13	5
1957	II 15	5
1958	II 8	1
1959	II 13	3
1960	II 13	2
1961	II 11	q-f
1962	II 4	2
1963	II 9	2
1964	II 16	2
1965	II 10	p
1966	II 8	1
1967	II 13	1
1968	II 17	1
1969	II 18	p
1970	II 6	p
1971	II 16	3
1972	II 16	3
1973	II 12	2

P – promoted
R – relegated

ARBROATH

Founded: 1878
Address: Gayfield Park
Telephone: 02414 2157
Ground capacity: 15,000
Record attendance: 13,510 v Rangers, Scottish Cup 3rd round, 23.2.52
Record victory: 36-0 v Bon Accord, Scottish Cup 1st round, 12.9.85
Record defeat: 0-8 v Kilmarnock, Division II, 1948–49
Most League points: 57, Division II, 1966–67
Most League goals: 87, Division II, 1967–68
League scoring record: 45, Dave Easson, Division II, 1958-59
Record League aggregate: 120, Jimmy Jack, 1966-1971
Most League appearances: 319, Ian Stirling, 1960-1971
Most capped player: 2 (6 in all), Ned Doig, Scotland

THE ARBROATH RECORD

Year	Division & place	Cup round reached	Year	Division & place	Cup round reached
1922	II 16	1	1952	II 16	3
1923	II 20	1	1953	II 7	1
1924	II 17	2	1954	II 14	2
1925	II 5	3	1955	II 12	5
1926	II 10	2	1956	II 18	5
1927	II 19	1	1957	II 10	5
1928	II 10	1	1958	II 3	2
1929	II 3	3	1959	II 2P	2
1930	II 9	2	1960	I 18R	2
1931	II 15	3	1961	II 12	2
1932	II 11	2	1962	II 6	2
1933	II 10	1	1963	II 6	2
1934	II 3	2	1964	II 3	2
1935	II 2P	1	1965	II 7	1
1936	I 12	1	1966	II 6	p
1937	I 14	2	1967	II 3	1
1938	I 11	1	1968	II 2P	2
1939	I 17R	1	1969	I 18R	1
1947	II 12	s-f	1970	II 5	1
1948	II 13	2	1971	II 3	3
1949	II 7	1	1972	II 2P	3
1950	II 14	1	1973	I 15	3
1951	II 13	1			

P – promoted
R – relegated
p – preliminary round

THE AYR RECORD

Year	Division & place	Cup round reached	Year	Division & place	Cup round reached
1899*	II 8	p	1933	I 16	2
1900*	II 8	p	1934	I 8	2
1901*	II 6	2	1935	I 18	2
1902*	II 8	1	1936	I 20R	1
1903*	II 3	2	1937	II 1P	1
1904*	II 3	1	1938	I 17	q-f
1905*	II 5	1	1939	I 14	1
1906*	II 7	p	1947	II 11	2
1907*	II 8	2	1948	II 10	1
1908*	II 3	p	1949	II 9	2
1909*	II 6	1	1950	II 13	1
1910*	II 6	2	1951	II 3	q-f
1911	II 2	p	1952	II 3	1
1912	II 1	1	1953	II 5	3
1913	II 1P	2	1954	II 9	2
1914	I 10	1	1955	II 8	5
1915	I 5		1956	II 2P	6
1916	I 4		1957	I 18R	5
1917	I 15		1958	II 5	1
1918	I 18		1959	II 1P	3
1919	I 6		1960	I 8	q-f
1920	I 10	3	1961	I 18R	2
1921	I 14	3	1962	II 9	1
1922	I 14	2	1963	II 13	2
1923	I 10	3	1964	II 14	q-f
1924	I 14	q-f	1965	II 18	1
1925	I 19R		1966	II 1P	1
1926	II 3	1	1967	I 18R	1
1927	II 8	1	1968	II 5	1
1928	II 1P	2	1969	II 2P	2
1929	I 16	2	1970	I 14	1
1930	I 9	2	1971	I 14	3
1931	I 18	3	1972	I 12	4
1932	I 17	1	1973	I 6	s-f

P—promoted
R—relegated
*—Ayr FC (combined with Ayr Parkhouse in 1910)
p—preliminary round

AYR UNITED

Founded: 1910
Address: Somerset Park, Ayr, Scotland
Telephone: Ayr 63435
Ground capacity: 25,000 (1,500 seated)
Record attendance: 25,225 v Rangers, Division I, 13.9.69
Record victory: 11-2 v Clackmannan, Scottish Cup 1st round, 17.1.31
Record defeat: 0-9 v Rangers, Division I, 16.11.29
Most League points: 60, Division II, 1958-59
Most League goals: 117, Division II, 1927-28
League scoring record: 66, J Smith, Division II, 1927-28
Most capped player: 1 (2 in all), John Crosbie, Scotland

BERWICK RANGERS

Founded: 1881
Address: Shielfield Park, Tweedmouth, Berwick-on-Tweed, Northumberland
Telephone: Berwick 7424
Ground capacity: 15,000
Record attendance: 13,365 v Rangers, Scottish Cup 1st round, 28.1.67
Record victory: 8-1 v Forfar Athletic
Record defeat: 1-9 v Dundee United
Most League points: 39, Division II, 1964-65
Most League goals: 83, Division II, 1961-62
League scoring record: 38, Ken Bowron, Division II, 1963-64
Record League aggregate: 98, Ken Bowron, 1963-1966 & 1968-1969
Most League appearances: 282, Alistair Campbell, 1955-1962

THE BERWICK RECORD

Year	Division & place	Cup round reached	Year	Division & place	Cup round reached
1956	II 14	1	1964	II 12	1
1957	II 18	1	1965	II 8	1
1958	II 19	1	1966	II 11	1
1959	II 10	1	1967	II 10	2
1960	II 9	1	1968	II 14	1
1961	II 11	1	1969	II 16	1
1962	II 8	1	1970	II 9	1
1963	II 17	1	1971	II 13	2
			1972	II 13	2
			1973	II 9	3

BRECHIN CITY

Founded: 1906
Address: Glebe Park, Brechin, Angus
Telephone: Brechin 2856
Ground capacity: 7,000 (250 seated)
Record attendance: 8,022 v Dundee, Scottish Cup, 2nd round, 1964
Record victory: 12-1 v Thornhill, Scottish Cup, 1st round, 28.1.26
Record defeat: 1-10 v Dunfermline Athletic, Division II, 1929-30
Most League points: 42, Division II, 1955-56, 1958-59
Most League goals: 80, Division II, 1957-58
Most capped player: None

THE BRECHIN RECORD

	Division & place	Cup round reached		Division & place	Cup round reached
1924		1	1951	*	2
1925		1	1952	*	1
1926		3	1953	*	1
1927		2	1954	*	2
1928		2	1955	II 16	4
1929		2	1956	II 6	6
1930	II 20	1	1957	II 6	5
1931	II 16	1	1958	II 7	1
1932	II 19	1	1959	II 5	2
1933	II 15	1	1960	II 12	1
1934	II 14	2	1961	II 14	3
1935	II 15	3	1962	II 19	2
1936	II 16	1	1963	II 19	2
1937	II 16	1	1964	II 15	2
1938	II 18	1	1965	II 19	p
1939	II 10	1	1966	II 16	p
1947	*	p	1967	II 20	1
1948	*	p	1968	II 16	1
1949	*	p	1969	II 17	p
1950	*	1	1970	II 14	p
			1971	II 19	3
			1972	II 15	2
			1973	II 19	3

p – preliminary
* – Brechin competed in Division 'C'

CELTIC

Founded: 1888
Address: Celtic Park (Parkhead), Glasgow SE
Telephone: (041) 554 2710
Ground capacity: 80,000
Record attendance: 92,000 v Rangers, Division I, 1.1.38
Record victory: 11-0 v Dundee, Division I, 26.10.95
Record defeat: 0-8 v Motherwell, Division I, 1936-37
Most League points: 67, Division I, 1915-16 & 1921-22
Most League goals: 111, Division I, 1966-67
League scoring record: 50, Jimmy McGrory, Division I, 1935-36
Record League aggregate: 397, Jimmy McGrory, 1922-23 & 1924-1938
Most League appearances: 378, Jimmy McGrory, 1922-23 & 1924-1938
Most capped player: 45 (48 in all), Bobby Evans, Scotland

Scottish Cup

	Year	Opponents	Score	Scorers
Winners	1892	Queen s Park	†5-1	Campbell 2, McMahon 2, og
	1899	Rangers	2-0	Hodge, McMahon
	1900	Queen's Park	4-3	Divers 3, McMahon
	1904	Rangers	3-2	Quinn 3
	1907	Hearts	3-0	Orr (pen), Somers 2
	1908	St Mirren	5-1	Bennett 2, Quinn, Hamilton, Somers
	1911	Hamilton A.	0-0	
			2-0	Quinn, McAtee
	1912	Clyde	2-0	McMenemy, Gallagher
	1914	Hibernian	0-0	
			4-1	McColl 2, Browning, McAtee
	1923	Hibernian	1-0	Cassidy
	1925	Dundee	2-1	Gallagher, McGrory
	1927	East Fife	3-1	McLean, Connelly, og
	1931	Motherwell	2-2	McGrory, og
			4-2	Thomson 2, McGrory 2
	1933	Motherwell	1-0	McGrory
	1937	Aberdeen	2-1	Crum, Buchan
	1951	Motherwell	1-0	McPhail
	1954	Aberdeen	2-1	Fallon, og
	1965	Dunfermline A.	3-2	Auld 2, McNeill
	1967	Aberdeen	2-0	Wallace 2
	1969	Rangers	4-0	McNeill, Lennox, Connelly, Chalmers
	1971	Rangers	1-1	Lennox
			2-1	Macari, Hood (pen)
	1972	Hibernian	6-1	McNeill, Deans 3, Macari 2
Runners-up	1889	Third Lanark	†1-2	McCallum
	1893	Queen's Park	1-2	Blessington
	1894	Rangers	1-3	Maley
	1901	Hearts	3-4	McOustra 2, McMahon
	1902	Hibernian	0-1	
	1909	Rangers	2-2	
			‡1-1	
	1926	St Mirren	0-2	
	1928	Rangers	0-4	
	1955	Clyde	1-1	Walsh
			0-1	
	1956	Hearts	1-3	Haughney
	1961	Dunfermline A.	0-0	
			0-2	
	1963	Rangers	1-1	Murdoch
			0-3	
	1966	Rangers	0-0	
			0-1	
	1970	Aberdeen	1-3	Lennox
	1973	Rangers	2-3	Dalglish, Connelly (pen)

Scottish League Cup

	Year	Opponents	Score	Scorers
Winners	1957	Partick Thistle	0-0	
			3-0	McPhail 2, Collins
	1958	Rangers	7-1	Wilson, Mochan 2, McPhail 3, Fernie
	1966	Rangers	2-1	Hughes (2 pen)
	1967	Rangers	1-0	Lennox
	1968	Dundee	5-3	Chalmers 2, Wallace, Lennox, Hughes
	1969	Hibernian	6-2	Wallace, Auld, Lennox 3, Craig
	1970	St Johnstone	1-0	Auld
Runners-up	1965	Rangers	1-2	Johnstone
	1971	Rangers	0-1	
	1972	Partick T.	1-4	Dalglish
	1973	Hibernian	1-2	Dalglish

THE CELTIC RECORD

	Division & place	Cup round reached		Division & place	Cup round reached
1889		Final	1928	I 2	Final
1890		1	1929	I 2	s-f
1891	I 3	s-f	1930	I 4	3
1892	I 2	Winners	1931	I 2	Winners
1893	I 1C	Final	1932	I 3	3
1894	I 1C	Final	1933	I 4	Winners
1895	I 2	3	1934	I 3	4
1896	I 1C	1	1935	I 2	4
1897	I 4	1	1936	I 1C	2
1898	I 1C	2	1937	I 3	Winners
1899	I 3	Winners	1938	I 1C	3
1900	I 2	Winners	1939	I 2	4
1901	I 2	Final	1947	I 7	1
1902	I 2	Final	1948	I 12	s-f
1903	I 5	3	1949	I 6	1
1904	I 3	Winners	1950	I 4	3
1905	I 1C	4	1951	I 7	Winners
1906	I 1C	3	1952	I 9	1
1907*	I 1C	Winners	1953	I 8	4
1908*	I 1C	Winners	1954	I 1C	Winners
1909	I 1C	Final	1955	I 2	Final
1910	I 1C	4	1956	I 5	Final
1911	I 5	Winners	1957	I 5	s-f
1912	I 2	Winners	1958	I 3	3
1913	I 2	3	1959	I 6	s-f
1914*	I 1C	Winners	1960	I 9	s-f
1915	I 1C		1961	I 4	Final
1916	I 1C		1962	I 3	s-f
1917	I 1C		1963	I 4	Final
1918	I 2		1964	I 3	4
1919	I 1C		1965	I 8	Winners
1920	I 2	3	1966	I 1C	Final
1921	I 2	3	1967*	I 1C	Winners
1922	I 1C	3	1968	I 1C	1
1923	I 3	Winners	1969	I 1C	Winners
1924	I 3	1	1970	I 1C	Final
1925	I 4	Winners	1971*	I 1C	Winners
1926	I 1C	Final	1972	I 1C	Winners
1927	I 3	Winners	1973	I 1C	Final

C – Scottish League champions
* – League and Cup double

CLYDE

Founded: 1877
Address: Shawfield Park, Glasgow C.5
Telephone: (041) 647 6329
Ground capacity: 25,000 (2,000 seated)
Playing area: 110 by 70 yards
Record attendance: 52,000 v Rangers, Division I, 21.11.08
Record victory: 11-1 v Cowdenbeath, Division II, 6.10.51
Record defeat: 0-11 v Rangers, Scottish Cup 4th round, 1880-81
Most League points: 64, Division II, 1956-57
Most League goals: 122, Division II, 1956-57
League scoring record: 32, Bill Boyd, Division I, 1932-33
Most capped player: 12, Tommy Ring, Scotland

Scottish Cup	Year	Opponents	Score	Scorers
Winners	1939	Motherwell	4-0	Martin 2, Wallace, Noble
	1955	Celtic	1-1	Robertson
		Replay	1-0	Ring
	1958	Hibernian	1-0	Coyle
Runners-up	1910	Dundee	2-2	Chalmers, Booth
		First replay	0-0	
		Second replay	1-2	Chalmers
	1912	Celtic	0-2	
	1949	Rangers	1-4	Galletly

CLYDEBANK

Founded: 1965 (new club)
Address: New Kilbowie Park, Clydebank
Telephone: Clydebank 2887
Ground capacity: 13,500 (seated 200)
Playing area: 110 by 68 yards
Record attendance: 14,900 v Hibernian, Scottish Cup 1st round, 10.2.65
Record victory: 7-1 v Hamilton, Division II, 20.11.71
Record defeat: 5-0 v Celtic, Scottish League Cup, 8.9.71
Most League points: 42, Division II, 1970-71
Most League goals: 62, Division II, 1967-68

THE CLYDEBANK RECORD

	Division & place		Cup round reached			Division & place		Cup round reached
1918	I	9			1965†	II	5	1
1919	I	10			1966‡			p
1920	I	5			1967§	II	18	p
1921	I	20			1968	II	9	p
1922	I	22R			1969	II	13	p
1923	II	2P			1970	II	13	2
1924	I	20R			1971	II	5	3
1925	II	2P			1972	II	9	4
1926	I	20R			1973	II	17	1
1927	II	3						
1928	II	14			P — promoted		R — relegated	
1929	II	16			p — preliminary round			
1930	II	18			*Old Clydebank disbanded			
1931*	II	19			†East Stirlingshire Clydebank			
					‡Clydebank juniors			
					§Clydebank			

COWDENBEATH

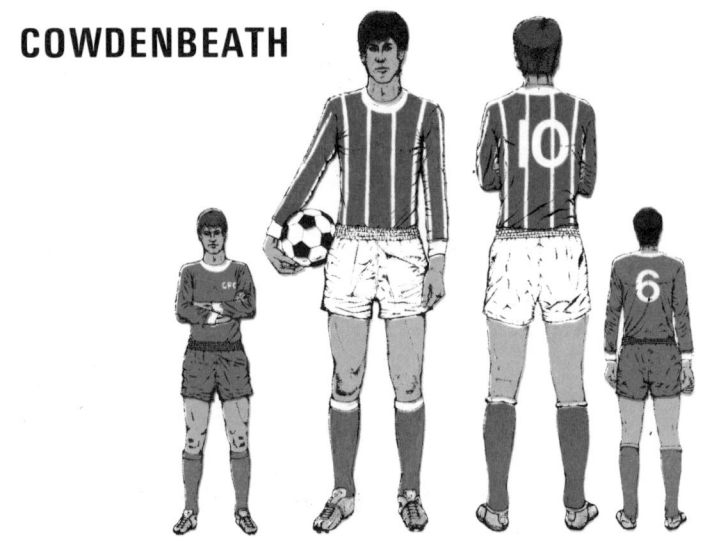

Founded: 1881
Address: Central Park, Cowdenbeath, Fife, Scotland
Telephone: Cowdenbeath 3205
Ground capacity: 25,000
Playing area: 110 by 70 yards
Record attendance: 25,586 v Rangers, League Cup quarter-final, 21.9.49
Record victory: 12-0 v Johnstone, Scottish Cup 1st round, 21.1.28
Record defeat: 1-11 v Clyde, Division II, 6.10.51
Most League points: 60, Division II, 1938-39
Most League goals: 120, Division II, 1938-39
League scoring record: 40, Willie Devlin, 1925-26
Most capped player: 1 (3 in all), Alec Venters, Scotland

THE CLYDE RECORD

	Division & place		Cup round reached			Division & place		Cup round reached
1892	I	7	p		1929	I	17	3
1893	I	10	1		1930	I	11	2
1894	II	3P	3		1931	I	12	2
1895	I	7	3		1932	I	13	q-f
1896	I	9	2		1933	I	12	s-f
1897	I	9	1		1934	I	14	1
1898	I	10	1		1935	I	10	2
1899	I	8	3		1936	I	18	s-f
1900	I	10R	2		1937	I	10	s-f
1901	II	5	2		1938	I	15	1
1902	II	12	p		1939	I	9	Winners
1903	II	12	1		1947	I	10	1
1904	II	2	1		1948	I	6	3
1905	II	1	1		1949	I	14	Final
1906	II	2P	1		1950	I	13	2
1907	I	8	1		1951	I	15R	3
1908	I	17	p		1952	II	1P	2
1909	I	3	s-f		1953	I	5	q-f
1910	I	5	Final		1954	I	8	2
1911	I	7	q-f		1955	I	7	Winners
1912	I	3	Final		1956	I	17R	s-f
1913	I	9	s-f		1957	II	1P	q-f
1914	I	9	2		1958	I	4	Winners
1915	I	17			1959	I	15	2
1916	I	15			1960	I	6	s-f
1917	I	13			1961	I	17R	1
1918	I	17			1962	II	1P	2
1919	I	17			1963	I	17R	2
1920	I	16	1		1964	II	2P	2
1921	I	7	2		1965	I	7	1
1922	I	10	3		1966	I	11	1
1923	I	16	1		1967	I	3	s-f
1924	I	19R	3		1968	I	8	2
1925	II	3	2		1969	I	13	2
1926	II	2P	3		1970	I	16	1
1927	I	17	3		1971	I	15	4
1928	I	15	1		1972	I	17R	3
					1973	II	1P	3
					P — promoted		R — relegated	
					p — preliminary round			

THE COWDENBEATH RECORD						
	Division & place	**Cup round reached**				
1906	II 9	p	1936	II 10	3
1907	II 7	1	1937	II 6	3
1908	II 12	p	1938	II 6	2
1909	II 11	p	1939	II 1	2
1910	II 11	p	1947	II 14	3
1911	II 5	p	1948	II 5	2
1912	II 4	p	1949	II 13	2
1913	II 5	p	1950	II 5	2
1914	II 1	p	1951	II 11	1
1915	II 1		1952	II 8	2
1916			1953	II 13	2
1917			1954	II 13	2
1918			1955	II 14	4
1919			1956	II 7	5
1920		1	1957	II 3	4
1921		p	1958	II 6	1
1922	II 2	2	1959	II 14	1
1923	II 11	2	1960	II 19	3
1924	II 2P	2	1961	II 8	2
1925	I 5	1	1962	II 14	1
1926	I 7	1	1963	II 8	2
1927	I 7	2	1964	II 17	1
1928	I 9	2	1965	II 12	1
1929	I 13	2	1966	II 10	2
1930	I 16	2	1967	II 6	1
1931	I 7	q-f	1968	II 12	1
1932	I 12	2	1969	II 14	1
1933	I 17	1	1970	II 2P	p
1934	I 20R	3	1971	I 18R	4
1935	II 12	1	1972	II 5	3
			1973	II 7	3

P – promoted
R – relegated
p – preliminary round

THE DUMBARTON RECORD						
	Division & place	**Cup round reached**				
1891	I 1C†	Final	1930	II 16	1
1892	I 1C	3	1931	II 10	1
1893	I 7	2	1932	II 12	1
1894	I 5	2	1933	II 9	2
1895	I 10	2	1934	II 6	1
1896	I 10R	1	1935	II 16	2
1897	II 10	Final	1936	II 18	3
1898	*	1	1937	II 15	2
1899	*	1	1938	II 7	1
1900	*	p	1939	II 11	1
1901	*	p	1947	II 13	q-f
1902	*	p	1948	II 11	3
1903	*	p	1949	II 15	3
1904	*	p	1950	II 15	2
1905	*	p	1951	II 9	1
1906	*	p	1952	II 10	3
1907	II 4	p	1953	II 10	1
1908	II 2	p	1954	II 16L	1
1909	II 4	p	1955	*	4
1910	II 4	1	1956	II 4	4
1911	II 1	p	1957	II 9	q-f
1912	II 3	1	1958	II 4	1
1913	II 6E	q-f	1959	II 4	2
1914	I 19	2	1960	II 6	1
1915	I 12		1961	II 10	2
1916	I 9		1962	II 17	1
1917	I 10		1963	II 12	1
1918	I 8		1964	II 6	2
1919	I 15		1965	II 14	1
1920	I 11	1	1966	II 12	q-f
1921	I 21	4	1967	II 14	1
1922	I 20R	1	1968	II 10	p
1923	II 4	1	1969	II 14	1
1924	II 10	1	1970	II 7	1
1925	II 8	2	1971	II 4	2
1926	II 11	q-f	1972	II 1P	4
1927	II 18	2	1973	I 16	4
1928	II 11	1			
1929	II 14	3			

† shared jointly with Rangers
* not members of League
P – promoted   R – relegated
L – not re-elected to League
E – elected to First Division
C – Scottish League Champions

DUMBARTON

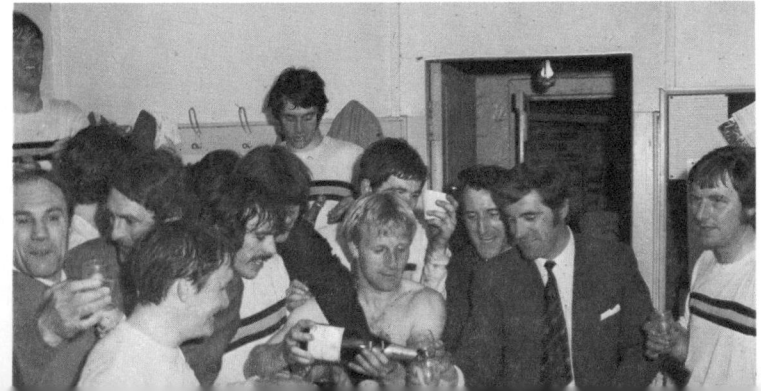

Founded: 1872 (as Dumbarton Athletic)
Address: Boghead Park, Dumbarton, Dunbartonshire
Telephone: Dumbarton 2569
Ground capacity: 18,000
Record attendance: 18,000 v Raith Rovers, Scottish Cup quarter-final, 2.3.57
Record victory: 8-0 v Cowdenbeath, Division II, 28.3.64
Record defeat: 0-8 v Dundee United, Division II, 1935-36
      v Morton, Division II, 1953-54
      v Third Lanark, Scottish Cup 3rd round, 22.2.36
Most League points: 52, Division II, 1971-72
Most League goals: 101, Division II, 1956-57
League scoring record: 38, Kenny Wilson, Division II, 1971-72
Most capped player: 18, John Lindsay, Scotland
      18, James McAulay, Scotland

Scottish Cup	Year	Opponents	Score
Winners	1883	Vale of Leven	2-2
		Replay	2-1
Runners-up	1881	Queen's Park	1-3
	1882	Queen's Park	2-2
		Replay	1-4
	1887	Hibernian	1-2
	1891	Hearts	0-1
	1897	Rangers	1-5

Promotion in 1972, the first excuse for a Dumbarton celebration in 80 years.

DUNDEE

Founded: 1893
Address: Dens Park, Dundee, Angus
Telephone: Dundee 86104
Ground capacity: 45,000 (5,000 seated)
Playing area: 110 by 75 yards
Record attendance: 43,024 v Rangers, Scottish Cup 2nd round, 7.2.53
Record victory: 10-0 v Alloa Athletic, Division II, 8.3.47
      10-0 v Dunfermline Athletic, Division II, 22.3.47
Record defeat: 0-11 v Celtic, Division I, 26.10.1895
Most League points: 54, Division I, 1961-62
Most League goals: 113, Division II, 1946-47
League scoring record: 38, David Halliday, Division I, 1923-24
Record League aggregate: 111, Alan Gilzean, 1960-1964
Most League appearances: 341, Doug Cowie, 1947-1961
Most capped player: 24, Alex Hamilton, Scotland

Scottish Cup	Year	Opponents	Score	Scorers
Winners	1910	Clyde	2-2	Hunter, Langlands
			0-0	
			2-1	Bellamy, Hunter
Runners-up	1925	Celtic	1-2	McLean (D)
	1952	Motherwell	0-4	
	1964	Rangers	1-3	Cameron
League Cup				
Winners	1952	Rangers	3-2	Flavell, Pattillo, Boyd
	1953	Kilmarnock	2-0	Flavell 2
Runners-up	1968	Celtic	3-5	McLean (G) 2, McLean (J)

THE DUNDEE RECORD

Year	Division & place	Cup round reached
1894	I 8	p
1895	I 8	s-f
1896	I 5	2
1897	I 5	q-f
1898	I 7	s-f
1899	I 10	1
1900	I 6	q-f
1901	I 7	q-f
1902	I 9	2
1903	I 2	s-f
1904	I 5	q-f
1905	I 7	1
1906	I 7	1
1907	I 2	2
1908	I 4	2
1909	I 2	2
1910	I 6	Winners
1911	I 6	s-f
1912	I 8	2
1913	I 14	q-f
1914	I 7	2
1915	I 15	
1916	I 8	
1917	I 16R	
1918†		
1919†		
1920	I 4	2
1921	I 4	q-f
1922	I 4	3
1923	I 7	1-f
1924	I 5	2
1925	I 8	Final
1926	I 10	2
1927	I 5	3
1928	I 14	3
1929	I 18	3
1930	I 14	q-f
1931	I 8	3
1932	I 11	2
1933	I 15	3
1934	I 12	2
1935	I 8	1
1936	I 13	3
1937	I 9	3
1938	I 19R	1
1939	II 6	2
1947	II 1P	q-f
1948	I 4	1
1949	I 2	s-f
1950	I 6	1
1951	I 3	q-f
1952	I 8	Final
1953	I 7	2
1954	I 7	3
1955	I 8	5
1956	I 13	6
1957	I 10	5
1958	I 11	3
1959	I 4	1
1960	I 4	2
1961	I 10	2
1962	I 1C	1
1963	I 9	q-f
1964	I 6	Final
1965	I 6	1
1966	I 9	2
1967	I 6	1
1968	I 9	2
1969	I 9	1
1970	I 6	s-f
1971	I 5	q-f
1972	I 5	4
1973	I 5	s-f

C – Scottish League champions
P – promoted   R – relegated
† No Second Division

THE DUNDEE UNITED RECORD

Year	Division & place	Cup round reached
1911*	II 8	p
1912*	II 10	p
1913*	II 10	2
1914*	II 4	1
1915*	II 11	
1920*	†	p
1921*	†	p
1922*	II 19	1
1923‡		2
1924	II 9	1
1925	II 1P	2
1926	I 17	1
1927	I 20R	q-f
1928	II 6	2
1929	II 1P	q-f
1930	I 19R	2
1931	II 2P	2
1932	I 19R	3
1933	II 13	2
1934	II 17	1
1935	II 4	3
1936	II 7	2
1937	II 14	1
1938	II 14	2
1939	II 9	2
1947	II 10	1
1948	II 15	2
1949	II 8	2
1950	II 8	2
1951	II 4	1
1952	II 4	3
1953	II 8	1
1954	II 15	1
1955	II 13	4
1956	II 8	5
1957	II 13	6
1958	II 9	2
1959	II 17	2
1960	II 2P	2
1961	I 9	2
1962	I 10	2
1963	I 7	s-f
1964	I 8	1
1965	I 9	2
1966	I 5	2
1967	I 9	s-f
1968	I 11	2
1969	I 5	q-f
1970	I 5	2
1971	I 6	4
1972	I 9	3
1973	I 7	3

P – promotion p – preliminary rounds
R – relegation
*as Dundee Hibernians
† Scottish Second Division not reformed until 1921
‡ Name changed to Dundee United. Dundee Hibernians did not compete in the League 1922-23.

DUNDEE UNITED

Founded: 1910*
Address: Tannadice Park, Dundee, Angus
Telephone: Dundee 862289
Ground capacity: 28,500 (2,500 seated)
Playing area: 110 by 74 yards
Record attendance: 28,000 v Barcelona, Fairs Cup 2nd round, 16.11.66
Record victory: 14-0 v Nithsdale Wanderers, Scottish Cup 1st round, 17.1.31
Record defeat: 1-12 v Motherwell, Division II, 23.1.54
Most League points: 51, Division II, 1928-29
Most League goals: 99, Division II, 1928-29
League scoring record: 41, John Coyle, Division II, 1955-56
Record League aggregate: 202, Peter McKay, 1947-1954
Most League appearances: *Not available*
Most capped player: 3 (11 in all) Orjan Persson, Sweden
*As Dundee Hibernians. Name changed to Dundee United in 1923

DUNFERMLINE ATHLETIC

Founded: 1885
Address: East End Park, Dunfermline
Telephone: Dunfermline 24295
Ground capacity: 27,000 (3,100 seated)
Playing area: 115 by 75 yards
Record attendance: 27,816 v Celtic, Division I, 1968-69
Record victory: 11-2 v Stenhousemuir, Division II, 1930-31
Record defeat: 0-10 v Dundee, Division II, 22.3.47
Most League points: 59, Division II, 1925-26
Most League goals: 120, Division II, 1957-58
League scoring record: 53, Bobby Skinner, Division II, 1925-26
Record League aggregate: 154, Charlie Dickson, 1955-64
Most League appearances: 301, George Peebles, 1956-66
Most capped player: 6 (12 in all), Andy Wilson, Scotland

Scottish Cup	Year	Opponents	Score	Scorers
Winners	1961	Celtic	0-0	
			2-0	Thomson, Dickson
	1968	Hearts	3-1	Gardner 2, Lister (pen)
Runners-up	1965	Celtic	2-3	Melrose, McLaughlin
Scottish League Cup				
Runners-up	1950	East Fife	0-3	

THE DUNFERMLINE RECORD

Year	Division & place	Cup round reached
1922	II 8	2
1923	II 13	3
1924	II 7	1
1925	II 13	1
1926	II 1P	1
1927	I 18	3
1928	I 20R	4
1929	II 11	1
1930	II 10	1
1931	II 3	1
1932	II 10	q-f
1933	II 3	1
1934	II 2P	1
1935	I 15	q-f
1936	I 10	1
1937	I 19R	1
1938	II 9	1
1939	II 5	3
1947	II 8	1
1948	II 7	2
1949	II 4	1
1950	II 4	3
1951	II 10	1
1952	II 6	3
1953	II 11	1
1954	II 8	2
1955	II 2P	6
1956	I 16	5
1957	I 17R	6
1958	II 2P	3
1959	I 16	q-f
1960	I 13	2
1961	I 12	Winners
1962	I 4	q-f
1963	I 8	3
1964	I 5	s-f
1965	I 3	Final
1966	I 4	s-f
1967	I 8	q-f
1968	I 4	Winners
1969	I 3	2
1970	I 9	1
1971	I 16	4
1972	I 18R	3
1973	II 2	3

P – promoted
R – relegated

EAST FIFE

Founded: 1903
Address: Bayview Park, Methil, Fife, Scotland
Telephone: Leven 2323
Ground capacity: 22,000
Record attendance: 21,515 v Raith Rovers, Division I, 2.1.50
Record victory: 13-2 v Edinburgh City, Division II, 11.12.37
Record defeat: 0-9 v Hearts, Division I, 5.10.57
Most League points: 57, Division II, 1929-30
Most League goals: 114, Division II, 1929-30
League scoring record: 33, Alex McGauchie, Division II, 1929-30
Most capped player: 5 (8 in all), George Aitken, Scotland

Scottish Cup	Year	Opponents	Score	Scorers
Winners	1938	Kilmarnock	1-1	McLeod
		Replay	4-2	McKerrell 2, McLeod Miller
Runners-up	1927	Celtic	1-3	Wood
	1950	Rangers	0-3	
Scottish League Cup				
Winners	1948	Falkirk	0-0	
		Replay	4-1	Duncan 3, Adams
	1950	Dunfermline	3-0	Fleming, Duncan, Morris
	1954	Partick Thistle	3-2	Gardiner, Fleming, Christie

THE EAST FIFE RECORD

Year	Division & place	Cup round reached
1921		3
1922	II 12	1
1923	II 9	3
1924	II 13	2
1925	II 9	1
1926	II 4	1
1927	II 6	Final
1928	II 4	1
1929	II 8	1
1930	II 2P	1
1931	I 20R	1
1932	II 8	1
1933	II 7	1
1934	II 13	1
1935	II 9	1
1936	II 6	1
1937	II 5	3
1938	II 5	Winners
1939	II 3	1
1947	II 3	q-f
1948	II 1P	q-f
1949	I 4	s-f
1950	I 4	Final
1951	I 10	1
1952	I 3	2
1953	I 3	2
1954	I 6	1
1955	I 11	5
1956	I 12	5
1957	I 15	6
1958	I 17R	1
1959	II 8	1
1960	II 18	1
1961	II 13	2
1962	II 10	3
1963	II 11	2
1964	II 4	2
1965	II 9	2
1966	II 4	1
1967	II 5	2
1968	II 3	2
1969	II 3	1
1970	II 10	q-f
1971	II 2P	3
1972	I 16	3
1973	I 9	3

P – promoted
R – relegated

EAST STIRLINGSHIRE

Founded: 1881
Address: Firs Park, Falkirk, Stirlingshire
Telephone: Falkirk 23583
Ground capacity: 9,000 (500 seated)
Record attendance: 10,000 v St Mirren, Division II, 16.11.35
Record victory: 8-2 v Brechin City, Division II, 31.3.62
Record defeat: 0-10 v Dundee United, Division II, 25.3.39
Most League points: 55, Division II, 1931-32
Most League goals: 111, Division II, 1931-32
League scoring record: 36, Malcolm Morrison, Division II, 1938-39
Record League aggregate: Not available
Most League appearances: Not available
Most capped player: 2, David Alexander, Scotland

THE EAST STIRLINGSHIRE RECORD

Year	Division & place	Cup round reached
1902	II 9	p
1903	II 8	p
1904	II 6	p
1905	II 9	p
1906	II 12	p
1907	II 10	p
1908	II 5	p
1909	II 9	p
1910	II 8	p
1911	II 7	1
1912	II 9	2
1913	II 3	2
1914	II 8	2
1915	II 4	
1920	†	2
1921	†	3
1922	II 15	3
1923	II 19	1
1924	*	3
1925	II 18	2
1926	II 18	1
1927	II 5	1
1928	II 9	1
1929	II 12	2
1930	II 12	1
1931	II 7	1
1932	II 1P	1
1933	I 20R	1
1934	II 9	3
1935	II 14	1
1936	II 8	1
1937	II 7	1
1938	II 13	1
1939	II 17	1
1947	‡	2
1948	‡	2
1949	‡	1
1950	‡	1
1951	‡	2
1952	‡	1
1953	‡	2
1954	‡	1
1955	‡	4
1956	II 16	4
1957	II 19	4
1958	II 15	1
1959	II 15	1
1960	II 15	3
1961	II 16	1
1962	II 11	2
1963	II 2P	3
1964	I 18R	3
1965††	II 5	p
1966	II 17	1
1967	II 19	p
1968	II 15	1
1969	II 9	2
1970	II 12	p
1971	II 17	2
1972	II 8	1
1973	II 13	2

P—promoted
R—relegated
p—preliminary round
* – Did not compete
† – No Second Division
‡ – Competed in Division 'C'
†† – as East Stirlingshire Clydebank

The industrial backcloth to East Stirlingshire's ground, Firs Park.

95

FALKIRK

Founded: 1876
Address: Brockville Park, Falkirk, Scotland
Telephone: Falkirk 24121
Ground capacity: 24,000 (2,750 seated)
Playing area: 110 by 70 yards
Record attendance: 23,100 v Celtic, Scottish Cup 3rd round, 21.2.53
Record victory: 10-0 v Breadalbane, Scottish Cup 1st round, 13.1.23 and 23.1.26
Record defeat: 1-11 v Airdrieonians, Division I, 28.4.51
Most League points: 59, Division II, 1935-36
Most League goals: 132, Division II, 1935-36
League scoring record: 43, Edward Morrison, Division I, 1928-29
Most capped player: 14 (15 in all), Alec Parker, Scotland

Scottish Cup

	Year	Opponents	Score	Scorers
Winners	1913	Raith Rovers	2-0	Robertson, Logan
	1957	Kilmarnock	1-1	Prentice
	Replay		2-1	Merchant, Moran

Scottish League Cup

	Year	Opponents	Score	Scorers
Runners-up	1948	East Fife	0-0	
	Replay		1-4	Aikman

THE FALKIRK RECORD

Year	Division & place	Cup round reached	Year	Division & place	Cup round reached
1902		q-f	1934	I 10	3
1903	II 7	q	1935	I 20R	1
1904	II 4	q	1936	II 1P	s-f
1905	II 2P	q	1937	I 7	2
1906	I 13	1	1938	I 4	q-f
1907	I 5	1	1939	I 5	3
1908	I 2	1	1947	I 11	3
1909	I 9	s-f	1948	I 7	2
1910	I 2	2	1949	I 5	1
1911	I 3	2	1950	I 14	2
1912	I 7	2	1951	I 16R	1
1913	I 5	Winners	1952	II 2P	q-f
1914	I 5	1	1953	I 13	3
1915	I 6		1954	I 13	2
1916	I 12		1955	I 12	7
1917	I 12		1956	I 14	5
1918	I 14		1957	I 14	Winners
1919	I 16		1958	I 10	q-f
1920	I 20	2	1959	I 17R	2
1921	I 18	1	1960	II 8	2
1922	I 5	2	1961	II 2P	1
1923	I 4	3	1962	I 14	1
1924	I 15	s-f	1963	I 13	1
1925	I 16	3	1964	I 14	q-f
1926	I 8	3	1965	I 16	1
1927	I 6	s-f	1966	I 10	1
1928	I 10	3	1967	I 14	2
1929	I 11	3	1968	I 15	1
1930	I 7	q-f	1969	I 17R	1
1931	I 14	3	1970	II 1P	q-f
1932	I 18	1	1971	I 7	3
1933	I 11	2	1972	I 14	3
			1973	I 14	4

P – promoted
R – relegated
q – qualifying rounds

FORFAR ATHLETIC

Founded: 1885
Address: Station Park, Forfar, Angus
Telephone: Forfar 3576
Ground capacity: 10,800 (850 seated)
Record attendance: 10,800 v Rangers, Scottish Cup 2nd round, 7.2.70
Record victory: 8-1 v Stenhousemuir, Division II, 1936-37
v Alloa Athletic, Division II, 1970-71
Record defeat: 2-10 v Dundee, Division II, 1938-39
Most League points: 47, Division II, 1968-69
Most League goals: 90, Division II, 1931-32
League scoring record: 45, Davie Kilgour, Division II, 1929-30

THE FORFAR RECORD

Year	Division & place	Cup round reached	Year	Division & place	Cup round reached
1922	II 14	1	1951	II 14	1
1923	II 15	1	1952	II 12	1
1924	II 14	2	1953	II 15	2
1925	II 20	1	1954	II 12	2
1926	*	2	1955	II 10	5
1927	II 9	2	1956	II 15	5
1928	II 5	2	1957	II 16	4
1929	II 7	1	1958	II 12	2
1930	II 8	2	1959	II 12	1
1931	II 12	1	1960	II 16	2
1932	II 6	1	1961	II 18	3
1933	II 14	1	1962	II 16	1
1934	II 11	2	1963	II 18	1
1935	II 11	1	1964	II 18	3
1936	II 13	1	1965	II 17	1
1937	II 12	1	1966	II 19	p
1938	II 15	2	1967	II 16	p
1939	II 15	1	1968	II 7	1
1947	*	1	1969	II 6	p
1948	*	1	1970	II 18	2
1949	*	1	1971	II 15	3
1950	II 10	1	1972	II 17	3
			1973	II 16	2

* – Competed in Division 'C'
p – preliminary round

HAMILTON ACADEMICALS

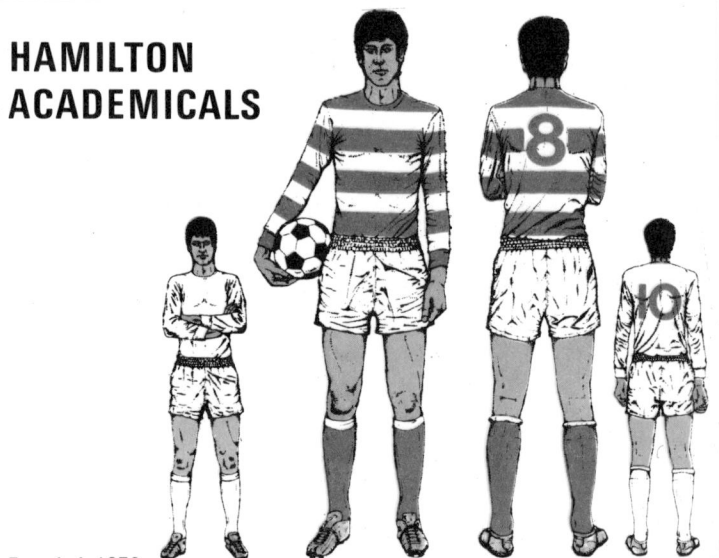

Founded: 1870
Address: Douglas Park, Hamilton, Lanarkshire
Telephone: Hamilton 23108
Ground capacity: 24,000
Record attendance: 28,281 v Heart of Midlothian, Scottish Cup 3rd round, 3.3.37
Record victory: 10-2 v Cowdenbeath, Division I, 1932-33
Record defeat: 1-11 v Hibernian, Division I, 6.11.65
Most League points: 50, Division II, 1964-65
Most League goals: 87, Division I, 1934-35
League scoring record: 34, David Wilson, Division I, 1936-37
Record League aggregate: 246, David Wilson, 1928-1939
Most League appearances: *Not available*
Most capped player: 2, Jimmie King, Scotland

Scottish Cup

Runners-up	Year	Opponents	Score	Scorer
	1911	Celtic	0-0	
			0-2	
	1935	Rangers	1-2	Harrison

THE HAMILTON RECORD

Year	Division & place	Cup round reached
1899	II 5	p
1900	II 7	1
1901	II 10	p
1902	II 5	p
1903	II 6	2
1904	II 1	p
1905	II 3	p
1906	II 4P	2
1907	I 16	p
1908	I 11	1
1909	I 16	1
1910	I 15	p
1911	I 16	Final
1912	I 12	1
1913	I 10	2
1914	I 18	2
1915	I 7	
1916	I 7	
1917	I 11	
1918	I 12	
1919	I 14	
1920	I 21	1
1921	I 15	3
1922	I 18	4
1923	I 18	3
1924	I 12	3
1925	I 13	s-f
1926	I 12	2
1927	I 15	3
1928	I 18	2
1929	I 12	2
1930	I 13	s-f
1931	I 10	2
1932	I 10	s-f
1933	I 8	1
1934	I 11	2
1935	I 4	Final
1936	I 6	1
1937	I 8	q-f
1938	I 13	3
1939	I 7	2
1947	I 16R	1
1948	II 3	1
1949	II 10	1
1950	II 6	1
1951	II 7	2
1952	II 9	2
1953	II 2P	3
1954	I 16R	q-f
1955	II 3	q-f
1956	II 11	5
1957	II 11	6
1958	II 10	1
1959	II 7	3
1960	II 4	1
1961	II 6	3
1962	II 13	2
1963	II 4	3
1964	II 13	2
1965	II 2P	1
1966	I 18R	1
1967	II 4	q-f
1968	II 11	1
1969	II 15	p
1970	II 19	1
1971	II 18	2
1972	II 19	3
1973	II 8	4

P – promoted   R – relegated
p – preliminary rounds

THE HEARTS RECORD

Year	Division & place	Cup round reached
1876	2	
1877	1	
1878	1	
1879	4	
1880	3	
1881	5	
1882	1	
1883	3	
1884	3	
1885	2	
1886	2	
1887	3	
1888	4	
1889	4	
1890	5	
1891	I 6	Winners
1892	I 3	3
1893	I 5	3
1894	I 2	1
1895	I 1C	s-f
1896	I 4	Winners
1897	I 1C	2
1898	I 4	3
1899	I 2	1
1900	I 4	s-f
1901	I 10	Winners
1902	I 3	3
1903	I 4	Final
1904	I 2	1
1905	I 8	2
1906	I 2	Winners
1907	I 9	Final
1908	I 12	3
1909	I 12	2
1910	I 12	3
1911	I 14	1
1912	I 4	s-f
1913	I 3	s-f
1914	I 3	2
1915	I 2	
1916	I 6	
1917	I 14	
1918	I 10	
1919	I 7	
1920	I 15	3
1921	I 3	s-f
1922	I 19	3
1923	I 12	4
1924	I 9	4
1925	I 10	2
1926	I 3	3
1927	I 13	1
1928	I 4	3
1929	I 4	1
1930	I 10	s-f
1931	I 5	2
1932	I 8	3
1933	I 3	s-f
1934	I 6	3
1935	I 3	s-f
1936	I 5	1
1937	I 5	3
1938	I 2	1
1939	I 4	3
1947	I 4	q-f
1948	I 9	2
1949	I 8	q-f
1950	I 3	2
1951	I 4	3
1952	I 4	s-f
1953	I 4	s-f
1954	I 2	q-f
1955	I 4	q-f
1956	I 3	Winners
1957	I 2	5
1958	I 1C	3
1959	I 2	2
1960	I 1C	2
1961	I 8	q-f
1962	I 6	3
1963	I 5	2
1964	I 4	3
1965	I 2	q-f
1966	I 7	q-f
1967	I 11	1
1968	I 12	Final
1969	I 8	2
1970	I 4	2
1971	I 11	4
1972	I 6	q-f
1973	I 10	3

C—Scottish League Champions

HEART OF MIDLOTHIAN

Founded: 1873
Address: Tynecastle Park, Gorgie Road, Edinburgh 11
Telephone: (031) 337 6132
Ground capacity: 49,000 (4,000 seated)
Record attendance: 53,496 v Rangers, Scottish Cup 2nd round, 13.2.32
Record victory: 15-0 v King's Park, Scottish Cup 2nd round, 13.2.37
Record defeat: 1-7 v Dundee, Division I, 27.2.65
Most League points: 62, Division I, 1957-58
Most League goals: 132, Division I, 1957-58
League scoring record: 44, Barney Battles, Division I, 1930-31
Record League aggregate: 206, Jimmy Wardhaugh, 1946-1959
Most capped player: 29, Bobby Walker, Scotland

Scottish Cup

	Year	Opponents	Score	Scorers
Winners	1891	Dumbarton	1-0	Mason
	1896	Hibernian	3-1	Baird (pen), King, Michael
	1901	Celtic	4-3	Walker (R), Bell 2, Thomson
	1906	Third Lanark	1-0	Wilson
	1956	Celtic	3-1	Crawford 2, Conn
Runners-up	1903	Rangers	1-1	Walker (R)
			0-0	
			0-2	
	1907	Celtic	0-3	
	1968	Dunfermline Athletic	1-3	Lunn og

Scottish League Cup

	Year	Opponents	Score	Scorers
Winners	1955	Motherwell	4-2	Bauld 3, Wardhaugh
	1959	Partick Thistle	5-1	Bauld 2, Murray 2, Hamilton
	1960	Third Lanark	2-1	Hamilton, Young
	1963	Kilmarnock	1-0	Davidson
Runners-up	1962	Rangers	1-1	Cumming
			1-3	Davidson

HIBERNIAN

Founded: 1875
Address: Easter Road, Edinburgh
Telephone: 031 661 2159
Ground capacity: 60,000 (3,000 seated)
Playing area: 112 by 74 yards
Record attendance: 65,850 v Hearts, Division I, 2.1.1950
Record victory: 15-1 v Peebles Rovers, Scottish Cup 2nd round, 11.2.61
Record defeat: 2-9 v Morton, Division I, 1918-19
Most League points: 54, Division II, 1932-33
Most League goals: 106, Division I, 1959-60
League scoring record: 42, Joe Baker, Division I, 1959-60
Record League aggregate: 185, Lawrie Reilly, 1946-58
Most League appearances: 348, Eddie Turnbull, 1946-59
Most capped player: 39, Lawrie Reilly, Scotland

Scottish Cup

	Year	Opponents	Score	Scorers
Winners	1887	Dumbarton	2-1	Not known
	1902	Celtic	1-0	McGeachan
Runners-up	1896	Hearts	1-3	O'Neill
	1914	Celtic	0-0	
			1-4	Smith
	1923	Celtic	0-1	
	1924	Airdrieonians	0-2	
	1947	Aberdeen	1-2	Cuthbertson
	1958	Clyde	0-1	
	1972	Celtic	1-6	Gordon

Scottish League Cup

	Year	Opponents	Score	Scorers
Winners	1973	Celtic	2-1	Stanton, O'Rourke
Runners-up	1951	Motherwell	0-3	
	1969	Celtic	2-6	O'Rourke, Stevenson

THE HIBERNIAN RECORD

Year	Division & place	Cup round reached
1894	II 1	p
1895	II 1P	2
1896	I 3	Final
1897	I 2	2
1898	I 3	q-f
1899	I 4	2
1900	I 3	2
1901	I 3	s-f
1902	I 6	Winners
1903	I 1C	q-f
1904	I 10	2
1905	I 5	1
1906	I 11	q-f
1907	I 11	s-f
1908	I 5	q-f
1909	I 6	1
1910	I 8	s-f
1911	I 9	1
1912	I 13	1
1913	I 6	3
1914	I 14	Final
1915	I 11	
1916	I 19	
1917	I 17	
1918	I 16	
1919	I 18	
1920	I 18	2
1921	I 13	1
1922	I 7	2
1923	I 8	Final
1924	I 7	Final
1925	I 3	1
1926	I 16	2
1927	I 9	1
1928	I 12	s-f
1929	I 14	1
1930	I 17	3
1931	I 19R	3
1932	II 7	1
1933	II 1P	q-f
1934	I 16	3
1935	I 11	3
1936	I 17	2
1937	I 17	2
1938	I 10	1
1939	I 13	s-f
1947	I 2	Final
1948	I 1C	s-f
1949	I 3	q-f
1950	I 2	1
1951	I 1C	s-f
1952	I 1C	1
1953	I 2	q-f
1954	I 5	3
1955	I 5	5
1956	I 4	5
1957	I 9	5
1958	I 9	Final
1959	I 10	q-f
1960	I 7	q-f
1961	I 7	q-f
1962	I 8	1
1963	I 16	3
1964	I 10	1
1965	I 4	s-f
1966	I 6	2
1967	I 5	q-f
1968	I 3	2
1969	I 12	1
1970	I 3	1
1971	I 12	s-f
1972	I 4	Final
1973	I 3	4

P—promoted R—relegated
C—Scottish League Champions
p—preliminary round

THE KILMARNOCK RECORD

Year	Division & place	Cup round reached
1896	II 4	1
1897	II 3	s-f
1898	II 1	Final
1899	II 1P	q-f
1900	I 5	q-f
1901	I 5	2
1902	I 7	3
1903	I 9	2
1904	I 14	q-f
1905	I 9	1
1906	I 14	2
1907	I 17	2
1908	I 14	s-f
1909	I 10	1
1910	I 11	1
1911	I 10	1
1912	I 16	2
1913	I 11	3
1914	I 12	3
1915	I 13	
1916	I 10	
1917	I 6	
1918	I 3	
1919	I 9	
1920	I 9	Winners
1921	I 12	2
1922	I 17	2
1923	I 15	2
1924	I 16	2
1925	I 12	q-f
1926	I 9	1
1927	I 16	2
1928	I 8	4
1929	I 10	Winners
1930	I 8	2
1931	I 11	s-f
1932	I 9	Final
1933	I 14	q-f
1934	I 7	2
1935	I 9	2
1936	I 8	2
1937	I 11	1
1938	I 18	Final
1939	I 10	2
1947	I 15R	1
1948	II 6	1
1949	II 11	1
1950	II 7	1
1951	II 12	1
1952	II 5	2
1953	II 4	2
1954	II 2P	2
1955	I 10	6
1956	I 8	6
1957	I 3	Final
1958	I 5	3
1959	I 8	q-f
1960	I 2	Final
1961	I 2	2
1962	I 5	q-f
1963	I 2	2
1964	I 2	s-f
1965	I 1C	q-f
1966	I 3	q-f
1967	I 7	1
1968	I 7	1
1969	I 4	q-f
1970	I 7	s-f
1971	I 13	q-f
1972	I 11	s-f
1973	I 17R	4

P — promoted
R — relegated
C — Scottish League Champions

KILMARNOCK

Founded: 1869
Address: Rugby Park, Kilmarnock
Telephone: Kilmarnock 25184
Ground capacity: 34,500 (4,200 seated)
Playing area: 115 by 75 yards
Record attendance: 34,246 v Rangers, League Cup, August 1963
Record victory: 11-1 v Paisley Academicals, Scottish Cup 1st round, 18.1.30
Record defeat: 0-8 v Hibernian, Division I, 1925-26
0-8 v Rangers, Division I, 1936-37
Most League points: 50, Division I, 1959-60, 1960-61 & 1964-65
Most League goals: 92, Division I, 1962-63
League scoring record: 35, Peerie Cunningham, Division I, 1927-28
Record League aggregate: 102, Jimmy Maxwell, 1931-1934
Most League appearances: 424, Frank Beattie, 1954-1971
Most capped player: 9, Joe Nibloe, Scotland

Scottish Cup	Year	Opponents	Score	Scorers
Winners	1920	Albion Rovers	3-2	Culley, J R Smith, Shortt
	1929	Rangers	2-0	Aitken, Williamson
Runners-up	1898	Rangers	0-2	
	1932	Rangers	1-1	Maxwell
			0-3	
	1938	East Fife	1-1	McAvoy
			2-4	Thomson (pen), McGrogan
	1957	Falkirk	1-1	Curlett
			1-2	Curlett
	1060	Rangers	0-2	
Scottish League Cup				
Runners-up	1953	Dundee	0-2	
	1961	Rangers	0-2	
	1963	Hearts	0-1	

MONTROSE

Founded: 1879
Address: Links Park, Montrose
Telephone: Montrose 573/375
Ground capacity: 9,000 (350 seated)
Playing area: 114 by 66 yards
Record attendance: 6,389 v Celtic, Scottish Cup 2nd round, 1938-39
Record victory: 8-0 v Solway Star, Scottish Cup 1st round, 18.1.30
Record defeat: 4-9 v Stenhousemuir, Division II, 1934-35
Most League points: 41, Division II, 1961-62
Most League goals: 78, Division II, 1970-71
Most capped player: 2 (6 in all), A Keiller, Scotland

THE MONTROSE RECORD

Year	Division & place	Cup round reached
1930	II 11	q-f
1931	II 8	3
1932	II 17	1
1933	II 17	2
1934	II 16	1
1935	II 17	1
1936	II 12	1
1937	II 13	1
1938	II 16	1
1939	II 14	2
1947	*	p
1948	*	q-f
1949	*	1
1950	*	1
1951	*	1
1952	*	1
1953	*	3
1954	*	1
1955	*	4
1956	II 19	4
1957	II 17	5
1958	II 14	2
1959	II 19	2
1960	II 7	2
1961	II 7	2
1962	II 5	2
1963	II 15	2
1964	II 5	1
1965	II 16	1
1966	II 9	1
1967	II 12	p
1968	II 13	p
1969	II 10	2
1970	II 8	1
1971	II 6	2
1972	II 10	3
1973	II 6	q-f

p—preliminary
*—Montrose compete in C Division

MORTON

Founded: 1874
Address: Cappielow Park, Greenock
Telephone: Greenock 23571
Ground capacity: 25,000 (2,900 seated)
Playing area: 110 by 71 yards
Record attendance: 23,500 v Celtic, Division I, 1921
and v Rangers, Scottish Cup 3rd round, 21.2.53
Record victory: 11-1 v Blairgowrie, Scottish Cup 1st round, 1.2.36
Record defeat: 2-8 v Rangers, Division I, 15.3.27
Most League points: 69, Division II, 1966-67
Most League goals: 135, Division II, 1963-64
League scoring record: 51, Allan McGraw, Division II, 1963-64
Most capped player: 25, Jimmy Cowan, Scotland

Scottish Cup	Year	Opponents	Score	Scorers
Winners	1922	Rangers	1-0	Gourlay
Runners-up	1948	Rangers	1-1	Whyte
		Replay	0-1	
Scottish League Cup				
Runners-up	1964	Rangers	0-5	

THE MORTON RECORD

	Division & place	Cup round reached				
1894	II 8	p	1930	I 18	1	
1895	II 5	p	1931	I 16	3	
1896	II 9	1	1932	I 15	1	
1897	II 5	s-f	1933	I 19R	1	
1898	II 3	2	1934	II 5	1	
1899	II 7	2	1935	II 6	2	
1900	II 2E	1	1936	II 3	q-f	
1901	I 4	q-f	1937	II 2P	s-f	
1902	I 10	1	1938	I 20R	3	
1903	I 12	1	1939	II 12E	1	
1904	I 11	s-f	1947	I 6	3	
1905	I 13	2	1948	I 14	Final	
1906	I 10	2	1949	I 15R	3	
1907	I 13	2	1950	II 1P	2	
1908	I 13	2	1951	I 12	2	
1909	I 17	1	1952	I 15R	3	
1910	I 17	1	1953	II 6	3	
1911	I 13	2	1954	II 5	3	
1912	I 6	q-f	1955	II 9	5	
1913	I 13	2	1956	II 9	5	
1914	I 4	2	1957	II 4	5	
1915	I 4		1958	II 13	2	
1916	I 3		1959	II 11	3	
1917	I 2		1960	II 14	1	
1918	I 4		1961	II 19	2	
1919	I 3		1962	II 3	2	
1920	I 6	s-f	1963	II 3	1	
1921	I 9	2	1964	II 1P	2	
1922	I 12	Winners	1965	I 10	2	
1923	I 14	1	1966	I 17R	1	
1924	I 11	1	1967	II 1P	1	
1925	I 14	1	1968	I 6	s-f	
1926	I 15	q-f	1969	I 10	s-f	
1927	I 19R	1	1970	I 10	2	
1928	II 18	2	1971	I 8	4	
1929	II 2P	1	1972	I 13	4	
			1973	I 12	3	

P—promoted
R—relegated
E—elected to First Division

MOTHERWELL

Founded: 1885*
Address: Fir Park, Motherwell, Lanarkshire
Telephone: Motherwell 63229
Ground capacity: 35,000 (3,500 seated)
Record attendance: 35,632 v Rangers, Scottish Cup 4th round replay, 12.3.52
Record victory: 12-1 v Dundee United, Division II, 1953-54
Record defeat: 0-10 v St Mirren, Scottish Southern League, 1945-46
Most League points: 66, Division I, 1931-32
Most League goals: 119, Division I, 1931-32
League scoring record: 52, Bill McFadyen, Division I, 1931-32
Record League aggregate: 283, Hugh Ferguson, 1916-1925
Most League appearances: 626, Bob Ferrier, 1918-1937
Most capped player: 12, George Stevenson, Scotland
*As Wee Alpha. Changed name to Motherwell in 1886.

Scottish Cup	Year	Opponents	Score	Scorers
Winners	1952	Dundee	4-0	Watson, Redpath, Humphries, Kelly
Runners-up	1931	Celtic	2-2	Stevenson, McMenemy
			2-4	Murdoch, Stevenson
	1933	Celtic	0-1	
	1939	Clyde	0-4	
	1951	Celtic	0-1	
League Cup				
Winners	1951	Hibernian	3-0	Kelly, Forrest, Watters
Runners-up	1955	Hearts	2-4	Redpath (pen), Bain

THE MOTHERWELL RECORD

	Division & place	Cup round reached				
1904	I 13	2	1935	I 7	q-f	
1905	I 14	2	1936	I 4	q-f	
1906	I 9	1	1937	I 4	q-f	
1907	I 10	1	1938	I 5	q-f	
1908	I 10	2	1939	I 12	Final	
1909	I 14	2	1947	I 8	s-f	
1910	I 10	3	1948	I 8	3	
1911	I 17	3	1949	I 12	2	
1912	I 15	3	1950	I 10	1	
1913	I 7	2	1951	I 9	Final	
1914	I 17	4	1952	I 7	Winners	
1915	I 18		1953	I 15R	3	
1916	I 13		1954	II 1P	s-f	
1917	I 8		1955	I 15	q-f	
1918	I 5		1956	I 10	5	
1919	I 5		1957	I 7	6	
1920	I 3	1	1958	I 8	s-f	
1921	I 5	q-f	1959	I 3	3	
1922	I 13	3	1960	I 5	3	
1923	I 13	s-f	1961	I 5	q-f	
1924	I 10	3	1962	I 9	s-f	
1925	I 18	3	1963	I 10	2	
1926	I 5	1	1964	I 11	q-f	
1927	I 2	1	1965	I 14	s-f	
1928	I 3	q-f	1966	I 13	2	
1929	I 3	q-f	1967	I 10	1	
1930	I 2	3	1968	I 17R	1	
1931	I 3	Final	1969	II 1P	1	
1932	I 1C	q-f	1970	I 11	q-f	
1933	I 2	Final	1971	I 9	3	
1934	I 2	s-f	1972	I 10	q-f	
			1973	I 8	4	

P – promoted
R – relegated
C – Champions

PARTICK THISTLE

Founded: 1876
Address: Firhill Park, Glasgow
Telephone: 041-946 2673
Ground capacity: 36,000 (3,500 seated)
Playing area: 110 by 71 yards
Record attendance: 49,838 v Rangers, Division I, 18.2.22
Record victory: 16-0 v Royal Albert, Scottish Cup 1st round, 17.1.31
Record defeat: 1-10 v Dunfermline Athletic, Division I, 1958-59
Most League points: 56, Division II, 1970-71
Most League goals: 91, Division I, 1928-29
League scoring record: 41, Alec Hair, Division I, 1926-27
Most capped player: 9, John McKenzie, Scotland

Scottish Cup	Year	Opponents	Score	Scorers
Winners	1921	Rangers	1-0	Blair
Runners-up	1930	Rangers	0-0	
		Replay	1-2	Torbet
Scottish League Cup				
Winners	1972	Celtic	4-1	Rae, Lawrie, McQuade, Bone
Runners-up	1954	East Fife	2-3	Walker, McKenzie
	1957	Celtic	0-0	
		Replay	0-3	
	1959	Hearts	1-5	Smith

THE PARTICK RECORD

	Division & place	Cup round reached
1894	II 5	p
1895	II 7	p
1896	II 6	p
1897	II 1P	1
1898	I 8	1
1899	I 9R	q-f
1900	II 1P	q-f
1901	I 11R	1
1902	II 2P	1
1903	I 8	q-f
1904	I 7	1
1905	I 6	q-f
1906	I 5	2
1907	I 14	1
1908	I 15	2
1909	I 18	2
1910	I 16	1
1911	I 4	2
1912	I 5	1
1913	I 17	3
1914	I 15	q-f
1915	I 8	
1916	I 5	
1917	I 9	
1918	I 6	
1919	I 4	
1920	I 13	3
1921	I 6	Winners
1922	I 6	s-f
1923	I 11	1
1924	I 8	q-f
1925	I 7	3
1926	I 14	3
1927	I 11	s-f
1928	I 7	q-f
1929	I 6	2
1930	I 6	Final
1931	I 4	2
1932	I 6	q-f
1933	I 10	3
1934	I 13	2
1935	I 13	2
1936	I 9	1
1937	I 13	3
1938	I 7	3
1939	I 11	1
1947	I 5	1
1948	I 3	3
1949	I 11	q-f
1950	I 7	s-f
1951	I 6	1
1952	I 6	1
1953	I 9	2
1954	I 3	q-f
1955	I 9	5
1956	I 9	q-f
1957	I 8	5
1958	I 6	2
1959	I 9	3
1960	I 10	q-f
1961	I 11	3
1962	I 7	2
1963	I 3	3
1964	I 7	3
1965	I 11	2
1966	I 12	1
1967	I 12	2
1968	I 10	q-f
1969	I 14	1
1970	I 18R	1
1971	II 1P	3
1972	I 7	3
1973	I 13	q-f

P – promoted
R – relegated
p – preliminary round

QUEEN OF THE SOUTH

Founded: 1919
Address: Palmerston Park, Dumfries
Telephone: Dumfries 4853
Ground capacity: 24,000 (1,500 seated)
Record attendance: 25,000 v Hearts, Scottish Cup 3rd round, 23.2.52
Record victory: 11-1 v Stranraer, Scottish Cup 1st round, 16.1.32
Record defeat: 2-10 v Dundee, Division I, 1.12.62
Most League points: 53, Division II, 1961-62
Most League goals: 94, Division II, 1959-60
League scoring record: 26, Jim Patterson, Division I, 1955-56
Most capped player: 3, Billy Houliston, Scotland

THE QUEEN OF THE SOUTH RECORD

	Division & place	Cup round reached
1926	II 17	1
1927	II 11	1
1928	II 12	1
1929	II 9	2
1930	II 7	2
1931	II 5	1
1932	II 9	2
1933	II 2P	1
1934	I 4	q-f
1935	I 17	1
1936	I 15	3
1937	I 18	q-f
1938	I 16	2
1939	I 6	q-f
1947	I 12	1
1948	I 13	3
1949	I 10	2
1950	I 15R	s-f
1951	II 1P	1
1952	I 10	3
1953	I 10	q-f
1954	I 10	3
1955	I 13	5
1956	I 6	q-f
1957	I 16	5
1958	I 15	q-f
1959	I 18R	1
1960	II 3	3
1961	II 5	2
1962	II 2P	2
1963	I 15	q-f
1964	I 17R	2
1965	II 3	1
1966	II 3	2
1967	II 9	1
1968	II 6	2
1969	II 5	1
1970	II 3	1
1971	II 11	3
1972	II 7	3
1973	II 11	3

P – promoted
R – relegated

Below Queen of the South defend at their impressive Palmerston Park stadium.
Right Queen's Park can never hope to fill their home at Hampden Park.

QUEEN'S PARK

Founded: 1867
Address: Hampden Park, Glasgow
Telephone: 041 632 1275/4090
Ground capacity: 135,000
Record attendance: 97,000 v Rangers, Scottish Cup 2nd round, 18.2.33
(*Ground record:* 149,547, Scotland v England, 17.4.37)
Record victory: 16-0 v St Peter's, Scottish Cup 1st round, 1885-86
Record defeat: 0-9 v Motherwell, Division I, 26.4.30
Most League points: 57, Division II, 1922-23
Most League goals: 100, Division I, 1928-29
League scoring record: 30, Willie Martin, Division I, 1937-38
Most capped player: 14, Watty Arnott, Scotland

Scottish Cup

	Year	Opponents	Score
Winners	1874	Clydesdale	2-0
	1875	Renton	3-0
	1876	Third Lanark	1-1
	Replay		2-0
	1880	Thornlibank	3-0
	*1881	Dumbarton	3-1
	1882	Dumbarton	2-2
	Replay		4-1
	†1884	Vale of Leven	
	1886	Renton	3-1
	1890	Vale of Leven	1-1
	Replay		2-1
	1893	Celtic	2-1
Runners-up	‡1892	Celtic	1-5
	1900	Celtic	3-4

*After a protested game which Queen's Park won 2-1
†Queen's Park awarded the cup after Vale of Leven failed to appear
‡After protested game which Celtic won 1-0

FA Cup

			Score	Scorer
Runners-up	1884	Blackburn Rovers	1-2	Christie
	1885	Blackburn Rovers	0-2	

THE QUEEN'S PARK RECORD

Division & place	Cup round reached
1872	(s-f†)
1873	(s-f†)
1874	Winners
1875	Winners
1876	Winners
1877	q-f (3†)
1878	3 (1†)
1879	q-f
1880	Winners
1881	Winners
1882	Winners
1883	q-f
1884	Winners (Final†)
1885	3 (Final†)
1886	Winners
1887	s-f
1888	s-f
1889	3
1890	Winners
1891	q-f
1892	Final
1893	Winners
1894	s-f
1895	1
1896	q-f
1897	1
1898	q-f
1899	q-f
1900	Final

Year	Division & place	Cup round reached
1901	I 8	2
1902	I 8	q-f
1903	I 10	1
1904	I 8	1
1905	I 12	1
1906	I 16	2
1907	I 15	s-f
1908	I 16	q-f
1909	I 15	q-f
1910	I 14	q-f
1911	I 18	2
1912	I 17	p
1913	I 18	3
1914	I 16	q-f
1915	I 20	
1916	I 18	
1917	I 18	
1918	I 7	
1919	I 8	
1920	I 12	3
1921	I 19	1
1922	I 21R	2
1923	II 1P	3
1924	I 17	3
1925	I 17	2
1926	I 13	2
1927	I 12	2
1928	I 16	s-f
1929	I 5	2
1930	I 15	1
1931	I 13	2
1932	I 16	2
1933	I 9	2
1934	I 15	2
1935	I 12	2
1936	I 14	1
1937	I 15	2
1938	I 12	2
1939	I 19	2
1947	I 13	3
1948	I 16R	3
1949	II 5	1
1950	II 9	1
1951	II 6	2
1952	II 15	2
1953	II 3	2
1954	II 10	1
1955	II 4	4
1956	II 1P	6
1957	I 13	6
1958	I 18R	3
1959	II 18	2
1960	II 11	3
1961	II 15	1
1962	II 12	1
1963	II 14	3
1964	II 7	2
1965	II 4	2
1966	II 13	1
1967	II 7	q-f
1968	II 4	p
1969	II 11	1
1970	II 15	p
1971	II 14	3
1972	II 12	2
1973	II 14	2

P—promoted
R—relegated
p—preliminary round
(†)—progress in the FA Cup

RAITH ROVERS

Founded: 1883
Address: Stark's Park, Pratt Street, Kirkcaldy, Fife
Telephone: Kirkcaldy 3514
Ground capacity: 35,000
Record attendance: 32,000 v Hearts, Scottish Cup 2nd round, 7.2.53
Record victory: 10-1 v Coldstream, Scottish Cup 2nd round, 13.2.54
Record defeat: 1-11 v Morton, Division II, 1935-36
Most League points: 59, Division II, 1937-38
Most League goals: 142, Division II, 1937-38
League scoring record: 35, Willie Penman, Division II, 1948-49
Most capped player: 6, Dave Morris, Scotland

Scottish Cup

	Year	Opponents	Score
Runners-up	1913	Falkirk	0-2

Scottish League Cup

	Year	Opponents	Score
Runners-up	1949	Rangers	0-2

THE RAITH ROVERS RECORD

Division & place	Cup round reached
1903	II 11	p
1904	II 5	p
1905	II 10	p
1906	II 8	p
1907	II 9	q-f
1908	II 1	q-f
1909	II 2	p
1910	II 2P	p
1911	I 15	p
1912	I 14	1
1913	I 16	Final
1914	I 11	3
1915	I 19	
1916	I 20	
1917	I 19	
1918	*	
1919	*	
1920	I 19	3
1921	I 16	1
1922	I 3	1
1923	I 9	q-f
1924	I 4	3
1925	I 9	3
1926	I 19R	2
1927	II 2P	1
1928	I 17	2
1929	I 20R	q-f
1930	II 5	1
1931	II 4	1
1932	II 3	2
1933	II 6	1
1934	II 8	1
1935	II 13	2

Year	Division & place	Cup round reached
1936	II 17	1
1937	II 8	1
1938	II 1P	q-f
1939	I 20R	1
1947	II 6	3
1948	II 4	3
1949	II 1P	2
1950	I 9	q-f
1951	I 8	s-f
1952	I 5	2
1953	I 12	2
1954	I 12	3
1955	I 14	6
1956	I 11	s-f
1957	I 4	s-f
1958	I 7	2
1959	I 14	1
1960	I 11	1
1961	I 16	3
1962	I 13	3
1963	I 18R	s-f
1964	II 10	1
1965	II 13	p
1966	II 5	p
1967	II 2P	1
1968	I 16	1
1969	I 16	1
1970	I 17R	1
1971	II 8	
1972	II 11	5
1973	II 3	3

p—preliminary rounds
P—promoted
R—relegated
*Raith Rovers did not compete

RANGERS

Founded: 1873
Address: Ibrox Stadium, Glasgow SW1
Telephone: (041) 427 0159
Ground capacity: 95,000 (10,125 seated)
Record attendance: 118,567 v Celtic, Division I, 2.1.39
Record victory: 14-2 v Blairgowrie, Scottish Cup 1st round, 20.1.34
Record defeat: 1-7 v Celtic, Scottish League Cup final, 19.10.57
Most League points: 76, Division I, 1920-21
Most League goals: 118, Division I, 1931-32 & 1933-34
League scoring record: 44, Sam English, Division I, 1931-32
Record League aggregate: 233, Bob McPhail, 1927-1939
Most League appearances: 492, Davie Meiklejohn, 1920-1936
Most capped player: 53, George Young, Scotland

Scottish Cup

	Year	Opponents	Score	Scorers
Winners	1894	Celtic	3-1	McCreadie, Barker, McPherson
	1897	Dumbarton	5-1	Miller, Hyslop, McPherson 2, Smith
	1898	Kilmarnock	2-0	Smith, Hamilton
	1903	Heart of Midlothian	1-1	
			0-0	
			2-0	Mackie, Campbell
	1928	Celtic	4-0	Meiklejohn (pen), McPhail, Archibald 2
	1930	Partick Thistle	0-0	
			2-1	Marshall, Craig
	1932	Kilmarnock	1-1	McPhail
			3-0	Fleming, McPhail, English
	1934	St Mirren	5-0	Nicholson 2, McPhail, Smith, Main
	1935	Hamilton	2-1	Smith 2
	1936	Third Lanark	1-0	McPhail
	1948	Morton	1-1	Gillick
			1-0	Williamson
	1949	Clyde	4-1	Young (2 pens), Williamson, Duncanson
	1950	East Fife	3-0	Findlay, Thornton 2
	1953	Aberdeen	1-1	Prentice
			1-0	Simpson
	1960	Kilmarnock	2-0	Millar 2
	1962	St Mirren	2-0	Brand, Wilson
	1963	Celtic	1-1	Brand
			3-0	Wilson, Brand 2
	1964	Dundee	3-1	Millar 2, Brand
	1966	Celtic	0-0	
			1-0	Johansen
	1973	Celtic	3-2	Parlane, Conn, Forsyth
Runners-up	1877	Vale of Leven	0-0	
			1-1	
			2-3	Campbell, McNeil
	1879	Vale of Leven	*1-1	Struthers
	1899	Celtic	0-2	
	1904	Celtic	2-3	Speedie 2
	1905	Third Lanark	0-0	
			1-3	
	1909	Celtic	2-2	Gilchrist, Bennett
			†1-1	Gordon
	1921	Partick Thistle	0-1	
	1922	Morton	0-1	
	1929	Kilmarnock	0-2	
	1969	Celtic	0-4	
	1971	Celtic	1-1	Johnstone
			1-2	og

Scottish League Cup

	Year	Opponents	Score	Scorers
Winners	1947	Aberdeen	4-0	Duncanson 2, Williamson, Gillick
	1949	Raith Rovers	2-0	Gillick, Paton
	1961	Kilmarnock	2-0	Brand, Scott
	1962	Heart of Midlothian	1-1	Millar
			3-1	Millar, Brand, McMillan
	1964	Morton	5-0	Forrest 4, Willoughby
	1965	Celtic	2-1	Forrest 2
	1971	Celtic	1-0	Johnstone
Runners-up	1952	Dundee	2-3	Findlay, Thornton
	1958	Celtic	1-7	Simpson
	1966	Celtic	1-2	og
	1967	Celtic	0-1	

*Vale of Leven awarded the Cup after Rangers failed to appear for replay
†trophy withheld after riots

THE RANGERS RECORD

	Division & place	Cup round reached
1875		2
1876		2
1877		Final
1878		4
1879		Final
1880		1
1881		q-f
1882		q-f
1883		2
1884		s-f
1885		q-f
1886		1
1887		3
1888		2
1889		2
1890		3
1891	I 1†	1
1892	I 4	4
1893	I 2	3
1894	I 4	Winners
1895	I 3	1
1896	I 2	3
1897	I 3	Winners
1898	I 2	Winners
1899	I 1C	Final
1900	I 1C	s-f
1901	I 1C	1
1902	I 1C	s-f
1903	I 3	Winners
1904	I 4	Final
1905	I 2	Final
1906	I 4	3
1907	I 3	3
1908	I 3	2
1909	I 4	Final
1910	I 3	2
1911	I 1C	3
1912	I 1C	2
1913	I 1C	3
1914	I 2	3
1915	I 3	
1916	I 2	
1917	I 3	
1918	I 1C	
1919	I 2	
1920	I 1C	s-f
1921	I 1C	Final
1922	I 2	Final
1923	I 1C	2
1924	I 1C	3
1925	I 1C	s-f
1926	I 6	s-f
1927	I 1C	q-f
1928*	I 1C	Winners
1929	I 1C	Final
1930*	I 1C	Winners
1931	I 1C	2
1932	I 2	Winners
1933	I 1C	3
1934*	I 1C	Winners
1935*	I 1C	Winners
1936	I 2	Winners
1937	I 1C	1
1938	I 3	s-f
1939	I 1C	3
1947	I 1C	3
1948	I 2	
1949*	I 1C	Winners
1950*	I 1C	Winners
1951	I 2	2
1952	I 2	q-f
1953*	I 1C	Winners
1954	I 4	s-f
1955	I 3	6
1956	I 1C	q-f
1957	I 1C	6
1958	I 2	s-f
1959	I 1C	3
1960	I 3	Winners
1961	I 1C	3
1962	I 2	Winners
1963*	I 1C	Winners
1964*	I 1C	Winners
1965	I 5	q-f
1966	I 2	Winners
1967	I 2	1
1968	I 2	q-f
1969	I 2	Final
1970	I 2	q-f
1971	I 4	Final
1972	I 3	s-f
1973	I 2	Winners

C — Scottish League Champions
† Joint champions
*League and Cup double

Willie Thornton, inherited by manager and former team-mate Willie Waddell as his assistant manager in 1969.

ST JOHNSTONE

Founded: 1884
Address: Muirton Park, Perth
Telephone: Perth 26961
Ground capacity: 28,000 (2,500 seated)
Playing area: 115 by 74 yards
Record attendance: 29,972 v Dundee, Scottish Cup 2nd round, 10.2.52
Record victory: 8-1 v Partick Thistle, Scottish League Cup, 16.8.69
Record defeat: 1-10 v Third Lanark, Scottish Cup 1st round, 24.1.03
Most League points: 56, Division II, 1923-24
Most League goals: 102, Division II, 1931-32
League scoring record: 28, John Munro, 1926-27
28, Andrew McCall, 1936-37
Most capped player: 2, Alex McLaren, Scotland

Scottish League Cup

	Year	Opponents	Score
Runners-up	1970	Celtic	0-1

THE ST JOHNSTONE RECORD

Year	Division & place	Cup round reached
1912	II 5	1
1913	II 11	3
1914	II 5	1
1915	II 8	
1916		
1917		
1918		
1919		
1920		2
1921		p
1922	II 13	1
1923	II 3	1
1924	II 1P	2
1925	I 11	1
1926	I 18	3
1927	I 14	1
1928	I 11	1
1929	I 9	2
1930	I 20R	2
1931	II 6	2
1932	II 2P	2
1933	I 5	3
1934	I 9	s-f
1935	I 5	q-f
1936	I 7	3
1937	I 12	2
1938	I 8	2
1939	I 8	1
1947	II 9	1
1948	II 9	2
1949	II 6	1
1950	II 3	2
1951	II 5	2
1952	II 11	2
1953	II 14	2
1954	II 6	1
1955	II 7	6
1956	II 3	5
1957	II 12	5
1958	II 11	2
1959	II 6	3
1960	II 1P	1
1961	I 15	1
1962	I 17R	2
1963	II 1P	2
1964	I 13	2
1965	I 13	2
1966	I 14	q-f
1967	I 15	2
1968	I 14	s-f
1969	I 6	q-f
1970	I 13	1
1971	I 3	3
1972	I 8	3
1973	I 11	3

P—promoted
R—relegated
p—preliminary round

ST MIRREN

Founded: 1876
Address: St Mirren Park, Love Street, Paisley, Renfrewshire
Telephone: 041 889 2558
Ground capacity: 46,500 (1,500 seated)
Playing area: 112 by 75 yards
Record attendance: 47,428 v Celtic, Scottish Cup 4th round, 7.3.25
Record victory: 15-0 v Glasgow University, Scottish Cup 1st round, 30.1.60
Record defeat: 2-9 v Dundee, Division I, 29.2.64
Most League points: 62, Division II, 1967-68
Most League goals: 114, Division II, 1935-36
League scoring record: 45, Dunky Walker, Division I, 1921-22
Most capped player: 6, Tommy Jackson, Scotland

Scottish Cup

	Year	Opponents	Score	Scorers
Winners	1926	Celtic	2-0	McCrae, Harrison
	1959	Aberdeen	3-1	Bryceland, Miller, Baker
Runners-up	1908	Celtic	1-5	Cunningham
	1934	Rangers	0-5	
	1962	Rangers	0-2	

Scottish League Cup

	Year	Opponents	Score	Scorers
Runners-up	1956	Aberdeen	1-2	Holmes

THE ST MIRREN RECORD

Year	Division & place	Cup round reached
1891	I 8	5
1892	I 10	1
1893	I 3	q-f
1894	I 6	2
1895	I 5	2
1896	I 8	2
1897	I 6	2
1898	I 6	2
1899	I 5	2
1900	I 8	1
1901	I 9	s-f
1902	I 5	s-f
1903	I 6	1
1904	I 6	q-f
1905	I 10	q-f
1906	I 8	s-f
1907	I 7	q-f
1908	I 7	Final
1909	I 7	q-f
1910	I 13	2
1911	I 12	1
1912	I 18	1
1913	I 12	q-f
1914	I 20	s-f
1915	I 9	
1916	I 17	
1917	I 7	
1918	I 11	
1919	I 11	
1920	I 14	2
1921	I 22	1
1922	I 8	q-f
1923	I 6	2
1924	I 6	2
1925	I 6	q-f
1926	I 4	Winners
1927	I 10	2
1928	I 6	3
1929	I 8	s-f
1930	I 5	q-f
1931	I 15	s-f
1932	I 5	1
1933	I 7	2
1934	I 17	Final
1935	I 19R	3
1936	II 2P	3
1937	I 16	q-f
1938	I 14	2
1939	I 18	3
1947	I 14	1
1948	I 5	q-f
1949	I 9	2
1950	I 11	1
1951	I 11	1
1952	I 14	2
1953	I 6	2
1954	I 11	1
1955	I 6	5
1956	I 15	6
1957	I 12	q-f
1958	I 13	2
1959	I 7	Winners
1960	I 14	2
1961	I 14	s-f
1962	I 16	Final
1963	I 12	q-f
1964	I 12	3
1965	I 15	1
1966	I 16	1
1967	I 17R	2
1968	II 1P	1
1969	I 11	2
1970	I 15	2
1971	I 17R	4
1972	II 4	4
1973	II 5	3

P—promoted
R—relegated

Left Rangers' Scottish international Willie Johnston climbs prodigiously to challenge Aberdeen's goalkeeper Georgehan and his covering defenders.
Below No love lost at Love Street, the home of St Mirren. The St Mirren defence is put at full stretch by the threat of two hovering Rangers forwards.

STENHOUSEMUIR

Founded: 1884
Address: Ochilview Park, Stenhousemuir, Scotland
Telephone: Larbert 2992
Ground capacity: 16,000 (500 seated)
Record attendance: 13,000 v East Fife, Scottish Cup 4th round, 11.3.50
Record victory: 9-2 v Dundee United, Division II, 1936-37
Record defeat: 2-11 v Dunfermline Athletic, Division II, 1930-31
Most League points: 50, Division II, 1960-61
Most League goals: 99, Division II, 1960-61

THE STENHOUSEMUIR RECORD			1950	II 12	q-f
	Division	*Cup round*	1951	II 15	1
	& place	*reached*	1952	II 13	1
1922	II 10	1	1953	II 12	1
1923	II 14	1	1954	II 4	1
1924	II 4	2	1955	II 6	5
1925	II 11	1	1956	II 5	q-f
1926	II 5	2	1957	II 14	5
1927	II 10	1	1958	II 16	2
1928	II 16	2	1959	II 3	2
1929	II 18	2	1960	II 5	3
1930	II 17	1	1961	II 3	1
1931	II 17	1	1962	II 15	3
1932	II 4	1	1963	II 16	1
1933	II 4	q-f	1964	II 11	1
1934	II 4	1	1965	II 15	1
1935	II 5	1	1966	II 18	p
1936	II 11	2	1967	II 17	p
1937	II 10	1	1968	II 18	p
1938	II 8	2	1969	II 19	1
1939	II 8	1	1970	II 16	p
1947	II 7	1	1971	II 10	2
1948	II 14	1	1972	II 14	1
1949	II 12	q-f	1973	II 10	2
				p — preliminary round	

STIRLING ALBION

Founded: 1945
Address: Annfield Park, Stirling
Telephone: Stirling 3584
Ground capacity: 25,000 (900 seated)
Record attendance: 26,400 v Celtic, Scottish Cup, 4th round, 14.3.59
Record victory: 7-0 v Albion Rovers, Division II, 1947-48
7-0 v Montrose, Division II, 1957-58
7-0 v St Mirren, Division I, 1959-60
7-0 v Arbroath, Division II, 1960-61
Record defeat: 0-9 v Dundee United, Division I, 30.12.67
Most League points: 59, Division II, 1964-65
Most League goals: 105, Division II, 1957-58
League scoring record: 22, Bobby Gilmour, Division I, 1958-59
Most capped player: None

THE STIRLING ALBION RECORD			1959	I 12	q-f
			1960	I 17R	2
	Division	*Cup round*	1961	II 1P	1
	& place	*reached*	1962	I 18R	q-f
1947		p	1963	II 10	1
1948	II 8	2	1964	II 19	1
1949	II 2P	1	1965	II 1P	q-f
1950	I 16R	q-f	1966	I 15	2
1951	II 2P	1	1967	I 16	1
1952	I 16R	2	1968	I 18R	1
1953	II 1P	2	1969	II 4	1
1954	I 14	3	1970	II 4	1
1955	I 16	5	1971	II 12	4
1956	I 18R	6	1972	II 3	2
1957	II 8	5	1973	II 4	4
1958	II 1P	2			

STRANRAER

Founded: 1870
Address: Stair Park, Stranraer, Wigtownshire, Scotland
Telephone: Stranraer 3271
Ground capacity: 5,000
Record attendance: 6,500 v Rangers, Scottish Cup 1st round, 24.1.48
Record victory: 7-0 v Brechin City, Division II, 1964-65
Record defeat: 1-11 v Queen of the South, Scottish Cup 1st round, 1931-32
Most League points: 44, Division II, 1960-61 and 1971-72
Most League goals: 83, Division II, 1960-61
Most capped player: None

THE STRANRAER RECORD			1963	II 5	1
			1964	II 8	2
	Division	*Cup round*	1965	II 6	p
	& place	*reached*	1966	II 15	1
1956	II 12	4	1967	II 15	p
1957	II 7	5	1968	II 19	p
1958	II 18	2	1969	II 8	2
1959	II 16	2	1970	II 17	1
1960	II 17	1	1971	II 9	3
1961	II 4	2	1972	II 6	2
1962	II 7	3	1973	II 15	4
				p—preliminary round	

Stranraer entertain their old rivals Queen of the South in 1972 at their Stair Park ground, the most southern outpost in senior football in Scotland.

The Home Countries

Does charity begin at home?

Below This goal by player-manager Terry Neill in 1972 gave Ireland only their second win over England since the War. But perhaps more important to Irish football than the prestige of victory was the Irish FA's cut of television rights and the large Wembley gate.
Right Midfield rivals Billy Bremner and Peter Storey in a tense moment in England's 1-0 win over Scotland in 1972. For Scotsmen, the annual encounter with England was still the highlight of the season.

'It's got to the stage where apart from the England-Scotland game nobody wants to know. The whole thing is a relic from the past. It's out of date, and let's face it, it ought to be scrapped.'

The view of that former First Division manager on the Home International Championship was one which was becoming more and more widespread even before the tournament was moved into eight days at the end of the season in 1968-69. There was a strong feeling among Englishmen and some Scots that it was obsolete and, far worse, irrelevant.

The recent developments in football had meant that the disparity between England and Scotland and the other two associations had grown even wider; and, though the brave fights put up by the Welsh and the Irish against their privileged enemies have always possessed some of the romance of giant-killing, the actual facts of life over the years offer little defence or comfort.

Northern Ireland's victory at Wembley in 1972 was only her second over England since the War —and in that time Wales had beaten England just once, in 1955.

FIFA threaten to end the Home Championship

The disparity had, of course, always been there—England beat Ireland 13-0 when the countries first met, in 1882—and Ireland's only outright success in the Championship was in 1913-14, and then without gaining the full six points. Wales last won it outright in 1937 and England and Scotland had a share in all but eight of the first 77 contests.

In any reassessment of the Championship, it has to be remembered that, for many years, it provided the only means of international expression for Scotland, Wales and Ireland. England had been playing foreign opposition in full internationals for 22 years when Scotland first ventured outside the fold to play France in 1930. Wales followed suit three years later, but they managed only two games before the War, and in Belfast the decision was not taken until 1951. So, for a very long time, the Home Championship *was* international football in these quarters.

But in 1974 it looked increasingly likely that the old situation would return, whether the Home Countries decided that way or not. Sections of both the South American and the Afro-Asian blocks in FIFA were campaigning strongly for the United Kingdom's representation both in

FIFA and the World Cup qualifying rounds to be cut from four to one, thus virtually eliminating each of the Home Countries as an individual international force. And it was certain that the main outcome in that event, a unified United Kingdom team, would not exactly be unacceptable to many of the game's leading figures in England, if nowhere else in the British Isles.

The Home International Championship started in 1884, when the Ireland-Scotland fixture, arranged two years earlier, completed the six-match circle. England and Scotland had already been playing for 14 years, officially for 12, and the Scots continued the dominance they had established in that period. Between 1874 and 1883 England

managed only one win over Scotland, and suffered three crushing defeats. The Scots, ahead in the development of tactics and the passing game, won four outright titles in the first seven years.

England, reaping the rewards from the legalising of professionalism, then took over, with seven clear wins in 11 years. Ireland, with their first win over Scotland, shared the honours in 1903, but it was Wales in 1906-07, who first really broke the duopoly.

A win over Scotland at Wrexham, a draw at Fulham and a 3-2 victory over Ireland in Belfast gave them the five points, and their outright title was assured when Scotland held England 1-1 at Newcastle.

Ireland's turn came in 1914. The

pinnacle of their season came on 14 February at Middlesbrough, when they proved the previous season's shock 2-1 win over England in Belfast was no fluke by winning 3-0 with Billy Gillespie of Sheffield United scoring a magnificent second goal. The Irish had never beaten Wales or England away and now, while still not able to call on all their best players, they accomplished both feats in one season.

The tournament still provides some classic games

It was a remarkable swansong for Ireland. By the time football began again after the First World War the civil war that had been brewing had boiled over and there was never to be a genuinely united Irish team again. It was not, however, until after the next War that the practice of the North choosing players from the Irish Free State for Championship matches finally ceased.

England had made a relatively small impact between the Wars— winning outright only in 1930, 1932 and 1938—but when the Championship restarted in 1946 they and then Scotland started to pull away. Wales, who had won six clear titles between 1920 and 1937, were now struggling to hold their own, despite discovering a mine of talent down at Swansea. In the next quarter-century

SUMMARY OF HOME INTERNATIONALS

	†First match	Matches played
England v Scotland	1872	90
Scotland v Wales	1876	86
England v Wales	1879	83
England v Ireland	1882	80
Wales v Ireland	1882	80
Scotland v Ireland	1884	78

Wins	Goals
England 33, Scotland 35, drawn 22	England 161, Scotland 156
Scotland 52, Wales 15, drawn 19	Scotland 221, Wales 39
England 55, Wales 11, drawn 17	England 223, Wales 78
England 62, Ireland 6, drawn 12	England 288, Ireland 77
Wales 37, Ireland 25, drawn 18	Wales 171, Ireland 121
Scotland 55, Ireland 12, drawn 11	Scotland 238, Ireland 74

Correct to the end of 1972-73 season.
†The championship itself did not start until 1883-84

SYNDICATION INTERNATIONAL

neither they nor the Irish ever looked likely champions.

The outright titles all went to England (12) and Scotland (5). The great games between them were all at Wembley: 7-2 to England in 1955, the 9-3 thrashing of 1961, and Scotland's 3-2 win over the world champions in 1967—a match of much drama, but little genuine importance.

The 1955 game is best remembered for the four goals scored by Dennis Wilshaw. This was not, however, a record for the Championship: Joe Bambrick had managed six in Northern Ireland's 7-0 win over Wales in February 1930. Bambrick's feat was all the odder for the fact that Ireland scored only one more goal and obtained not a single point in their other two games that season.

By the late sixties the only fixture that commanded real interest was England versus Scotland. But the Championship as a whole—despite its use as a qualifying group for the European Championship in 1966-68 (it had been used for the World Cup in 1950 and 1954)—was fast becoming an anachronism.

With an increasing number of sides involved in Europe, the League clubs (after EUFA had discarded the use of the Home Championship as a qualifying tournament) protested at the swelling number of internationals England played during the season. In 1968 the League's agreement with the FA stated that this figure should not exceed four and this left Alf Ramsey on a very tight rein indeed.

An unwanted chore or a financial necessity?

The reaction of Ramsey and the FA was understandable if drastic—they suggested the abolition of the Home Internationals, rather than allow England to be left out of European competition. The other three associations predictably fought that idea, and the compromise suggestion was to play the tournament in eight days *after* the end of the season. The Irish and Welsh were not keen, but assurances that all their players would be released by the clubs helped to persuade them—assurances which, with English clubs involved in vital European games, eventually proved to be somewhat shallow. The continuation of the Championship was vital to the Irish and Welsh FAs simply on financial terms. They survive on the money they make from these games —which in a good season will come to nearly three-quarters of their total income. To abolish the Home Internationals would be virtually to abolish the Welsh and Irish Associations.

Even with blanket television coverage offering Ireland and Wales considerable compensation, the experiment was not a success. Attendances at Wembley were healthy, but on a rain-soaked evening only 8,000 paid at Hampden to see Scotland and Northern Ireland draw 1-1; and the millions who watched on television saw a game totally devoid of international flavour, atmosphere—or class.

The system was retained, though it was rather an embarrassment. In the next few years the closing stages of European competitions and the postponement of vital League games meant that players who had already played 50 or more matches still had pressing engagements—or so their clubs would reasonably claim. For some English players and managers, the Home Internationals, squeezed into eight days around the time of the Cup Final and European semi-finals, was little more than a nuisance. The television companies and most of the press battled hopefully to inject enthusiasm, to make out it was one of the great annual events in football, but for all that it was increasingly a tired anti-climax.

Would it keep going on in its solid tradition? There was not much else to help it. It was pointless pretending, certainly for England and possibly for Scotland, that playing Wales and Ireland was adequate preparation for the rigours of world-class competition. It had become a duty, like spending Christmas with relations. But then if charity begins at home . . .

Perfidious Albion

Above *Bobby Moore, at the ready to meet a Scottish raid at Hampden.*
Above right *Spurs forward George Robb (extreme left), playing his first and last game for England. He probably owed his cap to a campaign by the London press. With Alf Ramsey's appointment, selection was taken out of the hands of the Selection Committee, and the press was powerless to influence the choice of the team.*
Below right *Rodney Marsh suggesting, perhaps, that the Scots' idea of ten yards is a bit on the short side.*

'The Football Association requires applications from young men who would be prepared to play in an international match against Scotland in Glasgow on November 23.' Imagine the effect of that in the small ad column of a daily paper!

The applications would begin pouring in at once—not only from Bobby Moore, Malcolm Macdonald and Mick Channon, but from every Fourth Division reserve and public parks amateur—and then the task of choosing the final team would begin.

This massive labour would be accomplished single-handed by the FA Secretary. He would consult nobody and select himself as captain of the side. And, because FA funds would be low, he would suddenly find himself wondering how the visit to Scotland would be financed.

So there would be another newspaper advertisement, and a circular letter to every club in membership of the FA: 'Contributions are required from interested parties to pay the railway and hotel expenses of the England team to play Scotland.' Fantastic as it may seem, that

was exactly what happened when Charles Alcock, the FA Secretary, first put forward the idea of an England v Scotland match in 1872.

Today, over a century later, an international is planned more like a military operation. The players will meet at least four days in advance at a luxury hotel. When Sir Alf Ramsey is satisfied that all his party has arrived, they will dine with the FA Councillors appointed to accompany the team. Then they will retire early in preparation for training the following morning.

For the privilege of playing for England, the players will have all expenses paid, receive £100 for playing, and be entitled to a share of the revenue from the television companies. All they need to bring are their boots, a personal towel, and, of course, themselves. As one FA official put it: 'All we really need is a body. We provide the rest.'

How different it all was in the far-off days of the first international when, on a cold, wet, windy night in 1872, a group of officers and gentlemen gathered in the Royal Garrick

Hotel in Glasgow. Instead of the frugal glasses of orangeade or coca-cola, and the starchless main meals, they tucked into a gargantuan feast with all the gusto of men who had endured the rigours of a train journey from London.

It had been a journey with nothing of the cushioned plushness of a modern Inter-City line. Limbs ached from the buffeting on the wooden austerity of the seats, and the acrid smell of smoke had the travellers still heavy with catarrh.

The game itself ended in a scoreless draw, a surprising result for the Englishmen, who had arranged the fixture, in the words of the FA minutes, 'In order to further the interests of the Association in Scotland'. There was to be ample opportunity to regret the condescending tone of that statement.

In the next 19 years England were to beat Scotland only twice but at least the significance of those defeats was not lost on 'Pa' Jackson, assistant secretary of the FA, who determined that England should create a team on the Queen's Park pattern.

So, in 1882, Jackson formed his Corinthians from former public schools and university men and, in the next seven years, of the 88 players capped by England, '52 were Corinthians. On three occasions when the FA agreed to play Ireland and Wales on the same day, the entire Corinthians side was sent to represent England.

Yet the death of the Corinthians and the true-blue amateur tradition they represented was assured almost from birth. Professionalism was already taking root in the North, and by the end of the century it had completely changed the complexion of international football.

The FA, mainly through the influence of the perceptive Charles Alcock, bowed to the inevitable and, in 1885, James Forrest of Blackburn Rovers became the first acknowledged professional to play for England. Forrest's fee was 10 shillings per match—£99.50 less than the FA offered their players in 1974.

At the start of professionalism, the paid players were treated with suspicion, and the amateur captain would always dine alone to avoid being tainted. At one Birmingham hotel, the manager even asked for guarantees from the FA ensuring that they would pay for any damage caused by professional members of the England team.

But from the day of Forrest's arrival in 1885, the eventual disappearance of the amateur player from the international scene was inevitable. The odd exception, such as Bernard Joy of Casuals and later Arsenal, served only to prove the point.

The amateur player might have had his day, but the amateur administrator most certainly had not. The first England team manager, Walter Winterbottom, did not emerge until after the Second World War and, even then, he was never accorded the right of selection. Perhaps that was not surprising, for the whole process had been haphazard from the beginning.

After the strange 'volunteering' process which selected the team for the original match, clubs were asked by the FA to nominate men for the second. A series of trial matches was held, during which a small army of 71 players was whittled down to the final eleven. As a result, only three men survived from the first international to the second.

The International Selection Committee, later to hold so much sway, was not formed until 1888. Originally it was composed of seven men. This was increased to nine (six from the northern and midland clubs and three from the south) in 1897. The Committee expanded as the years went by. By the fifties there were over 30 members, who were split into sections, one responsible for full internationals, one for amateur internationals and one for youth internationals etc. It was not until Alf Ramsey took over in 1963 that the team selection for full and Under-23 internationals was taken out of the hands of a committee, but certain members still remained responsible for amateur internationals.

Players were not so much selected as voted for. A committee enthusiast from, for example, south-east London would report that he had seen a promising player with Millwall, then a Third Division club. If he could lobby enough support, his discovery would go in to the exclusion of an established star. If the system were still in operation today, it would be technically possible for Bobby Moore's place in the England team to go to the Workington centre-half, who had impressed in a Fourth Division match!

Caps were won with all the unpredictability of pools dividends. In 1923, Bromley, the London amateur club, had a promising centre-forward called Frank Osborne, a clerk at Thomas Cooks, the travel agents. Fulham persuaded the youngster to join them as an amateur and, within a month, he was playing for England against France in Paris.

'Of course I was proud,' recalled Osborne, years later when he was manager of Fulham, 'but the whole thing was crazy. I was not nearly ready. Today I would have had to wait six years for a cap.'

The statistics tell the whole story. In eleven seasons before the Second

War, England used 99 players; in the following eleven they used 145, 66 of whom never gained a second cap.

Ironically enough, there was much more continuity during the War itself when, with so many leading players serving abroad, the pool of stars available for internationals was restricted.

That meant that the same players —Swift, Scott, Hardwick, Denis and Leslie Compton, Soo, Franklin, Mercer, Matthews, Carter, Lawton, Finney—came up for selection time

after time. In a sense they were the harbingers of the squad system of the 1960s. This historic departure did not, however, set a formal pattern for the future. Sir Alf Ramsey later recalled that when he began playing for England in the 1950s he was barely introduced to his colleagues.

But at least there had been some measure of progress, and a further important step came later in the War when Sir Stanley Rous, later to become President of FIFA, proposed to the FA, of which he was then secretary, that England should have a team manager.

The choice fell upon Walter Winterbottom, a schoolteacher who had been centre-half for Manchester United. A man of charm and insight, Winterbottom was well qualified, but he was to learn unhappily that he had been given responsibility without power. Winterbottom was asked merely to coach and prepare players, while the actual selection remained firmly in the hands of the selection committee. To have a team manager was one thing, but to allow him the license to decide who should play for England was quite different.

It was in this pantomime atmosphere that England, grievously under-prepared, embarked on her first World Cup sortie to Brazil in 1950. The inglorious defeat at the hands of the USA was just one in a whole catalogue of disasters. Things had gone wrong from the very start when two of the England players— Matthews and Taylor—both missed the first game because they had been touring with an FA team in Canada when the England party arrived in Brazil.

That, however, was but one of Walter Winterbottom's problems. When the party took a dislike to the Brazilian food, he even found himself entrusted with the task of cooking. That defeat by the USA and Hungary's historic 6-3 win at Wembley three years later taught the FA what the world has long suspected—that the British were no longer the masters of football.

Something drastic should have been done, but the only significant change came during the 1954 World Cup when some of the senior players were invited to advise on team selection.

Preparations were still as chaotic as ever. The England party arrived in Sweden for the 1958 World Cup finals to find that no training camp had been laid on. The harassed Winterbottom, whose experience of World Cups seemed never less than horrific, was left to chase around for accommodation only days before the first game.

Chile was hardly any better. Incredibly, the England party travelled to the tournament without a team doctor, and the result was that Peter Swan fell ill and, after receiving the wrong treatment, almost died.

The man who has done more than anyone to create a professional and realistic environment within England's international soccer is, of course, Sir Alf Ramsey. As the successful and unequivocal manager of Ipswich, he did not need to seek the England job when Winterbottom lost, as he was bound to do, his vain battle against administrative incom-

PRESS ASSOCIATION

FULL INTERNATIONALS PLAYED BY ENGLAND 1870–JANUARY 1974

Date		Venue	Opponents	Score
*19 November	1870	Kennington Oval	Scotland	1-0
*28 February	1871	Kennington Oval	Scotland	1-1
*18 November	1871	Kennington Oval	Scotland	2-1
*24 February	1872	Kennington Oval	Scotland	1-0
30 November	1872	Glasgow	Scotland	0-0
8 March	1873	Kennington Oval	Scotland	4-2
7 March	1874	Glasgow	Scotland	1-2
6 March	1875	Kennington Oval	Scotland	2-2
4 March	1876	Glasgow	Scotland	0-3
3 March	1877	Kennington Oval	Scotland	1-3
2 March	1878	Glasgow	Scotland	2-7
18 January	1879	Kennington Oval	Wales	2-1
5 April	1879	Kennington Oval	Scotland	5-4
13 March	1880	Glasgow	Scotland	4-5
15 March	1880	Wrexham	Wales	3-2
26 February	1881	Blackburn	Wales	0-1
12 March	1881	Kennington Oval	Scotland	1-6
18 February	1882	Belfast	Ireland	13-0
11 March	1882	Glasgow	Scotland	1-5
13 March	1882	Wrexham	Wales	3-5
3 February	1883	Kennington Oval	Wales	5-0
24 February	1883	Liverpool	Ireland	7-0
10 March	1883	Sheffield	Scotland	2-3
23 February	1884	Belfast	Ireland	8-1
15 March	1884	Glasgow	Scotland	0-1
17 March	1884	Wrexham	Wales	4-0
28 February	1885	Manchester	Ireland	4-0
14 March	1885	Blackburn	Wales	1-1
21 March	1885	Kennington Oval	Scotland	1-1
13 March	1886	Belfast	Ireland	6-1
29 March	1886	Wrexham	Wales	3-1
31 March	1886	Glasgow	Scotland	1-1
5 February	1887	Sheffield	Ireland	7-0
26 February	1887	Kennington Oval	Wales	4-0
19 March	1887	Blackburn	Scotland	2-3
4 February	1888	Crewe	Wales	5-1
17 March	1888	Glasgow	Scotland	5-0
31 March	1888	Belfast	Ireland	5-1
23 February	1889	Stoke-on-Trent	Wales	4-1
2 March	1889	Everton	Ireland	6-1
13 April	1889	Kennington Oval	Scotland	2-3
†15 March	1890	Belfast	Ireland	9-1
†15 March	1890	Wrexham	Wales	3-1
5 April	1890	Glasgow	Scotland	1-1
† 7 March	1891	Sunderland	Wales	4-1
† 7 March	1891	Wolverhampton	Ireland	6-1
6 April	1891	Blackburn	Scotland	2-1
† 5 March	1892	Wrexham	Wales	2-0
† 5 March	1892	Belfast	Ireland	2-0
2 April	1892	Glasgow	Scotland	4-1
25 February	1893	Birmingham	Ireland	6-1
13 March	1893	Stoke-on-Trent	Wales	6-0
1 April	1893	Richmond	Scotland	5-2
3 March	1894	Belfast	Ireland	2-2
12 March	1894	Wrexham	Wales	5-1
7 April	1894	Glasgow	Scotland	2-2
9 March	1895	Derby	Ireland	9-0
18 March	1895	Queen's Club, Kensington	Wales	1-1
6 April	1895	Everton	Scotland	3-0
7 March	1896	Belfast	Ireland	2-0
16 March	1896	Cardiff	Wales	9-1
4 April	1896	Glasgow	Scotland	1-2
20 February	1897	Nottingham	Ireland	6-0
29 March	1897	Sheffield	Wales	4-0
3 April	1897	Crystal Palace	Scotland	1-2
5 March	1898	Belfast	Ireland	3-2
28 March	1898	Wrexham	Wales	3-0
2 April	1898	Glasgow	Scotland	3-1
18 February	1899	Sunderland	Ireland	13-2
20 March	1899	Bristol	Wales	4-1
8 April	1899	Birmingham	Scotland	2-1
17 March	1900	Dublin	Ireland	2-0
26 March	1900	Cardiff	Wales	1-1
7 April	1900	Glasgow	Scotland	1-4
9 March	1901	Southampton	Ireland	3-0
18 March	1901	Newcastle	Wales	6-0
30 March	1901	Crystal Palace	Scotland	2-2
3 March	1902	Wrexham	Wales	0-0
22 March	1902	Belfast	Ireland	1-0
‡ 5 April	1902	Glasgow	Scotland	1-1
3 May	1902	Birmingham	Scotland	2-2
14 February	1903	Wolverhampton	Ireland	4-0
2 March	1903	Portsmouth	Wales	2-1
4 April	1903	Sheffield	Scotland	1-2
29 February	1904	Wrexham	Wales	2-2
12 March	1904	Belfast	Ireland	3-1
9 April	1904	Glasgow	Scotland	1-0
25 February	1905	Middlesbrough	Ireland	1-1
27 March	1905	Liverpool	Wales	3-1
1 April	1905	Crystal Palace	Scotland	1-0
17 February	1906	Belfast	Ireland	5-0
19 March	1906	Cardiff	Wales	1-0
7 April	1906	Glasgow	Scotland	1-2
16 February	1907	Everton	Ireland	1-0
18 March	1907	Fulham	Wales	1-1
6 April	1907	Newcastle	Scotland	1-1
15 February	1908	Belfast	Ireland	3-1
16 March	1908	Wrexham	Wales	7-1
4 April	1908	Glasgow	Scotland	1-1
6 June	1908	Vienna	Austria	6-1
8 June	1908	Vienna	Austria	11-1
10 June	1908	Budapest	Hungary	7-0
13 June	1908	Prague	Bohemia	4-0
13 February	1909	Bradford	Ireland	4-0
15 March	1909	Nottingham	Wales	2-0
3 April	1909	Crystal Palace	Scotland	2-0
29 May	1909	Budapest	Hungary	4-2
31 May	1909	Budapest	Hungary	8-2
1 June	1909	Vienna	Austria	8-1
12 February	1910	Belfast	Ireland	1-1
14 March	1910	Cardiff	Wales	1-0
2 April	1910	Glasgow	Scotland	0-2
C29 June	1910	Durban	South Africa	3-0
C23 July	1910	Johannesburg	South Africa	6-2
C30 July	1910	Capetown	South Africa	6-3
11 February	1911	Derby	Ireland	2-1
13 March	1911	Millwall	Wales	3-0
1 April	1911	Everton	Scotland	1-1
10 February	1912	Dublin	Ireland	6-1
11 March	1912	Wrexham	Wales	2-0
23 March	1912	Glasgow	Scotland	1-1
15 February	1913	Belfast	Ireland	1-2
17 March	1913	Bristol	Wales	4-3
5 April	1913	Stamford Bridge	Scotland	1-0
14 February	1914	Middlesbrough	Ireland	0-3
16 March	1914	Cardiff	Wales	2-0
4 April	1914	Glasgow	Scotland	1-3
V26 April	1919	Everton	Scotland	2-2
V 3 May	1919	Glasgow	Scotland	4-3
V11 October	1919	Cardiff	Wales	1-2
V18 October	1919	Stoke-on-Trent	Wales	2-0
25 October	1919	Belfast	Ireland	1-1
15 March	1920	Highbury	Wales	1-2
10 April	1920	Sheffield	Scotland	5-4
23 October	1920	Sunderland	Ireland	2-0
C26 June	1920	Durban	South Africa	3-1
C17 July	1920	Johannesburg	South Africa	3-1
C19 July	1920	Capetown	South Africa	9-1
14 March	1921	Cardiff	Wales	0-0
9 April	1921	Glasgow	Scotland	0-3
21 May	1921	Brussels	Belgium	2-0
22 October	1921	Belfast	N Ireland	1-1
13 March	1922	Liverpool	Wales	1-0
8 April	1922	Villa Park	Scotland	0-1
21 October	1922	West Bromwich	N Ireland	2-0
5 March	1923	Cardiff	Wales	2-2
19 March	1923	Highbury	Belgium	6-1
14 April	1923	Glasgow	Scotland	2-2
10 May	1923	Paris	France	4-1
21 May	1923	Stockholm	Sweden	4-2
24 May	1923	Stockholm	Sweden	3-1
20 October	1923	Belfast	N Ireland	1-2
1 November	1923	Antwerp	Belgium	2-2
3 March	1924	Blackburn	Wales	1-2
12 April	1924	Wembley	Scotland	1-1
17 May	1924	Paris	France	3-1
22 October	1924	Everton	N Ireland	3-1
8 December	1924	West Bromwich	Belgium	4-0
28 February	1925	Swansea	Wales	2-1
4 April	1925	Glasgow	Scotland	0-2
21 May	1925	Paris	France	3-2
C27 June	1925	Brisbane	Australia	5-1
C 4 July	1925	Sydney	Australia	2-1
C11 July	1925	Maitland	Australia	8-2
C18 July	1925	Sydney	Australia	5-0
C25 July	1925	Melbourne	Australia	2-0
24 October	1925	Belfast	N Ireland	0-0
1 March	1926	Crystal Palace	Wales	1-3
17 April	1926	Manchester	Scotland	1-0
24 May	1926	Antwerp	Belgium	5-3
20 October	1926	Liverpool	N Ireland	3-3
12 February	1927	Wrexham	Wales	3-3
2 April	1927	Glasgow	Scotland	2-1
11 May	1927	Brussels	Belgium	9-1
21 May	1927	Luxembourg	Luxembourg	5-2
26 May	1927	Paris	France	6-0
22 October	1927	Belfast	N Ireland	0-2
28 November	1927	Burnley	Wales	1-2
31 March	1928	Wembley	Scotland	1-5
17 May	1928	Paris	France	5-1
19 May	1928	Antwerp	Belgium	3-1
22 October	1928	Everton	N Ireland	2-1
17 November	1928	Swansea	Wales	3-2
13 April	1929	Glasgow	Scotland	0-1
9 May	1929	Paris	France	4-1
11 May	1929	Brussels	Belgium	5-1
15 May	1929	Madrid	Spain	3-4
C15 June	1929	Durban	South Africa	3-2
C13 July	1929	Johannesburg	South Africa	2-1
C17 July	1929	Capetown	South Africa	3-1
19 October	1929	Belfast	N Ireland	3-0
20 November	1929	Stamford Bridge	Wales	6-0
5 April	1930	Wembley	Scotland	5-2
10 May	1930	Berlin	Germany	3-3
14 May	1930	Vienna	Austria	0-0
20 October	1930	Sheffield	N Ireland	5-1
22 November	1930	Wrexham	Wales	4-0
28 March	1931	Glasgow	Scotland	0-2
14 May	1931	Paris	France	2-5
16 May	1931	Brussels	Belgium	4-1
17 October	1931	Belfast	Ireland	6-2
18 November	1931	Liverpool	Wales	3-1
9 December	1931	Highbury	Spain	7-1
9 April	1932	Wembley	Scotland	3-0
17 October	1932	Blackpool	N Ireland	1-0
16 November	1932	Wrexham	Wales	0-0
7 December	1932	Stamford Bridge	Austria	4-3
1 April	1933	Glasgow	Scotland	1-2
13 May	1933	Rome	Italy	1-1
20 May	1933	Berne	Switzerland	4-0
14 October	1933	Belfast	N Ireland	3-0
15 November	1933	Newcastle	Wales	1-2
6 December	1933	Tottenham	France	4-1
14 April	1934	Wembley	Scotland	3-0
10 May	1934	Budapest	Hungary	1-2
16 May	1934	Prague	Czechoslovakia	1-2
29 September	1934	Cardiff	Wales	4-0
14 November	1934	Highbury	Italy	3-2
6 February	1935	Everton	N Ireland	2-1
6 April	1935	Glasgow	Scotland	0-2
18 May	1935	Amsterdam	Netherlands	1-0
J21 August	1935	Glasgow	Scotland	2-4
19 October	1935	Belfast	N Ireland	3-1
4 December	1935	Tottenham	Germany	3-0
5 February	1936	Wolverhampton	Wales	1-2
4 April	1936	Wembley	Scotland	1-1
6 May	1936	Vienna	Austria	1-2
9 May	1936	Brussels	Belgium	2-3
17 October	1936	Cardiff	Wales	1-2
18 November	1936	Stoke-on-Trent	N Ireland	3-1
2 December	1936	Highbury	Hungary	6-2
17 April	1937	Glasgow	Scotland	1-3
14 May	1937	Oslo	Norway	6-0
17 May	1937	Stockholm	Sweden	4-0
20 May	1937	Helsinki	Finland	8-0
23 October	1937	Belfast	N Ireland	5-1
17 November	1937	Middlesbrough	Wales	2-1
1 December	1937	Tottenham	Czechoslovakia	5-4
9 April	1938	Wembley	Scotland	0-1
14 May	1938	Berlin	Germany	6-3
21 May	1938	Zurich	Switzerland	1-2
26 May	1938	Paris	France	4-2
22 October	1938	Cardiff	Wales	2-4
26 October	1938	Highbury	FIFA	3-0
9 November	1938	Newcastle	Norway	4-0
16 November	1938	Manchester	N Ireland	7-0
15 April	1939	Glasgow	Scotland	2-1
13 May	1939	Milan	Italy	2-2
18 May	1939	Belgrade	Yugoslavia	1-2
24 May	1939	Bucharest	Rumania	2-0
C17 June	1939	Johannesburg	South Africa	3-0
C24 June	1939	Durban	South Africa	8-2
C 1 July	1939	Johannesburg	South Africa	2-1
WT11 November	1939	Cardiff	Wales	1-1
WT18 November	1939	Wrexham	Wales	3-2
WT 2 December	1939	Newcastle	Scotland	2-1
WT13 April	1940	Wembley	Wales	0-1
WT11 May	1940	Glasgow	Scotland	1-1
WT 8 February	1941	Newcastle	Scotland	2-3
WT26 April	1941	Nottingham	Wales	4-1
WT 3 May	1941	Glasgow	Scotland	3-1
WT 7 June	1941	Cardiff	Wales	3-2
WT 4 October	1941	Wembley	Scotland	2-0
WT25 October	1941	Birmingham	Wales	2-1
WT17 January	1942	Wembley	Scotland	3-0
WT18 April	1942	Glasgow	Scotland	4-5
WT 9 May	1942	Cardiff	Wales	0-1
WT10 October	1942	Wembley	Scotland	0-0
WT24 October	1942	Wolverhampton	Wales	1-2
WT27 February	1943	Wembley	Wales	5-3
WT17 April	1943	Glasgow	Scotland	4-0
WT 8 May	1943	Cardiff	Wales	1-1
WT29 May	1943	Wembley	Wales	8-3
WT16 October	1943	Manchester	Scotland	8-0
WT19 February	1944	Wembley	Scotland	6-2
WT22 April	1944	Glasgow	Scotland	3-2
WT 6 May	1944	Cardiff	Wales	2-0
WT16 September	1944	Liverpool	Wales	2-2
WT14 October	1944	Wembley	Scotland	6-2
WT13 February	1945	Birmingham	Scotland	3-2
WT14 April	1945	Glasgow	Scotland	6-1
WT 5 May	1945	Cardiff	Wales	3-2
WT26 May	1945	Wembley	France	2-2
V15 September	1945	Belfast	N Ireland	1-0

KEYSTONE

Walter Winterbottom, in Ron Greenwood's judgement, 'the instigator of all new ideas in English football'. The first England team manager, he held the post from 1946 to 1962.

petence and selectorial vanity in 1962.

Although he was said to have been only third choice for the job, Ramsey could take the job on his own terms. He would not countenance the intolerable pressure which had been laid upon his hamstrung predecessor. He would pick the players and, if the selectors *had* to remain in existence, they would do so only as a rubber stamp.

Ramsey decided that, if a man was selected to play for England, the player had to be the first to be told. The Committee, the press and the world could wait. How different from the days when the most frequent morning paper story was how Stanley Accrington came out of the cinema and read in the evening paper that he had been chosen for England!

It was a sign of the times when, in 1964, Bobby Moore complained of the strain of England's pre-match training. Ten years earlier they would hardly have tired a nicotine besotten parks player, but, come Ramsey, those days were clearly over. Stalag Lilleshall was the players' description of their training camp for the 1966 World Cup.

Ten to four thirty, Monday to Thursday, Ramsey would be in his Lancaster Gate office, and he expected the same discipline and punctuality from everyone else. The awesome combination of Harold Sheperdson and Les Cocker—'as

Date	Venue	Opponents	Score
V20 October 1945	West Bromwich	Wales	0-1
V19 January 1946	Wembley	Belgium	2-0
V13 April 1946	Glasgow	Scotland	0-1
V11 May 1946	Stamford Bridge	Switzerland	4-1
28 September 1946	Belfast	N Ireland	7-2
30 September 1946	Dublin	Eire	1-0
13 November 1946	Manchester	Wales	3-0
27 November 1946	Huddersfield	Netherlands	8-2
12 April 1947	Wembley	Scotland	1-1
3 May 1947	Highbury	France	3-0
18 May 1947	Zurich	Switzerland	0-1
25 May 1947	Lisbon	Portugal	10-0
21 September 1947	Brussels	Belgium	5-2
18 October 1947	Cardiff	Wales	3-0
5 November 1947	Everton	N Ireland	2-2
19 October 1947	Highbury	Sweden	4-2
10 April 1948	Glasgow	Scotland	2-0
16 May 1948	Turin	Italy	4-0
26 September 1948	Copenhagen	Denmark	0-0
9 October 1948	Belfast	N Ireland	6-2
10 November 1948	Birmingham	Wales	1-0
2 December 1948	Highbury	Switzerland	6-0
9 April 1949	Wembley	Scotland	1-3
13 May 1949	Stockholm	Sweden	1-3
18 May 1949	Oslo	Norway	4-1
22 May 1949	Paris	France	3-1
21 September 1949	Everton	Eire	0-2
WC15 October 1949	Cardiff	Wales	4-1
WC16 November 1949	Manchester	N Ireland	9-2
30 November 1949	Tottenham	Italy	2-0
WC15 April 1950	Glasgow	Scotland	1-0
14 May 1950	Lisbon	Portugal	5-3
18 May 1950	Brussels	Belgium	4-1
WC25 June 1950	Rio de Janeiro	Chile	2-0
WC29 June 1950	Belo Horizonte	USA	0-1
WC 2 July 1950	Rio de Janeiro	Spain	0-1
7 October 1950	Belfast	N Ireland	4-1
15 November 1950	Sunderland	Wales	4-2
22 November 1950	Highbury	Yugoslavia	2-2
14 April 1951	Wembley	Scotland	2-3
9 May 1951	Wembley	Argentina	2-1
19 May 1951	Everton	Portugal	5-2
C26 May 1951	Sydney	Australia	4-1
C30 June 1951	Sydney	Australia	17-0
C 7 July 1951	Brisbane	Australia	4-1
C14 July 1951	Sydney	Australia	6-1
C21 July 1951	Newcastle NSW	Australia	5-0
3 October 1951	Highbury	France	2-2
20 October 1951	Cardiff	Wales	1-1
14 November 1951	Birmingham	N Ireland	2-0
28 November 1951	Wembley	Austria	2-2
5 April 1952	Glasgow	Scotland	2-1
18 May 1952	Florence	Italy	1-1
25 May 1952	Vienna	Austria	3-2
28 May 1952	Zurich	Switzerland	3-0
4 October 1952	Belfast	N Ireland	2-2
12 November 1952	Wembley	Wales	5-2
26 November 1952	Wembley	Belgium	5-0
18 April 1953	Wembley	Scotland	2-2
A17 May 1953	Buenos Aires	Argentina	0-0
24 May 1953	Santiago	Chile	2-1
31 May 1953	Montevideo	Uruguay	1-2
8 June 1953	New York	USA	6-3
WC10 October 1953	Cardiff	Wales	4-1
21 October 1953	Wembley	FIFA	4-4
C11 November 1953	Liverpool	N Ireland	3-1
25 November 1953	Wembley	Hungary	3-6
C 3 April 1954	Glasgow	Scotland	4-2
16 May 1954	Belgrade	Yugoslavia	0-1
23 May 1954	Budapest	Hungary	1-7
C17 June 1954	Basle	Belgium	4-4
C20 June 1954	Berne	Switzerland	2-0
C26 June 1954	Basle	Uruguay	2-4
2 October 1954	Belfast	N Ireland	2-0
10 November 1954	Wembley	Wales	3-2
1 December 1954	Wembley	West Germany	3-1
2 April 1955	Wembley	Scotland	7-2
15 May 1955	Paris	France	0-1
18 May 1955	Madrid	Spain	1-1
22 May 1955	Oporto	Portugal	1-3
2 October 1955	Copenhagen	Denmark	5-1
22 October 1955	Cardiff	Wales	1-2
2 November 1955	Wembley	N Ireland	3-0
30 November 1955	Wembley	Spain	4-1
14 April 1956	Glasgow	Scotland	1-1
9 May 1956	Wembley	Brazil	4-2
16 May 1956	Stockholm	Sweden	0-0
20 May 1956	Helsinki	Finland	5-1
26 May 1956	Berlin	West Germany	3-1
6 October 1956	Belfast	N Ireland	1-1
14 November 1956	Wembley	Wales	3-1
28 November 1956	Wembley	Yugoslavia	3-0
WC 5 December 1956	Wolverhampton	Denmark	5-2
6 April 1957	Wembley	Scotland	2-1
WC 8 May 1957	Wembley	Eire	5-1
WC15 May 1957	Copenhagen	Denmark	4-1
WC19 May 1957	Dublin	Eire	1-1
19 October 1957	Cardiff	Wales	4-0
6 November 1957	Wembley	N Ireland	2-3
27 November 1957	Wembley	France	4-0
19 April 1958	Glasgow	Scotland	4-0
7 May 1958	Wembley	Portugal	2-1
11 May 1958	Belgrade	Yugoslavia	0-5
18 May 1958	Moscow	USSR	1-1
WC 8 June 1958	Gothenburg	USSR	2-2
WC11 June 1958	Gothenburg	Brazil	0-0
WC15 June 1958	Boras	Austria	2-2
WC17 June 1958	Gothenburg	USSR	0-1
4 October 1958	Belfast	N Ireland	3-3
22 October 1958	Wembley	USSR	5-0
26 November 1958	Birmingham	Wales	2-2
11 April 1959	Wembley	Scotland	1-0
6 May 1959	Wembley	Italy	2-2
13 May 1959	Rio de Janeiro	Brazil	0-2
17 May 1959	Lima	Peru	1-4
24 May 1959	Mexico City	Mexico	1-2
28 May 1959	Los Angeles	USA	8-1
17 October 1959	Cardiff	Wales	1-1
28 October 1959	Wembley	Sweden	2-3
18 November 1959	Wembley	N Ireland	2-1
9 April 1960	Glasgow	Scotland	1-1
11 May 1960	Wembley	Yugoslavia	3-3
15 May 1960	Madrid	Spain	0-3
22 May 1960	Budapest	Hungary	0-2
8 October 1960	Belfast	N Ireland	5-2
WC19 October 1960	Luxembourg	Luxembourg	9-0
26 October 1960	Wembley	Spain	4-2
23 November 1960	Wembley	Wales	5-1
15 April 1961	Wembley	Scotland	9-3
10 May 1961	Wembley	Mexico	8-0
WC21 May 1961	Lisbon	Portugal	1-1
24 May 1961	Rome	Italy	3-2
27 May 1961	Vienna	Austria	1-3
WC28 September 1961	Highbury	Luxembourg	4-1
14 October 1961	Cardiff	Wales	1-1
WC25 October 1961	Wembley	Portugal	2-0
22 November 1961	Wembley	N Ireland	1-1
4 April 1962	Wembley	Austria	3-1
14 April 1962	Glasgow	Scotland	0-2
9 May 1962	Wembley	Switzerland	3-1
20 May 1962	Lima	Peru	4-0
WC31 May 1962	Rancagua	Hungary	1-2
WC 2 June 1962	Rancagua	Argentina	3-1
WC 7 June 1962	Rancagua	Bulgaria	0-0
WC10 June 1962	Vina del Mar	Brazil	1-3
ENC 3 October 1962	Sheffield	France	1-1
20 October 1962	Belfast	N Ireland	3-1
21 November 1962	Wembley	Wales	4-0
ENC27 February 1963	Paris	France	2-5
6 April 1963	Wembley	Scotland	1-2
8 May 1963	Wembley	Brazil	1-1
29 May 1963	Bratislava	Czechoslovakia	4-2
2 June 1963	Leipzig	East Germany	2-1
5 June 1963	Basle	Switzerland	8-1
12 October 1963	Cardiff	Wales	4-0
23 October 1963	Wembley	FIFA	2-1
20 November 1963	Wembley	N Ireland	8-3
11 April 1964	Glasgow	Scotland	0-1
6 May 1964	Wembley	Uruguay	2-1
17 May 1964	Lisbon	Portugal	4-3
24 May 1964	Dublin	Eire	3-1
27 May 1964	New York	USA	10-0
30 May 1964	Rio de Janeiro	Brazil	1-5
4 June 1964	Sao Paulo	Portugal	1-1
6 June 1964	Rio de Janeiro	Argentina	0-1
3 October 1964	Belfast	N Ireland	4-3
21 October 1964	Wembley	Belgium	2-2
18 November 1964	Wembley	Wales	2-1
9 December 1964	Amsterdam	Netherlands	1-1
10 April 1965	Wembley	Scotland	2-2
5 May 1965	Wembley	Hungary	1-0
9 May 1965	Belgrade	Yugoslavia	1-1
12 May 1965	Nurnberg	West Germany	1-0
16 May 1965	Gothenburg	Sweden	2-1
2 October 1965	Cardiff	Wales	0-0
20 October 1965	Wembley	Austria	2-3
10 November 1965	Wembley	N Ireland	2-1
8 December 1965	Madrid	Spain	2-0
5 January 1966	Everton	Poland	1-1
23 February 1966	Wembley	West Germany	1-0
2 April 1966	Glasgow	Scotland	4-3
4 May 1966	Wembley	Yugoslavia	2-0
26 June 1966	Helsinki	Finland	3-0
29 June 1966	Oslo	Norway	6-1
3 July 1966	Copenhagen	Denmark	2-0
5 July 1966	Chorzow	Poland	1-0
WC11 July 1966	Wembley	Uruguay	0-0
WC16 July 1966	Wembley	Mexico	2-0
WC20 July 1966	Wembley	France	2-0
WC23 July 1966	Wembley	Argentina	1-0
WC26 July 1966	Wembley	Portugal	2-1
WC30 July 1966	Wembley	West Germany	4-2
EC22 October 1966	Belfast	N Ireland	2-0
2 November 1966	Wembley	Czechoslovakia	0-0
EC16 November 1966	Wembley	Wales	5-1
EC15 April 1967	Wembley	Scotland	2-3
24 May 1967	Wembley	Spain	2-0
27 May 1967	Vienna	Austria	1-0
EC21 October 1967	Cardiff	Wales	3-0
EC22 November 1967	Wembley	N Ireland	2-0
6 December 1967	Wembley	USSR	2-2
EC24 February 1968	Glasgow	Scotland	1-1
3 April 1968	Wembley	Spain	1-0
8 May 1968	Madrid	Spain	2-1
22 May 1968	Wembley	Sweden	3-1
1 June 1968	Hanover	West Germany	0-1
EC 5 June 1968	Florence	Yugoslavia	0-1
EC 8 June 1968	Rome	USSR	2-0
6 November 1968	Bucharest	Rumania	0-0
11 December 1968	Wembley	Bulgaria	1-1
15 January 1969	Wembley	Rumania	1-1
12 March 1969	Wembley	France	5-0
3 May 1969	Belfast	N Ireland	3-1
7 May 1969	Wembley	Wales	2-1
10 May 1969	Wembley	Scotland	4-1
1 June 1969	Mexico City	Mexico	0-0
8 June 1969	Montevideo	Uruguay	2-1
12 June 1969	Rio de Janeiro	Brazil	1-2
5 November 1969	Amsterdam	Netherlands	1-0
10 December 1969	Wembley	Portugal	1-0
14 January 1970	Wembley	Netherlands	0-0
25 February 1970	Brussels	Belgium	3-1
18 April 1970	Cardiff	Wales	1-1
21 April 1970	Wembley	N Ireland	3-1
25 April 1970	Glasgow	Scotland	0-0
24 May 1970	Quito	Ecuador	2-0
WC 2 June 1970	Guadalajara	Rumania	1-0
WC 7 June 1970	Guadalajara	Brazil	0-1
WC11 June 1970	Guadalajara	Czechoslovakia	1-0
WC14 June 1970	Leon	West Germany	2-3
25 November 1970	Wembley	East Germany	3-1
EC 3 February 1971	Valetta	Malta	1-0
EC21 April 1971	Wembley	Greece	3-0
EC12 May 1971	Wembley	Malta	5-0
15 May 1971	Belfast	N Ireland	1-0
19 May 1971	Wembley	Wales	0-0
22 May 1971	Wembley	Scotland	3-1
EC13 October 1971	Basle	Switzerland	3-2
EC10 November 1971	Wembley	Switzerland	1-1
EC 1 December 1971	Athens	Greece	2-0
EC29 April 1972	Wembley	West Germany	1-3
EC13 May 1972	Berlin	West Germany	0-0
20 May 1972	Cardiff	Wales	3-0
23 May 1972	Wembley	N Ireland	0-1
27 May 1972	Glasgow	Scotland	1-0
11 October 1972	Wembley	Yugoslavia	1-1
WC15 November 1972	Cardiff	Wales	1-0
WC24 January 1973	Wembley	Wales	1-1
14 February 1973	Glasgow	Scotland	5-0
12 May 1973	Everton	N Ireland	2-1
15 May 1973	Wembley	Wales	3-0
19 May 1973	Wembley	Scotland	1-0
27 May 1973	Prague	Czechoslovakia	1-1
WC 6 June 1973	Katowice	Poland	0-2
10 June 1973	Moscow	USSR	2-1
14 June 1973	Turin	Italy	0-2
26 September 1973	Wembley	Austria	7-0
WC17 October 1973	Wembley	Poland	1-1
14 November 1973	Wembley	Italy	0-1

*These four games were all between an England XI and a team of Scots resident in England. The FA does not regard them as official matches
†On each of these days England played two internationals. The FA asked the Corinthian Casuals to provide the teams against Wales, while they themselves selected the sides to play Ireland. Corinthians are the only club side to have represented England in toto
‡This match was abandoned owing to a disaster at the ground. The FA does not regard it as an official match
V – Victory internationals (not regarded as official)
J – Jubilee game (not regarded as official)
WT – War-time internationals (not regarded as official)
WC – World Cup games
ENC – European Nations Cup games
EC – European Championship games
C – Commonwealth tour games. Though billed as 'England' these teams were usually FA Touring XIs. One cap was awarded to each of the players who went on the tour but individual games are not regarded as official internationals
A – Abandoned after 20 minutes owing to torrential rain

cuddly as a sack of cobblestones' said Max Marquis—were brought in as trainers and strict rules of conduct were laid down for the players.

What Ramsey has done for England needs little reiteration. He promised that England would win the World Cup in 1966 and they did. Consciously or otherwise, he succeeded by going back to 'Pa' Jackson's concept of running an international side on the same lines as a club.

But Ramsey was to learn, a little bitterly, that triumph is more transient than failure. Despite what he did for England, like Winterbottom, he was to find that the knives are always being sharpened in dark corners. There were those who claimed that the 1966 triumph was achieved despite him and that the failures in 1970, 1972 and, of course, 1974 came because of him.

The accusations only touch the fringes of the situation. If Winterbottom had to grapple with a crippling selection system, Ramsey faced something quite as bad: a club fixture list so congested that it frequently turned his selected teams into dead husks of what was intended. For example, for the friendly against Yugoslavia in 1972, Ramsey was left nine players short of his original selection because of players' club committments. The day of that advertisement for 'young men to play in an international match' did not, perhaps, seem so far away.

Alf Ramsey, at his best and happiest, in training with the players. Unlike Winterbottom, Ramsey had full control over the selection and supervision of the England team.

PRESS ASSOCIATION

A hard road for Scotland

The advertisement appeared in all the Scottish national newspapers. It was, in fact, in the 'Situations Vacant' column. And the vacant situation was that of Scottish international team manager. There is, of course, nothing particularly wrong about advertising for a team manager. It may not be the accepted custom, for the usual practice is to work very much behind the scenes in such circumstances. Even so, the Scottish Football Association's idea was sound enough, for who could be sure what unexpected names might apply?

Sound enough, that is, in all respects but one. Journalists and fans stared disbelievingly at the advert. For the wording made it very clear indeed that the SFA would be willing to hire a team manager on a *part-time basis*.

The storm duly broke. What on earth was happening at Park Gardens, home of the SFA? Did they really think Scotland could compete with the world's greatest football nations without the guidance of a full-time professional

PRESS ASSOCIATION

manager? How far could the amateur outlook go?

As it happened, wiser minds prevailed and the job did become full-time again. But that advertisement, appearing as it did between the managerships of Jock Stein and John Prentice, is something the SFA will take years to live down.

The incident typified the kind of thinking which has been mainly responsible for Scotland's comparatively poor international record since the War. It is true that, considering the size of her population, Scotland should not be allowed on the same field as nations like England, West Germany, Italy and Russia, countries with a vastly greater number of registered players.

But over the years Scotland has still proved that quality matters far more than quantity. She has produced dozens of players of world class, players whose hallmark has always been pure, natural ability, and the source shows no sign of drying up.

It is this natural feeling of the Scots for football, both in playing the game and watching it, which

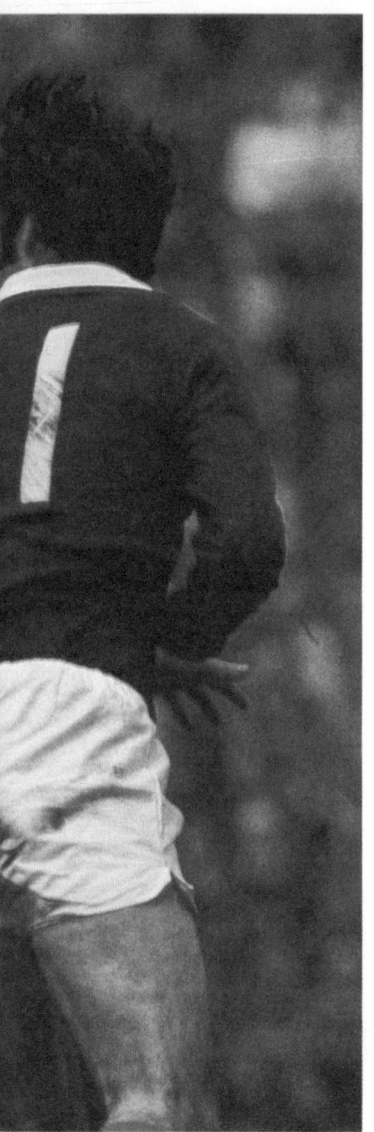

forced the SFA to bow to the demands of the present, in spite of a strong desire in some quarters to stay safely, comfortably and non-competitively in pre-War days. For while some countries might have grown apathetic about continual failure, the Scots instead became angry.

After the failure to qualify in the summer of 1971 for the European Championship, the uproar reached frightening proportions. Bobby Brown, a man probably far too gentle and likeable for a job which demanded toughness to the point of inflexibility, was sacked. Soon after, the SFA let it be known that they were willing to take on the best man available at a suitable salary—popularly quoted at £7,500.

That autumn, the task was offered to Willie Cunningham, manager of Falkirk, who turned it down. There was a brief period of worry in case the SFA should think that they could do no more and return to their old ways. But then, happily, Tommy Docherty appeared on the scene. He took the job on a trial basis, but there was never any real doubt that he would stay on. His impact on public and players alike was immediate and impressive and the side played confident, thoughtful football in the remaining European Championship qualifying games against Portugal and Belgium.

At last it seemed Scotland had a fighting chance. The conditions and salary of the managership guaranteed some much needed permanency where it mattered. The manager himself was a man of wide experience and excellent ability. But perhaps most significant of all were the signs, of which Docherty's

Top Tommy Docherty's appointment in 1971 saw the return to favour of the Anglos. Denis Law (10) and George Graham were but two who found themselves recalled. His squad for the first World Cup qualifying match in 1972 contained 11 Anglos out of 18.
Far left Pele's protestations did him little good in Scotland's match with Brazil in 1966. Billy Bremner marked him tightly and Scotland earned a 1-1 draw. In the Brazilian Independence Tournament six years later the Scots came close to repeating that result but a late goal by Jairzinho gave Brazil a win they hardly deserved.
Left Tommy Docherty, who gave way to Willie Ormond at the end of 1972.

appointment was but one, that the progressive voices at the SFA were at last making themselves heard.

Change was certainly long overdue. Before Docherty's appointment few people doubted that the SFA Selection Committee—later called the International Committee—wielded far more power than was good for the game in Scotland. Jock Stein's decision to turn down the full-time job and the £10,000 that was said to go with it, made it quite clear that the conditions of the job were very, very wrong.

Thus, the arrival of Tommy Docherty was generally interpreted as the start of a revolution in Park Gardens. Only a few years previously the appointment of so uncompromising, so determined a man would have been unthinkable.

Even Scottish clubs refuse to release their players

But, of course, only the most naive could have sat back to await with confidence a sudden, irresistible upsurge of Scottish football into the topmost strata of the game. The presence of Tommy Docherty solved one problem. Another remained—one which has bedevilled Scotland's ambitions at least as persistently as the eccentricities of the SFA. For if it is one thing to pick eleven players, it can be quite another thing to get these eleven on the field in the dark blue jerseys of Scotland. Players are not employed by international associations but by clubs. No country, with the possible exception of Northern Ireland, has been worse hit than Scotland by this simple fact of football life.

For Jock Stein was referring not only to any SFA shortcomings when he expressed his dissatisfaction with the conditions of the Scotland job. Crippling as that was, it seemed at times to be only a slight handicap compared to the difficulties in securing the release of players from their clubs. For example, the team Stein eventually fielded in Naples in 1965, for a game in which Scotland had to avoid defeat to stand a chance of qualifying for the World Cup finals, contained barely half of the players he had originally selected. Mackay, Stevenson, Crerand, Baxter, Law and Gilzean were all unavailable. Injuries and the dictates of Football League clubs gave Stein—and Scotland—no chance.

But the root of the problem lies in the economics of Scottish domestic football which have made regular selling of star players a pre-requisite of solvency. Admittedly, lack of imagination and vision at board level in these clubs has contributed to this unenviable situation, but that is another, larger question. The fact remains that English football is liberally sprinkled with high-calibre Scots who are allowed to play for their country by the grace and favour of their employers. On a great many occasions, neither the grace nor the favour have been forthcoming.

The reasons have varied from diplomatic injuries to more open selfishness. And there is nothing,

absolutely nothing, that Scotland has ever been able to do about it. The SFA cannot even guarantee the release of players with Scottish clubs. Bobby Brown had more than his share of troubles in the release of Scottish-based players, for selfishness knows no natural boundaries, and excuses are easy to invent, almost impossible to disprove. Sir Alf Ramsey has been similarly plagued in England. Tommy Docherty never did expect exemption, nor did he get it.

It is cruelly ironic that Docherty probably had more trouble with the release of players from the Scottish League than from the Football League. Apart from the Derby County players, the most conspicuous absentees from the squad for the Brazil Independence Tournament were from Scottish League clubs. Hay, Johnstone and Dalglish of Celtic, Jardine of Rangers, Stanton of Hibs all dropped out at one stage or another. It was left largely to the Anglos to earn Scotland their success.

Tommy Docherty could usually be relied upon to figure in controversy but by the seventies his forthright approach was also tempered by a measure of flexibility. Nevertheless his drive lifted the head of Scottish football until, in the eyes of the SFA, he could not combine his national team duties with those of managing Manchester United. He gave way to Willie Ormond, who overcame the depression of a 5-0 thrashing by England in his first match to lead Scotland into the finals of the 1974 World Cup. It was a feat which softened some of Scotland's tragedies of the past.

56 years pass before Scotland play abroad

It is a past in which the lessons are quite as outstanding as the memories. We have already noted that amateurism—and amateurishness—was long a characteristic of the SFA. At one time, this was not only understandable but quite forgivable. The Association was formed, after all, in 1873, the year after what was nearly a complete Queen's Park side had represented Scotland in the first-ever international game against England and had achieved a creditable goal-less draw. Apart from 'missionary' tours to such underdeveloped football areas as North America, the SFA were happy enough to keep the international side within these islands for the next 56 years. There was not, true, an extensive choice of opposition in the first two decades of this century—international associations being relatively scarce—but England were always rather more adventurous. In 1928, just as Scotland were at long last paying more attention to European competition, they joined the other home countries in withdrawing from FIFA over a dispute as to how an amateur should be defined. And so it was that the World Cup started in 1930 without any representatives from the UK.

Immediately after the War, however, the British countries rejoined

Above A bird's eye view of Hunter and Bremner fighting for the ball at Hampden in 1972. The game was another disappointment—the Scots lost 1-0.

Left The 3-2 win at Wembley gave Scotsmen a rare moment of joy in 1967. But they were still looking for their next win over England in 1974.

SYNDICATION INTERNATIONAL

PRESS ASSOCIATION

FIFA and were invited to send the top two in the Home International Championship to compete in Rio for the 1950 World Cup. Scotland finished second, but refused to go. They had already decided they would take part only as outright winners; it was a silly decision.

Even so, the challenge of the ever-growing world of football could not be ignored forever. In February of 1954, the SFA did appoint a team manager of a kind. They chose Andy Beattie, a man of stature and experience who soon found the job, with all its limitations, far too small for him. The SFA still persisted with their time-worn system of selection by committee. At the time Beattie claimed he had no real backing from the authorities and, in retrospect, that can hardly be questioned.

Just before the World Cup finals of 1954, held in Switzerland, Beattie resigned. He was bitter about being allowed only the bare minimum of players—one of whom was Tommy Docherty—and there was also trouble over expenses. Beattie did fulfil a moral obligation by going with his men to Switzerland, but that campaign was lost before it started. Scotland lost 1-0 to Austria and took a terrible thrashing, 7-0, from Uruguay. One of the players recalled that on his return a selector greeted him with the words: 'Forget about what happened in Switzer-

land, just so long as we beat England in April.'

Incredibly, the next three years passed in argument . . . not over what sort of team manager was needed but whether any manager was needed at all. At length, in January 1958, Sir Matt Busby was appointed—still, of course, on a part-time basis, but that plan was soon destroyed by the Munich disaster. The team's trainer, Dawson Walker, took charge during the 1958 World Cup in Sweden—where Scotland finished bottom of their section with one point from a possible six. Sir Matt Busby's return that September was short-lived. He simply was not fit enough, and he resigned three months later.

Then back came Andy Beattie in the spring of the following year. Bygones, hopefully, would be bygones. Yet the selectors and the permanent administration remained all-powerful, and their attitude to the manager was unchanged. The selectors, themselves club directors, had never permitted their own managers too much control, and they could see no reason why the national side should be any different, especially since the English, even then, were little further advanced. Thus Beattie's second chance was no chance at all. He was sacked in the autumn of 1960 on the eve of a match in Cardiff, when he had asked to be excused so he might watch his new club, Nottingham Forest. But who

could blame Beattie for putting his bread and butter before the jam?

Beattie's successor, Ian McColl, a former Rangers player of distinction, was still on the Ibrox staff when, in November 1960, he moved in to one of the most dubious jobs in football. Control stayed where it always had been—with the amateurs.

McColl was given neither the power nor the time. He stuck to his task for five years before he was fired in 1965 while training with his players at Largs. Then came Jock Stein, attempting vainly to pick up the pieces for the 1966 World Cup. And, on his exit, that infamous advertisement . . . 'might suit a man with other business interests'. No wonder Willie Waddell and Eddie Turnbull, two of Scotland's most successful club managers, turned down approaches from the SFA. John Prentice, however, took the gamble—and at long last the job was full-time. But with what reluctance was that apparently progressive decision reached by the SFA! Contract negotiations dragged on from March to September 1966. The next month out went Prentice, to be replaced by Bobby Brown.

Those were bad, bad days for Scottish international football, days which lasted until on a night of national passion a header from Joe Jordan beat Czechoslovakia and took them to Munich. It was a rare but welcome moment of sweetness.

FULL INTERNATIONALS PLAYED BY SCOTLAND 1870–JANUARY 1974

Date		Venue	Opponents	Score
*19 November	1870	Kennington Oval	England	0-1
*28 February	1871	Kennington Oval	England	1-1
*18 November	1871	Kennington Oval	England	1-2
*24 February	1872	Kennington Oval	England	0-1
30 November	1872	Glasgow	England	0-0
8 March	1873	London	England	2-4
7 March	1874	Glasgow	England	2-1
6 March	1875	London	England	2-2
4 March	1876	Glasgow	England	3-0
25 March	1876	Glasgow	Wales	4-0
3 March	1877	London	England	3-1
15 March	1877	Wrexham	Wales	2-0
2 March	1878	Glasgow	England	7-2
23 March	1878	Glasgow	Wales	9-0
5 April	1879	London	England	4-5
7 April	1879	Wrexham	Wales	3-0
13 March	1880	Glasgow	England	5-4
27 March	1880	Glasgow	Wales	5-1
12 March	1881	London	England	6-1
14 March	1881	Wrexham	Wales	5-1
11 March	1882	Glasgow	England	5-1
25 March	1882	Glasgow	Wales	5-0
10 March	1883	Sheffield	England	3-2
12 March	1883	Wrexham	Wales	3-0
15 March	1884	Glasgow	England	1-0
26 March	1884	Belfast	Ireland	5-0
29 March	1884	Glasgow	Wales	4-1
14 March	1885	Glasgow	Ireland	8-2
21 March	1885	London	England	1-1
23 March	1885	Wrexham	Wales	8-1
20 March	1886	Belfast	Ireland	7-2
27 March	1886	Glasgow	England	1-1
10 April	1886	Glasgow	Wales	4-1
19 February	1887	Glasgow	Ireland	4-1
19 March	1887	Blackburn	England	3-2
21 March	1887	Wrexham	Wales	2-0
10 March	1888	Edinburgh	Wales	5-1
17 March	1888	Glasgow	England	0-5
24 March	1888	Belfast	Ireland	10-2
9 March	1889	Glasgow	Ireland	7-0
13 April	1889	London	England	3-2
15 April	1889	Wrexham	Wales	0-0
22 March	1890	Paisley	Wales	5-0
29 March	1890	Belfast	Ireland	4-1
5 April	1890	Glasgow	England	1-1
21 March	1891	Wrexham	Wales	4-3
28 March	1891	Glasgow	Ireland	2-1
4 April	1891	Blackburn	England	1-2
19 March	1892	Belfast	Ireland	3-2
26 March	1892	Edinburgh	Wales	6-1
2 April	1892	Glasgow	England	1-4
18 March	1893	Wrexham	Wales	8-0
25 March	1893	Glasgow	Ireland	6-1
1 April	1893	London	England	2-5
24 March	1894	Kilmarnock	Wales	5-2
31 March	1894	Belfast	Ireland	2-1
7 April	1894	Glasgow	England	2-2
23 March	1895	Wrexham	Wales	2-2
30 March	1895	Glasgow	Ireland	3-1
6 April	1895	Liverpool	England	0-3
21 March	1896	Dundee	Wales	4-0
28 March	1896	Belfast	Ireland	3-3
4 April	1896	Glasgow	England	2-1
20 March	1897	Wrexham	Wales	2-2
27 March	1897	Glasgow	Ireland	5-1
3 April	1897	London	England	2-1
19 March	1898	Motherwell	Wales	5-2
26 March	1898	Belfast	Ireland	3-0
2 April	1898	Glasgow	England	1-3
18 March	1899	Wrexham	Wales	6-0
25 March	1899	Glasgow	Ireland	9-1
8 April	1899	Birmingham	England	1-2
3 February	1900	Aberdeen	Wales	5-2
3 March	1900	Belfast	Ireland	3-0
7 April	1900	Glasgow	England	4-1
23 February	1901	Glasgow	Ireland	11-0
2 March	1901	Wrexham	Wales	1-1
30 March	1901	London	England	2-2
1 March	1902	Belfast	Ireland	5-1
15 March	1902	Greenock	Wales	5-1
†5 April	1902	Glasgow	England	1-1
3 May	1902	Birmingham	England	2-2
9 March	1903	Cardiff	Wales	1-0
21 March	1903	Glasgow	Ireland	0-2
4 April	1903	Sheffield	England	2-1
12 March	1904	Dundee	Wales	1-1
26 March	1904	Dublin	Ireland	1-1
9 April	1904	Glasgow	England	0-1
6 March	1905	Wrexham	Wales	1-3
18 March	1905	Glasgow	Ireland	4-0
1 April	1905	London	England	0-1
3 March	1906	Edinburgh	Wales	0-2
17 March	1906	Dublin	Ireland	1-0
7 April	1906	Glasgow	England	2-1
4 March	1907	Wrexham	Wales	0-1
16 March	1907	Glasgow	Ireland	3-0
6 April	1907	Newcastle	England	1-1
7 March	1908	Dundee	Wales	2-1
14 March	1908	Dublin	Ireland	5-0
4 April	1908	Glasgow	England	1-1
1 March	1909	Wrexham	Wales	2-3
27 March	1909	Glasgow	Ireland	5-0
3 April	1909	London	England	0-2
5 March	1910	Kilmarnock	Wales	1-0
19 March	1910	Belfast	Ireland	0-1
2 April	1910	Glasgow	England	2-0
6 March	1911	Cardiff	Wales	2-2
18 March	1911	Glasgow	Ireland	2-0
1 April	1911	Liverpool	England	1-1
2 March	1912	Edinburgh	Wales	1-0
16 March	1912	Belfast	Ireland	4-1
23 March	1912	Glasgow	England	1-1
3 March	1913	Wrexham	Wales	0-0
15 March	1913	Dublin	Ireland	2-1
5 April	1913	London	England	0-1
28 February	1914	Glasgow	Wales	0-0
14 March	1914	Belfast	Ireland	1-1
4 April	1914	Glasgow	England	3-1
V26 April	1919	Everton	England	2-2
V 3 May	1919	Glasgow	England	3-4
26 February	1920	Cardiff	Wales	1-1
13 March	1920	Glasgow	Ireland	3-0
10 April	1920	Sheffield	England	4-5
12 February	1921	Aberdeen	Wales	2-1
26 February	1921	Belfast	Ireland	2-0
9 April	1921	Glasgow	England	3-0
4 February	1922	Wrexham	Wales	1-2
4 March	1922	Glasgow	Ireland	2-1
8 April	1922	Birmingham	England	1-0
3 March	1923	Belfast	Ireland	1-0
17 March	1923	Paisley	Wales	2-0
14 April	1923	Glasgow	England	2-2
16 February	1924	Cardiff	Wales	0-2
1 March	1924	Glasgow	N Ireland	2-0
12 April	1924	Wembley	England	1-1
14 February	1925	Edinburgh	Wales	3-1
28 February	1925	Belfast	N Ireland	3-0
4 April	1925	Glasgow	England	2-0
31 October	1925	Cardiff	Wales	3-0
27 February	1926	Glasgow	N Ireland	4-0
17 April	1926	Manchester	England	1-0
30 October	1926	Glasgow	Wales	3-0
26 February	1927	Belfast	N Ireland	2-0
2 April	1927	Glasgow	England	1-2
29 October	1927	Wrexham	Wales	2-2
25 February	1928	Glasgow	N Ireland	0-1
31 March	1928	Wembley	England	5-1
27 October	1928	Glasgow	Wales	4-2
23 February	1929	Belfast	N Ireland	7-3
13 April	1929	Glasgow	England	1-0
1 June	1929	Berlin	Germany	1-1
4 June	1929	Amsterdam	Netherlands	2-0
26 October	1929	Cardiff	Wales	4-2
22 February	1930	Glasgow	N Ireland	3-1
5 April	1930	Wembley	England	2-5
18 May	1930	Paris	France	2-0
25 October	1930	Glasgow	Wales	1-1
21 February	1931	Belfast	N Ireland	0-0
28 March	1931	Glasgow	England	2-0
16 May	1931	Vienna	Austria	0-5
20 May	1931	Rome	Italy	0-3
24 May	1931	Geneva	Switzerland	3-2
19 September	1931	Glasgow	N Ireland	3-1
31 October	1931	Wrexham	Wales	3-2
9 April	1932	Wembley	England	0-3
8 May	1932	Paris	France	3-1
17 September	1932	Belfast	N Ireland	4-0
26 October	1932	Edinburgh	Wales	2-5
1 April	1933	Glasgow	England	2-1
16 September	1933	Glasgow	N Ireland	1-2
4 October	1933	Cardiff	Wales	2-3
29 November	1933	Glasgow	Austria	2-2
14 April	1934	Wembley	England	0-3
20 October	1934	Belfast	N Ireland	1-2
21 November	1934	Aberdeen	Wales	3-2
6 April	1935	Glasgow	England	2-0
J21 August	1935	Glasgow	England	4-2
5 October	1935	Cardiff	Wales	1-1
13 November	1935	Edinburgh	N Ireland	2-1
4 April	1936	Wembley	England	1-1
14 October	1936	Glasgow	Germany	2-0
31 October	1936	Belfast	N Ireland	3-1
2 December	1936	Dundee	Wales	1-2
17 April	1937	Glasgow	England	3-1
9 May	1937	Vienna	Austria	1-1
15 May	1937	Prague	Czechoslovakia	3-1
30 October	1937	Cardiff	Wales	1-2
10 November	1937	Aberdeen	N Ireland	1-1
8 December	1937	Glasgow	Czechoslovakia	5-0
9 April	1938	Wembley	England	1-0
21 May	1938	Amsterdam	Netherlands	3-1
8 October	1938	Belfast	N Ireland	2-0
9 November	1938	Edinburgh	Wales	3-2
7 December	1938	Glasgow	Hungary	3-1
15 April	1939	Glasgow	England	1-2
WT 2 December	1939	Newcastle	England	1-2
WT11 May	1940	Glasgow	England	1-1
WT 8 February	1941	Newcastle	England	3-2
WT 3 May	1941	Glasgow	England	1-3
WT 4 October	1941	Wembley	England	0-2
WT17 January	1942	Wembley	England	0-3
WT18 April	1942	Glasgow	England	5-4
WT10 October	1942	Wembley	England	0-0
WT17 April	1943	Glasgow	England	0-4
WT16 October	1943	Manchester	England	0-8
WT19 February	1944	Wembley	England	2-6
WT22 April	1944	Glasgow	England	2-3
WT14 October	1944	Wembley	England	2-6
WT 3 February	1945	Villa Park	England	3-2
WT14 April	1945	Glasgow	England	1-6
V13 April	1946	Glasgow	England	1-0
23 January	1946	Glasgow	Belgium	2-2
15 May	1946	Glasgow	Switzerland	3-1
19 October	1946	Wrexham	Wales	1-3
27 November	1946	Glasgow	N Ireland	0-0
12 April	1947	Wembley	England	1-1
18 May	1947	Brussels	Belgium	1-2
24 May	1947	Luxembourg	Luxembourg	6-0
4 October	1947	Belfast	N Ireland	0-2
12 November	1947	Glasgow	Wales	1-2
10 April	1948	Glasgow	England	0-2
28 April	1948	Glasgow	Belgium	2-0
17 May	1948	Berne	Switzerland	1-2
23 May	1948	Paris	France	0-3
23 October	1948	Cardiff	Wales	3-1
17 November	1948	Glasgow	N Ireland	3-2
9 April	1949	Wembley	England	3-1
27 April	1949	Glasgow	France	2-0
WC 1 October	1949	Belfast	N Ireland	8-2
WC 9 November	1949	Glasgow	Wales	2-0
WC15 April	1950	Glasgow	England	0-1
26 April	1950	Glasgow	Switzerland	3-1
21 May	1950	Lisbon	Portugal	2-2
27 May	1950	Paris	France	1-0
21 October	1950	Cardiff	Wales	3-1
1 November	1950	Glasgow	N Ireland	6-1
13 December	1950	Glasgow	Austria	0-1
14 April	1951	Wembley	England	3-2
12 May	1951	Glasgow	Denmark	3-1
16 May	1951	Glasgow	France	1-0
20 May	1951	Brussels	Belgium	5-0
27 May	1951	Vienna	Austria	0-4
6 October	1951	Belfast	N Ireland	3-0
14 November	1951	Glasgow	Wales	0-1
5 April	1952	Glasgow	England	1-2
30 April	1952	Glasgow	USA	6-0
25 May	1952	Copenhagen	Denmark	2-1
30 May	1952	Stockholm	Sweden	1-3
18 October	1952	Cardiff	Wales	2-1
5 November	1952	Glasgow	N Ireland	1-1
18 April	1953	Wembley	England	2-2
6 May	1953	Glasgow	Sweden	1-2
WC 3 October	1953	Belfast	N Ireland	3-1
WC 4 November	1953	Glasgow	Wales	3-3
WC 3 April	1954	Glasgow	England	2-4
5 May	1954	Glasgow	Norway	1-0
19 May	1954	Oslo	Norway	1-1
25 May	1954	Helsinki	Finland	2-1
WC16 June	1954	Zurich	Austria	0-1
WC19 June	1954	Basle	Uruguay	0-7
16 October	1954	Cardiff	Wales	1-0
3 November	1954	Glasgow	N Ireland	2-2
8 December	1954	Glasgow	Hungary	2-4
2 April	1955	Wembley	England	2-7
4 May	1955	Glasgow	Portugal	3-0
15 May	1955	Belgrade	Yugoslavia	2-2
19 May	1955	Vienna	Austria	4-1
29 May	1955	Budapest	Hungary	1-3
8 October	1955	Belfast	N Ireland	1-2
9 November	1955	Glasgow	Wales	2-0
14 April	1956	Glasgow	England	1-1
2 May	1956	Glasgow	Austria	1-1
20 October	1956	Cardiff	Wales	2-2
7 November	1956	Glasgow	N Ireland	1-0
21 November	1956	Glasgow	Yugoslavia	2-0
6 April	1957	Wembley	England	1-2
WC 8 May	1957	Glasgow	Spain	4-2
WC19 May	1957	Basle	Switzerland	2-1
22 May	1957	Stuttgart	West Germany	3-1
WC26 May	1957	Madrid	Spain	1-4
5 October	1957	Belfast	N Ireland	1-1
WC 6 November	1957	Glasgow	Switzerland	3-2
13 November	1957	Glasgow	Wales	1-1
19 April	1958	Glasgow	England	0-4
7 May	1958	Glasgow	Hungary	1-1
1 June	1958	Warsaw	Poland	2-1
WC 8 June	1958	Vasteras	Yugoslavia	1-1
WC11 June	1958	Norrkoping	Paraguay	2-3
WC15 June	1958	Orebro	France	1-2
18 October	1958	Cardiff	Wales	3-0
5 November	1958	Glasgow	N Ireland	2-2
11 April	1959	Wembley	England	0-1
6 May	1959	Glasgow	West Germany	3-2
27 May	1959	Amsterdam	Netherlands	2-1
3 June	1959	Lisbon	Portugal	0-1
3 October	1959	Belfast	N Ireland	4-0
4 November	1959	Glasgow	Wales	1-1
9 April	1960	Glasgow	England	1-1
4 May	1960	Glasgow	Poland	2-3
29 May	1960	Vienna	Austria	1-4
5 June	1960	Budapest	Hungary	3-3
8 June	1960	Ankara	Turkey	2-4
22 October	1960	Cardiff	Wales	0-2
9 November	1960	Glasgow	N Ireland	5-2
15 April	1961	Wembley	England	3-9
WC 3 May	1961	Glasgow	Eire	4-1
WC 7 May	1961	Dublin	Eire	3-0
WC14 May	1961	Bratislava	Czechoslovakia	0-4
WC26 September	1961	Glasgow	Czechoslovakia	3-2
7 October	1961	Belfast	N Ireland	6-1
8 November	1961	Glasgow	Wales	2-0
WC29 November	1961	Brussels	Czechoslovakia	2-4
14 April	1962	Glasgow	England	2-0
2 May	1962	Glasgow	Uruguay	2-3
20 October	1962	Cardiff	Wales	3-2
7 November	1962	Glasgow	N Ireland	5-1
6 April	1963	Wembley	England	2-1
‡8 May	1963	Glasgow	Austria	4-1
4 June	1963	Bergen	Norway	3-4
9 June	1963	Dublin	Eire	0-1
13 June	1963	Madrid	Spain	6-2
12 October	1963	Belfast	N Ireland	1-2
7 November	1963	Glasgow	Norway	6-1
20 November	1963	Glasgow	Wales	2-1
11 April	1964	Glasgow	England	1-0
12 May	1964	Hanover	West Germany	2-2
3 October	1964	Cardiff	Wales	2-3
WC21 October	1964	Glasgow	Finland	3-1
25 November	1964	Glasgow	N Ireland	3-2
10 April	1965	Wembley	England	2-2
8 May	1965	Glasgow	Spain	0-0
WC23 May	1965	Chorzow	Poland	1-1
WC27 May	1965	Helsinki	Finland	2-1
2 October	1965	Belfast	N Ireland	2-3
WC13 October	1965	Glasgow	Poland	1-2
WC 9 November	1965	Glasgow	Italy	1-0
24 November	1965	Glasgow	Wales	4-1
WC 7 December	1965	Naples	Italy	0-3
2 April	1966	Glasgow	England	3-4
11 May	1966	Glasgow	Holland	0-3
18 June	1966	Glasgow	Portugal	0-1
25 June	1966	Glasgow	Brazil	1-1
22 October	1966	Cardiff	Wales	1-1
16 November	1966	Glasgow	N Ireland	2-1
15 April	1967	Wembley	England	3-2
10 May	1967	Glasgow	Russia	0-2
21 October	1967	Belfast	N Ireland	0-1
22 November	1967	Glasgow	Wales	3-2
24 February	1968	Glasgow	England	1-1
30 May	1968	Amsterdam	Holland	0-0
16 October	1968	Copenhagen	Denmark	1-0
WC 6 November	1968	Glasgow	Austria	2-1
WC11 December	1968	Nicosia	Cyprus	5-0
WC16 April	1969	Glasgow	West Germany	1-1
3 May	1969	Wrexham	Wales	5-3
6 May	1969	Glasgow	N Ireland	1-1
10 May	1969	Wembley	England	1-4
WC12 May	1969	Glasgow	Cyprus	8-0
21 September	1969	Dublin	Eire	1-1
WC22 October	1969	Hamburg	West Germany	2-3
WC 5 November	1969	Vienna	Austria	0-2
18 April	1970	Belfast	N Ireland	1-0
22 April	1970	Glasgow	Wales	0-0
25 April	1970	Glasgow	England	0-0
EC11 November	1970	Glasgow	Denmark	1-0
EC 3 February	1971	Liege	Belgium	0-3
EC21 April	1971	Lisbon	Portugal	0-2
15 May	1971	Cardiff	Wales	0-0
18 May	1971	Glasgow	N Ireland	0-1
22 May	1971	Wembley	England	1-3
EC 9 June	1971	Copenhagen	Denmark	0-1
14 June	1971	Moscow	Russia	0-1
EC13 October	1971	Glasgow	Portugal	2-1
EC10 November	1971	Glasgow	Belgium	1-0
1 December	1971	Rotterdam	Holland	1-2
26 April	1972	Glasgow	Peru	2-0
20 May	1972	Glasgow	N Ireland	2-0
24 May	1972	Glasgow	Wales	1-0
28 May	1972	Glasgow	England	0-1
28 June	1972	Belo Horizonte	Yugoslavia	2-2
2 July	1972	Porto Alegre	Czechoslovakia	0-0
5 July	1972	Rio de Janeiro	Brazil	0-1
WC18 October	1972	Copenhagen	Denmark	4-1
WC15 November	1973	Glasgow	Denmark	2-0
14 February	1973	Glasgow	England	0-5
12 May	1973	Wrexham	Wales	2-0
16 May	1973	Glasgow	N Ireland	1-2
19 May	1973	Wembley	England	0-1
22 June	1973	Berne	Switzerland	0-1
30 June	1973	Glasgow	Brazil	0-1
WC26 September	1973	Glasgow	Czechoslovakia	2-1
WC17 October	1973	Bratislava	Czechoslovakia	0-1
14 November	1973	Glasgow	West Germany	1-1

* These matches were played by a team of Scots resident in London. They are not regarded as official.
†This match was abandoned after a disaster at the ground. It is not regarded as official.
‡Abandoned after 79 minutes. V – Victory games. J – Jubilee game. WT – War-time game. WC – World Cup. EC – European Championship.

A funny thing happened on the way to Windsor Park

Vanishing Best keeps Ireland waiting again

MANCHESTER UNITED'S vanishing super-star George Best scored an international hat-trick when he failed to report on schedule for Northern Ireland in Glasgow yesterday.

It is the third time in 12 months that he has broken the rules of the game for his country.

He was a late-comer exactly a year ago when he missed the first training session for the England game in Belfast.

By ALEX TONER

disappointed but guarded a hint of 'I hav No te

'The whole thing,' Peter Doherty once said of Irish international football, 'is a complete joke.' There was no trace of vindictiveness in that comment. There was nothing the manager liked better than a laugh, and if Irish football has been a joke, it certainly has never been a bad one.

Besides, Doherty's contribution to the comic side of Irish football has been as rich as anyone's. There was the time when he was up until the late hours playing cards with his players before a match with Scotland. A worried supporter pointed out the time, mentioning that the Scots, like all good footballers, were safely tucked up in bed. 'Ah yes,' came the reply, 'but are they sleeping?'

Doherty talks with fond nostalgia about his eleven years spell as Ireland's manager, but he is not without his regrets. 'At times when I look back, I feel ashamed of what went on. I am convinced that if we had been organized we would have done much much better.'

Haphazard administration as well as circumstances outside any Irishman's control have long blighted Ireland's record. For years there was not even the chance for players to meet each other before the day of the match. Tom Priestley, the Chelsea and Coleraine winger of the 1930s recalled his introduction to the national team.

What would the FA have done to George Best?

'Elisha Scott, one of the world's greatest ever goalkeepers was then captain. To me and most fans of Irish football Scott had seemed like a God. I was really looking forward to meeting him, but it wasn't until we were in the dressing room before the kick-off that I actually spoke to him. Although he was my captain, I barely talked to him for five minutes. There was nothing unusual about that in those days. That was the way things were.'

Things had clearly changed for the better by the time Terry Neill took over the managership in 1971. But the cavalier approach to international football still remained. No one actually missed the boat for the Home Championship in 1972, but there was still one conspicuous absentee from the Irish party. For the third time in a year George Best failed to report on time for the Irish team. In England, where the punishments for Alan Hudson and Colin Todd showed how harsh the disciplinary machine could be, Best's international career would surely

have been finished. Yet so far from being censorious, Terry Neill generously kept Best's place in the team open until the last possible minute and even after the magnificent victory over England at Wembley, he was prepared to say how much he wished Best had been there to share his pleasure.

But then anyone whose task it is to get eleven Irish footballers to appear together at any one place has to be unusually tolerant. The history of Irish international football, if not quite a comedy of errors, is certainly littered with episodes which could only have happened to Irishmen.

Even in 1913-14, the season of Ireland's outright win in the Home Championship, there was the usual last minute chase for that elusive eleventh man. Ireland's right-winger at the time was a Manchester United player by the name of Hamill, whose reputation was for whole hearted effort at all times. Well . . . not quite at all times for on the Saturday before the crucial match against England, United officials noted an unusual lethargy about Hamill's play. Asked for an explanation, the unfortunate winger admitted that he had been conserving his energy in anticipation of the international. His patriotism cost him dear for he was promptly forbidden to play for his country. But, as so often, Ireland triumphed in adversity, winning against England and Wales and drawing with Scotland for the fifth point that gave them the Championship outright.

That success was to be an isolated one. Ireland did not win another international until 1923 and only won another eleven in the years before the Second World War. The poor record is largely attributable to the partition in 1921 and the formation of the breakaway Football Association of Ireland in the same year.

The years between the partition and the appointment of Doherty in 1951 are not recalled by Ulstermen with relish. It was left to Eire to provide the two highlights of the era. Against Belgium in a 1934 World Cup qualifying game, the Aberdeen centre-forward, Paddy Moore, scored all four goals in a remarkable comeback with which Eire pulled back a four goal deficit to draw 4-4. As the FAI Annual put it: 'This was Paddy Moore's finest hour, despite the honours he won afterwards. We were behind. Paddy brought his total of goals to four, to earn a draw, when we seemed to be licked.' That game may well have been Moore's finest hour, but Eire's was definitely on 21 September 1949 when, with a team that

included a carpenter and a printer of a Dublin newspaper, they became the first ever 'foreign' side to beat England at home. Eire's 2-0 win was a personal triumph for captain Johnny Carey, who in the absence of any team manager, worked out the tactics and took care of the pre-match training session.

Carey's contribution to Irish football was as great as anyone's. Before the Second World War the northern Irish Football Association regularly selected players from the Free State for its international sides,

and Carey was one of several to play for both Northern Ireland and Eire. In one week he actually managed to play for both sides —on September 26 and 28 1946— against the full England side.

The fault of Northern Ireland's poor record between the Wars did not lie with the players so much as the system under which they played. One anecdote, told by Hugh Davey, throws some light on what was wrong. Davey and his Reading colleague, Billy McConnell, had travelled up to Belfast via London.

RADIO TIMES HULTON PICTURE LIBRARY

SYNDICATION INTERNATIONAL

OWEN BARNES

Top left In May 1972, for the third time in twelve months, George Best failed to report on time for an Irish international. This time he had taken to the Spanish beaches, threatening to give up the game.
Top Without Best and forced to play away from home, the Irish defence conceded two goals to the Scots, but a 1-0 win against England in the next game was ample consolation for that. It was only Ireland's third ever win in England.
Above Port Vale's Sammy Morgan scores Northern Ireland's equalizing goal against Spain at Hull City's Boothferry Park. Unable to play in Ireland, the Irish settled instead for the club ground of manager Terry Neill.
Left Manchester United's Johnny Carey, winner of 28 caps for Eire and seven for Northern Ireland.

As usual they put in for their expenses: 'Three bob for a taxi and half a crown for a meal. As soon as we sent in the bill the officials were on to us, saying that that was far too much and that we'd have to cut down for the next game or we wouldn't be sure of our places in the team. We just laughed.'

The renaissance began in August 1951, when the international selectors wisely, if rather belatedly, decided that it was time to introduce professionalism at the top and appointed Peter Doherty as manager.

Why Doherty? There could have been no other choice. The man who had decorated the game with his magical artistry and was rated by Sepp Herberger, the wily West German team manager, as 'one of the greatest all-round players' was steeped in football.

He had all the qualities, but his main assets were his fierce dedication, honesty, sense of humour, hypnotic homespun eloquence and stern, sensibly imposed, discipline. He was the saviour of Irish football. But the revival was not instant. It took years of hard work, patience and the enthusiasm of the players to change Northern Ireland's image from that of 'Aunt Sallies' to a team that was to prove itself of true international stature.

Doherty was a players' man. He shared their jokes, their triumphs, their disasters and he never lost his sense of humour. Only once did he lose his temper. That was in Bologna in 1961, when Northern Ireland were playing Italy in a tour friendly. Peter had persuaded Wilbur Cush, than a Portadown player, to abandon his idea of retiring and had earmarked him for the job of marking Omar Sivori, the great inside-

forward. The selectors, who still selfishly clung to the job of picking the team, omitted Cush from the side.

'I don't think I have ever been so mad in my life,' said Doherty. 'I went to my hotel to pack my bags, I inquired about planes back home and I would have left on the spot. I stayed on only because it would have broken my heart to leave the players.'

Under the guidance of Doherty and his chief lieutenant, Danny Blanchflower, and with the infectious good humour of the late Gerry Morgan, a former international centre-half and one of the last of the traditional cloth cap trainers, results began to improve. Victories were still hard to come by, but the horrible hidings from England, which had been all too regular since the 13-0 catastrophe in the first ever

Irish international in 1882, were happily things of the past. There were meritorious draws, occasional victories against Scotland and above all the 3-2 win of 1957 on Ireland's second visit to Wembley.

That match was a tribute to Blanchflower's captaincy. Twice he ordered new tactical dispositions on the field in response to the changing phases of the game. Ireland took the lead with a Jimmy McIlroy penalty which went into the net via a post and the back of the diving England goalkeeper. 'Brother, when we do it, we do it clever,' Blanchflower commented after the game. The second goal was scored by Sammy McCrory, the Southend United inside-forward. In the morning papers Duncan Edwards had asked: 'What is an old man like McCrory doing in a game like this.' 'Not bad for an old man, eh!' McCrory said as he passed Edwards on his way back to the centre after the goal.

That match was the prelude to what was Ireland's golden era—the 1958 World Cup finals in Sweden. For the Irish it was a carnival as well as the most important competition in the world. They became the heroes of Sweden and the darlings of the world's press. While the Germans, Brazilians, Argentinians, Czechs and even the English had strict security and 'no interview' rules, the Irish camp, in a dreamy little seaside haunt at Tylosand, was open to all.

'We like to train on whiskey and potato bread'

The lovable Gerry Morgan, with his Jimmy Durante profile, and rakishly worn head gear, was the most photographed and most quoted character in Sweden. He had an unlimited supply of stories, most of them unadulterated blarney. He told one credulous scribe that the Irish trained on whisky and potato bread. Another went away with the story that the players would each receive a £1,000 bonus for each victory, and to cap that he said Jimmy McIlroy would be knighted if Northern Ireland won the cup.

It was all good, clean fun and valuable publicity for the 'mad Irish' who won thousands of supporters and were 'adopted' by the residents of Halmstad, where they played their first two matches. A goal from Wilbur Cush gave the team an encouraging 1-0 win against Czechoslovakia but that was soon followed by a 3-1 defeat by Argentina.

Even in defeat the Irish won friends. After the game the Irish party made their way, as usual, to 'The Black Kat', Halmstad's one night club. As one player put it: 'Well, you can never miss a chance to drown your sorrows can you.' For once the Argentinians were there, but they were closeted in an upstairs reception room. The revelry, meanwhile, was all downstairs, where the defeated Irish team were drinking to finer prospects in the next game.

A stirring 2-2 draw against West Germany meant a sectional play-off with Czechoslovakia, which the

FULL INTERNATIONALS PLAYED BY IRELAND AND NORTHERN IRELAND FEBRUARY 1882–JANUARY 1974

Date		Venue	Opponents	Score
18 February	1882	Belfast	England	0-13
25 February	1882	Wrexham	Wales	1-7
24 February	1883	Liverpool	England	0-7
17 March	1883	Belfast	Wales	1-1
9 February	1884	Wrexham	Wales	0-6
23 February	1884	Belfast	England	1-8
26 March	1884	Belfast	Scotland	0-5
28 February	1885	Manchester	England	0-4
14 March	1885	Glasgow	Scotland	2-8
11 April	1885	Belfast	Wales	2-8
27 February	1886	Wrexham	Wales	0-5
13 March	1886	Belfast	England	1-6
20 March	1886	Belfast	Scotland	2-7
5 February	1887	Sheffield	England	0-7
19 February	1887	Glasgow	Scotland	1-4
12 March	1887	Belfast	Wales	4-1
3 March	1888	Wrexham	Wales	0-11
24 March	1888	Belfast	Scotland	2-10
31 March	1888	Belfast	England	1-5
2 March	1889	Liverpool	England	1-6
9 March	1889	Glasgow	Scotland	0-7
27 April	1889	Belfast	Wales	1-3
8 February	1890	Shrewsbury	Wales	2-5
15 March	1890	Belfast	England	1-9
29 March	1890	Belfast	Scotland	1-4
7 February	1891	Belfast	Wales	7-2
7 March	1891	Wolverhampton	England	1-6
28 March	1891	Glasgow	Scotland	1-2
27 February	1892	Bangor (Wales)	Wales	1-1
5 March	1892	Belfast	England	0-2
19 March	1892	Belfast	Scotland	2-3
25 February	1893	Birmingham	England	1-6
25 March	1893	Glasgow	Scotland	1-6
8 April	1893	Belfast	Wales	4-3
24 February	1894	Swansea	Wales	1-4
3 March	1894	Belfast	England	2-2
31 March	1894	Belfast	Scotland	1-2
9 March	1895	Derby	England	0-9
16 March	1895	Belfast	Wales	2-2
30 March	1895	Glasgow	Scotland	1-3
29 February	1896	Wrexham	Wales	1-6
7 March	1896	Belfast	England	0-2
28 March	1896	Belfast	Scotland	3-3
20 February	1897	Nottingham	England	0-6
6 March	1897	Belfast	Wales	4-3
27 March	1897	Glasgow	Scotland	1-5
19 February	1898	Llandudno	Wales	1-0
5 March	1898	Belfast	England	2-3
26 March	1898	Belfast	Scotland	0-3
18 February	1899	Sunderland	England	2-13
4 March	1899	Belfast	Wales	1-0
25 March	1899	Glasgow	Scotland	1-9
24 February	1900	Llandudno	Wales	0-2
3 March	1900	Belfast	Scotland	0-3
17 March	1900	Dublin	England	0-2
23 February	1901	Glasgow	Scotland	0-11
9 March	1901	Southampton	England	0-3
23 March	1901	Llandudno	Wales	0-1
1 March	1902	Belfast	Scotland	1-5
22 March	1902	Belfast	England	0-1
22 March	1902	Cardiff	Wales	3-0
14 February	1903	Wolverhampton	England	0-4
21 March	1903	Glasgow	Scotland	2-0
28 March	1903	Belfast	Wales	2-0
12 March	1904	Belfast	England	1-3
21 March	1904	Bangor (Wales)	Wales	1-0
26 March	1904	Dublin	Scotland	1-1
25 February	1905	Middlesbrough	England	1-1
18 March	1905	Glasgow	Scotland	0-4
8 April	1905	Belfast	Wales	2-2
17 February	1906	Belfast	England	0-5
17 March	1906	Dublin	Scotland	0-1
2 April	1907	Wrexham	Wales	4-4
16 February	1907	Liverpool	England	0-1
23 February	1908	Belfast	Wales	2-3
16 March	1908	Glasgow	Scotland	0-3
15 February	1908	Belfast	England	1-3
14 March	1908	Dublin	Scotland	0-5
11 April	1908	Aberdare	Wales	1-0
13 February	1909	Bradford	England	0-4
20 March	1909	Belfast	Wales	2-3
27 March	1909	Glasgow	Scotland	0-5
12 February	1910	Belfast	England	1-1
11 March	1910	Wrexham	Wales	1-4
19 March	1910	Belfast	Scotland	1-0
11 February	1911	Derby	England	1-2
18 March	1911	Glasgow	Scotland	0-2
28 March	1911	Belfast	Wales	1-2
10 February	1912	Dublin	England	1-6
16 March	1912	Belfast	Scotland	1-4
13 April	1912	Cardiff	Wales	3-2
18 January	1913	Belfast	Wales	0-1
15 February	1913	Belfast	England	2-1
15 March	1913	Dublin	Scotland	1-2
19 January	1914	Wrexham	Wales	2-1
14 February	1914	Middlesbrough	England	3-0
14 March	1914	Belfast	Scotland	1-1

Date		Venue	Opponents	Score
25 October	1919	Belfast	England	1-1
14 February	1920	Belfast	Wales	2-2
13 March	1920	Glasgow	Scotland	0-3
23 October	1920	Sunderland	England	0-2
26 February	1921	Belfast	Scotland	0-2
9 April	1921	Swansea	Wales	1-2
22 October	1921	Belfast	England	1-1
4 March	1922	Glasgow	Scotland	1-2
1 April	1922	Belfast	Wales	1-1
21 October	1922	West Bromwich	England	0-2
3 March	1923	Belfast	Scotland	0-1
14 April	1923	Wrexham	Wales	3-0
20 October	1923	Belfast	England	2-1
1 March	1924	Glasgow	Scotland	0-2
15 March	1924	Belfast	Wales	0-1
22 October	1924	Liverpool	England	1-3
28 February	1925	Belfast	Scotland	0-3
18 April	1925	Wrexham	Wales	0-0
24 October	1925	Belfast	England	0-0
13 January	1926	Belfast	Wales	3-0
27 February	1926	Glasgow	Scotland	0-4
20 October	1926	Liverpool	England	3-3
26 February	1927	Belfast	Scotland	0-2
9 April	1927	Cardiff	Wales	2-2
22 October	1927	Belfast	England	2-0
4 February	1928	Belfast	Wales	1-2
25 February	1928	Glasgow	Scotland	1-0
22 October	1928	Liverpool	England	1-2
2 February	1929	Wrexham	Wales	2-2
23 February	1929	Belfast	Scotland	3-7
19 October	1929	Belfast	England	0-3
1 February	1930	Belfast	Wales	7-0
22 February	1930	Glasgow	Scotland	1-3
20 October	1930	Sheffield	England	1-5
21 February	1931	Belfast	Scotland	0-0
22 April	1931	Wrexham	Wales	2-3
19 September	1931	Glasgow	Scotland	1-3
17 October	1931	Belfast	England	2-6
5 December	1931	Belfast	Wales	4-0
17 September	1932	Belfast	Scotland	0-4
17 October	1932	Blackpool	England	0-1
7 December	1932	Wrexham	Wales	1-4
16 September	1933	Glasgow	Scotland	2-1
14 October	1933	Belfast	England	0-3
4 November	1933	Belfast	Wales	1-1
20 October	1934	Belfast	Scotland	2-1
6 February	1935	Liverpool	England	1-2
27 March	1935	Wrexham	Wales	1-3
19 October	1935	Belfast	England	1-3
13 November	1935	Edinburgh	Scotland	1-2
11 March	1936	Belfast	Wales	3-2
31 October	1936	Belfast	Scotland	1-3
18 November	1936	Stoke	England	1-3
17 March	1937	Wrexham	Wales	1-4
23 October	1937	Belfast	England	1-5
10 November	1937	Aberdeen	Scotland	1-1
16 March	1938	Belfast	Wales	1-0
8 October	1938	Belfast	Scotland	0-2
16 November	1938	Manchester	England	0-7
15 March	1939	Wrexham	Wales	1-3
V15 September	1945	Belfast	England	0-1
28 September	1946	Belfast	England	2-7
27 November	1946	Glasgow	Scotland	0-0
16 April	1947	Belfast	Wales	2-1
4 October	1947	Belfast	Scotland	2-0
5 November	1947	Liverpool	England	2-2
10 March	1948	Wrexham	Wales	0-2
9 October	1948	Belfast	England	2-6
17 November	1948	Glasgow	Scotland	2-3
9 March	1949	Belfast	Wales	0-2
WC 1 October	1949	Belfast	Scotland	2-8
WC16 November	1949	Manchester	England	2-9
WC 8 March	1950	Wrexham	Wales	0-0
7 October	1950	Belfast	England	1-4
1 November	1950	Glasgow	Scotland	1-6
7 March	1951	Belfast	Wales	1-2
12 May	1951	Belfast	France	2-2
6 October	1951	Belfast	Scotland	0-3
14 November	1951	Birmingham	England	0-2
19 March	1952	Swansea	Wales	0-3
4 October	1952	Belfast	England	2-2
5 November	1952	Glasgow	Scotland	1-1
11 November	1952	Paris	France	1-3
15 April	1953	Belfast	Wales	2-3
WC 3 October	1953	Belfast	Scotland	1-3
WC11 November	1953	Liverpool	England	1-3
WC31 March	1954	Wrexham	Wales	2-1
2 October	1954	Belfast	England	0-2
3 November	1954	Glasgow	Scotland	2-2
20 April	1955	Belfast	Wales	2-3
8 October	1955	Belfast	Scotland	2-1
2 November	1955	Wembley	England	0-3
11 April	1956	Cardiff	Wales	1-1
6 October	1956	Belfast	England	1-1
7 November	1956	Glasgow	Scotland	0-1
WC16 January	1957	Lisbon	Portugal	1-1
10 April	1957	Belfast	Wales	0-0

Date		Venue	Opponents	Score
WC25 April	1957	Rome	Italy	0-1
WC 1 May	1957	Belfast	Portugal	3-0
5 October	1957	Belfast	Scotland	1-1
6 November	1957	Wembley	England	3-2
4 December	1957	Belfast	Italy	2-2
WC15 January	1958	Belfast	Italy	2-1
16 April	1958	Cardiff	Wales	1-1
WC 8 June	1958	Halmstad	Czechoslovakia	1-0
WC11 June	1958	Halmstad	Argentina	1-3
WC15 June	1958	Malmo	West Germany	2-2
WC17 June	1958	Malmo	Czechoslovakia	2-1
WC19 June	1958	Norrkoping	France	0-4
4 October	1958	Belfast	England	3-3
15 October	1958	Madrid	Spain	2-6
5 November	1958	Glasgow	Scotland	2-2
22 April	1959	Belfast	Wales	4-1
3 October	1959	Belfast	Scotland	0-4
18 November	1959	Wembley	England	1-2
6 April	1960	Wrexham	Wales	2-3
8 October	1960	Belfast	England	2-5
WC26 October	1960	Belfast	West Germany	3-4
9 November	1960	Glasgow	Scotland	2-5
12 April	1961	Belfast	Wales	1-5
25 April	1961	Bologna	Italy	2-3
WC 3 May	1961	Athens	Greece	1-2
WC10 May	1961	West Berlin	West Germany	1-2
7 October	1961	Belfast	Scotland	1-6
WC17 October	1961	Belfast	Greece	2-0
22 November	1961	Wembley	England	1-1
11 April	1962	Cardiff	Wales	0-4
9 May	1962	Rotterdam	Netherlands	0-4
ENC10 October	1962	Katowice	Poland	2-0
20 October	1962	Belfast	England	1-3
7 November	1962	Glasgow	Scotland	1-5
ENC28 November	1962	Belfast	Poland	2-0
3 April	1963	Belfast	Wales	1-4
30 May	1963	Bilbao	Spain	1-1
12 October	1963	Belfast	Scotland	2-1
30 October	1963	Belfast	Spain	0-1
20 November	1963	Wembley	England	3-8
15 April	1964	Swansea	Wales	3-2
29 April	1964	Belfast	Uruguay	3-0
3 October	1964	Belfast	England	3-4
WC14 October	1964	Belfast	Switzerland	1-0
WC14 November	1964	Lausanne	Switzerland	1-2
25 November	1964	Glasgow	Scotland	2-3
WC17 March	1965	Belfast	Holland	2-1
31 March	1965	Belfast	Wales	0-5
WC 7 April	1965	Rotterdam	Holland	0-0
WC 7 May	1965	Belfast	Albania	4-1
2 October	1965	Belfast	Scotland	3-2
10 November	1965	Wembley	England	1-2
WC24 November	1965	Tirana	Albania	1-1
30 March	1966	Cardiff	Wales	4-1
7 May	1966	Belfast	West Germany	0-2
22 June	1966	Belfast	Mexico	4-1
22 October	1966	Belfast	England	0-2
16 November	1966	Glasgow	Scotland	1-2
12 April	1967	Belfast	Wales	0-0
21 October	1967	Belfast	Scotland	1-0
22 November	1967	Wembley	England	0-2
28 February	1968	Wrexham	Wales	0-2
10 September	1968	Jaffa	Israel	3-2
WC23 October	1968	Belfast	Turkey	4-1
WC11 December	1968	Istanbul	Turkey	3-0
3 May	1969	Belfast	England	1-3
6 May	1969	Glasgow	Scotland	1-1
10 May	1969	Belfast	Wales	0-0
WC10 September	1969	Belfast	Russia	0-0
WC22 October	1969	Moscow	Russia	0-2
18 April	1970	Belfast	Scotland	0-1
21 April	1970	Wembley	England	1-3
25 April	1970	Swansea	Wales	0-1
EC11 November	1970	Seville	Spain	0-3
EC 3 February	1971	Nicosia	Cyprus	3-0
EC21 April	1971	Belfast	Cyprus	5-0
15 May	1971	Belfast	England	0-1
18 May	1971	Glasgow	Scotland	1-0
22 May	1971	Belfast	Wales	1-0
EC22 September	1971	Moscow	Russia	0-1
EC13 October	1971	Belfast	Russia	1-1
EC16 February	1972	Hull	Spain	1-1
20 May	1972	Glasgow	Scotland	0-2
24 May	1972	Wembley	England	1-0
27 May	1972	Wrexham	Wales	0-0
WC18 October	1972	Sofia	Bulgaria	0-3
WC14 February	1973	Nicosia	Cyprus	0-1
WC28 March	1973	Coventry	Portugal	1-1
WC 8 May	1973	Fulham	Cyprus	3-0
12 May	1973	Everton	England	1-2
16 May	1973	Glasgow	Scotland	2-1
19 May	1973	Everton	Wales	1-0
WC26 September	1973	Sheffield	Bulgaria	0-0
WC14 November	1973	Lisbon	Portugal	1-1

ENC – European Nations Cup games
EC – European Championship games
WC – World Cup games
V – Victory International

Irish won 2-1 despite playing with a goalkeeper with a broken hand and an injured ankle. Unbelievably they had reached the quarter finals, but their tired, injury-ridden side had to surrender to the French, who sauntered to a 4-0 win at Norkopping.

When the Doherty regime ended with his retirement in 1961, Bertie Peacock, left-half in the Irish team in Sweden, and then player manager of Coleraine, took over after Danny Blanchflower had turned down the job.

Peacock it was who introduced George Best to international football. 'Harry Gregg was really responsible, for he kept telling me what a wonderful player Best was. After his first game against Wales at Swansea it was easy to see that he was going to be one of the world's great players,' he said.

Equally self-effacing was his admission that he was to blame for failure to qualify for the 1966 World Cup finals. A win against nonentities Albania would have meant a play-off with Switzerland.

'I made a terrible mistake,' Peacock confessed. 'I watched Albania in Holland and Switzerland, but I should have gone to see them in Albania. We were not prepared for the conditions. If I had known we would have taken our own food, because the players couldn't eat the food they got and they were not in the right mood for the game.' A 1-1 draw in a comic-opera game, ruined by a fussy Bulgarian referee, who made George Best stand to attention when he spoke to him, put the Irish out.

Even then the team kept their high spirits. They tried to hold a sing-song in the only hotel in Tirana, a mausoleum of a place, but were silenced by a stern-faced Chinese hotel official who announced that singing was strictly forbidden.

Peacock's resignation was followed in 1967 by the appointment of Billy Bingham, another Doherty old boy, who was later to manage the Greek national team. After resounding victories against Turkey and Cyprus and a draw against Russia in Belfast hopes of a World Cup trip to Mexico were shattered when George Best was injured and could not play against the Russians, who won 2-0 in Moscow.

And so on to the appointment of Terry Neill, who played for and managed Hull City besides taking care of the Irish team. The humour was there as ever—after he had scored the goal that gave Ireland their second ever win over England at Wembley Neill was quick to remark that it doubled his tally.

But while the North succeeded, the South was not sleeping. When Alan Kelly played his 42nd international in goal against Russia in October 1972, he admitted that he had not received a cap since 1967. Apparently the firm that manufactures the headgear was having problems. 'The matter is in hand' was the FA of Ireland's weighty comment.

Above *Derek Dougan and Bobby Moore, old rivals in the English League and international football, contend a high ball. By 1972 Dougan had been playing for Northern Ireland for 15 years.*

COLORSPORT

FULL INTERNATIONALS PLAYED BY EIRE 1924–OCTOBER 1973

Date		Venue	Opponents	Score
28 May	1924	Paris	Bulgaria	1-0
2 June	1924	Paris	Netherlands	1-2
3 June	1924	Paris	Estonia	3-1
16 June	1925	Dublin	USA	3-1
21 March	1926	Turin	Italy	0-3
23 April	1927	Dublin	Italy	1-2
12 February	1928	Liege	Belgium	4-2
20 April	1929	Dublin	Belgium	4-0
11 May	1930	Brussels	Belgium	3-1
26 April	1931	Barcelona	Spain	1-1
13 December	1931	Dublin	Spain	0-5
8 May	1932	Amsterdam	Netherlands	2-0
WC 25 February	1934	Dublin	Belgium	4-4
WC 8 April	1934	Amsterdam	Netherlands	2-5
15 December	1934	Dublin	Hungary	2-4
5 May	1935	Basle	Switzerland	0-1
8 May	1935	Dortmund	Germany	1-3
8 December	1935	Dublin	Netherlands	3-5
17 March	1936	Dublin	Switzerland	1-0
3 May	1936	Budapest	Hungary	3-3
9 May	1936	Luxembourg	Luxembourg	5-1
17 October	1936	Dublin	Germany	5-2
6 December	1936	Dublin	Hungary	2-3
17 May	1937	Berne	Switzerland	1-0
23 May	1937	Paris	France	2-0
WC 10 October	1937	Oslo	Norway	2-3
WC 7 November	1937	Dublin	Norway	3-3
18 May	1938	Prague	Czechoslovakia	2-2
22 May	1938	Warsaw	Poland	0-6
18 September	1938	Dublin	Switzerland	4-0
13 November	1938	Dublin	Poland	3-2
19 March	1939	Cork	Hungary	2-2
18 May	1939	Budapest	Hungary	2-2
23 May	1939	Bremen	Germany	1-1
16 June	1946	Lisbon	Portugal	1-3
23 June	1946	Madrid	Spain	1-0
30 September	1946	Dublin	England	0-1
2 March	1947	Dublin	Spain	3-2
4 May	1947	Dublin	Portugal	0-2
23 May	1948	Lisbon	Portugal	0-2
30 May	1948	Barcelona	Spain	1-2
5 December	1948	Dublin	Switzerland	0-1
24 April	1949	Dublin	Belgium	0-2
22 May	1949	Dublin	Portugal	1-0
WC 2 June	1949	Stockholm	Sweden	1-3
12 June	1949	Dublin	Spain	1-4
WC 8 September	1949	Dublin	Finland	3-0
21 September	1949	Everton	England	2-0
WC 9 October	1949	Helsinki	Finland	1-1
WC 13 November	1949	Dublin	Sweden	1-3
10 May	1950	Brussels	Belgium	1-5
26 November	1950	Dublin	Norway	2-2
13 May	1951	Dublin	Argentina	0-1
30 May	1951	Oslo	Norway	3-2
17 October	1951	Dublin	West Germany	3-2
4 May	1952	Cologne	West Germany	0-3
7 May	1952	Vienna	Austria	0-6
1 June	1952	Madrid	Spain	0-6
16 November	1952	Dublin	France	1-1
25 March	1953	Dublin	Austria	4-0
WC 4 October	1953	Dublin	France	3-5
WC 28 October	1953	Dublin	Luxembourg	4-0
WC 25 November	1953	Paris	France	0-1
WC 7 March	1954	Luxembourg	Luxembourg	1-0
8 November	1954	Dublin	Norway	2-1
1 May	1955	Dublin	Netherlands	1-0
25 May	1955	Oslo	Norway	3-1
28 May	1955	Hamburg	West Germany	1-2
19 September	1955	Dublin	Yugoslavia	1-4
27 November	1955	Dublin	Spain	2-2
10 May	1956	Rotterdam	Netherlands	4-1
WC 3 October	1956	Dublin	Denmark	2-1
25 November	1956	Dublin	West Germany	3-0
WC 8 May	1957	Wembley	England	1-5
WC 19 May	1957	Dublin	England	1-1
WC 2 October	1957	Copenhagen	Denmark	2-0
11 May	1958	Katowice	Poland	2-2
14 May	1958	Vienna	Austria	1-3
5 October	1958	Dublin	Poland	2-2
ENC 5 May	1959	Dublin	Czechoslovakia	2-0
ENC 10 May	1959	Bratislava	Czechoslovakia	0-4
1 November	1959	Dublin	Sweden	3-2
30 March	1960	Dublin	Chile	2-0
11 May	1960	Dusseldorf	West Germany	1-0
18 May	1960	Malmo	Sweden	1-4
28 September	1960	Dublin	Wales	2-3
6 November	1960	Dublin	Norway	3-2
WC 3 May	1961	Glasgow	Scotland	1-4
WC 7 May	1961	Dublin	Scotland	0-3
WC 8 October	1961	Dublin	Czechoslovakia	1-3
WC 29 October	1961	Prague	Czechoslovakia	1-7
8 April	1962	Dublin	Austria	2-3
ENC 12 August	1962	Dublin	Iceland	4-2
ENC 2 September	1962	Reykjavik	Iceland	1-1
9 June	1963	Dublin	Scotland	1-0
25 September	1963	Vienna	Austria	0-0
13 October	1963	Dublin	Austria	3-2
11 March	1964	Seville	Spain	1-5
8 April	1964	Dublin	Spain	0-2
10 May	1964	Cracow	Poland	1-3
13 May	1964	Oslo	Norway	4-1
24 May	1964	Dublin	England	1-3
25 October	1964	Dublin	Poland	3-2
24 March	1965	Dublin	Belgium	0-2
WC 5 May	1965	Dublin	Spain	1-0
WC 21 October	1965	Seville	Spain	1-4
WC 10 November	1965	Paris	Spain	0-1
4 May	1966	Dublin	West Germany	0-4
22 May	1966	Vienna	Austria	0-1
25 May	1966	Liege	Belgium	3-2
ENC 23 October	1966	Dublin	Spain	0-0
16 November	1966	Dublin	Turkey	2-1
ENC 7 December	1966	Valencia	Spain	0-2
22 February	1967	Ankara	Turkey	1-2
21 May	1967	Dublin	Czechoslovakia	0-2
22 November	1967	Prague	Czechoslovakia	2-1
30 October	1968	Katowice	Poland	0-1
10 November	1968	Dublin	Austria	2-2
4 December	1968	Dublin	Denmark	1-1
WC 4 May	1969	Dublin	Czechoslovakia	1-2
WC 27 May	1969	Copenhagen	Denmark	2-0
21 September	1969	Dublin	Scotland	1-1
WC 7 October	1969	Prague	Czechoslovakia	0-3
6 May	1970	Dublin	Poland	1-2
9 May	1970	Berlin	West Germany	1-2
23 September	1970	Dublin	Poland	0-2
EC 14 October	1970	Dublin	Sweden	1-1
EC 28 October	1970	Malmo	Sweden	0-1
EC 8 December	1970	Rome	Italy	0-3
EC 10 May	1971	Dublin	Italy	1-2
EC 30 May	1971	Dublin	Austria	1-4
EC 10 October	1971	Linz	Austria	0-6
11 June	1972	Recife	Iran	2-1
18 June	1972	Natal (Brazil)	Equador	3-2
21 June	1972	Recife	Chile	1-2
25 June	1972	Recife	Portugal	1-2
WC 18 October	1972	Dublin	Russia	1-2
WC 15 November	1972	Dublin	France	2-1
WC 13 May	1973	Moscow	USSR	0-1
16 May	1973	Wroclaw	Poland	0-2
WC 19 May	1973	Paris	France	1-1
6 June	1973	Oslo	Norway	1-1
21 October	1973	Dublin	Poland	1-0

ENC – European Nations Cup games   WC – World Cup games
EC – European Championship games

Jonahs in Wales?

August 1972 was a critical month in the century-long history of soccer in Britain. A South American move, led by Uruguay, to merge the four home associations into one was defeated only by intensive back-stage lobbying.

Had the resolution been put to FIFA and succeeded Britain would have been left with only one vote on committees and one team in tournaments. The idea of a United Kingdom team, with Best and Bremner, for example, free to help England in the World Cup, had some appeal.

But this would have been a small gain to set against the loss of four proudly independent nations to world football. Each of the four British associations has contributed much to the growth of the game and its legends—the story of Welsh international football is a story of constant, often glorious, battling against huge odds.

From the very earliest days Wales have been confined to an inferior status. On three occasions in the 1890s England even sent a second team to play Wales on the *same day* as the fixture with Ireland.

This derisory treatment, which continued for some years, was not immediately justified by results. In the first three matches against England, played between 1879 and 1881, Wales lost two by the odd goal and won the third.

Wales' first international matches were against Scotland and, from the start in 1876, they represented a devastating run of failure. In the first 11 years, Scotland scored 54 goals against five.

International football became a little like the law of the ocean where the big fish eat the smaller fish and the smaller ones eat the tiny ones. Wales turned to Ireland for her whipping boys, winning 7-1, 6-0, 8-2, 5-0 and 11-0 during the first six years and losing only once—1-4 in Belfast in 1887.

With the creation of the FA in 1863 and the commencement of the England v Scotland series, it became inevitable that organized football would spread to the hills of Wales and across the sea to Ireland.

In 1873 the Wrexham club was formed and they have the reputation of being the first organized club to emerge in the Principality. There is, however, considerable evidence that the Druids, who played at Plasmadoc Park, Ruabon, were formed even earlier.

Soon Chirk, Aberystwyth, Newtown, Corwen, Bala, Bangor and Caernarvon had clubs. So did Oswestry who, although just across the border in England, played their part in the development of Welsh football.

The earliest clubs were exclusively in the North of Wales where the gentlemen farmers and university graduates had the leisure to take up sport.

The original idea of an international match came from G A Clay-Thomas, a London Welshman, who made the proposal to the *Field* magazine. In February 1876, a meeting was arranged and the 'Cambrian FA', which was the Welsh body's first title, advertised for players in the *Field*.

The inaugural match, played on 25 March 1876, resulted in a 4-0 defeat. This first team contained two Davieses, a Jones, an Evans and a Williams. For nearly 100 years, scarcely a Welsh team would take the field without the possessor of at least one of these names in the side.

The earliest Welsh team did not contain any representatives from the South. Welsh football was North Wales football, and they were to guard that tradition into the 20th century, when the professionals of the industrial south had left the northern amateurs far behind.

'The parish pump politics of Welsh football'

But the first professional clubs were from the South: Merthyr, Aberdare, later followed by Cardiff in 1910 and Newport and Swansea in 1911. All of them later gained election to the Football League.

Despite this, the Northerners regarded these clubs as upstarts, and the international team had a preponderance of northerners until the 1920s. Whatever the current form of individuals, there was an insistence that there should be at least a 6-5 bias in favour of northern-born players. This idiotic system, perpetuated by generations of unwieldy selection committees—who far outnumbered the players—persisted even until after the First World War.

Not only soccer suffered from this stubborn parochialism. In rugby union selection committees the same divisions arose. The representatives of the east always demanded their quota of players from Cardiff and Newport, while the men from the west insisted that Swansea and Llanelli should provide the bulk of the team.

Incredibly, the soccer selectors persisted with their parish pump politics even when all the player-candidates were members of English football league clubs. 'You can't have Dai Astley of Aston Villa *and* Leslie Jones of Arsenal in the forward line', someone would say. 'They're

POPPERFOTO

Top left *Terry Medwin, the Spurs reserve winger, scores the first of the two goals that beat Hungary in the play-off for a place in the quarter-final of the 1958 World Cup. Drawn against Brazil, Wales were only beaten by a last minute goal from Pele.*
Bottom left *Mike England (left) in his usual commanding form in the middle of the Welsh defence. It was the attack that gave manager Dave Bowen his main problems. Between 1970 and 1972 Wales could only muster seven goals in fifteen internationals.*

both South Walians and you've already got four from there.'

Apart from this internal warfare, Welsh international football had another cross to bear. While the English selectors could demand the release of any player in the Football League, the Welsh, like the Irish and Scots, had to rely on the generosity of the English.

Some, like Arsenal, believed that any man had the right to play for the country of his birth and put few difficulties in the way. But others were totally unco-operative, and the burden has been carried right up to modern times.

Dave Bowen, the Welsh team manager, has claimed that only twice in his long period in control was he able to field his chosen side. Small wonder that Wales, despite producing some of the most outstanding players in the world, has never been able to produce results commensurate with her potential.

The selfishness of the English clubs did, however, produce one memorable moment of glory. It came in 1930 when the Football League banned the release of all League players for Saturday afternoon internationals played by Wales, Ireland and Scotland.

The situation provided few problems for the Scots. At the time their domestic football had never been of a higher standard and they could call upon a powerful team of home-based players. But Wales, who had to play them at Hampden, could demand players only from the four clubs affiliated to the Welsh FA.

These were Cardiff, already sliding from the greatness which had won them the FA Cup in 1927 and in the Second Division, Swansea, also in the Second Division, Wrexham (Third Division North) and Newport (Third Division South).

The harrassed Welsh selectors realized that even these clubs did not have sufficient players of quality. So they were forced to delve deeply into the amateur ranks. So emerged, under the captaincy of Fred Keenor, 'the Welsh unknowns'.

By any standards the team looked a strange one with Dewey of Cardiff Corinthians, Ellis of Oswestry and Collins of Llanelli all amateurs. Rightly, the team was dubbed Fred Keenor and 10 others.

Incredibly, Wrexham's Bamford shot Wales into the lead in five minutes but, when Battles put Scotland level in the 50th minute, everyone expected an avalanche of goals. But Wales, gallant little Wales, defending majestically, hung on to achieve one of the most remarkable results in soccer history.

How did it happen? Apart from the inspiring Keenor, one man

COLORSPORT

deserves the credit: Ted Robbins, the doyen of football secretaries, who, from 1910, had guided the fortunes of what had often been a motley collection of players.

Robbins, with his white hair, astrakhan coat and Edwardian wing collar, did not appear, on the face of it, the man to establish a rapport with professional footballers. Yet, somehow, he injected fire and brimstone into the most ordinary players. A Third Division nonentity would go out like the traditional Welsh dragon.

Robbins and the red shirt of Wales worked a strange alchemy which turned pigmies into giants. But perhaps it was that Welsh dragon too. One of the oldest Welsh proverbs is 'Y draig goch d dyry gychwen' (The Red Dragon gives impetus).

Robbins, the human dynamo, devoted his life to the cause of Wales. He travelled everywhere pleading in his soft North Walian voice for a more open handed attitude from the English clubs. Ivan Sharpe, that great journalist, once recalled how Robbins would ring up on a Friday and say 'I'm still two short for tomorrow's international. But I'm not worried. Wales are never whacked.'

Nor were they. The inspiration of that Hampden triumph—for, in the context, triumph it was—set the pattern for the arrival of the great Welsh side of the thirties which won the Home Championship three times (1933, 1934 and 1937) and was undefeated from 1932 to 1934.

The names are worth recalling. Individually, few of them have gone into history as all-time greats, but collectively, as members of a team inspired by Robbins, they were legendary: Roy John (Stoke), Ben Williams (Everton), Ben Ellis (Motherwell), Syd Lawrence (Swansea), Bob John (Arsenal), Dai Jones (Leicester), Jimmy Murphy (WBA), Fred Keenor (Cardiff and Crewe), Albert Day (Spurs), Tommy Griffith (Middlesbrough), Harry Hanford (Swansea), Dai Richards (Wolves), Fred Warren (Middlesbrough), Charlie Phillips (Wolves), Bill Richards and Taffy O'Callaghan (Fulham), Dai Astley (Villa), Ted Glover (Grimsby), Wally Robbins (WBA), Willie Evans (Spurs) and Ernie Curtis (Birmingham).

This group of players came at the worst-ever period in Wales' economic history. Unemployment was rife and those who were in work—and there was only the mines—came home with a pittance.

Welsh football thrives as Wales suffers

Ted Robbins and his men brought back a little of the pride to these men. The Welsh football team, triumphing over the English, was something in which they could believe.

It used to be said that Robbins only had to shout down a pitshaft and up would come a ready-made international. There was almost a grain of truth in it. For men with no money to spare, football and rugby were the only recreations.

Dai Astley, whose football weight became well over 12 stone—he was over 6 feet tall—was nine stone when he left the mines. In the mid-thirties, Cardiff signed two forwards who had been unemployed since they left school. Both had suffered so long from an inadequate diet that they had to be 'enormously fattened-up' before they could be tried in the reserve team.

It says much for the tenacity of the Welsh, and the insight of the talent scouts, that these boys were able to show they had something even when they were on the edge of malnutrition.

In 1934 came a grim reminder of what life was like when the Gresford colliery disaster in North Wales took the lives of hundreds of Welshmen. England agreed to play Wales at Ninian Park for the disaster fund. It was one of Stanley Matthews' earliest internationals and Wales were beaten 4-0.

Before the Second World War began in 1939, Wales had one more moment of glory when England sent their star-studded team to Ninian Park with a new name in the ranks—Tommy Lawton, the 19-year-old Everton centre-forward. Wales confounded everyone by winning the match 4-2.

The day that Stanley Mortensen played for Wales

Ted Robbins remained at the helm during the War when the authorities recognized that international football was essential for morale. Wales, barely able to raise a team, suffered a number of humiliating defeats and once, if you please, had to field an Englishman at Wembley.

When Ivor Powell, the Villa half-back, was injured early in the game, Wales were down to ten men. In the interests of making it a fair contest, Wales were invited to send on one of their reserves. But, from the Welsh bench, came an embarrassing shaking of heads. They had only brought the bare eleven players!

So, Stanley Mortensen of Blackpool, the England reserve, was asked to make up the number. In the most curious circumstances, he made his first international appearance.

The post-War years brought an upsurge in the talent available to Wales. Cardiff City won promotion to the Second Division in 1947 and Swansea did likewise two years later. With them, stars like Alf Sherwood, Roy Clarke and Roy Paul began to emerge.

So did Trevor Ford, a former Swansea reserve, who became a highly priced firebrand centre-forward with Aston Villa, Sunderland and Cardiff. Later there were the brilliant Allchurch brothers, Ivor and Len, and, of course, Cliff Jones, all of whom were the product of a brilliant Swansea schools' side.

But the greatest of them all was another Swansea boy, John Charles, who, having moved to Leeds as a youngster, became, simultaneously, a profoundly gifted centre-half and centre-forward.

With his £65,000 transfer to Juventus in 1957, Charles became the forerunner of the British born

FULL INTERNATIONALS PLAYED BY WALES: 1876–JANUARY 1974

Date		Venue	Opponents	Score
25 March	1876	Glasgow	Scotland	0-4
15 March	1877	Wrexham	Scotland	0-2
23 March	1878	Glasgow	Scotland	0-9
18 January	1879	London	England	1-2
7 April	1879	Wrexham	Scotland	0-3
15 March	1880	Wrexham	England	2-3
27 March	1880	Glasgow	Scotland	1-5
26 February	1881	Blackburn	England	1-0
14 March	1881	Wrexham	Scotland	1-5
25 February	1882	Wrexham	Ireland	7-1
13 March	1882	Wrexham	England	5-3
25 March	1882	Glasgow	Scotland	0-5
3 February	1883	London	England	0-5
12 March	1883	Wrexham	Scotland	0-3
17 March	1883	Belfast	Ireland	1-1
9 February	1884	Wrexham	Ireland	6-0
17 March	1884	Wrexham	England	0-4
29 March	1884	Glasgow	Scotland	1-4
14 March	1885	Blackburn	England	1-1
23 March	1885	Wrexham	Scotland	1-8
11 April	1885	Belfast	Ireland	8-2
27 February	1886	Wrexham	Ireland	5-0
29 March	1886	Wrexham	England	1-3
10 April	1886	Glasgow	Scotland	1-4
26 February	1887	London	England	0-4
12 March	1887	Belfast	Ireland	1-4
21 March	1887	Wrexham	Scotland	0-2
4 February	1888	Crewe	England	1-5
3 March	1888	Wrexham	Ireland	11-0
10 March	1888	Edinburgh	Scotland	1-5
23 February	1889	Stoke	England	1-4
15 April	1889	Wrexham	Scotland	0-0
27 April	1889	Belfast	Ireland	3-1
8 February	1890	Shrewsbury	Ireland	5-2
15 March	1890	Wrexham	England	1-3
22 March	1890	Paisley	Scotland	0-5
7 February	1891	Belfast	Ireland	2-7
7 March	1891	Sunderland	England	1-4
21 March	1891	Wrexham	Scotland	3-4
27 February	1892	Bangor (Wales)	Ireland	1-1
5 March	1892	Wrexham	England	0-2
26 March	1892	Edinburgh	Scotland	1-6
13 March	1893	Stoke	England	0-6
18 March	1893	Wrexham	Scotland	0-8
8 April	1893	Belfast	Ireland	3-4
24 February	1894	Swansea	Ireland	4-1
12 March	1894	Wrexham	England	1-5
24 March	1894	Kilmarnock	Scotland	2-5
16 March	1895	Belfast	Ireland	2-2
18 March	1895	London	England	1-1
23 March	1895	Wrexham	Scotland	2-2
29 February	1896	Wrexham	Ireland	6-1
16 March	1896	Cardiff	England	1-9
21 March	1896	Dundee	Scotland	0-4
6 March	1897	Belfast	Ireland	3-4
20 March	1897	Wrexham	Scotland	2-2
29 March	1897	Sheffield	England	0-4
19 February	1898	Llandudno	Ireland	0-1
19 March	1898	Motherwell	Scotland	2-5
28 March	1898	Wrexham	England	0-3
4 March	1899	Belfast	Ireland	0-1
18 March	1899	Wrexham	Scotland	0-6
20 March	1899	Bristol	England	1-4
3 February	1900	Aberdeen	Scotland	2-5
24 February	1900	Llandudno	Ireland	2-0
26 March	1900	Cardiff	England	1-1
2 March	1901	Wrexham	Scotland	1-1
18 March	1901	Newcastle	England	0-6
23 March	1901	Llandudno	Ireland	1-0
3 March	1902	Wrexham	England	0-0
15 March	1902	Greenock	Scotland	1-5
22 March	1902	Cardiff	Ireland	0-3
2 March	1903	Portsmouth	England	1-2
9 March	1903	Cardiff	Scotland	0-1
28 March	1903	Belfast	Ireland	0-2
29 February	1904	Wrexham	England	2-2
12 March	1904	Dundee	Scotland	1-1
21 March	1904	Bangor (Wales)	Ireland	0-1
6 March	1905	Wrexham	Scotland	3-1
27 March	1905	Liverpool	England	1-3
8 April	1905	Belfast	Ireland	2-2
3 March	1906	Edinburgh	Scotland	2-0
19 March	1906	Cardiff	England	0-1
2 April	1906	Wrexham	Ireland	4-4
23 February	1907	Belfast	Ireland	3-2
4 March	1907	Wrexham	Scotland	1-0
18 March	1907	London	England	1-1
7 March	1908	Dundee	Scotland	1-2
16 March	1908	Wrexham	England	1-7
11 April	1908	Aberdare	Ireland	0-1
1 March	1909	Wrexham	Scotland	3-2
15 March	1909	Nottingham	England	0-2
20 March	1909	Belfast	Ireland	3-2
5 March	1910	Kilmarnock	Scotland	0-1
11 March	1910	Wrexham	Ireland	4-1
14 March	1910	Cardiff	England	0-1
6 March	1911	Cardiff	Scotland	2-2
13 March	1911	London	England	0-3
28 March	1911	Belfast	Ireland	2-1
2 March	1912	Edinburgh	Scotland	0-1
11 March	1912	Wrexham	England	0-2
13 April	1912	Cardiff	Ireland	2-3
18 January	1913	Belfast	Ireland	1-0
3 March	1913	Wrexham	Scotland	0-0
17 March	1913	Bristol	England	3-4
19 January	1914	Wrexham	Ireland	1-2
28 February	1914	Glasgow	Scotland	0-0
16 March	1914	Cardiff	England	0-2
V11 October	1919	Cardiff	England	2-1
V18 October	1919	Stoke	England	0-2
14 February	1920	Belfast	Ireland	2-2
26 February	1920	Cardiff	Scotland	1-1
15 March	1920	London	England	2-1
12 February	1921	Aberdeen	Scotland	1-2
14 March	1921	Cardiff	England	0-0
9 April	1921	Swansea	Ireland	2-1
4 February	1922	Wrexham	Scotland	2-1
13 March	1922	Liverpool	England	0-1
1 April	1922	Belfast	Ireland	1-1
5 March	1923	Cardiff	England	2-2
17 March	1923	Paisley	Scotland	0-2
14 April	1923	Wrexham	Ireland	0-3
16 February	1924	Cardiff	Scotland	2-0
3 March	1924	Blackburn	England	2-1
15 March	1924	Belfast	N Ireland	1-0
14 February	1925	Edinburgh	Scotland	1-3
28 February	1925	Swansea	England	1-2
18 April	1925	Wrexham	N Ireland	0-0
31 October	1925	Cardiff	Scotland	0-3
13 January	1926	Belfast	N Ireland	0-3
1 March	1926	London	England	3-1
30 October	1926	Glasgow	Scotland	0-3
12 February	1927	Wrexham	England	3-3
9 April	1927	Cardiff	N Ireland	2-2
29 October	1927	Wrexham	Scotland	2-2
28 November	1927	Burnley	England	2-1
4 February	1928	Belfast	N Ireland	2-1
27 October	1928	Glasgow	Scotland	2-4
17 November	1928	Swansea	England	2-3
2 February	1929	Wrexham	N Ireland	2-2
26 October	1929	Cardiff	Scotland	2-4
20 November	1929	London	England	0-6
1 February	1930	Belfast	N Ireland	0-7
25 October	1930	Glasgow	Scotland	1-1
22 November	1930	Wrexham	England	0-4
22 April	1931	Wrexham	N Ireland	3-2
31 October	1931	Wrexham	Scotland	2-3
18 November	1931	Liverpool	England	1-3
5 December	1931	Belfast	N Ireland	0-4
26 October	1932	Edinburgh	Scotland	5-2
16 November	1932	Wrexham	England	0-0
7 December	1932	Wrexham	N Ireland	4-1
25 May	1933	Paris	France	1-1
4 October	1933	Cardiff	Scotland	3-2
4 November	1933	Belfast	N Ireland	1-1
15 November	1933	Newcastle	England	2-1
29 September	1934	Cardiff	England	0-4
21 November	1934	Aberdeen	Scotland	2-3
27 March	1935	Wrexham	N Ireland	3-1
5 October	1935	Cardiff	Scotland	1-1
5 February	1936	Wolverhampton	England	2-1
11 March	1936	Belfast	N Ireland	2-3
17 October	1936	Cardiff	England	2-1
2 December	1936	Dundee	Scotland	2-1
17 March	1937	Wrexham	N Ireland	4-1
30 October	1937	Cardiff	Scotland	2-1
17 November	1937	Middlesbrough	England	1-2
16 March	1938	Belfast	N Ireland	0-1
22 October	1938	Cardiff	England	4-2
9 November	1938	Edinburgh	Scotland	2-3
15 March	1939	Wrexham	N Ireland	3-1
20 May	1939	Paris	France	1-2
WT11 November	1939	Cardiff	England	1-1
WT18 November	1939	Wrexham	England	3-2
WT13 April	1940	Wembley	England	1-0
WT26 April	1941	Nottingham	England	1-4
WT 7 June	1941	Cardiff	England	2-3
WT25 October	1941	Birmingham	England	1-2
WT 9 May	1942	Cardiff	England	1-0
WT24 October	1942	Wolverhampton	England	2-1
WT27 February	1943	Wembley	England	3-5
WT 8 May	1943	Cardiff	England	1-1
WT25 September	1943	Wembley	England	3-8
WT 6 May	1944	Cardiff	England	0-2
WT16 September	1944	Liverpool	England	2-2
WT 5 May	1945	Cardiff	England	2-3
V20 October	1945	West Bromwich	England	1-0
19 October	1946	Wrexham	Scotland	3-1
13 November	1946	Manchester	England	0-3
16 April	1947	Belfast	N Ireland	1-2
18 October	1947	Cardiff	England	0-3
12 November	1947	Glasgow	Scotland	2-1
10 March	1948	Wrexham	N Ireland	2-0
23 October	1948	Cardiff	Scotland	1-3
10 November	1948	Birmingham	England	0-1
9 March	1949	Belfast	N Ireland	2-0
15 May	1949	Lisbon	Portugal	2-3
22 May	1949	Liege	Belgium	1-3
26 May	1949	Berne	Switzerland	0-4
WC15 October	1949	Cardiff	England	1-4
WC 9 November	1949	Glasgow	Scotland	0-2
23 November	1949	Cardiff	Belgium	5-1
WC 8 March	1950	Wrexham	N Ireland	0-0
21 October	1950	Cardiff	Scotland	1-3
15 November	1950	Sunderland	England	2-4
7 March	1951	Belfast	N Ireland	2-1
12 May	1951	Cardiff	Portugal	2-1
16 May	1951	Wrexham	Switzerland	3-2
20 October	1951	Cardiff	England	1-1
14 November	1951	Glasgow	Scotland	1-0
19 March	1952	Swansea	N Ireland	3-0
18 October	1952	Cardiff	Scotland	1-2
12 November	1952	Wembley	England	2-5
15 April	1953	Belfast	N Ireland	3-2
14 May	1953	Paris	France	1-6
21 May	1953	Belgrade	Yugoslavia	2-5
WC10 October	1953	Cardiff	England	1-4
WC 4 November	1953	Glasgow	Scotland	3-3
WC31 March	1954	Wrexham	N Ireland	1-2
9 May	1954	Vienna	Austria	0-2
22 September	1954	Cardiff	Yugoslavia	1-3
16 October	1954	Cardiff	Scotland	0-1
10 November	1954	Wembley	England	2-3
20 April	1955	Belfast	N Ireland	3-2
22 October	1955	Cardiff	England	2-1
9 November	1955	Glasgow	Scotland	0-2
23 November	1955	Wrexham	Austria	1-2
11 April	1956	Cardiff	N Ireland	1-1
20 October	1956	Cardiff	Scotland	2-2
14 November	1956	Wembley	England	1-3
10 April	1957	Belfast	N Ireland	0-0
WC 1 May	1957	Cardiff	Czechoslovakia	1-0
WC19 May	1957	Leipzig	East Germany	1-2
WC26 May	1957	Prague	Czechoslovakia	0-2
WC25 September	1957	Cardiff	East Germany	4-1
19 October	1957	Cardiff	England	0-4
13 November	1957	Glasgow	Scotland	1-1
WC15 January	1958	Tel-Aviv	Israel	2-0
WC 5 February	1958	Cardiff	Israel	2-0
16 April	1958	Cardiff	N Ireland	1-1
WC 8 June	1958	Sandviken	Hungary	1-1
WC11 June	1958	Stockholm	Mexico	1-1
WC15 June	1958	Stockholm	Sweden	0-0
WC17 June	1958	Stockholm	Hungary	2-1
WC19 June	1958	Gothenburg	Brazil	0-1
18 October	1958	Cardiff	Scotland	0-3
26 November	1958	Birmingham	England	2-2
22 April	1959	Belfast	N Ireland	1-4
17 October	1959	Cardiff	England	1-1
4 November	1959	Glasgow	Scotland	1-1
6 April	1960	Wrexham	N Ireland	3-2
28 September	1960	Dublin	Eire	3-2
22 October	1960	Cardiff	Scotland	2-0
23 November	1960	Wembley	England	1-5
12 April	1961	Belfast	N Ireland	5-1
WC19 April	1961	Cardiff	Spain	1-2
WC18 May	1961	Madrid	Spain	1-1
28 May	1961	Budapest	Hungary	2-3
14 October	1961	Cardiff	England	1-1
8 November	1961	Glasgow	Scotland	0-2
11 April	1962	Cardiff	N Ireland	4-0
12 May	1962	Rio de Janeiro	Brazil	1-3
16 May	1962	Sao Paulo	Brazil	1-3
22 May	1962	Mexico City	Mexico	1-2
20 October	1962	Cardiff	Scotland	2-3
ENC 7 November	1962	Budapest	Hungary	1-3
21 November	1962	Wembley	England	0-4
ENC20 March	1963	Cardiff	Hungary	1-1
3 April	1963	Belfast	N Ireland	4-1
12 October	1963	Cardiff	England	0-4
20 November	1963	Glasgow	Scotland	1-2
15 April	1964	Swansea	N Ireland	3-2
3 October	1964	Cardiff	Scotland	3-2
WC21 October	1964	Copenhagen	Denmark	0-1
18 November	1964	Wembley	England	1-2
WC 9 December	1964	Athens	Greece	0-2
WC17 March	1965	Cardiff	Greece	4-1
31 March	1965	Belfast	N Ireland	5-0
1 May	1965	Florence	Italy	1-4
WC30 May	1965	Moscow	Russia	1-2
2 October	1965	Cardiff	England	0-0
WC27 October	1965	Cardiff	Russia	2-1
24 November	1965	Glasgow	Scotland	1-4
WC 1 December	1965	Wrexham	Denmark	4-2
30 March	1966	Cardiff	N Ireland	1-4
14 May	1966	Rio de Janeiro	Brazil	1-3
18 May	1966	Belo Horizonte	Brazil	0-1
22 May	1966	Santiago	Chile	0-2
22 October	1966	Glasgow	Scotland	1-1
16 November	1966	Wembley	England	1-5
12 April	1967	Belfast	N Ireland	0-0
21 October	1967	Cardiff	England	0-3
22 November	1967	Glasgow	Scotland	2-3
28 February	1968	Wrexham	N Ireland	2-0
8 May	1968	Cardiff	West Germany	1-1
WC23 October	1968	Cardiff	Italy	0-1
26 March	1969	Frankfurt	West Germany	1-1
WC16 April	1969	Dresden	East Germany	1-2
3 May	1969	Wrexham	Scotland	3-5
7 May	1969	Wembley	England	1-2
10 May	1969	Belfast	N Ireland	0-0
28 July	1969	Cardiff	Rest of Britain	0-1
WC22 October	1969	Cardiff	East Germany	1-3
WC 4 November	1969	Rome	Italy	1-4
18 April	1970	Cardiff	England	1-1
22 April	1970	Glasgow	Scotland	0-0
25 April	1970	Swansea	N Ireland	1-0
EC11 November	1970	Cardiff	Rumania	0-0
EC21 April	1971	Swansea	Czechoslovakia	1-3
15 May	1971	Cardiff	Scotland	0-0
18 May	1971	Wembley	England	0-0
22 May	1971	Belfast	N Ireland	0-1
EC26 May	1971	Helsinki	Finland	1-0
EC13 October	1971	Swansea	Finland	3-0
EC27 October	1971	Prague	Czechoslovakia	0-1
EC24 November	1971	Bucharest	Rumania	0-2
20 May	1972	Cardiff	England	0-3
24 May	1972	Glasgow	Scotland	0-1
28 May	1972	Wrexham	N Ireland	0-0
WC15 November	1972	Cardiff	England	0-1
WC24 January	1973	Wembley	England	1-1
WC28 March	1973	Cardiff	Poland	2-0
12 May	1973	Wrexham	Scotland	0-2
15 May	1973	Wembley	England	0-3
19 May	1973	Everton	N Ireland	0-1
WC26 September	1973	Katowice	Poland	0-3

WC – World Cup games
EC – European Championship games
V – Victory International WT – War-time International
ENC – European Nations Cup games

players who succumbed to the blandishments of Gigi Peronace, that irrepressible agent, and moved to Italy before the removal of the maximum wage.

Although in Italy, Charles came back to join the Welsh party for the 1958 World Cup in Sweden. They qualified in their group with draws against Hungary, Sweden, the eventual finalists, and Mexico. And then, their finest hour, Wales beat Hungary, finalists in 1954, in the group play-off.

In the quarter-final, they came up against the powerful Brazil side. John Charles had been injured earlier in the tournament, but his brother Mel came in at centre-half, with Colin Webster of Manchester United at centre-forward.

Wales would have gained another draw, but for the late arrival of a Brazilian substitute of 17 who scored the only goal with only minutes to go. His name? Pele.

Jack Kelsey, the Arsenal goal-keeper, was named the best custodian in the tournament, and he was to grace Wales' goal for several years. Then he would be replaced by a young man who lived in the same street as Kelsey in the tiny Welsh hamlet of Winch Wen—Gary Sprake of Leeds United.

But the World Cup of 1958 remains the last real impact Wales made on the international scene. The demands of clubs seeking success in domestic and European competitions means that Wales can never again rely on obtaining the release of her best players.

Even so, under Dave Bowen they have had their moments. A side thrown together at the last minute through late withdrawals has frequently given England, in particular, a run for her money. The Robbins spirit still lingers, though, regrettably, only fitfully. Gallant little Wales.

The Major Competitions

Third time lucky for Leeds and Norman Hunter (number 6) as Allan Clarke heads home Mick Jones's cross for the only goal of the Centenary Final.

THE MAJOR COMPETITIONS

The story of the FA Cup

'I've got a League Championship medal, a Fairs Cup medal, a League Cup medal and dozens of caps—but sometimes I think I'd swap the lot for a place in a Cup winning side.' The words were those of Billy Bremner before Leeds United's long-awaited success at Wembley in 1972, but they could have come from any of a large number of professionals, that enormous group who have never been lucky enough to carry the Cup around the arena after the highlight of the English season.

The FA Cup has an undeniable aura about it. Not only is it the oldest football competition in the world, not only is its Final watched by hundreds of millions of people *outside* Britain, not only is it the annual showpiece for Britain's national sport, but it has been elevated far beyond that. It is now a ritual, different from a royal wedding or a moon-landing only in that it occurs at more predictable intervals.

In 1971 the BBC published a list of the biggest audiences for single programmes in the history of British television. Four of the top ten were Cup Finals. And despite all the protestations about the League Championship being the ultimate test of professional ability, there is the sneaking suspicion that no-one would sacrifice an FA Cup winners medal for a League Championship equivalent.

For, in the last resort, football must be a game about eleven men against eleven, about one team leaving the field victorious and the other vanquished, about a packed stadium saluting just one team—

just one winner.

In its ultimate simplicity the FA Cup is the forerunner of competitions all over the world. But in a sense it is a lot more than that, for the hundred-year history of the FA Cup is also the history of English football.

It was in the offices of *The Sportsman*, a London newspaper, on 20 July 1871, that seven men took a hesitant step and made football history. The central figure was 29-year-old Charles Alcock, secretary of the FA and the man who suggested that: '. . . it is desirable that a Challenge Cup shall be established in connection with the Association . . .' Among the other six present were M P Betts, who scored the first ever Cup Final goal, and Captain Francis Marindin, later president of the FA, who appeared in two Finals and refereed another eight.

The Harrow School competition that inspired the FA Cup

Alcock had pinched the idea for his competition from his old school, Harrow, where there was a simple knock-out tournament among the houses, the winner being known as the 'Cock House'. The FA ordered a Cup from Martin, Hall and Company; it cost a mere £20 and stood just 18 inches high.

Fifteen clubs entered the first year—all but Donington School, Spalding, and the great Queen's Park of Glasgow coming from the

home counties. In fact Donington scratched without playing a game and never entered again—thus establishing some kind of record—while Queen's Park, thanks to the kindness of the organizing committee, managed to reach the semi-final without kicking a ball.

The strict knock-out principle was not yet in operation; four clubs played in the third round and four in the next, in part through byes and in part through a rule which allowed teams which drew to both go through to the next round.

The Cup's beginnings were undoubtedly humble. Just 2,000 people turned out for the Final to see men dressed in trousers and caps (Royal Engineers wore 'dark blue serge knickerbockers'), who changed ends every time a goal was scored and who won throw-ins by touching the ball down in rugby fashion if it went out of play. The Kennington Oval pitch would have hardly been recognizable to present-day supporters—there was no centre-circle, no half-way line, no penalty area and a tape instead of a cross-bar. Alcock's team, the Wanderers, beat the Engineers 1-0.

The century that followed can be roughly divided into four phases—largely determined by the geographical location of the Final. Firstly there was the amateur era, then the Northern takeover, the Crystal Palace period and, finally, the post-1923 Wembley era.

Ten years after that first Final the Old Etonians beat Blackburn Rovers at the Oval. When the final whistle blew, the victorious captain, A F

Kinnaird, of the red beard and long white trousers, stood on his head in front of the pavilion. It was appropriate that his should be the final gesture of an age ready to be confined to the history books; he appeared in 9 of the first 12 Finals, five times on the winning side. Only James Forrest of Blackburn Rovers and C H R Wollaston of the Wanderers received so many winner's medals.

The Wanderers played one game —and won the Cup

Kinnaird's winning appearances were with Old Etonians in 1879 and 1882, and Wanderers, in 1873, 1877 and 1878. His first for the Wanderers was the only occasion on which the Final was contested on the challenge basis that was written into both the competition's title and its original rules. The Wanderers, being the holders, not only had the solitary game to play—the Challenge Final in which they beat Oxford University 2-0—but they were also allowed to choose the venue of that match, which is the reason for Lillie Bridge's one moment of sporting significance.

The Wanderers also entered the records in a unique way in 1878—they won the Cup for the third consecutive time and thus, according to the rules, outright. It was, however, returned with the proviso that it should never again be handed to one team in perpetuity. In fact the scene was a little more comical than that. Charles Alcock, as secretary of the Wanderers, handed back the Cup and asked that it should never be won outright. Charles Alcock, now in his role as secretary of the FA, was only too happy to agree.

In the years that followed only one club—Blackburn Rovers between 1884 and 1886—has repeated the feat, and they were presented with a special shield which still hangs in their boardroom.

It was to Blackburn, in fact, that the Cup fled when it left the gentlemen amateurs of the South. That Lancastrian cotton-weaving town had two fine clubs in the 1880s—Olympic, who became the first side from outside the home counties to win the trophy, in 1883, and Rovers, who won it in the subsequent three seasons.

But the Blackburn clubs were not the first 'outsiders' to make their mark on the competition. In 1879 Nottingham Forest became the first of England's northern sides to reach the semi-finals—and at their first attempt—but more significant was the performance of Darwen, a neighbour of Blackburn, the same year. In the previous round they had held Old Etonians to two draws, the first by scoring four times in the last 15 minutes, but had gone down 6-2 on their third visit to the capital.

Darwen were unlucky that the rule under which all ties after the second round had to be played at the Oval was still in force. No semi-final was contested outside London

124

until 1882, when Blackburn Rovers drew with Sheffield's The Wednesday at Huddersfield and beat them in Manchester, but for the next few years—before the Irish and Scottish FAs banned their clubs from entering—ties were played all over the United Kingdom. As a result Linfield captured the unique record of never having lost a Cup tie. They drew 2-2 with Nottingham Forest in 1889, and then withdrew before the replay, never to enter again.

Forest had actually arrived in Ireland and played a friendly instead, but it helped create an odd record for them as well, for they are the only club to have been drawn to play FA Cup ties in all four home countries. In 1885, after a drawn game at Derby, Forest had replayed a semi-final with Glasgow's Queen's Park at Merchiston Castle School, Edinburgh, the only semi-final ever contested outside England.

But to return to Darwen, whose performance was in no small way due to the presence of two Scots, Fergus Suter and James Love, both of whom had been 'mislaid' by Partick Thistle on a tour of England. They were, of course, among the first of the professionals that were soon to take over the competition and football south of the border.

The issue of payment did not actually come to a head until January 1884, when Preston North End drew with mighty Upton Park, one of the original entrants in 1872 and still staunch supporters of the lily-white amateur game. The Londoners protested that Preston had included professionals in their team, North End admitted as much, and were disqualified.

Just over a year later the FA sensibly bowed to the inevitable and professionals were allowed provided, among other clauses, they were: '. . . annually registered in a book to be kept by the committee of the FA . . .'

'The Cup'll never go back to London' —and it never did

At least Preston had the satisfaction of seeing Upton Park humbled in the next round by neighbours Blackburn Rovers, on their triumphant march to the first of a hat-trick of wins. At the time Blackburn were also midway through a record of 24 Cup games without defeat, which lasted from a 1-0 setback at the hands of Darwen in the second round of the 1882-83 competition to the December of 1886.

But it was not Rovers who first brought the Cup to Lancashire, rather a long since defunct outfit called Blackburn Olympic. When

Top 100,000 people watch, one cannot as Ronnie Allen tries to put West Bromwich back into the 1954 Cup Final from a penalty. Goalkeeper Sanders missed the moment that brought his club level with Preston North End. *Centre* The incident from a camera at the other end. Sanders is ringed. *Bottom* Forty years before and a dozen miles away, Liverpool attack the Burnley goal during the last Final to be played at the Crystal Palace.

UNITED PRESS INTERNATIONAL

UNITED PRESS INTERNATIONAL

TOPIX

their captain, Warburton, got back to a deserved civic reception in 1883, he declared to the crowd: 'The Cup is very welcome to Lancashire. It'll have a good home and it'll never go back to London.' He was quite right. In the next twelve years it went no further south than Birmingham where, in 1895, it was stolen from the window of a football-boot manufacturer William Shillcock and was never seen again.

In an edition of the *Sunday Pictorial* in February 1958 one Harry Burge, at the age of 83, admitted to having stolen the Cup and melted it down for counterfeit half-crowns. If that is true it is a sad commentary on the economics of the times—the Cup contained less than £20 worth of silver and could hardly have justified the effort.

When Villa won it for a year—and lost it forever

Fortunately for the FA the chairman of Wolverhampton Wanderers had presented his players with scaled-down replicas when they won the trophy in 1893, and it was therefore possible to create an exact reproduction of the original.

That same Wolves victory was on the occasion of the first Final to be contested outside the capital. Surrey CCC, alarmed at the size of the crowd for the 1892 Final, withdrew the Oval as a venue and, in recognition of Lancashire's supremacy, the game's premier event switched to the country's second city, Manchester. There the Fallowfield ground was besieged by a crowd which broke down the barriers and fell through the wooden terracing in a remarkable harbinger of both the first Wembley Final, 30 years later, and the Ibrox disaster, then less than ten years away.

A week earlier Everton's reserve team had thrashed Wolves 4-2 in a First Division game but this time it was a different story with the Midlanders' captain Allen scoring the only goal of the match. The next season saw an equally surprising result. Second Division Notts County beat Bolton, 4-1 at Goodison Park, after reasonably protesting that it was virtually a home game for Bolton, and their centre-forward Jimmy Logan scored a hat-trick to equal William Townley's 1890 feat for Blackburn Rovers.

After the 1894 Final the FA must have concluded that London was the only rightful place for the showpiece of the season, and it has been played there with only one exception (1915) ever since. The obvious choice was Crystal Palace—though the FA's decision to move the game to London can be viewed a little cynically in the light of the fact that only one of the finalists who ever played at the Palace was a London club—Spurs, in 1901—and only two others, Southampton and Bristol City, came from south of Birmingham.

Crystal Palace in 1895 was already a Victorian weekend playground—something like a cross between Battersea Fun Fair and Brighton beach—and it had a huge natural bowl which was used for

sporting events. Terracing as it is known today was never built there; most of the eighty or so thousand who attended Finals stood on the steep grassy slopes of the east side.

The first Final at the Palace (not, incidentally, the present home of Crystal Palace) was the third clash between Birmingham rivals West Bromwich and Aston Villa—they are still the only clubs to have met each other three times in a Final. At kick-off both had won once each, but Villa went on to take the Cup this time, promptly lost it to Mr Burge, but were back again two years later to carry off the new trophy after a Final which must rank along with 1948 and 1953 as one of the greatest ever.

It was also a particularly significant game for it gave Villa a League-Cup double which looked, for 64 years, like being the last of all time. Villa had won the League by the massive margin of 11 points (there were only 16 clubs in the division) and at the Palace defeated Everton 3-2, all the goals coming in the 25 minutes before half-time.

The club that took Villa's mantle of 'the team of all the talents' was Newcastle United—possessors of what is surely the oddest of all Cup Final records. In five Finals at the Crystal Palace they did not win a single game, in five appearances at Wembley they did not lose one!

The Geordies' record between 1905 and 1911 is startling in its consistency. They reached the Final in 1905, 1906, 1908, 1910 and 1911. In 1910 they admittedly managed to draw with Second Division Barnsley, and beat them in the replay at Goodison to record their only pre-First World War win. In 1909 they lost a semi-final by the game's only goal to Manchester United, so the only year in the seven between 1905 and 1911 that they did not reach the last four was 1907.

Newcastle's strange relationship with the name Crystal Palace

That season—one in which they won the League—Newcastle suffered a first round knock-out at St James' Park to a club then languishing at the bottom of the Southern League. And the name of that club whose feat must rank alongside the giant-killing exploits of Walsall and Colchester? Irony of ironies . . . Crystal Palace. It was almost as if the very name made the Northumbrians go weak at the knees.

When the two great sides of the era—Villa and Newcastle—met in 1905 they drew a crowd of 101,117 to a game that seemed to have little appeal for the Londoner—but even this figure had been surpassed four years earlier for a game that will surely remain unique for all time.

Since the Final returned in 1895 Londoners had regarded it, more than a little disdainfully, as an affair for provincials—rather like the Agricultural Exhibition at Earls Court is regarded today. In fact London had only one League club—Arsenal—at the turn of the century and had never had a professional interest in the Final.

Then, in the first year of the new century, came a record-breaking Final. 1901 saw Tottenham become the only non-League club to win the Cup since the Football League was founded, though they needed a replay against Sheffield United—winners two years before—to do it. The attendance printed in the following day's papers—114,815—was the largest ever at a football match and has been surpassed in England only twice since—at the 1913 and 1923 Finals.

Sandy Brown, who scored twice at Crystal Palace and once in the replay at Bolton, became the first man to score in every round of the Cup (a feat not equalled until 1935) and his total of 15 Cup goals has yet to be surpassed.

And on top of all this was a violently disputed goal which only the referee and the Sheffield United team of the hundred thousand present thought was justified. The incident was no doubt quite comical to non-partisan spectators. Clawley, the Spurs goalkeeper, clashed with Bennett, a Sheffield forward, and the ball ran behind. Clawley appealed for a goal-kick, Bennett for a corner and the referee silenced them both by awarding a goal. He apparently judged Clawley to have been *behind* his own goal-line before carrying the ball out and being challenged by Bennett.

London's star fell as quickly as it had risen and the capital did not have another representative in the Final until 1915, when Chelsea lost in the muted atmosphere of a war-time Old Trafford, to the side their fellow Londoners had defeated—Sheffield United.

The Yorkshiremen, however, did not carry off the same trophy Spurs

had deprived them of. The design of the latter had been pirated for another competition in Manchester and so the second of the three FA Cups was presented to Lord Kinnaird—whose nine Final appearances is still a record—to mark his 21 years as President of the Football Association.

The present trophy, weighing 175 oz and nineteen inches high, was ordered from Fattorini and Sons of Bradford and, appropriately if strangely, Bradford City were its first holders. Strangely, because neither Bradford club had been near a Final before and neither has been near one since.

As remarkable as the ability of some clubs to keep coming back and taking the Cup is the inability of others to get near it. Take Sunderland for instance. By the time they finally took the trophy back to

Opposite top *The programme for the second of the meetings between West Bromwich and Aston Villa, the last Final to be played at Kennington Oval. No other clubs have ever met in three Cup Finals as Villa and Albion did in 1887, 1892 and 1897.*
Opposite centre *Villa are back, this time at Crystal Palace where Hampton scored the two goals that beat unfortunate Newcastle in 1905.*
Opposite bottom *Villa again but yet another venue for the Final of 1920. The dreary Stamford Bridge produced equally dreary games; in 1920 Villa won with a centre which went in off the back of Kirton's neck.*
Above top *What fans were doing to get into a brand new Wembley in 1923.*
Above *Ricky George scores and Hereford become the first non-League club to defeat First Division opposition (the Newcastle United of 1972) since Yeovil beat Sunderland in 1949.*

Wearside in 1937, they had won the League Championship six times. But near neighbours and rivals Newcastle already had seven Final appearances to their credit—and another three soon to follow. Sunderland's only previous Final was another of the classics—the 1913 game that attracted a crowd even bigger than at the 1901 Final. It assembled for a decisive game, for it was the only Final in the first hundred years of the Cup to be contested by the clubs that finished first and second in the League. In the end honours were shared, Sunderland winning the League and Villa the Cup.

Villa went into the Final, just as they did in 1957, intent on defending their title as the last winners of the double. The Midlanders came very near to making a mess of it though. First their right-winger Charlie Wallace missed a penalty kick—the only time this has happened in a Final—then their England goalkeeper Sam Hardy left the field injured for ten minutes. In the end Barber fulfilled a remarkable prophecy of Clem Stephenson—who had turned to Sunderland's Charlie Buchan early in the match and recounted a dream he had had the night before. 'We won 1-0,' Stephenson is reputed to have said, 'with a goal headed by Barber.' And so it was.

Seven years later Stephenson, Wallace and Hardy provided an illusion of continuity when they again collected winners medals. In the interim Europe had been at war for four years and the Crystal Palace had been requisitioned as a service depot. There was no prospect of it being available before 1923 and the FA had to look elsewhere for a venue for the highlight of the season.

The year Chelsea nearly played the Final at home

Having decided that London was still the only possible home for the Cup Final—a contentious conclusion that was not particularly well received in Manchester, Birmingham or Liverpool—the FA were left with only one choice. The White Hart Lane and Highbury of 1919 were far from the imposing stadiums they are today, and the dreary Stamford Bridge was alone in being large enough.

So Chelsea's impersonal arena it was—a decision that nearly caused the FA a lot more criticism. By the semi-final stage the arrangements for the Final itself were far too advanced for the venue to be changed—but the Chelsea side that had reached the last pre-War Final were alive and well, third in the League, and favourites to reach the first post-War Final as well. The Pensioners went to Bramall Lane for their semi-final against Aston Villa with the prospect of a home tie in the Final—though it was technically against the rules of the competition.

It was Billy Walker who saved the FA's face. He scored two goals, Villa won 3-1 and went on to beat Huddersfield at Stamford Bridge.

The three Stamford Bridge Finals were among the most anonymous

ever. All three were won by the only goal of the match, and the attendances in 1920 and 1922 were among the lowest of the century, coming nowhere near to filling the ground.

The 1922 game was called the most forgettable of all time, but suddenly acquired a new significance after a sequel of 16 years later. The earlier game was a lamentable affair—even the FA minutes commented on the conduct of the players. It was appropriate that it should be decided by a disputed penalty when Preston's right-back Hamilton brought down Huddersfield's winger Billy Smith on the edge of the area, though many said outside it. After a lengthy and heated discussion between the Preston players and the referee, Smith himself took it and scored.

The 1938 game was equally drab, and the contestants were—Huddersfield and Preston. At least it was better tempered and had reached the last minute of extra-time without a goal when Huddersfield's centre-half Young tripped George Mutch and Mutch himself converted the penalty. The story goes that Bill Shankly—then playing for Preston—told Mutch to 'shut your eyes and hit it'. He had obviously been coached in something like that vein, for the ball hit the bar on its way in.

How a white horse disturbed the dreams of West Ham United

But back in 1923 no doubt everyone was glad to get away from Stamford Bridge to Wembley, where the FA had co-operated in a scheme to incorporate a vast new stadium in the British Empire Exhibition, scheduled to open in 1924. The Empire Stadium was ready a year earlier and public enthusiasm was enormous. Unfortunately the FA were lulled by the below capacity crowds at Stamford Bridge and thought that Wembley—capable of holding 127,000 according to the Exhibition authorities—would be more than big enough.

They were perhaps unlucky in that one of the contestants was West Ham, then leading the Second Division and the darlings of East London. In the end the FA publicly thanked a policeman called George Scorey and his white horse Billy that the game took place at all. West Ham were less pleased with the behaviour of the FA's equine saviour. Their game relied on the use of fast-running wingers Richards and Ruffell and, as trainer Charlie Paynter said afterwards: 'It was that white horse thumping its big feet into the pitch that made it hopeless. Our wingers were tumbling all over the place, tripping up in great ruts and holes.' Maybe, but it did not stop Ted Vizard having an excellent game on the left-wing for Bolton. The FA were more generous to PC Scorey, regularly sending him tickets for later Finals—but he was not much interested in football and, in fact, never went to another match. There must have been many who would have given much for a place at the Wembley Finals which followed.

RAY GREEN

Grief and glory on the way to Wembley

When Arsenal returned to Wembley for the centenary Cup Final in 1972 they at least had statistics on their side. Newcastle had won in 1951 and 1952, Spurs in 1961 and 1962 and Arsenal had taken the trophy in 1971. But the portents were to be overcome by Leeds in their third FA Cup Final, for Allan Clarke scored the only goal of the match and Arsenal became the first holders to return to Wembley and lose.

It was a defeat which reminded their followers of the inter-War period. Mighty Arsenal were the giants who strode across the thirties, winning the League five times but having a strangely chequered history in the Cup. True, they did win it twice, but far better remembered are the two occasions when they lost. The first of these was in 1927, when a Cardiff with eight internationals and only one Englishman in their side took the Cup out of England for the first and only time. The solitary goal of the game came from a speculative shot by Cardiff's centre-forward Ferguson. The ball seemed to be easily gathered by Arsenal's Welsh international goalkeeper Dan Lewis, but he seemed to indulge in a grotesque parody of his trade, the ball slipping away from his fumblings and rolling slowly over the line.

Lewis blamed the incident on his new jersey, and to this day Arsenal always wash goalkeepers' jerseys before they are used, to get rid of

any surplus grease. It was a pity that they could not wash away their Cup luck as easily.

Still, there was nothing contentious about Arsenal's 2-0 win over Huddersfield in the 1930 Final, a game remembered for the moment when the *Graf Zeppelin* appeared over the Stadium. The airship—pride of a re-emergent Germany—dipped in salute and passed on sedately.

Two years later Arsenal were back to suffer the greatest of all Cup Final controversies. Their opponents were eternal Cup runners-up Newcastle, and the losers medals seemed destined to make their familiar trek to the North East as early as the fifteenth minute when John put Arsenal ahead. But it was not to be.

Davidson, the Newcastle centre-half, sent a long ball along the right, Richardson went for it but it appeared to be hit too hard for him and looked to have bounced out of play before he hooked it back across the goal. The Arsenal defence stopped and Allen was left free to flick the ball into the net.

The referee, a Mr Harper, carved himself an everlasting niche in soccer history by allowing the goal and Newcastle went on to win via another by Allen. That particular incident—and the photographs of the day tended to support the view of the Arsenal defence rather than that of the referee—probably ranks as the

most arguable Cup Final goal ever.

For a time it was quite impossible to keep Arsenal out of the Cup headlines. In the third round the following season they went to Walsall, a club of no great pretensions, and lost 2-0 in a game that still ranks above Yeovil-Sunderland and Colchester-Leeds as the greatest of all the giant-killing acts. The reasons are emotional rather than analytical. What more needs to be said than that Arsenal spent more on their boots in 1933 than Walsall had paid in transfer fees for their whole team?

The little clubs can indeed add drama, and one of the most appealing things about the Cup is the periodic appearance of the giantkillers. On occasions it has even gained a club admission to the League—Peterborough after their successes in the 1950s and Hereford after their defeat of Newcastle in 1972 are perhaps the best examples. Often enough it has cost managers of League clubs their positions. When amateur Blyth Spartans defeated both Crewe and Stockport in successive rounds of the 1971-72 competition, the managers of both the Fourth Division clubs lost their jobs the following week.

Victories by non-League clubs over their League brothers are common enough of course—in 1956-57 it happened as many as eleven times. But since the League added a Third Division in 1920 there have been

The blood runs from Emlyn Hughes' face during his side's vain attempt to prevent Arsenal's double in 1971.

only four instances of a non-League club beating a First Division side, none away from home. Hereford came nearest in the third round of 1972, drawing at Newcastle and winning the replay. *Old Moore's Almanac* for the year had predicted that a non-League side would win the Cup and Hereford certainly did their best to oblige—drawing with West Ham in the next round before going down 3-1.

Superstition seems to play a big part in the Cup, where Portsmouth were the arch-adherents. In 1934 they employed manager Jack Tinn's lucky spats to bring them fortune and comedian Bud Flanagan to tell them jokes in the dressing room before the game with Manchester City. It did no good, City coming back to win 2-1 after losing the 1933 Final. City did the same thing in 1956, beating Birmingham with the 'Revie plan' after losing to Newcastle in 1955.

The 1934 Final was the occasion on which Frank Swift fainted. He said that the tension of the last few minutes, when he spent his time between the posts musing on how difficult it would be to clean the Cup and listening to the photographers counting down the seconds, was simply too much and he collapsed as

FOOTBALL ASSOCIATION CHALLENGE CUP FINALS 1872-1973

Year	Venue	Winners		Scorers	Runners-up		Scorers	Attendance
1872	Kennington Oval	Wanderers	1	*Betts*	Royal Engineers	0		2,000
1873[1]	Lillie Bridge	Wanderers	2	*Kinnaird, Wollaston*	Oxford University	0		3,000
1874	Kennington Oval	Oxford University	2	*Mackarness, Patton*	Royal Engineers	0		2,000
1875*	Kennington Oval	Royal Engineers	1	*Scorer not known*	Old Etonians	1	*Bonsor*	3,000
Replay	Kennington Oval	Royal Engineers	2	*Renny-Tailyour, A N Other*	Old Etonians	0		3,000
1876	Kennington Oval	Wanderers	0		Old Etonians	0		3,000
Replay	Kennington Oval	Wanderers	3	*Hughes (2), Wollaston*	Old Etonians	0		3,500
1877*	Kennington Oval	Wanderers	2	*Scorers not known*	Oxford University	0		3,000
1878[2]	Kennington Oval	Wanderers	3	*Scorers not known*	Royal Engineers	1	*Scorer not known*	4,500
1879	Kennington Oval	Old Etonians	1	*Scorer not known*	Clapham Rovers	0		5,000
1880	Kennington Oval	Clapham Rovers	1	*Lloyd-Jones*	Oxford University	0		6,000
1881	Kennington Oval	Old Carthusians	3	*Scorers not known*	Old Etonians	0		4,500
1882	Kennington Oval	Old Etonians	1	*Anderson*	Blackburn Rovers	0		6,500
1883*	Kennington Oval	Blackburn Olympic	2	*Matthews, Costley*	Old Etonians	1	*Goodhart*	8,000
1884	Kennington Oval	Blackburn Rovers	2	*Brown, Forrest*	Queen's Park (Glasgow)	1	*Christie*	4,000
1885	Kennington Oval	Blackburn Rovers	2	*Brown, Forrest*	Queen's Park (Glasgow)	0		12,500
1886	Kennington Oval	Blackburn Rovers	0		West Bromwich Albion	0		15,000
Replay[3]	The Racecourse, Derby	Blackburn Rovers	2	*Brown, Sowerbutts*	West Bromwich Albion	0		12,000
1887	Kennington Oval	Aston Villa	2	*Hunter, Hodgetts*	West Bromwich Albion	0		15,500
1888	Kennington Oval	West Bromwich Albion	2	*Woodhall, Bayliss*	Preston North End	1	*Dewhurst*	19,000
1889	Kennington Oval	Preston North End	3	*Gordon, Goodall, Thompson*	Wolverhampton Wanderers	0		22,000
1890	Kennington Oval	Blackburn Rovers	6	*Townley (3), Lofthouse, Southworth, Walton*	The Wednesday	1	*Bennett*	20,000
1891	Kennington Oval	Blackburn Rovers	3	*Southworth, Townley, Dewar*	Notts County	1	*Oswald*	23,000
1892	Kennington Oval	West Bromwich Albion	3	*Nicholls, Geddes, Reynolds*	Aston Villa	0		25,000
1893	Fallowfield, Manchester	Wolverhampton Wanderers	1	*Allen*	Everton	0		45,000
1894	Goodison Park	Notts County	4	*Logan (3), Watson*	Bolton Wanderers	1	*Cassidy*	37,000
1895	Crystal Palace	Aston Villa	1	*Devey*	West Bromwich Albion	0		42,560
1896[4]	Crystal Palace	The Wednesday	2	*Spiksley (2)*	Wolverhampton Wanderers	1	*Black*	48,836
1897	Crystal Palace	Aston Villa	3	*Campbell, Devey, Crabtree*	Everton	2	*Bell, Hartley*	65,891
1898	Crystal Palace	Nottingham Forest	3	*Capes (2), McPherson*	Derby County	1	*Bloomer*	62,017
1899	Crystal Palace	Sheffield United	4	*Bennett, Beers, Priest, Almond*	Derby County	1	*Boag*	78,833
1900	Crystal Palace	Bury	4	*McLuckie (2), Wood, Plant*	Southampton	0		68,945
1901	Crystal Palace	Tottenham Hotspur	2	*Brown (2)*	Sheffield United	2	*Bennett, Priest*	114,815
Replay	Burnden Park, Bolton	Tottenham Hotspur	3	*Cameron, Smith, Brown*	Sheffield United	1	*Priest*	20,740
1902	Crystal Palace	Sheffield United	1	*Common*	Southampton	1	*Wood*	76,914
Replay	Crystal Palace	Sheffield United	2	*Hedley, Barnes*	Southampton	1	*Brown*	33,068
1903	Crystal Palace	Bury	6	*Leeming (2), Ross, Sagar, Plant, Wood*	Derby County	0		63,102
1904	Crystal Palace	Manchester City	1	*Meredith*	Bolton Wanderers	0		61,374
1905	Crystal Palace	Aston Villa	2	*Hampton (2)*	Newcastle United	0		101,117
1906	Crystal Palace	Everton	1	*Young*	Newcastle United	0		75,609
1907	Crystal Palace	The Wednesday	2	*Stewart, Simpson*	Everton	1	*Sharp*	84,584
1908	Crystal Palace	Wolverhampton Wanderers	3	*Hunt, Hedley, Harrison*	Newcastle United	1	*Howie*	74,967
1909	Crystal Palace	Manchester United	1	*Turnbull A*	Bristol City	0		71,401
1910	Crystal Palace	Newcastle United	1	*Rutherford*	Barnsley	1	*Tufnell*	77,747
Replay	Goodison Park	Newcastle United	2	*Shepherd (2 inc a penalty)*	Barnsley	0		69,000
1911[5]	Crystal Palace	Bradford City	0		Newcastle United	0		69,098
Replay	Old Trafford	Bradford City	1	*Spiers*	Newcastle United	0		58,000
1912	Crystal Palace	Barnsley	0		West Bromwich Albion	0		54,556
Replay*	Bramall Lane	Barnsley	1	*Tufnell*	West Bromwich Albion	0		38,555
1913	Crystal Palace	Aston Villa	1	*Barber*	Sunderland	0		120,081
1914	Crystal Palace	Burnley	1	*Freeman*	Liverpool	0		72,778
1915	Old Trafford	Sheffield United	3	*Simmons, Kitchen, Fazackerley*	Chelsea	0		49,557
1916-1919	*Competition suspended*							
1920*	Stamford Bridge	Aston Villa	1	*Kirton*	Huddersfield Town	0		50,018
1921	Stamford Bridge	Tottenham Hotspur	1	*Dimmock*	Wolverhampton Wanderers	0		72,805
1922	Stamford Bridge	Huddersfield Town	1	*Smith (penalty)*	Preston North End	0		53,000
1923[6]	Wembley	Bolton Wanderers	2	*Jack, Smith J R*	West Ham United	0		126,047
1924	Wembley	Newcastle United	2	*Harris, Seymour*	Aston Villa	0		91,695
1925	Wembley	Sheffield United	1	*Tunstall*	Cardiff City	0		91,763
1926	Wembley	Bolton Wanderers	1	*Jack*	Manchester City	0		91,447
1927	Wembley	Cardiff City	1	*Ferguson*	Arsenal	0		91,206
1928	Wembley	Blackburn Rovers	3	*Roscamp (2), McLean*	Huddersfield Town	1	*Jackson*	92,041
1929	Wembley	Bolton Wanderers	2	*Butler, Blackmore*	Portsmouth	0		92,576
1930	Wembley	Arsenal	2	*James, Lambert*	Huddersfield Town	0		92,448
1931	Wembley	West Bromwich Albion	2	*Richardson W G (2)*	Birmingham	1	*Bradford*	92,406
1932	Wembley	Newcastle United	2	*Allen (2)*	Arsenal	1	*John*	92,298
1933	Wembley	Everton	3	*Stein, Dean, Dunn*	Manchester City	0		92,950
1934	Wembley	Manchester City	2	*Tilson (2)*	Portsmouth	1	*Rutherford*	93,258
1935	Wembley	Sheffield Wednesday	4	*Rimmer (2), Palethorpe, Hooper*	West Bromwich Albion	2	*Boyes, Sandford*	93,204
1936	Wembley	Arsenal	1	*Drake*	Sheffield United	0		93,384
1937	Wembley	Sunderland	3	*Gurney, Carter, Burbanks*	Preston North End	1	*O'Donnell*	93,495
1938*	Wembley	Preston North End	1	*Mutch (penalty)*	Huddersfield Town	0		93,497
1939	Wembley	Portsmouth	4	*Parker (2), Barlow, Anderson*	Wolverhampton Wanderers	1	*Dorsett*	99,370
1940-1945	*Competition suspended*							
1946*	Wembley	Derby County	4	*Turner H (og), Doherty, Stamps (2)*	Charlton Athletic	1	*Turner H*	98,000
1947*	Wembley	Charlton Athletic	1	*Duffy*	Burnley	0		99,000
1948	Wembley	Manchester United	4	*Rowley (2), Pearson, Anderson*	Blackpool	2	*Shimwell (penalty), Mortensen*	99,000
1949	Wembley	Wolverhampton Wanderers	3	*Pye (2), Smyth*	Leicester City	1	*Griffiths*	99,500
1950	Wembley	Arsenal	2	*Lewis (2)*	Liverpool	0		100,000
1951	Wembley	Newcastle United	2	*Milburn (2)*	Blackpool	0		100,000
1952	Wembley	Newcastle United	1	*Robledo G*	Arsenal	0		100,000
1953	Wembley	Blackpool	4	*Mortensen (3), Perry*	Bolton Wanderers	3	*Lofthouse, Moir, Bell*	100,000
1954	Wembley	West Bromwich Albion	3	*Allen (2 inc a penalty), Griffin*	Preston North End	2	*Morrison, Wayman*	100,000
1955	Wembley	Newcastle United	3	*Milburn, Mitchell, Hannah*	Manchester City	1	*Johnstone*	100,000
1956	Wembley	Manchester City	3	*Hayes, Dyson, Johnstone*	Birmingham City	1	*Kinsey*	100,000
1957	Wembley	Aston Villa	2	*McParland (2)*	Manchester United	1	*Taylor*	100,000
1958	Wembley	Bolton Wanderers	2	*Lofthouse (2)*	Manchester United	0		100,000
1959	Wembley	Nottingham Forest	2	*Dwight, Wilson*	Luton Town	1	*Pacey*	100,000
1960	Wembley	Wolverhampton Wanderers	3	*McGrath (og), Deeley (2)*	Blackburn Rovers	0		100,000
1961	Wembley	Tottenham Hotspur	2	*Smith, Dyson*	Leicester City	0		100,000
1962	Wembley	Tottenham Hotspur	3	*Greaves, Smith, Blanchflower (penalty)*	Burnley	1	*Robson*	100,000
1963	Wembley	Manchester United	3	*Law, Herd (2)*	Leicester City	1	*Keyworth*	100,000
1964	Wembley	West Ham United	3	*Sissons, Hurst, Boyce*	Preston North End	2	*Holden, Dawson*	100,000
1965*	Wembley	Liverpool	2	*Hunt, St John*	Leeds United	1	*Bremner*	100,000
1966	Wembley	Everton	3	*Trebilcock (2), Temple*	Sheffield Wednesday	2	*McCalliog, Ford*	100,000
1967[7]	Wembley	Tottenham Hotspur	2	*Robertson, Saul*	Chelsea	1	*Tambling*	100,000
1968*	Wembley	West Bromwich Albion	1	*Astle*	Everton	0		100,000
1969	Wembley	Manchester City	1	*Young*	Leicester City	0		100,000
1970	Wembley	Chelsea	2	*Houseman, Hutchinson*	Leeds United	2	*Charlton, Jones*	100,000
Replay*	Old Trafford	Chelsea	2	*Osgood, Webb*	Leeds United	1	*Jones*	62,000
1971*	Wembley	Arsenal	2	*Kelly, George*	Liverpool	1	*Heighway*	100,000
1972	Wembley	Leeds United	1	*Clarke*	Arsenal	0		100,000
1973	Wembley	Sunderland	1	*Porterfield*	Leeds United	0		100,000

*After half-an-hour's extra time. Extra time became compulsory in 1913. [1]Challenge system. The holders, Wanderers, were exempt until the Final.
[2]Wanderers won the trophy outright but restored it to the Association. [3]Blackburn Rovers were also awarded a special shield to mark their third consecutive win.
[4]After the Cup had been stolen in 1895, the FA ordered a replica. The 1896 Final was the first time it was awarded.
[5]After the Cup's design had been duplicated for another competition, it was withdrawn and presented to Lord Kinnaird on his completing 21 years as President of the Football Association. The present trophy was first awarded in 1911.
[6]Official attendance figure. Actual attendance was probably in excess of 200,000. [7]Substitutes allowed for the first time.

the final whistle went.

Portsmouth's rituals proved luckier five years later. Their opponents Wolves arrived at Wembley as the hottest favourites of the century and full of a publicity seeking course of 'monkey glands'. Portsmouth preferred to rely on the spats again and, when the signature book came round, were heartened to see that the Wolves players were so nervous that their signatures were barely legible.

Portsmouth won the Cup easily and proceeded to hold it for the longest period ever—seven years. This, however, was less due to their prowess than the outbreak of the Second World War.

After that lengthy intermission the Cup re-appeared in unfamiliar form. Because of the lack of a League programme, the FA decided to hold the Cup on a home-and-away basis—for the first and only time. It was not really a success, but it created its talking points.

Bradford PA lost 3-1 at home to Manchester City in the fourth round and then went on to win 8-2 at Maine Road, while Charlton became only the third team to *lose* a Cup game and still reach the Final. Fulham beat them 2-1 in the third round at Craven Cottage but Charlton had already won the first leg 3-1 and went through. One previous occasion when this had happened was the second part of a three-match quarter-final fiasco in 1890. Wednesday beat Notts County 5-0 in the first part. County protested to the FA, the game was replayed and County won 3-2. This time it was Sheffield's turn to protest and the eventual result was a 2-1 win for Wednesday—who went on to lose the Final rather ingnominiously 6-1 to Blackburn Rovers.

The 1946 Final was almost as high scoring a game—Derby winning 4-1. That surprised no one for it took

Derby's tally for the competition to 37, the highest aggregate since 1887-88 when Preston beat Hyde 26-0. Charlton's Bert Turner was the central figure of the game, scoring an own goal for Derby and within a minute equalizing with a free-kick which went in off Doherty's legs. He remains the only man to have scored for both sides in a Cup Final.

There followed two years later one of a pair of great Finals that have to be regarded in tandem. In the first the League runners-up, Manchester United, beat Blackpool 4-2 in what has always been regarded as the 'purest' of the Wembley games. Blackpool reached Wembley twice more in the next five years, losing to Newcastle in 1951 and facing Bolton

in 1953, a game consigned to legend as 'the Matthews Final'. Blackpool came back from 3-1 down 20 minutes from time and 3-2 down with just three minutes of normal time left to win 4-3 in the game which will probably always rank—whatever its merits—as *the* Cup Final.

It was a game in keeping with the heady atmosphere of 1953, of the Coronation, of Everest, of Gordon Richards' Derby win, of the Hungarians visit to Wembley. Yet tacticians point to Bolton's strange response to left-half Eric Bell's injury in the first half. Bell moved to the left-wing. Inside-left Harry Hassall, no great tackler, moved to left-half and, when left-back Ralph Banks went down with cramp twenty

Above 'The FA Cup is for the fans,' says Danny Blanchflower. Mansfield Town, average attendance around 5,000, found difficulty accommodating everyone who wanted to watch their sixth round tie with Leicester in 1969. *Left* An over-enthusiastic Evertonian at Wembley in 1966 annoys Brian Labone but gives Brian Harris (far left) the chance to see if the cap fits.

minutes from the end, he was left marking Matthews. As a result, Matthews' right-wing was left as open as the proverbial barn door and Bolton paid the price.

Bell's injury was a portent for the next decade. Between 1952 and 1961 only two Finals—1954 and 1958—were not marred by some vital injury. And, significantly, only two of the teams that suffered —Manchester City in 1956 and Nottingham Forest in 1959— eventually won the Cup. The phenomenon, dubbed 'the Wembley hoodoo', was generally attributed to the turf.

Danny Blanchflower explained after the 1961 Final: 'It was a lush trap; the ideal pitch should have a little give in it. But Wembley is too soft. It pulls at the lower muscles of the leg, braking some efforts and ruining the natural timing.' After that particular game—in which Len Chalmers of Leicester suffered torn ligaments—the hoodoo seemed to die away. Substitutes were first introduced in 1967 and it was never an issue again. Perhaps cutting the grass a little shorter made the difference.

Wolverhampton were the great team of the fifties, winning three Championships, yet their two Cup wins were in the last year of the previous decade and the first of the next. And they were against, perhaps, the two worst post-War finalists. In 1949 Leicester arrived at Wembley with the sole distinction of being the worst placed League

SYNDICATION INTERNATIONAL

PRESS ASSOCIATION

Right *Tension in the tunnel before the 1956 Final. Birmingham's skipper Len Boyd bounces the ball against a wall while the Manchester City players huddle round the man with the plan—nominal number 9 Don Revie.* **Below** *Wembley 1930 and the black shadow of Germany's Graf Zeppelin.*

club (they finished nineteenth in the Second Division) ever to reach the Final. In fact with one point less they would have been playing Third Division football in the August of the same year. Leicester's 3-1 defeat was the prelude to three more in the next 20 years—leaving them with the undisputed position of chief bridesmaid.

Wolves' 1960 opponents were in some ways even more ragged. Blackburn Rovers received a transfer request from centre-forward Derek Dougan on the morning of the match, left-back Dave Whelan broke a leg and right-half McGrath scored an own goal. It was the most one-sided of all the Wembley Finals and, while promising to herald in an even more successful decade than the one before for the Midlanders, it was in fact manager Cullis's swansong. Five years later Wolves were playing Second Division football.

Manchester United's record is far sadder. Despite their wins in 1948 and 1963 it is the games of 1957 and 1958 that they must be remembered by. Not only did United become the first club to lose successive Finals at Wembley, but they did so in tragic circumstances.

United approached Wembley in 1957 as League Champions, having reached the semi-final of the European Cup, and on the verge of becoming perhaps the best British club side ever. Real Madrid had beaten them in the European Cup, but it had disheartened nobody, and Busby had said: '. . . the only difference between the teams was in their experience, and we shall soon acquire that . . .' To add spice to the Cup Final their opponents were Aston Villa, the last club to do the double that United seemed to have so firmly in their grasp.

But within minutes Villa's outside-left McParland had crashed into the United keeper Ray Wood and fractured his cheekbone. Wood went off, Jackie Blanchflower had to take over, and the machine was disturbed. McParland scored two goals to give Villa a record seventh win. As one journalist put it the next day: 'McParland was the man of the match—bagging two goals and one goalkeeper.'

But if 1957 could be called tragic for United, then 1958 was cataclysmic. That was, of course, the year of Munich. Six of the 1957 Wembley side—Byrne, Colman, Edwards, Whelan, Taylor and Pegg—were dead. Two—Johnny Berry and Jackie Blanchflower—survived but never kicked a ball again. And what happened next has become a legend.

POPPERFOTO

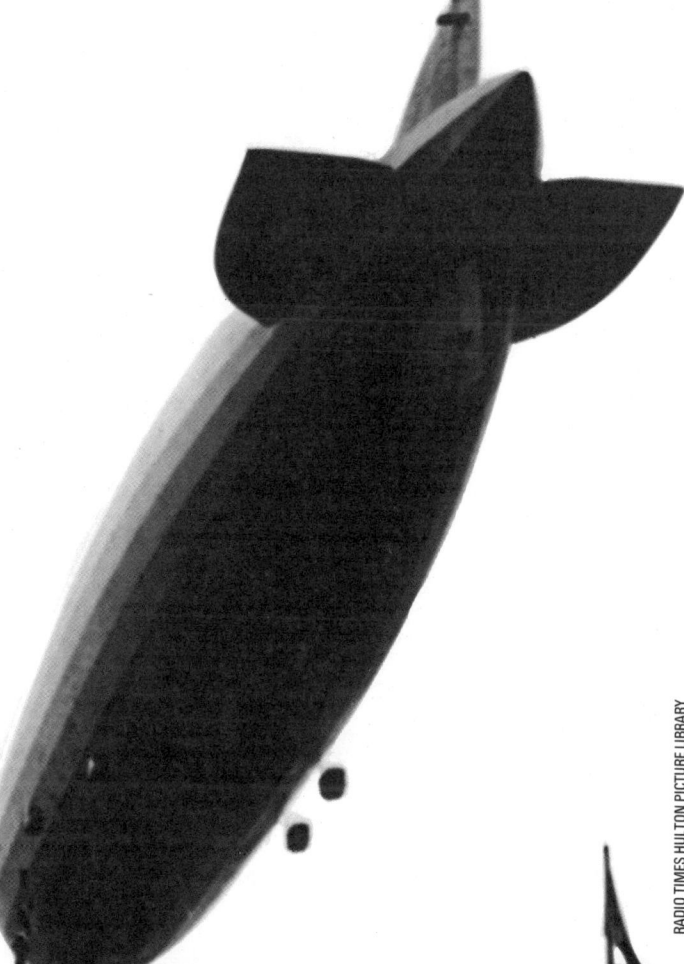

RADIO TIMES HULTON PICTURE LIBRARY

FA CUP 1872-1973

The Cup and League Double

1888-89	Preston North End
1896-97	Aston Villa
1960-61	Tottenham Hotspur
1970-71	Arsenal

Cup winners and League runners-up

1903-04	Manchester City
1912-13	Aston Villa
1947-48	Manchester United
1953-54	West Bromwich Albion
1959-60	Wolverhampton Wanderers
1971-72	Leeds United

League Champions and Cup runners-up

1904-05	Newcastle United
1912-13	Sunderland
1956-57	Manchester United

Runners-up in Cup and League

1927-28	Huddersfield Town
1931-32	Arsenal
1938-39	Wolverhampton Wanderers
1961-62	Burnley
1964-65	Leeds United
1969-70	Leeds United

Second Division Cup winners

1893-94	Notts County
1907-08	Wolverhampton Wanderers
1911-12	Barnsley
1930-31	West Bromwich Albion
1972-73	Sunderland

Second Division Cup runners-up

1903-04	Bolton Wanderers
1909-10	Barnsley
1919-20	Huddersfield Town (promoted)
1920-21	Wolverhampton Wanderers
1922-23	West Ham United (promoted)
1935-36	Sheffield United
1946-47	Burnley (promoted)
1948-49	Leicester City
1963-64	Preston North End

Non-League Cup winners since 1888

1900-01	Tottenham Hotspur

Non-League Cup runners-up since 1888

1889-90	The Wednesday
1899-00	Southampton
1901-02	Southampton

Relegated Cup Winners

None

Relegated Cup runners-up

1914-15	Chelsea*
1925-26	Manchester City
1968-69	Leicester City

*Chelsea finished next to bottom but were elected straight back to the extended First Division after the War.

Hat-trick of Cup wins

1876, 1877, 1878	Wanderers
1884, 1885, 1886	Blackburn Rovers

Consecutive Cup wins

1872, 1873	Wanderers
1890, 1891	Blackburn Rovers
1951, 1952	Newcastle United
1961, 1962	Tottenham Hotspur

Goalscorers in every round

1900-01	A Brown (Tottenham Hotspur)
1934-35	E Rimmer (The Wednesday)
1936-37	F O'Donnell (Preston)
1947-48	S Mortensen (Blackpool)
1950-51	J Milburn (Newcastle)
1952-53	N Lofthouse (Bolton)
1953-54	C Wayman (Preston North End)
1967-68	J Astle (West Bromwich)
1969-70	P Osgood (Chelsea)

The FA waived its rules to allow Stan Crowther, a member of the Villa side that had beaten United in 1957, to play for United after having turned out for Villa already in the competition. Ernie Taylor, already a successful Cup Finalist with Blackpool and Newcastle, was brought to hold the team together. And as if partaking in some medieval ritual, the crowd support bordered on religious fanaticism. Wherever the new United appeared gates were closed. In the Cup Sheffield Wednesday were the first to fall before this uncanny force, then the favourites West Bromwich, then Second Division Fulham after two semi-final games which ended at 2-2 and 5-3.

And so they arrived at the gates of Wembley, where their opponents were to be Bolton. Poor Bolton. Five years earlier every uncommitted observer had wanted them to lose so that Stanley Matthews could get his winner's medal. This time they must have had a sneaking suspicion that even their own fans would not have minded too much if the Cup had ended up just five miles down the road at Old Trafford.

But the fates had let things go far enough. Within three minutes a very unghostly Nat Lofthouse put Bolton one up and, early in the second half, made it two with a charge that bundled both the ball and goalkeeper Gregg into the back of the net.

The myth has grown up that it was Lofthouse's charge that lost United the game. That is unlikely. In many ways they had looked what they were —a team carried along on a wave of fanaticism that could not, in the end, disguise the makeshift nature of the effort. After all, only Foulkes and Charlton had played in both Finals. In the space of six years and three Finals in the 1920s Bolton had used just 17 players. United had been forced to use 20 in successive appearances.

Leeds—the better team that lost a unique replay

Manchester's Yorkshire counterpart—Leeds—have a record almost as sad. The team that Don Revie brought from the shadows became the first to take second place in both major competitions on two separate occasions, 1965 and 1970. What was sadder was the universal opinion that, in the latter Final, Leeds were the better of the two sides. But then the best side is surely the one that scores most goals and Chelsea did precisely that in the first replay since the Final moved to Wembley.

The Cup had long been something of a problem for this team that so much wanted to be loved as well as respected. Between the fifth round in 1952 and the third round in 1963 Leeds had established something of a record, going through 16 Cup games without a win. This included a remarkable spell (1956, 1957 and 1958) when they lost 2-1 at home to Cardiff City in three consecutive third rounds. No doubt they were delighted to get away to a 5-1 defeat at Luton in 1959.

In actual fact Rochdale's record is even worse—they reached the

second round in the 1927-28 season but did not appear there again until 1945-46. For eleven consecutive seasons this unfortunate club was knocked out in the first round.

One club with a very satisfactory post-War Cup record is Tottenham. They have won three Finals, to bring their total to five appearances and five wins. The third, fourth and fifth of these came within the space of six years—1961, 1962 and 1967—and the first of those, a 2-0 win against Leicester, earned Spurs the first double for 64 years.

The first season of the decade seems to have a fascination for White Hart Lane. Spurs won the Cup first in 1901, next in 1921, the League for the first time in 1951, the double in 1961 and the League Cup in 1971.

Newcastle have been even more successful than Tottenham at Wembley. In five appearances they have yet to be beaten and they share with the North Londoners the distinction of being the only club to win in consecutive seasons there. The Magpies were successful in 1924, 1932, 1951, 1952 and 1955, and were not particularly stretched on any of their post-Second World War appearances. The fact that they beat Arsenal twice—1932 and 1952—only serves to stress how poor London's record has been in an event that the FA have always insisted should be held there.

A rare spell of success for the capital's supporters

But Spurs' double in 1961 was the precursor of a remarkable run of success for the capital—the more so in comparison with what had gone before—culminating in the Arsenal double of 1971. In the decade 1961-1971 London clubs took six of the eleven Finals; in the previous 60 years of the century they had won precisely the same number.

Arsenal's double was the more remarkable of the two if only for its unpredictability. With Spurs in 1961 the possibility had been discussed from very early on in the season, though that might have reflected the paucity of the opposition as much as anything else. Arsenal came through at the last moment in both competitions—overhauling Leeds after being six points behind with just six weeks to go, and taking 27 points from their last 16 matches, and scoring a last-minute penalty to draw with Stoke in the semi-final.

On the Monday of Cup Final week they beat Spurs—appropriately as their North London neighbours were then the only twentieth-century double winners—to take the League, and five days later squeezed past Liverpool at Wembley to deprive Spurs of their uniqueness. It was Arsenal's 64th game of the season.

Strangely it was left to Arsenal to try and prevent yet another double the following season. They failed, after a dour game which, if nothing else, epitomized the football of the early seventies and ended in its most familiar score—1-0. Leeds were in no way dispirited by the manner of their victory—it was third time lucky both for the club and for Allan Clarke, the man who scored

GIANT-KILLING BY NON-LEAGUE CLUBS 1919-1973

Victories over First Division sides

*Cardiff City	2	Oldham Athletic	0		1919-20
*Sheffield Wednesday	0	Darlington	2	(after 0-0 draw)	1919-20
†Corinthians	1	Blackburn Rovers	0		1923-24
Colchester United	1	Huddersfield Town	0		1947-48
Yeovil Town	2	Sunderland	1		1948-49
Hereford United	2	Newcastle United	1	(after 2-2 draw)	1971-72

Victories over Second Division sides

*Coventry City	0	Luton Town	1	(after 2-2 draw)	1919-20
*Fulham	1	Swindon Town	2		1919-20
*Plymouth Argyle	4	Barnsley	1		1919-20
*Wolverhampton W	1	Cardiff City	2		1919-20
Wolverhampton W	0	Mansfield Town	1		1928-29
Chelmsford City	4	Southampton	1		1938-39
Colchester United	3	Bradford PA	2		1947-48
Yeovil Town	3	Bury	1		1948-49
†Bishop Auckland	3	Ipswich Town	1	(after 2-2 draw)	1954-55
Lincoln City	4	Peterborough United	5	(after 2-2 draw)	1956-57
Notts County	1	Rhyl	3		1956-57
Worcester City	2	Liverpool	1		1958-59
Ipswich Town	2	Peterborough United	3		1959-60
Newcastle United	1	Bedford Town	2		1963-64

Biggest victories over League sides

Carlisle United	1	Wigan Athletic	6		1934-35
†Walthamstow Avenue	6	Northampton Town	1		1936-37
Derby County	1	Boston United	6		1955-56
Hereford United	6	Queen's Park Rangers	1		1957-58
Barnet	6	Newport County	1		1970-71

Progress to last sixteen (present fifth round)

*1919-20 Cardiff City
*1919-20 Plymouth Argyle
 1947-48 Colchester United
 1948-49 Yeovil Town

*The Third Division did not come into being until 1920. In the 1919-20 season the best Southern League clubs were of a comparable standard with Second Division sides.
†Amateur club.

CENTRAL PRESS

the only goal of the Final.

Having won the one that had eluded them for so long however, Leeds went to Wolverhampton just two days later needing a single point for the elusive double. But they lost 2-1.

That Centenary Final at Wembley was the end of a story which had started over seven months earlier. For it was way back in the autumn of 1971 that teams like Guinness Exports and Rawmarsh Welfare had started on the long trek to Wembley. Nowadays, there are initially 36 groups comprised of eight, nine or ten local teams which set the competition rolling.

A club like Boden Colliery Welfare, playing in the North-Eastern Geographical Division in September 1974, is faced with 15 rounds before reaching Wembley. Of course, hardly any of the clubs which start at this early stage even reach the First Round proper. Twenty-four of the best non-League sides are exempt until the Fourth (the last) Qualifying

Round, and the winners from that round go on to the First Round proper where they are joined by the Third and Fourth Division clubs and the previous season's Amateur Cup finalists.

After two rounds this number has been cut to twenty, who are joined by the 44 big boys—the First and Second Division clubs.

It is a system which obviously favours the bigger clubs. The success of Third Division clubs in the League Cup has been attributed, in part, to the fact that bigger clubs have to compete at an earlier stage than they do in the FA Cup.

The FA Cup, however, has a place for the likes of Abergavenny Thursdays and Irthlingborough Diamonds. It started, and remains, a competition for all the clubs affiliated to the Football Association—and it is a place they guard manfully.

But just as the FA Cup is not only for the big clubs and great names, neither, perhaps, is it for the little clubs and the amateur player.

RADIO TIMES HULTON PICTURE LIBRARY

SUNDAY TELEGRAPH

FA CUP SUCCESS 1872–1973

	Cup Final wins	Cup Final appearances	Semi-final appearances
Aston Villa	7	9	17
Newcastle United	6	10	12
Blackburn Rovers	6	8	16
West Bromwich Albion	5	10	17
*Tottenham Hotspur	5	5	9
*Wanderers	5	5	5
Arsenal	4	8	12
Wolverhampton Wanderers	4	8	11
Bolton Wanderers	4	7	12
Manchester City	4	7	9
Sheffield United	4	6	10
Everton	3	7	16
Sheffield Wednesday	3	5	13
Manchester United	3	5	12
Preston North End	2	7	10
Old Etonians	2	6	6
Sunderland	2	3	10
*Nottingham Forest	2	2	9
*Bury	2	2	2
Huddersfield Town	1	5	7
Derby County	1	4	12
Liverpool	1	4	9
Leeds United	1	4	6
Oxford University	1	4	6
Royal Engineers	1	4	4
Chelsea	1	3	10
Burnley	1	3	7
Portsmouth	1	3	4
Blackpool	1	3	3
Notts County	1	2	4
Cardiff City	1	2	3
Clapham Rovers	1	2	3
West Ham United	1	2	3
Barnsley	1	2	2
Charlton Athletic	1	2	2
*Old Carthusians	1	1	3
*Blackburn Olympic	1	1	2
*Bradford City	1	1	1
Leicester City	–	4	5
Birmingham City	–	2	8
Southampton	–	2	7
Queen's Park (Glasgow)	–	2	4
Bristol City	–	1	2
Luton Town	–	1	1
Fulham	–	–	4
Millwall	–	–	3
Stoke City	–	–	3
Swifts	–	–	3
Darwen	–	–	2
Grimsby Town	–	–	2
Swansea City	–	–	2
Swindon Town	–	–	2
Cambridge University	–	–	1
Crewe Alexandra	–	–	1
Crystal Palace	–	–	1
Derby Junction	–	–	1
Glasgow Rangers	–	–	1
Hull City	–	–	1
Marlow	–	–	1
Norwich City	–	–	1
Old Harrovians	–	–	1
Oldham Athletic	–	–	1
Port Vale	–	–	1
Reading	–	–	1
Shropshire Wanderers	–	–	1
Watford	–	–	1
York City	–	–	1

*Undefeated in Finals

Opposite page Geoff Barnett clears from Allan Clarke in 1972. After appearing on the losing side with Leicester in 1969 and with Leeds in 1970, it was third time lucky for Clarke in 1972 when he scored the only goal of the game and was voted 'Man of the Match', just as he was in 1969.

Above Two Welsh international goalkeepers, two sadly similar mistakes; **top** Dan Lewis fumbles Ferguson's shot in the 1927 Final and Arsenal have lost to Cardiff while **bottom** 43 years later Gary Sprake dives over the top of Houseman's speculative effort and allows Chelsea to draw level.

Right All the ballyhoo and excitement is over for 1969, the losers have retired to lick their wounds, Manchester City have won the Cup for the fourth time; Tony Book holds the trophy, Glyn Pardoe his hard-earned medal.

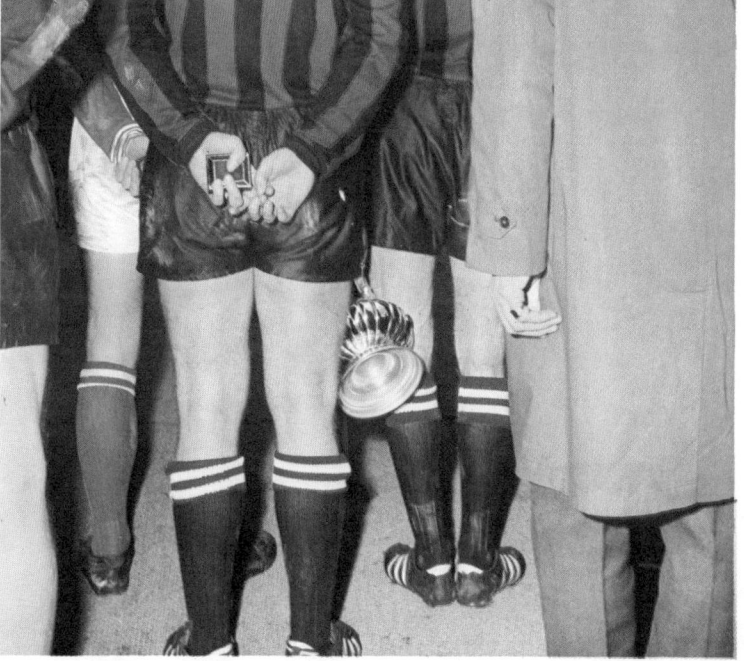

SYNDICATION INTERNATIONAL

Really it is a competition—and most certainly a Final—for the fan. It is the fan who pays £30 for black market tickets, who turns mortals into immortals simply because they scored a goal, who talks about it, dreams about it and relives it for months, who would not give away a Final ticket for a fortune, because the most valuable thing a fortune can buy is a Cup Final ticket.

Danny Blanchflower puts it the players' way: 'In truth we are brainwashed about the Cup Final. A player hears so much about it before he gets there . . . the "majestic" twin towers . . . the "hallowed" green turf . . . the "royal" greeting . . . the crowd singing "Abide With Me" . . . It all sounds like some distant religious ceremony that takes place at the end of the season in the promised land. The reality of it can never live up to the dream. The dream is not for the player, it is for the fan . . . the lover of the game who doesn't really know what it is like out there and never *will* know. It is the fan's day, which is why some 400 million of them all over the world tune in on Cup Final day. But long may it prosper.'

The League Championship

This page Goal number one for Mike Summerbee and Manchester City at Newcastle on 11 May 1968. City's 4-3 victory in this, their last game of the season, gave them the Championship by two points over their Manchester rivals, United.

Opposite page The goal that won the Championship and its aftermath; *top* John McGovern's shot enters the Liverpool net during Derby's last game of the season on Mayday 1972. Putting out distress signals *bottom* Ray Clemence contemplates and Tommy Smith recriminates while Derby celebrate. Even at this stage Derby's chances of actually taking the Championship seemed slight and it was a week before success was confirmed.

PRESS ASSOCIATION

It is not what you do, but what your contemporaries do that brings the difference between success and failure. Hence Leeds could win the 1969 League Championship by scoring 66 times, while forty or so years before, Manchester City mustered 23 goals more and were relegated!

The Yorkshiremen's 66 goal tally—one less than the record 67 points they amassed—was perfectly respectable in a climate of defensive football. City's 1926 total of 89, however, was not—unfortunately for them—as extraordinary then as it would have been forty years on.

For those years saw the decline and fall of positive, attacking football. Preventing goals is easier than scoring them, and the 'smash-and-grab' type of football, with goals on the quick break out of defence as introduced by Herbert Chapman during his reign at Arsenal, rapidly became the favoured tactic.

That style of play was perhaps best seen at its peak when the Gunners themselves played against Aston Villa in 1935. Territorially outplayed, Arsenal were restricted to just nine shots at goal, eight of them from their England centre-forward, Ted Drake. The score? Aston Villa 1 Arsenal 7. Drake scored all seven Arsenal goals and struck the crossbar with his eighth shot.

In the early days of the League, Sunderland, for example, won the 1893 title with 100 goals—and 48 points—from just 30 matches. But defences quickly became more sophisticated and the offside trap, brought to a fine art by Bill McCracken of Newcastle in the middle twenties, showed itself as early as 1909. In that year, Newcastle won the title with only 65 goals.

It is interesting to speculate what might have happened had the Football League's original intention to award points only for wins had been carried through. The mind boggles at the goals there might have been had a drawn game remained valueless in terms of points! However, it was not to be, for after 10 weeks of the first season it was decided that drawn games should be worth a point to each side. There had already been a number of these, notably the 5-5 draw between Blackburn and Accrington in September, and the 4-4 stalemate involving Accrington and Wolves early the following month.

At the end of the first season, Preston North End were champions. That inaugural season, 1888-89, when Preston also won the FA Cup without conceding a goal, their League record was so outstanding that it remains an imperishable landmark in soccer history.

In their 22 League matches, they won 18 times and drew four, scoring 74 goals against 15. They are the only British club ever to have gone through a season without a defeat in either League or Cup.

Preston were champions again in the League's second season, though they were beaten four times. In 1890-91, however, they finished second. It was Everton who took the title away from them, and who were to become the most consistent League club, spending all but five of the next 74 seasons in the top division. The record for unbroken membership belongs to Sunderland who, up to their relegation in 1958, had been 57 consecutive seasons in the top bracket.

The League Championship —the preserve of the North and the Midlands

Considering that the North East has produced only three major clubs, Sunderland, Newcastle and Middlesbrough, the area has done well in terms of First Division membership—at least one of the three was there until 1962—especially as none of those was an original member of the League.

There were twelve of those: Wolves, Everton, Preston, Burnley, Derby, Notts County, Blackburn Rovers, Bolton, Stoke, Accrington, Aston Villa and West Bromwich Albion. The North East was not the only region with no representative in the first League. Not one of that dozen came from London or the South.

By 1972-73, the story was a different one. London had five clubs in the First Division, the Midlands was seven-strong, while Lancashire, a comparative shadow of its former greatness, had only four—two Manchester clubs and the Merseyside pair. Leeds and Sheffield United represented Yorkshire, and Newcastle the North East.

The three remaining clubs—Ipswich, Norwich and Southampton—came, needless to say, from elsewhere. But that fact is important. Very few First Division teams have come from elsewhere. In the League's first 74 seasons, just eight clubs

have been situated outside the traditional areas of football power—London, the Midlands, Lancashire, Yorkshire and the North East—areas which contain some 80% of the country's population.

They are Grimsby (who joined Division One in 1901), Bristol City (1906), Cardiff (1921), Portsmouth (1927), Luton (1955), Ipswich (1961), Southampton (1966) and Norwich (1972). No more than three have ever been in the First Division at the same time.

But if that signifies any shift in the balance of power, it has been so slight as to be negligible. After all, apart from Portsmouth in 1949 and 1950, and Alf Ramsey's Ipswich in 1962, the Championship has never left the pockets of soccer strength.

This is not because the industrial areas produce the best players, but because they provide more spectators. Crowds paying money at the gate means money to spend on new players. It is a harsh fact of football life that the clubs with the best support tend to get the best players. There are exceptions—of which Aston Villa must be the prime example.

It was different in 1888 when the League started. Professionalism had been legal for only three years; money was not yet all important. Then, the best players came from those parts of the country where there were most young men. And with Lancashire and the Midlands centres of heavy industry, they were able to attract young men from Scotland, Ireland and Wales, where jobs were few. Many a skilful footballer emerged from kickabouts with his workmates.

But as industry began to spread, so did the quality and scope of the game. It is no coincidence that the first team from the South to join the League was a works team—Woolwich Arsenal. The Boer War had made a munitions factory on the banks of the Thames important to the country's war effort. More was to come from that factory than shells.

Not that Arsenal were the first 'outside' club to penetrate the monopoly of the Midlands and Lancashire. Arsenal did not really emerge until 1904, when the League was 16 years old.

The first 'newcomers' were Sunderland, in 1890, who won the Championship in 1891 and 1892, when Sheffield's Wednesday joined the First Division, a year ahead of the other Sheffield club, United.

The arrival of these three was no surprise. Sunderland had a fine team drawn from a mixture of local Northerners and Scotsmen who had been tempted over the border, while Sheffield was one of the first towns in which organized football was played. Indeed, the Sheffield amateur club, formed in 1857, is the oldest in the world.

Sunderland had been champions six times when they were relegated in 1958, which, when added to Newcastle's four, gives the North East an impressive record considering its population. Lancashire, of course, boasting the Liverpool and Manchester clubs in addition to earlier giants of the League such as Blackburn, Preston and Burnley, have easily the best record with 30 of the first 75 Championships.

There have been few discernable patterns with regard to the winning of the League, except perhaps for the years 1963-1970. Then the title seemed to be the preserve of the North. Champions in those years were Everton, Liverpool, Manchester United, Liverpool, United again, Manchester City, Leeds and Everton. Eight Cham-

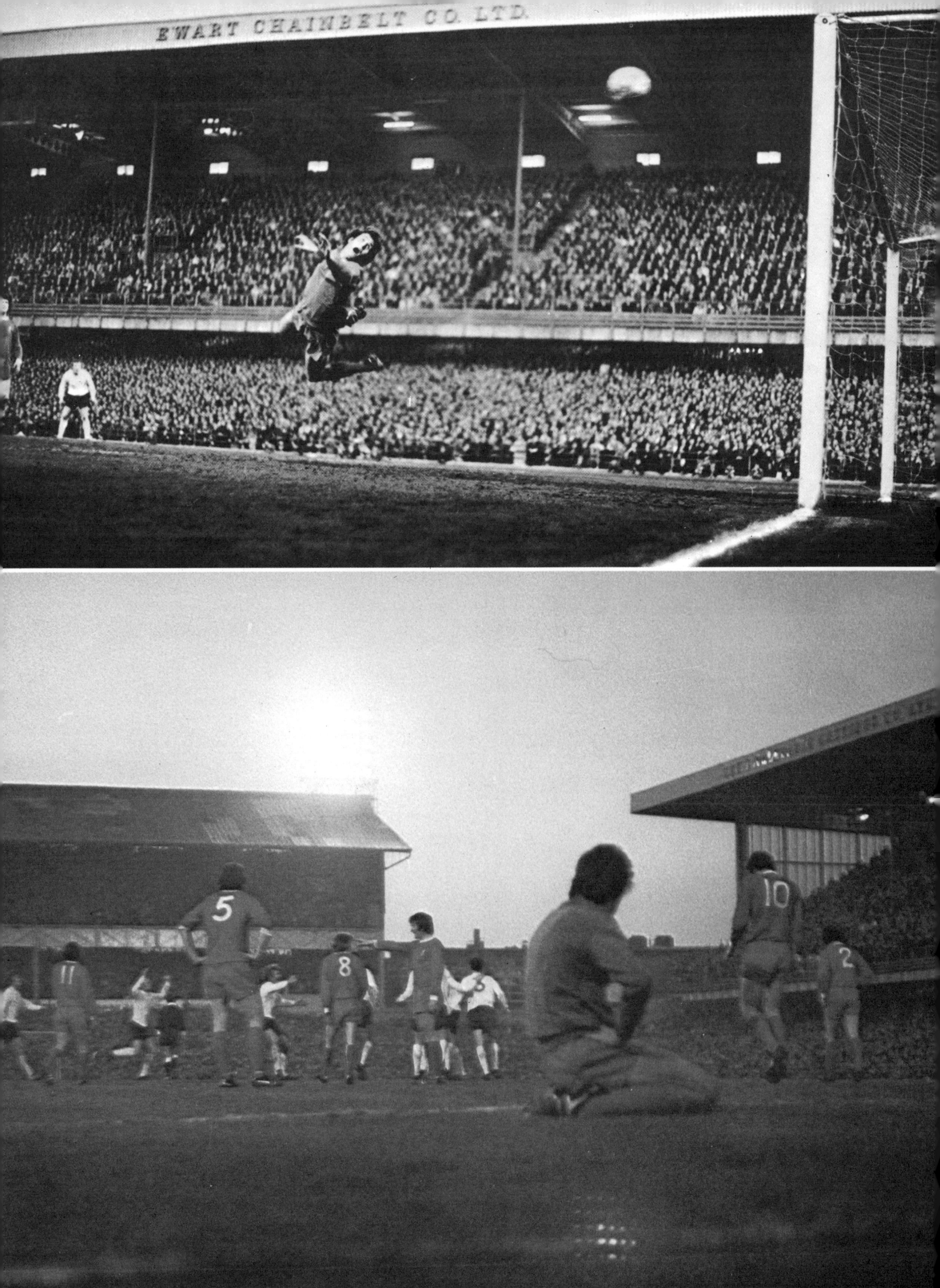

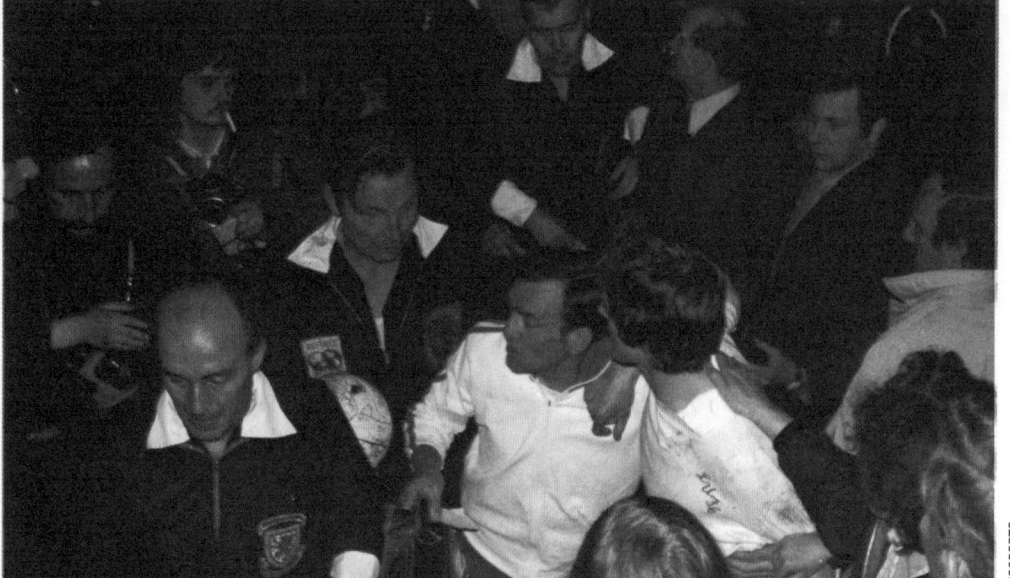

FOTOSPORTS

FOTOSPORTS

FOOTBALL LEAGUE CHAMPIONSHIP

	Winners	Runners-up
1888-89	Preston North End	Aston Villa
1889-90	Preston North End	Everton
1890-91	Everton	Preston North End
1891-92	Sunderland	Preston North End
1892-93	Sunderland	Preston North End
1893-94	Aston Villa	Sunderland
1894-95	Sunderland	Everton
1895-96	Aston Villa	Derby County
1896-97	Aston Villa	Sheffield United
1897-98	Sheffield United	Sunderland
1898-99	Aston Villa	Liverpool
1899-1900	Aston Villa	Sheffield United
1900-01	Liverpool	Sunderland
1901-02	Sunderland	Everton
1902-03	The Wednesday	Aston Villa
1903-04	The Wednesday	Manchester City
1904-05	Newcastle United	Everton
1905-06	Liverpool	Preston North End
1906-07	Newcastle United	Bristol City
1907-08	Manchester United	Aston Villa
1908-09	Newcastle United	Everton
1909-10	Aston Villa	Liverpool
1910-11	Manchester United	Aston Villa
1911-12	Blackburn Rovers	Everton
1912-13	Sunderland	Aston Villa
1913-14	Blackburn Rovers	Aston Villa
1914-15	Everton	Oldham Athletic
1915-19	No competition	
1919-20	West Bromwich Albion	Burnley
1920-21	Burnley	Manchester City
1921-22	Liverpool	Tottenham Hotspur
1922-23	Liverpool	Sunderland
1923-24	**Huddersfield Town	Cardiff City
1924-25	Huddersfield Town	West Bromwich Albion
1925-26	Huddersfield Town	Arsenal
1926-27	Newcastle United	Huddersfield Town
1927-28	Everton	Huddersfield Town
1928-29	Sheffield Wednesday	Leicester City
1829-30	Sheffield Wednesday	Derby County
1930-31	Arsenal	Aston Villa
1931-32	Everton	Arsenal
1932-33	Arsenal	Aston Villa
1933-34	Arsenal	Huddersfield Town
1934-35	Arsenal	Sunderland
1935-36	Sunderland	Derby County
1936-37	Manchester City	Charlton Athletic
1937-38	Arsenal	Wolverhampton Wanderers
1938-39	Everton	Wolverhampton Wanderers
1939-46	No competition	
1946-47	Liverpool	Manchester United
1947-48	Arsenal	Manchester United
1948-49	Portsmouth	Manchester United
1949-50	**Portsmouth	Wolverhampton Wanderers
1950-51	Tottenham Hotspur	Manchester United
1951-52	Manchester United	Tottenham Hotspur
1952-53	**Arsenal	Preston North End
1953-54	Wolverhampton Wanderers	West Bromwich Albion
1954-55	Chelsea	Wolverhampton Wanderers
1955-56	Manchester United	Blackpool
1956-57	Manchester United	Tottenham Hotspur
1957-58	Wolverhampton Wanderers	Preston North End
1958-59	Wolverhampton Wanderers	Manchester United
1959-60	Burnley	Wolverhampton Wanderers
1960-61	Tottenham Hotspur	Sheffield Wednesday
1961-62	Ipswich Town	Burnley
1962-63	Everton	Tottenham Hotspur
1963-64	Liverpool	Manchester United
1964-65	**Manchester United	Leeds United
1965-66	Liverpool	Leeds United
1966-67	Manchester United	Nottingham Forest
1967-68	Manchester City	Manchester United
1968-69	Leeds United	Liverpool
1969-70	Everton	Leeds United
1970-71	Arsenal	Leeds United
1971-72	Derby County	Leeds United
1972-73	Liverpool	Arsenal

**League title won on goal average

Above *Despair after Leeds had failed to beat Wolves in their last game of the 1971-72 season and had thus been relegated to the runners-up spot for the third consecutive year and the fifth time in eight seasons. The frustration of having failed to gain the single point necessary to become only the fifth ever double-winners is clear in* **bottom** *the faces of Billy Bremner and Terry Yorath and* **top** *in Les Cocker's need to restrain Allan Clarke from discussions with referee Bill Gow.* **Opposite** *Burnley's Colin Waldron scores at Maine Road.*

pionships, and seven of them won by Lancashire's two major cities.

Leeds' 1968-69 success was their first. Yorkshire neighbours Huddersfield, however, collected three in consecutive seasons during the twenties, under the guidance of the famous Herbert Chapman, later to build the Arsenal team that became the only club to emulate Huddersfield's feat.

Huddersfield's first Championship they won dramatically. For at the end of the 1923-24 season Cardiff City also had 57 points, and the two clubs' goal averages were remarkably similar. Huddersfield had scored 60 goals against 33, Cardiff 61 against 34. That in fact gave Huddersfield a microscopic advantage.

Cardiff—a penalty away from the title in 1924, re-election in 1934

And that was tragic for Cardiff. For in their last game of the season, the Welshmen had been awarded a penalty in the last minute at Birmingham. No one wanted to take it, but eventually Len Davies stepped up. He missed it, the game ended in a goalless draw and Huddersfield were champions.

If Huddersfield's climb to the top had been dramatic, Cardiff's rise—and their subsequent decline—was even more spectacular. Admitted to the Second Division in 1920, they won promotion

in their first season. Curiously, they were then only a 200th part of a goal behind Birmingham in first place.

Within seven years, Cardiff had been Championship runners-up, beaten FA Cup Finalists, and Cup winners in 1927. Within another seven, they were seeking re-election after finishing bottom of the Third Division South.

That same season, 1933-34, Huddersfield scored more goals than any of their First Division rivals. Perhaps that was some atonement for their poor tally that had deprived Cardiff of what would have been their first and only Championship success. For those 60 goals Huddersfield scored in 1923-24 comprised the lowest aggregate since the War.

The War seemed momentarily to have arrested the trend of fewer and fewer goals, and even the advent of the 'policeman' centre-half, the result of the offside law change in 1925 and exemplified by Arsenal's Herbie Roberts, could do little to stop the surge in goalscoring. In 1931, when the Championship was Arsenal's, they scored 127 goals, while Aston Villa, runners up that season, themselves scored a record 128.

After the Second World War, football boomed but goals like everything else were in short supply. That was until the great young Manchester United side of the mid-fifties. In 1957, just before the Munich disaster, they scored 103 goals, as did Wolves the next year. In 1959, Wolves surpassed

themselves with 110.

But with the Spurs team that won the double in 1960-61 came one of the last centuries before the massed defences took over. Though Tottenham scored a conspicuous 111 goals in 1962-63, Everton's 84 gave them six more points and thus the title. That Spurs total was to be the last three-figure total in the First Division for a long time.

The fall-off in goalscoring can be clearly seen at the other end of the table. While Spurs won the double, Newcastle went down with 86 goals to their credit. Compared with the miserable 27 Huddersfield scraped together when they were relegated just over a decade later, Newcastle might well curse their misfortune.

Relegated—with a better defensive record than the champions . . .

So too might Cardiff have done in the middle of that chequered spell which took them zooming up and down the League like a car on the big dipper. For back in 1928-29, Wednesday, the champions, conceded 62 goals, Cardiff let in a mere 59, the lowest in the division, and were sent down to Division Two. A little harsh, maybe, but Cardiff's fate bears witness to the fact that no matter how a team's statistics stand in isolation, that is not how the final placings are decided.

The history of the Football League mirrors that truth, but adds an important rider. That the money a club has or has not can change everything. Money comes from crowds, and crowds come from the promise of goals and success. The lesson is clear.

The League Cup – still unwanted & unloved?

'It's a joke. It can never get off the ground. Within three years it'll be scrapped.' That was the reaction of one First Division manager to the news that the move for a Football League Cup had been given official approval.

The millions who saw the passion, excitement and urgency generated by Stoke and West Ham in the four-match semi-final of 1972, or saw the expressions on the faces of the Stoke and Chelsea players as they climbed the Wembley steps a few weeks later, would find it difficult to believe that remark had been made only 12 years before.

'The League Cup has become one of the highlights of the domestic soccer calendar,' asserts Football League secretary Alan Hardaker, who initiated the idea. And the statistics back him up.

Yet for some time it appeared that the pessimists were the realists. The Cup, voted in at the annual meeting of the League in 1960 by a majority of only 15, was a very sickly infant, and the reception it received in some quarters was, to put it kindly, lukewarm. British managers, players and crowds were just beginning to adjust to the thought of European competition and here was another tournament, created to help the smaller sides and not particularly lucrative, to clog up the fixture list still further. It was not right to expect footballers to play 60 times a season.

Five clubs, including those who had finished second, third, fourth and fifth in the First Division the previous season, refused to enter, thus devaluing the competition before it had even started. The following year the number of absentees swelled to 10, including seven of the top ten.

The early, two-legged finals were hardly affairs to shake the football world and in 1962, when it was played out between a Second and a Fourth Division side, the two games pulled in barely 30,000 spectators. So, as the big clubs continued to view it with contempt and the smaller ones entered almost as a matter of form, as the press and the public looked on with detachment, the League Cup went stuttering on.

Hardaker remained the most ardent of its few committed supporters. He had always been obsessed with what was essentially his idea though, as he points out, he could not and did not implement it. 'It's been called Hardaker's baby and even Hardaker's folly,' he explains, 'but I did not take the decision to introduce it. Like everything else done by the League it was a matter for the clubs to vote on.'

Hardaker's early optimism was based on comparisons with the com-petition's much older sister, the FA Cup. 'Every worthwhile development in football has faced initial problems and criticism, and the League Cup was no exception. The early history of the FA Cup shows that it too had to face a variety of problems for several years, not least lack of interest. It was strongly criticised on its inception because it introduced a competitive element into amateur football, namely the winning of a trophy. There were 15 entries. After ten seasons there were 73.'

But the FA Cup was the first national competition. It was the natural result of the enthusiasm and aspirations of an emerging sport. The League Cup, by contrast, was anything but; money was its motivating force. It had to be created, and then it took several severe changes—with more commercial carrots being dangled—to drag it from a struggling child into a promising adolescent. They came in 1966.

The previous season the eight absent clubs had included seven from the top eight in the First Division—among them League Champions Manchester United, FA Cup holders Liverpool and, most indicative of all, Chelsea, the holders of the League Cup itself. Tommy Docherty apparently thought the Fairs Cup a good deal more important. Attendances, though slightly improved, remained mediocre.

A new League Cup —with Wembley and European entry

There were two major changes. First, the awkward home and away final was abolished in favour of a more romantic (and lucrative) Saturday climax at Wembley. Second, the Fairs Cup committee decided to accept the winners as entrants for its competition the following year—provided they were a First Division side. (Though an obvious incentive this move never actually promoted an entrant: in 1967 and 1969 the winners, Queen's Park Rangers and Swindon, were both Third Division sides, in 1968 Leeds—who were to win the Fairs Cup later that season—qualified by coming fourth in the League, and in 1970 Manchester City went on to win the Cup Winners Cup, thus defending that trophy the following year. Spurs, in 1971, were the first club able to take up the offer, and by then the actual Fairs Cup was no more.)

The changes completely revitalized a flagging League Cup. All but League Champions Liverpool and Cup winners Everton now entered, and the converts included four sides who had remained aloof from the

start—Arsenal, Sheffield Wednesday, Spurs and Wolves. Perhaps there was a certain justice in the fact that all four of them went out to sides of lesser standing in the League, and not one of them reached the last 16—that is, won more than one game.

In fact West Ham, who had seen something in the League Cup from the start, were responsible for the elimination of the two North London sides who had just joined the fold. They then beat Leeds (7-0) and Blackpool but were stopped short of Wembley by WBA—in a repeat of the previous year's two-legged final —after crashing 4-0 at The Hawthorns.

Albion's opponents were QPR, then running away with the Third

Top Ron Harris, David Webb, Alan Hudson, John Dempsey and Paddy Mulligan can only stand and watch as Terry Conroy heads Stoke in front in the 1972 League Cup final.

Above Jimmy Greenhoff and friends after Conroy's goal. It was Stoke's twelfth game of the competition and their very first success in a major competition—after a 109 year history.

Top right Arsenal's Bobby Gould (10) equalizes in 1969 against Swindon. But Don Rogers scored twice in extra-time and Third Division Swindon, like QPR in 1967, had beaten First Division opposition in the final.

Right Football League secretary Alan Hardaker, the most ardent advocate of the competition. But it took six years, a Wembley final and a place in Europe before it succeeded.

Division championship. Rangers had started as they meant to go on with a 5-0 win over Colchester, but they had only one game against a First Division club on the way, beating Leicester 4-2. The match at Wembley, in danger of being a one-sided anti-climax, proved to be the opposite. Lowly QPR, down two goals by an ex-player of their's, Clive Clark, were faced with an apparently impossible task against a club separated from them by about 30 places in the League. But they did do it, with goals from Roger Morgan, Rodney Marsh (a splendid effort that, with the help of television, made him a household name by the Monday morning) and Mark Lazarus.

Had the League Cup come of age? From some quarters came an honest conversion, from others came grudging acknowledgement. Cynics pointed out the fact that no Third Division club had reached the FA Cup Final in the 47 years that section had been in existence, let alone won it, and said that the big sides were still loath to take it at all seriously. But 98,000 at Wembley and millions more in their armchairs thought differently.

The moves had apparently done the trick. Though some clubs committed in Europe continued to opt out—notably Manchester United—the competition grew in stature over the next few years and the average attendance (all for midweek games except the final) soared from just over 11,000 in 1965-66 to over 19,000 in 1971-72.

In 1968 Leeds at last won a domestic honour, with a laboured 1-0 victory over a re-emerging Arsenal on a dreadful Wembley pitch. The following year Arsenal were back (this time on an even worse Wembley surface, thanks to the Horse of the Year Show) to face Swindon, who had played 11 matches to reach the final.

Swindon were trying to repeat Queen's Park Rangers' double of

League Cup and promotion to the Second Division, and they succeeded. Brilliant goalkeeping from Peter Downsborough and two goals from Don Rogers helped them to a 3-1 win, though the effects of a recent 'flu epidemic at Highbury took its toll of the Arsenal players during extra time. Nine of the Arsenal squad appeared in both 1968 and 1969, among them Frank McLintock, who thus finished on the losing side at Wembley for the fourth time.

Extra time was again required in 1970, this time for Manchester City's 2-1 win over West Bromwich Albion. The tie of the competition, however, was the semi-final between the Manchester giants. City—promoted in 1966, League Champions in 1968, FA Cup winners in 1969, and now on their way to a European triumph—had been severely challenging the supremacy of a Manchester United side desperately trying to maintain the status achieved by the European Cup win over Benfica at Wembley in 1968, and a side competing in the League Cup for the first time since 1960-61.

For the first time, perhaps, a League Cup match apart from the final took on a significance outside the competition. The edited versions of both games were televised, and millions saw City confirm their suspicions with a 2-1 win at Maine Road and a 2-2 draw at Old Trafford, the second leg being played in front of 63,418—a record for the League Cup away from Wembley. 'Perhaps now they'll bloody well believe us,' said City wing-half Mick Doyle after the tie. The final, a dull, grinding affair, was a disappointment.

For those who thought the age of the lower clubs was over in the League Cup the 1970-71 competition was something of a revelation. Aston Villa, like QPR and Swindon chasing escape from the Third Division, reached Wembley. They were fortunate in meeting only one

First Division side in their first five ties—a struggling Burnley in the second round—but when they did meet opponents of renown and calibre in Manchester United they proved nothing was missing. First they secured a 1-1 draw at Old Trafford and then, in front of 62,500, beat United 2-1 at Villa Park. But Wembley, Tottenham and Martin Chivers proved to be more difficult. Villa held Spurs for 80 minutes, but then two goals from the England man kept the League Cup firmly in the First Division.

There it was to stay in 1972, when Stoke beat Chelsea at Wembley in the final of what had been the first competition it had been compulsory for all 92 clubs to enter—a rather late and empty gesture at the 1971 annual general meeting. But, like the previous two seasons, it was the semi-final stage that stole the headlines.

The semi-final story dominated by penalty kicks

While Chelsea and Spurs were battling out their tie, West Ham were trying to make the final an all-London affair by beating Stoke. They got off to a good start with a 2-1 win at the Victoria Ground, but John Ritchie pulled a goal back at Upton Park in the return and, in the dying minutes of extra time Gordon Banks (who had been beaten by a Geoff Hurst penalty in the first leg) made a brilliant save to stop his England colleague repeating the feat. A fine replay at Hillsborough produced no goals, and then in the second replay at Old Trafford there was the strange sight of Bobby Moore donning the goalkeeper's jersey while the injured Ferguson was off the field.

Stoke beat him once, with Bernard following up a penalty kick Moore had managed to save first time; then, with Ferguson restored,

139

Above *West Brom's Jeff Astle after scoring against Manchester City in the 1970 final. His joy was short-lived: City won 2-1 in extra-time*
Top right *Tempers fray during the 1969 final, won by Leeds United (in white), lost by Arsenal.*
Bottom right *Leeds' Gary Sprake and goalscorer Terry Cooper with the Cup after their defeat of Arsenal.*

West Ham took the lead through Bonds and Brooking; Dobing pulled Stoke level before half-time and, as the two sides approached seven hours of battle, Conroy scored the winner.

The final didn't stand a chance. Three of the Stoke-West Ham clashes and both Chelsea-Spurs games had been covered by television and, though the pre-match publicity was as great as for any FA Cup Final, the match was almost inevitably a come-down. Stoke, by no means standing on ceremony or overawed by Wembley, absorbed all Chelsea's subtle pressure and took their chances well to win 2-1. After 12 matches in the tournament that year they deserved some reward.

The statistics for the 1971-72 competition reflected the status the League Cup had reached. For one thing the aggregate attendance leapt by over 300,000 to nearly 2,400,000, with the average rising by almost 2,000 a match. For the first time the four semi-finalists were all First Division sides. That is hardly a shattering fact in itself, but in the FA Cup over the same period (since 1961) that situation had

come about on six of the 12 occasions. Even allowing for the absence of some First Division sides in most years, it showed how much more influence the lower clubs enjoyed in the League Cup.

By the congested standards of the seventies it seemed ludicrous that one of the strongest objections to the League Cup in the early years was the fear of playing too much football —though rich clubs such as Spurs must have felt that a 92nd part of a 20% net pool just was not worth the effort.

When even Second Division Liverpool stayed out

It was ironic that the League Cup should gain in popularity just as the fixture list was becoming congested, with an increasing number of clubs entering Europe and the emergence of peripheral competitions: the Watney Cup, the Texaco Cup and the Anglo-Italian Tournament.

It may be that the League Cup provided the incentive; that officials and administrators saw the financial rewards to be reaped from competitive matches outside the two established folds. Certainly for a club stuck in the middle of the Third or Fourth Division and eliminated from the first round of the FA Cup in November, a run to the last eight or four can provide the only financial and psychological release during a mundane season.

No exercise can have started so

badly as the League Cup. As Walter Pilkington, one of its most ardent advocates, was to put it later: 'It arrived as an apparent weakling, unwanted and shunned by the rich relations, regarded as an unnecessary affliction, derided by critics who gave it little or no chance of survival.'

It had not even been really intended. The idea was gently mooted in the 'Pattern of Football', published in 1957 by the Football League, with the main proposal being five divisions of 20 clubs. That, pointed out the smaller 'big' clubs who could not afford to lose a single fixture—Preston, Bolton, and the rest—would mean losing four valuable matches. The League Cup then gained favour as a compensation but, somewhere along the line, while that idea was accepted, the restructuring of the League went by the board.

The early tournaments did little or nothing to undermine the conviction that it would die an early death. The first season, for instance, the figures were arranged by mutual agreement of the clubs concerned— an arrangement that proved so cumbersome that the competition dragged on, in front of meagre crowds, for 11 long months, with the final being resolved in the September of 1961. The lowest attendance was 1,737 for a first round tie between Lincoln City and Bradford Park Avenue—a dismal record that still stood in 1972. The 20% pool produced £29,982, or £354 for each competing club.

There were, however, more

memorable events: such as Bradford City's 2-1 defeat of Manchester United, Chelsea's 18 goals in three games (including seven against both Millwall and Doncaster), and Gerry Hitchens' 11 goals for Villa before he joined Inter-Milan.

The second season, with the number of absentees doubling—Bill Shankly even kept his Second Division Liverpool out, and they won the title—the result was almost total apathy. The final was an irrelevant affair between Second Division Norwich and Fourth Division Rochdale. This was the only season when all the competing First Division clubs (bar Leicester, who won a bye) competed from the first round.

The fixture pile-up —is it the League Cup's fault?

In the third season the First Division, though still represented by only twelve clubs, at last asserted its authority, Birmingham City beating Villa in the final. The top section retained their monopoly on finalists until 1967, despite the fact that their maximum presence in any year was only 14. Ironically in 1966-67, when all but Liverpool and Everton entered, the League Cup went to a Third Division side.

The competitions up till then were unlikely to have provided standard items for the serious reminiscences of football journalists. Goalscoring, perhaps, was the one thing that caught the eye: Tony

Hateley's 10 in six games for Villa in 1964-65; West Ham's 25 in eight games on the way to the 1966 final, including two fives against Cardiff in the semi-final and 11 of them to Hurst; WBA's 28 in nine games the same season, with 11 to Tony Brown; Orient's 9-2 win over Chester in 1962-63; Workington's 9-1 victory over neighbours Barrow in 1964-65; and Leicester's 8-1 triumph against Coventry the same year.

The rise in popularity of the League Cup after 1966 cannot be put down solely to the introduction of a Wembley final and a promise of a place in Europe. For one thing there was a general stimulation of interest in the game after the World Cup; television coverage was becoming more and more frequent and the League Cup, with its important rounds being played between October and March, plugged the mid-week gaps left by a lack of FA Cup replays and European games; and the League Cup proved it produced goals, averaging 3.49 a game up to 1967 and keeping above three for the rest of the decade—well over the figures for the League and the FA Cup. As it rose in popularity the little clubs benefited: the share-out from the 20% pool was £327 for every participating club in 1963-64, but by 1972 it was over £2,000.

The League Cup was bound to cause controversy. It upset a domestic balance that had been carefully evolved and constructed over 72 years. But the eventual success paved the way for other tournaments— though none of them had its logic of

a cup for the League clubs.

The first was the Watney Cup, the first sponsored competition in the British game. Introduced in 1970 and played out in the ten days before the start of the League programme, it received a warm welcome—if only because the invited clubs were the two highest-scoring sides from each division the previous season. Derby won the first, Colchester the second, beating WBA at The Hawthorns in the final.

Though only 19,000 saw that game and the average attendance was 12,000 the competing clubs did well financially: Third Division Halifax, who beat Manchester United before losing to Albion, pulled £7,700 and substantial television fees for their two games, including £4,000 from the sponsors. While they didn't exactly get drunk for weeks, it was a more than fair return after 25% of the net receipts had gone to the county associations of the competing clubs and 10% to the FA fund for the development of youth football.

Following a few weeks behind beer came petrol—in the form of the Texaco Cup. A much bigger and bolder concept—involving the six English First Division sides, six Scottish First Division sides, and two top sides from both Northern Ireland and Eire—its most common criticism was that it was the sides not quite qualifying for Europe, the also-rans, who were the 'attractions'. There was no logic in having second-best clubs playing out a British club championship.

Yet the first competition, taking most of the season to complete, was a reasonable success. Over 333,000 people watched the games—28,000 saw Wolves beat Hearts in the second leg of the final at Molineux—and the average of 3.33 goals per game was high. 'Viewpoint', in the Football League Review, was among the columns defending Texaco: 'The inference that the competition is a "second-rate" tournament for "second-rate" clubs is totally misleading and inaccurate. Wolverhampton Wanderers, first winners of the Texaco Cup, found the grounding they received last season has stood them in good stead for their entry into Europe through the EUFA Cup this season.

Will the FA Cup ever be challenged by its imitator?

'Let us not forget that the Texaco Cup has provided a new arena for clubs, players and spectators. It has proved itself to be an integral part of the football calendar, an important source of revenue for clubs, a change from domestic routine for players and spectators, and an opportunity to watch teams and players they would not normally come across during the course of the season.'

Nevertheless it could not be said that the Watney Cup, the Texaco Cup or the ill-tempered and meaningless Anglo-Italian Tournament, which sprouted at the end of the

Main picture *Ian Bowyer scores for City in the second leg of the 1970 all-Manchester semi-final.*
Inset left *The days when the final was not held at Wembley: Bobby Tambling puts Chelsea in front in 1965.*
Inset right *The Stoke-West Ham semi-final in 1972 had everything, including Mick Bernard's goal after Bobby Moore had saved his penalty.*

1969-70 season, carried anything like the attraction of even the League Cup.

The criticisms still levelled at the League Cup, however, were on the theme of fixture congestion and its two main problems: that of clashing dates and that of 'too much football'. Alf Ramsey had often had players arriving late, or not at all, for preparation for an Under-23 international—a situation already there because the best players were too often involved in European club competitions.

But those who continued to suggest a return to the duopoly of League and Cup were deluding themselves. The League Cup had arrived. What was clearly also true was that it was nowhere near to actually challenging the supremacy of the FA Cup itself. That competition's entrenched tradition and giant-killing romanticism put it on a plane of its own— on a match for match basis far beyond the League Championship itself. The League Cup remained a clearly second string attraction. A quick look at the clubs appearing in the finals confirms precisely this argument.

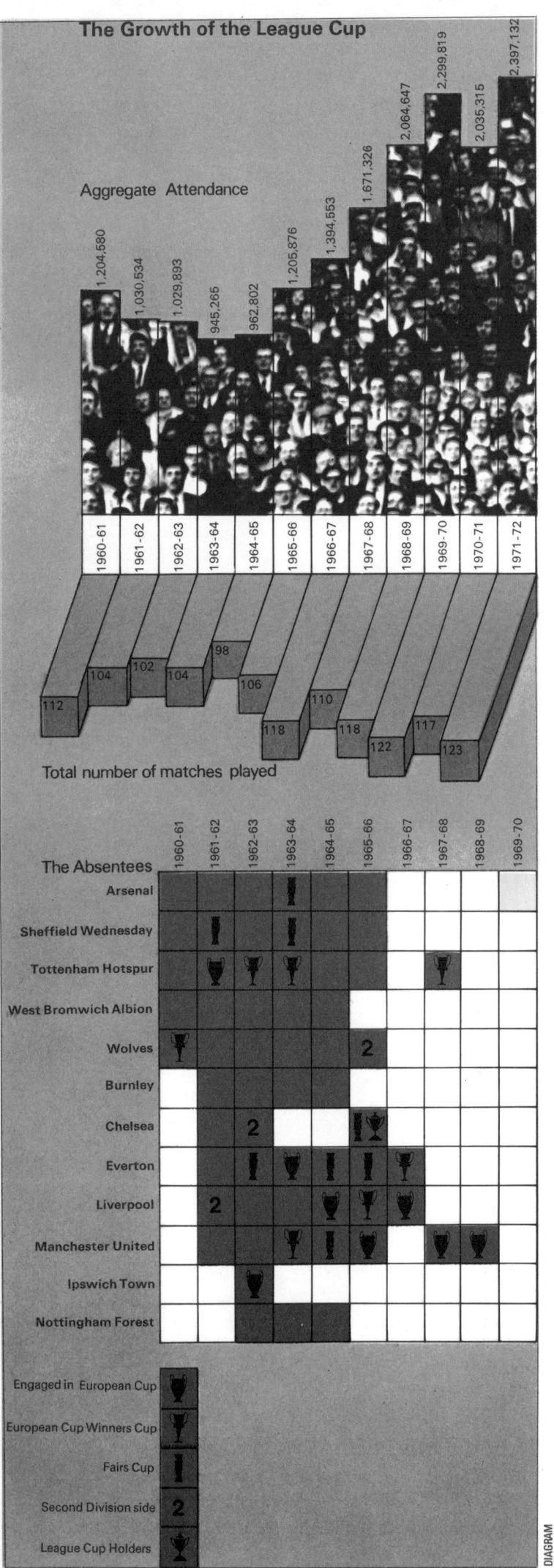

FOOTBALL LEAGUE CUP FINALS

1960-61	ASTON VILLA			
First leg:	*Rotherham 22 August 1961* Attendance 12,226			
	†Rotherham United	2	Aston Villa	0
	Webster, Kirkman			
Second leg:	*Villa Park 5 September 1961* Attendance 27,000			
	Aston Villa	3	†Rotherham United	0
	O'Neill, Burrows, McParland			

1961-62	†NORWICH CITY			
First leg:	*Rochdale 26 April 1962* Attendance 11,123			
	§Rochdale	0	†Norwich City	3
			Lythgoe 2, Punton	
Second leg:	*Norwich 1 May 1962* Attendance 19,708			
	†Norwich City	1	§Rochdale	0
	Hill			

1962-63	BIRMINGHAM CITY			
First leg:	*St Andrew's 23 May 1963* Attendance 31,850			
	Birmingham City	3	Aston Villa	1
	Leek 2, Bloomfield		Thomson	
Second leg:	*Villa Park 27 May 1963* Attendance 37,921			
	Aston Villa	0	Birmingham City	0

1963-64	LEICESTER CITY			
First leg:	*Stoke 15 April 1964* Attendance 22,309			
	Stoke City	1	Leicester City	1
	Bebbington		Gibson	
Second leg:	*Leicester 22 April 1964* Attendance 25,372			
	Leicester City	3	Stoke City	2
	Stringfellow, Gibson, Riley		Viollet, Kinnell	

1964-65	CHELSEA			
First leg:	*Stamford Bridge 15 March 1965* Attendance 20,690			
	Chelsea	3	Leicester City	2
	Tambling, Venables (pen),		Appleton, Goodfellow	
	McCreadie			
Second leg:	*Leicester 5 April 1965* Attendance 26,957			
	Leicester City	0	Chelsea	0

1965-66	WEST BROMWICH ALBION			
First leg:	*Upton Park 9 March 1966* Attendance 28,341			
	West Ham United	2	West Bromwich Albion	1
	Moore, Byrne		Astle	
Second leg:	*The Hawthorns 23 March 1966* Attendance 31,925			
	West Bromwich Albion	4	West Ham United	1
	Kaye, Brown, Clark, Williams		Peters	

1966-67	‡QUEEN'S PARK RANGERS			
Final:	*Wembley 4 March 1967* Attendance 97,952			
	‡Queen's Park Rangers	3	West Bromwich Albion	2
	Morgan (R), Marsh, Lazarus		Clark 2	

1967-68	LEEDS UNITED			
Final:	*Wembley 2 March 1968* Attendance 97,887			
	Leeds United	1	Arsenal	0
	Cooper			

1968-69	‡SWINDON TOWN			
Final:	*Wembley 15 March 1969* Attendance 98,189			
	‡Swindon Town	3	Arsenal	1
	Smart, Rogers 2		Gould	

1969-70	MANCHESTER CITY			
Final:	*Wembley 7 March 1970* Attendance 97,963			
	Manchester City	2	West Bromwich Albion	1
	Doyle, Pardoe		Astle	

1970-71	TOTTENHAM HOTSPUR			
Final:	*Wembley 27 February 1971* Attendance 98,096			
	Tottenham Hotspur	2	‡Aston Villa	0
	Chivers 2			

1971-72	STOKE CITY			
Final:	*Wembley 4 March 1972* Attendance 99,998			
	Stoke City	2	Chelsea	1
	Conroy, Eastham		Osgood	

1972-73	TOTTENHAM HOTSPUR			
Final:	*Wembley 3 March 1973* Attendance 100,000			
	Tottenham Hotspur	1	Norwich City	0
	Coates			

*After extra time †Second Division club
‡Third Division club §Fourth Division club

In 1970 Manchester City and West Bromwich, the finalists, were 10th and 16th in the First Division respectively. In 1971 Spurs did come third but their final opponents, Aston Villa, were a Third Division club. In 1972 Stoke were 17th and Chelsea 7th, and in 1973, while Spurs were 8th, opponents Norwich just escaped relegation in 20th place. In none of these seasons did either of the finalists win another domestic competition.

Norwich, in fact, reached the 1973 final (their first Wembley appearance) despite not having won any of their previous 12 League matches. After the final it was to be another 8 before they recorded a success. Just ten days earlier they had sold their star forward, Jimmy Bone, and the Wembley occasion could almost have killed the League Cup on its own, so dreadful a spectacle was it. Spurs, whose appearance in the final two years earlier had also been strongly criticised, played a thoroughly cautious game and won only with a goal from midfield substitute Ralph Coates. If the League Cup was to inspire support at all, it could scarcely afford finals like that.

Left *The growth of the Football League Cup: since 1960 total attendances have grown from just over one million to nearly two and a half million. The variation in the number of games played each season is caused by different methods of organising the draw, replays and the number of absentees. Those clubs which did not compete are shown in the lower part of the diagram. The first season in which every League club took part was 1969-70.*

RAY GREEN

Fourth to First: the difference?

THE MAJOR COMPETITIONS

'When I moved from Albion to Villa it naturally seemed like a step down. But I'd been playing in front of 20,000 in West Bromwich and suddenly there I was performing before twice that number. At Albion we often used to look at Villa and envy them their gates and atmosphere. There was no doubt about it, they were the big club round here. When I played my first game for them the difference was tremendous. The main problem was trying to find a shot to save!'
Jimmy Cumbes (West Bromwich Albion to Aston Villa).

'Moving to the Second at least gave me something to dream about. I want to be back in the First Division scoring at Maine Road. Then I can do a lap of honour giving a double two-finger salute to the crowd who made me feel so unwelcome when I was in City's colours.'
Ian Bowyer (Manchester City to Orient)

'The average side in the Third Division is made up of hard-working and hard-running players and, although there is a bit more skill in the Second Division, the top half-dozen clubs in the Third would do well enough. I don't believe there is that big a gap between the two. Here at Bolton they are all triers. If anything they tend to forsake skill for effort. But there are a lot of good players in our side and in the Third Division generally.'
Charlie Wright (Charlton Athletic to Bolton Wanderers)

'It's a heck of a sight quicker in the First.'
Rodney Marsh (Queen's Park Rangers to Manchester City)

'There were times when the glamour of the First Division attracted me, but now I'm more or less settled.'
Don Rogers (Swindon Town)

'When we were in the Third I preferred playing away from home. Third Division teams get used to playing in front of small crowds so when they came to Villa Park it was like a Cup Final to them. The atmosphere helped them raise their game and this made it all the more difficult for us.'
Ray Graydon (Aston Villa)

'There's a big gap between the Third and Fourth. They're both very hard, very physical, but there's much more skill the higher you go. You don't get a chance to play football in the lower Divisions but you do in the First and Second. The top players are that much quicker on their toes —looking all the time for these quick one-twos. You don't get many wall-passes in the Third Division, but you get them all the time in the First so when you go in for a tackle you've got to watch that they don't get it away first.'
Norman Gall (Brighton)

'We are not frightened of Division One but I realize that I'd probably have to add a few to the squad. We do have a good side now and I feel that we can give a very good account of ourselves in the First Division. Not so very long ago West Ham were a Second Division club, but they went up and established themselves with the same type of public, crowds and atmosphere.'
Benny Fenton (manager of Millwall)

'My big mistake when I first came here was still thinking in terms of the First Division. I couldn't adapt to the differing problems of the Third. We had no money to rebuild with, and the players just didn't seem good enough. But in the end it *was* thinking in terms of being a First Division outfit that did the trick. If you don't think big you'll never win anything.'
Pat Saward (manager of Brighton)

'When you look at the ground, the facilities, the history and the potential of the area, Third Division football at Bolton is ridiculous. If they could only have just a little success I'm sure they'd win back the support they've lost to the Manchester clubs.'
Roger Hunt (after retiring)

'Of course I feel the difference between the First and Fourth. But here at Liverpool it was made easier for me because they are all good players. Still, if you believe you're good and people keep telling you you're good it doesn't come as any surprise when you do make it.'
Kevin Keegan (Scunthorpe to Liverpool)

'There's nothing difficult in explaining what most clubs are doing miles away from the First Division. It's much more complicated trying to explain how clubs like Aston Villa ever managed to get *out* of it.'
First Division manager

'The Third is the most competitive in the League. You've got three out at the top and four out at the bottom. That means that one team in three will be playing somewhere else the following season. The pressures are much greater than in any of the other divisions.'
Gordon Lee (manager of Port Vale)

'When we had Stan Bowles he used to be kicked off the park match after match. It's the only way Fourth Division defenders could deal with him. I was often worried for the player's safety so frightening were some games. Stan wasn't used to it —he had a terrible time keeping

Above A painful readjustment for Rodney Marsh as he receives treatment on his debut for Manchester City against Chelsea in March 1972 after transferring from Second Division Queen's Park Rangers. For Marsh one clear difference between the two Divisions was the pace of the game.

Promoted from the Second Division

Season	First	Second
1892-93[1]	Small Heath	Sheffield United
1893-94[2]	Liverpool	Small Heath
1894-95[3]	Bury	Notts County
1895-96[4]	Liverpool	Manchester City
1896-97[5]	Notts County	Newton Heath
1897-98[6]	Burnley	Newcastle United
1898-99[7]	Manchester City	Glossop North End
1899-1900	The Wednesday	Bolton Wanderers
1900-01	Grimsby	Small Heath
1901-02	West Bromwich	Middlesbrough
1902-03	Manchester City	Small Heath
1903-04	Preston North End	Woolwich Arsenal
1904-05	Liverpool	Bolton Wanderers
1905-06	Bristol City	Manchester United
1906-07	Nottingham Forest	Chelsea
1907-08	Bradford City	Leicester Fosse
1908-09	Bolton Wanderers	Tottenham Hotspur
1909-10	Manchester City	Oldham Athletic
1910-11	West Bromwich	Bolton Wanderers
1911-12	Derby County	Chelsea
1912-13	Preston North End	Burnley
1913-14	Notts County	Bradford PA
1914-15	Derby County	Preston North End
1919-20	Tottenham Hotspur	Huddersfield Town
1920-21	Birmingham	Cardiff City
1921-22	Nottingham Forest	Stoke City
1922-23	Notts County	West Ham United
1923-24	Leeds United	Bury
1924-25	Leicester City	Manchester United
1925-26	The Wednesday	Derby County
1926-27	Middlesbrough	Portsmouth
1927-28	Manchester City	Leeds United
1928-29	Middlesbrough	Grimsby
1929-30	Blackpool	Chelsea
1930-31	Everton	West Bromwich
1931-32	Wolverhampton	Leeds United
1932-33	Stoke City	Tottenham Hotspur
1933-34	Grimsby Town	Preston North End
1934-35	Brentford	Bolton Wanderers
1935-36	Manchester United	Charlton Athletic
1936-37	Leicester City	Blackpool
1937-38	Aston Villa	Manchester United
1938-39	Blackburn Rovers	Sheffield United
1946-47	Manchester City	Burnley
1947-48	Birmingham City	Newcastle United
1948-49	Fulham	West Bromwich
1949-50	Tottenham Hotspur	Sheffield Wednesday
1950-51	Preston North End	Manchester City
1951-52	Sheffield Wednesday	Cardiff City
1952-53	Sheffield United	Huddersfield Town
1953-54	Leicester City	Everton
1954-55	Birmingham City	Luton Town
1955-56	Sheffield Wednesday	Leeds United
1956-57	Leicester City	Nottingham Forest
1957-58	West Ham United	Blackburn Rovers
1958-59	Sheffield Wednesday	Fulham
1959-60	Aston Villa	Cardiff City
1960-61	Ipswich Town	Sheffield United
1961-62	Liverpool	Leyton Orient
1962-63	Stoke City	Chelsea
1963-64	Leeds United	Sunderland
1964-65	Newcastle United	Northampton Town
1965-66	Manchester City	Southampton
1966-67	Coventry City	Wolverhampton
1967-68	Ipswich Town	Queen's Park Rangers
1968-69	Derby County	Crystal Palace
1969-70	Huddersfield Town	Blackpool
1970-71	Leicester City	Sheffield United
1971-72	Norwich City	Birmingham City
1972-73	Burnley	Queen's Park Rangers

[1]Promotion by a series of test matches between the top clubs in the Second Division and the bottom clubs in the First. Small Heath and Darwen (who finished third) promoted.
[2]After test matches Liverpool and Small Heath promoted.
[3]After test matches Bury promoted.
[4]After test matches Liverpool promoted.
[5]After test matches Notts County promoted.
[6]After test matches Burnley promoted.
[7]Automatic promotion of first two clubs introduced in 1899.

Promoted from the Third Division

Season	Third Division	
†1920-21	Crystal Palace	

Season	Third South	Third North
1921-22	Southampton	Stockport County
1922-23	Bristol City	Nelson
1923-24	Portsmouth	Wolverhampton
1924-25	Swansea Town	Darlington
1925-26	Reading	Grimsby
1926-27	Bristol City	Stoke City
1927-28	Millwall	Bradford PA
1928-29	Charlton Athletic	Bradford City
1929-30	Plymouth Argyle	Port Vale
1930-31	Notts County	Chesterfield
1931-32	Fulham	Lincoln City
1932-33	Brentford	Hull City
1933-34	Norwich City	Barnsley
1934-35	Charlton Athletic	Doncaster Rovers
1935-36	Coventry City	Chesterfield
1936-37	Luton Town	Stockport County
1937-38	Millwall	Tranmere Rovers
1938-39	Newport County	Barnsley
1946-47	Cardiff City	Doncaster Rovers
1947-48	Queen's Park Rangers	Lincoln City
1948-49	Swansea Town	Hull City
1949-50	Notts County	Doncaster Rovers
1950-51	Nottingham Forest	Rotherham United
1951-52	Plymouth Argyle	Lincoln City
1952-53	Bristol Rovers	Oldham Athletic
1953-54	Ipswich Town	Port Vale
1954-55	Bristol City	Barnsley
1955-56	Leyton Orient	Grimsby
1956-57	Ipswich Town	Derby County
1957-58	Brighton	Scunthorpe United

Season	Third Division First	Second
1958-59	Plymouth Argyle	Hull City
1959-60	Southampton	Norwich City
1960-61	Bury	Walsall
1961-62	Portsmouth	Grimsby Town
1962-63	Northampton Town	Swindon Town
1963-64	Coventry City	Crystal Palace
1964-65	Carlisle	Bristol City
1965-66	Hull City	Millwall
1966-67	Queen's Park Rangers	Middlesbrough
1967-68	Oxford United	Bury
1968-69	Watford	Swindon Town
1969-70	Orient	Luton Town
1970-71	Preston North End	Fulham
1971-72	Aston Villa	Brighton
1972-73	Bolton Wanderers	Notts County

†Only one club promoted

Promoted from the Fourth Division

Season	First	Second	Third	Fourth
1958-59	Port Vale	Coventry City	York City	Shrewsbury
1959-60	Walsall	Notts County	Torquay	Watford
1960-61	Peterborough	Crystal Palace	Northampton	Bradford PA
1961-62	Millwall	Colchester	Wrexham	Carlisle
1962-63	Brentford	Oldham	Crewe Alexandra	Mansfield Town
1963-64	Gillingham	Carlisle	Workington	Exeter City
1964-65	Brighton	Millwall	York City	Oxford United
1965-66	Doncaster	Darlington	Torquay	Colchester
1966-67	Stockport	Southport	Barrow	Tranmere
1967-68	Luton Town	Barnsley	Hartlepools	Crewe Alexandra
1968-69	Doncaster	Halifax	Rochdale	Bradford City
1969-70	Chesterfield	Wrexham	Swansea City	Port Vale
1970-71	Notts County	Bournemouth	Oldham	York City
1971-72	Grimsby	Southend	Brentford	Scunthorpe
1972-73	Southport	Hereford	Cambridge	Aldershot

Opposite page Colchester United's Eric Burgess keeps a close watch on West Bromwich Albion's Jeff Astle during the 1971 Watney Cup final which the Fourth Division side won on penalties after a 4-4 draw. Colchester lived up to skipper Bobby Cram's boast that a lot of good football is played in the Fourth.
Below Albion's goalkeeper in that match was Jim Cumbes. Later that year he moved down to the Third Division when he joined Aston Villa, but from playing in front of 20,000 people at The Hawthorns, he found that these gates were doubled at Villa Park. His only problem—'trying to find a shot to save'.

TERRY WEIR

COLORSPORT

his temper but you have to accept it coming from the First to the Fourth.'
Ernie Tagg (general manager at Crewe)

'I hadn't played First Division football for six years and on television some of the leading defenders had appeared unbeatable but I quickly discovered that, good though many of them are, they are only human. And playing for a team of top class professionals makes the game that much easier. If you are in the right place in the First Division the ball will come to you—right to your feet.'
Freddie Hill (Halifax Town to Manchester City)

'It's all a matter of time. In the middle of the field First Division players can take it slower, but in the penalty area they've got to act immediately. There's no second chance because the defenders are that much quicker and the marking is that much tighter.'
Joe Mercer

'I don't want to play in the Second Division.'
Peter Cormack (Nottingham Forest)

'We had a long struggle to get out of the Second. That must be the most competitive division of all. Clubs always seem to go up with about 56 points—there are so many who are potentially good enough that they all keep beating each other. In 1971 for instance Bolton took three points off us but we went up and they went down. Once you're up there it's not as difficult as it sometimes appears. Most clubs go back because they're not ambitious.'
Tony Currie (Sheffield United)

'I've got this theory which, unfortunately, can't be tested. If you put all the First Division managers in charge of Fourth Division clubs and all the Fourth Division managers in charge of First Division clubs, what do you think would happen. I'll tell you; nothing! They would all stay exactly where they were.'
Alec Stock (when manager of Luton)

'The pace is much faster in the Second Division than the Third, although I didn't think there was too much difference between the two when Rotherham were relegated from the Second. It was much harder

going back, but it's not so physical now.'
David Watson (Rotherham United to Sunderland)

'Well the crowds are bigger for a start.'
Roy McFarland (Tranmere Rovers to Derby County)

'I'm just glad to be playing in the First Division.'
Bobby Kellard (Crystal Palace)

'It's hard to score goals anywhere . . . even in practice matches. There are no easy goals anywhere, the Fourth, Third, Second or First Divisions. And it always will be.'
Tony Hateley

'You have to think and act more quickly. Players are on you all the time. Another big difference is concentration. I reckon that in defence, concentration is every bit as important as skill. When the pressure's on, you've got to stay cool and not get flustered.'
Micky Droy (Chelsea)

'The marking was much tighter in the Second Division and defenders give more stick.'
Tony Currie (Sheffield United)

'Anything other than First Division football is second best.'
Ken Knighton (Blackburn Rovers)

'Three goals in the First Division equal twelve in the Fourth.'
John O'Rourke (Coventry City to Queen's Park Rangers)

'The game is much more physical in the Fourth Division, and you have to get rid of the ball fast because defenders come at you very quickly.'
Albert Johanneson (Leeds United to York City)

'The difference between the First and the Second is speed. The game is so much quicker in the First and you do not have time to think about what you're going to do with the ball. You have to make the time of course, but there is always someone on you.'
Keith Weller (Millwall to Chelsea)

'Full-backs in the First Division give you more time to play football. Their tackling is not so crude, and yet more decisive. At Reading I was given a lot of punishment by tough full-backs who tackled first and thought second.'
Tom Jenkins (Reading to Southampton)

'The Third is a very physical League, compared with the Second. But that doesn't mean to say that there is a lack of skill. Several of the clubs we have met produce some really impressive displays.'
Gerry Ingram (Preston North End)

'All this talk about the Third Division being harder than the Second is nonsense. I don't find it any different at all.'
Dick Edwards (Torquay United)

'The transfer business is like a cattle market'

'In my opinion there is little between the First and Second Division in terms of skill and style. It may look this way when teams are promoted, but given time the promoted sides usually prove their worth as First Division outfits.'
Ian MacFarlane (when manager of Carlisle United)

'I'm perfectly happy at Bournemouth and that's the main thing. I weighed up everything, including personal ambition, and decided I didn't really want to leave, either the place or the club. I know people will say I lack the self-confidence to accept the challenge of First Division football, but that doesn't matter.

'I get the impression that the whole transfer business is much too like a cattle market and some managers have been seeking the super-star who doesn't exist. Cash doesn't come into it. I'm settling for peace of mind.'
Ted Macdougall (Bournemouth)

'I've played in the top three Divisions of the League and there's no doubt about it. Goals are much harder to come by in the Third. Sometimes I seem to have four men marking me and the game is much more physical. In the top flight it was one against one. Here in the Third the tackling is sharper and harder—not so well-timed, but definitely harder.'
Andy Lochhead (Aston Villa)

'There's a lot of kick-and-rush in the Second'

'You're allowed to play football in Division One. And it is nowhere near as physical, despite the impression you might get from the terraces. I'm not trying to condemn Second Division football, but there's a great deal of kick-and-rush stuff going on. When it comes to real constructiveness, there's nothing like playing against top sides.'
Trevor Cherry (when with Huddersfield Town)

'Fourth Division players are as skilled as those in the First. The difference is that they are not so consistent. A midfield player in the Fourth might play like Alan Ball for five or ten minutes in maybe one match out of six.'
Dave Bowen (Wales team manager)

'I think it's going to be harder for older players to stay in the Fourth Division. Players are leaving First Division clubs much earlier these days. Whereas a few years ago a player could drop down to the Second and expect to play a few years there before moving on to the Third or Fourth, today many of them are dropping down to the Fourth only a season or two after leaving the First.

'This has helped to raise the standard of play in the Fourth. It's not all clog down there. Some good football is played.'
Bobby Cram (Colchester United)

'If a goalkeeper is good enough, he often finds it easier to play in the First Division than in the lower grade. For top-class forwards shoot with greater accuracy, and a keeper has more chance of anticipating where a ball is going.

'But in a lower standard of football, a forward often mis-hits or slices a shot and a goalkeeper can move the "right" way only to find the ball has gone the "wrong" way into the net.'
Bill Shankly (Liverpool manager talking about signing Frank Lane from Tranmere Rovers)

Soccer's ghost towns

Accrington, Gateshead and New Brighton are still thriving northern towns. The wind does not whistle through empty stores, the eerie slamming of doors cannot be heard in the early hours, and casual visitors do not flee from inexplicable whisperings—but in one vital sense they are ghost towns.

For they are haunted by the phantoms of once thriving League football clubs; the banshees of tens of thousands of supporters still wail on the now overgrown terraces, the hopes and fears of long-gone managers still pervade the atmosphere of derelict grandstands. They are towns deprived of more than a football club—they are towns bereft of their fantasies, their hopes of a mass exodus to the shrine of Wembley, even their pub conversations.

By and large clubs leave the League for one of three reasons. The least common is their own resignation, usually forced by financial circumstances such as those that drove Accrington Stanley out in 1962. The second is a straightforward refusal to re-elect after a club has struggled over a protracted period. Bradford Park Avenue's disappearance in 1970—after four consecutive applications—certainly falls into this class.

The most unfortunate—and potentially unfair—cause is simply the need to admit an outstanding outsider. The classic case here is Peterborough's admission in 1960, at the cost of an unlucky Gateshead.

The reasons behind a club losing its League place

In fact it is not the teams that play in the Third and Fourth Divisions that vote their fellows out of the League. Each of the First and Second Division clubs are allowed to cast one vote for each of four applicants. The 48 Third and Fourth Division clubs, however, have only four voting representatives, each of which has the same four votes as, say, Arsenal or Everton. In fact the leading clubs do tend to canvass the opinions of their lesser brothers before voting and, in that sense at least, a representative opinion usually emerges.

It is not always clear precisely what influences the voters. Geographical location, for one, must be important. A club should obviously have a reasonably fertile catchment area and be quite accessible—which is why Workington's election was such a surprise. It should also be able to show evidence of potential crowd support

—as Peterborough, Cambridge and Oxford were all able to do—but not at the expense of other League clubs, which is why Wigan Athletic are not as popular as they might expect.

No-one would pretend that the acquisition of first class status by a non-League club is easy, but then it was never intended to be. Twice in a matter of just over 30 years two clubs, Wigan Borough and Accrington Stanley, folded in mid-season, and this figure would have been higher if the Football League had thrown open its doors to all the clubs who have applied to join it. There was, for example, a ludicrous case in 1928, when a bunch of amateur enthusiasts formed a club they called The Argonauts and asked for a place in the Third Division South. The fact they had never played a single match deterred them not; it had, after all, not dissuaded Chelsea in 1905, when they gained admission to the Second Division without ever having played a competitive game of football.

Clubs in associate membership (ie Third and Fourth Division clubs) of the League who have had a bad season or even a bad spell of seasons, are entitled to some protection for their manifold undertakings as a first class outfit.

One of the ideals of the Football League has always been to grant their status to all the major areas of population the length and breadth of the land and their competition embraces places as far apart as Carlisle and Plymouth. They have been elastic in their interpretation of the term 'major areas of population', as the presence among the 92 competing clubs of places like Workington, Wrexham and Shrewsbury proves. But once they have admitted a club the League is generally loath to write it off. Not only is that place and surrounding area deprived of League football, but players and staff lose employment, guarantees to banks and club property are placed in jeopardy, and old friends are betrayed.

The League, however, is not prepared to condone prolonged failure as they showed in the summer of 1970 when they dismissed, in favour of Cambridge United of the Southern League, a club who had played in all four divisions and held First Division status for seven years —Bradford Park Avenue. Bradford had finished bottom by wide margins for three successive seasons and were making their fourth application in a row for another chance.

In the 80 year period from 1892, when the League added a Second Division, up to 1972, a total of 23 clubs lost League status never to regain it. And a dozen of those fell

between 1923 and 1970—a short span of time in the eyes of any historian.

These figures do not give a true indication of the risk of losing status spread over the 80 years, since they disguise the fact that many existing League clubs have lost their place and been voted back, some of them more than once. The League's main period of expansion was between 1892 and 1922, and in those 30 years a situation not far short of 'musical chairs' existed.

After the founding of the Football League in 1888 there were only four of the next 30 seasons in which the competition did not show change in some form or other, from the inclusion of one new club to the addition of whole divisions, as in 1892, 1920 and 1921.

Lincoln City had an extraordinarily chequered early career. Elected to the Second Division in 1892, they were kicked out in 1908 to make room for Tottenham Hotspur. A year later they got back

Opposite page Cathkin Park, ex-home of Third Lanark, one of the Scottish FA's original eight members. When they finally went into liquidation in 1967, Thirds left Queen's Park as the sole survivor of the eight.
Below Discovered at the deserted Peel Park was the shield presented to Accrington after 60 years football.
Bottom Ian Gibson (right) who was transferred to Bradford Park Avenue shortly before Stanley went out of business, just missing being 'acquired' by the Football League.

APPLICATIONS FOR RE-ELECTION

(to Third and Fourth Divisions only. Clubs that have applied more than twice 1920-1973.)

The League's official re-election records only take into account the seasons after 1920. It was not until that date that the present procedure of election was adopted.

Barrow	11
Hartlepool	10
Newport County	9
Southport	8
Exeter City	7
Halifax Town	7
Walsall	7
Chester	6
Rochdale	6
Accrington Stanley	5
Bradford Park Avenue	5
Crewe Alexandra	5
Darlington	5
Gillingham	5
Lincoln City	5
New Brighton	5
Norwich City	4
York City	4
Aldershot	3
Bradford City	3
Colchester	3
Crystal Palace	3
Merthyr Town	3
Swindon Town	3
Workington	3

RAY GREEN

COLORSPORT

at the expense of Chesterfield. After another two seasons they finished bottom and out they went again in favour of near neighbours Grimsby Town. They bobbed up smiling again just 12 months later and took the place of Gainsborough Trinity. In 1920 they were booted out yet again, this time for Cardiff City, but were founder members of the Third Division North in 1921. Since then they have remained a League club for over 50 years, but they regained and lost Second Division status three times and also suffered relegation to the Fourth Division, in which they made five successful bids for re-election! A fine ground with a good playing surface, handy to the city centre and with good potential support when they are successful have helped them keep their status in modern times.

The fourteen clubs who came back with another chance

Other current League clubs who were given another chance after losing their status include Gillingham, Newport County, Blackpool, Walsall, Crewe Alexandra, Port Vale, Rotherham United, Luton Town, Doncaster Rovers, Stockport County, Stoke City, Chesterfield and Grimsby Town—a surprising baker's dozen.

The economic slump of the mid-twenties and early thirties had a disastrous effect on League football in South Wales. The first club to fall was Aberdare Athletic, who came into the Third South in its second season. In 1927 they fell from ninth to bottom and for the first time in the history of the League there was a tie at the ballot. Aberdare received 21 votes but so did Southern League club Torquay United, and when a second vote was taken the Devon side got in by a majority of seven. Aberdare carried on for a time in the Welsh League, but the club soon passed out of existence.

Three years later Merthyr Town joined Aberdare after a disastrous season on the field and at the turnstiles. They finished nine points adrift in the Third South and conceded 135 goals in 42 matches. Coventry City played a 2-2 draw at Penydarren Park in a re-arranged midweek fixture in April 1930, and on their boardroom wall still hangs the framed copy of the cheque they received as their share of the gate—eighteen shillings and four pence.

A new club called Thames Association were given Merthyr's place. They played at the West Ham Speedway Stadium, Prince Regent's Lane, London E16; but they failed dismally and, when they finished bottom in their second season, they did not even bother to apply for re-election. In 1931 Newport County had become the third South Wales club in four years to be dismissed from the Third South section. They were voted out for Mansfield Town, but a year later they applied for another chance and, when Thames did not come to the poll, there was an automatic vacancy and Newport got it. This was indeed a terrible time for the industrially prostrate principality; even Cardiff City,

runners up in Division I in 1924—when they lost the title only on goal average—and Cup winners in 1927, finished rock bottom of Division III in 1934, with gates at Ninian Park down to 5,000.

The paralysis in Britain's coal-fields also hit the North-East, and two of the original members of the Third North disappeared in 1928 and 1929. They were Durham City, who produced George Camsell, the great England and Middlesbrough centre-forward of the thirties, and Ashington, birthplace of the world famous Charlton brothers, Bobby and Jack. Both went out only the second time they sought re-election, but even unluckier were poor Gateshead.

That club had always had an ill-starred history. Founded in 1899 as South Shields Adelaide, they were elected to Division II as South Shields in 1919. The club, another slump victim, were relegated in 1928 and two years later they moved from Horsley Hill Road in South Shields to Redheugh Park, Gateshead, changing their name accordingly.

In 1932 and again in 1950 Gateshead finished runners-up in the Third North, and as late as 1953 they reached the quarter-finals of the FA Cup. Seven years later, in 1959–60, they had a bad season, finishing 22nd in Division IV, two places off the bottom. For some seasons Peterborough United had been applying unsuccessfully for a chance in the League and each time they were beaten at the ballot the outcry grew louder. They had won the Midland League five seasons running and their reputation as Cup giant-killers matched that of clubs like Yeovil Town and Colchester United.

There was a ceaseless press campaign on their behalf and tremendous lobbying among the First and Second Division clubs. Clearly a guilt complex had grown up in the minds of many of these clubs at failing to vote for Peterborough in the fifties. 'The Posh' certainly deserved their chance, but nobody foresaw it would be at the expense of Gateshead, a club with a record no worse than most Fourth Division sides and with only one previous application—and that on goal average over 20 years earlier—to their name.

No-one who attended the annual meeting at the Cafe Royal, London, in 1960 will ever forget the sight of the Gateshead representatives walking out of the room ashen-faced when it was announced they had received only 18 votes and had been cast out. Gateshead struggled on and even tried, unsuccessfully, to gain membership of the Second Division of the Scottish League. They could not even make a go of the Northern Premier League, a competition in which Bradford have also performed without distinction and, although both clubs remain in existence with League standard grounds, the prospects of them regaining first class status are too negligible to warrant discussion. In 1972 Gateshead, in fact, were struggling to maintain face against the likes of Heanor Town and Frickley Colliery in the Midland League.

Even when they were doing well,

Gateshead inevitably suffered, being in the geographical shadow of Newcastle and Sunderland. Football fans living in the town had only to cross the bridge over the Tyne and walk up the hill to see First Division football at St James' Park, and weeks when Newcastle were away a short ride on the electric train costing two bob return took them to Roker Park.

The Gateshead story, as well as being an unusually sad one, is a very significant pointer to the re-election hustings. Six points below them in 1960 were Hartlepools United, from the same area but with an infinitely worse record over the years. Perhaps it was their regular proximity to the danger zone that had taught them the right tactics. With a very popular manager and hard-headed public relations work they managed to summon up enough votes to stay in. Poor Gateshead, inexperienced in such matters, had scarcely considered the possibility that they would be dismissed and had hardly bothered to canvass.

Non-League clubs now put tremendous effort into their campaigns. Cambridge United spent £2,500 in 1970 and it won them Bradford Park Avenue's place, but not so much because of their own claims as because Bradford had failed to show that they deserved yet another chance. The following year Wigan Athletic spent even more, but failed dismally. There was certainly a reaction against their methods—giving away expensive engraved pens, for instance—but the real reason was a solid reluctance to dismiss another member before the corpse of Bradford was even cold.

The FA Cup— a non-League club's open forum

In fact the best publicity a non-League club can get is impressive performances in the FA Cup. Peterborough showed this by their giant-killing in the fifties, and Hereford United enhanced their chances by knocking out Newcastle United and holding West Ham to a draw early in 1972. It was quite apparent that Hereford—equipped with a brand new grandstand—were going to capitalize on the situation with a really hard push for membership. The chance to humble two First Division clubs would not come again for a long, long time. And Hereford were no doubt as aware as anyone that in the first 25 seasons after the Second World War the League had voluntarily ejected only three of its members—New Brighton, Gateshead and Bradford.

Wigan Athletic, with a ground in Springfield Park which could be developed to house crowds in excess of 50,000, have been one of England's most successful non-League clubs in the past 40 years, both in terms of playing success and support. But two things have always gone against them and their continuing hopes of League status. First, Wigan is situated in the Lancashire-Cheshire area, which is already over-subscribed with 18 League clubs. The two Manchesters and the Merseyside clubs are among the greatest in Britain, but the decline

IMPACT

GATESHEAD FOOTBALL CLUB

Redheugh Park 1972; a ground which had been packed for a quarter-final FA Cup tie just twenty years earlier is deserted as Gateshead struggle to maintain a respectable position in the humble Midland League.

in position and support of sides like Bolton Wanderers, Blackburn Rovers, Preston North End, Bury, Oldham Athletic and Stockport, the struggle to exist experienced by such as Barrow, Southport, Rochdale and Tranmere Rovers, and the loss of First Division status by Burnley and Blackpool, makes the League understandably reluctant about bringing in another Lancashire club. Second, although Wigan changed its name to Athletic in 1932, the League find it hard to forget or forgive the way in which their forerunners, Wigan Borough, got into difficulties and renounced their commitments in the autumn of 1931, leaving the Third North to be decided on 40 matches that season.

New Brighton, who held Spurs to a draw in a Cup tie just before the War, were another club in this area who found there was not enough support to go round. In 1950 they won their first four matches and were top of the Third North in September. The following April they had dropped to bottom place and did not get as many votes as Workington, another non-League club which had a string of good FA Cup performances to their name. When the news came through to this Cumbrian outpost that the 67-year-old local club had gained League status few people in the town were prepared to believe it. With a population under 30,000 far off the beaten track, Workington's election represents the League's most generous and unlikely gamble to spread the gospel. Workington can never be anything but a shoe-string outfit, and their directors once outnumbered their playing staff, but they get a tremendous kick out of just belonging;

THE CLUBS THAT HAVE LEFT THE LEAGUE

Name	Seasons as members	Divisions
Aberdare Athletic	1921–1927	3S
[1]Accrington (Stanley)	1888–1893, 1921–1962	1, 3, 3N, 4
Ashington	1921–1929	3N
Barrow	1921–1972	3, 3N, 4
†Blackpool	1896–1899, 1900–	1, 2
Bootle	1892–1893	2
Bradford (Park Avenue)	1908–1970	1, 2, 3, 3N, 4
Burton United (Swifts)	1892–1907	2
Burton Wanderers	1894–1897	2
†Chesterfield (Town)	1899–1909, 1921–	2, 3, 3N, 4
†Crewe Alexandra	1892–1896, 1921–	2, 3, 3N, 4
Darwen	1891–1899	1, 2
†Doncaster Rovers	1901–1903, 1904–1905, 1923–	2, 3, 3N, 4
Durham City	1921–1928	3N
Gainsborough Trinity	1896–1912	2
*Gateshead	1930–1960	3N, 4
†Gillingham	1920–1938, 1950–	3, 3S, 4
[2]Glossop North End	1899–1915	1, 2
†Grimsby Town	1892–1910, 1911–	1, 2, 3, 3N, 4
[3]Leeds City	1905–1919	2
†Lincoln City	1892–1908, 1909–1911, 1912–1920, 1921–	2, 3, 2N, 4
Loughborough Town	1895–1900	2
†Luton Town	1897–1900, 1920–	1, 2, 3, 3S, 4
Merthyr Town	1920–1930	3, 3S
Middlesbrough Ironopolis	1893–1894	2
Nelson	1921–1931	2, 3N
[4]New Brighton (Tower)	1899–1901, 1923–1951	2, 3N
†Newport County	1920–1931, 1932–	2, 3, 3S, 4
Northwich Victoria	1892–1894	2
†(Burslem) Port Vale	1892–1896, 1898–1907, 1919–	2, 3, 3S, 3N, 4
†[8]Rotherham United (County & Town)	1893–1896, 1919–	2, 3, 3N
*South Shields (Adelaide)	1919–1930	
[5]Stalybridge Celtic	1921–1923	3N
†Stockport County	1900–1904, 1905–	2, 3, 3N, 4
†Stoke (City)	1888–1890, 1891–1908, 1919–	1, 2, 3N
[6]Thames	1930–1932	3S
†Walsall (Town Swifts)	1892–1895, 1896–1901, 1921–	2, 3, 3N, 3S, 4 3N
[7]Wigan Borough	1921–1931	

Alternative names in parentheses.

*South Shields moved to Gateshead in 1930 and the two are effectively the same club. There is no connection between the present non-League clubs South Shields and Gateshead.

†Members of the League, season 1974–75.

[1]Accrington Stanley resigned from the League on 6 March 1962. Their fixtures for the season were expunged.

[2]Glossop North End did not resign until the start of the 1919–20 season.

[3]Leeds City were expelled from the League on 4 October 1919 for making illegal payments. Leeds United were constituted soon afterwards but cannot be strictly considered the same club. Port Vale took over Leeds City's remaining fixtures.

[4]New Brighton Tower resigned from the League at the end of the 1900–01 season.

[5]Stalybridge Celtic resigned from the League at the end of the 1922–23 season.

[6]Thames did not apply for re-election after the 1931–32 season, and thus effectively resigned.

[7]Wigan Borough resigned from the League on 26 October 1931. Their fixtures for the season were expunged.

[8]Rotherham Town were members of the League from 1893 to 1896. Rotherham County were members of the League from 1919 to 1925. In 1925 these two clubs combined under the name Rotherham United.

and after coming of age as a League club they can with some justification say they put their unexpected chance to very good use.

Many towns and clubs who failed to maintain League status will, of course, never regain it. Wigan and Chelmsford have strong claims to be next in line but there is no hope for those such as Loughborough, who ended a five-season stretch in Division II in 1900 by winning only one match in the entire season—the worst League record of all time. Their total of eight points was shared by Doncaster Rovers in 1905.

The saddest little cameo of all was, in the words of the poet Newbolt, Bootle's 'Hope of a Season's Fame.' That is all they had, one campaign, but in it they beat Ardwick (later Manchester City) 5-3 and Walsall Town Swifts 7-1 in Division II. They finished with four clubs below them but they had poor support and a poor ground. With Arsenal, Liverpool, Newcastle United and Rotherham all waiting for places the League not only extended the Second Division from 12 clubs to 15, but slung Bootle out into the bargain.

Middlesbrough Ironopolis, Glossop North End, Darwen are dinosaurs from a forgotten century, tombstone names—dotting the route to football's Boot Hill, a reminder that sentiment in the game at professional level has its limitations.

Season in, season out, the press publishes stories on clubs about to go to the wall, yet it has actually happened so rarely that it is tempting to suggest that a League club is one of the most important assets any town can have. As the mayor of Accrington said when the town's club was forced to disband. 'It's a tragedy for Accrington. A town loses some of its identity if its football club dies. If people don't hear the name every Saturday night they begin to forget the place exists. After all, what else do they know about Accrington?'

The aftermath of the first ever goal scored in an FA Challenge Trophy final as the scorer, Dave Lyon, receives the attentions of a Macclesfield fan. The Cheshire side beat Telford 2-0.

In search of the Football League

MANCHESTER EVENING NEWS

THE MAJOR COMPETITIONS

Until the motorways stretched themselves across the country, football to all but the most dedicated fan meant the local team. Come Saturday and a large part of Bedford or Wisbech or Macclesfield would amble along to watch their town's non-League team, no matter who they were playing.

But all that changed with the motorways. 'Your team' no longer had to be the nearest. The grand names—Arsenal, Manchester United, Wolves—suddenly came within reach, as streams of fans bound for the First Division grounds quickly discovered. Progress had at one blow deprived the non-League clubs of support, finance and atmosphere. The tag 'non-League' took on a new, downgraded meaning.

Non-League football, in the larger perspective of the English game, means giant-killing and giant-killing means the FA Cup. But the real prize at the top of the beanstalk for the non-League clubs has been nothing so ambitious as the Cup

itself, but the elusive Holy Grail of Football League status. And, like the Holy Grail itself, such status was much sought after but rarely found.

At the bottom of this, in turn, lurks a peculiar irony. For in a sense, to pass from non-League football into the Football League has been to pass from a sort of special glamour into a dim respectability. It is not without significance that Colchester United, a mighty Jack of the 1940s in the FA Cup, should achieve nothing of real excitement after acquiring League status until 1971, when Leeds United were thrillingly knocked out...of the Cup.

Colchester United, Yeovil Town with their notoriously sloping pitch, Bedford Town and their defiance of the Arsenal, Peterborough and their achievements of the 1950s, Wigan Athletic and the assault on Maine Road, Hereford United and the humiliation of Newcastle in 1972; these are heroic tales indeed.

Yet once upon a time, Southern League clubs were wont to do better, were able to visualize and pursue not only a good run in the Cup, but the Cup itself. It was in 1901 that Tottenham Hotspur became the first and only Southern League—and indeed, non-League—club ever to capture the FA Cup.

Today, the non-League clubs have their own tournament, the FA Challenge Trophy, with its final at Wembley. But this is rather like grafting a rose on to a cabbage. Reality is still to be found in the FA Cup and the attempts to storm the fortress of the League which for years was so impregnable. The annual general meeting used to be such a boneyard for the election hopes of the non-League clubs, such a wretchedly closed shop for the clubs seeking re-election, that one sports magazine put up, year by year, the same headline: THE LEAGUE NO IT ALL. The FA Challenge Trophy has provided one talking point however. Three of the first four winners were from the Northern Premier League and there were claims that this League had replaced the Southern as the best of the 'Other Leagues'.

The Southern League came lustily to birth in early 1894. Creeping professionalism had made a new, more ambitious competition necessary. And so Clapton and Ilford, from Essex, joined Millwall and another seven clubs to make up the First Division, among them Luton Town,

Southern League Winners

1894-95	Millwall Athletic
1895-96	Millwall Athletic
1896-97	Southampton St Mary's
1897-98	Southampton
1898-99	Southampton
1899-1900	Tottenham Hotspur
1900-01	Southampton
1901-02	Portsmouth
1902-03	Southampton
1903-04	Southampton
1904-05	Bristol Rovers
1905-06	Fulham
1906-07	Fulham
1907-08	Queen's Park Rangers
1908-09	Northampton Town
1909-10	Brighton & Hove Albion
1910-11	Swindon Town
1911-12	Queen's Park Rangers
1912-13	Plymouth Argyle
1913-14	Swindon Town
1914-15	Watford
1919-20	Portsmouth
1920-21	Brighton & Hove Albion Reserves
1921-22	Plymouth Argyle Reserves
1922-23	Ebbw Vale
1923-24	Peterborough & Fletton United
1924-25	Southampton Reserves
1925-26	Plymouth Argyle Reserves
1926-27	Brighton & Hove Albion Reserves
1927-28	Kettering Town
1928-29	Plymouth Argyle Reserves
1929-30	Aldershot Town
1930-31	Dartford
1931-32	Dartford
1932-33	Norwich City Reserves
1933-34	Plymouth Argyle Reserves
1934-35	Norwich City Reserves
1935-36	Margate
1936-37	Ipswich Town
1937-38	Guildford City
1938-39	Colchester United
1939-40	{ Chelmsford City (Eastern Section) Lovell's Athletic (Western Section)
1945-46	Chelmsford City
1946-47	Gillingham
1947-48	Merthyr Tydfil
1948-49	Gillingham
1949-50	Merthyr Tydfil
1950-51	Merthyr Tydfil
1951-52	Merthyr Tydfil
1952-53	Headington United
1953-54	Merthyr Tydfil
1954-55	Yeovil Town
1955-56	Guildford City
1956-57	Kettering Town
1957-58	Gravesend & Northfleet
1958-59	Bedford Town
1959-60	Bath City
1960-61	Oxford United
1961-62	Oxford United
1962-63	Cambridge City
1963-64	Yeovil Town
1964-65	Weymouth
1965-66	Weymouth
1966-67	Romford
1967-68	Chelmsford City
1968-69	Cambridge United
1969-70	Cambridge United
1970-71	Yeovil Town
1971-72	Chelmsford City
1972-73	Kettering Town

usually credited to Bennett, to make the score 2-2, was nothing of the sort. It was awarded by a Mr Kingscott, a referee too far away to see that the ball could not have crossed the line, and too arrogant to consult his linesman. Spurs' morale was strong enough to ride that setback, and the shock of being dishearteningly 1-0 down at half-time in the replay to a goal by Priest. Cameron, Smith and Brown then scored the goals which properly gave the North Londoners the Cup.

There was something almost incestuous about what happened the following season, Spurs losing in the first round to Southampton, who again went on to the Final, where they lost to . . . Sheffield United. In their defence was the incomparable C B Fry, an international full-back, a great cricketer and a superb athlete. The first game was drawn 1-1, but this time the replay went the way of the League side by 2-1.

So impressive was the Southern League's cup record that it was logical enough when the Football League expanded to the extent of a new Third Division—the Southern section—in season 1920-21, that they should co-opt the Southern League, *en bloc*. This league's great days were over; from now onwards they would recruit their members from a lower, humbler stratum of the game. There would be no more Southern League clubs reaching semi-finals, though Millwall, intriguingly, would manage it again in 1937 as a Third Division side. Meanwhile, the Southern League became at once a repository for fading players from the Football League clubs, and a possible gateway to the Third Division South.

Elsewhere, the Welsh League flourished with several divisions, the Birmingham and District League was solid and healthy, while in the North, the Lancashire Combination would eventually form the basis for the Northern Premier League, which came to birth in 1968-69. The Midland League, too, has sturdily survived, with constituents like Frickley Colliery (later Athletic) providing regular sources of talent to the major clubs.

The inter-War period may have seen few distinguished Cup runs by non-League clubs, but from time to time they would throw up a major star; the more so as the big League clubs' scouting systems and youth schemes were in their infancy. The outstanding case was probably that of the great England left-back, Eddie Hapgood, who slipped through the grasp of his local club, Bristol Rovers, because they wanted him to drive a coal cart, rather than his preferred milk-cart, during the summer. So Hapgood turned down £8 a week at Eastville—and accepted an offer of £4 a week in winter, £3 out of season, from the Midland club, Kettering Town. As it transpired, Kettering had the 18-year-old Hapgood in their team for only a dozen or so matches before Herbert Chapman swooped down from Highbury.

That was in 1927, and some 30 years later Hapgood returned to non-League football when he became manager for several years of the Southern League's Bath City. One of his successors was Malcolm Allison, later Manchester City manager, while during the War, the illustrious Stanley Mortensen also made his name there. During those War years, clubs such as Bath and the Welsh works side, Lovell's Athletic, competed quite successfully with League teams. Mortensen was an RAF flyer who crashed, hurt himself badly, but recovered his form at Bath, where, rather than at Blackpool, it may truly be said that he established his reputation. Two decades later, there was the still more remarkable case of the locally born right-back, one Tony Book, approaching 30 when he ventured into League football with Plymouth Argyle.

The iniquitous maximum wage was not

Northern Premier League Winners

1968-69	Macclesfield Town
1969-70	Macclesfield Town
1970-71	Wigan Athletic
1971-72	Stafford Rangers
1972-73	Boston United

Swindon Town, Reading and Southampton. Indeed, there was enough interest for a Second Division to be created, too, with such clubs as Maidenhead, New Brompton and Sheppey United. Woolwich Arsenal, who in fact had taken the earliest initiative the previous year, had meanwhile been elected to the Second Division of the League. It is interesting to note that among the teams to whom Arsenal originally wrote regarding the formation were Old Etonians, Old Carthusians, Old Westminsters and the Casuals.

The Southern League clubs got away to a flying start in the FA Cup, actually going so far as to provide two semi-finalists in the 1899-1900 season; though unfortunately Millwall and Southampton were drawn against one another in that penultimate round. Southampton needed two matches to dispose of Millwall 0-0 and 3-0, the first at Crystal Palace, the second at Reading.

Alas, the Southern League's challenge petered out in the Final, with Southampton falling 4-0 to Bury at Crystal Palace, in front of the second highest crowd ever seen in England—68,945.

The following season, another Southern League club got to the Final and this time did the trick, though Tottenham Hotspur needed that replay to beat Sheffield United. The journey to Bolton should never have been necessary, for the 'goal',

Top left *Ray Williams' first goal for Stafford in the 1972 Trophy final. Stafford scored three times in eight minutes to beat Barnet 3-0.*

Top right *Flying attack from Chelmsford's substitute; Southern League champions in 1972, Chelmsford are one of the most persistent of those clubs attempting to gain entry to the League.*

Bottom left *The Southern League club that did succeed in 1972, despite finishing behind Chelmsford, was Hereford. Here Ricky George celebrates a goal by Brian Owen against Barnet.*

Bottom right *A Lancashire non-League derby; Wigan Athletic striker Jim Fleming sees his shot blocked by the South Liverpool goalkeeper.*

abolished by Football League clubs until 1961, and so it can be easily imagined that the non-League clubs, who had no transfer agreement with the League clubs until well after the Second World War, should be a haven and a refuge for dissident League stars. The terms of the draconian League contract meant that a player was bound to his club in perpetuity, virtually for whatever they wanted to pay him. The only escape was to play for a non-League club; where it was often possible, in fact, to earn more than in the Football League. Barry Town are reputed to have offered John Charles £50 per week long before the maximum wage was abolished.

But when it finally did go its inevitable way, the status of the non-League clubs could only be

TONY TWEEN

J. LEATHERBARROW

diminished. They could no longer match the wages the big boys in the League were able to offer. Where once the FA Cup would throw together League and non-League club, and create the attraction of seeing underdogs, who included among their number perhaps nine ex-professionals, popular players whose 'return' to top-class combat was eagerly anticipated, now the non-Leaguers brought with them just a name.

It was no longer necessary for the best League players to contemplate moving say, from Spurs to Millwall to Hereford. With better rewards, the game spawned soccer entrepreneurs, and so players could afford to leave the game earlier. Having set themselves up in business, fewer players were forced to cling to the game for as long as they possibly could. And so the non-League outfits were obliged to concern themselves with producing their own, homespun footballers instead of trying to acquire the once big names.

The non-League clubs were also an excellent nursery for managers. Some, like Alec Stock of Yeovil and Ted Fenton of Colchester, were player-managers. The most distinguished of them all, Arthur Rowe, was actually manager of Southern League Chelmsford City when in 1949, Tottenham Hotspur, his old club, suddenly whisked him back into the higher realms as their manager. Rowe responded by winning them the Second and First Division Championships in

consecutive seasons.

The first great Cup run by a non-League club after the War came in 1948, when Colchester United, under the managership of the former West Ham half-back, later that club's manager, Ted Fenton, put out two Yorkshire clubs. Huddersfield Town were their first victims. Colchester put them out 1-0 at Layer Road and Fenton, playing at centre-half, was an inspiration.

FA Challenge Trophy Winners

1969-70	Macclesfield Town
1970-71	Telford United
1971-72	Stafford Rangers
1972-73	Scarborough

It was only the second time since the Third Division was formed in 1920 that a non-League club had beaten a First Division side.

The next round brought a wonderfully intriguing draw, for to the picturesque little ground at Layer Road now came Bradford, who had just shocked the Arsenal, the season's eventual League Champions, by winning 1-0 at Highbury. Bradford did better than Huddersfield, their county neighbours, to the extent that they scored two goals; but Colchester got three. There was excited talk of Colchester's 'F' plans and 'M' plans, but none was to avail them up at Blackpool, who turned out to be finalists that year, and who

thrashed them 5-0.

The following year, it was the turn of little Yeovil Town, from distant Somerset. Yeovil were player managed by a West Country-born inside-forward in Alec Stock, who had been invalided out of the tank corps after he was wounded in Normandy, and applied for the job almost irascibly on a wet, boring afternoon when he could not garden. The wage bill was a maximum of eighty pounds, the players all part-time professionals in the non-League manner, and they beat Sunderland.

Sunderland then had an extremely expensive team with one of the game's outstanding inside-forwards in Len Shackleton. But Stock 'thought we had a chance', not least because there was no need to alter their normal tactics, with one defensive left-half, and Stock himself playing as a deep-lying inside-forward. Stock scored Yeovil's first goal, and then almost asked for the game to be stopped in extra time—then played in all ties—because of shrouding fog. A draw, he felt, was good enough, and the club could do with the gate money from a replay at Sunderland. But he changed his mind, Yeovil scored again, and the sun obligingly came out. An 8-0 annihilation at the hands of Manchester United was in store in the next round, but Yeovil had written their page in the history of the FA Cup.

It was in a different manner that Peterborough United of the Midland League made themselves a

In Search of Football League Status

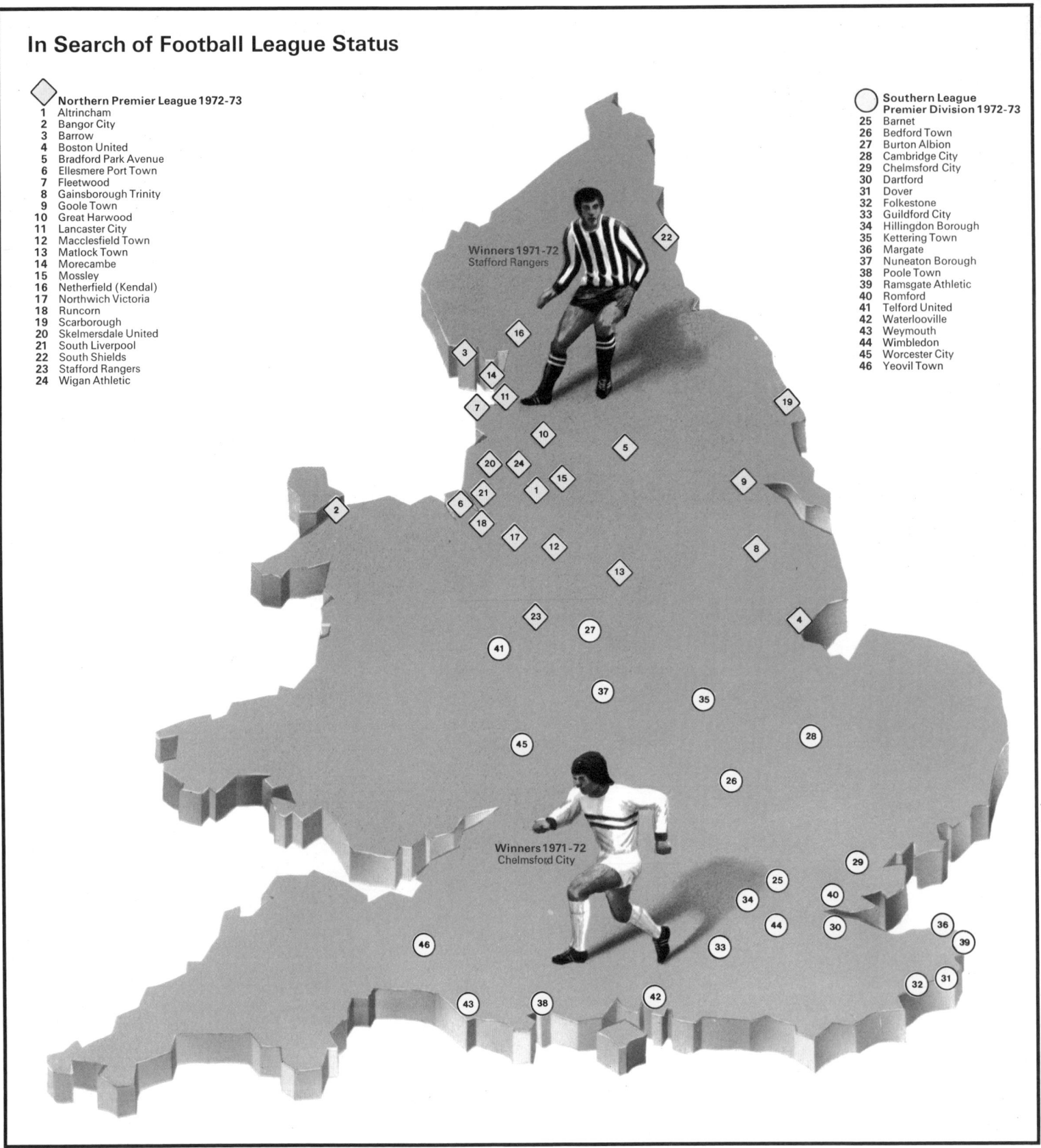

Northern Premier League 1972-73
1 Altrincham
2 Bangor City
3 Barrow
4 Boston United
5 Bradford Park Avenue
6 Ellesmere Port Town
7 Fleetwood
8 Gainsborough Trinity
9 Goole Town
10 Great Harwood
11 Lancaster City
12 Macclesfield Town
13 Matlock Town
14 Morecambe
15 Mossley
16 Netherfield (Kendal)
17 Northwich Victoria
18 Runcorn
19 Scarborough
20 Skelmersdale United
21 South Liverpool
22 South Shields
23 Stafford Rangers
24 Wigan Athletic

Southern League Premier Division 1972-73
25 Barnet
26 Bedford Town
27 Burton Albion
28 Cambridge City
29 Chelmsford City
30 Dartford
31 Dover
32 Folkestone
33 Guildford City
34 Hillingdon Borough
35 Kettering Town
36 Margate
37 Nuneaton Borough
38 Poole Town
39 Ramsgate Athletic
40 Romford
41 Telford United
42 Waterlooville
43 Weymouth
44 Wimbledon
45 Worcester City
46 Yeovil Town

Winners 1971-72 Stafford Rangers

Winners 1971-72 Chelmsford City

name and a host of eager friends, at first while under the managership of the former Newcastle United goalkeeper, Jack Fairbrother, later under another goalkeeper in Arsenal's George Swindin. They had a consistent record in the Cup but, looking back at the records of the 1950s, it is noticeable that Peterborough really never did anything great in giant-killing terms. Nothing as remarkable as Wigan Athletic for instance, who in 1954 had the temerity to hold Newcastle United to a 2-2 draw at St James' Park, then, unlike splendid Hereford in 1972, lose the return by a narrow 3-2 at home. Peterborough, that same year, did reach the third round, no small feat, but were despatched 3-1 at Cardiff.

But by the time of Peterborough's eventual League entry in 1960 a bleak wind of change was blowing. The suicidal de-zoning of the Third

The 24 Northern Premier League and 22 Southern League teams that formed the non-League elite in 1973. The most striking feature of the map is the cluster of hopefuls in the North West. In an area where League clubs such as Bolton, Bury, Blackburn and Burnley are all struggling to survive, how do the Wigans and the Altrinchams exist at all?
Opposite page *Dudley Tyler became the most expensive player to come out of non-League football when signed by West Ham in 1972.*

Division in 1958 coincided with new patterns in society and football; a desire to watch only the best, to desert even the local Third Division club, let alone the local non-League club, in favour of the nearest 'big' club.

Thus even when Hereford United brilliantly eliminated Newcastle United and then contained West Ham quite well in the 1972 Cup, elevation to the League meant a hugely increased amount of travelling, besides a wages bill. The Northern Premier League, the Southern League—now a two division affair with senior 'amateur' clubs steadily foresaking shamateurism to join them— were a hand-to-mouth affair, depending heavily on lotteries and the like, sometimes drawing crowds of no more than a few hundred, though Hereford averaged 6,500. Another intriguing change was a movement away from the broken-down League star towards the raising of young local talent, talent which might well spend all its time in non-League football. But it grows clearer year by year that what is needed to sustain the League's poor relations, in spirit at least, is the mirage of eventual League football in a multi-division national League.

Running Scotland's also-rans

'The only way Scottish Second Division clubs can survive', says the manager of one of their number, 'is by opting out of the rat-race. The less ambition you have, the more money you can tote up or, at least, the smaller overdrafts you accumulate. If you've got any sense you don't think about promotion or anything silly like that. You soldier on—that way you don't hit the highspots but you do stay alive.'

Despite appearances the Scottish Second Division is quite healthy. Income comes not so much from the gates but from associated ventures like social clubs and pools. But these are enough to keep clubs functioning, keep players in a job, and reassure committees that they are fulfilling some useful purpose in life. The real question mark against the Second Division is not whether it can survive as part of the Scottish League but whether it already exists as a completely separate entity.

There are some clubs, of course, who maintain a twilight existence on the edge of the First Division. They temper exceptional success in the Second with struggles in the First. But they tend to have little to show for their pride, tradition, and belief in their right to a First Division place other than financial worries and regular crushing defeats at the hands of Rangers and Celtic.

It is a guide to the strength of the Second Division that since its formation in 1893 only one club has ever managed to win the Scottish Cup while a member. That was back in 1938 when East Fife beat Kilmarnock—themselves 18th in the First Division—after five replays during the competition and not playing any club above sixth in the Scottish League.

At the end of the 1971-72 season there arose yet another of the periodic suggestions to reorganize Scottish football. Like most of the others this one was eminently sensible and totally without any chance of success. It involved cutting the First Division to just fourteen

clubs—about the highest number that could reasonably claim permanent first-class status—and dividing the other 23 League Clubs and 16 Highland League clubs into two divisions, north and south.

Such a suggestion could have little chance of success. The First Division members could not possibly take the loss of four home gates a season, and the likelihood of the Highland League members abandoning their independence was small, to say the least. In fact some of the First Division clubs would prefer the *addition* of four clubs, thus giving them an extra four home gates, and the cutting free of the Second Division jetsam to form some undefined independent league.

But while these ideas come and go the majority of the Second Division clubs continue in the traditional vein, just getting by and simply taking a pride in hearing their names mentioned on Sports Report every Saturday.

Stranraer are your Mr Average. Their's is an isolated town of only 10,000 inhabitants, they are happy with an attendance of four figures, but they pride themselves in being better off than they have been for a long time.

'We operate on a shoe-string budget—and we cut our cloth accordingly', says their committee vice-chairman, Mr Denis McColm, who also happens to be a school janitor through the week. 'Our gates average about 1,000,' he adds. 'And each week we are handed around £100 by our Club Pool. This does us nicely. We have no worries.

'We operate with about 15 players whose wages are average for the Second Division (this means something under £10—less than a good English "shamateur" would get) and we get along fine.' Like several other clubs, they do not even have to worry about a manager's wage. Stranraer are run by a 12-man committee who work entirely for

the love of it.

The fact that Stranraer is rather remote—away in the south-west of Scotland and over 100 miles from the Central Lowland belt of the country where the main action takes place—is not as much of a problem as might be expected. Most of their players are based in Glasgow and this centre is really the starting point for the coach to 'away' matches.

So cleverly do they cut their cloth, in fact, that they are not even forced to sell players regularly. 'We got £10,000 from Dundee United for Jackie Copland a couple of years ago,' says Mr McColm, 'but he was our first sale in a long time.' The sale of a player, therefore, is a bonus rather than an essential part of the club's income. In fact, discovering good players is probably the only real contribution the average Second Division side makes to Scottish football.

But how do they manage to sign players who later achieve greatness, and who, one would expect, should be holding out for a more glamorous offer? The answer is simple. Great footballers, like any other talent, can come from the unlikeliest corners. Second Division sides are able to sign them before the scouts from the big clubs even hear about them.

The secret of keeping heads above water, as practised so successfully by the Stranraers, the Brechins, the Stenhousemuirs, lies in these clubs' realistic attitude to life. They realize only too well that a town of 10,000 inhabitants—which is about average among the 'rabbits'—just could not support an ambitious football club.

Others, with even bigger populations, have tried to live with the Celtics and in the end all have failed spectacularly. Dunfermline Athletic are the latest and perhaps greatest example.

In the middle of the 1950s, the Fife club were determined to put themselves on the soccer map. By the end of the decade they had made it to the First Division.

In 1961, under the management of Jock Stein, they won the Scottish Cup, beating Celtic in the final. There was no turning back now. By 1968, when they again won the Scottish Cup, they had proved themselves one of the most progressive—and one of the most feared—provincial clubs in the country.

But the strain of having to maintain their status inevitably proved too much. By season 1971-72 they were reduced to calling for public aid, saying they needed an immediate £50,000 to save the club from extinction. At the end of the same season they were relegated to the Second

This page A thin yellow and black line of Berwick Rangers players defends its snowy and deserted territory against St Mirren, raiders from over the border, during the 1971-72 season. Berwick's strange position—an English club in the Scottish League—inspired both Gateshead and Wigan to apply for membership of the Scottish Second Division in the 1970s.

Opposite page The forty clubs that make up the lower-storey of Scottish soccer. The only major names missing are those of the 13 'traditional' First Division sides in the larger population centres viz: Aberdeen, Airdrie, Celtic,

Dundee, Dundee United, Falkirk, Hearts, Hibs, Kilmarnock, Motherwell, Partick, Rangers and St Johnstone (Perth).
The map shows clearly that the Second Division teams cluster round the Central Lowland belt—the only exceptions being the southern isolates, Stranraer, Queen of the South and Berwick, and the group of four to the north of the Firth of Tay. This is relevant in that it shows just how artificial any attempt to divide the Second Division into East/West or North/South sections would be. Only with the addition of the Highland

League would regionalization be a meaningful proposition.
The greatest distance between any two present League clubs is the 195 miles from Stranraer to Montrose—about the same distance as London to Leeds or Liverpool. But even this is less of a handicap than it appears as, in Stranraer's case, most of their players live in Glasgow and away journeys start from there.
For most clubs travel is no great problem. The clustering of clubs in the central belt certainly helps in saving travelling expenses—though it is also a problem in that people from all over

the area can travel to watch Rangers or Celtic almost as easily as their local club. Nevertheless teams like Falkirk and East Stirlingshire are within 60 miles of 28 of the Scottish League's other 36 teams.
The Highland League operates completely independently and has long resisted attempts to integrate it into a national network. The only League club which comes within 70 miles of its territory is Aberdeen, and attendances at Highland League games are often higher than those in the Second Division and, occasionally, those in the First.

Scotland's lower-storey

**'Bread-and-butter'
Second Division clubs**

1 Albion Rovers (Coatbridge)
2 Alloa Athletic
3 Berwick Rangers
4 Brechin City
5 Clydebank
6 East Stirlingshire (Falkirk)
7 Forfar Athletic
8 Hamilton Academicals
9 Montrose
10 Queen's Park (Glasgow)
11 Stenhousemuir
12 Stranraer

**'Fringe' First and
Second Division clubs**

13 Arbroath
14 Ayr United
15 Clyde (Glasgow)
16 Cowdenbeath
17 Dumbarton
18 Dunfermline Athletic
19 East Fife (Methil)
20 Morton (Greenock)
21 Queen of the South (Dumfries)
22 Raith Rovers (Kirkcaldy)
23 St. Mirren (Paisley)
24 Stirling Albion

Highland League clubs

25 Brora Rangers
26 Buckie Thistle
27 Caledonian (Inverness)
28 Clachnacuddin (Inverness)
29 Deveronvale (Banff)
30 Elgin City
31 Forres Mechanics
32 Fraserburgh
33 Huntly
34 Inverness Thistle
35 Keith
36 Lossiemouth
37 Nairn County
38 Peterhead
39 Ross County (Dingwall)
40 Rothes

DIAGRAM

Main picture *The limited appeal of a Brechin City match; the club's turnstiles are located in the hedge on the left!*
Inset left *Hampden Park, a ground which has held 150,000, is completely empty for a cup game between Rangers and impoverished Queen's Park, but*
inset right *when an Inverness team played Rangers things were very different.*

ABERDEEN JOURNALS LTD

Division from whence they had come.

Most of the others have learned from these fatal errors over the years, and it would not be unfair to say that every season, from the dozen and a half clubs which form the division, only a handful are seriously looking for, or are capable of, promotion. Of course it was not always so. In fact, the Second Division was formalized at the end of season 1921-22 through the desire of lesser clubs to enjoy the pickings of the First Division.

From the introduction of pro-fessionalism in 1893 until the beginning of the First World War the Second Division was only semi-recognized by the Scottish League and promotion to the First Division was by election only.

An aspiring Second Division club had to have plenty of friends to be elected. On the other hand, a club like Queen's Park, whose fortunes faded around 1910, were saved several times from dropping to the Second Division because they had plenty of friends who voted that they stayed where they were.

The system sowed the seeds of discontent. There grew a feeling that, as there were rewards for suc-cess, there should be a penalty for failure. That, in fact, there should be a promotion-relegation system between First and Second Division. But all was forgotten when the War began in 1914.

When hostilities ended four years later and football in Scotland began again the Second Division had vanished. In its place was the Central League, a rebel division comprised of clubs who had been in the pre-War lower grade and a few new-comers.

The break-away League was an immediate success, a real money spinner in Fife particularly and clubs like Dunfermline and Cowdenbeath were able to tempt players away from Celtic and Rangers.

Very quickly the Scottish League realized their First Division was threatened so the idea was hatched that the 'rebels' should be recog-nized as a Second Division.

'On our terms, though', said the Central League, who of course had been angling after a fair deal all along, anyway. And their terms were that there should be automatic

SCOTTISH SECOND DIVISION AND DIVISION B

Season	First	Second
1893-94[1]	Hibernian	Cowlairs
1894-95[2]	Hibernian	Motherwell
1895-96[3]	Abercorn	Leith Athletic
1896-97[4]	Partick Thistle	Leith Athletic
1897-98	Kilmarnock	Port Glasgow Athletic
1898-99[5]	Kilmarnock	Leith Athletic
1899-1900[6]	Partick Thistle	Morton
1900-01	St Bernard's	Airdrieonians
1901-02[7]	Port Glasgow Athletic	Partick Thistle
1902-03[8]	Airdrieonians	Motherwell
1903-04	Hamilton Academicals	Clyde
1904-05[9]	Clyde	Falkirk
1905-06[10]	Leith Athletic	Clyde
1906-07	St Bernard's	Vale of Leven
1907-08	Raith Rovers	Dumbarton
1908-09	Abercorn	Raith Rovers
1909-10[11]	Leith Athletic	Raith Rovers
1910-11	Dumbarton	Ayr United
1911-12	Ayr United	Abercorn
1912-13[12]	Ayr United	Dunfermline Athletic
1913-14	Cowdenbeath	Albion Rovers
1914-15	Cowdenbeath	St Bernard's
1915-1921	*Competition suspended*	
1921-22[13]	Alloa Athletic	Cowdenbeath
1922-23[14]	Queen's Park	Clydebank
1923-24	St Johnstone	Cowdenbeath
1924-25	Dundee United	Clydebank
1925-26	Dunfermline Athletic	Clyde
1926-27	Bo'ness	Raith Rovers
1927-28	Ayr United	Third Lanark
1928-29	Dundee United	Morton
1929-30	Leith Athletic	East Fife
1930-31	Third Lanark	Dundee United
1931-32	East Stirlingshire	St Johnstone
1932-33	Hibernian	Queen of the South
1933-34	Albion Rovers	Dunfermline Athletic
1934-35	Third Lanark	Arbroath
1935-36	Falkirk	St Mirren
1936-37	Ayr United	Morton
1937-38	Raith Rovers	Albion Rovers
1938-39[15]	Cowdenbeath	Alloa Athletic
1939-1946	*Competition suspended*	
1946-47	Dundee	Airdrieonians
1947-48	East Fife	Albion Rovers
1948-49	Raith Rovers	Stirling Albion
1949-50	Morton	Airdrieonians
1950-51	Queen of the South	Stirling Albion
1951-52	Clyde	Falkirk
1952-53	Stirling Albion	Hamilton Academicals
1953-54	Motherwell	Kilmarnock
1954-55	Airdrieonians	Dunfermline Athletic
1955-56	Queen's Park	Ayr United
1956-57	Clyde	Third Lanark
1957-58	Stirling Albion	Dunfermline Athletic
1958-59	Ayr United	Arbroath
1959-60	St Johnstone	Dundee United
1960-61	Stirling Albion	Falkirk
1961-62	Clyde	Queen of the South
1962-63	St Johnstone	East Stirlingshire
1963-64	Morton	Clyde
1964-65	Stirling Albion	Hamilton Academicals
1965-66	Ayr United	Airdrieonians
1966-67	Morton	Raith Rovers
1967-68	St Mirren	Arbroath
1968-69	Motherwell	Ayr United
1969-70	Falkirk	Cowdenbeath
1970-71	Partick Thistle	East Fife
1971-72	Dumbarton	Arbroath
1972-73	Clyde	Dunfermline Athletic

[1] Clyde (who finished third) elected to First Division
[2] Hibernian elected to First Division
[3] Abercorn elected to First Division
[4] Partick Thistle elected to First Division
[5] Kilmarnock elected to First Division
[6] Partick Thistle and Morton were elected to First Division. So were Queen's Park, but they had not been members of the Second Division
[7] Port Glasgow Athletic and Partick Thistle were elected to the First Division
[8] Airdrieonians and Motherwell elected to First Division
[9] Aberdeen (who finished seventh) and Falkirk elected to First Division
[10] Clyde and Hamilton Academicals (who finished fourth) elected to First Division
[11] Raith Rovers were elected to First Division
[12] Ayr United and Dumbarton (who finished sixth) elected to First Division
[13] Alloa Athletic elected to First Division. Three clubs were relegated to the Second
[14] From season 1922-23 onwards the first two clubs in the Second Division were automatically elected to the First
[15] No clubs were promoted at the end of 1938-39 because of the Second World War

promotion and relegation, rather than the vagaries of election.

The Scottish League agreed and in season 1921-22 the official Second Division came into being. The first movement came at the end of that term—Alloa were promoted and three clubs, including Queen's Park, were relegated in order to even up the numbers of teams in both Divisions. At the end of the following season began the two-up—two-down system. From then until the Second World War, the only changes in the Second Division were those prompted by clubs dropping out.

The number of clubs fluctuated but the overall set-up remained the same.

The entire League programme was suspended, of course, between 1939 and 1945. When normality was restored in season 1946-47 several changes had taken place.

For a start, the separate Leagues were called Divison A and Division B as opposed to I and II. And eight teams had dropped from the 1939 Second Division into the newly-formed Division C, which was composed of 'non-League' clubs and reserve teams of the established clubs in the top two divisions.

Stirling Albion, formed only in 1945, were the first champions of 'C' Division and they were promoted to Division B. During the next few years they proceeded to yo-yo their way up and down from 'B' to 'A' and back to 'B'.

In the late forties, with the inevitable 'boom' which followed the War allowing more clubs to run reserve teams, Division C was split into two regionalized groups—South-West and North-East. With the bisection of 'C' Division, it meant the end of promotion to 'B' from that table, as had happened to Stirling previously. It was not until 1955 that the set-up as it now is came into being.

The 'C' divisions were scrapped, and the Reserve League was formed. Five 'non-League' clubs from 'C' were elected to Division II as it now became known.

And the top two teams in Division II were promoted to the First Division. To even up the teams in each Division, the bottom two in the First Division in 1955 were not relegated.

Since then, there have been 19 teams in the Second Division, with just one exception. That was season 1966-67, when Clydebank, who had merged with East Stirlingshire the year before, gained independent membership after an internal row had seen the East Stirling part of the club return to their old home in Falkirk.

Why the Highland clubs are reluctant to join in

That gave a 20-team Second Division, but the collapse of Third Lanark the following year restored the balance. But for some time the feeling had been growing that the League should be re-constructed, with a smaller First Division, and possibly a Second and Third, each table consisting of around 12 clubs.

In season 1971-72, Scottish League President James Aitken asked the chairmen of all the clubs to meet him to discuss how best to put Scottish football back on its feet. The question of regionalization again came up, and again the Second Division clubs were against it.

Stranraer's Denis McColm says, 'We are not for regionalization of the Second Division. The present set-up suits us. After all, most of the games we play are in the central belt of Scotland. Only places like Montrose, Arbroath, Forfar and Brechin are distant, but they account for only four journeys in a year.'

It has been suggested in the past too, that Highland League clubs might be taken into the Second Division. But this is highly unlikely for the simple reason that the Highland League clubs are doing very nicely as they are.

Playing in a contained area they have few travelling worries nor competition from senior teams. Aberdeen, after all, are the only side within 100 miles of Inverness. In fact, the Highland Leaguers generally get better crowds than the Second Division sides. Most have more money. During the 1960s little Elgin City were able to fork out thousands for a new stand and most members have excellent floodlights. When Rangers played a friendly in Inverness in May 1972 they drew a crowd of close on 10,000. The interest is there in the Highlands and the clubs feel they would be foolish to do anything to jeopardize it.

The only time they want to be in the company of Scottish League sides is when Scottish Cup time comes around. Then the greater company they can be in, the happier they are. It is, after all, always more money to them. The same applies to the Second Division sides. The highlight of their year is a good run in the Scottish Cup, if possible. Certainly, it is the only real chance the players have of making any money.

'My club's not going anywhere—but I love playing football'

With very few exceptions, all the players in the division are part-time, with wages which can only be regarded as pin-money. These players live for the day when they are drawn against a crowd-pulling First Division outfit.

The men who turn out for the 'rabbits' week in, week out know there is little hope of their ever going places with their club. Most of them use the Second Division as a stepping-stone to greater things, if they have the talent.

One well-known player, who has spent all of his ten-year career there, says, 'I realized a long time ago I wasn't going to make the grade. But I enjoy playing in the Second Division. This is my level.

'I realize better than anybody that my club isn't going to achieve much. But it's a good way of getting extra pocket money. And I love playing football. And the standard's not so bad either you know. A lot of the top players come down here for a few years.

'All the lads who are in the same situation as I am feel the same thing. We look on it as being paid for doing something we enjoy a couple of times a week. That suits us fine. And why shouldn't it?'

'The club is often the town's major nightspot'

That suits the players, their attitude suits the clubs and really everybody in the Second Division is fairly contented with their lot. Perhaps they do not contribute a lot to the well-being of Scottish football, but they do have an important role to fulfil in their own communities. Says one committee member: 'The only time you ever hear names like Arbroath, Montrose, Forfar and Stranraer is in connection with their football clubs. They are desperately important to their towns. They provide a sort of focal point. Often enough the social club is the town's major nightspot.' As for the football clubs themselves their main concern is for their own well-being —and in the football of today there is little that is immoral about that.

The problems that beset the Irish

Right *Diagram showing the location of all the Northern and Southern Ireland League clubs. Not surprisingly, they cluster around the capitals, Belfast and Dublin, where the clubs tend to be better supported. Indeed, Waterford usually play the home legs of their European Cup ties in Dublin for that very reason. In the North too, clubs play games at grounds not their own, but for a different reason. Derry City and Distillery have been forced out of their own grounds by the violence that civil war has brought to Ireland.*

It probably surprised Spanish football fans to discover that their team's European Championship qualifying match against Northern Ireland early in 1972 was to be played in Hull. After all, Hull is as inaccessible from Northern Ireland as is Spain itself.

But then the Spaniards, racked by civil war so recently, should have understood as well as any European nation. The Irish were experiencing one of the irregular flarings of internecine conflict that have beset the Emerald Isle for nigh on four centuries. And in the climate of the 1970s, the world game—soccer—could not possibly avoid the danger of being dragged into the troubles.

The gate for Ards' League game with Distillery—£18

In the violent four years that followed the resurgence of Catholic feeling over civil rights in 1968, two of Ulster's Irish League clubs—Derry City and Distillery—were forced to leave their grounds. Derry—the Catholic name for Londonderry—abandoned Brandywell when terrorists seized a visiting team's bus and set it alight. They settled for playing all their home games at less troubled Coleraine.

But none of Northern Ireland's major sides could hope to avoid a conflict that had led to the deaths of hundreds of citizens and daily bombings of public and private targets. The reluctance to venture out to traditional forms of entertainment virtually curtailed football as a spectator sport, and in 1972 Ards reported receipts of just £18 for their League game with Distillery.

It is simply impossible to consider Irish football—either historically or currently—without including politics. Ireland is divided into two parts, the North, commonly known as Northern Ireland or (inaccurately) Ulster, and the South, commonly known as the Republic of Ireland or Eire, the English translation of the Gaelic name for Ireland. (Between 1921 and 1945 Eire was known as the Irish Free State.) Each of these two parts has its own football association and football league. In the North these are known as the Irish FA and the Irish League, in the South they are usually called the FA of Ireland and the League of Ireland.

Even the very names cause problems. In the 1950s FIFA insisted that the Irish FA call its international teams Northern Ireland, in recognition of the fact that they only draw on 6 of the 32 counties

Above *The programme for the 1972 Northern Ireland–Scotland game shows the kind of difficulties Irish football has had to face. For Ireland, at home to Scotland, were forced by the Belfast troubles to play the match at Hampden.*

of the island. The Belfast-centred organization refused, however, preferring to send out teams under the patently false name 'Ireland'. Technically Belfast is entitled to select players from the Republic of Ireland (FIFA's official name) for Home International matches—though in practice they never do.

And the southern Irish, while not so troubled by the civil war raging in the north at the turn of the 1970s, have been unable to avoid at least a share of an all-too familiar political history on the field.

Though it was abating in 1972, the main stumbling block to football in Eire over the years had long been the Gaelic Athletic Association. They imposed a weighty ban, under rule 27, stipulating that none of their members could play the 'alien' (ie English) games of football, cricket,

rugby or hockey, or could help promote those sports. Gaelic football and hurling, the national games, were considered the only acceptable sports, and for a long time there was tremendous animosity shown to anybody breaking that rule.

The youngsters bore the brunt of the Gaelic AA's dictum. The parish priest and the schoolteacher, urging them to involve themselves in religion and compelling them to speak Gaelic, made sure that to ignore the GAA's ruling meant a major decision of conscience, especially for a teenager.

Johnny Giles, an outstanding Gaelic footballer at school, could only play soccer at weekends, and then, in common with other youngsters, every effort had to be made to keep out of sight of the local priest or the schoolmaster. To be

spotted playing football meant a severe telling-off, for such actions bordered on treachery. Only at the start of the 1970s was this ban lifted.

But the real tragedy of Irish football is that for 50 years the Football Association of Ireland, controlling the game in 26 counties, and the Irish Football Association, with recognized jurisdiction over six, have gone their separate ways.

Unfortunately, other than the unlikely possibility of a major change on the political scene, there appears to be little chance of a fusion between the two associations and Ireland ever again fielding an international side representative of the whole island.

The pity is that, despite Northern Ireland's heartening success over England at Wembley in the 1972 Home Championship, if Ireland is ever again to become even a minor power in world soccer, she needs a team drawn from the 32 counties.

The honeymooner who introduced football to Ireland

Things, of course, were all so happily different in the last quarter of the nineteenth century when the infant game of soccer, introduced to the country by one John McAlery of Belfast, took its first unsteady steps in Ulster.

McAlery's part in the establishment of soccer in Ireland has been embellished by Celtic legend. He is reputed to have been on his honeymoon in Glasgow when he came across a group of youngsters playing football, a game which was then strange to him. He took the time to learn something of it and then, armed with the rules of the new sport, he set about introducing it to Ireland.

At McAlery's invitation, two of Scotland's leading clubs of the time, Queen's Park and Caledonians, came to Belfast on 24 October 1878 to play an exhibition match at the Ulster Cricket Club ground. Queen's Park won 3-2. The general reaction to the fixture seemed to be enthusiastic.

McAlery was there to capitalize on that enthusiasm. He went on a soccer pilgrimage throughout Ulster and the result of his fervent preaching was the establishment of Ireland's first club, Cliftonville FC. They were followed by Ulster FC, and gradually other clubs sprung up.

Cliftonville's first game, played on 11 October 1879, was, in fact, against a scratch side made up of 11 rugby players and the records show that Cliftonville lost by two goals to one. Despite this embarrass-

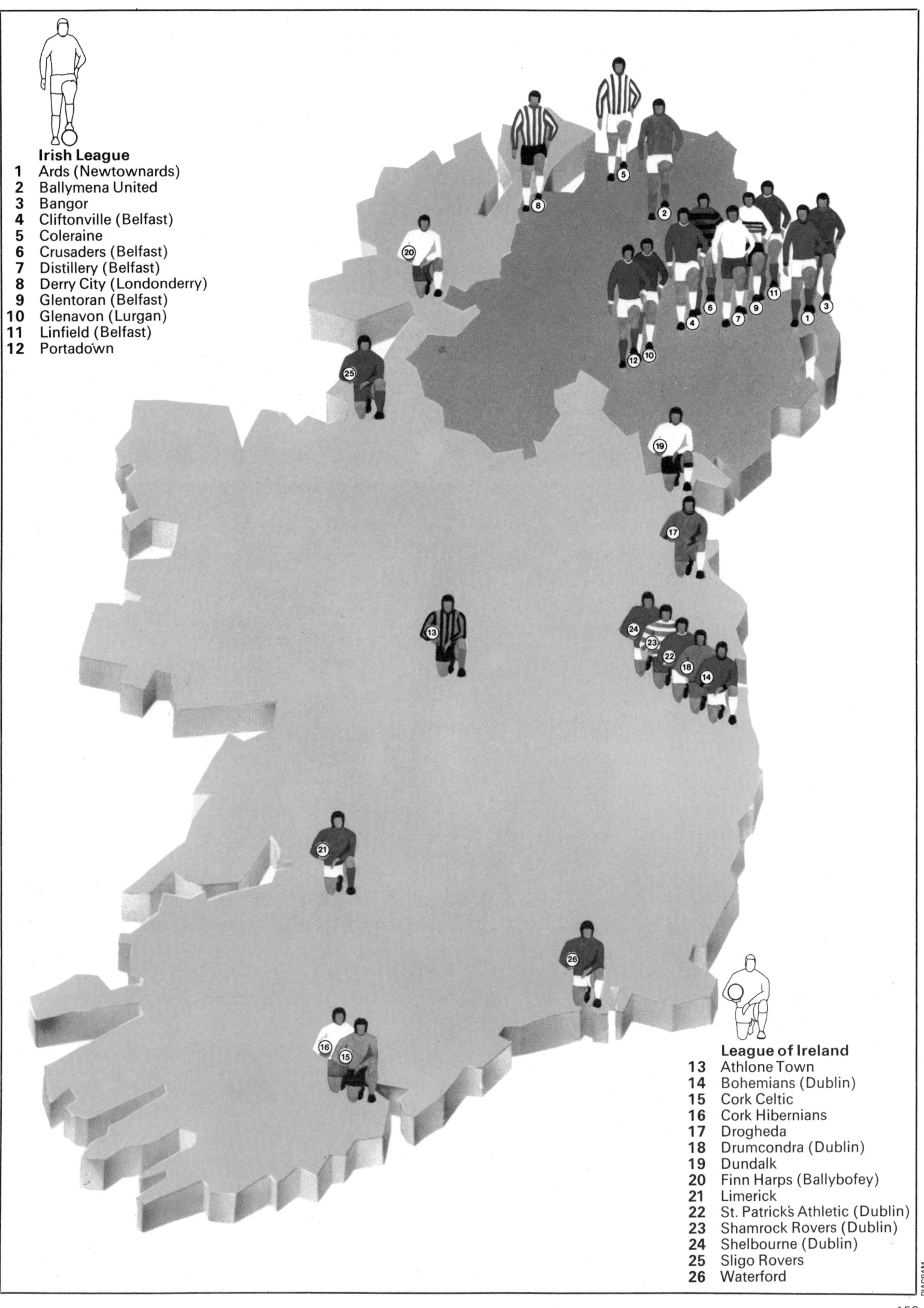

Irish League
1 Ards (Newtownards)
2 Ballymena United
3 Bangor
4 Cliftonville (Belfast)
5 Coleraine
6 Crusaders (Belfast)
7 Distillery (Belfast)
8 Derry City (Londonderry)
9 Glentoran (Belfast)
10 Glenavon (Lurgan)
11 Linfield (Belfast)
12 Portadown

League of Ireland
13 Athlone Town
14 Bohemians (Dublin)
15 Cork Celtic
16 Cork Hibernians
17 Drogheda
18 Drumcondra (Dublin)
19 Dundalk
20 Finn Harps (Ballybofey)
21 Limerick
22 St. Patrick's Athletic (Dublin)
23 Shamrock Rovers (Dublin)
24 Shelbourne (Dublin)
25 Sligo Rovers
26 Waterford

ing debut, both Cliftonville and football survived.

Its popularity eventually demanded further organization and once again McAlery stepped into the picture. He convened a major meeting at the Queen's Hotel, Belfast on 18 November 1880, and from this came the Irish Football Association. McAlery was the Association's first honorary secretary while its first President was a Major Spencer Chichester—a surname to be familiar in the area nearly a century later.

One of the major decisions of that first meeting was that a proper form of inter-club competition should be introduced immediately—and so began the IFA Cup championship. A trophy was subsequently purchased for £55.18.6 and seven clubs—Alexander, Avoniel, Cliftonville, Distillery, Knock, Oldpark and Moyola Park (the winners) competed for it.

The next significant milestone in Irish soccer came on 18 February 1882 when Ireland played their first international. They took on the might of England at the Knock FC ground, and met disaster. England romped to a 13-0 victory, still a record score for a Home International, and a chastening experience for Ireland's captain—the ubiquitous John McAlery. It did not deter—within eight years the Irish League had been formed.

By this time the game had spread slowly to the South, where it had to contend not only with rugby, but also with the national games of Gaelic football and hurling. The first southern club, Dublin Association, was formed in 1883. Shortly afterwards a club was started at Dublin University, and in November 1883, they provided Dublin with its first game of football, at University College Park. Progress, however, was slow and it was not until October 1892, that the game got its first and lasting recognition in southern Ireland with the introduction of the Leinster Senior Cup.

Ireland is traditionally divided into four regions—Leinster, Munster, Ulster and Connaught. Leinster comprises the counties around Dublin. The first title holders were Leinster Nomads who beat Dublin University 2-1 in the 1893 final. The game was watched by 900 spectators who had paid sixpence each, with ladies and soldiers in uniform admitted free!

Bohemians and Shelbourne were the first teams from the south to be admitted to the Irish League. Surprisingly, neither they nor any other southern team ever managed to take the League pennant, though it was Shelbourne who came closest to it in 1906-07 when they finished runners-up to the famous Linfield. The unfruitful tide eventually turned for the southern clubs in 1906 with Shelbourne's success in the Irish Cup. After losing to Distillery in the 1905 final, they returned the following year to beat Belfast Celtic and take the Cup out of the north for the first time.

Shelbourne were also to take the Irish Cup on another occasion—an unhappy moment in the history of Irish soccer.

In 1920, following an investiga-

tion into the Irish Cup semi-final between Belfast Celtic and Glentoran at which revolver shots were fired, causing near panic in a large crowd, the Celtic fans were held responsible and the Belfast team were removed from the competition.

A subsequent protest by Celtic against the fielding of an ineligible player by Glentoran was upheld, and they too were dismissed from the competition. This left Shelbourne, winners of the other semi-final, as the only qualified finalists and so they were awarded the Cup. It was the last time the Irish Cup would, in fact, go to Dublin.

The celebrated 'split' in Irish soccer was imminent. The seeds of discontent between officials in Dublin and those in the IFA in Belfast had been planted years earlier and were now unhappily beginning to sprout.

All over Ireland in 1920-21 armed men were making attacks on police barracks and carrying out ambushes. Owing to these outbreaks of violence, the Football League decided not to send a team to play the Irish League, but the Dublin teams, Bohemians, Shelbourne and St James' Gate, entered for the Irish Cup. Shelbourne reached the semi-final and went to Belfast to play the Lurgan club, Glenavon, but no goals were scored. In the other semi-final, Glentoran defeated Brantwood 4-3.

The North and the South go their separate ways

The Protest and Appeals Committee of the IFA decided, owing to conditions in Dublin and other parts of Ireland, that the Glenavon-Shelbourne tie should be replayed in Belfast—a decision which many in the north thought unwise. Shelbourne understandably refused to travel again to Belfast. This left Glenavon to fight out the final with Glentoran, who won 2-0.

For some time prior to 1920, the south had become extremely bitter about all Ireland's soccer affairs being ruled by the IFA in Belfast, and the bitterness had been fanned by several autocratic rulings from Belfast in regard to certain fixtures. This merely strengthened the already solid belief in Dublin that soccer affairs in the south now warranted separate control. The creation of an independent Irish Free State in 1921 inevitably concreted this feeling. Independent parliaments for north and south were established by June 1921 and the final treaty between the southern Irish and the rest of the United Kingdom was signed in December 1921. The rumblings and murmurings of separation eventually became reality at Dublin's Molesworth Hall on 1 September 1921 when the decision to create the Football Association of Ireland was taken. Among the clubs represented at the meeting were Shelbourne, Bohemians, Midland Athletic, Athlone YMCA, Frankfort, St James' Gate and Jacobs.

Plans were formulated to establish separate cup and league competitions and these began almost immediately. St James' Gate won both the FAI

27. Any member who plays, attends or helps to promote Rugby, Soccer, Hockey or Cricket thereby incurs automatic suspension from membership of the Association. Reinstatement of offenders may be granted only by Provincial Councils on the recommendation of County Committees concerned. Such reinstatements are subject to the following provisions, viz.,

(a) *Attending such games*: at least three months shall have elapsed from the date of last offence.

(b) *Playing or promoting such games*: At least six months in the case of a first offence, and two years in the case of a subsequent offence, shall have elapsed from date of last offence. Reinstatement under (b) be granted only between 1st January and Easter Sunday in each year.

This rule shall not apply to persons who were never previously members of the Association. Such persons may be admitted to membership upon personal application to the County Committee, provided they have not played or encouraged excluded games for three months prior to their application.

County Committees may also admit as members boys under 19 years of age who have played excluded games. In this case personal application shall be required.

GAELIC ATHLETIC ASSOCIATION

COLORSPORT

Top *The Gaelic Athletic Association's infamous Rule 27, forbidding its members to play football. Only revoked in 1970, the rule meant youngsters in the south had to oppose their schoolteachers and priests if they were keen to play the game.*
Centre *Irish international Bryan Hamilton. In 1972, Linfield turned a £13,000 deficit—the result of the civil war's effect on attendances—into a £7,000 profit by selling Hamilton to Ipswich.*
Above *Bobby Moore chats with soldiers keeping an eye on an Irish ground. Derry had to leave theirs after a visiting team's coach had been set alight.*

IRELAND'S LEAGUE AND CUP WINNERS

	Irish League	Irish Cup	League of Ireland (Eire)	FA of Ireland Cup (Eire)
1880-81		Moyola Park		
1881-82		Queen's Island		
1882-83		Cliftonville		
1883-84		Distillery		
1884-85		Distillery		
1885-86		Distillery		
1886-87		Ulster		
1887-88		Cliftonville		
1888-89		Distillery		
1889-90		Gordon Highlanders		
1890-91	Linfield	Linfield		
1891-92	Linfield	Linfield		
1892-93	Linfield	Linfield		
1893-94	Glentoran	Distillery		
1894-95	Linfield	Linfield		
1895-96	Distillery	Distillery		
1896-97	Glentoran	Cliftonville		
1897-98	Linfield	Linfield		
1898-99	Distillery	Linfield		
1899-00	Belfast Celtic	Cliftonville		
1900-01	Distillery	Cliftonville		
1901-02	Linfield	Linfield		
1902-03	Distillery	Distillery		
1903-04	Linfield	Linfield		
1904-05	Glentoran	Distillery		
1905-06	*	Shelbourne		
1906-07	Linfield	Cliftonville		
1907-08	Linfield	Bohemians		
1908-09	Linfield	Cliftonville		
1909-10	Cliftonville	Distillery		
1910-11	Linfield	Shelbourne		
1911-12	Glentoran	†Cup awarded to Linfield		
1912-13	Glentoran	Linfield		
1913-14	Linfield	Glentoran		
1914-15	Belfast Celtic	Linfield		
1915-16	No competition	Linfield		
1916-17	No competition	Glentoran		
1917-18	No competition	Belfast Celtic		
1918-19	No competition	Linfield		
1919-20	Belfast Celtic	‡Cup awarded to Shelbourne		
1920-21	Glentoran	Glentoran		
1921-22	Linfield	Linfield	St James' Gate	St James' Gate
1922-23	Linfield	Linfield	Shamrock Rovers	Alton United
1923-24	Queen's Island	Queen's Island	Bohemians	Athlone Town
1924-25	Glentoran	Distillery	Shamrock Rovers	Shamrock Rovers
1925-26	Belfast Celtic	Belfast Celtic	Shelbourne	Fordsons
1926-27	Belfast Celtic	Ards	Shamrock Rovers	Drumcondra
1927-28	Belfast Celtic	Willowfield	Bohemians	Bohemians
1928-29	Belfast Celtic	Ballymena	Shelbourne	Shamrock Rovers
1929-30	Linfield	Linfield	Bohemians	Shamrock Rovers
1930-31	Glentoran	Linfield	Shelbourne	Shamrock Rovers
1931-32	Linfield	Glentoran	Shamrock Rovers	Shamrock Rovers
1932-33	Belfast Celtic	Glentoran	Dundalk	Shamrock Rovers
1933-34	Linfield	Linfield	Bohemians	Cork
1934-35	Linfield	Glentoran	Dolphin	Bohemians
1935-36	Belfast Celtic	Linfield	Bohemians	Shamrock Rovers
1936-37	Belfast Celtic	Belfast Celtic	Sligo Rovers	Waterford
1937-38	Belfast Celtic	Belfast Celtic	Shamrock Rovers	St James' Gate
1938-39	Belfast Celtic	Linfield	Shamrock Rovers	Shelbourne
1939-40	No competition	Ballymena United	St James' Gate	Shamrock Rovers
1940-41	No competition	Belfast Celtic	Cork United	Cork United
1941-42	No competition	Linfield	Cork United	Dundalk
1942-43	No competition	Belfast Celtic	Cork United	Drumcondra
1943-44	No competition	Belfast Celtic	Shelbourne	Shamrock Rovers
1944-45	No competition	Linfield	Cork United	Shamrock Rovers
1945-46	No competition	Linfield	Cork United	Drumcondra
1946-47	Belfast Celtic	Belfast Celtic	Shelbourne	Cork United
1947-48	Belfast Celtic	Linfield	Drumcondra	Shamrock Rovers
1948-49	Linfield	Derry City	Drumcondra	Dundalk
1949-50	Linfield	Linfield	Cork Athletic	Transport
1950-51	Glentoran	Glentoran	Cork Athletic	Cork Athletic
1951-52	Glenavon	Ards	St Patrick's Athletic	Dundalk
1952-53	Glentoran	Linfield	Shelbourne	Cork Athletic
1953-54	Linfield	Derry City	Shamrock Rovers	Drumcondra
1954-55	Linfield	Dundela	St Patrick's Athletic	Shamrock Rovers
1955-56	Linfield	Distillery	St Patrick's Athletic	Shamrock Rovers
1956-57	Glenavon	Glenavon	Shamrock Rovers	Drumcondra
1957-58	Ards	Ballymena United	Drumcondra	Dundalk
1958-59	Linfield	Glentoran	Shamrock Rovers	St Patrick's Athletic
1959-60	Glenavon	Linfield	Limerick	Shelbourne
1960-61	Linfield	Glenavon	Drumcondra	St Patrick's Athletic
1961-62	Linfield	Linfield	Shelbourne	Shamrock Rovers
1962-63	Distillery	Linfield	Dundalk	Shelbourne
1963-64	Glentoran	Derry City	Shamrock Rovers	Shamrock Rovers
1964-65	Derry City	Coleraine	Drumcondra	Shamrock Rovers
1965-66	Linfield	Glentoran	Waterford	Shamrock Rovers
1966-67	Glentoran	Crusaders	Dundalk	Shamrock Rovers
1967-68	Glentoran	Crusaders	Waterford	Shamrock Rovers
1968-69	Linfield	Ards	Waterford	Shamrock Rovers
1969-70	Glentoran	Linfield	Waterford	Bohemians
1970-71	Linfield	Distillery	Cork Hibernians	Limerick
1971-72	Glentoran	Coleraine	Waterford	Cork Hibernians
1972-73	Crusaders	Glentoran	Waterford	Cork Hibernians

*Cliftonville and Distillery (shared).

†A dispute between several of the major clubs and the Irish FA and County Antrim FA resulted in the disruption of the Cup competition. Linfield won one of the semi-finals and were awarded the Cup in the absence of the other major clubs, who had gone on to organize their own version of the Irish Cup that year, which Belfast Celtic won by beating Glentoran 2-0.

‡After a riot at the Belfast Celtic v Glentoran semi-final both clubs were disqualified from the competition. In Celtic's case this was as a result of the referee's report, in Glentoran's because they included an ineligible player. Shelbourne had won the other semi-final and, in the absence of any opposition, were awarded the Cup.

Cup and FAI League in 1921-22. But Irish football was still very much in a state of confusion. Teams from the Falls and District League of Belfast (mainly composed of Catholic teams) were permitted to enter for the FAI Cup and in 1923, there was embarrassment all round when Alton United of Belfast succeeded in winning the Cup in the south.

The Alton United players were prevented from taking the Cup across the border into Northern Ireland, but at least they did get their winners medals. As a result of their success, there was a tacit agreement between the FAI and the IFA to respect each other's jurisdiction in matters relating to the running of their various domestic competitions.

For two years after its formation, the Football Association of Ireland remained an outlaw without recognition. However, following a meeting of the International Board, comprising England, Scotland, Wales and Ireland (meaning Belfast) the FAI were granted recognition on the condition that its name would be changed to the Football Association of the Irish Free State. Later that year, in August 1923, the association was accepted into membership of FIFA.

Six months later, at the Paris Olympic Games, the new association got off to a good start by beating Bulgaria 1-0, before losing to the Netherlands in the next round.

By now, the Irish Free State and Northern Ireland should have been separate entities as far as international competition was concerned. But, unfortunately, they were not. The Irish Football Association continued to select players from the Free State for its international sides and this unhappy state of affairs, a source of immense bitterness, continued until just after the Second World War.

Cardiff City's goalkeeper, Tom Farquharson, who had been capped for both the Irish Free State and Northern Ireland in the 1920s, was probably the first man to bring this particular issue into the open. In 1931, he publicly declared his allegiance to the Irish Free State and stated that he no longer wished to be selected for any Northern Ireland international side.

Johnny Carey plays for both Irelands within three days

However, his stand did not alter the situation and the IFA continued to pick southern players for international games. Even after the War, famous personalities from the south —Johnny Carey, Con Martin, Tommy Eglinton, Peter Farrell and Dave Walsh—regularly appeared on Northern Ireland sides. Carey actually managed to play for both sides within three days—both times against a full England side!

It was only in 1949 that the position resolved itself. With the south declaring itself a republic, the FA of Ireland was then able to get an undertaking from all its members that they would not play for any country other than the Republic of Ireland.

In September of that year, as if in celebration of their improved position, the Republic provided football with one of its most memorable upsets. Taking the field at Goodison Park on Wednesday 21st as rank outsiders, they left it after 90 minutes the first team from outside the Home Countries to defeat England on English soil. A 33rd minute penalty from Con Martin and a goal from Everton's Peter Farrell five minutes from time struck the blows.

Five years later FIFA cleared up a last bone of contention between the two Irish associations. There had been constant confusion and bitterness over the fact that both north and south insisted on being called Ireland. FIFA ruled that from then on the IFA would use the name 'Northern Ireland', and the FAI teams would be known as the 'Republic of Ireland'.

It was under their new name that the north achieved their greatest success. A few months before the 1958 World Cup in Sweden— Northern Ireland had qualified for the finals by beating Italy and Portugal—they had hinted at the good things to come with a 3-2 win over England at Wembley.

In Sweden, Northern Ireland beat Czechoslovakia 1-0, then lost to Argentina 3-1, drew 2-2 with West Germany and then beat Czechoslovakia again in the group play-off to move into the quarter-finals. Their 4-0 defeat in that round by France reflected the sad fact that they had little reserve strength in Sweden; they were forced to field two unfit players against the Frenchmen.

Why the Bests and the Conroys leave for England

For despite scoring a 1-0 win over England in the 1972 Home Championship, Northern Ireland have long suffered from a shortage of top-class players. It is a complaint that obviously affects the Republic too, and merely serves to illustrate the need for both Irelands to join forces.

'Divide and weaken' has all too much relevance to football in Ireland. But then the game there is necessarily second rate. Any good players like Best, Giles or Conroy, be they from north or south, emigrate to England as soon as the opportunity presents itself. Inevitably their allegiance is to the clubs that pay their wages and when Eire sent a side to Brazil's independence celebrations in 1972 it included none of the stars who had succeeded in England.

Clubs in the north and south of Ireland share one feature at least— they have to sell to survive. In 1972 Linfield made £7,000 profit. It would have been a £13,000 loss but for the sale of Bryan Hamilton to Ipswich.

And while civil war prowled the streets of this strangely medieval island there was little hope of the situation improving. 'An Irishman will do anything for his country except live in it,' said one emigre called George Bernard Shaw. As far as football was concerned that seemed to be an essential in the seventies for both the players and their long-suffering clubs.

The easy route to Europe

THE MAJOR COMPETITIONS

It has become the fashion in Britain to criticize other nations' domestic cup competitions. It is said, with undoubted justification, that in some countries they exist merely to provide a club side with entry to European competition. What is less readily recognized is that much closer to home there is a tournament which nowadays seems to exist for very similar reasons.

In the years between 1964 and 1972 one Football League club managed to gain entry to the European Cup Winners Cup every season but one. If that club were Manchester City or Chelsea, it would have been a remarkable achievement. But the club in question spent the whole of that period in the Second Division, and gained their valued entry ticket simply by virtue of winning the Welsh Cup.

The club was, of course, Cardiff City. In those eight years they played 15 home ties in European competitions—including games against teams like Sporting Lisbon, SV Hamburg and Real Madrid—and the income those ties represent would

not be sneered at by the best First Division managements. And while in the eight years after 1963, Cardiff failed to win only one of the eight Welsh Cups, in the previous thirty years they had won the competition just twice. It could only have been the appeal of Europe that sharpened Cardiff's interest.

Even so, they were slow to catch on. In 1962, Cheshire League club Bangor City took the trophy and then beat AC Napoli—of the Italian First Division—in the home leg of a European tie. Bangor took Napoli to a play-off before going out.

The following year, the Welsh representatives, Borough United were even more of an oddity. United came from Llandudno Junction, a small North Wales railway town with a population of 2,000. Yet despite their humble origins, these most inferior of underdogs held Slovan Bratislava to one goal in Wales and three in Czechoslovakia.

After that Cardiff took over the competition but, despite the added attraction of a place in Europe as a reward, public interest in the Welsh

Cup was on the decline. As late as 1956 nearly 40,000 watched Cardiff beat Swansea, yet by 1972 Wrexham and Cardiff could draw only 6,000 for a leg of their final.

The decline in attendances induced the Welsh FA to try and force more money from the competition by playing it on a home-and-away basis in 1962—and they also preferred not to decide the competition on an aggregate basis but to play a third game if the contestants won one game each.

When the Cup was first organized, the Welsh FA were obviously equally hampered by lack of funds. At the time of the first final, in 1878, they could not even afford a trophy. Thus the finalists, Wrexham and The Druids, in the words of one of the players, 'fought for something we were going to have, we hoped.'

They were the remainder of an entry of 19—all but Swansea coming from North Wales and the border country. That was indicative of the balance of power in Welsh football—not until 1912 did a southern club win the trophy. Welsh football, as

Opposite page The victorious Chirk team of 1890. Chirk, a small village on the River Dee, reached six Welsh Cup finals between 1887 and 1894 and lost only one. Billy Meredith is thought to be second from the right on the bottom row.
Above Cardiff score against SV Hamburg in a European Cup Winners Cup semifinal. Cardiff used the Welsh Cup as their means of entry to European competition.

WELSH CUP FINALS 1878-1973

Year	Venue	Winners		Runners-up	
1878	Wrexham	Wrexham	1	Druids	0
1879	Wrexham	Newtown	1	Wrexham	0
1880	Wrexham	Druids	2	Ruthin	1
1881	Wrexham	Druids	2	Newtown White Stars	0
1882	Wrexham	Druids	2	Northwich	1
1883	Wrexham	Wrexham	1	Druids	0
1884	Wrexham	Oswestry	3	Druids	2
1885	Wrexham	Druids	2	Oswestry	0
1886	Wrexham	Druids	5	Newtown	2
1887	Wrexham	Chirk	4	Davenham	2
1888	Wrexham	Chirk	5	Newtown	0
1889	Wrexham	Bangor	2	Northwich	1
1890	Wrexham	Chirk	1	Wrexham	0
1891	Oswestry	Shrewsbury	5	Wrexham	2
1892	Wrexham	Chirk	2	Westminster Rovers	1
1893	Oswestry	Wrexham	2	Chirk	1
1894	Ruabon	Chirk	2	Westminster Rovers	0
1895	Welshpool	Newtown	3	Wrexham	2
1896	Llandudno	Bangor	3	Wrexham	1
1897	Oswestry	Wrexham	2	Newtown	0
1898	Oswestry	Druids	1	Wrexham	1
Replay	Oswestry	Druids	2	Wrexham	1
1899	Chirk	Druids	2	Wrexham	2
Replay	Chirk	Druids	1	Wrexham	0
1900	Newtown	Aberystwyth	3	Druids	0
1901	Wrexham	Oswestry	1	Druids	0
1902	Wrexham	Wellington	1	Wrexham	0
1903	Wrexham	Wrexham	8	Aberaman	0
1904	Wrexham	Druids	3	Aberdare	2
1905	Wrexham	Wrexham	3	Aberdare	0
1906	Wrexham	Wellington	3	Whitchurch	2
1907	Wrexham	Oswestry	2	Whitchurch	0
1908	Wrexham	Chester	3	Connah's Quay	1
1909	Wrexham	Wrexham	1	Chester	0
1910	Wrexham	Wrexham	2	Chester	1
1911	Wrexham	Wrexham	6	Connah's Quay	0
1912	Cardiff	Cardiff City	0	Pontypridd	0
Replay	Aberdare	Cardiff City	3	Pontypridd	0
1913	Cardiff	Swansea	0	Pontypridd	0
Replay	Mid-Rhondda	Swansea	1	Pontypridd	0
1914	Swansea	Wrexham	1	Llanelli	1
Replay	Oswestry	Wrexham	1	Llanelli	0
1915	Wrexham	Wrexham	1	Swansea	1
Replay	Cardiff	Wrexham	1	Swansea	0
1916-1919	*Competition suspended*				
1920	Wrexham	Cardiff City	2	Wrexham	1
1921	Cardiff	Wrexham	1	Pontypridd	1
Replay	Shrewsbury	Wrexham	3	Pontypridd	1
1922	Pontypridd	Cardiff City	2	Ton Pentre	0
1923	Swansea	Cardiff City	3	Aberdare	2
1924	Pontypridd	Wrexham	2	Merthyr Town	2
Replay	Wrexham	Wrexham	1	Merthyr Town	0
1925	Wrexham	Wrexham	3	Flint Town	1
1926	Ebbw Vale	Ebbw Vale	3	Swansea Town	2
1927	Wrexham	Cardiff City	2	Rhyl	0
1928	Bangor	Cardiff City	2	Bangor City	0
1929	Wrexham	Connah's Quay	3	Cardiff City	0
1930	Shrewsbury	Cardiff City	0	Rhyl	0
Replay	Wrexham	Cardiff City	4	Rhyl	2
1931	Wrexham	Wrexham	7	Shrewsbury Town	0
1932	Wrexham	Swansea Town	1	Wrexham	1
Replay	Swansea	Swansea Town	2	Wrexham	0
1933	Chester	Chester	2	Wrexham	0
1934	Wrexham	Bristol City	1	Tranmere Rovers	1
Replay	Chester	Bristol City	3	Tranmere Rovers	0
1935	Chester	Tranmere Rovers	1	Chester	0
1936	Wrexham	Crewe Alexandra	2	Chester	0
1937	Chester	Crewe Alexandra	1	Rhyl	1
Replay	Chester	Crewe Alexandra	3	Rhyl	1
1938	Shrewsbury	Shrewsbury Town	2	Swansea Town	1
1939	Wrexham	South Liverpool	2	Cardiff City	1
1940	Shrewsbury	Wellington Town	4	Swansea Town	0
1941-1946	*Competition suspended*				
1947	Cardiff	Chester	0	Merthyr Tydfil	0
Replay	Wrexham	Chester	5	Merthyr Tydfil	1
1948	Wrexham	Lovell's Athletic	3	Shrewsbury Town	0
1949	Cardiff	Merthyr Tydfil	2	Swansea Town	0
1950	Cardiff	Swansea Town	4	Wrexham	1
1951	Swansea	Merthyr Tydfil	1	Cardiff City	1
Replay	Swansea	Merthyr Tydfil	3	Cardiff City	2
1952	Cardiff	Rhyl	4	Merthyr Tydfil	3
1953	Bangor	Rhyl	2	Chester	1
1954	Wrexham	Flint Town United	2	Chester	0
1955	Wrexham	Barry Town	1	Chester	1
Replay	Cardiff	Barry Town	4	Chester	3
1956	Cardiff	Cardiff City	3	Swansea Town	2
1957	Cardiff	Wrexham	2	Swansea Town	1
1958	Chester	Wrexham	1	Chester	1
Replay	Wrexham	Wrexham	2	Chester	1
1959	Newport	Cardiff City	2	Lovell's Athletic	0
1960	Cardiff	Wrexham	1	Cardiff City	1
Replay	Wrexham	Wrexham	1	Cardiff City	0
1961	Cardiff	Swansea Town	3	Bangor City	1
1962	*	Bangor City	0:2	Wrexham	3:0
Play-off	Rhyl	Bangor City	3	Wrexham	1
1963	*	Borough United	2:0	Newport County	1:0
1964	*	Cardiff City	0:3	Bangor City	2:1
Play-off	Wrexham	Cardiff City	2	Bangor City	0
1965	*	Cardiff City	5:0	Wrexham	1:1
Play-off	Shrewsbury	Cardiff City	3	Wrexham	0
1966	*	Swansea Town	3:0	Chester	0:1
Play-off	Chester	Swansea Town	2	Chester	1
1967	*	Cardiff City	2:2	Wrexham	2:1
1968	*	Cardiff City	2:4	Hereford United	0:1
1969	*	Cardiff City	3:2	Swansea Town	1:0
1970	*	Cardiff City	1:4	Chester	0:0
1971	*	Cardiff City	1:3	Wrexham	0:1
1972	*	Wrexham	2:1	Cardiff City	1:1
1973	*	Cardiff City	0:5	Bangor City	1:0

*Final played on a home-and-away basis *but* not decided on aggregate score.

opposed to South Wales rugby, started in Wrexham, and the headquarters of the Welsh Football Association have remained there ever since.

When a trophy was finally purchased it cost all of £100—five times the amount the English FA had paid for theirs in 1872. Appropriately, Wrexham became the first holders, when they defeated Druids 1-0. Captaining the losers was Llewelyn Kenrick, the founder of the Welsh FA.

Local teams dominated the competition right through to the twentieth century. Wrexham, Druids, Newtown and Chirk were the familiar names, and of those the last was certainly the most interesting.

The Welsh Cup— Cardiff's passport to Europe

Chirk is a small village—a genuine village as opposed to a small town—on the River Dee. But between 1887 and 1894 Chirk appeared in six finals and won all but one. The man behind the village's success was T E Thomas, headmaster at Chirk School and a man reputed to have introduced 49 future Welsh internationals to the game. Of that number, one stands head and shoulders above the rest—the legendary Billy Meredith.

It was the final of 1894, when Chirk beat Westminster Rovers 2-0, that attracted Manchester City to Meredith, and his goal for that club in the 1904 FA Cup Final made him the first Welshman to gain winner's medals in both cup competitions.

Just as the FA Cup is open to a number of Welsh clubs, it has always been the policy at Wrexham to encourage entries from the English clubs just across the border. Oswestry were the first to take the Cup out of Wales—in 1884—and it made occasional trips across the divide long before Cardiff finally managed to become the first club to bring it to South Wales in 1912.

Fifteen years later Cardiff

achieved a far more notable feat by removing the FA Cup from Wembley, and then completing a unique double by beating Rhyl in the Welsh Cup final. Ten of their players won two winner's medals.

English clubs were quick to retaliate. In the years of the depression the Welsh League clubs suffered as grievously as the coal mines and Merthyr, Aberdare and Newport all left the League, while even mighty Cardiff had to seek re-election in 1934. English clubs filled the vacuum and the Cup remained over the border from 1933 to 1948.

The 1934 final was surely the oddest ever for, after a drawn game, Bristol City and Tranmere Rovers, both English clubs, fought out the final on an English ground, Chester's Sealand Road. The game had as much relevance to its sponsoring association as the FA Cup Final would have if Wrexham contested it with Newport County in Swansea.

The Welsh Cup undoubtedly reached its zenith with that 40,000 crowd for the final in 1956. Semifinal and final receipts that year amounted to £7,643—about the same as could be expected 16 years later with two-legged finals and prices four times higher. The success of 1956 merely serves to highlight the sad decline since.

It is a sorry fact of life, but hardly a surprising one. The Welsh FA cannot even allocate a Saturday for the game as their four Football League clubs are always engaged in-season, and it appears to be little more than one of those peripheral competitions which are dying in the shadows of the mass publicity that only the very best competitions get.

Not even the lure of Europe seems able to save it, and that is perhaps appropriate, for it must devalue European competition to recognize tournaments which can be won by a club like Borough United. Perhaps if Wales possessed two or three First Division sides the story would be different . . . perhaps. Still, it would be interesting to see EUFA's reaction if Bristol City ever tried to enter the European Cup Winners Cup on the strength of having won the Welsh Cup the season before!

Whose Footballer of the year?

The choice of the Footballer of the Year, whether it be the European, English or Scottish award, often reveals more about the choosers than the chosen. That is to say, the choice tends to be arbitrary and whimsical. So far as the English award is concerned, for many years it was influenced, far beyond the bounds of duty and logic, by the Cup Final and which teams had reached it. The selection of the European Player of the Year—winner of the Ballon d'Or, the Golden Ball, awarded by *France Football* magazine—is seriously debased by the fact that it is made on an annual rather than a seasonal basis, which can lead to some non-sensical results.

Almost every major football-playing country—though Italy is a proud exception—now seems to elect its Footballer of the Year. Football journalists in Great Britain also elect their top twelve players from Great Britain. These receive the Rothmans Golden Boots Award —though of the twelve selected for the 1971-72 team, only four saw fit to turn up in London to receive their mementoes.

France Football initiated their Ballon d'Or in 1956, when it was won by Stanley Matthews; a fair enough choice both in terms of Matthews' incomparable prestige, and his astonishing performance the previous May at Wembley for England against Brazil, when he turned the famous left-back, Nilton Santos, virtually inside out.

The system of voting has always been the same. One representative, a journalist, of every football-playing European country is asked to cast five votes, in order of preference and merit.

Bobby Charlton is chosen as Europe's number one player

For this purpose, Britain counts as just one country, though the Republic of Ireland gets a vote too. When all the lists have been received, marks are awarded on a basis of five points for first place on any voting list, four points for second and so on, in descending order. The points are then added together, and naturally enough, the footballer with most of them wins.

In World Cup years, this works well enough, because most of the candidates for the award are gathered together under the gaze of journalists at the same time and place. It is interesting to look back over the years and see just how great a part World Cups have in fact played in determining who receives the award.

Thus, in 1958, after the World Cup in Sweden, it is no surprise to see that the prize alighted on Raymond Kopa, who had a marvellous World Cup for France and who for many people had ranked, with Didi, as the best player of the tournament.

In 1962, the winner was Josef Masopust, who had crowned a splendid personal showing in Chile, as left-half for Czechoslovakia, by scoring a cool and memorable first goal for his side against Brazil in the final. 1966 was the turn of Bobby Charlton. An ironic aspect of his being chosen Europe's player of that year, however, was that the assembled world journalists were asked, in their hordes, to vote for the outstanding player, and they selected not Charlton but Bobby Moore! And yet they also picked Charlton for what he had done during the previous summer at Wembley.

West Germany's Gerd Muller, leading goalscorer in the Mexico World Cup, emerged a clear winner in 1970. The second choice was Bobby Moore. If anything, Moore had a better World Cup in 1970

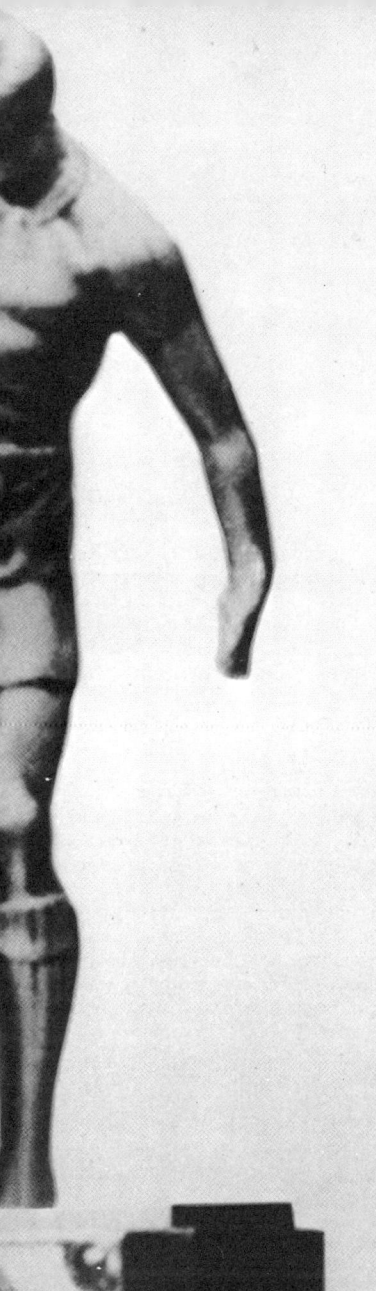

than he did when England won it in 1966 and he was voted the best player; but, not surprisingly, that fact was not relevant when the journalists in Mexico made their choice for the competition's best footballer.

Sometimes, again inevitably though not quite so acceptably, the European Cup plays a large part in the voting. This was seldom more evident than in 1968 when George Best became no less than the third Manchester United player and the fourth Briton to win the award. Best had had a superb match in the European Cup final at Wembley, when Manchester United overcame Benfica 4-1 thanks to his remarkable, individualist's goal early in extra time. But by the time he received his award, Best was not playing well. It was difficult to avoid the conclusion that he had been chosen on the basis of a single match, perhaps a legitimate philosophy when the match is a World Cup final, but scarcely so when it is a game below that level.

Alfredo di Stefano, centre-forward, motor and inspiration of the Real Madrid teams which dominated the European Cup for its first five seasons, very appropriately won the award in 1957 and in 1959; indeed he probably deserved to make it a hat-trick in 1960. That was the year di Stefano's former chief rival

Below Footballers of the Year. From left to right Stanley Matthews, first winner of the award in 1948, won it again fully 15 years later. Tom Finney was the first to win it twice, in 1954 and 1957, while Bert Trautmann, selected in 1956, was both the first foreigner and the first goalkeeper chosen. Danny Blanchflower collected two awards, in 1958 and 1961. The award was shared in 1969, by Dave Mackay and Tony Book.

in Spanish football, Luis Suarez, of Barcelona, was selected. It was an interesting choice in that Suarez, who would win so many honours in the ensuing years, did not win any in 1960. Five years later he would take third place, after Portugal's Eusebio, and his Internazionale colleague, Facchetti; but that was a long 22 points short of the black Benfica forward.

Written off one season, best in Europe the next

Denis Law has been the only Scotsman to win the European award so far; in 1964, as a Manchester United forward, having spent one season in Italy with Torino. The only goalkeeper to be chosen has been Russia's Lev Yashin, in 1963. That was a splendid vindication for Yashin, who only the previous year had been written off by many journalists—not least those of *France Football*—after an uncharacteristically poor and loose World Cup in Chile.

Apart from the problems presented by an annual rather than a seasonal basis of selection, the European Footballer of the Year poll is also seriously affected by the fact, made implicit in previous voting results, that few of the journalists concerned in the choice see most of the eligible players. Thus, even if the principle of a Player of the Year was acceptable, it could only really be reasonable to choose one within a given country.

The Scottish Player of the Year Award is perhaps the least blameworthy in this respect. The country is so much smaller an area to cover than Europe or England and Wales, and the Scottish League relatively so

limited, that it is quite feasible for the journalists who vote to regularly see and assess all the leading players.

The Scottish award, 17 years younger than its English counterpart, also seems rather less vulnerable to parochial pressure. Thus, when a Scot, Bobby Collins, won England's award in 1965, the opinion in the country at large was that this represented a deliberate attempt by a Northern block of journalists to get their man home by collusion. Leeds United, Collins' club, were at that time far from popular for their physical methods.

Billy McNeill, the first Scottish Footballer of the Year, was the first Celtic player to be honoured. Surprisingly only three of the first eight came from mighty Celtic.

The votes in the English poll have always been cast by members of the Football Writers' Association, the result being declared at about the time of the Cup Final. The award has always been taken very seriously in the game. Indeed, the story is told that as the Charlton brothers, Jackie and Bobby, stood side by side on the turf of Wembley, after helping England to win the 1966 World Cup final, Bobby almost tearfully asked his brother Jackie what more there was in football to strive for. Jackie sturdily replied that *he* was going to become Footballer of the Year; which he promptly did. Bobby himself had just won it in 1966; the only instance of brothers having both gained the honour, let alone in successive years.

The FA Cup Final has played a huge part in the naming of the English Footballer of the Year.

It was surely more than coincidence that the first Footballer of the Year award, in 1948, was made to Stanley Matthews, the year in which Blackpool reached the FA Cup Final

FOX PHOTOS

POPPERFOTO

for the first time. Three years later they were there again, and this time the award was given to another Blackpool player, the captain, Harry Johnston. Stanley Matthews—an extraordinary achievement—won a second Footballer of the Year award fully fifteen years later, in 1963. By this time he had returned to his original club, Stoke City, and, with high nostalgia, had helped them to climb back into the First Division. Though there may have been elements of nostalgia about the award as well, it was nevertheless a popular and most imaginative one; perhaps still more so than in 1948.

Matthews is in fact one of three players to have twice won the title. The first, oddly enough, was his rival and natural successor in the England team, Tom Finney, whose first Footballer of the Year honour also coincided with a Cup Final appearance, 1954, when Preston North End were beaten at Wembley by West Bromwich Albion. He succeeded again in 1957, by which time he had transformed himself from a superb two-footed winger into an equally brilliant, Kopa type of deep-lying, centre-forward.

Another Footballer of the Year whose award seemed influenced by the Cup Final was Joe Mercer, the veteran English international left-half, who was nominated in 1950, the year Arsenal won the Cup for the first time since the end of the War. 1955 and 1956, both years which saw Manchester City at Wembley, also saw the choice of Manchester City men. It was perhaps a little ironic that Don Revie should be chosen in 1955, when he ultimately finished on the losing side, while in 1956, belatedly recalled for the Final, he inspired City's victory over Birmingham City.

The link between the FA Cup and the award becomes clear

The choice that year in fact alighted on City's German goalkeeper, Bert Trautmann, deservedly considering Trautmann played on hampered by what was discovered after the Final to be a broken neck. Trautmann thus became the one foreigner to have been elected so far and the first goalkeeper. It would be another sixteen years before the England goalkeeper, Gordon Banks, a major star of the 1970 World Cup, became the second.

Footballer of the Year in 1958 was Danny Blanchflower. Blanchflower had given magnificent displays at right-half for Tottenham and Northern Ireland, captaining his country to their first Wembley success against England, and to a still greater victory over Italy, which qualified the Irish for the World Cup finals. Blanchflower in fact was to become the second player to win the Footballer of the Year award a second time when he led Spurs to their 1960-61 Cup and League double.

In between Blanchflower's coming top of the poll twice, Bill Slater emphasized the link between Cup and the award with his selection that followed his skippering Wolves to victory over Blackburn in 1960.

FOOTBALLER OF THE YEAR
Winners of the Football Writers Association poll

Season	Winner	Club
1947-48	Stanley Matthews	Blackpool
1948-49	Johnny Carey	Manchester United
1949-50	Joe Mercer	Arsenal
1950-51	Harry Johnston	Blackpool
1951-52	Billy Wright	Wolverhampton Wanderers
1952-53	Nat Lofthouse	Bolton Wanderers
1953-54	Tom Finney	Preston North End
1954-55	Don Revie	Manchester City
1955-56	Bert Trautmann	Manchester City
1956-57	Tom Finney	Preston North End
1957-58	Danny Blanchflower	Tottenham Hotspur
1958-59	Syd Owen	Luton Town
1959-60	Bill Slater	Wolverhampton Wanderers
1960-61	Danny Blanchflower	Tottenham Hotspur
1961-62	Jimmy Adamson	Burnley
1962-63	Stanley Matthews	Stoke City
1963-64	Bobby Moore	West Ham United
1964-65	Bobby Collins	Leeds United
1965-66	Bobby Charlton	Manchester United
1966-67	Jackie Charlton	Leeds United
1967-68	George Best	Manchester United
1968-69	Tony Book	Manchester City
1968-69	Dave Mackay	Derby County
1969-70	Billy Bremner	Leeds United
1970-71	Frank McLintock	Arsenal
1971-72	Gordon Banks	Stoke City
1972-73	Pat Jennings	Tottenham Hotspur

SCOTTISH PLAYER OF THE YEAR
Winners of the Scottish Football Writers Association poll

Season	Winner	Club
1964-65	Billy McNeill	Celtic
1965-66	John Greig	Rangers
1966-67	Ronnie Simpson	Celtic
1967-68	Gordon Wallace	Raith Rovers
1968-69	Bobby Murdoch	Celtic
1969-70	Pat Stanton	Hibernian
1970-71	Martin Buchan	Aberdeen
1971-72	David Smith	Rangers
1972-73	George Connelly	Celtic

EUROPEAN FOOTBALLER OF THE YEAR
Winners of the *France Football* poll

Year	Winner	Club & Country
1956	Stanley Matthews	Blackpool & England
1957	Alfredo di Stefano	Real Madrid & Spain
1958	Raymond Kopa	Real Madrid & France
1959	Alfredo di Stefano	Real Madrid & Spain
1960	Luis Suarez	Barcelona & Spain
1961	Enrique Sivori	Juventus & Italy
1962	Josef Masopust	Dukla Prague & Czechoslovakia
1963	Lev Yashin	Moscow Dynamo & USSR
1964	Denis Law	Manchester United & Scotland
1965	Eusebio	Benfica & Portugal
1966	Bobby Charlton	Manchester United & England
1967	Florian Albert	Ferencvaros & Hungary
1968	George Best	Manchester United & Northern Ireland
1969	Gianni Rivera	AC Milan & Italy
1970	Gerd Muller	Bayern Munich & West Germany
1971	Johann Cruyff	Ajax & Netherlands
1972	Franz Beckenbauer	Bayern Munich & West Germany
1973	Johann Cruyff	Barcelona & Netherlands

Above *Two winners, Dave Mackay and Billy Bremner.*

Bobby Moore, so dominant a player in English football for a decade, almost inevitably had to wait till he captained West Ham to a Cup Final, in 1964, before joining the roll call.

Two years previously, Jimmy Adamson had received the award after captaining Burnley to . . . the Cup Final of 1962! It was, for all that, a laudable choice, not least because Adamson, a solid and versatile right-half, never did win a cap for England. After the Cup Final, indeed, he went off to the Chilean World Cup as the England team's coach.

The veteran trio show up their younger rivals

Other players whose selection as the season's best player was plainly due to a large extent to their Cup Final appearances were Nat Lofthouse, the Bolton centre-forward, in 1953, and Syd Owen, the Luton Town centre-half, in 1959, exactly five years after he had played, with little success, in a World Cup series for England. Not surprisingly, the League Cup final was by the seventies accumulating similar prestige and influence, Gordon Banks, not being chosen until the year his club, Stoke City, won it, despite nine amazingly consistent years as England's goalkeeper!

Only once, so far, has the title been shared; by two veterans, Tony Book and Dave Mackay, in 1969. Mackay, a leading star with Spurs and Scotland, was enjoying an Indian summer with Derby County, whom he had just helped to win the Second Division. Tony Book, an extraordinary late developer, had not even played in the First Division till well into his thirties; but then he reached the all-important and influential Cup Final with Manchester City. In 1971, another veteran defender, playing in the Cup Final, was awarded the title; Frank McLintock, centre-half and captain of the double-winning Arsenal team.

The trophy, in principle, is awarded to 'the player who, by precept and example, on and off the field, shall have been considered to have done most for football during that season'. In the event, other, much more subjective criteria seem to enter into the judgement; though the proliferation of European competition, and its increasing importance, has done something to reduce the almost fetishistic importance of the FA Cup Final.

Nevertheless, it is hard to visualize the English Football Writers picking a player on the basis of sheer, all-round, objective excellence in local *club* football, as was the case when the choice of Scottish Footballer of the Year recently fell on Pat Stanton of Hibernian, when he was not even a regular member of the Scottish international side. But then no doubt it could be argued that a player can do as much for the game with a brilliant performance in a showpiece match, watched by millions, as he could in a seasonful of less noticeable club games.

All the Records Year by Year

The FA Cup
The Scottish FA Cup
The Football League
The Scottish League

FA CUP 1871-72

FIRST ROUND
Clapham Rovers v Upton Park	3-0
Crystal Palace v Hitchin	0-0*
Maidenhead v Great Marlow	2-0
Barnes v Civil Service	2-0
Wanderers v Harrow Chequers (scratched)	wo
Royal Engineers v Reigate Priory (scratched)	wo
Queen's Park	bye
Donington School	bye
Hampstead Heathens	bye

SECOND ROUND
Wanderers v Clapham Rovers	3-1
Crystal Palace v Maidenhead	3-0
Royal Engineers v Hitchin	3-1
Hampstead Heathens v Barnes	2-0
Queen's Park v Donington School (scratched)	wo

THIRD ROUND
Wanderers v Crystal Palace	†*
Royal Engineers v Hampstead Heathens	2-0
Queen's Park	‡bye

†Drawn game for which no score is available.
‡Queen's Park were granted a bye from the third round into the semi-final because of travelling.

SEMI-FINAL
Royal Engineers v Crystal Palace	3-0
Wanderers v Queen's Park (scratched)††	0-0, wo

††Queen's Park could not afford to travel to London for the replay.

FINAL AT KENNINGTON OVAL
Wanderers v Royal Engineers	1-0

*The progress of Crystal Palace and Hitchin into the second round and Crystal Palace and Wanderers into the semi-final round was covered by Rule 8 of the competition whereby in the case of a draw both clubs could compete in the next round.

FA CUP 1872-73

FIRST ROUND
Oxford University v Crystal Palace	3-2
Royal Engineers v Civil Service	3-0
1st Surrey Rifles v Upton Park	2-0
Maidenhead v Great Marlow	1-0
South Norwood v Barnes	1-0
Windsor Home Park v Reigate Priory	4-2
Clapham Rovers v Hitchin (scratched)	wo
Queen's Park	*bye
Wanderers	†bye

*Queen's Park, Glasgow, because of the travelling involved, were awarded byes to the semi-final round.
†This was the only occasion when the Cup holders were excused from taking part until the Final.

SECOND ROUND
Clapham Rovers v Oxford University	0-3
1st Surrey Rifles v Maidenhead	1-3
South Norwood v Windsor Home Park	0-3
Royal Engineers	bye
Queen's Park	bye
Wanderers	bye

THIRD ROUND
Oxford University v Royal Engineers	1-0
Maidenhead v Windsor Home Park	1-0
Queen's Park	bye
Wanderers	bye

FOURTH ROUND
Oxford University v Maidenhead	4-0
Queen's Park	bye
Wanderers	bye

SEMI-FINAL
Oxford University v Queen's Park (scratched)	*wo
Wanderers	bye

*Queen's Park apparently beat Oxford but could not afford to travel to London for the Final.

FINAL AT LILLIE BRIDGE*
Wanderers v Oxford University	2-0

*Wanderers, as Cup holders, had choice of ground.

FA CUP 1873-74

FIRST ROUND
Oxford University v Upton Park	4-0
Barnes v 1st Surrey Rifles	1-0
Cambridge University v South Norwood	1-0
Pilgrims v Great Marlow	1-0
Royal Engineers v Brondesbury	5-0
Uxbridge v Gitanos	3-0
Swifts v Crystal Palace	1-0
Woodford Wells v Reigate Priory	3-0
Sheffield v Shropshire Wanderers	††
Wanderers v Southall (scratched)	wo
Trojans v Farningham (scratched)	wo
Clapham Rovers v A A C (scratched)	wo
Maidenhead v Civil Service (scratched)	wo
High Wycombe v Old Etonians (scratched)	wo

††After two drawn games Sheffield won on the toss of a coin

SECOND ROUND
Oxford University v Barnes	2-1
Clapham Rovers v Cambridge University	4-1
Sheffield v Pilgrims	1-0
Royal Engineers v Uxbridge	2-1
Maidenhead v High Wycombe	1-0
Swifts v Woodford Wells	2-1
Wanderers v Trojans (scratched)	wo

THIRD ROUND
Oxford University v Wanderers	1-0
Clapham Rovers v Sheffield	2-1
Royal Engineers v Maidenhead	7-0
Swifts	bye

SEMI-FINAL
Oxford University v Clapham Rovers	1-0
Royal Engineers v Swifts	2-0

FINAL AT KENNINGTON OVAL
Oxford University v Royal Engineers	2-0

Top Queen's Park in 1874, still undefeated and the first winners of the Scottish Cup.
Bottom Royal Engineers in 1872, 7-4 on favourites for the FA Cup, but only runners-up.

SCOTTISH FA CUP 1873-74

FIRST ROUND
Queen's Park v Dumbreck	7-0
Clydesdale v Granville	6-0
Western v Blythwood	0-1
Alexandria Athletic v Callander	2-0
Eastern v Rovers	4-0
Renton v Kilmarnock	2-0
Dumbarton v Vale of Leven (scratched)	wo
3rd Lanark Rifle Volunteers v Southern (scratched)	wo

SECOND ROUND
Queen's Park v Eastern	1-0
Alexandria Athletic v Blythwood	0-2
Renton v Dumbarton	0-0, 1-0
Clydesdale v 3rd Lanark Rifle Volunteers	1-1, 0-0, 2-0

SEMI-FINAL
Queen's Park v Renton	2-0
Clydesdale v Blythwood	4-0

FINAL AT HAMPDEN PARK
Queen's Park v Clydesdale	2-0

The first FA Cup competitions were far less organised than those a century later. The first winners, Wanderers, won only one game before defeating Royal Engineers in the Final. They received a walk over in the first round, beat Clapham in the second, went through after only drawing in the third and received a walk-over in the semi-final after Queen's Park had been unable to pay for the long journey to London for a replay.

Wanderers' goal in the Final – the first in an FA Cup Final – was scored by M P Betts, who played under the name of A H Chequer, indicating that he had come from Harrow Chequers, who had scratched to Wanderers in the first round. Queen's Park had the same trouble the next year. After defeating Oxford they were unable to travel to the Final and Oxford took their place – thus being one of only three clubs to have reached a Final after losing an earlier match.

COURTESY OF DR PERCY YOUNG

FA CUP 1874-75

FIRST ROUND
Royal Engineers v Great Marlow	3-0
Cambridge University v Crystal Palace	†2-1
Clapham Rovers v Panthers	3-0
Pilgrims v South Norwood	2-1
Oxford University v Brondesbury	6-0
Wanderers v Farningham	16-0
Barnes v Upton Park	3-0
Old Etonians v Swifts	††3-0
Maidenhead v Hitchin	1-0
Woodford Wells v High Wycombe	1-0
Southall v Leyton	†5-0
Windsor Home Park v Uxbridge (scratched)	wo
Shropshire Wanderers v Sheffield (scratched)	wo
Civil Service v Harrow Chequers (scratched)	wo
Reigate Priory	bye

†Drawn game for which no score is available

SECOND ROUND
Royal Engineers v Cambridge University	5-0
Clapham Rovers v Pilgrims	2-0
Wanderers v Barnes	4-0
Maidenhead v Reigate Priory	2-1
Woodford Wells v Southall	3-0
Oxford University v Windsor Home Park (scratched)	wo
Shropshire Wanderers v Civil Service (scratched)	†two
Old Etonians	bye

†Drawn game for which no score is available

THIRD ROUND
Royal Engineers v Clapham Rovers	3-2
Oxford University v Wanderers	2-1
Old Etonians v Maidenhead	1-0
Shropshire Wanderers v Woodford Wells	†2-0

†Drawn game for which no score is available

SEMI-FINAL
Royal Engineers v Oxford University	†1-0
Old Etonians v Shropshire Wanderers	1-0

†Drawn game for which no score is available

FINAL AT KENNINGTON OVAL
Royal Engineers v Old Etonians	1-1, 2-0

SCOTTISH FA CUP 1874-75

FIRST ROUND
Helensburgh v 3rd Edinburgh Rifle Volunteers	3-0
Rangers v Oxford	2-0
West End v Star of Leven	3-0
Kilmarnock v Vale of Leven Rovers	4-0
Dumbreck v Alexandria Athletic	5-1
3rd Lanark Rifle Volunteers v Barrhead	1-0
Dumbarton v Arthurlie	3-0
Queen's Park v Western	1-0
Eastern v 23rd Renfrew Rifle Volunteers	3-0
Renton v Blythwood (scratched)	wo
Clydesdale v Vale of Leven (scratched)	wo
Rovers v Hamilton Academicals (scratched)	wo
Standard	bye

SECOND ROUND
Eastern v Kilmarnock	3-0
Renton v Helensburgh	2-0
3rd Lanark Rifle Volunteers v Standard	2-0
Queen's Park v West End	7-0
Clydesdale v Dumbreck	2-0
Dumbarton v Rangers	1-0
Rovers	bye

THIRD ROUND
Renton v Eastern	1-0
Dumbarton v 3rd Lanark Rifle Volunteers	1-0
Queen's Park v Rovers (scratched)	wo
Clydesdale	bye

SEMI-FINAL
Renton v Dumbarton	1-0
Queen's Park v Clydesdale	1-0

FINAL AT HAMPDEN PARK
Queen's Park v Renton	3-0

FA CUP 1875-76

FIRST ROUND
Wanderers v 1st Surrey Rifles	5-0
Crystal Palace v 105th Regiment	†3-0
Upton Park v Southall	1-0
Swifts v Great Marlow	2-0
Royal Engineers v High Wycombe	15-0
Panthers v Woodford Wells	1-0
Reigate Priory v Barnes	1-0
Oxford University v Forest School	6-0
Hertfordshire Rangers v Rochester	4-0
Old Etonians v Pilgrims	4-1
Maidenhead v Ramblers	2-0
Sheffield v Shropshire Wanderers (scratched)	wo
South Norwood v Clydesdale (scratched)	wo
Cambridge University v Civil Service (scratched)	wo
Clapham Rovers v Hitchin (scratched)	wo
Leyton v Harrow Chequers (scratched)	wo

†Drawn game for which no score is available

SECOND ROUND
Wanderers v Crystal Palace	3-0
Swifts v South Norwood	5-0
Reigate Priory v Cambridge University	0-8
Oxford University v Hertfordshire Rangers	8-2
Old Etonians v Maidenhead	8-0
Clapham Rovers v Leyton	12-0
Sheffield v Upton Park (scratched)	wo
Royal Engineers v Panthers (scratched)	wo

THIRD ROUND
Wanderers v Sheffield	2-0
Swifts v Royal Engineers	3-1
Cambridge University v Oxford University	0-4
Old Etonians v Clapham Rovers	1-0

SEMI-FINAL
Wanderers v Swifts	2-1
Oxford University v Old Etonians	0-1

FINAL AT KENNINGTON OVAL
Wanderers v Old Etonians	0-0, 3-0

SCOTTISH FA CUP 1875-76

SECOND ROUND
3rd Edinburgh Rifle Volunteers v Edinburgh Thistle	1-0
Levern v Hamilton Academicals	3-0
Drumpellier v Heart of Midlothian	2-0
Vale of Leven v Renton	3-0
Queen's Park v Northern	5-0
3rd Lanark Rifle Volunteers v Rangers	2-1
Helensburgh v 23rd Renfrew Rifle Volunteers	1-0
Clydesdale v Kilmarnock	6-0
Dumbarton v Renton Thistle	2-1
Western v Sandyford	3-0
Dumbreck v St Andrew's	2-0
Rovers v West End	6-0
Partick Thistle v Towerhill	2-0
Mauchline v Kilbirnie (scratched)	wo

THIRD ROUND
Queen's Park v Clydesdale	2-0
Vale of Leven v Mauchline	6-0
3rd Lanark Rifle Volunteers v Levern	3-0
Dumbreck v Partick Thistle	5-0
Rovers v 3rd Edinburgh Rifle Volunteers	4-0
Western v Helensburgh	2-0
Dumbarton v Drumpellier	5-1

FOURTH ROUND
Queen's Park v Dumbreck	2-0
3rd Lanark Rifle Volunteers v Western	5-0
Vale of Leven v Rovers	2-0
Dumbarton	bye

SEMI-FINAL
Queen's Park v Vale of Leven	3-1
3rd Lanark Rifle Volunteers v Dumbarton	3-0

FINAL AT HAMPDEN PARK
Queen's Park v 3rd Lanark Rifle Volunteers	1-1, 2-0

FA CUP 1876-77

FIRST ROUND
Pilgrims v Ramblers	4-1
Panthers v Wood Grange	3-0
Clapham Rovers v Reigate Priory	5-0
Rochester v Union	5-0
Swifts v Reading Hornets	2-0
Royal Engineers v Old Harrovians	2-1
South Norwood v Saxons	4-1
105th Regiment v 1st Surrey Rifles	3-0
Upton Park v Leyton	7-0
Great Marlow v Hertfordshire Rangers	2-1
Forest School v Gresham	4-1
Wanderers v Saffron Walden (scratched)	wo
Southall v Old Wykehamists (scratched)	wo
Cambridge University v High Wycombe (scratched)	wo
Shropshire Wanderers v Druids (scratched)	wo
Sheffield v Trojans (scratched)	wo
Oxford University v Old Salopians (scratched)	wo
Barnes v Old Etonians (scratched)	wo
Queen's Park	bye

SECOND ROUND
Wanderers v Southall	6-1
Pilgrims v Panthers	1-0
Cambridge University v Clapham Rovers	2-1
Rochester v Swifts	1-0
Royal Engineers v Shropshire Wanderers	3-0
Sheffield v South Norwood	7-0
Oxford University v 105th Regiment	6-1
Upton Park v Barnes	1-0
Great Marlow v Forest School	1-0
Queen's Park	bye

THIRD ROUND
Wanderers v Pilgrims	3-0
Cambridge University v Rochester	4-0
Royal Engineers v Sheffield	1-0
Upton Park v Great Marlow	†1-0
Oxford University v Queen's Park (scratched)	wo

†Drawn game for which no score is available.

FOURTH ROUND
Cambridge University v Royal Engineers	1-0
Oxford University v Upton Park	†1-0
Wanderers	bye

†Drawn game for which no score is available

SEMI-FINAL
Wanderers v Cambridge University	1-0
Oxford University	bye

FINAL AT KENNINGTON OVAL
Wanderers v Oxford University	2-0

SCOTTISH FA CUP 1876-77

FOURTH ROUND
Queen's Park v Northern	4-0
Vale of Leven v Busby	4-0
Lennox v Swifts	4-0
Lancefield v Hamilton	2-0
Rangers v Mauchline	3-0
Ayr Thistle v Partick Thistle (disqualified)	wo

FIFTH ROUND
Rangers v Lennox	3-0
Vale of Leven v Queen's Park	2-1
Ayr Thistle v Lancefield	1-0

SEMI-FINAL
Vale of Leven v Ayr Thistle	9-0
Rangers	bye

FINAL AT HAMPDEN PARK
Vale of Leven v Rangers	0-0, 1-1, 3-2

Queen's Park conceded their first ever goal in the Scottish Cup semi-final against Vale of Leven early in 1876. They had been in existence for almost nine years. Their first ever defeat in Scotland was also at the hands of Vale of Leven on 30 December 1876. The latter won a fifth round Scottish Cup tie 2-1.

FA CUP 1877-78

FIRST ROUND

Wanderers v Panthers	9-1
High Wycombe v Wood Grange	4-0
Great Marlow v Hendon	2-0
Sheffield v Notts County	3-0
Darwen v Manchester	3-1
Pilgrims v Ramblers	†1-0
Druids v Shropshire Wanderers	1-0
Oxford University v Hertfordshire Rangers	5-2
Clapham Rovers v Grantham	2-0
Swifts v Leyton	8-2
Old Harrovians v 105th Regiment	2-0
1st Surrey Rifles v Forest School	1-0
Cambridge University v Southill Park	3-1
Maidenhead v Reading Hornets	10-0
Upton Park v Rochester	3-0
Reading v South Norwood	2-0
Remnants v St Stephens	4-1
Hawks v Minerva	5-2
Barnes v St Marks (scratched)	wo
Royal Engineers v Union (scratched)	wo
Old Foresters v Old Wykehamists (scratched)	wo
Queen's Park	*bye

†Drawn game for which no score is available
*Queen's Park later withdrew

SECOND ROUND

Wanderers v High Wycombe	9-0
Barnes v Great Marlow	3-1
Sheffield v Darwen	1-0
Royal Engineers v Pilgrims	6-0
Oxford University v Old Foresters	1-0
Clapham Rovers v Swifts	4-0
Old Harrovians v 1st Surrey Rifles	6-0
Cambridge University v Maidenhead	4-2
Upton Park v Reading	1-0
Remnants v Hawks	2-0
Druids	bye

THIRD ROUND

Wanderers v Barnes	4-1
Royal Engineers v Druids	8-0
Oxford University v Clapham Rovers	3-2
Old Harrovians v Cambridge University	2-0
Upton Park v Remnants	3-0
Sheffield	bye

FOURTH ROUND

Wanderers v Sheffield	3-0
Royal Engineers v Oxford University	4-2
Old Harrovians v Upton Park	3-1

SEMI-FINAL

Royal Engineers v Old Harrovians	2-1
Wanderers	bye

FINAL AT KENNINGTON OVAL

Wanderers v Royal Engineers	3-1

SCOTTISH FA CUP 1877-78

FOURTH ROUND

Renton v Rovers	4-0
South Western v Glengowan	5-0
Mauchline v Kilbirnie	2-1
Parkgrove v Drumpellier	3-1
3rd Lanark Rifle Volunteers v Govan	7-0
Vale of Leven v Rangers	5-0
Thornliebank v Hibernian	**
Beith v Dundas St Clement's (scratched)	wo
Partick Thistle v Barrhead (disqualified)	wo
Jordanhill	bye
Renfrew	†bye

**After two draws, both teams went through to the next round
†Renfrew, who had earlier been beaten by Barrhead, were reinstated on the latter's disqualification

FIFTH ROUND

Vale of Leven v Jordanhill	10-0
Parkgrove v Partick Thistle	2-1
South Western v Hibernian	3-1
Renton v Thornliebank	2-1
3rd Lanark Rifle Volunteers v Beith	4-0
Mauchline v Renfrew (scratched)	wo

SIXTH ROUND

Vale of Leven v Parkgrove	5-0
3rd Lanark Rifle Volunteers v South Western	2-1
Renton v Mauchline	3-1

SEMI-FINAL

3rd Lanark Rifle Volunteers v Renton	1-0
Vale of Leven	bye

FINAL AT HAMPDEN PARK

Vale of Leven v 3rd Lanark Rifle Volunteers	1-0

SCOTTISH FA CUP 1878-79

FOURTH ROUND

Hibernian v Roy Roy	9-0
3rd Lanark Rifle Volunteers v Renfrew	4-0
Vale of Leven v Govan	11-1
Dumbarton v Portland	6-1
Queen's Park v Mauchline	5-0
Rangers v Alexandria Athletic	3-0
Beith v Kilmarnock Athletic	9-1
Helensburgh v Heart of Midlothian (scratched)	wo
Stonelaw v Thistle (disqualified)	wo
Partick Thistle	bye

FIFTH ROUND

Queen's Park v 3rd Lanark Rifle Volunteers	5-0
Rangers v Partick Thistle	4-0
Helensburgh v Hibernian	2-1
Dumbarton v Stonelaw	9-1
Vale of Leven v Beith	6-1

SIXTH ROUND

Rangers v Queen's Park	1-0
Vale of Leven v Dumbarton	3-1
Helensburgh	bye

SEMI-FINAL

Vale of Leven v Helensburgh	3-0
Rangers	bye

FINAL AT HAMPDEN PARK

Vale of Leven v Rangers	1-1*

*Cup awarded to Vale of Leven. Rangers refused to play the replay within the time allotted by the SFA. Rangers refused to turn up after the SFA had turned down a protest that they had scored a perfectly legitimate second goal in the first game.

FA CUP 1878-79

FIRST ROUND

Old Etonians v Wanderers	7-2
Reading v Hendon	1-0
Grey Friars v Great Marlow	2-1
Pilgrims v Brentwood	3-1
Nottingham Forest v Notts County	†1-0
Sheffield v Grantham	†3-1
Old Harrovians v Southill Park	8-0
Oxford University v Wednesbury Strollers	7-0
Royal Engineers v Old Foresters	3-0
Barnes v Maidenhead	†4-0
Upton Park v Saffron Walden	5-0
Forest School v Rochester	4-2
Cambridge University v Hertfordshire Rangers	2-0
Swifts v Hawks	2-1
Romford v Ramblers	3-1
Minerva v 105th Regiment (scratched)	wo
Darwen v Birch (scratched)	wo
Remnants v Unity (scratched)	wo
Panthers v Runnymede (scratched)	†two
Clapham Rovers v Finchley (scratched)	wo
South Norwood v Leyton (scratched)	wo
Eagley	bye

†Drawn game for which no score is available

SECOND ROUND

Old Etonians v Reading	1-0
Minerva v Grey Friars	3-0
Darwen v Eagley	4-1
Remnants v Pilgrims	6-2
Nottingham Forest v Sheffield	2-0
Old Harrovians v Panthers	3-0
Oxford University v Royal Engineers	4-0
Barnes v Upton Park	3-2
Clapham Rovers v Forest School	10-1
Cambridge University v South Norwood	3-0
Swifts v Romford	3-1

THIRD ROUND

Old Etonians v Minerva	5-2
Darwen v Remnants	3-2
Nottingham Forest v Old Harrovians	2-0
Oxford University v Barnes	2-1
Clapham Rovers v Cambridge University	1-0
Swifts	bye

FOURTH ROUND

Old Etonians v Darwen	5-5, 2-2, 6-2
Nottingham Forest v Oxford University	2-1
Clapham Rovers v Swifts	8-1

SEMI-FINAL

Old Etonians v Nottingham Forest	2-1
Clapham Rovers	bye

FINAL AT KENNINGTON OVAL

Old Etonians v Clapham Rovers	1-0

The first ever Welsh Cup tie was played on Saturday 30 October, 1877, between Druids of Ruabon and Newtown at Newtown. The founder of the Welsh FA, Llewelyn Kenrick, captained Druids that day; they won the game and eventually reached the final to meet Wrexham. Wrexham won 1-0, apparently using a 2-3-5 line up. If that is in fact correct, then it is the first recorded instance of what remained the standard formation for half a century. At the time the Welsh FA had not even purchased a trophy, but when they did it was a magnificent affair which dwarfed the FA Cup.

Because of the dearth of clubs in Wales, the Cup has always been open to English sides. This produced an English winner as early as 1884 when Oswestry defeated Druids 3-2. The situation became a little absurd in 1934, however, with a final replay which is surely unparalleled in any cup competition. The game was between two English clubs — Bristol City and Tranmere Rovers — and was played on an English ground, Chester's Sealand Road. City won 3-0 and it was not until 1948 that the Cup actually returned to a Welsh club.

The Scottish Cup of 1878-79 saw two scenes unfamiliar a century later. Hearts failed to turn up for their tie at Helensburgh and, later, mighty Rangers refused to play a final replay against Vale of Leven in a fit of pique over a disputed goal.

The 1878-79 Cup season was notable for the arrival of the northern teams. Nottingham Forest became the first northern side to reach the semi-finals (and the only one of the present League clubs to have got so far at the first attempt) but Darwen's displays were more newsworthy. In their fourth round tie against Old Etonians at the Oval, Darwen scored four times in the last 15 minutes to draw 5-5. Etonians refused to play extra time and it took a public subscription to bring Darwen back for a 2-2 draw. A third game was decisive, Etonians winning 6-2 and eventually taking the Cup.

Darwen had in their ranks two Scots — James Love and Fergus Suter — who were reputedly the first of the 'professionals' to find money in their boots. They had come down to Darwen as part of a touring Partick Thistle side, played a friendly, and been persuaded to stay. The tide was on the turn and the days of the gentlemen amateurs almost at an end. Wanderers, after a hat-trick of successes in 1876-78, were defeated in the very first round of the 1878-79 competition by Old Etonians, who went on to become their successors as Cup holders.

FA CUP 1879-80

SECOND ROUND
Clapham Rovers v South Norwood	4-0
Hendon v Mosquitoes	7-1
Wanderers v Old Carthusians	1-0
West End v Hotspurs	1-0
Oxford University v Birmingham	6-0
Aston Villa v Stafford Road Works	3-1
Maidenhead v Henley	3-1
Royal Engineers v Upton Park	4-1
Grey Friars v Gresham	9-0
Nottingham Forest v Turton	6-0
Blackburn Rovers v Darwen	3-1
Sheffield v Sheffield Providence	3-0
Pilgrims v Hertfordshire Rangers (scratched)	wo
Old Harrovians	bye
Old Etonians	bye

THIRD ROUND
Clapham Rovers v Pilgrims	7-0
Old Etonians v Wanderers	3-1
Royal Engineers v Old Harrovians	2-0
Nottingham Forest v Blackburn Rovers	6-0
Oxford University v Aston Villa (scratched)	wo
Hendon	bye
West End	bye
Maidenhead	bye
Grey Friars	bye
Sheffield	bye

FOURTH ROUND
Clapham Rovers v Hendon	2-0
Old Etonians v West End	5-1
Oxford University v Maidenhead	1-0
Royal Engineers v Grey Friars	1-0
Nottingham Forest v Sheffield	* 2-2

*Sheffield disqualified for refusing to play extra time

FIFTH ROUND
Clapham Rovers v Old Etonians	1-0
Oxford University v Royal Engineers	†1-0
Nottingham Forest	bye

†Drawn game for which no score is available

SEMI-FINAL
Oxford University v Nottingham Forest	1-0
Clapham Rovers	bye

FINAL AT KENNINGTON OVAL
Clapham Rovers v Oxford University	1-0

SCOTTISH FA CUP 1879-80

FOURTH ROUND
South Western v Arbroath	4-0
Pollockshields Athletic v Renfrew	2-1
Dumbarton v Clyde	11-1
Third Lanark v Kirkintilloch	5-1
Rob Roy v Johnstone Athletic	4-2
Thornliebank v Fossilpark	13-0
Mauchline v Hamilton Academicals	2-0
Cambuslang v Plains	3-0
Queen's Park v Strathblane	10-1
Parkgrove v Hibernian	**
Hurlford v Kilbirnie	**

**After two draws both teams went through to the next round

FIFTH ROUND
South Western v Parkgrove	3-2
Dumbarton v Kilbirnie	6-2
Queen's Park v Hurlford	15-1
Thornliebank v Rob Roy	12-0
Pollockshields Athletic v Cambuslang	4-0
Hibernian v Mauchline	2-0
Third Lanark	bye

SIXTH ROUND
Pollockshields Athletic v South Western	6-1
Dumbarton v Hibernian	6-2
Thornliebank v Third Lanark	2-1
Queen's Park	bye

SEMI-FINAL
Queen's Park v Dumbarton	1-0
Thornliebank v Pollockshields Athletic	2-1

FINAL AT CATHKIN PARK
Queen's Park v Thornliebank	3-0

SCOTTISH FA CUP 1880-81

FOURTH ROUND
Heart of Midlothian v Cambridge	3-0
Hurlford v Cartside	3-1
Central v Edinburgh University	1-0
Dumbarton v Glasgow University	9-0
Rangers v Clyde	11-0
Queen's Park v Beith	11-2
St Mirren v Cowlairs	1-0
Arthurlie v South Western (scratched)	wo
Mauchline v Clarkston (scratched)	wo
Vale of Leven v Arbroath (scratched)	wo
Thistle	bye

FIFTH ROUND
Vale of Leven v Thistle	7-1
Dumbarton v St Mirren	5-1
Arthurlie v Heart of Midlothian	4-0
Queen's Park v Mauchline	2-0
Rangers v Hurlford	3-0
Central	bye

SIXTH ROUND
Queen's Park v Central	10-0
Dumbarton v Rangers	3-1
Vale of Leven v Arthurlie	2-0

SEMI-FINAL
Dumbarton v Vale of Leven	2-0
Queen's Park	bye

FINAL AT KINNING PARK
Queen's Park v Dumbarton	2-1*, 3-1

*Dumbarton's protest about spectators on the pitch during the first game was upheld

FA CUP 1880-81

SECOND ROUND
Old Carthusians v Dreadnought	5-1
Royal Engineers v Pilgrims	1-0
Swifts v Reading	1-0
Upton Park v Weybridge	3-0
Darwen v Sheffield	5-1
The Wednesday v Blackburn Rovers	4-0
Turton v Astley Bridge	3-0
Reading Abbey v Acton	2-1
Great Marlow v West End	4-0
Old Etonians v Hendon	2-0
Grey Friars v Maidenhead	1-0
Stafford Road Works v Grantham	†7-1
Aston Villa v Nottingham Forest	2-1
Notts County	bye
Rangers	bye
Clapham Rovers	bye
Romford	bye
Hertfordshire Rangers	bye

†Drawn game for which no score is available

THIRD ROUND
Royal Engineers v Rangers	6-0
Clapham Rovers v Swifts	2-1
The Wednesday v Turton	2-0
Romford v Reading Abbey	2-0
Old Etonians v Hertfordshire Rangers	3-0
Aston Villa v Notts County	3-1
Old Carthusians	bye
Upton Park	bye
Darwen	bye
Great Marlow	bye
Stafford Road Works	bye
Grey Friars	bye

FOURTH ROUND
Old Carthusians v Royal Engineers	2-1
Clapham Rovers v Upton Park	5-4
Darwen v The Wednesday	5-1
Romford v Great Marlow	2-1
Old Etonians v Grey Friars	4-0
Stafford Road Works v Aston Villa	3-2

FIFTH ROUND
Old Carthusians v Clapham Rovers	4-1
Darwen v Romford	15-0
Old Etonians v Stafford Road Works	2-1

SEMI-FINAL
Old Carthusians v Darwen	4-1
Old Etonians	bye

FINAL AT KENNINGTON OVAL
Old Carthusians v Old Etonians	3-0

F H. AYRES
MANUFACTURER OF
SPORTS & GAMES
ii. Aldersgate St., London, E.C.

F O O T B A L L ' S
THE "INTERNATIONAL."

EVERY	FOR THE
REQUISITE	GAME.

TESTIMONIAL.
ROVERS' FOOTBALL CLUB.
Winners of the National Cup, 1884-5-6-8.
Lancashire Cup, 1884-5, 1885-6, 1886-7, 1887-8.
East Lancashire Charity Cup, 1885-6, 1886-7.
40, Oozehead Terrace, Blackburn, Jan. 23rd, 1889.

Dear Sir,

Please forward by return two Association Footballs same as one you sent on trial. Our players consider it a very good one.—Yours truly,

Mr. AYRES.   J. B. MITCHELL.

LA CROSSE, HOCKEY, GOLF, BILLIARDS, &c.

Above The reason Blackburn Rovers won the Cup so often? F H Ayres and Company ran this advertisement regularly for ten years, but 1879-80 was a little premature for it. In their first expedition into the Cup, which was that season, Rovers were rudely dismissed 6-0 by Nottingham Forest, who were at the time on the way to a second consecutive semi-final.

Old Carthusiass defeat of Old Etonians in the 1881 Cup Final was the first leg of a rare double. In 1894 they also won the first Amateur Cup final by defeating Casuals 2-1. In fact this oft repeated 'unique' record is not so: Royal Engineers, FA Cup winners in 1875, later went on to win the Amateur Cup in 1908 as Depot Battalion, Royal Engineers.

The two Scottish Cup finals of 1881 between Queen's Park and Dumbarton resulted in quite unprecedented scenes. The game was played at Rangers' home, Kinning Park, and the crowds were so great that many spent most of the game on the pitch. Because of this Dumbarton protested that Queen's second and winning goal was invalid, the pitch having virtually been invaded, and the SFA ordered a replay. Queen's threatened to withdraw from the Association, but eventually turned out and won 3-1. At the second game the gates had to be closed, the first time that this had happened in Scottish history. This was not really surprising for Dumbarton and Queen's were the Rangers and Celtic of pre-1900 Scotland.

The next year, 1882, there was even more trouble when the two met in the final. The crowd was bad-tempered and there were protests over yet another disputed goal — this time to level at 2-2. Queen's Park went on to win the replay, 4-1, before a record 15,000 crowd, but the two games left a remarkably bitter taste. Up to that point there had been a well-attended friendly every year between the clubs, but this was abandoned and, indeed, never reinstated. Dumbarton finally won the Cup the following year, beating Vale of Leven, after defeating Queen's Park in the sixth round.

FA CUP 1881-82

SECOND ROUND
Blackburn Rovers v Bolton Wanderers	6-2
Darwen v Accrington	3-1
Turton v Bootle	4-0
Wednesbury Old Alliance v Small Heath Alliance	6-0
Notts County v Wednesbury Strollers	11-1
Staveley v Grantham	3-1
Heeley v Sheffield	4-1
Upton Park v Hanover United	3-1
Hotspur v Reading Abbey	4-1
Reading Minster v Romford	3-1
Swifts v Old Harrovians	7-1
Maidenhead v Acton	2-1
Great Marlow v St Bartholomew's Hospital	2-0
Reading v West End (scratched)	*wo
Old Foresters v Pilgrims	3-1
Old Carthusians v Barnes	7-1
Aston Villa	bye
The Wednesday	bye
Old Etonians	bye
Dreadnought	bye
Royal Engineers	bye

*West End scratched after a drawn game

THIRD ROUND
Darwen v Turton	4-2
Aston Villa v Notts County	**4-1
The Wednesday v Staveley	**5-1
Hotspur v Reading Minster	2-0
Old Etonians v Swifts	3-0
Great Marlow v Dreadnought	2-1
Royal Engineers v Old Carthusians	2-0
Blackburn Rovers	bye
Wednesbury Old Alliance	bye
Heeley	bye
Upton Park	bye
Maidenhead	bye
Reading	bye
Old Foresters	bye

**two drawn games for which no scores are available

FOURTH ROUND
Blackburn Rovers v Darwen	5-1
Wednesbury Old Alliance v Aston Villa	4-2
The Wednesday v Heeley	3-1
Upton Park v Hotspur	5-0
Old Etonians v Maidenhead	6-3
Great Marlow v Reading (scratched)	wo
Old Foresters v Royal Engineers	2-1

FIFTH ROUND
Blackburn Rovers v Wednesbury Old Alliance	3-1
The Wednesday v Upton Park	6-0
Great Marlow v Old Foresters	*1-0
Old Etonians	bye

*drawn game for which no score is available

SEMI-FINAL
Blackburn Rovers v The Wednesday	0-0, 5-1
Old Etonians v Great Marlow	5-0

FINAL AT KENNINGTON OVAL
Old Etonians v Blackburn Rovers	1-0

The 1882 FA Cup Final was the real bridging point between the old 'gentlemen's' football and the new professionalism. It was the first appearance of a northern club — Blackburn Rovers — and the last time a Southern side was to win for 30 years. After the game Lord Kinnaird, the victorious captain, stood on his head in front of the pavillion. He had appeared in 8 Finals and won 5 winners medals, a record that was to be equalled but never surpassed. He also appeared in the following year's Final, when he collected a ninth medal.

Before a first round FA Cup tie against Everton late in 1881, Bootle discovered that they only had eight players. Three spectators were asked to play and Bootle won the tie. In the second round, with a full team, Bootle lost 4-0 to a team called Turton.

SCOTTISH FA CUP 1881-82

FOURTH ROUND
Falkirk v Milton of Campsie	3-1
Rangers v Thornliebank	2-0
Clyde v Edinburgh University	3-2
Kilmarnock v Our Boys	9-2
Queen's Park v Johnstone	3-2
Cartvale v Glasgow University	5-4
Hibernian v West Benhar	*8-0
Kilmarnock Athletic v Mauchline	3-2
Partick Thistle v Glasgow Athletic	1-0
Arthurlie v Helensburgh	*1-0
West Calder v Stranraer (scratched)	wo
South Western	bye
Dumbarton	bye
Beith	bye
Vale of Teith	bye
Shotts	bye

*after a drawn game

FIFTH ROUND
Arthurlie v Kilmarnock	4-1
West Calder v Falkirk	4-2
Queen's Park v Partick Thistle	10-0
Shotts v Vale of Teith	5-0
Kilmarnock Athletic v Beith	2-1
Cartvale v Clyde	5-4
Rangers v South Western	†6-4
Dumbarton v Hibernian	†4-1

†after a protested game

SIXTH ROUND
Queen's Park v Shotts	15-0
Kilmarnock Athletic v Arthurlie	5-2
Dumbarton v Rangers	†5-1
Cartvale v West Calder	5-3

†after a protested game

SEMI-FINAL
Queen's Park v Kilmarnock Athletic	3-2
Dumbarton v Cartvale	11-2

FINAL AT CATHKIN PARK
Queen's Park v Dumbarton	2-2, 4-1

SCOTTISH FA CUP 1882-83

FOURTH ROUND
Hurlford v Vale of Teith	3-2
Hibernian v Thistle	2-2, 4-1
Arthurlie v Queen of the South Wanderers	3-1
Dumbarton v Thornliebank	3-0
Queen's Park v Cambuslang	5-0
Lugar Boswell v Renton	5-3
Third Lanark v Dunblane	7-1
Kilmarnock Athletic v Abercorn	5-2
Pollockshields Athletic v Johnstone	3-1
Vale of Leven v Edinburgh University	2-0
Partick Thistle v Glasgow University (scratched)	wo

FIFTH ROUND
Vale of Leven v Lugar Boswell	5-0
Queen's Park v Hurlford	7-2
Arthurlie v Hibernian	†6-0
Third Lanark	bye
Dumbarton	bye
Kilmarnock Athletic	bye
Partick Thistle	bye
Pollockshields Athletic	bye

†after a protested game

SIXTH ROUND
Vale of Leven v Partick Thistle	4-0
Pollockshields Athletic v Third Lanark	5-2
Dumbarton v Queen's Park	3-1
Kilmarnock Athletic v Arthurlie	***1-0

***after three drawn games

SEMI-FINAL
Vale of Leven v Kilmarnock Athletic	*2-0
Dumbarton v Pollockshields Athletic	*5-0

*after a drawn game

FINAL AT HAMPDEN PARK
Dumbarton v Vale of Leven	2-2, 2-1

FA CUP 1882-83

SECOND ROUND
Blackburn Olympic v Lower Darwen	9-1
Darwen Ramblers v Haslingden	3-2
Darwen v Blackburn Rovers	1-0
Druids v Northwich Victoria	5-0
Bolton Wanderers v Liverpool Ramblers	3-0
Eagley v Halliwell	3-1
Old Carthusians v Etonian Ramblers	7-0
Royal Engineers v Reading	8-0
Clapham Rovers v Hanover United	7-1
Windsor v United Hospitals	3-1
Old Etonians v Brentwood	2-1
Swifts v Upton Park	*3-2
Hendon v Chatham	2-1
Great Marlow v Reading Minster (scratched)	wo
Phoenix Bessemer v Grimsby	8-1
The Wednesday v Lockwood Brothers	6-0
Nottingham Forest v Heeley	7-2
Aston Villa v Wednesbury Old Alliance	4-1
Aston Unity v Mitchell's St George's	3-0
Walsall Town v Stafford Road Works	4-1
Church	bye
Old Westminsters	bye
Rochester	bye
South Reading	bye
Notts County	bye

*drawn game for which no score is available

THIRD ROUND
Blackburn Olympic v Darwen Ramblers	8-0
Church v Darwen	*2-0
Druids v Bolton Wanderers	**1-0
Old Carthusians v Old Westminsters	3-2
Clapham Rovers v Windsor	3-0
Old Etonians v Rochester	7-0
Hendon v South Reading	11-1
Notts County v Phoenix Bessemer	*3-2
The Wednesday v Nottingham Forest	*3-2
Aston Villa v Aston Unity	3-1
Eagley	bye
Royal Engineers	bye
Swifts	bye
Great Marlow	bye
Walsall Town	bye

*drawn game for which no score is available
**two drawn games for which no scores are available

FOURTH ROUND
Blackburn Olympic v Church	2-0
Druids v Eagley	2-1
Old Carthusians v Royal Engineers	6-2
Old Etonians v Swifts	2-0
Hendon v Great Marlow	3-0
Notts County v The Wednesday	4-1
Aston Villa v Walsall Town	2-1
Clapham Rovers	bye

FIFTH ROUND
Blackburn Olympic v Druids	4-0
Old Carthusians v Clapham Rovers	5-3
Old Etonians v Hendon	4-2
Notts County v Aston Villa	4-3

SEMI-FINAL
Blackburn Olympic v Old Carthusians	4-0
Old Etonians v Notts County	2-1

FINAL AT KENNINGTON OVAL
Blackburn Olympic v Old Etonians	2-1

Blackburn Olympic, the first winners of the Cup to come from the North of England, and the first overtly professional winners, are perhaps the least known of all successful Cup Finalists. Their star rose suddenly and declined just as quickly. After reaching the semi-final the following season they were never heard of again. Olympic even had a manager, one Jack Hunter, whose earlier career had been with a travelling circus. He took his team away to Blackpool before the Final. Of his players, two were weavers, one a spinner, one a plumber, one a metal worker and two were unemployed other than football. A far cry from Old Etonians, last of the English amateur finalists.

WEST BROMWICH

Albion Football Club.

———

SEASON TICKET.

1883-1884.

To Admit to all Matches on the

FOUR ACRES,

SITUATE IN SEAGAR STREET.

PRICE :—THREE SHILLINGS.

Above *A West Bromwich Albion season ticket for 1883-84. For one third of the price of admission to the popular side for a single game in 1974, the Throstles fan could watch a whole season's football in the Midlands.*

Top *The first Blackburn Rovers side to win the FA Cup in 1884. Their opponents were the Scots side Queen's Park. If the latter had won they would have completed a remarkable double, for they had already won the Scottish Cup. In fact they returned to Glasgow extremely bitter at the game's refereeing. Under Scottish rules at the time the offside law only required two defenders between the ball and the goal, but English law required three. Queen's scored two goals that would have been allowed in Scotland and felt thoroughly deprived. They were also upset that Blackburn had four full-time professionals, payment of players still being illegal in Scotland.*

When Blackburn Rovers reached The Oval for the Cup Final in 1882 they had gone 35 consecutive games without defeat, still recognised to be the longest run of first-class

FA CUP 1883-84

THIRD ROUND

Blackburn Rovers v Padiham	3-0
Staveley v Lockwood Brothers	1-0
Upton Park v Reading	6-1
Eagley v Preston North End	1-9
Swifts v Clapham Rovers	2-1
Notts County v Grantham	4-1
Bolton Wanderers v Irwell Springs	8-1
Queen's Park v Oswestry	7-1
Aston Villa v Wednesbury Old Alliance	7-4
Wednesbury Town v Derby Midland	1-0
Romford v Brentwood	1-4
Old Foresters	bye
Old Westminsters	bye
Blackburn Olympic	bye
Old Wykehamists	bye
Northwich Victoria	bye

FOURTH ROUND

Blackburn Rovers v Staveley	5-0
Upton Park v Preston North End	1-1, wo*
Swifts v Old Foresters	2-1
Notts County v Bolton Wanderers	2-2, 2-1
Queen's Park v Aston Villa	6-1
Old Westminsters v Wednesbury Town	5-1
Blackburn Olympic v Old Wykehamists	9-1
Brentwood v Northwich Victoria	1-3

*Upton Park protested that Preston paid their players. The FA upheld the protest and disqualified Preston before the replay.

FIFTH ROUND

Blackburn Rovers v Upton Park	3-0
Swifts v Notts County	1-1, 0-1
Queen's Park v Old Westminsters	1-0
Blackburn Olympic v Northwich Victoria	9-1

SEMI-FINAL

Blackburn Rovers v Notts County	1-0
Queen's Park v Blackburn Olympic	4-1

FINAL AT KENNINGTON OVAL

Blackburn Rovers v Queen's Park	2-1

SCOTTISH FA CUP 1883-84

FOURTH ROUND

Mauchline v Royal Albert	4-0
St Bernard's v Thornliebank	2-0
Vale of Leven v Harp	6-0
Pollockshields Athletic v Our Boys	11-0
Dunblane v Rangers	0-6
Kilmarnock Athletic v Cambuslang	2-3
5th KRV v Hibernian	1-8
Partick Thistle v Queen's Park	0-4
Cartvale v Abercorn	4-2
Battlefield v Edinburgh University (scratched)	wo
Arthurlie	bye

FIFTH ROUND

Arthurlie v Vale of Leven	0-0, 1-3
Mauchline v Pollockshields Athletic	2-3
St Bernard's v Rangers	0-3
Queen's Park	bye
Battlefield	bye
Hibernian	bye
Cambuslang	bye
Cartvale	bye

SIXTH ROUND

Cambuslang v Rangers	2-5
Queen's Park v Cartvale	6-1
Vale of Leven v Pollockshields Athletic	4-2
Hibernian v Battlefield	6-1

SEMI-FINAL

Vale of Leven v Rangers	3-0
Hibernian v Queen's Park	1-5

FINAL

Cup awarded to Queen's Park	†

†Vale of Leven wanted to postpone the final because of the illness of two players and the family bereavement of another. But the FA, although sympathetic, decided that was impossible due to other engagements, such as the international against England. Vale did not turn up for the final and the Cup was awarded to Queen's Park.

fixtures without setback in English football. Since Darwen defeated them in the first round of the 1880-81 competition. Rovers had won 31 games and drawn four. One of

those victories was against mighty Preston North End in the latter's first ever professional game. Blackburn won reasonably convincingly, 16-0.

FA CUP 1884-85

THIRD ROUND
Blackburn Rovers v Witton	6-1
West Bromwich Albion v Aston Villa	††3-0
Druids v Chirk	4-1
Grimsby Town v Lincoln City	1-0
Chatham v Hanover United	2-0
Lower Darwen v Darwen Old Wanderers	4-2
Church v Southport	10-0
Queen's Park v Leek	3-2
Old Wykehamists v Upton Park	2-1
Notts County v Sheffield	9-0
Walsall Swifts v Mitchell's St George's	3-2
Nottingham Forest v The Wednesday	2-1
Swifts v Old Westminsters	2-1
Romford	bye
Old Carthusians	bye
Darwen	bye
Old Etonians	bye
Middlesbrough	bye

††Two drawn games (scores unavailable)

FOURTH ROUND
Blackburn Rovers v Romford	8-0
West Bromwich Albion v Druids	1-0*
Old Carthusians v Grimsby Town	3-0
Chatham v Lower Darwen	1-0
Church v Darwen	3-0
Queen's Park v Old Wykehamists	7-0
Notts County v Walsall Swifts	4-1
Nottingham Forest v Swifts	1-0
Old Etonians v Middlesbrough	5-2

*Druids arrived with only ten men and refused to take the field. West Bromwich therefore scored within five seconds of the kick-off, whereupon Druids decided to take part. This 'goal' is not normally recorded and West Bromwich scored again to 'officially' win 1-0

FIFTH ROUND
Old Carthusians v Chatham	3-0
Blackburn Rovers	bye
West Bromwich Albion	bye
Church	bye
Queen's Park	bye
Notts County	bye
Nottingham Forest	bye
Old Etonians	bye

SIXTH ROUND
Blackburn Rovers v West Bromwich Albion	2-0
Old Carthusians v Church	1-0
Queen's Park v Notts County	2-2, 2-1
Nottingham Forest v Old Etonians	2-0

SEMI-FINAL
Blackburn Rovers v Old Carthusians	5-0
Queen's Park v Nottingham Forest	1-1, 3-0

FINAL AT KENNINGTON OVAL
Blackburn Rovers v Queen's Park	2-0

SCOTTISH FA CUP 1884-85

FOURTH ROUND
Hibernian v Ayr	5-1
Morton v Wishaw Swifts	2-1
Vale of Leven v Arthurlie	2-1
Annbank v Queen of the South Wanderers	5-2
Battlefield v Pollockshields Athletic	3-0
Our Boys v West Benhar	3-3, 3-8
Renton v St Mirren	2-1
Rangers v Arbroath	3-4†, 8-1
Dumbarton v Partick Thistle	6-3
Cambuslang v Thornliebank	2-2, 0-0*

†Rangers protested the result and the SFA ordered a replay
*Both teams went through to the next round

FIFTH ROUND
Hibernian v Morton	4-0
Cambuslang v Dumbarton	4-1
Annbank v West Benhar	5-1
Rangers	bye
Renton	bye
Battlefield	bye
Vale of Leven	bye
Thornliebank	bye

SIXTH ROUND
Hibernian v Annbank	5-0
Vale of Leven v Thornliebank	4-3
Renton v Rangers	5-3
Cambuslang v Battlefield	3-1

SEMI-FINAL
Renton v Hibernian	3-2
Vale of Leven v Cambuslang	0-0, 3-1

FINAL AT HAMPDEN PARK
Renton v Vale of Leven	0-0, 3-1

SCOTTISH FA CUP 1885-86

FOURTH ROUND
Dumbarton v Partick Thistle	3-0
Queen of the South Wanderers v Arthurlie	†
Cambuslang v Wishaw Swifts	9-0
Hibernian v Arbroath	5-3
Renton v Cowlairs	4-0
Queen's Park v Airdrieonians	1-0
Third Lanark v Ayr	3-2*, 3-3, 5-1
Abercorn v Strathmore	7-2
Vale of Leven v Harp	6-0
Port Glasgow Athletic	bye

* replayed after Ayr protested
† Arthurlie won the tie. There is no record of the score

FIFTH ROUND
Renton v Vale of Leven	2-2, 3-0
Third Lanark v Port Glasgow Athletic	1-1, 1-1, 4-1
Arthurlie v Queen's Park	1-2
Abercorn v Cambuslang	0-1
Dumbarton v Hibernian	2-2, 3-4

SIXTH ROUND
Hibernian v Cambuslang	3-2
Third Lanark	bye
Renton	bye
Queen's Park	bye

SEMI-FINAL
Hibernian v Renton	0-2
Third Lanark v Queen's Park	0-3

FINAL AT CATHKIN PARK
Queen's Park v Renton	3-1

FA CUP 1885-86

THIRD ROUND
Blackburn Rovers v Darwen Old Wanderers	6-1
Staveley v Nottingham Forest	2-1
South Reading v Clapham Rovers*	wo
Burslem Port Vale v Leek (scratched)	wo
Swifts v Old Harrovians*	wo
Church v Rossendale	5-1
South Shore v Halliwell	6-1
Notts County v Notts Rangers	3-0
Wolverhampton Wanderers v Walsall Swifts	2-1
Old Westminsters v Romford	5-1
Preston North End* v Bolton Wanderers	3-2‡
Small Heath Alliance v Derby County	4-2
Davenham v Crewe Alexandra	2-1
Middlesbrough v Grimsby Town	2-1
Brentwood	bye
West Bromwich Albion	bye
Old Carthusians	bye
Redcar	bye

*disqualified
‡Preston disqualified after a protest

FOURTH ROUND
West Bromwich Albion v Wolverhampton Wanderers	3-1
Brentwood v South Reading	3-0
Blackburn Rovers	bye
Staveley	bye
Burslem Port Vale	bye
Swifts	bye
Church	bye
South Shore	bye
Notts County	bye
Old Carthusians	bye
Old Westminsters	bye
Bolton Wanderers	bye
Small Heath Alliance	bye
Davenham	bye
Redcar	bye
Middlesbrough	bye

FIFTH ROUND
Blackburn Rovers v Staveley	7-1
Brentwood v Burslem Port Vale †	wo
Swifts v Church	6-2
South Shore v Notts County	2-1
West Bromwich Albion v Old Carthusians	1-0
Old Westminsters v Bolton Wanderers*	wo
Small Heath Alliance v Davenham	2-1
Redcar v Middlesbrough	2-1

*disqualified
†Burslem Port Vale scratched after one drawn game

SIXTH ROUND
Blackburn Rovers v Brentwood	3-1
Swifts v South Shore	2-1
West Bromwich Albion v Old Westminsters	6-0
Small Heath Alliance v Redcar	2-0

SEMI-FINAL
Blackburn Rovers v Swifts	2-1
West Bromwich Albion v Small Heath Alliance	4-0

FINAL AT KENNINGTON OVAL
Blackburn Rovers v West Bromwich Albion	0-0, 2-0*

*replay at The Racecourse, Derby

Blackburn Rovers defeated Queen's Park in both the 1884 and 1885 FA Cup Finals. These remain the only occasions on which the same clubs have contested consecutive Finals. Queen's Park were also the last amateur club to appear in an English Cup Final.
On the way to the 1885 Cup Final Queen's Park defeated both the Nottingham clubs, then considered second only to Blackburn, after a replay. The second semi-final against Nottingham Forest is the only semi-final ever to be played outside England. It was staged at Merchiston Castle School in Edinburgh and it helped Forest set up their remarkable record of having been drawn to play Cup ties in all four home countries. In the first round of the 1888-89 competition they were drawn to play Linfield in Belfast. In fact by the time they arrived Linfield had withdrawn so the game become a friendly instead. No Scottish club ever reached the final again and three years later, the Scottish Football Association banned its members from entering competitions other than its own.

Rangers were drawn to play Arbroath in the Fourth Round of the 1884-85 Scottish Cup. Having lost 4-3 they sent home a telegram reading 'beaten on a back green'. Having measured the pitch they found it was only 49 yards 2 ft 1 in wide, 11 inches short of the minimum. They protested, the game was replayed, and Rangers won 8-1.

The 1886 Cup Final replay, played at The Racecourse, Derby, was the first Final ever played outside London. In winning the game Blackburn Rovers completed a hat-trick of successes never since repeated and were presented with a special shield – which still hangs in their boardroom – to mark the feat. The match is far more famous however, for the performance of the Blackburn captain Jimmy Brown. In his last ever game for the club, Brown dribbled the length of the pitch to score one of the greatest goals in the history of the Cup. In so doing he became the only man ever to score in three consecutive Cup Finals, and, more surprisingly, was immortalized in Arnold Bennett's 'The Card' for the feat.

FA CUP 1886-87†

THIRD ROUND
Aston Villa v Wolverhampton Wanderers	2-2, 3-3, 2-0
Horncastle v Grantham	2-0
Darwen v Bolton Wanderers	4-3
Chirk v Goldenhill (disqualified)	wo
Glasgow Rangers v Cowlairs	3-2
Lincoln City v Gainsborough Trinity	2-2, 1-0
Old Westminsters v Old Etonians	3-0
Partick Thistle v Cliftonville	11-1
Mitchell's St George's v Walsall Town	7-2
Lockwood Brothers v Nottingham Forest	2-1
Notts County v Staveley	3-0
Great Marlow v Dulwich	2-0
Preston North End v Renton	2-0
Old Foresters v Chatham	4-1
Old Carthusians v Caledonians (absent)	wo
Leek v Burslem Port Vale	2-2, 1-1, 3-1
Crewe Alexandra	bye
Swifts	bye
West Bromwich Albion	bye

FOURTH ROUND
Leek v Crewe Alexandra	1-0
Old Foresters v Swifts	2-0
West Bromwich Albion v Mitchell's St George's	1-0
Aston Villa	bye
Horncastle	bye
Darwen	bye
Chirk	bye
Glasgow Rangers	bye
Lincoln City	bye
Old Westminsters	bye
Partick Thistle	bye
Lockwood Brothers	bye
Notts County	bye
Great Marlow	bye
Preston North End	bye
Old Carthusians	bye

FIFTH ROUND
Aston Villa v Horncastle	5-0
Darwen v Chirk	3-1
Glasgow Rangers v Lincoln City	3-0
Old Westminsters v Partick Thistle	1-0
West Bromwich Albion v Lockwood Brothers	2-1*
Notts County v Great Marlow	5-2
Preston North End v Old Foresters	3-0
Old Carthusians v Leek	2-0
*after a disputed game	

SIXTH ROUND
Aston Villa v Darwen	3-2
Glasgow Rangers v Old Westminsters	5-1
West Bromwich Albion v Notts County	4-1
Preston North End v Old Carthusians	2-1

SEMI-FINAL
Aston Villa v Glasgow Rangers	3-1
West Bromwich Albion v Preston North End	3-1

FINAL AT KENNINGTON OVAL
Aston Villa v West Bromwich Albion	2-0

†There is some confusion as to the exact specification of the rounds. The *Football Annual for 1887*, edited by the honorary secretary of the Football Association, Charles Alcock, gives seven rounds and a Final. Later historys, such as the official *History of the Cup* give only three rounds and a Final after qualifying matches.

Hibernian's defeat of Dumbarton in the 1887 Scottish Cup final was the first time that an Edinburgh club had won the Scottish Cup. It was also the first and only time that the final was contested at Crosshills. The same year Hibs played and defeated Preston North End at their new ground, Easter Road, in what was billed as the 'Association Football Championship of the World'. More remotely Hibernian's success was one of the main promptings for the founding of Celtic in Glasgow.

SCOTTISH FA CUP 1886-87

FIFTH ROUND
Hibernian v Queen of the South Wanderers	7-3
Vale of Leven v Cambuslang Hibernians	2-0
Clyde v Third Lanark	0-0, 2-4
Queen's Park v Cambuslang	1-1, 5-4
Hurlford v Morton	5-1
Kilmarnock v Dunblane	6-0
Port Glasgow Athletic v St Bernard's	6-2
Dumbarton v Harp (scratched)	wo

SIXTH ROUND
Port Glasgow Athletic v Vale of Leven	1-3
Kilmarnock v Queen's Park	0-5
Third Lanark v Hibernian	1-2
Hurlford v Dumbarton	0-0, 2-1*, 1-3
*Hurlford insisted on playing on a frozen pitch; the result was declared null and void by the Scottish FA	

SEMI-FINAL
Hibernian v Vale of Leven	3-1
Queen's Park v Dumbarton	1-2

FINAL AT CROSSHILLS
Hibernian v Dumbarton	2-1

Below *The West Bromwich Albion side that won the FA Cup in 1888. It was their third consecutive Final but their first ever success. Billy Bassett is seated, second from the left. After defeating Preston North End at Trent Bridge in the 1887 semi-final, West Bromwich met them again in the actual Final in 1888. To say that Preston were confident is to put it mildly. One of their modest requests was that they might be photographed with the Cup before the game. They explained that they would be dirty afterwards and that this would spoil the picture. The referee, Major Marindin, who controlled eight Finals in all as well as playing in two, suggested that 'Had you not better win it first?' Apparently they had ten good scoring chances to Albion's two, but Albion converted 100% and Preston only 10%. It was called the greatest upset in the history of the Cup, and perhaps remained so until Sunderland defeated Leeds. West Bromwich's inspiration was 5ft 5in Billy Bassett, who went on to win eight consecutive caps against the Scots. Albion went on to beat Aston Villa in a series of three games to become the 'Champions of the Midlands'. Then then went to Scotland to play Scottish Cup winners Renton for the title of 'Champions of the World'. The game was played in a blinding snowstorm and Renton won.*

FA CUP 1887-88†

FIFTH ROUND
West Bromwich Albion v Stoke	4-1
Old Carthusians v Bootle	2-0
Derby Junction v Chirk	1-0
Darwen v Blackburn Rovers	0-3
Nottingham Forest v The Wednesday	2-4
Aston Villa v Preston North End	1-3
Middlesbrough v Old Foresters (scratched)	4-0*
Crewe Alexandra v Derby County	1-0

*Old Foresters protested at the state of the pitch and the FA ordered a replay. Meanwhile, Old Foresters scratched and Middlesbrough thus went through without a second game

SIXTH ROUND
West Bromwich Albion v Old Carthusians	4-2
Derby Junction v Blackburn Rovers	2-1
The Wednesday v Preston North End	1-3
Middlesbrough v Crewe Alexandra	0-2

SEMI-FINAL
West Bromwich Albion v Derby Junction	3-0
Preston North End v Crewe Alexandra	4-0

FINAL AT KENNINGTON OVAL
West Bromwich Albion v Preston North End	2-1

†There is confusion about the exact specification of the rounds. The *Football Annual for 1888* gives seven rounds and a Final, as do newspapers for that year.

SCOTTISH FA CUP 1887-88

FIFTH ROUND
Arbroath v Cowlairs	5-1
Cambuslang v Ayr	10-0
Thistle v Vale of Leven Wanderers	2-9
Abercorn v St Bernard's	9-0
Queen's Park v Partick Thistle	2-0
St Mirren v Renton	2-3
Our Boys v Albion Rovers	4-1
Dundee Wanderers v Carfin Shamrock	5-2

SIXTH ROUND
Abercorn v Arbroath	3-1
Renton v Dundee Wanderers	5-1
Cambuslang v Our Boys	6-0
Queen's Park v Vale of Leven Wanderers	7-1

SEMI-FINAL
Renton v Queen's Park	3-1
Abercorn v Cambuslang	1-1, 1-10

FINAL AT HAMPDEN PARK
Renton v Cambuslang	6-1

FA CUP 1888-89

FIRST ROUND

Grimsby Town v Sunderland Albion	3-1
Bootle v Preston North End	0-3
Halliwell v Crewe Alexandra	2-2, 5-1
Birmingham St George's v Long Eaton Rangers	3-2
Chatham v South Shore	2-1
Nottingham Forest v Linfield (scratched)	2-2, wo*
Small Heath v West Bromwich Albion	2-3
Burnley v Old Westminsters	4-3
Wolverhampton Wanderers v Old Carthusians	4-3
Walsall Town Swifts v Sheffield Heeley	5-1
The Wednesday v Notts Rangers	1-1, 3-0
Notts County v Old Brightonians	2-0
Blackburn Rovers v Accrington	1-1, 5-0
Swifts v Wrexham	3-1
Aston Villa v Witton	3-2
Derby County v Derby Junction	1-0

*Nottingham Forest travelled to Belfast for the replay but Linfield had scratched in the interim and the clubs played a friendly instead

SECOND ROUND

Grimsby Town v Preston North End	0-2
Halliwell v Birmingham St George's	2-3
Chatham v Nottingham Forest	1-1, 2-2, 3-2
West Bromwich Albion v Burnley	5-1
Wolverhampton Wanderers v Walsall Town Swifts	6-1
The Wednesday v Notts County	3-2
Blackburn Rovers v Swifts (scratched)	wo
Aston Villa v Derby County	5-3

THIRD ROUND

Preston North End v Birmingham St George's	2-0
Chatham v West Bromwich Albion	1-10
Wolverhampton Wanderers v The Wednesday	5-0
Blackburn Rovers v Aston Villa	8-1

SEMI-FINAL

Preston North End v West Bromwich Albion	1-0
Wolverhampton Wanderers v Blackburn Rovers	1-1, 3-1

FINAL AT KENNINGTON OVAL

Preston North End v Wolverhampton Wanderers	3-0

SCOTTISH FA CUP 1888-89

FIFTH ROUND

Third Lanark v Abercorn	5-4*, 2-2, 2-2, 3-1
Renton v Arbroath	3-3, 4-0
Celtic v Clyde	0-1†, 9-2
Dumbarton v Mossend Swifts	3-1
St Mirren v Queen of the South Wanderers	3-1
Campsie	bye
Dumbarton Athletic	bye
East Stirlingshire	bye

*Abercorn protested about bad light
†Celtic protested about bad light and the state of the pitch

SIXTH ROUND

Third Lanark v Campsie	6-0
Dumbarton v St Mirren	1-1, 2-2, 2-2, 3-1
Dumbarton Athletic v Renton	1-2
East Stirlingshire v Celtic	1-2

SEMI-FINAL

Dumbarton v Celtic	1-4
Third Lanark v Renton	2-0

FINAL AT HAMPDEN PARK

Third Lanark v Celtic	3-0‡, 2-1

‡The first game was declared unofficial because of a snowstorm. Third Lanark tried to claim the Cup but the SFA ordered a replay.

William Townley scored the first ever Cup Final hat-trick for Blackburn against The Wednesday in the 1890 Final. Rovers won 6-1 to record the highest score in a Final tie. Wednesday arrived for the Final having lost a disputed earlier tie against Notts County.

FOOTBALL LEAGUE 1888-89

		P	W	D	L	F	A	Pts
1	Preston	22	18	4	0	74	15	40
2	Aston Villa	22	12	5	5	61	43	29
3	Wolves	22	12	4	6	50	37	28
4	Blackburn	22	10	6	6	66	45	26
5	Bolton	22	10	2	10	63	59	22
6	WBA	22	10	2	10	40	46	22
7	Accrington	22	6	8	8	48	48	20
8	Everton	22	9	2	11	35	46	20
9	Burnley	22	7	3	12	42	62	17
10	Derby	22	7	2	13	41	60	16
11	Notts County	22	5	2	15	39	73	12
12	Stoke	22	4	4	14	26	51	12

Top *William McGregor of Aston Villa, whose open letter of 2 March 1888 led to the formation of the Football League. A meeting was held at Anderton's Hotel on the eve of the Cup Final (23 March 1888) and the idea was approved in principle. The details were finalized on 17 April at the Royal Hotel in Manchester by the twelve member clubs. With only 22 fixture dates available, other hopefuls—including Sheffield Wednesday and Nottingham Forest—had to be turned down. The League had grown in simple response to the need to guarantee fixtures. While there were only Cup competitions fixtures would always be called off at short notice for replays, and friendlies could never be guaranteed. Because of the uncertainty, spectators were increasingly reluctant to commit themselves to turning up to a match that might never be played—and so emerged McGregor's inevitable solution. Preston were the first winners of the League. Their performance in 1888-89 was unique for they remain the only side in England and Scotland to have gone a whole season without a League or or Cup defeat.*

FOOTBALL LEAGUE 1889-90

		P	W	D	L	F	A	Pts
1	Preston	22	15	3	4	71	30	33
2	Everton	22	14	3	5	65	40	31
3	Blackburn	22	12	3	7	78	41	27
4	Wolves	22	10	5	7	51	38	25
5	WBA	22	11	3	0	47	50	25
6	Accrington	22	9	6	7	53	56	24
7	Derby	22	9	3	10	43	55	21
8	Aston Villa	22	7	5	10	43	51	19
9	Bolton	22	9	1	12	54	65	19
10	Notts County	22	6	5	11	43	51	17
11	Burnley	22	4	5	13	36	65	13
12	Stoke	22	3	4	15	27	69	10

FA CUP 1889-90

FIRST ROUND

Preston North End v Newton Heath	6-1
Lincoln City v Chester	2-0
Bolton Wanderers v Belfast Distillery	10-1
Sheffield United v Burnley	2-1
The Wednesday v Swifts	6-1
Accrington v West Bromwich Albion	3-1
Notts County v Birmingham St George's	4-4, 6-2
South Shore v Aston Villa	2-4
Bootle v Sunderland Albion*	1-3
Derby Midland v Nottingham Forest	3-0
Blackburn Rovers v Sunderland	4-2
Newcastle West End v Grimsby Town	1-2
Wolverhampton Wanderers v Old Carthusians	2-0
Small Heath v Clapton	3-1
Stoke v Old Westminsters	3-0
Everton v Derby County	11-2

*Sunderland Albion were disqualified

SECOND ROUND

Preston North End v Lincoln City	4-0
Bolton Wanderers v Sheffield United	13-0
The Wednesday v Accrington	2-1
Notts County v Aston Villa	4-1
Bootle v Derby Midland	2-1
Blackburn Rovers v Grimsby Town	3-0
Wolverhampton Wanderers v Small Heath	2-1
Stoke v Everton	4-2

THIRD ROUND

Preston North End v Bolton Wanderers	2-3
The Wednesday v Notts County	5-0*, 2-3*, 2-1
Bootle v Blackburn Rovers	0-7
Wolverhampton Wanderers v Stoke	3-2

*replayed after protest on both occasions

SEMI-FINAL

Bolton Wanderers v The Wednesday	1-2
Blackburn Rovers v Wolverhampton Wanderers	1-0

FINAL AT KENNINGTON OVAL

Blackburn Rovers v The Wednesday	6-1

SCOTTISH FA CUP 1889-90

FOURTH ROUND

Aberdeen v Queen's Park	1-13
Airdrieonians v Abercorn	2-3
Grangemouth v Vale of Leven	1-7
Third Lanark v Linthouse	2-0
Lanemark v St Mirren	2-8
Moffat v Carfin Shamrock	4-2
Ayr v Leith Athletic	1-4
Cowdenbeath v Dunblane	†
Hibernian v Queen of the South Wanderers	†
Kilbirnie v East Stirlingshire	†
Heart of Midlothian v Alloa Athletic	†
East End v Cambuslang	†

†No scores are available. The first named team won in each case.

FIFTH ROUND

Queen's Park v St Mirren	1-0
Cowdenbeath v Abercorn	2-8
Vale of Leven v Heart of Midlothian	3-1
East End v Moffat	2-2*
Third Lanark	bye
Hibernian	bye
Leith Athletic	bye
Kilbirnie	bye

*East End won the replay

SIXTH ROUND

Queen's Park v Leith Athletic	1-0
Abercorn v Hibernian	6-2
Vale of Leven v East End	4-0
Third Lanark v Kilbirnie	4-1

SEMI-FINAL

Vale of Leven v Third Lanark	3-0
Queen's Park v Abercorn	2-0

FINAL AT IBROX PARK

Queen's Park v Vale of Leven	1-1, 2-1

FA CUP 1890-91

FIRST ROUND
Middlesbrough Ironopolis v Blackburn Rovers	
	1-2*, 0-3
Chester v Lincoln City	1-0
Accrington v Bolton Wanderers	2-2, 5-1
Long Eaton Rangers v Wolverhampton Wanderers	
	2-3
Royal Arsenal v Derby County	1-2
The Wednesday v Halliwell	12-0
Crusaders v Birmingham St George's	0-2
West Bromwich Albion v Old Westminsters	
(scratched)	wo
Darwen v Kidderminster	3-1*, 13-0
Sunderland v Everton	1-0
Clapton v Nottingham Forest	0-14
Sunderland Albion v 93rd Highlanders	2-0
Sheffield United v Notts County	1-9
Burnley v Crewe Alexandra	4-2
Stoke v Preston North End	3-0
Aston Villa v Casuals	13-1
*replayed after protest	

SECOND ROUND
Blackburn Rovers v Chester	7-0
Accrington v Wolverhampton Wanderers	2-3
Derby County v The Wednesday	2-3
Birmingham St George's v West Bromwich Albion	
	0-3
Darwen v Sunderland	0-2
Nottingham Forest v Sunderland Albion	
	1-1, 0-0, 5-0
Notts County v Burnley	2-1
Stoke v Aston Villa	3-0

THIRD ROUND
Blackburn Rovers v Wolverhampton Wanderers	2-0
The Wednesday v West Bromwich Albion	0-2
Sunderland v Nottingham Forest	4-0
Notts County v Stoke	1-0

SEMI-FINAL
Blackburn Rovers v West Bromwich Albion	3-2
Sunderland v Notts County	3-3, 0-2

FINAL AT KENNINGTON OVAL
Blackburn Rovers v Notts County	3-1

SCOTTISH FA CUP 1890-91

FIFTH ROUND
Dumbarton v 5th KRV	8-0
Heart of Midlothian v Morton	5-1
Royal Albert v Celtic	0-4*, 0-2
St Mirren v Queen's Park	2-3
Abercorn	bye
Third Lanark	bye
East Stirlingshire	bye
Leith Athletic	bye

*Crowd invaded the pitch 10 minutes before time and forced a replay, which was played at Ibrox.

SIXTH ROUND
Dumbarton v Celtic	3-0
Heart of Midlothian v East Stirlingshire	3-1
Third Lanark v Queen's Park	1-1, 2-2, 4-1
Leith Athletic v Abercorn	2-3

SEMI-FINAL
Dumbarton v Abercorn	3-1
Heart of Midlothian v Third Lanark	4-1

FINAL AT HAMPDEN PARK
Heart of Midlothian v Dumbarton	1-0

In the first round of the FA Cup in 1890–91, Nottingham Forest beat Clapton 14-0 at Clapton. This remains the highest away win in any English first-class fixture. In the same round Darwen scored 13 against Kidderminster, Villa 13 against Casuals and Sheffield Wednesday 12 against Halliwell. Forest's performance was part of a good day for Nottingham – County also won 9-1 away from home.

FOOTBALL LEAGUE 1890-91

		P	W	D	L	F	A	Pts
1	Everton	22	14	1	7	63	29	29
2	Preston	22	12	3	7	44	23	27
3	Notts County	22	11	4	7	52	35	26
4	Wolves	22	12	2	8	39	50	26
5	Bolton	22	12	1	9	47	34	25
6	Blackburn	22	11	2	9	52	43	24
7	Sunderland	22	10	5	7	51	31	23*
8	Burnley	22	9	3	10	52	63	21
9	Aston Villa	22	7	4	11	45	58	18
10	Accrington	22	6	4	12	28	50	16
11	Derby	22	7	1	14	47	81	15
12	WBA	22	5	2	15	34	57	12

*Two points deducted for fielding Ned Doig against WBA on 20 September 1890 before the League had approved his registration from Arbroath.

SCOTTISH LEAGUE 1890-91

		P	W	D	L	F	A	Pts
1=	Dumbarton†	18	13	3	2	61	21	29
1=	Rangers†	18	13	3	2	58	25	29
3	Celtic*	18	11	3	4	48	21	21
4	Cambuslang	18	8	4	6	47	42	20
5	Third Lanark*	18	8	3	7	38	39	15
6	Hearts	18	6	2	10	31	37	14
7	Abercorn	18	5	2	11	36	47	12
8	St Mirren	18	5	1	12	39	62	11
9	Vale of Leven	18	5	1	12	27	65	11
10	Cowlairs*	18	3	4	11	24	50	6

†Dumbarton and Rangers drew 2-2 in a play-off and were declared joint Champions.
*Each had four points deducted for infringements.

FOOTBALL LEAGUE 1891-92

		P	W	D	L	F	A	Pts
1	Sunderland	26	21	0	5	93	36	42
2	Preston	26	18	1	7	61	31	37
3	Bolton	26	17	2	7	51	37	36
4	Aston Villa	26	15	0	11	89	56	30
5	Everton	26	12	4	10	49	49	28
6	Wolves	26	11	4	11	59	46	26
7	Burnley	26	11	4	11	49	45	26
8	Notts County	26	11	4	11	55	51	26
9	Blackburn	26	10	6	10	58	65	26
10	Derby	26	10	4	12	46	52	24
11	Accrington	26	8	4	14	40	78	20
12	WBA	26	6	6	14	51	58	18
13	Stoke	26	5	4	17	38	61	14
14	Darwen	26	4	3	19	38	112	11

SCOTTISH LEAGUE 1891-92

		P	W	D	L	F	A	Pts
1	Dumbarton	22	18	1	3	81	26	37
2	Celtic	22	16	3	3	64	19	35
3	Hearts	22	15	4	3	64	36	34
4	Rangers	22	12	2	8	57	49	26
5	Leith	22	12	1	9	52	38	25
6	Third Lanark	22	9	4	9	44	38	22
7	Clyde	22	8	4	10	64	60	20
8	Renton	22	8	4	10	43	41	20
9	Abercorn	22	6	5	11	45	59	17
10	St Mirren	22	4	5	13	43	56	13
11	Cambuslang	22	2	6	14	21	79	10
12	Vale of Leven	22	0	5	17	24	101	5

During the 1890–91 FA Cup quarter-final between Notts County and Stoke at Trent Bridge a shot was punched off the line by County's left-back Hendry with his goalkeeper Toone well beaten. As the laws made no mention of penalties at the time, Stoke had to take a free-kick on the goal-line which Toone smothered easily. County won the match 1-0 and went on to the Final. The incident provoked so much comment that, partially as a result, penalties were introduced by the FA from September 1891. This led to another controversial incident in which Stoke were also the sufferers the next season. During a

FA CUP 1891-92

FIRST ROUND
Old Westminsters v West Bromwich Albion	2-3
Blackburn Rovers v Derby County	4-1
The Wednesday v Bolton Wanderers	4-1
Small Heath v Royal Arsenal	5-1
Sunderland Albion v Birmingham St George's	4-0
Nottingham Forest v Newcastle East End	2-1
Luton v Middlesbrough	0-3
Preston North End v Middlesbrough Ironopolis	
	2-2, 6-0
Crewe Alexandra v Wolverhampton Wanderers	
	2-2, 1-4
Blackpool v Sheffield United	0-3
Aston Villa v Heanor Town	4-1
Bootle v Darwen	0-2
Crusaders v Accrington	1-4
Sunderland v Notts County	4-0
Everton v Burnley	1-3
Stoke v Casuals	3-0

SECOND ROUND
West Bromwich Albion v Blackburn Rovers	3-1
The Wednesday v Small Heath	2-0
Sunderland Albion v Nottingham Forest	0-1
Middlesbrough v Preston North End	1-2
Wolverhampton Wanderers v Sheffield United	3-1
Aston Villa v Darwen	2-0
Accrington v Sunderland	1-3
Burnley v Stoke	1-3

THIRD ROUND
West Bromwich Albion v The Wednesday	2-1
Nottingham Forest v Preston North End	2-0
Wolverhampton Wanderers v Aston Villa	1-3
Sunderland v Stoke	2-2, 4-0

SEMI-FINAL
West Bromwich Albion v Nottingham Forest	
	1-1, 1-1, 6-2
Aston Villa v Sunderland	4-1

FINAL AT KENNINGTON OVAL
West Bromwich Albion v Aston Villa	3-0

SCOTTISH FA CUP 1891-92

SECOND ROUND
Rangers v Kilmarnock	0-0, 1-1, 3-1
Third Lanark v Dumbarton	1-3
Broxburn Shamrock v Heart of Midlothian	4-5
Annbank v Leith Athletic	2-1
Queen's Park v Bathgate Rovers	6-0
Arbroath v Renton	0-3
Celtic v Kilmarnock Athletic	3-0
Cowlairs v Mid-Annandale	11-2

THIRD ROUND
Celtic v Cowlairs	4-1
Rangers v Annbank	2-0
Renton v Heart of Midlothian	4-4, 1-1, 3-2
Dumbarton v Queen's Park	2-2, 1-4

SEMI-FINAL
Renton v Queen's Park	1-1, 0-3
Celtic v Rangers	5-3

FINAL AT IBROX PARK
Celtic v Queen's Park	1-0*, 5-1

*The final had to be replayed, the first game having been disrupted by an unexpectedly large crowd.

League game at Aston Villa, Stoke were losing 1-0 when a penalty was awarded them just two minutes from time. The Villa keeper picked up the ball and booted it out of the ground. By the time it had been found the referee had blown for full time. The law was soon changed to allow referees to add on time for penalties. The penalty law was changed again as late as 1892 when players were banned from touching the ball twice – and hence dribbling into the net.

FIRST DIVISION

		P	W	D	L	F	A	Pts
1	Sunderland	30	22	4	4	100	36	48
2	Preston	30	17	3	10	57	39	37
3	Everton	30	16	4	10	74	51	36
4	Aston Villa	30	16	3	11	73	62	35
5	Bolton	30	13	6	11	56	55	32
6	Burnley	30	13	4	13	51	44	30
7	Stoke	30	12	5	13	58	48	29
8	WBA	30	12	5	13	58	69	29
9	Blackburn	30	8	13	9	47	56	29
10	Nottm Forest	30	10	8	12	48	52	28
11	Wolves	30	12	4	14	47	68	28
12	Wednesday	30	12	3	15	55	65	27
13	Derby	30	9	9	12	52	64	27
14	Notts County	30	10	4	16	53	61	24
15	Accrington	30	6	11	13	57	81	23
16	Newton Heath	30	6	6	18	50	85	18

SCOTTISH FA CUP 1892-93

FIRST ROUND

Celtic v Linthouse		3-1
Airdrieonians v Third Lanark		3-6
Cowlairs v Queen's Park		1-4
Clyde v Dumbarton		1-6*
Motherwell v Campsie		9-2†, 6-4
St Mirren v Aberdeen		6-4
Dunblane v Broxburn Shamrock		0-3
Stenhousemuir v Heart of Midlothian		1-1, 0-8
Northern v Leith Athletic		1-3
Royal Albert v Cambuslang		6-1
Abercorn v Renton		6-0
St Bernard's v Queen of South Wanderers		5-1
Rangers v Annbank		7-0
King's Park v Monkcastle		6-1
5th KVR v Camelon		5-3
Albion Rovers v Kilmarnock		1-2

*The invasion of the pitch by the crowd caused the game to be abandoned with 25 minutes left to play. The SFA awarded the tie to Dumbarton.
†After a protest about the size of the pitch the tie was replayed.

SECOND ROUND

Celtic v 5th KVR	7-0
Leith Athletic v St Mirren	0-2
Abercorn v Third Lanark	4-5
St Bernard's v Royal Albert	5-2
Broxburn Shamrock v King's Park	3-0
Heart of Midlothian v Motherwell	4-2
Dumbarton v Rangers	0-1
Kilmarnock v Queen's Park	0-8

THIRD ROUND

Heart of Midlothian v Queen's Park	1-1, 2-5
Celtic v Third Lanark	5-1
St Bernard's v Rangers	3-2
Broxburn Shamrock v St Mirren	4-3

SEMI-FINAL

Queen's Park v Broxburn Shamrock	4-2
Celtic v St Bernard's	5-0

FINAL AT IBROX PARK

Queen's Park v Celtic	2-1

Right *Wolverhampton's 1893 team which won the only Final ever to be played at Fallowfield, Manchester, and the first to be initially contested outside London. An Everton reserve side had beaten the Wolves first team 4-2 the week before, but the underdogs won the real thing with a long-range headed goal from captain Harry Allen. The crowd, officially 45,000 but probably twice that number, broke down the gates and invaded the pitch and the match was played in near chaos.*

On 10 December 1892 Sheffield United defeated Burslem Port Vale 10-0 in a League fixture at Burslem. This remains the biggest away win in any Football League match. A contemporary report commented that: 'The Vale keeper lost his spectacles in the mud.'

SECOND DIVISION

		P	W	D	L	F	A	Pts
1	Small Heath	22	17	2	3	90	35	36
2	Sheff United	22	16	3	3	62	19	35
3	Darwen	22	14	2	6	60	36	30
4	Grimsby	22	11	1	10	42	41	23
5	Ardwick	22	9	3	10	45	40	21
6	Burton Swifts	22	9	2	11	47	47	20
7	Northwich Vic	22	9	2	11	42	58	20
8	Bootle	22	8	3	11	49	63	19
9	Lincoln	22	7	3	12	45	51	17
10	Crewe	22	6	3	13	42	69	15
11	Burslem PV	22	6	3	13	30	57	15
12	Walsall TS	22	5	3	14	37	75	13

TEST MATCHES 1892-93

Sheffield United 1 Accrington 0
Darwen 3 Notts County 2
Newton Heath 1 Small Heath 1

Play-off
Newton Heath 5 Small Heath 2

Sheffield United and Darwen promoted
Notts County relegated
Accrington resigned from the League

SCOTTISH LEAGUE

		P	W	D	L	F	A	Pts
1	Celtic	18	14	1	3	54	25	29
2	Rangers	18	12	4	2	41	27	28
3	St Mirren	18	9	2	7	40	39	20
4	Third Lanark	18	9	1	8	53	39	19
5	Hearts	18	8	2	8	39	42	18
6	Leith	18	8	1	9	36	31	17
7	Dumbarton	18	8	1	9	35	35	17
8	Renton	18	5	5	8	31	44	15
9	Abercorn	18	5	1	12	35	52	11
10	Clyde	18	2	2	14	25	55	6

1892-93 Champions Sunderland were the second side to be called 'The Team of all the Talents'. They became the first to score 100 goals or more in a single League season. In fact this total was not surpassed until after the First World War though, by then of course teams were playing far more games. Sunderland's winning margin of 11 points over the second club, Preston North End, has been equalled but never beaten in the division since. Aston Villa equalled it in 1897 as did Manchester United in 1956.

FA CUP 1892-93

FIRST ROUND

Everton v West Bromwich Albion	4-1
Nottingham Forest v Casuals	4-0
The Wednesday v Derby County	3-2*, 0-1†, 4-2
Burnley v Small Heath	2-0
Accrington v Stoke	2-1
Preston North End v Burton Swifts	9-2
Marlow v Middlesbrough Ironopolis	1-3
Notts County v Shankhouse	4-0
Wolverhampton Wanderers v Bolton Wanderers	1-1, 2-1
Newcastle United v Middlesbrough	2-3
Darwen v Aston Villa	5-4
Grimsby Town v Stockton	5-0
Blackburn Rovers v Newton Heath	4-0
Loughborough Town v Northwich Victoria	1-2
Blackpool v Sheffield United	1-3
Sunderland v Woolwich Arsenal	6-0

*Replay after protest
† Replay after second protest

SECOND ROUND

Everton v Nottingham Forest	4-2
The Wednesday v Burnley	1-0
Accrington v Preston North End	1-4
Middlesbrough Ironopolis v Notts County	3-2
Wolverhampton Wanderers v Middlesbrough	2-1
Darwen v Grimsby Town	2-0
Blackburn Rovers v Northwich Victoria	4-1
Sheffield United v Sunderland	1-3

THIRD ROUND

Everton v The Wednesday	3-0
Preston North End v Middlesbrough Ironopolis	2-2, 7-0
Wolverhampton Wanderers v Darwen	5-0
Blackburn Rovers v Sunderland	3-0

SEMI-FINAL

Everton v Preston North End	2-2, 0-0, 2-1
Wolverhampton Wanderers v Blackburn Rovers	2-1

FINAL AT FALLOWFIELD (MANCHESTER)

Wolverhampton Wanderers v Everton	1-0

With the introduction of a Second Division in 1892 – in fact the Football League simply absorbed the Football Alliance – a promotion/relegation system of test matches was instituted. This lasted until 1898 when Stoke and Burnley, realising that if they drew their match they would both be in the First Division, contrived a scoreless draw. Suspicions were aroused and a system of two up/two down was introduced.

COLORSPORT

Major Competitions in Season 1893-94

FIRST DIVISION

		P	W	D	L	F	A	Pts
1	Aston Villa	30	19	6	5	84	42	44
2	Sunderland	30	17	4	9	72	44	38
3	Derby	30	16	4	10	73	62	36
4	Blackburn	30	16	2	12	69	53	34
5	Burnley	30	15	4	11	61	51	34
6	Everton	30	15	3	12	90	57	33
7	Nottm Forest	30	14	4	12	57	48	32
8	WBA	30	14	4	12	66	59	32
9	Wolves	30	14	3	13	52	63	31
10	Sheff United	30	13	5	12	47	61	31
11	Stoke	30	13	3	14	65	79	29
12	Wednesday	30	9	8	13	48	57	26
13	Bolton	30	10	4	16	38	52	24
14	Preston	30	10	3	17	44	56	23
15	Darwen	30	7	5	18	37	83	19
16	Newton Heath	30	6	2	22	36	72	14

SECOND DIVISION

		P	W	D	L	F	A	Pts
1	Liverpool	28	22	6	0	77	18	50
2	Small Heath	28	21	0	7	103	44	42
3	Notts County	28	18	3	7	70	31	39
4	Newcastle	28	15	6	7	66	39	36
5	Grimsby	28	15	2	11	71	58	32
6	Burton Swifts	28	14	3	11	79	61	31
7	Burslem PV	28	13	4	11	66	64	30
8	Lincoln	28	11	6	11	59	58	28
9	Woolwich A	28	12	4	12	52	55	28
10	Walsall TS	28	10	3	15	51	61	23
11	Md Ironopolis	28	8	4	16	37	72	20
12	Crewe	28	6	7	15	42	73	19
13	Ardwick	28	8	2	18	47	71	18
14	Rotherham Twn	28	6	3	19	44	91	15
15	Northwich Vic	28	3	3	22	30	98	9

TEST MATCHES 1893-94

Preston North End 4 Notts County 0
Small Heath 3 Darwen 1
Liverpool 2 Newton Heath 0

Liverpool and Small Heath promoted
Darwen and Newton Heath relegated

At the beginning of the 1894-95 season Liverpool completed what remained the longest League run without defeat until Leeds broke it in 1969. They had joined the Second Division in 1893 and remained undefeated in the 28-game season. They then won their Test Match to gain promotion to the First, where they drew the first two games before suffering their first ever League defeat by Aston Villa. This was after a run of 31 games.

Aston Villa turned the tables on Sunderland in Season 1893-94 by taking the League Championship with a margin of 6 points. It was the start of an era in which they became the leading club in the land. Over a period of seven years Villa won five Championships and two FA Cup Finals. They also become only the second club to win the double (after Preston North End) in 1897. Yet as recently as 1891 they had finished fourth from bottom and had had to seek re-election to the League.

When the FA made Goodison the venue for the 1894 Cup Final Notts County protested that it was virtually a home tie for Bolton. They won anyway, with Jimmy Logan (seated centre) scoring a hat-trick to equal William Townley's feat of 1890. Only one man, Stan Mortensen in 1953, has done it since.

During the 1893-94 season Everton scored 22 goals in the space of four matches. Jack Southworth claimed 15 of these, including six on the trot against West Bromwich on 30 December 1893. Everton won 7-1.

FA CUP 1893-94

FIRST ROUND
Middlesbrough Ironopolis v Luton Town	2-1
Nottingham Forest v Heanor Town	1-0
Notts County v Burnley	1-0
Stockport County v Burton Wanderers	0-1
Leicester Fosse v South Shore	2-1
Derby County v Darwen	2-0
Newton Heath v Middlesbrough	4-0
West Bromwich Albion v Blackburn Rovers	2-3
Newcastle United v Sheffield United	2-0
Small Heath v Bolton Wanderers	3-4
Liverpool v Grimsby Town	3-0
Preston North End v Reading	18-0
Woolwich Arsenal v The Wednesday	1-2
Stoke v Everton	1-0
Sunderland v Accrington	3-0
Aston Villa v Wolverhampton Wanderers	4-2

SECOND ROUND
Middlesbrough Ironopolis v Nottingham Forest	0-2
Notts County v Burton Wanderers	2-1
Leicester Fosse v Derby County	0-0, 0-3
Newton Heath v Blackburn Rovers	0-0, 1-5
Newcastle United v Bolton Wanderers	1-2
Liverpool v Preston North End	3-2
The Wednesday v Stoke	1-0
Sunderland v Aston Villa	2-2, 1-3

THIRD ROUND
Nottingham Forest v Notts County	1-1, 1-4
Derby County v Blackburn Rovers	1-4
Bolton Wanderers v Liverpool	3-0
The Wednesday v Aston Villa	3-2

SEMI-FINAL
Notts County v Blackburn Rovers	1-0
Bolton Wanderers v The Wednesday	2-1

FINAL AT GOODISON PARK
Notts County v Bolton Wanderers	4-1

SCOTTISH FIRST DIVISION

		P	W	D	L	F	A	Pts
1	Celtic	18	14	1	3	53	32	29
2	Hearts	18	11	4	3	46	32	26
3	St Bernard's	18	11	1	6	53	39	23
4	Rangers	18	8	4	6	44	30	20
5	Dumbarton	18	7	5	6	32	35	19
6	St Mirren	18	7	3	8	49	47	17
7	Third Lanark	18	7	3	8	38	44	17
8	Dundee	18	6	3	9	47	59	15
9	Leith	18	4	2	12	36	46	10
10	Renton	18	1	2	15	23	57	4

Below *Notts County, the first Second Division side to win the FA Cup, in 1894.*

SCOTTISH FA CUP 1893-94

FIRST ROUND
Arbroath v Broxburn Shamrock	8-3
St Bernard's v Kilmarnock	3-1
Renton v Grangemouth	7-1
Cambuslang v East Stirlingshire	3-2
Port Glasgow Athletic v Airdrieonians	7-5
Dumbarton v Vale of Leven	2-1
Clyde v King's Park	5-2
Albion Rovers v 2nd Black Watch	6-0
Battlefield v Thistle	3-0
Leith Athletic v Orion	11-2
Queen's Park v Linthouse	5-1
Third Lanark v Inverness Thistle	9-3
Celtic v Hurlford	6-0
Abercorn v 5th KRV	2-1
St Mirren v Heart of Midlothian	1-0
Rangers v Cowlairs	8-0

SECOND ROUND
Abercorn v Battlefield	3-0
Port Glasgow Athletic v Renton	3-1
Queen's Park v Arbroath	3-0
Clyde v Cambuslang	6-0
Rangers v Leith Athletic	2-0
Third Lanark v St Mirren	3-2
Celtic v Albion Rovers	7-0
St Bernard's v Dumbarton	3-1

THIRD ROUND
Third Lanark v Port Glasgow Athletic	2-1
Celtic v St Bernard's	8-1
Clyde v Rangers	0-5
Abercorn v Queen's Park	3-3, 3-3, 0-2

SEMI-FINAL
Third Lanark v Celtic	3-5
Rangers v Queen's Park	1-1, 3-1

FINAL AT HAMPDEN PARK
Rangers v Celtic	3-1

SCOTTISH SECOND DIVISION

		P	W	D	L	F	A	Pts
1	Hibernian	18	13	3	2	72	27	29
2	Cowlairs	18	13	1	4	73	32	27
3	Clyde †	18	11	2	5	50	37	24
4	Motherwell	18	11	1	6	63	46	23
5	Partick	18	10	0	8	58	59	20
6	Port Glasgow	18	9	2	7	52	53	13*
7	Abercorn	18	5	2	11	42	60	12
8	Morton	18	4	1	13	36	63	9
9	Northern	18	3	3	12	34	62	9
10	Thistle	18	2	3	13	32	73	7

*Port Glasgow Athletic had 7 points deducted for fielding an ineligible player
† Clyde promoted to First Division

COLORSPORT

League Tables 1894-95

FIRST DIVISION

		P	W	D	L	F	A	Pts
1	Sunderland	30	21	5	4	80	37	47
2	Everton	30	18	6	6	82	50	42
3	Aston Villa	30	17	5	8	82	43	39
4	Preston	30	15	5	10	62	46	35
5	Blackburn	30	11	10	9	59	49	32
6	Sheff United	30	14	4	12	57	55	32
7	Nottm Forest	30	13	5	12	50	56	31
8	Wednesday	30	12	4	14	50	55	28
9	Burnley	30	11	4	15	44	56	26
10	Bolton	30	9	7	14	61	62	25
11	Wolves	30	9	7	14	43	63	25
12	Small Heath	30	9	7	14	50	74	25
13	WBA	30	10	4	16	51	66	24
14	Stoke	30	9	6	15	50	67	24
15	Derby	30	7	9	14	45	68	23
16	Liverpool	30	7	8	15	51	70	22

SECOND DIVISION

		P	W	D	L	F	A	Pts
1	Bury	30	23	2	5	78	33	48
2	Notts County	30	17	5	8	75	45	39
3	Newton Heath	30	15	8	7	78	44	38
4	Leicester Fosse	30	15	8	7	72	53	38
5	Grimsby	30	18	1	11	79	52	37
6	Darwen	30	16	4	10	74	43	36
7	Burton Wand	30	14	7	9	67	39	35
8	Woolwich A	30	14	6	10	75	58	34
9	Man City	30	14	3	13	82	72	31
10	Newcastle	30	12	3	15	72	84	27
11	Burton Swifts	30	11	3	16	52	74	25
12	Rotherham T	30	11	2	17	55	62	24
13	Lincoln	30	10	0	20	52	92	20
14	Walsall TS	30	10	0	20	47	92	20
15	Burslem PV	30	7	4	19	39	77	18
16	Crewe	30	3	4	23	26	103	10

FA CUP 1894-95

FIRST ROUND

Aston Villa v Derby County	2-1
Newcastle United v Burnley	2-1
Barnsley St Peter's v Liverpool	1-1, 0-4
Southampton St Mary's v Nottingham Forest	1-4
Sunderland v Fairfield	11-1
Luton Town v Preston North End	0-2
Bolton Wanderers v Woolwich Arsenal	1-0
Bury v Leicester Fosse	4-1
Sheffield United v Millwall Athletic	3-1
Small Heath v West Bromwich Albion	1-2
Darwen v Wolverhampton Wanderers	0-0, 0-2
Newton Heath v Stoke	2-3
The Wednesday v Notts County	5-1
Middlesbrough v Chesterfield	4-0
Southport Central v Everton	0-3
Burton Wanderers v Blackburn Rovers	1-2

SECOND ROUND

Aston Villa v Newcastle United	7-1
Liverpool v Nottingham Forest	0-2
Sunderland v Preston North End	2-0
Bolton Wanderers v Bury	1-0
Sheffield United v West Bromwich Albion	1-1, 1-2
Wolverhampton Wanderers v Stoke	2-0
The Wednesday v Middlesbrough	6-1
Everton v Blackburn Rovers	1-1, 3-2

THIRD ROUND

Aston Villa v Nottingham Forest	6-2
Sunderland v Bolton Wanderers	2-1
West Bromwich Albion v Wolverhampton Wanderers	1-0
The Wednesday v Everton	2-0

SEMI-FINAL

Aston Villa v Sunderland	2-1
West Bromwich Albion v The Wednesday	2-0

FINAL AT CRYSTAL PALACE

Aston Villa v West Bromwich Albion	1-0

SCOTTISH FIRST DIVISION

		P	W	D	L	F	A	Pts
1	Hearts	18	15	1	2	50	18	31
2	Celtic	18	11	4	3	50	29	26
3	Rangers	18	10	2	6	41	26	22
4	Third Lanark	18	10	1	7	51	39	21
5	St Mirren	18	9	1	8	34	34	19
6	St Bernard's	18	8	1	9	37	40	17
7	Clyde	18	8	0	10	38	47	16
8	Dundee	18	6	2	10	28	33	14
9	Leith	18	3	1	14	32	64	7
10	Dumbarton	18	3	1	14	27	58	7

SCOTTISH SECOND DIVISION

		P	W	D	L	F	A	Pts
1	Hibernian†	18	14	2	2	92	28	30
2	Motherwell	18	10	2	6	56	39	22
3	Port Glasgow	18	8	4	6	62	56	20
4	Renton*	17	10	0	7	46	44	20
5	Morton	18	9	1	8	59	63	19
6	Airdrieonians	18	8	2	8	68	45	18
7	Partick	18	8	2	8	51	59	18
8	Abercorn	18	7	3	8	48	66	17
9	Dundee Wand*	17	3	1	13	44	86	9*
10	Cowlairs	18	2	3	13	37	77	7

† Hibernian elected to First Division
*Dundee Wanderers and Renton played each other only once. Dundee were awarded two points when Renton failed to turn up for the return fixture.

TEST MATCHES 1894-95

Bury 1 Liverpool 0
Stoke 3 Newton Heath 0
Derby County 2 Notts County 1
Bury promoted. Liverpool relegated.

SCOTTISH FA CUP 1894-95

FIRST ROUND

St Bernard's v Airdrieonians	4-2
Slamannan Rovers v Renton	2-3*, 0-4
Ayr Parkhouse v Polton Vale	5-2
Clyde v Stevenston Thistle	7-2
Rangers v Heart of Midlothian	1-2
Orion v Dundee	1-5
Kilmarnock v East Stirlingshire	5-1
Raith Rovers v 5th KRV	6-3*, 3-4
Celtic v Queen's Park	4-1
Dumbarton v Galston	2-1
Leith Athletic v Abercorn	5-1*, 1-4
St Mirren v Battlefield	5-0*, 8-1
Annbank v Third Lanark	6-4
Hibernian v Forfar Athletic	6-1
Motherwell v Mossend Swifts	1-2
Lochee United v King's Park	2-5

*These four ties were replayed after various protests. For example the Slamannan crowd was unruly; Raith Rovers failed to provide goal nets.

SECOND ROUND

St Bernard's v Kilmarnock	3-1
Renton v 5th KRV	6-0
Dundee v St Mirren	2-0
Heart of Midlothian v Abercorn	6-1
Clyde v Annbank	4-2
Ayr Parkhouse v Mossend Swifts	3-1
King's Park v Dumbarton	2-1
Hibernian v Celtic	2-0†, 0-2

†Celtic protested that Hibs fielded an ineligible player and a replay was agreed.

THIRD ROUND

St Bernard's v Clyde	2-1
Ayr Parkhouse v Renton	2-3
Dundee v Celtic	1-0
Heart of Midlothian v King's Park	4-2

SEMI-FINAL

Dundee v Renton	1-1, 3-3, 0-3
Heart of Midlothian v St Bernard's	0-0, 0-1

FINAL AT IBROX PARK

St Bernard's v Renton	2-1

The 1895 Cup Final was the first ever to be held at the Crystal Palace, and it got off to a remarkable start. Within 30 seconds a shot from Bob Chatt had ricocheted off John Devey's knee past the helpless West Bromwich goalkeeper Reader and Villa had won the Cup. Because of confusion at the turnstiles—the crowd of 42,000 was then the largest ever seen in London—many spectators missed the game's only goal, which remains the quickest ever scored in a Cup Final. The match was the third Final between Villa and their neighbours in 8 years; Villa had won 2-0 in 1887 and West Brom 3-0 in 1892, so the aggregate was level at three goals each. They remain the only pair of clubs ever to have met each other in three Finals. Yet another oddity to emerge from this game was that both teams, West Bromwich and Aston Villa, lost the Cup. In the winners' case this was the result of its theft, on 11 September, from **below** the window of one William

Shillcock, a boot and shoe manufacturer, who was displaying it to help advertise his wares. The Cup was never recovered and Villa were fined £25, which was used to purchase a replica of the original from Vaughton's of Birmingham. The Monday after the Final, meanwhile, Albion played their last League match needing a five-goal victory to avoid the test matches. They beat Wednesday 6-0; allegations of 'fixing' were never substantiated. In 1958 one Harry Burge, then 83, confessed to having stolen the Cup and having melted it down to make half-crowns. It was probably worth about £20.

League Tables 1895-96

FIRST DIVISION

		P	W	D	L	F	A	Pts
1	Aston Villa	30	20	5	5	78	45	45
2	Derby	30	17	7	6	68	35	41
3	Everton	30	16	7	7	66	43	39
4	Bolton	30	16	5	9	49	37	37
5	Sunderland	30	15	7	8	52	41	37
6	Stoke	30	15	0	15	56	47	30
7	Wednesday	30	12	5	13	44	53	29
8	Blackburn	30	12	5	13	40	50	29
9	Preston	30	11	6	13	44	48	28
10	Burnley	30	10	7	13	48	44	27
11	Bury	30	12	3	15	50	54	27
12	Sheff United	30	10	6	14	40	50	26
13	Nottm Forest	30	11	3	16	42	57	25
14	Wolves	30	10	1	19	61	65	21
15	Small Heath	30	8	4	18	39	79	20
16	WBA	30	6	7	17	30	59	19

SECOND DIVISION

		P	W	D	L	F	A	Pts
1	Liverpool	30	22	2	6	106	32	46
2	Man City	30	21	4	5	63	38	46
3	Grimsby	30	20	2	8	82	38	42
4	Burton Wand	30	19	4	7	69	40	42
5	Newcastle	30	16	2	12	73	50	34
6	Newton Heath	30	15	3	12	66	57	33
7	Woolwich A	30	14	4	12	59	42	32
8	Leicester Fosse	30	14	4	12	57	44	32
9	Darwen	30	12	6	12	72	67	30
10	Notts County	30	12	2	16	57	54	26
11	Burton Swifts	30	10	4	16	39	69	24
12	Loughborough	30	9	5	16	40	67	23
13	Lincoln	30	9	4	17	53	75	22
14	Burslem PV	30	7	4	19	43	78	18
15	Rotherham Tn	30	7	3	20	34	97	17
16	Crewe	30	5	3	22	30	95	13

SCOTTISH FIRST DIVISION

		P	W	D	L	F	A	Pts
1	Celtic	18	15	0	3	64	25	30
2	Rangers	18	11	4	3	57	39	26
3	Hibernian	18	11	2	5	58	39	24
4	Hearts	18	11	0	7	67	36	22
5	Dundee	18	7	2	9	33	40	16
6	Third Lanark	18	7	1	10	47	51	15
7	St Bernard's	18	7	1	10	36	53	15
8	St Mirren	18	5	3	10	31	51	13
9	Clyde	18	4	3	11	39	59	11
10	Dumbarton	18	4	0	14	36	75	8

SCOTTISH SECOND DIVISION

		P	W	D	L	F	A	Pts
1	Abercorn*	18	12	3	3	53	31	27
2	Leith	18	11	1	6	55	37	23
3	Renton	18	9	3	6	40	28	21
4	Kilmarnock	18	10	1	7	51	45	21
5	Airdrieonians	18	7	4	7	48	44	18
6	Partick	18	8	2	8	46	54	18
7	Port Glasgow	18	6	4	8	40	41	16
8	Motherwell	18	5	3	10	31	52	13
9	Morton	18	4	4	10	42	50	12
10	Linthouse	18	5	1	12	25	49	11

*Abercorn elected to First Division

Below *Fred Spiksley, the Wednesday left-winger who scored both goals in the 2-1 win over Wolverhampton Wanderers which took the FA Cup to Sheffield for the first time. It was also the first time the new Cup, made after the original had been stolen from a Birmingham shop, had been presented.*

FA CUP 1895-96

SECOND ROUND

Wolverhampton Wanderers v Liverpool	2-0
Burnley v Stoke	1-1, 1-7
Derby County v Newton Heath	1-1, 5-1
Grimsby Town v West Bromwich Albion	1-1, 0-3
The Wednesday v Sunderland	2-1
Everton v Sheffield United	3-0
Blackpool v Bolton Wanderers	0-2
Newcastle United v Bury	1-3

THIRD ROUND

Wolverhampton Wanderers v Stoke	3-0
Derby County v West Bromwich Albion	1-0
The Wednesday v Everton	4-0
Bolton Wanderers v Bury	2-0

SEMI-FINAL

Wolverhampton Wanderers v Derby County	2-1
The Wednesday v Bolton Wanderers	1-1, 3-1

FINAL AT CRYSTAL PALACE

The Wednesday v Wolverhampton Wanderers	2-1

SCOTTISH FA CUP 1895-96

FIRST ROUND

Blantyre v Heart of Midlothian	1-12
East Stirlingshire v Hibernian	2-3
St Bernard's v Clackmannan	8-1
Renton v Cowdenbeath	1-0
Lochgelly United v Raith Rovers	2-1*, 2-5
Dumbarton v Rangers	1-1, 1-3
Celtic v Queen's Park	2-4
Third Lanark v Leith Athletic	6-0
Annbank v Kilmarnock	3-2
Ayr v Abercorn	3-2
Port Glasgow Athletic v Arthurlie	4-2
St Mirren v Alloa Athletic	7-0
Arbroath v King's Park	5-0
Morton v Dundee	2-3
Clyde v Polton Vale	3-0
St Johnstone v Dundee Wanderers	4-2

*A Lochgelly player, David 'Anderson', was in fact David McLaren of Lochee United and had already appeared for that club in an earlier round. After a protest from Raith the tie was replayed.

SECOND ROUND

Heart of Midlothian v Ayr	5-1
Hibernian v Raith Rovers	6-1
St Bernard's v Annbank	2-0
Renton v Clyde	2-1
Rangers v St Mirren	5-1
Third Lanark v Dundee	4-1
Queen's Park v Port Glasgow Athletic	8-1
Arbroath v St Johnstone	3-1

THIRD ROUND

Heart of Midlothian v Arbroath	4-0
Hibernian v Rangers	3-2
St Bernard's v Queen's Park	3-2
Renton v Third Lanark	3-3, 2-0

SEMI-FINAL

Heart of Midlothian v St Bernard's	1-0
Hibernian v Renton	2-1

FINAL AT LOGIE GREEN, EDINBURGH

Heart of Midlothian v Hibernian	3-1

TEST MATCHES 1895-96

Man City 1 WBA 1	Liverpool 2 WBA 0
Small Heath 0 Liverpool 0	Liverpool 4 Small Heath 0
WBA 6 Man City 1	Small Heath 8 Man City 0
Man City 3 Small Heath 0	WBA 2 Liverpool 0

	P	W	D	L	F	A	Pts
Liverpool	4	2	1	1	6	2	5
WBA	4	2	1	1	9	4	5
Small Heath	4	1	1	2	8	7	3
Man City	4	1	1	2	5	15	3

Liverpool promoted. Small Heath relegated.

Above left *John Reynolds, who played at half-back in the England team which defeated Scotland 3-0 at Everton in 1895. Reynolds, though born in Blackburn, had played five times for Ireland during a spell with Distillery in 1890 and 1891. He then moved to West Bromwich, with whom he won a cap for England against Scotland. He then moved to Villa, with whom he won another seven caps. Only one other player, R E Evans, has been known to play for two of the home countries.*

181

League Tables 1896-97

FIRST DIVISION

		P	W	D	L	F	A	Pts
1	Aston Villa	30	21	5	4	73	38	47
2	Sheff United	30	13	10	7	42	29	36
3	Derby	30	16	4	10	70	50	36
4	Preston	30	11	12	7	55	40	34
5	Liverpool	30	12	9	9	46	38	33
6	Wednesday	30	10	11	9	42	37	31
7	Everton	30	14	3	13	62	57	31
8	Bolton	30	12	6	12	40	43	30
9	Bury	30	10	10	10	39	44	30
10	Wolves	30	11	6	13	45	41	28
11	Nottm Forest	30	9	8	13	44	49	26
12	WBA	30	10	6	14	33	56	26
13	Stoke	30	11	3	16	48	59	25
14	Blackburn	30	11	3	16	35	62	25
15	Sunderland	30	7	9	14	34	47	23
16	Burnley	30	6	7	17	43	61	19

SECOND DIVISION

		P	W	D	L	F	A	Pts
1	Notts County	30	19	4	7	92	43	42
2	Newton Heath	30	17	5	8	56	34	39
3	Grimsby	30	17	4	9	66	45	38
4	Small Heath	30	16	5	9	69	47	37
5	Newcastle	30	17	1	12	56	52	35
6	Man City	30	12	8	10	58	50	32
7	Gainsborough	30	12	7	11	50	47	31
8	Blackpool	30	13	5	12	59	56	31
9	Leicester Fosse	30	13	4	13	59	56	30
10	Woolwich A	30	13	4	13	68	70	30
11	Darwen	30	14	0	16	67	61	28
12	Walsall	30	11	4	15	53	69	26
13	Loughborough	30	12	1	17	50	64	25
14	Burton Swifts	30	9	6	15	46	61	24
15	Burton Wand	30	9	2	19	31	67	20
16	Lincoln	30	5	2	23	27	85	12

TEST MATCHES 1896-97

Notts County 1 Sunderland 0
Newton Heath 2 Burnley 0
Burnley 0 Notts County 1
Sunderland 2 Newton Heath 0
Sunderland 0 Notts County 0
Newton Heath 1 Sunderland 1
Burnley 2 Newton Heath 0
Notts County 1 Burnley 1

	P	W	D	L	F	A	Pts
Notts County	4	2	2	0	3	1	6
Sunderland	4	1	2	1	3	2	4
Burnley	4	1	1	2	3	4	3
Newton Heath	4	1	1	2	3	5	3

Notts County promoted
Burnley relegated

FA CUP 1896-97

FIRST ROUND
Aston Villa v Newcastle United	5-0
Small Heath v Notts County	1-2
Preston North End v Manchester City	6-0
Stoke v Glossop North End	5-2
Burnley v Sunderland	0-1
Nottingham Forest v The Wednesday	1-0
Luton Town v West Bromwich Albion	0-1
Liverpool v Burton Swifts	4-3
Everton v Burton Wanderers	5-2
Stockton v Bury	0-0, 1-12
Blackburn Rovers v Sheffield United	2-1
Millwall Athletic v Wolverhampton Wanderers	1-2
Derby County v Barnsley St Peter's	8-1
Bolton Wanderers v Grimsby Town	0-0, 3-3, 3-2
Heanor Town v Southampton St Mary's	1-1, 0-1
Newton Heath v Kettering	5-1

SECOND ROUND
Aston Villa v Notts County	2-1
Preston North End v Stoke	2-1
Sunderland v Nottingham Forest	1-3
West Bromwich Albion v Liverpool	1-2
Everton v Bury	3-0
Blackburn Rovers v Wolverhampton Wanderers	2-1
Derby County v Bolton Wanderers	4-1
Southampton St Mary's v Newton Heath	1-1, 1-3

THIRD ROUND
Aston Villa v Preston North End	1-1, 0-0, 3-2
Nottingham Forest v Liverpool	1-1, 0-1
Everton v Blackburn Rovers	2-0
Derby County v Newton Heath	2-0

SEMI-FINAL
Aston Villa v Liverpool	3-0
Everton v Derby County	3-2

FINAL AT CRYSTAL PALACE
Aston Villa v Everton	3-2

SCOTTISH FA CUP 1896-97

FIRST ROUND
Arthurlie v Celtic	4-2
Third Lanark v Newton Stewart Athletic	8-1
Heart of Midlothian v Clyde	2-0
St Bernard's v Queen's Park	2-1
St Mirren v Renton	5-1
Partick Thistle v Rangers	2-4
Dumbarton v Raith Rovers	2-1
Duncrab Park v Hibernian	1-10
Motherwell v Kilmarnock	3-3, 2-5
Abercorn v Hurlford	4-0
Falkirk v Orion	2-0
Dundee v Inverness Thistle	7-1
Morton v Johnstone	3-1
Blantyre v Bathgate	5-0
Leith Athletic v Dunblane	5-1
Lochgelly United v King's Park	1-2

SECOND ROUND
Arthurlie v Morton	1-5
Kilmarnock v Falkirk	7-3
Third Lanark v Heart of Midlothian	5-2
Dumbarton v Leith Athletic	4-4, 3-3, 3-2
Rangers v Hibernian	3-0
Dundee v King's Park	5-0
St Bernard's v St Mirren	5-0
Abercorn v Blantyre	4-1

THIRD ROUND
Dumbarton v St Bernard's	2-0
Morton v Abercorn	2-2, 3-2
Dundee v Rangers	0-4
Kilmarnock v Third Lanark	3-1

SEMI-FINAL
Morton v Rangers	2-7
Dumbarton v Kilmarnock	4-3

FINAL AT HAMPDEN PARK
Rangers v Dumbarton	5-1

SCOTTISH FIRST DIVISION

		P	W	D	L	F	A	Pts
1	Hearts	18	13	2	3	47	22	28
2	Hibernian	18	12	2	4	50	20	26
3	Rangers	18	11	3	4	64	30	25
4	Celtic	18	10	4	4	42	18	24
5	Dundee	18	10	2	6	38	30	22
6	St Mirren	18	9	1	8	38	29	19
7	St Bernard's	18	7	0	11	32	40	14
8	Third Lanark	18	5	1	12	29	46	11
9	Clyde	18	4	0	14	27	65	8
10	Abercorn	18	1	1	16	21	88	3

SCOTTISH SECOND DIVISION

		P	W	D	L	F	A	Pts
1	Partick †	18	14	3	1	61	28	31
2	Leith	18	13	1	4	54	27	27
3	Kilmarnock	18	10	1	7	44	35	21
4	Airdrieonians	18	10	1	7	48	40	21
5	Morton	18	7	2	9	38	40	16
6	Renton	18	6	2	10	35	40	14
7	Linthouse	18	8	2	8	44	52	14*
8	Port Glasgow	18	4	5	9	39	50	13
9	Motherwell	18	6	1	11	40	55	13
10	Dumbarton	18	2	2	14	27	63	6

*Four points deducted for fielding an
    ineligible player.
†Partick elected to First Division

RILEY'S NOTED FOOTBALLS, &c.

THE "ROYAL RILEY."   THE "ROYAL RILEY."

The ROYAL RILEY Football, Buttonless, as illustration.
Best Selected Quality, Match Size.   Each, Post Free.   **8/3.**
The ROYAL WONDER Football, Buttonless, as Illustration
Superior Practice Quality, Full Size.   Each, Post Free   **6/6.**
The CUP-TIE Football, 8 Section, Button Ends.
    Selected Quality, Match Size,   Each, Post Free   **7/6.**
The CUP-TIE Football,   ditto.   Size 4, ONLY   **7/-.**
The SCOT FOOTBALL, Buttonless Pattern, Selected
CHROME Waterproof Leather, Match Size only.   Post Free,   **10/-.**
SPECIAL TERMS TO SHOPS. Fully Illustrated List of all Football Goods, Hockey, &c., FREE.   Telegrams: "Cricket," Accrington.
E. J. RILEY, Ltd., WILLOW MILLS, ACCRINGTON.

Above *Footballs from Lancashire, as used in the 1890s.*

Left *The Aston Villa side that won the double in 1897. Their eleven point margin over the second League club remains a record and the double was not repeated until the Spurs of 64 years later.*

League Tables 1897-98

FIRST DIVISION

		P	W	D	L	F	A	Pts
1	Sheff United	30	17	8	5	56	31	42
2	Sunderland	30	16	5	9	43	30	37
3	Wolves	30	14	7	9	57	41	35
4	Everton	30	13	9	8	48	39	35
5	Wednesday	30	15	3	12	51	42	33
6	Aston Villa	30	14	5	11	61	51	33
7	WBA	30	11	10	9	44	45	32
8	Nottm Forest	30	11	9	10	47	49	31
9	Liverpool	30	11	6	13	48	45	28
10	Derby	30	11	6	13	57	61	28
11	Bolton	30	11	4	15	28	41	26
12	Preston NE	30	8	8	14	35	43	24
13	Notts County	30	8	8	14	36	46	24
14	Bury	30	8	8	14	39	51	24
15	Blackburn	30	7	10	13	39	54	24
16	Stoke	30	8	8	14	35	55	24

SECOND DIVISION

		P	W	D	L	F	A	Pts
1	Burnley	30	20	8	2	80	24	48
2	Newcastle	30	21	3	6	64	32	45
3	Man City	30	15	9	6	66	36	39
4	Newton Heath	30	16	6	8	64	35	38
5	Woolwich A	30	16	5	9	69	49	37
6	Small Heath	30	16	4	10	58	50	36
7	Leicester Fosse	30	13	7	10	46	35	33
8	Luton	30	13	4	13	68	50	30
9	Gainsborough	30	12	6	12	50	54	30
10	Walsall	30	12	5	13	58	58	29
11	Blackpool	30	10	5	15	49	61	25
12	Grimsby	30	10	4	16	52	62	24
13	Burton Swifts	30	8	5	17	38	69	21
14	Lincoln	30	6	5	19	43	82	17
15	Darwen	30	6	2	22	31	76	14
16	Loughborough	30	6	2	22	24	87	14

SCOTTISH FIRST DIVISION

		P	W	D	L	F	A	Pts
1	Celtic	18	15	3	0	56	13	33
2	Rangers	18	13	3	2	71	15	29
3	Hibernian	18	10	2	6	47	29	22
4	Hearts	18	8	4	6	54	33	20
5	Third Lanark	18	9	1	8	39	41	19
6	St Mirren	18	8	2	8	30	37	18
7	Dundee*	18	5	3	10	29	36	13
8	Partick*	18	6	1	11	34	62	13
9	St Bernard's	18	4	1	13	35	67	9
10	Clyde	18	1	3	14	21	83	5

*Partick Thistle and Dundee played a test match to decide the bottom three and Dundee won 2-0

SCOTTISH SECOND DIVISION

		P	W	D	L	F	A	Pts
1	Kilmarnock	18	14	1	3	64	29	29
2	Port Glasgow	18	12	1	5	66	36	25
3	Morton	18	9	4	5	47	38	22
4	Leith	18	9	2	7	45	41	20
5	Linthouse	18	6	4	8	38	39	16
6	Abercorn	18	6	4	8	33	41	16
7	Ayr	18	7	2	9	36	45	16
8	Airdrieonians	18	6	2	10	44	56	14
9	Hamilton*	18	5	2	11	28	51	12
10	Motherwell	18	3	4	11	31	56	10

*Took the place of Renton, who resigned

Left *Ernest 'Nudger' Needham, who led his club, Sheffield United, to the League Championship, the first honour in their history.*

Below *Harry Linacre, the Nottingham Forest goalkeeper and an England cap in the early part of the twentieth century. Linacre came from a great footballing family in Aston-on-Trent, near Derby. His two uncles, Frank and Fred Forman, played in all the 1898-99 season internationals for England and remain the only brothers from the same professional club to have played together for England. They were also Forest regulars, like their nephew, and Frank Forman was captain of the Forest team that won the club's first honour with the FA Cup in 1898. Five days before the Final their opponents and local rivals Derby County had thrashed them 5-0 in a League match. But, despite this and a crippling injury to wing-half Wragg, Forest won the Final 3-1.*

COLORSPORT

FA CUP 1897-98

FIRST ROUND
Southampton St Mary's v Leicester Fosse	2-1
Preston North End v Newcastle United	1-2
Luton Town v Bolton Wanderers	0-1
Manchester City v Wigan County	2-1
West Bromwich Albion v New Brighton Tower	2-0
Sunderland v The Wednesday	0-1
Nottingham Forest v Grimsby Town	4-0
Long Eaton Rangers v Gainsborough Trinity	0-1
Liverpool v Hucknall St John's	2-0
Newton Heath v Walsall	1-0
Notts County v Wolverhampton Wanderers	0-1
Derby County v Aston Villa	1-0
Burnley v Woolwich Arsenal	3-1
Burslem Port Vale v Sheffield United	1-1, 2-1
Everton v Blackburn Rovers	1-0
Bury v Stoke	1-2

SECOND ROUND
Southampton St Mary's v Newcastle United	1-0
Bolton Wanderers v Manchester City	1-0
West Bromwich Albion v The Wednesday	1-0
Nottingham Forest v Gainsborough Trinity	4-0
Liverpool v Newton Heath	0-0, 2-1
Wolverhampton Wanderers v Derby County	0-1
Burnley v Burslem Port Vale	3-0
Everton v Stoke	0-0, 5-1

THIRD ROUND
Southampton St Mary's v Bolton Wanderers	0-0, 4-0
West Bromwich Albion v Nottingham Forest	2-3
Liverpool v Derby County	1-1, 1-5
Burnley v Everton	1-3

SEMI-FINAL
Southampton St Mary's v Nottingham Forest	1-1, 0-2
Derby County v Everton	3-1

FINAL AT CRYSTAL PALACE
Nottingham Forest v Derby County	3-1

SCOTTISH FA CUP 1897-98

SECOND ROUND
Dundee v St Mirren	2-0
Rangers v Cartvale	12-0
Third Lanark v Celtic	3-2
Kilmarnock v Leith Athletic	9-2
Dundee Wanderers v Ayr Parkhouse	3-6
Hibernian v East Stirlingshire	3-1
Heart of Midlothian v Morton	4-1
St Bernard's v Queen's Park	0-5

THIRD ROUND
Queen's Park v Rangers	1-3
Third Lanark v Hibernian	2-0
Ayr Parkhouse v Kilmarnock	2-7
Dundee v Heart of Midlothian	3-0

SEMI-FINAL
Rangers v Third Lanark	1-1, 2-2, 2-0
Kilmarnock v Dundee	3-2

FINAL AT HAMPDEN PARK
Rangers v Kilmarnock	2-0

TEST MATCHES 1897-98

Newcastle 2 Stoke 1	Blackburn 1 Burnley 3
Burnley 2 Blackburn 0	Stoke 1 Newcastle 0
Newcastle 4 Blackburn 0	Blackburn 4 Newcastle 3
Burnley 0 Stoke 2	Stoke 0 Burnley 0

	P	W	D	L	F	A	Pts
Stoke	4	2	1	1	4	2	5
Burnley	4	2	1	1	5	3	5
Newcastle	4	2	0	2	9	6	4
Blackburn	4	1	0	3	5	12	2

Burnley and Newcastle promoted
No clubs relegated

League Tables 1898-99

FIRST DIVISION

		P	W	D	L	F	A	Pts
1	Aston Villa	34	19	7	8	76	40	45
2	Liverpool	34	19	5	10	49	33	43
3	Burnley	34	15	9	10	45	47	39
4	Everton	34	15	8	11	48	41	38
5	Notts County	34	12	13	9	47	51	37
6	Blackburn	34	14	8	12	60	52	36
7	Sunderland	34	15	6	13	41	41	36
8	Wolves	34	14	7	13	54	48	35
9	Derby	34	12	11	11	62	57	35
10	Bury	34	14	7	13	48	49	35
11	Nottm Forest	34	11	11	12	42	42	33
12	Stoke	34	13	7	14	47	52	33
13	Newcastle	34	11	8	15	49	48	30
14	WBA	34	12	6	16	42	57	30
15	Preston	34	10	9	15	44	47	29
16	Sheff United	34	9	11	14	45	51	29
17	Bolton	34	9	7	18	37	51	25
18	Wednesday	34	8	8	18	32	61	24

SECOND DIVISION

		P	W	D	L	F	A	Pts
1	Man City	34	23	5	6	92	35	52
2	Glossop NE	34	20	6	8	76	38	46
3	Leicester Fosse	34	18	9	7	64	42	45
4	Newton Heath	34	19	5	10	67	43	43
5	New Brighton	34	18	7	9	71	52	43
6	Walsall	34	15	12	7	79	36	42
7	Woolwich A	34	18	5	11	72	41	41
8	Small Heath	34	17	7	10	85	50	41
9	Burslem PV	34	17	5	12	56	34	39
10	Grimsby	34	15	5	14	71	60	35
11	Barnsley	34	12	7	15	52	56	31
12	Lincoln	34	12	7	15	51	56	31
13	Burton Swifts	34	10	8	16	51	70	28
14	Gainsborough	34	10	5	19	56	72	25
15	Luton	34	10	3	21	51	95	23
16	Blackpool	34	8	4	22	49	90	20
17	Loughborough	34	6	6	22	38	92	18
18	Darwen	34	2	5	27	22	141	9

SCOTTISH FIRST DIVISION

		P	W	D	L	F	A	Pts
1	Rangers	18	18	0	0	79	18	36
2	Hearts	18	12	2	4	56	30	26
3	Celtic	18	11	2	5	51	33	24
4	Hibernian	18	10	3	5	42	43	23
5	St Mirren	18	8	4	6	46	32	20
6	Third Lanark	18	7	3	8	33	38	17
7	St Bernard's	18	4	4	10	30	37	12
8	Clyde	18	4	4	10	23	48	12
9	Partick	18	2	2	14	19	58	6
10	Dundee	18	1	2	15	23	65	4

SCOTTISH SECOND DIVISION

		P	W	D	L	F	A	Pts
1	Kilmarnock*	18	14	4	0	73	25	32
2	Leith	18	12	3	3	63	38	27
3	Port Glasgow	18	12	1	5	75	51	25
4	Motherwell	18	7	6	5	40	30	20
5	Hamilton	18	7	1	10	48	58	15
6	Airdrieonians	18	6	3	9	36	46	15
7	Morton	18	6	1	11	36	42	13
8	Ayr	18	5	3	10	35	51	13
9	Linthouse	18	5	1	12	20	62	11
10	Abercorn	18	4	1	13	42	65	9

*Kilmarnock elected to First Division

Below *The Aston Villa side which won the First Division Championship in 1899.*

Second Division Darwen are the only side to have suffered three 10-goal defeats in a single season. In 1898-99 they lost 10-0 to Manchester City, Walsall and Loughborough, all in the space of six weeks. Their 141 goals against was also a record.

Season 1898-99 provided one unique record. Glasgow Rangers won every single game they played in the Scottish League, the only time that this feat has been performed by a British club. Their only defeat in 1898-99 in fact was a shock collapse, 2-0, to Glasgow rivals Celtic in the Scottish Cup final. Only three other clubs — Celtic, Preston and Liverpool — have gone a League season without defeat.

FA CUP 1898-99

FIRST ROUND

Everton v Jarrow	3-1
Nottingham Forest v Aston Villa	2-1
Sheffield United v Burnley	2-2, 2-1
Preston North End v Grimsby Town	7-0
West Bromwich Albion v South Shore	8-0
Heanor Town v Bury	0-3
Liverpool v Blackburn Rovers	2-0
Glossop North End v Newcastle United	0-1
Notts County v Kettering Town	2-0
New Brompton v Southampton	0-1
Woolwich Arsenal v Derby County	0-6
Bolton Wanderers v Wolverhampton Wanderers	0-0, 0-1
Small Heath v Manchester City	3-2
Stoke v The Wednesday	2-2, 2-0
Newton Heath v Tottenham Hotspur	1-1, 3-5
Bristol City v Sunderland	2-4

SECOND ROUND

Everton v Nottingham Forest	0-1
Sheffield United v Preston North End	2-2, 2-1
West Bromwich Albion v Bury	2-1
Liverpool v Newcastle United	3-1
Notts County v Southampton	0-1
Derby County v Wolverhampton Wanderers	2-1
Small Heath v Stoke	2-2, 1-2
Tottenham Hotspur v Sunderland	2-1

THIRD ROUND

Nottingham Forest v Sheffield United	0-1
West Bromwich Albion v Liverpool	0-2
Southampton v Derby County	1-2
Stoke v Tottenham Hotspur	4-1

SEMI-FINAL

Sheffield United v Liverpool	2-2, 4-4, 0-1*, 1-0
Derby County v Stoke	3-1
*abandoned	

FINAL AT CRYSTAL PALACE

Sheffield United v Derby County	4-1

SCOTTISH FA CUP 1898-99

FIRST ROUND

Queen's Park v Kilsyth Wanderers	4-0
Hibernian v Royal Albert	2-1
6th G R V v Celtic	1-8
St Bernard's v Bo'ness	3-3, 4-2
Port Glasgow Athletic v Renton	3-2
Forfar Athletic v West Calder Swifts	4-5
Irvine v Partick Thistle	0-5
Morton v Annbank	3-1
St Mirren v Leith Athletic	7-1
Third Lanark v Arthurlie	4-1
Orion v Kilmarnock	0-2
East Stirlingshire v Dumbarton	4-1
Rangers v Heart of Midlothian	4-1
Ayr Parkhouse v Dundee	3-1
Clyde v Wishaw Thistle	3-0
Airdrieonians v Arbroath	3-3, 2-3

SECOND ROUND

Queen's Park v Hibernian	5-1
Celtic v St Bernard's	3-0
Port Glasgow Athletic v West Calder Swifts	3-1
Morton v Partick Thistle	2-2, 1-2
Third Lanark v St Mirren	1-2
East Stirlingshire v Kilmarnock	1-1, 0-0, 2-4
Ayr Parkhouse v Rangers	1-4
Clyde v Arbroath	3-1

THIRD ROUND

Celtic v Queen's Park	4-2*, 2-1
Port Glasgow Athletic v Partick Thistle	7-3
Kilmarnock v St Mirren	1-2
Rangers v Clyde	4-0
*abandoned	

SEMI-FINAL

Celtic v Port Glasgow Athletic	4-2
St Mirren v Rangers	1-2

FINAL AT HAMPDEN PARK

Celtic v Rangers	2-0

League Tables 1899-1900

FIRST DIVISION

		P	W	D	L	F	A	Pts
1	Aston Villa	34	22	6	6	77	35	50
2	Sheff United	34	18	12	4	63	33	48
3	Sunderland	34	19	3	12	50	35	41
4	Wolves	34	15	9	10	48	37	39
5	Newcastle	34	13	10	11	53	43	36
6	Derby	34	14	8	12	45	43	36
7	Man City	34	13	8	13	50	44	34
8	Nottm Forest	34	13	8	13	56	55	34
9	Stoke	34	10	10	14	37	45	34
10	Liverpool	34	14	5	15	49	45	33
11	Everton	34	13	7	14	47	49	33
12	Bury	34	13	6	15	40	44	32
13	WBA	34	11	8	15	43	51	30
14	Blackburn	34	13	4	17	49	61	30
15	Notts County	34	9	11	14	46	60	29
16	Preston	34	12	4	18	38	48	28
17	Burnley	34	11	5	18	34	54	27
18	Glossop NE	34	4	10	20	31	74	18

SECOND DIVISION

		P	W	D	L	F	A	Pts
1	Wednesday	34	25	4	5	84	22	54
2	Bolton	34	22	8	4	79	25	52
3	Small Heath	34	20	6	8	78	38	46
4	Newton Heath	34	20	4	10	63	27	44
5	Leicester Fosse	34	17	9	8	53	36	43
6	Grimsby	34	17	6	11	67	46	40
7	Chesterfield	34	16	6	12	65	60	38
8	Woolwich A	34	16	4	14	61	43	36
9	Lincoln	34	14	8	12	46	43	36
10	New Brighton	34	13	9	12	66	58	35
11	Burslem PV	34	14	6	14	39	49	34
12	Walsall	34	12	8	14	50	55	32
13	Gainsborough	34	9	7	18	47	75	25
14	Middlesbrough	34	8	8	18	39	69	24
15	Burton Swifts	34	9	6	19	43	84	24
16	Barnsley	34	8	7	19	46	79	23
17	Luton	34	5	8	21	40	75	18
18	Loughborough	34	1	6	27	18	100	8

SCOTTISH FIRST DIVISION

		P	W	D	L	F	A	Pts
1	Rangers	18	15	2	1	68	27	32
2	Celtic	18	9	7	2	46	27	25
3	Hibernian	18	9	6	3	43	24	24
4	Hearts	18	10	3	5	41	24	23
5	Kilmarnock	18	6	6	6	30	37	18
6	Dundee	18	4	7	7	36	40	15
7	Third Lanark	18	5	5	8	31	37	15
8	St Mirren	18	3	6	9	30	46	12
9	St Bernard's	18	4	4	10	29	47	12
10	Clyde	18	2	0	16	25	70	4

SCOTTISH SECOND DIVISION

		P	W	D	L	F	A	Pts
1	Partick*	18	14	1	3	56	26	29
2	Morton*†	17	13	0	4	63	25	26
3	Port Glasgow	18	10	0	8	50	41	20
4	Motherwell†	17	9	1	7	38	33	19
5	Leith	18	9	1	8	33	37	19
6	Abercorn	18	7	2	9	46	39	16
7	Hamilton	18	7	1	10	33	47	15
8	Ayr	18	6	2	10	39	48	14
9	Airdrieonians	18	4	3	11	27	49	11
10	Linthouse	18	2	5	11	28	68	9

*Partick Thistle and Morton were elected to the First Division.

†There is no record of Morton and Motherwell playing each other more than once.

The Manchester City keeper, C Williams, scored with a goal-kick against Sunderland on 14 April 1900 when his opposite number, Ned Doig, touched the ball on its way into the net. At that time full-backs used to tap goal-kicks into the keeper's hands and he would punt the ball from the 6-yard semi-circle.

Below *Part of the huge crowd at the 1900 Cup Final at Crystal Palace.*

FIRST DIVISION

		P	W	D	L	F	A	Pts
1	Liverpool	34	19	7	8	59	35	45
2	Sunderland	34	15	13	6	57	26	43
3	Notts County	34	18	4	12	54	46	40
4	Nottm Forest	34	16	7	11	53	36	39
5	Bury	34	16	7	11	53	37	39
6	Newcastle	34	14	10	10	42	37	38
7	Everton	34	16	5	13	55	42	37
8	Wednesday	34	13	10	11	52	42	36
9	Blackburn	34	12	9	13	39	47	33
10	Bolton	34	13	7	14	39	55	33
11	Man City	34	13	6	15	48	58	32
12	Derby	34	12	7	15	55	42	31
13	Wolves	34	9	13	12	39	55	31
14	Sheff United	34	12	7	15	35	52	31
15	Aston Villa	34	10	10	14	45	51	30
16	Stoke	34	11	5	18	46	57	27
17	Preston	34	9	7	18	49	75	25
18	WBA	34	7	8	19	35	62	22

SECOND DIVISION

		P	W	D	L	F	A	Pts
1	Grimsby	34	20	9	5	60	33	49
2	Small Heath	34	19	10	5	57	24	48
3	Burnley	34	20	4	10	53	29	44
4	New Brighton	34	17	8	9	57	38	42
5	Glossop NE	34	15	8	11	51	33	38
6	Middlesbrough	34	15	7	12	50	40	37
7	Woolwich A	34	15	6	13	39	35	36
8	Lincoln	34	13	7	14	43	39	33
9	Burslem PV	34	11	11	12	45	47	33
10	Newton Heath	34	14	4	16	42	38	32
11	Leicester Fosse	34	11	10	13	39	37	32
12	Blackpool	34	12	7	15	33	58	31
13	Gainsborough	34	10	10	14	45	60	30
14	Chesterfield	34	9	10	15	46	58	28
15	Barnsley	34	11	5	18	47	60	27
16	Walsall	34	7	13	14	40	56	27
17	Stockport	34	11	3	20	38	68	25
18	Burton Swifts	34	8	4	22	34	66	20

SCOTTISH FIRST DIVISION

		P	W	D	L	F	A	Pts
1	Rangers	20	17	1	2	60	25	35
2	Celtic	20	13	3	4	49	28	29
3	Hibernian	20	9	7	4	29	22	25
4	Morton	20	9	3	8	40	40	21
5	Kilmarnock	20	7	4	9	35	47	18
6	Third Lanark	20	6	6	8	20	29	18
7	Dundee	20	6	5	9	36	35	17
8	Queen's Park	20	7	3	10	33	37	17
9	St Mirren	20	5	6	9	33	43	16
10	Hearts	20	5	4	11	22	30	14
11	Partick	20	4	2	14	28	49	10

SCOTTISH SECOND DIVISION

		P	W	D	L	F	A	Pts
1	St Bernard's	18	11	4	3	43	26	26
2	Airdrieonians	18	11	1	6	43	32	23
3	Abercorn	18	9	3	6	37	33	21
4	Port Glasgow*	17	9	0	8	42	41	18
5	Clyde*	16	8	1	7	38	31	17
6	Ayr*	14	8	0	6	27	26	16
7	Leith*	17	5	2	10	21	29	12
8	E Stirlingshire*	14	5	2	7	19	29	12
9	Motherwell	18	4	3	11	26	42	11
10	Hamilton*	16	3	4	9	36	43	10

*no record available of these clubs having completed their fixtures

Below The legendary Fatty Foulke, Sheffield United's goalkeeper, fishes the ball out of the net after one of two goals scored against his team in the 1901 Cup Final by Sandy Brown of Tottenham Hotspur. Brown's goals earned the Londoners a 2-2 draw and won him a place in the record books. For Brown had become the first man to score in every round of the competition and the centre-forward's tally of 15 goals—including the one he got in the replay at Bolton—remains a record. Spurs were then members of the Southern League and are the only non-League club to have won the Cup since 1888.

FA CUP 1900-01

FIRST ROUND

Bolton Wanderers v Derby County	1-0
Reading v Bristol Rovers	2-0
Tottenham Hotspur v Preston North End	1-1, 4-2
The Wednesday v Bury	0-1
Middlesbrough v Newcastle United	3-1
Kettering Town v Chesterfield Town	1-1, 2-1
Woolwich Arsenal v Blackburn Rovers	2-0
West Bromwich Albion v Manchester City	1-0
Notts County v Liverpool	2-0
Wolverhampton Wanderers v New Brighton Tower	5-1
Sunderland v Sheffield United	1-2
Southampton v Everton	1-3
Stoke v Small Heath	1-1, 1-2
Newton Heath v Burnley	0-0, 1-7
Aston Villa v Millwall Athletic	5-0
Nottingham Forest v Leicester Fosse	5-1

SECOND ROUND

Bolton Wanderers v Reading	0-1
Tottenham Hotspur v Bury	2-1
Middlesbrough v Kettering Town	5-0
Woolwich Arsenal v West Bromwich Albion	0-1
Notts County v Wolverhampton Wanderers	2-3
Sheffield United v Everton	2-0
Small Heath v Burnley	1-0
Aston Villa v Nottingham Forest	0-0, 3-1

THIRD ROUND

Reading v Tottenham Hotspur	1-1, 0-3
Middlesbrough v West Bromwich Albion	0-1
Wolverhampton Wanderers v Sheffield United	0-4
Small Heath v Aston Villa	0-0, 0-1

SEMI-FINAL

Tottenham Hotspur v West Bromwich Albion	4-0
Sheffield United v Aston Villa	2-2, 3-0

FINAL AT CRYSTAL PALACE

Tottenham Hotspur v Sheffield United	2-2, 3-1*

*replay at Bolton

SCOTTISH FA CUP 1900-01

FIRST ROUND

Dundee Wanderers v Abercorn	0-3
Celtic v Rangers	1-0
Third Lanark v Douglas Wanderers	5-0
Kilmarnock v Airdrieonians	3-2
St Mirren v Kilwinning Eglinton	10-0
Morton v Bo'ness	10-0
Dundee v Arthurlie	3-1
Stenhousemuir v Queen's Park	1-3
St Bernard's v Partick Thistle	5-0
Heart of Midlothian v Mossend Swifts	7-0
Ayr v Orion	2-2, 3-1
Port Glasgow Athletic v Newton Stewart Athletic	9-1
Hibernian v Dumbarton	7-0
Royal Albert v St Johnstone	1-1, 2-2, 2-0
Forfar Athletic v Leith Athletic	0-4
Clyde v East Stirlingshire	6-0

SECOND ROUND

Clyde v Dundee	3-5
Heart of Midlothian v Queen's Park	2-1
Royal Albert v Hibernian	1-1, 0-1
Ayr v St Mirren	1-3
Celtic v Kilmarnock	6-0
Third Lanark v Abercorn	1-1, 1-0
Morton v St Bernard's	3-1
Leith Athletic v Port Glasgow Athletic	0-3

THIRD ROUND

Dundee v Celtic	0-1
St Mirren v Third Lanark	0-0, 1-1, 3-3, 1-0
Port Glasgow Athletic v Heart of Midlothian	1-5
Hibernian v Morton	2-0

SEMI-FINAL

Heart of Midlothian v Hibernian	1-1, 2-1
St Mirren v Celtic	0-1

FINAL AT IBROX PARK

Heart of Midlothian v Celtic	4-3

League Tables 1901-02

FIRST DIVISION

		P	W	D	L	F	A	Pts
1	Sunderland	34	19	6	9	50	35	44
2	Everton	34	17	7	10	53	35	41
3	Newcastle	34	14	9	11	48	34	37
4	Blackburn	34	15	6	13	52	48	36
5	Nottm Forest	34	13	9	12	43	43	35
6	Derby	34	13	9	12	39	41	35
7	Bury	34	13	8	13	44	38	34
8	Aston Villa	34	13	8	13	42	40	34
9	Wednesday	34	13	8	13	48	52	34
10	Sheff United	34	13	7	14	53	48	33
11	Liverpool	34	10	12	12	42	38	32
12	Bolton	34	12	8	14	51	56	32
13	Notts County	34	14	4	16	51	57	32
14	Wolves	34	13	6	15	46	57	32
15	Grimsby	34	13	6	15	44	60	32
16	Stoke	34	11	9	14	45	55	31
17	Small Heath	34	11	8	15	47	45	30
18	Man City	34	11	6	17	42	58	28

SECOND DIVISION

		P	W	D	L	F	A	Pts
1	WBA	34	25	5	4	82	29	55
2	Middlesbrough	34	23	5	6	90	24	51
3	Preston NE	34	18	6	10	71	32	42
4	Woolwich A	34	18	6	10	50	26	42
5	Lincoln	34	14	13	7	45	35	41
6	Bristol City	34	17	6	11	52	35	40
7	Doncaster	34	13	8	13	49	58	34
8	Glossop NE	34	10	12	12	36	40	32
9	Burnley	34	10	10	14	41	45	30
10	Burton United	34	11	8	15	46	54	30
11	Barnsley	34	12	6	16	51	63	30
12	Burslem PV	34	10	9	15	43	59	29
13	Blackpool	34	11		16	40	56	29
14	Leicester Fosse	34	12	5	17	38	56	29
15	Newton Heath	34	11	6	17	38	53	28
16	Chesterfield	34	11	6	17	47	68	28
17	Stockport	34	8	7	19	36	72	23
18	Gainsborough	34	4	11	19	30	80	19

SCOTTISH FIRST DIVISION

		P	W	D	L	F	A	Pts
1	Rangers	18	13	2	3	43	29	28
2	Celtic	18	11	4	3	38	28	26
3	Hearts	18	10	2	6	32	21	22
4	Third Lanark	18	7	5	6	30	26	19
5	St Mirren	18	8	3	7	29	28	19
6	Hibernian	18	6	4	8	36	23	16
7	Kilmarnock	18	5	6	7	21	25	16
8	Queen's Park	18	5	4	9	21	32	16
9	Dundee	18	4	5	9	15	31	13
10	Morton	18	1	5	12	18	40	7

SCOTTISH SECOND DIVISION

		P	W	D	L	F	A	Pts
1	Port Glasgow*	22	14	4	4	70	31	32
2	Partick*	22	14	3	5	56	26	31
3	Motherwell	22	12	2	8	50	44	26
4	Airdrieonians	22	10	5	7	41	32	25
5	Hamilton	22	11	3	8	46	40	25
6	St Bernard's	22	10	2	10	30	31	22
7	Leith	22	9	3	10	33	39	21
8	Ayr	22	8	5	9	27	33	21
9	E Stirlingshire	22	8	3	11	36	45	19
10	Arthurlie	22	6	5	11	32	42	17
11	Abercorn	22	4	5	13	27	57	13
12	Clyde	22	5	3	14	22	50	13

*Elected to First Division

On 5 April 1902, England met Scotland in an International Championship match at Ibrox Park, Glasgow. The day produced the worst disaster the game had known.

The ground was full by kick-off time, and latecomers, anxious not to miss too much of the game, made a dash from the packed East terrace to the West terrace. They charged up the staircases to the top, and settled to watch the match. Heavy rain was falling. Suddenly, rows of steel pylons at the back and front of the terrace shook and a yawning gap 70 feet by 14 feet wide appeared. People literally dropped through to the ground below, and others followed and fell

on top of them. Officially, 25 were killed, 24 dangerously injured, 153 injured, and 172 slightly injured. The match ended 1-1, but was deleted from international records, and later replayed at Birmingham.

Top The Aston Villa forwards attack Sunderland's goal in March 1902. Before the start of the following season, the curved line marking the goal area was replaced by the six-yard box.

Bottom 'Fatty' Foulke, Sheffield United's 21-stone goalkeeper, prepares to gather a tentative shot from the old-style lines during the 1902 Cup Final.

FA CUP 1901-02

FIRST ROUND

Tottenham Hotspur v Southampton	1-1, 2-2, 1-2
Liverpool v Everton	2-2, 2-0
Bury v West Bromwich Albion	5-1
Walsall v Burnley	1-0
Glossop North End v Nottingham Forest	1-3
Manchester City v Preston North End	1-1, 0-0, 4-2*
Stoke v Aston Villa	2-2, 2-1
Bristol Rovers v Middlesbrough	1-1, 1-0
Northampton Town v Sheffield United	0-2
Wolverhampton Wanderers v Bolton Wanderers	0-2
Woolwich Arsenal v Newcastle United	0-2
The Wednesday v Sunderland	0-1
Blackburn Rovers v Derby County	0-2
Lincoln City v Oxford City	0-0, 4-0
Portsmouth v Grimsby Town	1-1, 2-0
Notts County v Reading	1-2

*At Preston. Preston won the toss for choice of ground.

SECOND ROUND

Southampton v Liverpool	4-1
Walsall v Bury	0-5
Manchester City v Nottingham Forest	0-2
Bristol Rovers v Stoke	0-1
Sheffield United v Bolton Wanderers	2-1
Newcastle United v Sunderland	1-0
Lincoln City v Derby County	1-3
Reading v Portsmouth	0-1

THIRD ROUND

Bury v Southampton	2-3
Nottingham Forest v Stoke	2-0
Newcastle United v Sheffield United	1-1, 1-2
Derby County v Portsmouth	0-0, 6-3

SEMI-FINAL

Southampton v Nottingham Forest	3-1
Sheffield United v Derby County	1-1, 1-1, 1-0

FINAL AT CRYSTAL PALACE

Sheffield United v Southampton	1-1, 2-1†

†replay at Crystal Palace

SCOTTISH FA CUP 1901-02

FIRST ROUND

Arbroath v Kilwinning Eglinton (scratched)	wo
Third Lanark v Morton	0-0, 3-2
St Mirren v Airdrieonians	1-0
Ayr v Dundee	0-0, 0-2
Arthurlie v Port Glasgow Athletic	1-1, 1-3
Celtic v Thornliebank	3-0
Rangers v Johnstone	6-1
Queen's Park v Maxwelltown Volunteers	7-0
Partick Thistle v Kilmarnock	0-4
Falkirk	bye
Forfar Athletic	bye
Heart of Midlothian	bye
Hibernian	bye
Inverness Caledonian	bye
St Bernard's	bye
Stenhousemiur	bye

SECOND ROUND

Heart of Midlothian v Third Lanark	4-1
St Mirren v Stenhousemuir	6-0
Arbroath v Celtic	2-3
Rangers v Inverness Caledonian	5-1
Kilmarnock v Dundee	2-0
Falkirk v St Bernard's	2-0
Forfar Athletic v Queen's Park	1-4
Port Glasgow Athletic v Hibernian	1-5

THIRD ROUND

Falkirk v St Mirren	0-1
Heart of Midlothian v Celtic	1-1, 1-2
Hibernian v Queen's Park	7-1
Rangers v Kilmarnock	2-0

SEMI-FINAL

Rangers v Hibernian	0-2
St Mirren v Celtic	2-3

FINAL AT CELTIC PARK

Hibernian v Celtic	1-0

League Tables 1902-03

FIRST DIVISION

		P	W	D	L	F	A	Pts
1	Wednesday	34	19	4	11	54	36	42
2	Aston Villa	34	19	3	12	61	40	41
3	Sunderland	34	16	9	9	51	36	41
4	Sheff United	34	17	5	12	58	44	39
5	Liverpool	34	17	4	13	68	49	38
6	Stoke	34	15	7	12	46	38	37
7	WBA	34	16	4	14	54	53	36
8	Bury	34	16	3	15	54	43	35
9	Derby	34	16	3	15	50	47	35
10	Nottm Forest	34	14	7	13	49	47	35
11	Wolves	34	14	5	15	48	57	33
12	Everton	34	13	6	15	45	47	32
13	Middlesbrough	34	14	4	16	41	50	32
14	Newcastle	34	14	4	16	41	51	32
15	Notts County	34	12	7	15	41	49	31
16	Blackburn	34	12	5	17	44	63	29
17	Grimsby	34	8	9	17	43	62	25
18	Bolton	34	8	3	23	37	73	19

SECOND DIVISION

		P	W	D	L	F	A	Pts
1	Man City	34	25	4	5	95	29	54
2	Small Heath	34	24	3	7	74	36	51
3	Woolwich A	34	20	8	6	66	30	48
4	Bristol City	34	17	8	9	59	38	42
5	Man United	34	15	8	11	53	38	38
6	Chesterfield	34	14	9	11	67	40	37
7	Preston	34	13	10	11	56	40	36
8	Barnsley	34	13	8	13	55	51	34
9	Burslem PV	34	13	8	13	57	62	34
10	Lincoln	34	12	6	16	46	53	30
11	Glossop NE	34	11	7	16	43	58	29
12	Gainsborough	34	11	7	16	41	59	29
13	Burton United	34	11	7	16	39	59	29
14	Blackpool	34	9	10	15	44	59	28
15	Leicester Fosse	34	10	8	16	41	65	28
16	Doncaster	34	9	7	18	35	72	25
17	Stockport	34	7	6	21	39	74	20
18	Burnley	34	6	8	20	30	77	20

SCOTTISH FIRST DIVISION

		P	W	D	L	F	A	Pts
1	Hibernian	22	16	5	1	49	19	37
2	Dundee	22	13	5	4	31	12	31
3	Rangers	22	12	5	5	56	30	29
4	Hearts	22	11	6	5	46	28	28
5	Celtic	22	8	10	4	36	30	26
6	St Mirren	22	7	8	7	39	39	22
7	Third Lanark	22	8	5	9	34	27	21
8	Partick	22	6	7	9	34	50	19
9	Kilmarnock	22	6	4	12	24	43	16
10	Queen's Park	22	5	5	12	33	48	15
11	Port Glasgow	22	3	5	14	26	49	11
12	Morton	22	2	5	15	22	55	9

SCOTTISH SECOND DIVISION

		P	W	D	L	F	A	Pts
1	Airdrieonians*	22	15	5	2	43	19	35
2	Motherwell*	22	12	4	6	44	35	28
3	Ayr	22	12	3	7	34	24	27
4	Leith	22	11	5	6	43	42	27
5	St Bernard's	22	12	2	8	45	32	26
6	Hamilton	22	11	1	10	45	35	23
7	Falkirk	22	8	7	7	39	37	23
8	E Stirlingshire	22	9	3	10	46	41	21
9	Arthurlie	22	6	8	8	34	46	20
10	Abercorn	22	5	2	15	35	58	12
11	Raith	22	3	5	14	34	55	11
12	Clyde	22	2	7	13	22	40	11

*elected to First Division

FA CUP 1902-03

FIRST ROUND

Tottenham Hotspur v West Bromwich Albion	0-0, 2-0
Bolton Wanderers v Bristol City	0-5
Aston Villa v Sunderland	4-1
Barnsley v Lincoln City	2-0
Woolwich Arsenal v Sheffield United	1-3
Bury v Wolverhampton Wanderers	1-0
Grimsby Town v Newcastle United	2-1
Notts County v Southampton	0-0, 2-2, 2-1
Derby County v Small Heath	2-1
Blackburn Rovers v The Wednesday	0-0, 1-0
Nottingham Forest v Reading	0-0, 6-3
Glossop North End v Stoke	2-3
Millwall Athletic v Luton Town	3-0
Preston North End v Manchester City	3-1
Everton v Portsmouth	5-0
Manchester United v Liverpool	2-1

SECOND ROUND

Tottenham Hotspur v Bristol City	1-0
Aston Villa v Barnsley	4-1
Sheffield United v Bury	0-1
Grimsby Town v Notts County	0-2
Derby County v Blackburn Rovers	2-0
Nottingham Forest v Stoke	0-0, 0-2
Millwall Athletic v Preston North End	4-1
Everton v Manchester United	3-1

THIRD ROUND

Tottenham Hotspur v Aston Villa	2-3
Bury v Notts County	1-0
Derby County v Stoke	3-0
Millwall Athletic v Everton	1-0

SEMI-FINAL

Aston Villa v Bury	0-3
Derby County v Millwall Athletic	3-0

FINAL AT CRYSTAL PALACE

Bury v Derby County	6-0

SCOTTISH FA CUP 1902-03

FIRST ROUND

Celtic v St Mirren	0-0, 1-1, 4-0
St Johnstone v Third Lanark	1-10
Nithsdale Wanderers v Orion	1-0
Queen's Park v Motherwell	1-2
Abercorn v Douglas Wanderers	2-2, 1-3
Vale of Leven v Partick Thistle	0-4
Hamilton Academicals v Airdrieonians	5-0
Arbroath v Kilmarnock	1-3
Leith Athletic v Broxburn United	4-1
St Bernard's v Port Glasgow Athletic	1-2
Rangers v Auchterarder Thistle	7-0
Clyde v Heart of Midlothian	1-2
Hibernian v Morton	7-0
Ayr v Camelon	2-0
Dundee v Barholm Rovers	wo
Stenhousemuir v Inverness Caledonian	wo

SECOND ROUND

Celtic v Port Glasgow Athletic	2-0
Hamilton Academicals v Third Lanark	2-2, 1-3
Stenhousemuir v Douglas Wanderers	6-1
Motherwell v Partick Thistle	0-2
Dundee v Nithsdale Wanderers	7-0
Rangers v Kilmarnock	4-0
Ayr v Heart of Midlothian	2-4
Hibernian v Leith Athletic	4-1

THIRD ROUND

Celtic v Rangers	0-3
Dundee v Hibernian	0-0, 0-0, 1-0
Heart of Midlothian v Third Lanark	2-1
Stenhousemuir v Partick Thistle	3-0

SEMI-FINAL

Stenhousemuir v Rangers	1-4
Dundee v Heart of Midlothian	0-0, 0-1

FINAL AT CELTIC PARK

Rangers v Heart of Midlothian	1-1, 0-0, 2-0

Bury on the attack against Derby County on their way to the record win, 6-0, in an FA Cup Final.

CONWAY PICTURE LIBRARY

League Tables 1903-04

FIRST DIVISION

		P	W	D	L	F	A	Pts
1	Wednesday	34	20	7	7	48	28	47
2	Man City	34	19	6	9	71	45	44
3	Everton	34	19	5	10	59	32	43
4	Newcastle	34	18	6	10	58	45	42
5	Aston Villa	34	17	7	10	70	48	41
6	Sunderland	34	17	5	12	63	49	39
7	Sheff United	34	15	8	11	62	57	38
8	Wolves	34	14	8	12	44	66	36
9	Nottm Forest	34	11	9	14	57	57	31
10	Middlesbrough	34	9	12	13	46	47	30
11	Small Heath	34	11	8	15	39	52	30
12	Bury	34	7	15	12	40	53	29
13	Notts County	34	12	5	17	37	61	29
14	Derby	34	9	10	15	58	60	28
15	Blackburn	34	11	6	17	48	60	28
16	Stoke	34	10	7	17	54	57	27
17	Liverpool	34	9	8	17	49	62	26
18	WBA	34	7	10	17	36	60	24

SECOND DIVISION

		P	W	D	L	F	A	Pts
1	Preston	34	20	10	4	62	24	50
2	Woolwich A	34	21	7	6	91	22	49
3	Man United	34	20	8	6	65	33	48
4	Bristol City	34	18	6	10	73	41	42
5	Burnley	34	15	9	10	50	55	39
6	Grimsby	34	14	8	12	50	49	36
7	Bolton	34	12	10	12	59	41	34
8	Barnsley	34	11	10	13	38	57	32
9	Gainsborough	34	14	3	17	53	60	31
10	Bradford City	34	12	7	15	45	59	31
11	Chesterfield	34	11	8	15	37	45	30
12	Lincoln	34	11	8	15	41	58	30
13	Burslem PV	34	10	9	15	54	52	29
14	Burton United	34	11	7	16	45	61	29
15	Blackpool	34	11	5	18	40	67	27
16	Stockport	34	8	11	15	40	72	27
17	Glossop NE	34	10	6	18	57	64	26
18	Leicester Fosse	34	6	10	18	42	82	22

SCOTTISH FIRST DIVISION

		P	W	D	L	F	A	Pts
1	Third Lanark	26	20	3	3	61	26	43
2	Hearts	26	18	3	5	63	35	39
3	Celtic	26	18	2	6	69	28	38
4	Rangers	26	16	6	4	80	33	38
5	Dundee	26	13	2	11	54	45	28
6	St Mirren	26	11	5	10	45	38	27
7	Partick	26	10	7	9	43	40	27
8	Queen's Park	26	6	9	11	28	47	21
9	Port Glasgow	26	8	4	14	33	49	20
10	Hibernian	26	7	5	14	31	42	19
11	Morton	26	7	4	15	31	51	18
12	Airdrieonians	26	7	4	15	32	62	18
13	Motherwell	26	6	3	17	26	61	15
14	Kilmarnock	26	4	5	17	26	65	13

SCOTTISH SECOND DIVISION

		P	W	D	L	F	A	Pts
1	Hamilton	22	16	5	1	56	19	37
2	Clyde	22	12	5	5	51	36	29
3	Ayr	22	11	5	6	33	29	28
4	Falkirk	22	11	4	7	50	36	26
5	Raith	22	8	5	9	40	38	21
6	E Stirlingshire	22	8	5	9	33	40	21
7	Leith	22	8	4	10	42	40	20
8	St Bernard's	22	9	2	11	31	43	20
9	Albion*	22	8	5	9	41	37	19
10	Abercorn	22	6	4	12	40	54	16
11	Arthurlie	22	5	5	12	37	50	15
12	Ayr Parkhouse	22	3	4	15	22	54	10

*Two points deducted for fielding an unregistered player.

Below The Manchester City side that won the FA Cup in 1903-04. Seated in the centre is the captain and great Welsh right-winger, Billy Meredith of Chirk.

At Bradford, Sheffield FC, the oldest football club in the world, won their first and only honour when they beat Ealing 3-1 in the 1904 Amateur Cup final.

MANCHESTER CITY FOOTBALL CLUB.

WINNERS OF ENGLISH CUP, 1903-4.
RUNNERS-UP, FOOTBALL LEAGUE, 1903-4. ◆ JOINT HOLDERS MANCHESTER CUP, 1903-4.

RADIO TIMES HULTON PICTURE LIBRARY

FA CUP 1903-04

FIRST ROUND

Manchester City v Sunderland	3-2
Woolwich Arsenal v Fulham	1-0
Millwall Athletic v Middlesbrough	0-2
Preston North End v Grimsby Town	1-0
Plymouth Argyle v The Wednesday	2-2, 0-2
Notts County v Manchester United	3-3, 1-2
Everton v Tottenham Hotspur	1-2
Stoke v Aston Villa	2-3
Reading v Bolton Wanderers	1-1, 2-3
Southampton v Burslem Port Vale	3-0
Bristol City v Sheffield United	1-3
Bury v Newcastle United	2-1
Portsmouth v Derby County	2-5
Stockton v Wolverhampton Wanderers	1-4
Blackburn Rovers v Liverpool	3-1
West Bromwich Albion v Nottingham Forest	1-1, 1-3

SECOND ROUND

Woolwich Arsenal v Manchester City	0-2
Preston North End v Middlesbrough	0-3
The Wednesday v Manchester United	6-0
Tottenham Hotspur v Aston Villa	0-1*, 1-0
Bolton Wanderers v Southampton	4-1
Bury v Sheffield United	1-2
Derby County v Wolverhampton Wanderers	2-2, 2-2, 1-0
Blackburn Rovers v Nottingham Forest	3-1

*The Tottenham crowd invaded the pitch when Villa were leading 1-0 and the game was abandoned. Tottenham were fined £350 and the FA ordered the return to be played at Villa Park.

THIRD ROUND

Manchester City v Middlesbrough	0-0, 3-1
Tottenham Hotspur v The Wednesday	1-1, 0-2
Sheffield United v Bolton Wanderers	0-2
Derby County v Blackburn Rovers	2-1

SEMI-FINAL

Manchester City v The Wednesday	3-0
Bolton Wanderers v Derby County	1-0

FINAL AT CRYSTAL PALACE

Manchester City v Bolton Wanderers	1-0

SCOTTISH FA CUP 1903-04

FIRST ROUND

Abercorn v Maxwelltown Volunteers	2-2, 1-1, 2-1
Nithsdale Wanderers v Kilmarnock	2-2, 1-1, 1-2
Clyde v Arbroath	2-2, 0-4
Rangers v Heart of Midlothian	3-2
Dundee v Queen's Park	3-0
Hibernian v Airdrieonians	2-1
Motherwell v Partick Thistle	2-1
Ayr v St Mirren	0-2
St Johnstone v Hearts of Beath	2-0
Albion Rovers v Kilwinning Eglinton	2-1
St Bernard's v West Calder Swifts	1-1, 3-3, 2-1
Port Glasgow Athletic v Leith Athletic	1-2
Alloa Athletic v Aberdour	2-1
Third Lanark v Newton Stewart Athletic (scratched)	wo
Celtic v Stanley (scratched)	wo
Morton v Dalbeattie Star (scratched)	wo

SECOND ROUND

Kilmarnock v Albion Rovers	2-2, 1-0
St Bernard's v Celtic	0-4
Dundee v Abercorn	4-0
Third Lanark v Alloa Athletic	3-1
Hibernian v Rangers	1-2
Leith Athletic v Motherwell	3-1
Morton v Arbroath	2-0
St Mirren v St Johnstone	4-0

THIRD ROUND

Celtic v Dundee	1-1, 0-0, 5-0
Third Lanark v Kilmarnock	3-0
St Mirren v Rangers	0-1
Leith Athletic v Morton	1-3

SEMI-FINAL

Celtic v Third Lanark	2-1
Rangers v Morton	3-0

FINAL AT HAMPDEN PARK

Celtic v Rangers	3-2

League Tables 1904-05

FIRST DIVISION

		P	W	D	L	F	A	Pts
1	Newcastle	34	23	2	9	72	33	48
2	Everton	34	21	5	8	63	36	47
3	Man City	34	20	6	8	66	37	46
4	Aston Villa	34	19	4	11	63	43	42
5	Sunderland	34	16	8	10	60	44	40
6	Sheff United	34	19	2	13	64	56	40
7	Small Heath	34	17	5	12	54	38	39
8	Preston	34	13	10	11	42	37	36
9	Wednesday	34	14	5	15	61	57	33
10	Woolwich A	34	12	9	13	36	40	33
11	Derby	34	12	8	14	37	48	32
12	Stoke	34	13	4	17	40	58	30
13	Blackburn	34	11	5	18	40	51	27
14	Wolves	34	11	4	19	47	73	26
15	Middlesbrough	34	9	8	17	36	56	26
16	Nottm Forest	34	9	7	18	40	61	25
17	Bury	34	10	4	20	47	67	24
18	Notts County	34	5	8	21	36	69	18

SECOND DIVISION

		P	W	D	L	F	A	Pts
1	Liverpool	34	27	4	3	93	25	58
2	Bolton	34	27	2	5	87	32	56
3	Man United	34	24	5	5	81	30	53
4	Bristol City	34	19	4	11	66	45	42
5	Chesterfield	34	14	11	9	44	35	39
6	Gainsborough	34	14	8	12	61	58	36
7	Barnsley	34	14	5	15	38	56	33
8	Bradford City	34	12	8	14	45	49	32
9	Lincoln	34	12	7	15	42	40	31
10	WBA	34	13	4	17	56	48	30
11	Burnley	34	12	6	16	43	52	30
12	Glossop NE	34	10	10	14	37	46	30
13	Grimsby	34	11	8	15	33	46	30
14	Leicester Fosse	34	11	7	16	40	55	29
15	Blackpool	34	9	10	15	36	48	28
16	Burslem PV	34	10	7	17	47	72	27
17	Burton United	34	8	4	22	30	84	20
18	Doncaster	34	3	2	29	23	81	8

SCOTTISH FIRST DIVISION

		P	W	D	L	F	A	Pts
1	Celtic*	26	19	3	4	83	28	41
2	Rangers	26	18	5	3	68	31	41
3	Third Lanark	26	14	7	5	60	28	35
4	Airdrieonians	26	11	5	10	38	45	27
5	Hibernian	26	9	8	9	39	39	26
6	Partick	26	12	2	12	36	56	26
7	Dundee	26	10	5	11	38	32	25
8	Hearts	26	11	3	12	46	44	25
9	Kilmarnock	26	9	5	12	29	45	23
10	St Mirren	26	9	4	13	33	36	22
11	Port Glasgow	26	8	5	13	30	51	21
12	Queen's Park	26	6	8	12	28	45	20
13	Morton	26	7	4	15	27	50	18
14	Motherwell	26	6	2	18	28	53	14

*Celtic won a deciding match against Rangers

SCOTTISH SECOND DIVISION

		P	W	D	L	F	A	Pts
1	Clyde	22	13	6	3	38	22	32
2	Falkirk*	22	12	4	6	31	25	28
3	Hamilton	22	12	3	7	40	22	27
4	Leith	22	10	4	8	36	26	24
5	Ayr	22	11	1	10	46	37	23
6	Arthurlie	22	9	5	8	37	42	23
7	Aberdeen*	22	7	7	8	36	26	21
8	Albion	22	8	4	10	38	53	20
9	E Stirlingshire	22	7	5	10	38	38	19
10	Raith	22	9	1	12	30	34	19
11	Abercorn	22	8	1	13	31	45	17
12	St Bernard's	22	3	5	14	23	54	11

*Aberdeen and Falkirk were elected to the First Division

FA CUP 1904-05

FIRST ROUND
Lincoln City v Manchester City	1-2
Bolton Wanderers v Bristol Rovers	1-1, 3-0
Middlesbrough v Tottenham Hotspur	1-1, 0-1
Newcastle United v Plymouth Argyle	1-1, 1-1, 2-0
Woolwich Arsenal v Bristol City	0-0, 0-1
Derby County v Preston North End	0-2
Blackburn Rovers v The Wednesday	1-2
Small Heath v Portsmouth	0-2
Stoke v Grimsby Town	2-0
Liverpool v Everton	1-1, 1-2
Sunderland v Wolverhampton Wanderers	1-1, 0-1
Southampton v Millwall Athletic	3-1
Aston Villa v Leicester Fosse	5-1
Bury v Notts County	1-0
Fulham v Reading	0-0, 0-0, 1-0
Nottingham Forest v Sheffield United	2-0

SECOND ROUND
Manchester City v Bolton Wanderers	1-2
Tottenham Hotspur v Newcastle United	1-1, 0-4
Bristol City v Preston North End	0-0, 0-1
The Wednesday v Portsmouth	2-1
Stoke v Everton	0-4
Wolverhampton Wanderers v Southampton	2-3
Aston Villa v Bury	3-2
Fulham v Nottingham Forest	1-0

THIRD ROUND
Bolton Wanderers v Newcastle United	0-2
Preston North End v The Wednesday	1-1, 0-3
Everton v Southampton	4-0
Aston Villa v Fulham	5-0

SEMI-FINAL
Newcastle United v The Wednesday	1-0
Everton v Aston Villa	1-1, 1-2

FINAL AT CRYSTAL PALACE
Aston Villa v Newcastle United	2-0

SCOTTISH FA CUP 1904-05

FIRST ROUND
Rangers v Ayr	2-1
Dundee v Heart of Midlothian	1-3
Dumfries v Celtic	1-2
Port Glasgow Athletic v Stranraer	3-0
Airdrieonians v St Johnstone	7-0
Aberdeen v Queen's Park	2-1
St Mirren v Clyde	1-0
Third Lanark v Leith Athletic	4-1
Morton v Renton	2-0
Kilmarnock v Beith	2-2, 1-3
Bathgate v Arbroath	2-0
Arthurlie v Motherwell	0-0, 0-1
Hibernian v Partick Thistle	1-1, 2-4
Kirkcaldy United v Crieff Morrisonians	3-1
Cowdenbeath v 6th GRV	6-0
Lochgelly United v Inverness Caledonian	5-1

SECOND ROUND
Celtic v Lochgelly United	3-0
Aberdeen v Bathgate	1-1, 6-1
Kirkcaldy United v Partick Thistle	0-1
Morton v Rangers	0-6
Airdrieonians v Port Glasgow Athletic	3-0
Motherwell v Third Lanark	0-1
St Mirren v Heart of Midlothian	1-0
Beith v Cowdenbeath	4-0

THIRD ROUND
St Mirren v Airdrieonians	0-0, 1-3
Rangers v Beith	5-1
Celtic v Partick Thistle	3-0
Third Lanark v Aberdeen	4-1

SEMI-FINAL
Celtic v Rangers	0-2
Airdrieonians v Third Lanark	1-2

FINAL AT HAMPDEN PARK
Third Lanark v Rangers	0-0, 3-1

Doncaster Rovers had a disastrous spell in the Second Division and were voted out of the League in 1905 after gaining the fewest number of points (8) ever won by a League club in a single season. Not one of those 8 was won away from home. This equalled Loughborough Town's dreadful 1899-1900 season when they also accumulated just 8 points. Loughborough, however, established a record by winning only one of their 34 League games.

Below The only known panoramic view of Crystal Palace during a Cup Final. The event was played there from 1895 to 1914 but, apart from the small stands on the right, there was little accommodation available. The Crystal Palace itself, which had been moved from Hyde Park after the Great Exhibition of the 1850s, was on the hill above the funfair to the right. The 1905 Final attracted over 100,000 spectators, only the second time in history an English football match had drawn a six-figure crowd. Some fans can be seen clinging on to trees on the left as Aston Villa play Newcastle United.

RADIO TIMES HULTON PICTURE LIBRARY/ROY FLOOKS

League Tables 1905-06

FIRST DIVISION

		P	W	D	L	F	A	Pts
1	Liverpool	38	23	5	10	79	46	51
2	Preston NE	38	17	13	8	54	39	47
3	Wednesday	38	18	8	12	63	52	44
4	Newcastle	38	18	7	13	74	48	43
5	Man City	38	19	5	14	73	54	43
6	Bolton	38	17	7	14	81	67	41
7	Birmingham	38	17	7	14	65	59	41
8	Aston Villa	38	17	6	15	72	56	40
9	Blackburn	38	16	8	14	54	52	40
10	Stoke	38	16	7	15	54	55	39
11	Everton	38	15	7	16	70	66	37
12	Woolwich A	38	15	7	16	62	64	37
13	Sheff United	38	15	6	17	57	62	36
14	Sunderland	38	15	5	18	61	70	35
15	Derby	38	14	7	17	39	58	35
16	Notts County	38	11	12	15	55	71	34
17	Bury	38	11	10	17	57	74	32
18	Middlesbrough	38	10	11	17	56	71	31
19	Nottm Forest	38	13	5	20	58	79	31
20	Wolves	38	8	7	23	58	99	23

SECOND DIVISION

		P	W	D	L	F	A	Pts
1	Bristol City	38	30	6	2	83	28	66
2	Man United	38	28	6	4	90	28	62
3	Chelsea	38	22	9	7	90	37	53
4	WBA	38	22	8	8	79	36	52
5	Hull	38	19	6	13	67	54	44
6	Leeds City	38	17	9	12	59	47	43
7	Leicester Fosse	38	15	12	11	53	48	42
8	Grimsby	38	15	10	13	46	46	40
9	Burnley	38	15	8	15	42	53	38
10	Stockport	38	13	9	16	44	56	35
11	Bradford City	38	13	8	17	46	60	34
12	Barnsley	38	12	9	17	60	62	33
13	Lincoln	38	12	6	20	69	72	30
14	Blackpool	38	10	9	19	37	62	29
15	Gainsborough	38	12	4	22	44	57	28
16	Glossop NE	38	10	8	20	49	71	28
17	Burslem PV	38	12	4	22	49	82	28
18	Chesterfield	38	10	8	20	40	72	28
19	Burton United	38	10	6	22	34	67	26
20	Clapton Orient	38	7	7	24	35	78	21

SCOTTISH FIRST DIVISION

		P	W	D	L	F	A	Pts
1	Celtic	30	24	1	5	76	19	49
2	Hearts	30	18	7	5	64	27	43
3	Airdrieonians	30	15	8	7	53	31	38
4	Rangers	30	15	7	8	58	48	37
5	Partick	30	15	6	9	44	40	36
6	Third Lanark	30	16	2	12	62	37	34
7	Dundee	30	11	12	7	40	34	34
8	St Mirren	30	13	5	12	41	37	31
9	Motherwell	30	9	8	13	50	64	26
10	Morton	30	10	6	14	35	54	26
11	Hibernian	30	10	5	15	34	40	25
12	Aberdeen	30	8	8	14	37	49	24
13	Falkirk	30	9	5	16	54	69	23
14	Kilmarnock	30	8	4	18	46	68	20
15	Port Glasgow	30	6	8	16	38	68	20
16	Queen's Park	30	5	4	21	41	88	14

SCOTTISH SECOND DIVISION

		P	W	D	L	F	A	Pts
1	Leith	22	15	4	3	46	22	34
2	Clyde*	22	11	9	2	38	21	31
3	Albion	22	12	3	7	48	33	27
4	Hamilton*	22	12	2	8	45	33	26
5	St Bernard's	22	9	4	9	42	34	22
6	Arthurlie	22	10	2	10	45	45	22
7	Ayr	22	9	3	10	44	51	21
8	Raith	22	6	7	9	38	42	19
9	Cowdenbeath	22	7	3	12	27	39	17
10	Abercorn	22	6	5	11	31	46	17
11	Vale of Leven	22	6	4	12	33	50	16
12	E Stirlingshire	22	1	10	11	26	47	12

*Elected to First Division

Below *The Everton team that won the club's first ever FA Cup in 1906.*

FA CUP 1905-06

SECOND ROUND
Woolwich Arsenal v Watford	3-0
Sunderland v Gainsborough Trinity	1-1, 3-0
Manchester United v Norwich City	3-0
Aston Villa v Plymouth Argyle	0-0, 5-1
Derby County v Newcastle United	0-0, 1-2
Blackpool v Sheffield United	2-1
Tottenham Hotspur v Reading	3-2
Stoke v Birmingham	0-1
Chesterfield Town v Everton	0-3
Bradford City v Wolverhampton Wanderers	5-0
The Wednesday v Millwall Athletic	1-1, 3-0
Fulham v Nottingham Forest	1-3
Barnsley v Liverpool	0-1
Brentford v Lincoln City	3-0
New Brompton v Southampton	0-0, 0-1
Brighton v Middlesbrough	1-1, 1-1, 1-3

THIRD ROUND
Woolwich Arsenal v Sunderland	5-0
Manchester United v Aston Villa	5-1
Newcastle United v Blackpool	5-0
Tottenham Hotspur v Birmingham	1-1, 0-2
Everton v Bradford City	1-0
The Wednesday v Nottingham Forest	4-1
Liverpool v Brentford	2-0
Southampton v Middlesbrough	6-1

FOURTH ROUND
Manchester United v Woolwich Arsenal	2-3
Birmingham v Newcastle United	2-2, 0-3
Everton v The Wednesday	4-3
Liverpool v Southampton	3-0

SEMI-FINAL
Woolwich Arsenal v Newcastle United	0-2
Everton v Liverpool	2-0

FINAL AT CRYSTAL PALACE
Everton v Newcastle United	1-0

SCOTTISH FA CUP 1905-06

FIRST ROUND
Dundee v Celtic	1-2
Kilmarnock v Clyde	2-1
Beith v Inverness Thistle	2-0
Third Lanark v Galston	5-0
Forfar Athletic v Queen's Park	0-4
Falkirk v Hibernian	1-2
Leith Athletic v Partick Thistle	1-2
Heart of Midlothian v Nithsdale Wanderers	4-1
Motherwell v Hamilton Academicals	2-3
Airdrieonians v Maxwelltown Volunteers	9-2
Aberdeen v Dunfermline Athletic	3-0
Morton v Lochgelly United	4-3
St Mirren v Black Watch	7-2
Arthurlie v Rangers	1-7
Arbroath v Bo'ness	1-4
Port Glasgow Athletic v Dunblane	6-1

SECOND ROUND
Aberdeen v Rangers	2-3
Hibernian v Partick Thistle	1-1, 1-1, 2-1
Beith v Heart of Midlothian	0-3
Celtic v Bo'ness	3-0
Third Lanark v Hamilton Academicals	2-2, 3-1
St Mirren v Morton	3-1
Kilmarnock v Port Glasgow Athletic	2-2, 0-0, 0-0, 0-1
Queen's Park v Airdrieonians	1-2

THIRD ROUND
Celtic v Heart of Midlothian	1-2
Airdrieonians v St Mirren	0-0, 0-2
Port Glasgow Athletic v Rangers	1-0
Hibernian v Third Lanark	1-2

SEMI-FINAL
St Mirren v Third Lanark	1-1, 0-0, 0-1
Port Glasgow Athletic v Heart of Midlothian	0-2

FINAL AT IBROX PARK
Heart of Midlothian v Third Lanark	1-0

COLORSPORT

League Tables 1906-07

FIRST DIVISION

		P	W	D	L	F	A	Pts
1	Newcastle	38	22	7	9	74	46	51
2	Bristol City	38	20	8	10	66	47	48
3	Everton	38	20	5	13	70	46	45
4	Sheff United	38	17	11	10	57	55	45
5	Aston Villa	38	19	6	13	78	52	44
6	Bolton	38	18	8	12	59	47	44
7	Woolwich A	38	20	4	14	66	59	44
8	Man United	38	17	8	13	53	56	42
9	Birmingham	38	15	8	15	52	52	38
10	Sunderland	38	14	9	15	65	66	37
11	Middlesbrough	38	15	6	17	56	63	36
12	Blackburn	38	14	7	17	56	59	35
13	Wednesday	38	12	11	15	49	60	35
14	Preston	38	14	7	17	44	57	35
15	Liverpool	38	13	7	18	64	65	33
16	Bury	38	13	6	19	58	68	32
17	Man City	38	10	12	16	53	77	32
18	Notts County	38	8	15	15	46	50	31
19	Derby	38	9	9	20	41	59	27
20	Stoke	38	8	10	20	41	64	26

SECOND DIVISION

		P	W	D	L	F	A	Pts
1	Nottm Forest	38	28	4	6	74	36	60
2	Chelsea	38	26	5	7	80	34	57
3	Leicester Fosse	38	20	8	10	62	39	48
4	WBA	38	21	5	12	83	45	47
5	Bradford City	38	21	5	12	70	53	47
6	Wolves	38	17	7	14	66	53	41
7	Burnley	38	17	6	15	62	47	40
8	Barnsley	38	15	8	15	73	55	38
9	Hull	38	15	7	16	65	57	37
10	Leeds City	38	13	10	15	55	63	36
11	Grimsby	38	16	3	19	57	62	35
12	Stockport	38	12	11	15	42	52	35
13	Blackpool	38	11	11	16	33	51	33
14	Gainsborough	38	14	5	19	45	72	33
15	Glossop NE	38	13	6	19	53	79	32
16	Burslem PV	38	12	7	19	60	83	31
17	Clapton Orient	38	11	8	19	45	67	30
18	Chesterfield	38	11	7	20	50	66	29
19	Lincoln	38	12	4	22	46	73	28
20	Burton United	38	8	7	23	34	68	23

SCOTTISH FIRST DIVISION

		P	W	D	L	F	A	Pts
1	Celtic	34	23	9	2	80	30	55
2	Dundee	34	18	12	4	53	26	48
3	Rangers	34	19	7	8	69	33	45
4	Airdrieonians	34	18	6	10	60	43	42
5	Falkirk	34	17	7	10	73	58	41
6	Third Lanark	34	15	9	10	57	48	39
7	St Mirren	34	12	13	9	50	44	37
8	Clyde	34	15	6	13	47	52	36
9	Hearts	34	11	13	10	46	43	35
10	Motherwell	34	12	9	13	45	49	33
11	Hibernian	34	11	9	14	40	49	31
12	Aberdeen	34	10	10	14	50	55	30
13	Morton	34	11	6	17	41	50	28
14	Partick Thistle	34	9	8	17	40	61	26
15	Queen's Park	34	9	6	19	51	66	24
16	Hamilton	34	8	5	21	40	64	21
17	Kilmarnock	34	8	5	21	40	72	21
18	Port Glasgow	34	7	7	20	30	67	21

SCOTTISH SECOND DIVISION

		P	W	D	L	F	A	Pts
1	St Bernards†	21	13	4	4	39	25	30
2	Vale of Leven	22	13	1	8	54	35	27
3	Arthurlie	22	12	3	7	51	39	27
4	Dumbarton	22	11	3	8	52	35	25
5	Leith	22	10	4	8	40	35	24
6	Albion	22	10	3	9	43	37	23
7	Cowdenbeath†	21	10	5	6	36	37	23*
8	Ayr†	21	7	5	9	33	35	19
9	Raith	22	6	4	12	40	48	16
10	E Stirlingshire	22	6	4	12	36	49	16
11	Abercorn†	21	5	6	10	29	46	16
12	Ayr Parkhouse	22	5	2	15	31	63	12

*two points deducted for an irregularity
†no record exists of these clubs having completed their fixtures

Below A plate produced by The Wednesday to commemorate winning the Cup in 1907.

FA CUP 1906-07

SECOND ROUND

Burslem Port Vale v Notts County	2-2, 0-5
Blackburn Rovers v Tottenham Hotspur	1-1, 1-1, 1-2
West Bromwich Albion v Norwich City	1-0
Derby County v Lincoln City	1-0
Fulham v Crystal Palace	0-0, 0-1
Brentford v Middlesbrough	1-0
West Ham United v Everton	1-2
Bolton Wanderers v Aston Villa	2-0
Woolwich Arsenal v Bristol City	2-1
Bristol Rovers v Millwall	3-0
Barnsley v Portsmouth	1-0
Bury v New Brompton	1-0
Oldham Athletic v Liverpool	0-1
Bradford City v Accrington Stanley	1-0
Southampton v The Wednesday	1-1, 1-3
Luton Town v Sunderland	0-0, 0-1

THIRD ROUND

Notts County v Tottenham Hotspur	4-0
West Bromwich Albion v Derby County	2-0
Crystal Palace v Brentford	1-1, 1-0
Everton v Bolton Wanderers	0-0, 3-0
Woolwich Arsenal v Bristol Rovers	1-0
Barnsley v Bury	1-0
Liverpool v Bradford City	1-0
The Wednesday v Sunderland	0-0, 1-0

FOURTH ROUND

West Bromwich Albion v Notts County	3-1
Crystal Palace v Everton	1-1, 0-4
Barnsley v Woolwich Arsenal	1-2
The Wednesday v Liverpool	1-0

SEMI-FINAL

West Bromwich Albion v Everton	1-2
Woolwich Arsenal v The Wednesday	1-3

FINAL AT CRYSTAL PALACE

The Wednesday v Everton	2-1

SCOTTISH FA CUP 1906-07

FIRST ROUND

Third Lanark v St Johnstone	4-1
Falkirk v Rangers	1-2
Heart of Midlothian v Airdrieonians	0-0, 2-0
Dumfries v Port Glasgow Athletic	2-2, 0-2
Maxwelltown Volunteers v Morton	0-3
Ayr v Cowdenbeath	2-0
Raith Rovers v Aberdeen University	5-1
Arbroath v Queen's Park	1-1, 0-4
Renton v St Bernard's	0-0, 1-1, 2-0
Aberdeen v Johnstone	0-0, 1-2
Celtic v Clyde	2-1
Arthurlie v St Mirren	1-2
Partick Thistle v Dundee	2-2, 1-5
Galston v Motherwell	2-1
Kilmarnock v Clachnacuddin	4-0

SECOND ROUND

Queen's Park v Third Lanark	3-1
Raith Rovers v Ayr	4-0
St Mirren v Port Glasgow Athletic	4-1
Morton v Celtic	0-0, 1-1, 1-2
Hibernian v Johnstone	1-1, 5-0
Galston v Rangers	0-4
Kilmarnock v Heart of Midlothian	0-0, 1-2
Renton v Dundee	1-0

THIRD ROUND

Rangers v Celtic	0-3
St Mirren v Hibernian	1-1, 0-2
Queen's Park v Renton	4-1
Heart of Midlothian v Raith Rovers	2-2, 1-0

SEMI-FINAL

Celtic v Hibernian	0-0, 0-0, 3-0
Heart of Midlothian v Queen's Park	1-0

FINAL AT HAMPDEN PARK

Celtic v Heart of Midlothian	3-0

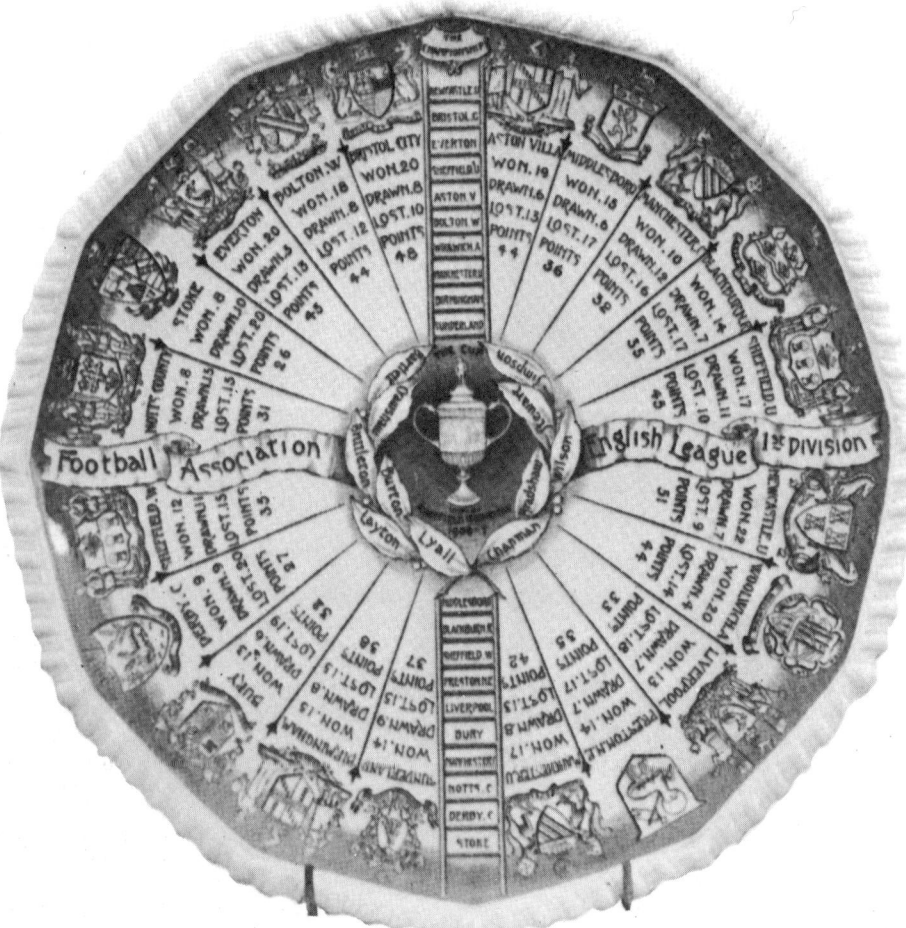

C PROCTOR: COURTESY OF J DANIELS, 20 SILVERTHORNE ROAD, S.W.8

League Tables 1907-08

FIRST DIVISION

		P	W	D	L	F	A	Pts
1	Man United	38	23	6	9	81	48	52
2	Aston Villa	38	17	9	12	77	59	43
3	Man City	38	16	11	11	62	54	43
4	Newcastle	38	15	12	11	65	54	42
5	Wednesday	38	19	4	15	73	64	42
6	Middlesbrough	38	17	7	14	54	45	41
7	Bury	38	14	11	13	58	61	39
8	Liverpool	38	16	6	16	68	61	38
9	Nottm Forest	38	13	11	14	59	62	37
10	Bristol City	38	12	12	14	58	61	36
11	Everton	38	15	6	17	58	64	36
12	Preston	38	12	12	14	47	53	36
13	Chelsea	38	14	8	16	53	62	36
14	Blackburn*	38	12	12	14	51	63	36
15	Woolwich A*	38	12	12	14	51	63	36
16	Sunderland	38	16	3	19	78	75	35
17	Sheff United	38	12	11	15	52	58	35
18	Notts County	38	13	8	17	39	51	34
19	Bolton	38	14	5	19	52	58	33
20	Birmingham	38	9	12	17	40	60	30

*equal

SECOND DIVISION

		P	W	D	L	F	A	Pts
1	Bradford City	38	24	6	8	90	42	54
2	Leicester Fosse	38	21	10	7	72	47	52
3	Oldham	38	22	6	10	76	42	50
4	Fulham	38	22	5	11	82	49	49
5	WBA	38	19	9	10	61	39	47
6	Derby	38	21	4	13	77	45	46
7	Burnley	38	20	6	12	67	50	46
8	Hull	38	21	4	13	73	62	46
9	Wolves	38	15	7	16	50	45	37
10	Stoke	38	16	5	17	57	52	37
11	Gainsborough	38	14	7	17	47	71	35
12	Leeds City	38	12	8	18	53	65	32
13	Stockport	38	12	8	18	48	67	32
14	Clapton Orient	38	11	10	17	40	65	32
15	Blackpool	38	11	9	18	51	58	31
16	Barnsley	38	12	6	20	54	68	30
17	Glossop NE	38	11	8	19	54	74	30
18	Grimsby	38	11	8	19	43	71	30
19	Chesterfield	38	6	11	21	46	92	23
20	Lincoln	38	9	3	26	46	83	21

SCOTTISH FIRST DIVISION

		P	W	D	L	F	A	Pts
1	Celtic	34	24	7	3	86	27	55
2	Falkirk	34	22	7	5	103	41	51
3	Rangers	34	21	8	5	74	40	50
4	Dundee	34	20	8	6	71	28	48
5	Hibernian	34	17	8	9	55	42	42
6	Airdrieonians	34	18	5	11	58	41	41
7	St Mirren	34	13	10	11	50	59	36
8	Aberdeen	34	13	9	12	45	44	35
9	Third Lanark	34	13	7	14	44	50	33
10	Motherwell	34	12	7	15	61	53	31
11	Hamilton	34	10	8	16	54	65	28
12	Hearts	34	11	6	17	50	61	28
13	Morton	34	9	9	16	43	66	27
14	Kilmarnock	34	6	13	15	38	61	25
15	Partick	34	8	9	17	43	69	25
16	Queen's Park	34	7	8	19	54	84	22
17	Clyde	34	5	8	21	37	75	18
18	Port Glasgow	34	5	7	22	39	99	17

SCOTTISH SECOND DIVISION

		P	W	D	L	F	A	Pts
1	Raith	22	14	2	6	37	23	30
2	Dumbarton	22	12	5	5	49	32	27*
3	Ayr	22	11	5	6	39	33	27
4	Abercorn	22	9	5	8	33	30	23
5	E Stirlingshire	22	9	5	8	30	31	23
6	Ayr Parkhouse	22	11	0	11	38	37	22
7	Leith	22	8	5	9	41	40	21
8	St Bernard's	22	8	5	9	31	32	21
9	Albion	22	7	5	10	36	48	19
10	Vale of Leven	22	5	8	9	25	31	18
11	Arthurlie	22	6	5	11	33	46	17
12	Cowdenbeath	22	5	4	13	26	35	14

*Two points deducted for a registration irregularity

Below *Wednesday goalkeeper Lyell, well backed up by his defence, repulses a Chelsea attack in a First Division match. It was Chelsea's first ever season in the First Division.*

FA CUP 1907-08

SECOND ROUND
Wolverhampton Wanderers v Bury	2-0
Swindon Town v Queen's Park Rangers	2-1
Stoke v Gainsborough Trinity	1-1, 2-2, 3-1
Portsmouth v Leicester Fosse	1-0
Notts County v Bolton Wanderers	1-1, 1-2
Oldham Athletic v Everton	0-0, 1-6
Southampton v West Bromwich Albion	1-0
Bristol Rovers v Chesterfield Town	2-0
Newcastle United v West Ham United	2-0
Liverpool v Brighton	1-1, 3-0
Grimsby Town v Carlisle United	6-2
Plymouth Argyle v Crystal Palace	2-3
Manchester City v New Brompton	1-1, 2-1
Norwich City v Fulham	1-2
Manchester United v Chelsea	1-0
Aston Villa v Hull City	3-0

THIRD ROUND
Wolverhampton Wanderers v Swindon Town	2-0
Portsmouth v Stoke	0-1
Bolton Wanderers v Everton	3-3, 1-3
Southampton v Bristol Rovers	2-0
Newcastle United v Liverpool	3-1
Grimsby Town v Crystal Palace	1-0
Manchester City v Fulham	1-1, 1-3
Aston Villa v Manchester United	0-2

FOURTH ROUND
Stoke v Wolverhampton Wanderers	0-1
Everton v Southampton	0-0, 2-3
Newcastle United v Grimsby Town	5-1
Fulham v Manchester United	2-1

SEMI-FINAL
Wolverhampton Wanderers v Southampton	2-0
Newcastle United v Fulham	6-0

FINAL AT CRYSTAL PALACE
Wolverhampton Wanderers v Newcastle United	3-1

SCOTTISH FA CUP 1907-08

FIRST ROUND
Falkirk v Rangers	2-2, 1-4
Heart of Midlothian v St Johnstone	2-1
Celtic v Peebles Rovers	4-0
Hibernian v Abercorn	5-1
St Bernard's v Queen's Park	1-1, 1-1, 0-1
Aberdeen v Albion Rovers	3-0
Dumfries v Motherwell	0-4
Partick Thistle v Bo'ness	4-0
Port Glasgow Athletic v Ayr Parkhouse	7-1
Dunblane v Elgin City	8-3
Kilmarnock v Hamilton Academicals	2-1
Raith Rovers v Inverness Thistle	2-0
Galston v Uphall	wo
St Mirren v Third Lanark	3-1
Morton v Vale of Atholl	7-1
Airdrieonians v Dundee	0-1

SECOND ROUND
Motherwell v St Mirren	2-2, 0-2
Heart of Midlothian v Port Glasgow Athletic	4-0
Rangers v Celtic	1-2
Partick Thistle v Raith Rovers	1-1, 1-2
Queen's Park v Galston	6-2
Kilmarnock v Dunblane	3-0
Hibernian v Morton	3-0
Aberdeen v Dundee	0-0, 2-2, 3-1

THIRD ROUND
Aberdeen v Queen's Park	3-1
Raith Rovers v Celtic	0-3
Hibernian v Kilmarnock	0-1
St Mirren v Heart of Midlothian	1-0*, 3-1

*abandoned

SEMI-FINAL
Aberdeen v Celtic	0-1
Kilmarnock v St Mirren	0-0, 0-2

FINAL AT HAMPDEN PARK
Celtic v St Mirren	5-1

RADIO TIMES HULTON PICTURE LIBRARY

League Tables 1908-09

FIRST DIVISION

		P	W	D	L	F	A	Pts
1	Newcastle	38	24	5	9	65	41	53
2	Everton	38	18	10	10	82	57	46
3	Sunderland	38	21	2	15	78	63	44
4	Blackburn	38	14	13	11	61	50	41
5	Wednesday	38	17	6	15	67	61	40
6	Woolwich A	38	14	10	14	52	49	38
7	Aston Villa	38	14	10	14	58	56	38
8	Bristol City	38	13	12	13	45	58	38
9	Middlesbrough	38	14	9	15	59	53	37
10	Preston	38	13	11	14	48	44	37
11	Chelsea	38	14	9	15	56	61	37
12	Sheff United	38	14	9	15	51	59	37
13	Man United	38	15	7	16	58	68	37
14	Nottm Forest	38	14	8	16	66	57	36
15	Notts County	38	14	8	16	51	48	36
16	Liverpool	38	15	6	17	57	65	36
17	Bury	38	14	8	16	63	77	36
18	Bradford City	38	12	10	16	47	47	34
19	Man City	38	15	4	19	67	69	34
20	Leicester Fosse	38	8	9	21	54	102	25

SECOND DIVISION

		P	W	D	L	F	A	Pts
1	Bolton	38	24	4	10	59	28	52
2	Tottenham	38	20	11	7	67	32	51
3	WBA	38	19	13	6	56	27	51
4	Hull	38	19	6	13	63	39	44
5	Derby	38	16	11	11	55	41	43
6	Oldham	38	17	6	15	55	43	40
7	Wolves	38	14	11	13	56	48	39
8	Glossop NE	38	15	8	15	57	53	38
9	Gainsborough	38	15	8	15	49	70	38
10	Fulham	38	13	11	14	58	48	37
11	Birmingham	38	14	9	15	58	61	37
12	Leeds City	38	14	7	17	43	53	35
13	Grimsby	38	14	7	17	41	54	35
14	Burnley	38	13	7	18	51	58	33
15	Clapton Orient	38	12	9	17	37	49	33
16	Bradford PA	38	13	6	19	51	59	32
17	Barnsley	38	11	10	17	48	57	32
18	Stockport	38	14	3	21	39	71	31
19	Chesterfield	38	11	8	19	37	67	30
20	Blackpool	38	9	11	18	46	68	29

SCOTTISH FIRST DIVISION

		P	W	D	L	F	A	Pts
1	Celtic	34	23	5	6	71	24	51
2	Dundee	34	22	6	6	70	33	50
3	Clyde	34	21	6	7	61	37	48
4	Rangers	34	19	7	8	90	37	45
5	Airdrieonians	34	16	9	9	67	46	41
6	Hibernian	34	16	7	11	41	32	39
7	St Mirren	34	15	6	13	53	45	36
8	Aberdeen	34	15	6	13	61	53	36
9	Falkirk	34	13	7	14	58	56	33
10	Kilmarnock	34	13	7	14	47	61	33
11	Third Lanark	34	11	10	13	56	49	32
12	Hearts	34	12	8	14	54	49	32
13	Port Glasgow	34	10	8	16	39	52	28
14	Motherwell	34	11	6	17	47	73	28
15	Queen's Park	34	6	13	15	41	64	25
16	Hamilton	34	6	12	16	42	74	24
17	Morton	34	8	7	19	39	90	23
18	Partick	34	2	4	28	38	102	8

SCOTTISH SECOND DIVISION

		P	W	D	L	F	A	Pts
1	Abercorn	22	13	5	4	39	16	31
2	Raith	22	11	6	5	46	21	28
3	Vale of Leven	22	12	4	6	38	25	28
4	Dumbarton	22	10	5	7	34	34	25
5	Leith	22	10	3	9	38	33	23
6	Ayr	22	10	3	9	40	36	23
7	Ayr Parkhouse	22	8	5	9	29	31	21
8	St Bernard's	22	9	3	10	34	37	21
9	E Stirlingshire	22	9	3	10	27	33	21
10	Albion	22	9	2	11	36	46	20
11	Cowdenbeath	22	4	4	14	19	43	12
12	Arthurlie	22	5	1	16	30	55	11

Below After a 1-1 draw, 1908 League Champions Manchester United, beat Queen's Park Rangers, the Southern League winners, 4-0 in September to become the first holders of **inset** the Charity Shield.

FA CUP 1908-09

SECOND ROUND

Manchester United v Everton	1-0
Blackburn Rovers v Chelsea	2-1
Tottenham Hotspur v Fulham	1-0
Crystal Palace v Burnley	0-0, 0-9
Newcastle United v Blackpool	2-1
Leeds City v West Ham United	1-1, 1-2
Preston North End v Sunderland	1-2
West Bromwich Albion v Bradford City	1-2
Bristol City v Bury	2-2, 1-0
Liverpool v Norwich City	2-3
Stockport County v Glossop North End	1-1, 0-1
Portsmouth v The Wednesday	2-2, 0-3
Leicester Fosse v Derby County	0-2
Plymouth Argyle v Exeter City	2-0
Nottingham Forest v Brentford	1-0
Woolwich Arsenal v Millwall Athletic	1-1, 0-1

THIRD ROUND

Manchester United v Blackburn Rovers	6-1
Tottenham Hotspur v Burnley	0-0, 1-3
West Ham United v Newcastle United	0-0, 1-2
Bradford City v Sunderland	0-1
Bristol City v Norwich City	2-0
The Wednesday v Glossop North End	0-1
Derby County v Plymouth Argyle	1-0
Nottingham Forest v Millwall Athletic	3-1

FOURTH ROUND

Burnley v Manchester United	1-0*, 2-3
Newcastle United v Sunderland	2-2, 3-0
Glossop North End v Bristol City	0-0, 0-1
Derby County v Nottingham Forest	3-0

*abandoned

SEMI-FINAL

Manchester United v Newcastle United	1-0
Bristol City v Derby County	1-1, 2-1

FINAL AT CRYSTAL PALACE

Manchester United v Bristol City	1-0

SCOTTISH FA CUP 1908-09

SECOND ROUND

Third Lanark v Aberdeen	4-1
Clyde v Hibernian	1-0
Airdrieonians v Heart of Midlothian	2-0
St Mirren v Beith	3-0
Dundee v Rangers	0-0, 0-1
Queen's Park v Partick Thistle	3-0
Motherwell v Falkirk	1-3
Celtic v Port Glasgow Athletic	4-0

THIRD ROUND

Celtic v Airdrieonians	3-1
Third Lanark v Falkirk	1-2
Clyde v St Mirren	3-1
Rangers v Queen's Park	1-0

SEMI-FINAL

Falkirk v Rangers	0-1
Celtic v Clyde	0-0, 2-0

FINAL AT HAMPDEN PARK

Rangers v Celtic	2-2, 1-1†

†Some newspapers had suggested that, if the first replay ended level, extra-time would be played. The rules, in fact, stated that extra-time could only be played after a third game. When the players left the field some sections of the crowd obviously felt cheated and started protesting. This led to a full-scale riot with pay-boxes burned and hundreds injured. Rangers and Celtic both refused to play a third game as a result, threatening that one or other would simply scratch, and the Scottish FA agreed that the Cup would be withheld.

RADIO TIMES HULTON PICTURE LIBRARY

In April 1909 Leicester Fosse, already relegated to the Second Division, were beaten 12-0 by neighbours Nottingham Forest in one of the last games of the season. As this was a record Division One score, and as those two points confirmed Forest's place in the First Division, a League Commission inquiry examined the circumstances surrounding the match. Their finding was quite simply that the Leicester Fosse players had been celebrating the wedding of a colleague the day before the game was played.

Broxburn and Beith met five times in a first-round Scottish Cup tie. The last three games were played on three consecutive days, Beith finally winning 4-2 on a Friday. The following day they met St Mirren in the next round, their fourth game in four days. They lost . . .

League Tables 1909-10

FIRST DIVISION

		P	W	D	L	F	A	Pts
1	Aston Villa	38	23	7	8	84	42	53
2	Liverpool	38	21	6	11	78	57	48
3	Blackburn	38	18	9	11	73	55	45
4	Newcastle	38	19	7	12	70	56	45
5	Man United	38	19	7	12	69	61	45
6	Sheff United	38	16	10	12	62	41	42
7	Bradford City	38	17	8	13	64	47	42
8	Sunderland	38	18	5	15	66	51	41
9	Notts County	38	15	10	13	67	59	40
10	Everton	38	16	8	14	51	56	40
11	Wednesday	38	15	9	14	60	63	39
12	Preston	38	15	5	18	52	58	35
13	Bury	38	12	9	17	62	66	33
14	Nottm Forest	38	11	11	16	54	72	33
15	Tottenham	38	11	10	17	53	69	32
16	Bristol City	38	12	8	18	45	60	32
17	Middlesbrough	38	11	9	18	56	73	31
18	Woolwich A	38	11	9	18	37	67	31
19	Chelsea	38	11	7	20	47	70	29
20	Bolton	38	9	6	23	44	71	24

SECOND DIVISION

		P	W	D	L	F	A	Pts
1	Man City	38	23	8	7	81	40	54
2	Oldham	38	23	7	8	79	39	53
3	Hull City	38	23	7	8	80	46	53
4	Derby	38	22	9	7	72	47	53
5	Leicester Fosse	38	20	4	14	79	58	44
6	Glossop NE	38	18	7	13	64	57	43
7	Fulham	38	14	13	11	51	43	41
8	Wolves	38	17	6	15	64	63	40
9	Barnsley	38	16	7	15	62	59	39
10	Bradford PA	38	17	4	17	64	59	38
11	WBA	38	16	5	17	58	56	37
12	Blackpool	38	14	8	16	50	52	36
13	Stockport	38	13	8	17	50	47	34
14	Burnley	38	14	6	18	62	61	34
15	Lincoln	38	10	11	17	42	69	31
16	Clapton Orient	38	12	6	20	37	60	30
17	Leeds City	38	10	7	21	46	80	27
18	Gainsborough	38	10	6	22	33	75	26
19	Grimsby	38	9	6	23	50	77	24
20	Birmingham	38	8	7	23	42	78	23

SCOTTISH FIRST DIVISION

		P	W	D	L	F	A	Pts
1	Celtic	34	24	6	4	63	22	54
2	Falkirk	34	22	8	4	71	28	52
3	Rangers	34	20	6	8	70	35	46
4	Aberdeen	34	16	8	10	44	29	40
5	Clyde	34	14	9	11	47	33	37
6	Dundee	34	14	8	12	52	44	36
7	Third Lanark	34	13	8	13	62	44	34
8	Hibernian	34	14	6	14	33	40	34
9	Airdrieonians	34	12	9	13	46	57	33
10	Motherwell	34	12	8	14	59	60	32
11	Kilmarnock	34	12	8	14	53	59	32
12	Hearts	34	12	7	15	59	57	31
13	St Mirren	34	13	5	16	48	58	31
14	Queen's Park	34	12	6	16	54	74	30
15	Hamilton	34	11	6	17	50	67	28
16	Partick	34	8	10	16	45	59	26
17	Morton	34	11	3	20	38	60	25
18	Port Glasgow	34	3	5	26	25	93	11

SCOTTISH SECOND DIVISION

		P	W	D	L	F	A	Pts
1	Leith	22	13	7	2	41	18	33
2	Raith*	22	14	5	3	35	20	33
3	St Bernard's	22	12	3	7	43	31	27
4	Dumbarton	22	9	5	8	44	37	23
5	Abercorn	22	7	8	7	38	39	22
6	Ayr	22	9	3	10	37	40	21
7	Vale of Leven	22	8	5	9	35	39	21
8	E Stirlingshire	22	9	2	11	38	43	20
9	Albion	22	7	5	10	34	39	19
10	Arthurlie	22	6	5	11	34	45	17
11	Cowdenbeath	22	7	3	12	22	34	17
12	Ayr Parkhouse	22	4	3	15	27	43	11

*Elected to First Division

Below *In 1910 Newcastle were the last club to win the second FA Cup. The design had been pirated for a minor competition and the old Cup was presented to Lord Kinnaird.*

COLORSPORT

FA CUP 1909-10

SECOND ROUND

Newcastle United v Fulham	4-0
Bradford City v Blackburn Rovers	1-2
Leicester Fosse v Bury	3-2
Stockport County v Leyton	0-2
Swindon Town v Burnley	2-0
Chelsea v Tottenham Hotspur	0-1
Southampton v Manchester City	0-5
Aston Villa v Derby County	6-1
Bristol Rovers v Barnsley	0-4
Bristol City v West Bromwich Albion	1-1, 2-4
Southend United v Queen's Park Rangers	0-0, 2-3
Wolverhampton Wanderers v West Ham United	1-5
Everton v Woolwich Arsenal	5-0
Sunderland v Bradford Park Avenue	3-1
Portsmouth v Coventry City	0-1
Northampton Town v Nottingham Forest	0-0, 0-1

THIRD ROUND

Newcastle United v Blackburn Rovers	3-1
Leicester Fosse v Leyton	1-0
Swindon Town v Tottenham Hotspur	3-2
Aston Villa v Manchester City	1-2
Barnsley v West Bromwich Albion	1-0
Queen's Park Rangers v West Ham United	1-1, 1-0
Everton v Sunderland	2-0
Coventry City v Nottingham Forest	3-1

FOURTH ROUND

Newcastle United v Leicester Fosse	3-0
Swindon Town v Manchester City	2-0
Barnsley v Queen's Park Rangers	1-0
Coventry City v Everton	0-2

SEMI-FINAL

Newcastle United v Swindon Town	2-0
Barnsley v Everton	0-0, 3-0

FINAL AT CRYSTAL PALACE

Newcastle United v Barnsley	1-1, 2-0*

*Replay at Goodison Park

SCOTTISH FA CUP 1909-10

FIRST ROUND

Rangers v Inverness Thistle	3-1
Queen's Park v Kirkcaldy United	0-0, 6-0
St Mirren v Elgin City	8-0
Kilmarnock v Third Lanark	0-0, 0-2
Dumbarton v Celtic	1-2
Morton v Partick Thistle	4-3
Airdrieonians v Douglas Wanderers	6-0
Leith Athletic v Clyde	0-1
Motherwell v Forfar Athletic	1-0
Bathgate v Heart of Midlothian	0-4
Hamilton v Hibernian	0-0, 0-2
Falkirk v Port Glasgow Athletic	3-0
Dundee v Beith	1-1, 1-0
Ayr v Alloa Athletic	3-2
Aberdeen v Bo'ness	3-0
East Fife v Hurlford	4-1

SECOND ROUND

Motherwell v Morton	3-0
Dundee v Falkirk	3-0
Clyde v Rangers	2-0
St Mirren v Heart of Midlothian	2-2, 0-0, 0-4
Ayr v Hibernian	0-1
Celtic v Third Lanark	3-1
Aberdeen v Airdrieonians	3-0
East Fife v Queen's Park	2-3

THIRD ROUND

Hibernian v Heart of Midlothian	0-1*, 1-0
Celtic v Aberdeen	2-1
Queen's Park v Clyde	2-2, 2-2, 1-2
Motherwell v Dundee	1-3

*abandoned

SEMI-FINAL

Clyde v Celtic	3-1
Hibernian v Dundee	0-0, 0-0, 0-1

FINAL AT IBROX PARK

Dundee v Clyde	2-2, 0-0, 2-1

FIRST DIVISION

		P	W	D	L	F	A	Pts
1	Man United	38	22	8	8	72	40	52
2	Aston Villa	38	22	7	9	69	41	51
3	Sunderland	38	15	15	8	67	48	45
4	Everton	38	19	7	12	50	36	45
5	Bradford City	38	20	5	13	51	42	45
6	Wednesday	38	17	8	13	47	48	42
7	Oldham	38	16	9	13	44	41	41
8	Newcastle	38	15	10	13	61	43	40
9	Sheff United	38	15	8	15	49	43	38
10	Woolwich A	38	13	12	13	41	49	38
11	Notts County	38	14	10	14	37	45	38
12	Blackburn	38	13	11	14	62	54	37
13	Liverpool	38	15	7	16	53	53	37
14	Preston	38	12	11	15	40	49	35
15	Tottenham	38	13	6	19	52	63	32
16	Middlesbrough	38	11	10	17	49	63	32
17	Man City	38	9	13	16	43	58	31
18	Bury	38	9	11	18	43	71	29
19	Bristol City	38	11	5	22	43	66	27
20	Nottm Forest	38	9	7	22	55	75	25

SECOND DIVISION

		P	W	D	L	F	A	Pts
1	WBA	38	22	9	7	67	41	53
2	Bolton	38	21	9	8	69	40	51
3	Chelsea	38	20	9	9	71	35	49
4	Clapton Orient	38	19	7	12	44	35	45
5	Hull	38	14	16	8	55	39	44
6	Derby	38	17	8	13	73	52	42
7	Blackpool	38	16	10	12	49	38	42
8	Burnley	38	13	15	10	45	45	41
9	Wolves	38	15	8	15	51	52	38
10	Fulham	38	15	7	16	52	48	37
11	Leeds City	38	15	7	16	58	56	37
12	Bradford PA	38	14	9	15	53	55	37
13	Huddersfield	38	13	8	17	57	58	34
14	Glossop NE	38	13	8	17	48	62	34
15	Leicester Fosse	38	14	5	19	52	62	33
16	Birmingham	38	12	8	18	42	64	32
17	Stockport	38	11	8	19	47	79	30
18	Gainsborough	38	9	11	18	37	55	29
19	Barnsley	38	7	14	17	52	62	28
20	Lincoln	38	7	10	21	28	72	24

SCOTTISH FIRST DIVISION

		P	W	D	L	F	A	Pts
1	Rangers	34	23	6	5	90	34	52
2	Aberdeen	34	19	10	5	53	28	44
3	Falkirk	34	17	10	7	65	42	44
4	Partick	34	17	8	9	50	41	42
5	Celtic	34	15	11	8	48	18	41
6	Dundee	34	18	5	11	54	42	41
7	Clyde	34	14	11	9	45	36	39
8	Third Lanark	34	16	7	11	59	53	39
9	Hibernian	34	15	6	13	44	48	36
10	Kilmarnock	34	12	10	12	42	45	34
11	Airdrieonians	34	12	9	13	49	53	33
12	St Mirren	34	12	7	15	46	57	31
13	Morton	34	9	11	14	49	51	29
14	Hearts	34	8	8	18	42	59	24
15	Raith	34	7	10	17	36	55	24
16	Hamilton	34	8	5	21	31	51	21
17	Motherwell	34	8	4	22	37	66	20
18	Queen's Park	34	5	4	25	28	80	14

SCOTTISH SECOND DIVISION

		P	W	D	L	F	A	Pts
1	Dumbarton	22	15	1	6	52	30	31
2	Ayr	22	12	3	7	54	36	27
3	Albion	22	10	5	7	26	21	25
4	Leith	22	10	5	7	44	43	25
5	Cowdenbeath	22	9	5	8	31	27	23
6	St Bernard's	22	10	2	10	36	41	22
7	E Stirlingshire	22	7	6	9	28	34	20
8	Dundee Hibs	22	7	5	10	29	35	19
9	Abercorn	22	9	1	12	39	50	19
10	Arthurlie	22	7	5	10	26	33	19
11	Port Glasgow	22	8	2	12	27	32	18
12	Vale of Leven	22	4	8	10	21	29	16

Below *Bradford City defend in depth as Newcastle threaten their goal in the 1911 Cup Final at Crystal Palace. The game, which ended 0-0, was the Tynesiders' fifth appearance at Crystal Palace in seven years.*

FA CUP 1910-11

SECOND ROUND

Bradford City v Norwich City	2-1
Crewe Alexandra v Grimsby Town	1-5
Burnley v Barnsley	2-0
Brighton v Coventry City	0-0, 0-2
Blackburn Rovers v Tottenham Hotspur	0-0, 2-1
Middlesbrough v Leicester Fosse	0-0, 2-1
West Ham United v Preston North End	3-0
Manchester United v Aston Villa	2-1
Newcastle United v Northampton Town	1-1, 1-0†
Hull City v Oldham Athletic	1-0
Derby County v West Bromwich Albion	2-0
Everton v Liverpool	2-1
Chesterfield Town v Chelsea	1-4
Wolverhampton Wanderers v Manchester City	1-0
Swindon Town v Woolwich Arsenal	1-0
Darlington v Bradford Park Avenue	2-1

† Both games played at Newcastle. Northampton sold their rights to a replay at home for £900.

THIRD ROUND

Bradford City v Grimsby Town	1-0
Burnley v Coventry City	5-0
Middlesbrough v Blackburn Rovers	0-3
West Ham United v Manchester United	2-1
Newcastle United v Hull City	3-2
Derby County v Everton	5-0
Wolverhampton Wanderers v Chelsea	0-2
Darlington v Swindon Town	0-3

FOURTH ROUND

Bradford City v Burnley	1-0
West Ham United v Blackburn Rovers	2-3
Newcastle United v Derby County	4-0
Chelsea v Swindon Town	3-1

SEMI-FINAL

Bradford City v Blackburn Rovers	3-0
Newcastle United v Chelsea	3-0

FINAL AT CRYSTAL PALACE

Bradford City v Newcastle United	0-0, 1-0*

*Replay at Old Trafford

SCOTTISH FA CUP 1910-11

FIRST ROUND

Aberdeen v Brechin City	3-0
Airdrieonians v Bo'ness	2-0
Celtic v St Mirren	2-0
Heart of Midlothian v Clyde	1-1, 0-1
Dundee v Hibernian	2-1
Leith Athletic v Falkirk	2-2, 1-4
Forfar Athletic v 5th KOSB	3-0
Galston v Lochgelly United	8-0
Rangers v Kilmarnock	2-1
East Stirlingshire v Morton	1-4
Third Lanark v Hamilton Academicals	0-1
Inverness Thistle v Johnstone	0-1
Motherwell v Annbank	5-0
Nithsdale Wanderers v Inverness Caledonian	3-1
Partick Thistle v St Bernard's	7-2
Stanley v Queen's Park	1-6

SECOND ROUND

Aberdeen v Airdrieonians	1-0
Clyde v Queen's Park	4-1
Partick Thistle v Dundee	0-3
Forfar Athletic v Falkirk	2-0
Celtic v Galston	1-0
Rangers v Morton	3-0
Hamilton Academicals v Johnstone	1-1, 3-1
Nithsdale Wanderers v Motherwell	0-0, 0-1

THIRD ROUND

Aberdeen v Forfar Athletic	6-0
Celtic v Clyde	1-0
Dundee v Rangers	2-1
Hamilton Academicals v Motherwell	2-1

SEMI-FINAL

Celtic v Aberdeen	1-0
Hamilton Academicals v Dundee	3-2

FINAL AT IBROX PARK

Celtic v Hamilton Academicals	0-0, 2-1

RADIO TIMES HULTON PICTURE LIBRARY

FIRST DIVISION

		P	W	D	L	F	A	Pts
1	Blackburn	38	20	9	9	60	43	49
2	Everton	38	20	6	12	46	42	46
3	Newcastle	38	18	8	12	64	50	44
4	Bolton	38	20	3	15	54	43	43
5	Wednesday	38	16	9	13	69	49	41
6	Aston Villa	38	17	7	14	76	63	41
7	Middlesbrough	38	16	8	14	56	45	40
8	Sunderland	38	14	11	13	58	51	39
9	WBA	38	15	9	14	43	47	39
10	Woolwich A	38	15	8	15	55	59	38
11	Bradford City	38	15	8	15	46	50	38
12	Tottenham	38	14	9	15	53	53	37
13	Man United	38	13	11	14	45	60	37
14	Sheff United	38	13	10	15	63	56	36
15	Man City	38	13	9	16	56	58	35
16	Notts County	38	14	7	17	46	63	35
17	Liverpool	38	12	10	16	49	55	34
18	Oldham	38	12	10	16	46	54	34
19	Preston	38	13	7	18	40	57	33
20	Bury	38	6	9	23	32	59	21

SECOND DIVISION

		P	W	D	L	F	A	Pts
1	Derby	38	23	8	7	74	28	54
2	Chelsea	38	24	6	8	64	34	54
3	Burnley	38	22	8	8	77	41	52
4	Clapton Orient	38	21	3	14	61	44	45
5	Wolves	38	16	10	12	57	33	42
6	Barnsley	38	15	12	11	45	42	42
7	Hull	38	17	8	13	54	51	42
8	Fulham	38	16	7	15	66	58	39
9	Grimsby	38	15	9	14	48	55	39
10	Leicester Fosse	38	15	7	16	49	66	37
11	Bradford PA	38	13	9	16	44	45	35
12	Birmingham	38	14	6	18	55	59	34
13	Bristol City	38	14	6	18	41	60	34
14	Blackpool	38	13	8	17	32	52	34
15	Nottm Forest	38	13	7	18	46	48	33
16	Stockport	38	11	11	16	47	54	33
17	Huddersfield	38	13	6	19	50	64	32
18	Glossop NE	38	8	12	18	42	56	28
19	Leeds City	38	10	8	20	50	78	28
20	Gainsborough	38	5	13	20	30	64	23

SCOTTISH FIRST DIVISION

		P	W	D	L	F	A	Pts
1	Rangers	34	24	3	7	86	34	51
2	Celtic	34	17	11	6	58	33	45
3	Clyde	34	19	4	11	56	32	42
4	Hearts	34	16	8	10	54	40	40
5	Partick	34	16	8	10	47	40	40
6	Morton	34	14	9	11	44	44	37
7	Falkirk	34	15	6	13	46	43	36
8	Dundee	34	13	9	12	52	41	35
9	Aberdeen	34	14	7	13	44	44	35
10	Airdrieonians	34	12	8	14	31	41	32
11	Third Lanark	34	12	7	15	40	57	31
12	Hamilton	34	11	8	15	32	44	30
13	Hibernian	34	12	5	17	44	47	29
14	Raith	34	9	9	16	48	59	27
15	Motherwell	34	11	5	18	34	44	27
16	Kilmarnock	34	11	4	19	38	60	26
17	Queen's Park	34	8	9	17	29	53	25
18	St Mirren	34	7	10	17	32	59	24

SCOTTISH SECOND DIVISION

		P	W	D	L	F	A	Pts
1	Ayr	22	16	3	3	54	24	35
2	Abercorn	22	13	4	5	43	23	30
3	Dumbarton	22	13	1	8	47	31	27
4	Cowdenbeath	22	12	2	8	39	31	26
5	St Johnstone	22	10	4	8	29	27	24
6	St Bernard's	22	9	5	8	39	36	23
7	Leith	22	9	4	9	31	34	22
8	Arthurlie	22	7	5	10	30	30	19
9	E Stirlingshire	22	7	3	12	22	31	17
10	Dundee Hibs	22	5	5	12	21	41	15
11	Vale of Leven	22	6	1	15	26	51	13
12	Albion	22	6	1	15	19	41	13

Below *Spurs entertain the Football League champions, Blackburn Rovers, at White Hart Lane. Bob Crompton (right of goalkeeper), Blackburn's captain, watches anxiously as his keeper is challenged by a Tottenham forward.*

FA CUP 1911-12

SECOND ROUND

Coventry City v Manchester United	1-5
Aston Villa v Reading	1-1, 0-1
Derby County v Blackburn Rovers	1-2
Wolverhampton Wanderers v Lincoln City	2-1
Leeds City v West Bromwich Albion	0-1
Crystal Palace v Sunderland	0-0, 0-1
Fulham v Liverpool	3-0
Darlington v Northampton Town	1-1, 0-2
Swindon Town v Notts County	2-0
Middlesbrough v West Ham United	1-1, 1-2
Everton v Bury	1-1, 6-0
Manchester City v Oldham Athletic	0-1
Bradford City v Chelsea	2-0
Bradford Park Avenue v Portsmouth	2-0
Barnsley v Leicester Fosse	1-0
Bolton Wanderers v Blackpool	1-0

THIRD ROUND

Reading v Manchester United	1-1, 0-3
Blackburn Rovers v Wolverhampton Wanderers	3-2
Sunderland v West Bromwich Albion	1-2
Fulham v Northampton Town	2-1
West Ham United v Swindon Town	1-1, 0-4
Oldham Athletic v Everton	0-2
Bradford Park Avenue v Bradford City	0-1
Bolton Wanderers v Barnsley	1-2

FOURTH ROUND

Manchester United v Blackburn Rovers	1-1, 2-4
West Bromwich Albion v Fulham	3-0
Swindon Town v Everton	2-1
Barnsley v Bradford City	0-0, 0-0, 0-0, 3-2

SEMI-FINAL

Blackburn Rovers v West Bromwich Albion	0-0, 0-1
Swindon Town v Barnsley	0-0, 0-1

FINAL AT CRYSTAL PALACE

Barnsley v West Bromwich Albion	0-0, 1-0*

*Replay at Bramall Lane

SCOTTISH FA CUP 1911-12

FIRST ROUND

St Mirren v Aberdeen	3-3, 0-4
Raith Rovers v Airdrieonians	0-0, 1-3
Armadale v Peterhead	2-1
Broxburn Athletic v Beith	6-0
Celtic v Dunfermline Athletic	1-0
Clyde v Abercorn	2-0
Partick Thistle v Dundee	2-2, 0-3
East Stirlingshire v Dumbarton	3-1
Falkirk v King's Park	2-2, 6-1
Rangers v Stenhousemuir	3-0
Morton v Clachnacuddin	2-0
Hibernian v Heart of Midlothian	1-1, 0-0, 1-2
Kilmarnock v Hamilton Academicals	1-0
Leith v Ayr United	3-0
St Johnstone v Motherwell	0-2
Third Lanark v Renton	5-0

SECOND ROUND

Aberdeen v Armadale	3-0
Celtic v East Stirlingshire	3-0
Clyde v Rangers	3-1
Heart of Midlothian v Dundee	1-0
Leith Athletic v Kilmarnock	0-2
Falkirk v Morton	0-0, 1-3
Motherwell v Airdrieonians	5-1
Third Lanark v Broxburn Athletic	6-1

THIRD ROUND

Aberdeen v Celtic	2-2, 0-2
Kilmarnock v Clyde	1-6
Morton v Heart of Midlothian	0-1
Third Lanark v Motherwell	3-1

SEMI-FINAL

Celtic v Heart of Midlothian	3-0
Clyde v Third Lanark	3-1

FINAL AT IBROX PARK

Celtic v Clyde	2-0

RADIO TIMES HULTON PICTURE LIBRARY

League Tables 1912-13

FIRST DIVISION

		P	W	D	L	F	A	Pts
1	Sunderland	38	25	4	9	86	43	54
2	Aston Villa	38	19	12	7	86	52	50
3	Wednesday	38	21	7	10	75	55	49
4	Man United	38	19	8	11	69	43	46
5	Blackburn	38	16	13	9	79	43	45
6	Man City	38	18	8	12	53	37	44
7	Derby	38	17	8	13	69	66	42
8	Bolton	38	16	10	12	62	63	42
9	Oldham	38	14	14	10	50	55	42
10	WBA	38	13	12	13	57	50	38
11	Everton	38	15	7	16	48	54	37
12	Liverpool	38	16	5	17	61	71	37
13	Bradford City	38	12	11	15	50	60	35
14	Newcastle	38	13	8	17	47	47	34
15	Sheff United	38	14	6	18	56	70	34
16	Middlesbrough	38	11	10	17	55	69	32
17	Tottenham	38	12	6	20	45	72	30
18	Chelsea	38	11	6	21	51	73	28
19	Notts County	38	7	9	22	28	56	23
20	Woolwich A	38	3	12	23	26	74	18

SECOND DIVISION

		P	W	D	L	F	A	Pts
1	Preston	38	19	15	4	56	33	53
2	Burnley	38	21	8	9	88	53	50
3	Birmingham	38	18	10	10	59	44	46
4	Barnsley	38	19	7	12	57	47	45
5	Huddersfield	38	17	9	12	66	40	43
6	Leeds City	38	15	10	13	70	64	40
7	Grimsby	38	15	10	13	51	50	40
8	Lincoln	38	15	10	13	50	52	40
9	Fulham	38	17	5	16	65	55	39
10	Wolves	38	14	10	14	56	54	38
11	Bury	38	15	8	15	53	57	38
12	Hull	38	15	6	17	60	56	36
13	Bradford PA	38	14	8	16	60	60	36
14	Clapton Orient	38	10	14	14	34	47	34
15	Leicester Fosse	38	13	7	18	50	65	33
16	Bristol City	38	9	15	14	46	72	33
17	Nottm Forest	38	12	8	18	58	59	32
18	Glossop NE	38	12	8	18	49	68	32
19	Stockport	38	8	10	20	56	78	26
20	Blackpool	38	9	8	21	39	69	26

SCOTTISH FIRST DIVISION

		P	W	D	L	F	A	Pts
1	Rangers	34	24	5	5	76	41	53
2	Celtic	34	22	5	7	53	28	49
3	Hearts	34	17	7	10	71	43	41
4	Airdrieonians	34	15	11	8	64	46	41
5	Falkirk	34	14	12	8	56	38	40
6	Hibernian	34	16	5	13	63	54	37
7	Motherwell	34	12	13	9	47	39	37
8	Aberdeen	34	14	9	11	47	40	37
9	Clyde	34	13	9	12	41	44	35
10	Hamilton	34	12	8	14	44	47	32
11	Kilmarnock	34	10	11	13	37	54	31
12	St Mirren	34	10	10	14	50	60	30
13	Morton	34	11	7	16	50	59	29
14	Dundee	34	8	13	13	38	46	29
15	Third Lanark	34	8	12	14	31	41	28
16	Raith	34	8	10	16	46	60	26
17	Partick	34	10	4	20	40	55	24
18	Queen's Park	34	5	3	26	34	88	13

SCOTTISH SECOND DIVISION

		P	W	D	L	F	A	Pts
1	Ayr*	26	13	8	5	45	19	34
2	Dunfermline	26	13	7	6	45	27	33
3	E Stirlingshire	26	12	8	6	43	27	32
4	Abercorn	26	12	7	7	33	31	31
5	Cowdenbeath	26	12	6	8	36	27	30
6	Dumbarton*	26	12	5	9	38	30	29
7	St Bernard's	26	12	3	11	36	34	27
8	Johnstone	26	9	6	11	31	43	24
9	Albion	26	10	3	13	38	40	23
10	Dundee Hibs	26	6	10	10	34	43	22
11	St Johnstone	26	7	7	12	29	38	21
12	Vale of Leven	26	8	5	13	28	45	21
13	Arthurlie	26	7	5	14	38	49	19
14	Leith	26	5	8	13	26	47	18

*Ayr United and Dumbarton were elected to the First Division. Nevertheless, no clubs were demoted from the First Division.

FA CUP 1912-13

SECOND ROUND
Aston Villa v West Ham United	5-0
Crystal Palace v Bury	2-0
Bradford Park Avenue v Wolverhampton Wanderers	3-0
Chelsea v The Wednesday	1-1, 0-6
Oldham Athletic v Nottingham Forest	5-1
Plymouth Argyle v Manchester United	0-2
Brighton v Everton	0-0, 0-1
Bristol Rovers v Norwich City	1-1, 2-2, 1-0
Sunderland v Manchester City	2-0
Huddersfield Town v Swindon Town	1-2
Hull City v Newcastle United	0-0, 0-3
Woolwich Arsenal v Liverpool	1-4
Burnley v Gainsborough Trinity	4-1
Middlesbrough v Queen's Park Rangers	3-2
Barnsley v Blackburn Rovers	2-3
Reading v Tottenham Hotspur	1-0

THIRD ROUND
Aston Villa v Crystal Palace	5-0
Bradford Park Avenue v The Wednesday	2-1
Oldham Athletic v Manchester United	0-0, 2-1
Bristol Rovers v Everton	0-4
Sunderland v Swindon Town	4-2
Liverpool v Newcastle United	1-1, 0-1
Burnley v Middlesbrough	3-1
Reading v Blackburn Rovers	1-2

FOURTH ROUND
Bradford Park Avenue v Aston Villa	0-5
Everton v Oldham Athletic	0-1
Sunderland v Newcastle United	0-0, 2-2, 3-0
Blackburn Rovers v Burnley	0-1

SEMI-FINAL
Aston Villa v Oldham Athletic	1-0
Sunderland v Burnley	0-0, 3-2

FINAL AT CRYSTAL PALACE
Aston Villa v Sunderland	1-0

SCOTTISH FA CUP 1912-13

SECOND ROUND
Ayr United v Airdrieonians	0-2
Celtic v Arbroath	4-0
East Stirlingshire v Clyde	1-1, 0-0, 0-1
Dumbarton v Aberdeen	2-1
Dundee v Thornhill	5-0
Morton v Falkirk	2-2, 1-3
Hamilton Academicals v Rangers	1-1, 0-2
Heart of Midlothian v Dunfermline Athletic	3-1
Hibernian v Motherwell	0-0, 1-1, 2-1
Kilmarnock v Abercorn	5-1
Partick Thistle v Inverness Caledonian	4-1
Aberdeen University v Peebles Rovers	0-3
Queen's Park v Dundee Hibernians	4-2
Raith Rovers v Broxburn United	5-0
St Johnstone v East Fife	3-0
St Mirren v Third Lanark	0-0, 2-0

THIRD ROUND
Celtic v Peebles Rovers	3-0
Clyde v Queen's Park	1-0
Dumbarton v St Johnstone	1-0
Partick Thistle v Dundee	0-1
Rangers v Falkirk	1-3
Kilmarnock v Heart of Midlothian	0-2
Raith Rovers v Hibernian	2-2, 1-0
St Mirren v Airdrieonians	1-0

FOURTH ROUND
Clyde v Dundee	1-1, 0-0, 2-1
Falkirk v Dumbarton	1-0
Celtic v Heart of Midlothian	0-1
Raith Rovers v St Mirren	2-1

SEMI-FINAL
Falkirk v Heart of Midlothian	1-0
Raith Rovers v Clyde	1-1, 1-0

FINAL AT CELTIC PARK
Falkirk v Raith Rovers	2-0

Above Aston Villa's one goal victory over Oldham in the semi-final of the FA Cup meant that for the only time in the history of the competition the Finalists — Villa and Sunderland — were also the clubs that finished first and second in the League. Here, a Villa attack against Oldham comes to nothing but Villa did win the Cup, 1-0.

RADIO TIMES HULTON PICTURE LIBRARY

League Tables 1913-14

FIRST DIVISION

		P	W	D	L	F	A	Pts
1	Blackburn	38	20	11	7	78	42	51
2	Aston Villa	38	19	6	13	65	50	44
3	Oldham	38	17	9	12	55	45	43
4	Middlesbrough	38	19	5	14	77	60	43
5	WBA	38	15	13	10	46	42	43
6	Bolton	38	16	10	12	65	52	42
7	Sunderland	38	17	6	15	63	52	40
8	Chelsea	38	16	7	15	46	55	39
9	Bradford City	38	12	14	12	40	40	38
10	Sheff United	38	16	5	17	63	60	37
11	Newcastle	38	13	11	14	39	48	37
12	Burnley	38	12	12	14	61	53	36
13	Man City	38	14	8	16	51	53	36
14	Man United	38	15	6	17	52	62	36
15	Everton	38	12	11	15	46	55	35
16	Liverpool	38	14	7	17	46	62	35
17	Tottenham	38	12	10	16	50	62	34
18	Wednesday	38	13	8	17	53	70	34
19	Preston	38	12	6	20	52	69	30
20	Derby	38	8	11	19	55	71	27

SECOND DIVISION

		P	W	D	L	F	A	Pts
1	Notts County	38	23	7	8	77	36	53
2	Bradford PA	38	23	3	12	71	47	49
3	Arsenal	38	20	9	9	54	38	49
4	Leeds City	38	20	7	11	76	46	47
5	Barnsley	38	19	7	12	51	45	45
6	Clapton Orient	38	16	11	11	47	35	43
7	Hull	38	16	9	13	53	37	41
8	Bristol City	38	16	9	13	52	50	41
9	Wolves	38	18	5	15	51	52	41
10	Bury	38	15	10	13	39	40	40
11	Fulham	38	16	6	16	46	43	38
12	Stockport	38	13	10	15	55	57	36
13	Huddersfield	38	13	8	17	47	53	34
14	Birmingham	38	12	10	16	48	60	34
15	Grimsby	38	13	8	17	42	58	34
16	Blackpool	38	9	14	15	33	44	32
17	Glossop NE	38	11	6	21	51	67	28
18	Leicester Fosse	38	11	4	23	45	61	26
19	Lincoln	38	10	6	22	36	66	26
20	Nottm Forest	38	7	9	22	37	76	23

SCOTTISH FIRST DIVISION

		P	W	D	L	F	A	Pts
1	Celtic	38	30	5	3	81	14	65
2	Rangers	38	27	5	6	79	31	59
3	Hearts	38	23	8	7	70	39	54
4	Morton	38	26	2	10	76	51	54
5	Falkirk	38	20	9	9	69	51	49
6	Airdrieonians	38	18	12	8	71	43	48
7	Dundee	38	19	5	14	65	53	43
8	Third Lanark	38	13	10	15	42	51	36
9	Clyde	38	11	11	16	44	44	33
10	Ayr	38	13	7	18	56	72	33
11	Raith	38	13	6	19	56	57	32
12	Kilmarnock	38	11	9	18	48	68	31
13	Aberdeen	38	10	10	18	47	55	30
14	Hibernian	38	12	6	20	58	75	30
15	Partick	38	10	9	19	37	51	29
16	Queen's Park	38	10	9	19	52	84	29
17	Motherwell	38	11	6	21	49	65	28
18	Hamilton	38	11	6	21	46	65	28
19	Dumbarton	38	10	7	21	45	87	27
20	St Mirren	38	8	6	24	38	73	22

SCOTTISH SECOND DIVISION

		P	W	D	L	F	A	Pts
1	Cowdenbeath	22	13	5	4	34	17	31
2	Albion	22	10	7	5	38	33	27
3	Dunfermline	22	11	4	7	46	28	26
4	Dundee Hibs	22	11	4	7	36	31	26
5	St Johnstone	22	9	5	8	48	38	23
6	Abercorn	22	10	3	9	32	32	23
7	St Bernard's	22	8	6	8	39	31	22
8	E Stirlingshire	22	7	8	7	40	36	22
9	Arthurlie	22	8	4	10	35	37	20
10	Leith	22	5	9	8	31	37	19
11	Vale of Leven	22	5	3	14	23	47	13
12	Johnstone	22	4	4	14	20	55	12

FA CUP 1913-14

SECOND ROUND

Sheffield United v Bradford Park Avenue	3-1
Millwall Athletic v Bradford City	1-0
Manchester City v Tottenham Hotspur	2-1
Blackburn Rovers v Bury	2-0
Burnley v Derby County	3-2
Bolton Wanderers v Swindon Town	4-2
Sunderland v Plymouth Argyle	2-1
Glossop North End v Preston North End	0-1
Exeter City v Aston Villa	1-2
Leeds City v West Bromwich Albion	0-2
Wolverhampton Wanderers v The Wednesday	1-1, 0-1
Brighton v Clapton Orient	3-1
Liverpool v Gillingham	2-0
West Ham United v Crystal Palace	2-0
Swansea Town v Queen's Park Rangers	1-2
Birmingham v Huddersfield Town	1-0

THIRD ROUND

Millwall Athletic v Sheffield United	0-4
Blackburn Rovers v Manchester City	1-2
Burnley v Bolton Wanderers	3-0
Sunderland v Preston North End	2-0
Aston Villa v West Bromwich Albion	2-1
The Wednesday v Brighton	3-0
West Ham United v Liverpool	1-1, 1-5
Birmingham v Queen's Park Rangers	1-2

FOURTH ROUND

Manchester City v Sheffield United	0-0, 0-0, 0-1
Sunderland v Burnley	0-0, 1-2
The Wednesday v Aston Villa	0-1
Liverpool v Queen's Park Rangers	2-1

SEMI-FINAL

Sheffield United v Burnley	0-0, 0-1
Aston Villa v Liverpool	0-2

FINAL AT CRYSTAL PALACE

Burnley v Liverpool	1-0

Below *September 1913 and Woolwich Arsenal play Hull at Highbury. It had been a rush removal to what were then the grounds of a theological college, and in Arsenal's first match there, earlier in the month, the players washed in bowls of water, while an injured player was taken away on a milk-cart.*

SCOTTISH FA CUP 1913-14

SECOND ROUND

Aberdeen v Albion Rovers	4-1
Airdrieonians v Dundee Hibernian	5-0
Broxburn United v Dumfries	5-1
Celtic v Clyde	0-0, 2-0
Morton v Hibernian	1-1, 1-2
East Stirlingshire v Forfar Athletic	1-1, 0-2
Kilmarnock v Hamilton Academicals	3-1
Leith Athletic v Motherwell	1-1, 2-5
Partick Thistle v Nithsdale Wanderers	1-0
Forres Mechanics v Peebles Rovers	0-4
Queen's Park v Arthurlie	1-0
Raith Rovers v Heart of Midlothian	2-0
Rangers v Alloa Athletic	5-0
St Mirren v Dundee	2-1
Kirkcaldy United v Stevenston United	0-4
Third Lanark v Dumbarton	2-0

THIRD ROUND

Forfar Athletic v Celtic	0-5
Hibernian v Rangers	2-1
Broxburn United v Motherwell	0-2
Kilmarnock v Partick Thistle	1-4
Airdrieonians v Queen's Park	1-1, 1-2
Aberdeen v St Mirren	1-2
Stevenston United v Peebles Rovers	3-2
Third Lanark v Raith Rovers	4-1

FOURTH ROUND

Motherwell v Celtic	1-3
Queen's Park v Hibernian	1-3
St Mirren v Partick Thistle	1-0
Third Lanark v Stevenston United	1-1, 0-0, 1-0

SEMI-FINAL

Celtic v Third Lanark	2-0
Hibernian v St Mirren	3-1

FINAL AT IBROX PARK

Celtic v Hibernian	0-0, 4-1

RADIO TIMES HULTON PICTURE LIBRARY

The War Years

FIRST DIVISION 1914-15

		P	W	D	L	F	A	Pts
1	Everton	38	19	8	11	76	47	46
2	Oldham	38	17	11	10	70	56	45
3	Blackburn	38	18	7	13	83	61	43
4	Burnley	38	18	7	13	61	47	43
5	Man City	38	15	13	10	49	39	43
6	Sheff United	38	15	13	10	49	41	43
7	Wednesday	38	15	13	10	61	54	43
8	Sunderland	38	18	5	15	81	72	41
9	Bradford PA	38	17	7	14	69	65	41
10	Bradford City	38	13	14	11	55	49	40
11	WBA	38	15	10	13	49	43	40
12	Middlesbrough	38	13	12	13	62	74	38
13	Aston Villa	38	13	11	14	62	72	37
14	Liverpool*	38	14	9	15	65	75	37
15	Newcastle	38	11	10	17	46	48	32
16	Notts County	38	9	13	16	41	57	31
17	Bolton	38	11	8	19	68	84	30
18	Man United*	38	9	12	17	46	62	30
19	Chelsea	38	8	13	17	51	65	29
20	Tottenham	38	8	12	18	57	90	28

*A commission concluded that the Manchester United–Liverpool game on 2 April 1915 had been 'fixed' but the result (2-0) was allowed to stand. No points were deducted.

SCOTTISH DIVISION 'A' 1914-15

		P	W	D	L	F	A	Pts
1	Celtic	38	30	5	3	91	25	65
2	Hearts	38	27	7	4	83	32	61
3	Rangers	38	23	4	11	74	47	50
4	Morton	38	18	12	8	74	48	48
5	Ayr	38	20	8	10	55	40	48
6	Falkirk	38	16	7	15	48	48	39
7	Hamilton	38	16	6	16	60	55	38
8	Partick	38	15	8	15	56	58	38
9	St Mirren	38	14	8	16	56	65	36
10	Airdrieonians	38	14	7	17	54	60	35
11	Hibernian	38	12	11	15	59	66	35
12	Dumbarton	38	13	8	17	51	66	34
13	Kilmarnock	38	15	4	19	55	59	34
14	Aberdeen	38	11	11	16	39	52	33
15	Dundee	38	12	9	17	43	61	33
16	Third Lanark	38	10	12	16	51	57	32
17	Clyde	38	12	6	20	44	59	30
18	Motherwell	38	10	10	18	49	66	30
19	Raith	38	9	10	19	53	68	28
20	Queen's Park	38	4	5	29	27	90	13

SECOND DIVISION 1914-15

		P	W	D	L	F	A	Pts
1	Derby	38	23	7	8	71	33	53
2	Preston	38	20	10	8	61	42	50
3	Barnsley	38	22	3	13	51	51	47
4	Wolves	38	19	7	12	77	52	45
5	Birmingham	38	17	9	12	62	39	43
6	Arsenal	38	19	5	14	69	41	43
7	Hull	38	19	5	14	65	54	43
8	Huddersfield	38	17	8	13	61	42	42
9	Clapton Orient	38	16	9	13	50	48	41
10	Blackpool	38	17	5	16	58	57	39
11	Bury	38	15	8	15	61	56	38
12	Fulham	38	15	7	16	53	47	37
13	Bristol City	38	15	7	16	62	56	37
14	Stockport	38	15	7	16	54	60	37
15	Leeds City	38	14	4	20	65	64	32
16	Lincoln	38	11	9	18	46	65	31
17	Grimsby	38	11	9	18	48	76	31
18	Nottm Forest	38	10	9	19	43	77	29
19	Leicester Fosse	38	10	4	24	47	88	24
20	Glossop NE	38	6	6	26	31	87	18

SCOTTISH DIVISION 'B' 1914-15

		P	W	D	L	F	A	Pts
1	Cowdenbeath	26	16	5	5	49	17	37
2	St Bernard's	26	18	1	7	66	34	37
3	Leith	26	15	7	4	54	31	37
4	E Stirlingshire	26	13	5	8	51	37	31
5	Clydebank	26	13	4	9	67	37	30
6	Dunfermline	26	13	2	11	49	39	28
7	Johnstone	26	11	5	10	41	51	27
8	St Johnstone*	25	10	6	9	54	50	26
9	Albion	26	9	7	10	37	42	25
10	Lochgelly	26	9	3	14	37	59	21
11	Dundee Hibs	26	8	3	15	48	61	19
12	Abercorn	26	5	7	14	34	65	17
13	Arthurlie*	25	5	4	16	33	64	14
14	Vale of Leven	26	4	5	17	33	66	13

*There is no record of St Johnstone and Arthurlie playing each other more than once.

WINNERS 1914-15

Southern League Watford
Central League Huddersfield Town
Irish Cup Linfield
Irish League Belfast Celtic
Welsh Cup Wrexham

FA CUP 1914-15

FIRST ROUND
Blackpool v Sheffield United	1-2
Liverpool v Stockport County	3-0
Bradford Park Avenue v Portsmouth	1-0
Bury v Plymouth Argyle	1-1, 2-1
Croydon Common v Oldham Athletic	0-3
Rochdale v Gillingham	2-0
Birmingham v Crystal Palace	2-2, 3-0
Brighton v Lincoln City	2-1
Bolton Wanderers v Notts County	2-1
Millwall Athletic v Clapton Orient	2-1
Burnley v Huddersfield Town	3-1
Bristol Rovers v Southend United	0-0, 0-3
Hull City v West Bromwich Albion	1-0
Grimsby Town v Northampton Town	0-3
Southampton v Luton Town	3-0
South Shields v Fulham	1-2
Chelsea v Swindon	1-1, 5-2
Arsenal v Merthyr Town	3-0
Preston North End v Manchester City	0-0, 0-3
Aston Villa v Exeter City	2-0
West Ham United v Newcastle United	2-2, 2-3
Swansea Town v Blackburn Rovers	1-0
The Wednesday v Manchester United	1-0
Reading v Wolverhampton Wanderers	0-1
Everton v Barnsley	3-0
Bristol City v Cardiff City	2-0
Queen's Park Rangers v Glossop North End	2-1
Derby County v Leeds City	1-2
Darlington v Bradford City	0-1
Middlesbrough v Goole Town	9-3
Nottingham Forest v Norwich City	1-4
Tottenham Hotspur v Sunderland	2-1

SECOND ROUND
Sheffield United v Liverpool	1-0
Bury v Bradford Park Avenue	0-1
Oldham Athletic v Rochdale	3-0
Brighton v Birmingham	0-0*, 0-3
Bolton Wanderers v Millwall Athletic	0-0*, 2-2*, 4-1
Burnley v Southend United	6-0
Hull City v Northampton Town	2-1
Fulham v Southampton	2-3*
Chelsea v Arsenal	1-0
Manchester City v Aston Villa	1-0
Newcastle United v Swansea Town	1-1*, 2-0
The Wednesday v Wolverhampton Wanderers	2-0
Everton v Bristol City	4-0
Queen's Park Rangers v Leeds City	1-0
Bradford City v Middlesbrough	1-0
Norwich City v Tottenham Hotspur	3-2

THIRD ROUND
Sheffield United v Bradford Park Avenue	1-0*
Birmingham v Oldham Athletic	2-3
Bolton Wanderers v Burnley	2-1*
Southampton v Hull City	2-2*, 0-4
Manchester City v Chelsea	0-1
The Wednesday v Newcastle United	1-2
Queen's Park Rangers v Everton	1-2
Bradford City v Norwich City	1-1*, 0-0*, 2-0

FOURTH ROUND
Oldham Athletic v Sheffield United	0-0*, 0-3
Bolton Wanderers v Hull City	4-2
Chelsea v Newcastle United	1-1*, 1-0
Bradford City v Everton	0-2

SEMI-FINAL
Sheffield United v Bolton Wanderers	2-1
Chelsea v Everton	2-0

FINAL AT OLD TRAFFORD
Sheffield United v Chelsea	3-0

*Extra time played

Left A heatwave in London during August 1914 prompts this St John's Ambulance man to supply the crowd with drinking water.

There was such a rush of games at the end of season 1915-16 that Celtic played two League games on 15 April. They beat Raith Rovers 6-0 and, in the evening, Motherwell 3-1.

WINNERS 1915-16

Lancashire Regional Tournament Manchester City
Lancashire Tournament Northern Division Burnley
Lancashire Tournament Southern Division Manchester City
Midland Regional Tournament Nottingham Forest
Midland Tournament Southern Division Nottingham Forest
Midland Tournament Northern Division Leeds City
Midland Tournament Midland Division Grimsby Town
London Combination Chelsea
London Supplementary Tournament 'A' Chelsea
London Supplementary Tournament 'B' West Ham United
South Western Combination Portsmouth
Irish Cup Linfield

WINNERS 1916-17

Lancashire Regional Tournament Liverpool
Lancashire Subsidiary Tournament Rochdale
Midland Regional Tournament Leeds City
Midland Subsidiary Tournament Bradford PA
London Combination West Ham United
Irish Cup Glentoran
Belfast and District League Glentoran

WINNERS 1917-18

Lancashire Regional Tournament Stoke
Lancashire Subsidiary Tournament Liverpool
Midland Regional Tournament Leeds City
Midland Subsidiary Tournament Grimsby Town
League Championship Play-off Leeds City
London Combination Chelsea
Irish Cup Belfast Celtic
Belfast and District League Linfield

WINNERS 1918-19

Lancashire Regional Tournament Everton
Lancashire Subsidiary Tournament 'A' Blackpool
Lancashire Subsidiary Tournament 'B' Oldham Athletic
Lancashire Subsidiary Tournament 'C' Manchester City
Lancashire Subsidiary Tournament 'D' Liverpool
Midland Regional Tournament Nottingham Forest
Midland Subsidiary Tournament 'A' Sheffield United
Midland Subsidiary Tournament 'B' Birmingham
Midland Subsidiary Tournament 'C' Bradford PA
Midland Subsidiary Tournament 'D' Hull City
League Championship Play-off Nottingham Forest
London Combination Brentford
Irish Cup Linfield

Right *George Utley leads Sheffield United out for their semi-final FA Cup tie with Bolton Wanderers in 1915. United won 2-1, going on to the only Final this century initially played outside London. That Final, in which they beat Chelsea 3-0, was played at Old Trafford, and has always been known as the 'Khaki Final' because of the large number of soldiers in the crowd.*

The only first-class game in English football played without spectators was the 1915 Bradford City-Norwich second Cup replay. Questions had been raised in the Commons about British-made shells failing to explode in France. The Government decided that the people making the shells were being distracted, and banned football matches during working hours in the vicinity of munitions factories. The game, at Lincoln, was played behind locked doors.

SCOTTISH LEAGUE 1915-16

		P	W	D	L	F	A	Pts
1	Celtic	38	32	3	3	116	23	67
2	Rangers	38	25	6	7	87	39	56
3	Morton*	37	22	7	8	86	35	51
4	Ayr	38	20	8	10	72	45	48
5	Partick	38	19	8	11	65	41	46
6	Hearts*	37	20	6	11	66	45	46
7	Hamilton	38	19	3	16	68	76	41
8	Dundee	38	18	4	16	56	49	40
9	Dumbarton	38	13	11	14	53	64	37
10	Kilmarnock	38	12	11	15	46	49	35
11	Aberdeen	38	11	12	15	51	64	34
12	Falkirk	38	12	9	17	45	61	33
13	Motherwell	38	11	8	19	55	81	30
14	Airdrieonians	38	11	8	19	44	74	30
15	Clyde	38	11	7	20	49	71	29
16	Third Lanark	38	9	11	18	40	56	28
17	St Mirren	38	12	4	22	50	67	28
18	Queen's Park	38	11	6	21	53	100	28
19	Hibernian	38	9	7	22	44	71	25
20	Raith	38	9	5	24	30	65	23

*Morton and Hearts only played each other once.

SCOTTISH LEAGUE 1916-17

		P	W	D	L	F	A	Pts
1	Celtic	38	27	10	1	79	17	64
2	Morton	38	24	6	8	72	89	54
3	Rangers	38	24	5	9	68	32	53
4	Airdrieonians	38	21	8	9	71	38	50
5	Third Lanark	38	19	11	8	53	37	49
6	Kilmarnock	38	18	7	13	69	45	43
7	St Mirren	38	15	10	13	49	43	40
8	Motherwell	38	16	6	16	57	59	38
9	Partick	38	14	7	17	44	43	35
10	Dumbarton	38	12	11	15	56	73	35
11	Hamilton	38	13	9	16	54	73	35
12	Falkirk	38	12	10	16	57	57	34
13	Clyde	38	10	14	14	41	53	34
14	Hearts	38	14	4	20	44	59	32
15	Ayr	38	12	7	19	47	59	31
16	Dundee	38	13	4	21	58	71	30
17	Hibernian	38	10	10	18	57	72	30
18	Queen's Park	38	11	7	20	56	81	29
19	Raith	38	8	7	23	42	91	23
20	Aberdeen	38	7	7	24	36	63	21

SCOTTISH LEAGUE 1917-18

		P	W	D	L	F	A	Pts
1	Rangers	34	25	6	3	66	24	56
2	Celtic	34	24	7	3	66	26	55
3	Kilmarnock	34	19	5	10	69	41	43
4	Morton	34	17	9	8	53	42	43
5	Motherwell	34	16	9	9	70	51	41
6	Partick	34	14	12	8	51	37	40
7	Queen's Park	34	14	6	14	64	63	34
8	Dumbarton	34	13	8	13	48	49	34
9	Clydebank	34	14	5	15	55	56	33
10	Hearts	34	14	4	16	41	58	32
11	St Mirren	34	11	7	16	42	50	29
12	Hamilton	34	11	6	17	52	63	28
13	Third Lanark	34	10	7	17	56	62	27
14	Falkirk	34	9	9	16	36	68	27
15	Airdrieonians	34	10	6	18	46	58	26
16	Hibernian	34	8	9	17	42	57	25
17	Clyde	34	9	2	23	37	72	20
18	Ayr	34	5	9	20	32	61	19

SCOTTISH LEAGUE 1918-19

		P	W	D	L	F	A	Pts
1	Celtic	34	26	6	2	71	22	58
2	Rangers	34	26	5	3	86	16	57
3	Morton	34	18	11	5	76	40	47
4	Partick	34	17	7	10	62	43	41
5	Motherwell	34	14	10	10	51	40	38
6	Ayr	34	15	8	11	62	53	38
7	Hearts	34	14	9	11	59	52	37
8	Queen's Park	34	15	5	14	59	57	35
9	Kilmarnock	34	14	7	13	61	59	35
10	Clydebank	34	12	8	14	54	65	32
11	St Mirren	34	10	12	12	43	55	32
12	Third Lanark	34	11	9	14	60	62	31
13	Airdrieonians	34	9	11	14	45	54	29
14	Hamilton	34	11	5	18	49	75	27
15	Dumbarton	34	7	8	19	31	58	22
16	Falkirk	34	6	8	20	46	73	20
17	Clyde	34	7	6	21	45	75	20
18	Hibernian	34	5	3	26	30	91	13

League Tables 1919-20

FIRST DIVISION

		P	W	D	L	F	A	Pts
1	WBA	42	28	4	10	104	47	60
2	Burnley	42	21	9	12	65	59	51
3	Chelsea	42	22	5	15	56	51	49
4	Liverpool	42	19	10	13	59	44	48
5	Sunderland	42	22	4	16	72	59	48
6	Bolton	42	19	9	14	72	65	47
7	Man City	42	18	9	15	71	62	45
8	Newcastle	42	17	9	16	44	39	43
9	Aston Villa	42	18	6	18	75	73	42
10	Arsenal	42	15	12	15	56	58	42
11	Bradford PA	42	15	12	15	60	63	42
12	Man United	42	13	14	15	54	50	40
13	Middlesbrough	42	15	10	17	61	65	40
14	Sheff United	42	16	8	18	59	69	40
15	Bradford City	42	14	11	17	54	63	39
16	Everton	42	12	14	16	69	68	38
17	Oldham	42	15	8	19	49	52	38
18	Derby	42	13	12	17	47	57	38
19	Preston	42	14	10	18	57	73	38
20	Blackburn	42	13	11	18	64	77	37
21	Notts County	42	12	12	18	56	74	36
22	Wednesday	42	7	9	26	28	64	23

SECOND DIVISION

		P	W	D	L	F	A	Pts
1	Tottenham	42	32	6	4	102	32	70
2	Huddersfield	42	28	8	6	97	38	64
3	Birmingham	42	24	8	10	85	34	56
4	Blackpool	42	21	10	11	65	47	52
5	Bury	42	20	8	14	60	44	48
6	Fulham	42	19	9	14	61	50	47
7	West Ham	42	19	9	14	47	40	47
8	Bristol City	42	13	17	12	46	43	43
9	South Shields	42	15	12	15	58	48	42
10	Stoke	42	18	6	18	60	54	42
11	Hull	42	18	6	18	78	72	42
12	Barnsley	42	15	10	17	61	55	40
13	Port Vale*	42	16	8	18	59	62	40
14	Leicester	42	15	10	17	41	61	40
15	Clapton Orient	42	16	6	20	51	59	38
16	Stockport	42	14	9	19	52	61	37
17	Rotherham Co	42	13	8	21	51	83	34
18	Nottm Forest	42	11	9	22	43	73	31
19	Wolves	42	10	10	22	55	80	30
20	Coventry	42	9	11	22	35	73	29
21	Lincoln	42	9	9	24	44	101	27
22	Grimsby	42	10	5	27	34	75	25

*Leeds City were expelled from the League
on 4 October 1919, when their record
was P8 W4 D2 L2 F17 A10 Pts10.
Port Vale took over their remaining fixtures

SCOTTISH LEAGUE

		P	W	D	L	F	A	Pts
1	Rangers	42	31	9	2	106	25	71
2	Celtic	42	29	10	3	89	31	68
3	Motherwell	42	23	11	8	73	53	57
4	Dundee	42	22	6	14	79	65	50
5	Clydebank	42	20	8	14	60	54	48
6	Morton	42	16	13	13	71	48	45
7	Airdrieonians	42	17	10	15	57	43	44
8	Third Lanark	42	16	11	15	57	62	43
9	Kilmarnock	42	20	3	19	59	74	43
10	Ayr	42	15	10	17	72	69	40
11	Dumbarton	42	13	13	16	57	65	39
12	Queen's Park	42	14	10	18	67	73	38
13	Partick	42	13	12	17	51	62	38
14	St Mirren	42	15	8	19	63	81	38
15	Hearts	42	14	9	19	57	72	37
16	Clyde	42	14	9	19	64	71	37
17	Aberdeen	42	11	13	18	46	64	35
18	Hibernian	42	13	7	22	60	79	33
19	Raith	42	11	10	21	61	82	32
20	Falkirk	42	10	11	21	45	74	31
21	Hamilton	42	11	7	24	56	86	29
22	Albion	42	10	7	25	42	77	27

SCOTTISH FA CUP 1919-20

FIRST ROUND
Cowdenbeath v Aberdeen	0-1
Albion Rovers v Dykehead	0-0, 2-1
Dunfermline Harp v Alloa Athletic	0-0, 0-1
Armadale v Clyde	1-0
Dundee v Airdrieonians	1-0
East Fife v Arthurlie	4-0
East Stirlingshire v Thornhill	6-0
St Bernard's v Bathgate	2-0
Heart of Midlothian v Nithsdale Wanderers	5-1
Galston v Hibernian	0-0, 1-2
Lochgelly United v Clachnacuddin	2-0
Morton v Forfar Athletic	4-0
Partick Thistle v Motherwell	3-1
Queen's Park v Hamilton Academicals	2-0
Rangers v Dumbarton	0-0, 1-0
Royal Albert v Forres Mechanics	7-0
Stevenston United v St Mirren	1-2
Third Lanark v Inverness Caledonian	4-1

SECOND ROUND
Aberdeen v Gala Fairydean	2-0
Albion Rovers v Huntingtower (scratched)	w o
Armadale v Hibernian	1-0
Ayr United v St Mirren	2-1
Broxburn United v Queen of the South Wanderers	1-0
Dundee v Celtic	1-3
St Bernard's v Bathgate	2-0
Heart of Midlothian v Falkirk	2-0
Alloa Athletic v Kilmarnock	0-2
Lochgelly United v Royal Albert	2-1
St Johnstone v Morton	1-1, 3-5
Partick Thistle v East Fife	5-0
Queen's Park v Vale of Leithen	3-0
Raith Rovers v East Stirlingshire	0-0, 1-1, 0-0, 4-0
Rangers v Arbroath	5-0
Third Lanark v Vale of Leven	2-1

THIRD ROUND
Aberdeen v Heart of Midlothian	1-0
St Bernard's v Albion Rovers	1-1, 1-4
Ayr United v Armadale	1-1, 0-1
Celtic v Partick Thistle	2-0
Kilmarnock v Queen's Park	4-1
Raith Rovers v Morton	2-2, 0-3
Rangers v Broxburn United	3-0
Lochgelly United v Third Lanark	0-3

FOURTH ROUND
Albion Rovers v Aberdeen	2-1
Morton v Third Lanark	3-0
Armadale v Kilmarnock	1-2
Rangers v Celtic	1-0

SEMI-FINAL
Kilmarnock v Morton	3-2
Albion Rovers v Rangers	0-0, 1-1, 2-0

FINAL AT HAMPDEN PARK
Kilmarnock v Albion Rovers	3-2

FA CUP 1919-20

FIRST ROUND
Aston Villa v Queen's Park Rangers	2-1
Port Vale v Manchester United	1-2
Sunderland v Hull City	6-2
Thorneycroft's Wanderers v Burnley	0-0, 0-5
Bristol Rovers v Tottenham Hotspur	1-4
West Stanley v Gillingham	3-1
Southampton v West Ham United	0-0, 1-3
Bury v Stoke	2-0
Bolton Wanderers v Chelsea	0-1
Fulham v Swindon Town	1-2
Newport County v Leicester City	0-0, 0-2
Manchester City v Clapton Orient	4-1
Bradford Park Avenue v Nottingham Forest	3-0
Castleford Town v Hednesford Town	2-0
Notts County v Millwall Athletic	2-0
Middlesbrough v Lincoln City	4-1
Grimsby Town v Bristol City	1-2
Arsenal v Rochdale	4-2
Cardiff City v Oldham Athletic	2-0
Blackburn Rovers v Wolverhampton Wanderers	2-2, 0-1
Bradford City v Portsmouth	2-2*, 2-0
Sheffield United v Southend United	3-0
Preston North End v Stockport County	3-1
Blackpool v Derby County	0-0, 4-1
Huddersfield Town v Brentford	5-1
Newcastle United v Crystal Palace	2-0
Plymouth Argyle v Reading	2-0
West Bromwich Albion v Barnsley	0-1
South Shields v Liverpool	1-1, 0-2
Luton Town v Coventry City	2-2, 1-0
Birmingham v Everton	2-0
Darlington v The Wednesday	0-0, 2-0

*abandoned

SECOND ROUND
Manchester United v Aston Villa	1-2
Burnley v Sunderland	1-1, 0-2
Tottenham Hotspur v West Stanley	4-0
West Ham United v Bury	6-0
Chelsea v Swindon Town	4-0
Leicester City v Manchester City	3-0
Bradford Park Avenue v Castleford Town	3-2
Notts County v Middlesbrough	1-0
Bristol City v Arsenal	1-0
Wolverhampton Wanderers v Cardiff City	1-2
Bradford City v Sheffield United	2-1
Preston North End v Blackpool	2-1
Newcastle United v Huddersfield Town	0-1
Plymouth Argyle v Barnsley	4-1
Luton Town v Liverpool	0-2
Birmingham v Darlington	4-0

THIRD ROUND
Aston Villa v Sunderland	1-0
Tottenham Hotspur v West Ham United	3-0
Chelsea v Leicester City	3-0
Notts County v Bradford Park Avenue	3-4
Bristol City v Cardiff City	2-1
Preston North End v Bradford City	0-3
Huddersfield Town v Plymouth Argyle	3-1
Liverpool v Birmingham	2-0

FOURTH ROUND
Tottenham Hotspur v Aston Villa	0-1
Chelsea v Bradford Park Avenue	4-1
Bristol City v Bradford City	2-0
Huddersfield Town v Liverpool	2-1

SEMI-FINAL
Aston Villa v Chelsea	3-1
Huddersfield Town v Bristol City	2-1

FINAL AT STAMFORD BRIDGE
Aston Villa v Huddersfield Town	1-0

Far left *Billy Walker, the Aston Villa forward whose two goals in Villa's 3-1 win over Chelsea in the FA Cup semi-final saved the Football Association an embarrassing situation. If Chelsea had won they would have played the Final on their own ground, Stamford Bridge. This was against the rules of the competition but arrangements were too far advanced to be changed.*

League Tables 1920-21

FIRST DIVISION

		P	W	D	L	F	A	Pts
1	Burnley	42	23	13	6	79	36	59
2	Man City	42	24	6	12	70	50	54
3	Bolton	42	19	14	9	77	53	52
4	Liverpool	42	18	15	9	63	35	51
5	Newcastle	42	20	10	12	66	45	50
6	Tottenham	42	19	9	14	70	48	47
7	Everton	42	17	13	12	66	55	47
8	Middlesbrough	42	17	12	13	53	53	46
9	Arsenal	42	15	14	13	59	63	44
10	Aston Villa	42	18	7	17	63	70	43
11	Blackburn	42	13	15	14	57	59	41
12	Sunderland	42	14	13	15	57	60	41
13	Man United	42	15	10	17	64	68	40
14	WBA	42	13	14	15	54	58	40
15	Bradford City	42	12	15	15	61	63	39
16	Preston	42	15	9	18	61	65	39
17	Huddersfield	42	15	9	18	42	49	39
18	Chelsea	42	13	13	16	48	58	39
19	Oldham	42	9	15	18	49	86	33
20	Sheff United	42	6	18	18	42	68	30
21	Derby	42	5	16	21	32	58	26
22	Bradford PA	42	8	8	26	43	76	24

SECOND DIVISION

		P	W	D	L	F	A	Pts
1	Birmingham	42	24	10	8	79	38	58
2	Cardiff	42	24	10	8	59	32	58
3	Bristol City	42	19	13	10	49	29	51
4	Blackpool	42	20	10	12	54	42	50
5	West Ham	42	19	10	13	51	30	48
6	Notts County	42	18	11	13	55	40	47
7	Clapton Orient	42	16	13	13	43	42	45
8	South Shields	42	17	10	15	61	46	44
9	Fulham	42	16	10	16	43	47	42
10	Wednesday	42	15	11	16	48	48	41
11	Bury	42	15	10	17	45	49	40
12	Leicester	42	12	16	14	39	46	40
13	Hull	42	10	20	12	43	53	40
14	Leeds	42	14	10	18	40	45	38
15	Wolves	42	16	6	20	49	66	38
16	Barnsley	42	10	16	16	48	50	36
17	Port Vale	42	11	14	17	43	49	36
18	Nottm Forest	42	12	12	18	48	55	36
19	Rotherham Co	42	12	12	18	37	53	36
20	Stoke	42	12	11	19	46	56	35
21	Coventry	42	12	11	19	39	70	35
22	Stockport	42	9	12	21	42	75	30

THIRD DIVISION

		P	W	D	L	F	A	Pts
1	Crystal Palace	42	24	11	7	70	34	59
2	Southampton	42	19	16	7	64	28	54
3	QPR	42	22	9	11	61	32	53
4	Swindon	42	21	10	11	73	49	52
5	Swansea	42	18	15	9	56	45	51
6	Watford	42	20	8	14	59	44	48
7	Millwall Ath	42	18	11	13	42	30	47
8	Merthyr Town	42	15	15	12	60	49	45
9	Luton	42	16	12	14	61	56	44
10	Bristol Rovers	42	18	7	17	68	57	43
11	Plymouth	42	11	21	10	35	34	43
12	Portsmouth	42	12	15	15	46	48	39
13	Grimsby	42	15	9	18	49	59	39
14	Northampton	42	15	8	19	59	75	38
15	Newport	42	14	9	19	43	64	37
16	Norwich	42	10	16	16	44	53	36
17	Southend	42	14	8	20	44	61	36
18	Brighton	42	14	8	20	42	61	36
19	Exeter	42	10	15	17	39	54	35
20	Reading	42	12	7	23	42	59	31
21	Brentford	42	9	12	21	42	67	30
22	Gillingham	42	8	12	22	34	74	28

SCOTTISH LEAGUE

		P	W	D	L	F	A	Pts
1	Rangers	42	35	6	1	91	24	76
2	Celtic	42	30	6	6	86	35	66
3	Hearts	42	20	10	12	74	49	50
4	Dundee	42	19	11	12	54	48	49
5	Motherwell	42	19	10	13	75	51	48
6	Partick	42	17	12	13	53	39	46
7	Clyde	42	21	3	18	63	62	45
8	Third Lanark	42	19	6	17	74	61	44
9	Morton	42	15	14	13	66	58	44
10	Airdrieonians	42	17	9	16	71	64	43
11	Aberdeen	42	14	14	14	53	54	42
12	Kilmarnock	42	17	8	17	62	68	42
13	Hibernian	42	16	9	17	58	57	41
14	Ayr	42	14	12	16	62	69	40
15	Hamilton	42	14	12	16	44	57	40
16	Raith	42	16	5	21	54	58	37
17	Albion	42	11	12	19	57	68	34
18	Falkirk	42	11	12	19	54	72	34
19	Queen's Park	42	11	11	20	45	80	33
20	Clydebank	42	7	14	21	47	72	28
21	Dumbarton	42	10	4	28	41	89	24
22	St Mirren	42	7	4	31	43	92	18

FA CUP 1920-21

SECOND ROUND
Southend United v Blackpool	1-0
Tottenham Hotspur v Bradford City	4-0
Notts County v Aston Villa	0-0, 0-1
Bradford Park Avenue v Huddersfield Town	0-1
Crystal Palace v Hull City	0-2
Burnley v Queen's Park Rangers	4-2
South Shields v Luton Town	0-4
Preston North End v Watford	4-1
Everton v The Wednesday	1-1, 1-0
Newcastle United v Liverpool	1-0
Lincoln City v Fulham	0-0, 0-1
Derby County v Wolverhampton Wanderers	1-1, 0-1
Grimsby Town v Southampton	1-3
Brighton v Cardiff City	0-0, 0-1
Swansea Town v Plymouth Argyle	1-2
Swindon Town v Chelsea	0-2

THIRD ROUND
Southend United v Tottenham Hotspur	1-4
Aston Villa v Huddersfield Town	2-0
Hull City v Burnley	3-0
Luton Town v Preston North End	2-3
Everton v Newcastle United	3-0
Fulham v Wolverhampton Wanderers	0-1
Southampton v Cardiff City	0-1
Plymouth Argyle v Chelsea	0-0, 0-0, 1-2

FOURTH ROUND
Tottenham Hotspur v Aston Villa	1-0
Hull City v Preston North End	0-0, 0-1
Everton v Wolverhampton Wanderers	0-1
Cardiff City v Chelsea	1-0

SEMI-FINAL
Tottenham Hotspur v Preston North End	2-1
Wolverhampton Wanderers v Cardiff City	0-0, 3-1

FINAL AT STAMFORD BRIDGE
Tottenham Hotspur v Wolverhampton Wanderers	1-0

SCOTTISH FA CUP 1920-21

SECOND ROUND
Kilmarnock v Aberdeen	1-2
Albion Rovers v Mid-Annandale	3-1
Clydebank v Alloa Athletic	0-0, 1-1, 0-1
Bo'ness v Armadale	0-0, 0-2
Ayr United v Dykehead	4-0
Vale of Leven v Celtic	0-3
Dumbarton v Elgin City	3-0
Dundee v Stenhousemuir	1-0
Stevenston United v East Fife	0-0, 1-2
East Stirlingshire v Solway Star	5-1
Broxburn United v Hamilton Academicals	1-2
Clyde v Heart of Midlothian	0-0, 1-1, 2-3
Motherwell v Renton	3-0
Queen of the South v Nithsdale Wanderers	1-3
Partick Thistle v Hibernian	0-0, 0-0, 1-0
Rangers v Morton	2-0

THIRD ROUND
Armadale v Albion Rovers	0-0, 0-0, 2-2, 0-2
East Fife v Celtic	1-3
Dumbarton v Nithsdale Wanderers	5-0
Aberdeen v Dundee	1-1, 0-0, 0-2
Hamilton Academicals v Heart of Midlothian	0-1
Motherwell v Ayr United	1-1, 1-1, 3-1
East Stirlingshire v Partick Thistle	1-2
Rangers v Alloa Athletic	0-0, 4-1

FOURTH ROUND
Dundee v Albion Rovers	0-2
Celtic v Heart of Midlothian	1-2
Partick Thistle v Motherwell	0-0, 2-2, 2-1
Dumbarton v Rangers	0-3

SEMI-FINAL
Partick v Heart of Midlothian	0-0, 0-0, 2-0
Rangers v Albion Rovers	4-1

FINAL AT CELTIC PARK
Partick Thistle v Rangers	1-0

Burnley's Championship side which went 30 games without defeat in 1920-21.

RADIO TIMES HULTON PICTURE LIBRARY

FIRST DIVISION

		P	W	D	L	F	A	Pts
1	Liverpool	42	22	13	7	63	36	57
2	Tottenham	42	21	9	12	65	39	51
3	Burnley	42	22	5	15	72	54	49
4	Cardiff	42	19	10	13	61	53	48
5	Aston Villa	42	22	3	17	74	55	47
6	Bolton	42	20	7	15	68	59	47
7	Newcastle	42	18	10	14	59	45	46
8	Middlesbrough	42	16	14	12	79	69	46
9	Chelsea	42	17	12	13	40	43	46
10	Man City	42	18	9	15	65	70	45
11	Sheff United	42	15	10	17	59	54	40
12	Sunderland	42	16	8	18	60	62	40
13	WBA	42	15	10	17	51	63	40
14	Huddersfield	42	15	9	18	53	54	39
15	Blackburn	42	13	12	17	54	57	38
16	Preston	42	13	12	17	42	65	38
17	Arsenal	42	15	7	20	47	56	37
18	Birmingham	42	15	7	20	48	60	37
19	Oldham	42	13	11	18	38	50	37
20	Everton	42	12	12	18	57	55	36
21	Bradford City	42	11	10	21	48	72	32
22	Man United	42	8	12	22	41	73	28

SECOND DIVISION

		P	W	D	L	F	A	Pts
1	Nottm Forest	42	22	12	8	51	30	56
2	Stoke	42	18	16	8	60	44	52
3	Barnsley	42	22	8	12	67	52	52
4	West Ham	42	20	8	14	52	39	48
5	Hull	42	19	10	13	51	41	48
6	South Shields	42	17	12	13	43	38	46
7	Fulham	42	18	9	15	57	38	45
8	Leeds	42	16	13	13	48	38	45
9	Leicester	42	14	17	11	39	34	45
10	Wednesday	42	15	14	13	47	50	44
11	Bury	42	15	10	17	54	55	40
12	Derby	42	15	9	18	60	64	39
13	Notts County	42	12	15	15	47	51	39
14	Crystal Palace	42	13	13	16	45	51	39
15	Clapton Orient	42	15	9	18	43	50	39
16	Rotherham Co	42	14	11	17	32	43	39
17	Wolves	42	13	11	18	44	49	37
18	Port Vale	42	14	8	20	43	57	36
19	Blackpool	42	15	5	22	44	57	35
20	Coventry	42	12	10	20	51	60	34
21	Bristol City	42	12	9	21	37	58	33
22	Bradford PA	42	12	9	21	46	62	33

THIRD DIVISION (NORTH)

		P	W	D	L	F	A	Pts
1	Stockport	38	24	8	6	60	21	56
2	Darlington	38	22	6	10	81	37	50
3	Grimsby	38	21	8	9	72	47	50
4	Hartlepools	38	17	8	13	52	39	42
5	Accrington	38	19	3	16	73	57	41
6	Crewe	38	18	5	15	60	56	41
7	Stalybridge Cel	38	18	5	15	62	63	41
8	Walsall	38	18	3	17	66	65	39
9	Southport	38	14	10	14	55	44	38
10	Ashington	38	17	4	17	59	66	38
11	Durham City	38	17	3	18	68	67	37
12	Wrexham	38	14	9	15	51	56	37
13	Chesterfield	38	16	3	19	48	67	35
14	Lincoln	38	14	6	18	48	59	34
15	Barrow	38	14	5	19	42	54	33
16	Nelson	38	13	7	18	48	66	33
17	Wigan Borough	38	11	9	18	46	72	31
18	Tranmere	38	9	11	18	51	61	29
19	Halifax	38	10	9	19	56	76	29
20	Rochdale	38	11	4	23	52	77	26

THIRD DIVISION (SOUTH)

		P	W	D	L	F	A	Pts
1	Southampton	42	23	15	4	68	21	61
2	Plymouth	42	25	11	6	63	24	61
3	Portsmouth	42	18	17	7	62	39	53
4	Luton	42	22	8	12	64	35	52
5	QPR	42	18	13	11	53	44	49
6	Swindon	42	16	13	13	72	60	45
7	Watford	42	13	18	11	54	48	44
8	Aberdare Ath	42	17	10	15	57	51	44
9	Brentford	42	16	11	15	52	43	43
10	Swansea	42	13	15	14	50	47	41
11	Merthyr Town	42	17	6	19	45	56	40
12	Millwall Ath	42	10	18	14	38	42	38
13	Reading	42	14	10	18	40	47	38
14	Bristol Rovers	42	14	10	18	52	67	38
15	Norwich	42	12	13	17	50	62	37
16	Charlton	42	13	11	18	43	56	37
17	Northampton	42	13	11	18	47	71	37
18	Gillingham	42	14	8	20	47	60	36
19	Brighton	42	13	9	20	45	51	35
20	Newport	42	11	12	19	44	61	34
21	Exeter	42	11	12	19	38	59	34
22	Southend	42	8	11	23	34	74	27

SCOTTISH FIRST DIVISION

		P	W	D	L	F	A	Pts
1	Celtic	42	27	13	2	83	20	67
2	Rangers	42	28	10	4	83	26	66
3	Raith	42	19	13	10	66	43	51
4	Dundee	42	19	11	12	57	40	49
5	Falkirk	42	16	17	9	48	38	49
6	Partick	42	20	8	14	57	53	48
7	Hibernian	42	16	14	12	55	44	46
8	St Mirren	42	17	12	13	71	61	46
9	Third Lanark	42	17	12	13	58	52	46
10	Clyde	42	16	12	14	60	51	44
11	Albion	42	17	10	15	55	51	44
12	Morton	42	16	10	16	58	57	42
13	Motherwell	42	16	7	19	63	58	39
14	Ayr	42	13	12	17	55	63	38
15	Aberdeen	42	13	9	20	48	54	35
16	Airdrieonians	42	12	11	19	46	56	35
17	Kilmarnock	42	13	9	20	56	83	35
18	Hamilton	42	9	16	17	51	62	34
19	Hearts	42	11	10	21	50	60	32
20	Dumbarton*	42	10	10	22	46	81	30
21	Queen's Park*	42	9	10	23	38	82	28
22	Clydebank*	42	6	8	28	34	103	20

* Three clubs relegated to Second Division

SCOTTISH SECOND DIVISION

		P	W	D	L	F	A	Pts
1	Alloa*	38	26	8	4	81	32	60
2	Cowdenbeath	38	19	9	10	56	30	47
3	Armadale	38	20	5	13	64	49	45
4	Vale of Leven	38	17	10	11	56	43	44
5	Bathgate	38	16	11	11	56	41	43
6	Bo'ness	38	16	7	15	57	49	39
7	Broxburn	38	14	11	13	43	43	39
8	Dunfermline	38	14	10	14	56	42	38
9	St Bernard's	38	15	8	15	50	49	38
10	Stenhousemuir	38	14	10	14	50	51	38
11	Johnstone	38	14	10	14	46	59	38
12	East Fife	38	15	7	16	55	54	37
13	St Johnstone	38	12	11	15	41	52	35
14	Forfar	38	11	12	15	44	53	34
15	E Stirlingshire	38	12	10	16	43	60	34
16	Arbroath	38	11	11	16	45	56	33
17	King's Park	38	10	12	16	47	65	32
18	Lochgelly Utd	38	11	9	18	46	56	31
19	Dundee Hibs	38	10	8	20	47	65	28
20	Clackmannan	38	10	7	21	41	75	27

* Only Alloa promoted

FA CUP 1921-22

SECOND ROUND

Crystal Palace v Millwall Athletic	0-0, 0-2
Southend United v Swansea Town	0-1
Swindon Town v Blackburn Rovers	0-1
Brighton v Huddersfield Town	0-0, 0-2
Aston Villa v Luton Town	1-0
Northampton Town v Stoke	2-2, 0-3
Liverpool v West Bromwich Albion	0-1
Bradford City v Notts County	1-1, 1-1, 0-1
Bradford Park Avenue v Arsenal	2-3
Leicester City v Fulham	2-0
Barnsley v Oldham Athletic	3-1
Preston North End v Newcastle United	3-1
Southampton v Cardiff City	1-1, 0-2
Nottingham Forest v Hull City	3-0
Bolton Wanderers v Manchester City	1-3
Tottenham Hotspur v Watford	1-0

THIRD ROUND

Millwall Athletic v Swansea Town	4-0
Blackburn Rovers v Huddersfield Town	1-1, 0-5
Stoke v Aston Villa	0-0, 0-4
West Bromwich Albion v Notts County	1-1, 0-2
Arsenal v Leicester City	3-0
Barnsley v Preston North End	1-1, 0-3
Cardiff City v Nottingham Forest	4-1
Tottenham Hotspur v Manchester City	2-1

FOURTH ROUND

Huddersfield Town v Millwall Athletic	3-0
Notts County v Aston Villa	2-2, 4-3
Arsenal v Preston North End	1-1, 1-2
Cardiff City v Tottenham Hotspur	1-1, 1-2

SEMI-FINAL

Huddersfield Town v Notts County	3-1
Preston North End v Tottenham Hotspur	2-1

FINAL AT STAMFORD BRIDGE

Huddersfield Town v Preston North End	1-0

SCOTTISH FA CUP 1921-22

SECOND ROUND

Aberdeen v Queen's Park	1-1, 2-1
Cowdenbeath v Airdrieonians	0-0, 1-4
Vale of Leven v Alloa Athletic	0-0, 0-1
Bathgate v Falkirk	1-0
Celtic v Third Lanark	1-0
Clyde v Bo'ness	5-1
Royal Albert v Dundee	0-1
East Stirlingshire v Dunfermline Athletic	2-1
Morton v Clydebank	1-1, 3-1
Hamilton Academicals v King's Park	4-1
Broxburn United v Heart of Midlothian	2-2, 2-2, 1-3
Motherwell v Hibernian	3-2
Ayr United v Partick Thistle	0-1
Inverness Citadel v Queen of the South	2-2, 1-2
Albion Rovers v Rangers	1-1, 0-4
Kilmarnock v St Mirren	1-4

THIRD ROUND

Aberdeen v Dundee	3-0
Morton v Clyde	4-1
Celtic v Hamilton Academicals	1-3
Motherwell v Alloa Athletic	1-0
Partick Thistle v Bathgate	3-0
Queen of the South v East Stirlingshire	2-0
Heart of Midlothian v Rangers	0-4
St Mirren v Airdrieonians	3-0

FOURTH ROUND

Hamilton Academicals v Aberdeen	0-0, 0-2
Motherwell v Morton	1-2
Partick Thistle v Queen of the South	1-0
Rangers v St Mirren	1-1, 2-0

SEMI-FINAL

Morton v Aberdeen	3-1
Rangers v Partick Thistle	2-0

FINAL AT HAMPDEN PARK

Morton v Rangers	1-0

On Boxing Day 1921, Aston Villa's winning goal in their Division One fixture with Sheffield United was a spectacular 30-yard header. Frank Barson, Villa's centre-half, was the man responsible. Another Villa player, Billy Walker, had also done the unusual in a League match that season. In November, he had scored three penalties against Bradford City—a record for one game.

Jimmy Evans, Southend United's full-back, scored a total of 10 goals in the Third Division South in 1921-22. All were from penalties, and meant that Evans became the first full-back to finish a season as a club's top League scorer.

The Scottish Second Division restarted in 1921-22, with promotion by position.

League Tables 1922-23

FIRST DIVISION

	P	W	D	L	F	A	Pts
1 Liverpool	42	26	8	8	70	31	60
2 Sunderland	42	22	10	10	72	54	54
3 Huddersfield	42	21	11	10	60	32	53
4 Newcastle	42	18	12	12	45	37	48
5 Everton	42	20	7	15	63	59	47
6 Aston Villa	42	18	10	14	64	51	46
7 WBA	42	17	11	14	58	49	45
8 Man City	42	17	11	14	50	49	45
9 Cardiff	42	18	7	17	73	59	43
10 Sheff United	42	16	10	16	68	64	42
11 Arsenal	42	16	10	16	61	62	42
12 Tottenham	42	17	7	18	50	50	41
13 Bolton	42	14	12	16	50	58	40
14 Blackburn	42	14	12	16	47	62	40
15 Burnley	42	16	6	20	58	59	38
16 Preston	42	13	11	18	60	64	37
17 Birmingham	42	13	11	18	41	57	37
18 Middlesbrough	42	13	10	19	57	63	36
19 Chelsea	42	9	18	15	45	53	36
20 Nottm Forest	42	13	8	21	41	70	34
21 Stoke	42	10	10	22	47	67	30
22 Oldham	42	10	10	22	35	65	30

SECOND DIVISION

	P	W	D	L	F	A	Pts
1 Notts County	42	23	7	12	46	34	53
2 West Ham	42	20	11	11	63	38	51
3 Leicester	42	21	9	12	65	44	51
4 Man United	42	17	14	11	51	36	48
5 Blackpool	42	18	11	13	60	43	47
6 Bury	42	18	11	13	55	46	47
7 Leeds	42	18	11	13	43	36	47
8 Wednesday	42	17	12	13	54	47	46
9 Barnsley	42	17	11	14	62	51	45
10 Fulham	42	16	12	14	43	32	44
11 Southampton	42	14	14	14	40	40	42
12 Hull	42	14	14	14	43	45	42
13 South Shields	42	15	10	17	35	44	40
14 Derby	42	14	11	17	46	50	39
15 Bradford City	42	12	13	17	41	45	37
16 Crystal Palace	42	13	11	18	54	62	37
17 Port Vale	42	14	9	19	39	51	37
18 Coventry	42	15	7	20	46	63	37
19 Clapton Orient	42	12	12	18	40	50	36
20 Stockport	42	14	8	20	43	58	36
21 Rotherham Co	42	13	9	20	44	63	35
22 Wolves	42	9	9	24	42	77	27

FA CUP 1922-23

SECOND ROUND

Bolton Wanderers v Leeds United	3-1
Millwall Athletic v Huddersfield Town	0-0, 0-3
Charlton Athletic v Preston North End	2-0
West Bromwich Albion v Sunderland	2-1
Middlesbrough v Sheffield United	1-1, 0-3
Wolverhampton Wanderers v Liverpool	0-2
Wigan Borough v Queen's Park Rangers	2-4
South Shields v Blackburn Rovers	0-0, 1-0
Bury v Stoke	3-1
Chelsea v Southampton	0-0, 0-1
Brighton v West Ham United	1-1, 0-1
Plymouth Argyle v Bradford Park Avenue	4-1
Bristol City v Derby County	0-3
The Wednesday v Barnsley	2-1
Tottenham Hotspur v Manchester United	4-0
Leicester City v Cardiff City	0-1

THIRD ROUND

Huddersfield Town v Bolton Wanderers	1-1, 0-1
Charlton Athletic v West Bromwich Albion	1-0
Liverpool v Sheffield United	1-2
Queen's Park Rangers v South Shields	3-0
Bury v Southampton	0-0, 0-1
West Ham United v Plymouth Argyle	2-0
Derby County v The Wednesday	1-0
Cardiff City v Tottenham Hotspur	2-3

FOURTH ROUND

Charlton Athletic v Bolton Wanderers	0-1
Queen's Park Rangers v Sheffield United	0-1
Southampton v West Ham United	1-1, 1-1, 0-1
Tottenham Hotspur v Derby County	0-1

SEMI-FINAL

Bolton Wanderers v Sheffield United	1-0
West Ham United v Derby County	5-2

FINAL

Bolton Wanderers v West Ham United	2-0

THIRD DIVISION (SOUTH)

	P	W	D	L	F	A	Pts
1 Bristol City	42	24	11	7	66	40	59
2 Plymouth	42	23	7	12	61	29	53
3 Swansea	42	22	9	11	78	45	53
4 Brighton	42	20	11	11	52	34	51
5 Luton	42	21	7	14	68	49	49
6 Portsmouth	42	19	8	15	58	52	46
7 Millwall Ath	42	14	18	10	45	40	46
8 Northampton	42	17	11	14	54	44	45
9 Swindon	42	17	11	14	62	56	45
10 Watford	42	17	10	15	57	54	44
11 QPR	42	16	10	16	54	49	42
12 Charlton	42	14	14	14	55	51	42
13 Bristol Rovers	42	13	16	13	35	36	42
14 Brentford	42	13	12	17	41	51	38
15 Southend	42	12	13	17	49	54	37
16 Gillingham	42	15	7	20	51	59	37
17 Merthyr Town	42	11	14	17	39	48	36
18 Norwich	42	13	10	19	51	71	36
19 Reading	42	10	14	18	36	55	34
20 Exeter	42	13	7	22	47	84	33
21 Aberdare Ath	42	9	11	22	42	70	29
22 Newport	42	8	11	23	40	70	27

THIRD DIVISION (NORTH)

	P	W	D	L	F	A	Pts
1 Nelson	38	24	3	11	61	41	51
2 Bradford PA	38	19	9	10	67	38	47
3 Walsall	38	19	8	11	51	44	46
4 Chesterfield	38	19	7	12	68	52	45
5 Wigan Borough	38	18	8	12	64	39	44
6 Crewe	38	17	9	12	48	38	43
7 Halifax	38	17	7	14	53	46	41
8 Accrington	38	17	7	14	59	65	41
9 Darlington	38	15	10	13	59	46	40
10 Wrexham	38	14	10	14	38	48	38
11 Stalybridge Cel	38	15	6	17	42	47	36
12 Rochdale	38	13	10	15	42	53	36
13 Lincoln	38	13	10	15	39	55	36
14 Grimsby	38	14	5	19	55	52	33
15 Hartlepools	38	10	12	16	48	54	32
16 Tranmere	38	12	8	18	49	59	32
17 Southport	38	12	7	19	32	46	31
18 Barrow	38	13	4	21	50	60	30
19 Ashington	38	11	8	19	51	77	30
20 Durham City	38	9	10	19	43	59	28

SCOTTISH FA CUP 1922-23

SECOND ROUND

Airdrieonians v Aberdeen	1-1, 0-2
Ayr United v Rangers	2-0
Bo'ness v Heart of Midlothian	3-2
Celtic v Hurlford	4-0
Dundee v St Bernard's	0-0, 3-2
Dunfermline Athletic v Clydebank	1-0
Hibernian v Peebles Rovers	0-0, 3-0
Kilmarnock v East Fife	1-1, 0-1
Johnstone v Falkirk	0-1
Hamilton Academicals v King's Park	1-0
Motherwell v St Mirren	2-1
Dundee Hibernians v Nithsdale Wanderers	0-1
Peterhead v Galston	1-0
Queen's Park v Bathgate	1-1, 2-0
Raith Rovers v Cowdenbeath	2-0
Vale of Leven v Third Lanark	2-2, 1-2

THIRD ROUND

Aberdeen v Peterhead	13-0
Bo'ness v Nithsdale Wanderers	2-0
Celtic v East Fife	2-1
Dundee v Hamilton Academicals	0-0, 1-0
Hibernian v Queen's Park	2-0
Motherwell v Falkirk	3-0
Dunfermline Athletic v Raith Rovers	0-3
Third Lanark v Ayr United	2-0

FOURTH ROUND

Celtic v Raith Rovers	1-0
Hibernian v Aberdeen	2-0
Motherwell v Bo'ness	4-2
Dundee v Third Lanark	0-0, 1-1, 0-1

SEMI-FINAL

Celtic v Motherwell	2-0
Hibernian v Third Lanark	1-0

FINAL AT HAMPDEN PARK

Celtic v Hibernian	1-0

SCOTTISH FIRST DIVISION

	P	W	D	L	F	A	Pts
1 Rangers	38	23	9	6	67	29	55
2 Airdrieonians	38	20	10	8	58	38	50
3 Celtic	38	19	8	11	52	39	46
4 Falkirk	38	14	17	7	44	32	45
5 Aberdeen	38	15	12	11	46	34	42
6 St Mirren	38	15	12	11	54	44	42
7 Dundee	38	17	7	14	51	45	41
8 Hibernian	38	17	7	14	45	40	41
9 Raith	38	13	13	12	31	43	39
10 Ayr	38	13	12	13	43	44	38
11 Partick	38	14	9	15	51	48	37
12 Hearts	38	11	15	12	51	50	37
13 Motherwell	38	13	10	15	59	60	36
14 Morton	38	12	11	15	44	47	35
15 Kilmarnock	38	14	7	17	57	66	35
16 Clyde	38	12	9	17	36	44	33
17 Third Lanark	38	11	8	19	40	59	30
18 Hamilton	38	11	7	20	43	59	29
19 Albion	38	8	10	20	38	64	26
20 Alloa	38	6	11	21	27	52	23

SCOTTISH SECOND DIVISION

	P	W	D	L	F	A	Pts
1 Queen's Park	38	24	9	5	73	31	57
2 Clydebank	38	21	10	7	69	29	52
3 St Johnstone	38	19	12	7	60	39	48*
4 Dumbarton	38	17	8	13	61	40	42
5 Bathgate	38	16	9	13	67	55	41
6 Armadale	38	15	11	12	63	52	41
7 Bo'ness	38	12	17	9	48	46	41
8 Broxburn	38	14	12	12	40	43	40
9 East Fife	38	16	7	15	48	42	39
10 Lochgelly	38	16	5	17	41	64	37
11 Cowdenbeath	38	16	6	16	56	52	36*
12 King's Park	38	14	6	18	46	60	34
13 Dunfermline	38	11	11	16	47	44	33
14 Stenhousemuir	38	13	7	18	53	67	33
15 Forfar	38	13	7	18	51	73	33
16 Johnstone	38	13	6	19	41	62	32
17 Vale of Leven	38	11	8	19	50	59	30
18 St Bernard's	38	8	15	15	39	50	29*
19 E Stirlingshire	38	10	8	20	48	69	28
20 Arbroath	38	8	12	18	45	69	28

*Two points deducted for fielding an ineligible player.

In Division Two, 1922-23, Southampton had an uneventful season, finishing in the middle of the table. But their final record is something of a curiosity. It reads, P42, W14, D14, L14, F40, A40, Pts42.

Liverpool won the League Championship for the second successive season.

The most goals a player has scored in an FA Cup game and yet finished on the losing side is seven. Billy Minter of St Albans City scored seven times against Dulwich Hamlet in a replayed Fourth Round qualifying tie on 22 November 1922. But despite poor Minter's monumental contribution, his side eventually lost the match 8-7.

FIRST DIVISION

		P	W	D	L	F	A	Pts
1	Huddersfield	42	23	11	8	60	33	57
2	Cardiff	42	22	13	7	61	34	57
3	Sunderland	42	22	9	11	71	54	53
4	Bolton	42	18	14	10	68	34	50
5	Sheff United	42	19	12	11	69	49	50
6	Aston Villa	42	18	13	11	52	37	49
7	Everton	42	18	13	11	62	53	49
8	Blackburn	42	17	11	14	54	50	45
9	Newcastle	42	17	10	15	60	54	44
10	Notts County	42	14	14	14	44	49	42
11	Man City	42	15	12	15	54	71	42
12	Liverpool	42	15	11	16	49	48	41
13	West Ham	42	13	15	14	40	43	41
14	Birmingham	42	13	13	16	41	49	39
15	Tottenham	42	12	14	16	50	56	38
16	WBA	42	12	14	16	51	62	38
17	Burnley	42	12	12	18	55	60	36
18	Preston	42	12	10	20	52	67	34
19	Arsenal	42	12	9	21	40	63	33
20	Nottm Forest	42	10	12	20	42	64	32
21	Chelsea	42	9	14	19	31	53	32
22	Middlesbrough	42	7	8	27	37	60	22

SECOND DIVISION

		P	W	D	L	F	A	Pts
1	Leeds	42	21	12	9	61	35	54
2	Bury	42	21	9	12	63	35	51
3	Derby	42	21	9	12	75	42	51
4	Blackpool	42	18	13	11	72	47	49
5	Southampton	42	17	14	11	52	31	48
6	Stoke	42	14	18	10	44	42	46
7	Oldham	42	14	17	11	45	52	45
8	Wednesday	42	16	12	14	54	51	44
9	South Shields	42	17	10	15	49	50	44
10	Clapton Orient	42	14	15	13	40	36	43
11	Barnsley	42	16	11	15	57	61	43
12	Leicester	42	17	8	17	64	54	42
13	Stockport	42	13	16	13	44	52	42
14	Man United	42	13	14	15	52	44	40
15	Crystal Palace	42	13	13	16	53	65	39
16	Port Vale	42	13	12	17	50	66	38
17	Hull	42	10	17	15	46	51	37
18	Bradford City	42	11	15	16	35	48	37
19	Coventry	42	11	13	18	52	68	35
20	Fulham	42	10	14	18	45	56	34
21	Nelson	42	10	13	19	40	74	33
22	Bristol City	42	7	15	20	32	65	29

FA CUP 1923-24

SECOND ROUND

Derby County v Newcastle United	2-2, 2-2, 2-2, 3-5
Exeter City v Watford	0-0, 0-1
Southampton v Blackpool	3-1
Bolton Wanderers v Liverpool	1-4
Manchester City v Halifax Town	2-2, 0-0, 3-0
Brighton v Everton	5-2
Cardiff City v Arsenal	1-0
The Wednesday v Bristol City	1-1, 0-2
Swansea Town v Aston Villa	0-2
West Ham United v Leeds United	1-1, 0-1
West Bromwich Albion v Corinthians	5-0
Charlton Athletic v Wolverhampton Wanderers	0-0, 0-1
Swindon Town v Oldham Athletic	2-0
Crystal Palace v Notts County	0-0, 0-0, 0-0, 2-1
Burnley v Fulham	0-0, 1-0
Manchester United v Huddersfield Town	0-3

THIRD ROUND

Watford v Newcastle United	0-1
Southampton v Liverpool	0-0, 0-2
Brighton v Manchester City	1-5
Cardiff City v Bristol City	3-0
Aston Villa v Leeds United	3-0
West Bromwich Albion v Wolverhampton Wanderers	1-1, 2-0
Crystal Palace v Swindon Town	1-2
Burnley v Huddersfield Town	1-0

FOURTH ROUND

Newcastle United v Liverpool	1-0
Manchester City v Cardiff City	0-0, 1-0
West Bromwich Albion v Aston Villa	0-2
Swindon Town v Burnley	1-1, 1-3

SEMI-FINAL

Newcastle United v Manchester City	2-0
Aston Villa v Burnley	3-0

FINAL

Newcastle United v Aston Villa	2-0

THIRD DIVISION (SOUTH)

		P	W	D	L	F	A	Pts
1	Portsmouth	42	24	11	7	87	30	59
2	Plymouth	42	23	9	10	70	34	55
3	Millwall Ath	42	22	10	10	64	38	54
4	Swansea	42	22	8	12	60	48	52
5	Brighton	42	21	9	12	68	37	51
6	Swindon	42	17	13	12	58	44	47
7	Luton	42	16	14	12	50	44	46
8	Northampton	42	17	11	14	64	47	45
9	Bristol Rovers	42	15	13	14	52	46	43
10	Newport	42	17	9	16	56	64	43
11	Norwich	42	16	8	18	60	59	40
12	Aberdare Ath	42	12	14	16	45	58	38
13	Merthyr Town	42	11	16	15	45	65	38
14	Charlton	42	11	15	16	38	45	37
15	Gillingham	42	12	13	17	43	58	37
16	Exeter	42	15	7	20	37	52	37
17	Brentford	42	14	8	20	54	71	36
18	Reading	42	13	9	20	51	57	35
19	Southend	42	12	10	20	53	84	34
20	Watford	42	9	15	18	45	54	33
21	Bournemouth	42	11	11	20	40	65	33
22	QPR	42	11	9	22	37	77	31

THIRD DIVISION (NORTH)

		P	W	D	L	F	A	Pts
1	Wolves	42	24	15	3	76	27	63
2	Rochdale	42	25	12	5	60	26	62
3	Chesterfield	42	22	10	10	70	39	54
4	Rotherham Co	42	23	6	13	70	43	52
5	Bradford PA	42	21	10	11	69	43	52
6	Darlington	42	20	8	14	70	53	48
7	Southport	42	16	14	12	44	42	46
8	Ashington	42	18	8	16	59	61	44
9	Doncaster	42	15	12	15	59	53	42
10	Wigan Borough	42	14	14	14	55	53	42
11	Grimsby	42	14	13	15	49	47	41
12	Tranmere	42	13	15	14	51	60	41
13	Accrington	42	16	8	18	48	61	40
14	Halifax	42	15	10	17	42	59	40
15	Durham City	42	15	9	18	59	60	39
16	Wrexham	42	10	18	14	37	44	38
17	Walsall	42	14	8	20	44	59	36
18	New Brighton	42	11	13	18	40	53	35
19	Lincoln	42	10	12	20	48	59	32
20	Crewe	42	7	13	22	32	58	27
21	Hartlepools	42	7	11	24	33	70	25
22	Barrow	42	8	9	25	35	80	25

SCOTTISH FA CUP 1923-24

SECOND ROUND

Airdrieonians v St Johnstone	4-0
Forfar Athletic v Motherwell	1-3
Ayr United v Kilmarnock	1-0
Clydebank v Arbroath	4-0
Falkirk v East Fife	2-0
Queen's Park v Armadale	3-1
Heart of Midlothian v Galston	6-0
Clyde v Vale of Leven	2-0
Cowdenbeath v Aberdeen	0-2
East Stirlingshire v Mid-Annandale	1-0
St Bernard's v Stenhousemuir	0-0, 0-0, 2-0
Dundee v Raith Rovers	0-0, 0-1
Hibernian v Alloa Athletic	1-1, 5-0
St Mirren v Rangers	0-1
Partick Thistle v Bo'ness	3-0
Hamilton Academicals v Queen of the South	2-1

THIRD ROUND

Motherwell v Airdrieonians	0-5
Clydebank v Ayr United	2-3
Falkirk v Queen's Park	0-0, 2-0
Heart of Midlothian v Clyde	3-1
Aberdeen v East Stirlingshire	2-0
Raith Rovers v St Bernard's	0-1
Rangers v Hibernian	1-2
Partick Thistle v Hamilton Academicals	1-1, 2-1

FOURTH ROUND

Airdrieonians v Ayr United	1-1, 0-0, 1-0
Heart of Midlothian v Falkirk	1-2
Aberdeen v St Bernard's	3-0
Hibernian v Partick Thistle	2-2, 1-1, 2-1

SEMI-FINAL

Airdrieonians v Falkirk	2-1
Aberdeen v Hibernian	0-0, 0-0, 0-1

FINAL AT IBROX PARK

Airdrieonians v Hibernian	2-0

SCOTTISH FIRST DIVISION

		P	W	D	L	F	A	Pts
1	Rangers	38	25	9	4	72	22	59
2	Airdrieonians	38	20	10	8	72	46	50
3	Celtic	38	17	12	9	56	33	46
4	Raith	38	18	7	13	56	38	43
5	Dundee	38	15	13	10	70	57	43
6	St Mirren	38	15	12	11	53	45	42
7	Hibernian	38	15	11	12	66	52	41
8	Partick	38	15	9	14	58	55	39
9	Hearts	38	14	10	14	61	50	38
10	Motherwell	38	15	7	16	58	63	37
11	Morton	38	16	5	17	48	54	37
12	Hamilton	38	15	6	17	52	57	36
13	Aberdeen	38	13	10	15	37	41	36
14	Ayr	38	12	10	16	38	60	34
15	Falkirk	38	13	6	19	46	53	32
16	Kilmarnock	38	12	8	18	48	65	32
17	Queen's Park	38	11	9	18	43	60	31
18	Third Lanark	38	11	8	19	54	78	30
19	Clyde	38	10	9	19	40	70	29
20	Clydebank	38	10	5	23	42	71	25

SCOTTISH SECOND DIVISION

		P	W	D	L	F	A	Pts
1	St Johnstone	38	22	12	4	79	33	56
2	Cowdenbeath	38	23	9	6	78	33	55
3	Bathgate	38	16	12	10	58	49	44
4	Stenhousemuir	38	16	11	11	58	45	43
5	Albion	38	15	12	11	67	53	42
6	King's Park	38	16	10	12	67	56	42
7	Dunfermline	38	14	11	13	52	45	39
8	Johnstone	38	16	7	15	60	56	39
9	Dundee United	38	12	15	11	41	41	39
10	Dumbarton	38	17	5	16	55	58	39
11	Armadale	38	16	6	16	56	63	38
12	Bo'ness	38	13	11	14	45	52	37
13	East Fife	38	14	9	15	54	47	37
14	Forfar	38	14	7	17	43	68	35
15	Broxburn	38	13	8	17	50	56	34
16	Alloa	38	14	6	18	44	53	34
17	Arbroath	38	12	8	18	49	51	32
18	St Bernard's	38	11	10	17	49	54	32
19	Vale of Leven	38	11	9	18	41	67	31
20	Lochgelly	38	4	4	30	20	86	12

The only player to have scored two goals for each side in a single Football League game is Sammy Wynne of Oldham. In the Division Two match with Manchester United on 6 October 1923, Wynne scored for his own side with a free-kick and a penalty, but also put two through his own goal. Those four goals probably give poor Wynne the dubious record for the most goals scored by a full-back in one League game.

A Birch, Chesterfield's goalkeeper, set a League goalscoring record for a keeper in 1923-24. Birch, who played in every one of his club's Division Three North fixtures, scored from five penalties.

During the Third Division North match between Crewe and Bradford Park Avenue on 8 March 1924, four penalties were awarded in five minutes, a League record.

League Tables 1924-25

FIRST DIVISION

		P	W	D	L	F	A	Pts
1	Huddersfield	42	21	16	5	69	28	58
2	WBA	42	23	10	9	58	34	56
3	Bolton	42	22	11	9	76	34	55
4	Liverpool	42	20	10	12	63	55	50
5	Bury	42	17	15	10	54	51	49
6	Newcastle	42	16	16	10	61	42	48
7	Sunderland	42	19	10	13	64	51	48
8	Birmingham	42	17	12	13	49	53	46
9	Notts County	42	16	13	13	42	31	45
10	Man City	42	17	9	16	76	68	43
11	Cardiff	42	16	11	15	56	51	43
12	Tottenham	42	15	12	15	52	43	42
13	West Ham	42	15	12	15	62	60	42
14	Sheff United	42	13	13	16	55	63	39
15	Aston Villa	42	13	13	16	58	71	39
16	Blackburn	42	11	13	18	53	66	35
17	Everton	42	12	11	19	40	60	35
18	Leeds	42	11	12	19	46	59	34
19	Burnley	42	11	12	19	46	75	34
20	Arsenal	42	14	5	23	46	58	33
21	Preston	42	10	6	26	37	74	26
22	Nottm Forest	42	6	12	24	29	65	24

SECOND DIVISION

		P	W	D	L	F	A	Pts
1	Leicester	42	24	11	7	90	32	59
2	Man United	42	23	11	8	57	23	57
3	Derby	42	22	11	9	71	36	55
4	Portsmouth	42	15	18	9	58	50	48
5	Chelsea	42	16	15	11	51	37	47
6	Wolves	42	20	6	16	55	51	46
7	Southampton	42	13	18	11	40	36	44
8	Port Vale	42	17	8	17	48	56	42
9	South Shields	42	17	7	13	42	38	41
10	Hull	42	15	11	16	50	49	41
11	Clapton Orient	42	14	12	16	42	42	40
12	Fulham	42	15	10	17	41	56	40
13	Middlesbrough	42	10	19	13	36	44	39
14	Wednesday	42	15	8	19	50	56	38
15	Barnsley	42	13	12	17	46	59	38
16	Bradford City	42	13	12	17	37	50	38
17	Blackpool	42	14	9	19	65	61	37
18	Oldham	42	13	11	18	35	51	37
19	Stockport	42	13	11	18	37	57	37
20	Stoke	42	12	11	19	34	46	35
21	Crystal Palace	42	12	10	20	38	54	34
22	Coventry	42	11	9	22	45	84	31

THIRD DIVISION (SOUTH)

		P	W	D	L	F	A	Pts
1	Swansea	42	23	11	8	68	35	57
2	Plymouth	42	23	10	9	77	38	56
3	Bristol City	42	22	9	11	60	41	53
4	Swindon	42	20	11	11	66	38	51
5	Millwall Ath	42	18	13	11	58	38	49
6	Newport	42	20	9	13	62	42	49
7	Exeter	42	19	9	14	59	48	47
8	Brighton	42	19	8	15	59	45	46
9	Northampton	42	20	6	16	51	44	46
10	Southend	42	19	5	18	51	61	43
11	Watford	42	17	9	16	38	47	43
12	Norwich	42	14	13	15	53	51	41
13	Gillingham	42	13	14	15	35	44	40
14	Reading	42	14	10	18	37	38	38
15	Charlton	42	13	12	17	46	48	38
16	Luton	42	10	17	15	49	57	37
17	Bristol Rovers	42	12	13	17	42	49	37
18	Aberdare Ath	42	14	9	19	54	67	37
19	QPR	42	14	8	20	42	63	36
20	Bournemouth	42	13	8	21	40	58	34
21	Brentford	42	9	7	26	38	91	25
22	Merthyr Town	42	8	5	29	35	77	21

THIRD DIVISION (NORTH)

		P	W	D	L	F	A	Pts
1	Darlington	42	24	10	8	78	33	58
2	Nelson	42	23	7	12	79	50	53
3	New Brighton	42	23	7	12	75	50	53
4	Southport	42	22	7	13	59	37	51
5	Bradford PA	42	19	12	11	84	42	50
6	Rochdale	42	21	7	14	75	53	49
7	Chesterfield	42	17	11	14	60	44	45
8	Lincoln	42	18	8	16	53	58	44
9	Halifax	42	16	11	15	56	52	43
10	Ashington	42	16	10	16	68	76	42
11	Wigan Borough	42	15	11	16	62	65	41
12	Grimsby	42	15	9	18	60	60	39
13	Durham City	42	13	13	16	50	68	39
14	Barrow	42	16	7	19	51	74	39
15	Crewe	42	13	13	16	53	78	39
16	Wrexham	42	15	8	19	53	61	38
17	Accrington	42	15	8	19	60	72	38
18	Doncaster	42	14	10	18	54	65	38
19	Walsall	42	13	11	18	44	53	37
20	Hartlepools	42	12	11	19	45	63	35
21	Tranmere	42	14	4	24	59	78	32
22	Rotherham Co	42	7	7	28	42	88	21

SCOTTISH FIRST DIVISION

		P	W	D	L	F	A	Pts
1	Rangers	38	25	10	3	77	27	60
2	Airdrieonians	38	25	7	6	85	31	57
3	Hibernian	38	22	8	8	78	43	52
4	Celtic	38	18	8	12	76	43	44
5	Cowdenbeath	38	16	10	12	76	65	42
6	St Mirren	38	18	4	16	65	63	40
7	Partick	38	14	10	14	60	61	38
8	Dundee	38	14	8	16	48	55	36
9	Raith	38	14	8	16	52	60	36
10	Hearts	38	12	11	15	65	69	35
11	St Johnstone	38	12	11	15	56	71	35
12	Kilmarnock	38	12	9	17	53	64	33
13	Hamilton	38	15	3	20	50	63	33
14	Morton	38	12	9	17	46	69	33
15	Aberdeen	38	11	10	17	46	56	32
16	Falkirk	38	12	8	18	44	54	32
17	Queen's Park	38	12	8	18	50	71	32
18	Motherwell	38	10	10	18	55	64	30
19	Ayr	38	11	8	19	43	65	30
20	Third Lanark	38	11	8	19	53	84	30

SCOTTISH SECOND DIVISION

		P	W	D	L	F	A	Pts
1	Dundee United	38	20	10	8	58	44	50
2	Clydebank	38	20	8	10	65	42	48
3	Clyde	38	20	7	11	72	39	47
4	Alloa	38	17	11	10	57	41	45
5	Arbroath	38	16	10	12	47	46	42
6	Bo'ness	38	16	9	13	71	48	41
7	Broxburn	38	16	9	13	48	54	41
8	Dumbarton	38	15	10	13	45	45	40
9	East Fife	38	17	5	16	66	58	39
10	King's Park	38	15	8	15	54	46	38
11	Stenhousemuir	38	15	7	16	51	58	37
12	Arthurlie	38	14	8	16	56	60	36
13	Dunfermline	38	14	7	17	62	57	35
14	Albion	38	15	5	18	58	64	35
15	Armadale	38	15	5	18	55	62	35
16	Bathgate	38	12	10	16	58	74	34
17	St Bernard's	38	14	4	20	52	71	32
18	E Stirlingshire	38	11	8	19	58	72	30
19	Johnstone	38	12	4	22	53	85	28
20	Forfar	38	10	7	21	46	67	27

Merthyr Town, who finished bottom of the Third Division South, suffered 29 defeats in their 42 matches, the greatest number ever lost in a single season in that division.

Manchester United conceded only 23 goals in their 42 Second Division matches. This is the lowest number of goals ever recorded against a club in that division.

Arthur Chandler, of Second Division champions Leicester City, not only led that division's scoring lists with 33 goals, but also established a record by finding the net in sixteen consecutive League games.

Huddersfield, in winning their second consecutive Championship, did not concede more than two goals in any League game.

FA CUP 1924-25

SECOND ROUND
Cardiff City v Fulham	1-0
Notts County v Norwich City	4-0
Hull City v Crystal Palace	3-2
Newcastle United v Leicester City	2-2, 0-1
Bradford Park Avenue v Blackpool	1-1, 1-2
Nottingham Forest v West Ham United	0-2
Tottenham Hotspur v Bolton Wanderers	1-1, 1-0
Blackburn Rovers v Portsmouth	0-0, 0-0, 1-0
Southampton v Brighton	1-0
Barnsley v Bradford City	0-3
Birmingham v Stockport County	1-0
Bristol City v Liverpool	0-1
West Bromwich Albion v Preston North End	2-0
Swansea Town v Aston Villa	1-3
Sunderland v Everton	0-0, 1-2
Sheffield United v The Wednesday	3-2

THIRD ROUND
Notts County v Cardiff City	0-2
Hull City v Leicester City	1-1, 1-3
West Ham United v Blackpool	1-1, 0-3
Tottenham Hotspur v Blackburn Rovers	2-2, 1-3
Southampton v Bradford City	2-0
Liverpool v Birmingham	2-1
West Bromwich Albion v Aston Villa	1-1, 2-1
Sheffield United v Everton	1-0

FOURTH ROUND
Cardiff City v Leicester City	2-1
Blackburn Rovers v Blackpool	1-0
Southampton v Liverpool	1-0
Sheffield United v West Bromwich Albion	2-0

SEMI-FINAL
Cardiff City v Blackburn Rovers	3-1
Sheffield United v Southampton	2-0

FINAL
Sheffield United v Cardiff City	1-0

SCOTTISH FA CUP 1924-25

SECOND ROUND
Celtic v Alloa Athletic	2-1
Vale of Leven v Solway Star	2-2, 3-3, 1-2
St Mirren v Ayr United	1-0
Partick Thistle v Dundee United	5-1
Montrose v Rangers	0-2
Arbroath v Clyde	3-0
Kilmarnock v Heart of Midlothian	2-1
Dykehead v Peebles Rovers	3-1
Dundee v Lochgelly United	2-1
Airdrieonians v Queen's Park	4-0
Royal Albert v Broxburn United	1-3
Falkirk v Dumbarton	3-0
Hamilton Academicals v East Stirlingshire	4-0
Raith Rovers v Bo'ness	0-0, 3-1
Armadale v Aberdeen	1-1, 0-2
Motherwell v Arthurlie	2-0

THIRD ROUND
Celtic v Solway Star	2-0
St Mirren v Partick Thistle	2-0
Rangers v Arbroath	5-3
Kilmarnock v Dykehead	5-3
Dundee v Airdrieonians	3-1
Broxburn United v Falkirk	2-1
Hamilton Academicals v Raith Rovers	1-0
Aberdeen v Motherwell	0-0, 2-1

FOURTH ROUND
St Mirren v Celtic	0-0, 1-1, 0-1
Kilmarnock v Rangers	1-2
Dundee v Broxburn United	1-0
Aberdeen v Hamilton Academicals	0-2

SEMI-FINAL
Celtic v Rangers	5-0
Dundee v Hamilton Academicals	1-1, 2-0

FINAL
Celtic v Dundee	2-1

League Tables 1925-26

FIRST DIVISION

	P	W	D	L	F	A	Pts
1 Huddersfield	42	23	11	8	92	60	57
2 Arsenal	42	22	8	12	87	63	52
3 Sunderland	42	21	6	15	96	80	48
4 Bury	42	20	7	15	85	77	47
5 Sheff United	42	19	8	15	102	82	46
6 Aston Villa	42	16	12	14	86	76	44
7 Liverpool	42	14	16	12	70	63	44
8 Bolton	42	17	10	15	75	76	44
9 Man United	42	19	6	17	66	73	44
10 Newcastle	42	16	10	16	84	75	42
11 Everton	42	12	18	12	72	70	42
12 Blackburn	42	15	11	16	91	80	41
13 WBA	42	16	8	18	79	78	40
14 Birmingham	42	16	8	18	66	81	40
15 Tottenham	42	15	9	18	66	79	39
16 Cardiff	42	16	7	19	61	76	39
17 Leicester	42	14	10	18	70	80	38
18 West Ham	42	15	7	20	63	76	37
19 Leeds	42	14	8	20	64	76	36
20 Burnley	42	13	10	19	85	108	36
21 Man City	42	12	11	19	89	100	35
22 Notts County	42	13	7	22	54	74	33

SECOND DIVISION

	P	W	D	L	F	A	Pts
1 Wednesday	42	27	6	9	88	48	60
2 Derby	42	25	7	10	77	42	57
3 Chelsea	42	19	14	9	76	49	52
4 Wolves	42	21	7	14	84	60	49
5 Swansea	42	19	11	12	77	57	49
6 Blackpool	42	17	11	14	76	69	45
7 Oldham	42	18	8	16	74	62	44
8 Port Vale	42	19	6	17	79	69	44
9 South Shields	42	18	8	16	74	65	44
10 Middlesbrough	42	21	2	19	77	68	44
11 Portsmouth	42	17	10	15	79	74	44
12 Preston	42	18	7	17	71	84	43
13 Hull	42	16	9	17	63	61	41
14 Southampton	42	15	8	19	63	63	38
15 Darlington	42	14	10	18	72	77	38
16 Bradford City	42	13	10	19	47	66	36
17 Nottm Forest	42	14	8	20	51	73	36
18 Barnsley	42	12	12	18	58	84	36
19 Fulham	42	11	12	19	46	77	34
20 Clapton Orient	42	12	9	21	50	65	33
21 Stoke	42	12	8	22	54	77	32
22 Stockport	42	8	9	25	51	97	25

FA CUP 1925-26

FOURTH ROUND

Bournemouth v Bolton Wanderers	2-2, 2-6
South Shields v Birmingham	2-1
Nottingham Forest v Swindon Town	2-0
Southend United v Derby County	4-1
Swansea Town v Stoke City	6-3
Bury v Millwall	3-3, 0-2
Arsenal v Blackburn Rovers	3-1
West Bromwich Albion v Aston Villa	1-2
Manchester City v Huddersfield Town	4-0
Crystal Palace v Chelsea	2-1
Clapton Orient v Middlesbrough	4-2
Cardiff City v Newcastle United	0-2
Tottenham Hotspur v Manchester United	2-2, 0-2
Sheffield United v Sunderland	1-2
Fulham v Liverpool	3-1
Notts County v New Brighton	2-0

FIFTH ROUND

Bolton Wanderers v South Shields	3-0
Southend United v Nottingham Forest	0-1
Millwall v Swansea Town	0-1
Aston Villa v Arsenal	1-1, 0-2
Manchester City v Crystal Palace	11-4
Clapton Orient v Newcastle United	2-0
Sunderland v Manchester United	3-3, 1-2
Notts County v Fulham	0-1

SIXTH ROUND

Nottingham Forest v Bolton Wanderers	2-2, 0-0, 0-1
Swansea Town v Arsenal	2-1
Clapton Orient v Manchester City	1-6
Fulham v Manchester United	1-2

SEMI-FINAL

Bolton Wanderers v Swansea Town	3-0
Manchester City v Manchester United	3-0

FINAL

Bolton Wanderers v Manchester City	1-0

THIRD DIVISION (NORTH)

	P	W	D	L	F	A	Pts
1 Grimsby	42	26	9	7	91	40	61
2 Bradford PA	42	26	8	8	101	43	60
3 Rochdale	42	27	5	10	104	58	59
4 Chesterfield	42	25	5	12	100	54	55
5 Halifax	42	17	11	14	53	50	45
6 Hartlepools	42	18	8	16	82	73	44
7 Tranmere	42	19	6	17	73	83	44
8 Nelson	42	16	11	15	89	71	43
9 Ashington	42	16	11	15	70	62	43
10 Doncaster	42	16	11	15	80	72	43
11 Crewe	42	17	9	16	63	61	43
12 New Brighton	42	17	8	17	69	67	42
13 Durham City	42	18	6	18	63	70	42
14 Rotherham	42	17	7	18	69	92	41
15 Lincoln	42	17	5	20	66	82	39
16 Coventry	42	16	6	20	73	82	38
17 Wigan Borough	42	13	11	18	68	74	37
18 Accrington	42	17	3	22	81	105	37
19 Wrexham	42	11	10	21	63	92	32
20 Southport	42	11	10	21	62	92	32
21 Walsall	42	10	6	26	58	107	26
22 Barrow	42	7	4	31	50	98	18

THIRD DIVISION (SOUTH)

	P	W	D	L	F	A	Pts
1 Reading	42	23	11	8	77	52	57
2 Plymouth	42	24	8	10	107	67	56
3 Millwall	42	21	11	10	73	39	53
4 Bristol City	42	21	9	12	72	51	51
5 Brighton	42	19	9	14	84	73	47
6 Swindon	42	20	6	16	69	64	46
7 Luton	42	18	7	17	80	75	43
8 Bournemouth	42	17	9	16	75	91	43
9 Aberdare	42	17	8	17	74	66	42
10 Gillingham	42	17	8	17	53	49	42
11 Southend	42	19	4	19	78	73	42
12 Northampton	42	17	7	18	82	80	41
13 Crystal Palace	42	19	3	20	75	79	41
14 Merthyr Town	42	14	11	17	69	75	39
15 Watford	42	15	9	18	73	89	39
16 Norwich	42	15	9	18	58	73	39
17 Newport	42	14	10	18	64	74	38
18 Brentford	42	16	6	20	69	94	38
19 Bristol Rovers	42	15	6	21	66	69	36
20 Exeter	42	15	5	22	72	70	35
21 Charlton	42	11	13	18	48	68	35
22 QPR	42	6	9	27	37	84	21

SCOTTISH FA CUP 1925-26

SECOND ROUND

Arbroath v St Mirren	0-0, 0-3
Partick Thistle v King's Park	4-1
Hibernian v Airdrieonians	2-3
Bo'ness v Bathgate	1-1, 1-3
Rangers v Stenhousemuir	1-0
Falkirk v Montrose	5-1
Morton v Raith Rovers	3-1
Albion Rovers v Peebles Rovers	1-1, 4-0
Celtic v Hamilton Academicals	4-0
Alloa Athletic v Heart of Midlothian	2-5
Forfar Athletic v Dumbarton	2-2, 1-4
Arthurlie v Clyde	2-2, 0-1
Aberdeen v Dundee	0-0, 3-0
St Johnstone v Queen's Park	7-2
Third Lanark v Leith Athletic	6-1
Solway Star v Brechin City	0-3

THIRD ROUND

St Mirren v Partick Thistle	2-1
Bathgate v Airdrieonians	2-5
Falkirk v Rangers	0-2
Morton v Albion Rovers	1-0
Heart of Midlothian v Celtic	0-4
Dumbarton v Clyde	3-0
Aberdeen v St Johnstone	2-2, 1-0
Third Lanark v Brechin City	4-0

FOURTH ROUND

St Mirren v Airdrieonians	2-0
Morton v Rangers	0-4
Celtic v Dumbarton	6-1
Third Lanark v Aberdeen	1-1, 0-3

SEMI-FINAL

St Mirren v Rangers	1-0
Celtic v Aberdeen	1-0

FINAL

St Mirren v Celtic	2-0

SCOTTISH FIRST DIVISION

	P	W	D	L	F	A	Pts
1 Celtic	38	25	8	5	97	40	58
2 Airdrieonians	38	23	4	11	95	54	50
3 Hearts	38	21	8	9	87	56	50
4 St Mirren	38	20	7	11	62	52	47
5 Motherwell	38	19	8	11	67	46	46
6 Rangers	38	19	6	13	79	55	44
7 Cowdenbeath	38	18	6	14	87	68	42
8 Falkirk	38	14	14	10	61	57	42
9 Kilmarnock	38	17	7	14	79	77	41
10 Dundee	38	14	9	15	47	59	37
11 Aberdeen	38	13	10	15	49	54	36
12 Hamilton	38	13	9	16	68	79	35
13 Queen's Park	38	15	4	19	70	81	34
14 Partick	38	10	13	15	64	73	33
15 Morton	38	12	7	19	57	84	31
16 Hibernian	38	12	6	20	72	77	30
17 Dundee United	38	11	6	21	52	74	28
18 St Johnstone	38	9	10	19	43	78	28
19 Raith	38	11	4	23	46	81	26
20 Clydebank	38	7	8	23	55	92	22

SCOTTISH SECOND DIVISION

	P	W	D	L	F	A	Pts
1 Dunfermline	38	26	7	5	109	43	59
2 Clyde	38	24	5	9	87	51	53
3 Ayr	38	20	12	6	77	39	52
4 East Fife	38	20	9	9	98	73	49
5 Stenhousemuir	38	19	10	9	74	52	48
6 Third Lanark	38	19	8	11	72	47	46
7 Arthurlie	38	17	5	16	81	75	39
8 Bo'ness	38	17	5	16	65	70	39
9 Albion	38	16	6	16	78	71	38
10 Arbroath	38	17	4	17	80	73	38
11 Dumbarton	38	14	10	14	54	78	38
12 Nithsdale	38	15	7	16	79	82	37
13 King's Park	38	14	9	15	67	73	37
14 St Bernard's	38	15	5	18	86	82	35
15 Armadale	38	14	5	19	82	101	33
16 Alloa	38	11	8	19	54	63	30
17 Queen of the S	38	10	8	20	64	88	28
18 E Stirlingshire	38	10	7	21	59	89	27
19 Bathgate	38	7	6	25	60	105	20
20 Broxburn	38	4	6	28	55	126	14

Manchester City had a distressing end to the 1925-26 season. After losing the Cup Final 1-0 to Bolton, City went to Newcastle for their last League game. They missed a penalty, lost 3-2, and were relegated. Had they scored from the penalty they would have remained in the First Division. City thus became the first club to reach the Cup Final and be relegated in the same season.

Huddersfield created a League record by playing 18 consecutive First Division games away from home without defeat. This run lasted from 15 November 1924 to 14 November 1925 and included 12 wins.

Louis Page scored a double hat-trick in his first game as centre-forward for Burnley, against Birmingham, on 10 April 1926.

FIRST DIVISION

		P	W	D	L	F	A	Pts
1	Newcastle	42	25	6	11	96	58	56
2	Huddersfield	42	17	17	8	76	60	51
3	Sunderland	42	21	7	14	98	70	49
4	Bolton	42	19	10	13	84	62	48
5	Burnley	42	19	9	14	91	80	47
6	West Ham	42	19	8	15	86	70	46
7	Leicester	42	17	12	13	85	70	46
8	Sheff United	42	17	10	15	74	86	44
9	Liverpool	42	18	7	17	69	61	43
10	Aston Villa	42	18	7	17	81	83	43
11	Arsenal	42	17	9	16	77	86	43
12	Derby	42	17	7	18	86	73	41
13	Tottenham	42	16	9	17	76	78	41
14	Cardiff	42	16	9	17	55	65	41
15	Man United	42	13	14	15	52	64	40
16	Wednesday	42	15	9	18	75	92	39
17	Birmingham	42	17	4	21	64	73	38
18	Blackburn	42	15	8	19	77	96	38
19	Bury	42	12	12	18	68	77	36
20	Everton	42	12	10	20	64	90	34
21	Leeds	42	11	8	23	69	88	30
22	WBA	42	11	8	23	65	86	30

SECOND DIVISION

		P	W	D	L	F	A	Pts
1	Middlesbrough	42	27	8	7	122	60	62
2	Portsmouth	42	23	8	11	87	49	54
3	Man City	42	22	10	10	108	61	54
4	Chelsea	42	20	12	10	62	52	52
5	Nottm Forest	42	18	14	10	80	55	50
6	Preston	42	20	9	13	63	52	49
7	Hull	42	20	7	15	63	52	47
8	Port Vale	42	16	13	13	88	78	45
9	Blackpool	42	18	8	16	95	80	44
10	Oldham	42	19	6	17	74	84	44
11	Barnsley	42	17	9	16	88	87	43
12	Swansea	42	16	11	15	68	72	43
13	Southampton	42	15	12	15	60	62	42
14	Reading	42	16	8	18	64	72	40
15	Wolves	42	14	7	21	73	75	35
16	Notts County	42	15	5	22	70	96	35
17	Grimsby	42	11	12	19	74	91	34
18	Fulham	42	13	8	21	58	92	34
19	South Shields	42	11	11	20	71	96	33
20	Clapton Orient	42	12	7	23	60	96	31
21	Darlington	42	12	6	24	79	98	30
22	Bradford City	42	7	9	26	50	88	23

FA CUP 1926-27

FOURTH ROUND

Chelsea v Accrington Stanley	7-2
Fulham v Burnley	0-4
Leeds United v Bolton Wanderers	0-0, 0-3
Darlington v Cardiff City	0-2
The Wednesday v South Shields	1-1, 0-1
Barnsley v Swansea Town	1-3
Reading v Portsmouth	3-1
West Ham United v Brentford	1-1, 0-2
Port Vale v Arsenal	2-2, 0-1
Liverpool v Southport	3-1
Wolverhampton Wanderers v Nottingham Forest	2-0
Hull City v Everton	1-1, 2-2, 3-2
Derby County v Millwall	0-2
Preston North End v Middlesbrough	0-3
Southampton v Birmingham	4-1
Corinthians v Newcastle United	1-3

FIFTH ROUND

Chelsea v Burnley	2-1
Bolton Wanderers v Cardiff City	0-2
South Shields v Swansea Town	2-2, 1-2
Reading v Brentford	1-0
Arsenal v Liverpool	2-0
Wolverhampton Wanderers v Hull City	1-0
Millwall v Middlesbrough	3-2
Southampton v Newcastle United	2-1

SIXTH ROUND

Chelsea v Cardiff City	0-0, 2-3
Swansea Town v Reading	1-3
Arsenal v Wolverhampton Wanderers	2-1
Millwall v Southampton	0-0, 0-2

SEMI-FINAL

Cardiff City v Reading	3-0
Arsenal v Southampton	2-1

FINAL

Cardiff City v Arsenal	1-0

THIRD DIVISION (NORTH)

		P	W	D	L	F	A	Pts
1	Stoke	42	27	9	6	92	40	63
2	Rochdale	42	26	6	10	105	65	58
3	Bradford PA	42	24	7	11	101	59	55
4	Halifax	42	21	11	10	70	53	53
5	Nelson	42	22	7	13	104	75	51
6	Stockport	42	22	7	13	93	69	49*
7	Chesterfield	42	21	5	16	92	68	47
8	Doncaster	42	18	11	13	81	65	47
9	Tranmere	42	19	8	15	85	67	46
10	New Brighton	42	18	10	14	79	67	46
11	Lincoln	42	15	12	15	90	78	42
12	Southport	42	15	9	18	80	85	39
13	Wrexham	42	14	10	18	65	73	38
14	Walsall	42	14	10	18	68	81	38
15	Crewe	42	14	9	19	71	81	37
16	Ashington	42	12	12	18	60	90	36
17	Hartlepools	42	14	6	22	66	81	34
18	Wigan Borough	42	11	10	21	66	83	32
19	Rotherham	42	10	12	20	70	92	32
20	Durham City	42	12	6	24	58	105	30
21	Accrington	42	10	7	25	62	98	27
22	Barrow	42	7	8	27	34	117	22

*Two points deducted for fielding Joe Smith without FA permission on 26 March 1927.

THIRD DIVISION (SOUTH)

		P	W	D	L	F	A	Pts
1	Bristol City	42	27	8	7	104	54	62
2	Plymouth	42	25	10	7	95	61	60
3	Millwall	42	23	10	9	89	51	56
4	Brighton	42	21	11	10	79	50	53
5	Swindon	42	21	9	12	100	85	51
6	Crystal Palace	42	18	9	15	84	81	45
7	Bournemouth	42	18	8	16	78	66	44
8	Luton	42	15	14	13	68	66	44
9	Newport	42	19	6	17	57	71	44
10	Bristol Rovers	42	16	9	17	78	80	41
11	Brentford	42	13	14	15	70	61	40
12	Exeter	42	15	10	17	76	73	40
13	Charlton	42	16	8	18	60	61	40
14	QPR	42	15	9	18	65	71	39
15	Coventry	42	15	7	20	71	86	37
16	Norwich	42	12	11	19	59	71	35
17	Merthyr Town	42	13	9	20	63	80	35
18	Northampton	42	15	5	22	59	83	35
19	Southend	42	14	6	22	64	77	34
20	Gillingham	42	11	10	21	54	72	32
21	Watford	42	12	8	22	57	87	32
22	Aberdare Ath	42	9	7	26	62	101	25

SCOTTISH FA CUP 1926-27

SECOND ROUND

Buckie Thistle v Beith	2-0
Bo'ness v Cowdenbeath	2-1
Kilmarnock v Dundee	1-1, 1-5
Brechin City v Celtic	3-6
Falkirk v Queen's Park	6-3
Mid-Annandale v Forfar Athletic	3-0
Rangers v St Mirren	6-0
Hamilton Academicals v Clydebank	5-1
Alloa Athletic v Dumbarton	1-1, 4-0
St Bernard's v Arthurlie	0-3
East Fife v Aberdeen	1-1, 2-1
Dunfermline Athletic v Airdrieonians	2-1
Elgin City v Clyde	2-4
Partick Thistle v King's Park	4-2
Dundee United v Vale of Leven	4-1
Broxburn United v Montrose	2-2, 0-1

THIRD ROUND

Buckie Thistle v Bo'ness	0-3
Dundee v Celtic	2-4
Falkirk v Mid-Annandale	3-0
Rangers v Hamilton Academicals	4-0
Alloa Athletic v Arthurlie	0-0, 0-3
East Fife v Dunfermline Athletic	2-0
Clyde v Partick Thistle	0-1
Dundee United v Montrose	2-2, 3-1

FOURTH ROUND

Bo'ness v Celtic	2-5
Falkirk v Rangers	2-2, 1-0
Arthurlie v East Fife	0-3
Partick Thistle v Dundee United	5-0

SEMI-FINAL

Celtic v Falkirk	1-0
East Fife v Partick Thistle	2-1

FINAL

Celtic v East Fife	3-1

SCOTTISH FIRST DIVISION

		P	W	D	L	F	A	Pts
1	Rangers	38	23	10	5	85	41	56
2	Motherwell	38	23	5	10	81	52	51
3	Celtic	38	21	7	10	101	55	49
4	Airdrieonians	38	18	9	11	97	64	45
5	Dundee	38	17	9	12	77	51	43
6	Falkirk	38	16	10	12	77	60	42
7	Cowdenbeath	38	18	6	14	74	60	42
8	Aberdeen	38	13	14	11	73	72	40
9	Hibernian	38	16	7	15	62	71	39
10	St Mirren	38	16	5	17	78	76	37
11	Partick	38	15	6	17	89	74	36
12	Queen's Park	38	15	6	17	74	84	36
13	Hearts	38	12	11	15	65	64	35
14	St Johnstone	38	13	9	16	55	69	35
15	Hamilton	38	13	9	16	60	85	35
16	Kilmarnock	38	12	8	18	54	71	32
17	Clyde	38	10	9	19	54	85	29
18	Dunfermline	38	10	8	20	53	85	28
19	Morton	38	12	4	22	56	101	28
20	Dundee United	38	7	8	23	56	101	22

SCOTTISH SECOND DIVISION

		P	W	D	L	F	A	Pts
1	Bo'ness	38	23	10	5	86	41	56
2	Raith	38	21	7	10	92	52	49
3	Clydebank	38	18	9	11	94	75	45
4	Third Lanark	38	17	10	11	67	48	44
5	E Stirlingshire	38	18	8	12	93	75	44
6	East Fife	38	19	4	15	103	91	42
7	Arthurlie	38	18	5	15	90	83	41
8	Ayr	38	13	15	10	67	68	41
9	Forfar	38	15	7	16	66	79	37
10	Stenhousemuir	38	12	12	14	69	75	36
11	Queen of the S	38	16	4	18	72	80	36
12	King's Park	38	13	9	16	76	75	35
13	St Bernard's	38	14	6	18	70	77	34
14	Armadale	38	12	10	16	69	78	34
15	Alloa	38	11	11	16	70	78	33
16	Albion	38	11	11	16	74	87	33
17	Bathgate	38	13	7	18	76	98	33
18	Dumbarton	38	13	6	19	69	84	32
19	Arbroath	38	13	6	19	64	82	32
20	Nithsdale	38	7	9	22	59	100	23

Middlesbrough's George Camsell established an individual scoring record with his 59 Second Division goals in 1926-27. William Dean beat it by just one the following season, 1927-28. Camsell also established a record for the number of League hat-tricks in a season with his nine in 1926-27.

The highest number of goals scored by a recognized half-back in a League match is three. T McDonald of Newcastle grabbed a hat-trick against Cardiff on Christmas Day 1926.

FIRST DIVISION

		P	W	D	L	F	A	Pts
1	Everton	42	20	13	9	102	66	53
2	Huddersfield	42	22	7	13	91	68	51
3	Leicester	42	18	12	12	96	72	48
4	Derby	42	17	10	15	96	83	44
5	Bury	42	20	4	18	80	80	44
6	Cardiff	42	17	10	15	70	80	44
7	Bolton	42	16	11	15	81	66	43
8	Aston Villa	42	17	9	16	78	73	43
9	Newcastle	42	15	13	14	79	81	43
10	Arsenal	42	13	15	14	82	86	41
11	Birmingham	42	13	15	14	70	75	41
12	Blackburn	42	16	9	17	66	78	41
13	Sheff United	42	15	10	17	79	86	40
14	Wednesday	42	13	13	16	81	78	39
15	Sunderland	42	15	9	18	74	76	39
16	Liverpool	42	13	13	16	84	87	39
17	West Ham	42	14	11	17	81	88	39
18	Man United	42	16	7	19	72	87	39
19	Burnley	42	16	7	19	82	98	39
20	Portsmouth	42	16	7	19	66	90	39
21	Tottenham	42	15	8	19	74	86	38
22	Middlesbrough	42	11	15	16	81	88	37

SECOND DIVISION

		P	W	D	L	F	A	Pts
1	Man City	42	25	9	8	100	59	59
2	Leeds	42	25	7	10	98	49	57
3	Chelsea	42	23	8	11	75	45	54
4	Preston	42	22	9	11	100	66	53
5	Stoke	42	22	8	12	78	59	52
6	Swansea	42	18	12	12	75	63	48
7	Oldham	42	19	8	15	75	51	46
8	WBA	42	17	12	13	90	70	46
9	Port Vale	42	18	8	16	68	57	44
10	Nottm Forest	42	15	10	17	83	84	40
11	Grimsby	42	14	12	16	69	83	40
12	Bristol City	42	15	9	18	76	79	39
13	Hull	42	12	15	15	41	54	39
14	Barnsley	42	14	11	17	65	85	39
15	Notts County	42	13	12	17	68	74	38
16	Wolves	42	13	10	19	63	91	36
17	Southampton	42	14	7	21	68	77	35
18	Reading	42	11	13	18	53	75	35
19	Blackpool	42	13	8	21	83	101	34
20	Clapton Orient	42	11	12	19	55	85	34
21	Fulham	42	13	7	22	68	89	33
22	South Shields	42	7	9	26	56	111	23

THIRD DIVISION (SOUTH)

		P	W	D	L	F	A	Pts
1	Millwall	42	30	5	7	127	50	65
2	Northampton	42	23	9	10	102	64	55
3	Plymouth	42	23	7	12	85	54	53
4	Brighton	42	19	10	13	81	69	48
5	Crystal Palace	42	18	12	12	79	72	48
6	Swindon	42	19	9	14	90	69	47
7	Southend	42	20	6	16	80	64	46
8	Exeter	42	17	12	13	70	60	46
9	Newport	42	18	9	15	81	84	45
10	QPR	42	17	9	16	72	71	43
11	Charlton	42	15	13	14	60	70	43
12	Brentford	42	16	8	18	76	74	40
13	Luton	42	16	7	19	94	87	39
14	Bournemouth	42	13	12	17	72	79	38
15	Watford	42	14	10	18	68	78	38
16	Gillingham	42	13	11	18	62	81	37
17	Norwich	42	10	16	16	66	70	36
18	Walsall	42	12	9	21	75	101	33
19	Bristol Rovers	42	14	4	24	67	93	32
20	Coventry	42	11	9	22	67	96	31
21	Merthyr Town	42	9	13	20	53	91	31
22	Torquay	42	8	14	20	53	103	30

THIRD DIVISION (NORTH)

		P	W	D	L	F	A	Pts
1	Bradford PA	42	27	9	6	101	45	63
2	Lincoln	42	24	7	11	91	66	55
3	Stockport	42	23	8	11	89	51	54
4	Doncaster	42	23	7	12	80	44	53
5	Tranmere	42	22	9	11	105	72	53
6	Bradford City	42	18	12	12	85	60	48
7	Darlington	42	21	5	16	89	74	47
8	Southport	42	20	5	17	79	70	45
9	Accrington	42	18	8	16	76	67	44
10	New Brighton	42	14	14	14	72	62	42
11	Wrexham	42	18	6	18	64	67	42
12	Halifax	42	13	15	14	73	71	41
13	Rochdale	42	17	7	18	74	77	41
14	Rotherham	42	14	11	17	65	69	39
15	Hartlepools	42	16	6	20	69	81	38
16	Chesterfield	42	13	10	19	71	78	36
17	Crewe	42	12	10	20	77	86	34
18	Ashington	42	11	11	20	77	103	33
19	Barrow	42	10	11	21	54	102	31
20	Wigan Borough	42	10	10	22	56	97	30
21	Durham City	42	11	7	24	53	100	29
22	Nelson	42	10	6	26	76	136	26

SCOTTISH FIRST DIVISION

		P	W	D	L	F	A	Pts
1	Rangers	38	26	8	4	109	36	60
2	Celtic	38	23	9	6	93	39	55
3	Motherwell	38	23	9	6	92	46	55
4	Hearts	38	20	7	11	89	50	47
5	Aberdeen	38	20	5	13	71	61	45
6	St Mirren	38	18	8	12	77	76	44
7	Partick	38	18	7	13	85	67	43
8	Kilmarnock	38	15	10	13	68	78	40
9	Cowdenbeath	38	16	7	15	66	68	39
10	Falkirk	38	16	5	17	76	69	37
11	St Johnstone	38	14	8	16	66	67	36
12	Hibernian	38	13	9	16	73	75	35
13	Airdrieonians	38	12	11	15	59	69	35
14	Dundee	38	14	7	17	65	80	35
15	Clyde	38	10	11	17	46	72	31
16	Queen's Park	38	12	6	20	69	80	30
17	Raith	38	11	7	20	60	89	29
18	Hamilton	38	11	6	21	67	86	28
19	Bo'ness	38	9	8	21	48	86	26
20	Dunfermline	38	4	4	30	41	126	12

SCOTTISH SECOND DIVISION

		P	W	D	L	F	A	Pts
1	Ayr	38	24	6	8	117	60	54
2	Third Lanark	38	18	9	11	99	66	45
3	King's Park	38	16	12	10	84	68	44
4	East Fife	38	18	7	13	87	73	43
5	Forfar	38	18	7	13	83	73	43
6	Dundee United	38	17	9	12	81	73	43
7	Arthurlie	38	18	4	16	84	90	40
8	Albion	38	17	4	17	79	69	38
9	E Stirlingshire	38	14	10	14	84	76	38
10	Arbroath	38	16	4	18	84	86	36
11	Dumbarton	38	16	4	18	66	72	36
12	Queen of the S	38	15	6	17	92	106	36
13	Leith	38	13	9	16	76	71	35
14	Clydebank	38	16	3	19	78	80	35
15	Alloa	38	12	11	15	72	76	35
16	Stenhousemuir	38	15	5	18	75	81	35
17	St Bernard's	38	15	5	18	75	101	35
18	Morton	38	13	8	17	65	82	34
19	Bathgate	38	10	11	17	62	81	31
20	Armadale	38	8	8	22	53	112	24

On 3 March 1928 Ronnie Dix became the youngest person to score in the League. Dix, aged 15 years and 180 days, scored for Bristol Rovers against Norwich in a Division Three South match. Dix had made his League debut just seven days earlier against Charlton.

Dixie Dean's 60 goals in 39 League games for Everton set a League scoring record.

1927-28 saw the keenest relegation struggle in the League's history. Of the last nine clubs in Division One, seven finished the season with 39 points, one had 38, and one 37. Spurs and Middlesbrough were demoted. Spurs' 38 points meant that they were relegated with the highest number of points ever secured by a club removed from either the First or Second Division.

FA CUP 1927-28

FOURTH ROUND

Exeter City v Blackburn Rovers	2-2, 1-3
Port Vale v New Brighton	3-0
Bury v Manchester United	1-1, 0-1
Wrexham v Birmingham	1-3
Arsenal v Everton	4-3
Aston Villa v Crewe Alexandra	3-0
Sunderland v Manchester City	1-2
Stoke City v Bolton Wanderers	4-2
Huddersfield Town v West Ham United	2-1
Southport v Middlesbrough	0-3
Reading v Leicester City	0-1
Tottenham Hotspur v Oldham Athletic	3-0
Sheffield United v Wolverhampton Wanderers	3-1
Swindon Town v The Wednesday	1-2
Derby County v Nottingham Forest	0-0, 0-2
Cardiff City v Liverpool	2-1

FIFTH ROUND

Blackburn Rovers v Port Vale	2-1
Manchester United v Birmingham	1-0
Arsenal v Aston Villa	4-1
Manchester City v Stoke City	0-1
Huddersfield Town v Middlesbrough	4-0
Leicester City v Tottenham Hotspur	0-3
The Wednesday v Sheffield United	1-1, 1-4
Nottingham Forest v Cardiff City	2-1

SIXTH ROUND

Blackburn Rovers v Manchester United	2-0
Arsenal v Stoke City	4-1
Huddersfield Town v Tottenham Hotspur	6-1
Sheffield United v Nottingham Forest	3-0

SEMI-FINAL

Blackburn Rovers v Arsenal	1-0
Huddersfield Town v Sheffield United	2-2, 0-0, 1-0

FINAL

Blackburn Rovers v Huddersfield Town	3-1

SCOTTISH FA CUP 1927-28

SECOND ROUND

Rangers v Cowdenbeath	4-2
Armadale v King's Park	2-4
Brechin City v Albion Rovers	1-4
Airdrieonians v Hamilton Academicals	2-1
Third Lanark v Hibernian	0-2
Ayr United v Falkirk	2-4
Dunfermline Athletic v Leith Amateurs	3-1
Dundee United v Dundee	3-3, 0-1
Keith v Celtic	1-6
Stenhousemuir v Alloa Athletic	1-2
Motherwell v Raith Rovers	2-2, 2-1
Heart of Midlothian v Forres Mechanics	7-0
Queen's Park v Morton	4-1
Forfar Athletic v Kilmarnock	1-2
Partick Thistle v Nithsdale Wanderers	4-0
St Mirren v Vale of Atholl	5-1

THIRD ROUND

Rangers v King's Park	3-1
Albion Rovers v Airdrieonians	3-1
Hibernian v Falkirk	0-0, 1-0
Dundee v Dunfermline Athletic	1-2
Celtic v Alloa Athletic	2-0
Heart of Midlothian v Motherwell	1-2
Kilmarnock v Queen's Park	4-4, 0-1
St Mirren v Partick Thistle	0-5

FOURTH ROUND

Albion Rovers v Rangers	0-1
Dunfermline Athletic v Hibernian	0-4
Motherwell v Celtic	0-2
Queen's Park v Partick Thistle	1-0

SEMI-FINAL

Rangers v Hibernian	3-0
Celtic v Queen's Park	2-1

FINAL

Rangers v Celtic	4-0

League Tables 1928-29

FIRST DIVISION

		P	W	D	L	F	A	Pts
1	Wednesday	42	21	10	11	86	62	52
2	Leicester	42	21	9	12	96	67	51
3	Aston Villa	42	23	4	15	98	81	50
4	Sunderland	42	20	7	15	93	75	47
5	Liverpool	42	17	12	13	90	64	46
6	Derby	42	18	10	14	86	71	46
7	Blackburn	42	17	11	14	72	63	45
8	Man City	42	18	9	15	95	86	45
9	Arsenal	42	16	13	13	77	72	45
10	Newcastle	42	19	6	17	70	72	44
11	Sheff United	42	15	11	16	86	85	41
12	Man United	42	14	13	15	66	76	41
13	Leeds	42	16	9	17	71	84	41
14	Bolton	42	14	12	16	73	80	40
15	Birmingham	42	15	10	17	68	77	40
16	Huddersfield	42	14	11	17	70	61	39
17	West Ham	42	15	9	18	86	96	39
18	Everton	42	17	4	21	63	75	38
19	Burnley	42	15	8	19	81	103	38
20	Portsmouth	42	15	6	21	56	80	36
21	Bury	42	12	7	23	62	99	31
22	Cardiff	42	8	13	21	43	59	29

SECOND DIVISION

		P	W	D	L	F	A	Pts
1	Middlesbrough	42	22	11	9	92	57	55
2	Grimsby	42	24	5	13	82	61	53
3	Bradford PA	42	22	4	16	88	70	48
4	Southampton	42	17	14	11	74	60	48
5	Notts County	42	19	9	14	78	65	47
6	Stoke	42	17	12	13	74	51	46
7	WBA	42	19	8	15	80	79	46
8	Blackpool	42	19	7	16	92	76	45
9	Chelsea	42	17	10	15	64	65	44
10	Tottenham	42	17	9	16	75	81	43
11	Nottm Forest	42	15	12	15	71	70	42
12	Hull	42	13	14	15	58	63	40
13	Preston	42	15	9	18	78	79	39
14	Millwall	42	16	7	19	71	86	39
15	Reading	42	15	9	18	63	86	39
16	Barnsley	42	16	6	20	69	66	38
17	Wolves	42	15	7	20	77	81	37
18	Oldham	42	16	5	21	54	75	37
19	Swansea	42	13	10	19	62	75	36
20	Bristol City	42	13	10	19	58	72	36
21	Port Vale	42	15	4	23	71	86	34
22	Clapton Orient	42	12	8	22	45	72	32

FA CUP 1928-29

FOURTH ROUND

Blackburn Rovers v Derby County	1-1, 3-0
Manchester United v Bury	0-1
Leicester City v Swansea Town	1-0
Liverpool v Bolton Wanderers	0-0, 2-5
West Bromwich Albion v Middlesbrough	1-0
Plymouth Argyle v Bradford Park Avenue	0-1
Huddersfield Town v Leeds United	3-0
Millwall v Crystal Palace	0-0, 3-5
Chelsea v Birmingham	1-0
Portsmouth v Bradford City	2-0
Bournemouth v Watford	6-4
West Ham United v Corinthians	3-0
Reading v The Wednesday	1-0
Aston Villa v Clapton Orient	0-0, 8-0
Burnley v Swindon Town	3-3, 2-3
Arsenal v Mansfield Town	2-0

FIFTH ROUND

Blackburn Rovers v Bury	1-0
Leicester City v Bolton Wanderers	1-2
West Bromwich Albion v Bradford Park Avenue	6-0
Huddersfield Town v Crystal Palace	5-2
Chelsea v Portsmouth	1-1, 0-1
Bournemouth v West Ham United	1-1, 1-3
Reading v Aston Villa	1-3
Swindon Town v Arsenal	0-0, 0-1

SIXTH ROUND

Blackburn Rovers v Bolton Wanderers	1-1, 1-2
West Bromwich Albion v Huddersfield Town	1-1, 1-2
Portsmouth v West Ham United	3-2
Aston Villa v Arsenal	1-0

SEMI-FINAL

Bolton Wanderers v Huddersfield Town	3-1
Portsmouth v Aston Villa	1-0

FINAL

Bolton Wanderers v Portsmouth	2-0

THIRD DIVISION (SOUTH)

		P	W	D	L	F	A	Pts
1	Charlton	42	23	8	11	86	60	54
2	Crystal Palace	42	23	8	11	81	67	54
3	Northampton	42	20	12	10	96	57	52
4	Plymouth	42	20	12	10	83	51	52
5	Fulham	42	21	10	11	101	71	52
6	QPR	42	19	14	9	82	61	52
7	Luton	42	19	11	12	89	73	49
8	Watford	42	19	10	13	79	74	48
9	Bournemouth	42	19	9	14	84	77	47
10	Swindon	42	15	13	14	75	72	43
11	Coventry	42	14	14	14	62	57	42
12	Southend	42	15	11	16	80	75	41
13	Brentford	42	14	10	18	56	60	38
14	Walsall	42	13	12	17	73	79	38
15	Brighton	42	16	6	20	58	76	38
16	Newport	42	13	9	20	69	86	35
17	Norwich	42	14	6	22	69	81	34
18	Torquay	42	14	6	22	66	84	34
19	Bristol Rovers	42	13	7	22	60	79	33
20	Merthyr Town	42	11	8	23	55	103	30
21	Exeter	42	9	11	22	67	88	29
22	Gillingham	42	10	9	23	43	83	29

THIRD DIVISION (NORTH)

		P	W	D	L	F	A	Pts
1	Bradford City	42	27	9	6	128	43	63
2	Stockport	42	28	6	8	111	58	62
3	Wrexham	42	21	10	11	91	69	52
4	Wigan Borough	42	21	9	12	82	49	51
5	Doncaster	42	20	10	12	76	66	50
6	Lincoln	42	21	6	15	91	67	48
7	Tranmere	42	22	3	17	79	77	47
8	Carlisle	42	19	8	15	86	77	46
9	Crewe	42	18	8	16	80	68	44
10	South Shields	42	18	8	16	83	74	44
11	Chesterfield	42	18	5	19	71	77	41
12	Southport	42	16	8	18	75	85	40
13	Halifax	42	13	13	16	63	62	39
14	New Brighton	42	15	9	18	64	71	39
15	Nelson	42	17	5	20	77	90	39
16	Rotherham	42	15	9	18	60	77	39
17	Rochdale	42	13	10	19	79	96	36
18	Accrington	42	13	8	21	68	82	34
19	Darlington	42	13	7	22	64	88	33
20	Barrow	42	10	8	24	64	93	28
21	Hartlepools	42	10	6	26	59	112	26
22	Ashington	42	8	7	27	45	115	23

SCOTTISH FA CUP 1928-29

SECOND ROUND

Celtic v East Stirlingshire	3-0
Murrayfield Amateurs v Arbroath	1-1, 2-5
Cowdenbeath v Airdrieonians	0-0, 2-3
St Johnstone v Motherwell	2-3
Bathgate v Raith Rovers	1-1, 2-5
Fraserburgh v Dumbarton	0-3
Albion Rovers v Clackmannan	8-1
Kilmarnock v Bo'ness	3-2
Rangers v Partick Thistle	5-1
Clyde v Hamilton Academicals	1-1, 2-1
Dundee v Brechin City	6-1
Stenhousemuir v Dundee United	1-1, 0-2
Aberdeen v Queen's Park	4-0
Queen of the South v Falkirk	1-2
Ayr United v Armadale	5-1
Third Lanark v St Mirren	0-1

THIRD ROUND

Celtic v Arbroath	4-1
Airdrieonians v Motherwell	1-1, 1-3
Raith Rovers v Dumbarton	3-2
Albion Rovers v Kilmarnock	0-1
Clyde v Rangers	0-2
Dundee v Dundee United	1-1, 0-1
Falkirk v Aberdeen	3-5
Ayr United v St Mirren	0-2

FOURTH ROUND

Celtic v Motherwell	0-0, 2-1
Raith Rovers v Kilmarnock	2-3
Rangers v Dundee United	3-1
St Mirren v Aberdeen	4-3

SEMI-FINAL

Celtic v Kilmarnock	0-1
Rangers v St Mirren	3-2

FINAL

Kilmarnock v Rangers	2-0

SCOTTISH FIRST DIVISION

		P	W	D	L	F	A	Pts
1	Rangers	38	30	7	1	107	32	67
2	Celtic	38	22	7	9	67	44	51
3	Motherwell	38	20	10	8	85	66	50
4	Hearts	38	19	9	10	91	57	47
5	Queen's Park	38	18	7	13	100	69	43
6	Partick Thistle	38	17	7	14	91	70	41
7	Aberdeen	38	16	8	14	81	68	40
8	St Mirren	38	16	8	14	78	74	40
9	St Johnstone	38	14	10	14	57	70	38
10	Kilmarnock	38	14	8	16	79	74	36
11	Falkirk	38	14	8	16	68	86	36
12	Hamilton	38	13	9	16	58	83	35
13	Cowdenbeath	38	14	5	19	55	69	33
14	Hibernian	38	13	6	19	54	62	32
15	Airdrieonians	38	12	7	19	56	65	31
16	Ayr	38	12	7	19	65	84	31
17	Clyde	38	12	6	20	47	71	30
18	Dundee	38	9	11	18	58	59	29
19	Third Lanark	38	10	6	22	71	102	26
20	Raith	38	9	6	23	52	105	24

SCOTTISH SECOND DIVISION

		P	W	D	L	F	A	Pts
1	Dundee United	36	24	3	9	99	55	51
2	Morton	36	21	8	7	85	49	50
3	Arbroath	36	19	9	8	90	60	47
4	Albion	36	18	8	10	95	67	44
5	Leith	36	18	7	11	78	56	43
6	St Bernard's	36	16	9	11	77	55	41
7	Forfar	35	14	10	11	69	75	38
8	East Fife	35	15	6	14	88	77	36
9	Queen of the S	36	16	4	16	86	79	36
10	Bo'ness	35	15	5	15	62	62	35
11	Dunfermline	36	13	7	16	66	72	33
12	E Stirlingshire	36	14	4	18	71	75	32
13	Alloa	36	12	7	17	64	77	31
14	Dumbarton	36	11	9	16	59	78	31
15	King's Park	36	8	13	15	60	84	29
16	Clydebank	36	11	5	20	70	86	27
17	Arthurlie *	32	9	7	16	51	73	25
18	Stenhousemuir	35	9	6	20	52	90	24
19	Armadale	36	8	7	21	47	99	23

*Arthurlie resigned towards the end of the season—but their record was allowed to stand.

The worst kind of record

During the 1928-29 season, Rotherham United became only the second side to have had at least 10 goals scored against them in more than one Football League game in the same season. Rotherham, of Division Three North, first lost 11-1 at Bradford City on 25 August 1928, and then 10-1 away to South Shields on 16 March 1929.

The Scottish team in the Football League

In the First Division, the record for fielding a side containing the most Scotsmen belongs to Newcastle United. In the Newcastle side that faced Leeds United on 6 October 1928, only Wood, the centre-half, came from outside Scotland. In 1955-56 Accrington went one better by fielding a team of 11 Scots in several Third Division North fixtures.

FIRST DIVISION

		P	W	D	L	F	A	Pts
1	Sheff Wed	42	26	8	8	105	57	60
2	Derby	42	21	8	13	90	82	50
3	Man City	42	19	9	14	91	81	47
4	Aston Villa	42	21	5	16	92	83	47
5	Leeds	42	20	6	16	79	63	46
6	Blackburn	42	19	7	16	99	93	45
7	West Ham	42	19	5	18	86	79	43
8	Leicester	42	17	9	16	86	90	43
9	Sunderland	42	18	7	17	76	80	43
10	Huddersfield	42	17	9	16	63	69	43
11	Birmingham	42	16	9	17	67	62	41
12	Liverpool	42	16	9	17	63	79	41
13	Portsmouth	42	15	19	17	66	62	40
14	Arsenal	42	14	11	17	78	66	39
15	Bolton	45	15	9	18	74	74	39
16	Middlesbrough	42	16	6	20	82	84	38
17	Man United	42	15	8	19	67	88	38
18	Grimsby	42	15	7	20	73	89	37
19	Newcastle	42	15	7	20	71	92	37
20	Sheff United	42	15	6	21	91	96	36
21	Burnley	42	14	8	20	79	97	36
22	Everton	42	12	11	19	80	92	35

SECOND DIVISION

		P	W	D	L	F	A	Pts
1	Blackpool	42	27	4	11	98	67	58
2	Chelsea	42	22	11	9	74	46	55
3	Oldham	42	21	11	10	90	51	53
4	Bradford PA	42	19	12	11	91	70	50
5	Bury	42	22	5	15	78	67	49
6	WBA	42	21	5	16	105	73	47
7	Southampton	42	17	11	14	77	76	45
8	Cardiff	42	18	8	16	61	59	44
9	Wolves	42	16	9	17	77	79	41
10	Nottm Forest	42	13	15	14	55	69	41
11	Stoke	42	16	8	18	74	72	40
12	Tottenham	42	15	9	18	59	61	39
13	Charlton	42	14	11	17	59	63	39
14	Millwall	42	12	15	15	57	73	39
15	Swansea	42	14	9	19	57	61	37
16	Preston	42	13	11	18	65	80	37
17	Barnsley	42	14	8	20	56	71	36
18	Bradford City	42	12	12	18	60	77	36
19	Reading	42	12	11	19	54	67	35
20	Bristol City	42	13	9	20	61	83	35
21	Hull	42	14	7	21	51	78	35
22	Notts County	42	9	15	18	54	70	33

THIRD DIVISION (SOUTH)

		P	W	D	L	F	A	Pts
1	Plymouth	42	30	8	4	98	38	68
2	Brentford	42	28	5	9	94	44	61
3	QPR	42	21	9	12	80	68	51
4	Northampton	42	21	8	13	82	58	50
5	Brighton	42	21	8	13	87	63	50
6	Coventry	42	19	9	14	88	73	47
7	Fulham	42	18	11	13	87	83	47
8	Norwich	42	18	10	14	88	77	46
9	Crystal Palace	42	17	12	13	81	74	46
10	Bournemouth	42	15	13	14	72	61	43
11	Southend	42	15	13	14	69	59	43
12	Clapton Orient	42	14	13	15	55	62	41
13	Luton	42	14	12	16	64	78	40
14	Swindon	42	13	12	17	73	83	38
15	Watford	42	15	8	19	60	73	38
16	Exeter	42	12	11	19	67	73	35
17	Walsall	42	13	8	21	71	78	34
18	Newport	42	12	10	20	74	85	34
19	Torquay	42	10	11	21	64	94	31
20	Bristol Rovers	42	11	8	23	67	93	30
21	Gillingham	42	11	8	23	51	80	30
22	Merthyr Town	42	6	9	27	60	135	21

THIRD DIVISION (NORTH)

		P	W	D	L	F	A	Pts
1	Port Vale	42	30	7	5	103	37	67
2	Stockport	42	28	7	7	106	44	63
3	Darlington	42	22	6	14	108	73	50
4	Chesterfield	42	22	6	14	76	56	50
5	Lincoln	42	17	14	11	83	61	48
6	York	42	15	16	11	77	64	46
7	South Shields	42	18	10	14	77	74	46
8	Hartlepools	42	17	11	14	81	74	45
9	Southport	42	15	13	14	81	74	43
10	Rochdale	42	18	7	17	89	91	43
11	Crewe	42	17	8	17	82	71	42
12	Tranmere	42	16	9	17	83	86	41
13	New Brighton	42	16	8	18	69	79	40
14	Doncaster	42	15	9	18	62	69	39
15	Carlisle	42	16	7	19	90	101	39
16	Accrington	42	14	9	19	84	81	37
17	Wrexham	42	13	8	21	67	88	34
18	Wigan Borough	42	13	7	22	60	88	33
19	Nelson	42	13	7	22	51	80	33
20	Rotherham	42	11	8	23	67	113	30
21	Halifax	42	10	8	24	44	79	28
22	Barrow	42	11	5	26	41	98	27

SCOTTISH FIRST DIVISION

		P	W	D	L	F	A	Pts
1	Rangers	38	28	4	6	94	32	60
2	Motherwell	38	25	5	8	104	48	55
3	Aberdeen	38	23	7	8	85	61	53
4	Celtic	38	22	5	11	88	46	49
5	St Mirren	38	18	5	15	73	56	41
6	Partick	38	16	9	13	72	61	41
7	Falkirk	38	16	9	13	62	64	41
8	Kilmarnock	38	15	9	14	77	73	39
9	Ayr	38	16	6	16	70	92	38
10	Hearts	38	14	9	15	69	69	37
11	Clyde	38	13	11	14	64	69	37
12	Airdrieonians	38	16	4	18	60	66	36
13	Hamilton	38	14	7	17	76	81	35
14	Dundee	38	14	6	18	51	58	34
15	Queen's Park	38	15	4	19	67	80	34
16	Cowdenbeath	38	13	7	18	64	74	33
17	Hibernian	38	9	11	18	45	62	29
18	Morton	38	10	7	21	67	95	27
19	Dundee United	38	7	8	23	56	109	22
20	St Johnstone	38	6	7	25	48	96	19

SCOTTISH SECOND DIVISION

		P	W	D	L	F	A	Pts
1	Leith Athletic	38	23	11	4	92	42	57
2	East Fife	38	26	5	7	114	58	57
3	Albion	38	24	6	8	101	60	54
4	Third Lanark	38	23	6	9	92	53	52
5	Raith	38	18	8	12	94	67	44
6	King's Park	38	17	8	13	109	80	42
7	Queen of the S	38	18	6	14	65	63	42
8	Forfar	38	18	5	15	98	95	41
9	Arbroath	38	16	7	15	83	87	39
10	Dunfermline	38	16	6	16	99	85	38
11	Montrose	38	14	10	14	79	87	38
12	E Stirlingshire	38	16	4	18	83	75	36
13	Bo'ness	38	15	4	19	67	95	34
14	St Bernard's	38	13	6	19	65	65	32
15	Armadale	38	13	5	20	56	91	31
16	Dumbarton	38	14	2	22	77	95	30
17	Stenhousemuir	38	11	5	22	75	108	27
18	Clydebank	38	7	10	21	66	92	24
19	Alloa	38	9	6	23	55	104	24
20	Brechin	38	7	4	27	57	125	18

FA CUP 1929-30

FOURTH ROUND

West Ham United v Leeds United	4-1
Millwall v Doncaster Rovers	4-0
Arsenal v Birmingham	2-2, 1-0
Middlesbrough v Charlton Athletic	1-1, 1-1, 1-0
Hull City v Blackpool	3-1
Swindon Town v Manchester City	1-1, 1-10
Newcastle United v Clapton Orient	3-1
Portsmouth v Brighton	0-1
Aston Villa v Walsall	3-1
Blackburn Rovers v Everton	4-1
Huddersfield Town v Sheffield United	2-1
Wrexham v Bradford City	0-0, 1-2
Nottingham Forest v Fulham	2-1
Sunderland v Cardiff City	2-1
Oldham Athletic v Sheffield Wednesday	3-4
Derby County v Bradford Park Avenue	1-1, 1-2

FIFTH ROUND

West Ham United v Millwall	4-1
Middlesbrough v Arsenal	0-2
Manchester City v Hull City	1-2
Newcastle United v Brighton	3-0
Aston Villa v Blackburn Rovers	4-1
Huddersfield Town v Bradford City	2-1
Sunderland v Nottingham Forest	2-2, 1-3
Sheffield Wednesday v Bradford Park Avenue	5-1

SIXTH ROUND

West Ham United v Arsenal	0-3
Newcastle United v Hull City	1-1, 0-1
Aston Villa v Huddersfield Town	1-2
Nottingham Forest v Sheffield Wednesday	2-2, 1-3

SEMI-FINAL

Arsenal v Hull City	2-2, 1-0
Huddersfield Town v Sheffield Wednesday	2-1

FINAL

Arsenal v Huddersfield Town	2-0

SCOTTISH FA CUP 1929-30

SECOND ROUND

Rangers v Cowdenbeath	2-2, 3-0
Motherwell v Clyde	3-0
Montrose v Citadel	3-1
Albion Rovers v Beith	2-1
Dundee v St Johnstone	4-1
Airdrieonians v Murrayfield Amateurs	8-3
Heart of Midlothian v St Bernard's	0-0, 5-1
Ayr United v Hibernian	1-3
Forfar Athletic v St Mirren	0-0, 0-3
Celtic v Arbroath	5-0
Hamilton Academicals v Kilmarnock	4-2
Vale of Leithen v King's Park	2-7
Falkirk v Queen of the South	1-1, 4-3
Leith Athletic v Clachnacuddin	2-0
Dundee United v Partick Thistle	0-3
Aberdeen v Nithsdale Wanderers	5-1

THIRD ROUND

Motherwell v Rangers	2-5
Albion Rovers v Montrose	2-2, 1-3
Dundee v Airdrieonians	0-0, 0-0, 1-0
Hibernian v Heart of Midlothian	1-3
Celtic v St Mirren	1-3
Hamilton Academicals v King's Park	4-0
Falkirk v Leith Athletic	0-0, 1-1, 1-1, 1-0
Partick Thistle v Aberdeen	3-2

FOURTH ROUND

Rangers v Montrose	3-0
Dundee v Heart of Midlothian	2-2, 0-4
St Mirren v Hamilton Academicals	3-4
Partick Thistle v Falkirk	3-1

SEMI-FINAL

Rangers v Heart of Midlothian	4-1
Partick Thistle v Hamilton Academicals	3-1

FINAL

Rangers v Partick Thistle	0-0, 2-1

Jim Barrett of West Ham United made his international debut for England against Northern Ireland on 19 October 1929. After only eight minutes he was injured and carried off, and as he never played for England again, his became the shortest international career on record.

Sheffield Wednesday won the League Championship for the second successive season.

Albert Geldard of Bradford Park Avenue became the youngest footballer to play in the League when, aged 15 years and 156 days, he played against Millwall in a Division Two match on 16 September 1929.

Joe Bambrick's six goals in Northern Ireland's 7-0 win over Wales in February 1930 made him the highest individual scorer in an international match between Home Countries.

FIRST DIVISION

	P	W	D	L	F	A	Pts
1 Arsenal	42	28	10	4	127	59	66
2 Aston Villa	42	25	9	8	128	78	59
3 Sheff Wed	42	22	8	12	102	75	52
4 Portsmouth	42	18	13	11	84	67	49
5 Huddersfield	42	18	12	12	81	65	48
6 Derby	42	18	10	14	94	79	46
7 Middlesbrough	42	19	8	15	98	90	46
8 Man City	42	18	10	14	75	70	46
9 Liverpool	42	15	12	15	86	85	42
10 Blackburn	42	17	8	17	83	84	42
11 Sunderland	42	16	9	17	89	85	41
12 Chelsea	42	15	10	17	64	67	40
13 Grimsby	42	17	5	20	82	87	39
14 Bolton	42	15	9	18	68	81	39
15 Sheff United	42	14	10	18	78	84	38
16 Leicester	42	16	6	20	80	95	38
17 Newcastle	42	15	6	21	78	87	36
18 West Ham	42	14	8	20	79	94	36
19 Birmingham	42	13	10	19	55	70	36
20 Blackpool	42	11	10	21	71	125	32
21 Leeds	42	12	7	23	68	81	31
22 Man United	42	7	8	27	53	115	22

SECOND DIVISION

	P	W	D	L	F	A	Pts
1 Everton	42	28	5	9	121	66	61
2 WBA	42	22	10	10	83	49	54
3 Tottenham	42	22	7	13	88	55	51
4 Wolves	42	21	5	16	84	67	47
5 Port Vale	42	21	5	16	67	61	47
6 Bradford PA	42	18	10	14	97	66	46
7 Preston	42	17	11	14	83	64	45
8 Burnley	42	17	11	14	81	77	45
9 Southampton	42	19	6	17	74	62	44
10 Bradford City	42	17	10	15	61	63	44
11 Stoke	42	17	10	15	64	71	44
12 Oldham	42	16	10	16	61	72	42
13 Bury	42	19	3	20	75	82	41
14 Millwall	42	16	7	19	71	80	39
15 Charlton	42	15	9	18	59	86	39
16 Bristol City	42	15	8	19	54	82	38
17 Nottm Forest	42	14	9	19	80	85	37
18 Plymouth	42	14	8	20	76	84	36
19 Barnsley	42	13	9	20	59	79	35
20 Swansea	42	12	10	20	51	74	34
21 Reading	42	12	6	24	72	96	30
22 Cardiff	42	8	9	25	47	87	25

FA CUP 1930-31

FOURTH ROUND

Birmingham v Port Vale	2-0
Watford v Brighton	2-0
Chelsea v Arsenal	2-1
Blackburn Rovers v Bristol Rovers	5-1
Bolton Wanderers v Sunderland	1-1, 1-3
Sheffield United v Notts County	4-1
Bury v Exeter City	1-2
Leeds United v Newcastle United	4-1
Crystal Palace v Everton	0-6
Grimsby Town v Manchester United	1-0
Southport v Blackpool	2-1
Bradford Park Avenue v Burnley	2-0
Brentford v Portsmouth	0-1
West Bromwich Albion v Tottenham Hotspur	1-0
Barnsley v Sheffield Wednesday	2-1
Bradford City v Wolverhampton Wanderers	0-0, 2-4

FIFTH ROUND

Birmingham v Watford	3-0
Chelsea v Blackburn Rovers	3-0
Sunderland v Sheffield United	2-1
Exeter City v Leeds United	3-1
Everton v Grimsby Town	5-3
Southport v Bradford Park Avenue	1-0
Portsmouth v West Bromwich Albion	0-1
Barnsley v Wolverhampton Wanderers	1-3

SIXTH ROUND

Birmingham v Chelsea	2-2, 3-0
Sunderland v Exeter City	1-1, 4-2
Everton v Southport	9-1
West Bromwich Albion v Wolverhampton Wanderers	1-1, 2-1

SEMI-FINAL

Birmingham v Sunderland	2-0
Everton v West Bromwich Albion	0-1

FINAL

West Bromwich Albion v Birmingham	2-1

THIRD DIVISION (SOUTH)

	P	W	D	L	F	A	Pts
1 Notts County	42	24	11	7	97	46	59
2 Crystal Palace	42	22	7	13	107	71	51
3 Brentford	42	22	6	14	90	64	50
4 Brighton	42	17	15	10	68	53	49
5 Southend	42	22	5	15	76	60	49
6 Northampton	42	18	12	12	77	59	48
7 Luton	42	19	8	15	76	51	46
8 QPR	42	20	3	19	82	75	43
9 Fulham	42	18	7	17	77	75	43
10 Bournemouth	42	15	13	14	72	73	43
11 Torquay	42	17	9	16	80	84	43
12 Swindon	42	18	6	18	89	94	42
13 Exeter	42	17	8	17	84	90	42
14 Coventry	42	16	9	17	75	65	41
15 Bristol Rovers	42	16	8	18	75	92	40
16 Gillingham	42	14	10	18	61	76	38
17 Walsall	42	14	9	19	78	95	37
18 Watford	42	14	7	21	72	75	35
19 Clapton Orient	42	14	7	21	63	91	35
20 Thames	42	13	8	21	54	93	34
21 Norwich	42	10	8	24	47	76	28
22 Newport	42	11	6	25	69	111	28

THIRD DIVISION (NORTH)

	P	W	D	L	F	A	Pts
1 Chesterfield	42	26	6	10	102	57	58
2 Lincoln	42	25	7	10	102	59	57
3 Tranmere	42	24	6	12	111	74	54
4 Wrexham	42	21	12	9	94	62	54
5 Southport	42	22	9	11	88	56	53
6 Hull	42	20	10	12	99	55	50
7 Stockport	42	20	9	13	77	61	49
8 Carlisle	42	20	5	17	98	81	45
9 Gateshead	42	16	13	13	71	73	45
10 Wigan Borough	42	19	5	18	76	86	43
11 Darlington	42	16	10	16	71	59	42
12 York	42	18	6	18	85	82	42
13 Accrington	42	15	9	18	84	108	39
14 Rotherham	42	13	12	17	81	83	38
15 Doncaster	42	13	11	18	65	65	37
16 Barrow	42	15	7	20	68	89	37
17 Halifax	42	13	9	20	55	89	35
18 Crewe	42	14	6	22	66	93	34
19 New Brighton	42	13	7	22	49	76	33
20 Hartlepools	42	12	6	24	67	86	30
21 Rochdale	42	12	6	24	62	107	30
22 Nelson	42	6	7	29	43	113	19

SCOTTISH FA CUP 1930-31

SECOND ROUND

Dundee United v Celtic	2-3
Queen's Park v Morton	0-1
Aberdeen v Partick Thistle	1-1, 3-0
Rangers v Dundee	1-2
Kilmarnock v Heart of Midlothian	3-2
Montrose v Civil Service Strollers	2-0
Bo'ness v Alloa Athletic	4-2
Murrayfield Amateurs v Ayr United	0-1
Motherwell v Albion Rovers	4-1
Hamilton Academicals v Hibernian	2-2, 2-5
Cowdenbeath v St Johnstone	1-1, 4-0
King's Park v St Bernard's	1-1, 0-1
St Mirren v Clyde	3-1
Inverness Caledonian v Falkirk	2-7
Third Lanark v Airdrieonians	1-0
Arbroath v Edinburgh City	1-0

THIRD ROUND

Morton v Celtic	1-4
Dundee v Aberdeen	1-1, 0-2
Montrose v Kilmarnock	0-3
Bo'ness v Ayr United	1-0
Hibernian v Motherwell	0-3
Cowdenbeath v St Bernard's	3-0
St Mirren v Falkirk	2-0
Third Lanark v Arbroath	4-2

FOURTH ROUND

Celtic v Aberdeen	4-0
Bo'ness v Kilmarnock	1-1, 0-5
Cowdenbeath v Motherwell	0-1
Third Lanark v St Mirren	1-1, 0-3

SEMI-FINAL

Celtic v Kilmarnock	3-0
Motherwell v St Mirren	1-0

FINAL

Celtic v Motherwell	2-2, 4-2

SCOTTISH FIRST DIVISION

	P	W	D	L	F	A	Pts
1 Rangers	38	27	6	5	96	29	60
2 Celtic	38	24	10	4	101	34	58
3 Motherwell	38	24	8	6	102	42	56
4 Partick	38	24	5	9	76	44	53
5 Hearts	38	19	6	13	90	63	44
6 Aberdeen	38	17	7	14	79	63	41
7 Cowdenbeath	38	17	7	14	58	65	41
8 Dundee	38	17	5	16	65	63	39
9 Airdrieonians	38	17	5	16	59	66	39
10 Hamilton	38	16	5	17	59	57	37
11 Kilmarnock	38	15	5	18	59	60	35
12 Clyde	38	15	4	19	60	87	34
13 Queen's Park	38	13	7	18	71	72	33
14 Falkirk	38	14	4	20	77	87	32
15 St Mirren	38	11	8	19	49	72	30
16 Morton	38	11	7	20	58	83	29
17 Leith	38	8	11	19	52	85	27
18 Ayr	38	8	11	19	53	92	27
19 Hibernian	38	9	7	22	49	81	25
20 East Fife	38	8	4	26	45	113	20

SCOTTISH SECOND DIVISION

	P	W	D	L	F	A	Pts
1 Third Lanark	38	27	7	4	107	42	61
2 Dundee United	38	21	8	9	93	54	50
3 Dunfermline	38	20	7	11	83	50	47
4 Raith	38	20	6	12	93	72	46
5 Queen of the S	38	18	6	14	83	66	42
6 St Johnstone	38	18	6	14	73	64	42
7 E Stirlingshire	38	17	7	14	85	74	41
8 Montrose	38	19	3	16	75	90	41
9 Albion	38	14	11	13	83	84	39
10 Dumbarton	38	15	8	15	73	72	38
11 St Bernard's	38	14	9	15	85	66	37
12 Forfar	38	15	6	17	78	83	36
13 Alloa	38	15	5	18	65	87	35
14 King's Park	38	14	6	18	78	70	34
15 Arbroath	38	15	4	19	83	94	34
16 Brechin	38	13	7	18	52	84	33
17 Stenhousemuir	38	13	6	19	78	98	32
18 Armadale	38	13	2	23	74	99	28
19 Clydebank	38	10	2	26	61	108	22
20 Bo'ness	38	9	4	25	54	100	22

The outstanding example of each member of a forward line scoring in a single game was when all five Everton forwards scored against Charlton Athletic at the Valley in an 18 minute spell. The Everton forwards were Stein, Dean, Dunn, Critchley and Johnson. The match, a Division Two League fixture played on 7 February 1931, ended as a convincing 7-0 victory for the Merseysiders, who went on to win the Division Two Championship.

The famous occasion when a referee was 'sent off' occurred in the annual Sheffield versus Glasgow match on 22 September 1930. Sheffield were playing in white shirts and black shorts, and the referee, Mr J Thomson of Burnbank, wore a white shirt without a jacket. When Sheffield's captain, Jimmy Seed, found that he was passing to the referee in error, he asked him to stop the game and put on a jacket. Mr Thomson obliged.

FIRST DIVISION

		P	W	D	L	F	A	Pts
1	Everton	42	26	4	12	116	64	56
2	Arsenal	42	22	10	10	90	48	54
3	Sheff Wed	42	22	6	14	96	82	50
4	Huddersfield	42	19	10	13	80	63	48
5	Aston Villa	42	19	8	15	104	72	46
6	WBA	42	20	6	16	77	55	46
7	Sheff United	42	20	6	16	80	75	46
8	Portsmouth	42	19	7	16	62	62	45
9	Birmingham	42	18	8	16	78	67	44
10	Liverpool	42	19	6	17	81	93	44
11	Newcastle	42	18	6	18	80	87	42
12	Chelsea	42	16	8	18	69	73	40
13	Sunderland	42	15	10	17	67	73	40
14	Man City	42	13	12	17	83	73	38
15	Derby	42	14	10	18	71	75	38
16	Blackburn	42	16	6	20	89	95	38
17	Bolton	42	17	4	21	72	80	38
18	Middlesbrough	42	15	8	19	64	89	38
19	Leicester	42	15	7	20	74	94	37
20	Blackpool	42	12	9	21	65	102	33
21	Grimsby	42	13	6	23	67	98	32
22	West Ham	42	12	7	23	62	107	31

SECOND DIVISION

		P	W	D	L	F	A	Pts
1	Wolves	42	24	8	10	115	49	56
2	Leeds	42	22	10	10	78	54	54
3	Stoke	42	19	14	9	69	48	52
4	Plymouth	42	20	9	13	100	66	49
5	Bury	42	21	7	14	70	58	49
6	Bradford PA	42	21	7	14	72	63	49
7	Bradford City	42	16	13	13	80	61	45
8	Tottenham	42	16	11	15	87	78	43
9	Millwall	42	17	9	16	61	61	43
10	Charlton	42	17	9	16	61	66	43
11	Nottm Forest	42	16	10	16	77	72	42
12	Man United	42	17	8	17	71	72	42
13	Preston	42	16	10	16	75	77	42
14	Southampton	42	17	7	18	66	77	41
15	Swansea	42	16	7	19	73	75	39
16	Notts County	42	13	12	17	75	75	38
17	Chesterfield	42	13	11	18	64	86	37
18	Oldham	42	13	10	19	62	84	36
19	Burnley	42	13	9	20	59	87	35
20	Port Vale	42	13	7	22	58	89	33
21	Barnsley	42	12	9	21	55	91	33
22	Bristol City	42	6	11	25	39	78	23

THIRD DIVISION (SOUTH)

		P	W	D	L	F	A	Pts
1	Fulham	42	24	9	9	111	62	57
2	Reading	42	23	9	10	97	67	55
3	Southend	42	21	11	10	77	53	53
4	Crystal Palace	42	20	11	11	74	63	51
5	Brentford	42	19	10	13	68	52	48
6	Luton	42	20	7	15	95	70	47
7	Exeter	42	20	7	15	77	62	47
8	Brighton	42	17	12	13	73	58	46
9	Cardiff	42	19	8	15	87	73	46
10	Norwich	42	17	12	13	76	67	46
11	Watford	42	19	8	15	81	79	46
12	Coventry	42	18	8	16	108	97	44
13	QPR	42	15	12	15	79	73	42
14	Northampton	42	16	7	19	69	69	39
15	Bournemouth	42	13	12	17	70	78	38
16	Clapton Orient	42	12	11	19	77	90	35
17	Swindon	42	14	6	22	70	84	34
18	Bristol Rovers	42	13	8	21	65	92	34
19	Torquay	42	12	9	21	72	106	33
20	Mansfield	42	11	10	21	75	108	32
21	Gillingham	42	10	8	24	40	82	28
22	Thames	42	7	9	26	53	109	23

THIRD DIVISION (NORTH)

		P	W	D	L	F	A	Pts
1	Lincoln	40	26	5	9	106	47	57
2	Gateshead	40	25	7	8	94	48	57
3	Chester	40	21	8	11	78	60	50
4	Tranmere	40	19	11	10	107	58	49
5	Barrow	40	24	1	15	86	59	49
6	Crewe	40	21	6	13	95	66	48
7	Southport	40	18	10	12	58	53	46
8	Hull	40	20	5	15	82	53	45
9	York	40	18	7	15	76	81	43
10	Wrexham	40	18	7	15	64	69	43
11	Darlington	40	17	4	19	66	69	38
12	Stockport	40	13	11	16	55	53	37
13	Hartlepools	40	16	5	19	78	100	37
14	Accrington	40	15	6	19	75	80	36
15	Doncaster	40	16	4	20	59	80	36
16	Walsall	40	16	3	21	57	85	35
17	Halifax	40	13	8	19	61	87	34
18	Carlisle	40	11	11	18	64	79	33
19	Rotherham	40	14	4	22	63	72	32
20	New Brighton	40	8	8	24	38	76	24
21	Rochdale	40	4	3	33	48	135	11
22	Wigan Borough resigned from the League							

SCOTTISH FIRST DIVISION

		P	W	D	L	F	A	Pts
1	Motherwell	38	30	6	2	119	31	66
2	Rangers	38	28	5	5	118	42	61
3	Celtic	38	20	8	10	94	50	48
4	Third Lanark	38	21	4	13	92	81	46
5	St Mirren	38	20	4	14	77	56	44
6	Partick	38	19	4	15	58	59	42
7	Aberdeen	38	16	9	13	57	49	41
8	Hearts	38	17	5	16	63	61	39
9	Kilmarnock	38	16	7	15	68	70	39
10	Hamilton	38	16	6	16	84	65	38
11	Dundee	38	14	10	14	61	72	38
12	Cowdenbeath	38	15	8	15	66	78	38
13	Clyde	38	13	9	16	58	70	35
14	Airdrieonians	38	13	6	19	74	81	32
15	Morton	38	12	7	19	78	87	31
16	Queen's Park	38	13	5	20	59	79	31
17	Ayr	38	11	7	20	70	90	29
18	Falkirk	38	11	5	22	70	76	27
19	Dundee United	38	6	7	25	40	118	19
20	Leith	38	6	4	28	46	137	16

SCOTTISH SECOND DIVISION

		P	W	D	L	F	A	Pts
1	E Stirlingshire	38	26	3	9	111	55	55
2	St Johnstone	38	24	7	7	102	52	55
3	Raith	38	20	6	12	83	65	46
4	Stenhousemuir	38	19	8	11	88	76	46
5	St Bernard's	38	19	7	12	81	62	45
6	Forfar	38	19	7	12	90	79	45
7	Hibernian	38	18	8	12	73	52	44
8	East Fife	38	18	5	15	107	77	41
9	Queen of the S	38	18	5	15	99	91	41
10	Dunfermline	38	17	6	15	78	73	40
11	Arbroath	38	17	5	16	82	78	39
12	Dumbarton	38	14	10	14	70	68	38
13	Alloa	38	14	7	17	73	74	35
14	Bo'ness	38	15	4	19	70	103	34
15	King's Park	38	14	5	19	97	93	33
16	Albion	38	13	2	23	81	104	28
17	Montrose	38	11	6	21	60	96	28
18	Armadale	38	10	5	23	68	102	25
19	Brechin	38	9	7	22	52	97	25
20	Edinburgh City	38	5	7	26	78	146	17

There is thought to have been only one League game without a corner kick. That was a Division One match between Newcastle United and Portsmouth, 5 December 1931, which ended as it began, 0-0.

On 26 October 1931, Wigan Borough became the first League club to resign during a season. Their record was expunged.

Rochdale break all the wrong records
Rochdale had a grim season in Division Three North. They set a League record by losing 17 games in succession: on 7 November 1931, they beat New Brighton 3-2, but then failed to gain another point until their 1-1 draw with the same team on 9 March 1932. Their 33 defeats in 40 matches were also a record for the division.

FA CUP 1931-32

FOURTH ROUND

Huddersfield Town v Queen's Park Rangers	5-0
Preston North End v Wolverhampton Wanderers	2-0
Portsmouth v Aston Villa	1-1, 1-0
Arsenal v Plymouth Argyle	4-2
Bury v Sheffield United	3-1
Sunderland v Stoke City	1-1, 1-1, 1-2
Manchester City v Brentford	6-1
Derby County v Blackburn Rovers	3-2
Chesterfield v Liverpool	2-4
Grimsby Town v Birmingham	2-1
Sheffield Wednesday v Bournemouth	7-0
Chelsea v West Ham United	3-1
Newcastle United v Southport	1-1, 1-1, 9-0
Port Vale v Leicester City	1-2
Watford v Bristol City	2-1
Bradford Park Avenue v Northampton Town	4-2

FIFTH ROUND

Huddersfield Town v Preston North End	4-0
Portsmouth v Arsenal	0-2
Bury v Stoke City	3-0
Manchester City v Derby County	3-0
Liverpool v Grimsby Town	1-0
Sheffield Wednesday v Chelsea	1-1, 0-2
Newcastle United v Leicester City	3-1
Watford v Bradford Park Avenue	1-0

SIXTH ROUND

Huddersfield Town v Arsenal	0-1
Bury v Manchester City	3-4
Liverpool v Chelsea	0-2
Newcastle United v Watford	5-0

SEMI-FINAL

Arsenal v Manchester City	1-0
Chelsea v Newcastle United	1-2

FINAL

Newcastle United v Arsenal	2-1

SCOTTISH FA CUP 1931-32

SECOND ROUND

Raith Rovers v Rangers	0-5
Heart of Midlothian v Cowdenbeath	4-1
Queen's Park v Motherwell	0-2
St Johnstone v Celtic	2-4
Hamilton Academicals v Armadale	5-2
Clyde v Arbroath	1-0
Edinburgh City v St Bernard's	2-3
Kilmarnock v Albion Rovers	2-0
Queen of the South v Dundee United	2-2, 1-1, 1-2
Dunfermline Athletic v Dundee	1-0
Airdrieonians v King's Park	2-2, 3-1
Bo'ness v Partick Thistle	2-2, 1-5

THIRD ROUND

Heart of Midlothian v Rangers	0-1
Motherwell v Celtic	2-0
Clyde v St Bernard's	2-0
Dundee United v Kilmarnock	1-1, 0-3
Hamilton Academicals	bye
Dunfermline Athletic	bye
Airdrieonians	bye
Partick Thistle	bye

FOURTH ROUND

Rangers v Motherwell	2-0
Clyde v Hamilton Academicals	0-2
Dunfermline Athletic v Kilmarnock	1-3
Airdrieonians v Partick Thistle	4-1

SEMI FINAL

Rangers v Hamilton Academicals	5-2
Kilmarnock v Airdrieonians	3-2

FINAL

Rangers v Kilmarnock	1-1, 3-0

League Tables 1932-33

FIRST DIVISION

		P	W	D	L	F	A	Pts
1	Arsenal	42	25	8	9	118	61	58
2	Aston Villa	42	23	8	11	92	67	54
3	Sheff Wed	42	21	9	12	80	68	51
4	WBA	42	20	9	13	83	70	49
5	Newcastle	42	22	5	15	71	63	49
6	Huddersfield	42	18	11	13	66	53	47
7	Derby	42	15	14	13	76	69	44
8	Leeds	42	15	14	13	59	62	44
9	Portsmouth	42	18	7	17	74	76	43
10	Sheff United	42	17	9	16	74	80	43
11	Everton	42	16	9	17	81	74	41
12	Sunderland	42	15	10	17	63	80	40
13	Birmingham	42	14	11	17	57	57	39
14	Liverpool	42	14	11	17	79	84	39
15	Blackburn	42	14	10	18	76	102	38
16	Man City	42	16	5	21	68	71	37
17	Middlesbrough	42	14	9	19	63	73	37
18	Chelsea	42	14	7	21	63	73	35
19	Leicester	42	11	13	18	75	89	35
20	Wolves	42	13	9	20	80	96	35
21	Bolton	42	12	9	21	78	92	33
22	Blackpool	42	14	5	23	69	85	33

SECOND DIVISION

		P	W	D	L	F	A	Pts
1	Stoke	42	25	6	11	78	39	56
2	Tottenham	42	20	15	7	96	51	55
3	Fulham	42	20	10	12	78	65	50
4	Bury	42	20	9	13	84	59	49
5	Nottm Forest	42	17	15	10	67	59	49
6	Man United	42	15	13	14	71	68	43
7	Millwall	42	16	11	15	59	57	43
8	Bradford PA	42	17	8	17	77	71	42
9	Preston	42	16	10	16	74	70	42
10	Swansea	42	19	4	19	50	54	42
11	Bradford City	42	14	13	15	65	61	41
12	Southampton	42	18	5	19	66	66	41
13	Grimsby	42	14	13	15	79	84	41
14	Plymouth	42	16	9	17	63	67	41
15	Notts County	42	15	10	17	67	78	40
16	Oldham	42	15	8	19	67	80	38
17	Port Vale	42	14	10	18	66	79	38
18	Lincoln	42	12	13	17	72	87	37
19	Burnley	42	11	14	17	67	79	36
20	West Ham	42	13	9	20	75	93	35
21	Chesterfield	42	12	10	20	61	84	34
22	Charlton	42	12	7	23	60	91	31

THIRD DIVISION (SOUTH)

		P	W	D	L	F	A	Pts
1	Brentford	42	26	10	6	90	49	62
2	Exeter	42	24	10	8	88	48	58
3	Norwich	42	22	13	7	88	55	57
4	Reading	42	19	13	10	103	71	51
5	Crystal Palace	42	19	8	15	78	64	46
6	Coventry	42	19	6	17	106	77	44
7	Gillingham	42	18	8	16	72	61	44
8	Northampton	42	18	8	16	76	66	44
9	Bristol Rovers	42	15	14	13	61	56	44
10	Torquay	42	16	12	14	72	67	44
11	Watford	42	16	12	14	66	63	44
12	Brighton	42	17	8	17	66	65	42
13	Southend	42	15	11	16	65	82	41
14	Luton	42	13	13	16	78	78	39
15	Bristol City	42	12	13	17	83	90	37
16	QPR	42	13	11	18	72	87	37
17	Aldershot	42	13	10	19	61	72	36
18	Bournemouth	42	12	12	18	60	81	36
19	Cardiff	42	12	7	23	69	99	31
20	Clapton Orient	42	8	13	21	59	93	29
21	Newport	42	11	7	24	61	105	29
22	Swindon	42	9	11	22	60	105	29

THIRD DIVISION (NORTH)

		P	W	D	L	F	A	Pts
1	Hull	42	26	7	9	100	45	59
2	Wrexham	42	24	9	9	106	51	57
3	Stockport	42	21	12	9	99	58	54
4	Chester	42	22	8	12	94	66	52
5	Walsall	42	19	10	13	75	58	48
6	Doncaster	42	17	14	11	77	79	48
7	Gateshead	42	19	9	14	78	67	47
8	Barnsley	42	19	8	15	92	80	46
9	Barrow	42	18	7	17	60	60	43
10	Crewe	42	20	3	19	80	84	43
11	Tranmere	42	17	8	17	70	66	42
12	Southport	42	17	7	18	70	67	41
13	Accrington	42	15	10	17	78	76	40
14	Hartlepools	42	16	7	19	87	116	39
15	Halifax	42	15	8	19	71	90	38
16	Mansfield	42	14	7	21	84	100	35
17	Rotherham	42	14	6	22	60	84	34
18	Rochdale	42	13	7	22	58	80	33
19	Carlisle	42	13	7	22	51	75	33
20	York	42	13	6	23	72	92	32
21	New Brighton	42	11	10	21	63	88	32
22	Darlington	42	10	8	24	66	109	28

SCOTTISH FIRST DIVISION

		P	W	D	L	F	A	Pts
1	Rangers	38	26	10	2	113	43	62
2	Motherwell	38	27	5	6	114	53	59
3	Hearts	38	21	8	9	84	51	50
4	Celtic	38	20	8	10	75	44	48
5	St Johnstone	38	17	10	11	70	57	44
6	Aberdeen	38	18	6	14	85	58	42
7	St Mirren	38	18	6	14	73	60	42
8	Hamilton	38	18	6	14	92	78	42
9	Queen's Park	38	17	7	14	78	79	41
10	Partick	38	17	6	15	75	55	40
11	Falkirk	38	15	6	17	70	70	36
12	Clyde	38	15	5	18	69	75	35
13	Third Lanark	38	14	7	17	70	80	35
14	Kilmarnock	38	13	9	16	72	86	35
15	Dundee	38	12	9	17	58	74	33
16	Ayr	38	13	4	21	62	96	30
17	Cowdenbeath	38	10	5	23	65	111	25
18	Airdrieonians	38	10	3	25	55	102	23
19	Morton	38	6	9	23	49	97	21
20	E Stirlingshire	38	7	3	28	55	115	17

SCOTTISH SECOND DIVISION

		P	W	D	L	F	A	Pts
1	Hibernian	34	25	4	5	80	29	54
2	Queen of the S	34	20	9	5	93	59	49
3	Dunfermline	34	20	7	7	89	44	47
4	Stenhousemuir	34	18	6	10	67	58	42
5	Albion	34	19	2	13	82	57	40
6	Raith	34	16	4	14	83	67	36
7	East Fife	34	15	4	15	85	71	34
8	King's Park	34	13	8	13	85	80	34
9	Dumbarton	34	14	6	14	69	67	34
10	Arbroath	34	14	5	15	65	62	33
11	Alloa	34	14	5	15	60	58	33
12	St Bernard's	34	13	6	15	67	64	32
13	Dundee United	34	14	4	16	65	67	32
14	Forfar	34	12	4	18	68	87	28
15	Brechin	34	11	4	19	65	95	26
16	Leith	34	10	5	19	43	81	25
17	Montrose	34	8	5	21	63	89	21
18	Edinburgh City	34	4	4	26	39	133	12

Reduced to ten men after 10 minutes, Wales did well to beat Scotland 5-2 at Tynecastle, Edinburgh, in October 1932. It was their first win on Scottish soil since 1906.

Everton capped a memorable three seasons by winning the FA Cup. In 1931-32, they were League champions, the season before, they had won the Second Division Championship.

The international Rangers

Towards the end of 1932-33, Glasgow Rangers had 13 internationals on their books. They were: Archibald, Brown, Craig, Fleming, Gray, T Hamilton, McPhail, Marshall, Meiklejohn and Morton, all Scotsmen, and English, R Hamilton and McDonald, who were Irish internationals. This considerable array of Scots and Irish talent helped Rangers finish the season at the top of the Scottish First Division, three points clear of Motherwell.

FA CUP 1932-33

FOURTH ROUND

Burnley v Sheffield United	3-1
Darlington v Chesterfield	0-2
Bolton Wanderers v Grimsby Town	2-1
Manchester City v Walsall	2-0
Southend United v Derby County	2-3
Aldershot v Millwall	1-0
Aston Villa v Sunderland	0-3
Blackpool v Huddersfield Town	2-0
Everton v Bury	3-1
Tranmere Rovers v Leeds United	0-0, 0-4
Chester v Halifax Town	0-0, 2-3
Luton Town v Tottenham Hotspur	2-0
Brighton v Bradford Park Avenue	2-1
West Ham United v West Bromwich Albion	2-0
Middlesbrough v Stoke City	4-1
Birmingham v Blackburn Rovers	3-0

FIFTH ROUND

Burnley v Chesterfield	1-0
Bolton Wanderers v Manchester City	2-4
Derby County v Aldershot	2-0
Sunderland v Blackpool	1-0
Everton v Leeds United	2-0
Halifax Town v Luton Town	0-2
Brighton v West Ham United	2-2, 0-1
Middlesbrough v Birmingham	0-0, 0-3

SIXTH ROUND

Burnley v Manchester City	0-1
Derby County v Sunderland	4-4, 1-0
Everton v Luton Town	6-0
West Ham United v Birmingham	4-0

SEMI-FINAL

Manchester City v Derby County	3-2
Everton v West Ham United	2-1

FINAL

Everton v Manchester City	3-0

SCOTTISH FA CUP 1932-33

SECOND ROUND

Celtic v Falkirk	2-0
Partick Thistle v Ayr United	1-1, 2-0
Albion Rovers v Dumbarton	2-1
Heart of Midlothian v Airdrieonians	6-1
St Johnstone v Dundee United	4-3
Hibernian v Aberdeen	1-1, 1-0
Motherwell v Montrose	7-1
Dundee v Bo'ness	4-0
Kilmarnock v St Mirren	1-0
Rangers v Queen's Park	1-1, 1-1, 3-1
Clyde v Leith Athletic	1-1, 5-0
Stenhousemuir v Third Lanark	2-0

THIRD ROUND

Celtic v Partick Thistle	2-1
Heart of Midlothian v St Johnstone	2-0
Motherwell v Dundee	5-0
Kilmarnock v Rangers	1-0
Albion Rovers	bye
Hibernian	bye
Clyde	bye
Stenhousemuir	bye

FOURTH ROUND

Celtic v Albion Rovers	1-1, 3-1
Heart of Midlothian v Hibernian	2-0
Motherwell v Kilmarnock	3-3, 8-3
Clyde v Stenhousemuir	3-2

SEMI-FINAL

Celtic v Heart of Midlothian	0-0, 2-1
Motherwell v Clyde	2-0

FINAL

Celtic v Motherwell	1-0

FIRST DIVISION

	P	W	D	L	F	A	Pts
1 Arsenal	42	25	9	8	75	47	59
2 Huddersfield	42	23	10	9	90	61	56
3 Tottenham	42	21	7	14	79	56	49
4 Derby	42	17	11	14	68	54	45
5 Man City	42	17	11	14	65	72	45
6 Sunderland	42	16	12	14	81	56	44
7 WBA	42	17	10	15	78	70	44
8 Blackburn	42	18	7	17	74	81	43
9 Leeds	42	17	8	17	75	66	42
10 Portsmouth	42	15	12	15	52	55	42
11 Sheff Wed	42	16	9	17	62	67	41
12 Stoke	42	15	11	16	58	71	41
13 Aston Villa	42	14	12	16	78	75	40
14 Everton	42	12	16	14	62	63	40
15 Wolves	42	14	12	16	74	86	40
16 Middlesbrough	42	16	7	19	68	80	39
17 Leicester	42	14	11	17	59	74	39
18 Liverpool	42	14	10	18	79	87	38
19 Chelsea	42	14	8	20	67	69	36
20 Birmingham	42	12	12	18	54	56	36
21 Newcastle	42	10	14	18	68	77	34
22 Sheff United	42	12	7	23	58	101	31

SECOND DIVISION

	P	W	D	L	F	A	Pts
1 Grimsby	42	27	5	10	103	59	59
2 Preston	42	23	6	13	71	52	52
3 Bolton	42	21	9	12	79	55	51
4 Brentford	42	22	7	13	85	60	51
5 Bradford PA	42	23	3	16	86	67	49
6 Bradford City	42	20	6	16	73	67	46
7 West Ham	42	17	11	14	78	70	45
8 Port Vale	42	19	7	16	60	55	45
9 Oldham	42	17	10	15	72	60	44
10 Plymouth	42	15	13	14	69	70	43
11 Blackpool	42	15	13	14	62	64	43
12 Bury	42	17	9	16	70	73	43
13 Burnley	42	18	6	18	60	72	42
14 Southampton	42	15	8	19	54	58	38
15 Hull	42	13	12	17	52	68	38
16 Fulham	42	15	7	20	48	67	37
17 Nottm Forest	42	13	9	20	73	74	35
18 Notts County	42	12	11	19	53	62	35
19 Swansea	42	10	15	17	51	60	35
20 Man United	42	14	6	22	59	85	34
21 Millwall	42	11	11	20	39	68	33
22 Lincoln	42	9	8	25	44	75	26

THIRD DIVISION (NORTH)

	P	W	D	L	F	A	Pts
1 Barnsley	42	27	8	7	118	61	62
2 Chesterfield	42	27	7	8	86	43	61
3 Stockport	42	24	11	7	115	52	59
4 Walsall	42	23	7	12	97	60	53
5 Doncaster	42	22	9	11	83	61	53
6 Wrexham	42	23	5	14	102	73	51
7 Tranmere	42	20	7	15	84	63	47
8 Barrow	42	19	9	14	116	94	47
9 Halifax	42	20	4	18	80	91	44
10 Chester	42	17	6	19	89	86	40
11 Hartlepools	42	16	7	19	89	93	39
12 York	42	15	8	19	71	74	38
13 Carlisle	42	15	8	19	66	81	38
14 Crewe	42	15	6	21	81	97	36
15 New Brighton	42	14	8	20	62	87	36
16 Darlington	42	13	9	20	70	101	35
17 Mansfield	42	11	12	19	81	88	34
18 Southport	42	8	17	17	63	90	33
19 Gateshead	42	12	9	21	76	110	33
20 Accrington	42	13	7	22	65	101	33
21 Rotherham	42	10	8	24	53	91	28
22 Rochdale	42	9	6	27	53	103	24

THIRD DIVISION (SOUTH)

	P	W	D	L	F	A	Pts
1 Norwich	42	25	11	6	88	49	61
2 Coventry	42	21	12	9	100	54	54
3 Reading	42	21	12	9	82	50	54
4 QPR	42	24	6	12	70	51	54
5 Charlton	42	22	8	12	83	56	52
6 Luton	42	21	10	11	83	61	52
7 Bristol Rovers	42	20	11	11	77	47	51
8 Swindon	42	17	11	14	64	68	45
9 Exeter	42	16	11	15	68	57	43
10 Brighton	42	15	13	14	68	60	43
11 Clapton Orient	42	16	10	16	75	69	42
12 Crystal Palace	42	16	9	17	71	67	41
13 Northampton	42	14	12	16	71	78	40
14 Aldershot	42	13	12	17	52	71	38
15 Watford	42	15	7	20	71	63	37
16 Southend	42	12	10	20	51	74	34
17 Gillingham	42	11	11	20	75	96	33
18 Newport	42	8	17	17	49	70	33
19 Bristol City	42	10	13	19	58	85	33
20 Torquay	42	13	7	22	53	93	33
21 Bournemouth	42	9	9	24	60	102	27
22 Cardiff	42	9	6	27	57	105	24

SCOTTISH FIRST DIVISION

	P	W	D	L	F	A	Pts
1 Rangers	38	30	6	2	118	41	66
2 Motherwell	38	29	4	5	97	45	62
3 Celtic	38	18	11	9	78	53	47
4 Queen of the S	38	21	3	14	75	78	45
5 Aberdeen	38	18	8	12	90	57	44
6 Hearts	38	17	10	11	86	59	44
7 Kilmarnock	38	17	9	12	73	64	43
8 Ayr	38	16	10	12	87	92	42
9 St Johnstone	38	17	6	15	74	53	40
10 Falkirk	38	16	6	16	73	68	38
11 Hamilton	38	15	8	15	65	79	38
12 Dundee	38	15	6	17	68	64	36
13 Partick	38	14	5	19	73	78	33
14 Clyde	38	10	11	17	56	70	31
15 Queen's Park	38	13	5	20	65	85	31
16 Hibernian	38	12	3	23	51	69	27
17 St Mirren	38	9	9	20	46	75	27
18 Airdrieonians	38	10	6	22	59	103	26
19 Third Lanark	38	8	9	21	62	103	25
20 Cowdenbeath	38	5	5	28	58	118	15

SCOTTISH SECOND DIVISION

	P	W	D	L	F	A	Pts
1 Albion	34	20	5	9	74	47	45
2 Dunfermline	34	20	4	10	90	52	44
3 Arbroath	34	20	4	10	83	53	44
4 Stenhousemuir	34	18	4	12	70	73	40
5 Morton	34	17	5	12	67	64	39
6 Dumbarton	34	17	3	14	67	68	37
7 King's Park	34	14	8	12	78	70	36
8 Raith	34	15	5	14	71	55	35
9 E Stirlingshire	34	14	7	13	65	74	35
10 St Bernard's	34	15	4	15	75	56	34
11 Forfar	34	13	7	14	77	71	33
12 Leith	34	12	8	14	63	60	32
13 East Fife	34	12	8	14	71	76	32
14 Brechin	34	13	5	16	60	70	31
15 Alloa	34	11	9	14	55	68	31
16 Montrose	34	11	4	19	53	81	26
17 Dundee United	34	10	4	20	81	88	24
18 Edinburgh City	34	4	6	24	37	111	14

FA CUP 1933-34

FOURTH ROUND

Portsmouth v Grimsby Town	2-0
Bury v Swansea Town	1-1, 0-3
Liverpool v Tranmere Rovers	3-1
Brighton v Bolton Wanderers	1-1, 1-6
Workington v Preston North End	1-2
Huddersfield Town v Northampton Town	0-2
Birmingham v Charlton Athletic	1-0
Millwall v Leicester City	3-6
Aston Villa v Sunderland	7-2
Tottenham Hotspur v West Ham United	4-1
Derby County v Wolverhampton Wanderers	3-0
Arsenal v Crystal Palace	7-0
Stoke City v Blackpool	3-0
Chelsea v Nottingham Forest	1-1, 3-0
Oldham Athletic v Sheffield Wednesday	1-1, 1-6
Hull City v Manchester City	2-2, 1-4

FIFTH ROUND

Swansea Town v Portsmouth	0-1
Liverpool v Bolton Wanderers	0-3
Preston North End v Northampton Town	4-0
Birmingham v Leicester City	1-2
Tottenham Hotspur v Aston Villa	0-1
Arsenal v Derby County	1-0
Stoke City v Chelsea	3-1
Sheffield Wednesday v Manchester City	2-2, 0-2

SIXTH ROUND

Bolton Wanderers v Portsmouth	0-3
Preston North End v Leicester City	0-1
Arsenal v Aston Villa	1-2
Manchester City v Stoke City	1-0

SEMI-FINAL

Portsmouth v Leicester City	4-1
Manchester City v Aston Villa	6-1

FINAL

Manchester City v Portsmouth	2-1

SCOTTISH FA CUP 1933-34

SECOND ROUND

Third Lanark v Rangers	0-3
Queen's Park v Heart of Midlothian	1-2
Hibernian v Alloa Athletic	6-0
Aberdeen v Dundee	2-0
Vale of Leithen v St Johnstone	1-3
Cowdenbeath v St Bernard's	2-1
Brechin City v St Mirren	0-4
Ayr United v Celtic	2-3
Hamilton Academicals v Falkirk	2-4
Albion Rovers v Kilmarnock	2-1
Ross County v Galston	3-1
Partick Thistle v Motherwell	3-3, 1-2
East Stirlingshire v Arbroath	1-1, 3-0
Queen of the South	bye

THIRD ROUND

Rangers v Heart of Midlothian	0-0, 2-1
Hibernian v Aberdeen	0-1
Queen of the South v Cowdenbeath	3-0
Celtic v Falkirk	3-1
Albion Rovers v Ross County	6-1
Motherwell v East Stirlingshire	5-0
St Johnstone	bye
St Mirren	bye

FOURTH ROUND

Rangers v Aberdeen	1-0
St Johnstone v Queen of the South	2-0
St Mirren v Celtic	2-0
Albion Rovers v Motherwell	1-1, 0-6

SEMI-FINAL

Rangers v St Johnstone	1-0
St Mirren v Motherwell	3-1

FINAL

Rangers v St Mirren	5-0

The record number of goals scored by a conventional half-back in a Football League game is three. The record was set in 1926 by a Newcastle player, T McDonald, and equalled against Wolves on 21 April 1934 by another Newcastle player, W Imrie.

In June 1934, Stanley Rous was appointed secretary of the Football Association.

S Milton had surely one of the unhappiest Football League debuts on record. A goalkeeper, Milton was picked to play in that position for Halifax Town against Stockport County in a Third Division North League match on 6 January 1934. Milton was faced with a Stockport attack in fine fettle, and he had to retrieve the ball from his net 13 times, an unenviable record. The score—13-0—also set a record, for the highest score in a League match.

FIRST DIVISION

		P	W	D	L	F	A	Pts
1	Arsenal	42	23	12	7	115	46	58
2	Sunderland	42	19	16	7	90	51	54
3	Sheff Wed	42	18	13	11	70	64	49
4	Man City	42	20	8	14	82	67	48
5	Grimsby	42	17	11	14	78	60	45
6	Derby	42	18	9	15	81	66	45
7	Liverpool	42	19	7	16	85	88	45
8	Everton	42	16	12	14	89	88	44
9	WBA	42	17	10	15	83	83	44
10	Stoke	42	18	6	18	71	70	42
11	Preston	42	15	12	15	62	67	42
12	Chelsea	42	16	9	17	73	82	41
13	Aston Villa	42	14	13	15	74	88	41
14	Portsmouth	42	15	10	17	71	72	40
15	Blackburn	42	14	11	17	66	78	39
16	Huddersfield	42	14	10	18	76	71	38
17	Wolves	42	15	8	19	88	94	38
18	Leeds	42	13	12	17	75	92	38
19	Birmingham	42	13	10	19	63	81	36
20	Middlesbrough	42	10	14	18	70	91	34
21	Leicester	42	12	9	21	61	86	33
22	Tottenham	42	10	10	22	54	93	30

SECOND DIVISION

		P	W	D	L	F	A	Pts
1	Brentford	42	26	9	7	93	48	61
2	Bolton	42	26	4	12	96	48	56
3	West Ham	42	26	4	12	80	63	56
4	Blackpool	42	21	11	10	79	57	53
5	Man United	42	23	4	15	76	55	50
6	Newcastle	42	22	4	16	89	68	48
7	Fulham	42	17	12	13	76	56	46
8	Plymouth	42	19	8	15	75	64	46
9	Nottm Forest	42	17	8	17	76	70	42
10	Bury	42	19	4	19	62	73	42
11	Sheff United	42	16	9	17	79	70	41
12	Burnley	42	16	9	17	63	73	41
13	Hull	42	16	8	18	63	74	40
14	Norwich	42	14	11	17	71	61	39
15	Bradford PA	42	11	16	15	55	63	38
16	Barnsley	42	13	12	17	60	83	38
17	Swansea	42	14	8	20	56	67	36
18	Port Vale	42	11	12	19	55	74	34
19	Southampton	42	11	12	19	46	75	34
20	Bradford City	42	12	8	22	50	68	32
21	Oldham	42	10	6	26	56	95	26
22	Notts County	42	9	7	26	46	97	25

THIRD DIVISION (SOUTH)

		P	W	D	L	F	A	Pts
1	Charlton	42	27	7	8	103	52	61
2	Reading	42	21	11	10	89	65	53
3	Coventry	42	21	9	12	86	50	51
4	Luton	42	19	12	11	92	60	50
5	Crystal Palace	42	19	10	13	86	64	48
6	Watford	42	19	9	14	76	49	47
7	Northampton	42	19	8	15	65	67	46
8	Bristol Rovers	42	17	10	15	73	77	44
9	Brighton	42	17	9	16	69	62	43
10	Torquay	42	18	6	18	81	75	42
11	Exeter	42	16	9	17	70	75	41
12	Millwall	42	17	7	18	57	62	41
13	QPR	42	16	9	17	63	72	41
14	Clapton Orient	42	15	10	17	65	65	40
15	Bristol City	42	15	9	18	52	68	39
16	Swindon	42	13	12	17	67	78	38
17	Bournemouth	42	15	7	20	54	71	37
18	Aldershot	42	13	10	19	50	75	36
19	Cardiff	42	13	9	20	62	82	35
20	Gillingham	42	11	13	18	55	75	35
21	Southend	42	11	9	22	65	78	31
22	Newport	42	10	5	27	54	112	25

THIRD DIVISION (NORTH)

		P	W	D	L	F	A	Pts
1	Doncaster	42	26	5	11	87	44	57
2	Halifax	42	25	5	12	76	67	55
3	Chester	42	20	14	8	91	58	54
4	Lincoln	42	22	7	13	87	58	51
5	Darlington	42	21	9	12	80	59	51
6	Tranmere	42	20	11	11	74	55	51
7	Stockport	42	22	3	17	90	72	47
8	Mansfield	42	19	9	14	75	62	47
9	Rotherham	42	19	7	16	86	73	45
10	Chesterfield	42	17	10	15	71	52	44
11	Wrexham	42	16	11	15	76	69	43
12	Hartlepools	42	17	7	18	80	78	41
13	Crewe	42	14	11	17	66	86	39
14	Walsall	42	13	10	19	81	72	36
15	York	42	15	6	21	76	82	36
16	New Brighton	42	14	8	20	59	76	36
17	Barrow	42	13	9	20	58	87	35
18	Accrington	42	12	10	20	63	89	34
19	Gateshead	42	13	8	21	58	96	34
20	Rochdale	42	11	11	20	53	71	33
21	Southport	42	10	12	20	55	85	32
22	Carlisle	42	8	7	27	51	102	23

SCOTTISH FIRST DIVISION

		P	W	D	L	F	A	Pts
1	Rangers	38	25	5	8	96	46	55
2	Celtic	38	24	4	10	92	45	52
3	Hearts	38	20	10	8	87	51	50
4	Hamilton	38	19	10	9	87	67	48
5	St Johnstone	38	18	10	10	66	46	46
6	Aberdeen	38	17	10	11	68	54	44
7	Motherwell	38	15	10	13	83	64	40
8	Dundee	38	16	8	14	63	63	40
9	Kilmarnock	38	16	6	16	76	68	38
10	Clyde	38	14	10	14	71	69	38
11	Hibernian	38	14	8	16	59	70	36
12	Queen's Park	38	13	10	15	61	80	36
13	Partick	38	15	5	18	61	68	35
14	Airdrieonians	38	13	7	18	64	72	33
15	Dunfermline	38	13	5	20	56	96	31
16	Albion	38	10	9	19	62	77	29
17	Queen of the S	38	11	7	20	52	72	29
18	Ayr	38	12	5	21	61	112	29
19	St Mirren	38	11	5	22	49	70	27
20	Falkirk	38	9	6	23	58	82	24

SCOTTISH SECOND DIVISION

		P	W	D	L	F	A	Pts
1	Third Lanark	34	23	6	5	94	43	52
2	Arbroath	34	23	4	7	78	42	50
3	St Bernard's	34	20	7	7	103	47	47
4	Dundee United	34	18	6	10	105	65	42
5	Stenhousemuir	34	17	5	12	86	80	39
6	Morton	34	17	4	13	88	64	38
7	King's Park	34	18	2	14	86	71	38
8	Leith	34	16	5	13	69	71	37
9	East Fife	34	16	3	15	79	73	35
10	Alloa	34	12	10	12	68	61	34
11	Forfar	34	13	8	13	77	73	34
12	Cowdenbeath	34	13	6	15	84	75	32
13	Raith	34	13	3	18	68	73	29
14	E Stirlingshire	34	11	7	16	57	76	29
15	Brechin	34	10	6	18	51	98	26
16	Dumbarton	34	9	4	21	60	105	22
17	Montrose	34	7	6	21	58	105	20
18	Edinburgh City	34	3	2	29	45	134	8

FA CUP 1934-35

FOURTH ROUND

Wolverhampton Wanderers v Sheffield Wednesday	1-2
Norwich City v Leeds United	3-3, 2-1
Reading v Millwall	1-0
Leicester City v Arsenal	0-1
Southampton v Birmingham	0-3
Blackburn Rovers v Liverpool	1-0
Nottingham Forest v Manchester United	0-0, 3-0
Burnley v Luton Town	3-1
Plymouth Argyle v Bolton Wanderers	1-4
Tottenham Hotspur v Newcastle United	2-0
Derby County v Swansea Town	3-0
Sunderland v Everton	1-1, 4-6
Swindon Town v Preston North End	0-2
Portsmouth v Bristol City	0-0, 0-2
Bradford City v Stockport County	0-0, 2-3
West Bromwich Albion v Sheffield United	7-1

FIFTH ROUND

Norwich City v Sheffield Wednesday	0-1
Reading v Arsenal	0-1
Blackburn Rovers v Birmingham	1-2
Nottingham Forest v Burnley	0-0, 0-3
Tottenham Hotspur v Bolton Wanderers	1-1, 1-1, 0-2
Everton v Derby County	3-1
Bristol City v Preston North End	0-0, 0-5
Stockport County v West Bromwich Albion	0-5

SIXTH ROUND

Sheffield Wednesday v Arsenal	2-1
Burnley v Birmingham	3-2
Everton v Bolton Wanderers	1-2
West Bromwich Albion v Preston North End	1-0

SEMI-FINAL

Sheffield Wednesday v Burnley	3-0
Bolton Wanderers v West Bromwich Albion	1-1, 0-2

FINAL

Sheffield Wednesday v West Bromwich Albion	4-2

SCOTTISH FA CUP 1934-35

SECOND ROUND

Motherwell v Morton	7-1
Rangers v Third Lanark	2-0
St Mirren v Forfar Athletic	3-0
Airdrieonians v Rosyth Dockyard	1-0
Ayr United v King's Park	1-1, 2-2, 4-4, 1-2
Heart of Midlothian v Kilmarnock	2-0
Dundee United v Queen's Park	6-3
Aberdeen v Albion Rovers	4-0
Hibernian v Clachnacuddin	7-1
Celtic v Partick Thistle	1-1, 3-1
Brechin City v Raith Rovers	1-1, 4-2
Clyde v Hamilton Academicals	3-3, 3-6
St Johnstone v Dumbarton	4-0
Buckie Thistle	bye

THIRD ROUND

Rangers v St Mirren	1-0
Airdrieonians v King's Park	6-2
Heart of Midlothian v Dundee United	2-2, 4-2
Aberdeen v Hibernian	0-0, 1-1, 3-2
Brechin City v Hamilton Academicals	2-4
Buckie Thistle v St Johnstone	0-1
Motherwell	bye
Celtic	bye

FOURTH ROUND

Motherwell v Rangers	1-4
Airdrieonians v Heart of Midlothian	2-3
Aberdeen v Celtic	3-1
Hamilton Academicals v St Johnstone	3-0

SEMI-FINAL

Rangers v Heart of Midlothian	1-1, 2-0
Aberdeen v Hamilton Academicals	1-2

FINAL

Rangers v Hamilton Academicals	2-1

The famous occasion when a player headed a goal from a penalty-kick took place on 5 January 1935. Anfield was the setting for a North-South clash between Liverpool and Arsenal. In the course of the game, Arsenal were awarded a penalty which their full-back, Eddie Hapgood, elected to take. Liverpool's goalkeeper, Riley, fisted Hapgood's spot-kick back out, and Hapgood headed home the rebound. Arsenal won the match 2-0.

The record gate for an English League match was broken on 23 February 1935, when 77,582 people paid to see Manchester City play Arsenal at Maine Road, Manchester. Season-ticket holders brought the total number of spectators present to 80,000.

S Raleigh, Gillingham's centre-forward, died from concussion sustained in a match with Brighton, 1 December 1934.

League Tables 1935-36

FIRST DIVISION

		P	W	D	L	F	A	Pts
1	Sunderland	42	25	6	11	109	74	56
2	Derby	42	18	12	12	61	52	48
3	Huddersfield	42	18	12	12	59	56	48
4	Stoke	42	20	7	15	57	57	47
5	Brentford	42	17	12	13	81	60	46
6	Arsenal	42	15	15	12	78	48	45
7	Preston	42	18	8	16	67	64	44
8	Chelsea	42	15	13	14	65	72	43
9	Man City	42	17	8	17	68	60	42
10	Portsmouth	42	17	8	17	54	67	42
11	Leeds	42	15	11	16	66	64	41
12	Birmingham	42	15	11	16	61	63	41
13	Bolton	42	14	13	15	67	76	41
14	Middlesbrough	42	15	10	17	84	70	40
15	Wolves	42	15	10	17	77	76	40
16	Everton	42	13	13	16	89	89	39
17	Grimsby	42	17	5	20	65	73	39
18	WBA	42	16	6	20	89	88	38
19	Liverpool	42	13	12	17	60	64	38
20	Sheff Wed	42	13	12	17	63	77	38
21	Aston Villa	42	13	9	20	81	110	35
22	Blackburn	42	12	9	21	55	96	33

SECOND DIVISION

		P	W	D	L	F	A	Pts
1	Man United	42	22	12	8	85	43	56
2	Charlton	42	22	11	9	85	58	55
3	Sheff United	42	20	12	10	79	50	52
4	West Ham	42	22	8	12	90	68	52
5	Tottenham	42	18	13	11	91	55	49
6	Leicester	42	19	10	13	79	57	48
7	Plymouth	42	20	8	14	71	57	48
8	Newcastle	42	20	6	16	88	79	46
9	Fulham	42	15	14	13	76	52	44
10	Blackpool	42	18	7	17	93	72	43
11	Norwich	42	17	9	16	72	65	43
12	Bradford City	42	15	13	14	55	65	43
13	Swansea	42	15	9	18	67	76	39
14	Bury	42	13	12	17	66	84	38
15	Burnley	42	12	13	17	50	59	37
16	Bradford PA	42	14	9	19	62	84	37
17	Southampton	42	14	9	19	47	65	37
18	Doncaster	42	14	9	19	51	71	37
19	Nottm Forest	42	12	11	19	69	76	35
20	Barnsley	42	12	9	21	54	80	33
21	Port Vale	42	12	8	22	56	106	32
22	Hull	42	5	10	27	47	111	20

THIRD DIVISION (SOUTH)

		P	W	D	L	F	A	Pts
1	Coventry	42	24	9	9	102	45	57
2	Luton	42	22	12	8	81	45	56
3	Reading	42	26	2	14	87	62	54
4	QPR	42	22	9	11	84	53	53
5	Watford	42	20	9	13	80	54	49
6	Crystal Palace	42	22	5	15	96	74	49
7	Brighton	42	18	8	16	70	63	44
8	Bournemouth	42	16	11	15	60	56	43
9	Notts County	42	15	12	15	60	57	42
10	Torquay	42	16	9	17	62	62	41
11	Aldershot	42	14	12	16	53	61	40
12	Millwall	42	14	12	16	58	71	40
13	Bristol City	42	15	10	17	48	59	40
14	Clapton Orient	42	16	6	20	55	61	38
15	Northampton	42	15	8	19	62	90	38
16	Gillingham	42	14	9	19	66	77	37
17	Bristol Rovers	42	14	9	19	69	95	37
18	Southend	42	13	10	19	61	62	36
19	Swindon	42	14	8	20	64	73	36
20	Cardiff	42	13	10	19	60	73	36
21	Newport	42	11	9	22	60	111	31
22	Exeter	42	8	11	23	59	93	27

THIRD DIVISION (NORTH)

		P	W	D	L	F	A	Pts
1	Chesterfield	42	24	12	6	92	39	60
2	Chester	42	22	11	9	100	45	55
3	Tranmere	42	22	11	9	93	58	55
4	Lincoln	42	22	10	9	91	51	53
5	Stockport	42	20	8	14	65	49	48
6	Crewe	42	19	9	14	80	76	47
7	Oldham	42	18	9	15	86	73	45
8	Hartlepools	42	15	12	15	57	61	42
9	Accrington	42	17	8	17	63	72	42
10	Walsall	42	16	9	17	79	59	41
11	Rotherham	42	16	9	17	69	66	41
12	Darlington	42	17	6	19	74	79	40
13	Carlisle	42	14	12	16	56	62	40
14	Gateshead	42	13	14	15	56	76	40
15	Barrow	42	13	12	17	58	65	38
16	York	42	13	12	17	62	95	38
17	Halifax	42	15	7	20	57	61	37
18	Wrexham	42	15	7	20	66	75	37
19	Mansfield	42	14	9	19	80	91	37
20	Rochdale	42	10	13	19	58	88	33
21	Southport	42	11	9	22	48	90	31
22	New Brighton	42	9	6	27	43	102	24

SCOTTISH FIRST DIVISION

		P	W	D	L	F	A	Pts
1	Celtic	38	32	2	4	115	33	66
2	Rangers	38	27	7	4	110	43	61
3	Aberdeen	38	26	9	3	96	50	61
4	Motherwell	38	18	12	8	77	58	48
5	Hearts	38	20	7	11	88	55	47
6	Hamilton	38	15	7	16	77	74	37
7	St Johnstone	38	15	7	16	70	81	37
8	Kilmarnock	38	14	7	17	69	64	35
9	Partick	38	12	10	16	64	72	34
10	Dunfermline	38	13	8	17	73	92	34
11	Third Lanark	38	14	5	19	63	71	33
12	Arbroath	38	11	11	16	46	69	33
13	Dundee	38	11	10	17	67	80	32
14	Queen's Park	38	11	10	17	58	75	32
15	Queen of the S	38	11	9	18	54	72	31
16	Albion	38	13	4	21	69	92	30
17	Hibernian	38	11	7	20	56	82	29
18	Clyde	38	10	8	20	63	84	28
19	Airdrieonians	38	9	9	20	68	91	27
20	Ayr	38	11	3	24	53	98	25

SCOTTISH SECOND DIVISION

		P	W	D	L	F	A	Pts
1	Falkirk	34	28	3	3	132	34	59
2	St Mirren	34	25	2	7	114	41	52
3	Morton	34	21	6	7	117	60	48
4	Alloa	34	19	6	9	65	51	44
5	St Bernard's	34	18	4	12	106	78	40
6	East Fife	34	16	6	12	86	79	38
7	Dundee United	34	16	5	13	108	81	37
8	E Stirlingshire	34	13	8	13	70	75	34
9	Leith	34	15	3	16	67	77	33
10	Cowdenbeath	34	13	5	16	76	77	31
11	Stenhousemuir	34	13	3	18	59	78	29
12	Montrose	34	13	3	18	58	82	29
13	Forfar	34	10	7	17	60	81	27
14	King's Park	34	11	5	18	55	109	27
15	Edinburgh City	34	8	9	17	57	83	25
16	Brechin	34	8	6	20	57	96	22
17	Raith	34	9	3	22	60	96	21
18	Dumbarton	34	5	6	23	52	121	16

FA CUP 1935-36

FOURTH ROUND

Liverpool v Arsenal	0-2
Sheffield Wednesday v Newcastle United	1-1, 1-3
Tranmere Rovers v Barnsley	2-4
Stoke City v Manchester United	0-0, 2-0
Port Vale v Grimsby Town	0-4
Manchester City v Luton Town	2-1
Middlesbrough v Clapton Orient	3-0
Leicester City v Watford	6-3
Fulham v Blackpool	5-2
Chelsea v Plymouth Argyle	4-1
Bradford City v Blackburn Rovers	3-1
Derby County v Nottingham Forest	2-0
Preston North End v Sheffield United	0-0, 0-2
Leeds United v Bury	2-1*, 3-2
Tottenham Hotspur v Huddersfield Town	1-0
Bradford Park Avenue v West Bromwich Albion	1-1, 1-1, 2-0

*abandoned

FIFTH ROUND

Newcastle United v Arsenal	3-3, 0-3
Barnsley v Stoke City	2-1
Grimsby Town v Manchester City	3-2
Middlesbrough v Leicester City	2-1
Chelsea v Fulham	0-0, 2-3
Bradford City v Derby County	0-1
Sheffield United v Leeds United	3-1
Bradford Park Avenue v Tottenham Hotspur	0-0, 1-2

SIXTH ROUND

Arsenal v Barnsley	4-1
Grimsby Town v Middlesbrough	3-1
Fulham v Derby County	3-0
Sheffield United v Tottenham Hotspur	3-1

SEMI-FINAL

Arsenal v Grimsby Town	1-0
Fulham v Sheffield United	1-2

FINAL

Arsenal v Sheffield United	1-0

SCOTTISH FA CUP 1935-36

SECOND ROUND

Aberdeen v King's Park	6-0
Celtic v St Johnstone	1-2
Dalbeattie Star v St Mirren	0-1
Albion Rovers v Rangers	1-3
Clyde v Hibernian	4-1
Dundee v Airdrieonians	2-1
Cowdenbeath v Dundee United	5-3
Motherwell v St Bernard's	3-0
Falkirk v Kilmarnock	1-1, 3-1
Dunfermline Athletic v Galston	5-2
Morton v Stenhousemuir	3-0
Elgin City v Queen of the South	0-3
Third Lanark v Leith Athletic	2-0
Dumbarton	bye

THIRD ROUND

Aberdeen v St Johnstone	1-1, 1-0
St Mirren v Rangers	1-2
Clyde v Dundee	1-1, 3-0
Cowdenbeath v Motherwell	1-3
Morton v Queen of the South	2-0
Third Lanark v Dumbarton	8-0
Falkirk	bye
Dunfermline Athletic	bye

FOURTH ROUND

Aberdeen v Rangers	0-1
Clyde v Motherwell	3-2
Falkirk v Dunfermline Athletic	5-0
Morton v Third Lanark	3-5

SEMI-FINAL

Rangers v Clyde	3-0
Falkirk v Third Lanark	1-3

FINAL

Rangers v Third Lanark	1-0

The loneliness of long-distance football

On Good Friday, 10 April 1936, Swansea Town defeated Plymouth by two goals to one in a Second Division match at Home Park, Plymouth. The following day, Swansea met Newcastle at St James' Park, Newcastle, losing 2-0. Between the two games, Swansea travelled 400 miles, a record distance for a League club to travel between games played on consecutive days.

Footballing fatality

James Thorpe, Sunderland's goalkeeper, died a few days after his team had met Chelsea on 1 February 1936. His death was due to diabetes, but a coroner's jury found that the illness had been accelerated by rough usage of the goalkeeper. They criticized the referee (who was not called as a witness), and urged all referees to exercize stricter control. An FA commission later exonerated the referee, adding that he had acted totally in accordance with his instructions.

FIRST DIVISION

	P	W	D	L	F	A	Pts
1 Man City	42	22	13	7	107	61	57
2 Charlton	42	21	12	9	58	49	54
3 Arsenal	42	18	16	8	80	49	52
4 Derby	42	21	7	14	96	90	49
5 Wolves	42	21	5	16	84	67	47
6 Brentford	42	18	10	14	82	78	46
7 Middlesbrough	42	19	8	15	74	71	46
8 Sunderland	42	19	6	17	89	87	44
9 Portsmouth	42	17	10	15	62	66	44
10 Stoke	42	15	12	15	72	57	42
11 Birmingham	42	13	15	14	64	60	41
12 Grimsby	42	17	7	18	86	81	41
13 Chelsea	42	14	13	15	52	55	41
14 Preston	42	14	13	15	56	67	41
15 Huddersfield	42	12	15	15	62	64	39
16 WBA	42	16	6	20	77	98	38
17 Everton	42	14	9	19	81	78	37
18 Liverpool	42	12	11	19	62	84	35
19 Leeds	42	15	4	23	60	80	34
20 Bolton	42	10	14	18	43	66	34
21 Man United	42	10	12	20	55	78	32
22 Sheff Wed	42	9	12	21	53	69	30

SECOND DIVISION

	P	W	D	L	F	A	Pts
1 Leicester	42	24	8	10	89	57	56
2 Blackpool	42	24	7	11	88	53	55
3 Bury	42	22	8	12	74	55	52
4 Newcastle	42	22	5	15	80	56	49
5 Plymouth	42	18	13	11	71	53	49
6 West Ham	42	19	11	12	73	55	49
7 Sheff United	42	18	10	14	66	54	46
8 Coventry	42	17	11	14	66	54	45
9 Aston Villa	42	16	12	14	82	70	44
10 Tottenham	42	17	9	16	88	66	43
11 Fulham	42	15	13	14	71	61	43
12 Blackburn	42	16	10	16	70	62	42
13 Burnley	42	16	10	16	57	61	42
14 Barnsley	42	16	9	17	50	64	41
15 Chesterfield	42	16	8	18	84	89	40
16 Swansea	42	15	7	20	50	65	37
17 Norwich	42	14	8	20	63	71	36
18 Nottm Forest	42	12	10	20	68	90	34
19 Southampton	42	11	12	19	53	77	34
20 Bradford PA	42	12	9	21	52	88	33
21 Bradford City	42	9	12	21	54	94	30
22 Doncaster	42	7	10	25	30	84	24

THIRD DIVISION (NORTH)

	P	W	D	L	F	A	Pts
1 Stockport	42	23	14	5	84	39	60
2 Lincoln	42	25	7	10	103	57	57
3 Chester	42	22	9	11	87	57	53
4 Oldham	42	20	11	11	77	59	51
5 Hull	42	17	12	13	68	69	46
6 Hartlepools	42	19	7	16	75	69	45
7 Halifax	42	18	9	15	68	63	45
8 Wrexham	42	16	12	14	71	57	44
9 Mansfield	42	18	8	16	91	76	44
10 Carlisle	42	18	8	16	65	68	44
11 Port Vale	42	17	10	15	58	64	44
12 York	42	16	11	15	79	70	43
13 Accrington	42	16	9	17	76	69	41
14 Southport	42	12	13	17	73	87	37
15 New Brighton	42	13	11	18	55	70	37
16 Barrow	42	13	10	19	70	86	36
17 Rotherham	42	14	7	21	78	91	35
18 Rochdale	42	13	9	20	69	86	35
19 Tranmere	42	12	9	21	71	88	33
20 Crewe	42	10	12	20	55	83	32
21 Gateshead	42	11	10	21	63	98	32
22 Darlington	42	8	14	20	66	96	30

THIRD DIVISION (SOUTH)

	P	W	D	L	F	A	Pts
1 Luton	42	27	4	11	103	53	58
2 Notts County	42	23	10	9	74	52	56
3 Brighton	42	24	5	13	74	43	53
4 Watford	42	19	11	12	85	60	49
5 Reading	42	19	11	12	76	60	49
6 Bournemouth	42	20	9	13	65	59	49
7 Northampton	42	20	6	16	85	68	46
8 Millwall	42	18	10	14	64	54	46
9 QPR	42	18	9	15	73	52	45
10 Southend	42	17	11	14	78	67	45
11 Gillingham	42	18	8	16	52	66	44
12 Clapton Orient	42	14	15	13	52	52	43
13 Swindon	42	14	11	17	75	73	39
14 Crystal Palace	42	13	12	17	62	61	38
15 Bristol Rovers	42	16	4	22	71	80	36
16 Bristol City	42	15	6	21	58	70	36
17 Walsall	42	13	10	19	62	84	36
18 Cardiff	42	14	7	21	54	87	35
19 Newport	42	12	10	20	67	98	34
20 Torquay	42	11	10	21	57	80	32
21 Exeter	42	10	12	20	59	88	32
22 Aldershot	42	7	9	26	50	89	23

SCOTTISH FIRST DIVISION

	P	W	D	L	F	A	Pts
1 Rangers	38	26	9	3	88	32	61
2 Aberdeen	38	23	8	7	89	44	54
3 Celtic	38	22	8	8	89	58	52
4 Motherwell	38	22	7	9	96	54	51
5 Hearts	38	24	3	11	99	60	51
6 Third Lanark	38	20	6	12	79	61	46
7 Falkirk	38	19	6	13	98	66	44
8 Hamilton	38	18	5	15	91	96	41
9 Dundee	38	12	15	11	58	69	39
10 Clyde	38	16	6	16	59	70	38
11 Kilmarnock	38	14	9	15	60	70	37
12 St Johnstone	38	14	8	16	74	68	36
13 Partick	38	11	12	15	73	68	34
14 Arbroath	38	13	5	20	57	84	31
15 Queen's Park	38	9	12	17	51	77	30
16 St Mirren	38	11	7	20	68	81	29
17 Hibernian	38	6	13	19	54	83	25
18 Queen of the S	38	8	8	22	49	95	24
19 Dunfermline	38	5	11	22	65	98	21
20 Albion	38	5	6	27	53	116	16

SCOTTISH SECOND DIVISION

	P	W	D	L	F	A	Pts
1 Ayr	34	25	4	5	122	49	54
2 Morton	34	23	5	6	110	42	51
3 St Bernard's	34	22	4	8	102	51	48
4 Airdrieonians	34	18	8	8	85	60	44
5 East Fife	34	15	8	11	76	51	38
6 Cowdenbeath	34	14	10	10	75	59	38
7 E Stirlingshire	34	18	2	14	81	78	38
8 Raith	34	16	4	14	72	66	36
9 Alloa	34	13	7	14	64	65	33
10 Stenhousemuir	34	14	4	16	82	86	32
11 Leith	34	13	5	16	62	65	31
12 Forfar	34	11	8	15	73	89	30
13 Montrose	34	11	6	17	65	100	28
14 Dundee United	34	9	9	16	72	97	27
15 Dumbarton	34	11	5	18	57	83	27
16 Brechin	34	8	9	17	64	98	25
17 King's Park	34	11	3	20	61	106	25
18 Edinburgh City	34	2	3	29	42	120	7

Ted Harston of Mansfield Town set a record for goals scored in a season in Division Three North. In the 41 games he played during the season, Harston found the net 55 times.

On 30 January 1937, there was not one away win in all the 35 FA Cup and League matches played.

On 17 April 1937, 149,547 people watched Scotland beat England 3-1 at Hampden Park in the last match of the Home Championship. This was both a British and a world record attendance. The receipts totalled £24,303. Seven days later, at the same ground, 144,303 people paid £11,000 to watch Celtic triumph 2-1 over Aberdeen in the Scottish Cup final. Both the attendance and the receipts broke all previous records for the Scottish Cup final.

FA CUP 1936-37

FOURTH ROUND

Luton Town v Sunderland	2-2, 1-3
Swansea Town v York City	0-0, 3-1
Grimsby Town v Walsall	5-1
Wolverhampton Wanderers v Sheffield United	2-2, 2-1
Millwall v Chelsea	3-0
Derby County v Brentford	3-0
Bolton Wanderers v Norwich City	1-1, 2-1
Manchester City v Accrington Stanley	2-0
Tottenham Hotspur v Plymouth Argyle	1-0
Everton v Sheffield Wednesday	3-0
Preston North End v Stoke City	5-1
Exeter City v Leicester City	3-1
Coventry City v Chester	2-0
West Bromwich Albion v Darlington	3-2
Burnley v Bury	4-1
Arsenal v Manchester United	5-0

FIFTH ROUND

Sunderland v Swansea Town	3-0
Grimsby Town v Wolverhampton Wanderers	1-1, 2-6
Millwall v Derby County	2-1
Bolton Wanderers v Manchester City	0-5
Everton v Tottenham Hotspur	1-1, 3-4
Preston North End v Exeter City	5-3
Coventry City v West Bromwich Albion	2-3
Burnley v Arsenal	1-7

SIXTH ROUND

Wolverhampton Wanderers v Sunderland	1-1, 2-2, 0-4
Millwall v Manchester City	2-0
Tottenham Hotspur v Preston North End	1-3
West Bromwich Albion v Arsenal	3-1

SEMI-FINAL

Sunderland v Millwall	2-1
Preston North End v West Bromwich Albion	4-1

FINAL

Sunderland v Preston North End	3-1

SCOTTISH FA CUP 1936-37

SECOND ROUND

Inverness Caledonian v East Fife	1-6
Albion Rovers v Celtic	2-5
Duns v Dumbarton	2-0
Falkirk v Motherwell	0-3
St Mirren v Brechin City	1-0
Cowdenbeath v Solway Star	9-1
Clyde v St Johnstone	3-1
Dundee v Queen's Park	2-0
Hamilton Academicals v Hibernian	2-1
Heart of Midlothian v King's Park	15-0
Aberdeen v Third Lanark	4-2
Partick Thistle v Arbroath	4-1
Queen of the South v Airdrieonians	2-0
Morton	bye

THIRD ROUND

East Fife v Celtic	0-3
Duns v Motherwell	2-5
St Mirren v Cowdenbeath	1-0
Clyde v Dundee	0-0, 1-0
Hamilton Academicals v Heart of Midlothian	2-1
Morton v Partick Thistle	1-1, 2-1
Aberdeen	bye
Queen of the South	bye

FOURTH ROUND

Celtic v Motherwell	4-4, 2-1
St Mirren v Clyde	0-3
Hamilton Academicals v Aberdeen	1-2
Morton v Queen of the South	4-1

SEMI-FINAL

Celtic v Clyde	2-0
Aberdeen v Morton	2-0

FINAL

Celtic v Aberdeen	2-1

League Tables 1937-38

FIRST DIVISION

		P	W	D	L	F	A	Pts
1	Arsenal	42	21	10	11	77	44	52
2	Wolves	42	20	11	11	72	49	51
3	Preston	42	16	17	9	64	44	49
4	Charlton	42	16	14	12	65	51	46
5	Middlesbrough	42	19	8	15	72	65	46
6	Brentford	42	18	9	15	69	59	45
7	Bolton	42	15	15	12	64	60	45
8	Sunderland	42	14	16	12	55	57	44
9	Leeds	42	14	15	13	64	69	43
10	Chelsea	42	14	13	15	65	65	41
11	Liverpool	42	15	11	16	65	71	41
12	Blackpool	42	16	8	18	61	66	40
13	Derby	42	15	10	17	66	87	40
14	Everton	42	16	7	19	79	75	39
15	Huddersfield	42	17	5	20	55	68	39
16	Leicester	42	14	11	17	54	75	39
17	Stoke	42	13	12	17	58	59	38
18	Birmingham	42	10	18	14	58	62	38
19	Portsmouth	42	13	12	17	62	68	38
20	Grimsby	42	13	12	17	51	68	38
21	Man City	42	14	8	20	80	77	36
22	WBA	42	14	8	20	74	91	36

SECOND DIVISION

		P	W	D	L	F	A	Pts
1	Aston Villa	42	25	7	10	73	35	57
2	Man United	42	22	9	11	82	50	53
3	Sheff United	42	22	9	11	73	56	53
4	Coventry	42	20	12	10	66	45	52
5	Tottenham	42	19	6	17	76	54	44
6	Burnley	42	17	10	15	54	54	44
7	Bradford PA	42	17	9	16	69	56	43
8	Fulham	42	16	11	15	61	57	43
9	West Ham	42	14	14	14	53	52	42
10	Bury	42	18	5	19	63	60	41
11	Chesterfield	42	16	9	17	63	63	41
12	Luton	42	15	10	17	89	86	40
13	Plymouth	42	14	12	16	57	65	40
14	Norwich	42	14	11	17	56	75	39
15	Southampton	42	15	9	18	55	77	39
16	Blackburn	42	14	10	18	71	80	38
17	Sheff Wed	42	14	10	18	49	56	38
18	Swansea	42	13	12	17	45	73	38
19	Newcastle	42	14	8	20	51	58	36
20	Nottm Forest	42	14	8	20	47	60	36
21	Barnsley	42	11	14	17	50	64	36
22	Stockport	42	11	9	22	43	70	31

THIRD DIVISION (NORTH)

		P	W	D	L	F	A	Pts
1	Tranmere	42	23	10	9	81	41	56
2	Doncaster	42	21	12	9	74	49	54
3	Hull	42	20	13	9	80	43	53
4	Oldham	42	19	13	10	67	46	51
5	Gateshead	42	20	11	11	84	59	51
6	Rotherham	42	20	10	12	68	56	50
7	Lincoln	42	19	8	15	66	50	46
8	Crewe	42	18	9	15	71	53	45
9	Chester	42	16	12	14	77	72	44
10	Wrexham	42	16	11	15	58	63	43
11	York	42	16	10	16	70	68	42
12	Carlisle	42	15	9	18	57	67	39
13	New Brighton	42	15	8	19	60	61	38
14	Bradford City	42	14	10	18	66	69	38
15	Port Vale	42	12	14	16	65	73	38
16	Southport	42	12	14	16	53	82	38
17	Rochdale	42	13	11	18	67	78	37
18	Halifax	42	12	12	18	44	66	36
19	Darlington	42	11	10	21	54	79	32
20	Hartlepools	42	10	12	20	53	80	32
21	Barrow	42	11	10	21	41	71	32
22	Accrington	42	11	7	24	45	75	29

THIRD DIVISION (SOUTH)

		P	W	D	L	F	A	Pts
1	Millwall	42	23	10	9	83	37	56
2	Bristol City	42	21	13	8	68	40	55
3	QPR	42	22	9	11	80	47	53
4	Watford	42	21	11	10	73	43	53
5	Brighton	42	21	9	12	64	44	51
6	Reading	42	20	11	11	71	63	51
7	Crystal Palace	42	18	12	12	67	47	48
8	Swindon	42	17	10	15	49	49	44
9	Northampton	42	17	9	16	51	57	43
10	Cardiff	42	15	12	15	67	54	42
11	Notts County	42	16	9	17	50	50	41
12	Southend	42	15	10	17	70	68	40
13	Bournemouth	42	14	12	16	56	57	40
14	Mansfield	42	15	9	18	62	67	39
15	Bristol Rovers	42	13	13	16	46	61	39
16	Newport	42	11	16	15	43	52	38
17	Exeter	42	13	12	17	57	70	38
18	Aldershot	42	15	5	22	39	59	35
19	Clapton Orient	42	13	7	22	42	61	33
20	Torquay	42	9	12	21	38	73	30
21	Walsall	42	11	7	24	52	88	29
22	Gillingham	42	10	6	26	36	77	26

During the season, Jimmy Richardson, the Millwall inside-right, appeared in all three divisions of the Football League, playing with Huddersfield, Newcastle and Millwall.

Raith Rovers, with 142 goals from 34 games, amassed the highest aggregate of goals in a League season in British League football. On their way to this record, they set another, by losing only two of their League matches, the fewest number in any post-1919 division.

SCOTTISH FIRST DIVISION

		P	W	D	L	F	A	Pts
1	Celtic	38	27	7	4	114	42	61
2	Hearts	38	26	6	6	90	50	58
3	Rangers	38	18	13	7	75	49	49
4	Falkirk	38	19	9	10	82	52	47
5	Motherwell	38	17	10	11	78	69	44
6	Aberdeen	38	15	9	14	74	59	39
7	Partick	38	15	9	14	68	70	39
8	St Johnstone	38	16	7	15	78	81	39
9	Third Lanark	38	11	13	14	68	73	35
10	Hibernian	38	11	13	14	57	65	35
11	Arbroath	38	11	13	14	58	79	35
12	Queen's Park	38	11	12	15	59	74	34
13	Hamilton	38	13	7	18	81	76	33
14	St Mirren	38	14	5	19	58	66	33
15	Clyde	38	10	13	15	68	78	33
16	Queen of the S	38	11	11	16	58	71	33
17	Ayr	38	9	15	14	66	85	33
18	Kilmarnock	38	12	9	17	65	91	33
19	Dundee	38	13	6	19	70	74	32
20	Morton	38	6	3	29	64	127	15

SCOTTISH SECOND DIVISION

		P	W	D	L	F	A	Pts
1	Raith	34	27	5	2	142	54	59
2	Albion	34	20	8	6	97	50	48
3	Airdrieonians	34	21	5	8	100	53	47
4	St Bernard's	34	20	5	9	75	49	45
5	East Fife	34	19	5	10	104	61	43
6	Cowdenbeath	34	17	9	8	115	71	43
7	Dumbarton	34	17	5	12	85	66	39
8	Stenhousemuir	34	17	5	12	87	78	39
9	Dunfermline	34	17	5	12	82	76	39
10	Leith	34	16	5	13	71	56	37
11	Alloa	34	11	4	19	78	106	26
12	King's Park	34	11	4	19	64	96	26
13	E Stirlingshire	34	9	7	18	55	95	25
14	Dundee United	34	9	5	20	69	104	23
15	Forfar	34	8	6	20	67	100	22
16	Montrose	34	7	8	19	56	88	22
17	Edinburgh City	34	7	3	24	77	135	17
18	Brechin	34	5	2	27	53	139	12

The only Second Division Scottish club to win the Scottish Cup is East Fife, who achieved this distinction in 1937-38. East Fife, who had two players on loan because of injuries to their regular players, took part in five replays during the course of the competition. This included the final, when after a 1-1 draw, East Fife disposed of Kilmarnock by four goals to two.

FA CUP 1937-38

FOURTH ROUND

Preston North End v Leicester City	2-0
Wolverhampton Wanderers v Arsenal	1-2
Barnsley v Manchester United	2-2, 0-1
Brentford v Portsmouth	2-1
Manchester City v Bury	3-1
Luton Town v Swindon Town	2-1
Charlton Athletic v Leeds United	2-1
Aston Villa v Blackpool	4-0
Everton v Sunderland	0-1
Bradford Park Avenue v Stoke City	1-1, 2-1
Chesterfield v Burnley	3-2
New Brighton v Tottenham Hotspur	0-0, 2-5
York City v West Bromwich Albion	3-2
Nottingham Forest v Middlesbrough	1-3
Sheffield United v Liverpool	1-1, 0-1
Huddersfield Town v Notts County	1-0

FIFTH ROUND

Arsenal v Preston North End	0-1
Brentford v Manchester United	2-0
Luton Town v Manchester City	1-3
Charlton Athletic v Aston Villa	1-1, 2-2, 1-4
Sunderland v Bradford Park Avenue	1-0
Chesterfield v Tottenham Hotspur	2-2, 1-2
York City v Middlesbrough	1-0
Liverpool v Huddersfield Town	0-1

SIXTH ROUND

Brentford v Preston North End	0-3
Aston Villa v Manchester City	3-2
Tottenham Hotspur v Sunderland	0-1
York City v Huddersfield Town	0-0, 1-2

SEMI-FINAL

Preston North End v Aston Villa	2-1
Sunderland v Huddersfield Town	1-3

FINAL

Preston North End v Huddersfield Town	1-0

SCOTTISH FA CUP 1937-38

SECOND ROUND

Rangers v Queen of the South	3-1
Falkirk v St Mirren	3-2
Ross County v Albion Rovers	2-5
Larbert Amateurs v Morton	2-3
Queen's Park v Ayr United	1-1, 1-2
Celtic v Nithsdale Wanderers	5-0
St Bernard's v King's Park	1-1, 4-3
Stenhousemuir v Motherwell	1-1, 1-6
Hamilton Academicals v Forfar Athletic	5-1
Raith Rovers v Edinburgh City	9-2
Partick Thistle v Cowdenbeath	1-0
Aberdeen v St Johnstone	5-1
East Fife v Dundee United	5-0
Kilmarnock	bye

THIRD ROUND

Falkirk v Albion Rovers	4-0
Morton v Ayr United	1-1, 1-4
Celtic v Kilmarnock	1-2
Motherwell v Hamilton Academicals	2-0
Partick Thistle v Raith Rovers	1-2
East Fife v Aberdeen	1-1, 2-1
Rangers	bye
St Bernard's	bye

FOURTH ROUND

Falkirk v Rangers	1-2
Kilmarnock v Ayr United	1-1, 5-0
St Bernard's v Motherwell	3-1
East Fife v Raith Rovers	2-2, 3-2

SEMI FINAL

Rangers v Kilmarnock	3-4
St Bernard's v East Fife	1-1, 1-1, 1-2

FINAL

Kilmarnock v East Fife	1-1, 2-4

League Tables 1938-39

FIRST DIVISION

	P	W	D	L	F	A	Pts
1 Everton	42	27	5	10	88	52	59
2 Wolves	42	22	11	9	88	39	55
3 Charlton	42	22	6	14	75	59	50
4 Middlesbrough	42	20	9	13	93	74	49
5 Arsenal	42	19	9	14	55	41	47
6 Derby	42	19	8	15	66	55	46
7 Stoke	42	17	12	13	71	68	46
8 Bolton	42	15	15	12	67	58	45
9 Preston	42	16	12	14	63	59	44
10 Grimsby	42	16	11	15	61	69	43
11 Liverpool	42	14	14	14	62	63	42
12 Aston Villa	42	15	11	16	71	60	41
13 Leeds	42	16	9	17	59	67	41
14 Man United	42	11	16	15	57	65	38
15 Blackpool	42	12	14	16	56	68	38
16 Sunderland	42	13	12	17	54	67	38
17 Portsmouth	42	12	13	17	47	70	37
18 Brentford	42	14	8	20	53	74	36
19 Huddersfield	42	12	11	19	58	64	35
20 Chelsea	42	12	9	21	64	80	33
21 Birmingham	42	12	8	22	62	84	32
22 Leicester	42	9	11	22	48	82	29

SECOND DIVISION

	P	W	D	L	F	A	Pts
1 Blackburn	42	25	5	12	94	60	55
2 Sheff United	42	20	14	8	69	41	54
3 Sheff Wed	42	21	11	10	88	59	53
4 Coventry	42	21	8	13	62	45	50
5 Man City	42	21	7	14	96	72	49
6 Chesterfield	42	20	9	13	69	52	49
7 Luton	42	22	5	15	82	66	49
8 Tottenham	42	19	9	14	67	62	47
9 Newcastle	42	18	10	14	61	48	46
10 WBA	42	18	9	15	89	72	45
11 West Ham	42	17	10	15	70	52	44
12 Fulham	42	17	10	15	61	55	44
13 Millwall	42	14	14	14	64	53	42
14 Burnley	42	15	9	18	50	56	39
15 Plymouth	42	15	8	19	49	55	38
16 Bury	42	12	13	17	65	74	37
17 Bradford PA	42	12	11	19	61	82	35
18 Southampton	42	13	9	20	56	82	35
19 Swansea	42	11	12	19	50	83	34
20 Nottm Forest	42	10	11	21	49	82	31
21 Norwich	42	13	5	24	50	91	31
22 Tranmere	42	6	5	31	39	99	17

THIRD DIVISION (SOUTH)

	P	W	D	L	F	A	Pts
1 Newport	42	22	11	9	58	45	55
2 Crystal Palace	42	20	12	10	71	52	52
3 Brighton	42	19	11	12	68	49	49
4 Watford	42	17	12	13	62	51	46
5 Reading	42	16	14	12	69	59	46
6 QPR	42	15	14	13	68	49	44
7 Ipswich	42	16	12	14	62	52	44
8 Bristol City	42	16	12	14	61	63	44
9 Swindon	42	18	8	16	72	77	44
10 Aldershot	42	16	12	14	53	66	44
11 Notts County	42	17	9	16	59	54	43
12 Southend	42	16	9	17	61	64	41
13 Cardiff	42	15	11	16	61	65	41
14 Exeter	42	13	14	15	65	82	40
15 Bournemouth	42	13	13	16	52	58	39
16 Mansfield	42	12	15	15	44	62	39
17 Northampton	42	15	8	19	51	58	38
18 Port Vale	42	14	9	19	52	58	37
19 Torquay	42	14	9	19	54	70	37
20 Clapton Orient	42	11	13	18	53	55	35
21 Walsall	42	11	11	20	68	69	33
22 Bristol Rovers	42	10	13	19	55	61	33

THIRD DIVISION (NORTH)

	P	W	D	L	F	A	Pts
1 Barnsley	42	30	7	5	94	34	67
2 Doncaster	42	21	14	7	87	47	56
3 Bradford City	42	22	8	12	89	56	52
4 Southport	42	20	10	12	75	54	50
5 Oldham	42	22	5	15	76	59	49
6 Chester	42	20	9	13	88	70	49
7 Hull	42	18	10	14	83	74	46
8 Crewe	42	19	6	17	82	70	44
9 Stockport	42	17	9	16	91	77	43
10 Gateshead	42	14	14	14	74	67	42
11 Rotherham	42	17	8	17	64	64	42
12 Halifax	42	13	16	13	52	54	42
13 Barrow	42	16	9	17	66	65	41
14 Wrexham	42	17	7	18	66	79	41
15 Rochdale	42	15	9	18	92	82	39
16 New Brighton	42	15	9	18	68	73	39
17 Lincoln	42	12	9	21	66	92	33
18 Darlington	42	13	7	22	62	92	33
19 Carlisle	42	13	7	22	64	111	33
20 York	42	12	8	22	66	92	32
21 Hartlepools	42	12	7	23	55	94	31
22 Accrington	42	7	6	29	49	103	20

SCOTTISH FIRST DIVISION

	P	W	D	L	F	A	Pts
1 Rangers	38	25	9	4	112	55	59
2 Celtic	38	20	8	10	99	53	48
3 Aberdeen	38	20	6	12	91	61	46
4 Hearts	38	20	5	13	98	70	45
5 Falkirk	38	19	7	12	73	63	45
6 Queen of the S	38	17	9	12	69	64	43
7 Hamilton	38	18	5	15	67	71	41
8 St Johnstone	38	17	6	15	85	82	40
9 Clyde	38	17	5	16	78	70	39
10 Kilmarnock	38	15	9	14	73	86	39
11 Partick Thistle	38	17	4	17	74	87	38
12 Motherwell	38	16	5	17	82	86	37
13 Hibernian	38	14	7	17	68	69	35
14 Ayr	38	13	9	16	76	83	35
15 Third Lanark	38	12	8	18	80	96	32
16 Albion	38	12	6	20	65	90	30
17 Arbroath	38	11	8	19	54	75	30
18 St Mirren	38	11	7	20	57	80	29
19 Queen's Park	38	11	5	22	57	83	27
20 Raith	38	10	2	26	65	99	22

SCOTTISH SECOND DIVISION

	P	W	D	L	F	A	Pts
1 Cowdenbeath	34	28	4	2	120	45	60
2 Alloa	34	22	4	8	91	46	48
3 East Fife	34	21	6	7	99	61	48
4 Airdrieonians	34	21	5	8	85	57	47
5 Dunfermline	34	18	5	11	99	78	41
6 Dundee	34	15	7	12	99	63	37
7 St Bernard's	34	15	6	13	79	79	36
8 Stenhousemuir	34	15	5	14	74	69	35
9 Dundee United	34	15	3	16	78	69	33
10 Brechin	34	11	9	14	82	106	31
11 Dumbarton	34	9	12	13	68	76	30
12 Morton	34	11	6	17	74	88	28
13 King's Park	34	12	2	20	87	92	26
14 Montrose	34	10	5	19	82	96	25
15 Forfar	34	11	3	20	74	138	25
16 Leith	34	10	4	20	57	83	24
17 E Stirlingshire	34	9	4	21	89	130	22
18 Edinburgh	34	6	4	24	58	119	16

FA CUP 1938-39

FOURTH ROUND

Portsmouth v West Bromwich Albion	2-0
West Ham United v Tottenham Hotspur	3-3, 1-1, 2-1
Preston North End v Aston Villa	2-0
Cardiff City v Newcastle United	0-0, 1-4
Leeds United v Huddersfield Town	2-4
Notts County v Walsall	0-0, 0-4
Middlesbrough v Sunderland	0-2
Blackburn Rovers v Southend United	4-2
Wolverhampton Wanderers v Leicester City	5-1
Liverpool v Stockport County	5-1
Everton v Doncaster Rovers	8-0
Birmingham v Chelmsford City	6-0
Chelsea v Fulham	3-0
Sheffield Wednesday v Chester	1-1, 1-1, 2-0
Sheffield United v Manchester City	2-0
Millwall v Grimsby Town	2-2, 2-3

FIFTH ROUND

Portsmouth v West Ham United	2-0
Newcastle United v Preston North End	1-2
Huddersfield Town v Walsall	3-0
Sunderland v Blackburn Rovers	1-1, 0-0, 0-1
Wolverhampton Wanderers v Liverpool	4-1
Birmingham v Everton	2-2, 1-2
Chelsea v Sheffield Wednesday	1-1, 0-0, 3-1
Sheffield United v Grimsby Town	0-0, 0-1

SIXTH ROUND

Portsmouth v Preston North End	1-0
Huddersfield Town v Blackburn Rovers	1-1, 2-1
Wolverhampton Wanderers v Everton	2-0
Chelsea v Grimsby Town	0-1

SEMI-FINAL

Portsmouth v Huddersfield Town	2-1
Wolverhampton Wanderers v Grimsby Town	5-0

FINAL

Portsmouth v Wolverhampton Wanderers	4-1

SCOTTISH FA CUP 1938-39

SECOND ROUND

Dundee v Clyde	0-0, 0-1
Rangers v Hamilton Academicals	2-0
Blairgowrie v Buckie Thistle	3-3, 1-4
Third Lanark v Cowdenbeath	3-0
Dunfermline Athletic v Duns	2-0
Hibernian v Kilmarnock	3-1
Falkirk v Airdrieonians	7-0
Aberdeen v Queen's Park	5-1
Queen of the South v Babcock & Wilcox	5-0
Heart of Midlothian v Elgin City	14-1
Montrose v Celtic	1-7
Edinburgh City v St Mirren	1-3
Dundee United v Motherwell	1-5
Alloa Athletic	bye

THIRD ROUND

Rangers v Clyde	1-4
Buckie Thistle v Third Lanark	0-6
Dunfermline Athletic v Alloa Athletic	1-1, 2-3
Falkirk v Aberdeen	2-3
Heart of Midlothian v Celtic	2-2, 1-2
Motherwell v St Mirren	4-2
Hibernian	bye
Queen of the South	bye

FOURTH ROUND

Clyde v Third Lanark	1-0
Hibernian v Alloa Athletic	3-1
Aberdeen v Queen of the South	2-0
Motherwell v Celtic	3-1

SEMI-FINAL

Clyde v Hibernian	1-0
Aberdeen v Motherwell	1-1, 1-3

FINAL

Clyde v Motherwell	4-0

Dixie Dean goes West

On 25 January 1939, Dixie Dean, the most prolific goalscorer of the time, left Notts County and English football to join Sligo Rovers in Eire. In April of that year, he played centre-forward for Sligo in the FA of Ireland Cup final against Shelbourne. The game ended in a 1-1 draw, and Sligo lost the replay 1-0.

1938-39 was the last season when players went unidentified. In 1939-40, players wore numbers in League games for the first time.

In Division Two, Tranmere Rovers lost 31 of their 42 League games, a Division Two record. Wolves set a First Division record in 1938-39 by conceding only 39 goals in 42 games, a record under the new offside rule. Barnsley also set a record—in Division Three North—letting in only 34 goals in 42 games.

The War Years

FIRST DIVISION 1939-40

	P	W	D	L	F	A	Pts
Blackpool	3	3	0	0	5	2	6
Sheff United	3	2	1	0	3	1	5
Arsenal	3	2	1	0	8	4	5
Liverpool	3	2	0	1	6	3	4
Everton	3	1	2	0	5	4	4
Bolton	3	2	0	1	6	5	4
Charlton	3	2	0	1	3	4	4
Derby	3	2	0	1	3	3	4
Man United	3	1	1	1	5	3	3
Chelsea	3	1	1	1	4	4	3
Stoke	3	1	1	1	7	4	3
Brentford	3	1	1	1	3	3	3
Leeds	3	1	1	1	2	4	3
Grimsby	3	1	1	1	2	4	3
Sunderland	3	1	0	2	6	7	2
Aston Villa	3	1	0	2	3	3	2
Wolverhampton	3	0	2	1	3	4	2
Huddersfield	3	1	0	2	2	3	2
Preston	3	0	2	1	0	2	2
Portsmouth	3	1	0	2	3	5	2
Blackburn	3	0	1	2	3	5	1
Middlesbrough	3	0	1	2	3	8	1

SECOND DIVISION 1939-40

	P	W	D	L	F	A	Pts
Luton	3	2	1	0	7	1	5
Birmingham	3	2	1	0	5	1	5
West Ham	3	2	0	1	5	4	4
Coventry	3	1	2	0	8	6	4
Leicester	3	2	0	1	6	5	4
Nottm Forest	3	2	0	1	5	5	4
Plymouth	3	2	0	1	4	3	4
Tottenham	3	1	2	0	6	5	4
WBA	3	1	1	1	8	8	3
Bury	3	1	1	1	4	5	3
Newport	3	1	1	1	5	4	3
Millwall	3	1	1	1	5	4	3
Man City	3	1	1	1	6	5	3
Southampton	3	1	0	2	5	6	2
Swansea	3	1	0	2	5	11	2
Barnsley	3	1	0	2	7	8	2
Chesterfield	2	1	0	1	2	2	2
Newcastle	3	1	0	2	8	6	2
Sheff Wed	3	1	0	2	3	5	2
Bradford	3	0	1	2	2	7	1
Fulham	3	0	1	2	3	6	1
Burnley	2	0	1	1	1	3	1

THIRD DIVISION (NORTH) 1939-40

	P	W	D	L	F	A	Pts
Accrington	3	3	0	0	6	1	6
Halifax	3	2	1	0	6	1	5
Darlington	3	2	1	0	5	2	5
Chester	3	2	1	0	5	2	5
Rochdale	3	2	0	1	2	2	4
New Brighton	3	2	0	1	4	5	4
Tranmere	3	1	1	1	6	6	3
Rotherham	3	1	1	1	5	6	3
Wrexham	3	1	1	1	3	2	3
Lincoln	3	1	1	1	6	7	3
Crewe	2	1	1	0	3	0	3
Oldham	3	1	0	2	3	5	2
Doncaster	3	1	0	2	4	5	2
Gateshead	3	1	0	2	6	7	2
Southport	3	0	2	1	4	5	2
Hull	2	0	2	0	3	3	2
Hartlepools	3	0	2	1	1	4	2
Barrow	3	0	2	1	4	5	2
Carlisle	2	1	0	1	3	3	2
York	3	0	1	2	3	5	1
Bradford City	3	0	1	2	3	6	1
Stockport	2	0	0	2	0	5	0

THIRD DIVISION (SOUTH) 1939-40

	P	W	D	L	F	A	Pts
Reading	3	2	1	0	8	2	5
Exeter	3	2	1	0	5	3	5
Cardiff	3	2	0	1	5	5	4
Crystal Palace	3	2	0	1	8	9	4
Brighton	3	1	2	0	5	4	4
Ipswich	3	1	2	0	5	3	4
Notts County	2	2	0	0	6	3	4
Southend	3	1	1	1	3	3	3
Bristol City	3	1	1	1	5	5	3
Clapton Orient	3	0	3	0	3	3	3
Mansfield	3	1	1	1	8	8	3
Norwich	3	1	1	1	4	4	3
Torquay	3	0	3	0	4	4	3
Bournemouth	3	1	1	1	13	4	3
Walsall	3	1	1	1	3	3	3
Northampton	3	1	0	2	12	2	2
QPR	3	0	2	1	4	5	2
Watford	3	0	2	1	4	5	2
Bristol Rovers	3	0	1	2	2	7	1
Port Vale	2	0	1	1	0	1	1
Aldershot	3	0	1	2	3	4	1
Swindon	3	0	1	2	2	4	1

SCOTTISH DIVISION 'A' 1939-40

	P	W	D	L	F	A	Pts
Rangers	5	4	1	0	14	3	9
Falkirk	5	4	0	1	20	10	8
Aberdeen	5	3	0	2	9	6	6
Celtic	5	3	0	2	7	7	6
Hearts	5	2	2	1	13	9	6
Partick Thistle	5	2	2	1	7	7	6
Motherwell	5	2	1	2	14	12	5
Hamilton	5	2	1	1	7	11	5
Third Lanark	5	2	1	2	9	8	5
Queen of the S	5	2	1	2	10	9	5
Albion	5	2	1	2	12	7	5
St Mirren	5	1	3	1	8	8	5
Kilmarnock	5	2	1	2	10	9	5
Hibernian	5	2	0	3	11	13	4
Alloa	5	2	0	3	8	13	4
Arbroath	5	2	0	3	9	9	4
St Johnstone	5	2	0	3	7	8	4
Ayr	5	2	0	3	10	17	4
Clyde	5	1	0	4	10	14	2
Cowdenbeath	5	1	0	4	6	14	2

SCOTTISH DIVISION 'B' 1939-40

	P	W	D	L	F	A	Pts
Dundee	4	3	1	0	13	5	7
Dunfermline	4	2	2	0	10	5	6
King's Park	4	2	2	0	11	7	6
East Fife	4	2	1	1	12	6	5
Queen's Park	4	1	3	0	7	5	5
Stenhousemuir	4	2	1	1	6	5	5
Dundee United	4	2	1	1	8	7	5
Dumbarton	4	2	1	1	9	9	5
E Stirlingshire	4	1	2	1	7	7	4
St Bernard's	4	1	2	1	7	7	4
Airdrieonians	4	2	0	2	7	8	4
Edinburgh	4	1	1	2	9	8	3
Montrose	4	1	1	2	7	8	3
Raith	4	1	1	2	8	12	3
Morton	4	1	1	2	4	7	3
Leith	4	1	0	3	4	7	2
Brechin	4	0	2	2	3	8	2
Forfar	4	0	0	4	7	18	0

WINNERS 1939-40

League Cup West Ham United
Midland League Wolverhampton Wanderers
North East League Huddersfield Town
North West League Bury
South 'A' League Arsenal
South 'B' League Queen's Park Rangers
South 'C' League Tottenham Hotspur
South 'D' League Crystal Palace
West League Stoke City
South West League Plymouth Argyle
East Midland League Chesterfield
Scottish Emergency Cup Rangers
Scottish Regional League West & South Rangers
Scottish Regional League East & North Falkirk
Irish FA Cup Ballymena United
FA of Ireland Cup (Eire) Shamrock Rovers
League of Ireland (Eire) St James' Gate

WINNERS 1940-41

League Cup Preston North End
Football League South Watford
Northern Regional League Preston North End
Southern Regional League Crystal Palace
London Cup Reading
Lancashire Cup Manchester United
Midland Cup Leicester City
Combined Cities Cup Middlesbrough
Western Regional Cup Bristol City
Scottish Southern League Cup Rangers
Scottish Summer Cup Hibernian
Scottish Southern League Rangers
Irish FA Cup Belfast Celtic
FA of Ireland Cup (Eire) Cork United
League of Ireland (Eire) Cork United

WINNERS 1941-42

League Cup Wolverhampton Wanderers
League North Blackpool
League South Leicester City
London Cup Brentford
London League Arsenal
Scottish Southern League Cup Rangers
Scottish Summer Cup Rangers
Scottish Southern League Rangers
Scottish North Eastern League 1st series Rangers
Scottish North Eastern League 2nd series Aberdeen
Irish FA Cup Linfield
FA of Ireland Cup (Eire) Dundalk
League of Ireland (Eire) Cork United

WINNERS 1942-43

League North Cup Blackpool
League North Blackpool
League South Cup Arsenal
League South Arsenal
League West Cup Swansea Town
League West Lovells Athletic
Scottish Southern League Cup Rangers
Scottish Summer Cup St Mirren
Scottish Southern League Rangers
Scottish North Eastern League 1st series Aberdeen
Scottish North Eastern League 2nd series Aberdeen
Irish FA Cup Belfast Celtic
FA of Ireland Cup (Eire) Drumcondra
League of Ireland (Eire) Cork United

WINNERS 1943-44

League North Cup Aston Villa
League North Blackpool
League South Cup Charlton Athletic
League South Tottenham Hotspur
League West Cup Bath City
League West Lovells Athletic
Scottish Southern League Cup Hibernian
Scottish Summer Cup Motherwell
Scottish Southern League Rangers
Scottish North Eastern League 1st series Raith Rovers
Scottish North Eastern League 2nd series Aberdeen
Irish FA Cup Belfast Celtic
FA of Ireland Cup (Eire) Shamrock Rovers
League of Ireland (Eire) Shelbourne

Above When War broke out, the 1939-40 football season had hardly got under way. The tables above show the state of each division when the League programme was halted. Goal average has not been calculated, as at such an early stage in the season, the figures presented in these hitherto unpublished tables serve as a guide to each team's performance, rather than a means of listing the teams in order.

The Englishman who played for Wales
Stanley Mortensen made his war-time international debut against his own country. At Wembley, on 25 September 1943, England played Wales. Mortensen was reserve for England, but when the injured Welsh left-half, Ivor Powell, was unable to resume after the interval, it was agreed by both sides that Mortensen should take Powell's place. The game ended in an 8-3 victory for England.

WINNERS 1944-45

League North Cup **Bolton Wanderers**
League North **Huddersfield Town**
League South Cup **Chelsea**
League South **Tottenham Hotspur**
League West Cup **Bath City**
League West **Cardiff City**
Scottish Southern League Cup **Rangers**
Scottish Summer Cup **Partick Thistle**
Scottish Southern League **Rangers**
Scottish North Eastern League 1st series **Dundee**
Scottish North Eastern League 2nd series **Aberdeen**
Irish FA Cup **Linfield**
FA of Ireland Cup (Eire) **Shamrock Rovers**
League of Ireland (Eire) **Cork United**

WINNERS 1945-46

League North **Sheffield United**
League South **Birmingham City**
League Three North Cup **Rotherham United**
League Three North (West) **Accrington Stanley**
League Three North (East) **Rotherham United**
League Three South Cup **Bournemouth**
League Three South (North) **Queen's Park Rangers**
League Three South (South) **Crystal Palace**
Scottish Southern League 'A' **Rangers**
Scottish Southern League 'B' **Dundee**
Scottish Victory Cup **Rangers**
Irish FA Cup **Linfield**
FA of Ireland Cup (Eire) **Drumcondra**
League of Ireland (Eire) **Cork United**

SCOTTISH SOUTHERN LEAGUE CUP 1945-46 (LEAGUE CUP)

SECTION WINNERS

Division A	Division B
1 Heart of Midlothian	1 East Fife
2 Rangers	2 Ayr United
3 Aberdeen	3 Airdrieonians
4 Clyde	4 Dundee

QUARTER-FINAL

Aberdeen v Ayr United	2-0
Airdrieonians v Clyde	1-0
Heart of Midlothian v East Fife	3-0
Rangers v Dundee	3-1

SEMI-FINAL

Aberdeen v Airdrieonians	2-2, 5-3
Rangers v Hearts	2-1

FINAL

Aberdeen v Rangers	3-2

LEADING GOALSCORERS (ENGLAND) 1939-46

Albert Stubbins, Newcastle United	226
Jock Dodds, Blackpool	221
Tommy Lawton, Everton, Tranmere Rovers, Aldershot and Chelsea	212

FA CUP 1945-46

THIRD ROUND (two legs)

Stoke City v Burnley	3-1, 1-2
Huddersfield Town v Sheffield United	1-1, 0-2
Mansfield Town v Sheffield Wednesday	0-0, 0-5
Chesterfield v York City	1-1, 2-3
Bolton Wanderers v Blackburn Rovers	1-0, 3-1
Chester v Liverpool	0-2, 1-2
Wrexham v Blackpool	1-4, 1-4
Leeds United v Middlesbrough	4-4, 2-7
Accrington Stanley v Manchester United	2-2, 1-5
Preston North End v Everton	2-1, 2-2
Charlton Athletic v Fulham	3-1, 1-2
Lovells Athletic v Wolverhampton Wanderers	2-4, 1-8
Southampton v Newport County	4-3, 2-1
Queen's Park Rangers v Crystal Palace	0-0, 0-0*, 1-0
Bristol City v Swansea Town	5-1, 2-2
Tottenham Hotspur v Brentford	2-2, 0-2
Chelsea v Leicester City	1-1, 2-0
West Ham United v Arsenal	6-0, 0-1
Northampton Town v Millwall	2-2, 0-3
Coventry City v Aston Villa	2-1, 0-2
Norwich City v Brighton	1-2, 1-4
Aldershot v Plymouth Argyle	2-0, 1-0
Luton Town v Derby County	0-6, 0-3
Cardiff City v West Bromwich Albion	1-1, 0-4
Newcastle United v Barnsley	4-2, 0-3
Rotherham United v Gateshead	2-2, 2-0
Bradford Park Avenue v Port Vale	2-1, 1-1
Manchester City v Barrow	6-2, 2-2
Grimsby Town v Sunderland	1-3, 1-2
Bury v Rochdale	3-3, 4-2
Birmingham City v Portsmouth	1-0, 0-0
Nottingham Forest v Watford	1-1, 1-1*, 0-1

*abandoned

FOURTH ROUND (two legs)

Stoke City v Sheffield United	2-0, 2-3
Sheffield Wednesday v York City	5-1, 6-1
Bolton Wanderers v Liverpool	5-0, 0-2
Blackpool v Middlesbrough	3-2, 2-3, 0-1
Manchester United v Preston North End	1-0, 1-3
Charlton Athletic v Wolverhampton Wanderers	5-2, 1-1
Southampton v Queen's Park Rangers	0-1, 3-4
Bristol City v Brentford	2-1, 0-5
Chelsea v West Ham United	2-0, 0-1
Millwall v Aston Villa	2-4, 1-9
Brighton v Aldershot	3-0, 4-1
Derby County v West Bromwich Albion	1-0, 3-1
Barnsley v Rotherham United	3-0, 1-2
Bradford Park Avenue v Manchester City	1-3, 8-2
Sunderland v Bury	3-1, 4-5
Birmingham City v Watford	5-0, 1-1

FIFTH ROUND (two legs)

Stoke City v Sheffield Wednesday	2-0, 0-0
Bolton Wanderers v Middlesbrough	1-0, 1-1
Preston North End v Charlton Athletic	1-1, 0-6
Queen's Park Rangers v Brentford	1-3, 0-0
Chelsea v Aston Villa	0-1, 0-1
Brighton v Derby County	1-4, 0-6
Barnsley v Bradford Park Avenue	0-1, 1-1
Sunderland v Birmingham City	1-0, 1-3

SIXTH ROUND (two legs)

Stoke City v Bolton Wanderers	0-2, 0-0
Charlton Athletic v Brentford	6-3, 3-1
Aston Villa v Derby County	3-4, 1-1
Bradford Park Avenue v Birmingham City	2-2, 0-6

SEMI-FINAL

Bolton Wanderers v Charlton Athletic	0-2
Derby County v Birmingham City	1-1, 4-0

FINAL

Derby County v Charlton Athletic	4-1

Top *In 1945 Jack Tinn, manager of Portsmouth, proudly shows Field Marshal Montgomery the FA Cup won by Portsmouth six years earlier. There was no FA Cup competition during the War, so Pompey held the Cup until the competition restarted in 1945-46.*

Above *A shot by Duncan, deflected by Charlton's Bert Turner, enters the net for Derby's first goal in the 1946 Cup Final. During this game, the ball burst. Oddly enough, the chances of this happening were discussed in a BBC broadcast shortly before* the game, and the referee, Mr E D Smith of Cumberland, remarked that it was a million-to-one chance. Even more curiously, the ball also burst when Derby played Charlton in a League match just five days after their Wembley meeting.

League Tables 1946-47

FIRST DIVISION

		P	W	D	L	F	A	Pts
1	Liverpool	42	25	7	10	84	52	57
2	Man United	42	22	12	8	95	54	56
3	Wolves	42	25	6	11	98	56	56
4	Stoke	42	24	7	11	90	53	55
5	Blackpool	42	22	6	14	71	70	50
6	Sheff United	42	21	7	14	89	75	49
7	Preston	42	18	11	13	76	74	47
8	Aston Villa	42	18	9	15	67	53	45
9	Sunderland	42	18	8	16	65	66	44
10	Everton	42	17	9	16	62	67	43
11	Middlesbrough	42	17	8	17	73	68	42
12	Portsmouth	42	16	9	17	66	60	41
13	Arsenal	42	16	9	17	72	70	41
14	Derby	42	18	5	19	73	79	41
15	Chelsea	42	16	7	19	69	84	39
16	Grimsby	42	13	12	17	61	82	38
17	Blackburn	42	14	8	20	45	53	36
18	Bolton	42	13	8	21	57	69	34
19	Charlton	42	11	12	19	57	71	34
20	Huddersfield	42	13	7	22	53	79	33
21	Brentford	42	9	7	26	45	88	25
22	Leeds	42	6	6	30	45	90	18

SECOND DIVISION

		P	W	D	L	F	A	Pts
1	Man City	42	26	10	6	78	35	62
2	Burnley	42	22	14	6	65	29	58
3	Birmingham	42	25	5	12	74	33	55
4	Chesterfield	42	18	14	10	58	44	50
5	Newcastle	42	19	10	13	95	62	48
6	Tottenham	42	17	14	11	65	53	48
7	WBA	42	20	8	14	88	75	48
8	Coventry	42	16	13	13	66	59	45
9	Leicester	42	18	7	17	69	64	43
10	Barnsley	42	17	8	17	84	86	42
11	Nottm Forest	42	15	10	17	69	74	40
12	West Ham	42	16	8	18	70	76	40
13	Luton	42	16	7	19	71	73	39
14	Southampton	42	15	9	18	69	76	39
15	Fulham	42	15	9	18	63	74	39
16	Bradford PA	42	14	11	17	65	77	39
17	Bury	42	12	12	18	80	78	36
18	Millwall	42	14	8	20	56	79	36
19	Plymouth	42	14	5	23	79	96	33
20	Sheff Wed	42	12	8	22	67	88	32
21	Swansea	42	11	7	24	55	83	29
22	Newport	42	10	3	29	61	133	23

THIRD DIVISION (NORTH)

		P	W	D	L	F	A	Pts
1	Doncaster	42	33	6	3	123	40	72
2	Rotherham	42	29	6	7	114	53	64
3	Chester	42	25	6	11	95	51	56
4	Stockport	42	24	2	16	78	53	50
5	Bradford City	42	20	10	12	62	47	50
6	Rochdale	42	19	10	13	80	64	48
7	Wrexham	42	17	12	13	65	51	46
8	Crewe	42	17	9	16	70	74	43
9	Barrow	42	17	7	18	54	62	41
10	Tranmere	42	17	7	18	66	77	41
11	Hull	42	16	8	18	49	53	40
12	Lincoln	42	17	5	20	86	87	39
13	Hartlepools	42	15	9	18	64	73	39
14	Gateshead	42	16	6	20	62	72	38
15	York	42	14	9	19	67	81	37
16	Carlisle	42	14	9	19	70	93	37
17	Darlington	42	15	6	21	68	80	36
18	New Brighton	42	14	8	20	57	77	36
19	Oldham	42	12	8	22	55	80	32
20	Accrington	42	14	4	24	56	92	32
21	Southport	42	7	11	24	53	85	25
22	Halifax	42	8	6	28	43	92	22

THIRD DIVISION (SOUTH)

		P	W	D	L	F	A	Pts
1	Cardiff	42	30	6	6	93	30	66
2	QPR	42	23	11	8	74	40	57
3	Bristol City	42	20	11	11	94	56	51
4	Swindon	42	19	11	12	84	73	49
5	Walsall	42	17	12	13	74	59	46
6	Ipswich	42	16	14	12	61	53	46
7	Bournemouth	42	18	8	16	72	54	44
8	Southend	42	17	10	15	71	60	44
9	Reading	42	16	11	15	83	74	43
10	Port Vale	42	17	9	16	68	63	43
11	Torquay	42	15	12	15	52	61	42
12	Notts County	42	15	10	17	63	63	40
13	Northampton	42	15	10	17	72	75	40
14	Bristol Rovers	42	16	8	18	59	69	40
15	Exeter	42	15	9	18	60	69	39
16	Watford	42	17	5	20	61	76	39
17	Brighton	42	13	12	17	54	72	38
18	Crystal Palace	42	13	11	18	49	62	37
19	Leyton Orient	42	12	8	22	54	75	32
20	Aldershot	42	10	12	20	48	78	32
21	Norwich	42	10	8	24	64	100	28
22	Mansfield	42	9	10	23	48	96	28

SCOTTISH DIVISION 'A'

		P	W	D	L	F	A	Pts
1	Rangers	30	21	4	5	76	26	46
2	Hibernian	30	19	6	5	69	33	44
3	Aberdeen	30	16	7	7	58	41	39
4	Hearts	30	16	6	8	52	43	38
5	Partick Thistle	30	16	3	11	74	59	35
6	Morton	30	12	10	8	58	45	34
7	Celtic	30	13	6	11	53	55	32
8	Motherwell	30	12	5	13	58	54	29
9	Third Lanark	30	11	6	13	56	64	28
10	Clyde	30	9	9	12	55	65	27
11	Falkirk	30	8	10	12	62	61	26
12	Queen of the S	30	9	8	13	44	69	26
13	Queen's Park	30	8	6	16	47	60	22
14	St Mirren	30	9	4	17	47	65	22
15	Kilmarnock	30	6	9	15	44	66	21
16	Hamilton	30	2	7	21	38	85	11

SCOTTISH DIVISION 'B'

		P	W	D	L	F	A	Pts
1	Dundee	26	21	3	2	113	30	45
2	Airdrieonians	26	19	4	3	78	38	42
3	East Fife	26	12	7	7	58	39	31
4	Albion	26	10	7	9	50	54	27
5	Alloa	26	11	5	10	51	57	27
6	Raith	26	10	6	10	45	52	26
7	Stenhousemuir	26	8	7	11	43	53	23
8	Dunfermline	26	10	3	13	50	72	23
9	St Johnstone	26	9	4	13	45	47	22
10	Dundee United	26	9	4	13	53	60	22
11	Ayr	26	9	2	15	56	73	20
12	Arbroath	26	7	6	13	42	63	20
13	Dumbarton	26	7	4	15	41	54	18
14	Cowdenbeath	26	6	6	14	44	77	18

When Italy beat Hungary 3-2 on 11 May 1947, a record ten members of the victorious Italian team came from Juventus.

Hull City used 42 players in the Third Division North, 1946-47. This was only the third time in the history of the League that such a large pool of players had been used in one season by a single club.

Cardiff equalled a Division Three South record by winning 30 of their 42 matches. By contrast, Leeds set a First Division record by losing 30 of their 42 matches.

Doncaster Rovers enjoyed an enormously successful season in winning the Third Division North championship in 1946-47. They set four League records during the course of the season. Their points total (72) was the highest number of points ever won by a club in any division of the League; that total included 37 points won away from home, also a League record. By winning 18 of their 21 away games, Doncaster established a third League record, for the most games won away from home and, in all, Doncaster Rovers won 33 of their 42 Division Three North games to set another League record. They also equalled the record for the division by losing just three matches during the season.

FA CUP 1946-47

FOURTH ROUND

West Bromwich Albion v Charlton Athletic	1-2
Blackburn Rovers v Port Vale	2-0
Preston North End v Barnsley	6-0
Sheffield Wednesday v Everton	2-1
Newcastle United v Southampton	3-1
Brentford v Leicester City	0-0, 0-0, 1-4
Wolverhampton Wanderers v Sheffield United	0-0, 0-2
Chester v Stoke City	0-0, 2-3
Burnley v Coventry City	2-0
Luton Town v Swansea Town	2-0
Middlesbrough v Chesterfield	2-1
Manchester United v Nottingham Forest	0-2
Liverpool v Grimsby Town	2-0
Chelsea v Derby County	2-2, 0-1
Birmingham City v Portsmouth	1-0
Bolton Wanderers v Manchester City	3-3, 0-1

FIFTH ROUND

Charlton Athletic v Blackburn Rovers	1-0
Sheffield Wednesday v Preston North End	0-2
Newcastle United v Leicester City	1-1, 2-1
Stoke City v Sheffield United	0-1
Luton Town v Burnley	0-0, 0-3
Nottingham Forest v Middlesbrough	2-2, 2-6
Liverpool v Derby County	1-0
Birmingham City v Manchester City	5-0

SIXTH ROUND

Charlton Athletic v Preston North End	2-1
Sheffield United v Newcastle United	0-2
Middlesbrough v Burnley	1-1, 0-1
Liverpool v Birmingham City	4-1

SEMI-FINAL

Charlton Athletic v Newcastle United	4-0
Burnley v Liverpool	0-0, 1-0

FINAL

Charlton Athletic v Burnley	1-0

SCOTTISH FA CUP 1946-47

SECOND ROUND

Aberdeen v Ayr United	8-0
East Fife v East Stirlingshire	5-1
Morton	bye
Dundee	bye
Albion Rovers	bye
Arbroath	bye
Raith Rovers	bye
Heart of Midlothian	bye
Cowdenbeath	bye
Hibernian	bye
Rangers	bye
Dumbarton	bye
Third Lanark	bye
Motherwell	bye
Falkirk	bye
Queen's Park	bye

THIRD ROUND

Morton v Aberdeen	1-1, 1-2
Dundee v Albion Rovers	3-0
Arbroath v Raith Rovers	5-4
Heart of Midlothian v Cowdenbeath	2-0
Rangers v Hibernian	0-0, 0-2
Dumbarton v Third Lanark	2-0
Falkirk v Motherwell	0-0, 0-1
East Fife v Queen's Park	3-1

FOURTH ROUND

Dundee v Aberdeen	1-2
Arbroath v Heart of Midlothian	2-1
Hibernian v Dumbarton	2-0
East Fife v Motherwell	0-2

SEMI-FINAL

Aberdeen v Arbroath	2-0
Hibernian v Motherwell	2-0

FINAL

Aberdeen v Hibernian	2-1

League Tables 1947-48

FIRST DIVISION

		P	W	D	L	F	A	Pts
1	Arsenal	42	23	13	6	81	32	59
2	Man United	42	19	14	9	81	48	52
3	Burnley	42	20	12	10	56	43	52
4	Derby	42	19	12	11	77	57	50
5	Wolves	42	19	9	14	83	70	47
6	Aston Villa	42	19	9	14	65	57	47
7	Preston	42	20	7	15	67	68	47
8	Portsmouth	42	19	7	16	68	50	45
9	Blackpool	42	17	10	15	57	41	44
10	Man City	42	15	12	15	52	47	42
11	Liverpool	42	16	10	16	65	61	42
12	Sheff United	42	16	10	16	65	70	42
13	Charlton	42	17	6	19	57	66	40
14	Everton	42	17	6	19	52	66	40
15	Stoke	42	14	10	18	41	55	38
16	Middlesbrough	42	14	9	19	71	73	37
17	Bolton	42	16	5	21	46	58	37
18	Chelsea	42	14	9	19	53	71	37
19	Huddersfield	42	12	12	18	51	60	36
20	Sunderland	42	13	10	19	56	67	36
21	Blackburn	42	11	10	21	54	72	32
22	Grimsby	42	8	6	28	45	111	22

SECOND DIVISION

		P	W	D	L	F	A	Pts
1	Birmingham	42	22	15	5	55	24	59
2	Newcastle	42	24	8	10	72	41	56
3	Southampton	42	21	10	11	71	53	52
4	Sheff Wed	42	20	11	11	66	53	51
5	Cardiff	42	18	11	13	61	58	47
6	West Ham	42	16	14	12	55	53	46
7	WBA	42	18	9	15	63	58	45
8	Tottenham	42	15	14	13	56	43	44
9	Leicester	42	16	11	15	60	57	43
10	Coventry	42	14	13	15	59	52	41
11	Fulham	42	15	10	17	47	46	40
12	Barnsley	42	15	10	17	62	64	40
13	Luton	42	14	12	16	56	59	40
14	Bradford PA	42	16	8	18	68	72	40
15	Brentford	42	13	14	15	44	61	40
16	Chesterfield	42	16	7	19	54	55	39
17	Plymouth	42	9	20	13	40	58	38
18	Leeds	42	14	8	20	62	72	36
19	Nottm Forest	42	12	11	19	54	60	35
20	Bury	42	9	16	17	58	68	34
21	Doncaster	42	9	11	22	40	66	29
22	Millwall	42	9	11	22	44	74	29

FA CUP 1947-48

FOURTH ROUND

Queen's Park Rangers v Stoke City	3-0
Luton Town v Coventry City	3-2
Brentford v Middlesbrough	1-2
Crewe Alexandra v Derby County	0-3
Manchester United v Liverpool	3-0
Charlton Athletic v Stockport County	3-0
Manchester City v Chelsea	2-0
Portsmouth v Preston North End	1-3
Fulham v Bristol Rovers	5-2
Wolverhampton Wanderers v Everton	1-1, 2-3
Blackpool v Chester	4-0
Colchester United v Bradford Park Avenue	3-2
Southampton v Blackburn Rovers	3-2
Swindon Town v Notts County	1-0
Tottenham Hotspur v West Bromwich Albion	3-1
Leicester City v Sheffield Wednesday	2-1

FIFTH ROUND

Queen's Park Rangers v Luton Town	3-1
Middlesbrough v Derby County	1-2
Manchester United v Charlton Athletic	2-0
Manchester City v Preston North End	0-1
Fulham v Everton	1-1, 1-0
Blackpool v Colchester United	5-0
Southampton v Swindon Town	3-0
Tottenham Hotspur v Leicester City	5-2

SIXTH ROUND

Queen's Park Rangers v Derby County	1-1, 0-5
Manchester United v Preston North End	4-1
Fulham v Blackpool	0-2
Southampton v Tottenham Hotspur	0-1

SEMI-FINAL

Derby County v Manchester United	1-3
Blackpool v Tottenham Hotspur	3-1

FINAL

Manchester United v Blackpool	4-2

THIRD DIVISION (SOUTH)

		P	W	D	L	F	A	Pts
1	QPR	42	26	9	7	74	37	61
2	Bournemouth	42	24	9	9	76	35	57
3	Walsall	42	21	9	12	70	40	51
4	Ipswich	42	23	3	16	67	61	49
5	Swansea	42	18	12	12	70	52	48
6	Notts County	42	19	8	15	68	59	46
7	Bristol City	42	18	7	17	77	65	43
8	Port Vale	42	16	11	15	63	54	43
9	Southend	42	15	13	14	51	58	43
10	Reading	42	15	11	16	56	58	41
11	Exeter	42	15	11	16	55	63	41
12	Newport	42	14	13	15	61	73	41
13	Crystal Palace	42	13	13	16	49	49	39
14	Northampton	42	14	11	17	58	72	39
15	Watford	42	14	10	18	57	79	38
16	Swindon	42	10	16	16	41	46	36
17	Leyton Orient	42	13	10	19	51	73	36
18	Torquay	42	11	13	18	63	62	35
19	Aldershot	42	10	15	17	45	67	35
20	Bristol Rovers	42	13	8	21	71	75	34
21	Norwich	42	13	8	21	61	76	34
22	Brighton	42	11	12	19	43	73	34

THIRD DIVISION (NORTH)

		P	W	D	L	F	A	Pts
1	Lincoln	42	26	8	8	81	40	60
2	Rotherham	42	25	9	8	95	49	59
3	Wrexham	42	21	8	13	74	54	50
4	Gateshead	42	19	11	12	75	57	49
5	Hull	42	18	11	13	59	48	47
6	Accrington	42	20	6	16	62	59	46
7	Barrow	42	16	13	13	49	40	45
8	Mansfield	42	17	11	14	57	51	45
9	Carlisle	42	18	7	17	88	77	43
10	Crewe	42	18	7	17	61	63	43
11	Oldham	42	14	13	15	63	64	41
12	Rochdale	42	15	11	16	48	72	41
13	York	42	13	14	15	65	60	40
14	Bradford City	42	15	10	17	65	66	40
15	Southport	42	14	11	17	60	63	39
16	Darlington	42	13	13	16	54	70	39
17	Stockport	42	13	12	17	63	67	38
18	Tranmere	42	16	4	22	54	72	36
19	Hartlepools	42	14	8	20	51	73	36
20	Chester	42	13	9	20	64	67	35
21	Halifax	42	7	13	22	43	76	27
22	New Brighton	42	8	9	25	38	81	25

SCOTTISH FA CUP 1947-48

SECOND ROUND

Rangers v Leith Athletic	4-0
Partick Thistle v Dundee United	4-3
East Fife v St Johnstone	5-1
Peterhead v Dumbarton	1-2
Hibernian v Arbroath	4-0
Nithsdale Wanderers v Aberdeen	0-5
St Mirren v East Stirlingshire	2-0
Clyde v Dunfermline Athletic	2-1
Morton v Falkirk	3-2
Queen's Park v Deveronvale	8-2
Airdrieonians v Heart of Midlothian	2-1
Stirling Albion v Raith Rovers	2-4
Celtic v Cowdenbeath	3-0
Motherwell v Third Lanark	1-0
Montrose v Duns	2-0
Alloa Athletic v Queen of the South	0-1

THIRD ROUND

Rangers v Partick Thistle	3-0
Dumbarton v East Fife	0-1
Hibernian v Aberdeen	4-2
St Mirren v Clyde	2-1
Morton v Queen's Park	3-0
Airdrieonians v Raith Rovers	3-0
Celtic v Motherwell	1-0
Montrose v Queen of the South	2-1

FOURTH ROUND

Rangers v East Fife	1-0
Hibernian v St Mirren	3-1
Airdrieonians v Morton	0-3
Celtic v Montrose	4-0

SEMI-FINAL

Rangers v Hibernian	1-0
Morton v Celtic	1-0

FINAL

Rangers v Morton	1-1, 1-0

SCOTTISH DIVISION 'A'

		P	W	D	L	F	A	Pts
1	Hibernian	30	22	4	4	86	27	48
2	Rangers	30	21	4	5	64	28	46
3	Partick	30	16	4	10	61	42	36
4	Dundee	30	15	3	12	67	51	33
5	St Mirren	30	13	5	12	54	58	31
6	Clyde	30	12	7	11	52	57	31
7	Falkirk	30	10	10	10	55	48	30
8	Motherwell	30	13	3	14	45	47	29
9	Hearts	30	10	8	12	37	42	28
10	Aberdeen	30	10	7	13	45	45	27
11	Third Lanark	30	10	6	14	56	73	26
12	Celtic	30	10	5	15	41	56	25
13	Queen of the S	30	10	5	15	49	74	25
14	Morton	30	9	6	15	47	43	24
15	Airdrieonians	30	7	7	16	39	78	21
16	Queen's Park	30	9	2	19	45	75	20

SCOTTISH DIVISION 'B'

		P	W	D	L	F	A	Pts
1	East Fife	30	25	3	2	103	36	53
2	Albion	30	19	4	7	58	49	42
3	Hamilton	30	17	6	7	75	45	40
4	Raith	30	14	6	10	83	66	34
5	Cowdenbeath	30	12	8	10	56	53	32
6	Kilmarnock	30	13	4	13	72	62	30
7	Dunfermline	30	13	3	14	72	71	29
8	Stirling	30	11	6	13	85	66	28
9	St Johnstone	30	11	5	14	69	63	27
10	Ayr	30	9	9	12	59	61	27
11	Dumbarton	30	9	7	14	66	79	25
12	Alloa	30	10	6	14	53	77	24*
13	Arbroath	30	10	3	17	55	62	23
14	Stenhousemuir	30	6	11	13	53	83	23
15	Dundee United	30	10	2	18	58	88	22
16	Leith	30	6	7	17	45	84	19

*Two points deducted for fielding unregistered players.

In the 1947-48 FA Cup, Manchester United were drawn in turn against six Division One clubs. This was the first instance of this happening to any club. The teams United met were, in order, Aston Villa, Liverpool, Charlton Athletic, Preston North End, and Blackpool, whom they beat 4-2 in the Final.

Quick off the mark
William Sharp, of Partick Thistle, scored against Queen of the South just seven seconds after the Scottish Division 'A' match had kicked off on 20 December 1947.

Tommy Lawton became the first Third Division player since World War Two to represent England in the International Championship. Lawton, of Notts County, played at centre-forward in England's 2-0 win over Scotland at Hampden Park on 10 April 1948.

In January 1948, 83,260 people watched Manchester United play Arsenal in a First Division match at Maine Road, Manchester. This was a record for a League match.

FIRST DIVISION

		P	W	D	L	F	A	Pts
1	Portsmouth	42	25	8	9	84	42	58
2	Man United	42	21	11	10	77	44	53
3	Derby	42	22	9	11	74	55	53
4	Newcastle	42	20	12	10	70	56	52
5	Arsenal	42	18	13	11	74	44	49
6	Wolves	42	17	12	13	79	66	46
7	Man City	42	15	15	12	47	51	45
8	Sunderland	42	13	17	12	49	58	43
9	Charlton	42	15	12	15	63	67	42
10	Aston Villa	42	16	10	16	60	76	42
11	Stoke	42	16	9	17	66	68	41
12	Liverpool	42	13	14	15	53	43	40
13	Chelsea	42	12	14	16	69	68	38
14	Bolton	42	14	10	18	59	68	38
15	Burnley	42	12	14	16	43	50	38
16	Blackpool	42	11	16	15	54	67	38
17	Birmingham	42	11	15	16	36	38	37
18	Everton	42	13	11	18	41	63	37
19	Middlesbrough	42	11	12	19	46	57	34
20	Huddersfield	42	12	10	20	40	69	34
21	Preston	42	11	11	20	62	75	33
22	Sheff United	42	11	11	20	57	78	33

SECOND DIVISION

		P	W	D	L	F	A	Pts
1	Fulham	42	24	9	9	77	37	57
2	WBA	42	24	8	10	69	39	56
3	Southampton	42	23	9	10	69	36	55
4	Cardiff	42	19	13	10	62	47	51
5	Tottenham	42	17	16	9	72	44	50
6	Chesterfield	42	15	17	10	51	45	47
7	West Ham	42	18	10	14	56	58	46
8	Sheff Wed	42	15	13	14	63	56	43
9	Barnsley	42	14	12	16	62	61	40
10	Luton	42	14	12	16	55	57	40
11	Grimsby	42	15	10	17	72	76	40
12	Bury	42	17	6	19	67	76	40
13	QPR	42	14	11	17	44	62	39
14	Blackburn	42	15	8	19	53	63	38
15	Leeds	42	12	13	17	55	63	37
16	Coventry	42	15	7	20	55	64	37
17	Bradford PA	42	13	11	18	65	78	37
18	Brentford	42	11	14	17	42	53	36
19	Leicester	42	10	16	16	62	79	36
20	Plymouth	42	12	12	18	49	64	36
21	Nottm Forest	42	14	7	21	50	54	35
22	Lincoln	42	8	12	22	53	91	28

FA CUP 1948-49

FOURTH ROUND

Manchester United v Bradford Park Avenue	
	1-1, 1-1, 5-0
Yeovil Town v Sunderland	2-1
Hull City v Grimsby Town	3-2
Stoke City v Blackpool	1-1, 1-0
Wolverhampton Wanderers v Sheffield United	3-0
Liverpool v Notts County	1-0
West Bromwich Albion v Gateshead	3-1
Chelsea v Everton	2-0
Leicester City v Preston North End	2-0
Luton Town v Walsall	4-0
Brentford v Torquay United	1-0
Burnley v Rotherham United	1-0
Portsmouth v Sheffield Wednesday	2-1
Newport County v Huddersfield Town	3-3, 3-1
Derby County v Arsenal	1-0
Cardiff City v Aston Villa	2-1

FIFTH ROUND

Manchester United v Yeovil Town	8-0
Hull City v Stoke City	2-0
Wolverhampton Wanderers v Liverpool	3 1
West Bromwich Albion v Chelsea	3 0
Leicester City v Luton Town	5 5 5 3
Brentford v Burnley	4 2
Portsmouth v Newport County	3 2
Derby County v Cardiff City	2-1

SIXTH ROUND

Hull City v Manchester United	0-1
Wolverhampton Wanderers v	
West Bromwich Albion	1 0
Leicester City v Brentford	2 0
Portsmouth v Derby County	2 1

SEMI-FINAL

Manchester United v Wolverhampton Wanderers	
	1-1, 0-1
Leicester City v Portsmouth	3-1

FINAL

Wolverhampton Wanderers v Leicester City	3-1

THIRD DIVISION (SOUTH)

		P	W	D	L	F	A	Pts
1	Swansea	42	27	8	7	87	34	62
2	Reading	42	25	5	12	77	50	55
3	Bournemouth	42	22	8	12	69	48	52
4	Swindon	42	18	15	9	64	56	51
5	Bristol Rovers	42	19	10	13	61	51	48
6	Brighton	42	15	18	9	55	55	48
7	Ipswich	42	18	9	15	78	77	45
8	Millwall	42	17	11	14	63	64	45
9	Torquay	42	17	11	14	65	70	45
10	Norwich	42	16	12	14	67	49	44
11	Notts County	42	19	5	18	102	68	43
12	Exeter	42	15	10	17	63	76	40
13	Port Vale	42	14	11	17	51	54	39
14	Walsall	42	15	8	19	56	64	38
15	Newport	42	14	9	19	68	92	37
16	Bristol City	42	11	14	17	44	62	36
17	Watford	42	10	15	17	41	54	35
18	Southend	42	9	16	17	41	46	34
19	Leyton Orient	42	11	12	19	58	80	34
20	Northampton	42	12	9	21	51	62	33
21	Aldershot	42	11	11	20	48	59	33
22	Crystal Palace	42	8	11	23	38	76	27

THIRD DIVISION (NORTH)

		P	W	D	L	F	A	Pts
1	Hull	42	27	11	4	93	28	65
2	Rotherham	42	28	6	8	90	46	62
3	Doncaster	42	20	10	12	53	40	50
4	Darlington	42	20	6	16	83	74	46
5	Gateshead	42	16	13	13	69	58	45
6	Oldham	42	18	9	15	75	67	45
7	Rochdale	42	18	9	15	55	53	45
8	Stockport	42	16	11	15	61	56	43
9	Wrexham	42	17	9	16	56	62	43
10	Mansfield	42	14	14	14	52	48	42
11	Tranmere	42	13	15	14	46	57	41
12	Crewe	42	16	9	17	52	74	41
13	Barrow	42	14	12	16	41	48	40
14	York	42	15	9	18	74	74	39
15	Carlisle	42	14	11	17	60	77	39
16	Hartlepools	42	14	10	18	45	58	38
17	New Brighton	42	14	8	20	46	58	36
18	Chester	42	11	13	18	57	56	35
19	Halifax	42	12	11	19	45	62	35
20	Accrington	42	12	10	20	55	64	34
21	Southport	42	11	9	22	45	64	31
22	Bradford City	42	10	9	23	48	77	29

SCOTTISH DIVISION 'A'

		P	W	D	L	F	A	Pts
1	Rangers	30	20	6	4	63	32	46
2	Dundee	30	20	5	5	71	48	45
3	Hibernian	30	17	5	8	75	52	39
4	East Fife	30	16	3	11	64	46	35
5	Falkirk	30	12	8	10	70	54	32
6	Celtic	30	12	7	11	48	40	31
7	Third Lanark	30	13	5	12	56	52	31
8	Hearts	30	12	6	12	64	54	30
9	St Mirren	30	13	4	13	51	47	30
10	Queen of the S	30	11	8	11	47	53	30
11	Partick	30	9	9	12	50	63	27
12	Motherwell	30	10	5	15	44	49	25
13	Aberdeen	30	7	11	12	39	48	25
14	Clyde	30	9	6	15	50	67	24
15	Morton	30	7	8	15	39	51	22
16	Albion	30	3	2	25	30	105	8

SCOTTISH DIVISION 'B'

		P	W	D	L	F	A	Pts
1	Raith	30	20	2	8	80	44	42
2	Stirling	30	20	2	8	71	47	42
3	Airdrieonians	30	16	9	5	76	42	41
4	Dunfermline	30	16	9	5	80	58	41
5	Queen's Park	30	14	7	9	66	49	35
6	St Johnstone	30	14	4	12	58	51	32
7	Arbroath	30	12	8	10	62	56	32
8	Dundee United	30	10	7	13	60	67	27
9	Ayr	30	10	7	13	51	70	27
10	Hamilton	30	9	8	13	48	57	26
11	Kilmarnock	30	9	7	14	58	61	25
12	Stenhousemuir	30	8	8	14	50	54	24
13	Cowdenbeath	30	9	5	16	53	58	23
14	Alloa	30	10	3	17	42	85	23
15	Dumbarton	30	8	6	16	52	79	22
16	E Stirlingshire	30	6	6	18	38	67	18

SCOTTISH FA CUP 1948-49

SECOND ROUND

Motherwell v Rangers	0-3
Partick Thistle v Queen of the South	3-0
Cowdenbeath v East Fife	1-2
Hibernian v Raith Rovers	1-1, 4-3
Clyde v Alloa Athletic	3-1
Ayr United v Morton	0-2
Stenhousemuir v Albion Rovers	5-1
Dundee v St Mirren	0-0, 2-1
Heart of Midlothian v Third Lanark	3-1
Dumbarton v Dundee United	1-1, 3-1

THIRD ROUND

Clyde v Morton	2-0
Heart of Midlothian v Dumbarton	3-0
Rangers	bye
Partick Thistle	bye
East Fife	bye
Hibernian	bye
Stenhousemuir	bye
Dundee	bye

FOURTH ROUND

Rangers v Partick Thistle	4-0
Hibernian v East Fife	0-2
Stenhousemuir v Clyde	0-1
Heart of Midlothian v Dundee	2-4

SEMI-FINAL

Rangers v East Fife	3-0
Clyde v Dundee	2-2, 2-1

FINAL

Rangers v Clyde	4-1

On Saturday 18 September 1948, there were 9 drawn games in Division One of the Football League, a record for any division of the League in a single day.

In both Divisions One and Two, the tally of goals scored during the season was 1,303.

Portsmouth, 1948-49 League champions, and Swansea, who finished top of Division Three South, both completed the season without a home defeat. At Fratton Park, Portsmouth won 18 games and drew 3, while Swansea won 20 and drew one at Vetch Field.

Three honours for Bromley

Bromley won the FA Amateur Cup by beating Romford 1-0 at Wembley; they also won the Kent Amateur Cup with the highest score recorded in the final: 9-1. Bromley completed a magnificent season by capturing the Athenian League championship. George Brown, their centre-forward, scored 100 goals during the season. These included a 7, a 6, two 5's, three 4's and five hat-tricks.

In Scotland, Rangers became the first side to achieve the treble, winning the League, the Scottish Cup and the League Cup.

FIRST DIVISION

	P	W	D	L	F	A	Pts
1 Portsmouth	42	22	9	11	74	38	53
2 Wolves	42	20	13	9	76	49	53
3 Sunderland	42	21	10	11	83	62	52
4 Man United	42	18	14	10	69	44	50
5 Newcastle	42	19	12	11	77	55	50
6 Arsenal	42	19	11	12	79	55	49
7 Blackpool	42	17	15	10	46	35	49
8 Liverpool	42	17	14	11	64	54	48
9 Middlesbrough	42	20	7	15	59	48	47
10 Burnley	42	16	13	13	40	40	45
11 Derby	42	17	10	15	69	61	44
12 Aston Villa	42	15	12	15	61	61	42
13 Chelsea	42	12	16	14	58	65	40
14 WBA	42	14	12	16	47	53	40
15 Huddersfield	42	14	9	19	52	73	37
16 Bolton	42	10	14	18	45	59	34
17 Fulham	42	10	14	18	41	54	34
18 Everton	42	10	14	18	42	66	34
19 Stoke	42	11	12	19	45	75	34
20 Charlton	42	13	6	23	53	65	32
21 Man City	42	8	13	21	36	68	29
22 Birmingham	42	7	14	21	31	67	28

SECOND DIVISION

	P	W	D	L	F	A	Pts
1 Tottenham	42	27	7	8	81	35	61
2 Sheff Wed	42	18	16	8	67	48	52
3 Sheff United	42	19	14	9	68	49	52
4 Southampton	42	19	14	9	64	48	52
5 Leeds	42	17	13	12	54	45	47
6 Preston	42	18	9	15	60	49	45
7 Hull	42	17	11	14	64	72	45
8 Swansea	42	17	9	16	53	49	43
9 Brentford	42	15	13	14	44	49	43
10 Cardiff	42	16	10	16	41	44	42
11 Grimsby	42	16	8	18	74	73	40
12 Coventry	42	13	13	16	55	55	39
13 Barnsley	42	13	13	16	64	67	39
14 Chesterfield	42	15	9	18	43	47	39
15 Leicester	42	12	15	15	55	65	39
16 Blackburn	42	14	10	18	55	60	38
17 Luton	42	10	18	14	41	51	38
18 Bury	42	14	9	19	60	65	37
19 West Ham	42	12	12	18	53	61	36
20 QPR	42	11	12	19	40	57	34
21 Plymouth	42	8	16	18	44	65	32
22 Bradford PA	42	10	11	21	51	77	31

THIRD DIVISION (SOUTH)

	P	W	D	L	F	A	Pts
1 Notts County	42	25	8	9	95	50	58
2 Northampton	42	20	11	11	72	50	51
3 Southend	42	19	13	10	66	48	51
4 Nottm Forest	42	20	9	13	67	39	49
5 Torquay	42	19	10	13	66	63	48
6 Watford	42	16	13	13	45	35	45
7 Crystal Palace	42	15	14	13	55	54	44
8 Brighton	42	16	12	14	57	69	44
9 Bristol Rovers	42	19	5	18	51	51	43
10 Reading	42	17	8	17	70	64	42
11 Norwich	42	16	10	16	65	63	42
12 Bournemouth	42	16	10	16	57	56	42
13 Port Vale	42	15	11	16	47	42	41
14 Swindon	42	15	11	16	59	62	41
15 Bristol City	42	15	10	17	60	61	40
16 Exeter	42	14	11	17	63	75	39
17 Ipswich	42	12	11	19	57	86	35
18 Leyton Orient	42	12	11	19	53	85	35
19 Walsall	42	9	16	17	61	62	34
20 Aldershot	42	13	8	21	48	60	34
21 Newport	42	13	8	21	67	98	34
22 Millwall	42	14	4	24	55	63	32

THIRD DIVISION (NORTH)

	P	W	D	L	F	A	Pts
1 Doncaster	42	19	17	6	66	38	55
2 Gateshead	42	23	7	12	87	54	53
3 Rochdale	42	21	9	12	68	41	51
4 Lincoln	42	21	9	12	60	39	51
5 Tranmere	42	19	11	12	51	48	49
6 Rotherham	42	19	10	13	80	59	48
7 Crewe	42	17	14	11	68	55	48
8 Mansfield	42	18	12	12	66	54	48
9 Carlisle	42	16	15	11	68	51	47
10 Stockport	42	19	7	16	55	52	45
11 Oldham	42	16	11	15	58	63	43
12 Chester	42	17	6	19	70	79	40
13 Accrington	42	16	7	19	57	62	39
14 New Brighton	42	14	10	18	45	63	38
15 Barrow	42	14	9	19	47	53	37
16 Southport	42	12	13	17	51	71	37
17 Darlington	42	11	13	18	56	69	35
18 Hartlepools	42	14	5	23	52	79	33
19 Bradford City	42	12	8	22	61	76	32
20 Wrexham	42	10	12	20	39	54	32
21 Halifax	42	12	8	22	58	85	32
22 York	42	9	13	20	52	70	31

SCOTTISH DIVISION 'A'

	P	W	D	L	F	A	Pts
1 Rangers	30	22	6	2	58	26	50
2 Hibernian	30	22	5	3	86	34	49
3 Hearts	30	20	3	7	86	40	43
4 East Fife	30	15	7	8	58	43	37
5 Celtic	30	14	7	9	51	50	35
6 Dundee	30	12	7	11	49	46	31
7 Partick Thistle	30	13	3	14	55	45	29
8 Aberdeen	30	11	4	15	48	56	26
9 Raith	30	9	8	13	45	54	26
10 Motherwell	30	10	5	15	53	58	25
11 St Mirren	30	8	9	13	42	49	25
12 Third Lanark	30	11	3	16	44	62	25
13 Clyde	30	10	4	16	56	73	24
14 Falkirk	30	7	10	13	48	72	24
15 Queen of the S	30	5	6	19	31	63	16
16 Stirling	30	6	3	21	38	77	15

SCOTTISH DIVISION 'B'

	P	W	D	L	F	A	Pts
1 Morton	30	20	7	3	77	33	47
2 Airdrieonians	30	19	6	5	79	40	44
3 Dunfermline	30	16	4	10	71	57	36
4 St Johnstone	30	15	6	9	64	56	36
5 Cowdenbeath	30	16	3	11	63	56	35
6 Hamilton	30	14	6	10	57	44	34
7 Kilmarnock	30	14	5	11	50	43	33
8 Dundee United	30	14	5	11	74	56	33
9 Queen's Park	30	12	7	11	63	59	31
10 Forfar	30	11	8	11	53	56	30
11 Albion	30	10	7	13	49	61	27
12 Stenhousemuir	30	8	8	14	54	72	24
13 Ayr	30	8	6	16	53	80	22
14 Arbroath	30	5	9	16	47	69	19
15 Dumbarton	30	6	4	20	39	62	16
16 Alloa	30	5	3	22	47	96	13

FA CUP 1949-50

FOURTH ROUND

Arsenal v Swansea Town	2-1
Burnley v Port Vale	2-1
Leeds United v Bolton Wanderers	1-1, 3-2
Charlton Athletic v Cardiff City	1-1, 0-2
Chelsea v Newcastle United	3-0
Chesterfield v Middlesbrough	3-2
Watford v Manchester United	0-1
Portsmouth v Grimsby Town	5-0
Liverpool v Exeter City	3-1
Stockport County v Hull City	0-0, 2-0
Blackpool v Doncaster Rovers	2-1
Wolverhampton Wanderers v Sheffield United	0-0, 4-3
West Ham United v Everton	1-2
Tottenham Hotspur v Sunderland	5-1
Bury v Derby County	2-2, 2-5
Bournemouth v Northampton Town	1-1, 1-2

FIFTH ROUND

Arsenal v Burnley	2-0
Leeds United v Cardiff City	3-1
Chesterfield v Chelsea	1-1, 0-3
Manchester United v Portsmouth	3-3, 1-0
Stockport County v Liverpool	1-2
Wolverhampton Wanderers v Blackpool	0-0, 0-1
Everton v Tottenham Hotspur	1-0
Derby County v Northampton Town	4-2

SIXTH ROUND

Arsenal v Leeds United	1-0
Chelsea v Manchester United	2-0
Liverpool v Blackpool	2-1
Derby County v Everton	1-2

SEMI-FINAL

Arsenal v Chelsea	2-2, 1-0
Liverpool v Everton	2-0

FINAL

Arsenal v Liverpool	2-0

SCOTTISH FA CUP 1949-50

SECOND ROUND

Rangers v Cowdenbeath	8-0
Raith Rovers v Clyde	3-2
Queen of the South v Morton	1-1, 3-0
Aberdeen v Heart of Midlothian	3-1
Celtic v Third Lanark	1-1, 4-1
Partick Thistle v Dundee United	5-0
Stirling Albion v Dumbarton	2-2, 1-1, 6-2
Stenhousemuir v St Johnstone	2-2, 4-2
Dunfermline Athletic v Albion Rovers	2-1
Falkirk v East Fife	2-3

THIRD ROUND

Celtic v Aberdeen	0-1
Dunfermline Athletic v Stenhousemuir	1-4
Rangers	bye
Raith Rovers	bye
Queen of the South	bye
Partick Thistle	bye
Stirling Albion	bye
East Fife	bye

FOURTH ROUND

Rangers v Raith Rovers	1-1, 1-1, 2-0
Queen of the South v Aberdeen	3-3, 2-1
Partick Thistle v Stirling Albion	5-1
Stenhousemuir v East Fife	0-3

SEMI-FINAL

Rangers v Queen of the South	1-1, 3-0
Partick Thistle v East Fife	1-2

FINAL

Rangers v East Fife	3-0

Charlie Mortimore scored 15 goals for Aldershot in Division Three South during 1949-50. These made Mortimore the club's top scorer for the season, and meant that he became the second amateur to head a League club's scoring list since the First World War.

England lose to America
On 28 June 1950, an amazing scoreline came out of Brazil. For at Belo Horizonte, the United States had beaten England 1-0.

On 16 July 1950, 199,854 people watched the World Cup Final in Rio de Janeiro, the official record crowd for any football match.

The Third Division was extended from 44 to 48 clubs as a result of the clamour by minor professional clubs for first-class status. The League management committee proposed the enlargement of each section of the Third Division by two clubs, and this proposal was adopted at the 1950 AGM.

John Charles, Leeds United's centre-half, became Wales' youngest ever international when, on 8 March 1950, at the age of 18 years and 71 days, he played against Northern Ireland.

FIRST DIVISION

		P	W	D	L	F	A	Pts
1	Tottenham	42	25	10	7	82	44	60
2	Man United	42	24	8	10	74	40	56
3	Blackpool	42	20	10	12	79	53	50
4	Newcastle	42	18	13	11	62	53	49
5	Arsenal	42	19	9	14	73	56	47
6	Middlesbrough	42	18	11	13	76	65	47
7	Portsmouth	42	16	15	11	71	68	47
8	Bolton	42	19	7	16	64	61	45
9	Liverpool	42	16	11	15	53	59	43
10	Burnley	42	14	14	14	48	43	42
11	Derby	42	16	8	18	81	75	40
12	Sunderland	42	12	16	14	63	73	40
13	Stoke	42	13	14	15	50	59	40
14	Wolves	42	15	8	19	74	61	38
15	Aston Villa	42	12	13	17	66	68	37
16	WBA	42	13	11	18	53	61	37
17	Charlton	42	14	9	19	63	80	37
18	Fulham	42	13	11	18	52	68	37
19	Huddersfield	42	15	6	21	64	92	36
20	Chelsea	42	12	8	22	53	65	32
21	Sheff Wed	42	12	8	22	64	83	32
22	Everton	42	12	8	22	48	86	32

SECOND DIVISION

		P	W	D	L	F	A	Pts
1	Preston	42	26	5	11	91	49	57
2	Man City	42	19	14	9	89	61	52
3	Cardiff	42	17	16	9	53	45	50
4	Birmingham	42	20	9	13	64	53	49
5	Leeds	42	20	8	14	63	55	48
6	Blackburn	42	19	8	15	65	66	46
7	Coventry	42	19	7	16	75	59	45
8	Sheff United	42	16	12	14	72	62	44
9	Brentford	42	18	8	16	75	74	44
10	Hull	42	16	11	15	74	70	43
11	Doncaster	42	15	13	14	64	68	43
12	Southampton	42	15	13	14	66	73	43
13	West Ham	42	16	10	16	68	69	42
14	Leicester	42	15	11	16	68	58	41
15	Barnsley	42	15	10	17	74	68	40
16	QPR	42	15	10	17	71	82	40
17	Notts County	42	13	13	16	61	60	39
18	Swansea	42	16	4	22	54	77	36
19	Luton	42	9	14	19	57	70	32
20	Bury	42	12	8	22	60	86	32
21	Chesterfield	42	9	12	21	44	69	30
22	Grimsby	42	8	12	22	61	95	28

THIRD DIVISION (NORTH)

		P	W	D	L	F	A	Pts
1	Rotherham	46	31	9	6	103	41	71
2	Mansfield	46	26	12	8	78	48	64
3	Carlisle	46	25	12	9	79	50	62
4	Tranmere	46	24	11	11	83	62	59
5	Lincoln	46	25	8	13	89	58	58
6	Bradford PA	46	23	8	15	90	72	54
7	Bradford City	46	21	10	15	90	63	52
8	Gateshead	46	21	8	17	84	62	50
9	Crewe	46	19	10	17	61	60	48
10	Stockport	46	20	8	18	63	63	48
11	Rochdale	46	17	11	18	69	62	45
12	Scunthorpe	46	13	18	15	58	57	44
13	Chester	46	17	9	20	62	64	43
14	Wrexham	46	15	12	19	55	71	42
15	Oldham	46	16	8	22	73	73	40
16	Hartlepools	46	16	7	23	64	66	39
17	York	46	12	15	19	66	77	39
18	Darlington	46	13	13	20	59	77	39
19	Barrow	46	16	6	24	51	76	38
20	Shrewsbury	46	15	7	24	43	74	37
21	Southport	46	13	10	23	56	72	36
22	Halifax	46	11	12	23	50	69	34
23	Accrington	46	11	10	25	42	101	32
24	New Brighton	46	11	8	27	40	90	30

THIRD DIVISION (SOUTH)

		P	W	D	L	F	A	Pts
1	Nottm Forest	46	30	10	6	110	40	70
2	Norwich	46	25	14	7	82	45	64
3	Reading	46	21	15	10	88	53	57
4	Plymouth	46	24	9	13	85	55	57
5	Millwall	46	23	10	13	80	57	56
6	Bristol Rovers	46	20	15	11	64	42	55
7	Southend	46	21	10	15	92	69	52
8	Ipswich	46	23	6	17	69	58	52
9	Bournemouth	46	22	7	17	65	57	51
10	Bristol City	46	20	11	15	64	59	51
11	Newport	46	19	9	18	77	70	47
12	Port Vale	46	16	13	17	60	65	45
13	Brighton	46	13	17	16	71	79	43
14	Exeter	46	18	6	22	62	85	42
15	Walsall	46	15	10	21	52	62	40
16	Colchester	46	14	12	20	63	76	40
17	Swindon	46	18	4	24	55	67	40
18	Aldershot	46	15	10	21	56	88	40
19	Leyton Orient	46	15	8	23	53	75	38
20	Torquay	46	14	9	23	64	81	37
21	Northampton	46	10	16	20	55	67	36
22	Gillingham	46	13	9	24	69	101	35
23	Watford	46	9	11	26	54	88	29
24	Crystal Palace	46	8	11	27	33	84	27

SCOTTISH DIVISION 'A'

		P	W	D	L	F	A	Pts
1	Hibernian	30	22	4	4	78	26	48
2	Rangers	30	17	4	9	64	37	38
3	Dundee	30	15	8	7	47	30	38
4	Hearts	30	16	5	9	72	45	37
5	Aberdeen	30	15	5	10	61	50	35
6	Partick Thistle	30	13	7	10	57	48	33
7	Celtic	30	12	5	13	48	46	29
8	Raith	30	13	2	15	52	52	28
9	Motherwell	30	11	6	13	58	65	28
10	East Fife	30	10	8	12	48	66	28
11	St Mirren	30	9	7	14	35	51	25
12	Morton	30	10	4	16	47	59	24
13	Third Lanark	30	11	2	17	40	51	24
14	Airdrieonians	30	10	4	16	52	67	24
15	Clyde	30	8	7	15	37	57	23
16	Falkirk	30	7	4	19	35	81	18

SCOTTISH DIVISION 'B'

		P	W	D	L	F	A	Pts
1	Queen of the S	30	21	3	6	69	35	45
2	Stirling	30	21	3	6	78	44	45
3	Ayr	30	15	6	9	64	40	36
4	Dundee United	30	16	4	10	78	58	36
5	St Johnstone	30	14	5	11	68	53	33
6	Queen's Park	30	13	7	10	56	53	33
7	Hamilton	30	12	8	10	65	49	32
8	Albion	30	14	4	12	56	51	32
9	Dumbarton	30	12	5	13	52	53	29
10	Dunfermline	30	12	4	14	58	73	28
11	Cowdenbeath	30	12	3	15	61	57	27
12	Kilmarnock	30	8	8	14	44	49	24
13	Arbroath	30	8	5	17	46	78	21
14	Forfar	30	9	3	18	43	76	21
15	Stenhousemuir	30	9	2	19	51	80	20
16	Alloa	30	7	4	19	58	98	18

In their first season in the Football League, Scunthorpe United conceded only nine goals in their 23 home matches in Division Three North. In their 23 away games in the same division, Hartlepools United scored only nine times, failing to break a duck in their last 11 fixtures.

Nottingham Forest won the Third Division South championship with a record points total for that division—70.

Billingham Synthonia did not concede a single goal at home in their Northern League programme, though they scored 44.

On 15 November 1950, Leslie Compton, the Arsenal centre-half, played in that position for England against Wales. It was Compton's first international appearance, and at 38 years and 2 months, he is credited with making the oldest international debut in the Home Championship.

FA CUP 1950-51

FOURTH ROUND

Newcastle United v Bolton Wanderers	3-2
Stoke City v West Ham United	1-0
Luton Town v Bristol Rovers	1-2
Hull City v Rotherham United	2-0
Wolverhampton Wanderers v Aston Villa	3-1
Preston North End v Huddersfield Town	0-2
Sunderland v Southampton	2-0
Newport County v Norwich City	0-2
Blackpool v Stockport County	2-1
Sheffield United v Mansfield Town	0-0, 1-2
Exeter City v Chelsea	1-1, 0-2
Millwall v Fulham	0-1
Derby County v Birmingham City	1-3
Bristol City v Brighton	1-0
Manchester United v Leeds United	4-0
Arsenal v Northampton Town	3-2

FIFTH ROUND

Stoke City v Newcastle United	2-4
Bristol Rovers v Hull City	3-0
Wolverhampton Wanderers v Huddersfield Town	2-0
Sunderland v Norwich City	3-1
Blackpool v Mansfield Town	2-0
Chelsea v Fulham	1-1, 0-3
Birmingham City v Bristol City	2-0
Manchester United v Arsenal	1-0

SIXTH ROUND

Newcastle United v Bristol Rovers	0-0, 3-1
Sunderland v Wolverhampton Wanderers	1-1, 1-3
Blackpool v Fulham	1-0
Birmingham City v Manchester United	1-0

SEMI-FINAL

Newcastle United v Wolverhampton Wanderers	0-0, 2-1
Blackpool v Birmingham City	0-0, 2-1

FINAL

Blackpool v Newcastle United	0-2

SCOTTISH FA CUP 1950-51

SECOND ROUND

Celtic v Duns	4-0
East Stirlingshire v Heart of Midlothian	1-5
Aberdeen v Third Lanark	4-0
St Johnstone v Dundee	1-3
Raith Rovers v Brechin City	5-2
Morton v Airdrieonians	3-3, 1-2
Albion Rovers v Clyde	0-2
Rangers v Hibernian	2-3
Queen's Park v Ayr United	1-3
Motherwell v Hamilton Academicals	4-1

THIRD ROUND

Heart of Midlothian v Celtic	1-2
Airdrieonians v Clyde	4-0
Aberdeen	bye
Dundee	bye
Raith Rovers	bye
Hibernian	bye
Ayr United	bye
Motherwell	bye

FOURTH ROUND

Celtic v Aberdeen	3-0
Dundee v Raith Rovers	1-2
Airdrieonians v Hibernian	0-3
Ayr United v Motherwell	2-2, 1-2

SEMI-FINAL

Celtic v Raith Rovers	3-2
Hibernian v Motherwell	2-3

FINAL

Celtic v Motherwell	1-0

FIRST DIVISION

		P	W	D	L	F	A	Pts
1	Man United	42	23	11	8	95	52	57
2	Tottenham	42	22	9	11	76	51	53
3	Arsenal	42	21	11	10	80	61	53
4	Portsmouth	42	20	8	14	68	58	48
5	Bolton	42	19	10	13	65	61	48
6	Aston Villa	42	19	9	14	79	70	47
7	Preston	42	17	12	13	74	54	46
8	Newcastle	42	18	9	15	98	73	45
9	Blackpool	42	18	9	15	64	64	45
10	Charlton	42	17	10	15	68	63	44
11	Liverpool	42	12	19	11	57	61	43
12	Sunderland	42	15	12	15	70	61	42
13	WBA	42	14	13	15	74	77	41
14	Burnley	42	15	10	17	56	63	40
15	Man City	42	13	13	16	58	61	39
16	Wolves	42	12	14	16	73	73	38
17	Derby	42	15	7	20	63	80	37
18	Middlesbrough	42	15	6	21	64	88	36
19	Chelsea	42	14	8	20	52	72	36
20	Stoke	42	12	7	23	49	88	31
21	Huddersfield	42	10	8	24	49	82	28
22	Fulham	42	8	11	23	58	77	27

SECOND DIVISION

		P	W	D	L	F	A	Pts
1	Sheff Wed	42	21	11	10	100	66	53
2	Cardiff	42	20	11	11	72	54	51
3	Birmingham	42	21	9	12	67	56	51
4	Nottm Forest	42	18	13	11	77	62	49
5	Leicester	42	19	9	14	78	64	47
6	Leeds	42	18	11	13	59	57	47
7	Everton	42	17	10	15	64	58	44
8	Luton	42	16	12	14	77	78	44
9	Rotherham	42	17	8	17	73	71	42
10	Brentford	42	15	12	15	54	55	42
11	Sheff United	42	18	5	19	90	76	41
12	West Ham	42	15	11	16	67	77	41
13	Southampton	42	15	11	16	61	73	41
14	Blackburn	42	17	6	19	54	63	40
15	Notts County	42	16	7	19	71	68	39
16	Doncaster	42	13	12	17	55	60	38
17	Bury	42	15	7	20	67	69	37
18	Hull	42	13	11	18	60	70	37
19	Swansea	42	12	12	18	72	76	36
20	Barnsley	42	11	14	17	59	72	36
21	Coventry	42	14	6	22	59	82	34
22	QPR	42	11	12	19	52	81	34

THIRD DIVISION (SOUTH)

		P	W	D	L	F	A	Pts
1	Plymouth	46	29	8	9	107	53	66
2	Reading	46	29	3	14	112	60	61
3	Norwich	46	26	9	11	89	50	61
4	Millwall	46	23	12	11	74	53	58
5	Brighton	46	24	10	12	87	63	58
6	Newport	46	21	12	13	77	76	54
7	Bristol Rovers	46	20	12	14	89	53	52
8	Northampton	46	22	5	19	93	74	49
9	Southend	46	19	10	17	75	66	48
10	Colchester	46	17	12	17	56	77	46
11	Torquay	46	17	10	19	86	98	44
12	Aldershot	46	18	8	20	78	89	44
13	Port Vale	46	14	15	17	50	66	43
14	Bournemouth	46	16	10	20	69	75	42
15	Bristol City	46	15	12	19	58	69	42
16	Swindon	46	14	14	18	51	68	42
17	Ipswich	46	16	9	21	63	74	41
18	Leyton Orient	46	16	9	21	55	68	41
19	Crystal Palace	46	15	9	22	61	80	39
20	Shrewsbury	46	13	10	23	62	86	36
21	Watford	46	13	10	23	57	81	36
22	Gillingham	46	11	13	22	71	81	35
23	Exeter	46	13	9	24	65	86	35
24	Walsall	46	13	5	28	55	94	31

THIRD DIVISION (NORTH)

		P	W	D	L	F	A	Pts
1	Lincoln	46	30	9	7	121	52	69
2	Grimsby	46	29	8	9	96	45	66
3	Stockport	46	23	13	10	74	40	59
4	Oldham	46	24	9	13	90	61	57
5	Gateshead	46	21	11	14	66	49	53
6	Mansfield	46	22	8	16	73	60	52
7	Carlisle	46	19	13	14	62	57	51
8	Bradford PA	46	19	12	15	74	64	50
9	Hartlepools	46	21	8	17	71	65	50
10	York	46	18	13	15	73	52	49
11	Tranmere	46	21	6	19	76	71	48
12	Barrow	46	17	12	17	57	61	46
13	Chesterfield	46	17	11	18	65	66	45
14	Scunthorpe	46	14	16	16	65	74	44
15	Bradford City	46	16	10	20	61	68	42
16	Crewe	46	17	8	21	63	82	42
17	Southport	46	15	11	20	53	71	41
18	Wrexham	46	15	9	22	63	73	39
19	Chester	46	15	9	22	72	85	39
20	Halifax	46	14	7	25	61	97	35
21	Rochdale	46	11	13	22	47	79	35
22	Accrington	46	10	12	24	61	92	32
23	Darlington	46	11	9	26	64	103	31
24	Workington	46	11	7	28	50	91	29

SCOTTISH DIVISION 'A'

		P	W	D	L	F	A	Pts
1	Hibernian	30	20	5	5	92	36	45
2	Rangers	30	16	9	5	61	31	41
3	East Fife	30	17	3	10	71	49	37
4	Hearts	30	14	7	9	69	53	35
5	Raith	30	14	5	11	43	42	33
6	Partick	30	12	7	11	48	51	31
7	Motherwell	30	12	7	11	51	57	31
8	Dundee	30	11	6	13	53	52	28
9	Celtic	30	10	8	12	52	55	28
10	Queen of the S	30	10	8	12	50	60	28
11	Aberdeen	30	10	7	13	65	58	27
12	Third Lanark	30	9	8	13	51	62	26
13	Airdrieonians	30	11	4	15	54	69	26
14	St Mirren	30	10	5	15	43	58	25
15	Morton	30	9	6	15	49	56	24
16	Stirling	30	5	5	20	36	99	15

SCOTTISH DIVISION 'B'

		P	W	D	L	F	A	Pts
1	Clyde	30	19	6	5	100	45	44
2	Falkirk	30	18	7	5	80	34	43
3	Ayr	30	17	5	8	55	45	39
4	Dundee United	30	16	5	9	75	60	37
5	Kilmarnock	30	16	2	12	62	48	34
6	Dunfermline	30	15	2	13	74	65	32
7	Alloa	30	13	6	11	55	49	32
8	Cowdenbeath	30	12	8	10	66	67	32
9	Hamilton	30	12	6	12	47	51	30
10	Dumbarton	30	10	8	12	51	57	28
11	St Johnstone	30	9	7	14	62	68	25
12	Forfar	30	10	4	16	59	97	24
13	Stenhousemuir	30	8	6	16	57	74	22
14	Albion	30	6	10	14	39	57	22
15	Queen's Park	30	8	4	18	40	62	20
16	Arbroath	30	6	4	20	40	83	16

An Englishman from Wales
The first player to appear in an England representative side while not attached to an English club was Charlie Rutter, Cardiff City's right-back. Rutter played for the England 'B' side against the Netherlands 'B' side in Amsterdam, March 1952. England won the match—a kind of forerunner to the Under-23 international games—1-0.

Freddie Steele's move from Mansfield to Port Vale on 28 December 1951 was the first case of a player-manager being transferred from one Football League club to another.

Billy Foulkes of Newcastle United scored with his first kick in his first international appearance for Wales, against England at Cardiff in October 1951.

FA CUP 1951-52

FOURTH ROUND
Tottenham Hotspur v Newcastle United	0-3
Swansea Town v Rotherham United	3-0
Notts County v Portsmouth	1-3
Middlesbrough v Doncaster Rovers	1-4
Blackburn Rovers v Hull City	2-0
Gateshead v West Bromwich Albion	0-2
Burnley v Coventry City	2-0
Liverpool v Wolverhampton Wanderers	2-1
Arsenal v Barnsley	4-0
Birmingham City v Leyton Orient	0-1
Luton Town v Brentford	2-2, 0-0, 3-2
Swindon Town v Stoke City	1-1, 1-0
Chelsea v Tranmere Rovers	4-0
Leeds United v Bradford Park Avenue	2-0
West Ham United v Sheffield United	0-0, 2-4
Southend United v Bristol Rovers	2-1

FIFTH ROUND
Swansea Town v Newcastle United	0-1
Portsmouth v Doncaster Rovers	4-0
Blackburn Rovers v West Bromwich Albion	1-0
Burnley v Liverpool	2-0
Leyton Orient v Arsenal	0-3
Luton Town v Swindon Town	3-1
Leeds United v Chelsea	1-1, 1-1, 1-5
Southend United v Sheffield United	1-2

SIXTH ROUND
Portsmouth v Newcastle United	2-4
Blackburn Rovers v Burnley	3-1
Luton Town v Arsenal	2-3
Sheffield United v Chelsea	0-1

SEMI-FINAL
Newcastle United v Blackburn Rovers	0-0, 2-1
Arsenal v Chelsea	1-1, 3-0

FINAL
Newcastle United v Arsenal	1-0

SCOTTISH FA CUP 1951-52

SECOND ROUND
St Mirren v Motherwell	2-3
Clyde v Dunfermline Athletic	3-4
Rangers v Elgin City	6-1
Cowdenbeath v Arbroath	1-4
Heart of Midlothian v Raith Rovers	1-0
St Johnstone v Queen of the South	2-2, 1-3
Airdrieonians v East Fife	2-1
Clachnacuddin v Morton	1-2
Wigtown & Bladnoch v Dundee	1-7
Alloa Athletic v Berwick Rangers	0-0, 1-4
Aberdeen v Kilmarnock	2-1
Leith Athletic v Dundee United	1-4
Hamilton Academicals v Third Lanark	1-1, 0-4
Albion Rovers v Stranraer	1-1, 4-3
Falkirk v Stirling Albion	3-3, 2-1
Dumbarton v Queen's Park	1-0

THIRD ROUND
Dunfermline Athletic v Motherwell	1-1, 0-4
Arbroath v Rangers	0-2
Queen of the South v Heart of Midlothian	1-3
Airdrieonians v Morton	4-0
Dundee v Berwick Rangers	1-0
Dundee United v Aberdeen	2-2, 2-3
Albion Rovers v Third Lanark	1-3
Dumbarton v Falkirk	1-3

FOURTH ROUND
Rangers v Motherwell	1-1, 1-2
Airdrieonians v Heart of Midlothian	2-2, 4-6
Dundee v Aberdeen	4-0
Third Lanark v Falkirk	1-0

SEMI-FINAL
Motherwell v Heart of Midlothian	1-1, 1-1, 3-1
Dundee v Third Lanark	2-0

FINAL
Motherwell v Dundee	4-0

FIRST DIVISION

	P	W	D	L	F	A	Pts
1 Arsenal	42	21	12	9	97	64	54
2 Preston	42	21	12	9	85	60	54
3 Wolves	42	19	13	10	86	63	51
4 WBA	42	21	8	13	66	60	50
5 Charlton	42	19	11	12	77	63	49
6 Burnley	42	18	12	12	67	52	48
7 Blackpool	42	19	9	14	71	70	47
8 Man United	42	18	10	14	69	72	46
9 Sunderland	42	15	13	14	68	82	43
10 Tottenham	42	15	11	16	78	69	41
11 Aston Villa	42	14	13	15	63	61	41
12 Cardiff	42	14	12	16	54	46	40
13 Middlesbrough	42	14	11	17	70	77	39
14 Bolton	42	15	9	18	61	69	39
15 Portsmouth	42	14	10	18	74	83	38
16 Newcastle	42	14	9	19	59	70	37
17 Liverpool	42	14	8	20	61	82	36
18 Sheff Wed	42	12	11	19	62	72	35
19 Chelsea	42	12	11	19	56	66	35
20 Man City	42	14	7	21	72	87	35
21 Stoke	42	12	10	20	53	66	34
22 Derby	42	11	10	21	59	74	32

SECOND DIVISION

	P	W	D	L	F	A	Pts
1 Sheff United	42	25	10	7	97	55	60
2 Huddersfield	42	24	10	8	84	33	58
3 Luton	42	22	8	12	84	49	52
4 Plymouth	42	20	9	13	65	60	49
5 Leicester	42	18	12	12	89	74	48
6 Birmingham	42	19	10	13	71	66	48
7 Nottm Forest	42	18	8	16	77	67	44
8 Fulham	42	17	10	15	81	71	44
9 Blackburn	42	18	8	16	68	65	44
10 Leeds	42	14	15	13	71	63	43
11 Swansea	42	15	12	15	78	81	42
12 Rotherham	42	16	9	17	75	74	41
13 Doncaster	42	12	16	14	58	64	40
14 West Ham	42	13	13	16	58	60	39
15 Lincoln	42	11	17	14	64	71	39
16 Everton	42	12	14	16	71	75	38
17 Brentford	42	13	11	18	59	76	37
18 Hull	42	14	8	20	57	69	36
19 Notts County	42	14	8	20	60	88	36
20 Bury	42	13	9	20	53	81	35
21 Southampton	42	10	13	19	68	85	33
22 Barnsley	42	5	8	29	47	108	18

THIRD DIVISION (NORTH)

	P	W	D	L	F	A	Pts
1 Oldham	46	22	15	9	77	45	59
2 Port Vale	46	20	18	8	67	35	58
3 Wrexham	46	24	8	14	86	66	56
4 York	46	20	13	13	60	45	53
5 Grimsby	46	21	10	15	75	59	52
6 Southport	46	20	11	15	63	60	51
7 Bradford PA	46	19	12	15	75	61	50
8 Gateshead	46	17	15	14	76	60	49
9 Carlisle	46	18	13	15	82	68	49
10 Crewe	46	20	8	18	70	68	48
11 Stockport	46	17	13	16	82	69	47
12 Chesterfield*	46	18	11	17	65	63	47
13 Tranmere*	46	21	5	20	65	63	47
14 Halifax	46	16	15	15	68	68	47
15 Scunthorpe	46	16	14	16	62	56	46
16 Bradford City	46	14	18	14	75	80	46
17 Hartlepools	46	16	14	16	57	61	46
18 Mansfield	46	16	14	16	55	62	46
19 Barrow	46	16	12	18	66	71	44
20 Chester	46	11	15	20	64	85	37
21 Darlington	46	14	6	26	58	96	34
22 Rochdale	46	14	5	27	62	83	33
23 Workington	46	11	10	25	55	91	32
24 Accrington	46	8	11	27	39	89	27

*Equal

THIRD DIVISION (SOUTH)

	P	W	D	L	F	A	Pts
1 Bristol Rovers	46	26	12	8	92	46	64
2 Millwall	46	24	14	8	82	44	62
3 Northampton	46	26	10	10	109	70	62
4 Norwich	26	25	10	11	99	55	60
5 Bristol City	42	22	15	9	95	61	59
6 Coventry	46	19	12	15	77	62	50
7 Brighton	46	19	12	15	81	75	50
8 Southend	46	18	13	15	69	74	49
9 Bournemouth	46	19	9	18	74	69	47
10 Watford	46	15	17	14	62	63	47
11 Reading	46	19	8	19	69	64	46
12 Torquay	46	18	9	19	87	88	45
13 Crystal Palace	46	15	13	18	66	82	43
14 Leyton Orient	46	16	10	20	68	73	42
15 Newport	46	16	10	20	70	82	42
16 Ipswich	46	13	15	18	60	69	41
17 Exeter	46	13	14	19	61	71	40
18 Swindon	46	14	12	20	64	79	40
19 Aldershot	46	12	15	19	61	77	39
20 Gillingham	46	12	15	19	55	74	39
21 QPR	46	12	15	19	61	82	39
22 Colchester	46	12	14	20	59	76	38
23 Shrewsbury	46	12	12	22	68	91	36
24 Walsall	46	7	10	29	56	118	24

SCOTTISH DIVISION 'A'

	P	W	D	L	F	A	Pts
1 Rangers	30	18	7	5	80	39	43
2 Hibernian	30	19	5	6	93	51	43
3 East Fife	30	16	7	7	72	48	39
4 Hearts	30	12	6	12	59	50	30
5 Clyde	30	13	4	13	78	78	30
6 St Mirren	30	11	8	11	52	58	30
7 Dundee	30	9	11	8	44	37	29
8 Celtic	30	11	7	12	51	54	29
9 Partick	30	10	9	11	55	63	29
10 Queen of the S	30	10	8	12	43	61	28
11 Aberdeen	30	11	5	14	64	68	27
12 Raith Rovers	30	9	8	13	47	53	26
13 Falkirk	30	11	4	15	53	63	26
14 Airdrieonians	30	10	6	14	53	75	26
15 Motherwell	30	10	5	15	57	80	25
16 Third Lanark	30	8	4	18	52	75	20

SCOTTISH DIVISION 'B'

	P	W	D	L	F	A	Pts
1 Stirling	30	20	4	6	64	43	44
2 Hamilton	30	20	3	7	72	40	43
3 Queen's Park	30	15	7	8	70	46	37
4 Kilmarnock	30	17	2	11	74	48	36
5 Ayr	30	17	2	11	76	56	36
6 Morton	30	15	3	12	79	57	33
7 Arbroath	30	13	7	10	52	57	33
8 Dundee United	30	12	5	13	52	56	29
9 Alloa	30	12	5	13	63	68	29
10 Dumbarton	30	11	6	13	58	67	28
11 Dunfermline	30	9	9	12	51	58	27
12 Stenhousemuir	30	10	6	14	56	65	26
13 Cowdenbeath	30	8	7	15	37	54	23
14 St Johnstone	30	8	6	16	41	63	22
15 Forfar	30	8	4	18	54	88	20
16 Albion	30	5	4	21	44	77	14

FA CUP 1952-53

FOURTH ROUND

Blackpool v Huddersfield Town	1-0
Shrewsbury Town v Southampton	1-4
Arsenal v Bury	6-2
Burnley v Sunderland	2-0
Preston North End v Tottenham Hotspur	2-2, 0-1
Halifax Town v Stoke City	1-0
Sheffield United v Birmingham City	1-1, 1-3
Chelsea v West Bromwich Albion	1-1, 0-0, 1-1, 4-0
Bolton Wanderers v Notts County	1-1, 2-2, 1-0
Manchester City v Luton Town	1-1, 1-5
Hull City v Gateshead	1-2
Plymouth Argyle v Barnsley	1-0
Everton v Nottingham Forest	4-1
Manchester United v Walthamstow Avenue	1-1, 5-2
Aston Villa v Brentford	0-0, 2-1
Newcastle United v Rotherham United	1-3

FIFTH ROUND

Blackpool v Southampton	1-1, 2-1
Burnley v Arsenal	0-2
Halifax Town v Tottenham Hotspur	0-3
Chelsea v Birmingham City	0-4
Luton Town v Bolton Wanderers	0-1
Plymouth Argyle v Gateshead	0-1
Everton v Manchester United	2-1
Rotherham United v Aston Villa	1-3

SIXTH ROUND

Arsenal v Blackpool	1-2
Birmingham City v Tottenham Hotspur	1-1, 2-2, 0-1
Gateshead v Bolton Wanderers	0-1
Aston Villa v Everton	0-1

SEMI-FINAL

Blackpool v Tottenham Hotspur	2-1
Bolton Wanderers v Everton	4-3

FINAL

Blackpool v Bolton Wanderers	4-3

SCOTTISH FA CUP 1952-53

SECOND ROUND

Dundee v Rangers	0-2
Cowdenbeath v Morton	0-1
Forfar Athletic v Falkirk	2-4
Stirling Albion v Celtic	1-1, 0-3
Raith Rovers v Heart of Midlothian	0-1
St Johnstone v Montrose	1-2
Berwick Rangers v Queen of the South	2-3
Albion Rovers v East Stirlingshire	2-0
Partick Thistle v Clyde	0-2
Buckie Thistle v Ayr United	1-5
Wigtown & Bladnoch v Third Lanark	1-3
Hamilton Academicals v Kilmarnock	2-2, 2-0
Airdrieonians v East Fife	3-0
Hibernian v Queen's Park	4-2
Alloa Athletic v Motherwell	0-2
Aberdeen v St Mirren	2-0

THIRD ROUND

Morton v Rangers	1-4
Falkirk v Celtic	2-3
Heart of Midlothian v Montrose	3-1
Queen of the South v Albion Rovers	2-0
Clyde v Ayr United	8-3
Third Lanark v Hamilton Academicals	1-0
Airdrieonians v Hibernian	0-4
Aberdeen v Motherwell	5-5, 6-1

FOURTH ROUND

Rangers v Celtic	2-0
Heart of Midlothian v Queen of the South	2-1
Clyde v Third Lanark	1-2
Hibernian v Aberdeen	1-1, 0-2

SEMI-FINAL

Rangers v Heart of Midlothian	2-1
Third Lanark v Aberdeen	1-1, 1-2

FINAL

Aberdeen v Rangers	1-1, 0-1

A Division One match between Aston Villa and Sunderland in September 1952 produced a remarkable goal. It was scored by Peter Aldis, the Aston Villa full-back, who headed the ball into Sunderland's net from 35 yards. This goal, Aldis's first in the League, is reckoned to give Aldis the distance record for a headed goal in League football.

The footballing parson

The only post-War Football League professional who was also a parson was the Reverend Norman Hallam. A Methodist minister, Hallam was right-half for Port Vale in 1952-53. He later played for Barnsley and then Halifax before joining the Midland League club, Goole Town.

FIRST DIVISION

		P	W	D	L	F	A	Pts
1	Wolves	42	25	7	10	96	56	57
2	WBA	42	22	9	11	86	63	53
3	Huddersfield	42	20	11	11	78	61	51
4	Man United	42	18	12	12	73	58	48
5	Bolton	42	18	12	12	75	60	48
6	Blackpool	42	19	10	13	80	69	48
7	Burnley	42	21	4	17	78	67	46
8	Chelsea	42	16	12	14	74	68	44
9	Charlton	42	19	6	17	75	77	44
10	Cardiff	42	18	8	16	51	71	44
11	Preston	42	19	5	18	87	58	43
12	Arsenal	42	15	13	14	75	73	43
13	Aston Villa	42	16	9	17	70	68	41
14	Portsmouth	42	14	11	17	81	89	39
15	Newcastle	42	14	10	18	72	77	38
16	Tottenham	42	16	5	21	65	76	37
17	Man City	42	14	9	19	62	77	37
18	Sunderland	42	14	8	20	81	89	36
19	Sheff Wed	42	15	6	21	70	91	36
20	Sheff United	42	11	11	20	69	90	33
21	Middlesbrough	42	10	10	22	60	91	30
22	Liverpool	42	9	10	23	68	97	28

SECOND DIVISION

		P	W	D	L	F	A	Pts
1	Leicester	42	23	10	9	97	60	56
2	Everton	42	20	16	6	92	58	56
3	Blackburn	42	23	9	10	86	50	55
4	Nottm Forest	42	20	12	10	86	59	52
5	Rotherham	42	21	7	14	80	67	49
6	Luton	42	18	12	12	64	59	48
7	Birmingham	42	18	11	13	78	58	47
8	Fulham	42	17	10	15	98	85	44
9	Bristol Rovers	42	14	16	12	64	58	44
10	Leeds	42	15	13	14	89	81	43
11	Stoke	42	12	17	13	71	60	41
12	Doncaster	42	16	9	17	59	63	41
13	West Ham	42	15	9	18	67	69	39
14	Notts County	42	13	13	16	54	74	39
15	Hull	42	16	6	20	64	66	38
16	Lincoln	42	14	9	19	65	83	37
17	Bury	42	11	14	17	54	72	36
18	Derby	42	12	11	19	64	82	35
19	Plymouth	42	9	16	17	65	82	34
20	Swansea	42	13	8	21	58	82	34
21	Brentford	42	10	11	21	40	78	31
22	Oldham	42	8	9	25	40	89	25

THIRD DIVISION (SOUTH)

		P	W	D	L	F	A	Pts
1	Ipswich	46	27	10	9	82	51	64
2	Brighton	46	26	9	11	86	61	61
3	Bristol City	46	25	6	15	88	66	56
4	Watford	46	21	10	15	85	69	52
5	Northampton	46	20	11	15	82	55	51
6	Southampton	46	22	7	17	76	63	51
7	Norwich	46	20	11	15	73	66	51
8	Reading	46	20	9	17	86	73	49
9	Exeter	46	20	8	18	68	58	48
10	Gillingham	46	19	10	17	61	66	48
11	Leyton Orient	46	18	11	17	79	73	47
12	Millwall	46	19	9	18	74	77	47
13	Torquay	46	17	12	17	81	88	46
14	Coventry	46	18	9	19	61	56	45
15	Newport	46	19	6	21	61	81	44
16	Southend	46	18	7	21	69	71	43
17	Aldershot	46	17	9	20	74	86	43
18	QPR	46	16	10	20	60	68	42
19	Bournemouth	46	16	8	22	67	70	40
20	Swindon	46	15	10	21	67	70	40
21	Shrewsbury	46	14	12	20	65	76	40
22	Crystal Palace	46	14	12	20	60	86	40
23	Colchester	46	10	10	26	50	78	30
24	Walsall	46	9	8	29	40	87	26

THIRD DIVISION (NORTH)

		P	W	D	L	F	A	Pts
1	Port Vale	46	26	17	3	74	21	69
2	Barnsley	46	24	10	12	77	57	58
3	Scunthorpe	46	21	15	10	77	56	57
4	Gateshead	46	21	13	12	74	55	55
5	Bradford City	46	22	9	15	60	55	53
6	Chesterfield	46	19	14	13	76	64	52
7	Mansfield	46	20	11	15	88	67	51
8	Wrexham	46	21	9	16	81	68	51
9	Bradford PA	46	18	14	14	77	68	50
10	Stockport	46	18	11	17	77	67	47
11	Southport	46	17	12	17	63	60	46
12	Barrow	46	16	12	18	72	71	44
13	Carlisle	46	14	15	17	83	71	43
14	Tranmere	46	18	7	21	59	70	43
15	Accrington	46	16	10	20	66	74	42
16	Crewe	46	14	13	19	49	67	41
17	Grimsby	46	16	9	21	51	77	41
18	Hartlepools	46	13	14	19	59	65	40
19	Rochdale	46	15	10	21	59	77	40
20	Workington	46	13	14	19	59	80	40
21	Darlington	46	12	14	20	50	71	38
22	York	46	12	13	21	64	86	37
23	Halifax	46	12	10	24	44	73	34
24	Chester	46	11	10	25	48	67	32

SCOTTISH DIVISION 'A'

		P	W	D	L	F	A	Pts
1	Celtic	30	20	3	7	72	29	43
2	Hearts	30	16	6	8	70	45	38
3	Partick	30	17	1	12	76	54	35
4	Rangers	30	13	8	9	56	35	34
5	Hibernian	30	15	4	11	72	51	34
6	East Fife	30	13	8	9	55	45	34
7	Dundee	30	14	6	10	46	47	34
8	Clyde	30	15	4	11	64	67	34
9	Aberdeen	30	15	3	12	66	51	33
10	Queen of the S	30	14	4	12	72	53	32
11	St Mirren	30	12	4	14	44	54	28
12	Raith	30	10	6	14	56	60	26
13	Falkirk	30	9	7	14	47	61	25
14	Stirling	30	10	4	16	39	62	24
15	Airdrieonians	30	5	5	20	41	92	15
16	Hamilton	30	4	3	23	29	94	11

SCOTTISH DIVISION 'B'

		P	W	D	L	F	A	Pts
1	Motherwell	30	21	3	6	109	43	45
2	Kilmarnock	30	19	4	7	71	39	42
3	Third Lanark	30	13	10	7	78	48	36
4	Stenhousemuir	30	14	8	8	66	58	36
5	Morton	30	15	3	12	85	65	33
6	St Johnstone	30	14	3	13	80	71	31
7	Albion	30	12	7	11	55	63	31
8	Dunfermline	30	11	9	10	48	57	31
9	Ayr	30	11	8	11	50	56	30
10	Queen's Park	30	9	9	12	56	51	27
11	Alloa	30	7	10	13	50	72	24
12	Forfar	30	10	4	16	38	69	24
13	Cowdenbeath	30	9	5	16	67	81	23
14	Arbroath	30	8	7	15	53	67	23
15	Dundee United	30	8	6	16	54	79	22
16	Dumbarton	30	7	8	15	51	92	22

Since the offside rule was changed in 1925, the record number of League games which a club has played in any one season without conceding a goal is 30. Port Vale, with their unpopular yet effective brand of defensive football, set this record in Division Three North, 1953-54. That season, Vale lost but three games, also a record for that division, conceding just 21 goals, a League record.

Stalemate
On 9 January 1954, 15 of the 32 Third Round FA Cup ties played that day ended as draws, a record for the FA Cup competition.

The record Scottish FA Cup win away from home was set on 13 February 1954. Then, in the Second Round, Raith Rovers crumpled Coldstream 10-1 on their own ground.

FA CUP 1953-54

FOURTH ROUND

West Bromwich Albion v Rotherham United	4-0
Burnley v Newcastle United	1-1, 0-1
Blackburn Rovers v Hull City	2-2, 1-2
Manchester City v Tottenham Hotspur	0-1
Leyton Orient v Fulham	2-1
Plymouth Argyle v Doncaster Rovers	0-2
Cardiff City v Port Vale	0-2
West Ham United v Blackpool	1-1, 1-3
Sheffield Wednesday v Chesterfield	0-0, 4-2
Everton v Swansea Town	3-0
Headington United v Bolton Wanderers	2-4
Scunthorpe United v Portsmouth	1-1, 2-2, 0-4
Arsenal v Norwich City	1-2
Stoke City v Leicester City	0-0, 1-3
Lincoln City v Preston North End	0-2
Ipswich Town v Birmingham City	1-0

FIFTH ROUND

West Bromwich Albion v Newcastle United	3-2
Hull City v Tottenham Hotspur	1-1, 0-2
Leyton Orient v Doncaster Rovers	3-1
Port Vale v Blackpool	2-0
Sheffield Wednesday v Everton	3-1
Bolton Wanderers v Portsmouth	0-0, 2-1
Norwich City v Leicester City	1-2
Preston North End v Ipswich Town	6-1

SIXTH ROUND

West Bromwich Albion v Tottenham Hotspur	3-0
Leyton Orient v Port Vale	0-1
Sheffield Wednesday v Bolton Wanderers	1-1, 2-0
Leicester City v Preston North End	1-1, 2-2, 1-3

SEMI-FINAL

West Bromwich Albion v Port Vale	2-1
Sheffield Wednesday v Preston North End	0-2

FINAL

West Bromwich Albion v Preston North End	3-2

SCOTTISH FA CUP 1953-54

SECOND ROUND

Falkirk v Celtic	1-2
Stirling Albion v Arbroath	0-0, 3-1
Brechin City v Hamilton Academicals	2-3
Morton v Cowdenbeath	4-0
Tarff Rovers v Partick Thistle	1-9
Peebles Rovers v Buckie Thistle	1-1, 2-7
Motherwell v Dunfermline Athletic	5-2
Coldstream v Raith Rovers	1-10
Third Lanark v Deveronvale	7-2
Rangers v Kilmarnock	2-2, 3-1
Berwick Rangers v Ayr United	5-1
Albion Rovers v Dundee	1-1, 0-4
Queen of the South v Forfar Athletic	3-0
Fraserburgh v Heart of Midlothian	0-3
Hibernian v Clyde	7-0
Duns v Aberdeen	0-8

THIRD ROUND

Stirling Albion v Celtic	3-4
Hamilton Academicals v Morton	2-0
Partick Thistle v Buckie Thistle	5-3
Motherwell v Raith Rovers	4-1
Third Lanark v Rangers	0-0, 4-4, 2-3
Berwick Rangers v Dundee	3-0
Queen of the South v Heart of Midlothian	1-2
Hibernian v Aberdeen	1-3

FOURTH ROUND

Hamilton Academicals v Celtic	1-2
Partick Thistle v Motherwell	1-1, 1-2
Rangers v Berwick Rangers	4-0
Aberdeen v Heart of Midlothian	3-0

SEMI-FINAL

Celtic v Motherwell	2-2, 3-1
Rangers v Aberdeen	0-6

FINAL

Aberdeen v Celtic	1-2

FIRST DIVISION

		P	W	D	L	F	A	Pts
1	Chelsea	42	20	12	10	81	57	52
2	Wolves	42	19	10	13	89	70	48
3	Portsmouth	42	18	12	12	74	62	48
4	Sunderland	42	15	18	9	64	54	48
5	Man United	42	20	7	15	84	74	47
6	Aston Villa	42	20	7	15	72	73	47
7	Man City	42	18	10	14	76	69	46
8	Newcastle	42	17	9	16	89	77	43
9	Arsenal	42	17	9	16	69	63	43
10	Burnley	42	17	9	16	51	48	43
11	Everton	42	16	10	16	62	68	42
12	Huddersfield	42	14	13	15	63	68	41
13	Sheff United	42	17	7	18	70	86	41
14	Preston	42	16	8	18	83	64	40
15	Charlton	42	15	10	17	76	75	40
16	Tottenham	42	16	8	18	72	73	40
17	WBA	42	16	8	18	76	96	40
18	Bolton	42	13	13	16	62	69	39
19	Blackpool	42	14	10	18	60	64	38
20	Cardiff	42	13	11	18	62	76	37
21	Leicester	42	12	11	19	74	86	35
22	Sheff Wed	42	8	10	24	63	100	26

SECOND DIVISION

		P	W	D	L	F	A	Pts
1	Birmingham	42	22	10	10	92	47	54
2	Luton	42	23	8	11	88	53	54
3	Rotherham	42	25	4	13	94	64	54
4	Leeds	42	23	7	12	70	53	53
5	Stoke	42	21	10	11	69	46	52
6	Blackburn	42	22	6	14	114	79	50
7	Notts County	42	21	6	15	74	71	48
8	West Ham	42	18	10	14	74	70	46
9	Bristol Rovers	42	19	7	16	75	70	45
10	Swansea	42	17	9	16	86	83	43
11	Liverpool	42	16	10	16	92	96	42
12	Middlesbrough	42	18	6	18	73	82	42
13	Bury	42	15	11	16	77	72	41
14	Fulham	42	14	11	17	76	79	39
15	Nottm Forest	42	16	7	19	58	62	39
16	Lincoln	42	13	10	19	68	79	36
17	Port Vale	42	12	11	19	48	71	35
18	Doncaster	42	14	7	21	58	95	35
19	Hull	42	12	10	20	44	69	34
20	Plymouth	42	12	7	23	57	82	31
21	Ipswich	42	11	6	25	57	92	28
22	Derby	42	7	9	26	53	82	23

THIRD DIVISION (SOUTH)

		P	W	D	L	F	A	Pts
1	Bristol City	46	30	10	6	101	47	70
2	Leyton Orient	46	26	9	11	89	47	61
3	Southampton	46	24	11	11	75	51	59
4	Gillingham	46	20	15	11	77	66	55
5	Millwall	46	20	11	15	72	68	51
6	Brighton	46	20	10	16	76	63	50
7	Watford	46	18	14	14	71	62	50
8	Torquay	46	18	12	16	82	82	48
9	Coventry	46	18	11	17	67	59	47
10	Southend	46	17	12	17	83	80	46
11	Brentford	46	16	14	16	82	82	46
12	Norwich	46	18	10	18	60	60	46
13	Northampton	46	19	8	19	73	81	46
14	Aldershot	46	16	13	17	75	71	45
15	QPR	46	15	14	17	69	75	44
16	Shrewsbury	46	16	10	20	70	78	42
17	Bournemouth	46	12	18	16	57	65	42
18	Reading	46	13	15	18	65	73	41
19	Newport	46	11	16	19	60	73	38
20	Crystal Palace	46	11	16	19	52	80	38
21	Swindon	46	11	15	20	46	64	37
22	Exeter	46	11	15	20	47	73	37
23	Walsall	46	10	14	22	75	86	34
24	Colchester	46	9	13	24	53	91	31

THIRD DIVISION (NORTH)

		P	W	D	L	F	A	Pts
1	Barnsley	46	30	5	11	86	46	65
2	Accrington	46	25	11	10	96	67	61
3	Scunthorpe	46	23	12	11	81	53	58
4	York	46	24	10	12	92	63	58
5	Hartlepools	46	25	5	16	64	49	55
6	Chesterfield	46	24	6	16	81	70	54
7	Gateshead	46	20	12	14	65	69	52
8	Workington	46	18	14	14	68	55	50
9	Stockport	46	18	12	16	84	70	48
10	Oldham	46	19	10	17	74	68	48
11	Southport	46	16	16	14	47	44	48
12	Rochdale	46	17	14	15	69	66	48
13	Mansfield	46	18	9	19	65	71	45
14	Halifax	46	15	13	18	63	67	43
15	Darlington	46	14	14	18	62	73	42
16	Bradford PA	46	15	11	20	56	70	41
17	Barrow	46	17	6	23	70	89	40
18	Wrexham	46	13	12	21	65	77	38
19	Tranmere	46	13	11	22	55	70	37
20	Carlisle	46	15	6	25	78	89	36
21	Bradford City	46	13	10	23	47	55	36
22	Crewe	46	10	14	22	68	91	34
23	Grimsby	46	13	8	25	47	78	34
24	Chester	46	12	9	25	44	77	33

SCOTTISH DIVISION 'A'

		P	W	D	L	F	A	Pts
1	Aberdeen	30	24	1	5	73	26	49
2	Celtic	30	19	8	3	76	37	46
3	Rangers	30	19	3	8	67	33	41
4	Hearts	30	16	7	7	74	45	39
5	Hibernian	30	15	4	11	64	54	34
6	St Mirren	30	12	8	10	55	54	32
7	Clyde	30	11	9	10	59	50	31
8	Dundee	30	13	4	13	48	48	30
9	Partick Thistle	30	11	7	12	49	61	29
10	Kilmarnock	30	10	6	14	46	58	26
11	East Fife	30	9	6	15	51	62	24
12	Falkirk	30	8	8	14	42	54	24
13	Queen of the S	30	9	6	15	38	56	24
14	Raith	30	10	3	17	49	57	23
15	Motherwell	30	9	4	17	42	62	22
16	Stirling	30	2	2	26	29	105	6

SCOTTISH DIVISION 'B'

		P	W	D	L	F	A	Pts
1	Airdrieonians	30	18	10	2	103	61	46
2	Dunfermline	30	19	4	7	72	40	42
3	Hamilton	30	17	5	8	74	51	39
4	Queen's Park	30	15	5	10	65	36	35
5	Third Lanark	30	13	7	10	63	49	33
6	Stenhousemuir	30	12	8	10	70	51	32
7	St Johnstone	30	15	2	13	60	51	32
8	Ayr	30	14	4	12	61	73	32
9	Morton	30	12	5	13	58	69	29
10	Forfar	30	11	6	13	63	80	28
11	Albion	30	8	10	12	50	69	26
12	Arbroath	30	8	8	14	55	72	24
13	Dundee United	30	8	6	16	55	70	22
14	Cowdenbeath	30	8	5	17	55	72	21
15	Alloa	30	7	6	17	51	75	20
16	Brechin	30	8	3	19	53	89	19

FA CUP 1954-55

FOURTH ROUND

Everton v Liverpool	0-4
Torquay United v Huddersfield Town	0-1
Hartlepools United v Nottingham Forest	1-1, 1-2
Newcastle United v Brentford	3-2
Sheffield Wednesday v Notts County	1-1, 0-1
Bristol Rovers v Chelsea	1-3
Bishop Auckland v York City	1-3
Tottenham Hotspur v Port Vale	4-2
Swansea Town v Stoke City	3-1
Preston North End v Sunderland	3-3, 0-2
Wolverhampton Wanderers v Arsenal	1-0
West Bromwich Albion v Charlton Athletic	2-4
Birmingham City v Bolton Wanderers	2-1
Doncaster Rovers v Aston Villa	0-0, 2-2, 1-1, 0-0, 3-1
Rotherham United v Luton Town	1-5
Manchester City v Manchester United	2-0

FIFTH ROUND

Liverpool v Huddersfield Town	0-2
Nottingham Forest v Newcastle United	1-1, 2-2, 1-2
Notts County v Chelsea	1-0
York City v Tottenham Hotspur	3-1
Swansea Town v Sunderland	2-2, 0-1
Wolverhampton Wanderers v Charlton Athletic	4-1
Birmingham City v Doncaster Rovers	2-1
Luton Town v Manchester City	0-2

SIXTH ROUND

Huddersfield Town v Newcastle United	1-1, 0-2
Notts County v York City	0-1
Sunderland v Wolverhampton Wanderers	2-0
Birmingham City v Manchester City	0-1

SEMI-FINAL

Newcastle United v York City	1-1, 2-0
Sunderland v Manchester City	0-1

FINAL

Newcastle United v Manchester City	3-1

SCOTTISH FA CUP 1954-55

FIFTH ROUND

Clyde v Albion Rovers	3-0
Morton v Raith Rovers	1-3
Ayr United v Inverness Caledonian	1-1, 2-4
Heart of Midlothian v Hibernian	5-0
Stirling Albion v Aberdeen	0-6
Dundee v Rangers	0-0, 0-1
Airdrieonians v Forfar Athletic	4-3
Dunfermline Athletic v Partick Thistle	4-2
Third Lanark v Queen of the South	2-1
Forres Mechanics v Motherwell	3-4
East Fife v Kilmarnock	1-2
Alloa Athletic v Celtic	2-4
Arbroath v St Johnstone	0-4
Hamilton Academicals v St Mirren	2-1
Falkirk v Stenhousemuir	4-0
Buckie Thistle v Inverness Thistle	2-0

SIXTH ROUND

Clyde v Raith Rovers	3-1
Inverness Caledonian v Falkirk	0-7
Buckie Thistle v Heart of Midlothian	0-6
Aberdeen v Rangers	2-1
Airdrieonians v Dunfermline Athletic	7-0
Third Lanark v Motherwell	1-3
Celtic v Kilmarnock	1-1, 1-0
St Johnstone v Hamilton Academicals	0-1

SEVENTH ROUND

Clyde v Falkirk	5-0
Aberdeen v Heart of Midlothian	1-1, 2-0
Airdrieonians v Motherwell	4-1
Celtic v Hamilton Academicals	2-1

SEMI-FINAL

Aberdeen v Clyde	2-2, 0-1
Airdrieonians v Celtic	2-2, 0-2

FINAL

Celtic v Clyde	1-1, 0-1

A combined effort

Stan Milburn and Jack Froggatt, both Leicester City defenders, are officially recorded as 'sharing one own goal' on 18 December 1954. In the Division One game with Chelsea at Stamford Bridge, Froggatt and Milburn were involved in a misunderstanding in front of goal, and simultaneously booted the ball into the Leicester net, thus sharing the blame. Chelsea won the game by three goals to one.

Stoke City and Bury created an endurance record for an FA Cup match when they met five times in the Third Round in January 1955. Altogether they played for 9 hours and 22 minutes before Stoke won 3-2 at Old Trafford.

On 2 April 1955, Duncan Edwards of Manchester United became the youngest ever England international when, aged 18 years six months, he played against Scotland.

League Tables 1955-56

FIRST DIVISION

		P	W	D	L	F	A	Pts
1	Man United	42	25	10	7	83	51	60
2	Blackpool	42	20	9	13	86	62	49
3	Wolves	42	20	9	13	89	65	49
4	Man City	42	18	10	14	82	69	46
5	Arsenal	42	18	10	14	60	61	46
6	Birmingham	42	18	9	15	75	57	45
7	Burnley	42	18	8	16	64	54	44
8	Bolton	42	18	7	17	71	58	43
9	Sunderland	42	17	9	16	80	95	43
10	Luton	42	17	8	17	66	64	42
11	Newcastle	42	17	7	18	85	70	41
12	Portsmouth	42	16	9	17	78	85	41
13	WBA	42	18	5	19	58	70	41
14	Charlton	42	17	6	19	75	81	40
15	Everton	42	15	10	17	55	69	40
16	Chelsea	42	14	11	17	64	77	39
17	Cardiff	42	15	9	18	55	69	39
18	Tottenham	42	15	7	20	61	71	37
19	Preston	42	14	8	20	73	72	36
20	Aston Villa	42	11	13	18	52	69	35
21	Huddersfield	42	14	7	21	54	83	35
22	Sheff United	42	12	9	21	63	77	33

SECOND DIVISION

		P	W	D	L	F	A	Pts
1	Sheff Wed	42	21	13	8	101	62	55
2	Leeds	42	23	6	13	80	60	52
3	Liverpool	42	21	6	15	85	63	48
4	Blackburn	42	21	6	15	84	65	48
5	Leicester	42	21	6	15	94	78	48
6	Bristol Rovers	42	21	6	15	84	70	48
7	Nottm Forest	42	19	9	14	68	63	47
8	Lincoln	42	18	10	14	79	65	46
9	Fulham	42	20	6	16	89	79	46
10	Swansea	42	20	6	16	83	81	46
11	Bristol City	42	19	7	16	80	64	45
12	Port Vale	42	16	13	13	60	58	45
13	Stoke	42	20	4	18	71	62	44
14	Middlesbrough	42	16	8	18	76	78	40
15	Bury	42	16	8	18	86	90	40
16	West Ham	42	14	11	17	74	69	39
17	Doncaster	42	12	11	19	69	96	35
18	Barnsley	42	11	12	19	47	84	34
19	Rotherham	42	12	9	21	56	75	33
20	Notts County	42	11	9	22	55	82	31
21	Plymouth	42	10	8	24	54	87	28
22	Hull	42	10	6	26	53	97	26

THIRD DIVISION (NORTH)

		P	W	D	L	F	A	Pts
1	Grimsby	46	31	6	9	76	29	68
2	Derby	46	28	7	11	110	55	63
3	Accrington	46	25	9	12	92	57	59
4	Hartlepools	46	26	5	15	81	60	57
5	Southport	46	23	11	12	66	53	57
6	Chesterfield	46	25	4	17	94	66	54
7	Stockport	46	21	9	16	90	61	51
8	Bradford City	46	18	13	15	78	64	49
9	Scunthorpe	46	20	8	18	75	63	48
10	Workington	46	19	9	18	75	63	47
11	York	46	19	9	18	85	72	47
12	Rochdale	46	17	13	16	66	84	47
13	Gateshead	46	17	11	18	77	84	45
14	Wrexham	46	16	10	20	66	73	42
15	Darlington	46	16	9	21	60	73	41
16	Tranmere	46	16	9	21	59	84	41
17	Chester	46	13	14	19	52	82	40
18	Mansfield	46	14	11	21	84	81	39
19	Halifax	46	14	11	21	66	76	39
20	Oldham	46	10	18	18	76	86	38
21	Carlisle	46	15	8	23	71	95	38
22	Barrow	46	12	9	25	61	83	33
23	Bradford PA	46	13	7	26	61	122	33
24	Crewe	46	9	10	27	50	105	28

THIRD DIVISION (SOUTH)

		P	W	D	L	F	A	Pts
1	Leyton Orient	46	29	8	9	106	49	66
2	Brighton	46	29	7	10	112	50	65
3	Ipswich	46	25	14	7	106	60	64
4	Southend	46	21	11	14	88	80	53
5	Torquay	46	20	12	14	86	63	52
6	Brentford	46	19	14	13	69	66	52
7	Norwich	46	19	13	14	86	82	51
8	Coventry	46	20	9	17	73	60	49
9	Bournemouth	46	19	10	17	63	51	48
10	Gillingham	46	19	10	17	69	71	48
11	Northampton	46	20	7	19	67	71	47
12	Colchester	46	18	11	17	76	81	47
13	Shrewsbury	46	17	12	17	69	66	46
14	Southampton	46	18	8	20	91	81	44
15	Aldershot	46	12	16	18	70	90	40
16	Exeter	46	15	10	21	58	77	40
17	Reading	46	15	9	22	70	79	39
18	QPR	46	14	11	21	64	86	39
19	Newport	46	15	9	22	58	79	39
20	Walsall	46	15	8	23	68	84	38
21	Watford	46	13	11	22	52	85	37
22	Millwall	46	15	6	25	83	100	36
23	Crystal Palace	46	12	10	24	54	83	34
24	Swindon	46	8	14	24	34	78	30

SCOTTISH LEAGUE 'A'

		P	W	D	L	F	A	Pts
1	Rangers	34	22	8	4	85	27	52
2	Aberdeen	34	18	10	6	87	50	46
3	Hearts	34	19	7	8	99	47	45
4	Hibernian	34	19	7	8	86	50	45
5	Celtic	34	16	9	9	55	39	41
6	Queen of the S	34	16	5	13	69	73	37
7	Airdrieonians	34	14	8	12	85	96	36
8	Kilmarnock	34	12	10	12	52	45	34
9	Partick Thistle	34	13	7	14	62	60	33
10	Motherwell	34	11	11	12	53	59	33
11	Raith	34	12	9	13	58	75	33
12	East Fife	34	13	5	16	61	69	31
13	Dundee	34	12	6	16	56	65	30
14	Falkirk	34	11	6	17	58	75	28
15	St Mirren	34	10	7	17	57	70	27
16	Dunfermline	34	10	6	18	42	82	26
17	Clyde	34	8	6	20	50	74	22
18	Stirling	34	4	5	25	23	82	13

SCOTTISH LEAGUE 'B'

		P	W	D	L	F	A	Pts
1	Queen's Park	36	23	8	5	78	28	54
2	Ayr	36	24	3	9	103	55	51
3	St Johnstone	36	21	7	8	86	45	49
4	Dumbarton	36	21	5	10	83	62	47
5	Stenhousemuir	36	20	4	12	82	54	44
6	Brechin	36	18	6	12	60	56	42
7	Cowdenbeath	36	16	7	13	80	85	39
8	Dundee United	36	12	14	10	78	65	38
9	Morton	36	15	6	15	71	69	36
10	Third Lanark	36	16	3	17	80	64	35
11	Hamilton	36	13	7	16	86	84	33
12	Stranraer	36	14	5	17	77	92	33
13	Alloa	36	12	7	17	67	73	31
14	Berwick	36	11	9	16	52	77	31
15	Forfar	36	10	9	17	62	75	29
16	E Stirlingshire	36	9	10	17	66	94	28
17	Albion	36	8	11	17	58	82	27
18	Arbroath	36	10	6	20	47	67	26
19	Montrose	36	4	3	29	44	133	11

FA CUP 1955-56

FOURTH ROUND

Leyton Orient v Birmingham City	0-4
West Bromwich Albion v Portsmouth	2-0
Charlton Athletic v Swindon Town	2-1
Arsenal v Aston Villa	4-1
Fulham v Newcastle United	4-5
Leicester City v Stoke City	3-3, 1-2
Bolton Wanderers v Sheffield United	1-2
York City v Sunderland	0-0, 1-2
Bristol Rovers v Doncaster Rovers	1-1, 0-1
Tottenham Hotspur v Middlesbrough	3-1
West Ham United v Cardiff City	2-1
Barnsley v Blackburn Rovers	0-1
Port Vale v Everton	2-3
Burnley v Chelsea	1-1, 1-1, 2-2, 0-0, 0-2
Liverpool v Scunthorpe United	3-3, 2-1
Southend United v Manchester City	0-1

FIFTH ROUND

West Bromwich Albion v Birmingham City	0-1
Charlton Athletic v Arsenal	0-2
Newcastle United v Stoke City	2-1
Sheffield United v Sunderland	0-0, 0-1
Doncaster Rovers v Tottenham Hotspur	0-2
West Ham United v Blackburn Rovers	0-0, 3-2
Everton v Chelsea	1-0
Manchester City v Liverpool	0-0, 2-1

SIXTH ROUND

Arsenal v Birmingham City	1-3
Newcastle United v Sunderland	0-2
Tottenham Hotspur v West Ham United	3-3, 2-1
Manchester City v Everton	2-1

SEMI-FINAL

Birmingham City v Sunderland	3-0
Tottenham Hotspur v Manchester City	0-1

FINAL

Manchester City v Birmingham City	3-1

SCOTTISH FA CUP 1955-56

FIFTH ROUND

Heart of Midlothian v Forfar Athletic	3-0
Stirling Albion v St Johnstone	2-1
Rangers v Aberdeen	2-1
Dundee v Dundee United	2-2, 3-0
Hibernian v Raith Rovers	1-1, 1-3
Motherwell v Queen's Park	0-2
Partick Thistle v Alloa Athletic	2-0
Brechin City v Arbroath	1-1, 3-2
Falkirk v Kilmarnock	0-3
Queen of the South v Cowdenbeath	3-1
East Fife v Stenhousemuir	1-3
Clyde v Dunfermline Athletic	5-0
St Mirren v Third Lanark	6-0
Airdrieonians v Hamilton Academicals	7-1
Ayr United v Berwick Rangers	5-2
Morton v Celtic	0-2

SIXTH ROUND

Heart of Midlothian v Stirling Albion	5-0
Dundee v Rangers	0-1
Raith Rovers v Queen's Park	2-2, 2-1
Partick Thistle v Brechin City	3-1
Kilmarnock v Queen of the South	2-2, 0-2
Stenhousemuir v Clyde	0-1
St Mirren v Airdrieonians	4-4, 1-3
Ayr United v Celtic	0-3

SEVENTH ROUND

Heart of Midlothian v Rangers	4-0
Raith Rovers v Partick Thistle	2-1
Queen of the South v Clyde	2-4
Celtic v Airdrieonians	2-1

SEMI-FINAL

Heart of Midlothian v Raith Rovers	0-0, 3-0
Celtic v Clyde	2-0

FINAL

Heart of Midlothian v Celtic	3-1

Accrington Stanley set a League record early in the 1955-56 season by fielding a side composed entirely of Scottish-born players. During the season, this team appeared several times. Indeed, all but four of the first-team squad of 19 players the club used that season in the Third Division North were born in Scotland.

On 3 September 1955, Wolves beat Cardiff 9-1 away from home to equal the Division One record away win. Curiously, later in the season, Cardiff won 2-0 at Wolves.

All four countries in the Home Championship finished level with three points, the first time this had ever happened.

FIRST DIVISION

		P	W	D	L	F	A	Pts
1	Man United	42	28	8	6	103	54	64
2	Tottenham	42	22	12	8	104	56	56
3	Preston	42	23	10	9	84	56	56
4	Blackpool	42	22	9	11	93	65	53
5	Arsenal	42	21	8	13	85	69	50
6	Wolves	42	20	8	14	94	70	48
7	Burnley	42	18	10	14	56	50	46
8	Leeds	42	15	14	13	72	63	44
9	Bolton	42	16	12	14	65	65	44
10	Aston Villa	42	14	15	13	65	55	43
11	WBA	42	14	14	14	59	61	42
12	Birmingham*	42	15	9	18	69	69	39
13	Chelsea*	42	13	13	16	73	73	39
14	Sheff Wed	42	16	6	20	82	88	38
15	Everton	42	14	10	18	61	79	38
16	Luton	42	14	9	19	58	76	37
17	Newcastle	42	14	8	20	67	87	36
18	Man City	42	13	9	20	78	88	35
19	Portsmouth	42	10	13	19	62	92	33
20	Sunderland	42	12	8	22	67	88	32
21	Cardiff	42	10	9	23	53	88	29
22	Charlton	42	9	4	29	62	120	22

*Equal

SECOND DIVISION

		P	W	D	L	F	A	Pts
1	Leicester	42	25	11	6	109	67	61
2	Nottm Forest	42	22	10	10	94	55	54
3	Liverpool	42	21	11	10	82	54	53
4	Blackburn	42	21	10	11	83	75	52
5	Stoke	42	20	8	14	83	58	48
6	Middlesbrough	42	19	10	13	84	60	48
7	Sheff United	42	19	8	15	87	76	46
8	West Ham	42	19	8	15	59	63	46
9	Bristol Rovers	42	18	9	15	81	67	45
10	Swansea	42	19	7	16	90	90	45
11	Fulham	42	19	4	19	84	76	42
12	Huddersfield	42	18	6	18	68	74	42
13	Bristol City	42	16	9	17	74	79	41
14	Doncaster	42	15	10	17	77	77	40
15	Leyton Orient	42	15	10	17	66	84	40
16	Grimsby	42	17	5	20	61	62	39
17	Rotherham	42	13	11	18	74	75	37
18	Lincoln	42	14	6	22	54	80	34
19	Barnsley	42	12	10	20	59	89	34
20	Notts County	42	9	12	21	58	86	30
21	Bury	42	8	9	25	60	96	25
22	Port Vale	42	8	6	28	57	101	22

FA CUP 1956-57

FOURTH ROUND
Middlesbrough v Aston Villa	2-3
Bristol City v Rhyl	3-0
Burnley v New Brighton	9-0
Huddersfield Town v Peterborough United	3-1
Newport County v Arsenal	0-2
Bristol Rovers v Preston North End	1-4
Blackpool v Fulham	6-2
West Bromwich Albion v Sunderland	4-2
Wrexham v Manchester United	0-5
Everton v West Ham United	2-1
Wolverhampton Wanderers v Bournemouth	0-1
Tottenham Hotspur v Chelsea	4-0
Southend United v Birmingham City	1-6
Millwall v Newcastle United	2-1
Cardiff City v Barnsley	0-1
Portsmouth v Nottingham Forest	1-3

FIFTH ROUND
Aston Villa v Bristol City	2-1
Huddersfield Town v Burnley	1-2
Preston North End v Arsenal	3-3, 1-2
Blackpool v West Bromwich Albion	0-0, 1-2
Manchester United v Everton	1-0
Bournemouth v Tottenham Hotspur	3-1
Millwall v Birmingham City	1-4
Barnsley v Nottingham Forest	1-2

SIXTH ROUND
Burnley v Aston Villa	1-1, 0-2
West Bromwich Albion v Arsenal	2-2, 2-1
Bournemouth v Manchester United	1-2
Birmingham City v Nottingham Forest	0-0, 1-0

SEMI-FINAL
Aston Villa v West Bromwich Albion	2-2, 1-0
Manchester United v Birmingham City	2-0

FINAL
Aston Villa v Manchester United	2-1

THIRD DIVISION (SOUTH)

		P	W	D	L	F	A	Pts
1	Ipswich	46	25	9	12	101	54	59
2	Torquay	46	24	11	11	89	64	59
3	Colchester	46	22	14	10	84	56	58
4	Southampton	46	22	10	14	76	52	54
5	Bournemouth	46	19	14	13	88	62	52
6	Brighton	46	19	14	13	86	65	52
7	Southend	46	18	12	16	73	65	48
8	Brentford	46	16	16	14	78	76	48
9	Shrewsbury	46	15	18	13	72	79	48
10	QPR	46	18	11	17	61	60	47
11	Watford	46	18	10	18	72	75	46
12	Newport	46	16	13	17	65	62	45
13	Reading	46	18	9	19	80	81	45
14	Northampton	46	18	9	19	66	73	45
15	Walsall	46	16	12	18	80	74	44
16	Coventry	46	16	12	18	74	84	44
17	Millwall	46	16	12	18	64	84	44
18	Plymouth	46	16	11	19	68	73	43
19	Aldershot	46	15	12	19	79	92	42
20	Crystal Palace	46	11	18	17	62	75	40
21	Exeter	46	12	13	21	61	79	37
22	Gillingham	46	12	13	21	54	85	37
23	Swindon	46	15	6	25	66	96	36
24	Norwich	46	8	15	23	61	94	31

THIRD DIVISION (NORTH)

		P	W	D	L	F	A	Pts
1	Derby	46	26	11	9	111	53	63
2	Hartlepools	46	25	9	12	90	63	59
3	Accrington	46	25	8	13	95	64	58
4	Workington	46	24	10	12	93	63	58
5	Stockport	46	23	8	15	91	75	54
6	Chesterfield	46	22	9	15	96	79	53
7	York	46	21	10	15	75	61	52
8	Hull	46	21	10	15	84	69	52
9	Bradford City	46	22	8	16	78	68	52
10	Barrow	46	21	9	16	76	62	51
11	Halifax	46	21	7	18	65	70	49
12	Wrexham	46	19	10	17	97	74	48
13	Rochdale	46	18	12	16	65	65	48
14	Scunthorpe	46	15	15	16	71	69	45
15	Carlisle	46	16	13	17	76	85	45
16	Mansfield	46	17	10	19	91	90	44
17	Gateshead	46	17	10	19	72	90	44
18	Darlington	46	17	8	21	82	95	42
19	Oldham	46	12	15	19	66	74	39
20	Bradford PA	46	16	3	27	66	93	35
21	Chester	46	10	13	23	55	84	33
22	Southport	46	10	12	24	52	94	32
23	Tranmere	46	7	13	26	51	91	27
24	Crewe	46	6	9	31	43	110	21

SCOTTISH FA CUP 1956-57

FIFTH ROUND
Berwick Rangers v Falkirk	1-2
Hibernian v Aberdeen	3-4
Dundee v Clyde	0-0, 1-2
Queen's Park v Brechin City	3-0
Inverness Caledonian v Raith Rovers	2-3
Stenhousemuir v Dundee United	1-1, 0-4
Queen of the South v Dumbarton	2-2, 2-4
Stirling Albion v Motherwell	1-2
Dunfermline Athletic v Morton	3-0
St Mirren v Partick Thistle	1-1, 2-2, 5-1
Heart of Midlothian v Rangers	0-4
Forres Mechanics v Celtic	0-5
Hamilton Academicals v Alloa Athletic	2-2, 5-3
Stranraer v Airdrieonians	1-2
East Fife v St Johnstone	4-0
Kilmarnock v Ayr United	1-0

SIXTH ROUND
Falkirk v Aberdeen	3-1
Queen's Park v Clyde	1-1, 0-2
Raith Rovers v Dundee United	7-0
Motherwell v Dumbarton	1-3
St Mirren v Dunfermline Athletic	1-0
Celtic v Rangers	4-4, 2-0
Hamilton Academicals v Airdrieonians	1-2
East Fife v Kilmarnock	0-0, 0-2

SEVENTH ROUND
Falkirk v Clyde	2-1
Dumbarton v Raith Rovers	0-4
Celtic v St Mirren	2-1
Kilmarnock v Airdrieonians	3-1

SEMI-FINAL
Falkirk v Raith Rovers	2-2, 2-0
Celtic v Kilmarnock	1-1, 1-3

FINAL
Falkirk v Kilmarnock	1-1, 2-1

SCOTTISH FIRST DIVISION

		P	W	D	L	F	A	Pts
1	Rangers	34	26	3	5	96	48	55
2	Hearts	34	24	5	5	81	48	53
3	Kilmarnock	34	16	10	8	57	39	42
4	Raith	34	16	7	11	84	58	39
5	Celtic	34	15	8	11	58	43	38
6	Aberdeen	34	18	2	14	79	59	38
7	Motherwell	34	16	5	13	72	66	37
8	Partick Thistle	34	13	8	13	53	51	34
9	Hibernian	34	12	9	13	69	56	33
10	Dundee	34	13	6	15	55	61	32
11	Airdrieonians	34	13	4	17	77	89	30
12	St Mirren	34	12	6	16	58	72	30
13	Queen's Park	34	11	7	16	55	59	29
14	Falkirk	34	10	8	16	51	70	28
15	East Fife	34	10	6	18	59	82	26
16	Queen of the S	34	10	5	19	54	96	25
17	Dunfermline	34	9	6	19	54	74	24
18	Ayr	34	7	5	22	48	89	19

SCOTTISH SECOND DIVISION

		P	W	D	L	F	A	Pts
1	Clyde	36	29	6	1	122	39	64
2	Third Lanark	36	24	3	9	105	51	51
3	Cowdenbeath	36	20	5	11	87	65	45
4	Morton	36	18	7	11	81	70	43
5	Albion	36	18	6	12	98	80	42
6	Brechin	36	15	10	11	72	68	40
7	Stranraer	36	15	10	11	79	77	40
8	Stirling	36	17	5	14	81	64	39
9	Dumbarton	36	17	4	15	101	70	38
10	Arbroath	36	17	4	15	79	57	38
11	Hamilton	36	14	8	14	69	68	36
12	St Johnstone	36	14	6	16	79	80	34
13	Dundee United	36	14	6	16	75	80	34
14	Stenhousemuir	36	13	6	17	71	81	32
15	Alloa	36	11	5	20	66	99	27
16	Forfar	36	9	5	22	75	100	23
17	Montrose	36	7	7	22	54	124	21
18	Berwick	36	7	6	23	58	114	20
19	E Stirlingshire	36	5	7	24	66	121	17

New man in charge
On 1 January 1957, Alan Hardaker became secretary to the Football League. Hardaker, once an amateur footballer with Hull City, had been assistant secretary since 1951.

After beating Scunthorpe United 2-1, on 19 September 1956, Crewe Alexandra of the Third Division North did not win again until they beat Bradford City 1-0 on 13 April 1957, a League record of 30 games without a win.

FIRST DIVISION

		P	W	D	L	F	A	Pts
1	Wolves	42	28	8	6	103	47	64
2	Preston	42	26	7	9	100	51	59
3	Tottenham	42	21	9	12	93	77	51
4	WBA	42	18	14	10	92	70	50
5	Man City	42	22	5	15	104	100	49
6	Burnley	42	21	5	16	80	74	47
7	Blackpool	42	19	6	17	80	67	44
8	Luton	42	19	6	17	69	63	44
9	Man United	42	16	11	15	85	75	43
10	Nottm Forest	42	16	10	16	69	63	42
11	Chelsea	42	15	12	15	83	79	42
12	Arsenal	42	16	7	19	73	85	39
13	Birmingham	42	14	11	17	76	89	39
14	Aston Villa	42	16	7	19	73	86	39
15	Bolton	42	14	10	18	65	87	38
16	Everton	42	13	11	18	65	75	37
17	Leeds	42	14	9	19	51	63	37
18	Leicester	42	14	5	23	91	112	33
19	Newcastle	42	12	8	22	73	81	32
20	Portsmouth	42	12	8	22	73	88	32
21	Sunderland	42	10	12	20	54	97	32
22	Sheff Wed	42	12	7	23	69	92	31

SECOND DIVISION

		P	W	D	L	F	A	Pts
1	West Ham	42	23	11	8	101	54	57
2	Blackburn	42	22	12	8	93	57	56
3	Charlton	42	24	7	11	107	69	55
4	Liverpool	42	22	10	10	79	54	54
5	Fulham	42	20	12	10	97	59	52
6	Sheff United	42	21	10	11	75	50	52
7	Middlesbrough	42	19	7	16	83	74	45
8	Ipswich	42	16	12	14	68	69	44
9	Huddersfield	42	14	16	12	63	66	44
10	Bristol Rovers	42	17	8	17	85	80	42
11	Stoke	42	18	6	18	75	73	42
12	Leyton Orient	42	18	5	19	77	79	41
13	Grimsby	42	17	6	19	86	83	40
14	Barnsley	42	14	12	16	70	74	40
15	Cardiff	42	14	9	19	63	77	37
16	Derby	42	14	8	20	60	81	36
17	Bristol City	42	13	9	20	63	88	35
18	Rotherham	42	14	5	23	65	101	33
19	Swansea	42	11	9	22	72	99	31
20	Lincoln	42	11	9	22	55	82	31
21	Notts County	42	12	6	24	44	80	30
22	Doncaster	42	8	11	23	56	88	27

THIRD DIVISION (NORTH)

		P	W	D	L	F	A	Pts
1	Scunthorpe	46	29	8	9	88	50	66
2	Accrington	46	25	9	12	83	61	59
3	Bradford City	46	21	15	10	73	49	57
4	Bury	46	23	10	13	94	62	56
5	Hull	46	19	15	12	78	67	53
6	Mansfield	46	22	8	16	100	92	52
7	Halifax	46	20	11	15	83	69	51
8	Chesterfield	46	18	15	13	71	69	51
9	Stockport	46	18	11	17	74	67	47
10	Rochdale	46	19	8	19	79	67	46
11	Tranmere	46	18	10	18	82	76	46
12	Wrexham	46	17	12	17	61	63	46
13	York	46	17	12	17	68	76	46
14	Gateshead	46	15	15	16	68	76	45
15	Oldham	46	14	17	15	72	84	45
16	Carlisle	46	19	6	21	80	78	44
17	Hartlepools	46	16	12	18	73	76	44
18	Barrow	46	13	15	18	66	74	41
19	Workington	46	14	13	19	72	81	41
20	Darlington	46	17	7	22	78	89	41
21	Chester	46	13	13	20	73	81	39
22	Bradford PA	46	13	11	22	68	95	37
23	Southport	46	11	6	29	52	88	28
24	Crewe	46	8	7	31	47	93	23

THIRD DIVISION (SOUTH)

		P	W	D	L	F	A	Pts
1	Brighton	46	24	12	10	88	64	60
2	Brentford	46	24	10	12	82	56	58
3	Plymouth	46	25	8	13	67	48	58
4	Swindon	46	21	15	10	79	50	57
5	Reading	46	21	13	12	79	51	55
6	Southampton	46	22	10	14	112	72	54
7	Southend	46	21	12	13	90	58	54
8	Norwich	46	19	15	12	75	70	53
9	Bournemouth	46	21	9	16	81	74	51
10	QPR	46	18	14	14	64	65	50
11	Newport	46	17	14	15	73	67	48
12	Colchester	46	17	13	16	77	79	47
13	Northampton	46	19	6	21	87	79	44
14	Crystal Palace	46	15	13	18	70	72	43
15	Port Vale	46	16	10	20	67	58	42
16	Watford	46	13	16	17	59	77	42
17	Shrewsbury	46	15	10	21	49	71	40
18	Aldershot	46	12	16	18	59	89	40
19	Coventry	46	13	13	20	61	81	39
20	Walsall	46	14	9	23	61	75	37
21	Torquay	46	11	13	22	49	74	35
22	Gillingham	46	13	9	24	52	81	35
23	Millwall	46	11	9	26	63	91	31
24	Exeter	46	11	9	26	57	99	31

SCOTTISH FIRST DIVISION

		P	W	D	L	F	A	Pts
1	Hearts	34	29	4	1	132	29	62
2	Rangers	34	22	5	7	89	49	49
3	Celtic	34	19	8	7	84	47	46
4	Clyde	34	18	6	10	84	61	42
5	Kilmarnock	34	14	9	11	60	55	37
6	Partick Thistle	34	17	3	14	69	71	37
7	Raith Rovers	34	14	7	13	66	56	35
8	Motherwell	34	12	8	14	68	67	32
9	Hibernian	34	13	5	16	59	60	31
10	Falkirk	34	11	9	14	64	82	31
11	Dundee	34	13	5	16	49	65	31
12	Aberdeen	34	14	2	18	68	76	30
13	St Mirren	34	11	8	15	59	66	30
14	Third Lanark	34	13	4	17	69	88	30
15	Queen of the S	34	12	5	17	61	72	29
16	Airdrieonians	34	13	2	19	71	92	28
17	East Fife	34	10	3	21	45	88	23
18	Queen's Park	34	4	1	29	41	114	9

SCOTTISH SECOND DIVISION

		P	W	D	L	F	A	Pts
1	Stirling Albion	36	25	5	6	105	48	55
2	Dunfermline	36	24	5	7	120	42	53
3	Arbroath	36	21	5	10	89	72	47
4	Dumbarton	36	20	4	12	92	57	44
5	Ayr	36	18	6	12	98	81	42
6	Cowdenbeath	36	17	8	11	100	85	42
7	Brechin	36	16	8	12	80	81	40
8	Alloa	36	15	9	12	88	78	39
9	Dundee United	36	12	9	15	81	77	33
10	Hamilton	36	12	9	15	70	79	33
11	St Johnstone	36	12	9	15	67	85	33
12	Forfar	36	13	6	17	70	71	32
13	Morton	36	12	8	16	77	83	32
14	Montrose	36	13	6	17	55	72	32
15	E Stirlingshire	36	12	5	19	55	79	29
16	Stenhousemuir	36	12	5	19	68	98	29
17	Albion	36	12	5	19	53	79	29
18	Stranraer	36	9	7	20	54	83	25
19	Berwick	36	5	5	26	37	109	15

FA CUP 1957-58

FOURTH ROUND

Everton v Blackburn Rovers	1-2
Cardiff City v Leyton Orient	4-1
Liverpool v Northampton Town	3-1
Newcastle United v Scunthorpe United	1-3
Wolverhampton Wanderers v Portsmouth	5-1
Chelsea v Darlington	3-3, 1-4
Stoke City v Middlesbrough	3-1
York City v Bolton Wanderers	0-0, 0-3
Manchester United v Ipswich Town	2-0
Sheffield Wednesday v Hull City	4-3
West Bromwich Albion v Nottingham Forest	3-3, 5-1
Tottenham Hotspur v Sheffield United	0-3
Bristol Rovers v Burnley	2-2, 3-2
Notts County v Bristol City	1-2
West Ham United v Stockport County	3-2
Fulham v Charlton Athletic	1-1, 2-0

FIFTH ROUND

Cardiff City v Blackburn Rovers	0-0, 1-2
Scunthorpe United v Liverpool	0-1
Wolverhampton Wanderers v Darlington	6-1
Bolton Wanderers v Stoke City	3-1
Manchester United v Sheffield Wednesday	3-0
Sheffield United v West Bromwich Albion	1-1, 1-4
Bristol City v Bristol Rovers	3-4
West Ham United v Fulham	2-3

SIXTH ROUND

Blackburn Rovers v Liverpool	2-1
Bolton Wanderers v Wolverhampton Wanderers	2-1
West Bromwich Albion v Manchester United	2-2, 0-1
Fulham v Bristol Rovers	3-1

SEMI-FINAL

Blackburn Rovers v Bolton Wanderers	1-2
Manchester United v Fulham	2-2, 5-3

FINAL

Bolton Wanderers v Manchester United	2-0

SCOTTISH FA CUP 1957-58

SECOND ROUND

Celtic v Stirling Albion	7-2
Clyde v Arbroath	4-0
Falkirk v St Johnstone	6-3
Montrose v Buckie Thistle	2-2, 1-4
Motherwell v Partick Thistle	2-2, 4-0
Inverness Caledonian v Stenhousemuir	5-2
Morton v Aberdeen	0-1
Raith Rovers v Dundee	0-1
Forfar Athletic v Rangers	1-9
St Mirren v Dunfermline Athletic	1-4
Queen of the South v Stranraer	7-0
Kilmarnock v Vale of Leithen	7-0
Dundee United v Hibernian	0-0, 0-2
Heart of Midlothian v Albion Rovers	4-1
Third Lanark v Lossiemouth	6-1
Queen's Park v Fraserburgh	7-2

THIRD ROUND

Clyde v Celtic	2-0
Buckie Thistle v Falkirk	1-2
Inverness Caledonian v Motherwell	0-7
Dundee v Aberdeen	1-3
Dunfermline Athletic v Rangers	1-2
Kilmarnock v Queen of the South	2-2, 0-3
Heart of Midlothian v Hibernian	3-4
Third Lanark v Queen's Park	5-3

FOURTH ROUND

Clyde v Falkirk	2-1
Motherwell v Aberdeen	2-1
Queen of the South v Rangers	3-4
Hibernian v Third Lanark	3-2

SEMI-FINAL

Clyde v Motherwell	3-2
Rangers v Hibernian	2-2, 1-2

FINAL

Clyde v Hibernian	1-0

In Moscow on 18 May 1958, England played the USSR for the first time ever.

Before the start of the 1957-58 season, it was decided that four Divisions would be introduced in 1958-59. So at the end of the season, the top halves of both Third Divisions formed the new Division Three, and the rest of the teams made up Division Four.

Have boots, will travel

Tony McNamara, a right-winger, played in all four divisions of the Football League inside twelve months. On 12 October 1957, he played his last game for Everton in Division One, and on 27 September 1958 he made his debut for Bury in Division Three. In between, he played in Division Two for Liverpool, and in the Fourth Division for Crewe.

FIRST DIVISION

		P	W	D	L	F	A	Pts
1	Wolves	42	28	5	9	110	49	61
2	Man United	42	24	7	11	103	66	55
3	Arsenal	42	21	8	13	88	68	50
4	Bolton	42	20	10	12	79	66	50
5	WBA	42	18	13	11	88	68	49
6	West Ham	42	21	6	15	85	70	48
7	Burnley	42	19	10	13	81	70	48
8	Blackpool	42	18	11	13	66	49	47
9	Birmingham	42	20	6	16	84	68	46
10	Blackburn	42	17	10	15	76	70	44
11	Newcastle	42	17	7	18	80	80	41
12	Preston	42	17	7	18	70	77	41
13	Nottm Forest	42	17	6	19	71	74	40
14	Chelsea	42	18	4	20	77	98	40
15	Leeds	42	15	9	18	57	74	39
16	Everton	42	17	4	21	71	87	38
17	Luton	42	12	13	17	68	71	37
18	Tottenham	42	13	10	19	85	95	36
19	Leicester	42	11	10	21	67	98	32
20	Man City	42	11	9	22	64	95	31
21	Aston Villa	42	11	8	23	58	87	30
22	Portsmouth	42	6	9	27	64	112	21

SECOND DIVISION

		P	W	D	L	F	A	Pts
1	Sheff Wed	42	28	6	8	106	48	62
2	Fulham	42	27	6	9	96	61	60
3	Sheff United	42	23	7	12	82	48	53
4	Liverpool	42	24	5	13	87	62	53
5	Stoke	42	21	7	14	72	58	49
6	Bristol Rovers	42	18	12	12	80	64	48
7	Derby	42	20	8	14	74	71	48
8	Charlton	42	18	7	17	92	90	43
9	Cardiff	42	18	7	17	65	65	43
10	Bristol City	42	17	7	18	74	70	41
11	Swansea	42	16	9	17	79	81	41
12	Brighton	42	15	11	16	74	90	41
13	Middlesbrough	42	15	10	17	87	71	40
14	Huddersfield	42	16	8	18	62	55	40
15	Sunderland	42	16	8	18	64	75	40
16	Ipswich	42	17	6	19	62	77	40
17	Leyton Orient	42	14	8	20	71	78	36
18	Scunthorpe	42	12	9	21	55	84	33
19	Lincoln	42	11	7	24	63	93	29
20	Rotherham	42	10	9	23	42	82	29
21	Grimsby	42	9	10	23	62	90	28
22	Barnsley	42	10	7	25	55	91	27

THIRD DIVISION

		P	W	D	L	F	A	Pts
1	Plymouth	46	23	16	7	89	59	62
2	Hull	46	26	9	11	90	55	61
3	Brentford	46	21	15	10	76	49	57
4	Norwich	46	22	13	11	89	62	57
5	Colchester	46	21	10	15	71	67	52
6	Reading	46	21	8	17	78	63	50
7	Tranmere	46	21	8	17	82	67	50
8	Southend	46	21	8	17	85	80	50
9	Halifax	46	21	8	17	80	77	50
10	Bury	46	17	14	15	69	58	48
11	Bradford City	46	18	11	17	84	76	47
12	Bournemouth	46	17	12	17	69	69	46
13	QPR	46	19	8	19	74	77	46
14	Southampton	46	17	11	18	88	80	45
15	Swindon	46	16	13	17	59	57	45
16	Chesterfield	46	17	10	19	67	64	44
17	Newport	46	17	9	20	69	68	43
18	Wrexham	46	14	14	18	63	77	42
19	Accrington	46	15	12	19	71	87	42
20	Mansfield	46	14	13	19	73	98	41
21	Stockport	46	13	10	23	65	78	36
22	Doncaster	46	14	5	27	50	90	33
23	Notts County	46	8	13	25	55	96	29
24	Rochdale	46	8	12	26	37	79	28

FOURTH DIVISION

		P	W	D	L	F	A	Pts
1	Port Vale	46	26	12	8	110	58	64
2	Coventry	46	24	12	10	84	47	60
3	York	46	21	18	7	73	52	60
4	Shrewsbury	46	24	10	12	101	63	58
5	Exeter	46	23	11	12	87	61	57
6	Walsall	46	21	10	15	95	64	52
7	Crystal Palace	46	20	12	14	90	71	52
8	Northampton	46	21	9	16	85	78	51
9	Millwall	46	20	10	16	76	69	50
10	Carlisle	46	19	12	15	62	65	50
11	Gillingham	46	20	9	17	82	77	49
12	Torquay	46	16	12	18	78	77	44
13	Chester	46	16	12	18	72	84	44
14	Bradford PA	46	18	7	21	75	77	43
15	Watford	46	16	10	20	81	79	42
16	Darlington	46	13	16	17	66	68	42
17	Workington	46	12	17	17	63	78	41
18	Crewe	46	15	10	21	70	82	40
19	Hartlepools	46	15	10	21	74	88	40
20	Gateshead	46	16	8	22	56	85	40
21	Oldham	46	16	4	26	59	84	36
22	Aldershot	46	14	7	25	63	97	35
23	Barrow	46	9	10	27	51	104	28
24	Southport	46	7	12	27	41	86	26

SCOTTISH FIRST DIVISION

		P	W	D	L	F	A	Pts
1	Rangers	34	21	8	5	92	51	50
2	Hearts	34	21	6	7	92	51	48
3	Motherwell	34	18	8	8	83	50	44
4	Dundee	34	16	9	9	61	51	41
5	Airdrie	34	15	7	12	64	62	37
6	Celtic	34	14	8	12	70	53	36
7	St Mirren	34	14	7	13	71	74	35
8	Kilmarnock	34	13	8	13	58	51	34
9	Partick Thistle	34	14	6	14	59	66	34
10	Hibernian	34	13	6	15	68	70	32
11	Third Lanark	34	11	10	13	74	83	32
12	Stirling	34	11	8	15	54	64	30
13	Aberdeen	34	12	5	17	63	66	29
14	Raith	34	10	9	15	60	70	29
15	Clyde	34	12	4	18	62	66	28
16	Dunfermline	34	10	8	16	68	87	28
17	Falkirk	34	10	7	17	58	79	27
18	Queen of the S	34	6	6	22	38	101	18

SCOTTISH SECOND DIVISION

		P	W	D	L	F	A	Pts
1	Ayr United	36	28	4	4	115	48	60
2	Arbroath	36	23	5	8	86	59	51
3	Stenhousemuir	36	20	6	10	87	68	46
4	Dumbarton	36	19	7	10	94	61	45
5	Brechin	36	16	10	10	79	65	42
6	St Johnstone	36	15	10	11	54	44	40
7	Hamilton	36	15	8	13	76	62	38
8	East Fife	36	15	8	13	83	81	38
9	Berwick	36	16	6	14	63	66	38
10	Albion	36	14	7	15	84	79	35
11	Morton	36	13	8	15	68	85	34
12	Forfar	36	12	9	15	73	87	33
13	Alloa	36	12	7	17	76	81	31
14	Cowdenbeath	36	13	5	18	67	79	31
15	E Stirlingshire	36	10	8	18	50	77	28
16	Stranraer	36	8	11	17	63	76	27
17	Dundee United	36	9	7	20	62	86	25
18	Queen's Park	36	9	6	21	53	80	24
19	Montrose	36	6	6	24	49	96	18

FA CUP 1958-59

FOURTH ROUND

Nottingham Forest v Grimsby Town	4-1
Birmingham City v Fulham	1-1, 3-2
Wolverhampton W v Bolton W	1-2
Preston North End v Bradford City	3-2
Charlton Athletic v Everton	2-2, 1-4
Chelsea v Aston Villa	1-2
Blackburn Rovers v Burnley	1-2
Accrington Stanley v Portsmouth	0-0, 1-4
Colchester United v Arsenal	2-2, 0-4
Worcester City v Sheffield United	0-2
Tottenham Hotspur v Newport County	4-1
Norwich City v Cardiff City	3-2
Bristol City v Blackpool	1-1, 0-1
West Bromwich Albion v Brentford	2-0
Stoke City v Ipswich Town	0-1
Leicester City v Luton Town	1-1, 1-4

FIFTH ROUND

Birmingham City v Nottm Forest	1-1, 1-1, 0-5
Bolton W v Preston North End	2-2, 1-1, 1-0
Everton v Aston Villa	1-4
Burnley v Portsmouth	1-0
Arsenal v Sheffield United	2-2, 0-3
Tottenham Hotspur v Norwich City	1-1, 0-1
Blackpool v West Bromwich Albion	3-1
Ipswich Town v Luton Town	2-5

SIXTH ROUND

Nottingham Forest v Bolton Wanderers	2-1
Aston Villa v Burnley	0-0, 2-0
Sheffield United v Norwich City	1-1, 2-3
Blackpool v Luton Town	1-1, 0-1

SEMI-FINAL

Nottingham Forest v Aston Villa	1-0
Norwich City v Luton Town	1-1, 0-1

FINAL

Nottingham Forest v Luton Town	2-1

SCOTTISH FA CUP 1958-59

SECOND ROUND

St Mirren v Peebles Rovers	10-0
Airdrieonians v Motherwell	2-7
Montrose v Dunfermline Athletic	0-1
Ayr United v Stranraer	3-0
Fraserburgh v Stirling Albion	3-4
Babcock & Wilcox v Morton	0-5
Celtic v Clyde	1-1, 4-3
Rangers v Heart of Midlothian	3-2
Dundee United v Third Lanark	0-4
Brechin City v Alloa Athletic	3-3, 1-3
Hibernian v Falkirk	3-1
Stenhousemuir v Partick Thistle	1-3
St Johnstone v Queen's Park	3-1
Aberdeen v Arbroath	3-0
Coldstream v Hamilton Academicals	0-4
Dumbarton v Kilmarnock	2-8

THIRD ROUND

St Mirren v Motherwell	3-2
Dunfermline Athletic v Ayr United	2-1
Stirling Albion v Morton	3-1
Celtic v Rangers	2-1
Third Lanark v Alloa Athletic	3-2
Hibernian v Partick Thistle	4-1
St Johnstone v Aberdeen	1-2
Hamilton Academicals v Kilmarnock	0-5

FOURTH ROUND

St Mirren v Dunfermline Athletic	2-1
Stirling Albion v Celtic	1-3
Third Lanark v Hibernian	2-1
Aberdeen v Kilmarnock	3-1

SEMI-FINAL

St Mirren v Celtic	4-0
Third Lanark v Aberdeen	1-1, 0-1

FINAL

St Mirren v Aberdeen	3-1

Beginning with the game against France on 3 October 1951, Billy Wright made a world record 70 consecutive appearances for England, ending on 8 May 1959 with the match against the USA. In the Home Championship, he had a record run of 25 games between April 1951 and April 1959.

Denis Law became Scotland's youngest international, when on 18 October 1958, he played against Wales aged just 18 years and 236 days.

The most away wins in any division of the League on a single day is eight, in Division 3, 27 September 1958.

League Tables 1959-60

FIRST DIVISION

		P	W	D	L	F	A	Pts
1	Burnley	42	24	7	11	85	61	55
2	Wolves	42	24	6	12	106	67	54
3	Tottenham	42	21	11	10	86	50	53
4	WBA	42	19	11	12	83	57	49
5	Sheff Wed	42	19	11	12	80	59	49
6	Bolton	42	20	8	14	59	51	48
7	Man United	42	19	7	16	102	80	45
8	Newcastle	42	18	8	16	82	78	44
9	Preston	42	16	12	14	79	76	44
10	Fulham	42	17	10	15	73	80	44
11	Blackpool	42	15	10	17	59	71	40
12	Leicester	42	13	13	16	66	75	39
13	Arsenal	42	15	9	18	68	80	39
14	West Ham	42	16	6	20	75	91	38
15	Man City	42	17	3	22	78	84	37
16	Everton	42	13	11	18	73	78	37
17	Blackburn	42	16	5	21	60	70	37
18	Chelsea	42	14	9	19	76	91	37
19	Birmingham	42	13	10	19	63	80	36
20	Nottm Forest	42	13	9	20	50	74	35
21	Leeds	42	12	10	20	65	92	34
22	Luton	42	9	12	21	50	73	30

SECOND DIVISION

		P	W	D	L	F	A	Pts
1	Aston Villa	42	25	9	8	89	43	59
2	Cardiff	42	23	12	7	90	62	58
3	Liverpool	42	20	10	12	90	66	50
4	Sheff United	42	19	12	11	68	51	50
5	Middlesbrough	42	19	10	13	90	64	48
6	Huddersfield	42	19	9	14	73	52	47
7	Charlton	42	17	13	12	90	87	47
8	Rotherham	42	17	13	12	61	60	47
9	Bristol Rovers	42	18	11	13	72	78	47
10	Leyton Orient	42	15	14	13	76	61	44
11	Ipswich	42	19	6	17	78	68	44
12	Swansea	42	15	10	17	82	84	40
13	Lincoln	42	16	7	19	75	78	39
14	Brighton	42	13	12	17	67	76	38
15	Scunthorpe	42	13	10	19	57	71	36
16	Sunderland	42	12	12	18	52	65	36
17	Stoke	42	14	7	21	66	83	35
18	Derby	42	14	7	21	61	77	35
19	Plymouth	42	13	9	20	61	89	35
20	Portsmouth	42	10	12	20	59	77	32
21	Hull	42	10	10	22	48	76	30
22	Bristol City	42	11	5	26	60	97	27

FA CUP 1959-60

FOURTH ROUND

Wolverhampton v Charlton Athletic	2-1
Huddersfield Town v Luton Town	0-1
Leicester City v Fulham	2-1
West Bromwich Albion v Bolton Wanderers	2-0
Bristol Rovers v Preston North End	3-3, 1-5
Rotherham United v Brighton	1-1, 1-1, 0-6
Scunthorpe United v Port Vale	0-1
Chelsea v Aston Villa	1-2
Sheffield United v Nottingham Forest	3-0
Southampton v Watford	2-2, 0-1
Liverpool v Manchester United	1-3
Sheffield Wednesday v Peterborough United	2-0
Bradford City v Bournemouth	3-1
Swansea Town v Burnley	0-0, 1-2
Crewe Alexandra v Tottenham Hotspur	2-2, 2-13
Blackburn Rovers v Blackpool	1-1, 3-0

FIFTH ROUND

Luton Town v Wolverhampton	1-4
Leicester City v West Bromwich Albion	2-1
Preston North End v Brighton	2-1
Port Vale v Aston Villa	1-2
Sheffield United v Watford	3-2
Manchester United v Sheffield Wednesday	0-1
Bradford City v Burnley	2-2, 0-5
Tottenham Hotspur v Blackburn Rovers	1-3

SIXTH ROUND

Leicester City v Wolverhampton Wanderers	1-2
Aston Villa v Preston North End	2-0
Sheffield United v Sheffield Wednesday	0-2
Burnley v Blackburn Rovers	3-3, 0-2

SEMI-FINAL

Wolverhampton Wanderers v Aston Villa	1-0
Sheffield Wednesday v Blackburn Rovers	1-2

FINAL

Wolverhampton Wanderers v Blackburn Rovers	3-0

THIRD DIVISION

		P	W	D	L	F	A	Pts
1	Southampton	46	26	9	11	106	75	61
2	Norwich	46	24	11	11	82	54	59
3	Shrewsbury	46	18	16	12	97	75	52
4	Coventry	46	21	10	15	78	63	52
5	Grimsby	46	18	16	12	87	70	52
6	Brentford	46	21	9	16	78	61	51
7	Bury	46	21	9	16	64	51	51
8	QPR	46	18	13	15	73	54	49
9	Colchester	46	18	11	17	83	74	47
10	Bournemouth	46	17	13	16	72	72	47
11	Reading	46	18	10	18	84	77	46
12	Southend	46	19	8	19	76	74	46
13	Newport	46	20	6	20	80	79	46
14	Port Vale	46	19	8	19	80	79	46
15	Halifax	46	18	10	18	70	72	46
16	Swindon	46	19	8	19	69	78	46
17	Barnsley	46	15	14	17	65	66	44
18	Chesterfield	46	18	7	21	71	84	43
19	Bradford City	46	15	12	19	66	74	42
20	Tranmere	46	14	13	19	72	75	41
21	York	46	13	12	21	57	73	38
22	Mansfield	46	15	6	25	81	112	36
23	Wrexham	46	14	8	24	68	101	36
24	Accrington	46	11	5	30	57	123	27

FOURTH DIVISION

		P	W	D	L	F	A	Pts
1	Walsall	46	28	9	9	102	60	65
2	Notts County	46	26	8	12	107	69	60
3	Torquay	46	26	8	12	84	58	60
4	Watford	46	24	9	13	92	67	57
5	Millwall	46	18	17	11	84	61	53
6	Northampton	46	22	9	15	85	63	53
7	Gillingham	46	21	10	15	74	69	52
8	Crystal Palace	46	19	12	15	84	64	50
9	Exeter	46	19	11	16	80	70	49
10	Stockport	46	19	11	16	58	54	49
11	Bradford PA	46	17	15	14	70	68	49
12	Rochdale	46	18	10	18	65	60	46
13	Aldershot	46	18	9	19	77	74	45
14	Crewe	46	18	9	19	79	88	45
15	Darlington	46	17	9	20	63	73	43
16	Workington	46	14	14	18	68	60	42
17	Doncaster	46	16	10	20	69	76	42
18	Barrow	46	15	11	20	77	87	41
19	Carlisle	46	15	11	20	51	66	41
20	Chester	46	14	12	20	59	77	40
21	Southport	46	10	14	22	48	92	34
22	Gateshead	46	12	9	25	58	86	33
23	Oldham	46	8	12	26	41	83	28
24	Hartlepools	46	10	7	29	59	109	27

SCOTTISH FA CUP 1959-60

SECOND ROUND

Rangers v Arbroath	2-0
Dunfermline Athletic v Stenhousemuir	2-3
E Stirlingshire v Inverness Caledonian	2-2, 4-1
Hibernian v Dundee	3-0
Elgin City v Forfar Athletic	5-1
St Mirren v Celtic	1-1, 4-4, 2-5
Dundee United v Partick Thistle	2-2, 1-4
Stirling Albion v Queen of the South	3-3, 1-5
Peebles Rovers v Ayr United	1-6
Alloa Athletic v Airdrieonians	1-5
Aberdeen v Clyde	0-2
Montrose v Queen's Park	2-2, 1-1, 1-2
Eyemouth United v Albion Rovers	1-0
Cowdenbeath v Falkirk	1-0
Motherwell v Keith	6-0
Heart of Midlothian v Kilmarnock	1-1, 1-2

THIRD ROUND

Stenhousemuir v Rangers	0-3
East Stirlingshire v Hibernian	0-3
Elgin City v Celtic	1-2
Partick Thistle v Queen of the South	3-2
Ayr United v Airdrieonians	4-2
Clyde v Queen's Park	6-0
Eyemouth United v Cowdenbeath	3-0
Kilmarnock v Motherwell	2-0

FOURTH ROUND

Rangers v Hibernian	3-2
Celtic v Partick Thistle	2-0
Ayr United v Clyde	0-2
Eyemouth United v Kilmarnock	1-2

SEMI-FINAL

Rangers v Celtic	1-1, 4-1
Clyde v Kilmarnock	0-2

FINAL

Rangers v Kilmarnock	2-0

SCOTTISH FIRST DIVISION

		P	W	D	L	F	A	Pts
1	Hearts	34	23	8	3	102	51	54
2	Kilmarnock	34	24	2	8	67	45	50
3	Rangers	34	17	8	9	72	38	42
4	Dundee	34	16	10	8	70	49	42
5	Motherwell	34	16	8	10	71	61	40
6	Clyde	34	15	9	10	77	69	39
7	Hibernian	34	14	7	13	106	85	35
8	Ayr	34	14	6	14	65	73	34
9	Celtic	34	12	9	13	73	59	33
10	Partick Thistle	34	14	4	16	54	78	32
11	Raith Rovers	34	14	3	17	64	62	31
12	Third Lanark	34	13	4	17	75	83	30
13	Dunfermline	34	10	9	15	72	80	29
14	St Mirren	34	11	6	17	78	86	28
15	Aberdeen	34	11	6	17	54	72	28
16	Airdrieonians	34	11	6	17	56	80	28
17	Stirling Albion	34	7	8	19	55	72	22
18	Arbroath	34	4	7	23	38	106	15

SCOTTISH SECOND DIVISION

		P	W	D	L	F	A	Pts
1	St Johnstone	36	24	5	7	87	47	53
2	Dundee United	36	22	6	8	90	45	50
3	Queen of the S	36	21	7	8	94	52	49
4	Hamilton	36	21	6	9	91	62	48
5	Stenhousemuir	36	20	4	12	86	67	44
6	Dumbarton	36	18	7	11	67	53	43
7	Montrose	36	19	5	12	60	52	43
8	Falkirk	36	15	9	12	77	43	39
9	Berwick	36	16	5	15	62	55	37
10	Albion	36	14	8	14	71	78	36
11	Queen's Park	36	17	2	17	65	79	36
12	Brechin	36	14	6	16	66	66	34
13	Alloa	36	13	5	18	70	85	31
14	Morton	36	10	8	18	67	79	28
15	E Stirlingshire	36	10	8	18	68	82	28
16	Forfar	36	10	8	18	53	84	28
17	Stranraer	36	10	3	23	53	79	23
18	East Fife	36	7	6	23	50	87	20
19	Cowdenbeath	36	6	2	28	42	124	14

An expensive agreement
In July 1959, the Football League established the copyright on their fixture lists. As a result, the Pools Promoters agreed to pay the League a minimum of £245,000 each year for 10 years. In return, the Pools firms were to be allowed to reprint the fixtures on their coupons.

Cliff Holton of Watford, the 1959-60 Football League leading goalscorer, became the only player since the War to notch two hat-tricks in League matches in successive days. On Good Friday, 15 April 1960, Holton scored three times against Chester. A day later, he hit three more against Gateshead.

FIRST DIVISION

		P	W	D	L	F	A	Pts
1	Tottenham	42	31	4	7	115	55	66
2	Sheff Wed	42	23	12	7	78	47	58
3	Wolves	42	25	7	10	103	75	57
4	Burnley	42	22	7	13	102	77	51
5	Everton	42	22	6	14	87	69	50
6	Leicester	42	18	9	15	87	70	45
7	Man United	42	18	9	15	88	76	45
8	Blackburn	42	15	13	14	77	76	43
9	Aston Villa	42	17	9	16	78	77	43
10	WBA	42	18	5	19	67	71	41
11	Arsenal	42	15	11	16	77	85	41
12	Chelsea	42	15	7	20	98	100	37
13	Man City	42	13	11	18	79	90	37
14	Nottm Forest	42	14	9	19	62	78	37
15	Cardiff	42	13	11	18	60	85	37
16	West Ham	42	13	10	19	77	88	36
17	Fulham	42	14	8	20	72	95	36
18	Bolton	42	12	11	19	58	73	35
19	Birmingham	42	14	6	22	62	84	34
20	Blackpool	42	12	9	21	68	73	33
21	Newcastle	42	11	10	21	86	109	32
22	Preston	42	10	10	22	43	71	30

SECOND DIVISION

		P	W	D	L	F	A	Pts
1	Ipswich	42	26	7	9	100	55	59
2	Sheff United	42	26	6	10	81	51	58
3	Liverpool	42	21	10	11	87	58	52
4	Norwich	42	20	9	13	70	53	49
5	Middlesbrough	42	18	12	12	83	74	48
6	Sunderland	42	17	13	12	75	60	47
7	Swansea	42	18	11	13	77	73	47
8	Southampton	42	18	8	16	84	81	44
9	Scunthorpe	42	14	15	13	69	64	43
10	Charlton	42	16	11	15	97	91	43
11	Plymouth	42	17	8	17	81	82	42
12	Derby	42	15	10	17	80	80	40
13	Luton	42	15	9	18	71	70	39
14	Leeds	42	14	10	18	75	83	38
15	Rotherham	42	12	13	17	65	64	37
16	Brighton	42	14	9	19	61	75	37
17	Bristol Rovers	42	15	7	20	73	92	37
18	Stoke	42	12	12	18	51	59	36
19	Leyton Orient	42	14	8	20	55	78	36
20	Huddersfield	42	13	9	20	62	71	35
21	Portsmouth	42	11	11	20	64	91	33
22	Lincoln	42	8	8	26	48	95	24

THIRD DIVISION

		P	W	D	L	F	A	Pts
1	Bury	46	30	8	8	108	45	68
2	Walsall	46	28	6	12	98	60	62
3	QPR	46	25	10	11	93	60	60
4	Watford	46	20	12	14	85	72	52
5	Notts County	46	21	9	16	82	77	51
6	Grimsby	46	20	10	16	77	69	50
7	Port Vale	46	17	15	14	96	79	49
8	Barnsley	46	21	7	18	83	80	49
9	Halifax	46	16	17	13	71	78	49
10	Shrewsbury	46	15	16	15	83	75	46
11	Hull	46	17	12	17	73	73	46
12	Torquay	46	14	17	15	75	83	45
13	Newport	46	17	11	18	81	90	45
14	Bristol City	46	17	10	19	70	68	44
15	Coventry	46	16	12	18	80	83	44
16	Swindon	46	14	15	17	62	55	43
17	Brentford	46	13	17	16	56	70	43
18	Reading	46	14	12	20	72	83	40
19	Bournemouth	46	15	10	21	58	76	40
20	Southend	46	14	11	21	60	76	39
21	Tranmere	46	15	8	23	79	115	38
22	Bradford City	46	11	14	21	65	87	36
23	Colchester	46	11	11	24	68	101	33
24	Chesterfield	46	10	12	24	67	87	32

FOURTH DIVISION

		P	W	D	L	F	A	Pts
1	Peterborough	46	28	10	8	134	65	66
2	Crystal Palace	46	29	6	11	110	69	64
3	Northampton	46	25	10	11	90	62	60
4	Bradford PA	46	26	8	12	84	74	60
5	York	46	21	9	16	80	60	51
6	Millwall	46	21	8	17	97	86	50
7	Darlington	46	18	13	15	78	70	49
8	Workington	46	21	7	18	74	76	49
9	Crewe	46	20	9	17	61	67	49
10	Aldershot	46	18	9	19	79	69	45
11	Doncaster	46	19	7	20	76	78	45
12	Oldham	46	19	7	20	79	88	45
13	Stockport	46	18	9	19	57	66	45
14	Southport	46	19	6	21	69	67	44
15	Gillingham	46	15	13	18	64	66	43
16	Wrexham	46	17	8	21	62	56	42
17	Rochdale	46	17	8	21	60	66	42
18	Accrington	46	16	8	22	74	88	40
19	Carlisle	46	13	13	20	61	79	39
20	Mansfield	46	16	6	24	71	78	38
21	Exeter	46	14	10	22	66	94	38
22	Barrow	46	13	11	22	52	79	37
23	Hartlepools	46	12	8	26	71	103	32
24	Chester	46	11	9	26	61	104	31

SCOTTISH FIRST DIVISION

		P	W	D	L	F	A	Pts
1	Rangers	34	23	5	6	88	46	51
2	Kilmarnock	34	21	8	5	77	45	50
3	Third Lanark	34	20	2	12	100	80	42
4	Celtic	34	15	9	10	64	46	39
5	Motherwell	34	15	8	11	70	57	38
6	Aberdeen	34	14	8	12	72	72	36
7	Hibernian	34	15	4	15	66	69	34
8	Hearts	34	13	8	13	51	53	34
9	Dundee United	34	13	7	14	60	58	33
10	Dundee	34	13	6	15	61	53	32
11	Partick Thistle	34	13	6	15	59	69	32
12	Dunfermline	34	12	7	15	65	81	31
13	Airdrieonians	34	10	10	14	61	71	30
14	St Mirren	34	11	7	16	53	58	29
15	St Johnstone	34	10	9	15	47	63	29
16	Raith Rovers	34	10	7	17	46	67	27
17	Clyde	34	6	11	17	55	77	23
18	Ayr	34	5	12	17	51	81	22

SCOTTISH SECOND DIVISION

		P	W	D	L	F	A	Pts
1	Stirling Albion	36	24	7	5	89	37	55
2	Falkirk	36	24	6	6	100	40	54
3	Stenhousemuir	36	24	2	10	99	69	50
4	Stranraer	36	19	6	11	83	55	44
5	Queen of the S	36	20	3	13	77	52	43
6	Hamilton	36	17	7	12	84	80	41
7	Montrose	36	19	2	15	75	65	40
8	Cowdenbeath	36	17	6	13	71	65	40
9	Berwick	36	14	9	13	62	69	37
10	Dumbarton	36	15	5	16	78	82	35
11	Alloa	36	13	7	16	78	68	33
12	Arbroath	36	13	7	16	56	76	33
13	East Fife	36	14	4	18	70	80	32
14	Brechin	36	9	9	18	60	78	27
15	Queen's Park	36	10	6	20	61	87	26
16	E Stirlingshire	36	9	7	20	59	100	25
17	Albion	36	9	6	21	60	89	24
18	Forfar	36	10	4	22	65	98	24
19	Morton	36	5	11	20	56	93	21

Tottenham began the season with 11 consecutive wins, a record, and ended it having won 31 of their 42 games, a First Division record. Spurs' 16 away wins—including an unequalled 8 in a row—was another First Division record. Spurs also equalled Arsenal's Division One record points total of 66.

Burnley were fined £1000 by the Football League for fielding ten reserves in a League match against Chelsea.

The maximum wage restrictions were removed and Johnny Haynes of Fulham became the first British footballer to earn £100 a week.

FA CUP 1960-61

FOURTH ROUND

Leicester City v Bristol City	5-1
Birmingham City v Rotherham United	4-0
Huddersfield Town v Barnsley	1-1, 0-1
Luton Town v Manchester City	3-1
Newcastle United v Stockport County	4-0
Stoke City v Aldershot	0-0, 0-0, 3-0
Sheffield United v Lincoln City	3-1
Bolton Wanderers v Blackburn Rovers	3-3, 0-4
Southampton v Leyton Orient	0-1
Sheffield Wednesday v Manchester United	1-1, 7-2
Brighton v Burnley	3-3, 0-2
Swansea Town v Preston North End	2-1
Scunthorpe United v Norwich City	1-4
Liverpool v Sunderland	0-2
Peterborough United v Aston Villa	1-1, 1-2
Tottenham Hotspur v Crewe Alexandra	5-1

FIFTH ROUND

Birmingham City v Leicester City	1-1, 1-2
Barnsley v Luton Town	1-0
Newcastle United v Stoke City	3-1
Sheffield United v Blackburn Rovers	2-1
Leyton Orient v Sheffield Wednesday	0-2
Burnley v Swansea Town	4-0
Norwich City v Sunderland	0-1
Aston Villa v Tottenham Hotspur	0-2

SIXTH ROUND

Leicester City v Barnsley	0-0, 2-1
Newcastle United v Sheffield United	1-3
Sheffield Wednesday v Burnley	0-0, 0-2
Sunderland v Tottenham Hotspur	1-1, 0-5

SEMI-FINAL

Leicester City v Sheffield United	0-0, 0-0, 2-0
Burnley v Tottenham Hotspur	0-3

FINAL

Leicester City v Tottenham Hotspur	0-2

SCOTTISH FA CUP 1960-61

SECOND ROUND

Buckie Thistle v Raith Rovers	0-2
Celtic v Montrose	6-0
Queen of the South v Hamilton Academicals	0-2
Hibernian v Peebles Rovers	15-1
Brechin City v Duns	5-3
Ayr United v Airdrieonians	0-0, 1-3
Cowdenbeath v Motherwell	1-4
Dundee v Rangers	1-5
East Fife v Partick Thistle	1-3
Kilmarnock v Heart of Midlothian	1-2
Dundee United v St Mirren	0-1
Third Lanark v Arbroath	5-2
Aberdeen v Deveronvale	4-2
Stranraer v Dunfermline Athletic	1-3
Alloa Athletic v Dumbarton	2-0
Forfar Athletic v Morton	2-0

THIRD ROUND

Raith Rovers v Celtic	1-4
Hamilton Academicals v Hibernian	0-4
Brechin City v Airdrieonians	0-3
Motherwell v Rangers	2-2, 5-2
Partick Thistle v Heart of Midlothian	1-2
St Mirren v Third Lanark	3-3, 8-0
Aberdeen v Dunfermline Athletic	3-6
Alloa Athletic v Forfar Athletic	2-1

FOURTH ROUND

Celtic v Hibernian	1-1, 1-0
Motherwell v Airdrieonians	0-1
Heart of Midlothian v St Mirren	0-1
Dunfermline Athletic v Alloa Athletic	4-0

SEMI-FINAL

Celtic v Airdrieonians	4-0
Dunfermline Athletic v St Mirren	0-0, 1-0

FINAL

Celtic v Dunfermline Athletic	0-0, 0-2

League Tables 1961-62

FIRST DIVISION

		P	W	D	L	F	A	Pts
1	Ipswich	42	24	8	10	93	67	56
2	Burnley	42	21	11	10	101	67	53
3	Tottenham	42	21	10	11	88	69	52
4	Everton	42	20	11	11	88	54	51
5	Sheff United	42	19	9	14	61	69	47
6	Sheff Wed	42	20	6	16	72	58	46
7	Aston Villa	42	18	8	16	65	56	44
8	West Ham	42	17	10	15	76	82	44
9	WBA	42	15	13	14	83	67	43
10	Arsenal	42	16	11	15	71	72	43
11	Bolton	42	16	10	16	62	66	42
12	Man City	42	17	7	18	78	81	41
13	Blackpool	42	15	11	16	70	75	41
14	Leicester	42	17	6	19	72	71	40
15	Man United	42	15	9	18	72	75	39
16	Blackburn	42	14	11	17	50	58	39
17	Birmingham	42	14	10	18	65	81	38
18	Wolves	42	13	10	19	73	86	36
19	Nottm Forest	42	13	10	19	63	79	36
20	Fulham	42	13	7	22	66	74	33
21	Cardiff	42	9	14	19	50	81	32
22	Chelsea	42	9	10	23	63	94	28

SECOND DIVISION

		P	W	D	L	F	A	Pts
1	Liverpool	42	27	8	7	99	43	62
2	Leyton Orient	42	22	10	10	69	40	54
3	Sunderland	42	22	9	11	85	50	53
4	Scunthorpe	42	21	7	14	86	71	49
5	Plymouth	42	19	8	15	75	75	46
6	Southampton	42	18	9	15	77	62	45
7	Huddersfield	42	16	12	14	67	59	44
8	Stoke	42	17	8	17	55	57	42
9	Rotherham	42	16	9	17	70	76	41
10	Preston	42	15	10	17	55	57	40
11	Newcastle	42	15	9	18	64	58	39
12	Middlesbrough	42	16	7	19	76	72	39
13	Luton	42	17	5	20	69	71	39
14	Walsall	42	14	11	17	70	75	39
15	Charlton	42	15	9	18	69	75	39
16	Derby	42	14	11	17	68	75	39
17	Norwich	42	14	11	17	61	70	39
18	Bury	42	17	5	20	52	76	39
19	Leeds	42	12	12	18	50	61	36
20	Swansea	42	12	12	18	61	83	36
21	Bristol Rovers	42	13	7	22	53	81	33
22	Brighton	42	10	11	21	42	86	31

THIRD DIVISION

		P	W	D	L	F	A	Pts
1	Portsmouth	46	27	11	8	87	47	65
2	Grimsby	46	28	6	12	80	56	62
3	Bournemouth	46	21	17	8	69	45	59
4	QPR	46	24	11	11	111	73	59
5	Peterborough	46	26	6	14	107	82	58
6	Bristol City	46	23	8	15	94	72	54
7	Reading	46	22	9	15	77	66	53
8	Northampton	46	20	11	15	85	57	51
9	Swindon	46	17	15	14	78	71	49
10	Hull	46	20	8	18	67	54	48
11	Bradford PA	46	20	7	19	80	78	47
12	Port Vale	46	17	11	18	65	58	45
13	Notts County	46	17	9	20	67	74	43
14	Coventry	46	16	11	19	64	71	43
15	Crystal Palace	46	14	14	18	83	80	42
16	Southend	46	13	16	17	57	69	42
17	Watford	46	14	13	19	63	74	41
18	Halifax	46	15	10	21	62	84	40
19	Shrewsbury	46	13	12	21	73	84	38
20	Barnsley	46	13	12	21	71	95	38
21	Torquay	46	15	6	25	76	100	36
22	Lincoln	46	9	17	20	57	87	35
23	Brentford	46	13	8	25	53	93	34
24	Newport	46	7	8	31	46	102	22

FOURTH DIVISION

		P	W	D	L	F	A	Pts
1	Millwall	44	23	10	11	87	62	56
2	Colchester	44	23	9	12	104	71	55
3	Wrexham	44	22	9	13	96	56	53
4	Carlisle	44	22	8	14	64	63	52
5	Bradford City	44	21	9	14	94	86	51
6	York	44	20	10	14	84	53	50
7	Aldershot	44	22	5	17	81	60	49
8	Workington	44	19	11	14	69	70	49
9	Barrow	44	17	14	13	74	58	48
10	Crewe	44	20	6	18	79	70	46
11	Oldham	44	17	12	15	77	70	46
12	Rochdale	44	19	7	18	71	71	45
13	Darlington	44	18	9	17	61	73	45
14	Mansfield	44	19	6	19	77	66	44
15	Tranmere	44	20	4	20	70	81	44
16	Stockport	44	17	9	18	70	69	43
17	Southport	44	17	9	18	61	71	43
18	Exeter	44	13	11	20	62	77	37
19	Chesterfield	44	14	9	21	70	87	37
20	Gillingham	44	13	11	20	73	94	37
21	Doncaster	44	11	7	26	60	85	29
22	Hartlepools	44	8	11	25	52	101	27
23	Chester	44	7	12	25	54	96	26
24	Accrington Stanley resigned from the League							

SCOTTISH FIRST DIVISION

		P	W	D	L	F	A	Pts
1	Dundee	34	25	4	5	80	46	54
2	Rangers	34	22	7	5	84	31	51
3	Celtic	34	19	8	7	81	37	46
4	Dunfermline	34	19	5	10	77	46	43
5	Kilmarnock	34	16	10	8	74	58	42
6	Hearts	34	16	6	12	54	49	38
7	Partick Thistle	34	16	3	15	60	55	35
8	Hibernian	34	14	5	15	58	72	33
9	Motherwell	34	13	6	15	65	62	32
10	Dundee United	34	13	6	15	70	71	32
11	Third Lanark	34	13	5	16	59	60	31
12	Aberdeen	34	10	9	15	60	73	29
13	Raith Rovers	34	10	7	17	51	73	27
14	Falkirk	34	11	4	19	45	68	26
15	Airdrieonians	34	9	7	18	57	78	25
16	St Mirren	34	10	5	19	52	80	25
17	St Johnstone	34	9	7	18	35	61	25
18	Stirling Albion	34	6	6	22	34	76	18

SCOTTISH SECOND DIVISION

		P	W	D	L	F	A	Pts
1	Clyde	36	15	4	7	108	47	54
2	Queen of the S	36	24	5	7	78	33	53
3	Morton	36	19	6	11	78	64	44
4	Alloa	36	17	8	11	92	78	42
5	Montrose	36	15	11	10	63	50	41
6	Arbroath	36	17	7	12	66	59	41
7	Stranraer	36	14	11	11	61	62	39
8	Berwick	36	16	6	14	83	70	38
9	Ayr	36	15	8	13	71	63	38
10	East Fife	36	15	7	14	60	59	37
11	E Stirlingshire	36	15	4	17	70	81	34
12	Queen's Park	36	12	9	15	64	62	33
13	Hamilton	36	14	5	17	78	79	33
14	Cowdenbeath	36	11	9	16	65	77	31
15	Stenhousemuir	36	13	5	18	69	86	31
16	Forfar	36	11	8	17	68	76	30
17	Dumbarton	36	9	10	17	49	66	28
18	Albion	36	10	5	21	42	74	25
19	Brechin	36	5	2	29	44	123	12

Triple success
Only once since the War have three players hit hat-tricks for one side in the same League match. Ron Barnes, Roy Ambler and Wyn Davies did this in Wrexham's 10-1 thrashing of Hartlepools in a Fourth Division game on 3 March 1962.

The England player from the Third Division
Johnny Byrne, the Crystal Palace inside-right, became only the third footballer from the Third Division, to appear for England (v Ireland, 22 November 1961) in the Home Championship since the War.

FA CUP 1961-62

FOURTH ROUND
Burnley v Leyton Orient	1-1, 1-0
Everton v Manchester City	2-0
Peterborough United v Sheffield United	1-3
Norwich City v Ipswich Town	1-1, 2-1
Fulham v Walsall	2-2, 2-0
Sunderland v Port Vale	0-0, 1-3
Stoke City v Blackburn Rovers	0-1
Shrewsbury Town v Middlesbrough	2-2, 1-5
Oldham Athletic v Liverpool	1-2
Preston North End v Weymouth	2-0
Manchester United v Arsenal	1-0
Nottingham Forest v Sheffield Wednesday	0-2
Aston Villa v Huddersfield Town	2-1
Charlton Athletic v Derby County	2-1
Wolverhampton Wanderers v West Bromwich Albion	1-2
Plymouth Argyle v Tottenham Hotspur	1-5

FIFTH ROUND
Burnley v Everton	3-1
Sheffield United v Norwich City	3-1
Fulham v Port Vale	1-0
Blackburn Rovers v Middlesbrough	2-1
Liverpool v Preston North End	0-0, 0-0, 0-1
Manchester United v Sheffield Wednesday	0-0, 2-0
Aston Villa v Charlton Athletic	2-1
West Bromwich Albion v Tottenham Hotspur	2-4

SIXTH ROUND
Sheffield United v Burnley	0-1
Fulham v Blackburn Rovers	2-2, 1-0
Preston North End v Manchester United	0-0, 1-2
Tottenham Hotspur v Aston Villa	2-0

SEMI-FINAL
Burnley v Fulham	1-1, 2-1
Manchester United v Tottenham Hotspur	1-3

FINAL
Burnley v Tottenham Hotspur	1-3

SCOTTISH FA CUP 1961-62

SECOND ROUND
Rangers v Arbroath	6-0
Clyde v Aberdeen	2-2, 3-10
Brechin City v Kilmarnock	1-6
Dumbarton v Ross County	2-3
Stirling Albion v Partick Thistle	3-1
East Fife v Albion Rovers	1-0
Stranraer v Montrose	0-0, 1-0
Motherwell v St Johnstone	4-0
Vale of Leithen v Heart of Midlothian	0-5
Morton v Celtic	1-3
Hamilton Academicals v Third Lanark	0-2
Inverness Caledonian v East Stirlingshire	3-0
Dunfermline Athletic v Wigtown	9-0
Queen of the South v Stenhousemuir	0-2
Alloa Athletic v Raith Rovers	1-2
Dundee v St Mirren	0-1

THIRD ROUND
Aberdeen v Rangers	2-2, 5-1
Kilmarnock v Ross County	7-0
Stirling Albion v East Fife	4-1
Stranraer v Motherwell	1-3
Heart of Midlothian v Celtic	3-4
Third Lanark v Inverness Caledonian	6-1
Dunfermline Athletic v Stenhousemuir	0-0, 3-0
Raith Rovers v St Mirren	1-1, 0-4

FOURTH ROUND
Kilmarnock v Rangers	2-4
Stirling Albion v Motherwell	0-6
Celtic v Third Lanark	4-4, 4-0
Dunfermline Athletic v St Mirren	0-1

SEMI-FINAL
Rangers v Motherwell	3-1
Celtic v St Mirren	1-3

FINAL
Rangers v St Mirren	2-0

League Tables 1962-63

FIRST DIVISION

		P	W	D	L	F	A	Pts
1	Everton	42	25	11	6	84	42	61
2	Tottenham	42	23	9	10	111	62	55
3	Burnley	42	22	10	10	78	57	54
4	Leicester	42	20	12	10	79	53	52
5	Wolves	42	20	10	12	93	65	50
6	Sheff Wed	42	19	10	13	77	63	48
7	Arsenal	42	18	10	14	86	77	46
8	Liverpool	42	17	10	15	71	59	44
9	Nottm Forest	42	17	10	15	67	69	44
10	Sheff United	42	16	12	14	58	60	44
11	Blackburn	42	15	12	15	79	71	42
12	West Ham	42	14	12	16	73	69	40
13	Blackpool	42	13	14	15	58	64	40
14	WBA	42	16	7	19	71	79	39
15	Aston Villa	42	15	8	19	62	68	38
16	Fulham	42	14	10	18	50	71	38
17	Ipswich	42	12	11	19	59	78	35
18	Bolton	42	15	5	22	55	75	35
19	Man United	42	12	10	20	67	81	34
20	Birmingham	42	10	13	19	63	90	33
21	Man City	42	10	11	21	58	102	31
22	Leyton Orient	42	6	9	27	37	81	21

SECOND DIVISION

		P	W	D	L	F	A	Pts
1	Stoke	42	20	13	9	73	50	53
2	Chelsea	42	24	4	14	81	42	52
3	Sunderland	42	20	12	10	84	55	52
4	Middlesbrough	42	20	9	13	86	85	49
5	Leeds	42	19	10	13	79	53	48
6	Huddersfield	42	17	14	11	63	50	48
7	Newcastle	42	18	11	13	79	59	47
8	Bury	42	18	11	13	51	47	47
9	Scunthorpe	42	16	12	14	57	59	44
10	Cardiff	42	18	7	17	83	73	43
11	Southampton	42	17	8	17	72	67	42
12	Plymouth	42	15	12	15	76	73	42
13	Norwich	42	17	8	17	80	79	42
14	Rotherham	42	17	6	19	67	74	40
15	Swansea	42	15	9	18	51	72	39
16	Portsmouth	42	13	11	18	63	79	37
17	Preston	42	13	11	18	59	74	37
18	Derby	42	12	12	18	61	72	36
19	Grimsby	42	11	13	18	55	66	35
20	Charlton	42	13	5	24	62	94	31
21	Walsall	42	11	9	22	53	89	31
22	Luton	42	11	7	24	61	84	29

THIRD DIVISION

		P	W	D	L	F	A	Pts
1	Northampton	46	26	10	10	109	60	62
2	Swindon	46	22	14	10	87	56	58
3	Port Vale	46	23	8	15	72	58	54
4	Coventry	46	18	17	11	83	69	53
5	Bournemouth	46	18	16	12	63	46	52
6	Peterborough	46	20	11	15	93	75	51
7	Notts County	46	19	13	14	73	74	51
8	Southend	46	19	12	15	75	77	50
9	Wrexham	46	20	9	17	84	83	49
10	Hull	46	19	10	17	74	69	48
11	Crystal Palace	46	17	13	16	68	58	47
12	Colchester	46	18	11	17	73	93	47
13	QPR	46	17	11	18	85	76	45
14	Bristol City	46	16	13	17	100	92	45
15	Shrewsbury	46	16	12	18	83	81	44
16	Millwall	46	15	13	18	82	87	43
17	Watford	46	17	8	21	82	85	42
18	Barnsley	46	15	11	20	63	74	41
19	Bristol Rovers	46	15	11	20	70	88	41
20	Reading	46	16	8	22	74	78	40
21	Bradford PA	46	14	12	20	79	97	40
22	Brighton	46	12	12	22	58	84	36
23	Carlisle	46	13	9	24	61	89	35
24	Halifax	46	9	12	25	64	106	30

FOURTH DIVISION

		P	W	D	L	F	A	Pts
1	Brentford	46	27	8	11	98	64	62
2	Oldham	46	24	11	11	95	60	59
3	Crewe	46	24	11	11	86	58	59
4	Mansfield	46	24	9	13	108	69	57
5	Gillingham	46	22	13	11	71	49	57
6	Torquay	46	20	16	10	75	56	56
7	Rochdale	46	20	11	15	67	59	51
8	Tranmere	46	20	10	16	81	67	50
9	Barrow	46	19	12	15	82	80	50
10	Workington	46	17	13	16	76	68	47
11	Aldershot	46	15	17	14	73	69	47
12	Darlington	46	19	6	21	72	87	44
13	Southport	46	15	14	17	72	106	44
14	York	46	16	11	19	67	62	43
15	Chesterfield	46	13	16	17	70	64	42
16	Doncaster	46	14	14	18	64	77	42
17	Exeter	46	16	10	20	57	77	42
18	Oxford	46	13	15	18	70	71	41
19	Stockport	46	15	11	20	56	70	41
20	Newport	46	14	11	21	76	90	39
21	Chester	46	15	9	22	51	66	39
22	Lincoln	46	13	9	24	68	89	35
23	Bradford City	46	11	10	25	64	93	32
24	Hartlepools	46	7	11	28	56	104	25

SCOTTISH FIRST DIVISION

		P	W	D	L	F	A	Pts
1	Rangers	34	25	7	2	94	28	57
2	Kilmarnock	34	20	8	6	92	40	48
3	Partick Thistle	34	20	6	8	66	44	46
4	Celtic	34	19	6	9	76	44	44
5	Hearts	34	17	9	8	85	59	43
6	Aberdeen	34	17	7	10	70	47	41
7	Dundee United	34	15	11	8	67	52	41
8	Dunfermline	34	13	8	13	50	47	34
9	Dundee	34	12	9	13	60	49	33
10	Motherwell	34	10	11	13	60	63	31
11	Airdrieonians	34	14	2	18	52	76	30
12	St Mirren	34	10	8	16	52	72	28
13	Falkirk	34	12	3	19	54	69	27
14	Third Lanark	34	9	8	17	56	68	26
15	Queen of the S	34	10	6	18	36	75	26
16	Hibernian	34	8	9	17	47	67	25
17	Clyde	34	9	5	20	49	83	23
18	Raith	34	2	5	27	35	118	9

SCOTTISH SECOND DIVISION

		P	W	D	L	F	A	Pts
1	St Johnstone	36	25	5	6	83	37	55
2	E Stirlingshire	36	20	9	7	80	50	49
3	Morton	36	23	2	11	100	49	48
4	Hamilton	36	18	8	10	69	56	44
5	Stranraer	36	16	10	10	81	70	42
6	Arbroath	36	18	4	14	74	51	40
7	Albion	36	18	2	16	72	79	38
8	Cowdenbeath	36	15	7	14	72	61	37
9	Alloa	36	15	6	15	57	56	36
10	Stirling	36	16	4	16	74	75	36
11	East Fife	36	15	6	15	60	69	36
12	Dumbarton	36	15	4	17	64	64	34
13	Ayr	36	13	8	15	68	77	34
14	Queen's Park	36	13	6	17	66	72	32
15	Montrose	36	13	5	18	57	70	31
16	Stenhousemuir	36	13	5	18	54	75	31
17	Berwick	36	11	7	18	57	77	29
18	Forfar	36	9	5	22	73	99	23
19	Brechin	36	3	3	30	39	113	9

FA CUP 1962-63

FOURTH ROUND

Leicester City v Ipswich Town	3-1
Leyton Orient v Derby County	3-0
Manchester City v Bury	1-0
Norwich City v Newcastle United	5-0
Arsenal v Sheffield Wednesday	2-0
Burnley v Liverpool	1-1, 1-2
West Ham United v Swansea Town	1-0
Swindon Town v Everton	1-5
West Bromwich Albion v Nottingham Forest	0-0, 1-2
Middlesbrough v Leeds United	0-2
Southampton v Watford	3-1
Port Vale v Sheffield United	1-2
Portsmouth v Coventry City	1-1, 2-2, 1-2
Gravesend v Sunderland	1-1, 2-5
Charlton Athletic v Chelsea	0-3
Manchester United v Aston Villa	1-0

FIFTH ROUND

Leicester City v Leyton Orient	1-0
Manchester City v Norwich City	1-2
Arsenal v Liverpool	1-2
West Ham United v Everton	1-0
Nottingham Forest v Leeds United	3-0
Southampton v Sheffield United	1-0
Coventry City v Sunderland	2-1
Manchester United v Chelsea	2-1

SIXTH ROUND

Norwich City v Leicester City	0-2
Liverpool v West Ham United	1-0
Nottingham Forest v Southampton	1-1, 3-3, 0-5
Coventry City v Manchester United	1-3

SEMI-FINAL

Leicester City v Liverpool	1-0
Southampton v Manchester United	0-1

FINAL

Leicester City v Manchester United	1-3

SCOTTISH FA CUP 1962-63

SECOND ROUND

Airdrieonians v Rangers	0-6
East Stirlingshire v Motherwell	1-0
Dundee v Montrose	8-0
Brechin City v Hibernian	0-2
Queen's Park v Alloa Athletic	5-1
Ayr United v Dundee United	1-2
Kilmarnock v Queen of the South	0-0, 0-1
Hamilton Academicals v Nairn County	1-1, 2-1
East Fife v Third Lanark	1-1, 0-2
Raith Rovers v Clyde	3-2
St Johnstone v Aberdeen	1-2
Cowdenbeath v Dunfermline Athletic	2-3
Berwick Rangers v St Mirren	1-3
Partick Thistle v Arbroath	1-1, 2-2, 3-2
Gala Fairydean v Duns	1-1, 2-1
Celtic v Heart of Midlothian	3-1

THIRD ROUND

Rangers v East Stirlingshire	7-2
Dundee v Hibernian	1-0
Queen's Park v Dundee United	1-1, 1-3
Queen of the South v Hamilton Academicals	3-0
Third Lanark v Raith Rovers	0-1
Aberdeen v Dunfermline Athletic	4-0
St Mirren v Partick Thistle	1-1, 1-0
Celtic v Gala Fairydean	6-0

FOURTH ROUND

Dundee v Rangers	1-1, 2-3
Dundee United v Queen of the South	1-1, 1-1, 4-0
Raith Rovers v Aberdeen	2-1
St Mirren v Celtic	0-1

SEMI-FINAL

Rangers v Dundee United	5-2
Raith Rovers v Celtic	2-5

FINAL

Rangers v Celtic	1-1, 3-0

Terrible winter disrupts the football programme

The winter of 1962-63 broke all previous records for postponements and abandoned matches due to bad weather. For six weeks, the football programme was wrecked by impossible playing conditions and over 400 League and Cup games were postponed or abandoned in England, Wales and Scotland. The worst-hit day—in fact the worst-hit ever, except for the War years—in England and Scotland was 9 February. Then, 57 games were called off through snow and ice, and only seven were completed. As a result of the severe winter, the football season was extended.

FIRST DIVISION

		P	W	D	L	F	A	Pts
1	Liverpool	42	26	5	11	92	45	57
2	Man United	42	23	7	12	90	62	53
3	Everton	42	21	10	11	84	64	52
4	Tottenham	42	22	7	13	97	81	51
5	Chelsea	42	20	10	12	72	56	50
6	Sheff Wed	42	19	11	12	84	67	49
7	Blackburn	42	18	10	14	89	65	46
8	Arsenal	42	17	11	14	90	82	45
9	Burnley	42	17	10	15	71	64	44
10	WBA	42	16	11	15	70	61	43
11	Leicester	42	16	11	15	61	58	43
12	Sheff United	42	16	11	15	61	64	43
13	Nottm Forest	42	16	9	17	64	68	41
14	West Ham	42	14	12	16	69	74	40
15	Fulham	42	13	13	16	58	65	39
16	Wolves	42	12	15	15	70	80	39
17	Stoke	42	14	10	18	77	78	38
18	Blackpool	42	13	9	20	52	73	35
19	Aston Villa	42	11	12	19	62	71	34
20	Birmingham	42	11	7	24	54	92	29
21	Bolton	42	10	8	24	48	80	28
22	Ipswich	42	9	7	26	56	121	25

SECOND DIVISION

		P	W	D	L	F	A	Pts
1	Leeds	42	24	15	3	71	34	63
2	Sunderland	42	25	11	6	81	37	61
3	Preston	42	23	10	9	79	54	56
4	Charlton	42	19	10	13	76	70	48
5	Southampton	42	19	9	14	100	73	47
6	Man City	42	18	10	14	84	66	46
7	Rotherham	42	19	7	16	90	78	45
8	Newcastle	42	20	5	17	74	69	45
9	Portsmouth	42	16	11	15	79	70	43
10	Middlesbrough	42	15	11	16	67	52	41
11	Northampton	42	16	9	17	58	60	41
12	Huddersfield	42	15	10	17	57	64	40
13	Derby	42	14	11	17	56	67	39
14	Swindon	42	14	10	18	57	69	38
15	Cardiff	42	14	10	18	56	81	38
16	Leyton Orient	42	13	10	19	54	72	36
17	Norwich	42	11	13	18	64	80	35
18	Bury	42	13	9	20	57	73	35
19	Swansea	42	12	9	21	63	74	33
20	Plymouth	42	8	16	18	45	67	32
21	Grimsby	42	9	14	19	47	75	32
22	Scunthorpe	42	10	10	22	52	82	30

THIRD DIVISION

		P	W	D	L	F	A	Pts
1	Coventry	46	22	16	8	98	61	60
2	Crystal Palace	46	23	14	9	73	51	60
3	Watford	46	23	12	11	79	59	58
4	Bournemouth	46	24	8	14	79	58	56
5	Bristol City	46	20	15	11	84	64	55
6	Reading	46	21	10	15	79	62	52
7	Mansfield	46	20	11	15	76	62	51
8	Hull	46	16	17	13	73	68	49
9	Oldham	46	20	8	18	73	70	48
10	Peterborough	46	18	11	17	75	70	47
11	Shrewsbury	46	18	11	17	73	80	47
12	Bristol Rovers	46	19	8	19	91	79	46
13	Port Vale	46	16	14	16	53	49	46
14	Southend	46	15	15	16	77	78	45
15	QPR	46	18	9	19	76	78	45
16	Brentford	46	15	14	17	87	80	44
17	Colchester	46	12	19	15	70	68	43
18	Luton	46	16	10	20	64	80	42
19	Walsall	46	13	14	19	59	76	40
20	Barnsley	46	12	15	19	68	94	39
21	Millwall	46	14	10	22	53	67	38
22	Crewe	46	11	12	23	50	77	34
23	Wrexham	46	13	6	27	75	107	32
24	Notts County	46	9	9	28	45	92	27

FOURTH DIVISION

		P	W	D	L	F	A	Pts
1	Gillingham	46	23	14	9	59	30	60
2	Carlisle	46	25	10	11	113	58	60
3	Workington	46	24	11	11	76	52	59
4	Exeter	46	20	18	8	62	37	58
5	Bradford City	46	25	6	15	76	62	56
6	Torquay	46	20	11	15	80	54	51
7	Tranmere	46	20	11	15	85	73	51
8	Brighton	46	19	12	15	71	52	50
9	Aldershot	46	19	10	17	83	78	48
10	Halifax	46	17	14	15	77	77	48
11	Lincoln	46	19	9	18	67	75	47
12	Chester	46	19	8	19	65	60	46
13	Bradford PA	46	18	9	19	75	81	45
14	Doncaster	46	15	12	19	70	75	42
15	Newport	46	17	8	21	64	73	42
16	Chesterfield	46	15	12	19	57	71	42
17	Stockport	46	15	12	19	50	68	42
18	Oxford	46	14	13	19	59	63	41
19	Darlington	46	14	12	20	66	93	40
20	Rochdale	46	12	15	19	56	59	39
21	Southport	46	15	9	22	63	88	39
22	York	46	14	7	25	52	66	35
23	Hartlepools	46	12	9	25	54	93	33
24	Barrow	46	6	18	22	51	93	30

SCOTTISH FIRST DIVISION

		P	W	D	L	F	A	Pts
1	Rangers	34	25	5	4	85	31	55
2	Kilmarnock	34	22	5	7	77	40	49
3	Celtic	34	19	9	6	89	34	47
4	Hearts	34	19	9	6	74	40	47
5	Dunfermline	34	18	9	7	64	33	45
6	Dundee	34	20	5	9	94	50	45
7	Partick Thistle	34	15	5	14	55	54	35
8	Dundee United	34	13	8	13	65	49	34
9	Aberdeen	34	12	8	14	53	53	32
10	Hibernian	34	12	6	16	59	66	30
11	Motherwell	34	9	11	14	51	62	29
12	St Mirren	34	12	5	17	44	74	29
13	St Johnstone	34	11	6	17	54	70	28
14	Falkirk	34	11	6	17	54	84	28
15	Airdrieonians	34	11	4	19	52	97	26
16	Third Lanark	34	9	7	18	47	74	25
17	Queen of the S	34	5	6	23	40	92	16
18	E Stirlingshire	34	5	2	27	37	91	12

SCOTTISH SECOND DIVISION

		P	W	D	L	F	A	Pts
1	Morton	36	32	3	1	135	37	67
2	Clyde	36	22	9	5	81	44	53
3	Arbroath	36	20	6	10	79	46	46
4	East Fife	36	16	13	7	92	57	45
5	Montrose	36	19	6	11	79	57	44
6	Dumbarton	36	16	6	14	67	59	38
7	Queen's Park	36	17	4	15	57	54	38
8	Stranraer	36	16	6	14	71	73	38
9	Albion	36	12	12	12	67	71	36
10	Raith	36	15	5	16	70	61	35
11	Stenhousemuir	36	15	5	16	83	75	35
12	Berwick	36	10	10	16	68	84	30
13	Hamilton	36	12	6	18	65	81	30
14	Ayr	36	12	5	19	58	83	29
15	Brechin	36	10	8	18	61	98	28
16	Alloa	36	11	5	20	64	92	27
17	Cowdenbeath	36	7	11	18	46	72	25
18	Forfar	36	6	8	22	57	104	20
19	Stirling	36	6	8	22	47	99	20

FA CUP 1963-64

FOURTH ROUND

West Ham United v Leyton Orient	1-1, 3-0
Aldershot v Swindon Town	1-2
Burnley v Newport County	2-1
Chelsea v Huddersfield Town	1-2
Sunderland v Bristol City	6-1
Leeds United v Everton	1-1, 0-2
Barnsley v Bury	2-1
Manchester United v Bristol Rovers	4-1
Ipswich Town v Stoke City	1-1, 0-1
Sheffield United v Swansea Town	1-1, 0-4
West Bromwich Albion v Arsenal	3-3, 0-2
Liverpool v Port Vale	0-0, 2-1
Oxford United v Brentford	2-2, 2-1
Blackburn Rovers v Fulham	2-0
Bedford Town v Carlisle United	0-3
Bolton Wanderers v Preston North End	2-2, 1-2

FIFTH ROUND

West Ham United v Swindon Town	3-1
Burnley v Huddersfield Town	3-0
Sunderland v Everton	3-1
Barnsley v Manchester United	0-4
Stoke City v Swansea Town	2-2, 0-2
Arsenal v Liverpool	0-1
Oxford United v Blackburn Rovers	3-1
Carlisle United v Preston North End	0-1

SIXTH ROUND

West Ham United v Burnley	3-2
Manchester United v Sunderland	3-3, 2-2, 5-1
Liverpool v Swansea Town	1-2
Oxford United v Preston North End	1-2

SEMI-FINAL

West Ham United v Manchester United	3-1
Swansea Town v Preston North End	1-2

FINAL

West Ham United v Preston North End	3-2

SCOTTISH FA CUP 1963-64

SECOND ROUND

Rangers v Duns	9-0
Partick Thistle v St Johnstone	2-0
Morton v Celtic	1-3
Alloa Athletic v Airdrieonians	1-3
East Fife v East Stirlingshire	0-1
Dunfermline Athletic v Fraserburgh	7-0
Aberdeen v Queen's Park	1-1, 2-1
Buckie Thistle v Ayr United	1-3
Hamilton Academicals v Kilmarnock	1-3
Albion Rovers v Arbroath	4-3
St Mirren v Stranraer	2-0
Falkirk v Berwick Rangers	2-2, 5-1
Motherwell v Dumbarton	4-1
Queen of the South v Heart of Midlothian	0-3
Clyde v Forfar Athletic	2-2, 2-3
Brechin City v Dundee	2-9

THIRD ROUND

Rangers v Partick Thistle	3-0
Celtic v Airdrieonians	4-1
East Stirlingshire v Dunfermline Athletic	1-6
Aberdeen v Ayr United	1-2
Kilmarnock v Albion Rovers	2-0
St Mirren v Falkirk	0-1
Motherwell v Heart of Midlothian	3-3, 2-1
Dundee v Forfar Athletic	6-1

FOURTH ROUND

Rangers v Celtic	2-0
Dunfermline Athletic v Ayr United	7-0
Kilmarnock v Falkirk	2-1
Dundee v Motherwell	1-1, 4-2

SEMI-FINAL

Rangers v Dunfermline Athletic	1-0
Kilmarnock v Dundee	0-4

FINAL

Rangers v Dundee	3-1

On 12 October 1963, Tottenham Hotspur had seven players on international duty in the Home Championship, a record. Norman, Greaves and Smith were in the England side that met Wales. The Welsh team included Spurs' brilliant winger, Cliff Jones. Scotland paraded Brown, Mackay and White against Ireland.

Quick off the mark

The fastest goal in first-class football was scored by Jim Fryatt of Bradford Park Avenue on 25 April 1964. Just four seconds after the kick-off, Tranmere Rovers found themselves a goal down. Though a fantastic time, referee R. J. Simon's stop-watch confirmed it.

FIRST DIVISION

		P	W	D	L	F	A	Pts
1	Man United	42	26	9	7	89	39	61
2	Leeds	42	26	9	7	83	52	61
3	Chelsea	42	24	8	10	89	54	56
4	Everton	42	17	15	10	69	60	49
5	Nottm Forest	42	17	13	12	71	67	47
6	Tottenham	42	19	7	16	87	71	45
7	Liverpool	42	17	10	15	67	73	44
8	Sheff Wed	42	16	11	15	57	55	43
9	West Ham	42	19	4	19	82	71	42
10	Blackburn	42	16	10	16	83	79	42
11	Stoke	42	16	10	16	67	66	42
12	Burnley	42	16	10	16	70	70	42
13	Arsenal	42	17	7	18	69	75	41
14	WBA	42	13	13	16	70	65	39
15	Sunderland	42	14	9	19	64	74	37
16	Aston Villa	42	16	5	21	57	82	37
17	Blackpool	42	12	11	19	67	78	35
18	Leicester	42	11	13	18	69	85	35
19	Sheff United	42	12	11	19	50	64	35
20	Fulham	42	11	12	19	60	78	34
21	Wolves	42	13	4	25	59	89	30
22	Birmingham	42	8	11	23	64	96	27

SECOND DIVISION

		P	W	D	L	F	A	Pts
1	Newcastle	42	24	9	9	81	45	57
2	Northampton	42	20	16	6	66	50	56
3	Bolton	42	20	10	12	80	58	50
4	Southampton	42	17	14	11	83	63	48
5	Ipswich	42	15	17	10	74	67	47
6	Norwich	42	20	7	15	61	57	47
7	Crystal Palace	42	16	13	13	55	51	45
8	Huddersfield	42	17	10	15	53	51	44
9	Derby	42	16	11	15	84	79	43
10	Coventry	42	17	9	16	72	70	43
11	Man City	42	16	9	17	63	62	41
12	Preston	42	14	13	15	76	81	41
13	Cardiff	42	13	14	15	64	57	40
14	Rotherham	42	14	12	16	70	69	40
15	Plymouth	42	16	8	18	63	79	40
16	Bury	42	14	10	18	60	66	38
17	Middlesbrough	42	13	9	20	70	76	35
18	Charlton	42	13	9	20	64	75	35
19	Leyton Orient	42	12	11	19	50	72	35
20	Portsmouth	42	12	10	20	56	77	34
21	Swindon	42	14	5	23	63	81	33
22	Swansea	42	11	10	21	62	84	32

THIRD DIVISION

		P	W	D	L	F	A	Pts
1	Carlisle	46	25	10	11	76	53	60
2	Bristol City	46	24	11	11	92	55	59
3	Mansfield	46	24	11	11	95	61	59
4	Hull	46	23	12	11	91	57	58
5	Brentford	46	24	9	13	83	55	57
6	Bristol Rovers	46	20	15	11	82	58	55
7	Gillingham	46	23	9	14	70	50	55
8	Peterborough	46	22	7	17	85	74	51
9	Watford	46	17	16	13	71	64	50
10	Grimsby	46	16	17	13	68	67	49
11	Bournemouth	46	18	11	17	72	63	47
12	Southend	46	19	8	19	78	71	46
13	Reading	46	16	14	16	70	70	46
14	QPR	46	17	12	17	72	80	46
15	Workington	46	17	12	17	58	69	46
16	Shrewsbury	46	15	12	19	76	84	42
17	Exeter	46	12	17	17	51	52	41
18	Scunthorpe	46	14	12	20	65	72	40
19	Walsall	46	15	7	24	55	80	37
20	Oldham	46	13	10	23	61	83	36
21	Luton	46	11	11	24	51	94	33
22	Port Vale	46	9	14	23	41	76	32
23	Colchester	46	10	10	26	50	89	30
24	Barnsley	46	9	11	26	54	90	29

FOURTH DIVISION

		P	W	D	L	F	A	Pts
1	Brighton	46	26	11	9	102	57	63
2	Millwall	46	23	16	7	78	45	62
3	York	46	28	6	12	91	56	62
4	Oxford	46	23	15	8	87	44	61
5	Tranmere	46	27	6	13	99	56	60
6	Rochdale	46	22	14	10	74	53	58
7	Bradford PA	46	20	17	9	86	62	57
8	Chester	46	25	6	15	119	81	56
9	Doncaster	46	20	11	15	84	72	51
10	Crewe	46	18	13	15	90	81	49
11	Torquay	46	21	7	18	70	70	49
12	Chesterfield	46	20	8	18	58	70	48
13	Notts County	46	15	14	17	61	73	44
14	Wrexham	46	17	9	20	84	92	43
15	Hartlepools	46	15	13	18	61	85	43
16	Newport	46	17	8	21	85	81	42
17	Darlington	46	18	6	22	84	87	42
18	Aldershot	46	15	7	24	64	84	37
19	Bradford City	46	12	8	26	70	88	32
20	Southport	46	8	16	22	58	89	32
21	Barrow	46	12	6	28	59	105	30
22	Lincoln	46	11	6	29	58	99	28
23	Halifax	46	11	6	29	54	103	28
24	Stockport	46	10	7	29	44	87	27

SCOTTISH FIRST DIVISION

		P	W	D	L	F	A	Pts
1	Kilmarnock	34	22	6	6	62	33	50
2	Hearts	34	22	6	6	90	49	50
3	Dunfermline	34	22	5	7	83	36	49
4	Hibernian	34	21	4	9	75	47	46
5	Rangers	34	18	8	8	78	35	44
6	Dundee	34	15	10	9	86	63	40
7	Clyde	34	17	6	11	64	58	40
8	Celtic	34	16	5	13	76	57	37
9	Dundee United	34	15	6	13	59	51	36
10	Morton	34	13	7	14	54	54	33
11	Partick Thistle	34	11	10	13	57	58	32
12	Aberdeen	34	12	8	14	59	75	32
13	St Johnstone	34	9	11	14	57	62	29
14	Motherwell	34	10	8	16	45	54	28
15	St Mirren	34	9	6	19	38	70	24
16	Falkirk	34	7	7	20	43	85	21
17	Airdrieonians	34	5	4	25	48	110	14
18	Third Lanark	34	3	1	30	22	99	7

SCOTTISH SECOND DIVISION

		P	W	D	L	F	A	Pts
1	Stirling Albion	36	26	7	3	84	31	59
2	Hamilton	36	21	8	7	86	53	50
3	Queen of the S	36	16	13	7	84	50	45
4	Queen's Park	36	17	9	10	57	41	43
5	ES Clydebank	36	15	10	11	64	50	40
6	Stranraer	36	17	6	13	74	64	40
7	Arbroath	36	13	13	10	56	51	39
8	Berwick	36	15	9	12	73	70	39
9	East Fife	36	15	7	14	78	77	37
10	Alloa	36	14	8	14	71	81	36
11	Albion	36	14	5	17	56	60	33
12	Cowdenbeath	36	11	10	15	55	62	32
13	Raith	36	9	14	13	54	61	32
14	Dumbarton	36	13	6	17	55	67	32
15	Stenhousemuir	36	11	8	17	49	74	30
16	Montrose	36	10	9	17	80	91	29
17	Forfar	36	9	7	20	63	89	25
18	Ayr	36	9	6	21	49	67	24
19	Brechin	36	6	7	23	53	102	19

FA CUP 1964-65

FOURTH ROUND

Liverpool v Stockport County	1-1, 2-0
Preston North End v Bolton Wanderers	1-2
Leicester City v Plymouth Argyle	5-0
Charlton Athletic v Middlesbrough	1-1, 1-2
West Ham United v Chelsea	0-1
Tottenham Hotspur v Ipswich Town	5-0
Peterborough United v Arsenal	2-1
Swansea Town v Huddersfield Town	1-0
Wolverhampton Wanderers v Rotherham United	2-2, 3-0
Sheffield United v Aston Villa	0-2
Stoke City v Manchester United	0-0, 0-1
Reading v Burnley	1-1, 0-1
Southampton v Crystal Palace	1-2
Sunderland v Nottingham Forest	1-3
Millwall v Shrewsbury Town	1-2
Leeds United v Everton	1-1, 2-1

FIFTH ROUND

Bolton Wanderers v Liverpool	0-1
Middlesbrough v Leicester City	0-3
Chelsea v Tottenham Hotspur	1-0
Peterborough United v Swansea Town	0-0, 2-0
Aston Villa v Wolverhampton Wanderers	1-1, 0-0, 1-3
Manchester United v Burnley	2-1
Crystal Palace v Nottingham Forest	3-1
Leeds United v Shrewsbury Town	2-0

SIXTH ROUND

Leicester City v Liverpool	0-0, 0-1
Chelsea v Peterborough United	5-1
Wolverhampton Wanderers v Manchester United	3-5
Crystal Palace v Leeds United	0-3

SEMI-FINAL

Liverpool v Chelsea	2-0
Manchester United v Leeds United	0-0, 0-1

FINAL

Leeds United v Liverpool	1-2

SCOTTISH FA CUP 1964-65

FIRST ROUND

St Mirren v Celtic	0-3
Dumbarton v Queen's Park	0-0, 1-2
Aberdeen v East Fife	0-0, 0-1
Kilmarnock v Cowdenbeath	5-0
Motherwell v Stenhousemuir	3-2
St Johnstone v Dundee	1-0
Clyde v Morton	0-4
Falkirk v Heart of Midlothian	0-3
Hibernian v E S Clydebank	1-1, 2-0
Ayr United v Partick Thistle	1-1, 1-7
Forfar Athletic v Dundee United	0-3
Rangers v Hamilton Academicals	3-0
Stirling Albion v Arbroath	2-1
Airdrieonians v Montrose	7-3
Inverness Caledonian v Third Lanark	1-5
Queen of the South v Dunfermline Athletic	0-2

SECOND ROUND

Queen's Park v Celtic	0-1
East Fife v Kilmarnock	0-0, 0-3
Motherwell v St Johnstone	1-0
Morton v Heart of Midlothian	3-3, 0-2
Hibernian v Partick Thistle	5-1
Dundee United v Rangers	0-2
Stirling Albion v Airdrieonians	1-1, 2-0
Third Lanark v Dunfermline Athletic	1-1, 2-2, 2-4

THIRD ROUND

Celtic v Kilmarnock	3-2
Motherwell v Heart of Midlothian	1-0
Hibernian v Rangers	2-1
Dunfermline Athletic v Stirling Albion	2-0

SEMI-FINAL

Celtic v Motherwell	2-2, 3-0
Hibernian v Dunfermline Athletic	0-2

FINAL

Celtic v Dunfermline Athletic	3-2

Gillingham set the record for an undefeated run of home matches including Cup and League Cup games. From 9 April 1963, Gillingham had gone 52 games—48 of them in the League— at their Priestfield Stadium without a defeat, before losing 1-0 to Exeter on 10 April 1965.

Stan Lynn, Birmingham City's full-back, scored 10 goals (8 from penalties) and ended the 1964-65 season as his club's top League goal-scorer. Only one other full-back—Jimmy Evans of Southend United in 1921-2—has achieved this distinction among Football League clubs.

League Tables 1965-66

FIRST DIVISION

	P	W	D	L	F	A	Pts
1 Liverpool	42	26	9	7	79	34	61
2 Leeds	42	23	9	10	79	38	55
3 Burnley	42	24	7	11	79	47	55
4 Man United	42	18	15	9	84	59	51
5 Chelsea	42	22	7	13	65	53	51
6 WBA	42	19	12	11	91	69	50
7 Leicester	42	21	7	14	80	65	49
8 Tottenham	42	16	12	14	75	66	44
9 Sheff United	42	16	11	15	56	59	43
10 Stoke	42	15	12	15	65	64	42
11 Everton	42	15	11	16	56	62	41
12 West Ham	42	15	9	18	70	83	39
13 Blackpool	42	14	9	19	55	65	37
14 Arsenal	42	12	13	17	62	75	37
15 Newcastle	42	14	9	19	50	63	37
16 Aston Villa	42	15	6	21	69	80	36
17 Sheff Wed	42	14	8	20	56	66	36
18 Nottm Forest	42	14	8	20	56	72	36
19 Sunderland	42	14	8	20	51	72	36
20 Fulham	42	14	7	21	67	85	35
21 Northampton	42	10	13	19	55	92	33
22 Blackburn	42	8	4	30	57	88	20

SECOND DIVISION

	P	W	D	L	F	A	Pts
1 Man City	42	22	15	5	76	44	59
2 Southampton	42	22	10	10	85	56	54
3 Coventry	42	20	13	9	73	53	53
4 Huddersfield	42	19	13	10	62	36	51
5 Bristol City	42	17	17	8	63	48	51
6 Wolves	42	20	10	12	87	61	50
7 Rotherham	42	16	14	12	75	74	46
8 Derby	42	16	11	15	71	68	43
9 Bolton	42	16	9	17	62	59	41
10 Birmingham	42	16	9	17	70	75	41
11 Crystal Palace	42	14	13	15	47	52	41
12 Portsmouth	42	16	8	18	74	78	40
13 Norwich	42	12	15	15	52	52	39
14 Carlisle	42	17	5	20	60	63	39
15 Ipswich	42	15	9	18	58	66	39
16 Charlton	42	12	14	16	61	70	38
17 Preston	42	11	15	16	62	70	37
18 Plymouth	42	12	13	17	54	63	37
19 Bury	42	14	7	21	62	76	35
20 Cardiff	42	12	10	20	71	91	34
21 Middlesbrough	42	10	13	19	58	86	33
22 Leyton Orient	42	5	13	24	38	80	23

THIRD DIVISION

	P	W	D	L	F	A	Pts
1 Hull	46	31	7	8	109	62	69
2 Millwall	46	27	11	8	76	43	65
3 QPR	46	24	9	13	95	65	57
4 Scunthorpe	46	21	11	14	80	67	53
5 Workington	46	19	14	13	67	57	52
6 Gillingham	46	22	8	16	62	54	52
7 Swindon	46	19	13	14	74	48	51
8 Reading	46	19	13	14	70	63	51
9 Walsall	46	20	10	16	77	64	50
10 Shrewsbury	46	19	11	16	73	64	49
11 Grimsby	46	17	13	16	68	62	47
12 Watford	46	17	13	16	55	51	47
13 Peterborough	46	17	12	17	80	66	46
14 Oxford	46	19	8	19	70	74	46
15 Brighton	46	16	11	19	67	65	43
16 Bristol Rovers	46	14	14	18	64	64	42
17 Swansea	46	15	11	20	81	96	41
18 Bournemouth	46	13	12	21	38	56	38
19 Mansfield	46	15	8	23	59	89	38
20 Oldham	46	12	13	21	55	81	37
21 Southend	46	16	4	26	54	83	36
22 Exeter	46	12	11	23	53	79	35
23 Brentford	46	10	12	24	48	69	32
24 York	46	9	9	28	53	106	27

FOURTH DIVISION

	P	W	D	L	F	A	Pts
1 Doncaster	46	24	11	11	85	54	59
2 Darlington	46	25	9	12	72	53	59
3 Torquay	46	24	10	12	72	49	58
4 Colchester	46	23	10	13	70	47	56
5 Tranmere	46	24	8	14	93	66	56
6 Luton	46	24	8	14	90	70	56
7 Chester	46	20	12	14	79	70	52
8 Notts County	46	19	12	15	61	53	50
9 Newport	46	18	12	16	75	75	48
10 Southport	46	18	12	16	68	69	48
11 Bradford PA	46	21	5	20	102	92	47
12 Barrow	46	16	15	15	72	76	47
13 Stockport	46	18	6	22	71	70	42
14 Crewe	46	16	9	21	61	63	41
15 Halifax	46	15	11	20	67	75	41
16 Barnsley	46	15	10	21	74	78	40
17 Aldershot	46	15	10	21	75	84	40
18 Hartlepools	46	16	8	22	63	75	40
19 Port Vale	46	15	9	22	48	59	39
20 Chesterfield	46	13	13	20	62	78	39
21 Rochdale	46	16	5	25	71	87	37
22 Lincoln	46	13	11	22	57	82	37
23 Bradford City	46	12	13	21	63	94	37
24 Wrexham	46	13	9	24	72	104	35

SCOTTISH FIRST DIVISION

	P	W	D	L	F	A	Pts
1 Celtic	34	27	3	4	106	30	57
2 Rangers	34	25	5	4	91	29	55
3 Kilmarnock	34	20	5	9	73	46	45
4 Dunfermline	34	19	6	9	94	55	44
5 Dundee United	34	19	5	10	79	51	43
6 Hibernian	34	16	6	12	81	55	38
7 Hearts	34	13	12	9	56	48	38
8 Aberdeen	34	15	6	13	61	54	36
9 Dundee	34	14	6	14	61	61	34
10 Falkirk	34	15	1	18	48	72	31
11 Clyde	34	13	4	17	62	64	30
12 Partick Thistle	34	10	10	14	55	64	30
13 Motherwell	34	12	4	18	52	69	28
14 St Johnstone	34	9	8	17	58	81	26
15 Stirling Albion	34	9	8	17	40	68	26
16 St Mirren	34	9	4	21	44	82	22
17 Morton	34	8	5	21	42	84	21
18 Hamilton	34	3	2	29	27	117	8

SCOTTISH SECOND DIVISION

	P	W	D	L	F	A	Pts
1 Ayr	36	22	9	5	78	37	53
2 Airdrieonians	36	22	6	8	107	56	50
3 Queen of the S	36	18	11	7	83	53	47
4 East Fife	36	20	4	12	72	55	44
5 Raith	36	16	11	9	71	43	43
6 Arbroath	36	15	13	8	72	52	43
7 Albion	36	18	7	11	58	54	43
8 Alloa	36	14	10	12	65	65	38
9 Montrose	36	15	7	14	67	63	37
10 Cowdenbeath	36	15	7	14	69	68	37
11 Berwick	36	12	11	13	69	58	35
12 Dumbarton	36	14	7	15	63	61	35
13 Queen's Park	36	13	7	16	62	65	33
14 Third Lanark	36	12	8	16	55	65	32
15 Stranraer	36	9	10	17	64	83	28
16 Brechin	36	10	7	19	52	92	27
17 E Stirlingshire	36	9	5	22	59	91	23
18 Stenhousemuir	36	6	7	23	47	93	19
19 Forfar	36	7	3	26	61	120	17

FA CUP 1965-66

FOURTH ROUND

Bedford Town v Everton	0-3
Crewe Alexandra v Coventry City	1-1, 1-4
Manchester City v Grimsby Town	2-0
Birmingham City v Leicester City	1-2
Manchester United v Rotherham United	0-0, 1-0
Wolverhampton Wanderers v Sheffield United	3-0
Bolton Wanderers v Preston North End	1-1, 2-3
Tottenham Hotspur v Burnley	4-3
Chelsea v Leeds United	1-0
Shrewsbury Town v Carlisle United	0-0, 1-1, 4-3
Hull City v Nottingham Forest	2-0
Southport v Cardiff City	2-0
Norwich City v Walsall	3-2
West Ham United v Blackburn Rovers	3-3, 1-4
Plymouth Argyle v Huddersfield Town	0-2
Newcastle United v Sheffield Wednesday	1-2

FIFTH ROUND

Everton v Coventry City	3-0
Manchester City v Leicester City	2-2, 1-0
Wolverhampton Wanderers v Manchester United	2-4
Preston North End v Tottenham Hotspur	2-1
Chelsea v Shrewsbury Town	3-2
Hull City v Southport	2-0
Norwich City v Blackburn Rovers	2-2, 2-3
Huddersfield Town v Sheffield Wednesday	1-2

SIXTH ROUND

Manchester City v Everton	0-0, 0-0, 0-2
Preston North End v Manchester United	1-1, 1-3
Chelsea v Hull City	2-2, 3-1
Blackburn Rovers v Sheffield Wednesday	1-2

SEMI-FINAL

Everton v Manchester United	1-0
Chelsea v Sheffield Wednesday	0-2

FINAL

Everton v Sheffield Wednesday	3-2

SCOTTISH FA CUP 1965-66

FIRST ROUND

Celtic v Stranraer	4-0
Dundee v East Fife	9-1
Heart of Midlothian v Clyde	2-1
Hibernian v Third Lanark	4-3
Stirling Albion v Queen's Park	3-1
Dunfermline Athletic v Partick Thistle	3-1
Morton v Kilmarnock	1-1, 0-3
East Stirlingshire v Motherwell	0-0, 1-4
Dumbarton v Montrose	2-1
Queen of the South v Albion Rovers	3-0
Hamilton Academicals v Aberdeen	1-3
Dundee United v Falkirk	0-0, 2-1
Cowdenbeath v St Mirren	1-0
Ayr United v St Johnstone	1-1, 0-1
Alloa Athletic v Ross County	3-5
Rangers v Airdrieonians	5-1

SECOND ROUND

Dundee v Celtic	0-2
Heart of Midlothian v Hibernian	2-1
Stirling Albion v Dunfermline Athletic	0-0, 1-4
Kilmarnock v Motherwell	5-0
Dumbarton v Queen of the South	1-0
Aberdeen v Dundee United	5-0
Cowdenbeath v St Johnstone	3-3, 0-3
Ross County v Rangers	0-2

THIRD ROUND

Celtic v Heart of Midlothian	3-3, 3-1
Dunfermline Athletic v Kilmarnock	2-1
Dumbarton v Aberdeen	0-3
Rangers v St Johnstone	2-0

SEMI-FINAL

Celtic v Dunfermline Athletic	2-0
Aberdeen v Rangers	0-0, 1-2

FINAL

Celtic v Rangers	0-0, 0-1

On 1 January 1966, while they were beating Aldershot 3-2 in a Division Four game, Chester lost both their full-backs, Ray Jones and Bryn Jones, with broken legs.

The World Cup final receipts—£204,805—were a world record for a football match.

At the start of the season, Manchester United had 15 internationals on their staff. They were: Pat Dunne, Harry Gregg, Shay Brennan, Noel Cantwell, Pat Crerand, Bill Foulkes, Denis Law, Nobby Stiles, Tony Dunne, George Best, David Herd, John Connelly, Bobby Charlton, Graham Moore, and David Sadler, then an amateur cap.

FIRST DIVISION

		P	W	D	L	F	A	Pts
1	Man United	42	24	12	6	84	45	60
2	Nottm Forest	42	23	10	9	64	41	56
3	Tottenham	42	24	8	10	71	48	56
4	Leeds	42	22	11	9	62	42	55
5	Liverpool	42	19	13	10	64	47	51
6	Everton	42	19	10	13	65	46	48
7	Arsenal	42	16	14	12	58	47	46
8	Leicester	42	18	8	16	78	71	44
9	Chelsea	42	15	14	13	67	62	44
10	Sheff United	42	16	10	16	52	59	42
11	Sheff Wed	42	14	13	15	56	47	41
12	Stoke	42	17	7	18	63	58	41
13	WBA	42	16	7	19	77	73	39
14	Burnley	42	15	9	18	66	76	39
15	Man City	42	12	15	15	43	52	39
16	West Ham	42	14	8	20	80	84	36
17	Sunderland	42	14	8	20	58	72	36
18	Fulham	42	11	12	19	71	83	34
19	Southampton	42	14	6	22	74	92	34
20	Newcastle	42	12	9	21	39	81	33
21	Aston Villa	42	11	7	24	54	85	29
22	Blackpool	42	6	9	27	41	76	21

SECOND DIVISION

		P	W	D	L	F	A	Pts
1	Coventry	42	23	13	6	74	43	59
2	Wolves	42	25	8	9	88	48	58
3	Carlisle	42	23	6	13	71	54	52
4	Blackburn	42	19	13	10	56	46	51
5	Ipswich	42	17	16	9	70	54	50
6	Huddersfield	42	20	9	13	58	46	49
7	Crystal Palace	42	19	10	13	61	55	48
8	Millwall	42	18	9	15	49	58	45
9	Bolton	42	14	14	14	64	58	42
10	Birmingham	42	16	8	18	70	66	40
11	Norwich	42	13	14	15	49	55	40
12	Hull	42	16	7	19	77	72	39
13	Preston	42	16	7	19	65	67	39
14	Portsmouth	42	13	13	16	59	70	39
15	Bristol City	42	12	14	16	56	62	38
16	Plymouth	42	14	9	19	59	58	37
17	Derby	42	12	12	18	68	72	36
18	Rotherham	42	13	10	19	61	70	36
19	Charlton	42	13	9	20	49	53	35
20	Cardiff	42	12	9	21	61	87	33
21	Northampton	42	12	6	24	47	84	30
22	Bury	42	11	6	25	49	83	28

FA CUP 1966-67

FOURTH ROUND

Brighton & Hove Albion v Chelsea	1-1, 0-4
Fulham v Sheffield United	1-1, 1-3
Manchester United v Norwich City	1-2
Sheffield Wednesday v Mansfield Town	4-0
Sunderland v Peterborough United	7-1
Leeds United v West Bromwich Albion	5-0
Cardiff City v Manchester City	1-1, 1-3
Ipswich Town v Carlisle United	2-0
Rotherham United v Birmingham City	0-0, 1-2
Bolton Wanderers v Arsenal	0-0, 0-3
Tottenham Hotspur v Portsmouth	3-1
Bristol City v Southampton	1-0
Nottingham Forest v Newcastle United	3-0
Swindon Town v Bury	2-1
Wolverhampton Wanderers v Everton	1-1, 1-3
Liverpool v Aston Villa	1-0

FIFTH ROUND

Chelsea v Sheffield United	2-0
Norwich City v Sheffield Wednesday	1-3
Sunderland v Leeds United	1-1, 1-1, 1-2
Manchester City v Ipswich Town	1-1, 3-0
Birmingham City v Arsenal	1-0
Tottenham Hotspur v Bristol City	2-0
Nottingham Forest v Swindon Town	0-0, 1-1, 3-0
Everton v Liverpool	1-0

SIXTH ROUND

Chelsea v Sheffield Wednesday	1-0
Leeds United v Manchester City	1-0
Birmingham City v Tottenham Hotspur	0-0, 0-6
Nottingham Forest v Everton	3-2

SEMI-FINAL

Chelsea v Leeds United	1-0
Tottenham Hotspur v Nottingham Forest	2-1

FINAL

Chelsea v Tottenham Hotspur	1-2

THIRD DIVISION

		P	W	D	L	F	A	Pts
1	QPR	46	26	15	5	103	38	67
2	Middlesbrough	46	23	9	14	87	64	55
3	Watford	46	20	14	12	61	46	54
4	Reading	46	22	9	15	76	57	53
5	Bristol Rovers	46	20	13	13	76	67	53
6	Shrewsbury	46	20	12	14	77	62	52
7	Torquay	46	21	9	16	73	54	51
8	Swindon	46	20	10	16	81	59	50
9	Mansfield	46	20	9	17	84	79	49
10	Oldham	46	19	10	17	80	63	48
11	Gillingham	46	15	16	15	58	62	46
12	Walsall	46	18	10	18	65	72	46
13	Colchester	46	17	10	19	76	73	44
14	Leyton Orient	46	13	18	15	58	68	44
15	Peterborough	46	14	15	17	66	71	43
16	Oxford	46	15	13	18	61	66	43
17	Grimsby	46	17	9	20	61	68	43
18	Scunthorpe	46	17	8	21	58	73	42
19	Brighton	46	13	15	18	61	71	41
20	Bournemouth	46	12	17	17	39	57	41
21	Swansea	46	12	15	19	85	89	39
22	Darlington	46	13	11	22	47	81	37
23	Doncaster	46	12	8	26	58	117	32
24	Workington	46	12	7	27	55	89	31

FOURTH DIVISION

		P	W	D	L	F	A	Pts
1	Stockport	46	26	12	8	69	42	64
2	Southport	46	23	13	10	69	42	59
3	Barrow	46	24	11	11	76	54	59
4	Tranmere	46	22	14	10	66	43	58
5	Crewe	46	21	12	13	70	55	54
6	Southend	46	22	9	15	70	49	53
7	Wrexham	46	16	20	10	76	62	52
8	Hartlepools	46	22	7	17	66	64	51
9	Brentford	46	18	13	15	58	56	49
10	Aldershot	46	18	12	16	72	57	48
11	Bradford City	46	19	10	17	74	62	48
12	Halifax	46	15	14	17	59	68	44
13	Port Vale	46	14	15	17	55	58	43
14	Exeter	46	14	15	17	50	60	43
15	Chesterfield	46	17	8	21	60	63	42
16	Barnsley	46	13	15	18	60	64	41
17	Luton	46	16	9	21	59	73	41
18	Newport	46	12	16	18	56	63	40
19	Chester	46	15	10	21	54	78	40
20	Notts County	46	13	11	22	53	72	37
21	Rochdale	46	13	11	22	53	75	37
22	York	46	12	11	23	65	79	35
23	Bradford PA	46	11	13	22	52	79	35
24	Lincoln	46	9	13	24	58	82	31

SCOTTISH FA CUP 1966-67

FIRST ROUND

Celtic v Arbroath	4-0
Elgin City v Ayr United	2-0
Queen's Park v Raith Rovers	3-2
Stirling Albion v Airdrieonians	1-2
Morton v Clyde	0-1
Motherwell v East Fife	0-1
St Mirren v Cowdenbeath	1-1, 2-0
Inverness Caledonian v Hamilton Academicals	1-3
Heart of Midlothian v Dundee United	0-3
Falkirk v Alloa Athletic	3-1
Partick Thistle v Dumbarton	3-0
Kilmarnock v Dunfermline Athletic	2-2, 0-1
Hibernian v Brechin City	2-0
Berwick Rangers v Rangers	1-0
St Johnstone v Queen of the South	4-0
Aberdeen v Dundee	5-0

SECOND ROUND

Celtic v Elgin City	7-0
Queen's Park v Airdrieonians	1-1, 2-1
Clyde v East Fife	4-1
St Mirren v Hamilton Academicals	0-1
Dundee United v Falkirk	1-0
Partick Thistle v Dunfermline Athletic	1-1, 1-5
Hibernian v Berwick Rangers	1-0
St Johnstone v Aberdeen	0-5

THIRD ROUND

Celtic v Queen's Park	5-3
Clyde v Hamilton Academicals	0-0, 5-1
Dundee United v Dunfermline Athletic	1-0
Hibernian v Aberdeen	1-1, 0-3

SEMI-FINAL

Celtic v Clyde	0-0, 2-0
Dundee United v Aberdeen	0-1

FINAL

Celtic v Aberdeen	2-0

SCOTTISH FIRST DIVISION

		P	W	D	L	F	A	Pts
1	Celtic	34	26	6	2	111	33	58
2	Rangers	34	24	7	3	92	31	55
3	Clyde	34	20	6	8	64	48	46
4	Aberdeen	34	17	8	9	72	38	42
5	Hibernian	34	19	4	11	72	49	42
6	Dundee	34	16	9	9	74	51	41
7	Kilmarnock	34	16	8	10	59	46	40
8	Dunfermline	34	14	10	10	72	52	38
9	Dundee United	34	14	9	11	68	62	37
10	Motherwell	34	10	11	13	59	60	31
11	Hearts	34	11	8	15	39	48	30
12	Partick Thistle	34	9	12	13	49	68	30
13	Airdrieonians	34	11	6	17	41	53	28
14	Falkirk	34	11	4	19	33	70	26
15	St Johnstone	34	10	5	19	53	73	25
16	Stirling	34	5	9	20	31	85	19
17	St Mirren	34	4	7	23	25	81	15
18	Ayr	34	1	7	26	20	86	9

SCOTTISH SECOND DIVISION

		P	W	D	L	F	A	Pts
1	Morton	38	33	3	2	113	20	69
2	Raith	38	27	4	7	95	44	58
3	Arbroath	38	25	7	6	75	32	57
4	Hamilton	38	18	8	12	74	60	44
5	East Fife	38	19	4	15	70	63	42
6	Cowdenbeath	38	16	8	14	70	55	40
7	Queen's Park	38	15	10	13	78	68	40
8	Albion	38	17	6	15	66	62	40
9	Queen of the S	38	15	9	14	84	76	39
10	Berwick	38	16	6	16	63	55	38
11	Third Lanark	38	13	8	17	67	78	34
12	Montrose	38	13	8	17	63	77	34
13	Alloa	38	15	4	19	55	74	34
14	Dumbarton	38	12	9	17	56	64	33
15	Stranraer	38	13	7	18	57	73	33
16	Forfar	38	12	3	23	74	106	27
17	Stenhousemuir	38	9	9	20	62	104	27
18	Clydebank	38	8	8	22	59	92	24
19	E Stirlingshire	38	7	10	21	44	87	24
20	Brechin	38	8	7	23	58	93	23

A great year for Celtic

Celtic won the Scottish League, Cup and League Cup, the Glasgow Cup, and became the first British club to win the European Cup, thus completing a remarkable grand slam.

More directors than players

When Workington increased their board of directors by the addition of a 13th member in October 1966, they found themselves with more directors than full-time players.

League Tables 1967-68

FIRST DIVISION

		P	W	D	L	F	A	Pts
1	Man City	42	26	6	10	86	43	58
2	Man United	42	24	8	10	89	55	56
3	Liverpool	42	22	11	9	71	40	55
4	Leeds	42	22	9	11	71	41	53
5	Everton	42	23	6	13	67	40	52
6	Chelsea	42	18	12	12	62	68	48
7	Tottenham	42	19	9	14	70	59	47
8	WBA	42	17	12	13	75	62	46
9	Arsenal	42	17	10	15	60	56	44
10	Newcastle	42	13	15	14	54	67	41
11	Nottm Forest	42	14	11	17	52	64	39
12	West Ham	42	14	10	18	73	69	38
13	Leicester	42	13	12	17	64	69	38
14	Burnley	42	14	10	18	64	71	38
15	Sunderland	42	13	11	18	51	61	37
16	Southampton	42	13	11	18	66	83	37
17	Wolves	42	14	8	20	66	75	36
18	Stoke	42	14	7	21	50	73	35
19	Sheff Wed	42	11	12	19	51	63	34
20	Coventry	42	9	15	18	51	71	33
21	Sheff United	42	11	10	21	49	70	32
22	Fulham	42	10	7	25	56	98	27

SECOND DIVISION

		P	W	D	L	F	A	Pts
1	Ipswich	42	22	15	5	79	44	59
2	QPR	42	25	8	9	67	36	58
3	Blackpool	42	24	10	8	71	43	58
4	Birmingham	42	19	14	9	83	51	52
5	Portsmouth	42	18	13	11	68	55	49
6	Middlesbrough	42	17	12	13	60	54	46
7	Millwall	42	14	17	11	62	50	45
8	Blackburn	42	16	11	15	56	49	43
9	Norwich	42	16	11	15	60	65	43
10	Carlisle	42	14	13	15	58	52	41
11	Crystal Palace	42	14	11	17	56	56	39
12	Bolton	42	13	13	16	60	63	39
13	Cardiff	42	13	12	17	60	66	38
14	Huddersfield	42	13	12	17	46	61	38
15	Charlton	42	12	13	17	63	68	37
16	Aston Villa	42	15	7	20	54	64	37
17	Hull	42	12	13	17	58	73	37
18	Derby	42	13	10	19	71	78	36
19	Bristol City	42	13	10	19	48	62	36
20	Preston	42	12	11	19	43	65	35
21	Rotherham	42	10	11	21	42	76	31
22	Plymouth	42	9	9	24	38	72	27

THIRD DIVISION

		P	W	D	L	F	A	Pts
1	Oxford	46	22	13	11	69	47	57
2	Bury	46	24	8	14	91	66	56
3	Shrewsbury	46	20	15	11	61	49	55
4	Torquay	46	21	11	14	60	56	53
5	Reading	46	21	9	16	70	60	51
6	Watford	46	21	8	17	74	50	50
7	Walsall	46	19	12	15	74	61	50
8	Barrow	46	21	8	17	65	54	50
9	Swindon	46	16	17	13	74	51	49
10	Brighton	46	16	16	14	57	55	48
11	Gillingham	46	18	12	16	59	63	48
12	Bournemouth	46	16	15	15	56	51	47
13	Stockport	46	19	9	18	70	75	47
14	Southport	46	17	12	17	65	65	46
15	Bristol Rovers	46	17	9	20	72	78	43
16	Oldham	46	18	7	21	60	65	43
17	Northampton	46	14	13	19	58	72	41
18	Leyton Orient	46	12	17	17	46	62	41
19	Tranmere	46	14	12	20	62	74	40
20	Mansfield	46	12	13	21	51	67	37
21	Grimsby	46	14	9	23	52	69	37
22	Colchester	46	9	15	22	50	87	33
23	Scunthorpe	46	10	12	24	56	87	32
24	Peterborough	46	20	10	16	79	67	31†

†Peterborough had 19 points deducted for offering irregular bonuses to their players. They were automatically demoted to the Fourth Division.

FOURTH DIVISION

		P	W	D	L	F	A	Pts
1	Luton	46	27	12	7	87	44	66
2	Barnsley	46	24	13	9	68	46	61
3	Hartlepools	46	25	10	11	60	46	60
4	Crewe	46	20	18	8	74	49	58
5	Bradford City	46	23	11	12	72	51	57
6	Southend	46	20	14	12	77	58	54
7	Chesterfield	46	21	11	14	71	50	53
8	Wrexham	46	20	13	13	72	53	53
9	Aldershot	46	18	17	11	70	55	53
10	Doncaster	46	18	15	13	66	56	51
11	Halifax	46	15	16	15	52	49	46
12	Newport	46	16	13	17	58	63	45
13	Lincoln	46	17	9	20	71	68	43
14	Brentford	46	18	7	21	61	64	43
15	Swansea	46	16	10	20	63	77	42
16	Darlington	46	12	17	17	47	53	41
17	Notts County	46	15	11	20	53	79	41
18	Port Vale	46	12	15	19	61	72	39†
19	Rochdale	46	12	14	20	51	72	38
20	Exeter	46	11	16	19	45	65	38
21	York	46	11	14	21	65	68	36
22	Chester	46	9	14	23	57	78	32
23	Workington	46	10	11	25	54	87	31
24	Bradford PA	46	4	15	27	30	82	23

†Port Vale were expelled from the League at the end of the season for making unauthorised payments. They were re-elected immediately.

SCOTTISH FIRST DIVISION

		P	W	D	L	F	A	Pts
1	Celtic	34	30	3	1	106	24	63
2	Rangers	34	28	5	1	93	34	61
3	Hibernian	34	20	5	9	67	49	45
4	Dunfermline	34	17	5	12	64	41	39
5	Aberdeen	34	16	5	13	63	48	37
6	Morton	34	15	6	13	57	53	36
7	Kilmarnock	34	13	8	13	59	57	34
8	Clyde	34	15	4	15	55	55	34
9	Dundee	34	13	7	14	62	59	33
10	Partick Thistle	34	12	7	15	51	67	31
11	Dundee United	34	10	11	13	53	72	31
12	Hearts	34	13	4	17	56	61	30
13	Airdrieonians	34	10	9	15	45	58	29
14	St Johnstone	34	10	7	17	43	52	27
15	Falkirk	34	7	12	15	36	50	26
16	Raith Rovers	34	9	7	18	58	86	25
17	Motherwell	34	6	7	21	40	66	19
18	Stirling Albion	34	4	4	26	29	105	12

SCOTTISH SECOND DIVISION

		P	W	D	L	F	A	Pts
1	St Mirren	36	27	8	1	100	23	62
2	Arbroath	36	24	5	7	87	34	53
3	East Fife	36	21	7	8	71	47	49
4	Queen's Park	36	20	8	8	76	47	48
5	Ayr	36	18	6	12	69	48	42
6	Queen of the S	36	16	6	14	73	57	38
7	Forfar	36	14	10	12	57	63	38
8	Albion	36	14	9	13	62	55	37
9	Clydebank	36	13	8	15	62	73	34
10	Dumbarton	36	11	11	14	63	74	33
11	Hamilton	36	13	7	16	49	58	33
12	Cowdenbeath	36	12	8	16	57	62	32
13	Montrose	36	10	11	15	54	64	31
14	Berwick	36	13	4	19	34	54	30
15	E Stirlingshire	36	9	10	17	61	74	28
16	Brechin	36	8	12	16	45	62	28
17	Alloa	36	11	6	19	42	69	28
18	Stenhousemuir	36	7	6	23	34	93	20
19	Stranraer	36	8	4	24	41	80	20

FA CUP 1967-68

FOURTH ROUND

Carlisle United v Everton	0-2
Coventry City v Tranmere Rovers	1-1, 0-2
Aston Villa v Rotherham United	0-1
Manchester City v Leicester City	0-0, 3-4
Leeds United v Nottingham Forest	2-1
Middlesbrough v Bristol City	1-1, 1-2
Stoke City v West Ham United	0-3
Sheffield United v Blackpool	2-1
Swansea Town v Arsenal	0-1
Birmingham City v Leyton Orient	3-0
Sheffield Wednesday v Swindon Town	2-1
Chelsea v Norwich City	1-0
Fulham v Portsmouth	0-0, 0-1
West Bromwich Albion v Southampton	1-1, 3-2
Tottenham Hotspur v Preston North End	3-1
Walsall v Liverpool	0-0, 2-5

FIFTH ROUND

Everton v Tranmere Rovers	2-0
Rotherham United v Leicester City	1-1, 0-2
Leeds United v Bristol City	2-0
West Ham United v Sheffield United	1-2
Arsenal v Birmingham City	1-1, 1-2
Sheffield Wednesday v Chelsea	2-2, 0-2
Portsmouth v West Bromwich Albion	1-2
Tottenham Hotspur v Liverpool	1-1, 1-2

SIXTH ROUND

Everton v Leicester City	3-1
Leeds United v Sheffield United	1-0
Birmingham City v Chelsea	1-0
West Bromwich Albion v Liverpool	0-0, 1-1, 2-1

SEMI-FINAL

Everton v Leeds United	1-0
West Bromwich Albion v Birmingham City	2-0

FINAL

Everton v West Bromwich Albion	0-1

SCOTTISH FA CUP 1967-68

FIRST ROUND

Rangers v Hamilton Academicals	3-1
Cowdenbeath v Dundee	0-1
Dundee United v St. Mirren	3-1
Heart of Midlothian v Brechin City	4-1
East Fife v Alloa Athletic	3-0
Morton v Falkirk	4-0
Elgin City v Forfar Athletic	3-1
Ayr United v Arbroath	0-2
Celtic v Dunfermline Athletic	0-2
Aberdeen v Raith Rovers	1-1, 1-0
Partick Thistle v Kilmarnock	0-0, 2-1
Clyde v Berwick Rangers	2-0
Motherwell v Airdrieonians	1-1, 0-1
East Stirlingshire v Hibernian	3-5
St Johnstone v Hawick Royal Albert	3-0
Queen of the South v Stirling Albion	1-1, 3-1

SECOND ROUND

Dundee v Rangers	1-1, 1-4
Dundee United v Heart of Midlothian	5-6
East Fife v Morton	0-0, 2-5
Elgin City v Arbroath	2-0
Dunfermline Athletic v Aberdeen	2-1
Partick Thistle v Clyde	3-2
Airdrieonians v Hibernian	1-0
St Johnstone v Queen of the South	5-2

THIRD ROUND

Rangers v Heart of Midlothian	1-1, 0-1
Morton v Elgin City	2-1
Dunfermline Athletic v Partick Thistle	1-0
St Johnstone v Airdrieonians	2-1

SEMI-FINAL

Heart of Midlothian v Morton	1-1, 2-1
Dunfermline Athletic v St Johnstone	1-1, 2-1

FINAL

Dunfermline Athletic v Heart of Midlothian	3-1

FIRST DIVISION

		P	W	D	L	F	A	Pts
1	Leeds	42	27	13	2	66	26	67
2	Liverpool	42	25	11	6	63	24	61
3	Everton	42	21	15	6	77	36	57
4	Arsenal	42	22	12	8	56	27	56
5	Chelsea	42	20	10	12	73	53	50
6	Tottenham	42	14	17	11	61	51	45
7	Southampton	42	16	13	13	57	48	45
8	West Ham	42	13	18	11	66	50	44
9	Newcastle	42	15	14	13	61	55	44
10	WBA	42	16	11	15	64	67	43
11	Man United	42	15	12	15	57	53	42
12	Ipswich	42	15	11	16	59	60	41
13	Man City	42	15	10	17	64	55	40
14	Burnley	42	15	9	18	55	82	39
15	Sheff Wed	42	10	16	16	41	54	36
16	Wolves	42	10	15	17	41	58	35
17	Sunderland	42	11	12	19	43	67	34
18	Nottm Forest	42	10	13	19	45	57	33
19	Stoke	42	9	15	18	40	63	33
20	Coventry	42	10	11	21	46	64	31
21	Leicester	42	9	12	21	39	68	30
22	QPR	42	4	10	28	39	95	18

SECOND DIVISION

		P	W	D	L	F	A	Pts
1	Derby	42	26	11	5	65	32	63
2	Crystal Palace	42	22	12	8	70	47	56
3	Charlton	42	18	14	10	61	52	50
4	Middlesbrough	42	19	11	12	58	49	49
5	Cardiff	42	20	7	15	67	54	47
6	Huddersfield	42	17	12	13	53	46	46
7	Birmingham	42	18	8	16	73	59	44
8	Blackpool	42	14	15	13	51	41	43
9	Sheff United	42	16	11	15	61	50	43
10	Millwall	42	17	9	16	57	49	43
11	Hull	42	13	16	13	59	52	42
12	Carlisle	42	16	10	16	46	49	42
13	Norwich	42	15	10	17	53	56	40
14	Preston	42	12	15	15	38	44	39
15	Portsmouth	42	12	14	16	58	58	38
16	Bristol City	42	11	16	15	46	53	38
17	Bolton	42	12	14	16	55	67	38
18	Aston Villa	42	12	14	16	37	48	38
19	Blackburn	42	13	11	18	52	63	37
20	Oxford	42	12	9	21	34	55	33
21	Bury	42	11	8	23	51	80	30
22	Fulham	42	7	11	24	40	81	25

THIRD DIVISION

		P	W	D	L	F	A	Pts
1	Watford	46	27	10	9	74	34	64
2	Swindon	46	27	10	9	71	35	64
3	Luton	46	25	11	10	74	38	61
4	Bournemouth	46	21	9	16	60	45	51
5	Plymouth	46	17	15	14	53	49	49
6	Torquay	46	18	12	16	54	46	48
7	Tranmere	46	19	10	17	70	68	48
8	Southport	46	17	13	16	71	64	47
9	Stockport	46	16	14	16	67	68	46
10	Barnsley	46	16	14	16	58	63	46
11	Rotherham	46	16	13	17	56	50	45
12	Brighton	46	16	13	17	72	65	45
13	Walsall	46	14	16	16	50	49	44
14	Reading	46	15	13	18	67	66	43
15	Mansfield	46	16	11	19	58	62	43
16	Bristol Rovers	46	16	11	19	63	71	43
17	Shrewsbury	46	16	11	19	51	67	43
18	Orient	46	14	14	18	51	58	42
19	Barrow	46	17	8	21	56	75	42
20	Gillingham	46	13	15	18	54	63	41
21	Northampton	46	14	12	20	54	61	40
22	Hartlepool	46	10	19	17	40	70	39
23	Crewe	46	13	9	24	52	76	35
24	Oldham	46	13	9	24	50	83	35

FOURTH DIVISION

		P	W	D	L	F	A	Pts
1	Doncaster	46	21	17	8	65	38	59
2	Halifax	46	20	17	9	53	37	57
3	Rochdale	46	18	20	8	68	35	56
4	Bradford City	46	18	20	8	65	46	56
5	Darlington	46	17	18	11	62	45	52
6	Colchester	46	20	12	14	57	53	52
7	Southend	46	19	13	14	78	61	51
8	Lincoln	46	17	17	12	54	52	51
9	Wrexham	46	18	14	14	61	52	50
10	Swansea	46	19	11	16	58	54	49
11	Brentford	46	18	12	16	64	65	48
12	Workington	46	15	17	14	40	43	47
13	Port Vale	46	16	14	16	46	46	46
14	Chester	46	16	13	17	76	66	45
15	Aldershot	46	19	7	20	66	66	45
16	Scunthorpe	46	18	8	20	61	60	44
17	Exeter	46	16	11	19	66	65	43
18	Peterborough	46	13	16	17	60	57	42
19	Notts County	46	12	18	16	48	57	42
20	Chesterfield	46	13	15	18	43	50	41
21	York	46	14	11	21	53	75	39
22	Newport	46	11	14	21	49	74	36
23	Grimsby	46	9	15	22	47	69	33
24	Bradford PA	46	5	10	31	32	106	20

SCOTTISH FIRST DIVISION

		P	W	D	L	F	A	Pts
1	Celtic	34	23	8	3	89	32	54
2	Rangers	34	21	7	6	81	32	49
3	Dunfermline	34	19	7	8	63	45	45
4	Kilmarnock	34	15	14	5	50	32	44
5	Dundee United	34	17	9	8	61	49	43
6	St Johnstone	34	16	5	13	66	59	37
7	Airdrieonians	34	13	11	10	46	44	37
8	Hearts	34	14	8	12	52	54	36
9	Dundee	34	10	12	12	47	48	32
10	Morton	34	12	8	14	58	68	32
11	St Mirren	34	11	10	13	40	54	32
12	Hibernian	34	12	7	15	60	59	31
13	Clyde	34	9	13	12	35	50	31
14	Partick Thistle	34	9	10	15	39	53	28
15	Aberdeen	34	9	8	17	50	59	26
16	Raith	34	8	5	21	45	67	21
17	Falkirk	34	5	8	21	33	69	18
18	Arbroath	34	5	6	23	41	82	16

SCOTTISH SECOND DIVISION

		P	W	D	L	F	A	Pts
1	Motherwell	36	30	4	2	112	23	64
2	Ayr	36	23	7	6	82	31	53
3	East Fife	36	21	6	9	82	45	48
4	Stirling	36	21	6	9	67	40	48
5	Queen of the S	36	20	7	9	75	41	47
6	Forfar	36	18	7	11	71	56	47
7	Albion	36	19	5	12	60	56	43
8	Stranraer	36	17	7	12	57	45	41
9	E Stirlingshire	36	17	5	14	70	62	39
10	Montrose	36	15	4	17	59	71	34
11	Queen's Park	36	13	7	16	50	59	33
12	Cowdenbeath	36	12	5	19	54	67	29
13	Clydebank	36	6	15	15	52	67	27
14	Dumbarton	36	11	5	20	46	69	27
15	Hamilton	36	8	8	20	37	72	24
16	Berwick	36	7	9	20	42	70	23
17	Brechin	36	8	6	22	40	78	22
18	Alloa	36	7	7	22	45	79	21
19	Stenhousemuir	36	6	6	24	55	125	18

FA CUP 1968–69

FOURTH ROUND
Newcastle United v Manchester City	0-0, 0-2
Blackburn Rovers v Portsmouth	4-0
Tottenham Hotspur v Wolverhampton Wanderers	2-1
Southampton v Aston Villa	2-2, 1-2
Sheffield Wednesday v Birmingham City	2-2, 1-2
Manchester United v Watford	1-1, 2-0
Bolton Wanderers v Bristol Rovers	1-2
Coventry City v Everton	0-2
West Bromwich Albion v Fulham	2-1
Arsenal v Charlton Athletic	2-0
Preston North End v Chelsea	0-0, 1-2
Stoke City v Halifax Town	1-1, 3-0
Mansfield Town v Southend United	2-1
Huddersfield v West Ham United	0-2
Liverpool v Burnley	2-1
Millwall v Leicester City	0-1

FIFTH ROUND
Manchester City v Blackburn Rovers	4-1
Tottenham Hotspur v Aston Villa	3-2
Birmingham City v Manchester United	2-2, 2-6
Bristol Rovers v Everton	0-1
West Bromwich Albion v Arsenal	1-0
Chelsea v Stoke City	3-2
Mansfield Town v West Ham United	3-0
Liverpool v Leicester City	0-0, 0-1

SIXTH ROUND
Manchester City v Tottenham Hotspur	1-0
Manchester United v Everton	0-1
Chelsea v West Bromwich Albion	1-2
Mansfield Town v Leicester City	0-1

SEMI-FINAL
Manchester City v Everton	1-0
West Bromwich Albion v Leicester City	0-1

FINAL
Leicester City v Manchester City	0-1

SCOTTISH FA CUP 1968–69

FIRST ROUND
Rangers v Hibernian	1-0
Dundee v Hearts	1-2
Dumbarton v St Mirren	0-1
Stenhousemuir v Airdrieonians	0-3
Aberdeen v Berwick Rangers	3-0
Raith Rovers v Dunfermline Athletic	0-2
Montrose v Cowdenbeath	1-0
Kilmarnock v Glasgow University	6-0
Dundee United v Queen's Park	2-1
Ayr United v Queen of the South	1-0
Stranraer v East Fife	3-1
Falkirk v Morton	1-2
East Stirlingshire v Stirling Albion	2-0
St Johnstone v Arbroath	3-2
Motherwell v Clyde	1-1, 1-2
Partick Thistle v Celtic	3-3, 1-8

SECOND ROUND
Rangers v Hearts	2-0
St Mirren v Airdrieonians	1-1, 1-3
Aberdeen v Dunfermline Athletic	2-2, 2-0
Montrose v Kilmarnock	1-1, 1-4
Dundee United v Ayr United	6-2
Stranraer v Morton	1-3
East Stirlingshire v St Johnstone	1-1, 0-3
Clyde v Celtic	0-0, 0-3

THIRD ROUND
Rangers v Airdrieonians	1-0
Aberdeen v Kilmarnock	0-0, 3-0
Dundee United v Morton	2-3
Celtic v St Johnstone	3-2

SEMI-FINAL
Rangers v Aberdeen	6-1
Morton v Celtic	1-4

FINAL
Celtic v Rangers	4-0

On 6 May 1969 only 7,843 people were at Hampden Park to see Northern Ireland play Scotland, then the smallest ever crowd at a full home international. There were on average more people at each of Fourth Division Lincoln City's games during the same season.

On 24 August 1968 the main stand at Nottingham Forest's ground caught fire during the game with Leeds and was completely destroyed. Police evacuated the 34,000 crowd and Forest played out the year on neighbouring Notts County's pitch, three hundred yards away.

League Tables 1969-70

FIRST DIVISION

		P	W	D	L	F	A	Pts
1	Everton	42	29	8	5	72	34	66
2	Leeds	42	21	15	6	84	49	57
3	Chelsea	42	21	13	8	70	50	55
4	Derby	42	22	9	11	64	37	53
5	Liverpool	42	20	11	11	65	42	51
6	Coventry	42	19	11	12	58	48	49
7	Newcastle	42	17	13	12	57	35	47
8	Man United	42	14	17	11	66	61	45
9	Stoke	42	15	15	12	56	52	45
10	Man City	42	16	11	15	55	48	43
11	Tottenham	42	17	9	16	54	55	43
12	Arsenal	42	12	18	12	51	49	42
13	Wolves	42	12	16	14	55	57	40
14	Burnley	42	12	15	15	56	61	39
15	Nottm Forest	42	10	18	14	50	71	38
16	WBA	42	14	9	19	58	66	37
17	West Ham	42	12	12	18	51	60	36
18	Ipswich	42	10	11	21	40	63	31
19	Southampton	42	6	17	19	46	67	29
20	Crystal Palace	42	6	15	21	34	68	27
21	Sunderland	42	6	14	22	30	68	26
22	Sheff Wed	42	8	9	25	40	71	25

SECOND DIVISION

		P	W	D	L	F	A	Pts
1	Huddersfield	42	24	12	6	68	37	60
2	Blackpool	42	20	13	9	56	45	53
3	Leicester	42	19	13	10	64	50	51
4	Middlesbrough	42	20	10	12	55	45	50
5	Swindon	42	17	16	9	57	47	50
6	Sheff United	42	22	5	15	73	38	49
7	Cardiff	42	18	13	11	61	41	49
8	Blackburn	42	20	7	15	54	50	47
9	QPR	42	17	11	14	66	57	45
10	Millwall	42	15	14	13	56	56	44
11	Norwich	42	16	11	15	49	46	43
12	Carlisle	42	14	13	15	58	56	41
13	Hull	42	15	11	16	72	70	41
14	Bristol City	42	13	13	16	54	50	39
15	Oxford	42	12	15	15	35	42	39
16	Bolton	42	12	12	18	54	61	36
17	Portsmouth	42	13	9	20	66	80	35
18	Birmingham	42	11	11	20	51	78	33
19	Watford	42	9	13	20	44	57	31
20	Charlton	42	7	17	18	35	76	31
21	Aston Villa	42	8	13	21	36	62	29
22	Preston	42	8	12	22	43	63	28

THIRD DIVISION

		P	W	D	L	F	A	Pts
1	Orient	46	25	12	9	67	36	62
2	Luton	46	23	14	9	77	43	60
3	Bristol Rovers	46	20	16	10	80	59	56
4	Fulham	46	20	15	11	81	55	55
5	Brighton	46	23	9	14	57	43	55
6	Mansfield	46	21	11	14	70	49	53
7	Barnsley	46	19	15	12	68	59	53
8	Reading	46	21	11	14	87	77	53
9	Rochdale	46	18	10	18	69	60	46
10	Bradford City	46	17	12	17	57	50	46
11	Doncaster	46	17	12	17	52	54	46
12	Walsall	46	17	12	17	54	67	46
13	Torquay	46	14	17	15	62	59	45
14	Rotherham	46	15	14	17	62	54	44
15	Shrewsbury	46	13	18	15	62	63	44
16	Tranmere	46	14	16	16	56	72	44
17	Plymouth	46	16	11	19	56	64	43
18	Halifax	46	14	15	17	47	63	43
19	Bury	46	15	11	20	75	80	41
20	Gillingham	46	13	13	20	52	64	39
21	Bournemouth	46	12	15	19	48	71	39
22	Southport	46	14	10	22	48	66	38
23	Barrow	46	8	14	24	46	81	30
24	Stockport	46	6	11	29	27	71	23

FOURTH DIVISION

		P	W	D	L	F	A	Pts
1	Chesterfield	46	27	10	9	77	32	64
2	Wrexham	46	26	9	11	84	49	61
3	Swansea	46	21	18	7	66	45	60
4	Port Vale	46	20	19	7	61	33	59
5	Brentford	46	20	16	10	58	39	56
6	Aldershot	46	20	13	13	78	65	53
7	Notts County	46	22	8	16	73	62	52
8	Lincoln	46	17	16	13	66	52	50
9	Peterborough	46	17	14	15	77	69	48
10	Colchester	46	17	14	15	64	63	48
11	Chester	46	21	6	19	58	66	48
12	Scunthorpe	46	18	10	18	67	65	46
13	York	46	16	14	16	55	62	46
14	Northampton	46	16	12	18	64	55	44
15	Crewe	46	16	12	18	51	51	44
16	Grimsby	46	14	15	17	54	58	43
17	Southend	46	15	10	21	59	85	40
18	Exeter	46	14	11	21	57	59	39
19	Oldham	46	13	13	20	60	65	39
20	Workington	46	12	14	20	46	64	38
21	Newport	46	13	11	22	53	74	37
22	Darlington	46	13	10	23	53	73	36
23	Hartlepool	46	10	10	26	42	82	30
24	Bradford P A	46	6	11	29	41	96	23

SCOTTISH FIRST DIVISION

		P	W	D	L	F	A	Pts
1	Celtic	34	27	3	4	96	33	57
2	Rangers	34	19	7	8	67	40	45
3	Hibernian	34	19	6	9	65	40	44
4	Hearts	34	13	12	9	50	36	38
5	Dundee United	34	16	6	12	62	64	38
6	Dundee	34	15	6	13	49	44	36
7	Kilmarnock	34	13	10	11	62	57	36
8	Aberdeen	34	14	7	13	55	45	35
9	Dunfermline	34	15	5	14	45	45	35
10	Morton	34	13	9	12	52	52	35
11	Motherwell	34	11	10	13	49	51	32
12	Airdrieonians	34	12	8	14	59	64	32
13	St Johnstone	34	11	9	14	50	62	31
14	Ayr	34	12	6	16	37	52	30
15	St Mirren	34	8	9	17	39	54	25
16	Clyde	34	9	7	18	34	56	25
17	Raith	34	5	11	18	32	67	21
18	Partick Thistle	34	5	7	22	41	82	17

SCOTTISH SECOND DIVISION

		P	W	D	L	F	A	Pts
1	Falkirk	36	25	6	5	94	34	56
2	Cowdenbeath	36	24	7	5	81	35	55
3	Queen of the S	36	22	6	8	72	49	50
4	Stirling	36	18	10	8	70	40	46
5	Arbroath	36	20	4	12	76	39	44
6	Alloa	36	19	5	12	62	41	43
7	Dumbarton	36	17	6	13	55	46	40
8	Montrose	36	15	7	14	57	55	37
9	Berwick	36	15	5	16	67	55	35
10	East Fife	36	15	4	17	59	63	34
11	Albion	36	14	5	17	53	64	33
12	E Stirlingshire	36	14	5	17	58	75	33
13	Clydebank	36	10	10	16	47	65	30
14	Brechin	36	11	6	19	47	74	28
15	Queen's Park	36	10	6	20	38	62	26
16	Stenhousemuir	36	10	6	20	47	89	26
17	Stranraer	36	9	7	20	56	75	25
18	Forfar	36	11	1	24	55	83	23
19	Hamilton	36	8	4	24	42	92	20

FA CUP 1969-70

FOURTH ROUND

Chelsea v Burnley	2-2, 3-1
Tottenham Hotspur v Crystal Palace	0-0, 0-1
Charlton Athletic v Queen's Park Rangers	2-3
Derby County v Sheffield United	3-0
Watford v Stoke City	1-0
Gillingham v Peterborough United	5-1
Liverpool v Wrexham	3-1
Southampton v Leicester City	1-1, 2-4
Tranmere Rovers v Northampton Town	0-0, 1-2
Manchester United v Manchester City	3-0
Carlisle United v Aldershot	2-2, 4-1
Middlesbrough v York City	4-1
Swindon Town v Chester	4-2
Sheffield Wednesday v Scunthorpe United	1-2
Blackpool v Mansfield Town	0-2
Sutton United v Leeds United	0-6

FIFTH ROUND

Chelsea v Crystal Palace	4-1
Queen's Park Rangers v Derby County	1-0
Watford v Gillingham	2-1
Liverpool v Leicester City	0-0, 2-0
Northampton Town v Manchester United	2-8
Carlisle United v Middlesbrough	1-2
Swindon Town v Scunthorpe United	3-1
Mansfield Town v Leeds United	0-2

SIXTH ROUND

Queen's Park Rangers v Chelsea	2-4
Watford v Liverpool	1-0
Manchester United v Middlesbrough	1-1, 2-1
Swindon Town v Leeds United	0-2

SEMI-FINAL

Chelsea v Watford	5-1
Manchester United v Leeds United	0-0, 0-0, 0-1

THIRD PLACE PLAY-OFF

Manchester United v Watford	2-0

FINAL

Chelsea v Leeds United	2-2, 2-1

SCOTTISH FA CUP 1969-70

FIRST ROUND

Celtic v Dunfermline Athletic	2-1
Dundee United v Ayr United	1-0
Dumbarton v Forfar Athletic	1-2
Rangers v Hibernian	3-1
East Fife v Raith Rovers	3-0
Morton v Queen of the South	2-0
Albion Rovers v Dundee	1-2
Airdrieonians v Hamilton Academicals	5-0
Motherwell v St Johnstone	2-1
Stranraer v Inverness Caledonian	2-5
Kilmarnock v Partick Thistle	3-0
Montrose v Heart of Midlothian	1-1, 0-1
Falkirk v Tarff Rovers	3-0
St Mirren v Stirling Albion	2-0
Arbroath v Clydebank	1-2
Clyde v Aberdeen	0-4

SECOND ROUND

Celtic v Dundee United	4-0
Forfar Athletic v Rangers	0-7
East Fife v Morton	1-0
Dundee v Airdrieonians	3-0
Motherwell v Inverness Caledonian	3-1
Kilmarnock v Heart of Midlothian	2-0
Falkirk v St Mirren	2-1
Aberdeen v Clydebank	2-1

THIRD ROUND

Celtic v Rangers	3-1
East Fife v Dundee	0-1
Motherwell v Kilmarnock	0-1
Falkirk v Aberdeen	0-1

SEMI-FINAL

Celtic v Dundee	2-1
Kilmarnock v Aberdeen	0-1

FINAL

Celtic v Aberdeen	1-3

Leeds go marching on

Leeds United established a new First Division record for the number of consecutive League games played without a defeat. They completed a run of 34 home and away matches without losing a single game. Their unbeaten run finally ended on 30 August 1969 when they lost 3-2 to Everton, the club that was to take the League title from them.

Six of the Best

George Best scored a record number of goals in a Cup tie, notching six for Manchester United in their 8-2 win over Fourth Division Northampton Town in the fifth round of the FA Cup. Best's team-mate Denis Law, when with Manchester City, once scored six goals in a fourth round tie at Luton, but the match was abandoned and Luton won the replay.

League Tables 1970-71

FIRST DIVISION

		P	W	D	L	F	A	Pts
1	Arsenal	42	29	7	6	71	29	65
2	Leeds	42	27	10	5	72	30	64
3	Tottenham	42	19	14	9	54	33	52
4	Wolves	42	22	8	12	64	54	52
5	Liverpool	42	17	17	8	42	24	51
6	Chelsea	42	18	15	9	52	42	51
7	Southampton	42	17	12	13	56	44	46
8	Man United	42	16	11	15	65	66	43
9	Derby	42	16	10	16	56	54	42
10	Coventry	42	16	10	16	37	38	42
11	Man City	42	12	17	13	47	42	41
12	Newcastle	42	14	13	15	44	46	41
13	Stoke	42	12	13	17	44	48	37
14	Everton	42	12	13	17	54	60	37
15	Huddersfield	42	11	14	17	40	49	36
16	Nottm Forest	42	14	8	20	42	61	36
17	WBA	42	10	15	17	58	75	35
18	Crystal Palace	42	12	11	19	39	57	35
19	Ipswich	42	12	10	20	42	48	34
20	West Ham	42	10	14	18	47	60	34
21	Burnley	42	7	13	22	29	63	27
22	Blackpool	42	4	15	23	34	66	23

SECOND DIVISION

		P	W	D	L	F	A	Pts
1	Leicester	42	23	13	6	57	30	59
2	Sheff United	42	21	14	7	73	39	56
3	Cardiff	42	20	13	9	64	41	53
4	Carlisle	42	20	13	9	65	43	53
5	Hull	42	19	13	10	54	41	51
6	Luton	42	18	13	11	62	43	49
7	Middlesbrough	42	17	14	11	60	43	48
8	Millwall	42	19	9	14	59	42	47
9	Birmingham	42	17	12	13	58	48	46
10	Norwich	42	15	14	13	54	52	44
11	QPR	42	16	11	15	58	53	43
12	Swindon	42	15	12	15	61	51	42
13	Sunderland	42	15	12	15	52	54	42
14	Oxford	42	14	14	14	41	48	42
15	Sheff Wed	42	12	12	18	51	69	36
16	Portsmouth	42	10	14	18	46	61	34
17	Orient	42	9	16	17	29	51	34
18	Watford	42	10	13	19	38	60	33
19	Bristol City	42	10	11	21	46	64	31
20	Charlton	42	8	14	20	41	65	30
21	Blackburn	42	6	15	21	37	69	27
22	Bolton	42	7	10	25	35	74	24

THIRD DIVISION

		P	W	D	L	F	A	Pts
1	Preston	46	22	17	7	63	39	61
2	Fulham	46	24	12	10	68	41	60
3	Halifax	46	22	12	12	74	55	56
4	Aston Villa	46	19	15	12	54	46	53
5	Chesterfield	46	17	17	12	66	38	51
6	Bristol Rovers	46	19	13	14	69	50	51
7	Mansfield	46	18	15	13	64	62	51
8	Rotherham	46	17	16	13	64	60	50
9	Wrexham	46	18	13	15	72	65	49
10	Torquay	46	19	11	16	54	57	49
11	Swansea	46	15	16	15	59	56	46
12	Barnsley	46	17	11	18	49	52	45
13	Shrewsbury	46	16	13	17	58	62	45
14	Brighton	46	14	16	16	50	47	44
15	Plymouth	46	12	19	15	63	63	43
16	Rochdale	46	14	15	17	61	68	43
17	Port Vale	46	15	12	19	52	59	42
18	Tranmere	46	10	22	14	45	55	42
19	Bradford City	46	13	14	19	49	62	40
20	Walsall	46	14	11	21	51	57	39
21	Reading	46	14	11	21	48	85	39
22	Bury	46	12	13	21	52	60	37
23	Doncaster	46	13	9	24	45	66	35
24	Gillingham	46	10	13	23	42	67	33

FOURTH DIVISION

		P	W	D	L	F	A	Pts
1	Notts County	46	30	9	7	89	36	69
2	Bournemouth	46	24	12	10	81	46	60
3	Oldham	46	24	11	11	88	63	59
4	York	46	23	10	13	78	54	56
5	Chester	46	24	7	15	69	55	55
6	Colchester	46	21	12	13	70	54	54
7	Northampton	46	19	13	14	63	59	51
8	Southport	46	21	6	19	63	57	48
9	Exeter	46	17	14	15	67	68	48
10	Workington	46	18	12	16	48	49	48
11	Stockport	46	16	14	16	49	65	46
12	Darlington	46	17	11	18	58	57	45
13	Aldershot	46	14	17	15	66	71	45
14	Brentford	46	18	8	20	66	62	44
15	Crewe	46	18	8	20	75	76	44
16	Peterborough	46	18	7	21	70	71	43
17	Scunthorpe	46	15	13	18	56	61	43
18	Southend	46	14	15	17	53	66	43
19	Grimsby	46	18	7	21	57	71	43
20	Cambridge	46	15	13	18	51	66	43
21	Lincoln	46	13	13	20	70	71	39
22	Newport	46	10	8	28	55	85	28
23	Hartlepool	46	8	12	26	34	74	28
24	Barrow	46	7	8	31	51	90	22

SCOTTISH FIRST DIVISION

		P	W	D	L	F	A	Pts
1	Celtic	34	25	6	3	89	23	56
2	Aberdeen	34	24	6	4	68	18	54
3	St Johnstone	34	19	6	9	59	44	44
4	Rangers	34	16	9	9	58	34	41
5	Dundee	34	14	10	10	53	45	38
6	Dundee United	34	14	8	12	53	54	36
7	Falkirk	34	13	9	12	46	53	35
8	Morton	34	13	8	13	44	44	34
9	Motherwell	34	13	8	13	43	47	34
10	Airdrieonians	34	13	8	13	60	65	34
11	Hearts	34	13	7	14	41	40	33
12	Hibernian	34	10	10	14	47	53	30
13	Kilmarnock	34	10	8	16	43	67	28
14	Ayr	34	9	8	17	37	54	26
15	Clyde	34	8	10	16	33	59	26
16	Dunfermline	34	6	11	17	44	56	23
17	St Mirren	34	7	9	18	38	56	23
18	Cowdenbeath	34	7	3	24	33	77	17

SCOTTISH SECOND DIVISION

		P	W	D	L	F	A	Pts
1	Partick Thistle	36	23	10	3	78	26	56
2	East Fife	36	22	7	7	86	44	51
3	Arbroath	36	19	8	9	80	52	46
4	Dumbarton	36	19	6	11	87	46	44
5	Clydebank	36	17	8	11	57	43	42
6	Montrose	36	17	7	12	78	64	41
7	Albion	36	15	9	12	53	52	39
8	Raith	36	15	9	12	62	62	39
9	Stranraer	36	14	8	14	54	52	36
10	Stenhousemuir	36	14	8	14	64	70	36
11	Queen of the S	36	13	9	14	50	56	35
12	Stirling	36	12	8	16	61	61	32
13	Berwick	36	10	10	16	42	60	30
14	Queen's Park	36	13	4	19	51	72	30
15	Forfar	36	9	11	16	63	75	29
16	Alloa	36	9	11	16	56	86	29
17	E Stirlingshire	36	9	9	18	57	86	27
18	Hamilton	36	8	7	21	50	79	23
19	Brechin	36	6	7	23	30	73	19

The unnecessary goalkeeper

One of the strangest events in all football annals happened on 12 May 1971. In the course of the England–Malta game the ball did not cross the England goal-line once and the England goalkeeper, Gordon Banks, did not receive the ball direct from a Maltese player at any time during the game.

A pools punter's best friend

In the 1970-71 season, Tranmere Rovers of the Third Division broke Plymouth Argyle's 50-year-old record by drawing 22 of their 46 League matches, the most ever tied in a single season. In actual fact, Plymouth's drawn percentage was higher as they played 42 and tied 21 games in the 1920-21 season.

FA CUP 1970–71

FOURTH ROUND

Liverpool v Swansea City	3-0
York City v Southampton	3-3, 2-3
Carlisle United v Tottenham Hotspur	2-3
Nottingham Forest v Orient	1-1, 1-0
Everton v Middlesbrough	3-0
Derby County v Wolverhampton Wanderers	2-1
Rochdale v Colchester United	3-3, 0-5
Leeds United v Swindon Town	4-0
Hull City v Blackpool	2-0
Cardiff City v Brentford	0-2
Stoke City v Huddersfield Town	3-3, 0-0, 1-0
West Bromwich Albion v Ipswich Town	1-1, 0-3
Leicester City v Torquay United	3-0
Oxford United v Watford	1-1, 2-1
Chelsea v Manchester City	0-3
Portsmouth v Arsenal	1-1, 2-3

FIFTH ROUND

Liverpool v Southampton	1-0
Tottenham Hotspur v Nottingham Forest	2-1
Everton v Derby County	1-0
Colchester United v Leeds United	3-2
Hull City v Brentford	2-1
Stoke City v Ipswich Town	0-0, 1-0
Leicester City v Oxford United	1-1, 3-1
Manchester City v Arsenal	1-2

SIXTH ROUND

Liverpool v Tottenham Hotspur	0-0, 1-0
Everton v Colchester United	5-0
Hull City v Stoke City	2-3
Leicester City v Arsenal	0-0, 0-1

SEMI-FINAL

Liverpool v Everton	2-1
Stoke City v Arsenal	2-2, 0-2

THIRD PLACE PLAY-OFF

Stoke City v Everton	3-2

FINAL

Liverpool v Arsenal	1-2

SCOTTISH FA CUP 1970–71

THIRD ROUND

Celtic v Queen of the South	5-1
Hibernian v Forfar Athletic	8-1
East Fife v St Mirren	1-1, 1-1, 1-3
St Johnstone v Raith Rovers	2-2, 3-4
Clyde v Brechin City	2-0
Airdrieonians v Alloa Athletic	1-1, 2-0
Rangers v Falkirk	3-0
Aberdeen v Elgin City	5-0
Dundee v Partick Thistle	1-0
Clachnacuddin v Cowdenbeath	0-3
Clydebank v Dundee United	0-0, 1-5
Stirling Albion v Motherwell	3-1
Dunfermline v Arbroath	3-1
Morton v Ayr United	2-0
Queen's Park v Kilmarnock	0-1
Heart of Midlothian v Stranraer	3-0

FOURTH ROUND

Dundee United v Aberdeen	1-1, 0-2
Raith Rovers v Clyde	1-1, 2-0
Morton v Kilmarnock	1-2
Cowdenbeath v Airdrieonians	0-4
St Mirren v Rangers	1-3
Dundee v Stirling Albion	2-0
Celtic v Dunfermline	1-1, 1-0
Heart of Midlothian v Hibernian	1-2

FIFTH ROUND

Rangers v Aberdeen	1-0
Hibernian v Dundee	1-0
Celtic v Raith Rovers	7-1
Kilmarnock v Airdrieonians	2-3

SEMI-FINAL

Hibernian v Rangers	0-0, 1-2
Celtic v Airdrieonians	3-3, 2-0

FINAL

Rangers v Celtic	1-1, 1-2

FIRST DIVISION

	P	W	D	L	F	A	Pts
1 Derby	42	24	10	8	69	33	58
2 Leeds	42	24	9	9	73	31	57
3 Liverpool	42	24	9	9	64	30	57
4 Man City	42	23	11	8	77	45	57
5 Arsenal	42	22	8	12	58	40	52
6 Tottenham	42	19	13	10	63	42	51
7 Chelsea	42	18	12	12	58	49	48
8 Man United	42	19	10	13	69	61	48
9 Wolves	42	18	11	13	65	57	47
10 Sheff United	42	17	12	13	61	60	46
11 Newcastle	42	15	11	16	49	52	41
12 Leicester	42	13	13	16	41	46	39
13 Ipswich	42	11	16	15	39	53	38
14 West Ham	42	12	12	18	47	51	36
15 Everton	42	9	18	15	37	48	36
16 WBA	42	12	11	19	42	54	35
17 Stoke	42	10	15	17	39	56	35
18 Coventry	42	9	15	18	44	67	33
19 Southampton	42	12	7	23	52	80	31
20 Crystal Palace	42	8	13	21	39	65	29
21 Nottm Forest	42	8	9	25	47	81	25
22 Huddersfield	42	6	13	23	27	59	25

SECOND DIVISION

	P	W	D	L	F	A	Pts
1 Norwich	42	21	15	6	60	36	57
2 Birmingham	42	19	18	5	60	31	56
3 Millwall	42	19	17	6	64	46	55
4 QPR	42	20	14	8	57	28	54
5 Sunderland	42	17	16	9	67	57	50
6 Blackpool	42	20	7	15	70	50	47
7 Burnley	42	20	6	16	70	55	46
8 Bristol City	42	18	10	14	61	49	46
9 Middlesbrough	42	19	8	15	50	48	46
10 Carlisle	42	17	9	16	61	57	43
11 Swindon	42	15	12	15	47	47	42
12 Hull	42	14	10	18	49	53	38
13 Luton	42	10	18	14	43	48	38
14 Sheff Wed	42	13	12	17	51	58	38
15 Oxford	42	12	14	16	43	55	38
16 Portsmouth	42	12	13	17	59	68	37
17 Orient	42	14	9	19	50	61	37
18 Preston	42	12	12	18	52	58	36
19 Cardiff	42	10	14	18	56	69	34
20 Fulham	42	12	10	20	45	68	34
21 Charlton	42	12	9	21	55	77	33
22 Watford	42	5	9	28	24	75	19

THIRD DIVISION

	P	W	D	L	F	A	Pts
1 Aston Villa	46	32	6	8	85	32	70
2 Brighton	46	27	11	8	82	47	65
3 Bournemouth	46	23	16	7	73	37	62
4 Notts County	46	25	12	9	74	44	62
5 Rotherham	46	20	15	11	69	52	55
6 Bristol Rovers	46	21	12	13	75	56	54
7 Bolton	46	17	16	13	51	41	50
8 Plymouth	46	20	10	16	74	64	50
9 Walsall	46	15	18	13	62	57	48
10 Blackburn	46	19	9	18	54	57	47
11 Oldham	46	17	11	18	59	63	45
12 Shrewsbury	46	17	10	19	73	65	44
13 Chesterfield	46	18	8	20	57	57	44
14 Swansea	46	17	10	19	46	59	44
15 Port Vale	46	13	15	18	43	59	41
16 Wrexham	46	16	8	22	59	63	40
17 Halifax	46	13	12	21	48	61	38
18 Rochdale	46	12	13	21	57	83	37
19 York	46	12	12	22	57	66	36
20 Tranmere	46	10	16	20	50	71	36
21 Mansfield	46	8	20	18	41	63	36
22 Barnsley	46	9	18	19	32	64	36
23 Torquay	46	10	12	24	41	69	32
24 Bradford City	46	11	10	25	45	77	32

FOURTH DIVISION

	P	W	D	L	F	A	Pts
1 Grimsby	46	28	7	11	88	56	63
2 Southend	46	24	12	10	81	55	60
3 Brentford	46	24	11	11	76	44	59
4 Scunthorpe	46	22	13	11	56	37	57
5 Lincoln	46	21	14	11	77	59	56
6 Workington	46	16	19	11	50	34	51
7 Southport	46	18	14	14	66	46	50
8 Peterborough	46	17	16	13	82	64	50
9 Bury	46	19	12	15	73	59	50
10 Cambridge	46	17	14	15	62	60	48
11 Colchester	46	19	10	17	70	69	48
12 Doncaster	46	16	14	16	56	63	46
13 Gillingham	46	16	13	17	61	67	45
14 Newport	46	18	8	20	60	72	44
15 Exeter	46	16	11	19	61	68	43
16 Reading	46	17	8	21	56	76	42
17 Aldershot	46	9	22	15	48	54	40
18 Hartlepool	46	17	6	23	58	69	40
19 Darlington	46	14	11	21	64	82	39
20 Chester	46	10	18	18	47	56	38
21 Northampton	46	12	13	21	66	79	37
22 Barrow	46	13	11	22	40	71	37
23 Stockport	46	9	14	23	55	87	32
24 Crewe	46	10	9	27	43	69	29

SCOTTISH FIRST DIVISION

	P	W	D	L	F	A	Pts
1 Celtic	34	28	4	2	96	28	60
2 Aberdeen	34	21	8	5	80	26	50
3 Rangers	34	21	2	11	71	38	44
4 Hibernian	34	19	6	9	62	34	44
5 Dundee	34	14	13	7	59	38	41
6 Hearts	34	13	13	8	53	49	39
7 Partick	34	12	10	12	53	54	34
8 St Johnstone	34	12	8	14	52	58	32
9 Dundee United	34	12	7	15	55	70	31
10 Motherwell	34	11	7	16	49	69	29
11 Kilmarnock	34	11	6	17	49	64	28
12 Ayr	34	9	10	15	40	58	28
13 Morton	34	10	7	17	46	52	27
14 Falkirk	34	10	7	17	44	60	27
15 Airdrieonians	34	7	12	15	44	76	26
16 East Fife	34	5	15	14	34	61	25
17 Clyde	34	7	10	17	33	66	24
18 Dunfermline	34	7	9	18	31	50	23

SCOTTISH SECOND DIVISION

	P	W	D	L	F	A	Pts
1 Dumbarton	36	24	4	8	89	51	52
2 Arbroath	36	22	8	6	71	41	52
3 Stirling	36	21	8	7	75	37	50
4 St Mirren	36	24	2	10	84	47	50
5 Cowdenbeath	36	19	10	7	69	28	48
6 Stranraer	36	18	8	10	70	62	44
7 Queen of the S	36	17	9	10	56	38	43
8 E Stirlingshire	36	17	7	12	60	58	41
9 Clydebank	36	14	11	11	60	52	39
10 Montrose	36	15	6	15	73	54	36
11 Raith	36	13	8	15	56	56	34
12 Queen's Park	36	12	9	15	47	61	33
13 Berwick	36	14	4	18	53	50	32
14 Stenhousemuir	36	10	8	18	41	58	28
15 Brechin	36	8	7	21	41	79	23
16 Alloa	36	9	4	23	41	75	22
17 Forfar	36	6	9	21	32	84	21
18 Albion	36	7	6	23	36	61	20
19 Hamilton	36	4	8	24	31	93	16

FA CUP 1971-72

FOURTH ROUND

Liverpool v Leeds United	0-0, 0-2
Cardiff City v Sunderland	1-1, 1-1, 3-1
Everton v Walsall	2-1
Tottenham Hotspur v Rotherham United	2-0
Birmingham City v Ipswich Town	1-0
Portsmouth v Swansea City	2-0
Huddersfield Town v Fulham	3-0
Hereford United v West Ham United	0-0, 1-3
Preston North End v Manchester United	0-2
Millwall v Middlesbrough	2-2, 1-2
Tranmere Rovers v Stoke City	2-2, 0-2
Coventry City v Hull City	0-1
Leicester City v Orient	0-2
Chelsea v Bolton Wanderers	3-0
Derby County v Notts County	6-0
Reading v Arsenal	1-2

FIFTH ROUND

Cardiff City v Leeds United	0-2
Everton v Tottenham Hotspur	0-2
Birmingham City v Portsmouth	3-1
Huddersfield Town v West Ham United	4-2
Manchester United v Middlesbrough	0-0, 3-0
Stoke City v Hull City	4-1
Orient v Chelsea	3-2
Derby County v Arsenal	2-2, 0-0, 0-1

SIXTH ROUND

Leeds United v Tottenham Hotspur	2-1
Birmingham City v Huddersfield Town	3-1
Manchester United v Stoke City	1-1, 1-2
Orient v Arsenal	0-1

SEMI-FINAL

Leeds United v Birmingham City	3-0
Arsenal v Stoke City	1-1, 2-1

FINAL

Leeds United v Arsenal	1-0

SCOTTISH FA CUP 1971-72

THIRD ROUND

Celtic v Albion Rovers	5-0
Dundee v Queen of the South	3-0
Heart of Midlothian v St Johnstone	2-0
Clydebank v East Fife	1-1, 1-0
Dumbarton v Hamilton Academicals	3-1
Raith Rovers v Dunfermline Athletic	2-0
Elgin City v Inverness Caledonian	3-1
Kilmarnock v Alloa Athletic	5-1
Clyde v Ayr United	0-1
Motherwell v Montrose	2-0
Forfar Athletic v St Mirren	0-1
Falkirk v Rangers	2-2, 0-2
Dundee United v Aberdeen	0-4
Morton v Cowdenbeath	1-0
Arbroath v Airdrieonians	1-3
Partick Thistle v Hibernian	0-2

FOURTH ROUND

Celtic v Dundee	4-0
Heart of Midlothian v Clydebank	4-0
Dumbarton v Raith Rovers	0-3
Elgin City v Kilmarnock	1-4
Ayr United v Motherwell	0-0, 1-2
St Mirren v Rangers	1-4
Aberdeen v Morton	1-0
Hibernian v Airdrieonians	2-0

FIFTH ROUND

Celtic v Heart of Midlothian	1-1, 1-0
Raith Rovers v Kilmarnock	1-3
Motherwell v Rangers	2-2, 2-4
Hibernian v Aberdeen	2-0

SEMI-FINAL

Celtic v Kilmarnock	3-1
Rangers v Hibernian	1-1, 0-2

FINAL

Celtic v Hibernian	6-1

Mansfield Town did not score a League goal at home until the 23rd minute of their game against Plymouth Argyle on 18 December 1971. This unrewarded period of 833 minutes of Third Division football at Field Mill is thought to constitute a record-breaking start to any Football League club's season. Mansfield still lost the game 3-2.

Aldershot drew 22 of their Fourth Division fixtures to equal Tranmere Rovers' record of the 1970-71 season. Both Tranmere and Aldershot, however, played 46 games that season and their achievement does not, therefore, compare in percentage terms with Plymouth's feat of 1920-21. That year Argyle drew 21 of their 42 League games.

League Tables 1972-73

FIRST DIVISION

		P	W	D	L	F	A	Pts
1	Liverpool	42	25	10	6	72	42	60
2	Arsenal	42	23	11	8	57	43	57
3	Leeds	42	21	11	10	77	45	53
4	Ipswich	42	17	14	11	55	45	48
5	Wolves	42	18	11	13	66	54	47
6	West Ham	42	17	12	13	67	53	46
7	Derby	42	19	8	15	56	54	46
8	Tottenham	42	16	13	13	58	48	45
9	Newcastle	42	16	13	13	60	51	45
10	Birmingham	42	15	12	15	53	54	42
11	Man City	42	15	11	16	57	60	41
12	Chelsea	42	13	14	15	49	51	40
13	Southampton	42	11	18	13	47	52	40
14	Sheff United	42	15	10	17	51	59	40
15	Stoke	42	14	10	18	61	56	38
16	Leicester	42	10	17	15	40	46	37
17	Everton	42	13	11	18	41	49	37
18	Man United	42	12	13	17	44	60	37
19	Coventry	42	13	9	20	40	55	35
20	Norwich	42	11	10	21	36	63	32
21	Crystal Palace	42	9	12	21	41	58	30
22	WBA	42	9	10	23	38	62	28

SECOND DIVISION

		P	W	D	L	F	A	Pts
1	Burnley	42	24	14	4	72	35	62
2	QPR	42	24	13	5	81	37	61
3	Aston Villa	42	18	14	10	51	47	50
4	Middlesbrough	42	17	13	12	46	43	47
5	Bristol City	42	17	12	13	63	51	46
6	Sunderland	42	17	12	13	59	49	46
7	Blackpool	42	18	10	14	56	51	46
8	Oxford	42	19	7	16	52	43	45
9	Fulham	42	16	12	14	58	49	44
10	Sheff Wed	42	17	10	15	59	55	44
11	Millwall	42	16	10	16	55	47	42
12	Luton	42	15	11	16	44	53	41
13	Hull	42	14	12	16	64	59	40
14	Nottm Forest	42	14	12	16	47	52	40
15	Orient	42	12	12	18	49	53	36
16	Swindon	42	10	16	16	46	60	36
17	Portsmouth	42	12	11	19	42	59	35
18	Carlisle	42	11	12	19	50	52	34
19	Preston	42	11	12	19	37	64	34
20	Cardiff	42	11	11	20	43	58	33
21	Huddersfield	42	8	17	17	36	56	33
22	Brighton	42	8	13	21	46	83	29

FA CUP 1972-73

FOURTH ROUND

Arsenal v Bradford City	2-0
Bolton Wanderers v Cardiff City	2-2, 1-1, 1-0
Carlisle United v Sheffield United	2-1
Chelsea v Ipswich Town	2-0
Coventry City v Grimsby Town	1-0
Derby County v Tottenham Hotspur	1-1, 5-3
Everton v Millwall	0-2
Hull City v West Ham United	1-0
Leeds United v Plymouth Argyle	2-1
Liverpool v Manchester City	0-0, 0-2
Newcastle United v Luton Town	0-2
Oxford United v Queen's Park Rangers	0-2
Sheffield Wednesday v Crystal Palace	1-1, 1-1, 3-2
Sunderland v Reading	1-1, 3-1
West Bromwich Albion v Swindon Town	2-0
Wolverhampton Wanderers v Bristol City	1-0

FIFTH ROUND

Bolton Wanderers v Luton Town	0-1
Carlisle United v Arsenal	1-2
Coventry City v Hull City	3-0
Derby County v Queen's Park Rangers	4-2
Leeds United v West Bromwich Albion	2-0
Manchester City v Sunderland	2-2, 1-3
Sheffield Wednesday v Chelsea	1-2
Wolverhampton Wanderers v Millwall	1-0

SIXTH ROUND

Chelsea v Arsenal	2-2, 1-2
Derby County v Leeds United	0-1
Sunderland v Luton Town	2-0
Wolverhampton Wanderers v Coventry City	2-0

SEMI-FINAL

Arsenal v Sunderland	1-2
Leeds United v Wolverhampton Wanderers	1-0

FINAL

Leeds United v Sunderland	0-1

THIRD DIVISION

		P	W	D	L	F	A	Pts
1	Bolton	46	25	11	10	73	39	61
2	Notts County	46	23	11	12	67	47	57
3	Blackburn	46	20	15	11	57	47	55
4	Oldham	46	19	16	11	72	54	54
5	Bristol Rovers	46	20	13	13	77	56	53
6	Port Vale	46	21	11	14	56	69	53
7	Bournemouth	46	17	16	13	66	44	50
8	Plymouth	46	20	10	16	74	66	50
9	Grimsby	46	20	8	18	67	61	48
10	Tranmere	46	15	16	15	56	52	46
11	Charlton	46	17	11	18	69	67	45
12	Wrexham	46	14	17	15	55	54	45
13	Rochdale	46	14	17	15	48	54	45
14	Southend	46	17	10	19	61	54	44
15	Shrewsbury	46	15	14	17	46	54	44
16	Chesterfield	46	17	9	20	57	61	43
17	Walsall	46	18	7	21	56	66	43
18	York	46	13	15	18	42	46	41
19	Watford	46	12	17	17	43	48	41
20	Halifax	46	13	15	18	43	53	41
21	Rotherham	46	17	7	22	51	65	41
22	Brentford	46	15	7	24	51	69	37
23	Swansea	46	14	9	23	51	73	37
24	Scunthorpe	46	10	10	26	33	72	30

FOURTH DIVISION

		P	W	D	L	F	A	Pts
1	Southport	46	36	10	10	71	48	62
2	Hereford	46	23	12	11	56	38	58
3	Cambridge	46	20	17	9	67	57	57
4	Aldershot	46	22	12	12	60	38	56
5	Newport	46	22	12	12	64	44	56
6	Mansfield	46	20	14	12	78	51	54
7	Reading	46	17	18	11	51	38	52
8	Exeter	46	18	14	14	57	51	50
9	Gillingham	46	19	11	16	63	58	49
10	Lincoln	46	16	16	14	64	57	48
11	Stockport	46	18	12	16	53	53	48
12	Bury	46	14	18	14	58	51	46
13	Workington	46	17	12	17	59	61	46
14	Barnsley	46	14	16	16	58	60	44
15	Chester	46	14	15	17	61	52	43
16	Bradford	46	16	11	19	61	65	43
17	Doncaster	46	15	12	19	49	58	42
18	Torquay	46	12	17	17	44	47	41
19	Peterborough	46	14	13	19	71	76	41
20	Hartlepool	46	12	17	17	34	49	41
21	Crewe	46	9	18	19	38	61	36
22	Colchester	46	10	11	25	48	76	31
23	Northampton	46	10	11	25	40	73	31
24	Darlington	46	7	15	24	42	85	29

SCOTTISH FA CUP 1972-73

THIRD ROUND

Ayr United v Inverness Thistle	3-0
Berwick Rovers v Falkirk	1-3
Brechin City v Aberdeen	2-4
Celtic v East Fife	4-1
Clyde v Montrose	1-1, 2-4
Dumbarton v Cowdenbeath	4-1
Dunfermline Athletic v Dundee	0-3
Elgin City v Hamilton Academicals	0-1
Heart of Midlothian v Airdrieonians	0-0, 1-3
Hibernian v Morton	2-0
Kilmarnock v Queen of the South	2-1
Motherwell v Raith Rovers	2-1
Rangers v Dundee United	1-0
St Mirren v Partick Thistle	0-1
Stirling Albion v Arbroath	3-3, 1-0
Stranraer v St Johnstone	1-1, 2-1

FOURTH ROUND

Ayr United v Stirling Albion	2-1
Dumbarton v Partick Thistle	2-2, 1-3
Kilmarnock v Airdrieonians	0-1
Montrose v Hamilton Academicals	2-2, 1-0
Motherwell v Celtic	0-4
Rangers v Hibernian	1-1, 2-1
Stranraer v Dundee	2-9
Aberdeen v Falkirk	3-1

FIFTH ROUND

Celtic v Aberdeen	0-0, 1-0
Montrose v Dundee	1-4
Partick Thistle v Ayr United	1-5
Rangers v Airdrieonians	2-0

SEMI-FINAL

Ayr United v Rangers	0-2
Celtic v Dundee	0-0, 3-0

FINAL

Celtic v Rangers	2-3

SCOTTISH FIRST DIVISION

		P	W	D	L	F	A	Pts
1	Celtic	34	26	5	3	93	28	57
2	Rangers	34	26	4	4	74	30	56
3	Hibernian	34	19	7	8	74	33	45
4	Aberdeen	34	16	11	7	61	34	43
5	Dundee	34	17	9	8	68	43	43
6	Ayr	34	16	8	10	50	51	40
7	Dundee United	34	17	5	12	56	51	39
8	Motherwell	34	11	9	14	38	48	31
9	East Fife	34	11	8	15	46	54	30
10	Hearts	34	12	6	16	39	50	30
11	St Johnstone	34	10	9	15	52	67	29
12	Morton	34	10	8	16	47	53	28
13	Partick	34	10	8	16	40	53	28
14	Falkirk	34	7	12	15	38	56	26
15	Arbroath	34	9	8	17	39	63	26
16	Dumbarton	34	6	11	17	43	72	23
17	Kilmarnock	34	7	8	19	40	71	22
18	Airdrieonians	34	4	8	22	34	75	16

SCOTTISH SECOND DIVISION

		P	W	D	L	F	A	Pts
1	Clyde	36	23	10	3	68	28	56
2	Dunfermline	36	23	6	7	95	32	52
3	Raith	36	19	9	8	73	42	47
4	Stirling	36	19	9	8	70	39	47
5	St Mirren	36	19	7	10	79	50	45
6	Montrose	36	18	8	10	82	58	44
7	Cowdenbeath	36	14	10	12	57	53	38
8	Hamilton	36	16	6	14	67	63	38
9	Berwick	36	16	5	15	45	54	37
10	Stenhousemuir	36	14	8	14	44	41	36
11	Queen of the S	36	13	8	15	45	52	34
12	Alloa	36	11	11	14	45	49	33
13	E Stirlingshire	36	12	8	16	52	69	32
14	Queen's Park	36	9	12	15	44	61	30
15	Stranraer	36	13	4	19	56	78	30
16	Forfar	36	10	9	17	38	66	29
17	Clydebank	36	9	6	21	48	72	21
18	Albion	36	5	8	23	35	83	18
19	Brechin	36	5	4	27	46	99	14

Arsenal's defeat in the semi-final at Hillsborough prevented them from becoming the first club this century to appear in three consecutive Cup Finals. It also prevented the first 'repeat' Cup Final of the twentieth century as Leeds were their 1972 opponents.

Sunderland, by defeating Leeds 1-0 in the 1973 Cup Final became only the fifth Second Division side to win the FA Cup. On the way they defeated three of the previous holders — Manchester City, Arsenal and Leeds for a remarkably memorable win.

League Tables 1973-74

FIRST DIVISION

		P	W	D	L	F	A	Pts
1	Leeds	42	24	14	4	66	31	62
2	Liverpool	42	22	13	7	52	31	57
3	Derby	42	17	14	11	52	42	48
4	Ipswich	42	18	11	13	67	58	47
5	Stoke	42	15	16	11	54	42	46
6	Burnley	42	16	14	12	56	53	46
7	Everton	42	16	12	14	50	48	44
8	QPR	42	13	17	12	56	52	43
9	Leicester	42	13	16	13	51	41	42
10	Arsenal	42	14	14	14	49	51	42
11	Tottenham	42	14	14	14	45	50	42
12	Wolves	42	13	15	14	49	49	41
13	Sheff United	42	14	12	16	44	49	40
14	Man City†	42	14	12	16	39	46	40
15	Newcastle	42	13	12	17	49	48	38
16	Coventry	42	14	10	18	43	54	38
17	Chelsea	42	12	13	17	56	60	37
18	West Ham	42	11	15	16	55	60	37
19	Birmingham	42	12	13	17	52	64	37
20	Southampton*	42	11	14	17	47	68	36
21	Man United*†	42	10	12	20	38	48	32
22	Norwich*	42	7	15	20	37	62	29

* Three clubs relegated.
† Game at Old Trafford abandoned after 86 minutes. Manchester City, who were leading 1-0, awarded both points.

SECOND DIVISION

		P	W	D	L	F	A	Pts
1	Middlesbrough*	42	27	11	4	77	30	65
2	Luton*	42	19	12	11	64	51	50
3	Carlisle*	42	20	9	13	61	48	49
4	Orient	42	15	18	9	55	42	48
5	Blackpool	42	17	13	12	57	40	47
6	Sunderland	42	19	9	14	58	44	47
7	Nottm Forest	42	15	15	12	57	43	45
8	WBA	42	14	16	12	48	45	44
9	Hull	42	13	17	12	46	47	43
10	Notts County	42	15	13	14	55	60	43
11	Bolton	42	15	12	15	44	40	42
12	Millwall	42	14	14	14	51	51	42
13	Fulham	42	16	10	16	39	43	42
14	Aston Villa	42	13	15	14	48	45	41
15	Portsmouth	42	14	12	16	45	62	40
16	Bristol City	42	14	10	18	47	54	38
17	Cardiff	42	10	16	16	49	62	36
18	Oxford	42	10	16	16	35	46	36
19	Sheff Wed	42	12	11	19	51	63	35
20	Crystal Palace‡	42	11	12	19	43	56	34
21	Preston‡§	42	9	14	19	40	62	31
22	Swindon‡	42	7	11	24	36	72	25

* Three clubs promoted.
‡ Three clubs relegated.
§ Preston had one point deducted for fielding an ineligible player.

THIRD DIVISION

		P	W	D	L	F	A	Pts
1	Oldham‡	46	25	12	9	83	47	62
2	Bristol Rovers‡	46	22	17	7	65	33	61
3	York‡	46	21	19	6	67	38	61
4	Wrexham	46	22	12	12	63	43	56
5	Chesterfield	46	21	14	11	55	42	56
6	Grimsby	46	18	15	13	67	50	51
7	Watford	46	19	12	15	64	56	50
8	Aldershot	46	19	11	16	65	52	49
9	Halifax	46	14	21	11	48	51	49
10	Huddersfield	46	17	13	16	56	55	47
11	Bournemouth	46	16	15	15	54	58	47
12	Southend	46	16	14	16	62	62	46
13	Blackburn	46	18	10	18	62	64	46
14	Charlton	46	19	8	19	66	73	46
15	Walsall	46	16	13	17	57	48	45
16	Tranmere	46	15	15	16	50	44	45
17	Plymouth	46	17	10	19	59	54	44
18	Hereford	46	14	15	17	53	57	43
19	Brighton	46	16	11	19	52	58	43
20	Port Vale	46	14	14	18	52	58	42
21	Cambridge*	46	13	9	24	48	81	35
22	Shrewsbury*	46	10	11	25	41	62	31
23	Southport*	46	6	16	24	35	82	28
24	Rochdale*	46	2	17	27	38	94	21

‡ Three clubs promoted.
* Four clubs relegated.

FOURTH DIVISION

		P	W	D	L	F	A	Pts
1	Peterborough*	46	27	11	8	75	38	65
2	Gillingham*	46	25	12	9	90	49	62
3	Colchester*	46	24	12	10	73	36	60
4	Bury*	46	24	11	11	81	49	59
5	Northampton	46	20	13	13	63	48	53
6	Reading	46	16	19	11	58	37	51
7	Chester	46	17	15	14	54	55	49
8	Bradford	46	17	14	15	58	52	48
9	Newport‡	46	16	14	16	56	65	45
10	Exeter†	45	18	8	19	58	55	44
11	Hartlepool	46	16	12	18	48	47	44
12	Lincoln	46	16	12	18	63	67	44
13	Barnsley	46	17	10	19	58	64	44
14	Swansea	46	16	11	19	45	46	43
15	Rotherham	46	15	13	18	56	58	43
16	Torquay	46	13	17	16	52	57	43
17	Mansfield	46	13	17	16	62	69	43
18	Scunthorpe†	45	14	12	19	47	64	42
19	Brentford	46	12	16	18	48	50	40
20	Darlington	46	13	13	20	40	62	39
21	Crewe	46	14	10	22	43	71	38
22	Doncaster	46	12	11	23	47	80	35
23	Workington	46	11	13	22	43	74	35
24	Stockport	46	7	20	19	44	69	34

† Exeter failed to turn up for their fixture at Scunthorpe and the latter were awarded both points.
‡ Newport had one point deducted for fielding an ineligible player.
* Four clubs promoted.

SCOTTISH FIRST DIVISION

		P	W	D	L	F	A	Pts
1	Celtic	34	23	7	4	82	27	53
2	Hibernian	34	20	9	5	75	42	49
3	Rangers	34	21	6	7	67	34	48
4	Aberdeen	34	13	16	5	46	26	42
5	Dundee	34	16	7	11	67	48	39
6	Hearts	34	14	10	10	54	43	38
7	Ayr	34	15	8	11	44	40	38
8	Dundee United	34	15	7	12	55	51	37
9	Motherwell	34	14	7	13	45	40	35
10	Dumbarton	34	11	7	16	43	58	29
11	Partick	34	9	10	15	33	46	28
12	St Johnstone	34	9	10	15	41	60	28
13	Arbroath	34	10	7	17	52	69	27
14	Morton	34	8	10	16	37	49	26
15	Clyde	34	8	9	17	29	65	25
16	Dunfermline	34	8	8	18	43	65	24
17	East Fife	34	9	6	19	26	51	24
18	Falkirk	34	4	14	16	33	58	22

SCOTTISH SECOND DIVISION

		P	W	D	L	F	A	Pts
1	Airdrieonians	36	28	4	4	102	25	60
2	Kilmarnock	36	26	6	4	96	44	58
3	Hamilton	36	24	7	5	68	38	55
4	Queen of the S	36	20	7	9	73	41	47
5	Raith	36	18	9	9	69	48	45
6	Berwick	36	16	13	7	53	35	45
7	Stirling	36	17	6	13	76	50	40
8	Montrose	36	15	7	14	71	64	37
9	Stranraer	36	14	8	14	64	70	36
10	Clydebank	36	13	8	15	47	48	34
11	St Mirren	36	12	10	14	62	66	34
12	Alloa	36	15	4	17	47	58	34
13	Cowdenbeath	36	11	9	16	59	85	31
14	Queen's Park	36	12	4	20	42	64	28
15	Stenhousemuir	36	11	5	20	44	59	27
16	E Stirlingshire	36	9	5	22	47	73	23
17	Albion	36	7	6	23	38	72	20
18	Forfar	36	5	6	25	42	94	16
19	Brechin	36	5	4	27	33	99	14

FA CUP 1973-74

FOURTH ROUND

Arsenal v Aston Villa	1-1, 0-2
Coventry City v Derby County	0-0, 1-0
Everton v West Bromwich Albion	0-0, 0-1
Fulham v Leicester City	1-1, 1-2
Hereford United v Bristol City	0-1
Liverpool v Carlisle United	0-0, 2-0
Luton Town v Bradford City	3-0
Manchester United v Ipswich Town	0-1
Newcastle United v Scunthorpe United	1-1, 3-0
Nottingham Forest v Manchester City	4-1
Oldham Athletic v Burnley	1-4
Peterborough United v Leeds United	1-4
Portsmouth v Orient	0-0, 1-1, 2-0
Queen's Park Rangers v Birmingham City	2-0
Southampton v Bolton Wanderers	3-3, 2-0
Wrexham v Middlesbrough	1-0

FIFTH ROUND

Bristol City v Leeds United	1-1, 1-0
Burnley v Aston Villa	1-0
Coventry City v Queen's Park Rangers	0-0, 2-3
Liverpool v Ipswich Town	2-0
Luton Town v Leicester City	0-4
Nottingham Forest v Portsmouth	1-0
Southampton v Wrexham	0-1
West Bromwich Albion v Newcastle United	0-3

SIXTH ROUND

Bristol City v Liverpool	0-1
Burnley v Wrexham	1-0
Newcastle United v Nottingham Forest	4-3*, 0-0, 1-0
Queen's Park Rangers v Leicester City	0-2

*FA ordered replay because of crowd invasion. Second and third games both played at Goodison Park.

SEMI-FINAL

Burnley v Newcastle United	0-2
Leicester City v Liverpool	0-0, 1-3

FINAL

Liverpool v Newcastle United	3-0

SCOTTISH FA CUP 1973-74

THIRD ROUND

Aberdeen v Dundee	0-2
Arbroath v Dumbarton	1-0
Celtic v Clydebank	6-1
Cowdenbeath v Ayr United	0-5
Dundee United v Airdrieonians	4-1
Falkirk v Dunfermline Athletic	2-2, 0-1
Forfar Athletic v St Johnstone	1-6
Heart of Midlothian v Clyde	3-1
Hibernian v Kilmarnock	5-2
Montrose v Stirling Albion	1-1, 1-3
Motherwell v Brechin City	2-0
Partick Thistle v Ferranti Thistle	6-1
Queen of the South v East Fife	1-0
Raith Rovers v Morton	2-2, 0-0, 0-1
Rangers v Queen's Park	8-0
Stranraer v St Mirren	1-1, 1-1, 3-2

FOURTH ROUND

Arbroath v Motherwell	1-3
Celtic v Stirling Albion	6-1
Dundee United v Morton	1-0
Dunfermline Athletic v Queen of the South	1-0
Heart of Midlothian v Partick Thistle	1-1, 4-1
Rangers v Dundee	0-3
St Johnstone v Hibernian	1-3
Stranraer v Ayr United	1-7

FIFTH ROUND

Celtic v Motherwell	2-2, 1-0
Dunfermline Athletic v Dundee United	1-1, 0-4
Heart of Midlothian v Ayr United	1-1, 2-1
Hibernian v Dundee	3-3, 0-3

SEMI-FINAL

Celtic v Dundee	1-0
Heart of Midlothian v Dundee United	1-1, 2-4

FINAL

Celtic v Dundee United	3-0

EUROPEAN CHAMPION CLUBS' CUP

1955-56 REAL MADRID
Paris 12 June 1956 Attendance 38,329
Real Madrid (2) **4** **Reims** (2) **3**
di Stefano, Rial 2, Leblond, Templin,
Marquitos Hidalgo
Real: Alonso, Atienza, Lesmes, Munoz, Marquitos, Zaggara, Joseito,
Marchal, di Stefano, Rial, Gento
Reims: Jacquet, Zimny, Giraudo, Leblond, Jonquet, Siatka, Hidalgo,
Glovacki, Kopa, Bliard, Templin

1956-57 REAL MADRID
Madrid 30 May 1957 Attendance 125,000
Real Madrid (0) **2** **Fiorentina** (0) **0**
di Stefano, Gento
Real: Alonso, Torres, Lesmes, Munoz, Marquitos, Zaggara, Kopa,
Mateos, di Stefano, Rial, Gento
Fiorentina: Sarti, Magnini, Cervato, Scaramucci, Orzan, Segato,
Julinho, Gratton, Virgili, Montuori, Bizzarri

1957-58 REAL MADRID
Brussels 29 May 1958 Attendance 67,000
Real Madrid (0) (2) **3** **AC Milan** (0) (2) **2**
di Stefano, Rial, Gento Schiaffino, Grillo
Real: Alonso, Atienza, Lesmes, Santisteban, Santamaria, Zaggara,
Kopa, Joseito, di Stefano, Rial, Gento
AC Milan: Soldan, Fontana, Beraldo, Bergamaschi, Maldini, Radice,
Danova, Liedholm, Schiaffino, Grillo, Cucchiaroni

1958-59 REAL MADRID
Stuttgart 3 June 1959 Attendance 80,000
Real Madrid (1) **2** **Reims** (0) **0**
Mateos, di Stefano
Real: Dominguez, Marquitos, Zaggara, Santisteban, Santamaria, Ruiz,
Kopa, Mateos, di Stefano, Rial, Gento
Reims: Colonna, Rodzik, Giraudo, Penverne, Jonquet, Leblond,
Lamartine, Bliard, Fontaine, Piantoni, Vincent

1959-60 REAL MADRID
Glasgow 18 May 1960 Attendance 127,621
Real Madrid (3) **7** **Eintracht Frankfurt** (1) **3**
di Stefano 3, Puskas 4 Kress, Stein 2
Real: Dominguez, Marquitos, Pachin, Vidal, Santamaria, Zaggara,
Canario, Del Sol, di Stefano, Puskas, Gento
Eintracht: Loy, Lutz, Hoefer, Weilbacher, Eigenbrodt, Stinka,
Kress, Lindner, Stein, Pfaff, Meier

1960-61 BENFICA
Berne 31 May 1961 Attendance 33,000
Benfica (2) **3** **Barcelona** (1) **2**
Aguas, Ramallets (og), Coluna Kocsis, Czibor
Benfica: Costa Pereira, Joao, Angelo, Neto, Germano, Cruz,
Augusto, Santana, Aguas, Coluna, Cavem
Barcelona: Ramallets, Foncho, Gracia, Verges, Gensana, Garay,
Kubala, Kocsis, Evaristo, Suarez, Czibor

1961-62 BENFICA
Amsterdam 2 May 1962 Attendance 68,000
Benfica (2) **5** **Real Madrid** (3) **3**
Aguas, Cavem, Coluna, Puskas 3
Eusebio 2 (1 pen)
Benfica: Costa Pereira, Joao, Angelo, Cavem, Germano, Cruz,
Augusto, Eusebio, Aguas, Coluna, Simoes
Real: Araquistain, Casado, Miera, Felo, Santamaria, Pachin,
Tejada, Del Sol, di Stefano, Puskas, Gento

1962-63 AC MILAN
Wembley 22 May 1963 Attendance 45,000
AC Milan (0) **2** **Benfica** (1) **1**
Altafini 2 Eusebio
Milan: Ghezzi, David, Trebbi, Benitez, Maldini, Trapattoni,
Pivatelli, Dino Sani, Altafini, Rivera, Mora
Benfica: Costa Pereira, Cavem, Cruz, Humberto, Raul, Coluna,
Augusto, Santana, Torres, Eusebio, Simoes

1963-64 INTER MILAN
Vienna 27 May 1964 Attendance 72,000
Inter Milan (1) **3** **Real Madrid** (0) **1**
Mazzola 2, Milani Felo
Inter: Sarti, Burgnich, Facchetti, Tagnin, Guarneri, Picchi,
Jair, Mazzola, Milani, Suarez, Corso
Real: Vicente, Isidro, Pachin, Zoco, Santamaria, Muller, Amancio,
Felo, di Stefano, Puskas, Gento

1964-65 INTER MILAN
Milan 27 May 1965 Attendance 80,000
Inter Milan (1) **1** **Benfica** (0) **0**
Jair
Inter: Sarti, Burgnich, Facchetti, Bedin, Guarneri, Picchi,
Jair, Mazzola, Peiro, Suarez, Corso
Benfica: Costa Pereira, Cavem, Cruz, Neto, Germano, Raul,
Augusto, Eusebio, Torres, Coluna, Simoes

1965-66 REAL MADRID
Brussels 11 May 1966 Attendance 38,714
Real Madrid (0) **2** **Partizan Belgrade** (0) **1**
Amancio, Serena Vasovic
Real: Araquistain, Pachin, Sanchis, Pirri, De Felipe, Zoco, Serena,
Amancio, Grosso, Velasquez, Gento
Partizan: Soskic, Jusufi, Migailovic, Becejac, Rasovic, Vasovic,
Bajic, Kovacevic, Hasanagic, Galic, Pirmajer

1966-67 CELTIC
Lisbon 25 May 1967 Attendance 45,000
Celtic (0) **2** **Inter Milan** (1) **1**
Gemmell, Chalmers Mazzola (pen)
Celtic: Simpson, Craig, Gemmell, Murdoch, McNeill, Clark,
Johnstone, Wallace, Chalmers, Auld, Lennox
Inter: Sarti, Burgnich, Facchetti, Bedin, Guarneri, Picchi,
Domenghini, Mazzola, Cappellini, Biccli, Corso

1967-68 MANCHESTER UNITED
Wembley 29 May 1968 Attendance 100,000
Manchester United (0) (1) **4** **Benfica** (0) (1) **1**
Charlton 2, Best, Kidd Graca
United: Stepney, Brennan, Dunne, Crerand, Foulkes, Stiles, Best,
Kidd, Charlton, Sadler, Aston
Benfica: Henrique, Adolfo, Cruz, Graca, Humberto, Jacinto,
Augusto, Eusebio, Torres, Coluna, Simoes

1968-69 AC MILAN
Madrid 28 May 1969 Attendance 50,000
AC Milan (2) **4** **Ajax Amsterdam** (0) **1**
Prati 3, Sormani Vasovic
Milan: Cudicini, Anquiletti, Schnellinger, Maldera, Rosato,
Trapattoni, Hamrin, Lodetti, Sormani, Rivera, Prati
Ajax: Bals, Suurbier (sub Muller), Van Duivenbode, Pronk,
Hulsoff, Vasovic, Swart, Cruyff, Danielson, Groot (sub Nuninga), Keizer

1969-70 FEYENOORD
Milan 6 May 1970 Attendance 50,000
Feyenoord (1) (1) **2** **Celtic** (1) (1) **1**
Israel, Kindvall Gemmell
Feyenoord: Graafland, Romeyns, Laseroms, Israel, Van Duivenbode,
Hasil, Jansen, Van Hanegem, Wery, Kindvall, Mouljin (sub Haak)
Celtic: Williams, Hay, Gemmell, Murdoch, McNeill, Brogan, Johnstone,
Lennox, Wallace, Auld (sub Connolly), Hughes

1970-71 AJAX AMSTERDAM
Wembley 2 June 1971 Attendance 90,000
Ajax Amsterdam (1) **2** **Panathinaikos** (0) **0**
Van Dijk, Haan
Ajax: Stuy, Vasovic, Suurbier, Hulsoff, Rijinders (sub Haan),
Neeskens, Swart (sub Blankenburg), Muhren, Keizer, Van Dijk, Cruyff
Panathinaikos: Economopoulos, Tomaras, Vlahos, Elefetrakis, Kamaras,
Sourpis, Grammos, Filokouris, Antoniadis, Domazos, Kapsis

1971-72 AJAX AMSTERDAM
Rotterdam 31 May 1972 Attendance 67,000
Ajax Amsterdam (0) **2** **Inter Milan** (0) **0**
Cruyff 2
Ajax: Stuy, Suurbier, Blankenburg, Hulshoff, Krol, Neeskens, Haan,
Muhren, Swart, Cruyff, Keizer
Inter: Bordon, Burgnich, Bellugi, Oriali, Facchetti, Bedin, Mazzola,
Giubertoni (sub Bertini), Jair, Pellicarro, Boninsegna, Frustalupi

1972-73 AJAX AMSTERDAM
Belgrade 30 May 1973 Attendance 93,500
Ajax Amsterdam (0) **1** **Juventus** (0) **0**
Rep
Ajax: Stuy, Suurbier, Blankenburg, Hulshoff, Krol, Neeskens,
Haan, G. Muhren, Rep, Cruyff, Keizer
Juventus: Zoff, Longobucco, Marchetti, Furino, Morini,
Salvadore, Altafini, Causio (sub Cuccureddu), Anastasi,
Capello, Bettega (sub Haller)

ASSOCIATED PRESS

*The first European Cup entrants from the Football League, Manchester United,
defend against Real Madrid who beat them in the 1957 semi-final.*

FAIRS CUP WINNERS AND FINALS

1955-58 BARCELONA
First Leg: Stamford Bridge 5.3.58 Attendance 45,466
London (1) **2** **Barcelona** (2) **2**
Greaves, Langley (pen) Tajada, Martinez
Second Leg: Barcelona 1.5.58 Attendance 62,000
Barcelona (3) **6** **London** (0) **0**
Suarez 2, Evaristo 2,
Martinez, Verges
London: **First Leg:** Kelsey (Arsenal); Sillett P. (Chelsea), Langley (Fulham);
Blanchflower (Spurs), Norman (Spurs), Coote (Brentford);
Groves (Arsenal), Greaves (Chelsea), Smith (Spurs), Haynes
(Fulham), Robb (Spurs).
Second Leg: Kelsey (Arsenal); Wright (West Ham), Cantwell (West Ham);
Blanchflower (Spurs), Brown (West Ham), Bowen (Arsenal);
Medwin (Spurs), Groves (Arsenal), Smith (Spurs), Bloomfield
(Arsenal), Lewis (Chelsea).

1958-60 BARCELONA
First Leg: Birmingham 29.3.60 Attendance 40,500
Birmingham City (0) **0** **Barcelona** (0) **0**
Second Leg: Barcelona 4.5.60 Attendance 70,000
Barcelona (2) **4** **Birmingham City** (0) **1**
Martinez, Czibor 2, Coll Hooper

1960-61 AS ROMA
First Leg: Birmingham 27.9.61 Attendance 21,005
Birmingham City (0) **2** **AS Roma** (1) **2**
Hellawell, Orritt Manfredini 2
Second Leg: Rome 11.10.61 Attendance 60,000
AS Roma (0) **2** **Birmingham City** (0) **0**
Farmer (og), Pestrin

1961-62 VALENCIA

First Leg: Valencia 8.9.62 Attendance 65,000

Valencia	6	Barcelona	2

Second Leg: Barcelona 12.9.62 Attendance 60,000

Barcelona	1	Valencia	1

1962-63 VALENCIA

First Leg: Zagreb 12.6.63 Attendance 40,000

Dynamo Zagreb	(1) 1	Valencia	(0) 2
Zambata		Waldo, Urtiaga	

Second Leg: Valencia 26.6.63 Attendance 55,000

Valencia	2	Dynamo Zagreb	0
Mano, Nunez			

1963-64 REAL ZARAGOZA

Final: Barcelona 24.6.64 Attendance 50,000

Real Zaragoza	(1) 2	Valencia	(1) 1
Villa, Marcelino		Urtiaga	

1964-65 FERENCVAROS

Final: Turin 23.6.65 Attendance 25,000

Ferencvaros	(1) 1	Juventus	(0) 0
Fenyvesi			

1965-66 BARCELONA

First Leg: Barcelona 14.9.66 Attendance 70,000

Barcelona	(0) 0	Real Zaragoza	(1) 1
		Canario	

Second Leg: Zaragoza 21.9.66 Attendance 70,000

Real Zaragoza	(1) 2	Barcelona	(1) 4
Marcelino 2		Pujol 3, Zaballa	

1966-67 DYNAMO ZAGREB

First Leg: Zagreb 30.8.67 Attendance 40,000

Dynamo Zagreb	(1) 2	Leeds United	(0) 0
Cercer 2			

Second Leg: Leeds 6.9.67 Attendance 35,604

Leeds United	(0) 0	Dynamo Zagreb	(0) 0

1967-68 LEEDS UNITED

First Leg: Leeds 7.8.68 Attendance 25,368

Leeds United	(1) 1	Ferencvaros	(0) 0
Jones			

Second Leg: Budapest 11.9.68 Attendance 70,000

Ferencvaros	(0) 0	Leeds United	(0) 0

Leeds United: Sprake; Reaney, Cooper, Bremner, Charlton, Hunter, Lorimer, Madeley, Jones, Giles (sub Hibbitt), Gray (sub O'Grady).

1968-69 NEWCASTLE UNITED

First Leg: Newcastle 29.5.69 Attendance 60,000

Newcastle United	(0) 3	Ujpest Dozsa	(0) 0
Moncur 2, Scott			

Second Leg: Budapest 11.6.69 Attendance 37,000

Ujpest Dozsa	(2) 2	Newcastle United	(0) 3
Bene, Gorocs		Moncur, Arentoft, Foggon	

Newcastle United: McFaul; Craig, Clark, Gibb, Burton, Moncur, Scott, Robson, Davies, Arentoft, Sinclair. (Foggon substituted for Scott in first leg and for Sinclair in second leg).

1969-70 ARSENAL

First Leg: Brussels 22.4.70 Attendance 37,000

Anderlecht	(2) 3	Arsenal	(0) 1
Devrindt, Mulder 2		Kennedy	

Second Leg: London 28.4.70 Attendance 51,612

Arsenal	(1) 3	Anderlecht	(0) 0
Kelly, Radford, Sammels			

Arsenal: Wilson; Storey, McNab, Kelly, McLintock, Simpson, Armstrong, Sammels, Radford, George (sub Kennedy in first leg), Graham.

1970-71 LEEDS UNITED

First Leg: Turin 26.5.71 Attendance 65,000

Juventus	(0) 0	Leeds United	(0) 0

(game abandoned after 51 minutes)

Turin 28.5.71 Attendance 65,000

Juventus	(1) 2	Leeds United	(0) 2
Bettega, Capello		Madeley, Bates	

Second Leg: Leeds 3.6.71 Attendance 42,483

Leeds United	(1) 1	Juventus	(1) 1
Clarke		Anastasi	

Leeds United: Sprake; Reaney, Cooper, Bremner, Charlton, Hunter, Lorimer, Clarke, Jones (sub Bates in first leg), Giles, Madeley (sub Bates in second leg).
(Leeds won on the 'away goals count double' rule).

UEFA CUP WINNERS AND FINALS

1971-72 TOTTENHAM HOTSPUR

First Leg: Wolverhampton 3.5.72 Attendance 45,000

Wolverhampton Wanderers	(0) 1	Tottenham Hotspur	(0) 2
McCalliog		Chivers 2	

Second Leg: Tottenham 17.5.72 Attendance 48,000

Tottenham Hotspur	(1) 1	Wolverhampton Wanderers	(0) 1
Mullery		Wagstaffe	

Tottenham Hotspur: Jennings, Kinnear, Knowles, Mullery, England, Beal, Coates (sub Pratt in first leg), Perryman, Chivers, Peters, Gilzean.

1972-73 LIVERPOOL

First Leg: Liverpool 10.5.73 Attendance 41,169

Liverpool	(3) 3	Borussia Monchengladbach	(0) 0
Keegan 2, Lloyd			

Second Leg: Monchengladbach 23.5.73 Attendance 35,000

Borussia Monchengladbach	(2) 2	Liverpool	(0) 0

Liverpool: Clemence, Lawler, Lindsay, Smith, Lloyd, Hughes, Keegan, Cormack, Toshack, Heighway (sub Hall in first leg, Boersma in second leg), Callaghan.

EUROPEAN CUP WINNERS CUP FINALS

1960-61 FIORENTINA

First Leg: Glasgow 17.5.61 Attendance 80,000

Rangers	(0) 0	Fiorentina	(1) 2
		Milan 2	

Second Leg: Florence 27.5.61 Attendance 50,000

Fiorentina	(1) 2	Rangers	(1) 1
Milan, Hamrin		Scott	

Rangers: Ritchie, Shearer, Caldow, Davis, Paterson, Baxter, Wilson, McMillan, Scott, Brand, Hume (Millar in second leg).

1961-62 ATLETICO MADRID

Final: Glasgow 10.5.62 Attendance 27,389

Atletico Madrid	(1) 1	Fiorentina	(1) 1
Peiro		Hamrin	

Replay: Stuttgart 5.9.62 Attendance 45,000

Atletico Madrid	(2) 3	Fiorentina	(0) 0
Jones, Mendoca, Peiro			

1962-63 TOTTENHAM HOTSPUR

Final: Rotterdam 15.5.63 Attendance 25,000

Tottenham Hotspur	(2) 5	Atletico Madrid	(0) 1
Greaves 2, White, Dyson 2		Collar (pen)	

Tottenham Hotspur: Brown, Baker, Henry, Blanchflower, Norman, Marchi, Jones, White, Smith, Greaves, Dyson.

1963-64 SPORTING LISBON

Final: Brussels 13.5.64 Attendance 9,000

Sporting Lisbon	(1) (3) 3	MTK Budapest	(1) (3) 3
Figueiredo 2, Dansky (og)		Sandor 2, Kuti	

Replay: Antwerp 15.5.64 Attendance 18,000

Sporting Lisbon	(1) 1	MTK Budapest	(0) 0
Morais			

1964-65 WEST HAM UNITED

Final: Wembley 19.5.65 Attendance 100,000

West Ham United	(0) 2	TSV Munich 1860	(0) 0
Sealey 2			

West Ham United: Standen, Kirkup, Burkett, Peters, Brown, Moore, Sealey, Boyce, Hurst, Dear, Sissons.

1965-66 BORUSSIA DORTMUND

Final: Glasgow 5.5.66 Attendance 41,657

Borussia Dortmund	(0) (1) 2	Liverpool	(0) (1) 1
Held, Yeats (og)		Hunt	

Liverpool: Lawrence, Lawler, Byrne, Milne, Yeats, Stevenson, Callaghan, Hunt, St John, Smith, Thompson.

1966-67 BAYERN MUNICH

Final: Nuremberg 31.5.67 Attendance 69,480

Bayern Munich	(0) (0) 1	Rangers	(0) (0) 0
Roth			

Rangers: Martin, Johansen, Provan, Jardine, McKinnon, Greig, Henderson, Smith (A), Hynd, Smith (D), Johnston.

1967-68 AC MILAN

Final: Rotterdam 23.5.68

AC Milan	(2) 2	SV Hamburg	(0) 0
Hamrin 2			

1968-69 SLOVAN BRATISLAVA

Final: Basle 21.5.69

Slovan Bratislava	(3) 3	Barcelona	(1) 2
Cvetler, Hrivnak, Jan Capkovic		Zaldua, Rexach	

1969-70 MANCHESTER CITY

Final: Vienna 29.4.70 Attendance 10,000

Manchester City	(2) 2	Gornik Zabrze	(0) 1
Young, Lee penalty		Oslizlo	

Manchester City: Corrigan, Book, Pardoe, Doyle (Bowyer), Booth, Oakes, Heslop, Bell, Lee, Young, Towers.

1970-71 CHELSEA

Final: Athens 19.5.71 Attendance 42,000

Chelsea	(0) (1) 1	Real Madrid	(0) (1) 1
Osgood		Zoco	

Replay: Athens 21.5.71 Attendance 24,000

Chelsea	(2) 2	Real Madrid	(0) 1
Dempsey, Osgood		Fleitas	

Chelsea: *Final:* Bonetti, Boyle, Harris, Hollins (Mulligan), Dempsey, Webb, Weller, Cooke, Osgood (Baldwin), Hudson, Houseman.
Replay: Bonetti, Boyle, Harris, Cooke, Dempsey, Webb, Weller, Baldwin, Osgood (Smethurst), Hudson, Houseman.

1971-72 RANGERS

Final: Barcelona 24.5.72 Attendance 45,000

Rangers	(2) 3	Moscow Dynamo	(0) 2
Stein, Johnston 2		Eschtrekov, Makiovic	

Rangers: McCloy, Jardine, Mathieson, Greig, Johnstone, Smith, McLean, Conn, Stein, Macdonald, Johnston.

1972-73 AC MILAN

Final: Salonika 16.5.73 Attendance 45,000

AC Milan	(1) 1	Leeds United	(0) 0
Chiaguri			

AC Milan: Vecchi, Sabadini, Zignoli, Anquilletti, Turone, Rosato (sub Dolci), Sogliano, Benetti, Bigon, Rivera, Chiaguri.

Leeds United: Harvey, Reaney, Cherry, Bates, Madeley, Hunter, Lorimer, Jordan, Jones, Gray (F), Yorath (sub McQueen)

The World Cup 1930–1974

1930 (held in Uruguay)
Group winners:
Group One: Argentina
Group Two: Yugoslavia
Group Three: Uruguay
Group Four: United States
Semi-Finals:
Argentina 6 United States 1
Uruguay 6 Yugoslavia 1

Final:
Uruguay 4 Argentina 2

1934 (held in Italy)
Quarter-Finals:
Germany 2 Sweden 1
Czechoslovakia 3 Switzerland 2
Austria 2 Hungary 1
Italy 1 Spain 1
Quarter-Final Replay:
Italy 1 Spain 0
Semi-Finals:
Czechoslovakia 3 Germany 1
Italy 1 Austria 0
Match for Third Place:
Germany 3 Austria 2

Final:
Italy 2 Czechoslovakia 1

1938 (held in France)
Quarter-Finals:
Sweden 8 Cuba 0
Hungary 2 Switzerland 0
Italy 3 France 1
Brazil 1 Czechoslovakia 1
Quarter-Final Replay:
Brazil 2 Czechoslovakia 1
Semi-Finals:
Italy 2 Brazil 1
Hungary 5 Sweden 1
Match for Third Place:
Brazil 4 Sweden 2

Final:
Italy 4 Hungary 2

1950 (held in Brazil)
Group Winners:
Group One: Brazil
Group Two: Spain
Group Three: Sweden
Group Four: Uruguay
Final Group:
Uruguay 2 Spain 2
Brazil 7 Sweden 1
Uruguay 3 Sweden 2
Brazil 6 Spain 1
Sweden 3 Spain 1
Uruguay 2 Brazil 1

Winners: Uruguay

1954 (held in Switzerland)
Group Qualifiers:
Group One: Brazil, Yugoslavia
Group Two: Hungary, W. Germany
Group Three: Uruguay, Austria
Group Four: England, Switzerland
Quarter-Finals:
W. Germany 2 Yugoslavia 0
Hungary 4 Brazil 2
Austria 7 Switzerland 5
Uruguay 4 England 2
Semi-Finals:
W. Germany 6 Austria 1
Hungary 4 Uruguay 2
Match for Third Place:
Austria 3 Uruguay 1

Final:
West Germany 3 Hungary 2

1958 (held in Sweden)
Group Qualifiers:
Group One: W. Germany, N. Ireland
Group Two: France, Yugoslavia
Group Three: Sweden, Wales
Group Four: Brazil, USSR
Quarter-Finals:
France 4 N. Ireland 0
W. Germany 1 Yugoslavia 0
Sweden 2 USSR 0
Brazil 1 Wales 0
Semi-Finals:
Brazil 5 France 2
Sweden 3 W. Germany 1
Match for Third Place:
France 6 W. Germany 3

Final:
Brazil 5 Sweden 2

1962 (held in Chile)
Group Qualifiers:
Group One: USSR, Yugoslavia
Group Two: W. Germany, Chile
Group Three: Brazil, Czechoslovakia
Group Four: Hungary, England
Quarter-Finals:
Yugoslavia 1 W. Germany 0
Brazil 3 England 1
Chile 2 USSR 1
Czechoslovakia 1 Hungary 0
Semi-Finals:
Brazil 4 Chile 2
Czechoslovakia 3 Yugoslavia 1
Match for Third Place:
Chile 1 Yugoslavia 0

Final:
Brazil 3 Czechoslovakia 1

1966 (held in England)
Group Qualifiers:
Group One: England, Uruguay
Group Two: W. Germany, Argentina
Group Three: Portugal, Hungary
Group Four: USSR, N. Korea
Quarter-Finals:
England 1 Argentina 0
W. Germany 4 Uruguay 0
Portugal 5 N. Korea 3
USSR 2 Hungary 1
Semi-Finals:
W. Germany 2 USSR 1
England 2 Portugal 1
Match for Third Place:
Portugal 2 USSR 1

Final:
England 4 West Germany 2

1970 (held in Mexico)
Group Qualifiers:
Group One: USSR, Mexico
Group Two: Italy, Uruguay
Group Three: Brazil, England
Group Four: W. Germany, Peru
Quarter-Finals:
Uruguay 1 USSR 0
Italy 4 Mexico 1
Brazil 4 Peru 2
W. Germany 3 England 2
Semi-Finals:
Italy 4 W. Germany 3
Brazil 3 Uruguay 1
Match for Third Place:
W. Germany 1 Uruguay 0

Final:
Brazil 4 Italy 1

West Germany 1974

Group Qualifiers:
Group 1: East Germany,
          West Germany
Group 2: Yugoslavia, Brazil
Group 3: Netherlands, Sweden
Group 4: Poland, Argentina

Group A Results:
Brazil 1 East Germany 0
Netherlands 4 Argentina 0
Argentina 1 Brazil 2
East Germany 0 Netherlands 2
Argentina 1 East Germany 1
Netherlands 2 Brazil 0

Group B Results:
Yugoslavia 0 West Germany 2
Sweden 0 Poland 1
Poland 2 Yugoslavia 1
West Germany 4 Sweden 2
Poland 0 West Germany 1
Sweden 2 Yugoslavia 1

Third Place
Poland 1 Brazil 0

Final
West Germany 2 Netherlands 1